Paralegals in American Law

TITLES IN THE DELMAR LCP SERIES

Ransford C. Pyle, *Foundations of Law for Paralegals: Cases, Commentary, and Ethics,* 1992.

Peggy N. Kerley, Paul A. Sukys, Joanne Banker Hames, *Civil Litigation for the Paralegal,* 1992.

Jonathan Lynton, Donna Masinter, Terri Mick Lyndall, *Law Office Management for Paralegals,* 1992.

Daniel Hall, *Criminal Law and Procedure,* 1992.

Daniel Hall, *Survey of Criminal Law,* 1993.

Jonathan Lynton, Terri Mick Lyndall, *Legal Ethics and Professional Responsibility,* 1994.

Michael Kearns, *The Law of Real Property,* 1994.

Angela Schneeman, *The Law of Corporations, Partnerships, and Sole Proprietorships,* 1993.

William Buckley, *Torts and Personal Injury Law,* 1993.

Gordon W. Brown, *Administration of Wills, Trusts, and Estates,* 1993.

Richard Stim, *Intellectual Property: Patents, Copyrights, and Trademarks,* 1994.

Ransford C. Pyle, *Family Law,* 1994.

Jack Handler, *Ballentine's Law Dictionary: Legal Assistant Edition,* 1994.

Jonathan Lynton, *Ballentine's Thesaurus for Legal Research & Writing,* 1994.

Daniel Hall, *Administrative Law,* 1994.

Angela Schneeman, *Paralegals in American Law,* 1994.

Eric M. Gansberg, *Paralegals in New York Law,* 1994.

Paralegals in American Law

INTRODUCTION TO PARALEGALISM

ANGELA SCHNEEMAN

Lawyers Cooperative Publishing

Delmar
Publishers Inc.™

Cover design by Spiral Design Studio

Delmar Staff:

Administrative Editor: Jay Whitney
Developmental Editor: Christopher Anzalone
Project Editor: Andrea Edwards Myers
Production Coordinator: James Zayicek
Art/Design Coordinator: Karen Kunz Kemp

For information, address:

Delmar Publishers Inc.
3 Columbia Circle
P.O. Box 15015
Albany, New York 12212-5015

Printed in the United States of America

  2 3 4 5 6 7 8 9 10 XXX 00 99 98 97 96 95

Library of Congress Cataloging-in-Publication Data

Schneeman, Angela.
      Paralegals in American law / Angela Schneeman. — 1st ed.
         p. cm.
      Includes index.
      ISBN 0-8273-6078-9
1. Legal assistants—United States. I. Title.
   KF320.L4S36 1991
340'.023'73—dc20   93-38409
                                                                      CIP

DEDICATION

To my husband, Greg, and our children, Alex and Katherine.

CONTENTS

■ CHAPTER 4   The Law Office Environment   75

PART II
THE ROLES OF THE PARALEGAL

■ **CHAPTER 9** **The Tort Paralegal and Personal Injury Litigation 267**

■ **CHAPTER 10   The Paralegal and Criminal Law**
                and Procedure   335

▨ CHAPTER 11 The Paralegal and Business Organizations   397

CHAPTER 12   The Family Law Paralegal   453

■ CHAPTER 13 The Wills, Trusts, and Estates Paralegal   493

■ CHAPTER 14   The Real Estate Paralegal   551

CHAPTER 15   The Intellectual Property Paralegal   591

▧ CHAPTER 16   The Administrative Law Paralegal   629

▪ CHAPTER 17 The Bankruptcy Paralegal   663

■ **CHAPTER 18   Every Paralegal Is a
               Contracts Paralegal   687**

▦ APPENDIXES

DELMAR PUBLISHERS INC.

 AND

LAWYERS COOPERATIVE PUBLISHING

ARE PLEASED TO ANNOUNCE THEIR PARTNERSHIP
TO CO-PUBLISH COLLEGE TEXTBOOKS FOR
PARALEGAL EDUCATION.

DELMAR, WITH OFFICES AT ALBANY, NEW YORK, IS A PROFES-
SIONAL EDUCATION PUBLISHER. DELMAR PUBLISHES QUALITY
EDUCATIONAL TEXTBOOKS TO PREPARE AND SUPPORT INDI-
VIDUALS FOR LIFE SKILLS AND SPECIFIC OCCUPATIONS.

LAWYERS COOPERATIVE PUBLISHING (LCP), WITH OFFICES AT
ROCHESTER, NEW YORK, HAS BEEN THE LEADING PUBLISHER
OF ANALYTICAL LEGAL INFORMATION FOR OVER 100 YEARS. IT
IS THE PUBLISHER OF SUCH REKNOWNED LEGAL ENCYCLOPE-
DIAS AS **AMERICAN LAW REPORTS, AMERICAN JURIS-
PRUDENCE, UNITED STATES CODE SERVICE, LAW-
YERS EDITION,** AS WELL AS OTHER MATERIAL, AND
FEDERAL- AND STATE-SPECIFIC PUBLICATIONS. THESE PUBLICA-
TIONS HAVE BEEN DESIGNED TO WORK TOGETHER IN THE DAY-
TO-DAY PRACTICE OF LAW AS AN INTEGRATED SYSTEM IN WHAT
IS CALLED THE "TOTAL CLIENT-SERVICE LIBRARY®" (TCSL®). EACH
LCP PUBLICATION IS COMPLETE WITHIN ITSELF AS TO SUBJECT
COVERAGE, YET ALL HAVE COMMON FEATURES AND EXTEN-
SIVE CROSS-REFERENCING TO PROVIDE LINKAGE FOR HIGHLY
EFFICIENT LEGAL RESEARCH INTO VIRTUALLY ANY MATTER AN
ATTORNEY MIGHT BE CALLED UPON TO HANDLE.

INFORMATION IN ALL PUBLICATIONS IS CAREFULLY AND CON-
STANTLY MONITORED TO KEEP PACE WITH AND REFLECT
EVENTS IN THE LAW AND IN SOCIETY. UPDATING AND SUPPLE-
MENTAL INFORMATION IS TIMELY AND PROVIDED
CONVENIENTLY.

FOR FURTHER REFERENCE, SEE:

AMERICAN JURISPRUDENCE 2D: AN ENCY-
CLOPEDIC TEXT COVERAGE OF THE COMPLETE BODY
OF STATE AND FEDERAL LAW.

AM JUR LEGAL FORMS 2D: A COMPILATION OF
BUSINESS AND LEGAL FORMS DEALING WITH A VARI-
ETY OF SUBJECT MATTERS.

**AM JUR PLEADING AND PRACTICE FORMS,
REV:** MODEL PRACTICE FORMS FOR EVERY STAGE OF
A LEGAL PROCEEDING.

AM JUR PROOF OF FACTS: A SERIES OF ARTI-
CLES THAT GUIDE THE READER IN DETERMINING
WHICH FACTS ARE ESSENTIAL TO A CASE AND HOW
TO PROVE THEM.

AM JUR TRIALS: A SERIES OF ARTICLES DISCUSS-
ING EVERY ASPECT OF PARTICULAR SETTLEMENTS
AND TRIALS WRITTEN BY 180 CONSULTING
SPECIALISTS.

UNITED STATES CODE SERVICE: A COMPLETE
AND AUTHORITATIVE ANNOTATED FEDERAL CODE
THAT FOLLOWS THE EXACT LANGUAGE OF THE STAT-
UTES AT LARGE AND DIRECTS YOU TO THE COURT
AND AGENCY DECISIONS CONSTRUING EACH
PROVISION.

ALR AND ALR FEDERAL: SERIES OF ANNOTA-
TIONS PROVIDING IN-DEPTH ANALYSES OF ALL THE
CASE LAW ON PARTICULAR LEGAL ISSUES.

U.S. SUPREME COURT REPORTS, L ED 2D:
EVERY REPORTED U.S. SUPREME COURT DECISION
PLUS IN-DEPTH DISCUSSIONS OF LEADING ISSUES.

FEDERAL PROCEDURE, L ED: A COMPREHEN-
SIVE, A–Z TREATISE ON FEDERAL PROCEDURE—CIVIL,
CRIMINAL, AND ADMINISTRATIVE.

FEDERAL PROCEDURAL FORMS, L ED: STEP-
BY-STEP GUIDANCE FOR DRAFTING FORMS FOR FED-
ERAL COURT OR FEDERAL AGENCY PROCEEDINGS.

FEDERAL RULES SERVICE, 2D AND 3D:
REPORTS DECISIONS FROM ALL LEVELS OF THE FED-
ERAL SYSTEM INTERPRETING THE FEDERAL RULES
OF CIVIL PROCEDURE AND THE FEDERAL RULES OF
APPELLATE PROCEDURE.

STORIES ET CETERA — A COUNTRY LAWYER LOOKS AT LIFE AND THE LAW

SUMMARY OF AMERICAN LAW

THE TRIAL LAWYER'S BOOK: PREPARING AND WINNING CASES

TRIAL PRACTICE CHECKLISTS

2000 CLASSIC LEGAL QUOTATIONS

WILLISTON ON CONTRACTS, 3D AND 4TH

FEDERAL RULES OF EVIDENCE DIGEST: ORGANIZES HEADNOTES FOR THE DECISIONS REPORTED IN FEDERAL RULES OF EVIDENCE SERVICE ACCORDING TO THE NUMBERING SYSTEM OF THE FEDERAL RULES OF EVIDENCE.

ADMINISTRATIVE LAW: PRACTICE AND PROCEDURE

AGE DISCRIMINATION: CRITICAL ISSUES AND PROOFS

ALR CRITICAL ISSUES: DRUNK DRIVING PROSECUTIONS

ALR CRITICAL ISSUES: FREEDOM OF INFORMATION ACTS

ALR CRITICAL ISSUES: TRADEMARKS

ALR CRITICAL ISSUES: WRONGFUL DEATH

AMERICANS WITH DISABILITIES: PRACTICE AND COMPLIANCE MANUAL

ATTORNEYS' FEES

BALLENTINE'S LAW DICTIONARY

CONSTITUTIONAL LAW DESKBOOK

CONSUMER AND BORROWER PROTECTION: AM JUR PRACTICE GUIDE

CONSUMER CREDIT: ALR ANNOTATIONS

DAMAGES: ALR ANNOTATIONS

EMPLOYEE DISMISSAL: CRITICAL ISSUES AND PROOFS

FEDERAL RULES DIGEST, 3D: ORGANIZES HEADNOTES FOR THE DECISIONS REPORTED IN FEDERAL RULES SERVICE ACCORDING TO THE NUMBERING SYSTEMS OF THE FEDERAL RULES OF CIVIL PROCEDURE AND THE FEDERAL RULES OF APPELLATE PROCEDURE.

FEDERAL RULES OF EVIDENCE SERVICE: REPORTS DECISIONS FROM ALL LEVELS OF THE FEDERAL SYSTEM INTERPRETING THE FEDERAL RULES OF EVIDENCE.

FEDERAL RULES OF EVIDENCE NEWS

FEDERAL PROCEDURE RULES SERVICE

FEDERAL TRIAL HANDBOOK, 2D

FORM DRAFTING CHECKLISTS: AM JUR PRACTICE GUIDE

GOVERNMENT CONTRACTS: PROCEDURES AND FORMS

HOW TO GO DIRECTLY INTO YOUR OWN COMPUTERIZED SOLO PRACTICE WITHOUT MISSING A MEAL (OR A BYTE)

JONES ON EVIDENCE, CIVIL AND CRIMINAL, 7TH

LITIGATION CHECKISTS: AM JUR PRACTICE GUIDE

MEDICAL LIBRARY, LAWYERS EDITION

MEDICAL MALPRACTICE — ALR CASES AND ANNOTATIONS

MODERN APPELLATE PRACTICE: FEDERAL AND STATE CIVIL APPEALS

MODERN CONSTITUTIONAL LAW

NEGOTIATION AND SETTLEMENT

PATTERN DEPOSITION CHECKLISTS, 2D

QUALITY OF LIFE DAMAGES: CRITICAL ISSUES AND PROOFS

SHEPARD'S CITATIONS FOR ALR

SUCCESSFUL TECHNIQUES FOR CIVIL TRIALS, 2D

FOREWORD

By Chere B. Estrin

Not so very long ago, before formalized training surfaced in a brand new field called paralegalism, attorneys struggled along, attempting to train a new breed of professionals to manage portions of their workload. Not certain, exactly, what it was that paralegals were expected to do, attorneys and paralegals worked together forging a successful effort in defining the field, assignments, and expectations.

Although a variety of schools soon materialized, many major publishers were, for quite some time, unwilling to address the field with texts specifically aimed toward the paralegal, let alone the paralegal student. Instructors limped along, piecing together articles and work product derived from their firms and prior assignments. For many instructors, it was a "make-it-up-as-you-go" approach. They were able to add a few watered-down lawyer texts, but no real tools existed for teachers in this brand new and exciting profession.

Finally, a few very fine publishers, particularly Delmar, listened to the lawyers, paralegals, instructors, and students. Here was a reliable, professional response to "one of the fastest growing fields for the nineties," as the field was now heralded. In addition, the American Bar Association provided a definition and guidelines for paralegals which seriously emphasized that paralegals were here to stay. Acknowledgment of the field poured in. Excellent paralegal texts for the student began to emerge and *Paralegals in American Law: Introduction to Paralegalism* is one.

This text gives the student a comprehensive overview of the specialties available to the practicing paralegal. The book is a complete guide to the most popular areas of law with which the student is most likely to be involved. It allows readers to become familiar with common terms and procedures. It prepares you for decisions you will make when choosing a specialty. In an easy-to-read style, this book introduces the concepts and assignments you are most likely to encounter on the job.

I was particularly pleased to see the author's extensive use of Estrin Publishing's book, *How to Land Your First Paralegal Job* by Andrea Wagner. Finding that first job is an all-important search, and Wagner's tips have helped thousands of students find exactly the positions they desired.

Paralegals in American Law offers strong yet concise chapters on family law, real estate, business organizations, wills, trusts, and estates, and litigation, among others. These chapters are especially practical and helpful to the novice legal assistant. The sections on the role of the paralegal in each specialty are particularly valuable to the beginner.

The text should whet your appetite to find out more about the areas of law that interest you. Pay close attention to the chapters, which also outline what skills are important to do the job. It is obvious that the author is an experienced and dedicated professional—one who understands what it is like to be on the firing line, and precisely the type of individual who can carefully guide you in your quest to learn all about your new career.

Use this book wisely. Keep it with you as you march into your first job and well within easy reach as you progress throughout the years. Congratulations! You've chosen a field with many exciting and progressive opportunities. I wish you outrageous success!

Chere B. Estrin is President of the Quorum/Estrin Group which provides attorneys and paralegals to the legal community. She is CEO of Estrin Publishing, author of Where Do I Go From Here? Career Choices for the Legal Assistant *and* The Paralegal Career Guide, *a columnist for* Legal Assistant Today, *and a California Lawyer "LAMMIE" award winner. Estrin's paralegal education involvement is extensive: Clark Boardman Callaghan publishes a series of paralegal books with Estrin Publishing and Wiley Law Publications publishes the Estrin series, a library of books aimed specifically at legal assistants.*

PREFACE

Unlike other introductory textbooks for paralegal students, I have written this text to be both stimulating and informative. The text explores the role of the paralegal in the law office environment. It includes information on the latest trends and legal assistant salaries to pique the readers' interest. The text is also a comprehensive overview of the paralegal's role in substantive areas of law: litigation, criminal law and procedure, business organizations, family law, wills, trusts, estates, torts, real property law, intellectual property, administrative law, bankruptcy, and contracts. In summation, it explains what the paralegal must know and do to earn respect and the benefits of an exciting career in law.

Contents

The text is divided into two parts. Part I discusses paralegalism from the perspectives of career goals, ethical behavior, and the requisite skills generally needed to be a successful legal assistant. Part II covers the paralegal's role in substantive areas of law.

Chapter 1 defines what a paralegal is and the history of paralegalism. The reader learns about the greatest employment opportunities for paralegals and the typical salaries earned by general and specialized paralegals. Lastly, employment search strategies are provided.

Chapter 2 discusses the various *professional organizations* that support paralegal training, employment, and professional development. Criteria for choosing aparalegal educational program are also explored. State-by-state licensure and certification are examined.

Chapter 3 discusses *ethical behavior* of the employed paralegal. The National Federation of Paralegal Association's Affirmation and Model Code and the National Association of Legal Assistant's Code are discussed in detail. A succinct exploration of unauthorized practice of law, confidentiality, conflicts of interest, misrepresentation, and solicitation are given. Hypothetical ethical situations are used to challenge the reader.

Chapter 4 explores working in the *law office environment.* The roles of typical law office staff members are described. The reader will discover how to achieve the law office's goals with billing, budgeting, and records management procedures.

The fundamentals of *interviewing and investigation* are discussed in Chapter 5. Communication skills are the central focus of this chapter.

Chapter 6 introduces the reader to the *American legal system.* The concepts of federalism and separation of powers are explained. The structure and functions of the judicial branch are also detailed. Sources of American law are included. Lastly, a brief but essential examination of various legal areas is provided: civil versus criminal law, tort law, and contract law.

Chapter 7 explains how *legal research* is successfully performed by the paralegal. Practical tips on legal writing are also provided.

Part II explores paralegalism in a practical and relevant format by exploring the roles of the paralegal in various substantive law areas. The logical approach for students to determine which legal careers they most enjoy is to be exposed to overviews of major substantive areas: litigation, torts, criminal law and procedure, business organizations, family law, wills, trusts, estates, real property law, intellectual property, administrative law, bankruptcy, and contracts.

Chapter 8 addresses the role of the paralegal in *litigation.* Civil procedure is explored in detail.

The *tort* paralegal is the focus of Chapter 9. Intentional torts, negligence, products liability, defenses, and immunities are discussed in detail.

Chapter 10 explains *criminal law and procedure.* From crimes against persons and property through arrest, trial, and sentencing, the reader will understand the role of the legal assistant in criminal law.

Chapter 11 discusses the role of the paralegal in the formation and dissolution of *business organizations.* Sole proprietorships, partnerships (general and limited), and corporations are explained in detail. The student is exposed to the structure and conduct of each organization as well as their advantages and disadvantages.

Family law and the role of the paralegal is the topic of Chapter 12. Marriage, separation, annulment, divorce, child custody, and adoption are included in the chapter.

Chapter 13 explains the role of the paralegal with *wills, trusts, and estates.* Topics in this chapter include intestate succession, the model will, trusts, estate planning, and probating a will.

Chapter 14 explores the various facets of *real property law,* including title determination, ownership, and the acquisition and transfer of real property. The reader will learn how to process and record mortgage deeds and other related documents.

Intellectual property is the focus of Chapter 15. The role of the legal assistant in patents, trademarks, and copyrights is explored.

In Chapter 16, the student will learn about the role of the paralegal in *administrative law.* How federal governmental agencies investigate issues, promulgate rules, and adjudicate disputes is the central focus of this chapter.

In Chapter 17, the reader will be exposed to the role of the paralegal in *bankruptcy* proceedings. The various forms and petitions are discussed, especially Chapters 7, 11, and 13.

Chapter 18 focuses on contracts, a subject with which every paralegal, no matter what his or her specialty, must be thoroughly conversant.

Unique Features

Each chapter concludes with Summary Questions. In addition to a review of the chapter materials, these questions give students the opportunity to research their state-specific laws. This feature affords the students an opportunity to learn and become better acquainted with the laws of their particular jurisdiction (state).

A Practical Paralegal Skills feature also appears at the end of each chapter. This feature allows the student to apply and practice the key concepts learned in the chapter.

There are two glossaries to assist the student in retaining the meaning of key terminology. The first is the running glossary, found in a footnote style format at the bottom of any page where a term is first discussed. At the end of the text, a second, alphabetically arranged glossary is provided. The definitions in both glossaries are drawn from *Ballentine's Law Dictionary: Legal Assistant Edition* © 1994, so everything is authoritative and current.

Color charts, tables, and graphs are placed throughout the text to provide colorful visual emphasis of key points found in each chapter.

The ⦀ icon found throughout the text indicates special features of note.

The appendixes include information on employment guidance, paralegal associations, and a table of the cases cited in this text.

Ancillary Materials

A student study guide has been published to accompany this textbook. Terminology and quizzes provide a self-paced reinforcement of the contents of each chapter. The study guide is perfect for self-study or for the student who wants or needs more than class lectures and a text.

Paralegals in New York Law adapts substantive legal topics to New York state law and procedure. An extensive instructor's guide is also available with chapter summaries, teaching strategies, answers to chapter summary questions, and a Multiple Choice/True-False testbank with answers. A computerized testbank is available as well.

There is a series of videos to supplement course lectures. The series (four videos) is from the *American Bar Association Commission on*

Public Understanding About the Law. Each video features interviews with legal professionals who explain criminal law, civil litigation, the federal court system, and state courts in simple terminology. The videos have dramatizations of actual courtroom proceedings to illustrate key concepts.

ACKNOWLEDGMENTS

This book includes the work of many fine authors, whose research and hard work are much appreciated. Contributors include:

Gordon W. Brown, North Shore Community College, MA

William R. Buckley, Ball State University, IN

Daniel Hall, University of Central Florida, FL

Joanne Banker Hames, DeAnza Community College, CA

Michael P. Kearns, Concordia College, IL

Peggy N. Kerley, Southeastern Paralegal Institute, TX

Terri Mick Lyndall, Paralegal Institute, GA

Jonathan Lynton, Paralegal Institute, GA

Donna Masinter, Drew, Eckl & Farnham, Atlanta, GA

Ransford Pyle, University of Central Florida, FL

Richard W. Stim, San Francisco State University, CA

Paul A. Sukys, North Central Technical College, OH

Pamela Tepper, Southeastern Paralegal Institute, TX

Andrea Wagner, author of *How to Land Your First Paralegal Job,*
 published by Estrin Publishing, 1991.

My thanks go to Jay Whitney for his ideas, and to the staff at Delmar for their encouragement, advice, and assistance, especially Chris Anzalone and Glenna Stanfield. In addition, I would like to thank Graphics West and Brooke Graves at Graves Editorial Service for their input.

A personal word of thanks to my family and my friends for giving me the encouragement and support I needed to complete this project.

Lastly, I would like to acknowledge the contributions of the following reviewers, whose suggestions and insights helped me enormously:

Janet R. Covington
 Southwestern Paralegal Institute
 Houston, TX

T. Eric Evans
 Ball State University
 Muncie, IN

Dolores Grissom
Samford University
Birmingham, AL

Norman W. Holt
Daytona Beach Community College
Daytona Beach, FL

Jay D. Johnson, J.D.
College of Mount St. Joseph
Cincinnati, OH

Martha Alley Mathis
Miller-Motte Business College
Clarksville, TN

J. T. Meisel
Marshal University Community and Technical College
Huntington, WV

Lance C. Miller
The American Institute
Phoenix, AZ

Virginia C. Noonan, Esq.
Northern Essex Community College
Haverhill, MA

Cathy Okrent
Schenectady County Community College
Schenectady, NY

Kathleen Mercer Reed
University of Toledo
Toledo, OH

David A. Reichard
The Philadelphia Institute
Philadelphia, PA

Evelyn S. Riyhani
University of California Extension
Irvine, CA

Karen Schwartz, Esq.
Woodbury College
Montpelier, VT

Cynthia Weishapple
Chippewa Valley Technical College
Eau Claire, WI

PART I

The Paralegal in the Legal System

CHAPTER 1
Paralegal Careers and Employment

The paralegal profession has been one of the fastest growing professions of the 1980s and 1990s. In fact, in its 1987 and 1989 surveys, the United States Department of Labor ranked the paralegal profession as the fastest growing occupation in the United States. Even in times of economic adversity, the number of paralegals employed in the United States continues to climb. For attorneys, paralegals represent a way to assist in providing affordable, quality legal services to clients. For paralegals, the profession offers well-paid, interesting work that many find rewarding.

This chapter explores paralegal careers by examining the definitions of the term *paralegal* and the emergence of the paralegal profession in the United States. Next, this chapter focuses on what paralegals do and who paralegals work for by examining paralegal employers, paralegal specialties, and paralegal salaries and benefits. This chapter next discusses strategies for a successful paralegal career, including beginning the job search, preparing a résumé, preparing for an interview, and planning a career.

Paralegal Defined

Paralegals may broadly be described as individuals who perform legal services under the supervision of an attorney, without practicing law or giving legal advice. The terms **paralegal** and *legal assistant* are usually interchangeable. The National Federation of Paralegal Associations (NFPA) defines the term paralegal (or *legal assistant*) as:

> [A] person, qualified through education, training or work experience, to perform substantive legal work that requires knowledge of legal concepts and is customarily, but not exclusively, performed by a lawyer. This person may be retained or employed by a lawyer, law office, governmental agency or other entity, or may be authorized by administrative, statutory, or court authority to perform this work.

The American Bar Association's Standing Committee on Ethics and Responsibility prefers the term *legal assistant*, which it defines as follows:

> A legal assistant is a person, qualified through education, training, or work experience, who is employed or retained by a lawyer, law office, governmental agency, or other entity in a capacity or function which involves the performance, under the ultimate direction and supervision of an attorney, of specifically-delegated substantive legal work, which work, for the most part, requires a sufficient knowledge of legal concepts that, absent such assistant, the attorney would perform the task.

The National Association of Legal Assistants (NALA) also uses the term *legal assistant*. Note that the NALA definition (which follows) specifically states that legal assistants are qualified through their formal education, training and experience and that they do work of a legal nature "under the supervision of an attorney." NALA defines legal assistants as a group of persons

> who assist attorneys in the delivery of legal services. Through formal education, training, and experience legal assistants have knowledge and expertise regarding the legal system and substantive and procedural law which qualify them to do work of a legal nature under the supervision of an attorney.

Although by most definitions, paralegals are those who assist attorneys and work under their direction, under certain circumstances, freelance paralegals and legal technicians may work without attorney supervision in a limited manner.

BALLENTINESBALLENTINESBALLENTINESBALLENTINESBALLENTINESBALLENTINESBALLENTINESBALLENTINESBALLENTINESBALLENTINESBALLENTINESBALLENTINESBALLENTINESBALLENTINES

paralegal A person who, although not an attorney, performs many of the functions of an attorney under an attorney's supervision.

The variety of titles and definitions used to describe individuals who assist attorneys is just one indication of the changing paralegal profession.

In the years to come, more precise definitions to describe certain categories of paralegals will likely be agreed upon by the legal community.

The Emergence of the Paralegal Profession

Although lawyers have been around for centuries, paralegals are a relatively new phenomenon. This section examines the evolution of the paralegal profession and paralegal education, and the reasons for the rapid growth and expansion of the profession.

The Evolution of the Paralegal Profession

The paralegal profession had its formal beginning in the United States in the 1960s. Paralegals were hired in the mid-1960s to assist federally funded lawyers in poverty programs as part of President Lyndon Johnson's "War on Poverty."[1] Soon the benefits of hiring paralegals became apparent throughout the private sector of the legal community and law firms began hiring paralegals as well. These individuals were often either experienced legal secretaries or college graduates who were trained by the attorneys within the firm for which they worked.

In some respects, the emergence of the paralegal profession paralleled that of another "para" profession, paramedics. The paramedic profession evolved during the Vietnam War era when soldiers began returning to the work force and using medical training they received in the military.

Recognition by the Legal Community

In 1968, the American Bar Association first recognized the importance of paralegals with the creation of its Special Committee on Lay Assistants (now called the Standing Committee on Legal Assistants). In 1974, the National Federation of Paralegal Associations (NFPA) was formed, constituted of a group of state associations. The National Association of Legal Assistants (NALA) was formed for individual members in 1975.

By the 1980s, well-trained, experienced paralegals were a hot commodity, almost a status symbol among law firms. During the 1980s and 1990s the profession has continued to grow and mature, although not always without growing pains. Many paralegals were hired to work for law firms where the attorneys were unsure of how best to utilize their time and talent. Many paralegals have, in effect, had to educate the attorneys they work for on what they can do and what responsibilities they can handle. Over the years, paralegals in general have earned the respect of attorneys and the public alike. Their numbers and responsibilities have grown rapidly. Today, according to the Department of Labor, there are more than 115,000 paralegals in this country, up 359 percent since 1983.

The Evolution of Paralegal Education

Paralegal education has also evolved through the years. In the 1960s and early 1970s, most paralegals were experienced legal secretaries or college graduates who were trained by the attorneys they worked for. Gradually, colleges and business schools began offering paralegal programs, and in the early 1970s the American Bar Association began approving paralegal programs. In 1970 there were only four paralegal training programs throughout the United States. Today, there are more than 650 paralegal schools, 150 of which are approved by the American Bar Association.[2]

Reasons for the Rapid Growth and Expansion of the Profession

The emergence and growth of the paralegal profession in this country are due to many factors, including economic reasons, the changing demographics of the workforce, the changing practice of law, and the professionalization of the field. The need for individuals to fill the many roles now played by paralegals has continued to grow for many reasons, as has the number of paralegals to fill those needs.

Economic Reasons for Continued Growth

The main reasons for the increased hiring of paralegals are economic. Law firms have found that they can hire paralegals, get their work completed competently and efficiently, and bill their clients less, all the while retaining their profit. For example, if a client has been quoted $350 for a simple will, and it takes approximately 3.5 hours to meet with the client, draft the will, and see to its execution, the firm's time could be spent in one of two ways:

Meeting with client	1 hour	Attorney rate	$100/hr.	$100
Drafting simple will	2 hours	Attorney rate	$100/hr.	$200
Meeting with client for execution of will	1/2 hour	Attorney rate	$100/hr.	$50
Total cost of billable time to law firm:				$350

When an attorney who bills at $100 per hour handles the task exclusively, the firm might bill $350 to the client, which is exactly the amount of billable time that it costs the firm. However, when a paralegal is involved, the scenario can look quite different:

Meeting with client	1 hour	Attorney rate	$100/hr.	$100
Draft simple will	2 hours	Paralegal rate	$50/hr.	$100
Review simple will	1/2 hour	Attorney rate	$100/hr.	$50
Meeting with client for execution of will	1/2 hour	Paralegal rate	$50/hr.	$25
Total cost of billable time to law firm:				$275

In this case, the cost in billable time to the law firm is $275. The law firm can choose to pass the savings on to the client and bill at a more competitive rate of $275, or the firm can bill at the usual rate of $350 and enjoy the extra profit. The average billing rate of paralegals in the United States is around $60 per hour—less than half of the billing rate of many attorneys. The salary paid to the paralegal, though not unsatisfactory, is still substantially less than the attorney is paid. The attorney's time can be focused on matters that may be taken care of only by a licensed attorney, thus benefiting the lawyer, the law firm, and the client.

Other Reasons for Continued Growth

In addition to the economic reasons for the increased hiring of paralegals, other factors have added to the boom. Some of those factors include:

1. Growth in demand for legal services in this country
2. The need to keep legal services affordable for the general public
3. The need to utilize attorney time in a more effective manner
4. Computerization of the practice of law
5. Increased competition, leading to the need to give clients more personal and responsive attention
6. Increasing use of the systems approach to handle the complexities of modern law
7. Greater specialization in the practice of law

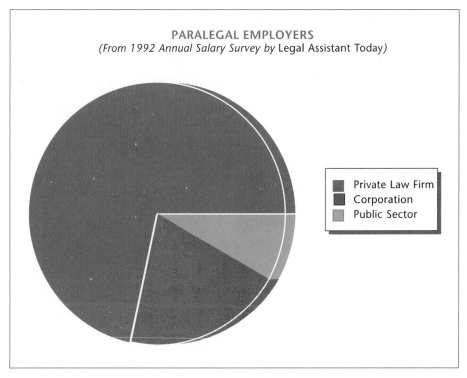

PARALEGAL EMPLOYERS
(From 1992 Annual Salary Survey by Legal Assistant Today)

Legend:
- ■ Private Law Firm
- ■ Corporation
- ■ Public Sector

Paralegal Employers Roughly 3/4 of all paralegals work at private law firms. Corporations employ about 16% of paralegals; the remaining 10% work for the public sector, generally in government agencies. (Adapted from the 1993 Annual Salary Survey by *Legal Assistant Today*.)

These factors are not fleeting in nature. All indications are that the paralegal profession will continue to grow throughout the end of this century, and probably into the next.

Paralegal Employers and Paralegal Specialties

One reason that it has been hard to define the term *paralegal* is because the work of paralegals is so diverse. The work of two paralegals with the same titles in different firms with different specialties can be incredibly different. Two important factors that determine the job description for a particular paralegal position are the type of employer and the specialty of the paralegal.

Paralegal Employers

Although the vast majority of paralegals work in private law firms, law firms are not the only employer of paralegals. Paralegals are employed by corporations and government agencies, as well as law firms of all sizes.

Law Firm Employers

In a 1993 survey of paralegals, more than 75 percent of the respondents indicated that they worked in private law firms. More than 70 percent of those paralegals indicated that they worked for law firms with fewer than 30 attorneys.[3] Both small and large law firms have their advantages and disadvantages.

One reason many paralegals prefer smaller law firms is that, unlike most large law firms, smaller law firms often do not have high billing requirements that necessitate long work hours. In addition, many paralegals feel that smaller law firms offer a more congenial, less stressful working atmosphere and a chance to experience working in more than just one area of law. Paralegals who work for small firms often experience more variety in their work and less specialization. One disadvantage, however, is that small firms are often unable to offer salaries and benefits that are competitive with those of large law firms.

In addition to enjoying what are often better pay and benefits, some paralegals find large law firms to be more exciting, challenging, and rewarding. Large law firms also can offer vast resources in comparison to smaller firms, including immense law libraries and additional support staff that are unavailable in smaller firms. However, paralegals in large law firms may have to meet demanding billing requirements that often commit the paralegal to long hours of hard work. Paralegals who work in medium-sized law firms report that their firms have some of the characteristics of both small and large firms.

The personnel of a law firm will vary depending on the size and structure of the firm. Typically, law firms with more than one attorney are owned and headed by the partners or shareholders of the firm. Reporting to them are attorneys within the firm who do not have an ownership stake, usually referred to as the firm's *associates.* If the firm employs law students who typically work on a part-time basis while finishing their education, those employees are referred to as *law clerks.* The law clerks typically report to one or more associates. In addition to law clerks and paralegals, the nonattorney personnel of law firms usually includes the office administrator, additional administrative staff, secretaries, word processing personnel, a receptionist, a records manager, and one or more file clerks. The non-attorney personnel generally report to the office administrator and the attorneys to whom they are assigned.

Larger law firms may have several more classifications and titles for their employees. They may have additional classes of attorneys, such as junior partners and senior associates. In addition, they may have an entire administrative staff instead of just a law office administrator. The clerical staff may include messengers and data entry personnel.

Although law firms all have many common elements, it is important that paralegals seeking employment realize that each law firm has its own distinct "personality" and culture. The success or failure of a first job can depend on the right match between the paralegal's personality and expectations and the personality and atmosphere of the law firm.

Government Employers

Thousands of paralegals are employed in all levels of government, including federal, state, and municipal. The federal government reports that it has more than 30,000 law-related positions for which paralegals may be qualified. Paralegals who work for the federal government are generally considered to be adequately paid and have great benefits. Paralegals usually qualify for a number of different types of positions, with varying titles, within the federal government. Some of these titles include Environmental Protection Specialist, Foreign Law Specialist, Intelligence Analyst, Civil Rights Analyst, Personnel Management Specialist, Paralegal Specialist, and Legal Clerk and Technician. The two positions most closely related to typical paralegal positions are the Legal Clerk/Technician series, which starts at a level GS-4, salary range between $15,171 and $19,725; and the Paralegal Specialist series, which starts at a level GS-5, salary range between $16,973 and $22,067. Descriptions of these positions are as follows:[4]

Legal Clerk and Technician Series

This series includes all classes of positions the duties of which are to perform or supervise legal clerical or technical work not classifiable in any other series in the Legal and Kindred Group, GS-900. The work requires: (1) a specialized knowledge of legal documents and processes; and (2) the ability to apply established instructions, rules, regulations, precedents, and procedures pertaining to legal activities.

Paralegal Specialist Series

This series includes positions which involve paralegal work not requiring professional legal competence [not requiring a law degree] where such work is of a type not classifiable in some other series. The work requires discretion and independent judgment in the application of specialized knowledge of particular laws, regulations, precedents, or agency practice based thereon. The work includes such activities as (a) legal research, analyzing legal decisions, opinions, rulings, memoranda, and other legal material, selecting principles of law, and preparing digests of the points of law involved; (b) selecting, assembling, summarizing, and compiling substantive information on statutes, treaties, contracts, other legal instruments and specific legal subjects; (c) case preparation for civil litigation, criminal law proceedings or agency hearings, including the collection, analysis, and evaluation of evidence, e.g. as to fraud and fraudulent, and other irregular activities or violations of laws; (d) analyzing facts and legal questions presented by personnel administering specific Federal Laws, answering the questions where they have been settled by interpretations of applicable legal provisions, regulations, precedents, and agency policy, and in some instances preparing informative and instructional material for general use; (e) adjudicating applications or cases on the basis of pertinent laws, regulations, policies, and precedent decisions; or (f) performing other paralegal duties. Work in this series may or may not be performed under the direction of a lawyer.

Application for employment with the federal government is made either through the United States Office of Personnel Management, or directly to the hiring agency. Additional information concerning federal jobs for paralegals can be found in *The Paralegal's Guide to U.S. Government Jobs*, available from Federal Reports, 1010 Vermont Avenue NW, Suite 408, Washington, DC 20005; (202) 293-3311.

The work of paralegals employed by the government is as diverse as the administrative agencies that employ them. In addition to the many federal positions available, state and county governments often have many opportunities. More information on state and local government employment can be obtained by contacting the appropriate government personnel office in your area.

Corporate Employers

In addition to law firms and governmental agencies, corporate legal departments are a major employer of paralegals. Roughly 20 percent of all employed paralegals work in corporate law departments. Corporate law departments tend to have low turnover, and paralegals working within corporations generally report high job satisfaction.[5] Some of the reasons for high job satisfaction are that corporate law departments typically offer better pay and benefits than law firms do. In addition, paralegals within a corporate law department do not have billing requirements and are usually not required to put in much overtime. Finally, there may be more advancement opportunities for paralegals employed by corporate legal departments. Even with all the advantages offered by corporations, many paralegals would not give up the fast pace and excitement unique to private law firms. Corporate legal departments may be considered more slow-paced, and paralegals who work within them are often expected to perform administrative functions not required of paralegals within large law firms.

A new national association of corporate paralegals is currently being formed to meet

THE SMALL LAW FIRM	
Advantages	*Disadvantages*
More variety in work	Fewer resources available
Lower billing requirements are common	Lower salaries are common
More congenial, relaxed working atmosphere	Fewer benefits are typically offered
	May not offer the fast-paced, exciting atmosphere associated with large firms
THE LARGE LAW FIRM	
Advantages	*Disadvantages*
Higher pay is common	Overspecialization
Better benefits are usually offered	High billable hour requirements
Vast resources in law firm	Possible stressful working conditions
Exciting fast-paced atmosphere	

Paralegals indicate that there are both advantages and disadvantages in small and large law firms. It is important to determine which size law firm you consider most rewarding.

the specific needs of paralegals employed by corporate legal departments. The American Corporate Legal Assistant Association (ACLAA) is forming in Houston, Texas, but its founders hope to have local chapters throughout the United States soon.

Freelance Paralegals

Freelance paralegals offer their services to law firms, corporate legal departments, and the public. Paralegals who sell their services directly to the public are often referred to as **legal technicians**. Freelance paralegals enjoy versatility and a certain amount of independence in their work. However, freelancing does have its drawbacks. Success as a freelance paralegal often depends on the paralegal's experience, technical skills, marketing skills, contacts, and the market for the services. Freelance paralegals are usually specialists in one or more areas of law; commonly, freelance paralegals specialize in complex litigation, probate, or corporate law. Legal technicians are restricted in the types of services they can provide by state statutes concerning the unauthorized practice of law and by ethical considerations.

Other Paralegal Employers

In addition to working for traditional paralegal employers and freelancing, there are alternative paths that paralegals can follow. During the 1980s and 1990s, many corporations and law firms instituted hiring freezes that left them in need of additional paralegal help when the firm or corporation was exceptionally busy. Temporary paralegal agencies have filled this need well. Many paralegals enjoy the flexible scheduling and variety available by working through temporary employment agencies. Other paralegals have found employment with nontraditional paralegal employers such as nonprofit agencies and legal clinics.

Paralegal Specialties

Because of the complexity of the practice of modern law, most paralegals specialize in one area of law. The majority of paralegals specialize in litigation,

---

BALLENTINESBALLENTINESBALLENTINESBALLENTINESBALLENTINESBALLENTINESBALLENTINESBALLENTINESBALLENTINESBALLENTINESBALLENTINESBALLENTINESBALLENTINESBALLENTINESBALLENTINESBALLENTINES

freelance paralegal   A self-employed paralegal who offers his or her services to law firms, corporate legal departments, or the public.

legal technician   A self-employed paralegal who offers services directly to the public, without the supervision of an attorney.

TOP TEN PARALEGAL EMPLOYERS AMONG FEDERAL AGENCIES
1. Department of Justice
2. Department of Health and Human Services
3. U.S. Court System
4. Department of Treasury
5. Department of the Army
6. Department of Transportation
7. Department of the Navy
8. Department of Labor
9. Department of State
10. Department of Energy

Examples of activities performed by administrative law paralegals include ensuring that corporations comply with labor and employment standards, reviewing health care claims by veterans, and evaluating environmental impact statements for nuclear storage facilities.

corporate law, or real estate. This section includes a brief description of several areas in which paralegals may specialize.

General Litigation

There is an abundance of work for paralegals in the area of litigation. Litigation paralegals can work in smaller law firms, where they are often an integral part of the entire litigation process, or they may specialize further in a certain area of litigation within larger law firms.

The duties of litigation paralegals often include the following:

Prelitigation Fact Investigation

1. Interviewing clients
2. Interviewing witnesses
3. Obtaining statements from witnesses
4. Gathering and reviewing evidence (police reports, photographs, etc.)
5. Organizing and indexing documentary evidence
6. Researching factual and legal issues

Commencing Litigation

1. Researching the substantive law of cases
2. Drafting pleadings
3. Coordinating service of process
4. Reviewing pleadings from opposing parties
5. Drafting motions
6. Preparing orders after motions

Discovery

1. Drafting written forms of discovery (interrogatories, requests to produce, requests for admissions)
2. Assisting clients in complying with discovery requests

ADVANTAGES AND DISADVANTAGES TO WORKING IN A CORPORATE LEGAL DEPARTMENT	
Advantages	*Disadvantages*
+ Better pay than average law firm	− Work may be more specialized and less interesting
+ Better benefits than law firms	− Expected to perform more administrative duties
+ No billing requirements	− May be slow-paced compared to law firms
+ No overtime usually required	
+ More advancement opportunities	

Twenty percent of the paralegals employed in corporate legal departments feel there are both advantages and disadvantages to their roles.

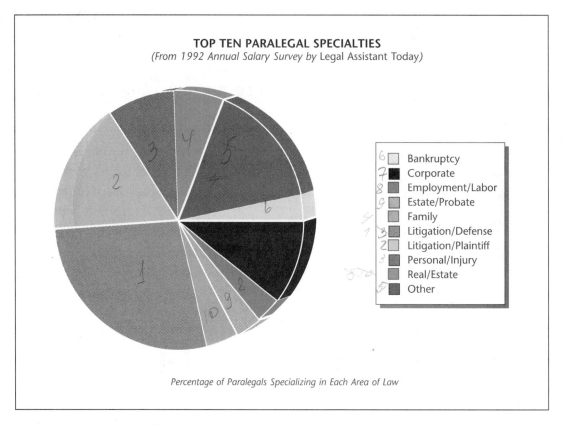

TOP TEN PARALEGAL SPECIALTIES
(From 1992 Annual Salary Survey by Legal Assistant Today)

Legend:
- Bankruptcy
- Corporate
- Employment/Labor
- Estate/Probate
- Family
- Litigation/Defense
- Litigation/Plaintiff
- Personal/Injury
- Real/Estate
- Other

Percentage of Paralegals Specializing in Each Area of Law

Top Ten Paralegal Specialties Nearly 27% of paralegals specialize in defense litigation. Bankruptcy, employment and labor, estate and probate law offices each employ about 3% of all paralegals. (Adapted from the 1993 Annual Salary Survey by *Legal Assistant Today*.)

3. Reviewing discovery obtained from opposing parties
4. Preparing clients for depositions
5. Digesting and summarizing depositions

Pretrial

1. Researching and recommending possible expert witnesses
2. Drafting briefs
3. Assisting with preparation of questions for jury selection
4. Drafting pretrial motions
5. Preparing trial notebooks

Trial

1. Organizing files and evidence for trial
2. Serving witnesses with subpoenas
3. Interviewing witnesses
4. Preparing the client
5. Drafting jury instructions
6. Drafting proposed judgments
7. Assisting with research and preparation of trial briefs
8. Preparing and organizing trial exhibits
9. Assisting attorneys during trial

Posttrial

1. Researching possible posttrial motions
2. Drafting posttrial motions
3. Drafting notices of appeal and requests for transcripts
4. Assisting with research and writing of appellate briefs

Miscellaneous

1. Maintaining firm's calendaring system
2. Organizing client files
3. Assisting with computerization of litigation
4. Preparing documents associated with enforcing judgments

Special skills that aid in a successful career as a litigation paralegal include interviewing skills, written and verbal communication skills, and organizational and analytical skills for reviewing and organizing evidence and pleadings. Legal research skills and computer proficiency are also very important to litigation paralegals.

Personal Injury (Plaintiff)

Personal injury is a branch of litigation that deals with actual injury to the person, typically resulting from an automobile accident or some other injury stemming from the negligence of another. Paralegals who work for plaintiff personal injury attorneys work with the attorneys to represent individuals who have been injured. Because

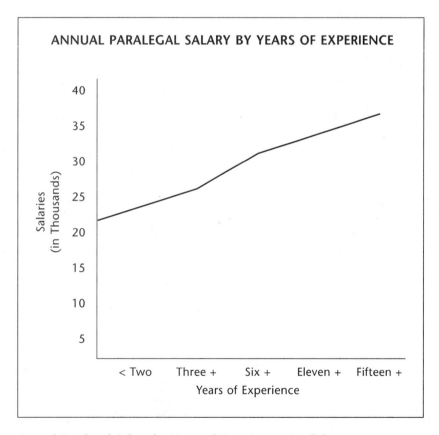

Annual Paralegal Salary by Years of Experience Paralleling most occupations, as paralegals gain more experience, their salaries rise.

this type of action frequently results in litigation, paralegals who specialize in personal injury often perform the same duties as general litigation paralegals. In addition, the personal injury paralegal may perform the following duties:

1. Interviewing clients to ascertain the extent of their injuries and to obtain consents for receiving medical information
2. Obtaining medical reports from doctors, hospitals, and other medical facilities
3. Obtaining reports regarding wage loss
4. Collecting other information concerning a client's out-of-pocket expenses stemming from the accident
5. Researching pertinent state laws concerning negligence and personal injury
6. Obtaining insurance information from opposing counsel

Skills important to the personal injury paralegal include all those important to the litigation paralegal plus a good knowledge of medical terminology. In addition, the personal injury paralegal may need a special ability to communicate with and interview individuals who have been (sometimes severely) injured.

Personal Injury (Defense)

Whereas personal injury paralegals who work on the plaintiff side work with the attorneys representing the injured party, the personal injury paralegal on the defense side works to represent the party who has been accused of the negligence causing the injury. In a personal injury suit, the defendant will often be covered by automobile or some other type of insurance, and this coverage usually includes legal defense. Personal injury defense paralegals may be employed by attorneys who represent insurance companies, either in private law firms or as in-house counsel. In addition to general litigation duties, personal injury defense paralegals may perform the following tasks:

1. Interviewing clients and witnesses to determine the facts of cases
2. Scheduling medical examinations of plaintiffs by doctors chosen by the defendants' attorneys
3. Reviewing insurance policies to determine the extent of coverage
4. Reviewing medical information and information concerning a plaintiff's expenses stemming from the accident
5. Reviewing police reports and witness statements

Paralegals working in the personal injury defense area need all of the skills required of other litigation and personal injury paralegals.

Workers' Compensation

The work of paralegals who specialize in workers' compensation matters resembles the work of personal injury paralegals in many respects, because workers' compensation involves personal injury. However, workers' compensation matters are not heard within the court system. Instead, they are heard by the Workers' Compensation Appeals Board, which has its own rules and regulations. Like other administrative agencies, in many states the Workers' Compensation Appeals Board allows paralegals to appear before it on behalf of clients, so long as the clients agree. Therefore, workers' compensation is an area where experienced, specialized paralegals are utilized to the fullest extent. The duties typically performed by a workers' compensation paralegal may include:

1. Interviewing clients
2. Obtaining medical information
3. Coordinating investigations regarding on-the-job accidents
4. Drafting pleadings and other documents
5. Interviewing potential witnesses

Workers' compensation paralegals require the same skills as most general litigation paralegals and personal injury paralegals. In addition, workers compensation paralegals who appear before the Workers' Compensation Appeals Board must have the ability to present themselves in a clear, concise, and professional manner before the Board.

Criminal Law (Defense)

Criminal law defense paralegals generally work for law firms or sole practitioners that specialize in criminal law, as well as for public defenders' offices and local, state, and federal agencies. Duties performed by criminal law defense paralegals may include:

1. Interviewing clients to determine facts relating to their cases
2. Reviewing police reports and other reports provided by prosecutors
3. Obtaining statements from witnesses to alleged crimes
4. Assisting with all aspects of discovery, including police reports and search warrants
5. Assisting with pretrial and trial procedures
6. Researching legal and factual issues
7. Assisting clients with obtaining information concerning bail
8. Organizing files and evidence for trial
9. Assisting with client preparation for trial
10. Assisting attorneys during trial
11. Researching and drafting posttrial motions
12. Drafting posttrial motions
13. Maintaining tickler files to remind attorneys and clients of important court dates and other deadlines

Skills important to criminal law paralegals who specialize in defense work include the ability to communicate well, both orally and in writing. The criminal law paralegal must have the ability to effectively interview clients and witnesses. The criminal law paralegal must also be able to perform detailed legal research on issues of law. An understanding of the court system and criminal procedures is critical to a criminal law defense paralegal.

In all areas of law, confidentiality is of utmost importance, but in criminal law it is especially so, and the paralegal must accept this responsibility. The criminal law defense paralegal must be able to put aside personal feelings and work *for* the client.

Criminal Law (Prosecution)

Criminal law paralegals who work in the prosecution area typically work for state or federal agencies in the office of the prosecutor. The duties typically performed by criminal law paralegals for the prosecution include:

1. Interviewing witnesses
2. Drafting complaints
3. Assisting with pretrial and trial procedures
4. Assisting crime victims by giving referrals to appropriate government agencies
5. Drafting subpoenas
6. Cataloging and preparing exhibits for trial

As with criminal law paralegals who specialize in the defense area, criminal law paralegals for the prosecution must have excellent interviewing, communication, and research skills.

Corporate Law

Corporate law paralegals typically work in the legal department of a corporation, but they may also work to serve several corporate clients in law firms that specialize in corporate law. The duties performed by corporate law paralegals often include:

1. Drafting all forms of corporate documents
2. Reviewing and updating corporate minute books
3. Incorporating and dissolving corporations
4. Preparing foreign qualification documents

5. Assisting with mergers and acquisitions

6. Assisting with compliance with SEC rules and regulations

7. Researching blue sky laws

Skills important to a successful career as a corporate paralegal include an ability to research corporate law and draft corporate documents with precision and clarity. Corporate paralegals must have a good understanding of business and finance as well. In addition, corporate paralegals must be very detail-oriented and have good organizational skills.

Partnership Law

Few paralegals specialize solely in partnership law, but often it is an integral part of the corporate paralegal's work. For paralegals, working in partnership law often involves several of the following duties:

1. Researching partnership law

2. Drafting partnership agreements

3. Overseeing the execution of partnership agreements

4. Drafting amendments to partnership agreements

5. Drafting partnership resolutions

Paralegals who work in the partnership area must be able to draft accurate and concise documentation and to perform thorough research. They must have the ability to read and understand financial statements.

Labor Law

Labor law is the area of law governing such matters as hours of work, minimum wages, unemployment insurance, and collective bargaining. Paralegals who work in this area may work for legal departments of unions, administrative agencies such as the National Labor Relations Board or the Equal Employment Opportunities Commission, or similar state agencies. Other paralegals who specialize in labor law work for law firms that represent private citizens in connection with labor law matters. Their duties may include:

1. Interviewing clients

2. Researching and compiling data for collective bargaining negotiations

3. Attending bargaining negotiations between labor and management

4. Preparing for hearings before administrative agencies such as the National Labor Relations Board

5. Interviewing witnesses in employment discrimination matters

6. Assisting with litigation involving labor law matters

Employee Benefits

Employers may elect any one of a wide variety of employee benefit plans to compensate their employees in addition to salaries. Some of these plans include pension plans, profit-sharing plans, stock option plans, and employee stock ownership plans. Many of these plans are covered under the Employee Retirement Income Security Act of 1974 (ERISA) and must comply with certain restrictions. Paralegals are often involved in drafting and administering employee benefit plans. Some of their specific duties include:

1. Drafting employee benefit plans

2. Drafting summary plan descriptions

3. Submitting employee benefit plans and supplemental documents to the Internal Revenue Service for approval

4. Assisting with the administration of employee benefit plans

BALLENTINESBALLENTINESBALLENTINESBALLENTINESBALLENTINESBALLENTINESBALLENTINESBALLENTINESBALLENTINESBALLENTINESBALLENTINESBALLENTINESBALLENTINESBALLENTINES

labor laws   Federal and state statutes and administrative regulations that govern such matters as hours of work, minimum wages, unemployment insurance, safety, and collective bargaining.

5. Drafting notices concerning employee benefit plans

Paralegals who work in this area must have excellent writing and organizational skills.

Bankruptcy Law

Bankruptcy has become a big business in recent years. *Bankruptcy* is the system under which a debtor may come into court or be brought into court by creditors, either seeking to have the debtor's assets administered and sold for the benefit of creditors and to be discharged from those debts (a straight bankruptcy), or to have those debts reorganized. Paralegals who specialize in bankruptcy work for law firms that act as trustees in bankruptcy court or represent the creditors or debtors. Paralegals who work in bankruptcy may perform the following duties:

Acting as Trustee

1. Preparing notices to banks and financial institutions requesting the release of debtors' funds
2. Coordinating appraisals of debtors' assets
3. Preparing newspaper notices regarding sale of debtors' assets
4. Preparing accounts of property sold
5. Reviewing claims for distribution of funds

Debtor

1. Interviewing clients regarding their financial situation
2. Drafting bankruptcy petitions
3. Preparing for first meeting of creditors
4. Attending hearings in bankruptcy

Creditor

1. Preparing claims of creditor
2. Filing claims of creditor with bankruptcy court

Paralegals who work in this area must have a thorough knowledge of bankruptcy court procedures and must be familiar with the forms required for bankruptcies.

Family Law

Paralegals who specialize in family law typically work in law firms that specialize in family law, or they work for administrative agencies, often serving as advocates for individuals experiencing financial hardships. The duties of a family law paralegal may include:

1. Interviewing clients
2. Completing client questionnaires from information gleaned in initial interviews
3. Researching family law and procedures
4. Coordinating service of process
5. Reviewing pleadings received on behalf of clients
6. Drafting pleadings and other legal documents, including summonses, petitions, motions, orders, stipulations, and decrees
7. Preparing for and attending depositions
8. Preparing deposition summaries
9. Preparing interrogatories
10. Assisting with preparation of answers to interrogatories
11. Assisting with pretrial preparation
12. Assisting with trial preparation

Excellent interpersonal skills are of great importance to the family law paralegal, who often must deal with emotional clients. Clients often regard paralegals as more approachable and less intimidating than the attorneys the paralegals work for, and will talk more freely with family law paralegals concerning their cases. Family law paralegals must deal with clients with a mix of empathy, objectivity, and professionalism. In addition to interpersonal skills, paralegals must have excellent organizational skills and the ability to communicate well in writing. Much of the family law paralegal's job involves keeping track of important court dates and other deadlines and drafting documents and correspondence.

Estate Planning and Probate

Estate planning and probate paralegals typically work in law firms that specialize in this area. However, a number of probate paralegals also work for administrative agencies, probate court services, and bank trust departments. The work of an estate planning and probate paralegal may include several of the following duties:

Estate Planning

1. Interviewing clients to determine facts relating to their potential estates
2. Reviewing financial information submitted by clients and preparing checklists for attorney review
3. Preparing drafts of wills, trusts, and related documents
4. Obtaining information regarding insurance policies and ensuring that the proper beneficiaries are designated to complement the estate plan
5. Overseeing the proper execution of wills by clients and witnesses
6. Preparing summaries of wills and other documents for clients

Probate

1. Attending client conferences to explain proper procedures following the death of a client or family member
2. Preparing and filing (when necessary) probate forms
3. Assisting with collection and inventory of the assets of the deceased, including contents of safety deposit boxes, bank accounts, and all real and personal property
4. Assisting with the clerical, bookkeeping, and accounting functions relating to estates
5. Preparing estate tax returns

6. Reviewing claims against estates
7. Assisting with the liquidation of assets
8. Maintaining communications with clients to advise them of the progress of settling the estate

The estate-planning paralegal must have effective interviewing skills to help gather all pertinent information regarding the client's estate. In addition, the estate-planning paralegal must possess the clear and concise writing skills associated with drafting wills, trusts, and other estate-planning documents.

The paralegal who specializes in probate must be able to communicate effectively with individuals who may be experiencing considerable grief. The probate process can take several months and sometimes may even take years. Because the paralegal often is the probate client's main link to the law firm, it is important that the paralegal communicate frequently and effectively with the client to assure that there are no misunderstandings. The probate paralegal must also have an ability to work with numbers. Paralegals are often responsible for the day-to-day bookkeeping matters concerning the estate, as well as the more complex accounting matters concerning estate tax returns.

Real Estate

Real estate paralegals can work in several different settings. They may work for law firms that specialize in real estate, they may work for title companies, realty companies, construction companies, or corporations that invest in real estate. The tasks common to real estate paralegals in all of these areas may include:

1. Researching zoning ordinances and other laws relating to the transfer and use of real estate
2. Preparing land sale contracts
3. Ordering title work from title companies
4. Reviewing abstracts or certificates of title
5. Preparing maps of property based on the legal description of property

6. Preparing drafts of title opinions
7. Scheduling closings
8. Preparing deeds
9. Preparing notes
10. Preparing mortgages
11. Reviewing documents prepared by other parties
12. Providing lenders with necessary documentation
13. Attending closings to assist with document review and execution and the transfer of funds
14. Reviewing title work
15. Disbursing funds
16. Filing the necessary documentation after closings

Real estate paralegals must be familiar with real estate law in the geographic areas in which they work. In addition, a successful real estate paralegal must be very detail-oriented and have the ability to communicate in writing very effectively and precisely. Organizational skills can be equally important to real estate paralegals, who often find themselves working on commercial real estate transactions that involve numerous documents.

Intellectual Property

The intellectual property paralegal typically works for a law firm that specializes in copyright, patent, and/or trademark law, or a company that deals with these legal matters on an ongoing basis, such as a manufacturer of patented devices that are sold under a trademark. The duties commonly performed by an intellectual property paralegal include:

Copyrights

1. Assisting with the preparation and filing of copyright applications
2. Researching pertinent copyright laws
3. Researching current copyrights

4. Researching possible copyright infringements
5. Assisting with all aspects of copyright infringement litigation

Trademarks

1. Researching existing trademarks
2. Assisting with the preparation and filing of trademark registration applications
3. Researching pertinent state and federal trademark laws
4. Assisting with all aspects of litigation dealing with trademarks

Patents

1. Researching existing patents
2. Assisting with the preparation and filing of patent applications
3. Assisting with patent infringement litigation

The skills that are important to intellectual property paralegals include excellent communication skills, both written and verbal. Forms completed by the paralegal must communicate with great detail and accuracy the exact intent of the client.

The intellectual property paralegal must also be a very organized individual. He or she is often responsible for handling numerous reports, applications, and exhibits for several clients at one time. Critical deadlines must be kept track of precisely. Intellectual property often must be protected internationally and the paralegal may be responsible for maintaining intellectual property rights around the world.

Finally, the intellectual property paralegal must have the ability to accurately research both federal and state laws, as well as international laws, dealing with copyrights, trademarks, and patents.

Administrative Law

Administrative law paralegals work for administrative agencies in federal, state, or local government. In addition, administrative law paralegals may work for private-practice law firms that specialize in the representation of clients in administrative law matters. The work of administrative law paralegals is especially diverse because administrative agencies themselves deal with so many different aspects of the law. Some duties typically performed by administrative law paralegals include:

1. Collecting information from citizens
2. Handling complaints and questions from citizens
3. Researching pertinent statutes and administrative rules and regulations
4. Appearing at administrative hearings
5. Drafting numerous types of legal documents

The skills important to successful administrative law paralegals will depend on the type of agencies or law firms they work for. Administrative law paralegals in all areas of law must be proficient at legal research. In addition, they must be able to communicate the results of their research in an effective manner, both verbally and in writing.

General Practice

Although more and more attorneys specialize in one or more areas of law, the general practice law firm has not become extinct. Many attorneys still have general practices that serve clients in a multitude of areas, and many paralegals are employed by them. Paralegals who work in general-practice law firms often perform several of the duties performed by paralegals who specialize in only one area of law, especially family law, estate planning and probate, real estate, bankruptcy, and criminal law.

Other Areas of Specialty

There are numerous other areas of law in which paralegals may specialize; in fact, paralegals may specialize in any area of law that exists. Over the years, the practice of law has become more and more specialized, with new specialties being introduced all the time. Computer law is one example of an expanding area of practice that did not exist just a few years ago. Some other areas of paralegal specialties include:

Admiralty law	Entertainment law
Advertising law	Environmental law
Antitrust law	Immigration law
Banking law	Insurance law
Charitable trusts	Military law
Collections law	Prisoners' Rights
Consumer protection	Securities
Contract law	Tax law

Alternative Careers for Paralegals

In general, paralegals must have a good basic understanding of the law in the state and local area in which they work, and of the legal system of the United States. Paralegals must be able to research, analyze, organize, and communicate well in writing and verbally, and, in addition, they must be very detail-oriented. The training that paralegals receive and the experience they gain can often be combined with the skills required of them and put to use in related careers. Individuals who have paralegal training may find positions as legislative assistants, librarians, law office administrators, private investigators, and numerous other jobs that utilize their unique skills and experience. They may also work in the growing legal publishing or legal services and product marketing industries.

Popular Areas of Specialization for the 1990s and Beyond

The needs of the legal community are constantly changing, as are the needs for paralegal specialists. Changing trends in society and law lead to certain paralegal specialties that are in more demand than others. Obviously, paralegals who specialize in those areas are in a better position when it comes to job selection, job security, and higher compensation. Some of the high-demand areas of specialization for the 1990s and beyond are bankruptcy, environmental law, intellectual property law, and litigation case management.

Hiring trends also vary in different geographical locations within the United States. According to responses of some of the top paralegal recruiters in the country in one *Legal Assistant Today* article,[6] some of the highest demand areas of specialization are as follows:

East

Boston, Massachusetts

- In-house positions in corporations and financial institutions
- Both state and federal securities
- Trusts and estates
- Real estate
- Intellectual property
- Bankruptcy
- Litigation support

Hartford, Connecticut

- Residential real estate
- Commercial litigation
- Some real estate foreclosures
- Temporary litigation positions

New York, New York

- Real estate
- Commercial litigation
- Environmental Litigation

Atlanta, Georgia

- Environmental
- Patent and trademark
- Employee benefits
- Litigation support managers
- Commercial litigation

- General in-house corporate
- Immigration
- Temporary positions for large litigation projects
- Bankruptcy

Midwest

Chicago, Illinois

- Claims-based litigation
- Intellectual property
- Environmental
- Music publishing disputes
- Reinsurance
- Asbestos claims
- Environmental claims

Dallas, Texas

- Intellectual property
- Labor
- In-house law departments at corporations
- Personal injury
- Workers' compensation

West

Santa Monica, California

- Intellectual property
- Bankruptcy
- Environmental
- Paralegals with a computer background or computer skills

San Francisco, California

- Multiple skills, multiple practice areas
- Real estate

Paralegal Salaries and Benefits

There is a wide range of salaries and benefits among paralegals. A paralegal's salary generally takes into account:

1. Experience
2. Education

3. Area of law
4. Type of employer
5. Geographic location

This section discusses how these factors affect the average salaries of paralegals across the country. The statistics used in this section are taken from the 1993 salary survey by *Legal Assistant Today* magazine, based on the responses of paralegals from across the nation.

Salaries by Years of Experience

As the paralegal's experience increases, so does his or her salary. Recent statistics indicate that the average annual salary of a paralegal with more than 15 years of experience is approximately 36 percent higher than that of paralegals with 0–2 years of experience.

Salaries by Education and Training

Education is also a factor in the salary of a paralegal. Paralegals who have a bachelor's degree, which is a requirement of some law firms and corporations, tend to earn a slightly higher annual salary than those who have associate degrees. According to the 1993 *Legal Assistant Today* salary survey, the average annual salary of a paralegal with a bachelor's degree was $29,343, in comparison to $26,933, the average salary of a paralegal with an associate degree.

Salaries by Area of Law

The area of law in which a paralegal specializes can also greatly affect his or her earning potential. In recent years, the highest paid positions tended to be in the areas of corporate law, employment/labor law, environmental law, real estate, and litigation defense. The area of family law is consistently near the bottom of the pay scale.

Salaries by Type of Employer

Not only does the type of law practiced have a bearing on the paralegal's salary, but the type of employer he or she works for can also significantly affect the paralegal's salary. Paralegals employed by corporations generally tend to earn the highest salaries, whereas those employed by the government sector typically earn the lowest. According to the 1993 *Legal Assistant Today* annual salary survey, the average annual salaries of paralegals employed by corporations was $32,939, followed by those employed by private law firms, at $29,071, and those employed by the public sector/government, at $27,954.

Salaries by Geographic Location

Just as the cost of living varies by geographic location, so does the average paralegal salary. In addition to the cost of living, other factors, such as demand and the type of law practiced, also affect the average salary in a given geographical area. Typically, the highest salaries are offered in the northeast states of Connecticut, Delaware, Maine, Massachusetts, New Hampshire, New Jersey, New York, Pennsylvania, Rhode Island, and Vermont, and in the states of California, Nevada, and Hawaii.

Paralegal Benefits

A vast array of benefits are offered by employers of paralegals. Traditionally the best benefits have been in government jobs and within corporate legal departments. Small law firms have typically been unable to offer competitive benefits, although in recent years some small law firms have offered unique benefits, such as flexible hours, that large law firms cannot always match.

According to a survey of 630 paralegals throughout the United States, taken by *Legal Assistant Today* magazine,[7] the benefit most commonly offered to paralegals is health insurance. More than 90 percent of the respondents to the survey stated that they received health insurance benefits from their employers. Following health insurance, the most commonly offered benefits were: employer contributions to retirement plans, travel allowances, life insurance, personal business cards, profit sharing, and paid

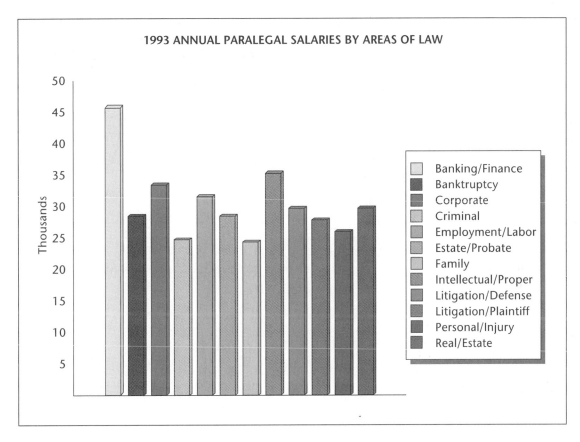

1993 Annual Paralegal Salaries by Area of Law Banking and finance paralegals, on average, command the greatest annual salaries. Although they may earn just under $25,000 per year, many family law paralegals consider the salary well worth the ever-changing drama of that specialty.

continuing legal education. The average number of days of vacation per year was reported to be 13, and the average number of sick days allowed annually was 9.

What Potential Employers Look For

Your first paralegal position is almost always the most difficult to come by. Paralegal employers usually prefer to hire experienced paralegals for most positions. However, there are ways to gain practical experience while completing your education. There are also ways to make yourself more attractive to paralegal employers who are willing to hire skilled, knowledgeable individuals with the right qualities but no experience. This section discusses some of the more important factors potential employers consider when hiring paralegals. In addition to a paralegal's education and experience, potential employers look for individuals who have good attitudes about work and about their careers. They want someone who will fit in well with the personality and culture of the firm or company and make a contribution to the organization as a whole.

Education Counts

At this time, no minimum educational requirements for paralegals have been set by law or state bar associations. In the past, many paralegals were legal secretaries who were trained in-house. In recent years, however, there appears to be a trend toward giving hiring preference to individuals who have graduated from four-year paralegal programs, or who have a related four-year degree plus a paralegal certificate. This is only an apparent trend, though, not a steadfast rule. The reputation of the school is also of importance to the potential employer. Although many of the best schools are approved by the American Bar Association, many other schools that are not ABA approved still have a fine reputation within the local legal community.

In addition to proof of graduation from a respected paralegal training program, many potential employers look for the following information regarding paralegal education in their prospective employees:

1. The student's grade point average
2. Courses taken
3. Extra scholastic activities in which the student participated
4. Participation in internship programs.

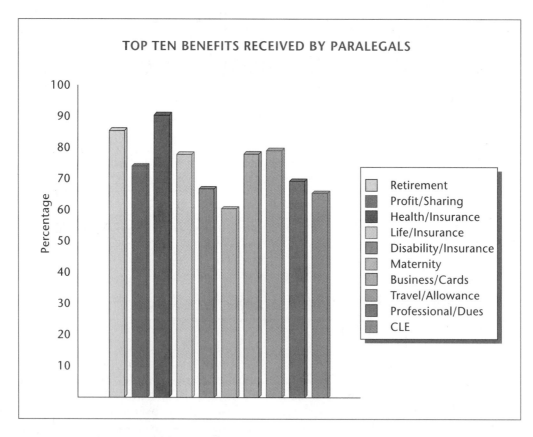

Top Ten Benefits Received by Paralegals   More than 90% of paralegals receive some sort of health insurance. About 60% receive business cards.

The Value of Practical Experience

The value of practical experience cannot be over-stressed. Many potential employers take the position that some aspects of paralegalism just cannot be learned in the classroom. Although it may seem difficult to get your initial paralegal experience, there are some ways for inexperienced paralegal students to gain experience before beginning a job search after graduation. The most common ways of gaining experience for students are internships, working temporary jobs, and working at entry-level positions within law firms or other related organizations.

Internships

Many paralegal programs offer paralegal internships to students who are nearing completion of their education. Often the students learn of opportunities through the paralegal programs or placement counseling offices in their schools. At other times, the paralegal student may be personally responsible for finding a position as an intern. Although paralegal internships usually do not pay well (if at all), they do offer many benefits to both the paralegal student and the potential employer. A paralegal internship can give the student a feel for what being a paralegal is really like. In addition, it will give the student some good practical experience and possible contacts for future employment. Paralegal internships frequently lead to permanent employment as a paralegal within the firm after graduation.

Working Temporary Positions

Working for temporary agencies is another way for a paralegal student to get a foot in the door. Temporary paralegal service agencies offer many positions that are considered to be entry-level, but work that students find through temporary agencies gives them practical experience and may possibly lead to permanent employment.

Entry-Level Positions with Potential Employers

Another route taken by some inexperienced paralegals is to take a position at a law firm, or with another potential employer, for which they may actually be overqualified. Law firms are often looking for individuals to fill entry-level positions such as case clerks or paralegal assistants. Paralegals with clerical experience may take a position as a legal secretary with the aim of moving into a paralegal position later. The paralegal who chooses this path to get a foot in the door should be candid and honest when taking the position, telling the hiring individual that the position is being accepted with the intention of moving up to a paralegal position when experience has been gained and a position is available within the firm. If you take an entry-level position with the intent of moving into a paralegal position, you should be careful to do the best job possible and not to let management forget what your goals are.

Beginning Your Job Search

When you begin your job search, there are two types of job sources: those that are advertised and those that are not. Some of the obvious places to begin looking for employment are with your school placement office, employment agencies, and in the classified ad sections of newspapers and other periodicals. There is, however, another type of opportunity, jobs that are never advertised to the public. Those positions can often be found by networking and by targeting specific paralegal employers.

School Placement Offices

School placement offices are a great place to begin looking for a job. Some schools boast of the percentage of paralegal graduates they place in jobs after graduation, and they are eager to keep that percentage high. The personnel within school placement offices often have an ongoing relationship with recruiters from corporations and law firms who appreciate their free service. They are in a good position to match individuals with particular jobs.

School placement offices can also be a valuable resource for experienced paralegals looking for a more advanced position. Experienced paralegals can often utilize the placement services of their alma maters when seeking employment.

Employment Agencies and Services

Employment agencies are also a valuable resource for those seeking employment as paralegals. Bar associations and paralegal associations often have their own employment agencies or placement services. In addition, private employment agencies that specialize in the placement of law office personnel operate in many cities.

Bar Associations and Paralegal Associations

Many state and local bar associations have their own employment agencies and services that specialize in the placement of law office personnel, including paralegals. These services may be free or charge a minimal fee. In addition, paralegal associations often offer their own job banks as a benefit to their members. Attorneys who are hiring paralegals often contact the local paralegal association to get the word out that they will be accepting résumés for a particular position.

Private Employment Agencies

There are a variety of private employment agencies in every major city in this country. These agencies may charge a fee to the individuals they place, or they may charge a fee to the employer who hires their candidates. Still other employment agencies are willing to negotiate the terms of payment as a condition of employment. Some employment agencies specialize in the placement of law firm personnel, including paralegals.

Newspapers and Other Periodicals

Your local newspaper is usually a good resource when seeking paralegal employment. Listings of available paralegal positions may be under "paralegal" or "legal assistant." Positions requiring paralegal skills may also be listed under various other titles. "Legal technician," "child support specialist," or "trademark specialist" are examples of some possibilities. Local bar association periodicals and other periodicals aimed at attorneys and law office personnel may also have classified ad sections that list paralegal positions. When answering a newspaper or periodical ad, be sure to follow the instructions in the ad. For example, when the ad requests résumés, send a résumé—do not call or appear in person.

Networking

Networking is an excellent way to get started in your paralegal career and to advance after you have some experience. *Networking* means getting out into the community and meeting people who share your background and interests. If you have the opportunity to get to know several paralegals and attorneys, you will have several contacts when you look for a job or need a personal reference. Paralegal associations are a great place for networking, and most associations accept student members. Joining a paralegal association allows you to meet and share concerns with other paralegals in your area. It can also lead to information about job opportunities that are never advertised. Paralegal and bar association continuing education seminars are also good places to meet individuals who share your interests. By attending seminars on topics that interest you, you can increase your knowledge in the field while forming future contacts. Performing voluntary work for legal clinics and other non-profit organizations can be very rewarding as well as a great way to gain experience and to network.

Targeting Potential Employers

Another approach to seeking paralegal employment is to target a specific law firm or group of firms or attorneys and to aggressively seek employment with those firms or corporations. If you have a specific law firm in mind that you would like to work for, you can call to find out the appropriate individual to whom to send your résumé and cover letter. Your résumé can be followed up by a telephone call a few days later. If you are willing to wait for an opening, let them know.

You may target specific firms by word of mouth—by talking with other paralegals who recommend the firms in which they are employed. Another approach is to target firms that specialize in a specific area of law. The *Martindale-Hubbell Law Directory* has a complete listing of all attorneys by state and city, including their names, addresses, and areas of specialty. Another source is the local news and newspapers. If you are interested in corporate law and mergers and acquisitions, you may want to target the legal departments of corporations that are in the news because of an upcoming merger or acquisition. If you are interested in a specific area of criminal law, you may want to target attorneys who are in the news because they are involved in highly visible criminal matters. Law firms that are involved in big projects and big cases may well be in need of additional paralegal help, and may have little time to act on that need.

Informational Interviews

After you have a list of potential employers to target, you may want to take your targeting strategy one step further by conducting informational interviews with the appropriate personnel managers from the law firms or corporations you have selected. An *informational interview* (in contrast to an employment interview) is an interview with the person responsible for hiring for an organization with the aim of obtaining general information about careers with the organization, even if no positions are currently available. Because of the time involved in informational interviews, this is an extraordinary measure that is not possible in every instance. Large law firms that have personnel departments and corporate personnel departments may be the most likely to grant informational interviews.

The informational interview can benefit the paralegal in at least three ways. First, the paralegal conducting the interview can gain valuable insight as to exactly what types of positions are or may become available within the firm or corporation and what qualifications the potential employer is looking for. Second, the informational interview is good practice for actual employment interviews as positions become available. Third, and probably most important, an informational interview could be a foot in the door when a position becomes available within the firm or corporation. An impressed personnel manager may remember an interested candidate with whom he or she has had an informational interview, and contact that individual for an employment interview when a position becomes available.

The interviewer at an informational interview is the paralegal; the interviewee is the personnel manager or the individual in charge of hiring for the organization. The questions put to the interviewee should include general questions about the organization, its practice, the number of paralegals it employs, the work it performs, its common practice for hiring paralegals, and the qualifications the organization looks for in potential paralegal employees.

The Résumé

How important is your résumé? Consider this: In a one- or two-page document, you have the opportunity to "sell" yourself to a potential employer. It may be the first step in a new career that could change your life. On the other hand, with a poorly written or constructed résumé, you will never get your foot in the door.

Some of the important factors that must be considered when preparing a résumé include its appearance, its content and style, and the items that often accompany a résumé—the cover letter, writing samples, and personal references.

Appearances

When you apply for a paralegal position, your résumé will usually be your first impression on a potential employer. First impressions are important! When a résumé lands on the desk of a busy attorney or law office administrator, who may have hundreds of résumés to review, it must have a neat, professional appearance even to get read.

Résumés should be no longer than one or two pages. They should be neatly typed or reproduced on high-quality bond paper—either white or another light color, not a bold or bright color. If possible, the résumé should be professionally printed. It should be carefully proofread several times. Enlist the help of a colleague or friend for this task. Many law firms have a collection of poorly written résumés containing typographical or grammatical errors that are maintained as a joke. Don't let your résumé become a joke!

Résumé Contents and Style

Your résumé is your opportunity to promote yourself, but you have only a maximum of two pages to do it in. Résumés must be concise, accurate, and to the point. Most résumés are prepared in a chronological style that contains the following sections:

Personal Information This section should include your name, address, and telephone number or numbers. It is not necessary to include personal information such as your height, weight, age, or marital status. Photographs are not recommended.

Career Objective This should be a specific objective to let your potential employer know that your objectives match the position being offered. If you are actively seeking two or more different types of positions, you may want to have more than one version of your résumé prepared, with appropriate career objectives for specific potential employers and jobs.

Work Experience This section is a description of your work experience, beginning with the most recent and working back in time. Usually, you need go back only two or three positions, unless you have earlier work experience that you would like to emphasize. Each entry in this section should include the dates that you were employed in that position, the title of your position, the name and address of your employer, and a brief job description. The job description you give at this point can be very important. Job descriptions should list your duties while emphasizing your accomplishments on the job. In addition, it may be appropriate at times to give a brief description of the company you worked for if it would not be apparent to your potential employer. Usually just one sentence will suffice. For example: "Investment Opportunities Incorporated is a multimillion-dollar real estate investment corporation." If your work experience is unrelated to the paralegal position you are applying for, stress any skills you have learned from those positions that could be helpful in a paralegal position. For example, if you have experience as an assistant manager in a restaurant, you might want to emphasize your organizational skills, your leadership skills, and your ability to manage others.

Educational Experience If you do not have impressive, pertinent work experience, but you do have a paralegal degree or certificate, your educational experience should be listed before your work experience. This section should include the name and address of each school you have attended since high school, the dates you attended that school, your graduation date or expected graduation date, any degrees or certificates awarded, and your major areas of study, including a short list of legal specialty classes that you would like to emphasize. You may also include your grade point average if you feel that it will work to your advantage, and any honors and distinctions that you have been awarded.

Special Skills and Qualities In this section you should list any special skills that may be pertinent to the position for which you are applying. Some of these skills may include:

1. Specific computer proficiencies
2. Foreign languages fluency
3. Sign language capability
4. Leadership and management qualities you possess

Memberships and Affiliations If you are a member of pertinent organizations, such as your state paralegal association, you may want to include that information as well.

Personal References and Transcripts Personal references and school transcripts should not be included in a résumé. However, you may want to note, at the end of your résumé, that such information is available upon request.

TIPS ON PREPARING A RÉSUMÉ
Prepare a separate résumé for each type of paralegal position you are applying for
One page is preferable—never more than two
Keep at least 3/4-inch margins
Use cover letter stationery that matches your résumé
Do not abbreviate
Use past tense for all previous activities. Use present tense for current ongoing activities
Use a "functional" résumé instead of a chronological résumé if there are gaps in your résumé that you do not choose to highlight
Do not list reasons for leaving past employment
Do not include past salary information or salary requirements
Never lie!

should never be in excess of two pages. If you have trouble fitting all the required information into two pages, you will have to be selective and leave out information that is not particularly relevant to the specific position you are applying for.

The importance of a good résumé cannot be overstated. If you are in doubt, seek help with your résumé. Numerous reference books on how to prepare résumés can be found in any bookstore or library. In addition, your school, your advisor, or a professional service can be of great help when assembling a résumé.

Customizing a Résumé

If there are gaps in your résumé that you do not care to point out to a potential employer, you may want to use a functional-style résumé instead of a chronological-style résumé. Again, your résumé

The Cover Letter

Your cover letter is yet another opportunity to sell yourself to a potential employer. It should be short and to the point. Résumés should always be accompanied by cover letters that include the following information:

1. The name of the position for which you are applying
2. How you learned of the position
3. A brief summary of your qualifications for the position
4. Why you would like the position
5. A request for an interview

Always be sure to obtain the correct name, title, and address of the individual to whom to send the letter.

JANET WILLIAMS
123 Elm Street
Maplewood, Minnesota 55117
(342) 435-2845

Objective: Position as a litigation paralegal in a litigation department of a large law firm.

Education

1992   The Paralegal Institute (ABA Approved); Minneapolis, MN
Legal Assistant Certificate Received May 1992
Legal Specialty Courses Completed: Fundamentals of American Law, Litigation, Advanced Litigation for Paralegals, Legal Writing and Research, Business Law, Contracts Law, Torts, Computers in the Law Firm

1991   University of Minnesota
Bachelor of Science in Business Administration Received June 1991

Work Experience

1992   Brown, McKinley and Johanson
Maplewood, Minnesota
Summer Legal Assistant Internship
Drafted pleadings and other legal documents; assisted with deposition summarizing

1989–1991 Top Temporary Service, Inc.
Minneapolis, Minnesota
Part-Time Temporary Clerical Worker
Assignments included: Secretarial—drafted and typed routine correspondence and reports; Receptionist—greeted clients, scheduled appointments, and handled busy switchboard

Professional Associations

Member of the Minnesota Association of Legal Assistants

References, transcripts, and writing samples available upon request.

Chronological Résumé   This résumé focuses first on educational background.

Writing Samples

Writing samples should not be included with your résumé and cover letter. However, if you get called for an interview, be sure to bring writing samples with you. Writing samples demonstrate both your ability to draft accurate and concise legal documents and your ability to communicate well to others. Therefore, your samples should include several different types of legal documents and pieces of correspondence or general writing.

NAME
ADDRESS
CITY, STATE, ZIP
AREA CODE/PHONE NUMBER

Objective: Legal Administrator for a Mid-sized Law Firm

Relevant Skills and Abilities

Management Expertise
- Train attorneys and support staff in the use of computers
- Monitor work flow for all support staff
- Hire and supervise management staff
- Research, organize and manage relocation of office

Computer Knowledge
- Installed Local Area Network computer system
- Research and purchase computer software
- Use WordPerfect 5.1, Westlaw, PC-File, MS-DOS, ZyIndex
- Wrote reference manual for hundreds of macros and dozens of forms and letters

Legal Experience
- Interview clients and witnesses
- Experience with federal and state courts
- Worked with collections, judgments, and real estate matters

Professional Experience

1985 to present   Smith & Smith, Oklahoma City, Oklahoma;
                   Systems and Office Manager/Paralegal
1980–1985   Legal secretary for various Oklahoma City small and
                   mid-sized law firms

Education

Bachelor of Arts Degree in Sociology, Stanford University; Stanford, California

Affiliations
- American Bar Association, Legal Assistants Division
- Oklahoma City Paralegal Association
- Association of Legal Administrators
- YWCA, National Fundraising Group
- Community Counsel Services, Board of Directors

Chronological Résumé This résumé focuses first on work experience. (Courtesy *Where Do I Go From Here?*, Estrin Publishing.)

You may use samples that were school assignments, and you may use samples gleaned from previous work experience. However, be sure to protect any former client's confidentiality by rewriting samples without actual names or personal information.

Personal References

You should also be prepared for interviews by having a list of personal references ready. Personal references should include the individual's name, address, and telephone number. Personal

---

JANET WILLIAMS
123 Elm Street
Maplewood, Minnesota 55117
(342) 435-2845

LITIGATION PARALEGAL

Education

The Paralegal Institute (ABA Approved); Minneapolis, MN
Legal Assistant Certificate
Legal Specialty Courses Completed: Fundamentals of American Law, Litigation, Advanced Litigation for Paralegals, Legal Writing and Research, Business Law, Contracts Law, Torts, Computers in the Law Firm

The University of Minnesota
Bachelor of Science in Business Administration
Grade Point Average 3.75

Work Experience

Brown, McKinley and Johanson
Maplewood, Minnesota
Legal Secretary
Assisted busy litigation attorney by drafting and typing correspondence, pleadings, and other legal documents; answered telepone calls from clients; scheduled depositions and other appointments; prepared client bills

Special Skills

- Knowledge of all types of law office procedures
- Fluent in Spanish, written and spoken
- Knowledge of several word processing and accounting software programs, including WordPerfect and Lotus 1-2-3
- Excellent communication skills
- Excellent organizational skills

Professional Associations

Member of the Minnesota Association of Legal Assistants

References, transcripts, and writing samples available upon request.

The Functional Résumé   The functional résumé can be used to downplay gaps in your educational background or work experience.

references should be people that have worked with you, or possibly school instructors. Those from whom you want references should always be consulted before their names are given out. This will give them some time to think about what they would like to say to your prospective employer, instead of sounding surprised when they get the call.

JANET WILLIAMS
123 Elm Street
Maplewood, Minnesota 55117
(342) 435-2845

January 10, 1994

Ms. Linda Evert
Felton, Lindloff and Richards
348 Mendota Road
Clarksville, Ohio 012345

Dear Ms. Evert:

I am very interested in the position you had advertised in the *Ohio Times*. My résumé is enclosed for your consideration.

I am a recent graduate of the Paralegal Institute, an ABA-approved institution. I also have a Bachelor of Science Degree in Business Administration from the University of Minnesota. As you will note from my résumé, I have completed an internship working in the area of litigation. I feel that with my education and litigation experience, I could make a significant contribution to your firm.

Please call me at (342) 435-2845 to schedule an interview at your convenience. I look forward to hearing from you soon.

Sincerely,

Janet Williams

Janet Williams

Enclosure

The Résumé Cover Letter The cover letter must express your interest in the position and should include a brief biography. Always include a telephone number so the interviewer can contact you.

The Interview

When you get a call for an interview, the most important thing to remember is to be prepared. You can be prepared by doing your research, knowing what you want to say and how you want to say it, and dressing for the part. In addition, you must know how you want to handle the initial interview and the second interview, and how to follow up after an interview.

Do Your Research

When you get called for an interview, the first thing you should do to prepare yourself is to find out what you can about the law firm or corporation with which you are interviewing. If you are interviewing with a law firm, you may want to begin with *Martindale-Hubbell* to find out how many attorneys work for the firm, who the attorneys are, and what their specialties are. Local libraries can be of assistance when you are looking for information on corporations. If you know anyone within the firm or corporation, ask them about the organization and the position. You are not expected to know everything there is to know about a firm before attending an interview, but being somewhat familiar with the firm will help you to ask intelligent questions during the interview.

Know What You Want to Say

Rehearse the interview in your mind. Think about the questions typically asked during interviews and how you want to answer those questions. One commonly asked question that interviewees often have trouble answering is "Where do you want to be five years from now?" Even if you are unsure, it is better to have a tentative answer than none at all. Remember, no one is going to hold you to your answer five years from now.

Keep in mind the important things about yourself that you would like to convey during the interview. Also, it is a good idea to bring a list of questions with you so that you are assured of finding out everything you want to know about the potential employer before the interview is over.

Know How You Want to Say It

Almost as important as what you say in an interview is the manner in which you say it. Interviewers try to spot certain traits during interviews—many times subconsciously. If you are well-prepared with what you want to say about yourself and what you want to find out about the firm, you can focus on your manner during the interview. Some traits that you should try to display include:

- Professionalism
- Friendliness
- Honesty
- Poise
- Enthusiasm
- Excellent communication skills
- Initiative
- Intelligence
- Resourcefulness
- Assertiveness
- Excellent listening skills

Dress the Part

When applying for a paralegal position, dress like a paralegal. Dress like a paralegal who is going to the most important business meeting of his or her career. Be sure to allow extra time to get to the interview, especially if you do not know exactly where the firm or corporation is located. You may also want to stop in the rest room for one last mirror check before entering the office right on time (not too early). Before you leave for the interview, be sure you have everything you need (preferably in a professional-looking briefcase), including: directions on how

RESOURCES FOR RESEARCHING LAW FIRMS AND CORPORATIONS
Martindale-Hubbell Law Directory Information on law firms and all lawyers admitted to state bars in the United States
The American Law Guide Information on the top 200 law firms and major legal centers in the United States
Lawyers Register by Specialties and Field of Law Listing of U.S. attorneys by specialty
Paralegal's Guide to U.S. Government Jobs
Standard and Poor's Description of publicly held corporations and their records
State bar association directories Many state bar associations publish directories of all admitted attorneys
Who's Who in American Law
Directory of Corporate Counsel
Dun's Marketing Service Books

These references can be found in most public, college, and law school libraries.

to get to the office (if necessary), the name of the person you will be meeting with, your writing samples, your list of personal references, and your list of questions and topics that you would like to discuss during the interview.

Handling the Interview

Try to relax. When you are introduced to the interviewer, greet him or her with a smile and a handshake. The first impression you want to make is that of being friendly and professional. Try to focus on what the interviewer tells you, especially his or her name.

Everyone is nervous during job interviews, and every interviewer will understand and expect a certain amount of nervousness. Do not let it control you to the point where you are unable to answer questions or ask the questions you would like to ask. That is where being prepared comes in.

Typically the interviewer will begin by telling you about the firm or the corporation in general. You can show that you have researched the firm by asking pertinent questions about the firm at this point.

Next, the interviewer will usually tell you about the position you are applying for. He or she will probably ask questions about you and your background as they apply to the firm and the position. You may be introduced to others in the firm with whom you might be working.

Be as open and honest as possible with the interviewer, without being overbearing or overfamiliar. If the interviewer asks you a question that you are uncomfortable about answering, keep your answer short and to the point. Do not feel that you have to explain every detail.

You can best answer tough questions by being prepared for them. Do not lay blame for any past failures or complain about former employers. Following is a list of sample questions that are commonly asked at interviews:

1. Tell me about yourself.
2. Why do you feel that you are a good candidate for this position?
3. What are you looking for in a position?
4. What particular strengths do you have to offer this firm?
5. What life accomplishments are you most proud of? Why?
6. What are your weaknesses?
7. Why did you decide to become a paralegal?
8. Why did you leave your last position?
9. How do you cope with pressure on the job?
10. What were your favorite courses in school? Your least favorite? Why?
11. What were your grades in school?
12. What are your salary requirements?
13. What do you plan on doing five years from now? Ten years?
14. Are you available to work overtime?

Illegal Interview Questions

Some interview questions are illegal. For instance, it is illegal for employers to discriminate against potential employees by asking questions concerning the applicant's marital status, number of children or child-care situation, age, health, religion, or political affiliations. If you are asked an illegal question, you have several options. First, do not be rude. Perhaps the interviewer is inexperienced and the turn of the conversation caused him or her to ask an inappropriate question without any intention of breaking the law. Second, do not feel obliged to answer the question if you do not want to. One way to handle an inappropriate question is by answering with a relatively positive statement concerning yourself. For example, if the interviewer asks if you plan on having any children, you may respond by saying that you are committed to a full-time career. You need say nothing further.

Questions for the Interviewer

After the interviewer has finished giving you all of the prepared information about the firm or company and the position, and has finished asking you the pertinent questions, he or she will probably ask if you have any questions. This is the time to show the interviewer that you are prepared by referring to your list of prepared questions. You will probably find that most of your questions have been answered during the interviewing process. If not, be sure to ask your questions now. Your questions should focus on the position and the firm, leaving questions regarding salary and benefits for a second interview. Don't forget to give the interviewer your writing samples and personal references if he or she has not asked for them already.

Closing the Interview

Try to leave the interview on a positive note. If you are interested in the position, be sure to say so and to say why you are interested. Find out when the interviewer expects a decision to be made on hiring for the position. Usually, promising first interviews are followed by second interviews with the same individual or with other individuals within the firm or company. If you have received other job offers, or expect that you will be receiving other offers, be honest with the interviewer. If they know that you have received another offer, interviewers will often do what they can to speed up the decision-making process and not keep you waiting.

The Second Interview

Rarely is a paralegal hired after just one interview. Second interviews are common in most law firms and corporations. This is often a chance for attorneys and paralegals who will be working with the new hire to meet the best candidates. The second interview may be a lunch meeting with several individuals from the firm, or you may be introduced to several individuals in the office. The second interview is the time for discussion of such matters as pay, benefits, and any other questions not answered during the first interview. If you are offered a position at the second interview, do not feel obligated to give your answer on the spot. It is reasonable to ask for a couple of days to think the offer over (but don't take too long).

TIPS FOR A SUCCESSFUL INTERVIEW
Be sure to bring accurate directions to the office
Leave in time to get there a few minutes early
Be conscious of your body language. Don't display any outward signs of nervousness, such as fidgeting
Begin each interview with a smile and a handshake
Listen to and concentrate on what is being said
Be confident but realistic
Maintain appropriate eye contact
Leave salary negotiations for a second interview

Communication skills, both verbal and written, are essential for a job applicant as well as an employed paralegal.

Following Up

Your part of the interview is not over when you walk out the office door. Every interview should be followed up with a personal letter to the individual who interviewed you, thanking that individual for the time and consideration. Again, be sure to tell the interviewer that you are interested in the position.

JANET WILLIAMS
123 Elm Street
Maplewood, Minnesota 55117
(342) 435-2845

January 10, 1994

Ms. Linda Evert
Felton, Lindloff and Richards
348 Mendota Road
Clarksville, Ohio 012345

Dear Ms. Evert:

Thank you for meeting with me last week. I thoroughly enjoyed our meeting and the tour of your offices. I am very interested in the paralegal position we discussed.

I feel that my education and litigation experience would be a good fit with your firm, and that I would be able to make a strong contribution to your paralegal department.

I look forward to hearing from you soon regarding the position you have available.

Sincerely,

Janet Williams

Janet Williams

The Thank-You Letter A follow-up letter thanking the interviewers for their time, as well as reiterating your interest in the position, is thoughtful and professional.

Planning Your Career

Now that you know a little about the paralegal profession, it may be time for you to make a personal assessment. Is the paralegal profession for you? This first chapter has discussed several of the qualities and skills necessary to successful paralegals. Are these qualities you possess? Are they skills that you possess or feel confident that you can learn? Every successful career starts out with a plan, even though that plan is subject to frequent revision. This section reviews some of the skills and qualities that make a successful paralegal, to assist you with a self-assessment. In addition, it suggests some possible paths that you may want to incorporate into your short- and long-term plans.

Qualities and Skills of Successful Paralegals

Not everyone is cut out to be a paralegal. Successful paralegals often possess the following personality traits:

1. Common sense
2. Good judgment
3. Assertiveness
4. Diplomacy
5. Patience
6. Perseverance
7. Self-motivation
8. Confidence

If you feel that you have these personality traits, you may want to reexamine the skills that successful paralegals must possess:

1. Excellent organizational skills
2. Excellent writing skills
3. Good telephone etiquette
4. Analytical skills
5. Computer skills
6. Ability to prioritize

7. Ability to work under pressure
8. Knowledge of pertinent legal concepts and procedure
9. Ability to work well with others
10. Ability to work well with minimal supervision

If you do not currently possess all these skills, are they skills that you are interested in working to obtain?

Short-Range Plan

If you have decided on a career as a paralegal, you will need a plan. Your short-range plan may include finishing your education and obtaining your first paralegal position. Your plan should include strategies for both of these events. Your plan may also include several of the following:

1. A specific type of employer to target
2. A specific area of law on which to concentrate, with the aim of specialization
3. An alternate area of law for concentration and specialization
4. An internship or other means for gaining experience

Your plan should take into account all the factors discussed in this chapter.

Long-Range Plans

Even before you land your first paralegal position, you may want to have a long-range plan. Do you intend to be a paralegal for an extended period of time, or do you plan on using the position as a stepping stone? There are three basic paths to take to get ahead once your paralegal career has begun. You can become an expert and specialist in one area of law as a paralegal; you can seek to move into management; or you can work toward independence by becoming a freelance paralegal or legal technician.

Specialization

Many paralegals have made successful and rewarding careers by specializing in a particular area of law. You can become an expert in an area of law by taking as many courses as possible in the area, gaining as much practical experience as possible, and by taking available continuing education courses on the subject after graduation. If you specialize in an area that is in demand, your skills and experience will also be very much in demand. Many firms make it possible to move up through the ranks as a paralegal, by having differing levels of paralegals on staff, such as Paralegal Assistant, Junior Paralegal, Paralegal I, Paralegal II, and Senior Paralegal. Each level offers increasing responsibility and pay.

Management

Other paralegals have found rewarding careers in law office management positions or management positions within a corporation. If management fits into your long-range plans, you can begin by taking management courses within your school. After you have landed your first paralegal position, let your employer know your interest in management. Act like a manager. You may begin by becoming a paralegal manager, a workload coordinator, a paralegal supervisor, and eventually even a law office administrator. The Legal Assistant Management Association (LAMA) has more than 550 legal assistant manager members. Within a government agency or a corporation, there are usually even more opportunities.

Independence

If your goal is independence, you may want to gain the necessary experience to strike out on your own as a freelance paralegal or a legal technician. A successful independent career as a freelance paralegal or legal technician will require experience, specialization, and as many contacts in the field as possible.

Summary Questions

1. What are some of the factors that contribute to the continued growth of the paralegal profession?
2. In what setting do the majority of paralegals work in the United States?
3. What are some of the possible advantages and disadvantages to working in a corporate legal department?
4. What are some of the factors that affect a paralegal's salary?
5. What education is required of paralegals under state laws?
6. What are some questions you may want to be prepared to ask a potential employer at an interview?
7. What are some ways to network in your area to find out about possible employment opportunities?

Practical Paralegal Skills

Research the paralegal job market in your area by scanning the newspaper or using other resources suggested in this chapter. After you have found an available position of a type that may be of interest to you at some point in the future, prepare a résumé, cover letter, list of references, and writing samples appropriate for the position.

Notes

[1] Wagner, Andrea, *How to Land Your First Paralegal Job* 3 (Santa Monica, Cal. Estrin Publishing 1992).

[2] Bruno, Carol, "Measuring Progress," *Legal Assistant Today* 38 (Nov./Dec. 1992).

[3] Milano, Carol, "1993 Salary Survey Results," *Legal Assistant Today* 48 (May/June 1993).

[4] *The Paralegal's Guide to U.S. Government Jobs* 4 (5th ed. Washington, D.C. 1991).

[5] Milano, Carol, "1992 Salary Survey Results," *Legal Assistant Today* 67 (May/June 1992).

[6] Patrick, Diane, "What's Hot What's Not," *Legal Assistant Today* 48 (March/April 1993).

[7] Milano, Carol, "Evaluating your Benefits," *Legal Assistant Today* 38 (July/Aug. 1993).

CHAPTER 2

Professional Associations and Paralegal Regulation

The bar associations and paralegal associations in the United States are both very influential groups that can greatly affect the paralegal profession. Although the issue of paralegal regulation remains unsettled, both the bar association and the paralegal associations will definitely be involved in deciding the issue. This chapter introduces the prominent attorney and paralegal associations of the United States and examines paralegal education requirements and the proposed regulation of paralegals.

Attorney and Paralegal Associations

The role of the American Bar Association and the state bar associations in the practice of law in this country cannot be overlooked. Bar associations are responsible for regulating attorneys, proposing new legislation, and overseeing the continuing education of attorneys. Although the paralegal associations in this country are not as influential in the practice of law as a whole, their effect on paralegals is substantial. This section focuses on the bar associations and paralegal associations in this country and the effect they have on the paralegal.

The American Bar Association

A **bar association** is a voluntary organization of members of the bar of the United States or of a state or county. The primary function of bar associations is to promote professionalism and enhance the administration of justice. The **American Bar Association** (ABA) is the country's largest voluntary professional association of attorneys. More than half of the attorneys in this country are members of the ABA. Its influence in lawmaking and the practice of law, particularly through the development of model codes and guidelines, is substantial.

The ABA has had a significant effect on the paralegal profession. Its recognition of the field in 1968, with the creation of its Special Committee on Lay Assistants (later renamed the Special Committee on Legal Assistants) gave authenticity to the profession in the eyes of many attorneys and the public. The American Bar Association now allows paralegals to become associate members of the ABA. Although paralegal members do not have all of the rights of attorney members, they are on the mailing list for publications that inform members about significant developments within the legal community. They are also notified of continuing legal education opportunities sponsored by the ABA.

State Bar Associations

Each state in the country has at least one bar association with the same general purpose as the national association. In many instances state bar associations are very prominent and influential within the legal community, and they are also very influential with regard to state legislation. A state bar association plays a major role in the regulation of attorneys who are licensed to practice law within that state.

Many state bar associations have also taken an interest in the regulation of paralegals within their states, and state bar associations' positions with regard to the utilization of paralegals vary

BALLENTINESBALLENTINESBALLENTINESBALLENTINESBALLENTINESBALLENTINESBALLENTINESBALLENTINESBALLENTINESBALLENTINESBALLENTINESBALLENTINESBALLENTINESBALLENTINESBALLENTINES

bar association   A voluntary organization of members of the bar of a state or county, or of the bar of every state, whose primary function is promoting professionalism and enhancing the administration of justice.

American Bar Association   The country's largest voluntary professional association of attorneys. Its purposes include enhancing professionalism and advancing the administration of justice.

from state to state. Some states have invited paralegals to become associate members, much like the American Bar Association.

Local Bar Associations

Larger communities also have local bar associations that can provide significant support to paralegals. Local bar associations may provide information, seminars, employment agencies, or job banks that may be of particular interest to paralegals.

Paralegal Associations

Although membership in a paralegal association is not mandatory for paralegals, the associations have done much to shape public opinion of paralegals, both with attorneys and with the public in general. The paralegal associations promote professionalism within the profession, offer continuing legal education to paralegals, set ethical guidelines for paralegals to follow, and offer assistance in many forms to paralegals. The two major national paralegal associations are the **National Federation of Paralegal Associations** (NFPA) and the **National Association of Legal Assistants** (NALA). In addition, most states have at least one state paralegal association.

The National Federation of Paralegal Associations

The National Federation of Paralegal Associations (NFPA) was formed in 1974, and its members consist primarily of state associations. The NFPA represents more than 17,500 paralegals nationwide. Membership in some state associations automatically constitutes membership in the NFPA.

The NFPA was organized in response to the following reasons:

1. the need for paralegal participation in the development, advancement, and promotion of the profession

2. the need to monitor and actively participate in educational matters

3. the need to keep informed about socioeconomic, political, judicial, and technological trends and developments across the country affecting the evolution of the profession and the delivery and availability of legal services.

The NFPA has five official goals:

1. To advance, foster, and promote the paralegal profession with absolute dedication;

2. To monitor and participate in developments in the paralegal profession;

3. To maintain a nationwide communication network among paralegal associations and other members of the legal community;

4. To advance the education standards of the paralegal profession; and

5. To participate in, carry on and conduct research, seminars, experiments, investigations, studies or other work concerning the paralegal profession.

The NFPA monitors and reports on developments in courts, bar associations, and legislation that may affect paralegals, and represents many paralegals in a national forum on the issues of paralegal education and paralegal licensing. The NFPA publishes the *National Reporter,* a quarterly journal for paralegals. The NFPA has also adopted a code of ethics for paralegals' guidance.

BALLENTINESBALLENTINESBALLENTINESBALLENTINESBALLENTINESBALLENTINESBALLENTINESBALLENTINESBALLENTINESBALLENTINESBALLENTINESBALLENTINESBALLENTINESBALLENTINES

National Federation of Paralegal Associations An association of paralegal and legal assistant organizations nationwide whose purpose is to enhance professionalism and the interests of those in the profession, as well as to advance the administration of justice.

National Association of Legal Assistants A national organization of legal assistants and paralegals whose purpose is to enhance professionalism and the interests of those in the profession, as well as to advance the administration of justice generally.

The National Association of Legal Assistants

The National Association of Legal Assistants (NALA) was formed in 1975, primarily for individual members, although it also has some state and local association members. NALA currently has approximately 15,000 members. NALA classifies its members as active, associate, student, or sustaining; active members are the only voting members of NALA. Student membership is available to students who are pursuing a course of study to become legal assistants. NALA also monitors events affecting paralegals and represents paralegals on some of the important national issues, including education and certification, although the positions of NALA vary significantly from those of the NFPA. NALA has adopted its own code of ethics and Model Standards and Guidelines for Utilization of Legal Assistants. *Facts and Findings*, a bimonthly magazine for paralegals, is the official NALA publication.

State and Local Paralegal Associations

Every state and most major cities have their own paralegal associations that are invaluable resources to paralegals. These associations provide continuing education, information on topics of significance to paralegals, job banks and job placement services, and excellent opportunities to network with other paralegals in the area. State, regional, and local paralegal associations also set the standards for ethics within their communities.

Other Associations Affecting Paralegals

In addition to the associations previously discussed, other associations within the United States also affect paralegals. The Legal Assistant Management Association (LAMA) is an association formed specifically for legal assistants in managerial positions. The **American Association for Paralegal Education** (AAfPE) is an association formed for paralegal educators and institutions that educate paralegals. Professional Legal Assistants, Inc. (PLA) is a group that represents the interests of paralegals, much like the NFPA and NALA, only on a smaller scale. The membership of PLA is approximately 500 members.

Other associations that may provide information of interest to paralegals include the Association of Legal Administrators (ALA) and the American Association of Law Libraries (AAL).

Paralegal Education Requirements

There are no formal education requirements for paralegals at this time. In fact, many competent paralegals began as legal secretaries who were trained as paralegals by the attorneys for whom they worked. The modern trend, however, is toward formal education and training. Paralegal training can be found in many different settings, including four-year colleges and universities, junior colleges, business schools, and specialized paralegal schools. Colleges and universities usually offer four-year paralegal degrees, often with accelerated programs for those who already have four-year degrees in other areas. Junior colleges usually offer two-year paralegal certificates accompanied by associate of arts degrees. Business school programs usually can be completed in two years or less, as can the programs offered by specialized paralegal schools.

BALLENTINESBALLENTINESBALLENTINESBALLENTINESBALLENTINESBALLENTINESBALLENTINESBALLENTINESBALLENTINESBALLENTINESBALLENTINESBALLENTINESBALLENTINESBALLENTINES

American Association for Paralegal Education   A national organization of paralegal teachers and educational institutions, which provides technical assistance and supports research in the paralegal field, promotes standards for paralegal instruction, and cooperates with the American Bar Association and others in developing an approval process for paralegal education.

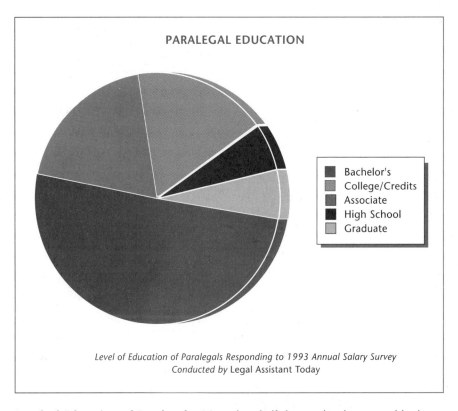

PARALEGAL EDUCATION

- Bachelor's
- College/Credits
- Associate
- High School
- Graduate

Level of Education of Paralegals Responding to 1993 Annual Salary Survey
Conducted by Legal Assistant Today

Level of Education of Paralegals More than half the paralegals surveyed had a bachelor's degree. More than 35% had at least an associate degree or some college education. (Adapted from the 1993 Annual Salary Survey by *Legal Assistant Today*.)

The curriculum offered in these programs depends on the school. However, most paralegal programs offer introductory courses that are required of all paralegal students, including the following:

1. *Introduction to Law.* This course includes an introduction to the basic concepts of American law.

2. *Introduction to Paralegal Careers.* This course includes an introduction to the work of the paralegal, including paralegal ethics.

3. *Legal Research and Legal Writing.* This course teaches basic legal research and legal writing skills, including computerized legal research.

In addition, paralegal programs offer specialty courses in specific areas of law. These courses teach the basic concepts surrounding the particular area of law as well as procedures for working in that area. Specialty courses are typically offered in:

1. Litigation
2. Criminal law
3. Family law
4. Wills, trusts, and probate
5. Real estate
6. Bankruptcy and collections
7. Business law/corporate law

Certain specialty courses may be required and others elective. Some schools offer specialty certificates for students who take a requisite number of courses in a certain area of law.

Criteria for Choosing a Paralegal Training Program

The American Association for Paralegal Education (AAfPE) suggests considering the following factors when deciding whether a paralegal training program might suit your needs[1]:

1. The educational objectives of the program should be stated clearly in the program literature, which should be available to you upon request. General and specific training objectives should be provided.

2. The reputations of both the umbrella institution and the program itself should be considered. Look to the educational standing of the program with the general public and legal community.

3. Admission standards and the level of education required for acceptance into the program will tell you the academic level of the program and whether you would be eligible.

4. ABA approval indicates that the program has met the standards prescribed by the organized bar. This gives some level of assurance of quality and reputation.

5. Membership in AAfPE shows that the program administration is interested in current developments in paralegal education and in offering a quality program.

6. The qualifications of the program administrator and whether the staff is on campus full- or part-time will give you an idea how much supervision and leadership the program has.

7. The placement record will tell you if graduates find legal assistant positions, what types of work they perform, and what firms employ them.

More information on choosing a paralegal school or paralegal program is available from the American Association for Paralegal Education, PO Box 40244, Overland Park, KS 66204; (913) 381-4458.

ABA-Approved Programs

Paralegal programs approved by the American Bar Association have advisory boards made up of attorneys and paralegals who provide input as to the perceived needs of the local bar and legal community. Schools that are approved by the ABA must meet specific requirements concerning types of courses offered by the program and the number of semester hours required for program completion. In addition, the program must meet the American Bar Association's guidelines. Those guidelines require a college-level program which:

- is part of an accredited educational institution
- offers *at least* 60 semester or 90 quarter units (or the equivalent) of classroom work. These units must include general education and at least 18 semester (or 27 quarter) units of legal specialty courses
- has an advisory committee with attorneys and legal assistants from the public and private sectors
- has qualified, experienced instructors
- has adequate financial support from the institution in which it is situated
- is accredited by, or eligible for accreditation by, an accrediting agency recognized by the Council on Post-Secondary Accreditation
- has adequate student services, including counseling and placement
- has an adequate library available
- has appropriate facilities and equipment

Future Trends in Paralegal Education

As the paralegal profession grows and expands, future regulation and minimum education requirements appear to be inevitable, but the full

Lawyers Cooperative Publishing

Paralegals in American Law

INTRODUCTION TO PARALEGALISM

Angela Schneeman

Legal research is the practice of finding and analyzing solutions to questions of law. Researching answers to legal problems is the primary reason clients hire attorneys and why attorneys employ paralegals. ‖‖

"Whether in the stacks or on-line with computer-assisted legal research, the satisfaction of finding that on-point case is personally and professionally rewarding."

INVESTIGATION

"Imagine my relief when the clerk-of-the-works offered his time and help with some very technical matters at the site. Once I understood exactly how our client injured himself, the case took a multi-million dollar turn and eventually settled."

Interviewing and investigating are two distinct skills that often go hand-in-hand. Both interviewing and investigating involve gathering facts for a lawsuit or for other legal services that will be performed for a client. Communication skills and persistence are the two qualities that a paralegal interviewer and investigator must possess. ▐▐▐▐

Only by understanding diverse jurisdictions, judicial procedures, burdens of proof, structures and functions of the three branches of government, as well as sources of law, and the politics that contribute to the American legal system, will a paralegal be successful. That success is both professionally and personally rewarding. ▌▌▌

"The cold nights we spent searching for records in a warehouse paid off. When the court ordered document production, our attorney was ready to comply."

PARALEGAL / ATTORNEY TEAM

"You actually become very close to your colleagues in a litigation team before trial because the days are always long and intense. When the three of us needed to consult with the lead attorney, we often took advantage of the firm's open door policy."

Paralegals are described as individuals who perform legal services under the supervision of an attorney, without practicing law or giving legal advice. Over 70 percent of paralegals work in private law firms and 70 percent of those paralegals work in firms with less than 30 attorneys. ▌▌

extent of those requirements is as yet unknown. In a survey taken by *Legal Assistant Today* magazine, as reported in the January/February 1993 issue, 95 percent of the responding paralegals felt that there should be minimum education requirements for all paralegals. Ninety-seven percent of the respondents felt that the institutions offering paralegal programs should have uniform minimum requirements. In its Model Standards and Guidelines for Utilization of Paralegals, the National Association of Legal Assistants sets forth specific standards for education.

Another trend coming from the educational institutions is the offering of more advanced degrees for paralegals. Records of the American Association for Paralegal Education indicate that the number of schools offering bachelor's degrees in paralegal studies jumped from 25 in 1986 to 62 in 1992. Postbaccalaureate certificate programs and master's degrees with a paralegal certificate are also becoming more common.

Paralegal Regulation

Attorneys must be licensed and admitted to the bar in the state in which they practice—but who sets the national standards for and regulates paralegals? At this time, the answer is no one. There are currently no minimum national requirements for education for paralegals, nor are there national guidelines for certification or licensing. Paralegals are subject to the same laws concerning the unauthorized practice of law that all nonattorneys are subject to. However, there is a movement underway in many states, and at the national level, to change this. Regulation by means of certification and licensing are some of the hot topics of the 1990s. Possibly by the time you read this text, some of these issues will have been resolved.

There are several different means by which paralegals might be regulated. In addition to minimum education requirements, they could be regulated by licensing requirements, certification requirements, codes of ethics, and laws concerning the unauthorized practice of law. Current positions on these regulation issues vary among the various states, bar associations, and even among the two top paralegal associations.

Licensing of Paralegals

A **license** is a privilege conferred on a person by the government to do something which he or she otherwise would not have the right to do. No form of licensing for paralegals is currently required in any state in this country. However, two types of licensing have been proposed and either or both may be adopted in several states in the near future.

The first type of proposed licensing covers a broader base of paralegals, and requires that all paralegals must meet certain requirements and be licensed in the state in which they work. The second type of licensing requires that paralegals who do not work under the supervision of an attorney meet certain requirements and be licensed by the state. This is the type of licensing that has been proposed in California for legal technicians.

Licensing of All Paralegals

NFPA has endorsed a two-tier regulation policy that includes licensing and specialty licensing. The NFPA endorsement includes implementation of regulation of all paralegals on a state-by-state

BALLENTINESBALLENTINESBALLENTINESBALLENTINESBALLENTINESBALLENTINESBALLENTINESBALLENTINESBALLENTINESBALLENTINESBALLENTINESBALLENTINESBALLENTINESBALLENTINES

license A special privilege, not a right common to everyone. ... A privilege conferred on a person by the government to do something he or she otherwise would not have the right to do.

basis. In 1993, NFPA passed a resolution stating that it can support licensing programs which contain minimum standards, provide for an expanded role of practice for qualifying paralegals, contain provisions for a method of consumer redress, require continuing education in a legal or specialty field, and contain character and fitness standards.

NALA, on the other hand, is strictly opposed to the licensing of paralegals. NALA promotes certification of legal assistants, as discussed later in this chapter.

Licensing Legal Technicians

Another type of licensing that has been proposed in some state legislatures is the required licensing of only those individuals who offer their services to the public without the supervision of an attorney. In 1986, the American Bar Association Commission on Professionalism released a report recommending limited licensing of paralegals who perform certain legal services independently. For its reasoning, the report stated in part: "[I]t can no longer be claimed that lawyers have the exclusive possession of the esoteric knowledge required and are therefore the only ones able to advise clients on any matter concerning the law."

In California and elsewhere around the country, those individuals are referred to as **legal technicians**. Strong arguments have been presented both in favor of and against the licensing of legal technicians in California. On one side are those who want to protect the public from unqualified legal service providers and reserve the performance of law-related duties to lawyers. On the other side are those who argue that the presence of legal technicians to perform routine legal services is necessary to keep costs down and make legal services affordable for everyone.

The state of Texas is also considering proposed legislation to certify the legal technician profession. Under the proposed legislation in Texas, legal technicians would be allowed to perform specified legal services directly for the public if they meet specific requirements, including passing an examination.

Most states have laws that strictly prohibit the practice of law by anyone other than a licensed attorney. There are those who feel that any service that could be construed as the practice of law should be confined to attorneys or, at the least, to paralegals who work under the direct supervision of an attorney. In contrast, others feel that many legal services can be well performed by nonattorneys, making needed legal services more affordable and more available to the public.

NFPA is currently participating in the ABA Commission on Nonlawyer Practice, the focus of which is to study the role of nonlawyers in the delivery of legal services. The Commission on Nonlawyer Practice (the Commission) is a newly created body of the American Bar Association that began a two-year study in December 1992. During the first year, the Commission was to hold seven public hearings concerning the role of nonlawyers in the delivery of legal services. During the Commission's second year, it is to compile the data, make findings and recommendations, and prepare a report on the topic.

Certification of Paralegals

The memberships of NALA and NFPA are in disagreement over the regulation of paralegals. Whereas NFPA prefers the licensing of paralegals under certain conditions, NALA is basically opposed to licensing and in favor of certification. As opposed to licensing, which involves permission from the state to perform certain functions, certification deals with self-regulation. A top priority of NALA since its formation has been the establishment of certain standards for the profession. NALA developed a voluntary certification program with a designation of **Certified Legal Assistant** (CLA) for those who successfully meet the requirements, which include successful completion

BALLENTINESBALLENTINESBALLENTINESBALLENTINESBALLENTINESBALLENTINESBALLENTINESBALLENTINESBALLENTINESBALLENTINESBALLENTINESBALLENTINESBALLENTINESBALLENTINESBALLENTINES

legal technician   A self-employed paralegal who offers services directly to the public, without the supervision of an attorney.

Certified Legal Assistant   A legal assistant who has been certified by the National Association of Legal Assistants.

of a two-day comprehensive examination covering communications, ethics, human relations and interviewing techniques, judgment and analytical ability, legal research, and legal terminology. In addition, the test covers substantive areas of law, including general practice, bankruptcy law, corporate law, estate planning and probate, contract law, real estate, litigation, criminal law, and administrative law. Paralegals taking the test can choose to be tested on four areas of substantive law.

Paralegals who have already received the CLA certification may obtain a specialty certification in their area of law by passing a four-hour exam focusing on their area of specialty. Specialty certification is available in the areas of civil litigation, probate and estate planning, corporate and business law, criminal law and procedure, and real estate. As of 1991, more than 4,300 legal assistants had received certification from NALA.

The members of NALA argue that paralegals who are certified have a competitive edge in the workplace. Potential employers who are aware of the certification process know the standards that have been met by a potential employee who is a certified paralegal. In addition, NALA argues that paralegals can increase their compensation and mobility by becoming certified. A 1989 survey of legal assistants by NALA indicated that certified paralegals earned an average of $2,000 more per year than their uncertified counterparts.

A certified paralegal should be distinguished from a certificated paralegal. *Certificated paralegals* are those who have graduated from a paralegal certificate program. *Certified paralegals* are those who have been certified by NALA.

Future Trends in Regulation of Paralegals

All signs point to more and more responsibilities being taken on by paralegals, both within law firms and independently. The acceptance of paralegals is growing rapidly. Already several administrative agencies allow paralegals to represent clients before their governing boards under certain circumstances. As the profession continues to expand, some type of regulation will be inevitable. Many paralegals and attorneys alike are anxiously awaiting the report of the ABA Commission on Nonlawyer Practice, due in 1994, as an indication of the direction of regulation of paralegals in the future.

NFPA has reported the following pending legislation and developments during 1993 concerning the regulation of paralegals[2]:

Alabama   NFPA has furnished comprehensive information on regulation and education for paralegals to paralegals affiliated with the Legal Services Corporation in Alabama. They are commencing a study of standards for and regulation of legal assistants.

Arizona   NFPA learned that a bill was introduced into the state senate to reinstate an unauthorized practice statute and make the **unauthorized practice of law** a Class 5 felony.

The Arizona Bar formed a task force to study the regulation of nonlawyers delivering legal services directly to the public. NFPA provided comprehensive materials to assist the task force in its study.

Arkansas   NFPA responded to a request from the Arkansas Bar Association for comprehensive information to assist its recently reactivated Paralegal Committee in the committee's study of regulation and credentialing of paralegals.

California   A task force was formed in California to study whether legal technicians should be allowed to deliver certain services directly to the public.

Connecticut   After studying associate membership for paralegals in the Connecticut Bar Association, the state bar voted to reject such membership for paralegals.

unauthorized practice of law   Engaging in the practice of law without the license required by law.

Colorado The Colorado Bar formed a committee that is studying standards for utilization of paralegals. NFPA furnished comprehensive information to the bar.

Delaware The Board of the Unauthorized Practice of Law of the Supreme Court recently issued an order stating that paralegals who attend mediation sessions in lieu of attorneys are not engaged in the unauthorized practice of law. The order expands the role of the paralegal in Delaware.

Florida In the wake of its Legal Technicians Study Committee report, the Florida State Bar formed an Implementation Committee to develop guidelines for the regulation of legal technicians.

Idaho An unauthorized practice of law case is pending against a former insurance adjuster who was functioning as an insurance adjuster/paralegal in Idaho. The paralegal is involved in negotiating claims to conclusion for insurance companies.

Illinois The Illinois State Bar Association sponsored a conference to examine ways to provide greater access to civil justice. A summary of the conference's debates and recommendations is contained in an article, "The 1992 Allerton House Conference on Access to Civil Justice," published in the December 1992 issue of the *Illinois Bar Journal,* (vol. 80).

Indiana NFPA learned that the Indiana State Bar Association's (ISBA) Paralegal Committee has prepared guidelines for the utilization of legal assistant services. The guidelines were presented to the ISBA House of Delegates for approval in November 1992, and are then to be considered by the Indiana Supreme Court. The Indiana Paralegal Association (IPA) and NFPA, working with the IPA, were able to furnish information to ISBA. The guidelines contain a definition of *paralegal / legal assistant* and state that the lawyer is ultimately responsible for all of the professional actions of a legal assistant performing

at the direction of the lawyer. Further, the guidelines address the lawyer's maintaining responsibility for work product and nonlawyers' not being responsible for establishing an attorney-client relationship, establishing fees, or rendering a legal opinion to a client. The guidelines further recommend that it should always be made clear that the legal assistant is not licensed to practice law. The guidelines permit a legal assistant's name and title to appear on the lawyer's letterhead and business cards. The guidelines state that the lawyer is responsible for ensuring that a legal assistant preserves all client confidences, that a lawyer may charge for work performed by a legal assistant, that a lawyer may not split legal fees with nor pay referral fees to a legal assistant, and that a lawyer should promote and facilitate a legal assistant's participation in continuing education and pro bono activities. The guidelines specifically preclude the practice of independent paralegals (legal technicians or what the report refers to as "store-front" legal assistants) because, as stated in the report, of current inadequate safeguards to quantify or assure competence, protect the public from harm, ensure confidentiality of communications, or ensure against conflicts of interest. NFPA continues to monitor the progress of the proposed guidelines.

Minnesota NFPA commented to the Minnesota State Bar Association Paralegal Task Force on its draft report recently released. The report will be presented to the Minnesota State Bar Association (MSBA) and when approved will be presented to the Minnesota Supreme Court Task Force, which was established to conduct a feasibility study concerning the regulation of nonlawyers to deliver legal services pursuant to Senate File 520. A summary of the four recommendations is:

- The MSBA should oppose licensing paralegals to practice without the supervision of an attorney
- The MSBA should continue to support increased funding for programs that provide

legal services to low-income, elderly, and disadvantaged clients

- The MSBA should take steps to increase the utilization of paralegals working under the supervision of attorneys through education and cooperative efforts. (The report lists specific examples)

- The MSBA should participate in the ABA Commission on Nonlawyer Practice at least to the extent of offering testimony at the regional hearing

Montana   NFPA filed testimony on Montana Senate Bill No. 9, which proposes to authorize nonlawyers to assist litigants in civil cases with advice on filing and litigating claims in court. The "court assistants" shall serve at the county's expense. In the alternative, county commissioners, in consultation with the county justices of the peace, may authorize individuals to act as court assistants and to charge fees. A court assistant is prohibited from representing a client in court and may only advise a client in the areas of court procedures, drafting pleadings, conducting discovery, and presentation of the case in the justice's court.

Nevada   The Nevada Supreme Court (NSC) directed the Nevada State Bar (NSB) to conduct a six-month study concerning the utilization of nonlawyers in the delivery of legal services and the question of whether qualifying standards or regulation may be appropriate. Paralegals and lawyers are represented on the committee, which met in January 1993. The NSB has applied to the NSC for an extension of time to complete the study and prepare a report. NFPA provided comprehensive materials concerning regulation and education criteria to the NSB committee.

New Jersey   NFPA learned that Assembly Bill 1922 was introduced into the New Jersey legislature in October 1992. The bill proposes to amend Chapter 170 of Title 2A of the New Jersey Statutes to increase the penalty for engaging in the unauthorized practice of law. The proposed bill does not attempt to clarify the practice of law by defining, for example, the practice of law, legal services, legal advice, proceedings, representation, or the role of nonlawyers in delivery of legal services. Rather, the bill addresses only the penalty for engaging in unauthorized practice. The bill proposes to increase the penalty from "a disorderly person" to "guilty of a crime of the fourth degree" for any person determined to have engaged in the unauthorized practice of law.

NFPA furnished information to a law firm concerning paralegals who attend § 341(a) creditors' meetings in bankruptcy cases. The firm has twice been questioned and received objections to a paralegal attending a § 341(a) hearing.

New Mexico   The New Mexico State Bar formed a work-study group composed of two subgroups. One subgroup is conducting a study on regulation of legal assistants; the other subgroup is focusing on legal assistant affiliation with the state bar. The composition of the regulation subgroup is three lawyers, eight legal assistants, and the chair, who is a professor and lawyer. NFPA furnished information to the regulation subgroup through the New Mexico legal assistants' group.

NFPA filed testimony on N.M. Senate Bill 804, which was introduced into the legislature proposing to authorize prescribed "legal assistant services" to be delivered directly to the public by nonlawyers. The legal assistant services were described as research of records and statistical research; investigation and analysis of records, documents, and facts; problem analysis; referral services; preparation of legal memoranda; assistance in drafting legal documents and completing legal forms; legal research, consisting of locating, citing, checking, and shepardizing reported decisions of courts or administrative adjudicatory bodies; and interviewing of witnesses. "Legal assistant services" does not mean representation of persons before judicial or administrative bodies; preparation of pleadings and other papers incident to actions or proceedings in a judicial or administrative forum; giving legal advice or counsel; rendering a service that requires legal knowledge or skill at a level commensurate with that of a licensed attorney; or preparing contracts and other documents without the use of forms and under which legal rights are created or secured.

South Dakota   NFPA filed testimony on S.D. Senate Bill No. 13, which was introduced to provide for regulation of a profession or occupation. The bill defines "registration," "certification," and "licensing" for purposes of the Act. The bill provides that any profession or occupation applying for regulation under the Act shall furnish a regulatory proposal containing considerations for a regulatory board, qualifications of practitioners, disciplinary procedures to be applied to practitioners, proposed requirements for continuing education, and draft legislation for the applicant profession or occupation. The bill provides that regulation may not be recommended unless it is necessary to protect the public; then, only the "least restrictive form of regulation consistent with the public interest" shall be a primary consideration.

Tennessee   The Tennessee Bar Association presented a proposal to the state supreme court whereby nonlawyers delivering legal services would come under the jurisdiction of the Board of Professional Responsibility with regard to the unauthorized practice of law. Tennessee has an unauthorized practice statute; this proposal merely places the responsibility for enforcement upon a different body.

Texas   Following months of public comment; the author of draft legislation to regulate legal technicians revised the proposed bill. The bill apparently has sponsors in both houses of the state legislature. The author intends to have the bill introduced into the current session of the legislature.

Traditional paralegals in San Antonio have drafted a bill to regulate traditional paralegals in Texas. A senator has agreed to sponsor the bill in the Texas legislature.

Utah   NFPA filed testimony on Utah Senate Bill 9, which proposes to authorize law-trained legal assistants to assist family court judges and court commissioners in the processing of family law matters. This case management pilot program would allow legal assistants to assist in conference calls between the parties and counsel; manage discovery; arrange telephone calls and meetings among the judge or court commissioner, the parties, and counsel; prepare final written orders of settlement; and perform any other related duties assigned by the judge or court commissioner. Results of the evaluation of the pilot program were to be provided to the Judiciary Interim Committee in October 1993 and to the Judiciary House and Senate Standing Committees by February 1994.

Vermont   NFPA furnished comprehensive information on paralegal responsibilities and standards for paralegals to the Vermont State Bar, which is studying a situation occurring in family court. Apparently, paralegals are accompanying otherwise pro se parties to court to assist the parties in preparing their financial disclosure statements and testimony in child support delinquency hearings. The paralegals do not make statements to the court, nor do they represent the parties.

Virginia   The Virginia Alliance of Legal Assistant Associations (VALAA) is conducting a study as to adopting standards and guidelines for the utilization of legal assistants. The National Capital Area Paralegal Association (NCAPA) and the Roanoke Valley Paralegal Association are members of the VALAA. NFPA is providing comments on the proposed standards and guidelines to VALAA through the NCAPA and Roanoke associations.

Summary Questions

1. What are the current licensing requirements for paralegals?
2. What is paralegal certification? Must all paralegals be certified?
3. What is the difference between a legal technician and a traditional paralegal?
4. What are the differing views of licensing of NFPA and NALA?

 ## Practical Paralegal Skills

Contact the paralegal association in your city or state to answer the following questions.

1. Is the association a member of NFPA or NALA?
2. What qualifications must members of the association have? Does the association accept student members?
3. What benefits does the association offer?
4. Does the association have a set of bylaws or guidelines to which its members subscribe?
5. Does the association have a formal position on the regulation issue?

 ## Notes

1 *How to Choose a Paralegal Education Program* (1990). A booklet provided by the American Association for Paralegal Education, with contributions from the American Association for Paralegal Education, the American Bar Association Standing Committee on Legal Assistants, the Association of Legal Administrators, the Legal Assistant Management Association, the National Association of Legal Assistants, and the National Federation of Paralegal Associations.

2 Shimko-Herman, Deanna, "NFPA Files Testimony, Monitors Case Law, Exempt/Nonexempt Status, and UPL," *National Paralegal Reporter* 25 (Summer 1993); "NFPA Files Testimony, Monitors Case Law and UPL," *National Paralegal Reporter* 15 (Spring 1993).

CHAPTER 3
Attorney and Paralegal Ethics

Ethics in the Legal Community

Ethics is the code of moral principles and standards of behavior for persons in professions such as law or medicine. **Legal ethics** is the code of conduct among lawyers which governs their moral and professional duties toward one another, toward their clients, and toward the courts. The role of legal ethics is to identify and remove inappropriate conduct from the legal profession. Legal ethics do not apply just to attorneys. Individuals employed by attorneys, especially paralegals, must also exercise ethical behavior. Although the concept of ethics may seem somewhat abstract, concrete choices concerning ethical behavior are constantly being made by paralegals.

This chapter discusses attorney ethics and possible sanctions against attorneys for unethical behavior. It also explores paralegal ethics and the possible consequences to paralegals who act unethically.

Attorney Ethics and Sanctions for Unethical Behavior

Attorneys are governed by the code of professional ethics adopted by each state. The American Bar Association (ABA) has promulgated its own sets of ethical regulations for attorneys. Currently it follows the Model Rules of Professional Conduct (Model Rules), which replaced its older Code of Professional Responsibility (CPR). Many state bars and courts have adopted the Model Rules and CPR as legally binding and enforceable regulations against attorneys and their employees. Thus, paralegals should become familiar with the provisions of the ABA Model Rules and the CPR.

Rule 5.3 of the Model Code of Professional Responsibility specifically addresses the attorney's responsibility for his or her nonlawyer assistants.

Model Code of Professional Responsibility Rule 5.3. Responsibilities Regarding Nonlawyer Assistants

With respect to a nonlawyer employed or retained by or associated with a lawyer:

(a) a partner in a law firm shall make reasonable efforts to ensure that the firm has in effect measures giving reasonable assurance that the person's conduct is compatible with the professional obligations of the lawyer;

(b) a lawyer having direct supervisory authority over the nonlawyer shall make reasonable efforts to ensure that the person's conduct is compatible with the professional obligations of the lawyer; and

(c) a lawyer shall be responsible for conduct of such a person that would be a violation of the Rules of Professional Conduct if engaged in by a lawyer if:

(1) the lawyer orders or ratifies the conduct involved; or

(2) the lawyer is a partner in the law firm in which the person is employed, or has direct supervisory authority over the person, and knows of the conduct at a time when its consequences can be avoided or mitigated but fails to take reasonable remedial action.

BALLENTINESBALLENTINESBALLENTINESBALLENTINESBALLENTINESBALLENTINESBALLENTINESBALLENTINESBALLENTINESBALLENTINESBALLENTINESBALLENTINESBALLENTINESBALLENTINESBALLENTINES

ethics   A code of moral principles and standards of behavior for people in professions such as law or medicine.

legal ethics   The code of conduct among lawyers which governs their moral and professional duties toward one another, toward their clients, and toward the courts.

ABA Code of Professional Responsibility and Model Rules of Professional Conduct

The CPR is divided into nine Canons, all of which broadly prescribe ethical conduct for lawyers. Within the Canons are Disciplinary Rules (DRs) and Ethical Considerations (ECs), which provide more detailed guidance on ethical issues. The DRs and ECs carefully discuss permissible attorney conduct in advertising; soliciting clients; contacting clients, adverse parties, or the public; protecting client confidences; establishing and sharing legal fees; withdrawing from representation; undertaking unauthorized practice of law; maintaining prohibited interactions with a client's interests; providing competent and zealous representation; and other ethical questions. The ABA Model Rules, although they use different phraseology, address identical concerns. Because the Model Rules are much longer and more specific, this discussion focuses on the nine Canons of the CPR, with references to the Model Rules where applicable.

Following are the nine Canons of the CPR, along with a brief explanation of each.

CANON 1: A LAWYER SHOULD ASSIST IN MAINTAINING THE INTEGRITY AND COMPETENCE OF THE LEGAL PROFESSION.

This subject is also addressed by Rule 8 of the Model Rules of Professional Conduct, on maintaining the integrity of the profession. This canon relates to the profession's duty to police itself. Rule 8.3 of the Model Rules specifically states that an attorney who has knowledge of another attorney's violation of the Rules of Professional Conduct shall inform the appropriate professional authority.

Example: The attorney you work for, Marvin Terry, is working on a personal injury lawsuit, representing the defendant. The plaintiff's attorney is constantly calling your client on the telephone. Even after Mr. Terry has specifically told the plaintiff's attorney that all contact with his client should be made through him, the plaintiff's attorney continues to contact Mr. Terry's client, trying to get him to make admissions over the telephone. This is clearly unethical behavior by the plaintiff's attorney. Mr. Terry has a duty under Canon 1 to report this behavior to the proper authority within your state.

CANON 2: A LAWYER SHOULD ASSIST THE LEGAL PROFESSION IN FULFILLING ITS DUTY TO MAKE LEGAL COUNSEL AVAILABLE.

This canon addresses the attorney's duty to perform pro bono services and to represent indigent clients when appointed. It is addressed more specifically in Rule 6 of the Model Rules, which states that a lawyer should render public interest legal service,[1] and that a lawyer shall not seek to avoid appointment by a tribunal to represent a person except for good cause.[2]

CANON 3: A LAWYER SHOULD ASSIST IN PREVENTING THE UNAUTHORIZED PRACTICE OF LAW.

This canon is of particular interest to paralegals, as it may directly concern them. It is also addressed in Model Rule 5.5, which states, in part, that an attorney shall not assist a person who is not a member of the bar in the performance of activity that constitutes the unauthorized practice of law.

Example: Attorney Christine Pearson specializes in real estate law, but occasionally she will bring in a family law case. Ms. Pearson knows very little about family law, but her paralegal, Wendy Roberts, has had extensive experience in the area. When Ms. Pearson brings in a family law case, she has Wendy handle the entire matter, including meeting with the clients, completing all pleadings, and settling the matter through mediation. When Wendy asks Ms. Pearson a question, the answer is usually, "I don't know, Wendy. You know more about family law than I do." When the case is over, Ms. Pearson bills the clients and collects the fee. Ms. Pearson is clearly in violation of Canon 3. She is encouraging the unauthorized practice of law by not supervising or taking any responsibility for the files handled by her paralegal.

CANON 4: A LAWYER SHOULD PRESERVE THE CONFIDENCES AND SECRETS OF A CLIENT.

This is another canon that is clearly applicable to paralegals. It is addressed in Rule 1.6 of the Model Rules, which states that a lawyer shall not reveal information relating to representation of a client except as otherwise stated in the Code.

Example: Attorney Bennet Brown has a client who is driving him nuts. Mr. Brown is representing Tony Calendar in a business litigation matter, but their case is weak. In addition to making unreasonable demands, Mr. Calendar is constantly hounding Mr. Brown on the telephone, even calling him at home at night and on weekends. Mr. Brown has had it. During a bar association social one evening (after a few cocktails), he confides in his good friend Janet Heland about Mr. Calendar. He complains in a rather loud voice about the fact that Mr. Calendar has no case, and explains the details to Janet. Janet has no relation to the case, and Mr. Brown knows she will keep anything he says confidential. However, he does not realize that the attorney standing directly behind Janet works for the law firm that is representing the opposing party in the Calendar case. This attorney picks up vital information that will help his client.

In this case, even if the attorney for the opposing party had not overheard Mr. Brown, Mr. Brown would still have been in violation of Canon 4. The fact that the other counsel did overhear only demonstrates the importance of strictly observing this canon.

CANON 5: A LAWYER SHOULD EXERCISE IN-DEPENDENT PROFESSIONAL JUDGMENT ON BEHALF OF A CLIENT.

This canon refers to sharing fees and the practice of law with nonlawyers. The related Rule 5.4 of the Model Rules specifically prohibits sharing legal fees with a nonlawyer (except under special circumstances) and forming a partnership with a nonlawyer if any of the partnership's activities includes the practice of law. In addition, Rule 5.4(c) states that a lawyer shall not let a person who recommends, employs, or pays the lawyer to render legal services for another to direct or regulate the lawyer's professional judgment in rendering such legal services.

CANON 6: A LAWYER SHOULD REPRESENT A CLIENT COMPETENTLY.

This canon really speaks for itself. Rule 1.1 of the Model Rules states that a lawyer shall provide competent representation to a client. Competent representation requires the legal knowledge, skill, thoroughness, and preparation reasonably necessary for the representation.

CANON 7: A LAWYER SHOULD REPRESENT A CLIENT ZEALOUSLY WITHIN THE BOUNDS OF THE LAW.

This canon states that attorneys must do everything reasonably in their power and within the bounds of the law to represent the best interests of their clients. Several rules within the Model Rules address this topic.

CANON 8: A LAWYER SHOULD ASSIST IN IMPROVING THE LEGAL SYSTEM.

This canon refers to the many ways in which lawyers can work to improve the legal system, including their personal practices and conduct and their services within the larger legal community, to assist in improving legal practices and procedures.

CANON 9: A LAWYER SHOULD AVOID EVEN THE APPEARANCE OF PROFESSIONAL IMPROPRIETY.

Again, this canon speaks for itself.

In addition to the CPR and Model Rules, the ABA and many state bar associations have adopted guidelines for the use of paralegals. Many of these guidelines are patterned after the Model Standards and Guidelines promoted by NALA, which are discussed later in this chapter.

Sanctions for Unethical Behavior

The codes of ethical behavior to which attorneys must adhere are enforced by a variety of sanctions, depending on the ethical codes and pertinent laws of the state where the violation occurred.

Some action may be merely unethical. Minor infractions which are not clearly illegal, but are violations of the state ethics code or rules of ethics, may be punished by a reprimand from the bar or by suspension of the attorney's license to practice. More serious infractions may result in criminal prosecution. The unauthorized practice of law is usually considered a misdemeanor. Other, more serious, unethical acts may result in felony charges for crimes such as fraud. When a serious infraction takes place, the state bar may move to have the attorney disbarred and to have his or her license to practice law revoked.

Notwithstanding any of the foregoing, any unethical behavior that results in harm to a client or a third party may result in civil actions being brought against the attorney for monetary damages in a malpractice or similar lawsuit.

The case of *People v. Macy*, 789 P.2d 188 (Colo. 1990), involved an attorney who aided another in the unauthorized practice of law (in violation of Canon 3 of the CPR and Rule 5.5 of the Model Rules). The offending attorney was suspended from the practice of law for a two-year period.

The PEOPLE of the State of Colorado, Complainant,
v.
Lloyd W. MACY, Attorney-Respondent.
No. 90SA9.
Supreme Court of Colorado,
En Banc.
April 2, 1990.

PER CURIAM.

This is an attorney discipline case in which a hearing panel of the Supreme Court Grievance Committee unanimously recommended that the respondent, Lloyd W. Macy, be suspended from practicing law for two years and be assessed the costs of the proceeding. We accept the panel's recommendation.

A hearing board of the grievance committee heard this matter, and a hearing panel approved the findings and conclusions of the hearing board. Macy elected not to file exceptions to the hearing panel's report. ... The hearing board's findings and conclusions were based on the amended complaint, the allegations of which were admitted by Macy; documentary evidence; stipulations of the parties; and Macy's testimony before the hearing board.

I.

Lloyd W. Macy was admitted to the bar of this court on April 5, 1967. He is therefore subject to the jurisdiction of this court and its grievance committee in all matters relating to the practice of law. ...

In 1986, Charles J. Taylor, who is not a lawyer, approached Macy for advice in connection with Taylor's desire to sell "living trust" packages to customers who wished to use them to avoid taxes or probate. In December of that year, Macy met with Taylor and reviewed a package of "living trust" documents prepared by Taylor for marketing through nonlawyer salespersons.

Taylor began selling "living trust" documents in January 1987. During the next several months, Macy reviewed several "living trust" packages prepared for individuals and answered questions addressed to him by nonlawyer salespersons regarding individual customers' concerns. Taylor paid Macy $75.00 per hour for his services.

II.

Macy's conduct violated two provisions of the Code of Professional Responsibility, DR 1-102(A)(1) (violating a disciplinary rule), and DR 3-101(A) (aiding a nonlawyer in the unauthorized practice of law). Aiding a nonlawyer in the unauthorized practice of law is a violation of a duty owed to the legal profession. ... The creation and sale of trust documents by nonlawyers constitutes the unauthorized practice of law. ... This court has suspended an attorney in the past for aiding a nonlawyer in marketing trusts to the public. *People v. Boyls*, 197 Colo. 242, 591 P.2d 1315 (1976) ... .

The *Standards for Lawyer Discipline* also suggest certain factors that aggravate or mitigate an attorney's misconduct and therefore increase or decrease the appropriate sanction. Several aggravating factors are present in this case. Macy has a prior disciplinary record. ... Macy has substantial experience in the practice of law. ... The evidence suggests that Macy may have acted out of a selfish desire to generate legal business for himself, rather than simply to receive legal fees from Taylor. ... Finally, Macy's disciplinary record reveals that he has repeatedly made errors of judgment, and that the advice he gave customers of Taylor's "living trust" operation was in part patently erroneous. Both these latter factors reflect adversely on Macy's fitness to practice law, *see Standards for Lawyer Discipline* 9.1, and the grave risk of serious financial harm to purchasers of Taylor's trust documents make Macy's professional misconduct especially serious. ...

The grievance committee has recommended that Macy be suspended for two years. ... After reviewing the findings of the hearing board of the grievance committee and the length of suspension recommended by the committee, we conclude that suspension for two years is appropriate.

Paralegal Ethics

Paralegals are usually considered to be bound by the ethical guidelines prescribed for attorneys. In addition, paralegals have been given guidelines for ethical behavior by the following:

1. The Affirmation of Professional Responsibility of the National Federation of Paralegal Associations (NFPA's Affirmation);

2. The National Federation of Paralegal Associations' Model Code of Ethics and Professional Responsibility (NFPA's Model Code);

3. The National Association of Legal Assistants' Code of Ethics and Professional Responsibility (NALA's Code); and

4. Model Standards and Guidelines for Utilization of Legal Assistants of the National Association of Legal Assistants (NALA's Model Standards).

Neither paralegal association has any authority to enforce these codes, standards, and guidelines, and paralegals cannot be brought before a bar for disciplinary action. However, there are always consequences to unethical behavior, as discussed later in this chapter.

NFPA's Affirmation of Professional Responsibility

In 1977, the NFPA approved its Affirmation of Professional Responsibility to "delineate the principles of purpose and conduct toward which paralegals should aspire." NFPA's Affirmation covers the six broad categories of professional responsibility, professional conduct, competency and integrity, client confidences, support of public interests, and professional development. The NFPA's Affirmation is, in a sense, a proclamation by the members of the NFPA. The NFPA has no power to sanction paralegals for failure to abide by the Affirmation. The NFPA's Affirmation has received criticism as being too vague and not addressing the specific concerns of paralegals and attorneys who employ paralegals.

AFFIRMATION OF PROFESSIONAL RESPONSIBILITY
of the National Federation of Paralegal Associations

Preamble

The National Federation of Paralegal Associations recognizes and accepts its commitment to the realization of the most basic right of a free society, equal justice under the law.

In examining contemporary legal institutions and systems, the members of the paralegal profession recognize that a redefinition of the traditional delivery of legal services is essential in order to meet the needs of the general public. The paralegal profession is committed to increasing the availability and quality of legal services.

The National Federation of Paralegal Associations has adopted this *Affirmation of Professional Responsibility* to delineate the principles of purpose and conduct toward which paralegals should aspire. Through this Affirmation, the National Federation of Paralegal Associations places upon each paralegal the responsibility to adhere to these standards and encourages dedication to the development of the profession.

I. Professional Responsibility

A paralegal shall demonstrate initiative in performing and expanding the paralegal role in the delivery of legal services within the parameters of the unauthorized practice of law statutes.

Discussion: Recognizing the professional and legal responsibility to abide by the unauthorized practice of law statutes, the Federation supports and encourages new interpretations as to what constitutes the practice of law.

II. Professional Conduct

A paralegal shall maintain the highest standards of ethical conduct.

Discussion: It is the responsibility of a paralegal to avoid conduct which is unethical or appears to be unethical. Ethical principles are aspirational in character and embody the fundamental rules of conduct by which every paralegal should abide. Observance of these standards is essential to uphold respect for the legal system.

III. Competency and Integrity

A paralegal shall maintain a high level of competence and shall contribute to the integrity of the paralegal profession.

Discussion: The integrity of the paralegal profession is predicated upon individual competence. Professional competence is each paralegal's responsibility and is achieved through continuing education, awareness of developments in the field of law and aspiring to the highest standards of personal performance.

IV. Client Confidences

A paralegal shall preserve client confidences and privileged communications.

Discussion: Confidential information and privileged communication are a vital part of the attorney, paralegal and client relationship. The importance of preserving confidential and privileged information is understood to be an uncompromising obligation of every paralegal.

V. Support of Public Interests

A paralegal shall serve the public interests by contributing to the availability and delivery of quality legal services.

Discussion: It is the responsibility of each paralegal to promote the development and implementation of programs that address the legal needs of the public. A paralegal shall strive to maintain a sensitivity to public needs and to educate the public as to the services that paralegals may render.

VI. Professional Development

A paralegal shall promote the development of the paralegal profession.

Discussion: This Affirmation of Professional Responsibility promulgates a positive attitude through which a paralegal may recognize the importance, responsibility and potential of the paralegal contribution to the delivery of legal services. Participation in professional associations enhances the ability of the individual paralegal to contribute to the quality and growth of the paralegal profession.

NFPA Model Code of Ethics and Professional Responsibility

In May of 1993, NFPA adopted a Model Code of Ethics and Professional Responsibility. The memberships of several associations that are members of NFPA are reviewing the NFPA Model Code for adoption. Even when adopted by a state or local association, the NFPA Model Code is considered to be a set of guidelines; it is not enforceable by any governing agency. The NFPA Model Code consists of eight broad Canons, each supplemented by more specific ethical considerations (ECs).

NFPA MODEL CODE OF ETHICS AND PROFESSIONAL RESPONSIBILITY

PREAMBLE

The National Federation of Paralegal Associations, Inc. ("NFPA") is a professional organization comprised of paralegal associations and individual paralegals throughout the United States. Members of NFPA have varying types of backgrounds, experience, education, and job responsibilities which reflect the diversity of the paralegal profession. NFPA promotes the growth, development and recognition of the paralegal profession as an integral partner in the delivery of legal services.

NFPA recognizes that the creation of guidelines and standards for professional conduct are important for the development and expansion of the paralegal profession. In May 1993, NFPA adopted this Model Code of Ethics and Professional Responsibility ("NFPA Model Code") to delineate the principles for ethics and conduct to which every paralegal should aspire. The Model Code expresses NFPA's commitment to increasing the quality and efficiency of legal services and recognizes the profession's responsibilities to the public, the legal community, and colleagues.

Paralegals perform many different functions, and these functions differ greatly among practice areas. In addition, each jurisdiction has its own unique legal authority and practices governing ethical conduct and professional responsibilities.

It is essential that each paralegal strive for personal and professional excellence and encourage the professional development of other paralegals as well as those entering the profession. Participation in professional associations intended to advance the quality and standards of the legal profession is of particular importance. Paralegals should possess integrity, professional skill and dedication to the improvement of the legal system and should strive to expand the paralegal role in the delivery of legal services.

CANON 1.
A PARALEGAL SHALL ACHIEVE AND MAINTAIN A HIGH LEVEL OF COMPETENCE.

EC-1.1   A paralegal shall achieve competency through education, training, and work experience.

EC-1.2   A paralegal shall participate in continuing education to keep informed of current legal, technical and general developments.

EC-1.3   A paralegal shall perform all assignments promptly and efficiently.

CANON 2.
A PARALEGAL SHALL MAINTAIN A HIGH LEVEL OF PERSONAL AND PROFESSIONAL INTEGRITY.

EC-2.1   A paralegal shall not engage in any ex parte communications involving the courts or any other adjudicatory body in an attempt to exert undue influence or to obtain advantage for the benefit of only one party.

EC-2.2   A paralegal shall not communicate, or cause another to communicate, with a party the paralegal knows to be represented by a lawyer in a pending matter without the prior consent of the lawyer representing such other party.

EC-2.3   A paralegal shall ensure that all timekeeping and billing records prepared by the paralegal are thorough, accurate, and honest.

EC-2.4   A paralegal shall be scrupulous, thorough and honest in the identification and maintenance of all funds, securities, and other assets of a client and shall provide accurate accountings as appropriate.

EC-2.5   A paralegal shall advise the proper authority of any dishonest or fraudulent acts by any person pertaining to the handling of the funds, securities or other assets of a client.

CANON 3.
A PARALEGAL SHALL MAINTAIN A HIGH STANDARD OF PROFESSIONAL CONDUCT.

EC-3.1   A paralegal shall refrain from engaging in any conduct that offends the dignity and decorum of proceedings before a court or other adjudicatory body and shall be respectful of all rules and procedures.

EC-3.2   A paralegal shall advise the proper authority of any action of another legal professional which clearly demonstrates fraud, deceit, dishonesty, or misrepresentation.

EC-3.3   A paralegal shall avoid impropriety and the appearance of impropriety.

CANON 4.
A PARALEGAL SHALL SERVE THE PUBLIC INTEREST BY CONTRIBUTING TO THE DELIVERY OF QUALITY LEGAL SERVICES AND THE IMPROVEMENT OF THE LEGAL SYSTEM.

EC-4.1   A paralegal shall be sensitive to the legal needs of the public and shall promote the development and implementation of programs that address those needs.

EC-4.2 A paralegal shall support bona fide efforts to meet the need for legal services by those unable to pay reasonable or customary fees; for example, participation in pro bono projects and volunteer work.

EC-4.3 A paralegal shall support efforts to improve the legal system and shall assist in making changes.

CANON 5.
A PARALEGAL SHALL PRESERVE ALL CONFIDENTIAL INFORMATION PROVIDED BY THE CLIENT OR ACQUIRED FROM OTHER SOURCES BEFORE, DURING, AND AFTER THE COURSE OF THE PROFESSIONAL RELATIONSHIP.

EC-5.1 A paralegal shall be aware of and abide by all legal authority governing confidential information.

EC-5.2 A paralegal shall not use confidential information to the disadvantage of the client.

EC-5.3 A paralegal shall not use confidential information to the advantage of the paralegal or of a third person.

EC-5.4 A paralegal may reveal confidential information only after full disclosure and with the client's written consent; or, when required by law or court order; or, when necessary to prevent the client from committing an act which could result in death or serious bodily harm.

EC-5.5 A paralegal shall keep those individuals responsible for the legal representation of a client fully informed of any confidential information the paralegal may have pertaining to that client.

EC-5.6 A paralegal shall not engage in any indiscreet communications concerning clients.

CANON 6.
A PARALEGAL'S TITLE SHALL BE FULLY DISCLOSED.

EC-6.1 A paralegal's title shall clearly indicate the individual's status and shall be disclosed in all business and professional communications to avoid misunderstandings and misconceptions about the paralegal's role and responsibilities.

EC-6.2 A paralegal's title shall be included if the paralegal's name appears on business cards, letterhead, brochures, directories, and advertisements.

CANON 7.
A PARALEGAL SHALL NOT ENGAGE IN UNAUTHORIZED PRACTICE OF LAW.

EC-7.1 A paralegal shall comply with the applicable legal authority governing the unauthorized practice of law.

CANON 8.
A PARALEGAL SHALL AVOID CONFLICTS OF INTEREST AND SHALL DISCLOSE ANY POSSIBLE CONFLICT TO THE EMPLOYER OR CLIENT, AS WELL AS TO THE PROSPECTIVE EMPLOYERS OR CLIENTS.

EC-8.1 A paralegal shall act within the bounds of the law, solely for the benefit of the client, and shall be free of compromising influences and loyalties. Neither the paralegal's personal or business interest, nor those of other clients or third persons, should compromise the paralegal's professional judgment and loyalty to the client.

EC-8.2 A paralegal shall avoid conflicts of interest which may arise from previous assignments whether for a present or past employer or client.

EC-8.3 A paralegal shall avoid conflicts of interest which may arise from family relationships and from personal and business interests.

EC-8.4 A paralegal shall create and maintain an effective recordkeeping system that identifies clients, matters, and parties with which the paralegal has worked, to be able to determine whether an actual or potential conflict of interest exists.

EC-8.5 A paralegal shall reveal sufficient non-confidential information about a client or former client to reasonably ascertain if an actual or potential conflict of interest exists.

EC-8.6 A paralegal shall not participate in or conduct work on any matter where a conflict of interest has been identified.

EC-8.7 In matters where a conflict of interest has been identified and the client consents to continued representation, a paralegal shall comply fully with the implementation and maintenance of an Ethical Wall.

NALA's Code of Ethics and Professional Responsibility

NALA's Code of Ethics and Professional Responsibility closely resembles the ABA Code of Professional Responsibility. It was adopted in 1975 and revised in 1979 and 1988. Canon 12 of NALA's Code specifically states that legal assistants are governed by the ABA Model Code of Professional Responsibility and the ABA Model Rules of Professional Conduct.

CODE OF ETHICS AND PROFESSIONAL RESPONSIBILITY
of the National Association of Legal Assistants

Preamble

It is the responsibility of every legal assistant to adhere strictly to the accepted standards of legal ethics and to live by general principles of proper conduct. The performance of the duties of the legal assistant shall be governed by specific canons as defined herein in order that justice will be served and the goals of the profession attained.

The canons of ethics set forth hereinafter are adopted by the National Association of Legal Assistants, Inc., as a general guide, and the enumeration of these rules does not mean there are not others of equal importance although not specifically mentioned.

Canon 1

A legal assistant shall not perform any of the duties that lawyers only may perform nor do things that lawyers themselves may not do.

Canon 2

A legal assistant may perform any task delegated and supervised by a lawyer so long as the lawyer is responsible to the client, maintains a direct relationship with the client, and assumes full professional responsibility for the work product.

Canon 3

A legal assistant shall not engage in the practice of law by accepting cases, setting fees, giving legal advice or appearing in court (unless otherwise authorized by court or agency rules).

Canon 4

A legal assistant shall not act in matters involving professional legal judgment as the services of a lawyer are essential in the public interest whenever the exercise of such judgment is required.

Canon 5

A legal assistant must act prudently in determining the extent to which a client may be assisted without the presence of a lawyer.

Canon 6

A legal assistant shall not engage in the unauthorized practice of law and shall assist in preventing the unauthorized practice of law.

Canon 7

A legal assistant must protect the confidences of a client, and it shall be unethical for a legal assistant to violate any statute now in effect or hereafter to be enacted controlling privileged communications.

Canon 8

It is the obligation of the legal assistant to avoid conduct which would cause the lawyer to be unethical or even appear to be unethical, and loyalty to the employer is incumbent upon the legal assistant.

Canon 9

A legal assistant shall work continually to maintain integrity and a high degree of competency throughout the legal profession.

Canon 10

A legal assistant shall strive for perfection through education in order to better assist the legal profession in fulfilling its duty of making legal services available to clients and the public.

Canon 11

A legal assistant shall do all other things incidental, necessary, or expedient for the attainment of the ethics or responsibilities imposed by statute or rule of court.

Canon 12

A legal assistant is governed by the *American Bar Association Model Code of Professional Responsibility* and the *American Bar Association Model Rules of Professional Conduct*.

NALA's Model Standards and Guidelines for Utilization of Legal Assistants

In 1984, NALA presented its Model Standards and Guidelines for Utilization of Legal Assistants. NALA's Model Standards differ from NALA's Code in several ways. First, NALA's Model Standards are much more specific; for instance, the Model Standards set forth specific standards for paralegal education. Second, NALA's Model Standards are written for both paralegals and attorneys, with the aim of more effective utilization of legal assistants. They include specific suggestions for tasks that may be performed by paralegals, within the guidelines. As with NFPA's Code, NFPA's Affirmation, and NALA's Code, the guidelines were designed to be followed in conjunction with the ABA's Code of Professional Conduct and the ABA's Model Rules for Professional Responsibility.

MODEL STANDARDS AND GUIDELINES FOR UTILIZATION OF LEGAL ASSISTANTS of the National Association of Legal Assistants

Preamble
  Proper utilization of the services of legal assistants affects the efficient delivery of legal services. Legal assistants and the legal profession should be assured that some measures exist for identifying legal assistants and their role in assisting attorneys in the delivery of legal services. Therefore, the National Association of Legal Assistants, Inc., hereby adopts these Model Standards and Guidelines as an educational document for the benefit of legal assistants and the legal profession.

Definition
  Legal assistants are a distinguishable group of persons who assist attorneys in the delivery of legal services. Through formal education, training, and experience, legal assistants have knowledge and expertise regarding the legal system and substantive and procedural law which qualify them to do work of a legal nature under the supervision of an attorney.

Standards
  A legal assistant should meet certain minimum qualifications. The following standards may be used to determine an individual's qualifications as a legal assistant:

1. Successful completion of the Certified Legal Assistant (CLA) examination of the National Association of Legal Assistants, Inc.;

2. Graduation from an ABA approved program of study for legal assistants;

3. Graduation from a course of study for legal assistants which is institutionally accredited but not ABA approved, and which requires not less than the equivalent of 60 semester hours of classroom study;

4. Graduation from a course of study for legal assistants, other than those set forth in (2) and (3) above, plus not less than six months of in-house training as a legal assistant;

5. A baccalaureate degree in any field, plus not less than six months in-house training as a legal assistant;

6. A minimum of three years of law-related experience under the supervision of an attorney, including at least six months of in-house training as a legal assistant; or

7. Two years of in-house training as a legal assistant.

  For purposes of these standards, "in-house training as a legal assistant" means attorney education of the employee concerning legal assistant duties and these Guidelines. In addition to review and analysis of assignments, the legal assistant should receive a reasonable amount of instruction directly related to the duties and obligations of the legal assistant.

Guidelines
  These guidelines relating to standards of performance and professional responsibility are intended to aid legal assistants and attorneys. The responsibility rests with an attorney who employs legal assistants to educate them with respect to the duties they are assigned and to supervise the manner in which such duties are accomplished.

Legal assistants should:

1. Disclose their status as legal assistants at the outset of any professional relationship with a client, other attorneys, a court or administrative agency or personnel thereof, or members of the general public;

2. Preserve the confidences and secrets of all clients; and

3. Understand the attorney's Code of Professional Responsibility and these Guidelines in order to avoid any action which would involve the attorney in a violation of that Code, or give the appearance of professional impropriety.

Legal assistants should not:

1. Establish attorney-client relationships; set legal fees; give legal opinions or advice; or represent a client before a court; nor

2. Engage in, encourage, or contribute to any act which could constitute the unauthorized practice of law.

Legal assistants may perform services for an attorney in the representation of a client, provided:

1. The services performed by the legal assistant do not require the exercise of independent professional legal judgment;

2. The attorney maintains a direct relationship with the client and maintains control of all client matters;

3. The attorney supervises the legal assistant;

4. The attorney remains professionally responsible for all work on behalf of the client, including any actions taken or not taken by the legal assistant in connection therewith; and

5. The services performed supplement, merge with and become the attorney's work product.

In the supervision of a legal assistant, consideration should be given to:

1. Designating work assignments that correspond to the legal assistant's abilities, knowledge, training and experience;

2. Educating and training the legal assistant with respect to professional responsibility, local rules and practices and firm policies;

3. Monitoring the work and professional conduct of the legal assistant to ensure that the work is substantively correct and timely performed;

4. Providing continuing education for the legal assistant in substantive matters through courses, institutes, workshops, seminars and in-house training; and

5. Encouraging and supporting membership and active participation in professional organizations.

Except as otherwise provided by statute, court rule or decision, administrative rule or regulation, or the attorney's Code of Professional Responsibility; and within the preceding parameters and proscriptions, a legal assistant may perform any function delegated by an attorney, including, but not limited to the following:

1. Conduct client interviews and maintain general contact with the client after the establishment of the attorney-client relationship, so long as the client is aware of the status and function of the legal assistant, and the client contact is under the supervision of the attorney.

2. Locate and interview witnesses, so long as the witnesses are aware of the status and function of the legal assistant.

3. Conduct investigations and statistical and documentary research for review by the attorney.

4. Conduct legal research for review by the attorney.

5. Draft legal documents for review by the attorney.

6. Draft correspondence and pleadings for review by and signature of the attorney.

7. Summarize depositions, interrogatories, and testimony for review by the attorney.

8. Attend executions of wills, real estate closings, depositions, court or administrative hearings and trials with the attorney.

9. Author and sign letters, provided the legal assistant's status is clearly indicated and the correspondence does not contain independent legal opinions or legal advice.

Ethics Topics of Special Concern to Paralegals

Paralegals must be concerned with every aspect of ethics. There are, however, special types of ethical dilemmas with which paralegals are most often confronted. This section briefly discusses some of the areas of ethics of particular concern to paralegals, including the unauthorized practice of law, confidentiality, conflicts of interest, misrepresentation, solicitation, and reporting unethical behavior.

The Unauthorized Practice of Law

The issue of unauthorized practice of law by paralegals was highlighted in the mid-1970s when a woman named Rosemary Furman, a former court reporter with more than 20 years' experience, opened a legal typing business in Jacksonville, Florida. Ms. Furman founded her business on her strong belief that it was not necessary to retain an attorney to perform simple, routine legal services. Ms. Furman and her service provided and typed divorce, name change, adoption, and bankruptcy forms. She claimed that she did not give legal advice, but rather left all

---

SUMMARY OF PARALEGAL ETHICS CODES AND GUIDELINES

1977	The Affirmation of Professional Responsibility of the National Federation of Paralegal Associations
1993	The National Federation of Paralegal Associations Model Code of Ethics and Professional Responsibility
*1975	The National Association of Legal Assistants Code of Ethics and Professional Responsibility
1984	Model Standards and Guidelines for Utilization of Legal Assistants of the National Association of Legal Assistants

*Amended in 1979 and 1988.

Summary of Paralegal Ethics Codes and Guidelines

---

decisions to her clients. The Florida State Bar Association did not agree, and in 1977 it charged Rosemary Furman with practicing without a license. In 1979, the Florida State Supreme Court affirmed a decision finding Ms. Furman guilty and sentenced her to four months in jail. The government then commuted her sentence with the understanding that she would shut her business down permanently.

Part of the problem with the whole concept of the unauthorized practice of law is that "practice of law" has not been precisely and uniformly defined. *Ballentine's Law Dictionary* (Delmar Publishers/Lawyers Cooperative Publishing, 1994) defines the *practice of law* as:

> The work of an attorney at law in the preparation of pleadings and other papers in connection with a lawsuit or other proceeding; the trial or management of such an action on behalf of clients before judges, courts, and administrative agencies; the preparation of legal instruments and documents of all kinds; and advising clients with respect to their legal rights and taking action for them in matters connected with the law.

Paralegals who draft legal documents and perform other law-related services may at first glance appear to be practicing law. However, most paralegals work under the supervision of an attorney who is ultimately responsible for their actions. These paralegals are merely assisting attorneys with their practice of law. Therefore, there is really no question of unauthorized practice of law. However, legal technicians and freelance paralegals often work without the supervision of an attorney, and then the question of unauthorized practice becomes a problem.

The statutes of most states specifically address the issue of unauthorized practice of law, which is usually a misdemeanor. Paralegals should be familiar with the unauthorized practice of law statutes in the state in which they work, as well as pertinent case law and the position of the state bar.

Although the unauthorized practice of law is typically of little concern to the paralegal who is employed by a law firm, or working under the supervision of an attorney, one rule can be applied to all paralegals: *Do not give legal advice.* Almost without exception, giving legal advice to another by anyone who is not licensed to practice law is considered to be the unauthorized practice of law. If you are in doubt as to where to draw the line, it is best to check with the attorney for whom you work.

Confidentiality

Confidentiality is another area addressed in all standards of ethical behavior for attorneys and paralegals. Information that is revealed by a client to an attorney during the course of a legal consultation is privileged and may be disclosed only with the consent of the client, or when special circumstances provide an exception to the rule. The Model Rules of Professional Conduct promoted by the ABA address the topic of confidentiality in Rule 1.6:

Rule 1.6 Confidentiality of information.

(a) A lawyer shall not reveal information relating to representation of a client except as stated in paragraphs (b), (c), and (d) unless the client consents after disclosure to the client.

(b) A lawyer shall reveal such information to the extent the lawyer believes necessary:

  (1) To prevent a client from committing a crime; or

  (2) To prevent a death or substantial bodily harm to another.

(c) A lawyer may reveal such information to the extent the lawyer believes necessary:

(1) To serve the client's interest unless it is information the client specifically requires not to be disclosed;

(2) To establish a claim or defense on behalf of the lawyer in a controversy between the lawyer and client;

(3) To establish a defense to a criminal charge or civil claim against the lawyer based upon conduct in which the client was involved;

(4) To respond to allegations in any proceeding concerning the lawyer's representation of the client; or

(5) To comply with the *Rules of Professional Conduct.*

(d) When required by a tribunal to reveal such information, a lawyer may first exhaust all appellate remedies.

The privilege of confidentiality clearly extends to the lawyer's employees and law firm staff, especially paralegals. Paralegals are often in a position to receive confidential information and must at all times resist the temptation to disclose this information, either to the media, as a matter of convenience when working on a client's file, or as a source of interesting gossip with friends and family. Although paralegals may not be sanctioned by the bar association, the attorneys they work for may be sanctioned for their paralegals' violations. In addition, they may be subject to lawsuits by clients who have been damaged by a paralegal's breach of confidentiality.

Conflicts of Interest

Another area of particular concern to paralegals and attorneys alike is conflict of interest. The term **conflict of interest** relates to the existence of a variance between the interests of the parties in a **fiduciary relationship**. Because attorneys act in a fiduciary capacity toward their clients, they must be sure that they have no other interests that

conflict of interest   The existence of a variance between the interests of the parties in a fiduciary relationship.

fiduciary relationship   A relationship between two persons in which one is obligated to act with the utmost good faith, honesty, and loyalty on behalf of the other.

would conflict with the interests of their clients, or even appear to so conflict.

A common situation in which a conflict of interest may arise is when an attorney leaves one law firm to work for another firm. If the first firm has represented clients who are involved in lawsuits with clients of the second firm, a potential conflict of interest arises. This can be a problem for attorneys leaving large law firms that represent hundreds of clients involved in litigation with numerous opposing parties. The risk of disclosure of confidential information creates some serious ethical questions.

This problem is often minimized by what is referred to as erecting a *Chinese wall* or an *ethical wall*. This means that the attorney who comes from another firm will have no exposure to or access to information about cases or situations in which his or her prior law firm may have been involved.

Rule 1.9 of the ABA Model Rules addresses the problem as follows:

> Rule 1.9 A lawyer who has formerly represented a client in a matter shall not thereafter:
>
> (a) represent another person in the same or a substantially related matter to which that person's interests are materially adverse to the interests of the former client unless the former client consents after consultation; or
>
> (b) use information relating to the representation to the disadvantage of the former client except as rule 1.6 would permit with respect to a client or when the information has become generally known.

Similar rules apply to paralegals. The New Jersey Supreme Court Advisory Committee on Professional Ethics ruled that a paralegal may move from one firm to another despite the fact that the two firms represented opposing parties in an ongoing lawsuit. As a condition of the hiring, the new firm had to construct an ethical wall to keep the paralegal from any contact with the case involving her former firm.[3]

All paralegals must work to prevent even the appearance of conflict of interest.

Misrepresentation

Paralegals must be careful not to divulge any confidential information. They must also be concerned with not giving out any false or misleading information to clients, opposing parties, or opposing parties' counsel. Misrepresentation, although not specifically addressed in the Code of Ethics of Paralegals, is clearly unethical.

Rule 3.4 of the ABA's Model Rules specifically states:

> Rule 3.4 A lawyer shall not:
>
> (a) unlawfully obstruct another party's access to evidence or unlawfully alter, destroy or conceal a document or other material having potential evidentiary value. A lawyer shall not counsel or assist another person to do any such act;
>
> (b) falsify evidence, counsel or assist a witness to testify falsely, or offer an inducement to a witness that is prohibited by law;
>
> (c) knowingly disobey an obligation under the rules of a tribunal except for an open refusal based on an assertion that no valid obligation exists;
>
> (d) in pretrial procedure, make a frivolous discovery request or fail to make a reasonably diligent effort to comply with a legally proper discovery request by an opposing party;
>
> (e) in trial, allude to any matter that the lawyer does not reasonably believe is relevant or that will not be supported by admissible evidence, assert personal knowledge of facts in issue except when testifying as a witness, or state a personal opinion as to the justness of a cause, the credibility of a witness, the culpability of a civil litigant or the guilt or innocence of an accused; or
>
> (f) request a person other than a client to refrain from voluntarily giving relevant information to another party unless:
>
> > (1) the person is a relative or an employee or other agent of a client; and
> >
> > (2) the lawyer reasonably believes that the person's interest will not be adversely affected by refraining from giving such information.

Paralegals who act in violation of this rule or who assist an attorney with any act in violation of this rule are clearly guilty of unethical behavior.

Solicitation

Years ago, advertisement of legal services by attorneys was considered unethical and thus was strictly prohibited. Obviously, as shown by the television, newspaper, and other advertisements that abound today, this is no longer the case. However, there are limits on an attorney's ethical solicitation of business. To thwart "ambulance chasers," the aggressive solicitation of individual clients is still prohibited. Rule 7.3 of the Model Rules addresses the situation as follows:

Rule 7.3 Direct contact with prospective clients.

A lawyer may not solicit professional employment from a prospective client with whom the lawyer has no family or prior professional relationship, in person or otherwise, when a significant motive for the lawyer's doing so is the lawyer's pecuniary gain. The term "solicit" includes contact in person, by telephone or telegraph, by letter or other writing, or by other communication directed to a specific recipient … .

A paralegal should not actively participate in the solicitation of individual clients, and especially should not encourage someone to switch from one attorney to the attorney who employs the paralegal. This action would be considered unethical under most circumstances.

Reporting Unethical Behavior

One ethical dilemma paralegals may encounter is discovering unethical behavior by the attorneys they work for. Reporting unethical behavior could mean the loss of status or of employment with the firm. Is it unethical to remain silent? Yes. Although it is not exceedingly clear from the codes of ethics and the NFPA Affirmation, when paralegals are held to the standards of attorneys, they must comply with Model Rule 8.3(a), which states:

Rule 8.3(a)   A lawyer having knowledge that another lawyer has committed a violation of the rules of professional conduct that raises a substantial question as to that lawyer's honesty, trustworthiness or fitness as a lawyer in other respects, shall inform the appropriate professional authority.

This rule leaves no doubt that it is the attorney's responsibility to report a violation of the Rules of Professional Conduct to the proper professional authority. Because paralegals are held to the same ethical standards as attorneys in many instances, this rule applies to paralegals as well.

There are measures short of reporting an attorney to the state's professional authority that can be taken by a paralegal who witnesses unethical behavior by an attorney employer. Before a paralegal reports unethical behavior, he or she may want to discuss the behavior with the attorney who appears to be acting unethically. Are there circumstances of which the paralegal is unaware? Possibly the action is not, in fact, unethical. If it becomes clear after addressing the attorney that the actions are unethical and/or illegal, perhaps the matter can be handled by others within the law firm. The paralegal may choose to bring the matter to the attention of the appropriate individual or committee within the law firm. If this still does not produce positive results, the attorney should be reported to the ethics committee of the state bar association.

To the date of this publication, there have been no cases involving a paralegal's duty to report unethical or illegal behavior. However, it remains clear that if questioned by a court or an ethics committee of the state bar, the paralegal has a duty to report the full truth concerning any actions of which he or she has knowledge. Any paralegal deciding to take this action must use the utmost care not to violate client confidences.

A paralegal who considers himself or herself in a serious ethical dilemma that may require reporting an attorney may want to seek independent legal advice on the proper steps to take—again, being careful not to violate client confidences.

Practical Applications of Paralegal Ethics

Although paralegal ethics may seem rather vague and abstract, paralegals are faced with tough ethical choices throughout their careers. In this section, several possible applications of the affirmations, codes, and standards and guidelines are applied to hypothetical situations that are similar to situations faced by working paralegals.

Situation 1

Sharon Knowlan is a legal assistant with Blakley, Barker & Crabtree. She works in the personal injury area with attorney Ann Blakley, and has had extensive experience in that area. One case Sharon has been working on is the *Redwell v. Greenly* case, wherein Ann Blakley represents Agnes Redwell in a personal injury suit. The case had been proceeding for 18 months, and Ann Blakley was out of town and unreachable when Agnes Redwell called Sharon Knowlan one morning.

"I've got to have my case settled," said Agnes. "My mother is very sick and I need the money to fly out to Washington to be with her."

After a brief discussion regarding the settlement negotiations that had taken place so far, Sharon Knowlan called the attorney for the defendant. She did not know the attorney personally, so she identified herself as "Sharon Knowlan with Blakley, Barker & Crabtree" and proceeded to negotiate a settlement on behalf of Agnes. After several telephone calls back and forth on that day, Sharon settled the case for $500 more than Ann Blakley had told her it was worth.

Were Sharon's actions unethical?

Yes. Sharon definitely overstepped the boundaries of work that should be performed by a paralegal by negotiating a settlement on behalf of a client. Sharon's actions would probably be in violation of the unauthorized practice of law statutes in her state. In addition, her action was in violation of several of the Model Rules and

Canons of the CPR, as well as sections of the NFPA's Model Code and Affirmations and NALA's Code. Specific violations include the facts that Sharon was not working under attorney supervision and that she did not identify herself as a paralegal when negotiating the settlement with the defendant's attorney. In all likelihood, the attorney for the defendant assumed that Sharon was an attorney employed by Blakley, Barker & Crabtree.

Situation 2

Martin Gerard is a paralegal specializing in family law with the firm of Elias, Schneider & Goldstrom. Martin had been working on the *Larkin v. Larkin* divorce case when he got a call concerning Mrs. Larkin (his firm's client). The call was from a woman named Susan Davis, who identified herself as a babysitter who had been retained by Mr. Larkin to watch the Larkin's three-year-old daughter.

"Little Bridgett fell down and she may need stitches," explained Ms. Davis. "Mr. Larkin is on his way home to get her, but I thought Mrs. Larkin would like to know. I have tried her apartment and her work number but I haven't gotten any answer. Do you know where I may reach her?"

Martin did know where Mrs. Larkin was. She had left town with her boyfriend last week to try to relax a little before her divorce hearing next week. She had given Martin her number in case of emergency.

"She went down to Florida with Jim Greenfield," said Martin. "Let me give you her number."

Did Martin act unethically?

Yes. By giving a babysitter who was retained by Mr. Larkin information about Mrs. Larkin's whereabouts and actions, Martin was violating the client's confidentiality. There were a number of other actions that Martin could have taken in this situation. For example, Martin could have taken the information from Susan Davis and called Mrs. Larkin himself, without betraying Mrs. Larkin's confidence by giving out her whereabouts and telephone number.

Situation 3

Sandy Meyers had just begun her first week at her job as a litigation paralegal, with the firm of Wendell & Jacobson, when she was confronted by a problem. She was assigned to work on the *Ace Manufacturing v. Diamond Supply* file, a case name that she recognized from her previous job. At her last job, her employer represented Ace Manufacturing. Sandy was not directly involved with the case, although she did help out one of the other paralegals at her last firm by summarizing a few depositions. Now Sandy's new job was with Wendell & Jacobson, and they were representing Diamond Supply; Sandy had been asked to oversee the entire litigation process. Sandy had a feeling that this might be considered a conflict of interest, but she wasn't really sure. She was still on probation at her new job and didn't want to rock the boat. Should she tell her new employer of her past involvement with the file?

Yes, definitely! Even the appearance of a conflict of interest such as this could cause severe problems for Sandy's new employers. At the least, they would be embarrassed if they knew nothing of Sandy's prior involvement and her former employer called them on it. At worst, Sandy's actions could be cause for an action by the state bar association's ethics committee. Her actions could also cause them to lose their client. Canon 8 of NFPA's Model Code clearly establishes Sandy's duty to disclose the possible conflict.

Situation 4

Brenda Jergens enjoyed her new position at the firm of Bremmer & Bremmer, a small law firm where everyone knew each other well and the atmosphere was very informal. Because the firm specialized in personal injury plaintiff litigation, it often incurred considerable costs on behalf of clients. These clients frequently gave the firm money to be deposited in trust accounts for expenditures on their behalf. Separate bank accounts were established for the deposit of funds delivered to the firm in its fiduciary capacity. One of Brenda's duties was to maintain the client trust accounts for the firm.

Brenda was, however, a bit nervous about a procedure that seemed to be the norm at Bremmer & Bremmer. Twice in the last month, the firm was short of cash on payday. Mr. Bremmer, the firm's senior partner, had asked Brenda to cut a check to the firm from the client trust account as a "loan" to the firm to make payroll. The first time, the money was repaid in a few days. Although the money borrowed from the trust account the second time hadn't been repaid yet, she was reasonably certain that it would be soon. However, the next payday was approaching and Brenda was uncomfortable with the situation. Brenda wasn't sure, but she thought that perhaps Mr. Bremmer's actions were unethical. Were they?

Yes. His actions were unethical. Rule 1.5 of the Model Rules of Professional Conduct mandates that an attorney hold client property separate from the attorney's own property. Client trust accounts consist of funds that belong to clients, not to the firm. Many lawyers and law firms have found themselves in trouble with state ethics committees, courts, and clients for misuse of client funds.

Brenda should talk to Mr. Bremmer or another appropriate individual within the firm about the situation, and explain her uneasiness. She should also refuse to cut any further checks from the trust account for firm expenses, as she may also be held partly responsible. If the unethical actions continue at Bremmer & Bremmer, she may even be forced to take the matter up with the ethics committee of the state bar, to protect the firm's clients in accordance with Canon 2, EC-2.5 of the NFPA's Model Code.

The Consequences of Unethical Paralegal Behavior

When a paralegal acts unethically, he or she is not in any danger of being disbarred or of being brought before a board for a reprimand. However, this does not mean that unethical behavior by a paralegal cannot cause serious consequences. A paralegal's unethical behavior can result in a loss of respect for the paralegal, the loss of a client to the firm, and disciplinary action against the responsible attorney. In addition, the paralegal may lose his or her employment and be subject to criminal prosecution or a civil lawsuit.

Loss of Respect

At a minimum, unethical behavior by a paralegal can lead to the loss of respect by the paralegal's superiors and co-workers and to a poor reputation with his or her peers. The legal community is often the target of negative stereotyping, and unethical behavior by one of its members reflects poorly on everyone. No one wants to be associated with an unethical paralegal.

Loss of Clients

In addition to losing the respect of your co-workers, unethical behavior can lead to the loss of clients of the paralegal's firm. Unethical behavior that jeopardizes a client's case will not be well thought of. Clients will hold their attorneys responsible for the behavior of their employees. If a paralegal breaks a client's trust by unethical behavior, the attorney may very well lose the client.

Disciplinary Action Against Responsible Attorney

As discussed earlier, unethical behavior by a paralegal can lead to disciplinary action against the attorney who is responsible for the paralegal. Attorneys can be disciplined or even disbarred for violations of the code of ethics in the state in which the attorney practices.

Loss of Employment

Behavior by a paralegal that is clearly unethical and damaging to a client, attorney, or the law firm often leads to loss of employment. Not only does the paralegal become unemployed, but the paralegal also probably will not receive any recommendation from the discharging employer.

Illegal Behavior

Unethical acts are unethical because they harm someone. Depending on the type of behavior, these same acts may also be criminal. Paralegals may find themselves facing criminal charges when their unethical behavior is also illegal behavior.

Lawsuits

When the unethical behavior of a paralegal causes a client or another party to be injured, the firm that employs the paralegal could be sued by the injured party. Although paralegals are typically covered under the law firm's malpractice insurance, no paralegal wants to be responsible for causing the employer to be sued. In addition, there is always the possibility that the paralegal's actions could cause him or her to be named personally in a lawsuit. If the paralegal's conduct is clearly outside the scope of employment, the paralegal may be personally responsible for any damages caused by his or her actions.

Summary Questions

1. What are some of the reasons that attorneys must adhere to strict ethical rules?

2. Do NFPA and NALA have any authority to enforce their Affirmation, Model Codes, and Model Standards?

3. What actions can individual states take, either through the state bar or through the courts, to enforce the states' ethical codes of professional conduct for attorneys?

4. What are some types of duties that may be considered the unauthorized practice of law when performed by a paralegal?

5. What is a *Chinese wall?* How could it affect a paralegal who is changing jobs?

6. What are some actions that a paralegal may take after witnessing unethical behavior in the law firm where he or she works?

7. What are some of the negative consequences that may be associated with unethical behavior by a paralegal?

8. Suppose that you are a new paralegal in the firm of Hanson & Birkemeyer, a small law firm that specializes in plaintiff personal injury. Since the beginning of your employment with Hanson & Birkemeyer six months ago, you have been working on the *Breyer v. Linden* personal injury file. You are familiar with all the facts of the case. Shortly after noon one day, Ms. Birkemeyer calls during the lunch recess of a court hearing she is attending.

   "I just overheard some interesting information in the hallway concerning the *Breyer v. Linden* lawsuit," says Ms. Birkemeyer. "I think today may be the day to settle. I won't be getting out of here until late this afternoon, but you are familiar with all the facts of the case. I want you to call Terry Small, the attorney for the defendant, tell him that you are with our firm, and tell him that you want to settle the case for $150,000, but it has to be today. Don't settle for less than $100,000. If you have any questions you can ask one of the attorneys in the office, but you know more about the case than anyone else."

   Do you see any problems with this? What would you do?

 ## Practical Paralegal Skills

What local guidelines apply to the attorneys in your home state? Have the Model Rules of Professional Conduct or the Code of Professional Responsibility been adopted? How are sanctions against attorneys for unethical behavior handled?

 ## Notes

[1] Rule 6.1, Model Rules of Professional Conduct.

[2] Rule 6.2, Model Rules of Professional Conduct.

[3] Cohn, Steven, "New Jersey Committee Allows 'Ethical Wall' for Paralegals Moving to New Firms," *Legal Assistant Today* 20 (Mar. 1993).

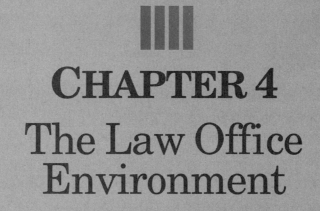

CHAPTER 4
The Law Office Environment

Each law firm has its own environment and its own team of personnel. However, some basics apply to almost all law offices. Some of the first things paralegals want to know when they land that first paralegal position are how the law firm functions and where they fit in. This chapter tries to answer those questions, as completely as possible, by focusing on law office personnel matters, law office administration, timekeeping and billing requirements, law firm accounting systems, law firm economics and zero-based budgeting, records management, suspense and diary systems, word and data processing systems, and the law library and other management systems.

Law Office Personnel Matters

The manner in which law office personnel matters are handled greatly affects both the law office environment and the paralegal. This section looks at the typical law firm staff, working with attorneys, dealing with difficult situations, performance reviews, and stress management, all topics of special concern to paralegals.

The Law Firm Staff

This section examines the role of each staff member and that person's typical relation to the law firm's paralegals.

The Law Firm Partners or Shareholders

Depending on whether the law firm is a professional corporation or a partnership, the firm's *shareholders* or *partners* are the attorneys who own the law firm. Sole practitioners are the only owners of their firms, but very large law firms may have dozens of partners or shareholders. The exact role played by the partners or shareholders will depend on the size and focus of the

TIPS ON TAKING ASSIGNMENTS FROM ATTORNEYS
▪ Be sure that you and the attorney agree on a realistic due date for the assignment
▪ Ask questions about any aspects of the assignment that are unclear to you
▪ Be sure to find out who to bill your time to
▪ Always take notes when an attorney is giving you an assignment. Keep the notes with the file while you are working
▪ If you need additional resources to complete your assignment efficiently and on time, say so
▪ Organize your questions while you are working, so that you can ask the attorney all of the pertinent questions at one or two meetings, instead of constantly asking the attorney questions
▪ When working on longer assignments, keep the attorney apprised of your progress. Progress reports in memo format are usually sufficient when the assignment is progressing as expected
▪ Volunteer to perform any related tasks that may present themselves and to tie up any loose ends to your assignment

To avoid ethical violations, paralegals must be supervised by an attorney. These tips will help to ensure a successful attorney-paralegal relationship.

TIMEKEEPING IN SIX-MINUTE INTERVALS	
0–12 MINUTES	= .2 HOURS
12–24 MINUTES	= .4 HOURS
24–36 MINUTES	= .6 HOURS
36–48 MINUTES	= .8 HOURS
48–60 MINUTES	= 1.0 HOURS

It is important to learn how the law office records time.

[CLIENT NAME]				DAILY TIME DIARY		
			DATE 7/2/93		ATTY. 999	

CLIENT #	MATTER #	DATE	TIME	ATTY.	CODE	SUB CODE
0001	10004	7/2	1.8	999	101	101
CLE - altered a motion to compel discovery						

CLIENT #	MATTER #	DATE	TIME	ATTY.	CODE	SUB CODE
0284	11006	7/2	2.5	999	101	101
Revised memo to file on Post Judgment collection.						

CLIENT #	MATTER #	DATE	TIME	ATTY.	CODE	SUB CODE
0284	11006	7/2	2.0	999	131	131
Documents to non-parties and cover letter.						

CLIENT #	MATTER #	DATE	TIME	ATTY.	CODE	SUB CODE
0365	14392	7/2	.3	999	101	101
Revise memo on whether the economic loss rule applies to installers as opposed to manufacturers.						

CLIENT #	MATTER #	DATE	TIME	ATTY.	CODE	SUB CODE
0284	11006	7/2	.5	999	116	116
Letter to opposing counsel informing her of pending actions and to urge payment						

CLIENT #	MATTER #	DATE	TIME	ATTY.	CODE	SUB CODE
0284	14418	7/2	.6	999	108	108
How to garnish the wages of a self-employed person (research).						

CLIENT #	MATTER #	DATE	TIME	ATTY.	CODE	SUB CODE

CLIENT #	MATTER #	DATE	TIME	ATTY.	CODE	SUB CODE

		TOTAL TIME	

A Daily Time Diary A typical factor in determining whether a paralegal deserves a promotion or raise is whether completed time sheets are submitted promptly for all billable hours.

law firm. In larger law firms, several partners or shareholders may constitute an executive committee. One of the partners may be designated the managing partner, to work with the office administrator and the executive committee to handle office administrative matters.

In many large firms, partners or shareholders devote the majority of their time to speaking engagements and courting new clients. Their actual practice of law and work on client files is reserved for the largest, most important cases or matters. In law firms where this is so, paralegals may have little involvement with the firm's partners or shareholders. Most of their contact will be with the firm's associates who are delegated to oversee the majority of the client files.

Law firms may also have attorneys who are "of counsel." Attorneys of counsel are usually semi-retired partners or shareholders who have maintained their contacts with the firm and usually work on a part-time basis.

The Law Firm Associates

Attorneys who do not have an ownership interest in a law firm are generally referred to as the firm's *associates*. These individuals are typically hired with the promise of becoming a partner or shareholder of the firm if their performance is adequate, within a set number of years.

The associates of the firm are the attorneys typically responsible for overseeing the daily work on client files. They may be in charge of files, or they may report to responsible partners or shareholders. The associates typically delegate assignments to the paralegals in the firm and work closely to supervise them. Associates in large law firms are often required to bill a very high number of hours per year, so they work under a certain amount of pressure from the partners to whom they report. Most associates are very appreciative of the efforts paralegals make to assist them, so long as the work is done correctly and on time. Remember, if you are a paralegal working with an associate on a particular file, the associate will be ultimately responsible for your work. A certain amount of scrutiny is certainly understandable when the associate is unfamiliar with your work. In addition, associates have a legal, ethical, and moral obligation to supervise your work.

Law Clerks

Law clerks are law students who work in a firm to gain experience before graduating from law school or passing the bar exam. Law students are often hired for summer positions and part-time positions during the school year, and often aim at being hired as associates after graduating and passing the bar exam. The utilization of law clerks varies significantly from firm to firm. In most firms, law clerks' work involves intensive legal research and writing. Paralegals and law clerks may be assigned to work together on certain projects, especially those involving legal research. Law clerks are seldom assigned client files, and they rarely meet with clients.

The Law Office Administrator

The position of the *law office administrator* or *law office manager* will depend on the size and management structure of the law firm. In most small to medium-size firms, the office administrator is responsible for all administrative functions of the law firm, including personnel, marketing, and budgeting. In larger firms, separate individuals may perform each of these functions. Paralegals typically report to the office administrator on all personnel matters and questions concerning office policy. The office administrator reports to the partners or shareholders of the firm, the managing partner, or the executive committee. The law office administrator is responsible for overseeing the entire nonattorney staff of the law firm. At times, the associates of a law firm also report to the law office administrator on certain matters.

Paralegal Manager

Larger law firms that employ several paralegals often have a *paralegal manager* on staff. Paralegal managers are responsible for coordinating the assignments of the paralegals in their departments and, at times, for acting as liaisons between the paralegals and the attorneys when problems arise. Paralegal managers may report to the law office administrator, directly to the law firm's partners or shareholders, to the managing partner, or to the management or executive committee.

The duties of a paralegal manager may include:

1. Hiring and supervising paralegal personnel

2. Delegating assignments and managing the work flow to the paralegals within the firm

3. Scheduling and conducting meetings of the paralegal personnel within a firm

4. Acting as liaison between the paralegals and the attorneys within a law firm

5. Designing and implementing policies and systems for the paralegal personnel within a law firm.

Paralegals

The number of paralegals in a firm will vary depending on the size of the firm. Paralegals may be departmentalized in terms of specialty, or they may all make up the "paralegal department" of a firm. Paralegals report to the paralegal manager (if there is one) or to the law office administrator and any attorneys who delegate assignments to them. This means that paralegals often must answer to several different individuals. Paralegal office space also depends on the office's situation. Some paralegals have their own small but private offices; in firms where office space is at a premium, paralegals may share offices or be located in modular office space.

The Law Office Librarian

Every law office has some type of law library, and every law library has at least one individual who performs the functions of a *law librarian*. A knowledgeable law librarian can be a valuable asset to all law firm personnel. If you are assigned several research projects, chances are that you will get to know the librarian very well. Don't be afraid to ask for help from the librarian when you need it. Law librarians are usually very knowledgeable and very willing to help. You can repay the favor to the librarian by carefully following all procedures for using the law firm library.

In many small to medium-sized law firms, no actual librarian is employed, and the task of library maintenance frequently falls to the firm's paralegals. In that event, it will be especially important for you to become familiar with the law firm library as soon as possible so that you can assist with library maintenance if you are asked to do so.

Case Assistants

Case assistants are relative newcomers to the law office. They are unique to large law firms and firms that do a significant amount of litigation. Case assistants help paralegals with the clerical tasks associated with large cases, including document organization and indexing. At times new paralegals will begin their careers as case assistants to get the experience to qualify for paralegal positions.

Legal Secretaries

Never underestimate the importance of a good *legal secretary*. If you are starting a new position within a law firm, a knowledgeable, experienced legal secretary can be an invaluable asset. He or she can help to familiarize you with office procedures, the firm's files and clients, and the basic procedures followed in preparing legal documents.

Typically, paralegals do not have their own personal secretaries, but instead share the services of a secretary with one or more other paralegals and/or associates. Sharing a secretary with a busy attorney can be a source of frustration to the paralegal when both the paralegal and the attorney have deadlines to meet and secretarial work to be done. Try to be courteous by always giving your secretary as much time as possible to complete assignments. Your secretary may be responsible for typing your correspondence and certain legal documents, or for sending them through the word processing department within the firm. He or she may also be responsible for taking your phone calls when you are out of the office or otherwise unavailable.

In many law firms that are fully automated, paralegals have little in the way of secretarial support. They are responsible for typing their own correspondence and short legal documents on terminals located in their offices. Longer legal documents are usually prepared by the word processing department.

The Word Processor

Most law firms have a designated *word processor* or *word processing department*. Because paralegals often prepare numerous legal documents, it is important that they understand the correct procedures for requesting documents from the word processing department. Experienced word processors can be extremely helpful in assisting you with finding the correct form to use for the particular document you need. Word processors may report to a word processing manager, or they may report directly to the law office administrator. Remember always to do your best to give the word processing department ample time to complete your assignments.

The Receptionist

The law firm *receptionist* works the "front line" for the firm, greeting clients in person as they come to the office. He or she is also responsible for answering the telephone and routing calls to the correct individual. It is, therefore, important that you let the receptionist know your whereabouts during the day in accordance with law office procedure.

The Records Manager

Another individual or department on which paralegals often rely heavily is the *records manager* or the *records department*. Records managers are often responsible for retrieving files for paralegals, replacing files when paralegals are through with them, and assisting with finding lost files in the law office. Each firm has its own procedure for file retrieval. It is important that procedures be followed as closely as possible, to make the records manager and the records department more

efficient. The records file clerk is often also responsible for duplicating and calendar/reminder systems.

Other Law Office Personnel

The staff members listed here are just a sampling of the personnel common to most law firms. Various other positions exist within law firms, including junior partners, senior associates, senior paralegals, messengers, bookkeepers, and data processors.

Working with Attorneys

Because there are as many different personalities as there are attorneys, it is difficult to generalize about rules to follow when working with attorneys. After you are on the job long enough to get to know the attorneys for whom you work, you will be the best judge of how to work with particular attorneys. However, if you are just starting out in a new position, and have never worked in a law firm environment before, here are some general rules to follow until you get your bearings.

1. Be courteous and professional
2. Be prepared when asking questions
3. Be assertive when necessary
4. Communicate!

Courtesy and Professionalism

When you begin working for an attorney, he or she will assess your ability to meet with other people, especially his or her clients. It is important that your manner remain courteous and professional. Be careful to use proper grammar, dress appropriately, and speak clearly.

Be Prepared When Asking Questions

Attorneys are taught to analyze facts. If you are working with an attorney on a file and you have a question, ask! Before you ask your question, however, review the situation carefully to be sure that you are aware of all the facts. Before the attorney can answer your question, he or she will need to know all of the circumstances surrounding the issue.

Be Assertive When Necessary

Busy attorneys can at times be very focused on their work. If you have a question or need to talk about something, it may take persistence to get the attorney's full attention. However, if there is a problem that the attorney must know about, it is up to you to be assertive enough to get the message across.

If you have performed research and come to a conclusion, don't be intimidated if the attorney starts to question you about your conclusion. Be assertive. Possibly the attorney is just playing devil's advocate and wants to make certain that you are sure of yourself and your position.

Being assertive also means knowing when to say no. If an attorney gives you an assignment and asks for it tomorrow morning, don't say yes unless you can have it ready by tomorrow morning. If you have other assignments that will prevent you from completing the task on time, say so by explaining the situation to the attorney. He or she can give you a different due date or give the assignment to someone else who has more time. Don't get caught in a power struggle. When an attorney wants you to give priority to his or her assignment, in preference to an assignment you have already received, ask him or her to discuss it with the other attorney and let them come to an agreement.

Communicate

One of the most important rules in dealing with attorneys and the practice of law is to communicate. When you are working on a file with a particular attorney, be sure to let him or her know of all developments. The type of communication you use will be determined by the type of message you are sending. If you just need to update an attorney as to routine progress on a file, perhaps you can combine it with the progress or status of other files and send a progress report, to save the attorney's time. When using a memo to communicate important facts to an attorney, you may want to follow up by mentioning it to him or her a few days later to make sure that the memo was received and reviewed. If, however, there is an emergency, you will need to speak face-to-face as soon as possible—even if it means locating an attorney at a meeting or in a court room.

Honesty is another important part of communication, including admitting to any mistakes you may make. In almost every instance, any mistake you make is best corrected by admitting it and looking for alternative solutions as soon as possible. Trying to cover up the mistake may only cause problems to escalate.

Dealing with Difficult Employers, Co-Workers, and Situations

Everyone at some point in his or her career must work with a difficult person. The problem may be a personality conflict or just a bad attitude on the part of one or more individuals. If you are involved in a conflict that causes you stress or impedes your progress on the job, it is best to deal quickly and directly with the problem. Address the person face-to-face and politely ask to talk it out. Often misunderstandings can be solved simply by communicating with the other individual.

There may be times when you are unhappy with managerial decisions within the office. Office policies may inadvertently make it more difficult for you to efficiently perform your duties. The best way to counteract this situation is by taking control whenever possible. If a policy or problem at your job is causing you to be unhappy, sit down and think it through logically. Here is one four-step process you can follow to get through problems with difficult situations at work:

1. Is there anything you can do on your own to change the situation? If not, you must decide to live with it or take it up with management. If you decide that it is not important enough to address management

with the problem, remember that that is your decision.

2. If you decide to bring the problem to the attention of the firm's management, be prepared with answers and suggestions for improving the situation.

3. At this point, management may recognize the problem, and perhaps fix it with one of your suggestions, or management may disagree with you and decide to do nothing. Perhaps they can explain their reasons to you. There may be circumstances surrounding the problem of which you were unaware.

4. If you are still unhappy with the situation, you can do one of two things. Live with it, knowing that you have done all that you can, or begin looking for other employment.

If you decide to discuss a difficult work situation with someone at work, keep in mind that the person in whom you confide should be one who is likely to offer positive advice that you can use.

Performance Reviews and Evaluations

Most law firms and legal departments conduct personnel evaluations annually, although it is typical to conduct the first evaluation six months after an employee has begun work. Your performance review is a time for management to let you know how they feel you are doing and to discuss your future with the firm. A good review is often accompanied by a better-than-average pay increase. Paralegals are usually evaluated on their billable hours, organizational skills, overall quality of work, writing skills, initiative, judgment, ability to complete assignments on time, ability to get along with others, punctuality, teamwork, and knowledge of their work.

The attorneys for whom the paralegal most often works and the paralegal manager (if there is one) will be asked to complete evaluation forms with their opinions on each of the skills and abilities to be evaluated for the paralegal.

These forms are then collected and reviewed by the law office administrator, who typically performs the reviews.

During your review, ask questions concerning the future goals and plans of the firm and how those plans may affect you. Remind management of your long-term goals and commitments, and listen carefully to suggestions for improvement in your performance. It is important that paralegals maintain accurate records of their own concerning time worked, case loads, and other responsibilities assigned to them. This information will be helpful to both the paralegal and management during the evaluation process.

Stress Management

Every job involves some level of stress. If the paralegal profession involved no stress whatsoever, it would not be very interesting or challenging. The goal of stress management is not to eliminate stress, but rather to learn to deal with it effectively. Everyone has personal methods of dealing with stress. Some, such as substance abuse and excessive absence from work, are destructive. Here, however, are suggestions on several constructive ways to deal with the stress you will encounter on your job.

1. If your workload looks overwhelming and it is causing you stress, make a list of the things you need to do and prioritize them. It may not be as bad as you think.

2. Tackle the problem. Stress can sometimes give you excess nervous energy. Use it to your advantage by working late to get caught up if you are stressed about getting behind with your workload.

3. If you are stressed about a particular assignment, talk it over with the responsible attorney, the paralegal manager, or someone else who might be able to help you with the problem.

4. Take a break. Leave the situation for a quick change of scenery and to regain control. Things should look better when you return.

5. Take a walk on your lunch break. Exercise and fresh air can do wonders to alleviate stress.

6. Talk the stress-causing problem over with someone. A friend or relative who will lend a sympathetic ear is usually preferable to a co-worker. Keep in mind the rules of confidentiality, though; never identify clients or specific legal problems outside the law office.

An Introduction to Law Office Administration

The law is a highly organized and systemized field of knowledge; the processes and procedures of the law are similarly highly organized and structured. Excellent attorneys are also characterized by a highly organized and efficient approach to the process of thought and analysis. It is of critical importance that the law office and the legal department (the place in which the work of the law is done) also be effectively organized and systematized.

The Systems Approach

One of the most common and most effective approaches to law office administration is the systems approach. Using a systems approach has several meanings for the administration of an office. It means that the tasks to be accomplished are each identified and systematized. This regularization of procedures assures accuracy and saves time, two major goals of a law firm. It also enables the law firm to maintain effective records over time; if a paralegal had his or her own system of recordkeeping, and left the firm, no one would be able to decipher the file's meaning once he or she had departed. A systematized approach to file maintenance, in contrast, ensures that information will be accessible no matter who the firm employs. The systems approach thereby assists in malpractice avoidance by providing a structure, complete with checks and balances, that fosters careful, effective legal work.

The systems approach, in addition to treating each separate area as a system, also treats the whole structure (in this case a law firm or legal department) as a system. This means that the whole system is made up of interdependent parts and that each part understands its place within the whole. Paralegals become involved with all the members of the law office team, from the courier to the associates to the partners. Paralegals are also a part of the legal team serving the client, and each member of the legal team—the senior lawyer, the junior lawyer, the paralegal, the legal secretary—has an important and unique role to play in providing quality services for the client. The law firm comprises not only the various groups specializing in specific areas of the law, but also the administrative section, the billing section, the word processing section, the courier/mailroom/copying center section, the accounting section, and other specialized sections, depending on the size and structure of the firm. By understanding the law firm as a system which demands that each part fulfill its role in harmony with the other parts, the paralegal can make the greatest contribution to effective administration of the firm.

Avoiding Malpractice Through Systems

In the practice of law, the possibility of being sued for **malpractice** or being brought before the bar for ethical violations is always a reality.

BALLENTINESBALLENTINESBALLENTINESBALLENTINESBALLENTINESBALLENTINESBALLENTINESBALLENTINESBALLENTINESBALLENTINESBALLENTINESBALLENTINESBALLENTINESBALLENTINES

malpractice   The failure of a professional to act with reasonable care; misconduct by a professional person in the course of engaging in the profession.

Lawyers and law offices open themselves to potential violations when they intentionally or negligently violate the law or legal ethics. A negligent violation does not require bad intent; it requires merely an error or a mistake—but in the practice of law a mistake can be devastating. For that reason, law offices need to minimize or eliminate any behavior that falls below the standard of what a reasonable attorney would do.

The systems approach, by breaking down and organizing the activities to be performed and the timetable in which they must be performed, helps a law office do its work in an efficient and organized manner, thus helping to prevent malpractice. No attorney intends to miss a court date, or to have an action barred because he or she failed to file a complaint before the running of the statute of limitations, but these things happen. A systems approach cannot guarantee perfection; no system can do that because the system must be used by fallible people. A systems approach will, however, create the kind of environment in which the work of the law can best be done: organized, accurate, and professional. For example, most firms have three methods for checking court dates. First, dates are published in the local legal news organ, which is then checked by firm personnel. Second, dates are sent to attorneys by calendar clerks for the judges. Third, computer systems are set up to remind attorneys of court deadlines. Having three methods prevents the possibility that a court date will be missed. Under the systems approach, the firm would have Paralegal A check the newspapers, Paralegal B open all mail for the litigation department and log court dates, and Paralegal C check the computer system. A system involving three different people regularly checking various sources for court dates is more consistent and less likely to result in an error than if such a system were not in place.

Timekeeping and Billing Requirements

The age-old saying, "Time is money," could not be more true than in the law office environment. Because time is an intangible, though, it is often elusive and hard to sell. Think of it this way: If you were a shopkeeper selling clocks, you would have a full range of styles, sizes, colors, manufacturers, and, of course, prices. A customer could come into your shop, look at the clock, touch it, and maybe even hear it chime. He or she could then determine how much the clock was worth to him or her.

In the law office, the professional staff (of which the paralegal is an integral part) sells ideas, expertise, and general services for an hourly rate. Because one cannot see or touch ideas, expertise, or service, it makes the item for sale an intangible. It is, therefore, much more difficult for the average client to determine the worth of the purchase.

In addition to the hourly rate, lawyers use other methods to charge clients for legal services. One approach is the **contingency fee**, where the client pays a percentage (usually a third) of what he or she collects in a lawsuit or settlement to the attorney. If the client does not collect anything in the lawsuit, he or she does not pay any legal fees, although the client must pay expenses such as court costs, filing fees, and court reporting fees.

Another type of charge is the **fixed fee**, which is most frequently used for standardized procedures such as real estate closings, bankruptcies, or preparation of wills. Standardized fees are used by attorneys for performing routine legal

BALLENTINESBALLENTINESBALLENTINESBALLENTINESBALLENTINESBALLENTINESBALLENTINESBALLENTINESBALLENTINESBALLENTINESBALLENTINESBALLENTINESBALLENTINESBALLENTINES

contingent fee   A fee for legal services, calculated on the basis of an agreed-upon percentage of the amount of money recovered for the client by the attorney.

fixed fee   A standardized fee used by attorneys for performing routine legal tasks.

Law Office Scenario

Jennifer Christopher, a paralegal in a busy law firm, raced into her office. She had gotten a late start this morning, and she knew her desk was piled with work to be done.

She looked around on the top of her desk, but couldn't find her daily time diary. Just then the phone rang. Before she had completed her telephone conference with a client, one of the associate attorneys was waiting in her office to discuss a file they were both working on. Jennifer had to cut their conversation short to make it to a meeting in the conference room with one of the partners and his client. The whole day proceeded like this. Jennifer went from the telephone to conferences to reviewing and drafting documents to meetings with attorneys. Before she knew it, the day was over, and Jennifer had not accounted for one minute of her time. She sat down and tried to reconstruct her day, and all of the files she had worked on, but came up with only six billable hours. "I know I worked more than that," Jennifer thought.

tasks that should take a predetermined amount of time. For example, the preparation of a basic will without any trust documents may cost $150. However, if the client wants a more specialized will, the extra services probably will not be covered by a fixed fee.

By thinking of the sale of legal services as an intangible rather than tangible thing, you can see how important it is to give the client quality service for a fair price. To do so, all timekeepers (attorneys, paralegals, and law clerks) must be efficient, effective, and accurate in timekeeping.

Billing Requirements

Most firms have annual hourly time goals or requirements. These goals are the firm's attempt to project and maintain its objectives by making sure that each contributor is appropriately productive. These time requirements are referred to as **billable hour requirements**. *Billable hours,* as the name denotes, are hours of work that can be billed directly to the client. Billable hours include any activity, from interviewing the client to making phone calls to doing legal research, necessary for that particular case.

The average billable time requirement for paralegals is approximately 1,500 hours per year,[1] but can vary significantly depending on the size of the firm and its location. With two weeks of vacation, one week of sick leave, and one week of paid holidays per year, the average hours to be billed per day is approximately 6.25 hours. Although this may not seem like much time to bill during an 8-hour day, keep in mind that these 6.25 hours consist only of time that can be billed directly to a client. Excellent time management skills are required to bill 6.25 hours per day without working many more hours than 8 per day. The average billable hour requirement for attorneys is even higher; in many firms, attorneys may be expected to bill a minimum of 2,000 hours per year.

As a paralegal, you will also be expected to spend a certain amount of time on nonbillable office matters, such as attendance at staff and committee meetings and continuing legal education courses. You will probably be asked to account for this time as well.

BALLENTINESBALLENTINESBALLENTINESBALLENTINESBALLENTINESBALLENTINESBALLENTINESBALLENTINESBALLENTINESBALLENTINESBALLENTINESBALLENTINESBALLENTINES

billable hour requirements   Number of hours required of each attorney, paralegal, or other timekeeper to be billed to a client on behalf of the law firm.

Overtime

There is a great deal of controversy in the legal community surrounding the issue of overtime pay for paralegals. Executives are typically exempt from labor laws that provide for overtime compensation for other types of employees. Clerical workers are considered nonexempt and are entitled to overtime pay for hours worked in excess of 40 hours per week. Paralegals may fall somewhere in between. Most paralegals feel that they should not be considered eligible for overtime pay. In a 1992 survey by *Legal Assistant Today*[2] 58 percent of the responding paralegals felt that paralegals should not be paid overtime. Only 37 percent actually were paid overtime. The respondents who did not favor overtime pay for paralegals stated that they want to be viewed as professionals and felt that they are adequately compensated as such without overtime pay.

In contrast, some paralegals feel that they should be fairly compensated for overtime with additional pay. Although they consider themselves to be professionals, they recognize that the attorneys in the office who are considered professionals earn considerably more than paralegals.

Many firms handle the overtime compensation issue by awarding year-end bonuses to paralegals, to reflect in some way the overtime worked by the paralegals.

Timekeeping and Billing Systems

With advances in technology and the increasing affordability of computers, most law firms now have automated timekeeping and billing systems. Most of these automated systems, however, follow the same principles as the manual systems that have been popular in law firms for years. For that reason, this section explores both manual and automated timekeeping and billing systems.

Timekeeping

Timekeepers, including attorneys, paralegals, law clerks, and any other personnel who bill for their time, often bill in tenths of an hour. One hour is generally represented by 1.0, a half hour by .5, and so forth. That means that timekeepers must track their activities over six-minute intervals. Another option is to keep time by quarters, with the smallest unit being a quarter of an hour. All attorneys and paralegals within a firm should use the same time unit system, for consistency of reporting. Most people generally do not monitor their time this carefully, so it is essential for the paralegal to wear a watch or have a desk clock that can be frequently checked and noted at the beginning of each task.

A *daily time diary* is the most commonly used method to record time. It contains the original data and is the source document for preparation of the final time slips, so naturally the recorded information must be clear and legible, to facilitate the transfer of this data to the final document. It is most effective to record your time on a daily time diary as each task is performed. Record each task when it is begun and give a description of the work. Immediately upon completion of the task, record the ending time. Keeping track of time in this way ensures that the majority of time during the day is accounted for. The law office scenario at the beginning of this chapter illustrates how easily billable time can get lost when it is not kept track of throughout the day. Supervising attorneys may review the timesheets of paralegals and offer valuable suggestions for managing and recording time effectively. Accounting for the majority of a paralegal's time increases productivity. In addition, keeping good, accurate time records permits the firm to collect for the majority of the time billed. Increasing productivity and recovery for most of the time worked are two important factors that keep a law firm in business.

In some large firms, where the cooperation of a large number of timekeepers is essential to effective billing, it is often the practice to distribute paychecks only to those timekeepers who are up to date with their timekeeping, pursuant to office procedure.

Manual Timekeeping and Billing Systems

Some firms, especially smaller firms, use manual timekeeping and billing systems. One that is popular among smaller firms is the *slip system.* Slips are printed on perforated paper or on pads, and attorneys and paralegals complete one slip for each activity they perform. The slip is then filed in a billing folder or envelope for each client. At the end of the billing period (i.e., monthly, quarterly, etc.), the slips are pulled out and tallied. From that information, bills are prepared and sent to the clients.

Another method, also used primarily in smaller firms, involves using a ledger sheet. A ledger sheet form enables the individual timekeeper to record, usually by hand, the activities he or she performed during the day, the time spent, and the amount to be billed. These ledgers are accumulated and used for billing at the appropriate time.

Manual bills may be typed on a typewriter or into a computer. They may display for the client a variety of information, such as (1) the timekeeper's name; (2) the tasks performed; (3) the date(s) the tasks were performed; (4) the length of time spent on the task(s); (5) the dollar value for each task. Today's clients generally prefer the maximum amount of information on their bills, and it is a good idea to provide as complete and thorough an accounting as possible, for both professional and economic reasons. Detailed bills are being used with more and more frequency, whereas general bills are becoming less common.

Automated Timekeeping and Billing Systems

In recent years great advances have been made in timekeeping and billing software designed specifically for law firms. As these systems have become more economical, more firms are automating their timekeeping and billing systems. Automated systems are often found to be more efficient, easier to use, and more effective at capturing and billing the time of attorneys and paralegals.

One automated timekeeping and billing system based on the manual timeslip system involves the direct input of timeslips by the timekeeper or a secretary into the computer. This system uses the processing capabilities and efficiency of the computer to record and analyze the use of time. These systems generally work as follows: The timekeeper manually records time and gives hard copies (slips) to the secretary or other designated person, who inputs the time into the billing system. The information put into the system usually includes the client name, the file number, the timekeeper's name and billing rate, the designation of the timekeeper (i.e., attorney, law clerk, or paralegal), the time spent on the specific task, the date the task was performed, and a narrative of what task was performed. From this data, the computer system can compile the complete bill for the client, as well as various reports for the firm.

After the bill is prepared, it is approved by the appropriate attorney and mailed to the client, often with a cover letter. A copy of the bill should be kept in the billing file for that particular client or matter, and a copy is typically sent to the bookkeeping or accounting department.

Timekeeping and Billing Reports

The use of systems for timekeeping and billing allows the generation of several useful reports regarding the timekeeping and billing practices of each timekeeper. The title and exact content of each report will depend on which type of system is used. Usually, fully automated timekeeping systems allow for the generation of several different types of reports that may or may not be used or circulated.

File Status Report

A file status report may display unbilled time, unbilled disbursements, and fee and disbursement receivable totals, as well as other status amounts used in calculating the investment in a client or matter. The report generally is sorted by billing attorney, but shows all timekeepers who were active on the matter for a given period.

Attorney Detail Report

The attorney detail report displays all billed and unbilled time for each client or matter for each attorney. The firm may decide to show both hour and dollar amounts, or hours only. This report may also reflect current month and year-to-date numbers.

Attorney and Paralegal Realization Reports

Realization reports may very well be the most important of all reports. They show the hours and dollars billed and/or written off for all timekeepers and the percentage of the timekeeper's time that was billed. If, for instance, a paralegal

---

GREGG & MICHAELS, LTD.
ATTORNEYS AT LAW
123 WASHINGTON PLAZA
ST. PAUL, MINNESOTA 12345
(612) 555-1212

To: Mr. Clark Jamison, President
Able Plastics Company
4567 Birch Avenue
St. Paul, MN 12345

Date	Timekeeper	Task	Time	Amount	Total
3/4/94	JDO	Client interview	1.5	$150	$225
3/5/94	TMT	Draft Articles of Incorporation	3.0	$ 75	$225
3/6/94	JDO	Review and revise Articles of Incorporation	1.0	$150	$150
3/6/94	TMT	Draft bylaws and stock certificates; Order Minute Book; Conference with JDO	4.0	$ 75	$300
3/6/94	JDO	Conference with TMT	1.0	$150	$150
			TOTAL		$1,050.00

Expenses:

Corporate Minute Book $50.00

TOTAL AMOUNT DUE: $1,100.00

A Detailed Bill   Most clients expect and request a detailed accounting of the legal services provided by a law firm.

works long hours, but because the work is considered inadequate, only a portion of it can be billed (the balance is written off), the paralegal's realization rate will be low.

Law Firm Accounting Systems

Law firms, depending upon their size and type, use a variety of accounting systems. Paralegals may be responsible for assisting with the accounting process. This section introduces the accounting processes most commonly used in law firms.

Accounts Receivable: One-Write System (Manual)

The one-write manual system of accounting may be used by smaller law firms and can be purchased from an office supply store. Each client or matter is assigned an individual ledger card. By using a special pegboard and various carbonized forms, information such as amount charged to client, date of charge, amount paid by client, date paid by client, and balance due may be easily reflected by recording information with a ballpoint pen onto the necessary forms. The information is recorded all at one time; hence the name *one-write system*. It is a very simplified system of bookkeeping, but for the smaller firm, it can be quite effective. It does not, however, allow for any complex recordation, and it requires a fair amount of storage space, such as file drawers, to maintain the ledger cards.

Similar to the one-write system, a general manual system for accounts payable and receivable can be used by very small law firms, usually

GREGG & MICHAELS, LTD.
ATTORNEYS AT LAW
123 WASHINGTON PLAZA
ST. PAUL, MINNESOTA 12345
(612) 555-1212

To: Mr. Clark Jamison, President
Able Plastics Company
4567 Birch Avenue
St. Paul, MN 12345

For Services Rendered from March 1, 1994 through March 31, 1994 regarding the incorporation of Able Plastics Company:

Legal Services:	$1,050.00
Costs Advanced:	50.00
TOTAL AMOUNT DUE:	$1,100.00

A General Bill General bills are becoming less common.

CONTROL NO: 4593
SYST. DATE: 10/31/83 14:23
REPORT NO.: 272-00504

BARRISTER - FINANCIAL MANAGEMENT SYSTEM
AGED WORK-IN-PROGRESS AND ACCOUNTS RECEIVABLE REPORT
FROM: 00/00/00   TO: 10/31/83
FOR BILLING ATTORNEY   301 MICHAELS

PAGE NO.: 1
ACCT DATE: 10/31/83
GROUP: SQ1

ID	CLIENT-MATTER	TOTAL AMOUNT	CURRENT	31 - 60 DAYS	61 - 90 DAYS	91 - 180 DAYS	OVER 180 DAYS
0123.001	MILLER PLASTICS — GENERAL						
	UNBILLED TIME	265.00	265.00	.00	.00	.00	.00
	UNBILLED DISBURSEMENTS	64.50	64.50	.00	.00	.00	.00
	ACCOUNTS RECEIVABLE - FEE	5535.00	535.00	.00	.00	5000.00	.00
	ACCOUNTS RECEIVABLE - DISB	76.25	76.25	.00	.00	.00	.00
	AMOUNT ON ACCOUNT	5000.00					
	PREPAYMENT	2000.00					
	INVESTMENT (TOTAL)	1059.25CR	940.75	.00	.00	5000.00	.00
0123.002	MILLER PLASTICS — PRODUCT LIABILITY						
	UNBILLED TIME	2188.00	706.75	1481.25	.00	.00	.00
	UNBILLED DISBURSEMENTS	233.98	231.12	2.86	.00	.00	.00
	ACCOUNTS RECEIVABLE - FEE	6948.00	.00	.00	4073.00	2875.00	.00
	ACCOUNTS RECEIVABLE - DISB	58.50	.00	.00	.00	58.50	.00
	AMOUNT ON ACCOUNT	3000.00					
	INVESTMENT (TOTAL)	6428.48	937.87	1484.11	4073.00	2933.50	.00
0123.003	MILLER PLASTICS — CLAIM OF J.K. MILLER						
	UNBILLED TIME	985.25	455.00	530.25	.00	.00	.00
	UNBILLED DISBURSEMENTS	110.88	68.58	42.30	.00	.00	.00
	ACCOUNTS RECEIVABLE - FEE	1279.50	.00	.00	.00	1279.50	.00
	INVESTMENT (TOTAL)	2375.63	523.58	572.55	.00	1279.50	.00
** TOTAL CLIENT 0123.	MILLER PLASTICS **						
	UNBILLED TIME	3438.25	1426.75	2011.50	.00	.00	.00
	UNBILLED DISBURSEMENTS	409.36	364.20	45.16	.00	.00	.00
	ACCOUNTS RECEIVABLE - FEE	13762.50	535.00	.00	4073.00	9154.50	.00
	ACCOUNTS RECEIVABLE - DISB	134.75	76.25	.00	.00	58.50	.00
	AMOUNT ON ACCOUNT	8000.00					
	PREPAYMENT	2000.00					
	INVESTMENT (TOTAL)	7744.86	2402.20	2056.66	4073.00	9213.00	.00
1100.006	HILL ELECTRONICS, INC. — VS. A. P. SAMUELS						
	UNBILLED TIME	1192.50	1192.50	.00	.00	.00	.00
	ACCOUNTS RECEIVABLE - FEE	4246.00	2092.00	.00	528.00	1626.00	.00
	ACCOUNTS RECEIVABLE - DISB	3.50	3.50	.00	.00	.00	.00
	PREPAYMENT	5000.00					
	INVESTMENT (TOTAL)	442.00	3288.00	.00	528.00	1626.00	.00
** TOTAL CLIENT 1100.	HILL ELECTRONICS, INC. **						
	UNBILLED TIME	1192.50	1192.50	.00	.00	.00	.00
	ACCOUNTS RECEIVABLE - FEE	4246.00	2092.00	.00	528.00	1626.00	.00
	ACCOUNTS RECEIVABLE - DISB	3.50	3.50	.00	.00	.00	.00
	PREPAYMENT	5000.00					
	INVESTMENT (TOTAL)	442.00	3288.00	.00	528.00	1626.00	.00

Aged Work-in-Progress and Accounts Receivable Report   Computerized accounts receivable and work-in-progress systems provide instantaneous reports to paralegals and their supervising attorneys on the status of client relationships. (Courtesy of Barrister Information Systems Corporation.)

those with no more than five attorneys and a low volume of monthly transactions. Using this method, the bookkeeper or person responsible for the accounting process issues checks for general office operations and client disbursements from the firm checking account. At the end of each month, all disbursements and receipts are posted in a general journal and allocated to the various income and expense accounts numbers. From that, balances are posted in a general ledger, a trial balance is run, and a financial statement is prepared.

Accounts Receivable: Computerized Systems

In a larger, more automated law firm, a bookkeeper is generally in charge of recording all accounts receivable. Automated timekeeping and billing are complemented by automated bookkeeping.

After a computerized bill has been sent to the client, it is logged into the system. The bookkeeper maintains copies of all statements to clients generated on the system, as well as copies of statements paid and the payment checks made within the calendar year. Any checks received in payment for services, reimbursements, or refunds must be forwarded to the bookkeeper for credit to the proper account.

On a monthly basis, all billing attorneys are provided with an aged work-in-progress report and a schedule of past due accounts. At any time during the month, though, updated information may be requested from the bookkeeper detailing the status of unpaid or delinquent statements. If an account is delinquent, the billing attorney may wish to send a reminder to the client.

It is becoming more and more prevalent for firms to actively pursue past due accounts, because once accounts are more than six months past due, it is often difficult to collect on them. By keeping in constant contact with clients who have past due accounts, via letters and subsequent reminders, the probability of collecting those accounts dramatically improves. Failing to collect past due accounts causes the firm to lose money, because it has spent time on an unprofitable file that could have been spent on a client whose accounts are current.

Accounts Payable

In a small law firm, one person is usually designated to pay bills, which may include rent, equipment leases, stationery, office supplies, utilities, salaries, and so forth. The person in charge usually works with a good adding machine with both a digital display and a tape. Bills are time-stamped as they arrive, with special attention to their terms, (the conditions under which the debt is to be repaid). For example, the bill might be due upon receipt, or it might be due within 30 days. All deadlines should be met so that the firm does not damage its credit rating. A company checking account often uses a system with duplicate copies of checks, so that detailed references are always at hand.

Checks also must be written for expenses that the firm is willing to pay on behalf of a client. As these bills are incurred, they must be charged to the client's file so that the client can repay the debt.

In larger firms, accounts payable are generally handled on the computer system. Information is entered into the computer on a screen that looks much like a check. Continuous-form checks may then be printed on laser printers. In either case, timeliness is highly important. Bills must be kept current so that the firm's credit reputation is not tarnished. Frequently, checks for client expenses are sent to the some vendors (i.e., courts, court reporters, and investigators), and it is important to keep those accounts current so that the firm can maintain a positive working relationship with these services.

If a check is written on behalf of a client, that information must be fed into the database as well as entered on the check. Generally, checks written for expenses for which the client is to reimburse the firm will have information about the client number and name, the matter number, the amount, the date, and an explanation of why the expense was incurred. Copies of these checks or computer printouts from inputting the information are then forwarded to the billing department so that the expenses can be billed to clients.

Payroll

In small law firms, payroll checks can be prepared by the bookkeeper or the individual chosen to perform the accounting process. Checks are usually issued either on a biweekly or semimonthly basis. Employee payroll deductions are calculated from federal, state, and, in some cases, city withholding charts, by using the employees' withholding allowance certificates. It is very important when preparing any payroll that all tax deposits and all quarterly and annual reports be made in a timely manner. Serious penalties are levied for failure to comply.

Larger law firms often use a payroll service, because it cuts the time spent by the payroll processor. Payroll services can usually be found to match the firm's needs at a relatively inexpensive cost. A small firm might choose to use a tele-data service or a phone-in procedure to transmit payroll data. Larger, more automated firms might use a personal computer payroll system that transmits data to the payroll service by modem. One of the major assets of a payroll service is that the firm is notified of all forthcoming payroll deposits and reportings by the service. Additionally, payroll services will, in most cases, prepare quarterly and annual reports, including W-2 forms. If prearranged, they will make tax deposits, thus alleviating any worry about failure to make timely filings.

Check Requests

To safeguard and control the flow of firm checks, one person is typically assigned the responsibility of writing (but not signing) the checks and balancing the accounts. In the small firm, a paralegal may be assigned to this task. In larger firms, a bookkeeper is usually in charge. Check requests are used so that all necessary information can be captured.

The Safe

Many firms have safes for important documents or checks that must be held for a period of time. Evidence, stock certificates, bonds, and original

wills and trust documents are other important papers that may be kept in a firm's safe. These items should be kept in envelopes with notations on the outside indicating the client/matter number, the attorney/paralegal who placed the package in the safe, and a brief description of the contents. The package should then be logged. Removal of items from the safe should require the signature of the responsible paralegal or attorney and the date of removal.

Trust Accounts

The bookkeeper or another responsible person within the law firm must be in charge of the firm's **trust accounts**, separate bank accounts established for deposit of funds delivered to the firm in its fiduciary capacity. For example, in some cases the firm is given money to hold in escrow until a case is finally completed or settled, or the firm receives money to hold until the client requests that it be disbursed. In another situation, the firm receives funds on prior written instructions from one party and disburses them to other parties when the funds clear.

Check Request

Circle One   Regular   Client Trust Account

Pay to the Order of: _____

Check to be charged to:

Firm Expense: _____

Client Name and Number: _____

Purpose: _____

Date: _____   Amount $_____

Attorney (Name and Number): _____

Comments: _____

Check Request Most law offices have specific procedures on who can request a check and for what amounts.

Funds received by the firm in its fiduciary capacity will be deposited in the firm's trust account when the attorney receiving the funds instructs the person responsible to do so. The firm will establish a trust account file for each trust account client.

Withdrawals from the trust account are made through a check request signed by the responsible attorney. This request must clearly identify the client and indicate that the funds are to be withdrawn from the trust account. Even funds to be paid directly to the firm from the trust account must be requested through a check request. The reason for the particularities of trust accounts are that the funds in these accounts belong to the clients, not to the firm. Therefore, every safeguard must be taken to ensure that the funds are used only for the benefit of the client and not the firm.

The policy of all firms should be that funds deposited into trust accounts cannot be disbursed until they have cleared the issuing bank and are credited to the firm's trust account. The procedure usually takes about two days, but can take substantially longer.

In some states, trust funds must be held in interest-bearing accounts, and the interest obtained on these accounts is forwarded to the bar association for indigent defense or other bar activities. If this is required, the firm must contact the local or state bar association to be sure that all procedures are complied with.

Reimbursable Expenses

A number of expenses incurred by paralegals and attorneys are reimbursed by the firm. Such expenses might include automobile mileage and travel expenses, such as hotel accommodations, airfare, taxis, long-distance telephone, food, and entertainment. The list varies depending on the law firm and its rules on reimbursement.

All supporting data concerning reimbursable expenses must be kept and filed in a logical manner. The Internal Revenue Service requires that special, detailed reporting of all business meals, client entertainment, out-of-town travel, and business gift expenses taken as deductions be shown separately on the firm's tax return. This calls for care in charging only appropriate items to these accounts. The reimbursement request forms for such expenses are detailed and require adequate substantiating information.

Items Typically Charged Back to Clients

A number of costs to the law firm are charged back to clients. These items are typically enumerated on a client's periodic statement. Some of these costs include file retrieval and storage costs; charges for long-distance telephone calls to or on behalf of the client; charges from WESTLAW, LEXIS, or other computerized research databases for research performed on behalf of the client; photocopying charges; courier charges; overtime expenses; and facsimile charges.

When costs are expended on behalf of a client, they must be carefully accounted for so that the firm can be reimbursed when the client is billed.

Law Firm Economics and Zero-Based Budgeting

One common approach to law firm accounting and economics is *zero-based budgeting*. Generally, zero-based budgeting requires a justification of all expenditures and develops a budget based on merit rather than the former year's allocations.

BALLENTINESBALLENTINESBALLENTINESBALLENTINESBALLENTINESBALLENTINESBALLENTINESBALLENTINESBALLENTINESBALLENTINESBALLENTINESBALLENTINESBALLENTINESBALLENTINES

trust account   A bank account created by a depositor for the benefit of a person or persons other than the depositor. The money in a trust account may not be commingled with other funds of the depositor or of the bank.

Zero-based budgeting has been applied, in recent years, to law firm accounting because the practice of law has changed greatly. Because of the competitive business environment in which law firms exist today, law firms must exhibit great fiscal control if they are to be successful. It has become very costly to run a law firm in a competitive way, so it is important that everyone, from the bottom up, be aware of the economics of the practice and contribute to the firm's economic goals.

Zero-based budgeting is a very specific budgeting process designed to maximize the firm's productivity by making all relevant employees accountable to an overall structure. Each person is accountable for his or her bottom line—that is, income versus expense. With zero-based budgeting, every attorney and paralegal plays a role to some degree with regard to his or her overhead and income. It is therefore imperative that all attorneys, paralegals, and other affected employees understand their own realization rates (work effort versus dollars earned). It is equally important that billing partners recognize the effective rates that their billing practices create.

Billing Predictions

In the zero-based budgeting process, firm members who bill their time commit to the number of billable hours they believe they will work in the forthcoming year and the quality of that work (proposed realization rate). *Realization rate* means the amount of time that is billed versus the amount of income the firm has received from that billed time. For example, an attorney may bill 3.0 hours on a timesheet for the drafting of a complaint, but the billing partner may bill only 1.5 hours to the client. Thus, the firm will only receive profits from 1.5 hours, rather than 3.0 hours, which would make the attorney's realization rate on that particular task 50 percent. A good realization rate is 80 percent or higher. This procedure gives the firm a potential gross revenue figure that all partners or shareholders have the responsibility to bill and collect in a timely fashion. After the budgeting process is completed,

someone with a firm grasp on reality must review the completed proposals to identify unrealistic estimates and bargain with the authors of those proposals.

Revenue Predictions

Revenue predictions are predictions of the actual dollars to be billed and collected—not just billable hours. There can be a huge difference. For example, you may work 1,600 hours at a rate of $60 per hour. If you could bill and collect at 100 percent realization, you would bring $96,000 to the firm. If, however, you worked 1,600 hours at a rate of $60, but because of write-offs, you only billed and collected 80 percent, then the revenue figure attributed to you would be $76,800. Uncollectible billed fees must also be taken into consideration.

Cost Predictions

The following costs must be estimated and balanced against expected revenue:

1. *Rental Expenses.* This figure is allocated to each billing member of the firm depending upon the amount of space he or she physically occupies. It is typically allocated by shares, which are units to measure space allocations. For instance, a partner-sized office may be worth five shares; an associate-sized office four shares; and a paralegal office two shares.

2. *General Overhead.* This is each firm member's share of the office expenses, such as electricity, equipment, water, maintenance, security, supplies, and the like.

3. *Administrative Overhead.* This is each firm member's share of services rendered by receptionists, couriers, word and data processers, accounting, and so on—administration in general.

4. *Secretarial Support.* This calculation includes salaries and rent of space for the secretaries and word processing staff, including temporaries. An attorney and

paralegal sharing a secretary may use a 75/25 percent allocation. Salaries must also take into account benefit packages offered to these employees.

5. *Personal Expenses.* These expenses can include dues, licenses, continuing education, and retirement contributions made on behalf of each billing member of the firm.

All of the preceding factors are taken into consideration to produce zero-based budget reports, one for each billing member of the firm, and one for the firm as a whole. This combined report will project the predicted net profit for the firm for the upcoming year.

It is easy to see that when all the expenses are added up, one must make a significant contribution through revenue to come out with a profit. The general rule of thumb is that a paralegal's salary is approximately one-third of his or her gross (not net) revenue figure. It has never been as important as it is now for paralegals to understand that the practice of law is a business and must be operated as one. Clients are acutely aware of the costs of legal services and no longer hesitate to shop around for the best service at the best price. Law firms must streamline their operations and become keenly aware of the competition, which now includes the many corporate clients that are broadening their in-house legal departments and thus reducing the need for outside counsel. The paralegal will play an extremely important role in the 1990s. Many firms are hiring large numbers of paralegals and reducing the numbers of young associate attorneys because (1) paralegals work for good but reasonable salaries compared to those of attorneys; (2) they will never have to be considered for partnership; and (3) they are well-trained professionals who can do a wide variety of tasks, including research, writing, and interviewing of clients.

Records Management

The operation of a law firm, and the effective representation of a legal client, generates a tremendous amount of written material. Legal paperwork can take many forms, from client correspondence to formal court documents. These records may also be stored in a variety of ways. Computers enable information to be stored on data diskettes, compact disks, or magnetic tape. Other information may be stored on microfiche or microfilm; computer-generated reports may be stored in special, oversized cabinets; and, of course, we still store millions of pieces of paper in file folders stored in file cabinets. *Records management* refers to the entire spectrum of activities necessary to generate, maintain, and close files.

In a large law firm, and in some medium-sized ones, one individual is in charge of records management. This individual may be called the *records manager* and usually handles the following tasks:

1. Assign file numbers (which may, in a centralized filing system, be different from the client/matter numbers)

2. Send either the file numbers or the actual labeled files to the person requesting them

3. Store and maintain all open records in a central file room (this may include microfilming materials and destroying duplicates)

4. Oversee the closing of records:
   a. Assign box numbers for files being sent to off-site storage;
   b. Maintain a computerized database of all closed records;
   c. Coordinate transport of boxes from secretarial, paralegal, and attorney work areas to the records management area and then to storage;

d. Retrieve files from storage as requested. Return files to storage and maintain records on file retrieval activity;

e. Send appropriate information to the bookkeeper regarding file storage and retrieval costs so that clients may be billed appropriately;

f. Monitor review/destruction dates for closed files that are in storage and arrange for stripping and destruction of files after receiving written approval from the attorney.

In large records rooms, the records manager is often assisted by a records clerk who sorts, indexes, stores, retrieves, and disposes of records, as well as a records center supervisor, who handles the day-to-day operation of the center and directs the clerks. This leaves the records manager free to develop and implement new policies and procedures.

In smaller firms, records management might be done by a variety of people. Paralegals are usually responsible for keeping accurate files and maintaining them in an organized, systematic manner. Some cases on which paralegals work may take years to complete, and several individuals must be able to retrieve and use the records filed. Recording systems must be logical so that others can learn to use them effectively.

Filing Systems in General

In almost all filing systems, each client file is given a client number and a matter number, both of which are collectively called the "client/matter" or "file" number. This is done only after a conflict-of-interest check has been performed to ensure that representation of the client, or use of certain persons on the case, will not violate ethical guidelines.

Client numbers are used to identify the specific client. That number may be strictly numeric (generally four or five digits), or it may be alphanumeric. For instance, in the first case, the client number could appear as 96586. In the latter, it could appear S2345, with the S denoting attorney

Stevens. The data processing or accounting departments are generally in charge of assigning file numbers after they have received the fully completed file record. Of course, in a smaller firm, paralegals, attorneys, and secretaries might share this responsibility.

Matter numbers (generally three or four digits) are added to the client number following a period or dash. The matter number is assigned to separate the many different types of business a law firm handles for any one client. As an example, XYZ Corporation has been assigned 9586 as its client number. The first case they send is *XYZ Corporation v. Kraft Manufacturing,* and that matter is given the number 001, which, of course, makes the client/matter number 9586.001. The next file opened on behalf of XYZ Corporation would have the same client number and the next matter number (9586.002).

In addition to client/matter numbers used specifically for clients, most firms use firm client/matter numbers. These numbers are used to record nonbillable time spent on behalf of the firm. An example of a numeric firm client/matter numbering system, which keeps track of firm (nonbillable) hour categories, is as follows:

0001.10001	Office Administration
0001.10002	Personal Time
0001.10003	Recruiting and Interviewing
0001.10004	Continuing Education
0001.10005	Business Development
0001.10006	Professional Activities
0001.10007	Memo Bank
0001.10008	Pro Bono
0001.10009	Writing of Articles
0001.10010	Computer Forms
0001.10011	Firm Newsletter
0001.10012	Client Seminars
0001.10013	Managing Partner's Time

Most law firms use client/matter numbers for their file system. This is called a *numeric system.* It means that files are placed in the drawers of the file cabinet (or on the shelf) in order, beginning with the client portion of the number.

Other law firms use an alphabetic system. Under this system, commonly referred to as a *direct access system,* files are placed in A-through-Z order. File folders may or may not be color-coded according to letter. Standard filing procedures must be followed by all if the system is to work. Standard procedures are published by the Association of Records Managers and Administrators (ARMA).

Opening a New File

When a new file needs to be opened, it is of the utmost importance that a form called a *file record, new matter memo,* or some similar name be completed with all of the necessary information. This record is the original source of data regarding matters undertaken by the firm. In addition, this information is used for the conflict-of-interest search.

When a file record is completed, every space in the file record form must be completed. If the file is a new matter for an existing client who has already been assigned a client number, the client number and the next matter number are assigned in the proper spaces. If the file is for a new client, that fact must be noted. Other information typically contained in the new file record includes:

1. *Date.* The date the file was opened.
2. *Client Name.* The name of the client being represented.
3. *Matter Name.* The matter or the style of the case.
4. *Name and Address.* The client's name and address.
5. *Responsible Attorney.* The attorney who has primary responsibility for the file. (Typically, the initials of the attorney and his or her personal number are used.)
6. *Billing Attorney.* The attorney who will be in charge of the billings to the client. The responsible and billing attorneys may be the same. Often, however, the billing attorney is senior to the working attorney.
7. *Referral.* The name of the person or company who referred the case to the firm.

8. *Case Type.* The kind of case (i.e., will, personal injury, etc.); there may be codes for each case type also.
9. *Bill Code.* The frequency with which the file will be billed (i.e., monthly, quarterly, upon completion).
10. *Referring Attorney.* The name of the attorney who received the file.
11. *Bill Format.* The manner in which invoices will be prepared for presentation to the client. Firms differ as to the format they use. For example, a firm may display time entries that include the timesheet date, the text, and the hours spent, as well as itemized disbursements. Another possibility lists all of the foregoing items plus the attorneys' names or initials.
12. *Client Reference Number.* Upon occasion, clients require that reference be made to a specific number that they use internally, such as their own file numbers, a court case number, or perhaps the claim or policy number.
13. *Client Rates.* If the file is opened for a new client, the rates must be decided upon. Often rates are set for the following classifications:

Senior Partner
Junior Partner
Senior Associate
Junior Associate
Law Clerk
Paralegal.

Conflicts of Interest

All new clients and cases which the law firm takes on must be scrutinized for potential conflicts of interest. Conflicts of interest occur when there is a personal or financial connection among the lawyer, the law firm, the client, and other clients, and there exist ethical guidelines that explain how conflicts should be handled. Potential conflicts of interest arise in many different forms and situations. Some of the more common conflict situations arise when the firm has sued a person or corporation who wishes to become a new client; when an attorney was an attorney in another firm when that firm represented the opposing party; and when the firm incorporated the defendant corporation and an employee of the firm is on the board of directors of the corporation to be sued, or is a majority shareholder.

To alert everyone within the firm to a possible conflict, firms may either:

1. Circulate copies of all new file records
2. Send a daily memo to all attorneys and paralegals
3. Send a daily newsletter that includes the conflict memo
4. Send an electronic message.

If a memo is used, it should list all new matters received the previous day. The firm's client may be underlined for easy reference. If a conflict or any questions exist, the person in charge of conflict searches, as well as the responsible attorney, should be contacted immediately.

Some firms still use manual systems for conflict searching, but the majority now use sophisticated computer databases. If the firm is automated, certain information from the file record or a separate conflict information form will be entered into the computer database to check it against possible conflicts. It will check (1) the name of the client, (2) all plaintiffs, (3) all plaintiffs' attorneys, (4) all defendants, (5) all defendants' attorneys, (6) the name of each parent or subsidiary corporation, the corporation's officers, a partnership's general partners, and other assorted information. A new file may not be opened if the conflict search discloses any potential conflict with any past or present client or adverse party. Any conflict must be immediately reported to the attorney who requested the new file number. It is importance that, as information becomes available on a client file, the information be sent to the data processing department and the person in charge of conflict searches. This may be accomplished by completing and submitting a file maintenance form, with the new information

clearly marked. The computer system is then updated and the conflict system is kept up-to-date.

If a firm is not automated, it is often the responsibility of a paralegal to handle conflict checks manually. The same items are checked—it just takes a bit longer.

Conflicts of interest are extremely important and must be done to avoid the possibility that the firm may be engaged by a new client whose problems could in some way adversely affect a current or former client. Conflicts can be checked in a number of ways, but conflict checking must always be viewed as a critical assignment. The system within each firm varies, but it is vital. A fundamental principle of ethical behavior is the avoidance of conflicts of interest. All parties in the law firm must work together to ensure that a present or former client's interests are not adversely affected by the representation of a new client.

Active Files

Depending upon the type of law practice, active files may be stored in a central file room, or, in the case of many litigation practices, in the file cabinets within each department (the cabinets line the hallways). Of course, some files that are used frequently will be kept in the attorney's, paralegal's, and secretary's offices or workspaces. With this plan, each person who removes a file is expected to complete an *out card*. The name of the working attorney and the location of the file must be given. The out card takes the place of the file in the corresponding alpha or numeric sequence.

If a central file room is used, indexes will be available so that files can be easily located. They will be filed numerically, alphabetically, or by a combination of the two.

Naturally, appropriate file security measures must be taken to protect a law firm's files and other important records, whether they are in individual offices, file cabinets, or central storage. The firm must protect against theft, water, and fire damage.

Internal File Organization

The manner of organization and filing of material within each separately numbered client file should be consistent. Each firm has particular ways of doing things, but typically each file contains several subfiles or subsections. These subfiles may be separate folders contained in an expandable file folder, or they may all be contained within the same folder. These subfiles or subsections of files may include:

- Correspondence
- Legal research
- Pleadings
- Discovery
- Billing
- Attorneys' notes
- Deposition file
- Witness file
- Client documents
- Memos

Paralegals are often responsible for keeping files in order so that information within the files can be quickly located by anyone reviewing the file.

File Storage

When a matter has been completed and billed, it is often prepared for storage, making room in the file drawers and file shelves for new matters. To do so, a file storage inventory form may be used, including pertinent information concerning the contents of the file and its location in storage. When the storage inventory form has been completed, it is submitted to the person in charge of records management and assigned an identifying number—the same number that is assigned to the box in which the file folder will be located.

Before files are sent to storage, they should be cleaned up by removing any legal pads, extra copies, and unnecessary documents and papers from the file. This is important to reduce unnecessary bulk in storage. Originals of certain documents (such as wills) should be kept in a vault within the firm or returned to the client rather than being sent to storage.

The firm may have its own space for closed files, or the firm may use an outside storage company to store closed files. It is imperative that firms be able to retrieve closed matters quickly and efficiently. Often clients have other matters for which information in the closed files will be helpful.

Micrographics

Technical advances have spurred the development of several forms of document storage and retrieval systems that can aid law firms in maximizing access to records and minimizing storage space requirements for records and documents. One commonly used method involves microfilming documents. In this method, information is stored in *microfilm*, a "piece" of film that is a photographic record of printed or graphic information on a reduced scale; or on *microfiche*, a "sheet" of film containing rows of printed or graphic information on a reduced scale. A microfilm or microfiche reader is the electronic equipment through which one views the film or the fiche. Firms may microfilm their own materials if they have the proper equipment, or they may hire an outside service to perform the microfilming. In addition to micrographics, other technologies, such as electronic document retrieval systems involving optical scanning, promise to revolutionize file storage by eliminating as much paper as possible.

Document Destruction

Generally, files are reviewed for destruction when they are a minimum of seven years old. Important exceptions to this guide are original wills, trust documents, final divorce decrees, and settlement papers. Law firms usually keep these documents in their safes. The records manager checks for any files with eligible review/destroy dates. The printout of these files, along with a memo, is sent to the responsible attorney. The memo encourages careful yet timely scrutiny of each file, allowing an average two-week review of the list. It is then sent back to the records manager with proper instructions. The attorney may wish to see the actual file before making a decision; in that event, a records request form must be completed and sent to the records manager.

When a file is to be destroyed, the firm's file destruction procedures must be followed. For security reasons, file contents are usually shredded rather than dumped. For confidential documents, document destruction assures the client that proper security measures are taken with his or her information. For other documents, paper recycling is appropriate.

Suspense and Diary Systems

An important system in any law office is the suspense and diary system. This system may be used on an individual or firm-wide basis.

The Suspense and Tickler System

There are a number of good ways to have a personal suspense system (often called a tickler system). A *suspense,* or *tickler, system* is a reminder system whose essential purpose is docket control. It is a means to keep track of follow-up dates for various activities or procedures. For example, when opposing counsel is served with interrogatories, the response to those interrogatories is due 30 days later. A note should be made to follow up in 30 days to be sure that a response has been received.

As its name suggests, a tickler system "tickles" the memory so that work can be tracked effectively. One method often used by paralegals is to purchase a legal-size, expandable envelope with individual pockets marked 1-31, or an index card holder with dividers marked 1-31. Each day of the month then has a pocket or divider for filing information about upcoming dates. As the paralegal works throughout the day, he or she marks the date on a copy of each item requiring follow-up and files it in the correct pocket of the tickler system. Each morning, the tickler system is checked for items that require follow-up on that particular day. This system must be checked daily to be effective.

The Diary System and Docket Control

A *diary,* or *docket control, system* is used to keep track of court dates and other important dates relating to a case. Its form can range from a date board to a computerized calendar. Life in a law firm is extremely busy and often hectic. Without the use of excellent control systems, important events can easily be missed. This, of course, could lead to malpractice. In fact, very specific questions regarding docket control are asked on malpractice insurance applications. The answers might make a difference in a firm's ability to obtain malpractice insurance, and they will certainly affect the premium paid.

Naturally, it is critical that the legal team working on a case be accurately apprised of the deadlines relative to that case. This is generally done in one of several ways, including paralegal research, computerized docket control, date boards, and backup services. Even though law firms have the types of systems discussed above, docket control is ultimately the obligation of the attorney and the paralegal. If the person in the firm who is responsible for reading the legal publication overlooks a hearing and does not notify the appropriate attorney and/or paralegal, or if the card from the backup service never reaches your office, it remains the inescapable obligation and duty of the attorney and the paralegal.

Paralegal Research

When paralegal research is the system used, a paralegal is assigned the task of reading all local legal publications (newspapers and journals), containing calendar information for various courts. The paralegal reviews court calendars on a daily basis for appearances by the firm's lawyers and notifies the attorneys as they appear. The attorneys are provided with a copy of the calendar a day or two before the pertinent date.

Computerized Docket Control

Some firms may use a computerized docket control system, also known as a computerized calendar, into which the responsible person enters all pertinent information, including that found on the tickler record. The computer then sorts the information, arranging it in date order. The responsible person calls up the information each day and notifies the attorneys and paralegals of their obligations. Additionally, this system allows the person in charge of docket control to send all docket information for that day to the timekeeper.

Date Boards

On the other end of the spectrum from computerized systems is the date board, which can be used to remind timekeepers of upcoming events. One person is generally assigned to accept the information, post it, send written reminders to the people affected, and then erase the information when the event has passed.

Backup Services

Law firms often use backup services, frequently provided by court reporting firms, to collect and copy information from legal publications (newspapers), court documents, and court records. These services send the attorney a card showing:

1. the name, address, and telephone number of the service
2. the date the card was printed and mailed
3. the date the information was published in the newspaper
4. the style of the case
5. the description of the action
6. the specific name of the court
7. the name of the judge
8. the court date and time
9. the names of the attorneys who are to appear
10. specific instructions (i.e., It will be necessary to be in court for oral argument on all motions unless specifically excused. Please direct all inquiries to this calendar to Smith (345-1234), Calendar Clerk for Judge P. Jones.)
11. filing deadlines
12. deposition dates
13. discovery deadlines
14. statute of limitations.

It is important to note that once these reminders have been received from these services, special attention must be paid to instructions that the court may publish in these notices. For example, many times court calendars may list thirty cases for a particular calendar but only require that the parties and attorneys for the first ten cases appear. Another example would be that the court may require all settlements to be finalized by a specific date or the case will be tried. Failure to follow these instructions could result in sanctions against the parties and/or their attorneys. Some services use the telephone to advise the firm of calendar dates, to determine readiness, and to ask for adjournment, but most people prefer a hard copy of this important information.

Word and Data Processing Systems

To say that word processing has fundamentally changed the way offices manage written information would be a gross understatement. For the paralegal, whose work involves internal and external communication with all members of the legal team and clients, word processing is the most important way to communicate in writing.

A *word processing program* is a software package that, when used in conjunction with appropriate hardware, gives the user certain writing capabilities. Sometimes the firm's word processing software is a popular off-the-shelf brand, but some firms use a customized program as part of an integrated system. Whatever the word processor, it will have certain features in common with most other word processors, and it will also have its own method of accessing those features.

Paralegals typically use word processors in a variety of ways: generating correspondence and memos, storing name and address records, and storing various forms and documents. The paralegal's direct involvement with word processing is also varied. In some instances, all paralegals, and even the attorneys in the firm, have terminals and keyboards on their desks to use for short correspondence and memos; only long documents are sent to the word processing department. In other offices, all correspondence, short documents, and memos are typed by secretaries, while longer documents are sent to a word processing department within the firm. Paralegals must know the basics about word processing to effectively interact with word processing departments.

Simple and Integrated Word Processors

In a small law office that does not have the sophisticated technology of a large firm, paralegals may find a simple word processing system, perhaps running on a single personal computer (PC) or dedicated word processing system. In a larger firm, totally integrated systems, in which word processing is linked to spreadsheets and legal research to produce presentation graphics, are common. In either case, the physical components may be very similar; the software creates the great differences in capability. Paralegals need a good working knowledge of the word processing system within the office, even if they have a secretary or word processing operator who inputs information into the computer.

Basic Word Processing Functions

At its most basic level, a word processor is an electronic typewriter, and it can be used for all functions associated with typewriting. All word processors enable the user to write, edit, and modify the text, as well as to save it so that it can be used in the future. Another typical feature is a spell checker, which goes through the document looking for spelling errors. Grammar programs indicate places with faulty grammar throughout the document. Most word processors also enable the user to merge texts, print in various type styles, known as *fonts,* and perform some basic graphics functions, such as line and box drawings.

More sophisticated word processing functions can be found in larger and more powerful programs. Fully integrated software packages include the capability to combine spreadsheet functions, word processing capabilities, graphics, and intercommunication between environments.

Integrated Word Processing Systems

In an integrated word processing system, the word processing functions previously described are combined with other programs to increase the flexibility and capability of the system. This means that a single system can perform a wide variety of functions, from word processing and generating mailing lists, to accounting and desktop publishing, to docket management, litigation support, and optical scanning. A single system, therefore, might have the following features in addition to basic word processing:

1. A spreadsheet program
2. A database management program
3. A desktop publishing program
4. Legal research applications.

Data Processing

Data processing refers to any and all activities that involve manipulating data electronically to give the user information. As a business that runs in an office, a law firm has many needs beyond the purely legal, and data processing helps meet many of those needs. Data processing handles functions previously done manually, and performs those functions more quickly, efficiently, and accurately than before. Data processing is also part of an integrated system, so its information can be used in a multiplicity of ways for a multiplicity of purposes.

Depending on the size of the law firm and the amount of specialization on the paralegal level, paralegals may be responsible for functions that use data processing, automated accounting and timekeeping, database management, and management information systems.

Accounting packages are able to perform the following functions:

Accounts payable/receivable

Timekeeping and billing

General ledger

Payroll (paying employees and keeping tax and deduction records)

Check reconciliation

Report writing (enables the user to write reports using generated data)

Internal auditing (enables the firm to provide security and controls on its financial transactions)

Database Management

A *database* is a list of information or data that, when input into a database management system, can be stored efficiently and made capable of retrieval in a number of different ways. For example, if the law firm has a client database, information and reports can be obtained on the referring attorney, geographic location, or date of disposition of the case. In other words, a database is an extremely efficient and flexible way of maintaining and retrieving data so that it can be used in a multiplicity of ways.

Complex litigation—often organized and managed by paralegals—usually involves the use of databases to index and retrieve documents related to the case. There are many different types of software designed especially for this purpose.

One excellent application of database principles is in marketing, where information of different types is distributed to selected people or organizations on the database. If the firm were offering a seminar on mortgage interest deductions, for instance, a database could easily select the firm's homeowner clients, integrate their names and addresses into announcements, and prepare envelopes. Databases are also used for conflict-of-interest checks, where the computer looks for matches between the initiating name and the existing database.

In a larger firm, there well might be a database administrator responsible for selecting, defining, and maintaining the database and providing reports to management. In a smaller firm, these functions might fall to an office administrator, paralegal, or secretary.

Management Information Systems

Management information systems (MIS) are computer-based systems that supply management with data, information, and reports that support management functions. In a law firm, MIS uses range from creating and analyzing productivity reports to analyzing zip code origins of the firm's clients. Management applications frequently require databases and therefore are interactive with databases and, of course, word processing.

The Law Library and Other Management Systems

The systems and procedures of law office administration discussed in the previous sections of this chapter represent the most significant areas for effective administration of a law practice. However, a number of other systems within a law office are also part of the law office environment. This section examines the law library system, committees, office manuals and handbooks, paralegal training and continuing legal education programs, the mailroom, and pro bono paralegal work.

The Law Library

Paralegals typically spend many hours in the law firm library, and certainly one of the characteristics of a good paralegal is the ability to do effective research. Paralegals must become acquainted with the law firm's library at the outset of their employment.

Law firm libraries differ widely in size and the scope of their resources. In most medium to large firms, the library will be maintained by a professional librarian and library staff. In a very small firm, a paralegal may be the librarian.

In smaller firms where librarians are not on staff, paralegals often do at least their share of library maintenance. Paralegals assigned tasks such as filing supplements or loose-leaf services must be sure that those tasks are completed in a timely fashion. Neglected, out-of-date publications are not only a research inconvenience but may also result in a serious error at trial, in briefs submitted to the court, or in advice given to clients.

No matter how large or small the law firm's library and its staff, paralegals must become familiar with local and area law libraries as well.

Courthouse and law school libraries are obvious sources for case law, law reviews, journal articles, and treatises. Public libraries can supply a wealth of information: city directories, out-of-state telephone directories, general periodicals, newspapers, and much more. There is often a telephone reference service. Some large public and university libraries are depositories for government documents, such as federal agency publications, census statistics, and legislative materials. There may be specialized libraries in the area that are maintained by state and federal government agencies, professional societies or associations, or large corporations. Many of these libraries provide research assistance to the general public. Attorneys routinely require information on a wide variety of subjects; a notebook (or well-annotated file) with telephone numbers, names, and sources is invaluable.

Law Library Resources

Most law firm libraries, regardless of size, will have at least some resources in the following categories:

1. Case law
2. Statutes/Regulations
3. Finding tools
4. Treatises, texts, and loose-leaf publications
5. Court rules, form books, and jury instructions
6. Periodicals
7. Encyclopedias, dictionaries, and directories.

The Law Librarian

It is important to understand the role of the law firm librarian, because his or her knowledge and expertise is invaluable. Most law firm librarians have, at a minimum, an M.L.S. (Master of Library Science) degree, and some have a law degree as well. Some of the responsibilities of a librarian or his or her staff are:

1. To provide research assistance, including online computer database searches

2. To recommend and purchase library materials required by the firm and to see that the collection is up-to-date and growing with the practice

3. To perform daily and weekly library maintenance functions, such as filing supplements and loose-leaf services, routing periodicals and other library materials, shelving, and binding periodicals

4. To catalog and process new acquisitions and maintain a catalog of the collection

5. To handle interlibrary loans with other law firms or area libraries

6. To organize and index the firm's internal work product in its various forms, such as legal memoranda, expert witness and other deposition files, microforms, brief banks, and any other documents the firm deems useful

7. To provide library orientation for new attorneys and paralegals

8. To keep attorneys and paralegals informed of recent acquisitions, new sources of information, and other developments

9. To plan space requirements that take into consideration future expansion of the library collection

10. To perform library bookkeeping and accounting functions, including approving and paying invoices and statements

11. To create bibliographies and other library utilization aids.

Computer Research

Computer-assisted legal and nonlegal research is rapidly becoming indispensable in many law firms; the LEXIS and WESTLAW services are commonly found even in small firms. In addition to these leaders, a growing number of other online database services are available to law firms. Some are legal in nature, such as Veralex, Information American, or ABA Net; others are nonlegal, such as Dialog, Vu-Text, Dow-Jones News Retrieval, or CompuServe. These databases may contain online versions of sources available in print. The firm may decide it is more practical or efficient to access an online service than to own the actual volumes. Various vendors offer databases that are indexing and abstraction tools only; others are full-text. Search techniques vary widely, and assistance from a reference librarian is advisable for efficiency and cost control.

Library Organization

Typically, law library materials are classified and catalogued according to the classification scheme used by the Library of Congress. In many instances, however, a small- to medium-sized collection will be grouped by general subject area: "bankruptcy," "real estate," "tax," and so on. The familiar card catalog is rapidly being replaced by computer-generated systems.

Committees

In most firms, depending upon the size, there are a number of committees, such as business development, summer associate program, associate orientation, forms, newsletter, CLE, library, and the like. The recruitment committee, for example, reviews resumes and recommends people for interviews; the forms committee reviews and standardizes forms for firm use. Paralegals are often asked to participate on such committees. Committee work is a great way for paralegals to make a real contribution to the firm, even though it is nonbillable time. It is also a way for paralegals to increase their knowledge and exposure.

Office Manuals and Handbooks

A good office manual includes a wide range of information, from employee benefits to working hours to vacations. It will also set forth the various procedures utilized by the law firm, such as mailing procedures, file closing procedures, and billing procedures.

In some cases, paralegals may be called upon to assist in the writing of an office manual. This is a major project, one that takes considerable time, thought, and work. It is also important to get advice relating to any issues that may be construed as discriminatory.

In addition to an office handbook or manual, many firms write and distribute a variety of specialized manuals. Orientation manuals for law clerks and paralegals may include information on local area judges, docket control, special mail procedures, court filing procedures, and rules on obtaining court opinions. Manuals for legal secretaries cover areas such as dealing with clients, general responsibilities, confidentiality, timekeeping, and reading files. The content of these manuals will vary considerably from law firm to law firm, but, regardless of their differences, they are essential in a well-organized, efficient law firm.

Paralegal Training Programs

The training procedures a firm uses represent another system. The completion of paralegal training is not the end of education for the effective legal assistant. Law firms, corporations, and the government all recognize that continuing legal education must exist for paralegals as well as attorneys.

Although attorneys in most states are required to participate in a certain number of continuing legal education hours per year to keep their standing with the bar, there is no such requirement for paralegals. Some law firms, however, strongly encourage or even require that their paralegals attend certain continuing legal education courses. Most law firms and other employers will pay the expense of continuing legal education.

There is great variation in the extent of training offered by firms. Some firms offer little guidance, whereas others offer an elaborate system for continuing paralegal training.

In-house training programs are available in many law firms for new paralegals as well as for paralegals with substantial experience. In-house training can be in the form of formal classes taught by attorneys or paralegals within the firm, which paralegals are required to attend, or it can be as informal as the information passed on from an experienced paralegal to a new employee. Organized in-house training programs may include:

1. Seminars given by attorneys or other specialists within the firm on new developments in law as they concern the firm's practice
2. Mentoring programs
3. Step-by-step procedural manuals
4. Standardized forms for preparation of legal documents
5. Checklists for completing legal procedures.

In-house training is a very valuable resource to paralegals because it typically focuses on practical information that is very useful to paralegals in their work.

Most firms have paralegal manuals that detail the paralegal's responsibilities and the firm's procedures and expectations. These manuals are generally written by experienced paralegals in various departments in the firm and cover a wide range of information that can help both new and experienced paralegals.

The Mailroom

The mailroom is an important law office system because it controls the flow of important legal documents and correspondence. Law firm mailroom procedures vary. The size of the mailroom and its number of employees depend largely upon the size of the firm. Typically, a room is set aside in a central area specifically for receipt, sorting, and distribution of mail. Each attorney, paralegal, and administrative employee is given a mailbox.

Schedules for mail pickup at the post office, intraoffice deliveries, and pickups and mail runs outside the office are posted and strictly adhered to. Mailroom personnel deliver and pick up intraoffice mail by use of an "in box/out box" system at each secretary's and paralegal's desk, at the receptionist's work area, or at central mailrooms located on each floor. They might also be responsible for fax pickups, which need to be done often.

Unless the law firm is quite small, mail is generally metered. A mail meter automatically applies the amount of postage necessary for mailing a particular letter or parcel. This is often more efficient than putting stamps on every piece of mail. If postage stamps are required, the bookkeeping department usually keeps a supply on hand. Sophisticated mail equipment incorporates scales connected electronically to the meter. The mailroom employees can place an envelope on the scale, which then automatically calculates the postage and activates the meter for the correct amount.

The mailroom is also responsible, in most cases, for administering air freight and express mail services. In a law firm, those services are frequently required, and requests for those services should be coordinated with the mailroom attendants. A client/matter number should be included on the air freight bill or the express mail form so that a proper charge can be made to the client's account. Many law firms have their own courier services to deliver and pick up documents, or runners to deliver local mail to other offices or to the courthouse.

Pro Bono Paralegal Work

The literal translation of the term *pro bono* is "for the good." It is the term used to describe work done by attorneys and paralegals for the public good at no cost. Attorneys have been performing pro bono services for decades. In recent years, paralegals have also found pro bono work to be a rewarding way of making a contribution to the community. Several programs exist, through paralegal associations and attorney associations, that allow paralegals to become involved in pro bono work. In addition to the good it can do for the community, performing pro bono work is also a good way to gain practical experience in an area of law that interests you, and it is a great way to make contacts within the community.

Paralegals who perform pro bono work often work with the homeless, disabled, elderly, abused or neglected children, or immigrants and refugees. They may offer their services in the area of court advocacy, literacy tutoring, mentoring, or crisis support. Paralegals interested in providing pro bono services should contact their local paralegal associations or bar associations for a list of organizations to which they can offer their services.

Summary Questions

1. To whom do the paralegals of a law firm typically report?
2. What are three important things to remember when taking an assignment from an attorney?
3. What is your preferred method of dealing with on-the-job stress?
4. Are most paralegals paid overtime? Are they considered exempt or nonexempt employees? Why?

ZERO-BASED BUDGET

	12/31/93	1994
REVENUE/INCOME:	_____	_____
COSTS/EXPENSES:		
1. SALARY		
A. BASE PAY	_____	_____
B. PAYROLL TAXES	_____	_____
C. BENEFITS	_____	_____
2. RENTAL EXPENSES	_____	_____
3. GENERAL OVERHEAD	_____	_____
4. ADMINISTRATIVE OVERHEAD	_____	_____
5. SECRETARIAL SUPPORT		
A. SECRETARIAL SALARY (INCLUDING TEMPS)	_____	_____
B. SECRETARIAL RENT	_____	_____
C. PENSION PLAN	_____	_____
TOTAL EXPENSES	_____	_____
NET	_____	_____

Zero-Based Budget Form   Zero-based budgeting is a very specific budgeting process designed to maximize the law firm's profit by making all the employees accountable to an overall structure of income versus expenses.

5. What are some advantages to using a systems approach to law office management?

6. You are asked to attend a paralegal recruitment committee meeting. Is this considered billable or nonbillable time?

7. What is a contingency fee?

FILE RECORD
SMITH, JONES & BLACK
ATTORNEYS AT LAW

FROM   Attorney Jones
DATE   01 / 18 / 87

0001	20001
CLIENT #	MATTER #

1. When was file received?   01 / 17 / 87   2. Which attorney will have primary responsibility for this file?

CMJ	999
Atty. Int.	Atty. #

3. Which attorney will have responsibility for billing this file?. . . . .

CMJ	999
Atty. Int.	Atty. #

4. Who referred the Client to DEF?   Leatha North

5. What type of case is this? (Supply One)   11

THIRD PARTY INSURANCE DEFENSE LITIGATION
11 Products Liability
12 Automobile Accidents
13 Medical Malpractice
14 Other Prof. Malpractice
15 Homeowners Liability
16 Business Liability
17 Civil Rights Litigation
18 Libel & Slander
19 Municipal Liability

WORKERS COMPENSATION
21 Defendants Self Insureds
22 Defendants Insurers
23 Claimants Cases
24 Stipulations

FIRST PARTY INSURANCE DEFENSE
31 Accident & Health Claims
32 Arson Claims
33 Property (Non-arson) Claims
34 Surety
35 Coverage Questions-Auto
36 Coverage Questions-Other

PLAINTIFF'S CLAIMS
41 Personal Injury
42 Major Subrogation Property (over $10,000)
43 Minor Subrogation Property (under $10,000)
44 Major Subrogation-Other (over $10,000)
45 Minor Subrogation-Other (under $10,000)

CONTRACTS
61 Contract Claim—Plaintiff
62 Contract Claim—Defendant
63 Lien Claim—Plaintiff
64 Lien Claim—Denfendant
65 Government Contract
66 General/Miscellaneous
67 Labor (OSHA Wage and Hour)
68 Contract Documents
69 Other

OTHERS
51 Corporate
52 Real Estate
53 Trusts & Estates
54 Bankruptcy
55 Divorce
56 Deposition for Out of State Counsel
57 Others (use only as a last resort)
58 Releases
59 Minor Settlements

6. When should this file be billed?
   (Supply One)   15

BILLING FREQUENCY CODES
01 Annually-January
02 Annually-February
03 Annually-March
04 Annually-April
05 Annually-May
06 Annually-June
07 Annually-July
08 Annually-August
09 Annually-September
10 Annually-October
11 Annually-November
12 Annually-December
13 Every month
14 End of Case (Hourly matters only)
15 End of Case (Contingent matters only)
16 Quarterly for matters opened Jan., April, July & Oct.
17 Quarterly for matters opened Feb., May, Aug. & Nov.
18 Quarterly for matters opened Mar., June, Sept. & Dec.
19 Semiannually for matters opened in Jan., July
20 Semiannually for matters opened in Feb., Aug.
21 Semiannually for matters opened in Mar., Sept.
22 Semiannually for matters opened in April, Oct.
23 Semiannually for matters opened in May, Nov.
24 Semiannually for matters opened in June, Dec.
25 Bi-annually (every two years)

7. To which attorney did this matter come?   CMJ   999
   Atty. Int.   Atty. #

8. In which format should this bill be printed?
   (Supply One)   42

9. Have we or will we need to set up special client rates? (Check special client rate label in your manual)   ☒ Yes   ☐ No

FORMAT PROVIDES
32 Date, Svcs.,, Item Disb.   42 Date, Svcs., Hrs., Item Disb.   52 Date, Atty., Svcs., Item Disb.   62 Date, Atty., Hrs., Item Disb.

10. Client Name: (36 Max.)
`Friendly Insurance Company`

11. How should we identify this matter? (ex: Jones vs. State Farm or in re:) (36 Max.)
`Baby Boutique v. Sheila Marie`

12. Where do we send bills? (30 Max.)
`Friendly Insurance Company`
`3300 Peachtree Street`
`Atlanta, Georgia 30357-1204`

13. What was the client's reference # or I.D. for this file?   `109-222`

14. If we need a special client rate for this client, what rates should be entered? **A RATE MUST BE SUPPLIED FOR EACH CLASSIFICATION.**

1) 105	2) 95	3) 90	4) 80	5) 70	6) 65	7) 60
Sr. Ptr.	Jr. Ptr.	Sr. Assoc.	Jr. Assoc.	Law Clrk.	Sr. p/t	Jr. p/t

Plaintiff(s)
Baby Boutique

Their Attorney(s)
T.L. Joe

Defendant(s)
Sheila Marie
Friendly Insurance Company

Their Attorney(s)
C.M. Jones

Court: In the Superior Court of Fair County
Civil Action No: CV-90-1987   Judge: Judge Ollie

DATA PROCESSING

File Record The file record provides all the information required when a new case is opened or when the firm is retained by a new client.

8. What is a realization rate in regard to billing clients?

9. Why is it important that all attorneys be informed of pertinent information regarding new clients and new matters when files are opened?

10. Why would a firm use more than one method for docket control?

 Practical Paralegal Skills

Consider and describe the type of environment in which you would prefer to work. Include the personnel who might be employed by such a firm and the firm's level of automation.

1. What billing requirements would be prevalent in such an environment?

2. What management systems might be in place?

3. Does such an environment exist? If so, where?

 Notes

For further reference, see *Law Office Management for Paralegals,* by Jonathan Lynton, Donna Masinter, and Terri Mick Lyndall (Lawyers Cooperative Publishing & Delmar Publishers, 1992).

[1] Milano, Carol, "Salary Survey Results," *Legal Assistant Today* 48 (May/June 1993).

[2] "Should Paralegals Be Paid Overtime?," *Legal Assistant Today* 36 (May/June 1992).

CHAPTER 5
Interviewing and Investigating

Although interviewing and investigating are two skills often associated only with litigation, they are in fact used in all areas of law by paralegals. This chapter gives a brief overview of the interviewing and investigating skills helpful to paralegals, including client interviewing, using communication skills for interviewing, conducting investigations, and coordinating investigations with the services of an in-house or private investigator.

An Introduction to Interviewing and Investigating

Interviewing and investigating are two distinct skills that often go hand in hand. Excellent interviewing skills are needed to conduct a thorough investigation in litigation matters. Both interviewing and investigating skills involve gathering facts for a lawsuit or for other legal services that will be performed for a client. Attorneys cannot represent their clients effectively without all pertinent facts.

Most paralegals, from time to time, will have to interview clients for any one of numerous reasons. The main goal of most paralegal/client interviews is to obtain the necessary facts and information to allow the attorney to properly analyze the situation and serve the client's legal needs. In addition, paralegals may be asked to interview witnesses and others to obtain pertinent facts and testimony regarding a client's case.

The term *investigating* may conjure up mental visions of trench coats and black fedoras. In fact, the term **investigate** means to inquire; to look into; to make an investigation. When the term is taken literally, much of any paralegal's work involves investigating. Whether they are searching for witnesses and evidence for a trial, or trying to locate the registered office of a corporation, paralegals must have excellent investigative skills.

The Client Interview

Most law firms and legal departments have established policies and procedures for the involvement of paralegals in client interviews. The client interview is an important process in providing legal service. Often both the attorney and the paralegal are involved. The objectives of the client interview are typically to gather information from the client, to answer questions from the client, and to build goodwill with the client.

This section discusses the basics of client interviewing, including scheduling the interview, preparing for the interview, and conducting the interview.

Scheduling Client Interviews

Often the scheduling of client interviews is the responsibility of the attorney's secretary. If a paralegal is to attend a client interview, he or she will be informed of the date, time, and topic of the meeting. At other times, when the attorney prefers that the paralegal be involved on a particular file from the outset, the paralegal may be asked to call the client to schedule the first client interview.

investigate   To inquire; to look into; to make an investigation.

Law Office Scenario

Toward the end of the second week of Andrea Smith's new paralegal job, she was called into attorney Barbara Kendall's office.

"Andrea," attorney Kendall began, "I have a phone message here from a Mr. Thomas Inderly who says he is calling about a personal injury matter. Would you please call him back, get the facts of the case, and schedule a meeting for him with me. Tell him to bring the usual information that we will need. I would like you to attend the interview

with me too. You'll need to check for potential conflicts of interest and get one of those client questionnaires ready. We'll also need the appropriate forms for him to sign at the interview."

"Sure," answered Andrea tentatively. "I'll call him right back and take care of it." Andrea left the office wondering to herself, "What should I ask Mr. Inderly? What forms was Ms. Kendall referring to? What role will I play at the interview?"

Checking for Potential Conflicts of Interest

Before scheduling an appointment for a potential litigation client, the firm's client list should be checked, or other firm procedures followed, to check for potential conflicts of interest. It is considered unethical for an attorney to represent a client when the attorney may have conflicting interests due to the attorney's representation of other clients or due to his or her own personal business matters. All law firms have procedures for screening new clients who come into the office to see if representation of the new client may present a conflict of interest to one or more of the attorneys in the office.

Before Scheduling an Interview

If you are asked by an attorney to schedule an appointment for a new client, you should have the attorney answer the following questions before you call the client:

1. Who will be at the meeting?
2. What is the purpose of the meeting?
3. Where will the meeting be held?
4. How long will the meeting take?

5. What materials and information should the client bring?
6. When would the attorney like the meeting to be held? Can the attorney suggest alternative dates and times?

After you have ascertained all this information from the attorney, you will be in a position to have an intelligent telephone conversation with the client and to relay all necessary information.

In the law office scenario at the beginning of this section, Andrea should find out from Ms. Kendall when Ms. Kendall would be available for the initial client interview and where she would like to meet the new client. Andrea should also find out exactly what she should ask Mr. Inderly to bring to the interview.

Scheduling the Interview

When a telephone call is made to a client to schedule an initial interview, the following should be accomplished:

1. The caller should introduce himself or herself to the client, being sure to inform the client of his or her position within the firm

2. The date, time, and place of the meeting should be agreed upon

3. Pertinent information should be obtained over the telephone to help the paralegal and attorney prepare for the initial meeting. This information may include the type of matter the client wishes to discuss (if not yet known), important deadlines that must be met (such as time to answer a complaint or file a claim), and the client's full name and address

4. Directions to the office should be given to the client, if necessary, including instructions on where to park

5. The client should be advised what to bring to the meeting, to help to expedite the information-gathering process

6. If the appointment is made more than one or two weeks in advance, it should be confirmed by the paralegal or the paralegal's secretary just prior to the meeting.

Because the attorney in the law office scenario does not know the client or anything about him, Andrea should determine who referred Mr. Inderly to Ms. Kendall. She should also get the basic facts concerning the type of personal injury suit that Mr. Inderly is contemplating. Is he a potential plaintiff, or the defendant? If he has been served with a summons and complaint, when must the response be served?

The Confirming Letter

If the client's interview is scheduled more than a day or two in advance, a confirming letter should be sent to the client. In the letter, the client should once again be reminded to bring to the meeting all materials and information necessary to begin work on the client's behalf. The materials and information that the client is asked to bring will depend on the type of matter involved. Each law firm should have a list of items to ask the client to bring for a particular matter. If not, the paralegal may want to prepare one for his or her own use. Following is a sample of some of the items that may be requested from a client for particular matters:

Possible Litigation Matter

- Copies of pertinent insurance policies
- Copies of any pleadings that have been served on the client
- Information relating to opposing party, such as name, address, insurance carrier, etc.
- Accident or incident reports
- Photographs and/or diagram of injury site, if available
- Newspaper clippings relating to accident or injury
- Description of automobiles involved in accident, including license numbers, owners, and amount of damage
- Medical bills and any other available medical information concerning treatment of the client's injuries resulting from the accident or incident
- Employment information concerning time lost because of accident or incident

Estate Planning

- Financial statements or lists of assets and long-term debts
- Copies of deeds for real property owned
- Copies of any available appraisals on insured items (for identification purposes)
- Information concerning life insurance policies and retirement plans
- Names and addresses of family members and potential beneficiaries

Criminal

- Copy of police report and any other information concerning charges against client
- Names and addresses of any potential witnesses

- Newspaper clippings relating to the alleged crime

Family Law (Divorce)

- List of assets and debts and any other financial information
- Copies of any pleadings that have been served on client

Real Estate

- Copy of purchase agreement
- Copy of any surveys done on property
- Abstract of title or certificate of title
- Copies of any mortgages or liens on the property

Bankruptcy

- Copies of all financial information concerning the client's assets and debts

Contract Law

- Copy of proposed contract
- Names and addresses of all interested parties and their attorneys

Corporate Law

- Copies of business plan (for new corporations)
- Corporate minute books
- Stock ledger books
- Copies of any other pertinent corporate documentation

If the interview is to be held in a conference room at the attorney's office, the paralegal or other individual scheduling the appointment should be certain to schedule the conference room for the meeting in accordance with office policy. If the appointment is to take place outside the office, the attorney should be notified and the proper address and directions to the place of meeting should be noted.

Background and Preparation

After the client's appointment has been scheduled, there may be background work for the paralegal. Everyone who is to attend the meeting should be informed by memo, and the meeting date and time should be confirmed.

Often the client will be asked to send information to the office for the attorney's and/or paralegal's review before the meeting. The paralegal should be sure to follow up to make sure that the information has been received and reviewed prior to the meeting. If the paralegal is asked to attend a meeting dealing with a specific area of law with which he or she is unfamiliar, he or she may want to do some simple research prior to the date of the appointment.

Prior to the appointment, a file should be assembled for the client interview, containing all notes regarding telephone conversations with the client and any background research that has been performed. In addition, any forms or agreements that the client will be asked to sign at the meeting should be placed in the file, including a retainer agreement form and any necessary authorizations.

Conducting the Initial Client Interview

The paralegal in a private law firm rarely conducts an initial interview on his or her own. At an initial client interview, the issue of attorney fees will have to be discussed with the client. In addition, the client will probably be seeking some form of legal advice. Both of these topics should be left exclusively to an attorney. The attorney will also be responsible for making a final determination as to whether to accept the individual as a client of the firm. Finally, the attorney may also feel that his or her presence is desirable to help build goodwill between the new client and the firm.

KENDALL & KENDALL, LTD.
Attorneys at Law
123 Main Street
Oakville, Iowa 45678
(612) 555-1212

January 5, 1995

Mr. Thomas Inderly
3487 Park Place
Oakville, Iowa 45678

Dear Mr. Inderly:

It was a pleasure talking with you on the telephone the other day. I would like to confirm your appointment with attorney Barbara Kendall which is scheduled for January 9, 1995, at 4:00 P.M. here at our offices.

To help make our meeting more efficient, please bring the following information with you concerning the accident on November 24, 1994, at the intersection of Fig and Elm Streets:

1. A copy of your automobile insurance policy

2. The name, address, and automobile insurance policy information of the other driver involved in the accident

3. Any available information concerning the property damage to your automobile and to the other driver's automobile, including the photographs you mentioned

4. Copies of all of your medical bills for treatment of your injuries stemming from the accident, to date.

If you have any questions, please feel free to call me.

Sincerely,

Andrea Smith

Andrea Smith
Paralegal

Letter Confirming Client's Initial Interview Many law offices have accumulated sample letters for virtually every occasion to be used as a resource when drafting letters to clients.

Short of conducting the client interview alone, the paralegal often participates in the initial client interview in one of the following ways:

1. The paralegal may meet with the client prior to the client's meeting with the attorney to gather the basic facts of the

case and to obtain the necessary detail information.

2. The paralegal may attend the entire client interview with the attorney to take notes and ask pertinent questions.

3. The paralegal may follow up with the client after the initial meeting with the attorney is over to obtain detailed information necessary to proceed with the client's case.

Meeting with Client Prior to Initial Attorney/Client Interview

When the paralegal meets with the client prior to the initial interview with the attorney, the paralegal greets the client when he or she arrives at the office and sits down with the client to gather pertinent information. Usually with the aid of a client interview form, the paralegal gathers the pertinent personal information and the basic facts about the case at hand from the client. The paralegal then relates the important facts to the attorney who will meet with the client for his or her initial consultation. By performing the important but time-consuming task of collecting pertinent information prior to the attorney's meeting, the paralegal saves the attorney's time and helps to keep down the legal fees for the client.

Attending the Initial Attorney/Client Interview

If you are asked to attend an initial client interview with an attorney, make sure the file is ready and arrive on time. The attorney will typically introduce you to the client and briefly explain your role. Both you and the attorney will listen to the facts as presented by the client, and you will probably be asked to take notes with a client interview questionnaire. If there are some points as to which you are unclear, be sure to ask questions. Your notes should be complete and accurate. At times it may be appropriate to wait until the conclusion of the meeting to get correct name spellings and other information that the attorney will not be immediately concerned with. Before the client leaves the office, however, that information should be obtained.

During the interview, the attorney will be assessing the facts as presented by the client. The attorney will then define the legal problem and describe to the client the manner in which the case would be handled by the law firm, including the firm's billing practices. After an agreement is reached between the attorney and client as to how to best proceed with the matter and how the firm will be paid, the client will be asked to sign a retainer agreement. The retainer agreement establishes the ground rules of the attorney's representation and the work to be performed by the law firm, including fees, billing rates, expenses incurred on behalf of the client, and retainer.

At an initial interview, a client may also be asked to sign authorization forms to allow the law firm to obtain information concerning the client's medical treatment, wage loss, tax, or income information.

The Client Interview Form

When first meeting with a new client, there is always an abundance of essential information to be obtained. The most effective way to collect all information needed to open a client's file and begin work on it is to use a new client interview form. This form serves as a checklist for the paralegal during the interview so that all information is obtained during the meeting.

The form used will depend on the type of matter the client is involved in. Law firms typically have many versions of client interview forms to fit particular needs. Most forms include both personal data about the client and information relating to the case or matter. The personal data typically includes:

- Name
- Home address
- Address for billing
- Home telephone
- Work telephone
- Fax number
- Date of birth

- Social Security number
- Spouse's name
- Spouse's work telephone
- Employer
- Address

Forms for many types of client interviews can be found in formbooks. At times, you may have to create your own client interview form to handle a unique situation. It is important to not feel restricted by the design of an interview form. Although interview forms are constructed to help

---

FEE AGREEMENT

I hereby retain the law firm of Kendall & Kendall, Ltd. to represent me in the matter of *Inderly v. Koehler*, a personal injury lawsuit involving an automobile accident at the intersection of Fig and Elm Streets in Oakville, Iowa.

The attorneys agree to perform all legal services called for under this agreement for a contingency fee equal to one-third (1/3) of the total amount recovered from the lawsuit of *Inderly v. Koehler*, either by way of out-of-court settlement or court-awarded damages.

Additionally, I agree to pay all actual out-of-pocket expenses incurred in connection with this matter. Actual expenses include, but are not limited to, such items as filing fees, service fees, long-distance telephone calls, photocopying, and travel. The attorneys agree to provide client with an itemized list of all actual expenses and costs.

_____
Thomas Inderly

Date: _____

KENDALL & KENDALL, LTD.

By _____

Date _____

Retainer Agreement   The discussion concerning fees is generally reserved to the attorney. Paralegals are not allowed to discuss fees unless supervised by an attorney.

gather all pertinent information, no form can encompass every situation. Often an initial client interview takes a completely unexpected turn, when a client reveals important facts that were completely unanticipated. The form is to be used merely as a checklist and a guideline to follow during an interview. A paralegal who is responsible for note-taking should always be prepared with plenty of extra paper and an open mind when gathering facts during an initial client interview.

Memorandum Regarding the Interview

Each firm has its own policy with regard to follow-up work after interviews. Often the attorney or paralegal dictates a memorandum summarizing each client interview, to be kept in the file. When this is the procedure, the paralegal may be delegated the task of preparing the memo for the attorney's approval. When a summary memo is prepared, it should include:

1. The date and time of the interview
2. Who was present at the interview

3. The client's full name
4. How the client was referred to the law firm
5. A brief background of the client's legal problem
6. A brief description of the work to be completed on behalf of the client
7. A description of the fee arrangement entered into with the client.

Other Client Interviews

Paralegals are frequently asked to meet with clients who have already been introduced to the firm. These client interviews may be to help a client answer interrogatories or to collect additional facts in one or more specific areas. If you are asked to conduct a client interview, find out specifically what information the attorney wants you to gather from the interview; then take notes and use all of the communication skills discussed in the next section.

Communication Skills for Interviewing

No other area of paralegal work requires excellent communication skills more than interviewing. Even when the paralegal knows all the mechanics of interviewing, only with excellent communication skills can he or she conduct an interview effectively. Communication skills that are helpful when interviewing include making a client feel comfortable, active listening, keeping the interview on track, and conducting a thorough interview.

Making the Client Feel Comfortable

The aim of the client interview is typically to gather facts from the client. Clients will be much more willing to answer questions and to volunteer pertinent information if they feel comfortable and at ease. To make the client feel comfortable with

you, you will want the client to view you as being friendly, professional, and approachable.

When you greet the client, do it with a handshake and a warm smile. If it is office policy to do so, be sure to offer the client a cup of coffee or other beverage. Take time for small talk before getting down to the business of collecting facts from the client. Begin the interview by asking an open-ended question that allows the client to say what is on his or her mind. When the client has finished his or her story, you can follow up by asking any relevant questions that the client has not already answered. Good open-ended questions to get the client talking might include, "So what can we do for you today?" "What can you tell me about the situation with ...?"

If you are meeting with a client in your office, your office should be cleared of clutter, and no

PERSONAL DATA

Name:
Home Address:
Address for Billing:
Home Telephone:
Work Telephone:
Fax Number:
Date of Birth:
Social Security No.:
Driver's License No.:
Spouse's Name:
Spouse's Work Phone:
Employer:
Address:

INFORMATION RELATING TO CLAIM:

Type of claim (EEOC, med. malpractice, etc.):
Date of incident leading to claim:
Brief statement of incident (or attach statement):

Itemize damages incurred to date:

Do you anticipate additional damages? If so, describe:

Name and address of any doctors you have seen:

Identity, address, and phone of any potential witnesses:

Description and location of any documents or correspondence pertinent
to litigation:

Have you made any statements to anyone (orally or in writing) regarding
this case? If so, describe.

Do you have any insurance which covers this claim? If so, please describe.

Have you been served with any papers relating to this case?
Have you heard from any lawyers concerning this case?

PRIOR LITIGATION:

Type of litigation:
Date and place of litigation:
Outcome of litigation:

Attorney representing you:

Client Interview Form The client interview form includes all the questions that must
be asked of a new client. Many law offices require additional information depending
on the legal area in which the firm will represent the client.

confidential material should be visible. The client can sit in a comfortable chair opposite your desk. If you are meeting in a conference room, choose a chair that is close to the client instead of at the opposite end of the table.

Your manner with the client should be professional but not too formal. Express yourself precisely, but try to avoid legalese that may intimidate the client. Maintain appropriate eye contact while speaking with the client—enough to show you are interested, without staring.

Active Listening

Active listening is important to build a good rapport with the client and to gather all facts without having to ask clients to repeat themselves. Not only is it important to listen well, but it is also important to show clients that you are listening, and to encourage them along the path you would like them to follow. Use these tips for active listening:

1. Don't interrupt the client when he or she is speaking, but show that you are listening by maintaining eye contact and nodding when appropriate.

2. Restate the facts and feelings that the client is trying to express to you in short and simple terms, and by making summary responses.

3. Avoid obviously correcting the client when he or she has misstated a fact or belief.

4. When you would like the client to expand on a statement, encourage the client by repeating the statement. For example, suppose that an estate-planning client is telling you about a family situation and says, "My daughter has four children." If you repeat the client's statement as a question, by saying "Your daughter has four children?," chances are that the client will continue by telling you the names and ages of the grandchildren.

5. When you have information as to the procedures that will be followed on the client's file, wait until the client is done relating all facts to you, then relate the procedures directly to the information given to you by the client.

6. Observe the client's body language to understand what the client is feeling, not just what the client is saying.

7. Keep an open mind. Don't presume that you know what the client is feeling or what he or she will say next. Ask questions.

8. Be sympathetic and sensitive without expressing an opinion.

9. Don't be judgmental.

Keeping the Interview on Track

Although it is important that clients feel free to talk to you, it is also important to remember that clients are paying the firm for your time spent during the interview. A certain amount of small talk is appropriate, but an hour's conversation about fishing or a recent vacation is not. Clients may ramble on without realizing how much time they are spending, only to be upset when they receive the bill from the firm.

There are several means for steering a conversation back to the topic to be addressed. When necessary, ask questions of the client that pertain to the facts. Use subtle body language, by looking at your client interview form with pen in hand. That may bring a client back to the task at hand.

Completing a Thorough Interview

Before the client leaves the office, be sure you have ascertained all of the necessary information. Have you recorded all information on the client interview form?

When concluding client interviews, you want to leave clients with a sense of satisfaction by letting them know what will be done on their behalf. The paralegal should outline to clients the procedural steps that will be taken on the file, giving clients as much detail as they seem to want. At this juncture, it is important to remember that it is not the paralegal's duty to give legal advice to clients. Educating a client on legal procedure is not giving legal advice, but advising a client on how to proceed with nonroutine matters is. It is clear that a paralegal's giving legal advice is unethical and probably illegal. If the client asks a question that requires a legal opinion or legal advice, explain that the attorney is in a much better position to answer that particular question and that you will ask the attorney to respond to the question as soon as possible.

An Introduction to Investigating

The term *investigation* is typically associated with litigation investigations to gather facts and evidence for an impending lawsuit. However, investigation can mean gathering facts for any type of legal work to be performed for a client. Investigating means asking questions and getting answers. One of the more important aspects of investigating is knowing who to ask what questions. This section briefly explores the basics of investigating that are commonly performed or coordinated by paralegals, including a discussion about facts and evidence, forms and types of evidence, and sources of evidence.

Facts and Evidence

In litigation, a fact is not a fact until it has been proven. The litigation investigation, then, is really a two-fold project: first to find the facts, then to find the evidence to prove the facts. **Evidence** is the means by which any matter of fact may be established or disproved, including testimony, documents, or physical objects. The law and rules of evidence determine what evidence is to be admitted or rejected in the trial of a civil action or a criminal prosecution and what weight is to be given to evidence which is admitted. For evidence to be admitted in a court of law, it must be material and relevant. **Material evidence** is evidence going to the substantive matters in a dispute or having a legitimate bearing and effective influence on the decision of the case. Evidence is considered to be **relevant** if it tends to make the existence of a material fact more or less probable.

Forms of Evidence

There are several forms of evidence, including testimonial evidence, documentary evidence, real evidence, and demonstrative evidence. A thorough litigation investigation seeks to uncover all forms of evidence that exist to support the facts concerning a matter.

Testimonial evidence is evidence elicited from a witness. The witness may be your client or someone who will testify as to what he or she perceived that is pertinent to a case.

In the law office scenario at the beginning of this chapter, Andrea should ask Mr. Inderly if there were any witnesses to the incident leading to his personal injury. For example, if Mr. Inderly was injured in a rear-end automobile collision, Andrea should ask who witnessed the accident. Were there passengers in either automobile or bystanders who saw what happened? Police reports

---

BALLENTINESBALLENTINESBALLENTINESBALLENTINESBALLENTINESBALLENTINESBALLENTINESBALLENTINESBALLENTINESBALLENTINESBALLENTINESBALLENTINESBALLENTINES

evidence The means by which any matter of fact may be established or disproved. Such means include testimony, documents, and physical objects. The law of evidence is made up of rules that determine what evidence is to be admitted or rejected in the trial of a civil action or a criminal prosecution and what weight is to be given to admitted evidence.

material evidence Evidence that goes to the substantive matters in dispute or has legitimate bearing and effective influence on the decision of the case; evidence which is pertinent.

relevant evidence Evidence that proves or disproves a fact, or that tends to prove or disprove a fact. Relevance is the basic measure of the admissibility of evidence.

typically include the names of any witnesses to accidents.

Documentary evidence is a written object, including documents, business records, and medical reports, that tends to establish the truth or untruth of a matter at issue. The type of document constituting documentary evidence will depend on the type of case. In a personal injury matter, a medical report concerning the injuries of the plaintiff may be considered documentary evidence. In a real estate matter, a deed or abstract of title may be used as documentary evidence.

Real evidence, also referred to as *physical evidence*, is evidence furnished by a substantive, tangible object. In a murder trial, the real evidence might be a knife or a gun.

Demonstrative evidence is evidence offered for viewing by the fact finder (judge or jury) to help the fact finder comprehend the events of a case. Demonstrative evidence may include photographs, maps, charts, diagrams, models, or other presentations.

Types of Evidence

A paralegal conducting or coordinating a litigation investigation must be aware of all of the forms of evidence that may exist, and must actively seek all of the testimonial, documentary, and physical evidence pertaining to the case at hand. Just as there are several forms of evidence, there are also several types of evidence, including direct evidence, circumstantial evidence, cumulative evidence, and corroborative evidence.

Direct evidence is proof that speaks directly to the issue at hand. It requires no support by other evidence. It may be proof based solely upon the witness's own knowledge, as distinguished from evidence from which inferences must be drawn if it is to have value as proof. Suppose that Mr. Inderly, from the law office scenario, was rear-ended while stopped at a stop sign, and that the driver of the car left the scene while Mr. Inderly was unconscious. An eyewitness who testifies that he or she saw Mr. Inderly stop at the stop sign, and saw the defendant's car hit the rear end of Mr. Inderly's car, would be presenting direct evidence to establish the circumstances of the collision.

Circumstantial evidence refers to facts and circumstances from which a jury or judge may reason and reach conclusions in a case. Contrary to popular belief, most criminal convictions are based exclusively on circumstantial evidence, unless there is a confession or an eyewitness. If a witness to the hypothetical collision involving Mr. Inderly were to testify that he or she was approximately one block from the alleged collision when it occurred, and that he or she heard a loud noise that sounded like a collision and then saw the defendant's car driving from the direction of the alleged collision with its front end smashed in, the witness would be providing circumstantial evidence.

Cumulative evidence is additional evidence of the same kind, or from the same source, on the same point. If the witness who only heard the collision and saw the damaged car drive away were also to testify that he or she noticed red

BALLENTINESBALLENTINESBALLENTINESBALLENTINESBALLENTINESBALLENTINESBALLENTINESBALLENTINESBALLENTINESBALLENTINESBALLENTINESBALLENTINESBALLENTINESBALLENTINES

documentary evidence   A document or other writing that tends to establish the truth or falsity of a matter at issue. When oral evidence is given, it is the person (i.e., the witness) who speaks; when documentary evidence is involved, it is the document that "speaks."

real evidence   Physical evidence, as opposed to testimony; demonstrative evidence.

demonstrative evidence   Physical evidence offered for viewing by the judge or jury.

direct evidence   Proof that speaks directly to the issue, requiring no support by other evidence; proof based solely upon the witness's own knowledge, as distinguished from evidence from which inferences must be drawn if it is to have value as proof.

circumstantial evidence   Facts and circumstances from which a jury or a judge may reason and reach conclusions in a case.

cumulative evidence   Additional evidence of the same kind, or from the same source, to the same point; evidence proving that which has already been proven. Cumulative evidence is to be contrasted with corroborating evidence, which always comes from a different source and is often different in kind or character.

paint (the color of Mr. Inderly's car) on the damaged car as it drove away, that testimony would be cumulative evidence.

In contrast to cumulative evidence, **corroborating evidence** always comes from a different source, and may be of a different character. Corroborating evidence also tends to show that prior evidence is true. In the previous examples, the testimony of the witness who heard the collision could be used as corroborating evidence to the evidence presented by the eyewitness to the collision.

Sources of Evidence

The source of evidence will depend on the type of evidence being sought and on the type of case. An experienced investigator will have his or her own list of contacts and sources of evidence. Following is a list of some of the more commonly used sources:

- Client statements
- Witness statements
- Photographs
- Police reports
- Documents obtained from the client
- All types of discovery
- Newspaper articles and notices
- Business records
- Government records
- Employment records
- Hospital records
- Court records
- Automobile registrations (Department of Motor Vehicles)
- Property tax records (County Assessor's Office)
- Public library resources.

Public and private records can be a very valuable source of evidence. Some pertinent private business records may already be in the hands of the firm's client. Others may be requested through discovery. Many public records are available to the general public, although it may take a little digging to find what you are looking for. Other public records require the permission of the client or other appropriate individual for disclosure.

Conducting the Investigation

When a paralegal is given the responsibility for investigation on a file, the investigation may be conducted in one of three ways:

1. The paralegal may personally conduct the investigation
2. The paralegal may enlist the services of an in-house investigator who is an employee of the law firm
3. The paralegal may retain the services of a private investigator on behalf of the client.

If the investigation will be limited or the budget for litigation is minimal, an experienced paralegal may decide to handle the investigation on his or her own. Investigatory tasks that are often handled by paralegals include obtaining documentary evidence, such as medical reports, police reports, and business records, and taking client and witness statements.

Persistence is one quality that a paralegal investigator must possess. An investigator may plan on calling an individual to obtain information,

BALLENTINESBALLENTINESBALLENTINESBALLENTINESBALLENTINESBALLENTINESBALLENTINESBALLENTINESBALLENTINESBALLENTINESBALLENTINESBALLENTINESBALLENTINESBALLENTINES

corroborating evidence   Evidence from another source which tends to show the probability that the testimony of a prior witness is truthful.

but in fact it may take 15 telephone calls to obtain the information sought. When you try to obtain evidence from an individual who does not have the answers to the questions you are asking, don't take "No" for an answer. Find out what the subject does know, including the name of someone who might be able to answer your questions, if possible.

The drawbacks to a paralegal's personally handling the investigation include the fact that investigation work can be very time-consuming. A paralegal who is working on an important, extensive investigation may have little time for anything else. Also, a paralegal's lack of investigatory experience could be a definite disadvantage; inexperience may lead to an unnecessarily lengthy investigation or missed evidence.

The Plan of Investigation

Creating a plan is one of the most important parts of the investigation process. A plan of investigation generally takes the following into consideration:

1. The purpose of the investigation
2. Potential sources of evidence
3. The resources available to conduct the investigation
4. The known facts of the case and the facts that must be ascertained
5. The evidence at hand and the evidence that needs to be obtained.

Purpose of the Investigation

The purpose of the investigation is usually to prove your client's claim and to find evidence to substantiate a settlement with the opposing party or a victory in court. The evidence to prove your client's case includes both evidence that substantiates his or her story and new evidence of which your client may be unaware. Another type of evidence that should not be disregarded is evidence that is harmful to your client's case. If you can find evidence that is damaging to your client's case, chances are that the opposing counsel will find it too. It is best to be prepared by having all relevant facts and evidence at hand.

Potential Sources of Evidence

The sources available to conduct an investigation will vary depending on the type of case and the known facts you have to begin your investigation. As discussed previously, the evidence can be in several forms, including testimonial, documentary, real, and demonstrative.

Available Resources

Another aspect of the case that must be taken into consideration is the extent of the resources available for conducting your investigation. If the case is one involving minimal damages and a minor potential award, an extensive, time-consuming, and costly investigation will not be practical. If, in contrast, the case has the potential for a major settlement, a larger investigation budget may be justified. Time is also a resource. If the paralegal responsible for conducting the investigation has several other pressing obligations, it may make sense in the planning stage to enlist help with the investigation, whether from another paralegal in the firm, an in-house investigator, or a private investigator. The responsible attorney and the paralegal responsible for planning and conducting or coordinating the investigation should agree on a tentative budget for the investigation during the planning process.

The Known Facts and Facts That Must Be Ascertained

The first step in conducting an investigation usually involves determining the facts of the situation. In most cases, an investigation with the initial aim of gathering every available form and type of evidence is probably unnecessary and almost always very expensive. For nonlitigation matters, evidence may be unnecessary. For example, when clients come in to a law office for estate planning, they will tell the attorney the facts about their families. An attorney will not ask that these facts be supported by evidence, such as birth and death certificates.

In other types of cases, *some* evidence may be required. If your corporate client is contemplating the purchase of real estate, the lender will probably want some evidence that your client is, in fact, a corporation. The lender may want to see the corporation's articles of incorporation. If they want more evidence than documents signed by your client, they may ask for a certificate of good standing issued by the Secretary of State, or other appropriate state official, as proof of the incorporation and good standing of your client.

In litigation matters, attorneys typically like to go into court armed with all available evidence of every form and every kind. However, that may be unnecessary too. Most lawsuits are settled before they ever reach a courtroom. The opposing counsel may also agree to admit to certain facts without the necessity of proving them with all available evidence.

Therefore, the first step in any investigation is to determine the facts of the matter. In litigation, you may also want to ascertain what evidence may be available. For example, if your law firm represents a personal injury client, the investigation will begin with the client interview. Certain evidence, such as medical reports and police reports, also helps define the facts of the case.

After the facts have been assembled from the client interview, the medical reports, and the police reports, an assessment is made to determine the next step in the investigation. The next step might involve having photographs taken of the accident scene and obtaining statements from the witnesses.

Evidence at Hand and Evidence That Must Be Obtained

As soon as the initial client interview has been completed, the investigating paralegal can begin to review the evidence at hand and plan the evidence that should be sought during the investigation. The paralegal should analyze each event described by the client to determine: (1) if there is evidence to substantiate the client's claim; (2) what type of evidence is needed to prove the client's claim concerning the event (if any); and (3) where this evidence can be obtained.

Although planning an investigation is important, it is also important to approach an investigation with an open mind and not to let your plan restrict the natural path the investigation may take. Often one phase of an investigation uncovers facts that were previously unknown and point to the need for more investigation in that area.

If the responsible attorney is not actively involved in preparing the investigation plan, it is important that the attorney be consulted at this stage to approve the plan and to give the paralegal any further information or instructions that may be useful during the investigation.

Interviewing Witnesses

Often the most important evidence presented at a trial is testimonial evidence introduced by witnesses. Both sides of a legal battle often use both lay witnesses and expert witnesses.

Long before a case ever comes to trial, it is important for the attorneys to know what lay witnesses exist and what their testimony will be. **Lay witnesses** are individuals who have witnessed an incident or who have personal knowledge of relevant facts concerning an incident. A very important part of an investigation is locating and interviewing potential witnesses.

Locating Witnesses

There are several sources for locating individuals who may have witnessed a particular incident. Some of the more common sources are:

BALLENTINESBALLENTINESBALLENTINESBALLENTINESBALLENTINESBALLENTINESBALLENTINESBALLENTINESBALLENTINESBALLENTINESBALLENTINESBALLENTINESBALLENTINESBALLENTINES

lay witness A witness, other than an expert witness, who possesses no expertise in the field about which he or she testifies. Except in limited circumstances in some jurisdictions, a lay witness is not permitted to testify as to his or her opinion, but only as to things he or she actually observed.

1. Names listed on police reports
2. Individuals named in newspaper articles concerning the event and journalists who covered the incident for news reports
3. Individuals personally known to the client
4. Individuals who were situated near the incident when it occurred (such as neighbors and those who work nearby)
5. Individuals who respond to posted or published notices requesting information concerning a particular event.

Witnesses listed in a police report are typically eyewitnesses to an incident. Both names and addresses are usually given in police reports, making these witnesses both important and easy to locate.

Names of witnesses may also be given in newspaper articles. Again, these witnesses are usually eyewitnesses. It may take a little work to locate these individuals, however, because newspaper articles may give the full name of an individual, but not the individual's address, and certainly not his or her telephone number.

Often the client is the best source for locating potential witnesses. He or she may have the names of individuals who were eyewitnesses to an incident or who have first-hand knowledge of an incident of which no one else is aware. In addition, the client is often able to furnish the full name, address, and telephone number of a witness.

How you locate witnesses who may have been in the vicinity of an incident will depend on the type of case you are working on. In a criminal matter, neighbors or individuals who work in the area may have heard or seen something. Locating these individuals may require door-to-door inquiries at times. In a personal injury matter such as an automobile accident, witnesses may include those who live or work in the vicinity of the accident, as well as those who were at nearby bus stops, or were driving by. Often, the best way to locate these individuals is to make an inspection of the scene of the accident at the time of day that the accident occurred, and talk to those who might have had an opportunity to witness the accident.

If witnesses cannot be found by talking to people at the scene of an accident, a notice may be posted at the scene asking for information from anyone who saw the incident. In addition, notices may be published in local newspapers asking for information from anyone with knowledge of a particular incident.

Locating witnesses is often one of the first steps to take when conducting an investigation. It is important that potential witnesses be identified, located, and interviewed as soon as possible. This is your best chance to find witnesses and to obtain their written testimony while their memories are still fresh as to the incident. Even when an individual's name is given in a newspaper article, the telephone number and address are not usually readily available for that potential witness. Some sources for locating telephone numbers and addresses for potential witnesses include:

1. The telephone directory
2. The city directory
3. The source for the witness's name (such as the client, the newspaper reporter, etc.)
4. The Department of Motor Vehicles
5. Employers.

Locating a witness generally involves both imagination and perseverance.

Elements of a Witness Interview

The decision as to how best to schedule an interview with a witness is a judgment call. After potential witnesses have been located, it is usually best to contact the witness by telephone to schedule the interview at a place and time convenient for the witness. At times, though, witnesses must be approached in person at their homes or their places of employment.

Before meeting with a witness, the investigator should have a clear plan for the interview and a list of questions to be answered. Again, investigators should remember to have both a plan and an open mind when interviewing witnesses. It is always possible that a witness will have relevant information to relay during an interview that the investigator could not possibly anticipate.

When interviewing a witness, the investigator should identify himself or herself and give a brief explanation of the purpose of the interview. Courtesy and professionalism are of the utmost importance, as is showing respect for the witness and the witness's knowledge and time. The paralegal should also clearly let the witness know how much his or her time and testimony are appreciated and just how important they are. The interview should begin with open-ended questions, letting the witness tell everything he or she knows that is relevant about the incident. After the witness has told the facts that he or she knows to the best of his or her recollection, the interviewer may ask specific questions to help prompt the witness's memory. It is, however, important not to lead the witness.

It is vital to get a record of the witnesses' statements. There are several methods for obtaining a written witness statement. One method is to mechanically record the witness's statement (with the permission of the witness). If the witness's statement is mechanically recorded, it may later be transcribed and signed by the witness. If the witness is fully cooperative, the investigator may take extensive notes during the interview and have the notes transcribed and sent to the witness for his or her signature. At other times, it is best not to leave the interview without having the witness sign a statement. In that case, the statement may be handwritten by the investigator and reviewed and signed by the witness at the conclusion of the interview. This method may be preferable when the investigator cannot be sure that the witness will sign and return a statement at a later date.

During the witness interview, the investigator will be assessing the potential strength of the witness to testify in court. When interviewing a witness, some questions to ask yourself are:

1. Does this witness seem sure of himself or herself?
2. Does this witness express himself or herself clearly and concisely?
3. Does this witness appear to be honest and believable?
4. How valuable are the facts of which this witness has first-hand knowledge?

The answers to these questions will be extremely important to the attorney who is preparing for a court trial. An attorney must learn not only what the witness knows, but also how the witness expresses himself or herself. The paralegal investigator's evaluations should go into a witness interview report to the attorney, which also includes the witness's statement and all other pertinent information concerning the interview.

Under most circumstances, lay witnesses may testify only as to matters of which they have first-hand knowledge. The testimony of a witness as to a statement made to him or her outside of court, or made to someone else who told the witness what was said, is referred to as **hearsay** and is generally inadmissible. In addition, the lay witness must be qualified by circumstances to give an opinion as to what he or she witnessed. For example, a lay witness who saw a head-on collision may give an opinion as to how fast the cars he or she observed were traveling at the time of the collision. The witness may testify that one of the cars crossed the center line, but any opinion as to the driver's carelessness or recklessness would be inadmissible.

Interviewing the Hostile Witness

Not all witnesses are eager or willing to talk to investigators; they may be reluctant or hostile witnesses. The witness may be a friend or relative of the opposing party in a lawsuit, or possibly the witness just does not want to get involved.

hearsay The testimony of a witness as to a statement made to him or her outside of court, or made to someone else who told the witness what was said, that is offered in court to prove the truth of the matter contained in the statement.

Extra care must be used when interviewing a potentially hostile witness. The first contact with such a witness may be in person and by surprise as soon after the incident as possible. Delay in interviewing potentially hostile witnesses may give them time to rehearse their statements or to consult with the attorney for the opposing party, who may advise that the witness talk to no one concerning the incident. If a reluctant or hostile witness does agree to talk with you and to give a statement, you will need all your excellent communication skills.

Although the same communication techniques generally work for friendly and hostile witnesses, to begin with, hostile witnesses typically require much more specific questioning than friendly witnesses. They are much less apt to open up and tell everything they know concerning the incident. At times hostile witnesses refuse to see or talk to the investigator, even when reminded that they could be subpoenaed to appear in court to give their testimony.

Expert Witnesses

As part of a thorough civil or criminal litigation investigation, it is common for the investigator to locate and interview expert witnesses. An **expert witness** is a person who is qualified, either by actual experience or careful study, to form a definite opinion respecting a subject about which persons having no particular training, experience, or special study are incapable of forming accurate opinions. Whereas the admissibility of opinions of lay witnesses is very restricted, expert witnesses are called on specifically to give their opinions. When an expert witness has personal knowledge of the facts in a particular case, he or she can give an opinion so long as it falls within the expert's established area of expertise. Expert witnesses are available in practically every area imaginable, including economics, medicine,

pathology, forensics, and psychology. In addition to presenting evidence at trial, it is not uncommon for an expert witness to assist the attorney by acting as a consultant on complex technical matters.

Locating an expert witness who is qualified to give an opinion that will further your client's case can be a time-consuming process. Law firms that specialize in litigation typically keep files with information on available expert witnesses. In addition, attorney referrals, referral services, and information provided by clients can be used to locate potential expert witnesses. There are also many subject-specific biographical resources that report on experts within a specific field. The following general biographical resources are available in bound volumes in libraries or as databases. Most of these resources contain information on experts in several different fields. This information may include names, addresses, telephone numbers, areas of expertise, education, licenses, and affiliations:[1]

- *ARBA Guide to Biographical Dictionaries* (Bohdan Wynar ed., Libraries Unlimited, Inc. 1986) (critical reviews of many biographical materials)

- *Who's Who in America* (Wilmette, IL: Marquis Who's Who, Macmillan Directory Division 1899) (biennial, with annual supplements). Also available on WESTLAW and DIALOG

- *Forensic Services Directory: The National Register of Experts, Engineers, Scientific Advisers, Medical Specialists, Technical Consultants and Sources of Specialized Consultants and Sources of Specialized Knowledge* (National Forensic Center, annual). Also available on WESTLAW and LEXIS

- ExpertNet (ExpertNet, Ltd.). Available on WESTLAW, LEXIS, and DIALOG

expert witness A person who is so qualified, either by actual experience or by careful study, as to enable him or her to form a definite opinion of his or her own respecting a subject about which persons having no particular training, experience, or special study are incapable of forming accurate opinions.

- TASA (Technical Advisory Service for Attorneys). Available on WESTLAW
- *Defense Research Institute's Expert Witness Index*, Chicago, IL: DRI; (312) 944-0575
- "IDEX," Overland Park, KS: IDEX, 1-800-521-5596
- *"Dissertation Abstracts On-line"* (University Microfilms International). Available on microform, CD-ROM, WESTLAW, DIALOG, BRS, or OCLC/ERIC.

After locating the names of several potential expert witnesses, a paralegal may have to perform further research to get a clear idea of the testimony likely to be given by a particular expert witness. Articles and books published by the expert witness can be reviewed, as can prior testimony by that expert witness from reported cases. Although investigating a potential expert witness is a task that paralegals may perform, the final decision as to whether to retain an expert witness typically rests with the responsible attorney. In addition to investigating potential expert witnesses for your client, you can use these same resources used to investigate the background of expert witnesses who may be called by the opposing counsel, after you learn those names through the discovery process.

Physical Evidence

Physical evidence may be obtained from several different sources, including the client, witnesses, or the scene of the incident or accident. To avoid charges by the opposition that evidence has been tampered with or replaced, each piece of physical evidence should be tracked from its receipt by the law firm from the moment it is obtained through its final introduction as a trial exhibit.

Demonstrative Evidence

Demonstrative evidence, including charts, graphs, and photographs, is often obtained through an investigation or prepared prior to trial for presentation to the jury or judge. Investigating paralegals may be responsible for preparing demonstrative evidence or arranging for its preparation by other qualified individuals.

Photographs depicting the scene of an incident or accident, property damage or personal injuries, or other pertinent visual images are often very important evidence. At times, a paralegal who is an experienced photographer and has access to an adequate camera and equipment may be responsible for taking photographs. At other times, the paralegal will be responsible for locating and directing a professional photographer or private investigator to take the necessary photographs.

Investigating Individuals

From time to time, it may be necessary to obtain background information on an individual. The investigation may be in connection with a divorce, or it may be to check on a potential defendant in a lawsuit or partner for a business client.

In this age of computers, a wealth of information is available on almost every individual in the United States. This information includes records of the individual's birth, marriages, divorces, death, driving records, and court judgments entered against the individual.

Every state in the country keeps records on the births, marriages, divorces, and deaths of its residents, and this information is generally available to the public. However, because procedures vary from state to state, it may take a little work and persistence to find it. The best place to start is in a telephone directory of state offices from the state in which you are interested. The department that can assist you may be called "Vital Statistics," "Department of Public Records," or another similar name.

After you have found the correct department, it will usually release copies or certified copies of birth and death certificates for a nominal fee. It may also issue marriage and divorce information, or it may refer you to the correct court.

In addition to vital statistics agencies, the state's motor vehicle records department may be of use. Most states will release to the public, for a nominal fee, information contained on an individual's driver's license application or renewal and information concerning automobiles registered by the subject. Some states will even release the subject's driving record, including any driving violations in recent years.

The local courthouse may also have a wealth of information on a subject. Most courts have indexing systems where you can easily check to see what lawsuits a subject has been involved in, and what the outcome of those lawsuits was. Systems for searching for judgments filed against an individual are also typically in place. In most instances, the court file can be reviewed. Because of the vast array of court systems and court departments within a small geographical area, it helps when performing courthouse searches if you know what you are looking for and where to look before you begin.

Information on real estate is usually readily available at the Register of Deeds or county recorder's office in the county where the property is located. Reviewing the county recorder's records can tell you whose name the property is in and what mortgages or other liens are filed against the property.

Investigating Corporations and Businesses

It is often necessary to find background information on a corporation or other business. The information you are looking for may be minimal, such as where the business is located, where it is incorporated, and who can accept service of process on behalf of the corporation. You might need this information if your client who is contemplating entering into a business venture with an alleged corporation, or if your client is planning to sue a corporation. Most of this information is easy to obtain with just one telephone call to the appropriate Secretary of State's office. Other information that may be needed concerning a corporation is who owns the corporation, what its financial status is, and what assets it owns. This information may be harder to come by, but should be available for publicly held corporations. An

abundance of information is generally available on publicly held corporations through the registration and disclosure statements they must file with the Securities Exchange Commission. Some of the information contained in SEC filings includes: balance sheets, lists of subsidiaries, biographies of officers and directors, major pending litigation, and disclosures of stock ownership of major shareholders. Some of the more accessible resources include the following.[2]

Resources for SEC Filing Information on Public Corporations

- The Securities and Exchange Commission in Washington, DC
- Disclosure (service offering fax or overnight delivery of information on file with the SEC)
- Betchel (service offering fax or overnight delivery of information on file with the SEC)
- DIALOG File 100 (Disclosure) (online service)
- LEXIS COMPANY library (online service)
- WESTLAW's SEC database

Resources for State of Incorporation and Principal Place of Business and Registered Agent

- Secretary of State or other appropriate state official (in state of incorporation or state where corporation is authorized to do business)
- *Directory of Corporate Affiliations* (available at many public libraries)
- *Dun's Million Dollar Directory* (available at many public libraries)
- *Moody's Manuals* (available at many public libraries)
- *Standard and Poor's Register* (available at many public libraries)

Resources on Smaller/Privately Held Companies

- *Dun's Million Dollar Directory* (available at many public libraries)

- *Ward's Business Directory* (available at many public libraries)

- *Register of American Manufacturers* (available at many public libraries).

Coordinating the Investigation

No matter who investigates a matter, the paralegal may be assigned to oversee and coordinate several individuals' work. However, the procedures may vary depending on who does what.

In-House Investigator

Large law firms that specialize in litigation may have their own investigators on staff. When a paralegal is responsible for coordinating an investigation, he or she should enlist the services of the in-house investigator in accordance with law firm policy. The paralegal should be careful to give the investigator all relevant information that could be of use, which may include:

1. The known relevant facts of the investigation
2. The purpose of the investigation
3. The extent of the requested investigation
4. The type of evidence sought
5. The budget for the investigation
6. Primary sources for the investigation.

Private Investigator

The third option for the paralegal is to enlist the services of a private investigator. The law firm may have the names and addresses of private investigators whose services the firm often uses. If not, the paralegal should seek referrals from the supervising attorney, other law firm personnel, other contacts in the legal community, or the local bar association or paralegal association.

A private investigator will need to know the same type of information as an in-house investigator before commencing the investigation. In addition, you should make it clear to the investigator

what the parameters of the investigation are to be, and at what point he or she should seek permission to continue the investigation. Some of the common tasks performed by private investigators include interviewing witnesses and securing their statements and testimony, locating evidence, locating missing persons or witnesses, searching for hidden assets, and doing background checks and financial histories.

Some information you may want to obtain when retaining an investigator that is new to your firm includes:

1. How long has the investigator been in business?
2. Does the investigator have a valid license in your state?
3. What is the investigator's educational and professional background?

Many reputable private investigators have legal backgrounds as police officers, paralegals, or attorneys. Experienced private investigators with good knowledge of the law will not waste time searching for evidence that will not be admissible. They also have a clear understanding of legal ethics and will do their best to protect the legal ethics of the attorney who employs them.

You may also want to check to see if the private investigator is certified. Although certification is not mandatory, many private investigators opt to comply with educational and testing requirements to gain Certified Legal Investigator (CLI), Certified Protection Professional (CPP), or Certified Fraud Examiner (CFE) designations. The CLI designation is awarded by the National Association of Legal Investigators and is granted to individuals who pass a half-day exam. The CPP designation is granted by the American Society of Industrial Security to those who pass tests on eight mandatory subjects and four optional subjects ranging from emergency planning and investigations to computer and nuclear security. Finally, the CFE designation is granted to members of the National Association of Certified Fraud Examiners who pass a two-day test or prove they have eight years' applicable experience, and meet other applicable requirements.[3]

Both in-house investigators and private investigators offer the advantages of being experienced and having a wealth of resources on which to draw.

 Summary Questions

1. Why is it important to check for potential conflicts of interest before scheduling an initial client interview?

2. What are some of the reasons that paralegals in private law firms rarely conduct initial client interviews on their own?

3. What are some methods that you can use during a client interview to keep the client talking about the topic at hand?

4. What are the four forms of evidence?

5. How are cumulative evidence and corroborative evidence similar? How are they different?

6. What are some of the advantages and disadvantages to using a private investigator?

7. Suppose that you are a paralegal in a law firm that represents the plaintiff in a personal injury lawsuit. When reviewing the information brought in by your client, you notice a newspaper clipping of an short article describing the accident. A witness named Janet Stepwisky was quoted in that article, but you cannot find her name anywhere else in that file. How might you attempt to contact Ms. Stepwisky for an interview and possibly a statement?

8. What important observations must be made by the investigator while the investigator is taking a witness statement?

 Practical Paralegal Skills

Assume that you are employed by a law firm who is representing a potential plaintiff in a personal injury lawsuit. Katherine Simpson claims that she was the victim of a hit-and-run accident on the street in front of a school. A partial client interview form might look like the following:

CLIENT INTERVIEW FORM
PERSONAL INJURY—PLAINTIFF

TYPE OF CLAIM: Personal Injury (Plaintiff)

DATE OF INCIDENT LEADING TO CLAIM: 3/5/94

BRIEF STATEMENT OF INCIDENT: Katherine Simpson was parked in her car in front of a school located at 123 Main Street, Hometown, Homestate, waiting for a friend, Bill Noble, to come out of school, when she was struck from behind by a light blue Grand Am automobile, possibly a

1991 or 1992 model. The driver of the Grand Am automobile did not stop at the scene of the accident, but drove away. Bill Noble was able to get its license plate number, a Homestate license plate number SHV893. The police were contacted and they told Katherine that they would locate the driver of the vehicle, who would probably be charged with the crime of leaving the scene of an accident.

As a result of the accident, Katherine Simpson has had chronic neck and back pain for which she is being treated by both a physician and a chiropractor. She has not been hospitalized. Her physician has indicated that her injuries may constitute a permanent partial disability.

ITEMIZE DAMAGES INCURRED TO DATE:

Damage to automobile:	$3,500
Lost wages due to Injury:	$4,000
Dr. Weldon Martin (physician)	$2,345
Dr. Elizabeth Hill (chiropractor)	$2,000
(Further medical expenses and wage loss are expected.)	

NAME AND ADDRESS OF ANY DOCTORS YOU HAVE SEEN:

Dr. Weldon Martin   Dr. Elizabeth Hill
135 1st Avenue   345 2nd Street
Hometown, Homestate 12345   Hometown, Homestate 12345

IDENTITY, ADDRESS, AND PHONE OF ANY POTENTIAL WITNESSES:

Bill Noble
321 Harmon Street
Hometown, Homestate 12345
(123) 555-1212

Names of other witnesses who were in or outside of the school and may have seen the incident are unknown.

Assume that you have been asked to begin an investigation into the possibility of initiating a lawsuit on behalf of Ms. Simpson. You are to obtain as much information as possible concerning the incident and the potential defendant. What are some of the specific steps you might take?

Notes

1 Shimpock-Vieweg, Kathy, "Unraveling the Mystery of Expert Witnesses," *Legal Assistant Today* 42 (July/August 1992).

2 Leiter, Richard A., and Bausch, Donna K., "The Goods on Corporate America," *Legal Assistant Today* 95 (March/April 1992).

3 Cook, Leroy, "How to Choose and Use Private Investigators," *The Practical Lawyer* 29 (April 1991).

CHAPTER 6
An Introduction to the American Legal System

All paralegals, as well as every citizen of the United States, are affected by the American legal system. The average citizen usually pays little attention to the workings of the American legal system, though, until he or she becomes personally involved with it.

Paralegals, whatever their specialties, must have a good knowledge of our legal system and our court systems. The work of a paralegal gives him or her a first-hand look at the inner workings of our legal system.

This section is a brief introduction to the organization and structure of the American legal system, starting with federalism. Our focus then moves to the separation of powers and each of the three branches of government, including an introduction to the court systems in this country and the sources of law. This chapter concludes with a look at certain categories of law, including civil and criminal law, tort law, and contract law.

Federalism

The United States is divided into two sovereign forms of government—the government of the United States and the governments of the many states. This division of power is commonly called **federalism**. It is also common to refer to this division as the *vertical division of power,* because the national government rests above the state governments in the hierarchy. The drafters of the Constitution of the United States established these two levels of government in an attempt to prevent the centralization of power, that is, too much power being vested in one group. The belief that "absolute power corrupts absolutely" was the catalyst for the division of governmental power.

In theory, the national and state governments each possess authority over their citizens (dual

| THE FEDERAL GOVERNMENT AND THE CONSTITUTION OF THE UNITED STATES OF AMERICA |
| STATE GOVERNMENTS AND THE CONSTITUTIONS OF THE INDIVIDUAL STATES |

Federalism—The Vertical Division of Power
Federalism is how the levels of government (local, state, and federal) interact with each other.

sovereignty), as well as over particular policy areas, free from the interference of the other government. The principle of federalism is found in the Tenth Amendment to the Constitution of the United States, which reads, "The powers not delegated to the United States by the Constitution, nor prohibited to it by the States, are reserved to the States respectively, or the people." In essence, the Constitution sets up a limited national government by giving the national government only those powers expressly or implicitly reserved to it by the Constitution. In contrast, the many state governments are not limited to those powers specifically reserved to them. States may legislate in areas not mentioned in the Constitution, provided that no other constitutional provision is violated by so doing. What this all means is that certain governmental powers and duties are vested in the national government, others belong to the states, and some are shared concurrently by the national and state governments.

When state and federal law directly conflict with each other, however, and both national and state governments possess jurisdiction over the matter in question, federal law is controlling. This control is due to the Supremacy Clause of the Constitution, which provides that the "Constitution, and the laws of the United States … shall be the supreme law of the land."[1] Neither state statutes nor state constitutions may conflict with the United States Constitution.

Separation of Powers

In addition to the division of power between the state and federal governments, another important division of governmental power exists, known as **separation of powers**. Separation of powers is the division of the power vested in the national government into three branches—the executive, legislative, and judicial branches—making a horizontal division of power, just as federalism is the vertical division. Each branch is vested with

THE THREE BRANCHES OF THE UNITED STATES GOVERNMENT		
THE EXECUTIVE BRANCH	THE LEGISLATIVE BRANCH	THE JUDICIAL BRANCH

The drafters of the federal constitution arranged to have power spread across three separate branches of government. In this way, no one individual or group of individuals has ultimate power over the government.

certain functions upon which the other two may not encroach.

The executive branch consists of the president of the United States, the president's staff, and the various administrative agencies that the president oversees.

The legislative branch consists of the United States Congress, which creates the laws of the United States.

The judicial branch comprises the various federal courts of the land, and is charged with the administration of justice.

Keep in mind that two levels of government exist, excluding local entities. Even though the United States Constitution does not establish three branches of government for the many states (the United States Constitution only specifies the structure of the federal government), all state constitutions do, in varying forms, follow the federal constitution as their model. The result is a two-tiered system, with each tier split into three parts.

The Executive Branch of Government

The executive branch of government is responsible for enforcing the laws made by the legislative branch. The executive branch of the United States government consists of the president of the United States, presidential appointees, and all administrative agencies. At the state level, it includes the governor, the governor's appointees, and all state administrative agencies. Administrative agencies include boards, commissions, and offices, or departments established to implement the law which generally originates with the legislative branch of government.

The authority of the president and the executive branch is granted by the Constitution of the United States, and it is likewise limited by the Constitution. For example, although the president has the authority to appoint several representatives of the United States, such as ambassadors, federal judges, and heads of several administrative agencies, many of those appointments must be approved by the legislative branch of government through an affirmative vote of at least two-thirds of the Senate. State constitutions place similar limitations on the executive branch of state governments.

BALLENTINESBALLENTINESBALLENTINESBALLENTINESBALLENTINESBALLENTINESBALLENTINESBALLENTINESBALLENTINESBALLENTINESBALLENTINESBALLENTINESBALLENTINES

federalism   The system by which the states of the United States relate to each other and to the federal government.

separation of powers   A fundamental principle of the Constitution, which gives exclusive power to the legislative branch to make the law, exclusive power to the executive branch to administer it, and exclusive power to the judicial branch to enforce it.

The executive branch of the federal government is divided into 14 main departments whose heads are appointed by the president. Heads (or "Secretaries") of 12 of these departments are members of the president's cabinet.

The Legislative Branch of Government

The legislative branch of government includes both federal and state lawmaking bodies. At the federal level, and in most states, the legislature is **bicameral** in structure (it consists of two parts). Typically, these divisions are referred to as the upper house (*Senate*) and the lower house (*House of Representatives*). In some states, these two groups may be referred to as the *Senate* and the *Assembly*. In addition to the federal and state levels, legislation also takes place at the local and city levels. These law-making bodies are often referred to as *committees* or *councils*.

Regardless of the level of the legislative body, its main function is **legislation**. The laws made by legislative bodies include federal and state statutes and local and city ordinances.

Typical Stages of Statutory Legislation

Statutes, whether federal or state, often follow a similar process, from the proposal stage to approval by the chief executive.

The Proposal

A statute typically begins with a proposal. This proposal may come from several sources, including the governor or president. Administrative agencies, special committees and task forces, and the bar association are also common sources of proposals. When a member of the house becomes interested in an idea, he or she may sponsor the bill. When the proposal for legislation is made by the legislature itself, that proposal is the form of a bill. The legislative council or another appointed committee or office of the legislature drafts the bill and circulates it throughout the legislative body.

Committee Consideration

After a proposal has been made for new legislation, a member of the legislature introduces the bill. The bill may be submitted to the lower house for approval before it is sent to the upper house, or it may be submitted simultaneously to both houses of the legislature. New bills are assigned consecutive numbers so that their progress may be easily tracked. Bills introduced to the Senate, begin with the prefix S. For example, S. 135 would be the 135th bill introduced to the Senate during the current session. Bills introduced to the House of Representatives begin with the prefix *H.R.*

After the bill has been introduced to the legislative body, it is usually sent to the committee with responsibility for that type of legislation, which then considers the bill. Hearings may be held in which citizens and public officials give testimony in support of or in opposition to the bill. The committee then issues its report regarding the bill.

Floor Debate

After the bill leaves the committee, it goes to the floor of the house for a full house debate. These debates are typically recorded or transcribed.

BALLENTINESBALLENTINESBALLENTINESBALLENTINESBALLENTINESBALLENTINESBALLENTINESBALLENTINESBALLENTINESBALLENTINESBALLENTINESBALLENTINESBALLENTINESBALLENTINES

bicameral Two-chambered, referring to the customary division of a legislature into two houses (a Senate and a House of Representatives).

legislation Laws enacted by a legislative body (such as Congress, a state legislature, or a city council).

Amendments may be made from the floor and voted on. Once the debate on the bill ends, a vote of the house is taken.

Conference Committee Consideration

When the bill has been introduced to both the lower and upper houses, debated on by both houses, and amended by both houses, quite different bills may emerge from each house. For that reason, **conference committees** are established to put together one coherent bill from the amended bills approved by each house. The conference committees consist of members of both houses, who work together to create a compromise bill that encompasses the intentions of both houses of the legislature. Identical bills can then be reintroduced to each house.

Floor Debate on Revisions

After the revised bills are reintroduced to each house of the legislature, the bills are again subject to floor debate and vote by both houses. If both houses pass the bill as it is, it is then submitted to the chief executive (the president or governor) for approval.

Approval or Veto of the Chief Executive

When a bill reaches the chief executive, he or she has the option of approving the bill and making it law, or vetoing the bill and sending it back to the legislature. A vetoed bill is often sent back to the legislature with an explanation of why the bill was disapproved, sometimes with the hope of getting a revised version of the bill. A chief executive veto can be overridden if approved by a designated number of legislators. Typically, the approval of two-thirds of the legislators is required to pass a bill over the objection of the chief executive.

Duties and Powers of the Judicial Branch

The judicial branch of government is charged with the administration of justice. The courts administer justice by acting as the conduit for dispute resolution. The courts are the place where civil and criminal disputes are resolved if the parties cannot reach a resolution themselves.

The judicial branch is independent from the other two branches of government. Often people think of the courts as enforcers of the law. Although true in a sense, this is also untrue, in that the judicial branch does not work with the executive branch in an attempt to achieve criminal convictions. It is the duty of the courts of this nation to remain neutral and apply the laws in a fair and impartial manner. The United States Constitution established a judiciary system shielded from interference from the other two branches. For example, the Constitution prohibits Congress from reducing the pay of federal judges after they are appointed. This prevents Congress from coercing the court into action under the threat of no pay. The Constitution also provides for lifetime appointments of federal judges, thereby keeping the judicial branch from being influenced by political concerns, which may cause judges to ignore the law and make decisions based on what is best for their political careers. Judicial independence permits courts to make decisions that are disadvantageous to the government, but required by law, without fear of retribution from the other two branches.

BALLENTINESBALLENTINESBALLENTINESBALLENTINESBALLENTINESBALLENTINESBALLENTINESBALLENTINESBALLENTINESBALLENTINESBALLENTINESBALLENTINESBALLENTINESBALLENTINES

conference committee   A meeting of representatives of both houses of a legislature to resolve differences in the versions of the same bill passed by each, by working out a compromise acceptable to both bodies.

DEPARTMENTS OF THE UNITED STATES EXECUTIVE BRANCH
▪ Department of State
▪ Department of Treasury
▪ Department of Defense
▪ Department of Justice
▪ Department of Interior
▪ Department of Agriculture
▪ Department of Commerce
▪ Department of Labor
▪ Department of Health and Human Services
▪ Department of Education
▪ Department of Housing and Urban Development
▪ Department of Transportation
▪ Department of Energy
▪ Department of Veterans Affairs

There are currently 14 major executive branch departments in the United States. The first was the Department of State and the most recent was the Department of Veterans Affairs.

In an effort to resolve disputes, courts must apply the laws of the land. To apply the law, judges must interpret legislation and the constitutions of the nation. To **interpret** means to read the law in an attempt to understand its meaning. All courts, whether local, state, or federal, are bound by the United States Constitution, and thus all courts have a duty to apply federal constitutional law.

This nation's courts are the final word in declaring the meaning of written law. If a court interprets a statute's meaning contrary to the intent of a legislature, then the legislature may later rewrite the statute to make its intent more clear, which has the effect of "reversing" the judicial interpretation of the statute. The process is much more difficult if a legislature desires to change a judicial interpretation of a constitution. At the national level, the federal Constitution has been amended 26 times. The amendment process, found in Article V of the Constitution, requires not only an action by the federal legislature but also action by the states. To amend a constitution is simply a more cumbersome and time-consuming endeavor than amending legislation.

In addition to interpreting the law, the judiciary has the power of **judicial review**, which permits it to review the actions of the executive and legislative branches and declare acts that are in violation of the Constitution **void**. Alexander Hamilton wrote of the power of judicial review, and of the importance of an independent judiciary, in the *Federalist Papers*, where he stated:

> Permanency in office frees the judges from political pressures and prevents invasions on judicial power by the president and Congress.

* * *

> The Constitution imposes certain restrictions on the Congress designed to protect individual liberties, but unless the courts are independent and have the power to declare the laws in violation of the Constitution null and void these protections amount to nothing. The power of the Supreme Court to declare laws unconstitutional leads some to assume that the judicial branch will be superior to the legislative branch.
>
> Only the Constitution is fundamental law; the Constitution establishes the principles and structure of the government. To argue that the Constitution is not superior to the laws suggests that the representatives of the people are superior to the people and that the Constitution is

interpret   To construe; to explain; to draw out meaning.

judicial review   Review by a court of a decision or ruling of an administrative agency; review by an appellate court of a determination by a lower court.

void   Null; without legal effect.

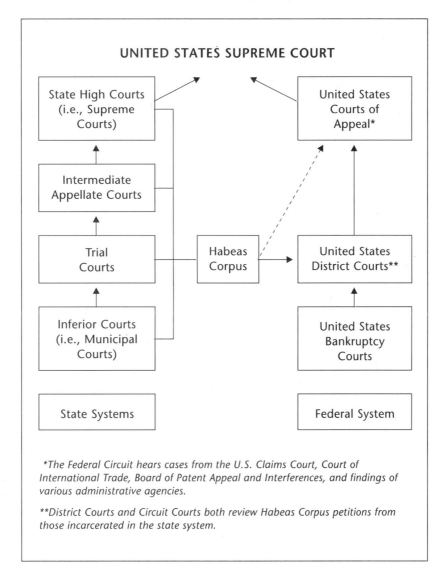

UNITED STATES SUPREME COURT

State High Courts (i.e., Supreme Courts)

United States Courts of Appeal*

Intermediate Appellate Courts

Trial Courts

Habeas Corpus

United States District Courts**

Inferior Courts (i.e., Municipal Courts)

United States Bankruptcy Courts

State Systems

Federal System

*The Federal Circuit hears cases from the U.S. Claims Court, Court of International Trade, Board of Patent Appeal and Interferences, and findings of various administrative agencies.

**District Courts and Circuit Courts both review Habeas Corpus petitions from those incarcerated in the state system.

Federal and State Court Systems In each system, there is a supreme court, the highest court to resolve disputes originating in the lower courts.

inferior to the government it gave birth to. The courts are the arbiters between the legislative branch and the people; the courts are to interpret the laws and prevent the legislative branch from exceeding the powers granted it. The courts must not only place the Constitution higher than the laws passed by Congress, they must also place the intentions of the people ahead of the intentions of the representatives.

The landmark case dealing with judicial review is *Marbury v. Madison*, 1 Cranch 137, 2 L. Ed. 60 (1803). Justice Marshall wrote the opinion for the Court and determined that, although the

Constitution does not contain explicit language providing for the power of judicial review, Article III of the Constitution indirectly endows the power in the judiciary. It is now well-established that courts possess the authority to review the actions of the executive and legislative branches and to declare any law, command, or other action void if such violates the United States Constitution. The power is held by both state and federal courts. Any state law that violates the United States Constitution may be struck down by either federal or state courts. Of course, state laws that violate state constitutions may be stricken for the same reason.

The power to invalidate statutes is used sparingly, for two reasons. First, members of the judiciary are aware of how awesome the power is, and are thus reluctant to use it. Second, many rules of statutory construction exist, which have the effect of preserving legislation. For example, if two interpretations of a statute are possible, one that violates the Constitution and one that does not, a basic rule of statutory construction requires that the statute be construed so that it is consistent with the Constitution.

The Structure of United States Court Systems

The duties of the judicial branch of a government are centered around the court systems. Numerous courts exist within the United States. Different court systems exist for each of the states and for the federal government. Furthermore, each court system contains many different courts. Although these court systems differ from one another in many ways, they do have some characteristics in common. All court systems have trial courts and courts of appeal or review. Many court systems have two levels of review courts, intermediate courts of appeal, and highest courts of appeal or courts of last resort, sometimes referred to as supreme courts. Furthermore, the function of all trial courts is similar, as are the functions of courts of appeal and courts of last resort.

This section examines the various types of courts, beginning with a look at trial courts, courts of appeal, and courts of last resort. Our focus then moves to the courts within the federal court system and the state court systems. This section concludes with a discussion of the jurisdiction and venue of the courts.

Trial Courts

The **trial court** is where a case begins. Trial courts are where witnesses are heard and evidence is presented, often to a jury as well as to a judge. Trial courts are also called **lower courts**. The primary function of any trial court is first to determine the facts and then to apply appropriate legal principles to those facts—principles that for the most part have been established by the legislature and by higher courts.

Trial courts have **original jurisdiction**. **Jurisdiction** refers to the power or authority of a court to hear a particular case. A court of original jurisdiction is the court in which a case begins and is tried.

Courts of Appeal

Courts of appeal are primarily courts of review. These courts examine what happened in the trial court to guarantee that the parties received

---

BALLENTINESBALLENTINESBALLENTINESBALLENTINESBALLENTINESBALLENTINESBALLENTINESBALLENTINESBALLENTINESBALLENTINESBALLENTINESBALLENTINESBALLENTINESBALLENTINES

trial court   A court that hears and determines a case initially, as opposed to an appellate court; a court of general jurisdiction.

lower court   An inferior court, usually a trial court; a court of limited jurisdiction.

original jurisdiction   The jurisdiction of a trial court, as distinguished from the jurisdiction of an appellate court.

jurisdiction   In a general sense, the right of a court to adjudicate lawsuits of a certain kind.

a fair **trial**. The appellate courts review the trial court's actions by examining a written, verbatim transcript or record of the lower court proceedings, along with **briefs** submitted by the attorneys for the parties. The attorneys are also normally allowed to argue orally. The appellate court's role is to determine if any legal errors occurred in the trial court. A *legal error* is an error in the way the law is interpreted or applied to a situation.

Because the authority of the courts of appeal is to review a trial court's actions rather than to resolve factual disputes, courts of appeal are sometimes called courts of **appellate jurisdiction**, or **higher courts**.

Courts of Last Resort

In addition to the courts of appeal, many court systems have a court of last resort, often referred to as a **supreme court**. Intermediate courts of appeal and the court of last resort are both primarily courts of appellate jurisdiction and review the proceedings at the trial level. However, one basic difference exists between intermediate courts of appeal and a court of last resort. Generally, intermediate courts of appeal must review cases in which the parties request a review. On the other hand, in most civil cases a court of last resort has a discretionary right to review the cases. In other words, this court hears only those appeals that it wants to hear. The parties do not have the right to have their appeal heard in that court.

Federal Court System

The federal court system was established in the United States Constitution, Article III, which created the "Supreme Court and such inferior courts as Congress may establish." Today those inferior courts include trial courts and appellate courts. The trial courts are most commonly known as the United States District Courts (or federal district courts), but also include various specialized courts such as federal bankruptcy courts, U.S. Court of Federal Claims, U.S. Court of International Trade, and the U.S. Tax Court. The appellate courts are known as United States Courts of Appeals (or federal courts of appeals).

United States District Courts

The United States and its territories are divided into 94 different districts, each one having a federal district court. Some larger districts are further subdivided into different divisions. Each state has at least one federal district court within its boundaries; depending on population, a state may have more. The number of judges assigned to each district varies according to need. District courts are the trial courts of the federal court system.

United States Courts of Appeal

The United States is divided into 12 appellate districts, including 11 numbered circuits (each one having jurisdiction over 3 or more states) and the District of Columbia. These courts have appellate jurisdiction, so they review the proceedings that took place in the district courts to determine if any substantial legal error was committed. In addition, the Court of Appeals for the Federal Circuit has national jurisdiction and hears appeals in patent, copyright, and trademark cases from any district court. This court also hears appeals from the Court of Federal Claims and U.S. Court of International Trade.

BALLENTINESBALLENTINESBALLENTINESBALLENTINESBALLENTINESBALLENTINESBALLENTINESBALLENTINESBALLENTINESBALLENTINESBALLENTINESBALLENTINESBALLENTINESBALLENTINES

trial   A hearing or determination by a court of the issues existing between the parties to an action; an examination by a court of competent jurisdiction, according to the law of the land, of the facts or law at issue in either a civil case or a criminal prosecution, for the purpose of adjudicating the matters in controversy.

brief   A written statement submitted to a court for the purpose of persuading it of the correctness of one's position. A brief argues the facts of the case and the applicable law, supported by citations of authority.

appellate jurisdiction   The authority of one court to review the proceedings of another court or of an administrative agency.

higher courts   Any court that is above a lower court, usually an appellate court.

supreme court   In most states, the highest appellate court of the state.

United States Supreme Court

The United States has only one federal Supreme Court, consisting of one Chief Justice and eight Associate Justices. Any six Justices constitute a quorum. The court is located in Washington, D.C., and holds its sessions from October through June. Primarily, the Supreme Court exercises appellate jurisdiction, and in most cases the exercise of that appellate jurisdiction is discretionary. In other words, the Supreme Court hears only those appeals that it wants to hear. In determining whether to grant a **hearing** in a case, the Court obviously considers the importance of the decision not only to the aggrieved parties, but also to society as a whole.

To request a hearing in the Supreme Court, a party files with the Court a document called a *petition for a* **writ of certiorari**. In this petition, the party explains to the court why the case is important enough for the Supreme Court to consider. The Justices then consider each petition and vote on whether to grant it. For a petition to be granted, at least four of the nine Justices must agree. If the petition for writ of certiorari is not granted, the decision of the court of appeals stands. If a petition for certiorari is granted, however, it does not mean that the party has won the case. The party has only managed to get a full hearing (review) by the Supreme Court. After the petition has been granted and the writ has been issued, the case proceeds much like an appeal in the appellate courts. The Justices consider the lower court transcripts. The attorneys submit legal briefs and are allowed to argue the case orally in front of the Court. Oral arguments before the Supreme Court, however, are very limited. By the time a case has reached the oral argument stage, the Justices know the legal arguments for both sides. Thus, the oral argument stage often serves as a chance for the Justices to ask questions about any legal arguments they want clarified.

To prevail before the Supreme Court, a party must have the vote of the majority of the Justices who have heard the case. When the Supreme Court renders its decision on a case, it is accompanied by the Court's opinion. Although the words *decision* and *opinion* are frequently used interchangeably, technically the term *decision* refers to the adjudication of the court, whereas an *opinion* states the reasons given by the court for that adjudication.

The opinion of the court must be approved by the majority of the Justices in support of the Supreme Court's decision. Often, any Justices who did not agree with the majority decision will submit **dissenting opinions**. In addition, Justices who agreed with the decision, but not with the reasoning behind the majority opinion, may submit **concurring opinions**.

Normally, the federal courts of appeal hear appeals from cases tried in federal district courts. The U.S. Supreme Court, however, can and does review cases originally tried in state courts as long as some federal or constitutional issue exists.

Although the Supreme Court is primarily a court of review, in certain cases it does have original jurisdiction, that is, the case is actually tried in the Supreme Court. Article III, § 2 of the U.S. Constitution provides:

BALLENTINESBALLENTINESBALLENTINESBALLENTINESBALLENTINESBALLENTINESBALLENTINESBALLENTINESBALLENTINESBALLENTINESBALLENTINESBALLENTINESBALLENTINESBALLENTINES

hearing A proceeding in which evidence is introduced and witnesses are examined so that findings of fact can be made and a determination rendered. Although, in a general sense, all trials can be said to be hearings, not all hearings are trials. The difference is in the degree of formality each requires, the rules of procedure being more relaxed in hearings.

writ of certiorari A writ issued by a higher court to a lower court requiring the certification of the record in a particular case so that the higher court can review the record and correct any actions taken in the case which are not in accordance with the law.

dissenting opinion A written opinion filed by a judge of an appellate court who disagrees with the decision of the majority of judges in a case, giving the reasons for his or her differing view. Often a dissenting opinion is written by one judge on behalf of one or more other dissenting judges.

concurring opinion An opinion issued by one or more judges which agrees with the result reached by the majority opinion rendered by the court, but reaches that result for different reasons.

In all cases affecting ambassadors, other public ministers and consuls, and those in which a state shall be a party, the Supreme Court shall have original jurisdiction. In all other cases before mentioned [Art. III, § 2.1] the Supreme Court shall have appellate jurisdiction, both as to law and fact, with such exception, and under such regulations as the Congress shall make.

State Court Systems

Each state has its own court system, established pursuant to the laws of the state. For the most part, however, the individual states have patterned their court structures after the federal system. All states have some sort of trial courts and some sort of appellate or review courts. Most states also have a state supreme court or a court of last resort. The role of each of these courts is also comparable to their equivalents in the federal system. The names, however, differ from state to state.

In addition, many state court systems today have something referred to as a *small claims court* (the people's court). In these courts, parties who are suing for small amounts of money go through a simplified litigation process. Attorneys are usually not involved, and all pleadings are extremely simple. These courts are intended to afford speedy legal relief in small cases where normal litigation costs would preclude the action.

Jurisdiction

Jurisdiction is the power or authority that a court has to hear a particular case. In determining whether a court has jurisdiction, two different issues arise. First, the case must be the kind of case that the court has power to hear. This is known as **subject matter jurisdiction**. Second, the court usually must have power or authority over the parties, and in particular, the defendant. This is usually known as **personal jurisdiction**, sometimes called **jurisdiction in personam**. At times, a court can hear a case if it lacks personal jurisdiction as long as it has jurisdiction in rem or jurisdiction quasi in rem. **Jurisdiction in rem** means that the property that is the subject of a lawsuit is located within the state. **Jurisdiction quasi in rem** sometimes exists when the defendant owns any property located within the state, even though that property is not the subject of the lawsuit. However, any judgment must be satisfied or collected from that property. To decide a case, a court must have subject matter *and* either personal jurisdiction, in rem jurisdiction, or quasi in rem jurisdiction.

Subject Matter Jurisdiction

Subject matter jurisdiction determines whether a court has the power to hear a particular type of case. Various laws dictate the kinds of cases that can be brought in federal courts and the kinds that can be brought in state courts.

A federal court has subject matter jurisdiction only when the Constitution, treaties, or some federal law specifically confers jurisdiction on that court. Generally, in criminal cases, the federal courts have jurisdiction where the offense is a crime under federal law. In civil cases, the federal courts have subject matter jurisdiction where the lawsuit revolves around some constitutional issue, a treaty, or some federal law, or if there is a diversity of citizenship (that is, the plaintiff and the defendant in the lawsuit are citizens of different states).

Even if the federal courts have subject matter jurisdiction, it does not always mean that the case must be brought in that court. Subject matter jurisdiction of the federal courts can be either

BALLENTINESBALLENTINESBALLENTINESBALLENTINESBALLENTINESBALLENTINESBALLENTINESBALLENTINESBALLENTINESBALLENTINESBALLENTINESBALLENTINESBALLENTINESBALLENTINES

subject matter jurisdiction   The jurisdiction of a court to hear and determine the type of case before it.

jurisdiction in personam   (personal jurisdiction) The jurisdiction a court has over the person of a defendant. It is acquired by service of process upon the defendant or by his or her voluntary submission to jurisdiction.

jurisdiction in rem   The jurisdiction a court has over property situated in the state.

jurisdiction quasi in rem   The jurisdiction a court has over the defendant's interest in property located within the jurisdiction.

exclusive or concurrent. **Exclusive jurisdiction** means that the action *must* be brought in federal court. **Concurrent jurisdiction** means that it may be brought either in federal court or in state court. Concurrent jurisdiction can also exist between two or more states. That is, when a case belongs in a state court system, more than one state may have subject matter jurisdiction. This would be determined by the facts of the case and the appropriate state laws.

Except for cases that must be brought in federal court, each state has the right to determine the jurisdictional limits of the courts within that state. States usually have at least one trial court with **general jurisdiction** in civil cases, that is, the power to hear any kind of case except those that must be brought in federal court. These courts are often known as county courts, circuit courts, superior courts, or courts of common pleas. However, unlike the federal system, where there is one level of trial courts, many states have created special trial courts with limited subject matter jurisdiction. A **court of limited jurisdiction** has authority to hear only certain kinds of cases. For example, some courts have authority to hear only juvenile proceedings, or family law matters, or cases in which the amount of money in dispute is below a specified amount. These courts are often known as municipal courts, district courts, or justice courts.

Appellate jurisdiction is the power of a court to review the decision of a court of original jurisdiction. In exercising appellate jurisdiction, a reviewing court has the power to **affirm** the decision (uphold the lower court), **reverse** the decision (change the lower courts decision), or **reverse and remand** the case (change the lower court's decision and send it back to the trial court to be retried). Appellate jurisdiction does not give a reviewing court power to retry a case.

Personal Jurisdiction

In addition to having jurisdiction over the subject matter of the case, a court must also have jurisdiction over the parties, which is known as *personal jurisdiction*. Personal jurisdiction means that the court has the power to render a judgment that affects the rights of the parties before the court.

The Fourteenth Amendment to the U.S. Constitution requires that "due process of law" be followed in civil as well as criminal cases. This has come to mean that a court can exercise jurisdiction over a nonresident defendant only when the defendant has some substantial connection or association with the state. State laws describing the circumstances under which the state may exercise jurisdiction over nonresident defendants are known as **long arm statutes**.

In Rem Jurisdiction

Sometimes, even though personal jurisdiction is questionable or even nonexistent, a court can still hear a case if it has jurisdiction over property

BALLENTINESBALLENTINESBALLENTINESBALLENTINESBALLENTINESBALLENTINESBALLENTINESBALLENTINESBALLENTINESBALLENTINESBALLENTINESBALLENTINESBALLENTINES

exclusive jurisdiction　Jurisdiction when only one court has the power to adjudicate the same class of cases or the same matter.

concurrent jurisdiction　Two or more courts having the power to adjudicate the same class of cases or the same matter.

general jurisdiction　The type of jurisdiction possessed by a trial court; that is, a court having jurisdiction to try all classes of civil and criminal cases except those which can be heard only by a court of limited jurisdiction.

court of limited jurisdiction　A court whose jurisdiction is limited to civil cases of a certain type or which involve a limited amount of money, or whose jurisdiction in criminal cases is confined to petty offenses and preliminary hearings.

affirm　In the case of an appellate court, to uphold the decision or judgment of the lower court after an appeal.

reversed　A term used in appellate court opinions to indicate that the court has set aside the judgment of the trial court.

reversed and remanded　An expression used in appellate court opinions to indicate that the court has reversed the judgment of the trial court and that the case has been returned to the trial court for a new trial.

long arm statutes　State statutes providing for substituted service of process on a nonresident corporation or individual. Long arm statutes permit a state's courts to take jurisdiction over a nonresident if he or she has done business in the state, or has committed a tort or owns property within the state.

that is the subject of the dispute. This jurisdiction is referred to as *in rem jurisdiction*, and it is a substitute in some cases for personal jurisdiction. In exercising in rem jurisdiction, a court is limited to rendering judgments that affect only the property. The court cannot render personal judgments against the defendant if the judgments do not concern that property.

Quasi In Rem Jurisdiction

Another substitute for personal jurisdiction is *quasi in rem jurisdiction*. For quasi in rem jurisdiction

to exist, various requirements must be met. First, a defendant must own some property within the state, although that property may not be the subject of the lawsuit. Second, the plaintiff can use only that property located within the state to satisfy a judgment awarded by the court. Third, that property is usually brought before the court at the beginning of the lawsuit through an **attachment** proceeding, in which the court usually orders that the property be seized and remain under the control of the court until the case is resolved.

Sources of American Law

American law is actually a body of many laws emanating from many sources. Sources of law include common law, statutory law, administrative law, court rules, and constitutional law.

Common Law, the Origin of American Law

The oldest form of law in the United States is the **common law**. The common law was developed in England and brought to the United States by the English colonists. The common law is judge-made law; in the United States, it is law that has been developed by the judges of both England and the United States. To comprehend how common law developed, you must understand the concepts of precedent and stare decisis. Whenever a court renders a legal decision, that decision becomes binding on the court and its inferior courts when

the same issue arises again in the future. The decision of the court is known as a **precedent**. The principle that inferior courts will comply with that decision when the issue is raised in the future is known as the doctrine of **stare decisis** from the Latin phrase *stare decisis et non queta overa* (meaning "stand by precedents and do not disturb settled points"). The rationale behind this policy is the need to promote certainty, stability, and predictability of the law.[2]

Common law is fluid, always changing with societal values and expectations. As one court stated, "The common law of the land is based upon human experience in the unceasing effort of an enlightened people to ascertain what is right and just between men."[3] For example, under ancient common law, ownership of land extended to the periphery of the universe. With the invention of the airplane, a change in this common law was

BALLENTINESBALLENTINESBALLENTINESBALLENTINESBALLENTINESBALLENTINESBALLENTINESBALLENTINESBALLENTINESBALLENTINESBALLENTINESBALLENTINESBALLENTINESBALLENTINESBALLENTINES

attachment   The process by which a person's property is figuratively brought into court to ensure satisfaction of a judgment that may be rendered against him or her. In the event judgment is rendered, the property may be sold to satisfy the judgment.

common law   Law found in the decisions of the courts rather than in statutes; judge-made law.

precedent   Prior decisions of the same court, or a higher court, which a judge must follow in deciding a subsequent case presenting similar facts and the same legal problem, even though different parties are involved and many years have elapsed.

stare decisis   Latin term for "standing by the decision." The doctrine that judicial decisions stand as precedents for cases arising in the future. It is a fundamental policy of our law that, except in unusual circumstances, a court's determination on a point of law will be followed by courts of the same or lower rank in later cases presenting the same legal issue, even though different parties are involved and many years have elapsed.

TYPES OF JURISDICTION	
Subject Matter Jurisdiction	Jurisdiction of the court to hear and decide the type of case before it.
Personal Jurisdiction	Jurisdiction over the person. Also referred to as jurisdiction in personam. Acquired by obtaining service of process upon the defendant or by the defendant's voluntary submission to jurisdiction.
In Rem Jurisdiction	Jurisdiction which a court has over property situated in the state that is subject of a dispute.
Quasi In Rem Jurisdiction	Jurisdiction which a court has over the defendant's interest in property located within the jurisdiction. The property need not be the subject of the lawsuit, but only the property within the jurisdiction can be awarded in the lawsuit.

For a court to decide a case, it must have subject matter *and* either personal jurisdiction, in rem jurisdiction, or quasi in rem jurisdiction.

needed. In *MacPherson v. Buick Motor Co.*, 217 N.Y. 382, 111 N.E. 1050 (1916), a new common law right was recognized in a purchaser against a manufacturer for injuries caused by latent defects in an article purchased at retail. Thus common law changes due to technological and social developments.

Initially, the 13 original states all adopted the common law. Today, only Louisiana has not adopted the common law in some form; most states have expressly adopted the common law either by statute or by constitutional authority, although many adopted only parts of the common law. However, approximately half of the states no longer recognize common-law crimes. Even in those states, though, the civil common law and portions of the criminal common law (i.e., defenses to criminal charges) continue in force.

Modifications to, and nullifications of, common law come about in many different manners. In some instances, courts have decided that the common law must be changed to meet contemporary conditions. In extreme situations, parts of the common law have been totally abolished. Because legislatures are charged with the duty of making laws, they have the final word, unless there is a state constitutional provision stating otherwise, on the status of the common law. Some legislatures, however, have expressly given their judiciaries the authority to modify, partially abolish, or wholly abolish the common law as long as the state constitution and the United States Constitution are not violated by so doing. The common law normally is inferior to legislation, so if a legislature acts in an area previously dealt with by common law, the new statute is controlling, absent a statement by the legislature to the contrary.

Statutory Law

The legislative branch is responsible for the creation of law. Legislatures possess the authority to modify, abolish, or adopt the common law, in whole or in part. During the 19th century, states began a major movement away from the common law and instead began codifying the law.

Although the power of the legislative branch is significant, there are limits. The constitutions of the United States and of the many states contain limits on such state and federal authority. Most of these limits are found in the Bill of Rights. For example, the First Amendment to the federal Constitution prohibits government from punishing an individual for exercising choice of religion. As discussed previously, if a legislature does enact law that violates a constitutional provision, it is the duty of the judicial branch to declare the law void. This is the power of judicial review.

The written laws of municipalities are **ordinances**. Ordinances are enacted by city councils and commonly regulate zoning, building, construction, and related matters. Many cities have criminal ordinances that mirror state statutes, only they apply to those acts that occur within the jurisdiction of the city. Ordinances may not conflict with state or federal law. Any ordinance that is inconsistent with higher law may be invalidated by a court. States limit the power of cities to punish for ordinance violations, and most city court trials are to the bench, not to a jury.

Administrative Law

Administrative agencies are governmental units—federal, state, and local—which administer the affairs of the government. Although often lumped together, there are actually two types of agencies, administrative and regulatory. The two names reflect the purposes behind each type. *Administrative* agencies put into effect government programs. For example, in Indiana, the State Department of Public Welfare administers the distribution of public money to those deemed needy. In contrast, state medical licensing boards are *regulatory*, because their duty is to oversee and regulate the practice of medicine in the various states. Both regulatory and administrative agencies receive their powers from the legislative branch.

Because legislatures do not possess the time or the expertise to write precise statutes, they often enact a very general statute which grants one or more administrative agencies the authority to make more precise laws. Just as legislative enactments are known as statutes (or codes), administrative laws are known as **regulations**.

SOURCES OF AMERICAN LAW
■ Common Law
■ Statutory Law
■ Administrative Law
■ Court Rules
■ Constitutional Law

Laws come from many different sources, but the ultimate law governing a state or the whole country is the federal Constitution.

Court Rules

Just as administrative agencies need the authority to fill in the gaps of legislation, because statutes are not specific enough to satisfy all of an agency's needs, so do courts. The United States Congress and all of the state legislatures have enacted some form of statute establishing general rules of civil and criminal procedure. However, to fill in the gaps left by legislatures, courts adopt **court rules** which also govern civil and criminal processes. Although court rules deal with the procedural issues (such as service of process, limits on the length of briefs and memoranda, and timing of filing) rather than substantive issues, they are nevertheless important. Of course, court rules may not conflict with legislative mandates. If a rule does conflict with a statute, the statute is controlling.

Most court rules are drafted under the direction of the highest court of the state and become effective either by vote of the court or after being presented to the state legislature for ratification. In the federal system, the rules are drafted by the Judicial Conference, under the direction of the Supreme Court, and then presented to Congress. If Congress fails to act to nullify the rules, they become law.

BALLENTINESBALLENTINESBALLENTINESBALLENTINESBALLENTINESBALLENTINESBALLENTINESBALLENTINESBALLENTINESBALLENTINESBALLENTINESBALLENTINESBALLENTINESBALLENTINES

ordinance   A law of a municipal corporation; a local law enacted by a city council, town council, board of supervisors, or the like. A rule established by authority.

regulation   A rule having the force of law, promulgated by an administrative agency.

rules of court   (court rules) Rules promulgated by the court, governing procedure or practice before it.

Constitutional Law

Constitutional law, particularly the United States Constitution and the Bill of Rights, has major a impact on our legal system and our society as a whole. The United States Constitution is the foundation of American law, and no laws may be passed or enforced if they are in conflict with the Constitution.

Although it is common to associate the study of constitutional law with study of the United States Constitution, it is important to remember that each state also has its own constitution, with its own body of case law interpreting its meaning.

Civil Versus Criminal Law

Civil law and criminal law are two broad categories of law with distinct differences. **Civil law** determines private rights and liabilities, whereas **criminal law** concerns offenses against the authority of the state.

Litigation is simply another term for a *lawsuit*, which is a dispute between two or more parties regarding civil or criminal law issues. Civil law involves disputes between private parties and defines legal rights and obligations between them. Civil litigation is the process of resolving private disputes through the court system. Unless the parties privately resolve their dispute, the litigation process usually results in a trial, or hearing, where the parties present their evidence to a judge or jury. The judge or jury then decides the dispute.

Not all cases that involve litigation are considered civil litigation. Our court system is designed to handle both civil and criminal cases. Criminal law defines conduct prohibited by legislative bodies, which also prescribe punishments for violations.

Parties in Civil Litigation and Criminal Actions

The parties to a civil lawsuit include the plaintiff, the defendant, and possibly third parties. The **plaintiff** is the party that has allegedly suffered some legal wrong at the hands of the **defendant**, the party responsible for infringing upon the plaintiff's legal rights. The plaintiff files a lawsuit against the defendant, using the courts as the forum to argue that the defendant should be held responsible for the plaintiff's injuries and should accordingly compensate the plaintiff for its losses.

The parties in a criminal lawsuit are different from those in a civil action. In criminal cases, the public, through the authority of the state (or, if federal, the United States), brings the accused criminal (the defendant) to court to determine his or her guilt or innocence. Of course, masses of citizens do not actually haul defendants bodily into the courtroom. Instead, the government provides a special officer, called the *prosecutor* or *district attorney* in many localities, who files criminal charges against the defendant on the public's behalf. At the state level, this official might be called the *attorney general*; at the federal tier, he or she would be the United States Attorney serving the Department of Justice under the United States Attorney General. Criminal lawsuits differ from their civil counterparts in that criminal prosecutions are intended to convict and punish the criminal offender, whereas civil

---

BALLENTINESBALLENTINESBALLENTINESBALLENTINESBALLENTINESBALLENTINESBALLENTINESBALLENTINESBALLENTINESBALLENTINESBALLENTINESBALLENTINESBALLENTINESBALLENTINESBALLENTINES

civil law   Law based upon a published code of statutes, as opposed to law found in the decisions of courts. Body of law that determines private rights and liabilities, as distinguished from criminal law.

criminal law   Branch of the law that specifies what conduct constitutes crime and establishes appropriate punishments for such conduct.

litigation   A legal action; a lawsuit.

plaintiff   A person who brings a lawsuit.

defendant   The person against whom an action is brought.

lawsuits are designed to settle disputes between private parties. In criminal actions, the convicted defendant may be punished by imprisonment or fined by the government. In civil suits, however, the defendant who loses judgment to the plaintiff must compensate the plaintiff directly.

Civil and Criminal Procedure

Civil litigation, which deals with private disputes between parties, is subject to the rules of civil litigation, sometimes referred to as **civil procedure**. Criminal cases, which deal with acts that are offenses against society as a whole, such as murder and robbery, are subject to the rules for criminal law, which are also known as the rules of **criminal procedure**.

Sometimes the same act results in both a civil dispute and a criminal action. For example, suppose that Maggie Applebee drives her car while under the influence of alcohol. As a result, she crashes into another vehicle and injures the driver of that car, Brian Watson. Maggie Applebee would be arrested for the crime of drunk driving, but Brian Watson might also sue civilly. The civil case (*Watson v. Applebee*) will proceed according to the rules of civil procedure. The criminal case (*People v. Applebee*) will proceed according to the rules of criminal procedure. In the criminal case, the government (in this case the state) would file an action against Maggie Applebee for the crime of drunk driving. If she were found guilty, the court could sentence her to jail or impose a fine payable to the state. In the civil case, Brian Watson would sue Maggie Applebee for money to compensate him for his medical bills, his lost wages, and his pain and suffering. Although the same act may spawn both a civil action and a criminal case, the two legal cases are always kept separate. They will never be tried together. In part, this is because a different standard or **burden of proof** is required in the criminal case. The standard of evidence used to judge the criminal case is higher than the standard applied in civil cases.

Burdens of Proof in Civil and Criminal Law

Civil and criminal law may be further distinguished in terms of burdens of proof. In a civil lawsuit, the plaintiff's case must be proved by a **preponderance of the evidence**, meaning that the plaintiff must convince the judge or jury that his or her version of the facts is more likely than not and that he or she is entitled to judgment. This degree of proof is sometimes called presenting a **prima facie case**, or "crossing the 51 percent line," because the plaintiff must outprove the defendant by more than half the evidence. In certain cases, such as those involving fraud, misrepresentation, intentional infliction of emotional distress, and probate contests, the plaintiff must prove his or her case by **clear and convincing evidence**, which is a higher standard and more difficult to meet than a mere preponderance.

BALLENTINESBALLENTINESBALLENTINESBALLENTINESBALLENTINESBALLENTINESBALLENTINESBALLENTINESBALLENTINESBALLENTINESBALLENTINESBALLENTINESBALLENTINESBALLENTINES

civil procedure   The rules of procedure by which private rights are enforced; the rules by which civil actions are governed.

criminal procedure   The rules of procedure by which criminal prosecutions are governed.

burden of proof   The duty of establishing the truth of a matter; the duty of proving a fact that is in dispute. In most instances the burden of proof, like the burden of going forward, shifts from one side to the other during the course of a trial as the case progresses and evidence is introduced by each side.

preponderance of the evidence   The degree of proof required in most civil actions. It means that the greater weight and value of the credible evidence, taken as a whole, belongs to one side in a lawsuit rather than to the other side. In other words, the party whose evidence is more convincing has a "preponderance of the evidence" on its side and must, as a matter of law, prevail in the lawsuit because it has met its burden of proof.

prima facie case   A cause of action or defense that is sufficiently established by a party's evidence to justify a verdict in his or her favor, provided the other party does not rebut that evidence; a case supported by sufficient evidence to justify its submission to the trier of fact and the rendition of a compatible verdict.

clear and convincing evidence   A degree of proof required in some civil cases, higher than the usual standard of preponderance of the evidence.

By contrast, in a criminal lawsuit the prosecutor must prove the case **beyond a reasonable doubt**. This means that the judge or jury must believe the defendant's guilt without significant reservations. This burden of proof is much more difficult than either of the proof levels required in civil cases. This heavier burden on the government exists to protect defendants from overzealous prosecutors who might succeed in convicting innocent individuals with less evidence if the proof requirements were easier to satisfy.

Tort Law

A **tort** is a wrongful injury to a person or his or her property. The person inflicting the harm is called the **tortfeasor**. Tort law considers the rights and remedies available to persons injured through other people's carelessness or intentional misconduct. Tort law also holds persons in certain circumstances responsible for other people's injuries regardless of blame. Torts are commonly subdivided into three broad categories: intentional torts, negligence, and strict (or absolute) liability.

Intentional Torts

Intentional torts are actions designed to injure another person or that person's property. The tortfeasor intends a particular harm to result from the misconduct. There are many specific types of intentional torts, including battery, assault, false imprisonment, infliction of emotional distress, fraud, misrepresentation, malicious prosecution, abuse of process, invasion of privacy, defamation (libel and slander), trespass, conversion, slander of title, disparagement of goods, and defamation by computer.

Negligence

Negligence is the failure to exercise reasonable care to avoid injuring others. It is distinguishable from intentional torts in that negligence does not require the intent to commit a wrongful action; instead, the wrongful action itself is sufficient to constitute negligence. What makes misconduct negligence is that (1) the behavior was not reasonably careful and (2) someone was injured as a result of this unreasonable carelessness.

Strict, or Absolute, Liability

Strict (or **absolute**) **liability** is the tortfeasor's responsibility for injuring another regardless of intent, negligence, or fault. The most important

---

BALLENTINESBALLENTINESBALLENTINESBALLENTINESBALLENTINESBALLENTINESBALLENTINESBALLENTINESBALLENTINESBALLENTINESBALLENTINESBALLENTINESBALLENTINES

beyond a reasonable doubt   The degree of proof required to convict a person of a crime. A reasonable doubt is a fair doubt based upon reason and common sense, not an arbitrary or possible doubt. To convict a criminal defendant, a jury must be persuaded of his or her guilt to a level beyond "apparently" or "probably." Proof beyond a reasonable doubt is the highest level of proof the law requires.

tort   A wrong involving a breach of duty and resulting in an injury to the person or property of another. A tort is distinguished from a breach of contract in that a tort is a violation of a duty established by law, whereas a breach of contract results from a failure to meet an obligation created by the agreement of the parties. … [T]he tort is a private wrong that must be pursued by the injured party in a civil action.

tortfeasor   A person who commits a tort.

intentional tort   An injury inflicted by positive, willful, and aggressive conduct, or by design, as opposed to an injury caused by negligence or resulting from an accident.

negligence   The failure to do something that a reasonable person would do in the same circumstances, or the doing of something a reasonable person would not do. Negligence is a wrong generally characterized by carelessness, inattentiveness, and neglectfulness rather than by a positive intent to cause injury.

strict liability   Liability for an injury whether or not there is fault or negligence; absolute liability.

type of strict liability is *products liability*, a legal theory under which the manufacturer or other seller of an unreasonably dangerous or defective product is held liable for injuries the product causes. Individuals in possession of wild and dangerous animals are also subject to absolute liability for injuries caused by those animals. Other activities found to be so dangerous that they impose absolute liability are the use of chemical sprays, the storage of a large amount of natural gas in a populated area, the storage of explosives, and the conducting of blasting operations which result in damage to adjoining property.[4]

Absolute liability is different from intentional torts in that intent to commit an absolute liability tort is irrelevant. Likewise, strict liability is distinguishable from negligence, because the tortfeasor is responsible under absolute liability regardless of how careful he or she might have been.

Public Policy Objectives in Tort Law

Like every aspect of our legal system, there are several purposes underlying tort principles. These include:

1. Protecting persons and property from unjust injury by providing legally enforceable rights
2. Compensating victims by holding accountable the persons responsible for causing such harm
3. Encouraging minimum standards of social conduct among society's members
4. Deterring violations of those standards of social conduct
5. Allocating losses among different participants in the social arena.

Protecting Persons and Property: Accountability

Modern tort law strives to prevent unjustified harm to innocent victims. Tort law enables private citizens to use the legal system to resolve disputes in which one party claims that the other

has acted improperly, resulting in harm. The system compels the tortfeasor to compensate the injured party for his or her losses. This accountability (or culpability) factor is crucial to our legal sense of fair play and equity. People should be held responsible for their actions, especially when they wreak havoc on others. Redress should be available for innocent victims of carelessness, recklessness, or intentional injury.

Minimum Standards of Social Conduct: Deterrence

To function meaningfully in American society, citizens must understand society's norms and values. One extremely important norm encourages the public to behave so as to avoid hurting others or their belongings. Tort law is largely composed of *minimum standards of conduct*; persons functioning below such thresholds are defined as tortfeasors, whereas individuals acting at/or above such criteria are acceptable to the community. However, the intention is not to ensure conformity; rather, the ideal is to inspire people to respect the dignity and integrity each individual possesses. Tort law is not designed to infringe heedlessly upon another's activities. Tort law discourages abuses by establishing a clear system of legal rights and remedies enforceable in court proceedings. We know that we can go to court when someone strikes us, invades our privacy, creates a nuisance, or acts negligently toward us. Likewise, we know that we might be hauled into court if we do those things to others. By establishing minimum standards of conduct, tort law sets the rules for living—the "rules of thumb" by which we try to get along with other people.

Allocating Losses

It is easy to grasp the idea that an individual tortfeasor should compensate the victim for the tortfeasor's wrongdoing. However, in modern society there are often many different participants in virtually any activity, and it is less clear who should be labeled as tortfeasor or victim. For example, at the time of the American Revolution, most Americans were fairly self-sufficient and dealt directly with other individuals for goods or services. If a colonist bought a broken plow or a poorly shod horse from the local blacksmith, he or she knew who to take to task. However, as the United States became more industrialized, commercial transactions ceased to be one-on-one interactions. Today, people buy canned produce from a local grocery that bought it from a wholesaler that bought it from a manufacturer that bought it from a grower. If the produce is spoiled, perhaps the purchaser's spouse or child, rather than the purchaser, will suffer the injury. The culpability lines become less clear as the producer of the defective item becomes more removed from the ultimate user. Tort law has evolved the legal theory of products liability to determine who is in the best position to bear the costs of defective products—the innocent user or the sellers and manufacturers. It is an economic decision that courts and legislatures have made in stating that industry can best afford the costs of injuries caused by dangerously made goods. In other words, the burden of shouldering the economic loss is placed upon commercial business instead of the individual who suffers the harm. This illustrates how tort law can be used to assign the expenses associated with misfortune even when fault is hazy. More commonly, though, a single tortfeasor can be identified and saddled with the financial obligation.

Contract Law and the Uniform Commercial Code

Another area of law underlying much litigation is the law of contracts. Most individuals in our society are participants in several different contracts during any given point of their adult life. It is important for paralegals to have an understanding of what a contract is, what makes a contract valid, and what the essential elements of a well-written contract are. Contracts appear in most, if not all, areas of law, including corporate law, employment law, family law, litigation, and real estate.

Elements

A **contract** has been defined as an agreement upon a sufficient consideration to do, or refrain from doing, a particular legal thing. This section focuses on this definition and the elements that comprise it. To have a **valid** contract, two or more parties with **capacity** must have an *agreement* involving valid **consideration** to do or refrain from doing some lawful act. A contract that comprises all of the necessary elements is considered to be valid. A contract that lacks one or more of the necessary elements is considered to be void; it is not a true contract and cannot be enforced. A contract that may be rejected by one of the parties on legal grounds is considered to be a **voidable** contract. There are important distinctions between a void contract and a voidable contract. A void contract is actually no contract at all—it binds no one, and an action cannot be maintained for its breach. A void contract does not require a disaffirmance to avoid it.

A voidable contract, in contrast, is valid and binding until it is avoided by the party entitled to avoid it. It has a defect which may be cured by ratification of the party entitled to avoid it.

BALLENTINESBALLENTINESBALLENTINESBALLENTINESBALLENTINESBALLENTINESBALLENTINESBALLENTINESBALLENTINESBALLENTINESBALLENTINESBALLENTINESBALLENTINESBALLENTINES

contract   An agreement entered into, for adequate consideration, to do, or refrain from doing, a particular thing.

valid   Effective; sufficient in law; legal; lawful; not void; in effect.

capacity   Compentency in law.

consideration   The reason a person enters into a contract; that which is given in exchange for performance or the promise to perform; the price bargained and paid; the inducement.

voidable   Avoidable; subject to disaffirmance; defective but valid unless disaffirmed by the person entitled to disaffirm.

ELEMENTS FOR A VALID CONTRACT
▪ The parties must have capacity to contract.
▪ There must be an offer.
▪ Consideration must be exchanged.
▪ There must be mutual agreement between the parties.
▪ The object or purpose of the contract must be legal.
▪ The legal requirements for form must be met (i.e., Statute of Frauds).

There are three basic elements to each contract: offer, consideration, and acceptance.

Capacity

For a contract to be valid, the parties to the contract must have *capacity*—the ability to know and understand the terms of the contract. It is usually assumed that all adults have the capacity to enter into binding contracts. Corporations also have the capacity to enter into contracts. Those lacking capacity include minors, mentally incompetent persons, and intoxicated persons.

In most states, individuals under the age of 18 are minors and lack capacity to enter into a contract. With few exceptions, contracts entered into by them are considered to be voidable. Minors who do enter into contracts have the right to cancel the contracts any time before reaching the age of 18. However, the minor who cancels a contract must return the benefits received from the contract if he or she cancels the contract.

A person who is so mentally incompetent that he or she does not know that a contract is being made, and does not understand the terms of the contract, is deemed to be insane and lacking capacity to enter into a contract. Contracts entered into by insane persons may be deemed voidable or possibly even void.

Persons who are so intoxicated that they cannot understand the terms of a contract, or even that they are entering into a contract, also lack capacity. Contracts entered into by them are also voidable or void.

Mutual Agreement

An agreement exists between two parties when they have a "meeting of the minds." This means that both parties understand the agreement and there are no misunderstandings or mistakes between them. A meeting of the minds generally occurs after an offer has been made by an **offeror** and accepted by an **offeree**. A valid offer is made with the intention of inviting another party (or several other parties) to enter into some defined contractual agreement. The offer constitutes a promise made by the offeror requesting from the offeree an act, restraint from performing some act which the offeree has the right to perform, or a return promise.

The offer must be definite and certain and it must be clearly communicated to the offeree. At times, an invitation may be made by an individual or a statement made that appears to be an offer, but actually is not. These exceptions to a valid offer include social invitations, offers made in excitement, and offers made in jest. A social invitation generally does not carry contractual intent. If Amy asks Bob if she can take him to a party, she is not making an offer to enter into a contract. If Bob compliments Amy on her new car after it has just been returned from the repair shop for the third time in a month, and she replies with, "Yeah, it's great. Do you want to buy it?", she has made the offer in jest, not to enter into a contractual agreement.

An offer may be made to a certain individual, or it may be made to the public (such as in an advertisement). After an offer is made, the next step is often negotiations between the offeror and the offeree. These negotiations may be conducted

---

BALLENTINESBALLENTINESBALLENTINESBALLENTINESBALLENTINESBALLENTINESBALLENTINESBALLENTINESBALLENTINESBALLENTINESBALLENTINESBALLENTINESBALLENTINES

offeror   A person who makes an offer.

offeree   A person to whom an offer is made.

personally or through agents. In any event, there can be no agreement between the offeror and the offeree (and no valid contract) until the offeree accepts the exact terms of the offer.

Consideration

A valid contract must include the exchange of consideration. Something of real value must be exchanged between the parties. The consideration may be cash or other tangible objects, the performance of an act, the agreement to refrain from performance of an act which the party has the right to perform, or a promise of future consideration. The exchange of consideration sets the valid contract apart from a *unilateral promise*. A promise to do something for someone in exchange for no consideration is not an enforceable contract. For example, if Jim tells Jerry he will mow Jerry's lawn while Jerry is out of town, Jim has made a promise. No consideration has been exchanged and a valid contract has not been made. If, on the other hand, Jim tells Jerry that he will mow Jerry's lawn while Jerry is out of town, and Jerry promises to mow Jim's lawn while Jim is out of town, consideration has been exchanged, namely, the promises to mow each other's lawns.

Legality of the Contract

A contract can be valid only if its object or purpose is legal. A contract may be void if its purpose is illegal because of statute or common law. If either the formation or the performance of the contract is illegal and would result in a crime and/or tort, or if it is opposed to public policy or interest, the contract is generally considered to be void. Some examples of contracts that would be considered void because they have an illegal purpose would be a contract to purchase a painting after it is stolen by a thief, a contract for the purchase of illegal narcotics, a contract that involves a fraudulent act on the part of both parties, or an agreement to harm or murder someone.

Breach of Contract

When one party fails to perform his or her obligations under a contract, he or she is said to be in **breach of contract**. The injured party generally has a variety of different remedies. The injured party may choose to **rescind** the contract or to **release** the other party from his or her obligations, or the parties may agree on **novation**. Typically, any of these resolutions to breach of contract may be achieved without litigation.

If the injured party chooses to sue the party who is in breach of contract, he or she may sue for money damages or for **specific performance**. The injured party may choose to sue for specific performance when the object or purpose of the breached contract is unique and the injured party feels that he or she cannot be fairly compensated by money damages. For example, if the parties have entered into a contract for the purchase of a race horse, and the seller breaches the contract by failing to deliver the horse, the buyer may sue for specific damages by requesting that the horse be delivered to him or her. In the alternative, the buyer may sue for money damages that total the sum paid to the seller under the

BALLENTINESBALLENTINESBALLENTINESBALLENTINESBALLENTINESBALLENTINESBALLENTINESBALLENTINESBALLENTINESBALLENTINESBALLENTINESBALLENTINESBALLENTINESBALLENTINES

breach of contract   Failure, without legal excuse, to perform any promise that forms a whole or a part of a contract, including the doing of something inconsistent with its terms.

rescind   To annul a contract from the beginning, not merely to terminate the contract as to future transactions.

release   The act of giving up or discharging a claim or right to the person against whom the claim exists or against whom the right is enforceable.

novation   The extinguishment of one obligation by another; a substituted contract that dissolves a previous contractual duty and creates a new one. Novation, which requires the mutual agreement of everyone concerned, replaces a contracting party with a new party who had no rights or obligations under the previous contract.

specific performance   The equitable remedy of compelling performance of a contract, as distinguished from an action at law for damages for breach of contract due to nonperformance. Specific performance may be ordered in circumstances where damages are an inadequate remedy.

contract, plus damages which may include lost profits and court costs.

At other times, it may be more appropriate for the injured party to a breached contract to sue for **injunctive relief**. Injunctive relief prohibits the other party to the contract from performing some specific act. Following the preceeding example, injunctive relief may be sought to prevent the sale of the race horse to a third party while the parties to the purchase agreement are settling their dispute.

There are a number of defenses to a claim of breach of contract. For example, the party who is accused of breaching the contract may claim that there never was a valid contract because the agreement lacked one of the necessary elements. In addition, at times a contract becomes impossible to perform. For instance, one of the parties may die, or the object of the contract may be lost or destroyed.

Transfer of Contract Rights and Duties

Under many circumstances, the rights and duties of the parties to a contract may be assigned to a third party. An **assignment** of contract rights may take place if it is not prohibited in the contract, if it does not involve the assignment of a personal duty, and if the assignment does not significantly affect the other original party to the contract.

The party who assigns his or her rights and/or duties is referred to as the **assignor**. The person receiving the rights and/or duties is referred to as the **assignee**. The assignee has all of the same rights and responsibilities as the assignor with regard to the rights and duties assigned to him or her.

For example, if Ron and Larry have a rental agreement, whereby Larry pays Ron $1,000 per month for rent, Ron can assign the rent to Mary (the assignee) to repay a debt he owes Mary. Mary then has the right to collect the rent from Larry per Larry's agreement with Ron. If agreed between Ron and Mary, Ron could also assign his duties under the contract with Larry, such as the duty to maintain the premises being rented to Larry. In that instance, Mary would have all of the rights and duties that were originally Ron's under the rental agreement. Larry may be required to consent to an assignment of Ron's duties under their original contract.

Contract Formalities

Contracts are subject to certain statutory formalities, including the Statute of Frauds and the parol evidence rule. Both of these statutory formalities must be followed for a contract to be valid and enforceable.

Statute of Frauds

The **Statute of Frauds**, which has been adopted in nearly every state in this country, requires that certain classes of contracts be in writing to be enforceable. Some examples of contracts that are subject to the Statute of Frauds include contracts involving the sale of goods for a price of $500 or more, contracts for the sale of real estate, and contracts that cannot be performed within one year. Any contracts that fall into these classes, and any other classes set forth in the Statute of Frauds as adopted by the pertinent state, must be in writing to be enforceable.

BALLENTINESBALLENTINESBALLENTINESBALLENTINESBALLENTINESBALLENTINESBALLENTINESBALLENTINESBALLENTINESBALLENTINESBALLENTINESBALLENTINESBALLENTINESBALLENTINES

injunctive relief   Relief resulting from an injunction.

assignment   A transfer of property, or a right in property, from one person to another.

assignor   A person who assigns a right.

assignee   A person to whom a right is assigned.

Statute of Frauds   A statute, existing in one or another form in every state, that requires certain classes of contracts to be in writing and signed by the parties. Its purpose is to prevent fraud or reduce the opportunities for fraud.

Parol Evidence Rule

The **parol evidence rule** complements the Statute of Frauds by requiring that when a written contract is in place between parties, the written contract must contain the entire agreement between the parties. If the parties decide to amend the contract, they must do so in writing. The reason for this is that in the event of a contract dispute, it would be impossible to prove the terms of a written contract if one party claimed that the contract had been amended by a verbal agreement.

The Uniform Commercial Code

The **Uniform Commercial Code** (UCC), which governs contracts and other commercial transactions, was drafted by the National Conference of Commissioners on Uniform State Laws and the American Law Institute. It has been adopted completely or substantially by all states. The Uniform Commercial Code was drafted to promote uniformity in contract and other laws among the states. As more and more commerce began to take place among the states, a certain amount of uniformity became necessary. The Uniform Commercial Code addresses such topics as sales, commercial paper, bank deposits and collections, letters of credit, bulk transfers, warehouse receipts, bills of lading and other documents of title, investment securities, and secured transactions, including sales of accounts, contract rights, and chattel paper.

 Summary Questions

1. If a state law conflicts with a federal law, which law controls?

2. What are the three branches of government and what are the main functions of each?

3. If there is an appeal on a matter that was heard in federal district court, where would the appeal be heard?

4. Where are appeals from a United States Court of Appeal heard?

5. Brandon Jenson and his neighbor, John Harrison, are involved in an altercation. Punches are thrown and John Harrison's nose is broken. Might this result in criminal litigation, civil litigation, or both? Who would the parties be?

6. In a products liability lawsuit involving faulty car brakes, must it be proven that the manufacturer was negligent in manufacture of the brakes? Why or why not?

7. Jim staggers out of a bar (after having several drinks) and tells his friend Bob that Bob may have Jim's Rolex watch if Bob will give Jim a ride home. Has a valid contract been made between Jim and Bob?

8. What is the difference between money damages and specific performance?

9. If Ted and Karen verbally agree that Karen will buy Ted's house for $250,000, can Ted sue Karen for that amount if Karen changes her mind?

BALLENTINESBALLENTINESBALLENTINESBALLENTINESBALLENTINESBALLENTINESBALLENTINESBALLENTINESBALLENTINESBALLENTINESBALLENTINESBALLENTINESBALLENTINES

parol evidence rule   Rule under which evidence of prior or contemporaneous oral agreements that would change the terms of a written contract are inadmissible.

Uniform Commercial Code (UCC)   One of the Uniform Laws, which has been adopted in much the same form in every state. It governs most aspects of commercial transactions including sales, leases, negotiable instruments, deposits and collections, letters of credit, bulk sales, warehouse receipts, bills of lading and other documents of title, investment securities, and secured transactions.

Practical Paralegal Skills

What is the structure of the state court system within your home state? Prepare a chart indicating the name and subject matter jurisdiction of each type of court within your state's court system.

Notes

For further reference, see *Criminal Law and Procedure*, by Daniel Hall (Lawyers Cooperative Publishing and Delmar Publishers Inc., 1992), and *Civil Litigation for the Paralegal*, by Peggy N. Kerley, Paul A. Sukys, and Joanne Banker Hames (Lawyers Cooperative Publishing and Delmar Publishers Inc., 1992).

[1] 20 Am Jur 2d. *Common Law* § 184 (1993).

[2] *Id.*

[3] *Helms v. American Sec. Co.*, 22 N.E.2d 822 (Ind. 1986).

[4] 74 Am Jur 2d. *Torts* § 15 (1993).

▐▐▐▐
CHAPTER 7
Legal Research and Legal Writing

Legal research and legal writing are two skills utilized by nearly every paralegal. That doesn't mean that paralegals spend all of their time with dusty old law books in law libraries, writing legal briefs and memorandums daily. Although this may be a factor in the work of many paralegals, legal research also encompasses research done by computer and over the telephone. It includes checking a simple procedure in a handbook or manual and writing a brief memorandum to the file or a letter to a client. Understanding the basics of what is required to perform adequate legal research and how to put your findings into writing are of the utmost importance to every paralegal.

This chapter gives a brief introduction to some of the numerous facets of legal research, including sources of law, court reporters, federal and state statutes and other legislation, shepardizing, secondary sources of law, and other resources for legal research. After a section on legal research techniques, this chapter concludes with an introduction to the basic concepts of legal writing and a discussion of certain types of legal writing.

An Introduction to Legal Research

Although it is important for paralegals to have a knowledge of the basic concepts of law, it is just as important that they know where to find the law. Considering the volumes of statutes and case law that have been written in this country, it is evident that paralegals cannot possibly know everything they need to know in their careers without legal research.

Paralegals beginning legal research often become frustrated when they are unable to draw a definite conclusion to a legal question after exhausting what seems to be every possible avenue of legal research. Don't lose heart. Although there are thousands of volumes of law in this country, not every question of law has been answered in every jurisdiction. Even after thorough research, it may still be impossible to determine an answer to a legal question without a judge's decision. If every aspect of law were so narrowly defined that every legal issue could be resolved without a doubt, there would be a lot less traffic through the court systems in this country. Legal research is the practice of finding and analyzing what there is to be found to answer a question of law. At times this also includes realizing what has not been found because it does not exist.

To decide where to begin your research, you must begin with an analysis of the problem at hand.

First, note the area of substantive law involved. In our law office scenario, the area is corporate law; more specifically, it is corporate director's liability. If Kate is not familiar with these areas, she may want to do preliminary research to get some background information before she begins the next step.

After defining the substantive area of law, determine the jurisdiction with which you are concerned. In the example in our law office scenario, the jurisdiction is the state of Minnesota, the state where the corporation is located and transacts its business. The laws of other states may also be pertinent if the corporation transacts business in other states where it is possible to be a target for litigation. For this preliminary research, the sources Kate will probably examine are Minnesota corporate statutes and Minnesota case law, both of which are considered primary sources of law.

Almost all of the vast materials available for legal research can be classified into one of three broad categories: primary sources of law, secondary sources of law, and finding tools. This section introduces the primary and secondary sources of law that paralegals may be concerned with, as well as the finding tools to locate those materials, and concludes with a brief discussion of the location of all of this information, the law library.

Law Office Scenario

|||| *Law Office Scenario* ||||

Kate Williams, a new paralegal with the Martin & Robertson law firm, was called in to Mr. Martin's office early one Monday morning.

"Kate," he said. "I have a research assignment for you. Our client, Andrea Bennigan, has been offered a new position with a hazardous waste disposal firm. She has been offered the position of controller, and they would also like her to be on the board of directors. Andrea is very interested in taking the position, but she is also concerned about her potential personal liability as a director with the corporation. There is a tremendous amount of potential liability for lawsuits in the hazardous waste area, and she wants to be sure that she cannot be held accountable personally for any negligent acts that the corporation may be accused of.

"The corporation is a Minnesota business corporation," continued attorney Martin. "I want you to research potential personal liability for a director of a Minnesota business corporation for acts of the corporation as they may apply to Andrea. I am meeting with her tomorrow afternoon and would like at least some preliminary information by that time."

"Okay," said Kate. "I can start working on it this afternoon."

What should Kate look for? Where should she start? These are the types of questions that accompany almost every legal research assignment.

Primary Sources of Law

Primary sources of law are the binding sources of law. The most common categories of primary sources of law include judicial decisions (cases), statutes, and administrative rules and regulations.

Judicial Decisions

The law in the United States is based on common law. The courts in this country abide by the doctrine of **stare decisis**, which binds the courts to stand by the **precedents** of decided cases. A **judicial decision** is binding on all other courts of equal or lesser authority in that jurisdiction unless and until a contrary decision is made by a higher court. Therefore, the importance of researching judicial decisions is readily apparent. Not only must case law be found, but it must also be the most current case law on the point of law you are researching.

Statutory Law

Statutory law is also a binding primary source of law. In many instances, the statutory law in this country has replaced common or case law. In many other instances, the two work hand in hand, with case law being used to interpret statutory law. State statutes control the residents of the state and others acting within the state. Federal statutes are binding on the entire country. In the

---

BALLENTINESBALLENTINESBALLENTINESBALLENTINESBALLENTINESBALLENTINESBALLENTINESBALLENTINESBALLENTINESBALLENTINESBALLENTINESBALLENTINESBALLENTINES

stare decisis Means "standing by the decision." … [T]he doctrine that judicial decisions stand as precedents for cases arising in the future. It is a fundamental policy of our law that, except in unusual circumstances, a court's determination on a point of law will be followed by courts of the same or lower rank in later cases presenting the same legal issue, even though different parties are involved and many years have elapsed.

precedent Prior decisions of the same court, or a higher court, which a judge must follow in deciding a subsequent case presenting similar facts and the same legal problem, even though different parties are involved and many years have elapsed.

judicial decision A decision by a court.

PRIMARY SOURCES OF LAW
▪ Case Law
▪ Statutory Law
▪ Administrative Rules and Regulations
▪ Constitutions
▪ Administrative Agency Decisions
▪ Rules of Court
▪ Executive Orders
▪ Treaties
▪ Ordinances
▪ Attorney General Opinions

Primary sources are the actual law.

event of a conflict between state and federal law, federal law takes priority. In the event of a conflict between case law and statutory law, statutory law is binding.

Administrative Law

A growing primary source of law in the United States is administrative law. With the ever-increasing complexity of our society and the need for more laws in specialized areas, the number of administrative rules and regulations is multiplying rapidly. Administrative agencies are given authority by the legislature or by statute to create binding rules and regulations at federal, state, and local levels.

Although other forms of law are appropriate for legal research under certain circumstances, the primary sources of law are the only sources of law that are binding on a court. When asked to prepare a trial brief or a legal memorandum, in almost every instance you will be seeking primary sources of law.

Secondary Sources of Law

Secondary sources of law are sources that discuss and analyze the law; they are *not* actual law

themselves. Although secondary sources of law are not binding, for three reasons they can be as important as primary law to a paralegal who is performing legal research.

First, secondary sources have educational value. When asked to research an area of law with which you are unfamiliar, often the best way to begin is to learn the basics of that area of law. A secondary source such as a legal encyclopedia is a logical place to start in that instance.

Second, secondary sources are often valuable finding tools. The same sources that seek to educate the reader on a specific topic can lead to other sources, including primary sources, on that topic.

Third, secondary law can be persuasive. When the primary sources of law fail to provide a definitive answer to a question of law, prestigious and well-respected secondary sources of law can be used to support your case.

Some of the more common secondary sources include law review articles, legal encyclopedias, restatements, and treatises.

Finding Tools

Finding tools are not really sources of law, but they are a means to find pertinent law. Because case law is constantly changing, with new court decisions being published every year, case law is organized chronologically. When you consider the

SECONDARY SOURCES
▪ Law Review Articles
▪ Legal Encyclopedias
▪ Treatises
▪ Legal Practice Manuals

Secondary sources are generally commentaries or reviews in law treatises and legal encyclopedias.

problem of finding a case that relates to the topic you are researching, when all cases for the last hundred years or so have been recorded in chronological order, with no regard to subject, it is easy to understand the importance of finding tools. Finding tools for case law include digests, indexes, and computerized research tools. Statutory finding tools include citators, indexes, and computerized systems. Finding tools for secondary sources of law include law library cataloging systems and indexes.

The Most Current Source of Law

In whatever area you are researching, it is important to be sure that you are always using the most current case, law, or other resource available. Using outdated materials can lead to very serious oversights and errors. Throughout this chapter, the different means for updating legal publications are discussed. One of the most popular means for updating a hardbound book is through the use of *pocket parts*, paperback pamphlets that fit into the back cover of a publication and are replaced periodically. The section numbers or the other numbering method used in the main volume of the text are the same in the pocket part, so that you can quickly check the pocket part for the pertinent section to see if it has been updated.

The Law Library

Nearly all legal research begins in a law library. If you are employed by a law firm or legal department with an extensive law library, most of your research will take place there. At other times, you will need to use other law libraries. Other law libraries generally available to the public include:

1. State law libraries
2. County law libraries
3. Bar association law libraries
4. Law school libraries
5. Courthouse law libraries.

Although most of these law libraries are usually open to the public, there may be restrictions on

FINDING TOOLS
■ Digests
■ Indexes
■ Annotations
■ Citators
■ Computerized Legal Research Systems

Finding tools are legal reference materials that help find both primary and secondary sources of law.

the circulation of their materials. For example, any individual may be free to use the resources of a law school library, but only students of the school may be allowed to check books out from the library and remove them from the premises.

Whenever you begin researching in a library that is unfamiliar to you, it is important that you find your way around. Don't be embarrassed to ask for a tour of the facility, or even a map; both are available at most law libraries. Even experienced attorneys need to familiarize themselves with a new law library.

Most law libraries are divided into sections that may resemble the following:

Court Reporters—State and Federal

Statutes—State and Federal

Periodicals

Treatises

Computer research

Loose-leaf services

Most law libraries contain the same types of resources, but they may be organized in totally different manners, so don't be afraid to ask.

The information you need within a law library can usually be found by browsing in the appropriate section of the library or by using the card catalog or computerized cataloging systems available at the library. When researching at a library that is new to you, you should also familiarize yourself with the library's system for locating specific materials.

Case Law and Court Reports

Case law is made when a judge issues an opinion that sets precedent. Although over the years more and more of our law has become statutory law or administrative law, the importance of case law has not diminished. Courts are still constantly making laws by setting new precedents and by interpreting statutory law.

Because courts are bound by the principle of stare decisis, and must follow precedent, the importance of finding precedent to support your case is obvious. The preferred type of precedent is a *mandatory authority*, one that the court will be required to follow. The court must follow prior decisions regarding cases that are substantially similar in both factual issues and issues of law and that are made by higher courts within the same court system.

If mandatory authority cannot be found, *persuasive authority* may be sought. Judges are not required to follow persuasive authority, although good persuasive authority may convince a judge to rule in the desired manner. Persuasive authority may come from court opinions from lower courts within the same court system, from court opinions from other jurisdictions, or from a secondary source of law.

MANDATORY VERSUS PERSUASIVE AUTHORITY	
Mandatory Authority	*Persuasive Authority*
A case with the same or similar facts and applicable rules of law decided by a higher court within the same court system	A case with the same or similar facts and applicable rules of law decided by a lower court within the same court system
	A case with the same or similar facts and applicable rules of law decided by the same court
	A case in a different state court with the same or similar facts and applicable rules of law
	A case within a different court system (federal or state) with the same or similar facts and applicable rules of law
	Secondary sources of law

Mandatory authority is a precedent that a court must follow; persuasive authority is a precedent that a court need not follow, but which may influence the ruling.

Elements of Researching Case Law

The first step in conducting case law research is to analyze the case at hand. It will be important to find cases that are similar in factual issues and issues of law, so you must first define these issues. Four elements to be analyzed are the subject matter of the case, the types of individuals involved in the case, the legal theories behind their claims and defenses, and the relief being sought.

The most preferable type of precedent is a case that is **on all fours**. This term refers to a judicial opinion in a case which is almost identical to your subject case with respect to both the facts and the applicable law. The next best type of case is one that is **on point**. A case on point is a judicial opinion which, with respect to the facts involved and the applicable law, is similar to but not on all fours with your subject case.

From Decision to Bound Court Reports

One of the reasons for the complexity of case law research is that case law must be current, and new cases are decided nearly every day. Obviously, there is a substantial delay between the time a decision is issued by the court and the time it is published in a bound volume. There are, however, publications in which a case will appear before it is published in a bound text.

The first published version of most decisions is the **slip opinion**, a pamphlet version of (usually) just one case issued shortly after a decision is reached. Slip opinions are usually issued by the court itself. Not many attorneys or law libraries subscribe to slip opinions because of the expense and difficulty in organizing them. However, it is important to know that they are available if you need the opinion in a particular case immediately.

After the slip opinion, an advance sheet containing several cases is published. The **advance sheet** is a pamphlet containing many of the features that appear in the permanent version of the decision. However, opinions in the advance sheet are still subject to revision by the judges who wrote them. Advance sheets are typically available in both commercial and official versions of decisions.

Finally, the bound volumes of the case reports are published. The information in the bound volumes is often a chronological compilation of advance sheets. Bound volumes are the most user-friendly source for researching case law, and by far the most widely distributed. However, it can take considerable time (often two to three years) before a decision appears in this form.

Certain court opinions, such as those from the United States Supreme Court and those on certain topics of law, may be available from loose-leaf services prior to publication in hardbound reporters. Loose-leaf services are discussed throughout this chapter.

Types of Court Reports

Case law is typically published in official, unofficial, and annotated court reports. Not all three types of court reports are available for every jurisdiction.

Official Court Reports

The official version of case law is usually published in a **court report** by the state or federal government. Unofficial versions may be published by commercial law book publishers.

Unofficial Reporters

In some jurisdictions, West Publishing or another private publishing company publishes an unofficial version of court opinions. In some jurisdictions, the commercial publisher version may also be considered an "official version." The official version and the unofficial version typically contain the same cases and are very similar. In some instances, the commercial version is published more frequently and may be easier to use.

The unofficial version of court reports, as distributed in bound volumes by West Publishing Company, is also available through the WEST-LAW and LEXIS computerized legal research systems.

BALLENTINESBALLENTINESBALLENTINESBALLENTINESBALLENTINESBALLENTINESBALLENTINESBALLENTINESBALLENTINESBALLENTINESBALLENTINESBALLENTINESBALLENTINESBALLENTINESBALLENTINES

case law   The law as laid down in the decisions of the courts in similar cases that have previously been decided.

on all fours   Refers to a judicial opinion in a case that is very similar to another case, both with respect to the facts they involve and the applicable law.

on point   Refers to a judicial opinion that, with respect to the facts involved and the applicable law, is similar to but not on all fours with another case.

slip opinion   A single judicial decision published shortly after it has been issued by the court and well before it is incorporated into a reporter.

advance sheets   Printed copies of judicial opinions published in loose-leaf form shortly after the opinions are issued. These published opinions are later collected and published in bound form with other reported cases which are issued over a longer period of time.

court reports   Official, published reports of cases decided by courts, giving the opinions rendered in the cases, with headnotes prepared by the publisher.

Annotated Law Reports

In addition to the official and unofficial versions of a reported case, often there is an annotated version. The *American Law Reports (ALR)* series produced by Lawyers Cooperative Publishing Company contains the text of selected cases, along with summaries of the briefs submitted to the court on those cases, and in-depth **annotations**.

The *ALR* series consists of *ALR1st, ALR2d, ALR3d, ALR4th, ALR5th,* and *ALR Fed. ALR3d, ALR4th, ALR5th,* and *ALR Fed.* are updated with pocket parts containing references to recent cases. *ALR2d* is supplemented by the *Later Case Service* and pamphlets. *ALR1st* is supplemented through the *Blue Book of Supplemental Decisions* and its pocket parts. The *annotation* included with each reported case is an encyclopedia-style overview of important issues within the case. It also contains cross-references to similar cases and to pertinent statutes and other resources. Annotated law reports can be especially useful to paralegals because the annotations aid in the understanding of the case's main issues. The annotations may also lead to similar cases which can be very helpful.

In addition, the *ALR* series contains cross-references to other cases, *American Jurisprudence 2d (Am. Jur. 2d), Proof of Facts,* and *ALR Digests. ALR5th* also contains cross-references to West's Key Number System and to queries for electronic searches. The annotations from the *ALR* series (with the exception of the first series) are now available on the LEXIS and Veralex computer systems. Each case may itself be used as a primary authority, whereas the annotation is considered a secondary authority.

The Format of an Opinion

The format of a judicial opinion, as printed in a court report, will vary depending on the court and the court report. Most published opinions include the official citation, the caption, the docket number, the names of the attorneys representing each party, the syllabus, headnotes, the opinion, the holding, and dicta. In addition, opinions in *ALRs* will include annotations and summaries of the briefs submitted to the courts.

The Citation   The official **citation**, or abbreviation of the name of the case, usually appears at the beginning of each reported decision. This citation includes the volume number and reporter series in which the case is reported, followed by the page number. For instance a case cite of "239 N.W.2d 761" means that the case is found in volume 239 of the *North Western Reporter, Second Series* beginning on page 761.

The Caption   The case *caption* is also the name of the case. It includes the names of the parties and their designations in the case—usually either plaintiff and defendant or appellant and appellee. The party bringing the action is typically named first.

The Court and Jurisdiction   The court hearing the case and rendering the decision is listed after the caption. For cases in appellate courts, there is often a reference to the court from which the case was appealed.

The Docket Number   When a case is initially filed with a court, it is assigned a **docket number** by the clerk of court. This number can be extremely useful for identifying and tracking cases within the court system.

Date of Case   The date the case was heard and the date a decision was rendered follow the docket number.

Syllabus or Synopsis   The **syllabus**, or *synopsis* as it is referred to in some reporters, is a brief summary of the facts of the case, which usually comes before the opinion itself. The syllabus or synopsis includes the decision of the court and may refer to dissenting opinions, if any. The case may include a syllabus by the publishing company's editorial staff as well as one by the court.

Headnotes   **Headnotes** that summarize the various points of law discussed in the opinion usually follow the syllabus or synopsis. In many instances, headnotes are an excellent way to quickly determine if the opinion to follow discusses the points of law in which you are interested. In many reporters, headnotes are designed to be an excellent cross-referencing tool.

Names of Attorneys   The names of the attorneys representing each party in the case are typically listed following the headnotes.

Names of Judges   The names of the judges who decided the case, and specifically the name of the judge writing the majority opinion, are usually listed immediately preceding the opinion.

The Opinion   The actual **majority opinion** of the court is reprinted in its entirety. In some instances, a majority opinion may be followed by one or more concurring opinions. A **concurring opinion** is written by one or more judges who feel that the correct decision was reached, but do not agree with the reasoning behind that decision as explained in the majority opinion. Dissenting opinions may follow the majority opinion or the concurring opinion, if there is one. A **dissenting opinion** is an opinion of one or more judges who disagreed with the majority opinion and felt compelled to write an opinion as to the reasons for their dissent. At times, there may be merely a notation following the majority opinion naming one or more judges who dissented from the majority opinion.

The Format of an Annotated Law Report

A decision appearing in an annotated law report will look very similar to a decision appearing in an official or unofficial court report, with a few additions. The case reported in an annotated law report begins with the caption, the name of the court and jurisdiction, the date of the decision, and the citation. The case citation is then followed by a summary of the decision which is prepared by the staff of the Lawyers Cooperative Publishing Company or other law report publisher. The summary of decision in an annotated law report replaces the syllabus or synopsis found in other court reports. The summary of decision is followed by headnotes, the names of the attorneys and judges, and the opinion itself. The annotation follows the opinions.

The Annotation

The annotation following a case focuses on one particular topic of law covered within the case. It may be only a couple of pages long, or more than 100 pages, depending on the importance and complexity of the topic.

The title of the annotation is not the same as the case it follows. Rather, it refers to the subject covered within the annotation. For instance, the name of the annotation for *Morgan v. Eaton's Dude Ranch* is "Personal Civil Liability of Officer or Director of Corporation for Negligence of Subordinate Corporate Employee Causing Personal

---

BALLENTINESBALLENTINESBALLENTINESBALLENTINESBALLENTINESBALLENTINESBALLENTINESBALLENTINESBALLENTINESBALLENTINESBALLENTINESBALLENTINESBALLENTINES

annotation   A notation, appended to any written work, which explains or comments upon its meaning.

citation   Reference to authority on a point of law, by name, volume, and page or section of the court report or other book in which it appears.

docket number   Number assigned to a case by the clerk of court when the case is initially filed with a court; useful for identifying and tracking cases within the court system.

syllabus   The headnote of a reported case.

headnote   A summary statement that appears at the beginning of a reported case to indicate the points decided by the case.

majority opinion   An opinion issued by an appellate court that represents the view of a majority of the members of the court.

concurring opinion   An opinion issued by one or more judges which agrees with the result reached by the majority opinion rendered by the court, but reaches that result for different reasons.

dissenting opinion   A written opinion filed by a judge of an appellate court who disagrees with the decision of the majority of judges in a case, giving the reaons for his or her differing view. Often a dissenting opinion is written by one judge on behalf of one or more other dissenting judges.

Injury or Death of Third Person." This annotation discusses the *Morgan v. Eaton's Dude Ranch* case plus several other cases dealing with the same topic. The name of the author of the annotation follows the title, as does a list of references to related material within the Lawyers Cooperative Publishing system.

An outline of the annotation and an index to specific subjects covered within the annotation are also included. Because annotations discuss the statutes and similar cases from several jurisdictions throughout the country as they relate to the topic, a "Table of Jurisdictions Represented" precedes the annotation itself. The section numbers following the jurisdictions indicate which section of the annotation contains references to those particular jurisdictions.

An annotation may have an introduction that discusses the scope of the annotation and a "Related Matters" paragraph that cross-references the user to other related annotations. It may also include a summary and comment section before the body of the annotation itself. The annotation may be broken into several individual subtopics, depending on the length and complexity of the subject covered.

Finding Cases

When you consider the volume of cases that are reported, and the fact that they are reported in chronological order, it becomes apparent that very efficient finding tools must be used to locate a specific case or a specific type of case. The main types of finding tools that assist with finding case decisions are digests, indexes to the reporters, computer services, headnotes and annotations within other cases, and legal encyclopedias.

Vast resources are available to assist in finding court opinions. The type of resource that you use will depend on the jurisdiction or jurisdictions in which you are searching, the amount of experience and knowledge you have on the specific topic that you are researching, and the amount of information you have to begin your search.

Digests

When you have narrowed your case search to a specific topic and jurisdiction, the digests to the corresponding reporter series are the place to begin your search for relevant decisions. A **digest** is a series of volumes designed to aid in finding cases in one or more series of case reports. Each set of volumes is arranged alphabetically by subject matter. Under each particular subject matter is a brief summary and description of the court opinions related to that subject, with a reference as to where to find each court opinion. The exact format followed depends on the type of digest and the publisher.

West Publishing Company digests follow a key topic and number system. Under this system, each topic and subtopic is assigned a key topic and number. These same key topics and numbers are used in West's legal encyclopedia, *Corpus Juris Secundum*, in all court reports published by West, and in all digests published by West. These key topics and numbers may also be found in other West publications and may be used for research on WESTLAW. Each topic in West's digests includes the pertinent headnotes that appear at the beginning of all reported cases for that reporter series under that specific topic and key number. You can also search for certain topics in the West digests and narrow your search by scanning the pertinent subtopics available.

Digests are also published by Lawyers Cooperative Publishing Company to assist in finding court opinions and annotations within the ALR series.

Indexes to Court Reporters

Indexes of specific subjects are another way to access court opinions. If you have a very specific question of law that does not fall neatly under one of the subjects in the digest system, the index

digest   A series of volumes containing summaries of cases organized by legal topics, subject areas, and so on.

Citation

Caption

Docket Number

Court Jurisdiction

Date of Case

Syllabus/ Synopsis

Headnotes

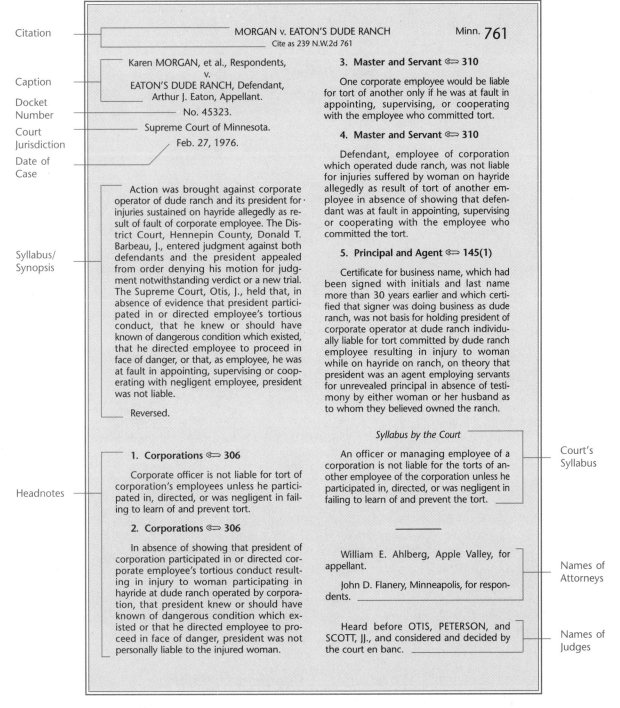

MORGAN v. EATON'S DUDE RANCH   Minn. **761**
Cite as 239 N.W.2d 761

Karen MORGAN, et al., Respondents,
v.
EATON'S DUDE RANCH, Defendant,
Arthur J. Eaton, Appellant.

No. 45323.

Supreme Court of Minnesota.

Feb. 27, 1976.

Action was brought against corporate operator of dude ranch and its president for injuries sustained on hayride allegedly as result of fault of corporate employee. The District Court, Hennepin County, Donald T. Barbeau, J., entered judgment against both defendants and the president appealed from order denying his motion for judgment notwithstanding verdict or a new trial. The Supreme Court, Otis, J., held that, in absence of evidence that president participated in or directed employee's tortious conduct, that he knew or should have known of dangerous condition which existed, that he directed employee to proceed in face of danger, or that, as employee, he was at fault in appointing, supervising or cooperating with negligent employee, president was not liable.

Reversed.

1. Corporations ⬅ 306

Corporate officer is not liable for tort of corporation's employees unless he participated in, directed, or was negligent in failing to learn of and prevent tort.

2. Corporations ⬅ 306

In absence of showing that president of corporation participated in or directed corporate employee's tortious conduct resulting in injury to woman participating in hayride at dude ranch operated by corporation, that president knew or should have known of dangerous condition which existed or that he directed employee to proceed in face of danger, president was not personally liable to the injured woman.

3. Master and Servant ⬅ 310

One corporate employee would be liable for tort of another only if he was at fault in appointing, supervising, or cooperating with the employee who committed tort.

4. Master and Servant ⬅ 310

Defendant, employee of corporation which operated dude ranch, was not liable for injuries suffered by woman on hayride allegedly as result of tort of another employee in absence of showing that defendant was at fault in appointing, supervising or cooperating with the employee who committed the tort.

5. Principal and Agent ⬅ 145(1)

Certificate for business name, which had been signed with initials and last name more than 30 years earlier and which certified that signer was doing business as dude ranch, was not basis for holding president of corporate operator at dude ranch individually liable for tort committed by dude ranch employee resulting in injury to woman while on hayride on ranch, on theory that president was an agent employing servants for unrevealed principal in absence of testimony by either woman or her husband as to whom they believed owned the ranch.

Syllabus by the Court

An officer or managing employee of a corporation is not liable for the torts of another employee of the corporation unless he participated in, directed, or was negligent in failing to learn of and prevent the tort.

———

William E. Ahlberg, Apple Valley, for appellant.

John D. Flanery, Minneapolis, for respondents.

Heard before OTIS, PETERSON, and SCOTT, JJ., and considered and decided by the court en banc.

Court's Syllabus

Names of Attorneys

Names of Judges

Court Opinion The legal dispute known as *Morgan v. Eaton's Dude Ranch* is reported at 239 N.W.2d 761. This is a primary source of law. Reprinted with permission of West Publishing Company.

FIRST TWO PAGES OF COURT OPINION FROM ALR3d

SUBJECT OF ANNOTATION

Beginning on page 916

Personal civil liability of officer or director of corporation for negligence of subordinate employee causing personal injury or death of third person

---

Karen MORGAN, et al., Respondents,

v

EATON'S DUDE RANCH, Defendant, Arthur J. Eaton, Appellant

Supreme Court of Minnesota
February 27, 1976
239 NW2d 761, 90 ALR3d 912

———

SUMMARY OF DECISION

The District Court of Hennepin County, Minnesota, Donald T. Barbeau, J., entered judgment on a jury verdict against the corporate operator of a dude ranch and its president for injuries sustained by a passenger on a hay wagon when a tree, which had fallen down with branches extending over the trail, caught her leg as the wagon drove past, injuring her seriously. The trial court held as a matter of law that both the corporate president and the corporation were responsible for the hay wagon driver's conduct. The trial court denied the corporate officer's motion for judgment notwithstanding the verdict or a new trial.

The Supreme Court of Minnesota, Otis, J., reversed the order of the trial court denying the individual defendant's motion for judgment notwithstanding the verdict. The court held that an officer or managing employee of a corporation is not liable for the torts of another employee of the corporation unless he participated in, directed, or was negligent in failing to learn of and prevent the tort. The court held that, although there was evidence that the corporation president managed the operation of the ranch, in the absence of evidence indicating that he participated in or directed the wagon driver's tortious conduct or that he knew or should have known of the dangerous condition that existed or that he directed the driver to proceed in the face of danger, there was no basis in law or fact for imposing liability upon him.

———

Court Opinion Analyzed in *ALR3d* *Morgan v. Eaton's Dude Ranch* is analyzed at 90 ALR3d 912.

may refer you to the appropriate digest topic. Both West Publishing Company and Lawyers Co-operative Publishing Company produce very specific indexes that lead to the topics covered in their digests.

Computer Searches

In recent years, online databases have become a very popular method of locating and retrieving court opinions. The two most popular legal research

90 ALR3d   Morgan V Eaton's Dude Ranch
                  (Minn) 239 NW2d 761, 90 ALR3d 912

HEADNOTES

Classified to ALR Digests

Corporations § 155 — officers and directors — duties and liabilities — for torts — for personal injury

1. A corporate officer is not liable for the torts of the corporation's employees unless he participated in, directed, or was negligent in failing to learn of and prevent the tort. Where no evidence was presented at trial indicating that the president of a corporation, doing business as a dude ranch, participated in or directed the tortious conduct of an employee of the ranch, who was driving a hay wagon at the time a tree, which had fallen down with branches extending over the trail, caught the passenger's leg as the wagon drove past, injuring her seriously, the president was not liable for the injuries suffered by the passenger. There was evidence that the president managed the operation of the ranch, but no evidence that he knew or should have known of the dangerous condition that existed or that he directed the driver of the hay wagon to proceed in the face of danger.
[Annotated]

Master and Servant § 475 — liability of servant — for tort of other servant

2. An officer of a corporation who was also an employee of the corporation was not liable, as an employee, for the tort of another employee in driving a hay wagon close to a tree which had fallen down, whose branches extending over the trail caught the leg of a passenger as the wagon drove past, injuring her seriously. There was no evidence that the officer, as an employee, was at fault in appointing the driver of the hay wagon, or in supervising or cooperating with him.

Syllabus by the Court

An officer or managing employee of a corporation is not liable for the torts of another employee of the corporation unless he participated in, directed, or was negligent in failing to learn of and prevent the tort.

APPEARANCES OF COUNSEL

William E. Ahlberg, Apple Valley, for appellant.

John D. Flanery, Minneapolis, for respondents.

Heard before Otis, Peterson, and Scott, JJ., and considered and decided by the court en banc.

OPINION OF THE COURT

Otis, Justice.

This is a personal injury action. The jury awarded plaintiff Karen Morgan $8,925 and her husband, plaintiff Phillip S. Morgan, $2,500 against defendants, Eaton's Dude Ranch and A. J. Eaton. A. J. Eaton appeals from the district court order denying his motion for judgment notwithstanding the verdict or a new trial.

This case presents the issue of whether an officer of a corporation is vicariously liable for the torts of a corporate employee when that officer neither participated in, nor directed, nor was negligent in failing to learn of and prevent the tort.

Court Opinion Analyzed in *ALR3d* (*Continued*)

databases are WESTLAW and LEXIS. Both services can access both federal and state cases. Often the opinions are available online much sooner than they are in print. Cases are accessed through both WESTLAW and LEXIS by first choosing the appropriate database (jurisdiction),

---

ANNOTATION

PERSONAL CIVIL LIABILITY OF OFFICER OR DIRECTOR OF CORPORATION FOR NEGLIGENCE OF SUBORDINATE CORPORATE EMPLOYEE CAUSING PERSONAL INJURY OR DEATH OF THIRD PERSON

by

W. A. Harrington, L.L.B.

I. PRELIMINARY MATTERS

§ 1. Introduction:
    [a] Scope
    [b] Related matters
§ 2. Summary

II. GROUNDS FOR LIABILITY

§ 3. Participation in or direction of tortious act
§ 4. Independent negligent acts
§ 5. Ultra vires acts
§ 6. Acts performed or undertaken as agent or employee of corporation

III. LIABILITY FOR DEATH OR INJURY RESULTING FROM PARTICULAR OPERATIONS OR ACTIVITIES

§ 7. Ownership, operation, or maintenance of land or premises:
    [a] In general
    [b] Injury from failure to correct or remedy condition known to be dangerous
    [c] Injury from activity involving management and participation of officer

---

TOTAL CLIENT-SERVICE LIBRARY® REFERENCES

19 Am Jur 2d, Corporations § 1383

8 Am Jur Proof of Facts 2d 193, Personal Liability of Corporate Officer on Promissory Note

ALR Digests, Corporations § 155.

ALR Quick Index, Corporate Officers, Directors, and AGents; Death; Subordinates; Third Persons; Vicarious Liability

---

Annotations from *ALR3d* Annotations that follow court opinions in *ALR* are generally commentary explaining the legal topics used to determine the case. This is a secondary source of law.

and then by choosing specific search words or phrases that will lead to pertinent court opinions.

Headnotes and Annotations Within Other Cases

One relevant case may contain important cross-references to other cases of potential value. Both West and *ALR* headnotes can also lead to related cases that may be of use in your research. The topic and key number can be looked up in any West Publishing digest to locate other cases discussing the topic of the headnote. *ALR* headnotes give topic and section numbers that can be tracked in *ALR* digests for similar cases concerning the

---

90 ALR3d   CORPORATE OFFICER'S TORT LIABILITY   § 1[b]
90 ALR 3d 916

[d] Injury or death from nonexecution of duties amounting to misfeasance
§ 8. —Outdoor displays or exhibitions
§ 9. Handling, operation, or maintenance of vehicles
§ 10. Activities in connection with sale or marketing of goods.

TABLE OF JURISDICTIONS REPRESENTED
Consult POCKET PART in this volume for later cases

US: §§ 3, 10
Cal: §§ 4, 7[b]
Fla: §§ 3, 9
Ill: §§ 3, 7[c]
Mass: §§ 3, 7[a]
Minn: §§ 3, 4, 6, 8, 9

Mont: §§ 4, 7[d]
Neb: §§ 3, 8
NM: §§ 3
NY: §§ 3, 7[a]
Tex: §§ 3, 5
Wash: §§ 3, 9

I. Preliminary matters

§ 1. Introduction

[a] Scope

This annotation collects and analyzes the cases in which the courts have decided whether or to what extent an officer or a director[1] of a corporation is or may become personally liable in damages for the negligence of a subordinate corporate employee[2] resulting in the personal injury or death of a third person.[3] Cases dealing with the criminal responsibility of corporate officers for torts or other wrongs committed by the corporation are treated elsewhere.[4]

Since relevant statutory provisions are included only insofar as they are reflected in the reported cases within the scope of the annotation, the reader is advised to consult the latest enactments of his or her jurisdiction.

[b] Related matters

Personal liability of officers or directors of corporation on corporate checks issued against insufficient funds. 47 ALR 3d 1250.

Liability of corporate officer or director for commission or compensation received from third person in connection with that person's transaction with corporation. 47 ALR3d 373.

Persons liable under statutes imposing upon directors, officers, or

---

1. For a discussion of the operative distinctions and similarities between the terms "officer" and "director," See 19 Am Jur 2d, Corporations § 1080.

2. As used in this annotation, the term "subordinate corporate employee" does not include other officers or directors, even those of lower rank in the corporate organization.

3. For the purposes of the annotation the term "third person" is not intended to embrace employees of the corpora-

tion involved, but is limited in usage to outsiders. As to liability for injuries caused by the negligence of a fellow servant, see 53 Am Jur 2d, Master and Servant §§ 295 et seq.

4. As to the law governing criminal liability of corporate directors and officers, see 19 Am Jur 2d, Corporations §§ 1391–1393.

Annotations from *ALR3d* (*Continued*)

same topic. In addition, the annotations in the *ALR* series usually contain several references to other cases that may be of interest.

Legal Encyclopedias

When your research includes *Corpus Juris Secundum* or *Am. Jur. 2d,* these sources will often refer you to pertinent cases concerning your topic.

References within Corpus Juris Secundum use the key topic method; Am. Jur. 2d makes reference to specific cases and topics covered within its digest systems.

Citing Case Law

To *cite* means to refer to a legal authority. With regard to case law, *citing* means referring to

~⊂ 306   CORPORATIONS   7 N W D 2d—174

For later cases see same Topic and Key Number in Pocket Part

Minn. 1982. Generally, officers of corporation are shielded from personal liability for interference with contracts if they merely cause corporation not to perform contract.—Furlev Sales and Associates, Inc. v. North American Automotive Warehouse, Inc., 325 N.W.2d 20.

Officer and principal shareholder of corporation was shielded from personal liability in tort for interference with corporation's contract, where there was no evidence that officer acted outside scope of best interests of corporation.—Id.

Attorney for corporate officer or for corporation who is acting outside scope of his authority does not possess immunity from personal tort liability which law affords corporate shareholder or officer acting for corporation.—Id.

Minn. 1982. A corporate officer is criminally liable for his own acts, even if done in his official capacity, and he is liable either directly as a principal or as an aider and abettor.—State v. Williams, 324 N.W.2d 154.

Minn. 1976. In absence of showing that president of corporation participated in or directed corporate employee's tortious conduct resulting in injury to woman participating in hayride at dude ranch operated by corporation, that president knew or should have known of dangerous condition which existed or that he directed employee to proceed in face of danger, president was not personally liable to the injured woman.—Morgan v. Eaton's Dude Ranch, 239 N.W.2d 761, 307 Minn. 280, 90 ALR3d 912.

Corporate officer is not liable for tort of corporation's employees unless he participated in, directed, or was negligent in failing to learn of and prevent tort.—Id.

Minn. 1969. When officers and only owners of closely held corporation use their holdings in that corporation to negotiate transaction, part of allegedly illegal scheme, they act also on behalf of that corporation, and corporation as well as individuals may be held responsible.—Hunt v. Nevada State Bank, 172 N.W.2d 292, 285 Minn. 77, certiorari denied Burke v. Hunt 90 S.Ct. 1239, 397 U.S. 1010, 25 L.Ed.2d 423.

Minn. 1966. In absence of showing that company was not a legal corporate entity or that special grounds existed for disregarding corporate entity for purpose of holding defendants personally liable, corporation only was liable on note signed by defendant in his capacity as president.—Ahlm v. Rooney, 143 N.W.2d 65, 274 Minn. 259.

Minn. 1943. Although a director or other officer of a corporation ordinarily is not liable for acts performed by other officers or agents, he is criminally liable for his own acts, although done in his official capacity, if he participated in the unlawful acts, either directly or as an aider, abettor, or accessory.—State v. McBride, 9 N.W.2d 416, 215 Minn. 123.

An officer or agent of corporation cannot avoid responsibility for his act on ground that it was done in his official capacity, nor can he assert that acts in corporate form are not his acts merely because they are carried on by him through instrumentality of corporation which he controls and dominates and which he has employed for that purpose.—Id.

Minn. App. 1985. President and owner of corporation was personally liable for his own fraudulent representation as agent of the corporation.—Sullivan v. Ouimet, 377 N.W.2d 24.

A Page from West's *Digest* The Note under Minn. 1976 is a discussion of *Morgan v. Eaton's Dude Ranch.* This is both a secondary source of law and a finding tool. Adapted with permission of West Publishing Company.

particular cases in a uniform manner. There is a prescribed manner in which to cite each type of case and each reporter. The exact manner is prescribed by *The University of Chicago Manual of Legal Citation* and *The Bluebook: A Uniform System of Citation* (15th ed. 1991).

Standard abbreviations and formats should be used for all case cites. These abbreviations are included in the *Chicago Manual* and *The Bluebook,* which are available in nearly every law library, if not in every office. These sources can also answer most questions regarding what to cite and how to cite it.

Federal Court Reports

Federal court reports include cases reported from the following federal courts:

1. United States Supreme Court
2. United States Courts of Appeals
3. United States District Courts
4. Temporary Court of Appeals
5. U.S. Court of Appeals for the Federal Circuit
6. Court of Federal Claims and its predecessor, the U.S. Court of Claims
7. U.S. Court of International Trade
8. Bankruptcy courts
9. Judicial Panel on Multidistrict Litigation
10. Special Court Regional Rail Reorganization
11. Tax Court
12. Court of Military Appeals
13. Court of Military Review
14. Other Courts that have been abolished.

Supreme Court Decisions

The decisions of the United States Supreme Court have been reported since 1790. Today the decisions of the Supreme Court are published in several different sources. The official reporter of United States Supreme Court decisions is the *U.S. Reports* (*U.S.*). Other useful versions include West's *Supreme Court Reporter* (*S. Ct.*) and Lawyers Cooperative Publishing's *United States Supreme Court Reports, Lawyers' Edition*, also referred to as the *Lawyers' Edition* (*L. Ed.*). Aside from their editorial features, these unofficial reports have the advantage of being published much more quickly than the official version—often within weeks of a Supreme Court decision. Because Supreme Court decisions have such significance, they are also reported in a number of loose-leaf services that reprint the entire opinion of the Court very quickly. In addition, several online computer services, including WESTLAW and LEXIS,

can be used to access Supreme Court decisions, often on the same day they are handed down.

Decisions within the *Supreme Court Reporter* may be accessed by subject and by name in the *U.S. Supreme Court Digest*. The *U.S. Supreme Court Digest* is organized by topic in bound volumes, with updated pocket-part pamphlets located in the back of each volume. Supreme Court decisions published in the *Lawyers' Edition* may be accessed through the *United States Supreme Court Digest, Lawyers' Edition*, which is also updated by pocket part.

The United States Courts of Appeals and U.S. District Courts

Unlike the United States Supreme Court, there is no official reporter for the United States Courts of Appeals or the United States District Courts. In addition, no commercial publisher publishes *all* of the opinions from the U.S. Courts of Appeals or the United States District Courts; only selected cases from both of these courts are published. However, slip opinions on any case may usually be obtained from the appropriate court authority.

Although no official reporter exists, West Publishing's *Federal Reporter*, in its first (*F.*), Second (*F.2d*), and third (*F.3d*) series, and *Federal Supplement* (*F. Supp.*) publish the most cases, and these sources are widely used for researching federal cases. At this time, selected cases from the U.S. District Courts are published in the *Federal Supplement* and selected cases from the Courts of Appeals are published in the *Federal Reporter*. Prior to 1932, cases from both the U.S. District Courts and the U.S. Circuit Courts were published in the *Federal Reporter*.

Decisions from the U.S. Temporary Emergency Court of Appeals are published in *Federal Reporter;* decisions from the U.S. Court of International Trade, the Special Court under the Regional Rail Reorganization Act, and the Judicial Panel on Multidistrict Litigation are published

18B Am Jur 2d   CORPORATIONS   § 1879

to have committed the tort (and which is thus the proper forum) may be brought within the court's long-arm jurisdiction on the theory that he is personally liable for the tort.[96]

§ 1878. Criteria for imposing personal liability; checklist

The following is a checklist of criteria for imposing individual liability for injuries or damage to third person:[97]

- The corporation owes a duty of care to the third person
- The corporation delegates that duty to the officer[98]
- The officer breaches that duty through personal fault (whether by malfeasance, misfeasance, or nonfeasance)
- The third person is injured as a proximate result of the officer's breach of that duty

2. LIABILITY FOR ACTS OF SUBORDINATE OFFICERS, AGENTS OR EMPLOYEES
[§§ 1879–1881]

a. IN GENERAL [§ 1879]

§ 1879. Generally

Ordinarily, a director is not liable for the tortious acts of officers, agents, or employees of the corporation, unless he participated therein or authorized the wrongful act.[99]

▐▐▐▐ *Observation:* This rule is not changed by a statute making an employee or agent of a professional service corporation personally liable for the negligent or wrongful act of any person under his direct supervision

96. Lee B. Stern & Co. v Green (**Fla** App D3) 398 So 2d 918.

97. Schaefer v D & J Produce, Inc., 62 **Ohio** App 2d 53, 16 Ohio Ops 3d 108, 403 NE2d 1015, motion overr.

98. The fact that a duty may by law be nondelegable affects only the liability of the corporation, not the liability of the individual officers. Schaefer v D & J Produce, Inc., 62 **Ohio** App 2d 53, 16 Ohio Ops 3d 108, 403 NE2d 1015, motion overr.

99. Martin v Wood (CA3 Pa) 400 F2d 310; Zubik v Zubik (CA3 Pa) 384 F2d 267, cert den 390 US 988, 19 L Ed 2d 1291, 88 S Ct 1183; Hagemeyer Chemical Co. v Insect-O-Lite Co. (CA6 Ky) 291 F2d 696, 130 USPQ 186; United States v. Appendagez, Inc., 5 CIT 74, 560 F Supp 50; Donner v Tams-Witmark Music Library, Inc. (ED Pa) 480 F Supp 1229, 208 USPQ 367; Lighting Systems, Inc. v International Merchandising Associates, Inc. (WD Pa) 464 F Supp 601; Teledyne Industries, Inc. v Eon Corp. (SD NY) 401 F Supp 729, affd (CA2 NY) 546 F2d 495; Jabczenski v Southern Pacific Memorial Hospital, Inc. (App) 119 **Ariz** 15, 579 P2d 53; Cahill v Hawaiian Paradise Park Corp., 56 **Hawaii** 522, 543 P2d 1356; Tedrow v Deskin, 265 **Md** 546, 290 A2d 799; Morgan v Eaton's Dude Ranch, 307 **Minn** 280, 239 NW2d 761, 90 ALR3d 912; Kreuger v Schmiechen, 364 **Mo** 568, 264 SW2d 311; Connell v Hayden (2d Dept) 83 App Div 2d 30, 443 NYS2d 383; Osborne v Hay, 284 **Or** 133, 585 P2d 674; Wicks v Milzoco Builders, Inc., 503 **Pa** 614, 470 A2d 86; Hunt v Rabon, 275 **SC** 475, 272 SE2d 643; Cato v Silling, 137 **W Va** 694, 73 SE2d 731, cert den 348 US 981, 99 L Ed 764, 75 S Ct 572, reh den 349 US 924, 99 L Ed 1256, 75 S Ct 659.

It is said that courts will treat directors with more leniency with respect to a single isolated act on the part of a subordinate officer or agent than where the practice appears to have been so habitually and openly committed as to have been easily detected upon proper supervision. Lowell Hoit & Co. v Detig, 320 **Ill.** App 179, 50 NE2d 602.

As to the liability of directors for mismanagement or defalcations by officers or employees of the corporation, see §§ 1721 et seq. And as to liability for personal injuries or death resulting from negligent acts of subordinates, see §§ 1880, 1881.

A Page from *Am. Jur. 2d* *Am. Jur.* is a legal encyclopedia. It is a useful secondary source to consult for understanding general legal topics.

in the *Federal Supplement*. In addition, several topical reporters cover special federal courts. Some of these topical reporters are *Federal Rules Decisions*, which includes opinions of the United States District Courts on the Federal Rules of Civil and Criminal Procedure, and the *Bankruptcy Reporter*, which contains opinions of the U.S. bankruptcy courts and selected opinions from other bankruptcy courts.

Court Opinions from These Courts	Court Reporter	Digests
United States Supreme Court	United States Reports (U.S.) Supreme Court Reporter (S. Ct.) United States Supreme Court Reports, Lawyers' Edition (L. Ed.) United States Law Week (U.S.L.W.) United States Supreme Court Bulletin (CCH)	American Digest System United States Supreme Court Digest (West) United States Supreme Court Digest, L. Ed. Federal Digest Modern Federal Practice Digest Federal Practice Digest 2d through Federal Practice Digest 4th
United States Courts of Appeals	Federal Reporter (F.2d, F.3d) ALR, ALR2d, ALR3d, ALR Fed	American Digest System Federal Digest Modern Federal Practice Digest Federal Practice Digest 2d through Federal Practice Digest 4th ALR Digest ALR2d Digest ALR Digest 3d, 4th, 5th & Fed.
United States District Courts and United States Court of International Trade	Federal Supplement (F. Supp.) ALR, ALR2d, ALR3d, ALR Fed.	American Digest System Federal Digest Modern Federal Practice Digest Federal Practice Digest 2d through Federal Practice Digest 4th ALR Digest ALR2d Digest ALR Digest 3d, 4th, 5th & Fed.

Federal Court Reporters and Digests Court reporters are primary sources of law; digests are secondary sources and finding tools.

Federal court cases from both the U.S. District Courts and the U.S. Courts of Appeals, as well as the U.S. Supreme Court, can be accessed by subject using the *Federal Practice Digest* series, currently in its fourth edition; the *Modern Federal Digest*, which covers cases from 1940 to 1960; or the *Federal Digest,* which covers cases prior to 1939.

In addition to the West Publishing case reporters, Lawyers Cooperative Publishing Company offers annotated law reports on federal court opinions in *ALR1st, ALR2d, ALR3d,* and *ALR Fed.* Federal cases within the *ALR* series may be accessed by subject through *ALR Digests* or through the *Index to Annotations*.

Federal cases can easily be accessed online through WESTLAW or LEXIS, which offer all of the cases published in the *Federal Reporter* and the *Federal Supplement*, in a much timelier fashion. WESTLAW and LEXIS also contain opinions from federal cases that are not published anywhere but in slip opinions available from the courts.

One other source of published federal court opinions are the loose-leaf reporters that publish opinions on specific topics of law. Some of the major publishers of loose-leaf services include the Bureau of National Affairs, Matthew Bender & Co., and Commerce Clearing House. These loose-leaf services publish cases on a variety of subjects, including accounting, banking, commercial law, estate planning, taxation, pension plans, and securities.

Citing Federal Cases

Citations to federal courts follow specific rules as set forth in the *Chicago Manual* and *The Bluebook*. Cites to U.S. Supreme Court decisions should be to the *United States Reports (U.S.), Supreme Court Reporter (S. Ct.), Lawyer's Edition (L. Ed.),* or *United States Law Week (U.S.L.W.),* in that order of preference. Cites to the lower federal courts should be to the reporter you are using. The cite to a federal court opinion should include the name of the case, the volume and name of the reporter, the page number, the name of the court rendering the decision, and the year. A cite to a federal court case may appear as: "*Mansell v. Mansell,* 490 U.S. 581 (1989)." In this example, the 1989 Supreme Court case entitled "*Mansell v. Mansell*" can be found in volume 490 of *United States Reports,* on page 581. Although the case was also reported in *Supreme Court Reporter, Lawyer's Edition,* and *United States Law Week,* it is not necessary to include those parallel cites.

State Court Reports

Selected court cases heard in state courts are published in state court reports, regional reports, and the *ALRs*. These reports contain the opinions of the highest court in each state and selected opinions from the lower state courts. Few states publish cases at the trial court level. Only selected appellate court decisions are published, whereas all decisions from the highest state court (the state supreme court, superior court, or court of last resort) are typically reported.

State court opinions may be found in official court reports published by the individual states, commercial state-specific court reports, regional court reports, or annotated law reports that cover cases at the state court level.

Official State Court Reports

In years past, almost every state in the country had its own official state court report. These court reports typically reported the cases from the highest court in the state, along with selected cases from the lower state courts. In recent years, many states have discontinued their official state reports, because of the high cost of producing them and the competition from commercial publishers, which usually publish the cases faster and with more attractive editorial features. Some states have adopted West Publishing's state reporter or regional reporter as their official report. Other states have no "official" report. It is important to know if there is an official report in the state in which you are working. When referring to a case in a document submitted to a state court, the official report must be cited. The most current edition of *The University of Chicago Manual of Legal Citation* or *The Bluebook* should be consulted to determine whether a particular state has an official report and how to cite cases within the official state report.

Regional and State Reporters

The most widely used source of state court opinions is the regional reporters published by West Publishing Company. Regional reporters are published for seven regions across the United States, which cover the following states:

Atlantic (A., A.2d)

Connecticut
Delaware
District Of Columbia
Maine
Maryland
New Hampshire
New Jersey
Pennsylvania
Rhode Island
Vermont

North Eastern (N.E., N.E.2d)

Illinois
Indiana
Massachusetts
New York
Ohio

North Western (N.W., N.W.2d)

Iowa
Michigan
Minnesota
Nebraska
North Dakota
South Dakota
Wisconsin

Pacific (P., P.2d)

Alaska
Arizona
California

Colorado
Hawaii
Idaho
Kansas
Montana
Nevada
New Mexico
Oklahoma
Oregon
Utah
Washington
Wyoming

South Eastern (S.E., S.E.2d)

Georgia
North Carolina
South Carolina
Virginia
West Virginia

South Western (S.W., S.W.2d)

Arkansas
Kentucky
Missouri
Tennessee
Texas

Southern (So., So. 2d)

Alabama
Florida
Louisiana
Mississippi

For certain of the larger states that hear an exceptionally large number of cases in their state courts, West Publishing has state-specific reporters that are not official. These states include California, Illinois, and New York.

Cases within the regional reporters may be accessed through the West *General Digest* system, or through the corresponding regional or state digests.

Annotated Law Reports

The annotated law reports published by Lawyers Cooperative Publishing Company include leading cases from the highest state courts as well as state appellate courts and state trial courts. Annotated cases from state courts can be found in the first *ALR*, as well as in *ALR2d*, *ALR3d*, *ALR4th*, and *ALR5th*. Each annotation contains a section at the beginning that lists the jurisdictions covered on the topic within the annotation. The number of state cases published in the *ALRs* cannot compare with the volume of state cases published in West's reporters; however, the annotations for cases covered by the *ALRs* can be very useful.

ALR3d, ALR4th, and *ALR5th* are updated by pocket parts in each volume that list new court decisions concerning the topic of the annotations within each volume. ALR2d is updated by *Later Case Service* volumes and the first edition of *ALR* is updated by the *ALR1st Blue Book of Supplemental Decisions*, a seven-volume set.

Computer Access to State Court Decisions

As with federal court opinions, accessing state court opinions through computer databases offers certain advantages. State appellate court decisions are available through WESTLAW or LEXIS before they are available elsewhere, and the coverage of these databases is extensive.

Digest Systems for State Court Reports

Efficient access to the state court reports almost always begins with the appropriate digest system. West's state and regional reporters are accessed through the *Comprehensive American Digest System*, regional digests, or state digests; the annotated law reports are accessed through their corresponding digests.

The Comprehensive *American Digest System*

The *American Digest System* is a national system followed by West to provide easy subject access to all of its reported court opinions. It includes the *General Digest*, the *Decennial Digest*, and the *Century Digest*. It is probably the easiest way to access court cases by subject within the regional reporters. Headnotes from all West *advance sheets* are collected and published in the *General Digest*, which is published approximately monthly. The headnotes, arranged and printed under topics and key numbers, refer the users of the *General Digest* to the corresponding court opinions.

Because each volume of the *General Digest* covers each topic reported on during the pertinent time period, when you are searching under a specific topic, you will have to check numerous volumes of the *General Digest*. There are two ways to get around this problem. First, the number of *General Digests* that must be searched is limited, because every five years the headnotes are recompiled into a single set of volumes called a *Decennial Digest*. (The *Decennial Digest* used to be published every ten years; however, because of the increasing volume of cases being reported on, each *Decennial Digest* is now published in two parts, five years apart.)

The other time-saver provided by West Publishing within the *General Digest,* is the cumulative tables that appear in certain West *General Digest* volumes. These cumulative tables indicate which volumes each key number appears in. Not all volumes contain headnotes for each key number, because there may have been no relevant cases published during the time period covered by that particular digest volume. Therefore, when you are searching for all cases within a particular key number, you can save yourself the time of looking through each of the volumes in the *General Digest* by searching through the *General Digest* cumulative tables to see which volumes contain headnotes with the key number you are searching for.

As mentioned previously, the headnotes in the *American Digest System* are arranged alphabetically by topic. Key number topics are arranged by number under the pertinent topic. Under each specific key number topic, the headnotes are arranged by jurisdiction. Each headnote indicates the jurisdiction where the case was heard, and gives a reference to the reporter where the headnote and corresponding court opinion can be found.

Regional and State Digests

In addition to the *General Digest* system, which encompasses all jurisdictions reported on by West Publishing, there are also digests available that are limited to a specific region, such as the *Atlantic, North Western, Pacific,* and *South Eastern*

digests, and for each specific state. These more limited digests may be more practical to use when you are concerned with cases only within a specific state or jurisdiction. Because each of these digests covers a much smaller area, they are much easier to use. The regional and state digests are updated by pocket parts.

Accessing American Law Reports

As mentioned earlier, the cases and annotations in the *ALR*s can be accessed either through the corresponding digests or through the multivolume set *Index to Annotations*. Both the digests and the indexes are updated by pocket parts.

The *ALR* digests are used in much the same way as the *American Digest System*. The appropriate set of digests must first be located. Currently,

CONVERSION	COPYRIGHTS AND INTELLEC-TUAL PROPERTY—Cont'd	CORPORATIONS—Cont'd	CORPORATIONS—Cont'd
⇐⇒	⇐⇒	⇐⇒	⇐⇒
15(1)—18	6—11, 14, 17	1.4(3)—12, 15, 16, 17, 18	202—12, 13, 14, 15, 16, 17, 18
19(1)—18	8—16	1.4(4)—11, 12, 13, 14, 15, 16, 17, 18	204—15
	10.1—16	2—18	206(1)—12, 15, 18
CONVICTS	10.2—15	3—11	206(2)—11, 14, 16, 17, 18
	10.4—11, 12, 15, 17, 18	4—17	206(4)—11, 12, 13, 14, 15, 16, 18
⇐⇒		14(1)—14, 18	207—12, 15, 16
1—11, 13, 18	CORONERS	15—15	207.1—13, 16, 18
2—11, 14, 15		18—15	207¹/₂—17
3—11, 16	⇐⇒	30(1)—11	210—15
5—11, 13, 14, 15, 16, 17	8—14	30(5)—17	300—18
6—11, 14, 15, 16, 17, 18	14—11	31—13	306—11, 12, 13, 14, 15, 16, 18
7(1)—12, 14, 15, 17	23—12, 14	34(2)—17	307—11, 12, 13, 15, 16, 17, 18
7(2)—14, 15		190—11, 12, 13, 15, 16, 17	308(1)—11, 13
8—14	CORPORATIONS	194—11, 12, 15, 18	308(2)—13
	⇐⇒	195—12	308(3)—18
COPYRIGHTS AND INTELLEC-TUAL PROPERTY	1—12	196—18	308(11)—16
	1.1(2)—11	197—16	310(1)—11, 12, 13, 14, 15, 18
⇐⇒	1.1(3)—17	198(2)—12	310(2)—15, 16, 17
1—11, 12, 17, 18	1.3—11, 13, 15, 17, 18	198(3)—15	312—16
2—17, 18	1.4(1)—11, 12, 13, 14, 15, 16, 17, 18	198(4)—12, 16	
4—11, 15, 17, 18	1.4(2)—11, 13, 15, 16, 17, 18	199—15	
4.5—11, 14, 15, 17, 18		201—12	
5—17, 18			

A Table of Headnotes in West Digests This table indicates which volumes within a set of the Decennial Digests include headnotes under certain key number topics. Adapted with permission of West Publishing Company.

State Courts	Reporters	Digests
Atlantic state courts (Connecticut, Delaware, District of Columbia, Maine, Maryland, New Hampshire, New Jersey, Pennsylvania, Rhode Island, and Vermont); The highest state courts and some appellate courts	Atlantic Reporter 2d (A.2d) ALR, ALR2d through ALR5th	American Digest System Atlantic Digest ALR Digests Connecticut, Delaware, District of Columbia, Maine, Maryland, New Hampshire, New Jersey, Pennsylvania, Rhode Island, and Vermont state digests
North Eastern state courts (Illinois, Indiana, Massachusetts, New York, and Ohio); The highest state court and some appellate courts	North Eastern Reporter 2d (N.E.2d) ALR, ALR2d through ALR5th	American Digest System Illinois, Indiana, Massachusetts, New York, and Ohio state digests ALR Digests
North Western state courts (Iowa, Michigan, Minnesota, Nebraska, North Dakota, South Dakota, and Wisconsin); The highest state court and some appellate courts	North Western Reporter 2d (N.W.2d) ALR, ALR2d through ALR5th	American Digest System Northwestern Digest Iowa, Michigan, Minnesota, Nebraska, North Dakota, South Dakota, and Wisconsin state digests ALR Digests
Pacific state courts (Alaska, Arizona, California, Colorado, Hawaii, Idaho, Kansas, Montana, Nevada, New Mexico, Oklahoma, Oregon, Utah, Washington, and Wyoming); The highest state courts and some appellate courts	Pacific Reporter 2d (P.2d) ALR, ALR2d through ALR5th	American Digest System Pacific Digest Alaska, Arizona, California, Colorado, Hawaii, Idaho, Kansas, Montana, Nevada, New Mexico, Oklahoma, Oregon, Utah, Washington, and Wyoming state digests ALR Digests
South Eastern state courts (Georgia, North Carolina, South Carolina, Virginia, and West Virginia); The highest state courts and some appellate courts	South Eastern Reporter 2d (S.E.2d) ALR, ALR2d through ALR 5th	American Digest System South Eastern Digest Georgia, North Carolina, South Carolina, Virginia, and West Virginia state digests ALR Digests
Southern state courts (Alabama, Florida, Louisiana, and Mississippi); The highest state courts and some appellate courts	Southern Reporter 2d (So. 2d) ALR, ALR2d through ALR5th	American Digest System Alabama, Florida, Louisiana, and Mississippi state digests ALR Digests
South Western state courts (Arkansas, Kentucky, Missouri, Tennessee, and Texas); The highest state courts and some appellate courts	South Western Reporter 2d (S.W.2d) ALR, ALR2d through ALR5th	American Digest System Arkansas, Kentucky, Missouri, Tennessee, and Texas state digests ALR Digests

State and Regional Court Reporters and Digests It is important to become familiar with the court reporters and digests used in your state.

one set of digests covers *ALR3d, ALR4th, ALR5th,* and *ALR Fed*; this set is updated by pocket part. Each volume of the digest set is arranged alphabetically by annotation topic. Each lengthy topic is broken down by sections. Under each section, the pertinent annotation titles and case summaries are listed. Each contain references to the correct reporter.

Citing Cases in Regional or State Reporters

A case heard in state court may have more than one citation, depending on the reporters in which the case appears. A case may have an "official" cite when it appears in an official report, as well as an "unofficial" cite if it also appears in an unofficial, commercial reporter. In addition, the case may have a different cite that refers to an annotated report. The general rule is to use the cite from the source you are using, unless you are citing a state court decision in a document to be submitted to the same court. In that event, the official report should be cited, followed by the cite for the unofficial reporter, if that is the reporter you are using.

The elements of a case cite include the case name; volume, reporter, and page; the court deciding the case; the state; and the year. If the case you are citing was decided in the highest court of the state, it is not necessary to include the name of the deciding court. For example, "*Morgan v. Eaton's Dude Ranch*, 239 N.W.2d 761 (Minn. 1976)" is the proper way to cite the case entitled *Morgan v. Eaton's Dude Ranch* that appears in the 239th volume of the North West 2d series of court reporters, on page 761, which was decided in the Minnesota Supreme Court in 1976. For documents to be submitted to a court within the Minnesota state court system, the cite would include the information for the official reporter, and would appear as follows: "*Morgan v. Eaton's Dude Ranch*, 307 Minn. 280, 239 N.W.2d 761 (1976)."

An Introduction to Statutory Research

Research involving court opinions frequently goes hand-in-hand with statutory research. Often, court opinions are merely an interpretation of the pertinent statutes. Therefore, it is important when beginning any research project to be aware of the statutes that apply to the situation at hand. When researching statutory law, it is always important to research the statutes for the appropriate jurisdiction and to find the most current applicable statutes.

Format of a Published Statute

The format of a statute, as published in codified statute books, will vary depending on the legislature and the publisher. Statutes may be annotated, although many official publications do not include annotations. The text of the law itself will be identical in both annotated and unannotated publications. However, annotated versions offer many more editorial features, which may be very useful.

Title or Section Number   All codified statute sections are located in numerical order within the statutes and begin with the title or section number (usually in boldface type). If you know the number of the statute section you are looking for, you can find it easily by looking for it in numerical order in the correct volume. If you do not know the section or title number of the statute section, you can ascertain it from the index to the statutes.

Statutory Text   The text of the statutory title or section follows the title or section number and title.

Statute History   The history of the statute immediately follows the statute section. The history includes the origin of the law, the effective date of the law, and any amendments to the law.

Reporter's Notes or Annotations The next section following the statutory text will vary greatly, depending on the statute and the publisher. The official statutes published by the states often have nothing following the statute history. Other versions of the statutes have annotations or "Reporter's Notes," which may include the source of the law, any former provisions, and the change of the former law. The Reporter's Notes also include general comments on the text of the statute.

Historical and Statutory Notes A historical notes section may or may not be included, depending on the source of the statute section you are reviewing. Such a section includes notes concerning the amendments that have been made to the statute section.

Cross-References Annotated statutes usually include cross-references to other pertinent statutes, cases, and treatises following the statute section, annotations, and history.

Citing Statutory Law

As with case law, there are standard rules for citing statutory law. The official version of the statute must be cited in documents submitted to courts. For all other cites, the volume you are using should be cited. The standard abbreviations and citation formats for each set of statutes, including proper citations for slip laws and sessions laws, can be found in *The University of Chicago Manual of Legal Citation* or *The Bluebook*.

Federal Statutes and Other Federal Legislation

As with court opinions, there is more than one source for federal statutes. This section examines the federal statutes from slip laws to bound volume. Next it discusses researching federal statutes by computer and other federal legislation, and it concludes with a brief discussion of how to cite federal statutes.

Slip Laws

During each annual session of the United States Congress, several hundred statutes may be enacted. Each law passed is designated by a number that identifies it as either a **public law** or a **private**

law and indicates the order in which the law was passed. The first published version of these statutes is the **slip law**. Slip laws are available through the U.S. Government Printing Office, although public laws are often available sooner through WESTLAW, LEXIS, or loose-leaf services that publish public laws on specific topics.

Session Laws

At the conclusion of each session, the slip laws are compiled into the official ***Statutes at Large***. The bound Statutes at Large supersedes the slip laws and becomes the official law. These laws are not

BALLENTINESBALLENTINESBALLENTINESBALLENTINESBALLENTINESBALLENTINESBALLENTINESBALLENTINESBALLENTINESBALLENTINESBALLENTINESBALLENTINESBALLENTINESBALLENTINES

public law Body of law dealing with the relationship between the people and their government, the relationship between agencies and branches of government, and the relationshp between governments themselves.

private law The rules of conduct that govern activities occurring among or between persons, as opposed to the rules of conduct governing the relationship between persons and their government.

slip law Printed copies of a legislative enactment published in loose-leaf or pamphlet form shortly after the legislation is passed.

Statutes at Large An official publication of the federal government, issued after each session of Congress, which includes all statutes enacted by the Congress and all congressional resolutions and treaties, as well as presidential proclamations and proposed or ratified amendments to the Constitution.

302A.251 STANDARD OF CONDUCT.

Subdivision 1. **Standard; liability**. A director shall discharge the duties of the position of director in good faith, in a manner the director reasonably believes to be in the best interests of the corporation, and with the care an ordinarily prudent person in a like position would exercise under similar circumstances. A person who so performs those duties is not liable by reason of being or having been a director of the corporation.

Subd. 2. **Reliance**. (a) A director is entitled to rely on information, opinions, reports, or statements, including financial statements and other financial data, in each case prepared or presented by:

(1) one or more officers or employees of the corporation whom the director reasonably believes to be reliable and competent in the matters presented;

(2) counsel, public accountants, or other persons as to matters that the director reasonably believes are within the person's professional or expert competence; or

(3) a committee of the board upon which the director does not serve, duly established in accordance with section 302A.241, as to matters within its designated authority, if the director reasonably believes the committee to merit confidence.

(b) Paragraph (a) does not apply to a director who has knowledge concerning the matter in question that makes the reliance otherwise permitted by paragraph (a) unwarranted.

Subd. 3. **Presumption of assent; dissent**. A director who is present at a meeting of the board when an action is approved by the affirmative vote of a majority of the directors present is presumed to have assented to the action approved, unless the director:

(a) Objects at the beginning of the meeting to the transaction of business because the meeting is not lawfully called or convened and does not participate thereafter in the meeting, in which case the director shall not be considered to be present at the meeting for any purpose of this chapter;

(b) Votes against the action at the meeting; or

(c) Is prohibited by section 302A.255 from voting on the action.

Subd. 4. **Elimination or limitation of liability**. A director's personal liability to the corporation or its shareholders for monetary damages for breach of fiduciary duty as a director may be eliminated or limited in the articles. The articles shall not eliminate or limit the liability of a director:

(a) for any breach of the director's duty of loyalty to the corporation or its shareholders;

(b) for acts or omissions not in good faith or that involve intentional misconduct or a knowing violation of law;

(c) under section 302A.559 or 80A.23;

(d) for any transaction from which the director derived an improper personal benefit; or

(e) for any act or omission occurring prior to the date when the provision in the articles eliminating or limiting liability becomes effective.

Subd. 5. **Considerations**. In discharging the duties of the position of director, a director may, in considering the best interests of the corporation, consider the interests of the corporation's employees, customers, suppliers, and creditors, the economy of the state and nation, community and societal considerations, and the long-term as well as short-term interests of the corporation and its shareholders including the possibility that these interests may be best served by the continued independence of the corporation.

History. *1981 c 270 s 44; 1982 c 497 s 29,30; 1987 c 2 s 2; 1Sp1987 c 1 s 18; 1989 c 172 s 6*

Statutory Format A *statute* is a law passed by the legislative branch and signed into law by the chief executive. It will be used by the court when resolving legal disputes and is a primary source of law.

codified, but rather are arranged in chronological order.

The unofficial versions of the **session laws** are available much earlier than the official versions. The *United States Code Congressional and Administrative News*, published by West Publishing, and the *USCS Advance,* a monthly service accompanying Lawyers' Cooperative Publishing Company's *United States Code Service,* have the advantages of appearing long before the official version, and offering helpful editorial features as well.

Official and Unofficial Versions of Bound Volumes of Statutes

The official *U.S. Code* (U.S.C.) has been published by the U.S. Government Printing Office since 1926. It replaces the *Statutes at Large* that was previously considered the official version of the federal statutes. The U.S. Code is divided by subject into 48 titles, and is accessed by title or by its *General Index*. A new edition of the U.S. Code is published approximately every six years, and additional cumulative supplements are issued for the years between editions. Significant time elapses from the passage of a new law in Congress until its appearance in the U.S. Code— sometimes up to three years. For that reason, and because of their editorial features, unofficial versions of the U.S. Code have become very popular.

West Publishing's *United States Code Annotated* (*USCA*), and Lawyers Cooperative Publishing Company's *United States Code Service* (*USCS*) are two very popular annotated versions of the U.S. Code. They are arranged by title, following the same system as the U.S. Code. Both of these unofficial versions include annotations and cross-references to pertinent case law and to other resources. They also have the advantage of being much more current than the U.S. Code, with pocket parts and supplements coming out quarterly or annually.

Federal statutes are usually accessed easily through the subject index that accompanies the statutes. In addition, popular name tables available in the U.S.C., USCA, and USCS give a list of popular names for statutes and their citations.

Federal statutes may also be found through loose-leaf services that publish federal statutes on certain topics with great speed.

Researching Federal Statutes by Computer

Both WESTLAW and LEXIS offer federal statutes online, and both services contain the full text of the U.S. Code. In addition, WESTLAW also contains the *USCA*; LEXIS contains case annotations from *USCS*.

Researching Other Federal Legislation

Federal law research does not end with federal court opinions and federal statutes. There is a vast array of federal law sources that must be researched from time to time. Some of those sources include the United States Constitution, federal administrative law, federal treaties, and federal rules of court.

The United States Constitution   The United States Constitution is an important basis for much of our law. The Constitution is included in the U.S. Code, *USCA*, and *USCS*. *USCA* and *USCS* also include annotations and references to important court opinions and other resources concerning the Constitution. In addition, numerous treatises have been written on the subject of constitutional law.

Federal Administrative Law   The administrative rules and regulations that comprise the administrative law of this country can be found in the **Code of Federal Regulations** (C.F.R.), which has been published since 1938, and in the ***Federal Register***. All proposed federal rules and regulations must

---

BALLENTINESBALLENTINESBALLENTINESBALLENTINESBALLENTINESBALLENTINESBALLENTINESBALLENTINESBALLENTINESBALLENTINESBALLENTINESBALLENTINESBALLENTINES

session laws   The collected statutes enacted during a session of a legislature.

United States Code   The official codification of the statutes enacted by Congress.

Code of Federal Regulations (C.F.R.)   An arrangement, by subject matter, of the rules and regulations issued by federal administrative agencies.

Federal Register   An official publication, printed daily, containing regulations and proposed regulations issued by administrative agencies, as well as other rulemaking and other official business of the executive branch of government. All regulations are ultimately published in the Code of Federal Regulations.

TITLES OF UNITED STATES CODE

*1. General Provisions.
2. The Congress.
*3. The President.
*4. Flag and Seal, Seat of Government, and the States.
*5. Government Organization and Employees; and Appendix.
†6. [Surety Bonds.]
7. Agriculture.
8. Aliens and Nationality.
*9. Arbitration.
*10. Armed Forces; and Appendix.
*11. Bankruptcy; and Appendix.
12. Banks and Banking.
*13. Census.
*14. Coast Guard.
15. Commerce and Trade.
16. Conservation.
*17. Copyrights.
*18. Crimes and Criminal Procedure; and Appendix.
19. Customs Duties.
20. Education.
21. Food and Drugs.
22. Foreign Relations and Intercourse.
*23. Highways.
24. Hospitals and Asylums.
25. Indians.
26. Internal Revenue Code; and Appendix.

27. Intoxicating Liquors.
*28. Judiciary and Judicial Procedure; and Appendix.
29. Labor.
30. Mineral Lands and Mining.
*31. Money and Finance.
*32. National Guard.
33. Navigation and Navigable Waters.
‡34. [Navy.]
*35. Patents.
36. Patriotic Societies and Observances.
*37. Pay and Allowances of the Uniformed Services.
*38. Veterans' Benefits; and Appendix.
*39. Postal Service.
40. Public Buildings, Property, and Works.
41. Public Contracts.
42. The Public Health and Welfare.
43. Public Lands.
*44. Public Printing and Documents.
45. Railroads.
*46. Shipping; and Appendix.
47. Telegraphs, Telephones, and Radiotelegraphs.
48. Territories and Insular Possessions.
*49. Transportation; and Appendix.
50. War and National Defense; and Appendix.

*This title has been enacted as law. However, any Appendix to this title has not been enacted as law.
†This title was enacted as law and has been repealed by the enactment of Title 31.
‡This title has been eliminated by the enactment of Title 10.

Titles of the United States Code Federal statutes are organized by title in the United States Code (U.S.C.). It is a primary source of law.

be published in the *Federal Register*, which is issued daily. After a rule or regulation becomes law, it is published in the C.F.R., which is organized by agency and by subject. Volumes of the Code of Federal Regulations are replaced annually and are updated by monthly supplements. The C.F.R. is also available through WESTLAW and LEXIS.

Federal Treaties Federal *treaties* are agreements or contracts between two or more nations or sovereigns, with a view to public welfare. United

States treaties are made by the president with the advice and consent of the Senate. The official source for federal treaties is United States Treaties and Other International Agreements (U.S.T.), which has been published since 1950. Before that time, the official source for federal treaties was the Statutes at Large. More current sources for United States treaties include *USTS Current Service*, published by William S. Hein & Company; and *Consolidated Treaties & International Agreements: Current Document Service*, published by Oceanna Publications.

Federal Rules of Court **Court rules** are rules adopted by courts to govern civil and criminal processes. The Federal Rules of Civil Procedure, the Federal Rules of Criminal Procedure, the Federal Rules of Appellate Procedure, and the Federal Rules of Evidence are the main rules of court adopted by federal courts. These rules are available in the U.S. Code, the *USCA*, and the *USCS*. They are also available online with WESTLAW and LEXIS.

Citing Federal Statutes

When citing federal statutes, cites should be made to the United States Code (U.S.C.), if possible. Otherwise cites may be made to the *United States Code Annotated* (USCA) or to the *United States Code Service* (USCS). Cites should include the title, the source, the section number, and the year. For example, "35 U.S.C. § 349 (1990)" is the correct cite for title 35 of the United States Code, section 349. The date refers to the date of the main volume or supplement where the statute is located.

State Statutes and Other State Legislation

The drafting and compilation of most state law are patterned after that of federal law. Many states have both official and unofficial compilations of the law in their states. As with federal law, the first available version of state laws is usually the slip laws, followed by session laws, and finally the bound volumes of statutes by subject. Annotated versions of state statutes exist for most states. When in doubt as to which version to cite, the most recent edition of *The University of Chicago Manual of Legal Citation* or *The Bluebook* are the authorities to consult.

In addition to the bound official and unofficial print versions of state statutes, both WESTLAW and LEXIS have state statutes from each state online.

Other State Legislation

Researching state law can encompass much more than state court opinions and state statutes. In addition, you may need to be familiar with techniques for researching your state's constitution, state administrative law, and state court rules.

State Constitutional Law

As with the United States Constitution, the constitution of each state is available within the statutes for that particular state. Annotated state statutes typically offer an annotated version of the state constitution, with comments and references to pertinent cases and other sources. Pamphlets containing state constitutions are also usually available from the state government.

State Administrative Law

A substantial portion of the law in this country is in the form of state administrative rules and regulations. The states differ in the compilation and organization of their administrative rules

court rules Rules adopted by courts to govern civil and criminal processes.

State	Official	Unofficial
Alabama	Code of Alabama	
Alaska	Alaska Statutes	
Arizona	Arizona Revised Statutes Annotated	
Arkansas	Arkansas Code Annotated	
California	West's Annotated California Code Deering's Annotated and Unannotated California Code	
Colorado	Colorado Revised Statutes West's Colorado Revised Statutes Annotated	
Connecticut	General Statutes of Connecticut	Connecticut General Statutes Annotated (West)
Delaware	Delaware Code Annotated	
District of Columbia	District of Columbia Code Annotated	
Florida	Florida Statutes	Florida Statutes Annotated (West) Florida Statutes Annotated (Harrison)
Georgia	Official Code of Georgia Annotated (Michie)	Code of Georgia Annotated (Harrison)
Hawaii	Hawaii Revised Statutes	
Idaho	Idaho Code	
Illinois	Illinois Revised Statutes	Smith-Hurd Illinois Annotated Statutes
Indiana	Indiana Code	Burns Indiana Statutes Annotated West's Annotated Indiana Code
Iowa	Code of Iowa	Iowa Code Annotated
Kansas	Kansas Statutes Annotated Vernon's Kansas Statutes Annotated	
Kentucky	Baldwin's Official Edition, Kentucky Revised Statutes Annotated Kentucky Revised Statutes Annotated, Official Edition (Michie/Bobbs-Merrill)	

State Statutory Compilations States organize their statutes in many ways, including by title, section, and number.

and regulations, however. Some states offer separate sets of administrative rules and regulations that are organized by subject and kept current by pocket parts and supplements. Other states

State	Official	Unofficial
Louisiana	West's Louisiana Revised Statutes Annotated West's Louisiana Civil Code Annotated West's Louisiana Code of Criminal Procedure Annotated West's Louisiana Code of Evidence Annotated West's Louisiana Code of Juvenile Procedure Annotated	
Maine	Maine Revised Statutes Annotated (West)	
Maryland	Annotated Code of Maryland	Annotated Code of Maryland (1957)
Massachusetts	General Laws of the Commonwealth of Massachusetts (Mass./Law. Co-op.)	Massachusetts General Laws Annotated (West) Annotated Laws of Massachusetts (Law. Co-op.)
Michigan	Michigan Compiled Laws	Michigan Compiled Laws Annotated (West) Michigan Statutes Annotated (Callaghan)
Minnesota	Minnesota Statutes	Minnesota Statutes Annotated (West)
Mississippi	Mississippi Code Annotated	
Missouri	Missouri Revised Statutes	Vernon's Annotated Missouri Statutes
Montana	Montana Code Annotated	
Nebraska	Revised Statutes of Nebraska	
Nevada	Nevada Revised Statutes	Nevada Revised Statutes Annotated (Michie)
New Hampshire	New Hampshire Revised Statutes Annotated	
New Jersey	New Jersey Revised Statutes	New Jersey Statutes Annotated (West)
New Mexico	New Mexico Statutes Annotated (Michie)	
New York	McKinney's Consolidated Laws of New York Annotated Consolidated Laws Service	
North Carolina	General Statutes of North Carolina	
North Dakota	North Dakota Century Code	

State Statutory Compilations *(Continued)*

State	Official	Unofficial
Ohio	Ohio Revised Code Annotated (Anderson) Ohio Revised Code Annotated (Baldwin)	
Oklahoma	Oklahoma Statutes	Oklahoma Statutes Annotated (West)
Oregon	Oregon Revised Statutes	
Pennsylvania	Pennsylvania Consolidated Statutes Purdon's Pennsylvania Consolidated Statutes Annotated	
Rhode Island	General Laws of Rhode Island	
South Carolina	Code of Laws of South Carolina 1976 Annotated (Law. Co-op.)	
South Dakota	South Dakota Codified Laws Annotated	
Tennessee	Tennessee Code Annotated	
Texas	Vernon's Texas Codes Annotated	
Utah	Utah Code Annotated	
Vermont	Vermont Statutes Annotated	
Virginia	Code of Virginia Annotated	
Washington	Revised Code of Washington	Revised Code of Washington Annotated
West Virginia	West Virginia Code	
Wisconsin	Wisconsin Statutes	West's Wisconsin Statutes Annotated
Wyoming	Wyoming Statutes	

State Statutory Compilations   *(Continued)*

have no such compilations, so pertinent rules and regulations must be obtained from the responsible agency.

Citing State Statutes

The general rule for citing state statutes is to cite the official publication of the statutes, if one exists, in documents to be submitted to state courts. In general, state statutory cites use the following format: abbreviated name of source of statute, section, and year. For example, the citation for section 302A.255 of the Minnesota Statutes is "Minn. Stat. § 302A.255 (1993)."

Shepardizing

No one wants to go through the experience of researching a particular issue and writing a lengthy memorandum based on the findings, only to be told that the case or statute on which the conclusion was based was superseded by another court decision or a new statute. It would be even worse to have the attorneys you work for rely on information from authorities that are no longer valid.

With all of the hardbound volumes, supplements, and pocket parts that have to be checked, how can you be sure that the statute or case you are using for authority is still current? By shepardizing.

Shepardizing is the process of looking up the cite of the case or statute with which you are concerned in the appropriate *Shepard's Citator* to determine the history of the case or statute. For cases, *Shepard's* gives you information such as parallel cites, the case history, appeals, other cases that have cited the case you are concerned with, and other sources that have referred to the case. For statutes, the appropriate volume of *Shepard's* gives you the session law cite, amendments, repeals (full or partial) of the statute, court opinions that have interpreted the statute, and other resources that discuss the statute. In addition to court opinions and statutes, there are methods for shepardizing other sources of law, including constitutions, certain administrative regulations and decisions, ordinances, rules of court, and restatements.

Shepardizing a Court Opinion

To shepardize a court opinion, you must first locate the current volumes and pamphlets of the appropriate set of *Shepard's Citators*. Then you must look up the case or statute in each appropriate volume and supplement of the citator.

Locating the Appropriate Set of Shepard's Citators

Nearly every law library includes a section with current *Shepard's Citators*. Individual sets of *Shepard's Citators* exist for almost every reporter and statutory compilation in the country. For example, *Shepard's United States Citations, Case Edition* is used for shepardizing Supreme Court opinions that are published in the *Federal Reporter 2d*.

When shepardizing a court opinion, you will need the entire corresponding set of *Shepard's*. After you have determined the appropriate set, your next task is to ensure that every needed pamphlet and hardbound volume is available. This is done by locating the most current pamphlet. Pamphlets are released monthly in most instances, so the most current pamphlet should be for the month and year just past. On the cover of this pamphlet is a list entitled "What Your Library Should Contain." You should have in front of you all the items from that list before you begin the task of shepardizing. At first glance, the information contained inside a volume of *Shepard's* might look confusing and not very useful. However, once you understand the abbreviations and the system, you will find that it is indeed very useful information. A list of abbreviations is included in the front of each volume or pamphlet of *Shepard's*.

Court opinions are listed within each volume or pamphlet by court reporter volume, and then by page. Under the appropriate volume, the page number of the beginning of each case is printed in bold type.

After you have found the correct court opinion in bold, the citing material follows in a column. As mentioned earlier, the citing material under a court opinion cite could include the parallel cite of the case, the case history, other cases that

shepardizing   Using a citator.

State	Administrative Compilation	Administrative Register
Alabama	Alabama Administrative Code	None
Alaska	Alaska Administrative Code	None
Arizona	Official Compilation Administrative Rules and Regulations	Administrative Digest
Arkansas	None	Arkansas Register
California	California Code of Regulations	California Regulatory Notice Register
Colorado	Code of Colorado Regulations	Colorado Register
Connecticut	Regulations of Connecticut State Agencies	Connecticut Law Journal
Delaware	None	None
District of Columbia	D.C. Municipal Regulations	District of Columbia Register
Florida	Florida Administrative Code Annotated	Florida Administrative Weekly
Georgia	Official Compilation Rules and Regulations of the State of Georgia	None
Hawaii	None	None
Idaho	None	None
Illinois	Illinois Administrative Code	Illinois Register
Indiana	Indiana Administrative Code	Indiana Register
Iowa	Iowa Administrative Code	Iowa Administrative Bulletin
Kansas	Kansas Administrative Regulations	Kansas Register
Kentucky	Kentucky Administrative Regulations Service	Kentucky Administrative Register
Louisiana	Louisiana Administrative Code	Louisiana Register
Maine	Code of Maine Rules	None
Maryland	Code of Maryland Regulations	Maryland Register
Massachusetts	Code of Massachusetts Regulations	Massachusetts Register
Michigan	Michigan Administrative Code (1979)	Michigan Register
Minnesota	Minnesota Rules	Minnesota State Register
Mississippi	None	Mississippi Register
Missouri	Missouri Code of State Regulations	Missouri Register
Montana	Administrative Rules of Montana	Montana Administrative Register
Nebraska	Nebraska Administrative Rules & Regulations	None

Table of State Administrative Compilations and Registers Administrative rules and regulations are promulgated by such executive branch departments as Motor Vehicles, Transportation, Education, and Welfare.

State	Administrative Compilation	Administrative Register
Nevada	Nevada Administrative Code	None
New Hampshire	New Hampshire Code of Administrative Rules	New Hampshire Rulemaking Register
New Jersey	New Jersey Administrative Code	New Jersey Register
New Mexico	None	New Mexico Register
New York	Official Compilation of Codes, Rules & Regulations of the State of New York	New York State Register
North Carolina	North Carolina Administrative Code	North Carolina Register
North Dakota	North Dakota Administrative Code	None
Ohio	Ohio Administrative Code	Ohio Monthly Record, Ohio Government Reports, Ohio Department Reports
Oklahoma	None	Oklahoma Register, Oklahoma Gazette
Oregon	Oregon Administrative Rules	Oregon Administrative Rules Bulletin
Pennsylvania	Pennsylvania Code	Pennsylvania Bulletin
Rhode Island	None	None
South Carolina	Administrative regulations appear in volumes 23–27 of the Code of Laws of South Carolina 1976 Annotated (Law. Co-op.)	South Carolina State Register
South Dakota	Administrative Rules of South Dakota	South Dakota Register
Tennessee	Official Compilation Rules & Regulations of the State of Tennessee	Tennessee Administrative Register
Texas	Texas Administrative Code	Texas Register
Utah	Administrative Rules of the State of Utah	Utah State Bulletin
Vermont	None	Vermont Administrative Procedures Bulletin
Virginia	None	Virginia Register of Regulations
Washington	Washington Administrative Code	Washington State Register
West Virginia	None	None
Wisconsin	Wisconsin Administrative Code	Wisconsin Administrative Register
Wyoming	None	None

Table of State Administrative Compilations and Registers *(Continued)*

have cited the case you are shepardizing, annotations that have discussed or mentioned the cited case, and other sources that have mentioned or discussed the cited case. The pamphlet or volume you are looking in may also contain no citing material for the subject case or statute. This means that there is no relevant information to report for the time period covered by that particular pamphlet or volume.

For example, a case is reported in volume 239 of the North Western Reporter 2d on page 197. If there were a parallel citation to a state court report, *Shepard's* would list that first. A small "d" in front of the first case cite indicates that this case was distinguished in that court opinion. To be distinguished from a cited case means that in the text of the citing court opinion, the subject case was found to be different either in law or in fact. The small numbers immediately before page numbers in these cites refer to headnotes; in our example, they indicate that the subject of headnote number 2 was discussed on page 507 of the case in *North Western 2d* volume 498. Any additional information desired on the topic of the headnotes referred to in the *Shepard's* cites may be found by looking up the case cites given.

After you have recorded the appropriate information from the most current pamphlet or volume of *Shepard's*, repeat this procedure for each of the remaining pamphlets or volumes in the entire set, working from the most current to the oldest included on the list. When your task is complete, you will know if the case is still valid, and you will have a list of other cases or resources to look to for further information.

Shepardizing Statutes

The process of sheparding statutes is very similar to that of sheparding court cases. First, locate all the necessary volumes and pamphlets for the appropriate set of *Shepard's*. Next, look up the statute by section or title number. For instance, cites under a statute heading show where that section has been cited. A listing may be broken down by subdivisions of the statute and include more cites. In addition, there may be entries for amendments to this statute section; the history of the statute section confirms this information. Finally, a last group of entries may contain cites to law review articles where the statute has been discussed.

Shepardizing statutes is particularly helpful for finding cases that discuss the statute and for checking the validity of a statute section, particularly if the statutory codification is not frequently updated.

Cite Checking

One task often delegated to paralegals is *cite checking*. This task involves reviewing cites within legal documents to verify case citations, check the history of the cases, and conform the cites to the proper form.

First, the cites must be checked for accuracy. All cites within documents must be looked up in the proper reporters. In addition, all quotations from the cases must be proofread to make sure they are correct.

Second, the history of the cites must be checked, either by shepardizing or through a computerized system. Any indications that a case has been reversed, overruled, modified, or vacated, or that a statute has been amended or repealed, must be checked immediately. If an authority cited in a legal document is no longer valid, this fact should be brought to the attention of the responsible attorney immediately, especially if the document is to be submitted to a court in the near future.

Finally, the cites in the legal document you are checking must be conformed precisely to the appropriate form. New editions of citation manuals are issued periodically, and courts may impose their own rules for citation style, so it is important that you have the current edition of the appropriate authority when performing this portion of the task.

Cite checking can be a time-consuming process, but computer cite-checking systems have been introduced to speed the process. The two most frequently used systems are Insta-Cite and Auto-Cite.

ABBREVIATIONS—ANALYSIS
CASES

History of Case

a	(affirmed)	Same case affirmed on appeal.
cc	(connected case)	Different case from case cited but arising out of same subject matter or intimately connected therewith.
D	(dismissed)	Appeal from same case dismissed.
m	(modified)	Same case modified on appeal.
r	(reversed)	Same case reversed on appeal.
s	(same case)	Same case as case cited.
S	(superseded)	Substitution for former opinion.
v	(vacated)	Same case vacated.
US	cert den	Certiorari denied by U. S. Supreme Court.
US	cert dis	Certiorari dismissed by U. S. Supreme Court.
US	reh den	Rehearing denied by U. S. Supreme Court.
US	reh dis	Rehearing dismissed by U. S. Supreme Court.
US	app pndg	Appeal pending before the U. S. Supreme Court.

Treatment of Case

c	(criticised)	Soundness of decision or reasoning in cited case criticised for reasons given.
d	(distinguished)	Case at bar different either in law or fact from case cited for reasons given.
e	(explained)	Statement of import of decision in cited case. Not merely a restatement of the facts.
f	(followed)	Cited as controlling.
h	(harmonized)	Apparent inconsistency explained and shown not to exist.
j	(dissenting opinion)	Citation in dissenting opinion.
L	(limited)	Refusal to extend decision of cited case beyond precise issues involved.
o	(overruled)	Ruling in cited case expressly overruled.
p	(parallel)	Citing case substantially alike or on all fours with cited case in its law or facts.
q	(questioned)	Soundness of decision or reasoning in cited case questioned.

Shepard's Abbreviations When preparing a legal history of a case, it is essential to begin with the abbreviations page. Reproduced with permission of Shepard's/McGraw-Hill, Inc. Further reproduction is strictly prohibited.

NORTHWESTERN REPORTER, 2d SERIES (Minnesota Cases)

Vol. 233

—770—
504NW³226

Vol. 234

—775—
Cir. 5
813FS489
Cir. 8
990F2d392
991F2d1406
808FS1410
811FS¹⁴1384
814FS774
815FS²⁴1275

Vol. 235

—187—
499NW¹³494

—597—
498NW⁷506

Vol. 236

—163—
498NW43
504NW⁸271

—592—
499NW511

Vol. 237

—76—
499NW⁸845
503NW⁸141

—365—
Cir. 8
983F2d⁸893

—375—
497NW³628

Vol. 238

—862—
498NW⁷33

—878—
d496NW¹416

Vol. 239

—197—
d498NW505
f498NW²507
Cir. 8
816FS²546

—227—
Case 2
503NW476

—445—
504NW244

—455—
f499NW⁸818

—472—
505NW³327

—768—
501NW⁴692
505NW³327

—892—
498NW759

Vol. 240

—500—
816FS547

—507—
499NW¹²489
503NW⁸809

—517—
f503NW¹139
503NW⁸139

—814—
502NW¹414

Vol. 241

—781—
505NW296
505NW³298
505NW⁴298

—788—
Cir. 8
815FS1276

—806—
j505NW618

Vol. 242

—78—
499NW¹483

Vol. 243

—157—
498NW¹450

—313—
497NW³620

—737—
502NW⁴787

Vol. 244

—51—
j504NW207

—147—
496NW¹846

—482—
504NW³72

—635—
499NW²508
499NW²838

—648—
Cir. 1
d808FS65
Cir. 3
d148BRW775
148BRW⁴776
d148BRW⁵
[777

—652—
499NW⁷818

Vol. 245

—242—
498NW50

—258—
504NW¹266

—844—
499NW³529
499NW⁴529

—848—
496NW851

Vol. 246

—48—
500NW⁴805

—170—
Cir. 8
f811FS1378

—176—
499NW¹⁰514

—565—
Case 2
497NW290
500NW⁴170
502NW⁴426
505NW⁴56
505NW²355

—637—
d499NW802
Cir. 8
149BRW⁶558

—858—
499NW²812

Vol. 247

—385—
e496NW⁸418
f499NW²841
f499NW⁴841
f499NW⁸841
504NW²213
504NW⁵213

—600—
502NW⁴799

—901—
497NW²291

—907—
498NW⁸50
498NW⁵505
503NW⁵160
503NW⁸497
Cir. 8
816FS⁵545

Vol. 248

—279—
500NW138

—281—
505NW⁷70

—291—
501NW701
Cir. 8
816FS1363
Cir. 10
810FS¹³1143

—310—
499NW⁸817
499NW³818

—733—
502NW²221
502NW³221

Vol. 251

—101—
500NW⁴156

—125—
497NW⁴252

—135—
Cir. 8
e149BRW561

—341—
Cir. 8
811FS1378

—620—
505NW¹296
505NW²298

—703—
501NW¹637

—707—
d498NW¹313

Vol. 252

—105—
504NW¹63

—124—
497NW¹628

—266—
500NW804

—852—
505NW297

Vol. 253

—133—
498NW⁸28

—835—
503NW476

Vol. 254

—75—
497NW¹241

—371—
498NW⁴779
500NW⁴499

Vol. 255

—22—
19WmM618
19WmM636

—42—
d504NW⁴763

Vol. 256

—82—
Cir. 11
816FS¹1573

—280—
498NW³440

—298—
502NW762

—485—
498NW307

—506—
61USLW
[4546

—803—
503NW¹483

—808—
497NW⁶628
499NW⁶831
500NW⁶498
501NW⁶648
502NW²207

Vol. 257

—324—
501NW⁶665

—343—
500NW499

—366—
f500NW500

—551—
501NW²692

—689—
Cir. 8
149BRW³557

—762—
502NW¹³207

—791—
502NW⁴799
502NW⁸800

—796—
d499NW²803

—804—
Cir. 8
e812FS⁸924
812FS³925

—816—
498NW264

Vol. 258

—96—
497NW⁸261
e497NW¹262
504NW266

—565—
f498NW¹303
f498NW³303
f498NW⁴304

—570—
500NW⁴160
Cir. 8
816FS¹1357
816FS³1358

—598—
500NW802

—774—
497NW288

—856—
499NW¹⁴484

—877—
498NW³315
498NW³778

—891—
498NW32
505NW56
505NW¹58
505NW²58

Vol. 259

—254—
503NW⁴484
505NW³297

—467—
Case 1
504NW²790

—567—
498NW¹⁴46

—896—
f496NW¹846

—898—
d504NW788

—904—
497NW³310
503NW⁵106
504NW⁸754

Vol. 260

—150—
505NW70
Cir. 8
986F2d¹⁰1195

—169—
L499NW¹518

—579—
497NW294
497NW⁴307
497NW⁴619
498NW⁴66
498NW⁴474
502NW⁴792
504NW⁴280
19WmM623

Vol. 261

—335—
Case 1
504NW⁷290

—335—
Case 2
499NW¹486

—581—
498NW¹315

—594—
497NW²288

—598—
497NW⁶304
504NW⁸468

Vol. 262

—157—
498NW²296
504NW²44

—163—
496NW³834
499NW847

—349—
e505NW⁵57

—366—
d498NW⁴73
Cir. 8
814FS¹³774
12.43460n

—426—
501NW³632

—684—
503NW¹⁹125
504NW³491

Vol. 263

—66—
497NW⁴322

—76—
505NW³69

—385—
d503NW¹¹139
d503NW140

—389—
503NW¹491

—395—
503NW808
Cir. 8
812FS923
814FS771
19WmM201

—603—
498NW¹60
c498NW⁸61

—803—
496NW¹822
499NW¹¹485
502NW74
504NW¹¹510

Vol. 264

—137—
500NW786

—152—
Cir. 8
814FS⁴773

—812—
503NW114

Vol. 265

—205—
d503NW³802

Shepard's Citator This page is a sample of a legal history of court opinions determined in Minnesota. Reproduced with permission of Shepard's/McGraw-Hill, Inc. Further reproduction is strictly prohibited.

Secondary Sources of Law

Although secondary sources of law are not considered to be binding authority, at times they can be just as useful as primary sources. Common secondary sources include legal encyclopedias, treatises, formbooks, and periodicals.

Legal Encyclopedias

The two most popular legal encyclopedias are the multivolume *Corpus Juris Secundum (C.J.S.)* and *American Jurisprudence 2d (Am. Jur. 2d)*. Both these sets offer comprehensive discussions on numerous topics, as well as references to pertinent court opinions, statutes, law review articles, formbooks, and annotations.

Corpus Juris Secundum is published by West Publishing Company, and most of the references in that text are to other West Publishing References. *Am. Jur. 2d* is published by Lawyers Cooperative Publishing, and the majority of its references are to other Lawyers Cooperative Publishing references, although it also references cases not included in the *ALR* series.

Both sets of encyclopedias are updated by pocket parts in the back of each volume, and by new volumes that are issued periodically. They are accessed by indexes found in the back of each volume or in separate volumes at the end of each set.

In addition to these two general sets of encyclopedias, many other sets of encyclopedias on specific topics are available. These encyclopedias summarize a specific area of law and provide cross-references to other sources.

Several states also have their own legal encyclopedia sets.

Treatises

A treatise is a book or set of books that provides an overview, analysis, or summary of a particular type of law. A treatise can be very helpful to give you an understanding of the area of law you are researching. In addition, treatises also cite and analyze cases which may aid in your research for primary case law. Formbooks and restatements are considered to be types of treatises.

Legal Formbooks

Legal formbooks can be of great assistance in drafting legal documents. These books contain forms for hundreds of types of documents, all of which can be found through the index or indexes of the set of formbooks. In addition, many legal formbooks are designed to be used in conjunction with other resources such as legal encyclopedias and case reporters. Many legal formbooks also include annotations with the forms, which include general information, checklists, and cross-references that can aid in your research. Some of the more popular formbooks include: *Am. Jur. Legal Forms 2d, Am. Jur. Pleadings and Practice Forms, West's Legal Forms (2d ed.), Federal Procedural Forms, Lawyers' Edition*, and *West's Federal Forms*. In addition, several formbooks and sets of formbooks are available on specific topics, many of which are state-specific.

Restatements

Restatements are a particular kind of treatise published by the American Law Institute (ALI). Restatements, in effect, restate and comment on the current law in a particular area of law. They are often used as secondary sources of law. Although not mandatory authority, they are considered one of the best sources of persuasive authority. Current restatements are available online on WESTLAW.

Legal Periodicals

Numerous legal periodicals are available in most law libraries. A majority of legal periodicals are *law reviews*, collections of articles on specific areas of law that are thoroughly researched and often contain good resources both for background information on a topic and for further research and primary sources of law. Law reviews are published by law schools and edited by law students.

Consulting a computerized catalog of periodical articles or your law librarian may be the best way to locate what you are looking for. Bound indexes to legal periodicals can also be used. The most popular indexes include *The Index to Legal Periodicals* and the *Index to Periodical Articles Related to Law*. Both of these resources are available in most law libraries, especially public law libraries.

Other Resources for Legal Research

In addition to the traditional sources for legal research discussed so far in this chapter, there are numerous other resources, including legal directories, computer databases, and government resources.

Legal Directories

Legal directories such as the *Martindale-Hubbell Law Directory* provide state-by-state listings of attorneys that may be useful for a multitude of purposes. When your task is to locate an attorney in another state who specializes in a certain area of law, or to set up a deposition in a distant city, *Martindale-Hubbell* can provide the names of the individuals you will need to contact. Another feature of *Martindale-Hubbell* that is often overlooked is its state-by-state summaries of statutory law. It can be an excellent place to begin a research project that involves researching the law of several states.

Loose-leaf Services

Loose-leaf services serve many different purposes in legal research. Most often they contain court opinions and statutes, as well as a general discussion of the law and cross-references. Loose-leaf services consist of sets of binders containing information that is replaced periodically to add new cases, statutes, or administrative rules and regulations, depending on the subject and format of the service. Because of their frequent updating, loose-leaf services are often an excellent source for the most current laws and court opinions. Most major areas of law are covered by at least one of these loose-leaf services, including tax law, securities law, criminal law, and family law. The publishers of these loose-leaf services include Commerce Clearing House (CCH), the Bureau of National Affairs (BNA), Prentice-Hall, and Matthew Bender.

Legal Dictionaries

Legal dictionaries can be great aids in legal research and legal writing. Numerous variations exist, including *Ballentine's Law Dictionary* and *Black's Law Dictionary*.

Computer Databases

Although LEXIS and WESTLAW are the two main computerized databases for researching case law, statutory law, and regulations, they are just the tip of the iceberg. Both of these sources have many more uses, and there are also many other databases available on a widespread basis. Computerized research can offer resources that are not otherwise available in your law library and they can offer much more efficient ways of retrieving that information. For example, shepardizing cases through *Shepard's* on WESTLAW can be much quicker than going through several pamphlets and volumes of text. When you begin a new position, or begin researching in a law library that is new to you, it is important to find out what is available through computerized legal research.

Read the available instructions and ask for training from someone who is experienced with the software. Adequate training can save a tremendous amount of time when you are accessing computerized databases. Remember, with most systems, time is money. Always have your research planned out before you begin your search on the computer. Know the parameters of your search and know when to stop.

Government Resources

Both the federal government and state governments have a wealth of information available to the public. Accessing that information can be a problem, however. Most government publications are not widely advertised or distributed. Finding out what exists and how to obtain it can involve several telephone calls.

Your search for government information may begin with a look in the telephone directory to find the name and number of the appropriate agency or division. Don't expect an answer from the first individual you speak with. The key to obtaining information over the telephone from government agencies or departments is persistence.

Whenever possible, when you begin your research on the telephone, try to end up with a hard copy of the information that you are seeking.

For example, the Internal Revenue Service has representatives who are well qualified to answer complex questions concerning the contents of the Internal Revenue Code. However, when you are completing your research memo, you will not want to say that "John Doe from the IRS said … ." Have whoever gives you the information give you the source of that information so that you can verify it and cite it.

Some good published resources available from the U.S. government to assist with obtaining government information include *The U.S. Government Manual* and *The Official Congressional Directory*, both available from the U.S. Government Printing Office. The *U.S. Government Manual* includes lists of principal officials and sources of information for each department or agency within the federal government. The *Official Congressional Directory* includes information and telephone numbers for Congress and its members. The federal information offices located in many cities also have a broad base of information available to the public, including referrals to the correct public agency to answer your questions concerning government information and government documents.

Putting It All Together: Legal Research Techniques

Even experienced legal researchers do not necessarily follow the same procedures when performing legal research, although their procedures may have much in common. The steps you follow when completing legal research will depend, at least in part, on the following:

1. What end result are you looking for? Are you seeking the answer to a specific question, or are you looking for general information?

2. How familiar are you with the topic being researched?

3. How much research information is available on the topic?

4. Is your research limited to one jurisdiction?

5. Where does your research lead you?

6. How much time are you expected to take to complete the task?

The method of research you use will depend on the results you are looking for. If you are looking for research to support your position in a court brief, you will be looking for mandatory authority. If, on the other hand, you simply wish to educate yourself before meeting with a client, a brief review of a secondary source of law may be sufficient.

If you are familiar with the topic being researched, your research may begin with either case law or statutory law. Being familiar with the topic means that you know what you are looking for and which topics and headings to look under.

In some instances, your research may be limited by the research materials available. You may find that there is no pertinent material in one or more of the sources that you would typically research.

If your task is to predict the outcome of a court case in a state court, it will do you little good to perform research on the issues at hand that would encompass the federal courts or the court systems of other states. In that situation, your research may be limited to state-specific sources.

When accepting a legal research assignment, it is important to find out the amount of time you are expected to spend on the project and the scope of the expected results. Taking into consideration the number of cross-references to statutes and court opinions, it is sometimes hard to know where to end your research. For example, if you find one case that is on point, shepardize that case, and thereby find three more, you could review those three cases, shepardize them, and have them lead you to even more cases. If the attorney is looking for some general information on a topic before a meeting with a client, he or she would probably not expect you to spend several hours researching the topic. If, on the other hand, the attorney is preparing a case for an important trial, several days of your time researching an issue may be justified.

For that reason, it is important to understand how much time you are expected to expend on a project and to understand what the scope of the expected end product is. An attorney who is expecting a quick verbal answer to a question will not be happy to receive a 20-page memorandum outlining every detail and several contingencies of the issue.

It is always important, when performing legal research, to keep an open mind. At times (especially when researching an area of law with which you are unfamiliar), your research may lead you to unexpected resources and unexpected conclusions.

Use the cross-references available in the sources in which you are researching. Don't make your research any harder than it has to be. When researching an area with which you are unfamiliar, it often pays to begin with secondary sources. Not only will it help you to understand the issue, but it will also refer you to pertinent primary sources of law that may be just what you are ultimately looking for.

Basic Concepts of Effective Legal Writing

The importance of effective legal writing skills for paralegals cannot be overemphasized. You may have a great knowledge of the subject you are working on or researching, but unless you can communicate what you have learned, it will do you no good.

The purpose of legal writing is effective communication. Regardless of your medium, your goal is to effectively communicate the necessary information to the reader. Effective communication must be accurate, concise, and well-organized.

Organization

One of the most crucial elements in effective legal writing is organization. A well-organized legal document or correspondence is much easier to read and will have a much bigger impact on the reader.

Organization begins with planning and with an outline. For short correspondence, your plan may not have to be in writing. However, even a short letter should be thought out before you begin. Outlining will help you to organize your thoughts and express them in an organized fashion. One method of outlining follows these steps:

1. Write down the major points that you would like to express in your writing

2. Decide which of these points should be lumped together, and which will constitute a new section or paragraph of your writing

3. Put the major points in the order in which they will be most effective

4. Add important facts and statements to support your major points.

Style

Your writing style for drafting legal documents, memoranda, or correspondence will depend at least in part on the recipient of your writing. There are, however, some general rules to be followed.

Be Concise It is important for your writing to be as concise as possible. No busy attorney or judge wants to read a 20-page memorandum when a 10-page memorandum can relay the same information.

Use Short Sentences Attorneys are notorious for using one-sentence paragraphs that take up half a page. Although this is easy to do when you are trying to express complex thoughts and situations, it is not necessary. When you find your sentences becoming too long and too complex, try to think about ways to turn those sentences into two or three sentences instead.

Avoid Legalese In recent years, there has been a trend to simplify the language and writing of the legal profession. Many clients and attorneys alike have determined that there is no "magic" to complex legal terminology. Especially when communicating with clients, don't use complex legal jargon if plain English will suffice. Clients do not want to be impressed with your knowledge of legal terminology—they want to understand what you are trying to communicate to them.

Obviously, at times it is necessary to use complex legal terminology. When using legal terms in communications with clients, you may want to define certain terms for them.

Use Correct Grammar and Punctuation
Improper grammar and punctuation can be very distracting in any type of writing. It is important that you be aware of your grammar and punctuation in every type of legal writing. There are several tools available to assist with grammar and punctuation. Don't assume that your secretary, transcriber, or word processor will know it all. If you are unsure, look it up.

Use Footnotes Use footnotes in your legal writing, but with discretion. When preparing a legal memorandum to attorneys or to a court, write footnotes with proper citations to the cases, statutes, and secondary sources of law that were used to prepare the memorandum. The attorneys or judges will want to know where you found your information so that they can determine the credibility of the source or find more information if they choose to. When writing to clients and others, however, footnotes to cases and other sources are almost always more distracting than helpful.

Proofreading Even short, seemingly unimportant correspondence or documents deserve to be proofread—at least once! Proofreading can eliminate errors that would be embarrassing, confusing, or even costly. Each document should be read once over quickly for content. Does it say what you want? Does it say it in the tone you want to express?

If the content is acceptable, the document should be proofread for typographical, spelling, grammar, and punctuation errors. You may want to do this with a dictionary in hand, as well as punctuation and grammar guides and a citation manual. Running a document through a computerized spell checker does not replace proofreading. Words used incorrectly but spelled correctly will not be caught by the computer.

Whenever possible, legal documents should be proofread by someone other than the individual who prepared them. It is much easier to find someone else's mistakes. Legal property descriptions and other complex, possibly confusing, legal verbiage should be proofread by two people; one person reads the original out loud while the other checks the copy.

Don't forget to proofread your titles and headings. Often mistakes are missed in these two obviously important areas because they are so easily overlooked in the proofreading process.

MINNESOTA STATUTES—MINNESOTA STATUTES ANNOTATED

1986, 325E.01

A1993C375	299F.04	Subd. 38	302A.401	302A.521	303.21	Subd. 45a	Subd. 3
Subd. 9a	Subd. 5	Subd. 1	Subd. 1	Subd. 1	Subd. 3	Ad1993C137	A1993C137
A1993C375	Ad1993C326	A1993C17	A1993C17	A1993C137	A1993C369		
Subd. 10		Subd. 53	Subd. 3	Subd. 6		322B.115	322B.80
A1993C375	299F.092	A1993C17	A1993C17	A1993C17	306.141	A1993C137	Subd. 1
	Subd. 9	Subd. 54			Ad1993C100	Subd. 2	A1993C137
298.296	R1993C337	Ad1993C17	302A.402	302A.551		A1993C137	Subd. 3
Subd. 1			Subd. 1	Subd. 1	306.99		Ad1993C137
A1993C369	299F.093	302A.105	A1993C17	(1993C17)	Ad1993C100	322B.20	
	Subd. 1	A1993C17	Subd. 2	A1993C17		Subd. 5	322B.873
298.75	A1993C337		A1993C17	Subd. 3	307.01	A1993C137	A1993C137
Subd. 4		302A.111	Subd. 4	A1993C137	et seq.	Subd. 7	
A1993C375	299F.097	Subd. 3	Ad1993C17		Sg1993C288	A1993C137	322B.901
Subd. 5	R1993C337	A1993C17		302A.553		Subd. 12	Ad1993C137
A1993C375		Subd. 4	302A.403	Subd. 1	307.08	A1993C137	
	299F.21	A1993C17	Subd. 2	(1993C17)	Subd. 2	Subd. 14	322B.91
299A.325	Subd. 2		A1993C17	A1993C17	A1993C326	A1993C137	Subd. 1
R1993C326	A1993C375	302A.115	Subd. 4			Subd. 21	A1993C137
		Subd. 1	A1993C17	302A.559	307.12	A1993C137	
299A.35	299F.23	A1993C17		Subd. 1	Ad1993C100		322B.92
Subd. 1	Subd. 2		302A.413	A1993C17		322B.30	A1993C137
A1993C326	A1993C375	302A.117	Subd. 4		308A.011	Subd. 2	
Subd. 2	Subd. 5	Subd. 1	A1993C17	302A.613	Subd. 1	A1993C137	322B.93
A1993C326	Ad1993C375	A1993C17	Subd. 9	Subd. 2	A1993C222	Subd. 3	A1993C137
			A1993C17	A1993C17		A1993C137	
299A.50	299F.362	302A.123		Subd. 3	309.501		322B.935
Subd. 3	Subd. 1	Subd. 3	302A.423	A1993C17	A1993C192	322B.306	Subd. 2
Ad1993C341	A1993C329	A1993C17	Subd. 2			Subd. 1	A1993C137
	Subd. 11		A1993C17	302A.621	309.502	A1993C137	Subd. 3
299C.01	Ad1993C329	302A.133		Subd. 6	R1993C192	Subd. 3	A1993C137
et seq.		A1993C17	302A.435	A1993C17		A1993C137	
Sg1993C266	299F.811		Subd. 1		317A.165		322B.960
	A1993C326	302A.135	A1993C17	302A.641	Subd. 1	322B.31	Subd. 4
299C.065		Subd. 1	Subd. 3	Subd. 1	498NW24	Subd. 3	Ad1993C131
Subd. 1	299F.815	A1993C17	A1993C17	A1993C17	Subd. 2	A1993C137	
A1993C326	Subd. 1	Subd. 3			498NW24		325D.01
	A1993C326	A1993C17	302A.437	302A.671	Subd. 3	322B.313	et seq.
299C.10			Subd. 2	Subd. 3	498NW24	A1993C137	Sg1993C375
A1993C266	299J.06	302A.137	A1993C17	A1993C17			
	Subd. 4	A1993C17			317A.823	322B.316	325D.33
299C.11	A1993C341		302A.447	302A.673	Subd. 1	A1993C137	Subd. 7
503NW483		302A.153	Subd. 2	Subd. 1	A1993C86		R1993C375
	299K.08	A1993C17	A1993C17	A1993C48		322B.323	Subd. 8
299C.46	Subd. 3		Subd. 3	A1993C86	317A.827	Subd. 2	Ad1993C375
Subd. 5	Ad1993C172	302A.161	A1993C17	Subd. 3	Subd. 3	A1993C137	
Ad1993C326	Subd. 4	Subd. 12		A1993C137	(1993C48)		325D.37
	Ad1993C172	A1993C137	302A.449	Subd. 3	A1993C48	322B.373	Subd. 3
299C.54			Subd. 1	A1993C17		Subd. 1	A1993C375
Subd. 3a	299K.10	302A.171	A1993C17		319A.02	A1993C137	
Ad1993C326	Subd. 9	Subd. 2		302A.711	Subd. 7		325D.43 to
	Ad1993C282	A1993C17	302A.461	Subd. 1	A1993C137	322B.54	325D.48
299C.61			Subd. 4	A1993C17		Subd. 3	500NW789
Subd. 5	299L.03	302A.231	A1993C17	Subd. 2	319A.11	A1993C137	
A1993C238	Subd. 11	Subd. 3		A1993C17	Subd. 1		325D.45
	Ad1993C351	A1993C17	302A.463		A1993C375	322B.693	Subd. 1
299C.64			A1993C17	302A.753		Subd. 1	500NW790
498NW506	300.045	302A.233		499NW810	322A.16	A1993C137	
	A1993C96	A1993C17	302A.471		A1993C369		325D.51
299D.03			Subd. 3	302A.821		322B.696	498NW275
Subd. 1	300.20	302A.237	A1993C17	Subd. 6	322A.70	A1993C137	
A1993C326	Subd. 2	A1993C17		A1993C48	A1993C48		325D.52
	A1993C257		302A.473			322B.699	498NW275
299D.06		302A.241	Subd. 4	302A.901	322B.03	Subd. 1	
A1993C326	300.21	Subd. 1	A1993C17	Subd. 2a	Subd. 17a	A1993C137	325D.53
	A1993C257	A1993C17	Subd. 7	Ad1993C17	Ad1993C137		498NW275
299F.011			A1993C17		Subd. 19a	322B.77	
Subd. 4c	302A.011	302A.255		303.13	Ad1993C137	Subd. 1	325E.01
A1993C327	Subd. 25	Subd. 2	302A.501	Subd. 1	Subd. 36a	A1993C137	et seq.
	A1993C137	A1993C17	Subd. 1	A1993C48	Ad1993C137		Sg1993C221
	Subd. 26		A1993C17	A1993C369	Subd. 41		
	A1993C17		A1993C137	Subd. 2	A1993C137		
				A1993C48			

Shepard's Citator This page is a sample of the legal history of statutes codified in Minnesota. Reproduced with permission of Shepard's/McGraw-Hill, Inc. Further reproduction is strictly prohibited.

Tools for Effective Legal Writing

There are several types of very useful resources for effective legal writing. Resources are available to assist with nearly every aspect of writing, including content, format, punctuation, and grammar. There are also texts and reference books designed specifically to aid in legal writing.

Formbooks and the Forms File

For assistance with content and format, you may need to look no further than your office. Is there a form file of previously drafted memoranda, pleadings, and correspondence? By using a form file from within the office, you can be assured that you are using a style that is accepted and encouraged within your office.

If you spend any time at all drafting a unique piece of correspondence or legal document, keep an extra copy where it will be readily available for future reference. If you remain in the same job for any length of time, chances are you will find yourself writing the same types of legal documents and correspondence repeatedly. Having a sample on hand can be a great time-saver.

Very few legal documents are totally unique. If you have been asked to draft a legal document, it will probably be very similar to a legal document that has been drafted by someone else before and put into a formbook. Legal formbooks, available in nearly every law library, contain standard language that can help save you time in drafting legal documents. In addition, formbooks often include checklists to help ensure that you have not forgotten to put crucial information in a legal document.

Court Rules and Statutes

When drafting legal documents, especially pleadings, the appropriate statutes and court rules should be consulted to be ensure that your documents contain all the necessary information in the appropriate format. Often, court rules specify very precisely what information must be included in documents to be submitted to the court, and what format should be used for those documents.

Dictionaries and Thesauruses

The legal dictionary and thesaurus can be very useful tools for any type of legal writing. If you are unsure whether the word you want to use is the correct word, whether it is spelled correctly, or whether it is used correctly, a good legal dictionary and thesaurus, such as *Ballentine's Law Dictionary* and *Ballentine's Thesaurus for Legal Research & Writing*, can answer these questions. A thesaurus can also help put a little variety in your vocabulary in lengthy documents.

Style Manuals

For assistance with correspondence and questions concerning spelling, punctuation, and grammar, several resources exist. In addition to the traditional resources, several computer programs include spelling and grammar programs and even thesauruses. Some useful style books to keep on hand are:

1. *The Chicago Manual of Style*
2. *The Gregg Reference Manual*
3. *Webster's New World Secretarial Manual*
4. *Ballentine's Law Dictionary: Legal Assistant Edition*
5. *Ballentine's Thesaurus for Legal Research & Writing.*

Effective Dictation

Depending on the setup of your office, you will probably be required to dictate at least some of your correspondence and legal documentation. Although it may seem uncomfortable at first, with a little practice your dictation can become very efficient. Here are a few tips to help.

1. Jot down notes outlining what you are going to say before you begin dictating. It will help to keep you organized and will be appreciated by the transcriber.

2. At the beginning of each tape, tell the transcriber what is on the tape and the approximate length of the documents.

3. Be sure to tell the transcriber if the correspondence or document you are dictating is to be in draft or final form. Often longer documents or correspondence will be produced first in draft form.

4. Speak slowly and enunciate clearly. Speaking fast will not get your work transcribed any faster—it will only cause frustration and confusion on the part of the transcriber, who may not be able to keep up with you or understand you.

5. Spell out any words that might be confusing, especially names.

6. Always indicate when you are ending a sentence or a paragraph.

7. Indicate which numbers you would like spelled out and which ones you would like in numerical form.

8. Be sure to indicate both the beginning and the end of special instructions within the text, such as indenting, bolding, and underlining.

9. Dictate in a quiet location, whenever possible, to avoid background noise.

10. Remember that, although you are talking into a machine, there is a person on the other end of the transcription process. Be courteous.

Types of Legal Writing

Most legal writing performed by paralegals is directed to the attorneys for whom they work, to clients, or to courts. The types of writing they most commonly work on are in-office memoranda, correspondence, and pleadings and other legal documents.

The In-Office Legal Memorandum

Nearly all legal research performed by paralegals is concluded with a memorandum regarding the findings to the attorney who assigned the research, or to the file. Hours of legal research would be pointless if the information was not accurately communicated to the individual who requested that information. When you begin drafting a legal memorandum, you must keep in mind its contents and form. You will probably want to use the notes from your legal research to prepare an outline before drafting the memo. A typical legal memorandum includes a heading, a brief statement of the facts and legal issues presented, a conclusion, discussion, and a summary.

The Heading

The heading of an in-office memorandum usually includes the name of the individual to whom the memo is addressed, the name of the author, the date, and the subject. Many law offices have a standard format to be followed within the office. A typical heading may look like the following:

IN-OFFICE MEMORANDUM

TO: James Gregory
FROM: Brent Allan
DATE: March 30, 1994
RE: Thompson Contract Dispute Research
         File No. 94-385729

Statement of the Facts and Legal Issues

This section is really just a brief restatement of the assignment for which you are writing the legal memorandum. It should restate the known facts of the case and the unanswered questions. The facts should be restated, in detail and with precision, with a brief statement as to the origin of the information. For example, "According to our client, Vern Thompson, ..." or "According to the police report ... ." Typically this section can be concluded with a question of law, such as "Is a contract for the purchase of real estate valid if no earnest money is given in consideration?" Usually this question will be provided for you in your assignment.

The Conclusion

At times, it is difficult to summarize your research into one "conclusion." However, try to be as brief as possible in this section, giving a short answer with as few qualifications as possible. Qualifications and exceptions can be explained in the discussion section of the memorandum.

The Discussion

The discussion may be the most important section of the memorandum. It will discuss the statutes, cases, and other authorities as they apply to the facts and issues of your research assignment. It should be organized by issue, using headings and subheadings for long discussions. When referencing statutes, administrative law, or case law, be sure to discuss their relevance to the issue at hand.

When you are relying on a statute for authority, it is important to know how that statute has been interpreted if its meaning is not clear when applied to the issues you are researching. Applicable cases must be reviewed and analyzed.

Your discussion should support your answer and your conclusion, but don't omit important contradictory information.

It is especially important to keep your writing well organized in this section. Be sure to follow your outline and use headings and subheadings for lengthy memorandums.

Also, be sure to include a list of the authorities on which you based your answer for the readers. This can be especially important when the attorney wants to check a particular point of your conclusion, or when the attorney wants to research a related question. The authorities listed will often include statutes, case law, and possibly secondary sources of law.

The Summary

The summary will parallel your conclusion toward the beginning of the memorandum, but it may be more in-depth, giving brief statements as to how and why your conclusion was reached, based on the information in your discussion and the authorities you have cited. If the memorandum leaves any questions unanswered, or if it brings up unanticipated questions of law, you may want to include in your summary an offer to perform follow-up research.

The External Legal Memorandum

In addition to the in-office legal memorandum, several types of memoranda may be prepared for presentation outside the office. These memoranda take many forms, but are usually submitted to courts to support your client's position. The format followed for these memoranda will depend on who they are intended for and what their exact purpose is. Typically, an external memo will include the same basic sections as an in-office legal memorandum, with a few exceptions. Most importantly, the discussion section may be referred to as an *argument section*. Its purpose is not to objectively discuss all aspects of the facts and issues of the case; rather, its objective is to present your client's argument. Information detrimental to your client is either not included or is explained as being irrelevant in this section.

As with the in-office memorandum, the external memorandum presents each question and issue separately and answers each question citing the available authorities.

It is also important that the conclusion and summary be strongly worded in an external memorandum. This is the basic conclusion that you wish to be reached for your client by the reader.

Correspondence

Correspondence is your means of communicating important information to clients and others and of documenting information that has been communicated verbally. Your goal in drafting correspondence should be to keep it clear, concise, and to the point (without being curt).

If you are addressing a legal issue with a client, write in a conversational tone, avoiding legalese.

If you are asked by an attorney to draft correspondence to clients advising them on legal matters, the letter should be drafted for the attorney's signature. Otherwise, you should be the signator, with your title listed below your name so as not to mislead the recipient. For example:

Sincerely,
Maggie Burton
Paralegal

Pleadings

Paralegals are often asked to draft pleadings for court proceedings. The most important resources for drafting pleadings include formbooks, form files within the law office, state statutes, and the applicable rules of court. Often statutes are very specific as to what information must be included in pleadings. Court rules may be equally specific about the format that must be followed when drafting pleadings.

Other Legal Documents

In addition to the pleadings used in litigation, there are numerous other legal documents that paralegals are responsible for drafting, including wills, contracts, and corporate documents. The general rules discussed herein for legal writing apply to all these documents. Each law office usually has its own form files to use when preparing these types of legal documents, so the paralegal does not have to reinvent the wheel each time he or she is assigned to draft a legal document. For assignments that are unique to the law firm, legal formbooks can be very useful tools.

Summary Questions

1. What are the three main primary sources of law?
2. What is meant by mandatory authority and persuasive authority? Give examples of each.
3. What are some possible advantages to using unofficial case reporters?
4. If you are unsure as to how to correctly cite a case, where could you look?
5. Where are U.S. Supreme Court decisions published?
6. What are some advantages to using annotated statutes over official statutes?

7. What are the two main reasons for shepardizing court opinions?
8. When might it be beneficial to begin a research project with secondary authority sources?
9. What is cite checking?
10. What advantages are offered by annotated law reporters over other types of court reporters?

Practical Paralegal Skills

Take another look at the law office scenario in this chapter. Assume that Andrea Bennigan is a client of the firm you work for, and perform the research assignment assuming that the corporation is organized under the laws of your home state. Prepare your answer in the form of an in-office legal memorandum.

PART II
The Roles of the Paralegal

CHAPTER 8
The Litigation Paralegal

More paralegals work in the litigation area than any other area of law. Litigation is often considered to be one of the most interesting and challenging areas in which to work. This chapter is an introduction to the role of the litigation paralegal and to civil litigation. It includes an examination of the litigation process, starting with preliminary considerations and initiating litigation. We then examine the discovery process and pretrial and trial procedures. The chapter concludes with a brief discussion of posttrial matters.

The Role of Paralegals in Litigation

Litigation paralegals are a very diverse group of individuals. The litigation paralegal may work in a variety of different settings, from the small law firm that specializes in personal injury to a complex commercial litigation department of a very large law firm. Litigation paralegals are set apart from other paralegals by the fact that they work with cases involving court procedures. The examination of the role of the litigation paralegal in this section includes a look at the number of paralegals who specialize in litigation, the work typically performed by litigation paralegals, and the skills important to them.

The Number of Litigation Paralegals in the United States

More paralegals work in the litigation area than any other single area of law. A 1993 *Legal Assistant Today* survey indicated that nearly 53 percent of all respondents worked in the area of litigation.[1] The salaries of litigation paralegals ranked about average, or slightly above average in comparison with paralegals in all areas of law. The national average salary for a defense litigation paralegal in 1993 was $30,039, followed by the salaries of plaintiff litigation paralegals and personal injury paralegals at $28,408 and $26,295. The highest reported salary was $65,000.

The Work of Litigation Paralegals in the United States

The work of litigation paralegals often includes considerable time spent gathering and analyzing the facts relevant to court cases, as well as researching the law. Formal legal documents must be prepared and filed with the court, witnesses must be interviewed, and other evidence must be identified and located.

The tasks performed by litigation paralegals vary greatly from firm to firm and from case to case. In a complex litigation case, the litigation paralegal may be part of a litigation team along with attorneys, other paralegals, and legal secretaries. The litigation paralegal's responsibilities may be limited to one aspect of the case. For example, one litigation paralegal might be responsible for organizing and indexing documentary evidence in a case (e.g., contracts, purchase orders, letters between parties), whereas another paralegal in the firm is responsible for researching legal issues. In smaller, less complex cases, one litigation paralegal may be involved in all aspects of the case.

The following is a list of some of the more common tasks that may be included in the job description of a litigation paralegal.

Prelitigation Facts Investigation

1. Interviewing clients
2. Interviewing witnesses
3. Obtaining statements from witnesses
4. Gathering evidence (police reports, photographs, etc.)
5. Organizing and indexing documentary evidence
6. Researching factual and legal issues

Commencing Litigation

1. Researching the substantive law of the case
2. Establishing a calendar to keep up with deadlines
3. Drafting pleadings
4. Coordinating service of process
5. Reviewing pleadings from opposing party
6. Drafting motions, including memoranda of points and authorities
7. Preparing orders after motions

Discovery

1. Drafting written forms of discovery (interrogatories, requests to produce, requests for admissions)
2. Assisting client in complying with discovery requests
3. Reviewing discovery obtained from opposing parties
4. Preparing client for deposition
5. Setting up, reviewing, and summarizing depositions

Trial

1. Organizing file and evidence for trial
2. Serving subpoenas on witnesses
3. Interviewing witnesses
4. Preparing the client
5. Drafting jury instructions
6. Drafting proposed judgments
7. Assisting with research and preparation of trial brief
8. Preparing and organizing trial exhibits
9. Assisting the attorney during trial

Posttrial

1. Researching possible posttrial motions
2. Drafting possible posttrial motions
3. Drafting notice of appeal and requests for transcripts

4. Assisting with research and writing of appellate briefs

Miscellaneous

1. Maintaining firm's calendaring system
2. Organizing client files
3. Assisting with computerization of litigation documents
4. Preparing documents associated with enforcing judgments.

These tasks are discussed in detail throughout this chapter. Tasks that may not be performed by a litigation paralegal include appearing in court on behalf of a client, asking questions at a deposition, and giving legal advice to a client.

Litigation paralegals may specialize in almost any subarea of law. Some paralegals work exclusively in the areas of plaintiff litigation, defense litigation or personal injury. Others work in the medical malpractice or commercial litigation areas. Even the areas of family law or probate often encompass extensive litigation to resolve matters.

Skills Important to Litigation Paralegals

Litigation paralegals need some very definite skills. The litigation paralegal must be able to communicate well, both orally and in writing. You cannot conduct intelligent interviews of clients or prospective witnesses without the ability to communicate orally. Litigation paralegals cannot help draft witness statements or pleadings without the ability to communicate well in writing.

Litigation paralegals must possess organizational and analytical skills. Reviewing and analyzing documentary evidence and pleadings are tasks often given to paralegals. Likewise, litigation paralegals are sometimes asked to organize documents, discovery, and pleadings.

The ability to do legal research, including a familiarity with formbooks and a knowledge of the court system, is also important. Drafting court documents and preparing memoranda of points and authorities (discussion or analysis of legal questions) require this skill.

In today's law office, a litigation paralegal must be computer-literate, that is, possess general knowledge of the computer, word processing, and database programs. This skill is particularly important in law firms that handle complex litigation.

Introduction to Civil Litigation

Civil litigation is the process of resolving disputes through the court system. Unless the parties privately resolve their dispute, the litigation process usually results in a trial or hearing where the parties present their evidence to a judge or jury. The judge or jury then decides the dispute.

This introduction to civil litigation includes a look at the distinction between procedural and substantive law and an examination of the sources of civil law.

Procedural versus Substantive Law

The rules of civil litigation deal primarily with how a civil case is handled in the court system. It consists of rules of procedure known as **procedural law**. Procedural law tells us the method to use to enforce our rights or to obtain redress for the violation of our rights.

However, litigation is not an area of law that can be practiced by itself. Before attorneys litigate a case, they must determine that there actually is a case to be litigated, or whether a question of **substantive law** exists. Substantive law is the area of law that creates, defines, or explains what our rights are. Areas of substantive law that frequently form the basis of civil lawsuits include torts, contracts, real estate, and commercial and business transactions.

Sources of Law

Answers to legal questions concerning civil litigation can be found in either primary sources, including statutes and case law, or secondary sources, including practice manuals, formbooks, and legal encyclopedias. In addition to the traditional sources of laws, rules relating to civil litigation are often adopted by individual courts. These are known as *local rules of court*. In the federal system, these rules can vary from district to district; in state systems, they can vary from one local area to another. In other words, even within one state some rules of procedure may be different from one court to another. Local rules of a court should always be checked before initiating any litigation within that court.

When questions arise relating to litigation, the primary sources of the law are not the only possible reference materials. In fact, it is often quicker and easier to use a secondary source. Many secondary sources exist for both state and federal procedure, including legal encyclopedias, practice manuals, and textbooks. They also include various legal periodicals.

A secondary source that is heavily relied upon in the area of litigation is the formbook. As the name suggests, formbooks contain sample forms for all aspects of litigation, from complaints to judgments. Better formbooks also contain explanations of the laws relating to the various forms, and thus also act as valuable research tools.

BALLENTINESBALLENTINESBALLENTINESBALLENTINESBALLENTINESBALLENTINESBALLENTINESBALLENTINESBALLENTINESBALLENTINESBALLENTINESBALLENTINESBALLENTINESBALLENTINESBALLENTINES

procedural law   The law governing the manner in which rights are enforced; the law prescribing the procedure to be followed in a case.

substantive law   Area of the law that defines right conduct, as opposed to procedural law, which governs the process by which rights are adjudicated.

Civil Litigation in United States Court Systems

Because civil litigation revolves around the courts, one of the first considerations in the litigation process is the selection of the proper court in which to proceed. A civil litigation case usually begins in a trial court, where the parties to a lawsuit file their pleadings and present evidence to a judge or jury. Before filing any lawsuit, an attorney must decide which of the many trial courts is the proper one for that lawsuit. To decide a case, a court must have subject matter jurisdiction and either personal jurisdiction, in rem jurisdiction, or quasi in rem jurisdiction.

An analysis of jurisdiction tells a party whether to file an action in federal court or state court. If a case belongs in a state court, jurisdiction also determines in which state or states the action can be filed. However, within the federal court system and within each state court system are a number of trial courts located in different geographical areas. Choosing the court in the proper geographical area is a question of **venue**. Lawsuits should be filed and heard in a court that has proper venue. However, unlike jurisdiction, a court's lack of proper venue does not render a judgment void. If a defendant does not object to improper venue, he or she waives the right to object to the judgment rendered by the court.

Venue in federal cases is governed by statute (28 U.S.C. § 1391). The United States Code provides that the proper geographical location for federal actions is the district in which the defendant resides or where the cause of action arises. If jurisdiction is based on diversity of citizenship, venue is also proper where the plaintiff resides.

Venue in state court actions is, of course, determined by state law. As a general rule, however, actions can usually be maintained in the county in which the defendant resides or where the cause of action arises.

Because venue does not relate to the basic power of a court to hear a case, under proper circumstances it can be changed. However, the place of trial can only be changed to another court that has jurisdiction. To change venue, a party makes a formal written request to the court where the lawsuit was filed. This is done by making a motion for **change of venue**.

Initiating Litigation

The type of lawsuit that may result from the following scenario is a personal injury lawsuit. Because personal injury lawsuits are very common in the United States, this scenario is used as an example in the discussions throughout the rest of this chapter.

The decision to commence litigation is not one to be taken lightly. Lawsuits involve a great deal of time on the part of the client, the attorney, and the attorney's staff. Lawsuits also involve a great deal of money. This section looks at some of the factors to be taken into consideration before

BALLENTINESBALLENTINESBALLENTINESBALLENTINESBALLENTINESBALLENTINESBALLENTINESBALLENTINESBALLENTINESBALLENTINESBALLENTINESBALLENTINESBALLENTINESBALLENTINES

venue   The county or judicial district in which a case is to be tried. In civil cases, venue may be based on where the events giving rise to the cause of action took place or where the parties live or work. The venue of a criminal prosecution is the place where the crime was committed.

change of venue   Moving the trial of a case from one county or judicial district to another … . A motion may be made requesting that the court transfer the case to a proper court when one party believes that the action has been commenced in the wrong judicial district, or when one party feels that there are extenuating circumstances concerning the venue, such as publicity concerning the case.

IIII	*Law Office Scenario*	IIII

Sarah Woodward is a litigation paralegal at the Jackson & Green law firm. She has just been asked to attend an initial client meeting with a new client. Sarah will be involved in every aspect of the case. Following is a portion of Sarah's notes taken during the meeting with Janet Jones, the new client:

> Six months ago, on February 12, 1994, Janet Jones was injured in an automobile

collision. The accident occurred when the driver of a florist's van failed to yield at a stop sign and hit the car that Janet Jones was driving. The van was owned by the Elegant Flowers Corporation, and it was driven by Daisy Martin. Janet Jones sustained severe injuries during the accident for which she was treated in the hospital for one week. Her physician has indicated that she may have permanent residual effects from her injuries.

a lawsuit is commenced, including preliminary considerations, interviewing, and investigating.

Preliminary Considerations

There are several important decisions to be made prior to initiating a lawsuit. First, a determination must be made as to whether a cause of action exists, and the time limitations concerning the case must be examined. The attorneys also study the feasibility of the lawsuit and the ethical considerations in accepting the case.

Determining the Existence of a Cause of Action

Not all damages suffered by individuals are compensable through the litigation process. The mere fact that a party has been injured or has sustained some monetary loss does not in itself give that person the right to sue. A legal right to recover damages must exist. This legally recognized right to relief is known as a **cause of action**. For example, using our law office scenario, suppose that Daisy Martin (the driver who failed to stop at the stop sign) was injured in the collision. Can she sue Janet Jones to recover her damages?

Because Janet Jones did nothing wrong to cause Daisy Martin's injuries, Daisy Martin has no cause of action nor right to sue her.

In determining whether a cause of action exists, both the law and the facts in the case must be examined. First, it must be determined what general area of substantive law applies to the case. For example, is it a contract case or a tort case? Or is it both? Second, the general substantive area of law must be narrowed and a more specific topic identified. Then the law of that specific area must be examined to determine what factors or elements must be present before a cause of action is created. Once the elements of a cause of action have been ascertained, the final step in determining whether a cause of action exists in a particular case is to review the case itself to see if facts exist to support each of the elements.

Identifying the elements of a cause of action is important in the litigation process for various reasons. Probably most important is that each of the elements must be proven at trial for the plaintiff to prevail. In other words, to win the case the attorney must present evidence that supports each element of the cause of action. Also, in some state jurisdictions, the initial pleading must allege facts that support each element of the cause of action.

cause of action Circumstances that give a person the right to bring a lawsuit and receive relief from the court.

Knowing the elements of the cause of action in a particular case is essential for any litigation paralegal to assist the attorney in pretrial preparation. The litigation paralegal must have an understanding of what the attorney must prove at trial in order to gather appropriate evidence and conduct relevant discovery. It also equips the paralegal to prepare pleadings that comply with legal requirements and to review opposing pleadings for legal deficiencies.

Identifying the elements of a cause of action in a particular case may take some research. You might have to review case law and statutes. Secondary source books, such as encyclopedias and practice manuals, are valuable references. Formbooks, which often contain explanations and legal analysis of the forms, are also helpful.

Time Limitations

Even when all the elements of a cause of action exist in a particular case, the parties have time limits within which to initiate their lawsuits. It is important that litigation paralegals be aware of these time limits in every case.

The basic time limit is known as a **statute of limitations**. Unless a case is filed within the time period set by the applicable statute of limitations, it will be dismissed, regardless of the merits of the case. Statutes of limitations are found in state and federal codes and may vary from one jurisdiction to another. These time limitations also differ depending on the type of case.

Missing a statute of limitations can result in a malpractice claim against the law firm. Therefore, all litigation firms have set up calendar or tracking systems to remind them of these and other important dates. These calendaring systems are known as *tickler systems*. Before the advent of computers in the law firm, reminders were kept by hand. A firm might use a special calendar or a small file box organized by date. Today, numerous software packages exist that help firms keep track of important dates.

ELEMENTS OF A CAUSE OF ACTION OF FRAUD, BREACH OF CONTRACT, AND NEGLIGENCE
Fraud
1. The defendant misrepresented, concealed, or failed to disclose a fact.
2. The defendant knew of the falsity of the statement.
3. The defendant intended to defraud.
4. The plaintiff justifiably relied on the statement.
5. Damages resulted.
Breach of Contract
1. A contract existed.
2. The plaintiff performed or was excused from performance of his or her duties under the contract.
3. The defendant breached or failed to perform.
4. Damages resulted.
Negligence
1. The defendant must have a duty of due care toward the victim.
2. That duty must have been breached (a careless act).
3. The defendant's careless act must be the actual cause of the damages.
4. The defendant's careless act must be the proximate cause of the damages (i.e., the damages must be foreseeable).
5. Damages must have been sustained.

Before an action can begin, the plaintiff must first determine if the defendant failed to perform a duty to the plaintiff, causing damages or injury.

BALLENTINESBALLENTINESBALLENTINESBALLENTINESBALLENTINESBALLENTINESBALLENTINESBALLENTINESBALLENTINESBALLENTINESBALLENTINESBALLENTINESBALLENTINESBALLENTINES

statutes of limitations   Federal and state statutes prescribing the maximum period of time during which various types of civil actions and criminal prosecutions can be brought after the occurrence of the injury or the offense.

Feasibility of the Lawsuit

Even if a cause of action exists, and it is possible to bring a case before the expiration of the prescribed time limitations, the responsible attorney must determine the feasibility of a lawsuit in each particular case. The attorney and potential client must consider the probable outcome of a lawsuit, the damages sustained by the plaintiff, and the potential cost before a lawsuit is initiated.

Interviews and Investigation Prior to Litigation

Successful litigation begins with proper preparation and investigation of both the facts and the law. This preparation often starts with the client interview. In most cases, the client is the most knowledgeable source of information about the facts of the case. During a client interview, these facts are communicated to the attorney handling the case. The attorney can then determine what aspects of the case need further investigation or research. Not only is the client interview an essential step in the fact-gathering process, but it also establishes the foundation for a long-term relationship between the client and the firm.

Locating Witnesses or Defendants

Prior to filing a lawsuit, all available facts should be accumulated and organized. These facts are normally derived from the client, other witnesses, or documents. In addition to locating fact witnesses, the defendant should be located prior to filing suit. Sometimes pending litigation causes potential defendants to become elusive, so litigation paralegals are often asked to research the opposing party's address for service of process. This effort should be made early in the investigation so that it does not hamper proper service of the complaint or petition.

If the defendant is a corporation, the legal name of the company and the name and address of the agent for service of process must be obtained. This information is available from the Secretary of State's office and may be obtained by telephone or use of a computer service such as NEXIS or INFORMATION AMERICA. In some states, if the defendant is a partnership or limited partnership, this information may also be available from the Secretary of State's office.

Techniques for Interviewing Fact Witnesses

Once a potential fact witness has been located, a telephone call should be made to determine what information the witness has and whether the witness is willing to be interviewed. The witness should clearly understand who the potential parties in litigation are and what claims are being made on behalf of the client represented by paralegal's firm. If the witness has information that may be relevant to the case, a personal visit should be arranged to take his or her statement. This interview is a task often performed by a litigation paralegal or an investigator hired by the law firm.

An interview form may be drafted to suit the circumstances surrounding the case and the witness, to expedite the interview and help elicit all pertinent facts from the witness. This form, a tape recorder, and a writing pad are necessary tools for the witness interview. Although a verbatim tape recording of the interview is preferable, the witness may be reluctant to have his or her statement taped. In that event, written notes should be taken of the interview and signed by the witness before the interview concludes. Even if the statement is tape-recorded, written notes should be taken in case the tape player malfunctions. Once the interview has been completed, a typed witness statement should be prepared and transmitted to the witness for review and signing. A witness's statement may not be tape-recorded, in person or over the phone, without the witness's knowledge and permission. In some jurisdictions, such a taping is a crime.

Thoroughness is critical in a witness interview. Failure to be thorough can result in a witness changing or adding to his or her testimony at the time of trial or deposition. The litigation paralegal must obtain the most complete information possible about the client's claim.

Methods for Locating and Preserving Evidence

Testimony from witnesses is only one kind of evidence that can be used to prove a case. Written documents, photographs, and items of personal property are often introduced as evidence at trial to prove the facts of the case. Documents relating to the client, such as his or her medical bills and records or employment records, are usually easy to obtain by sending a request to the appropriate person or business, along with a release or authorization signed by the client.

To avoid charges by the opposition that evidence has been tampered with or replaced, each piece of evidence should be tracked from the moment it is obtained by the law firm through its final introduction as a trial exhibit. Evidence must be marked to indicate its source, date of acquisition, and storage location. An *evidence log* enables the litigation paralegal to maintain an accurate record of any evidence, including any transfer of custody. Each time evidence is removed from its storage location, the removal is documented on the evidence log.

The method for preserving evidence varies depending on the nature of the evidence. Photographs tend to fade or suffer damage from handling. X-rays require special folders for preservation. An original $300,000 note might be maintained in the firm's vault, with a copy of the note retained in an envelope labeled with the location of the original.

Police Reports—Local, county, or state police and Department of Motor Vehicles

Automobile Ownership—Department of Motor Vehicles

Insurance Coverage—State Department of Insurance, Department of Motor Vehicles, individual insurance company

Weather Reports—United States Weather Bureau

Fire Reports—Fire Marshal

Aviation Records (on accidents or safety standards)—Federal Aviation Administration and National Transportation Safety Board

Property Ownership or Taxes—Local tax assessor's office, State Department of Revenue, and county clerk's office

Birth and Death Records—Bureau of Vital Statistics and local coroner's office

Medical Treatment—Doctor, hospital, ambulance company, x-ray firm, and physical therapist

Personal Data—Registrar of Voters, criss-cross directories, U.S. Post Office, Social Security Office, county court records (including judgments and/or liens, criminal, marriage and divorce), and computerized services such as NEXIS and INFORMATION AMERICA

Newspaper or Publicity—Local newspapers and television stations, archives of local library, and computerized services such as NEXIS and INFORMATION AMERICA

Types and Sources of Evidence in a Personal Injury Case These are just some of the sources that can be used by a paralegal when gathering evidence.

STYLE OF CASE: _____

EVIDENCE: _____

DATE ACQUIRED: _____   ACQUIRED BY: _____

MANNER BY WHICH ACQUIRED: _____

PARTICULAR IDENTIFYING MARKS: _____

LOCATIONS OF EVIDENCE: _____

EVIDENCE CUSTODIAN: _____

CHAIN OF EVIDENCE CUSTODY:

RELEASED TO   DATE   PURPOSE OF RELEASE

_____

_____

_____

_____

_____

An Example of an Evidence Log An evidence log is a document attached to physical evidence to record its chain of possession.

Some forms of evidence do not lend themselves to storage in the law firm during lengthy litigation because of their size or daily use on a job site. Photographs of these exhibits may be taken and retained in the client's file for use in preparing the case for trial, at which time the original piece of evidence may be introduced.

Expert Witnesses

In a case involving technical or medical issues, expert witnesses are often necessary. Experts can perform several functions in a case. They can be hired in an advisory capacity to explain the technical aspects of the case to the attorney. More often, they are hired to be witnesses during the trial. Before individuals are allowed to testify as experts, they must be qualified by the court to do so. In qualifying experts, the court looks at their education, skill, and experience in the subject field. If an individual is qualified as an expert, at trial he or she can explain and simplify complicated technical issues for the judge or jury.

The decision to hire an expert witness is made by the supervising attorney. However, the litigation paralegal is often asked to locate an expert. Suggested sources for locating potential experts include:

Professional organizations

Published court records of experts

Other attorneys in the office

Colleges or universities

Professional journals

Attorneys who have handled similar litigation.

Before deciding to use a particular expert, the expert's résumé should be reviewed to determine if he or she has testified in earlier cases. If the potential witness has qualified as an expert in other cases, he or she is likely to be qualified by the court in the case at hand. Previous cases should also be reviewed to make sure that the expert has not given testimony that would contradict the testimony he or she now expects to give.

The initial interview and investigation process often involves all of the foregoing procedures. For example, suppose that you, as a litigation paralegal, have just been given the Janet Jones file after her initial interview with the attorney you work for, and you have been asked to begin the preliminary interviews and investigation. You might take several steps to gather information immediately. Your first tasks might include obtaining as much information as possible about Janet Jones's medical condition and expenses, about the accident itself, and about the possible defendant or defendants. Janet Jones's doctors would be contacted for their medical records and evaluations, as well as any hospitals where Janet Jones was treated. In addition, you might contact her employer to obtain information concerning Janet Jones's lost wages. To obtain information concerning the accident, a police report (if one was completed), any accident reports filed with the parties' insurance companies, and statements from witnesses may be needed. You must ascertain the defendant's location, and you should call the Secretary of State to obtain information concerning the Elegant Flowers Corporation, the owner of the van and the employer of Daisy Martin. In addition, some thought might be given to using one or more of Janet Jones's doctors as expert witnesses.

The Initial Pleadings

After completing preliminary investigation, interviews, and research, the attorney and client determine whether to pursue the case. If the decision is made to proceed, the litigation process formally begins with the preparation and filing of appropriate pleadings. After a general discussion of pleadings, this section focuses on the specific types of pleadings, including the complaint and responses to the complaint (e.g., answers and counterclaims). The section concludes with a brief look at motions, another important type of document closely related to pleadings.

Pleadings in General

Pleadings are the various documents filed in a court proceeding that define the nature of the dispute between the parties. Not all documents filed with the court are pleadings. The term *pleading* technically refers only to papers that contain statements, or allegations, describing the contentions and defenses of the parties to the lawsuit. The pleadings set the framework for all of the following steps and proceedings; if an issue is not raised in the pleadings, the parties may be prevented from bringing it up at trial. The duties of litigation paralegals often include the drafting of these documents. They are also often asked to review pleadings prepared by the opposing side.

The content and format of the various pleadings are largely controlled by the appropriate statutory law. Cases filed in federal court are governed primarily by the **Federal Rules of Civil Procedure**. Cases filed in a state court are governed by the laws of the state and the individual rules of many county or area courts, known as local rules of court. Within the federal court system, various district courts may also have their own local rules.

pleadings   Formal statements by the parties to an action setting forth their claims or defenses.

Federal Rules of Civil Procedure   A comprehensive set of rules governing procedure in civil cases in United States District Courts.

Local rules can differ from one court to another, even if the courts are located in the same state. Before preparing or filing any pleading, therefore, check all local rules!

The Complaint

The initial pleading prepared and filed on behalf of the plaintiff in an action, which starts the court process, is generally known as a **complaint**, or in some cases a **petition**. The complaint is the pleading in which the plaintiff states the basis for the lawsuit. Generally, the complaint does the following:

1. Identifies the plaintiffs and defendants in the lawsuit and describes their status and capacity to sue and be sued

2. Contains a statement showing that the court in which it is filed has proper jurisdiction and venue

3. Describes the factual basis for the lawsuit

4. Makes a request or demand for some relief from the court.

The complaint itself usually follows a set format, with various parts:

1. The caption—the part of the complaint that identifies the court in which the complaint is filed, the names of the plaintiffs and defendants, and the title of the document

2. The allegations (or causes of action)—a description of the parties, statements showing proper jurisdiction and venue, the factual basis for the lawsuit, and a description of the loss or damages incurred

3. The prayer—a request for some relief or remedy from the court

4. The subscription and verification—the signature of the attorney filing the document, the date, and the plaintiff's statement, under penalty of perjury, that the contents of the complaint are true.

The Parties to a Lawsuit

The parties to the lawsuit are known as the **plaintiff**, the one who files the action, and the **defendant**, the one who is sued. They are identified in the caption by their names and an indication of whether they are plaintiffs or defendants. Most commonly, a party to a lawsuit will be an individual, a corporation, a partnership or other unincorporated business, or a governmental agency. Unless a party is simply an individual, the status of the party is usually described both in the caption and in a separate allegation within the body of the complaint. For example, in the Janet Jones case described in our law office scenario, the plaintiff is Janet Jones, and the defendants are Daisy Martin, an individual, and the Elegant Flower Corporation, an Oregon corporation.

The parties listed in the caption must have **capacity**, or the legal right to sue or be sued. Competent, adult individuals generally have the right to sue and be sued. However, children or **incompetent** adults do not have the capacity to pursue their own lawsuits. Unless a general guardian or conservator has already been appointed, the court will appoint a special person, referred to as a **guardian ad litem**, to pursue the case on behalf of the minor or incompetent person.

BALLENTINESBALLENTINESBALLENTINESBALLENTINESBALLENTINESBALLENTINESBALLENTINESBALLENTINESBALLENTINESBALLENTINESBALLENTINESBALLENTINESBALLENTINES

complaint The initial pleading in a civil action, in which the plaintiff alleges a cause of action and asks that the wrong done be remedied by the court.

petition The name given in some jurisdictions to a complaint or other pleading that alleges a cause of action.

plaintiff A person who brings a lawsuit.

defendant The person against whom an action is brought.

capacity Competency in law. A person's ability to understand the nature and effect of the act in which he or she is engaged.

incompetent person A person who is not legally qualified for a specific activity (such as giving testimony or entering into a contract) by reason of … mental incapacity.

guardian ad litem A person appointed by the court to represent and protect the interests of a minor or an incompetent person during litigation.

Pleading Jurisdiction and Venue

The complaint in any action must contain some allegation showing that the lawsuit is filed in the proper court. The court must have jurisdiction to hear the case, and the case must be filed in the proper venue.

Pleading the Claim or Cause of Action

Although the complaint or petition usually follows certain legal technicalities, its primary purpose is to show the factual basis for the lawsuit. It does not contain any discussion or analysis of legal theories. However, when reviewing the facts alleged in the complaint, the defendant's attorney and the court should be able to tell that there is a legal basis for the lawsuit, even though the legal basis need not be expressly stated in the complaint. How detailed this factual description must be depends on the jurisdiction in which the lawsuit is filed.

A complaint may contain any number of causes of action or counts. Whenever more than one cause of action arises out of the same general factual situation, the rules of pleading usually allow them to be joined in the same complaint.

Demand for Relief

Every complaint or petition filed in an action contains a demand for relief from the court, often called a **prayer**. Courts have the power to grant two different types of relief, money damages and equitable relief. *Money damages* usually means the award of money to the plaintiff as compensation for some loss. **Equitable relief**, on the other hand, is granted when the court orders the defendant to do something, or to stop doing something other than simply paying money damages. In some state jurisdictions, only certain courts have the power to grant equitable relief.

Money damages are the most common relief sought in civil lawsuits. The primary purpose of damages in a civil suit is to compensate plaintiffs for loss they have sustained. These damages are known as **compensatory damages**, although they may be referred to by other names in certain kinds of cases. For example, in personal injury cases such as the Janet Jones case, compensatory damages are categorized as either special damages or general damages. **Special damages** are actual out-of-pocket expenses incurred by the plaintiff, such as doctor's bills and lost earnings. **General damages** are not out-of-pocket expenses, but include other elements such as pain and suffering, loss of use of a limb, or disfigurement caused by a scar. Even though general damages do not reimburse the plaintiff for an economic expense, they do compensate the plaintiff for some loss.

Although money damages in most civil cases are compensatory in nature, sometimes a plaintiff is entitled to recover **punitive**, or exemplary, **damages**. These are meant to punish the defendant and are awarded only when the defendant has committed some extremely offensive act. Such damages are not favored by the courts and come under careful scrutiny by the appellate courts. Nevertheless, they are allowed in some cases.

BALLENTINESBALLENTINESBALLENTINESBALLENTINESBALLENTINESBALLENTINESBALLENTINESBALLENTINESBALLENTINESBALLENTINESBALLENTINESBALLENTINESBALLENTINESBALLENTINESBALLENTINES

prayer   Portion of a bill in equity or a petition [complaint] that asks for ... relief and specifies the relief sought.

equitable relief   A remedy available in equity rather than at law; generally relief other than money damages.

compensatory damages   Damages recoverable in a lawsuit for loss or injury suffered by the plaintiff as a result of the defendant's conduct.

special damages   Damages that may be added to the general damages in a case, and arise from the particular or special circumstances of the case.

general damages   Damages that are the natural and probable result of the wrongful acts complained of.

punitive damages   Damages that are awarded over and above compensatory damages or actual damages because of the wanton, reckless, or malicious nature of the wrong done by the plaintiff. Such damages bear no relation to the plaintiff's actual loss and are often called exemplary damages, because their purpose is to make an example of the plaintiff to discourage others from engaging in the same kind of conduct in the future.

In the course of any lawsuit, the parties will inevitably incur substantial expenses and costs for such items as filing fees, process server fees, deposition fees, and expert witness fees. Costs are not included in computing the plaintiff's damages. However, if the plaintiff wins the lawsuit, he or she is usually awarded certain costs in addition to the actual damages. In contrast, should the defendant win the case, he or she is normally awarded costs from the plaintiff. Unless the lawsuit is based on a contract that specifically provides for the payment of attorney fees in the event of a legal dispute, or unless there is some special law governing the situation, parties are expected to pay their own attorney fees.

Lawsuits in which equitable relief is sought are known as *actions in equity,* whereas lawsuits in which money damages are sought are known as *actions in law.* A complaint may combine a request for equitable relief and money damages.

The types of equitable relief that can be ordered by a court of equitable jurisdiction are varied. Some of the more common types of equitable relief are:

Specific performance—An order requiring a party to perform a contract

Rescission—An order rescinding or voiding a contract

Restitution—An order to return money or property, usually paid in connection with a contract that was subsequently rescinded

Declaratory relief—A court order defining or explaining the rights and obligations of the parties under some contract

Quiet title—An order clarifying ownership of real property

Injunction—An order requiring a party to stop doing something

Mandamus—An order requiring a party to do something.

When injunctive relief is the primary object of a lawsuit, the plaintiff will often request some immediate provisional remedy from the court as soon as a complaint is filed. Provisional remedies usually include a temporary restraining order and a preliminary **injunction**. A **temporary restraining order** may be granted without any formal hearing, based primarily on affidavits or declarations submitted to the court. Should the court decide to keep the restraining order in effect after a **hearing**, it will issue a **preliminary injunction**. A preliminary injunction remains in effect until the trial, at which time the injunction becomes permanent if the plaintiffs prove their case.

Drafting the Complaint

Once the parties to the lawsuit are identified, it must be determined what causes of action the plaintiff has and what relief is to be requested. Then the paralegal can draft the complaint for the attorney's review. Before actually preparing a document, however, check your local court rules regarding technical requirements for the pleading. Some local court rules require a certain kind or size of paper; others require a certain size of print or a special format that must be followed.

BALLENTINESBALLENTINESBALLENTINESBALLENTINESBALLENTINESBALLENTINESBALLENTINESBALLENTINESBALLENTINESBALLENTINESBALLENTINESBALLENTINESBALLENTINESBALLENTINES

injunction   A court order that commands or prohibits some act or course of conduct. It is preventive in nature and designed to protect a plaintiff from irreparable injury to his or her property or other rights by prohibiting or commanding the doing of certain acts.

temporary restraining order (TRO)   [I]njunctive relief that the court is empowered to grant, without notice to the opposite party and pending a hearing on the merits, upon a showing that failure to do so will result in "immediate and irreparable injury, loss, or damage."

hearing   A proceeding in which evidence is introduced and witnesses are examined so that findings of fact can be made and a determination rendered. Although, in a general sense, all trials can be said to be hearings, not all hearings are trials. The difference is in the degree of formality each requires, with the rules of procedure being more relaxed in hearings.

preliminary injunction   An injunction granted prior to a full hearing on the merits. Its purpose is to preserve the status quo until the final hearing.

Also, to save a great deal of time, use some of the various formbooks within the law firm or library containing sample complaints that deal with similar factual situations (as well as any form files kept by the law firm). Even the most experienced litigation attorneys and paralegals follow forms whenever possible. One formbook that is popular for assisting with the drafting of pleadings is *American Jurisprudence Pleading and Practice Forms Annotated (Am.Jur.),* published by The Lawyers Cooperative Publishing Company and Bancroft Whitney Company. Additionally, some illustrative form pleadings are included in an Appendix of Forms found with the Federal Rules of Civil Procedure.

The first part of any complaint or petition is known as the *caption*. The caption contains the name of the court in which the action is being filed, the names of the plaintiffs and defendants, and the title of the document. In some jurisdictions it also contains the name, address, and telephone number of the attorney and who the attorney represents. In other jurisdictions, the caption also contains the addresses of the plaintiff and defendant.

Below the caption is the body of the complaint, containing various jurisdictional and factual allegations that constitute the plaintiff's cause of action. These allegations are broken down into short, numbered paragraphs. Because there is no absolute method for paragraphing, the use of formbooks or other sample complaints is very helpful in setting up this part of the complaint. In the absence of a form to follow, normal paragraphing rules can be followed.

Even though there is no mandatory order in which paragraphing must be done, there are usual and customary ways in which it is done:

1. In most complaints, paragraphs on jurisdiction and venue appear first

2. If any of the parties are businesses, either corporate or otherwise, allegations concerning their status or capacity then follow

3. If there is more than one defendant in the lawsuit, it is standard to include an "agency" allegation, claiming that one or more of the defendants are agents or employees of one or more of the other defendants. Such an allegation refers to the substantive legal principle of vicarious liability or respondeat superior, a concept that imposes liability on an employer for certain acts of its employees

4. Following these standard allegations are various allegations describing the factual basis for the lawsuit and a description of the damages that were suffered.

All statements contained in a complaint, or any pleading, should be true. However, at times a plaintiff may not be certain about some facts that must be alleged in the complaint. For example, the plaintiff may not know for sure if the defendant business is a corporation or some other business entity, although the plaintiff may believe that it is incorporated. In such cases, the proper way to plead the facts is "on information and belief." For example, using the Janet Jones scenario, if the van driven by Daisy Martin was filled with flowers to be delivered at the time of the accident and it appears that Daisy Martin was driving the Elegant Flowers Van on business, but there is no other available evidence to support that fact, the following paragraph might be used:

On information and belief, Plaintiff alleges that at all times herein mentioned, the defendant Daisy Martin was the agent and employee of the Elegant Flowers Corporation.

Many complaints contain more than one cause of action. In such situations, it is important to remember that each cause of action should be sufficient in itself to constitute a legally sufficient complaint. Therefore, it is often necessary to restate many of the same allegations that were alleged in prior causes of action. It is not necessary, however, to expressly restate those allegations. If something is being repeated it may be referred to and incorporated by reference.

UNITED STATES DISTRICT COURT
FOR THE NORTHERN DISTRICT OF CALIFORNIA

JANET JONES

    PLAINTIFF,   CIVIL NO. 98765

VS.   COMPLAINT FOR NEGLIGENCE

DAISY MARTIN AND THE

ELEGANT FLOWERS CORPORATION,

AN OREGON CORPORATION,

    DEFENDANT

Plaintiff JANET JONES alleges:

JURISDICTION

1. Plaintiff JANET JONES is, and was at all times herein mentioned, domiciled in and a citizen of the state of California. Defendant DAISY MARTIN was at all times herein mentioned domiciled in and a citizen of the state of Oregon. Further, Defendant ELEGANT FLOWERS CORPORATION is an Oregon Corporation, qualified to do business in the state of California.

2. At all times herein mentioned, plaintiff was and now is a resident of the judicial district in which this action is filed.

3. At all times herein mentioned, defendant, ELEGANT FLOWERS CORPORATION, was the owner of a certain motor vehicle, Oregon license number 456 ABC.

4. At all times herein mentioned, defendant DAISY MARTIN was operating said motor vehicle with the permission and consent of defendant ELEGANT FLOWERS CORPORATION.

5. At all times herein mentioned, defendant DAISY MARTIN was the agent, employee, and servant of defendant ELEGANT FLOWERS CORPORATION, and at all times was acting within the course and scope of said agency and employment.

6. On December 3, 1994, defendant DAISY MARTIN negligently and carelessly drove the above mentioned motor vehicle, Oregon license 456 ABC, causing it to collide with another vehicle driven by plaintiff at the intersection of Market Street and Hill Street in San Francisco, California.

Complaint The complaint filed by Janet Jones against Daisy Martin and the Elegant Flowers Corporation is a cause of action for negligence. Each court has specific requirements on how legal documents are to be prepared and filed with the court.

7.   As a result, plaintiff was severely injured, having had her leg and arm broken and having suffered other bruises, contusions, and muscle strains. Also as a result, plaintiff was prevented from continuing her normal activities, suffered and continues to suffer great pain of body and mind, lost wages, and incurred expenses for medical attention and hospitalization in the sum of ten thousand dollars ($10,000) and will continue to incur such expenses in an amount as yet undetermined.

Wherefore plaintiff JANET JONES demands judgment against defendants and each of them in the sum of $100,000.00 and costs.

Dated January 4, 1995.

_____

Terry Alvarez

ALVAREZ & COE

100 Market Street

San Francisco, CA 94101

Attorney for Plaintiffs

Complaint   *(Continued)*

Remember that not all parties to the complaint must be parties to all causes of action. However, each of those named in the caption must be a party to at least one cause of action within the complaint.

The prayer is usually located after the allegations in the complaint. At the end of the prayer are the date, signature, and address of the attorney filing the complaint. This is sometimes referred to as the *subscription*. Whenever an attorney signs a pleading in federal court, that signature represents the attorney's affirmation that the allegations in the pleadings are made in good faith.

Filing the Complaint

After the complaint has been prepared, reviewed by the attorney, and properly signed, it can be filed in the proper court. *Filing* of a complaint means that the original of the document is given to the court. The court in turn assigns a number, known as a *docket number,* to the case and starts a file that will contain all subsequent pleadings and other documents dealing with the case. All subsequent pleadings and papers filed in connection with the case must contain the docket number to ensure proper filing. The court usually requires a fee for filing a complaint, which must be paid before the court will accept the document, although filing fees may be waived if the plaintiff can show financial hardship. The amount of the filing fee is usually determined by local rules or by statute. Whenever a complaint is filed with the court, copies of the complaint on which the docket number and date of filing can be noted should be kept. Many courts now accept filings by facsimile (fax), for an additional fee. Each court must be contacted for its own rules regarding fax filings.

Regardless of how a complaint is filed, the document must always be filed within the statute of limitations. Failure to file it on time will result in the lawsuit being dismissed.

The Summons

In some jurisdictions, the court issues a summons when the complaint is filed. A **summons** form notifies the defendant that he or she has been sued and should answer the complaint by a certain date. Issuing the summons simply involves the clerk of the court affixing his or her signature to the form. It is usually expected that the attorney for the plaintiff will have filled out the form for submission to the clerk at the time the complaint is filed. However, the original summons is not filed with the court at this time. The plaintiff retains it until after the defendants have been served. At that time the original summons can be returned to the court for filing, along with evidence that the defendants have been served. In some courts, if the summons is not returned to the court within a certain amount of time, the case can be dismissed.

Other jurisdictions may not require the signature of the clerk of court on the summons, or may not require that the complaint be filed before the summons and complaint are served on the defendant. In those jurisdictions, a copy of the summons and complaint are served on the defendant by an agent of the plaintiff's attorney or by the local sheriff. The original summons and complaint are filed with the court at a later date, along with an **affidavit of service**.

Service of the Complaint

The defendant in any lawsuit is entitled to receive notice of the action. This is accomplished by **service of process**. A copy of the summons and a copy of the complaint must be delivered to the defendant. It is the plaintiff's responsibility, rather than the court's, to see that the defendant is properly served. Litigation paralegals are often asked to arrange for service of the complaint.

All jurisdictions have rules regarding who can serve a complaint, how it can be served, and the time limits for service. Although there may be some differences among jurisdictions, the concepts are similar. Generally, plaintiffs cannot serve papers themselves; someone must do it for them. Various law enforcement agencies, such as the U.S. Marshal or a local sheriff, sometimes take responsibility for serving civil complaints. They may, however, charge the plaintiff a fee for providing these services. In other instances, the complaint is served by a *licensed process server,* an individual licensed by the state to serve papers. In some cases, a complaint can be served by any adult who is not a party to the action.

The litigation paralegal must be concerned not only about who serves the complaint, but also with how it is served. A common method is **personal service**. When personal service is required, a copy of the summons and complaint must be personally delivered to the defendant. Sometimes personal service is difficult, if not impossible. Some laws, such as Rule 4 of the Federal Rules of Civil Procedure, allow a copy of the summons and complaint to be left with a competent adult at the defendant's residence. Some states also allow the papers to be served by mail, or in some cases by publication. When personal service cannot be accomplished, the appropriate laws must be reviewed to determine alternatives. At issue in the *Trammel* case was whether service of process on a 12-year-old residing at the defendant's residence constituted proper service of process.

BALLENTINESBALLENTINESBALLENTINESBALLENTINESBALLENTINESBALLENTINESBALLENTINESBALLENTINESBALLENTINESBALLENTINESBALLENTINESBALLENTINESBALLENTINESBALLENTINES

summons   In a civil case, the process by which an action is commenced and the defendant is brought within the jurisdiction of the court.

affidavit of service   An affidavit that certifies that process has been served. Also referred to as a *return of service* or *proof of service*.

service of process   Delivery of a summons, writ, complaint, or other process to the opposite party, or other person entitled to receive it, in such manner as the law prescribes, whether by leaving a copy at his or her residence, by mailing a copy to his or her attorney, or by publication.

personal service of process   The actual or direct delivery of process (such as a writ or a summons) to the person to whom it is directed or to someone authorized to receive it on his or her behalf.

AO440 (Rev. 5/85) Summons in a Civil Action

United States District Court

_____ DISTRICT OF _____

SUMMONS IN A CIVIL ACTION

v.   CASE NUMBER:

TO: (Name and Address of Defendant)

YOU ARE HEREBY SUMMONED and required to file with the Clerk of this Court and serve upon

PLAINTIFF'S ATTORNEY (name and address)

an answer to the complaint which is herewith served upon you, within _____ days after service of this summons upon you, exclusive of the day of service. If you fail to do so, judgment by default will be taken against you for the relief demanded in the complaint.

_____   _____
CLERK   DATE

_____
BY DEPUTY CLERK

Summons A summons is a document that notifies a defendant that he or she has been sued and that an answer to the complaint should be filed with the court by a certain date.

If the defendant in the lawsuit is a corporation, service is usually accomplished by serving an officer or director of the corporation or by serving the agent for service of process. The names and addresses of corporate officers, directors, or agents for service can usually be obtained from the Secretary of State where the corporation is incorporated or does business.

In addition to the rules for the manner of service, there are also rules regarding time limits that may affect service. For example, in federal court the copy of the complaint and summons

---

TRAMMEL, et al.
v.
NATIONAL BANK OF GEORGIA
No. 62590
Court of Appeals of Georgia
Oct. 8, 1981
285 S.E.2d 590 (Ga. Ct. App. 1981)

Appellants appeal from adverse summary judgments in an action on a promissory note and a counterclaim for conversion of certain accessories attached to the truck securing the note.

On October 10, 1979, plaintiff/appellee National Bank of Georgia filed suit against defendants/appellants Robert D. and Kathy J. Trammel for the deficiency on the balance of a promissory note. The collateral for the note, a 1972 Ford pickup truck, had been previously repossessed and sold at a properly advertised public auction. The appellants had requested that the truck be sold at auction. They had also requested that they be reimbursed for the value of accessories added to the truck by the appellants.

In their answer and counterclaim, appellants raised the defenses of lack of personal jurisdiction, improper service, and partial failure of consideration ... .

After submission of affidavits the plaintiff moved for and was awarded summary judgment on the main action and on the defendant's counterclaim. Defendants appeal. Held:

1. The defendants, by affidavit, stated that service was left at their house with their twelve-year-old daughter. They contend that their twelve-year-old daughter is not "a person of suitable age and discretion" as required for alternative service in [the Georgia statutes]. In support of this theory defendants cite numerous statutes which limit the ability of twelve-year-olds to function as adults. This court is aware of the instances wherein the law deems a twelve-year-old [to be lacking] requisite capacity to perform certain acts.

* * *

Under the facts of this case summary judgment for the plaintiff on its complaint was proper unless, as a matter of law, the trial court lacked jurisdiction of the defendant. Thus, the first issue to be decided is whether the defendant's 12-year-old daughter was a person of suitable age and discretion.

Defendants argue that "the fact that the Trammels actually received the service copies intended for them and thereby gained actual knowledge of the pendency of this suit is irrelevant." We do not agree ... . We are aware of those decisions by our court that " '[w]here there has been no service of a suit, or waiver thereof, the necessity of service is not dispensed with by the mere fact that the defendant may in some way learn of the filing of the suit.' " ... Also, we are in complete agreement that "no case can proceed without service upon the defendant in one of the modes prescribed by law, unless service is waived" ... and "the necessity of service is not dispensed with by the mere fact that the defendant may in some way learn of or have actual knowledge of the filing of the action." ... However, in the instant case the return of service shows, and the contention of plaintiff is, that service was properly made at the home of the defendant, upon a person of suitable age and discretion, and is in a mode prescribed by law. The fact that the defendants received the service from the person served is some indication that that person was of suitable age and discretion and that service was effectuated in such a manner to reasonably accomplish it. ...

The only evidence that the appellant submits in support of his contention that the daughter of appellants was not of suitable age and discretion is that she is 12 years old. We refuse to hold as a matter of law that a 12-year-old is not "a person of suitable age and discretion." This is a factual matter and the presumption of valid service stands unless rebutted by the party which moves to set aside the service ... . We find evidence of service of process on a 12-year-old individual residing in the defendant's residence, without more, does not reflect insufficient service of process ... .

Judgment affirmed.

must be served within 120 days of the filing of the complaint. Failure to do so, without justification, can result in dismissal of the action. The law firm tickler or calendar is often used to track timely service. After service has been completed, the person serving the complaint must complete an affidavit of service, which is often on the reverse side of the summons. The affidavit of service should be filed with the court.

Responses to the Initial Pleadings

After the initial pleading has been filed and served, the next step in the litigation process is up to the defendants. At this point they have various options. The defendants can contest the lawsuit, negotiate a settlement with the plaintiff, or do nothing at all. If the defendants challenge the lawsuit, they can do so on two bases: they can either contest the facts of the case or they can challenge the action on some legal basis.

Time Limits

If the defendants choose to contest the action, they must act within certain time limitations. This time limit is normally fixed by the statutory laws or rules of procedure of the jurisdiction in which the action is pending, and can vary from one jurisdiction to another. In federal court, this time is normally 20 days, although there are some exceptions. Frequently, a substantial part of this time will already have elapsed before the defendant locates and retains an attorney. As a result, the attorney may have only a few days in which to evaluate the case, consider the possibility of an early settlement, or prepare a proper response to the complaint or petition.

Stipulations Enlarging Time

A stipulation enlarging time in which to respond is an agreement between the attorneys in an action that the defendant's attorney may take additional time in which to respond. In federal court, this agreement or stipulation must be approved by the court, although in some state courts it need not be. If the stipulation does not require court approval, a letter between the attorneys confirming their agreement will suffice.

Motions to Extend or Enlarge Time

If the defendant's attorney feels that more time is needed to prepare a response, and the plaintiff's attorney is unwilling to agree, an extension of time can be requested from the court. This is done by making a motion with the court. A **motion** is a formal request to the court for some kind of order. A motion to extend or enlarge time is usually made by filing papers with the court explaining the request and the reasons for it, serving these papers on the other attorneys in the action, and then possibly appearing in court for a brief hearing on the motion.

The Answer

An **answer** is a pleading that challenges the plaintiff's right to the relief requested in the initial pleading. Normally this is done by contesting all or some of the facts alleged in the complaint or petition. Answers are prepared using one of three main formats: the general denial, the specific denial, or the qualified denial.

The substance of a *general denial* is only one paragraph or allegation, in which the defendant denies all of the allegations contained in the complaint. In federal court, general denials are proper when the defendant is denying all of the factual contentions of the complaint, including the allegations of subject matter jurisdiction, personal jurisdiction, and venue. Some state courts severely limit the use of general denials. Moreover,

BALLENTINESBALLENTINESBALLENTINESBALLENTINESBALLENTINESBALLENTINESBALLENTINESBALLENTINESBALLENTINESBALLENTINESBALLENTINESBALLENTINESBALLENTINESBALLENTINESBALLENTINES

motion   An application made to a court for the purpose of obtaining an order or rule directing something to be done in favor of the applicant.

answer   A pleading in response to a complaint.

in some courts general denials cannot be used if the complaint has been verified.

A *specific denial* is an answer in which the defendant specifically replies to each of the contentions alleged in the complaint. The defendant replies to the various contentions by admitting them, denying them, or denying them on information and belief. Occasionally, a defendant may not be absolutely certain about a certain allegation or may not have sufficient knowledge of the facts. Just as the plaintiff is allowed to plead facts on information and belief, so also can the defendant deny allegations in the same way. Denials on information and belief should be used only when the pleader really does not have first-hand knowledge of the true facts.

A *qualified denial* is a combination of specific and general responses. In a qualified denial, the answering defendant expressly admits or denies certain allegations, then generally denies everything else.

An **affirmative defense** is a fact or circumstance that will defeat the plaintiff's claim even if the plaintiff can prove every contention alleged in the complaint. For example, suppose that the plaintiff has filed a lawsuit for breach of contract alleging that the plaintiff loaned the defendant $75,000, that when the loan came due the defendant refused to pay, and that the defendant continues to refuse to pay. If the plaintiff could prove these allegations at trial, the plaintiff would prevail and obtain a judgment for the amount of the unpaid loan. If the defendant, however, alleges and proves that he filed bankruptcy and that this debt was discharged in bankruptcy, the plaintiff will lose the case. The fact that the debt was discharged in bankruptcy is an affirmative defense and operates to defeat the plaintiff's claim.

True affirmative defenses must be alleged in the answer or they will generally be deemed waived. A partial list of affirmative defenses is found in Rule 8(c) of the Federal Rules of Civil Procedure. If any of those defenses are claimed in an action in federal court, they must be specifically alleged in the answer as an affirmative defense. Failure to do so could result in the defense being waived. The list in Rule 8, however, is not all-inclusive. Other affirmative defenses exist under different areas of substantive laws.

Drafting the Answer

An answer is a pleading that is filed in court; thus, it follows the same general format as the complaint or petition. It contains a caption, body or allegations, prayer or "wherefore" clause, and signature. Formbooks can be as helpful in drafting answers as they are in drafting complaints.

The content of the body of the answer depends on whether it is a specific, general, or qualified denial. A general denial contains only one paragraph, as discussed previously. A specific denial is more detailed. However, only a few different paragraphs or allegations are typically used in an answer, including:

1. Paragraphs specifically denying certain allegations contained in the complaint
2. Paragraphs denying on information and belief certain allegations contained in the complaint
3. Paragraphs admitting specific allegations contained in the complaint.

In a qualified denial, the following paragraph might appear in the body of the answer:

Defendant admits the allegations of Paragraphs 1, 2, and 3 of the complaint and denies each and every other allegation of plaintiff's complaint.

In a complaint containing more than one count or cause of action, it is common to find a paragraph incorporating paragraphs from previous counts.

affirmative defense   A defense that amounts to more than simply a denial of the allegations of the plaintiff's complaint. It sets up new matter which, if proven, could result in a judgment against the plaintiff even if all the allegations of the complaint are true.

Responding to this paragraph sometimes presents difficulties, especially when some of the incorporated paragraphs have been admitted and some denied. The following is an example of a possible response:

In answer to Paragraph 8 of Count Two of the complaint, wherein plaintiff incorporates by reference certain paragraphs of Count One of the complaint, defendant admits, denies, and alleges to the same effect and in the same manner as she admitted, denied, and alleged to those specific paragraphs previously in this answer.

When answering a complaint with more than one count or cause of action, each cause of action or count can be responded to as a whole in the answer, or the answer may contain replies to each allegation in the various counts.

Whether a defendant files a general denial or a specific denial, affirmative defenses might apply. When drafting an answer, you must review the substantive law of the case as well as the facts to determine whether an affirmative defense exists. Affirmative defenses appear in the body of the answer, following the paragraphs denying or admitting the allegations in the complaint.

The body of the answer is followed by a simple prayer, or "wherefore" clause; the date; and the attorney's signature. In some courts, including federal court, the attorney's signature is followed by the attorney's address. The prayer usually requests that the plaintiffs be allowed no recovery.

Service and Filing of the Answer

After the answer is prepared, it must be served on the plaintiff or the plaintiff's attorney and it must be filed in court. The procedures for serving an answer are usually very simple. If a party is represented by an attorney, service can be made on the attorney rather than the party. Although the answer can be personally served on the plaintiff's attorney, mailing a copy of the answer to the attorney usually suffices.

The answer is filed in court in the same way a complaint is filed. Courts may also require that a filing fee accompany the answer.

Counterclaims, Cross-Claims, and Third-Party Complaints

At times, defendants have their own claims and are entitled to some relief from the court. They may be asserting this claim against the plaintiff, a co-defendant, or a third party (someone who is not a party to the original action). In federal court, when defendants assert a claim against a plaintiff, it is known as a **counterclaim**. When the claim is asserted against a co-defendant, it is known as a **cross-claim**. When the claim is against a new party, it is known as a **third-party complaint**. Counterclaims and cross-claims are included with the answer. Third-party complaints are pleadings separate from the answer. Regardless of which form the defendants' claim takes, the content of the claim is the same. The content of the defendants' claim for relief is similar to the content of the plaintiff's claim in a complaint. Usually the defendants state the jurisdictional basis for the court's hearing the matter, unless the basis for the court's jurisdiction is the same as in the complaint. This statement is followed by numbered paragraphs describing the factual basis for the claim.

In some state jurisdictions, although defendants have the same rights to assert claims, the format

---

BALLENTINESBALLENTINESBALLENTINESBALLENTINESBALLENTINESBALLENTINESBALLENTINESBALLENTINESBALLENTINESBALLENTINESBALLENTINESBALLENTINESBALLENTINES

counterclaim   A cause of action on which a defendant in a lawsuit might have sued the plaintiff in a separate action. Such a cause of action, stated in a separate division of a defendant's answer, is a counterclaim.

cross-claim   A counterclaim against a coplaintiff or a codefendant.

third-party complaint   A complaint filed by the defendant in a lawsuit against a third person whom he or she seeks to bring into the action because of that person's alleged liability to the defendant.

AO 440 (Rev. 5/85) Summons in a Civil Action

RETURN OF SERVICE

Service of the Summons and Complaint was made by me[1]	DATE
NAME OF SERVER	TITLE

Check one box below to indicate appropriate method of service

☐ Served personally upon the defendant. Place where served: _____
_____

☐ Left copies thereof at the defendant's dwelling house or usual place of abode with a person of suitable age and discretion then residing therein.
Name of person with whom the summons and complaint were left: _____

☐ Returned unexecuted: _____
_____
_____

☐ Other (specify): _____
_____
_____

STATEMENT OF SERVICE FEES

TRAVEL	SERVICES	TOTAL

DECLARATION OF SERVER

I declare under penalty of perjury under the laws of the United States of America that the foregoing information contained in the Return of Service and Statement of Service Fees is true and correct.

Executed on _____   _____
         Date   *Signature of Server*

_____
Address of Server

1) As to who may serve a summons see Rule 4 of the Federal Rules of Civil Procedure.

Affidavit of Service This document, usually on the reverse side of the summons, is filed with the court by the server of the summons. It certifies that the complaint was in writing and specifies when, where, and how the service was accomplished.

and the names of the pleadings differ. For example, in some states, if defendants assert a claim, they do so in a pleading entitled a *cross-complaint*. This pleading, which is separate from the answer, is used against a plaintiff, co-defendant, or third party.

UNITED STATES DISTRICT COURT
FOR THE NORTHERN DISTRICT OF CALIFORNIA

JANET JONES,

    PLAINTIFF,   CIVIL NO. 98765

VS.   ANSWER OF DEFENDANT THE

                                  ELEGANT FLOWERS

DAISY MARTIN AND THE   CORPORATION

ELEGANT FLOWERS CORPORATION,

AN OREGON CORPORATION.

Defendant THE ELEGANT FLOWERS CORPORATION answers as follows:

    1. Defendant THE ELEGANT FLOWERS CORPORATION admits the allegations of Paragraphs 1, 2, 3, and 4 of the complaint.

    2. Defendant THE ELEGANT FLOWERS CORPORATION specifically denies the allegations of Paragraph 7 of the complaint.

    3. In answer to Paragraph 5 of the complaint, Defendant THE ELEGANT FLOWERS CORPORATION admits that defendant Daisy Martin was the employee of THE ELEGANT FLOWERS CORPORATION at the relevant time mentioned in the complaint, but specifically denies that, during the time relevant to the complaint, defendant DAISY MARTIN was acting within the course and scope of an employee, agent, or servant of the defendant THE ELEGANT FLOWERS CORPORATION.

    4. In answer to Paragraph 6 of the complaint, Defendant THE ELEGANT FLOWERS CORPORATION admits that an automobile collision occurred between plaintiff JANET JONES and defendant DAISY MARTIN at the intersection of Market Street and Hill Street in San Francisco, California on December 3, 1992, but specifically denies each and every other allegation contained in said paragraph.

Answer to a Complaint In the answer to the complaint, a defendant outlines his or her defenses.

Replies and Answers

Responses must be made to allegations contained in counterclaims, cross-claims, and third-party complaints. The response to a counterclaim is entitled a **reply**. Except for the title of the document, it resembles an answer in all respects. The responses to cross-claims and third-party complaints are entitled *answers* and do not differ

Wherefore defendant prays:

1. That the court enter a judgment dismissing the complaint against the plaintiff THE ELEGANT FLOWERS CORPORATION.

2. That defendant be awarded costs incurred herein; and

3. That defendant be awarded such other and further relief as the court may deem just.

Dated: January 14, 1995.

_____

TAYLOR MOORE

15 Plaza de Oro

Sacramento, CA 94813

(916) 555-1212

Attorney for Defendant

THE ELEGANT FLOWERS

CORPORATION

Answer to a Complaint   *(Continued)*

from an answer to a complaint. Under the Federal Rules of Civil Procedure, all responses are due 20 days after service of the pleading containing the claim.

Legal Challenges to the Complaint

The primary purpose of an answer is to challenge the factual basis for the plaintiff's claim. However, not all defenses or challenges to a complaint deal with the truth or falsity of the factual allegations. Sometimes defendants wish to challenge the action on a more technical, legal basis. For example, the defendants might claim that they were not properly served with the complaint. Some jurisdictions, including federal courts, allow this type of

defense to be raised in either the answer or a motion.

In federal court, many legal challenges to actions are raised by the defendants in motions to dismiss the case. A *motion to* **dismiss** is a request that the court immediately terminate the action without granting the plaintiff any of the relief requested in the complaint. Legal challenges or defenses that can be raised in a motion to dismiss under Rule 12 of the Federal Rules of Civil Procedure include:

1. Lack of jurisdiction over the subject matter

2. Lack of jurisdiction over the person

3. Improper venue

4. Insufficiency of process

BALLENTINESBALLENTINESBALLENTINESBALLENTINESBALLENTINESBALLENTINESBALLENTINESBALLENTINESBALLENTINESBALLENTINESBALLENTINESBALLENTINESBALLENTINES

reply   1. In pleading, the plaintiff's answer to the defendant's setoff or counterclaim. 2. A response; an answer.

dismiss   To order a case, motion, or prosecution to be terminated.

5. Insufficiency of service of process
6. Failure to state a claim upon which relief can be granted
7. Failure to join a party under Rule 19 (an indispensable party).

In some state jurisdictions, another type of pleading, known as a **demurrer**, is used to challenge the legal sufficiency of the complaint. The grounds for a demurrer are similar to those for a motion to dismiss the case. When a demurrer is filed, the court usually holds a hearing to decide on the issues that were raised. If the demurrer is sustained, either the case is dismissed or the plaintiff is given the opportunity to amend the complaint. If the demurrer is overruled, the defendant is given a short time in which to file an answer.

Failure to Answer

If a party fails to answer a pleading to which a response is requested (that is, the defendant fails to answer the complaint, or the plaintiff fails to reply to a counterclaim), then a **default judgment** may follow. In most jurisdictions, including federal court, obtaining a judgment is a two-step process. First, the plaintiff or the plaintiff's attorney files with the court an **affidavit**—a statement under penalty of perjury, sworn to before a notary—verifying that the opposing party has defaulted (not responded) and requesting that the clerk enter that party's default. Entry of default is not the same as a default judgment. Entry of default means that the failure to respond has been noted in the court's file. After the default has been entered, the claimant can then apply for a default judgment.

To obtain a default judgment, the plaintiff must prove the claim at a brief court hearing where evidence is presented to a judge. In lieu of a court hearing, many jurisdictions allow the plaintiff to submit affidavits to substantiate the claim. The laws of the jurisdiction determine the exact procedure to be followed, although generally a default judgment cannot be obtained if the defendant is a minor, incompetent, or in the military service. In federal court, the plaintiff may also request a hearing before a judge to determine the amount of damages.

Courts usually permit parties against whom a default judgment was entered to petition the court by making a motion to set aside the default judgment. The most common grounds for making and granting such a motion are that the judgment was entered through mistake, inadvertence, surprise, or excusable neglect.

Motion Practice

During the course of litigation, questions or problems regarding the case inevitably arise. Sometimes these questions or problems involve practical, procedural issues. Some problems, such as insufficient time to answer a complaint, may be easily solved informally. At other times, these problems involve more complicated and substantial legal issues. If the issue is more complicated, and the parties substantially disagree regarding the facts and the law, an application is often made to the court to settle the issue. The application for such a court order is a *motion*.

Except for motions made during the trial, motions are required to be written, filed in court, and served on the opposing attorneys (or parties, if they are not represented). If the motion is

demurrer   A method of raising an objection to the legal sufficiency of a pleading. A demurrer says, in effect, that the opposing party's complaint alleges facts which, even if true, do not add up to a cause of action and that, therefore, the case should be dismissed.

default judgment   A judgment rendered in favor of a plaintiff based upon a defendant's failure to take a necessary step in a lawsuit within the required time.

affidavit   Any voluntary statement reduced to writing and sworn to or affirmed before a person legally authorized to administer an oath.

UNITED STATES DISTRICT COURT
FOR THE NORTHERN DISTRICT OF CALIFORNIA

JANET JONES,

    PLAINTIFF,

VS.

DAISY MARTIN AND THE

ELEGANT FLOWERS CORPORATION,

AN OREGON CORPORATION.

CIVIL NO. 98765

AFFIDAVIT AND REQUEST

TO ENTER DEFAULT

State of California
County of San Francisco

    I, Terry Alvarez, being duly sworn say:

    1. I am the attorney for the plaintiff in the above action.

    2. A copy of the summons and complaint was served on defendants DAISY MARTIN and THE ELEGANT FLOWERS CORPORATION on January 5, 1995, and the return of service of John Smith, United States Marshal, is on file in this action.

    3. Defendants DAISY MARTIN and THE ELEGANT FLOWERS CORPORATION have not answered or otherwise appeared in this action, and the time within which defendants may appear has expired.

Terry Alvarez

ALVAREZ & COE

100 Market Street

San Francisco, CA 94101

(415) 555-1212

Attorney for Plaintiff

Affidavit and Request to Enter Default After the complaint is filed with the court and the summons is served, the defendant has the option of answering the complaint. If the defendant fails to answer the complaint, the plaintiff can request the court to enter a finding of default and give summary judgment to the plaintiff.

contested, the opposing attorneys will also file papers opposing the motion. Often the written documents are followed by a brief court hearing before the judge rules on the motion. Although they are not considered to be pleadings, in appearance motions do resemble pleadings. The

Subscribed and sworn to before me on March 5, 1995.

_____

Request to Clerk to Enter Default

To: Clerk

Defendants DAISY MARTIN and THE ELEGANT FLOWERS CORPORATION, having failed to answer or otherwise appear in the above-entitled action, and the time for appearance having expired, you are requested to enter their default pursuant to Rule 55(a) of the Federal Rules of Civil Procedure.

Dated March 5, 1995.

_____

Terry Alvarez

ALVAREZ & COE

100 Market Street

San Francisco, CA 94101

Attorney for Plaintiff

Affidavit and Request to Enter Default *(Continued)*

documents constituting a motion filing follow the same formalities required of pleadings and all contain the same caption as the pleadings. Litigation paralegals are often asked to research the law governing a particular motion or to prepare the written documents to be filed in court. They might also be requested to contact the court to set the hearing date for a motion.

The party making the motion, known as the **moving party**, begins by preparing written papers for service and filing. These papers, which all follow the same general format as pleadings, usually include the motion, the notice of hearing on the motion, affidavits in support of the motion, and a memorandum of points and authorities in support of the motion.

The document entitled "motion" describes the nature of the motion, the grounds for the motion, and the relief requested.

The notice of hearing on the motion is a simple document stating when and where the court hearing on the motion will take place.

Although not always required, motions are commonly supported by affidavits. An *affidavit* is a statement, under penalty of perjury, sworn to before a notary or other person authorized to administer an oath, by the moving party or individual making the affidavit. An affidavit usually describes the factual basis for making the motion and is made by the person having personal knowledge of those facts.

moving party A party who makes a motion.

In some courts a declaration is used in lieu of an affidavit. Like the affidavit, a declaration is a statement under penalty of perjury, but it is not sworn to before a notary.

Along with a supporting affidavit, most attorneys also support a motion with a memorandum of points and authorities. In some courts this document is required. A memorandum of points and authorities is a legal argument in the form of a discussion and analysis of the law (statutes, cases, or constitutional provisions) that applies to the case. Before preparing a memorandum of points and authorities, the law that governs the case must be thoroughly researched. This task is often delegated to litigation paralegals.

Service and Filing

The motion and supporting papers must be filed with the court and copies served on the other parties to the action. All jurisdictions impose some time limitations on the service of motions. Under the Federal Rules of Civil Procedure, unless changed by a specific statute or court order, the written motion and notice of hearing must be served not later than five days before the time set for the hearing.

Responding to a Motion

To oppose a motion, an attorney commonly serves and files papers in opposition. These usually consist of affidavits in opposition to the motion and a memorandum of points and authorities in opposition to the motion. These affidavits and the memorandum have the same technical requirements as do the moving papers. For most motions in federal court, opposing affidavits must be served not later than one day before the hearing.

Court Procedures Involving Motions

In addition to the written documents, motions often involve court hearings. Because a hearing on the motion is a court appearance, it must be handled by the attorney, although a litigation paralegal may be responsible for scheduling the hearing. In some courts, motions are heard at set times and in set departments (sometimes referred to as "law and motion"). In other courts, a specific time with the judge hearing the motion may have to be arranged.

The attorneys for the moving and responding parties appear before a judge and present **oral arguments** in support of or in opposition to the motion. The judge considers the written documents and the oral arguments and then makes a decision. After the judge rules on the motion, a written order reflecting that ruling must be submitted to the judge for signature. Most courts require that the prevailing party prepare the written order for the judge's signature. Litigation paralegals are often asked to prepare drafts of these orders for attorney approval. Some courts have local rules that require the moving party to submit a proposed order with the moving papers. Sometimes a judge's ruling on a case is not a simple grant or denial of the motion; at times, orders become very involved.

Pretrial Motions

Motions can be made at any time during the litigation process. Consequently, they deal with all aspects of litigation. Pretrial motions deal with issues or problems that arise before the trial occurs. Following are some typical pretrial motions:

A *motion to dismiss* the action is a request that the court terminate the lawsuit immediately, without a hearing on the merits of plaintiff's claim.

A *motion to amend* is a request that the court allow a party to a lawsuit to amend a pleading.

A *motion for change of venue* is a motion requesting that the court transfer the case to a proper court, when one party believes that the action was commenced in the

oral argument   A party, through his or her attorney, usually presents his or her case to an appellate court on appeal by arguing the case verbally to the court, in addition to submitting a brief. Oral argument may also be made in support of a motion.

UNITED STATES DISTRICT COURT
FOR THE NORTHERN DISTRICT OF CALIFORNIA

JANET JONES,

    PLAINTIFF,   CIVIL NO. 98765

VS.   MOTION TO DISMISS

DAISY MARTIN AND THE

ELEGANT FLOWERS CORPORATION,

AN OREGON CORPORATION.

    THE ELEGANT FLOWERS CORPORATION, by Taylor Moore, its attorney, moves the court to dismiss the complaint on file on the following grounds: the complaint in this action alleges that this action is filed in federal court because it involves a dispute between citizens of different states; however, the court lacks subject matter jurisdiction as alleged in the complaint in that plaintiff and both defendants are citizens of the same state as is more clearly stated in the affidavits hereto annexed as Exhibits A and B. A memorandum of Points and Authorities in support of this motion is served and filed with this motion.

Dated January 20, 1995.

TAYLOR MOORE

15 Plaza de Oro

Sacramento, CA 94813

(916) 555-1212

Attorney for Defendant

THE ELEGANT FLOWERS

CORPORATION

Motion to Dismiss The defendant may answer the complaint by filing a motion to dismiss which states that there is no cause of action for the complaint or that the court lacks jurisdiction over the complaint.

wrong judicial district, or when one party feels that there are extenuating circumstances concerning venue, such as publicity concerning the case.

A *motion to quash the return of service* may be made if the defendant claims that he or she was improperly served with the summons and complaint.

A *motion to compel* asks the court to compel a party to an action to respond to requested discovery.

A *motion for summary judgment* may be made when it appears from the pleadings that there really are no disputed factual issues in the case. The moving party can request a judgment on the case, or on a particular issue of the case, without a trial.

Discovery

Discovery is the legal process by which the parties to a lawsuit search for facts relevant to a particular case. This section is an introduction to discovery and an examination of the most common methods of discovery, including depositions, interrogatories, physical and mental examinations, requests for production of documents, and requests for admissions.

An Introduction to Discovery

Most people who have not been involved in litigation are surprised to learn that both sides in a lawsuit have the opportunity to gather all the facts relevant to that lawsuit. Accustomed as they are to the surprise witness produced at the last minute by Perry Mason and his imitators, most people believe that the attorney who wins a case is the one who manages to trap his or her opponent by concealing crucial evidence until the last possible second. The truth is exactly the opposite of this fiction. Pretrial discovery is allowed because the law supports the principle that lawsuits should be decided on the facts and legal merits of the case, rather than on the ability of one attorney to conceal evidence or ambush the other attorney with surprise witnesses.

The Federal Rules of Civil Procedure limit discovery to the subject matter of the litigation. Most states impose similar limitations. Nevertheless, the extent of the discovery process is quite broad—broader, in fact, than the extent to which evidence can be introduced in a case once it has reached the trial stage. There are, however, several limits on the discovery process. The **attorney-client privilege** prevents the forced disclosure of written or oral communications between an attorney and a client or a prospective client. The **work product rule** prevents the opposing party in a lawsuit from using the discovery process to obtain letters, memos, documents, records, and other tangible items that have been produced in anticipation of litigation or that have been prepared for the trial itself. In addition, certain information covered by confidentiality agreements and other types of agreements may be excluded from discovery if permitted by the pertinent rules of civil procedure.

It is to everyone's benefit to have the discovery process run as smoothly as possible. For this reason, most parties cooperate freely with discovery requests, but there are times when a party or parties refuse to cooperate. The rules of civil procedure provide methods for compelling discovery and sanctions for those who refuse to cooperate.

An attorney has five methods of discovery from which to choose: depositions, interrogatories, requests for the production of documents and entry upon land for inspection, requests for physical and/or mental examinations, and requests for admissions. In federal court, the discovery process

---

BALLENTINESBALLENTINESBALLENTINESBALLENTINESBALLENTINESBALLENTINESBALLENTINESBALLENTINESBALLENTINESBALLENTINESBALLENTINESBALLENTINESBALLENTINESBALLENTINES

discovery   A means for providing a party, in advance of trial, with access to facts that are within the knowledge of the other side, to enable the party to better try his or her case.

attorney-client privilege   Nothing a client tells his or her attorney in connection with his or her case can be disclosed by the attorney, or anyone employed by the attorney or the attorney's firm, without the client's permission.

work product rule   The rule that an attorney's work product is not subject to discovery.

is regulated by Rules 26 through 37 of the Federal Rules of Civil Procedure.

Depositions

A **deposition** is the written or oral testimony of a witness or party given under oath outside the courtroom. It is one of the most important and widely used pretrial discovery tools. The use of depositions in federal court is regulated by Rules 27 through 32 of the Federal Rules of Civil Procedure. The purpose of the deposition is to uncover and explore all facts known by a party to the lawsuit or by a nonparty witness involved in the lawsuit. An individual who is questioned during a deposition is called a **deponent**. Under Rule 26 of the Federal Rules, the scope of testimony during discovery is much broader than the scope of testimony during trial. During the taking of a deposition, an attorney is allowed to ask questions that could not be asked at trial because these questions seek evidence that is not admissible. During a deposition, the attorney may ask the deponent not only any question involving admissible evidence, but also any questions that could reasonably lead to the discovery of admissible evidence.

During an oral deposition, the deponent is actually present in the attorney's office, the courthouse, or some other convenient location to answer an attorney's questions aloud. Attorneys may be involved in an oral deposition in one of two ways. First, they may ask questions of the opposing party or a nonparty witness. In this situation, the attorney is said to be *taking the deposition*. If, in contrast, the attorney's client is being questioned, that attorney will be present at the deposition to protect the best interests of his or her client. That attorney is said to be *defending the deposition.*

Another individual who is always present at a deposition is the **court reporter** or certified shorthand reporter. The court reporter places the deponent under oath, takes a word-for-word account of the proceeding, and, if required, produces a written copy of the deposition. This written copy of the deposition is known as the *transcript*. An attorney taking a deposition can also videotape that deposition. Under certain circumstances, a videotaped deposition can be used at trial to dramatically demonstrate the credibility—or lack thereof—of a witness.

Notice Requirements

Professional courtesy dictates that the attorney taking a deposition should contact the defending attorney to schedule mutually acceptable dates and times for the depositions of the defending attorney's clients.

The federal rules and the rules of most other jurisdictions require that formal notice of a deposition be given to the deponent and to each party. Once an agreement on the deposition date has been reached, the paralegal may be asked to arrange for the preparation and service of a notice of intent to take oral deposition, or simply a **notice of deposition**. This notice sets the date, time, and place of the deposition, the name of the attorney taking the deposition, and the name and address of the person whose deposition is to be taken.

When the attorney taking the deposition is requesting a nonparty witness to testify, the legal means for securing the presence of such a witness is a **subpoena**, an official document issued by the clerk of court commanding a person to be present at a deposition. A nonparty witness can be subpoenaed to produce documents at his or her deposition, according to Rule 45 of the Federal

BALLENTINESBALLENTINESBALLENTINESBALLENTINESBALLENTINESBALLENTINESBALLENTINESBALLENTINESBALLENTINESBALLENTINESBALLENTINESBALLENTINESBALLENTINESBALLENTINES

deposition   The transcript of a witness's testimony given under oath outside of the courtroom, usually in advance of the trial or hearing, upon oral examination or in response to written interrogatories.

deponent   A person who gives a deposition. A person who gives sworn testimony in any form.

court reporter   A person who stenographically or by "voice writing" records court proceedings, from which he or she prepares a transcript that becomes a part of the record in the case.

notice of deposition   Written notice that a party to a lawsuit must give to all other parties before taking a deposition.

subpoena   A command in the form of written process requiring a witness to come to court to testify.

UNITED STATES DISTRICT COURT
FOR THE NORTHERN DISTRICT OF CALIFORNIA

JANET JONES,

    PLAINTIFF,   CIVIL NO. 98765

VS.   NOTICE OF INTENT TO

DAISY MARTIN AND THE   TAKE ORAL DEPOSITION

ELEGANT FLOWERS CORPORATION,

AN OREGON CORPORATION.

_____

To: Mark Henderson, attorney for defendant DAISY MARTIN and Taylor
    Moore, attorney for defendant ELEGANT FLOWERS CORPORATION

    PLEASE TAKE NOTICE that pursuant to the Rules of Civil Procedure, Terry
Alvarez will take the oral deposition of Daisy Martin before a notary public on February 12, 1995, at 4:00 p.m. and thereafter from day to day until completed, at
the law offices of Alvarez & Coe, 100 Market Street, San Francisco, CA 94101.

                                      Respectfully submitted,

                                      _____

                                      Terry Alvarez

                                      Attorney for Plaintiff

Certificate of Service

    I hereby certify that a true and correct copy of the foregoing Notice of Intent to Take Oral Deposition has been furnished to counsel of record on this
24th day of January, 1995.

                                        _____

Notice of Intent to Take Oral Deposition This document indicates an agreed-upon
date, time, and place for the deposition to be taken.

Rules of Civil Procedure, by serving the nonparty witness with a **subpoena duces tecum**. The subpoena duces tecum contains a specific listing of the documents that the nonparty witness must produce at the deposition.

The Paralegal's Role During Oral Deposition

The paralegal's job at the deposition will vary, based on experience, the complexity of the case, and the attorney's division of responsibilities. The litigation paralegal's duties will also vary depending on whether the attorney is taking or defending the deposition. In either case, the paralegal is usually asked to take notes and evaluate the witness. Paralegals may also be called upon to control or produce documents and exhibits.

The Paralegal's Role After Oral Deposition

Paralegal responsibilities in the deposition process do not end with the final question. Postdeposition tasks may include assuming responsibility for the transcript, which both the attorney taking the deposition and the attorney defending the deposition will probably want to see. To obtain copies of the transcript, the paralegal usually contacts the court reporter to find out when the transcript will be ready and to arrange for the appropriate number of copies to be delivered.

When the paralegal works for the attorney who defended the deposition, the job often involves arranging for the client to review and correct the transcript. Any errors in the transcript should be corrected by the deponent.

Another important aspect of the litigation paralegal's duties with regard to the deposition is preparation of a deposition summary. The *deposition summary* is a written record that reduces many hours of testimony to a few concisely drawn, easily read, and quickly understood pages. A properly written deposition summary can organize selected topics or subject matter into an orderly arrangement. Once the testimony has been arranged in the deposition summary according to a particular plan, inconsistent testimony may become evident. A well-drawn summary can also point out missing pieces of evidence that might lead the attorney to conduct further discovery. There are three types of deposition summaries from which to choose: the page-line deposition summary, the topical deposition summary, and the chronological deposition summary. The type of summary used in a case will depend not only on the facts involved, but also on the legal issues that the attorney wants to emphasize.

The *page-line deposition summary* covers the testimony as it unfolded in the deposition itself. Such a summary is helpful when the attorney is uncertain about just how to use the deponent's testimony. The page-line summary allows the attorney to review the testimony quickly and focus on areas that he or she wants to explore further. The *topical deposition summary* organizes the testimony into specific subject areas. Such a deposition is useful when the attorney already knows what areas to concentrate on in planning legal strategy. Finally, the *chronological deposition summary* organizes the testimony according to a particular time sequence. Such a summary is useful when the chronology of events is of critical importance to the case.

Interrogatories

Interrogatories are written questions submitted by one party in a lawsuit to another party in that suit. The responding party must answer these questions in writing and under oath. Rule 33 of the Federal Rules of Civil Procedures regulates the use of interrogatories in federal courts. Although many states have adopted the federal rules as their own, always check for variations in the state and local rules governing the use of interrogatories. Interrogatories can be served on any party to a lawsuit. However, unlike a notice of deposition, interrogatories cannot be served on nonparty witnesses involved in a lawsuit. A party served with interrogatories generally has 30 days to provide answers to the interrogatories.

All interrogatories sent to a party at one time constitute a *set*. Multiple sets of interrogatories, however, can be served on the parties to a lawsuit.

BALLENTINESBALLENTINESBALLENTINESBALLENTINESBALLENTINESBALLENTINESBALLENTINESBALLENTINESBALLENTINESBALLENTINESBALLENTINESBALLENTINESBALLENTINESBALLENTINESBALLENTINES

subpoena duces tecum A ... written command requiring a witness to come to court to testify and at that time to produce for use as evidence the papers, documents, books, or records listed in the subpoena.

interrogatories Written questions put by one party to another, or ... to a witness in advance of trial.

Page	Line	Topic	Summary
4	9	Test	Patient DeMarco was scheduled for an intravenous polygram
8	17	Antidote	The antidote had to be retrieved from the pharmacy.

Page-Line Deposition Summary This summary cross-references topics to page and line number.

In federal court there is no limit on the number of interrogatories per set or the number of sets that may be served on a party. However, in the interests of efficiency and economy, some state courts do set such limits.

Purposes of Interrogatories

The primary purpose of interrogatories is to obtain information on the basic facts in a case, including any other persons who may be involved in the lawsuit. Interrogatories may also be used to determine the party's contentions and to locate relevant documents. A set of interrogatories may also disclose the identities of both lay and expert witnesses that the other party intends to call to the stand at trial. This last point is especially critical in the identification of expert witnesses, because Rule 33 allows interrogatories to explore not only the opinions of an expert but also how he or she reached those opinions.

Properly drafted interrogatories can help to narrow the issues and facts in preparation for trial. Like the deposition, interrogatories can also be used to impeach a witness at the time of trial. Finally, interrogatories may facilitate settlement of the case.

Interrogatories offer substantial advantages over other discovery methods. They are simple,

Topic	Page	Summary
Education	1	He received an associate's degree from Hampton County Community College.
Employment Experience	1	Eckerson was employed by Hampton General Hospital 6/5/62 as a radiologic technologist.
Certification	2	He became a certified radiologic technologist in 1991.
Patient's Chart	6	Eckerson identifies contents of DeMarco's chart.
Patient's Condition	8	DeMarco suffered cardiac arrest.

Topical Deposition Summary This summary focuses on the topics discussed in the deposition.

Date	Event	Page
1990	Graduated from College.	1
1990	Employed at Hampton General	3
1991	Certified as R.T.	2

Chronological Deposition Summary This summary cross-references key events with dates.

inexpensive, and efficient. In addition, a set of interrogatories can be more thorough than a deposition and can complement the other discovery techniques.

Like the other discovery devices, though, interrogatories do have disadvantages. For example, they are limited to the parties to a lawsuit. Second, compared to depositions, interrogatories lack spontaneity. The party responding to a set of interrogatories has time to draft self-serving answers that may be edited by the attorney or paralegal before they are sent out. Further, because answers to interrogatories are submitted in writing, immediate follow-up on those answers is not possible. Finally, interrogatories may alert the opposition to the direction of the serving attorney's case.

Drafting Interrogatories

Paralegals are often asked to participate in drafting interrogatories, to free the attorney's time so that he or she can concentrate on other matters. The drafting of interrogatories is one of the most important jobs that paralegals perform during the litigation process, because properly drafted interrogatories not only provide information themselves, but also indicate the need to use other discovery devices. The paralegal's role in drafting interrogatories may later be expanded to include drafting a motion to compel the other party to respond to any interrogatories that have not been properly answered. A paralegal may also be responsible for reviewing the other party's response.

Before an effective set of interrogatories can be drafted, the paralegal must be familiar with the facts of the case. To accomplish this, paralegals review the pleadings, the correspondence file, the attorney's notes, and the research notebook. Notes are taken as the material is reviewed. The types of questions that should be asked of the other party are also noted. After a thorough review of all available information, the interrogatories are drafted.

The format used for interrogatories is mandated by federal or state rules. The appropriate court rules must be consulted to determine the form required in your particular jurisdiction. Most jurisdictions require a title that identifies the party serving the interrogatories, the party receiving the interrogatories, and the number of the set of interrogatories. Definitions to clear up discrepancies concerning words with several meanings, instructions for the answering party, the specific interrogatories, and the attorney's signature are also typically required. Following the signature block, a certificate of service sets out the date, type of service, and to whom service of the interrogatories was made.

Make a note regarding the deadline for receiving a response on the calendar or tickler system whenever interrogatories are served on the opposing party. If the interrogatories are not answered within a prescribed time period, a letter or telephone call to the opposing counsel usually prompts a quick response. If necessary, a motion to compel discovery may be made to the proper court.

Answering Interrogatories

Like all other forms of discovery, responding to interrogatories requires patient and careful planning. Because the attorney's client is responsible for answering the questions, it is essential that he or she be contacted immediately upon receipt of a set of interrogatories. Pay special attention to the due date of the interrogatories so that they can be answered within the prescribed time period.

The client normally supplies the information to the attorney or the paralegal, who then drafts the answers. Each interrogatory must be answered separately, in writing. A party answering interrogatories has a duty to make a reasonable investigation to obtain all information requested. Interrogatory answers must be straightforward and complete. On some occasions, however, the client may need to qualify a response or indicate that the answer is unknown at this time. If the answer to a question is unknown because of lack of sufficient information, the reason for failing to answer must be indicated.

Objections to interrogatories may be served with the answers or in a separate pleading. Objections may be made to certain interrogatories on the grounds that the information is protected by the attorney-client privilege or the work product privilege. In addition, objections may be made against interrogatories that involve inadmissible and irrelevant evidence or interrogatories that are overbroad, vague, or unintelligible.

Physical and Mental Examinations

A *physical or mental examination* is the examination of a party in a lawsuit to determine factual information about the physical or mental condition of that party. Such an examination is used when that physical or mental condition is an important factor in a lawsuit, such as in a personal injury, medical malpractice, or certain products liability cases. One party to a lawsuit can request that the other party undergo a physical or mental examination, even if the party who is to undergo the examination is a minor. Physical and mental examinations, by their very nature, invade the

TIPS FOR DRAFTING EFFECTIVE INTERROGATORIES
1. Review all pertinent information in the file carefully.
2. Understand what the attorney wishes to accomplish with the interrogatories.
3. Review pertinent court rules.
4. Use form files within the office and/or formbooks.
5. Prepare an outline.
6. Draft preliminary portions of the request, including: title of the document, introductory paragraph, definitions and instructions, time covered, continuing nature of interrogatories, procedure to be followed for objections, and permission for the party to provide a document instead of describing same.
7. Organize the interrogatories into categories.
8. Review and revise.
9. Proofread carefully.
10. Obtain attorney's review, approval, and signature.
11. Arrange for service of interrogatories. Prepare affidavit of service.
12. Make note of date for response on calendar or tickler system.

Interrogatories are written questions submitted by one party in a lawsuit to another party in that suit. The main purpose is to obtain information on basic facts involved in the lawsuit.

privacy of the person undergoing the examination. For this reason, among others, this discovery tool is typically used only to establish the truth about a plaintiff's allegation of physical or mental injuries.

The paralegal's role in the request for a physical or a mental examination depends upon whether the attorney he or she works for, or the opposing attorney, has requested the examination. If the paralegal works for the attorney who requested an examination of an opposing party, the paralegal may be asked to schedule the actual examination. In such a situation, the opposing counsel must be contacted to see if there are any objections to the examination. If the other party is not agreeable, a motion for compulsory physical exam and a proposed order may be drafted.

If the paralegal works for the attorney whose client has been requested to undergo a physical or mental examination, he or she may be asked to notify the client immediately. The attorney will have explained to the client in the initial interview that such an examination is possible. However, the client may be uneasy about the actual examination. Explaining the purpose and procedures to be utilized may give the client some comfort. This explanation may take the form of a letter to the client setting out the details concerning the examination.

After the examination has been completed, the paralegal is often responsible for obtaining copies of the physician's report for the attorney's review.

Request for Documents

A *request for documents* is a request by one party in a lawsuit to another party in that suit to allow the first party access to documents relevant to the subject matter of the suit. Besides the formal request for documents, there are other procedures for obtaining documents needed for litigation, including a request for documents at the deposition of a party, a subpoena duces tecum for a nonparty to produce documents at a deposition, and interrogatories that lead to the production of documents. However, the formal request for documents still remains the most efficient and effective way to obtain documents.

A request for documents to a party may be made when the party is originally served with process. In that event, the party has 45 days to respond to the request. Otherwise, the party has 30 days to respond. For the responding party to comply with the request as efficiently as possible, the request must specify with reasonable

particularity the general categories of documents or the particular documents that the requesting party wishes to inspect. The request should also specify a reasonable time, place, and manner of production.

As might be expected, the term *documents* has a wide variety of meanings. Rule 34(a) of the Federal Rules of Civil Procedure defines *documents* to include such diverse items as photographs, graphs, computer printouts, calendars, and accounting records, among others. The scope of the rule extends not only to documents in the actual custody of the party, but also to documents under the control of that party. In other words, the requesting party has the right to obtain some documents that are actually in the possession of a third individual, such as the other party's tax consultant. This rule also allows the requesting party to inspect and copy those documents.

The paralegal's role in a request for production of documents will depend on whether the attorney he or she works for made the request, or if the attorney must help his or her client respond to a request. Often the paralegal will have to fill both roles in the same lawsuit. Thus, the litigation paralegal must know how to review, organize, and analyze documents received from the other party. However, the paralegal must also know how to help clients to produce documents that the other party has requested.

Requesting the Production of Documents

Before drafting a request, the paralegal must develop a working knowledge of the case by reviewing the pleadings, the correspondence, the attorney's notes, and the research on the case. Once this has been done, the paralegal is ready to draft the request. First, sample requests for documents should be located in formbooks or the firm's word processing form file. Of course, because no two cases are exactly the same, the samples will have to be modified to fit the particular facts and issues in the subject case. Still, forms and samples can often be used for the basic areas of the request, such as the introductory paragraph and the definitions of terms. The paralegal must be familiar with the pertinent court rules involving discovery. Each court may have individual rules relating to the number of requests allowed, the time allowed for responding to requests, the manner for objecting to requests, and the availability of a motion to compel production of the requested documents.

Most requests for the production of documents include a title that identifies the party making the request, the party receiving the request, and the number of the request. In addition, the document will include definitions of any terms in the request that might be confusing or misleading to the responding party, instructions for responding to the request, and a list of the documents requested, with reasonable particularity. The request for production of documents also includes the signature of the requesting attorney and a certificate of service similar to the one used for interrogatories.

Responding to a Request for Documents

A document production is only as successful as the planning that precedes it. When responding to a document request, the attorney must decide on the organizational approach that will best serve his or her purposes. The attorney must also decide on the number of documents to be produced.

The Federal Rules of Civil Procedure provide that a party producing documents has a choice of two organizational approaches. The documents may be produced either as they are kept in the usual course of business, or according to the categories specified in the document request.

Producing the documents as they are kept in the usual course of business requires less time and effort by the responding party. However, producing the documents according to the categories and the request can be managed if relatively few documents are requested. Further, the party producing the documents may prefer this technique because it forces him or her to review all the requested documents, lessening the chance of inadvertently revealing privileged documents. A request for the production of certain documents may be objected to if the documents are protected. Grounds for

such objections include arguing that complying with the request will violate either the attorney-client privilege or the attorney-work product privilege. Other objections may allege that the request is overbroad, duplicative, or irrelevant.

Organizing and Indexing Documents After Production

The litigation paralegal may have several duties following the production of documents and review of the opposition's documents. As there will often be hundreds of documents involved in the litigation, control problems are very serious. The paralegal can aid in establishing tight control over these documents by organizing and indexing them.

Organizational plans vary from case to case. Some cases turn on chronological events; documents in such cases are ordered by date. Other cases may be broken down into several subject categories; the documents are therefore organized by those subjects. In other cases, the paralegal is asked to organize the documents in anticipation of upcoming depositions; in such a case, all documents related to the testimony of each deponent to be called must be put together.

If the case is to be managed manually, without the aid of a computer, several copies of each document should be made. One set can be placed in chronological order, a second set in subject order, and a third set in deponent order. Keep the copies separate from the original numbered set and limit access to the original set.

An index of the documents produced by all parties is critical to controlling the files throughout the lawsuit. This index can be limited to the document number, the date, the author, the recipient, the document type, and a brief summary of its contents. Preparing a comprehensive index may be a difficult job at the outset of the lawsuit, but it is much less difficult than trying to search blindly for a document later in the case.

Requests for Admissions

A **request for admissions** is filed by one party in a lawsuit on another party in that lawsuit, asking the second party to admit to the truthfulness of some fact or opinion. The request may also ask the party to authenticate the genuineness of a document. According to Rule 36 of the Federal Rules of Civil Procedure, a request for admissions may be served on any party in a lawsuit; however, the request may not be served on a nonparty. Rule 36 allows a request for admissions to be served at the same time the complaint is served. In such situations, the served party has 45 days to respond to the request. If the request for admissions is served after the complaint is served, the party has 30 days to respond. The federal rules place no limit on the number of requests that can be filed. However, some states (California, for example), do limit the number of requests that can be filed.

The primary purpose of a request for admissions is to simplify a lawsuit by reducing the number and nature of the points in controversy. The simplification of the points in controversy has a "ripple effect," simplifying many of the other matters involved in the suit. For example, if fewer points are in controversy, fewer witnesses will be necessary should the case reach the trial stage. Simplifying the points in controversy could also lead to early settlement of the case, because claims and defenses that have no legal merit evaporate quickly under the scrutiny of a well-drafted request for admissions. Finally, a carefully drafted request for admissions can emphasize important factual information that is buried in volumes of documents and testimony.

Drafting the Request for Admissions

Litigation paralegals are often called upon to draft requests for admissions. This responsibility is extremely important because, as mentioned previously, properly drafted requests can save time and money and can often lead to early settlement of the lawsuit. Consequently, great care must be taken in preparing the request.

Before drafting the request, all available information concerning the case and the applicable federal, state, and local court rules must be carefully reviewed so that the paralegal can accurately determine response deadlines and procedure details. Also, before actually drafting the request, a list of the desired admissions of the other party is usually prepared.

With the aid of the preliminary list of desired admissions and samples from formbooks or the firm's word processing form file, the request for admissions can be drafted. Obviously, no two situations are exactly the same, so the forms must be modified to fit the facts of the case at hand. Nevertheless, requests for admissions generally include a title that identifies the party making the request, the party receiving the request, the number of the request, and an introductory paragraph citing the applicable court rules. Definitions and instructions are also included to aid the responding party. The specific requests should be as simple as possible. The part of the request asking for authentication of the genuineness of documents should be very specific as to the identity of each of those documents; it is best to list each document separately. Copies of the documents in the list must be gathered together and attached to the request with an appropriate identifying heading.

The part of the request listing the facts and opinions to be admitted should also be very carefully worded. Each fact and opinion should be listed separately.

Responding to the Request for Admissions

A paralegal who works for an attorney whose client has been served with a request for admissions may be responsible for keeping track of the due date for the request and making sure it is answered in time. In addition, the paralegal may be responsible for meeting with the client to gather

request for admissions Written statements concerning a case, directed to an adverse party, that he or she is required to admit or deny. Such admissions or denials will be treated by the court as having been established, and need not be proven at trial.

information and for preparing a preliminary response to the request.

The paralegal who is responsible for drafting the response usually meets with the client to cover the alternatives available in response in to each request. The paralegal must also consider any objections that might be raised to the request. The alternatives available in responding to a request for admission are:

1. To admit
2. To deny
3. To refuse to either admit or deny
4. To object.

When drafting the response, each statement to which the client is responding must be copied exactly as it appears on the original request. If a statement is true, the response must admit that it is true. However, if reasonable doubt exists as to the truthfulness of a particular statement, it may be denied. A statement that has been admitted is called a *judicial admission*. A judicial admission is placed into evidence and can be presented to the court at the time of trial.

Any statement that is not truthful should be denied. However, the temptation to deny a statement on a technicality, such as a misspelled word or an obvious typographical error, must be resisted. The opposing party may ask the court to compel a client to pay the cost of proving a matter that should not have been denied in the first place.

The third alternative is to refuse to either admit or deny a request. However, the Federal Rules of Civil Procedure do not allow this alternative unless a reasonable inquiry into the subject has been made. Moreover, a lack of personal knowledge is not a proper basis for refusing to respond, unless the party has reason to doubt the credibility of the source of the information. A response to the request for admission does not require verification in federal court. However, because some state and local rules demand such verification, you must check the proper procedure for your area.

Basically, the same objections available in response to other discovery techniques are available in response to a request for admissions. The grounds for such objections include stating that complying with the request would violate the attorney-client privilege or the work product privilege. Other objections are that the request is overbroad, irrelevant, or duplicative. Objections may also be made on the grounds that the statement is a compound request, which asks a party to admit to two or more facts in one statement.

Pretrial, Trial, and Posttrial

Throughout the discovery process, the attorneys for all parties will be weighing the evidence and considering their options. Often, the parties to a lawsuit will agree to a settlement without ever having to appear in court. At other times, a **trial** may be the only way to resolve the dispute. Even after the normal trial process has been exhausted, one of the parties may appeal the court's decision. This section examines the disposition options of a lawsuit, including settlements, trial, and posttrial matters.

Settlements and Dismissals

Many civil cases end in **settlement**. Often settlement negotiations are conducted simultaneously with active preparation of a lawsuit. In fact, preparation of a lawsuit may actually lead to settlement

trial A hearing or determination by a court of the issues existing between the parties to an action; an examination by a court of competent jurisdiction, according to the law of the land, of the facts or law at issue in either a civil case or a criminal prosecution, for the purpose of adjudicating the matters in controversy.

settlement The ending of a lawsuit by agreement.

because, as the attorney gathers information about the suit, he or she may decide that settlement is in the client's best interests.

An attorney must consider a number of factors before deciding to recommend settlement to the client. Perhaps the two most obvious factors are time and money. Because the legal system is overburdened with a heavy case load, it is not uncommon for a court's calendar to be backed up for months. Some courts in large metropolitan areas have dockets that are backed up for years. This type of overcrowding means that a trial date cannot be set for months, or even years, after the original complaint is filed. If the client cannot afford to wait that long for a judgment, then the attorney may elect to settle the case without going to trial.

Also recall that a lengthy and involved discovery procedure may be necessary to gather the facts required to prove the client's case at trial. The more involved the discovery process, the more expensive the lawsuit.

Another settlement factor may be the particular court's decisions in similar cases. For example, if the attorney who represents the plaintiff finds that the court recently rendered a judgment favorable to the defendant in a suit very similar to the one at issue, it may be in the client's best interest to engage in settlement negotiations.

Finally, the subsequent tactics of the other party's attorney may motivate a client to seriously consider settlement. Recall, for example, that the defendant, in responding to a lawsuit, may elect to file a counterclaim against the plaintiff. The legitimacy of the counterclaim and the degree to which the defendant may succeed in presenting that counterclaim are critical factors in making any settlement decision.

Before a decision to make a settlement offer is finalized, preliminary investigative work must be completed so that the attorney can make an informed decision as to the advisability of settlement and the amount of the offer to be made. Much of this preliminary investigative work involves the paralegal, and it often includes gathering information concerning the client's personal history, the client's present health and medical history, and a calculation of the client's damages.

Settlement Offers

Once the preliminary investigative work has been completed, the information must be pulled together into a useful report. This report must convince the defendant that a settlement would be in his or her best interest. Depending on the situation, litigation paralegals may be charged with writing a settlement summary or settlement letter, the objective of which is to persuade the opponent to agree to the settlement terms. The choice of which format to use is based on the complexity of the case and the amount of money involved. Drafting settlement summaries and settlement letters is an important part of the paralegal's role in the overall settlement process. The law firm's form files and personal injury formbooks are often used to prepare initial drafts of settlement summaries or settlement letters. Items typically found in a settlement brochure for a personal injury case include:

1. Description of the accident
2. Witness statements
3. Photos of the accident scene
4. Photos of the plaintiff before the accident
5. Photos of the plaintiff after the accident
6. Statement of the facts
7. Plaintiff's personal history
8. Medical history of the plaintiff
9. Medical condition of the plaintiff
10. Medical expenses
11. Evaluation of the claim.

Settlement Agreements and Releases

If the parties reach an agreement based on the settlement offer, then it will be necessary to place the details of that settlement into some permanent written form. The complexity of the case

---

UNITED STATES DISTRICT COURT
FOR THE NORTHERN DISTRICT OF CALIFORNIA

JANET JONES,

     PLAINTIFF,   CIVIL NO. 98765

VS.   RELEASE

DAISY MARTIN AND THE

ELEGANT FLOWERS CORPORATION,

AN OREGON CORPORATION.

_____

     JANET JONES, plaintiff in the above case, hereby releases the defendants and all other persons, known or unknown, who may have contributed to the incident which forms the basis of this lawsuit, from all claims and demands for any act or matter whatsoever which may have arisen or may arise in the future.

     Signed and sealed this _____ day of June, 1995.

                                     _____

                                     Janet Jones

General Release A general release is a document filed by the plaintiff that releases the defendant from claims and demands stemming from a complaint.

and the settlement arrangements determines whether the parties will need a settlement agreement or a release.

A *settlement agreement* is actually a contract between the parties. As such, it must meet all the legal requirements of a contract. In other words, it must be created by the voluntary mutual assent of the parties, it must involve the give-and-take element of consideration, and it must be legal and entered into by parties with the capacity to contract.

If the facts and the legal issues involved in the lawsuit are not overly complex, the parties may be satisfied to settle the case by using a **release**, rather than a settlement agreement. A *general release* is used for full and final settlements. In a general release, all possible claims against all possible persons who might be liable for the plaintiff's injuries are settled. This type of release is advantageous for the defendant because he or she can be assured that no further action will be taken by the plaintiff relating to the subject matter of the lawsuit.

In a complex lawsuit involving multiple claims, a party may elect to relinquish some claims while retaining others. In such a situation, a *partial release* is appropriate. This type of release is advantageous to the plaintiff because it preserves

release A document or writing stating that a right or claim is given up or discharged.

some of the grounds he or she has for bringing a subsequent lawsuit against the defendant.

If the defendant in a lawsuit has filed a counterclaim against the plaintiff, and both parties in the case agree to relinquish part or all of their claims in the suit, a mutual release may be entered into. In a mutual release, each party relinquishes its claim against the other party. This type of release benefits both parties, because each of them can be assured that all potential liability in regard to this particular lawsuit has been eliminated.

Dismissals

Once a lawsuit has been settled, an order for dismissal is usually drawn up. There are three major types of dismissals: a stipulated dismissal, a voluntary dismissal on notice, and a court-ordered involuntary dismissal.

The parties to a lawsuit may stipulate to a dismissal at any time and on any terms. A stipulated dismissal may be either with prejudice or without prejudice. A stipulated dismissal with prejudice means that the claim cannot be brought to court again at any time in the future. In contrast, a stipulated dismissal without prejudice means that the lawsuit can be brought at another time in any court that has jurisdiction hear the case.

Rule 41 of the Federal Rules of Civil Procedure permits a plaintiff to voluntarily dismiss a claim without order of the court by filing a motion of dismissal "at any time before service by the adverse party of an answer or of a motion for summary judgment, whichever comes first." As with a stipulated dismissal, this dismissal can be with or without prejudice.

The court has authority to dismiss an action if a party has failed to proceed with an action, or if the party has failed to comply with a court order. A dismissal marks the end of a case, but it usually does not result in the court's entry of a judgment.

Consent Decrees

As an alternative to a dismissal, the parties may elect to use a **consent decree**. A consent decree outlines the details of the settlement agreed upon by the parties. The parties file the decree with the court, requesting that the judge examine the agreement and either approve or disapprove of the terms they have set forth. Most of the time judges do not hesitate in rendering approval. Once it has been approved by the court, the consent decree is just as effective as a judgment would have been had the case gone to trial.

Distribution of Funds

Distribution of funds is often accomplished when the stipulated dismissal is signed or when the court approves the consent decree. A settlement proceeds statement similar to the closing statement in a real estate transaction, should be prepared to account for the receipt of all proceeds. Such an accounting avoids later problems or questions as to the payment of any expense involved in the settlement.

Trial Techniques

The litigation paralegal plays a very important role in trial preparation. While the trial attorney concentrates on the substance of the trial, the paralegal concentrates on making sure that the attorney's case can be presented effectively. The litigation paralegal is instrumental in preliminary trial preparation, preparation of exhibits and briefs, coordination of trial logistics, and assistance with the jury selection process.

Preliminary Preparation for Trial

Preparation for trial actually begins at the initial client interview. It is at this point that the

consent decree 1. A judgment in an action brought by an administrative agency, in which the defendant declines to admit wrongdoing but agrees not to engage in the conduct alleged, in exchange for which the government's suit is dropped.
2. A decree entered in an equitable action suit upon the consent of the parties. Such a decree is binding on the parties; they cannot subsequently appeal it or go to trial on the matter.

attorney begins to assess the merits of the case to determine what course of action to take. Each of the processes and tasks examined thus far in this chapter advances the prosecution or defense of the case. Although most cases are settled or dismissed before reaching the trial stage, the attorney must proceed on the assumption that eventually the case will reach trial. Some preparation tasks may be performed several months in advance of trial; others must be handled at the last minute.

Whatever the situation, the attorney and his or her client will prevail only if they are thoroughly prepared for all eventualities. One tool often used by paralegals to aid in this preparation is a *trial checklist* that includes all the tasks to be performed before the trial and the time frame for completion of those tasks. When the checklist is monitored regularly and faithfully, the paralegal can be sure that the case is truly ready for trial.

One trial preparation task that can be completed during the preliminary stages is the organization of the litigation files. Naturally, it is best if the files are kept current as the case develops. For example, each time a pleading is filed by either side, it should immediately be placed in the pleadings binder. An early reviewing of the litigation files will reveal a number of items to add to the "to do" part of the trial preparation checklist.

The *trial notebook,* a vital part of any trial preparation, is usually the litigation paralegal's responsibility. The trial notebook binder contains, in complete or summary form, everything necessary to prosecute or defend a case. The form of the notebook is dictated by the type of case, the number of pleadings, the complexity of the legal issues, the number of exhibits and witnesses, and the anticipated length of the trial. However, most trial notebooks include the following sections:

1. The parties and the attorneys
2. The pleadings and motions
3. The witnesses
4. The expert witnesses
5. Document indexes

TRIAL PREPARATION CHECKLIST
1. Enter trial date and other significant trial preparation deadlines on tickler or calendar system.
2. Notify clients and witnesses of trial date and schedule meetings to prepare for trial testimony.
3. Review and organize file.
4. Prepare and serve trial subpoenas.
5. Review chronology and cast of characters, and update if necessary.
6. Review, update, and complete trial notebook.
7. Designate and organize trial exhibits. Prepare trial exhibit log.
8. Assist with trail brief.
9. Visit courtroom and diagram location of trial exhibits and documents.
10. Locate a "work room" at a nearby hotel (if trial is out of town).
11. Arrange travel and hotel for out-of-town clients and witnesses.
12. Arrange documents to be introduced by witnesses, according to the examination outline in the trial notebook. Assist with preparing witnesses for giving testimony at trial.
13. Assist with collecting jury demographics data. Help determine the juror profile for your case.

A case can be won or lost based on how well the attorney-paralegal team prepares for the trial. The best paralegals are prepared to resolve unanticipated problems during trial without excessively burdening the attorney.

6. Deposition summaries
7. A chronology of events
8. The cast of characters
9. Legal research
10. Jury profiles and instructions
11. The trial outline

12. The attorney's notes
13. The "things to do" list.

Preparation of Witnesses

Paralegals are often instrumental in preparing witnesses for trial. One task they frequently perform is arranging for subpoenas to be sent to certain witnesses. They may also be charged with communicating the details of the trial to the witnesses. Finally, they may be required to arrange and attend all witness preparation meetings.

The litigation paralegal must consult with his or her attorney to determine whether any witnesses will require a subpoena. In some instances, attorneys prefer to subpoena only witnesses who are not considered "friendly." However, a friendly witness may request a subpoena to present to an employer as evidence that he or she has been ordered to appear and testify.

Trial subpoenas require the same general procedure as deposition subpoenas. A trial subpoena must be personally served on the witness. In addition, all mileage and witness fees required must be tendered to the witness. Finally, the return-of-service information on the subpoena must be completed and filed with the court before the subpoena becomes valid.

Shortly before trial, the litigation paralegal often arranges a meeting between each witness and the attorney. Before the meeting, paralegals are often asked to collect all documents that pertain to the witness and to review the witness's deposition, noting any areas that give the witness difficulty or that may require further clarification. The paralegal may prepare an outline or actual questions that the attorney anticipates asking each witness during the trial. During the witness preparation meeting, the attorney is responsible for explaining the trial process to each witness. He or she will also explain what is expected from the witness. Many attorneys also conduct mock questioning sessions so that the witness will know exactly what questions will be asked during direct examination. Often this mock session is videotaped so that witnesses may view and critique themselves and their testimony prior to the trial.

Preparation of Exhibits and Briefs

The paralegal is often called upon to gather and organize the exhibits in a case. This responsibility may require obtaining enlarged exhibits or unusual graphics. The paralegal may also have to set up a chronology or organize a set of statistics. Whatever the situation, it helps to know what use is to be made of those exhibits. In some jurisdictions, court rules require that the parties exchange lists of all their trial exhibits before the trial. Once the documents and other materials the attorney will introduce at trial have been established, the litigation paralegal prepares a trial exhibit log to trace the exhibit's progress throughout the trial. This applies to enlarged exhibits, unusual graphics, a chronology of the case, and any other exhibits. It is important for the paralegal to know how to determine the effectiveness of a document that may be used as a trial exhibit. The following questions can help the paralegal to evaluate how effective a document will be as a trial exhibit:

1. Is the document relevant?
2. Is the document admissible?
3. Is the document necessary?
4. Does the document support the cause of action?
5. Is the document confusing?
6. Does the document contain repetitive information?
7. Will the document detract from the testimony of the witness?
8. Does the document increase the effectiveness of the witness's testimony?
9. Is the document easy to read from the jury box and counsel table?
10. Is the document accurate?
11. Does the document have an attractive appearance?
12. Is the document clear?
13. Can a clear and readable copy of the document be made?

14. Can the procedural foundation be laid for introduction of the document at trial?

If the document meets these tests, it is marked as a trial exhibit and entered on the trial exhibit log. The litigation paralegal is often responsible for making copies of the exhibits and placing those copies in manila folders. The files are most often labeled by trial exhibit number and by the name of the witness through whom the exhibit will be produced. Copies of each exhibit must be made for each of the attorneys, for the judge, and for the trial notebook.

Coordinating Trial Logistics

The paralegal is often responsible for coordinating the logistics of a trial. If the trial is held at the local court in the city or county where the attorney usually works, the logistics will be routine. However, when the trial is held in another district or another county, or when the attorney's client and many of the witnesses are from out of town, the paralegal may be asked to arrange for travel, hotel accommodations and food.

Also, for out-of-town trials the paralegal must often examine the courthouse to determine the location of telephones, photocopy machines, fax machines, rest rooms, and vending machines. He or she may also need to locate a work area for meeting with the client or witnesses during the trial. The paralegal could schedule a meeting with the court clerk and the court reporter before the trial and determine if the courtroom will be available the evening before or early on the morning of the trial for the delivery of exhibits and documents. Finally, the litigation paralegal may have to arrange for security clearance and access to courthouse elevators and the loading docks after hours.

The Jury Process

The jury system is a time-honored institution in this country. The Seventh Amendment to the U.S. Constitution guarantees the right to a jury trial in civil lawsuits at common law (as long as the amount in controversy exceeds $20). In the past, planning for, conducting, and winning a case before a jury were largely matters of chance. Today, however, attorneys have a wide variety of tools at their disposal to help maximize the effectiveness of a jury trial. One of the most important of these techniques is the *jury profile,* a composite description of the legal jurors for a particular case. Social psychologists and litigation specialists are equipped to provide law firms with valuable statistics and jury sampling information. These statistics and information are designed to create not only the image of the preferred jurors, but also a profile of the jurors that the paralegal's attorney will want to avoid. Although the cost of this is often prohibitive in smaller cases, if the expense results in a favorable decision or reduces the judgment against a client, the cost will certainly be justified.

Another important technique to maximize the effectiveness of a jury trial is holding a *mock jury trial* prior to the actual trial. A mock trial is a practice trial. Again, social psychologists and litigation specialists can be retained to arrange the mock trial. Legal directories are excellent sources for locating companies that specialize in conducting mock trials.

The jury selection process, *voir dire,* is an area in which litigation paralegals are often used. During **voir dire examination**, the attorneys for each side question potential jurors in an attempt to determine any biases they have that might affect their ability to be fair and impartial in the case. The litigation paralegal may assist by drafting questions for potential jurors. In addition, the paralegal may attend the jury selection to observe and take notes for the attorney.

The Paralegal's Role at Trial

The paralegal's role at the trial concerns the same general areas as during the preparation stages. The paralegal may be responsible for locating

voir dire examination Examination of a potential juror for the purpose of determining whether he or she is qualified and acceptable to act as a juror in the case.

and having the witnesses present in the courtroom for their testimony. The paralegal may also be asked to provide for transportation of witnesses, a task that may even include picking up out-of-town witnesses at the airport. The paralegal may be called upon to calm or reassure a nervous witness, and may have to work with hostile witnesses that the attorney is forced to call to the stand.

During the trial, the litigation paralegal often keeps track of the exhibits introduced by both sides. The exhibit log must be maintained to keep track of which exhibits have been offered and admitted, which exhibits have incurred objections, and whether the exhibit was ultimately admitted into evidence. During the trial, the paralegal confers with the attorney to determine which exhibits will be introduced the next day and reviews the exhibit files to make certain that adequate copies of these exhibits are ready for the next trial session.

The attorney's full energy and concentration must be directed toward the witness on the stand, on the objections raised by opposing counsel, and on the court's rulings on particular motions. The litigation paralegal, therefore, assumes responsibility for taking full and accurate notes of the trial proceedings. A lined notebook with a wide left margin is often used to note inconsistencies in testimony, incomplete answers to questions, and exhibits that have not yet been admitted into evidence. The paralegal often notes the beginning and ending times of each session and each break. These notations enable the paralegal to quickly locate a particular piece of information.

Posttrial Practice

Even the completion of a lengthy trial does not always signal the end of the litigation. There is always the possibility that one of the parties will make a motion for a **judgment notwithstanding the verdict**, which asks the court to have the verdict and its judgment set aside, or a motion for a **new trial**. In addition, there is always the possibility that the case will be appealed to a higher court.

Motion for Judgment Notwithstanding the Verdict

The motion for a judgment notwithstanding the verdict is permitted under Rule 50 of the Federal Rules of Civil Procedure, which allows the court to have the verdict and its judgment set aside when the court is convinced that a group of reasonable individuals would not have reached such a verdict and that the jury's decision is wrong as a matter of law.

Motion for a New Trial

Rule 59 of the Federal Rules of Civil Procedure allows a dissatisfied party to file a motion asking for a new trial. A motion for a new trial must state the legal grounds on which a new trial should be granted. The court may grant such a new trial on the following grounds: (1) a verdict contrary to law; (2) a totally defective verdict; (3) irregularity in the court proceeding; (4) excessive or insufficient damage awards; (5) jury misconduct; or (6) newly discovered evidence.

Appeals to Higher Courts

Litigation paralegals are often instrumental in preparing the appeal. An **appeal** is filed by a party who has lost a case or is dissatisfied with a judgment or a court order. The appeal asks that a higher court review the lower court's decision. A

BALLENTINESBALLENTINESBALLENTINESBALLENTINESBALLENTINESBALLENTINESBALLENTINESBALLENTINESBALLENTINESBALLENTINESBALLENTINESBALLENTINESBALLENTINESBALLENTINES

judgment notwithstanding the verdict A judgment rendered by the court in favor of a party, notwithstanding the fact that the jury has returned a verdict against that party.

new trial A trial that may be ordered by the trial court itself, or by an appellate court on appeal, when prejudicial error has occurred or when, for any other reason, a fair trial was prevented.

appeal The process by which a higher court is requested by a party to a lawsuit to review the decision of a lower court. Such reconsideration is normally confined to a review of the record from the lower court, with no new testimony taken or new issues raised.

person bringing an appeal is referred to as the **appellant**. The person who opposes an appeal is the **appellee**. The appellee may also file a **cross-appeal**, based on a different legal rationale than the appeal filed by the appellant. Only questions of law are subject to review. The appellate court has no authority to consider questions relating to the facts of a case.

In recent years the appellate process has been simplified in the federal courts. The clerk in the district court supervises the preparation of the court records—all pleadings and transcripts in the case—for an appeal. The clerk also provides the attorneys with the appropriate forms and copies of the local rules. In contrast, involvement in a state appellate process generally requires more attention to state court procedural rules.

To initiate an appeal, a **notice of appeal** is filed with the appellate court. The notice of appeal lists the party or parties taking the appeal, the judgment, the order or portion of the judgment appealed (including the caption of the case in the trial court), and the court to which the appeal is taken. According to Rule 4(a) of the Federal Rules of Appellate Procedure, the original of the notice of appeal must be filed with the clerk of the district court from which the appeal is taken within 30 days after entry of the judgment or order appealed.

Under Rule 10(b) of the Federal Rules of Appellate Procedure, within 10 days of the filing of the notice of appeal, the appellant is responsible for making a written request, on a form supplied by the district court clerk, to the court reporter for the complete transcript, the official daily record of the court proceeding, or desired portions of the transcript. A copy of the request is filed with the clerk of district court. The appellant must also notify the clerk of the appellate court that the transcript has been ordered.

The appellate brief is an integral part of the appeal. This formal document consists of the legal issues, the important facts, the legal arguments, and the legal authorities. The paralegal may be called upon to help draft several types of briefs: the appellant's brief, the appellee's brief, and the reply brief. Rules of the appellate court must be consulted with regard to the required format of the brief, the appellate brief colors, and other particularities of the appellate court with regard to briefs.

The requirements for the appellant's brief vary slightly among the federal circuit courts of appeal, but generally they include:

1. Certificate of interested persons
2. Statement regarding oral argument
3. Table of contents
4. Table of cases in alphabetical order
5. List of statutes, treatises, and law review articles, including the author's names where appropriate
6. Statement of jurisdiction
7. Statement of issues
8. Statement of the case, the nature of the case, the course of the proceedings, and the disposition in the court below. This section includes the statement of facts that are relevant to the legal issues, including appropriate references to the record
9. Summary of the argument
10. The argument, including the reasons for the contentions regarding issues, as well as citations to authorities, statutes, and parts of the record relied upon
11. A short conclusion listing the exact relief sought
12. Certificate of service

BALLENTINESBALLENTINESBALLENTINESBALLENTINESBALLENTINESBALLENTINESBALLENTINESBALLENTINESBALLENTINESBALLENTINESBALLENTINESBALLENTINESBALLENTINESBALLENTINESBALLENTINES

appellant   A party who appeals from a lower court to a higher court.

appellee   A party against whom a case is appealed from a lower court to a higher court.

cross-appeal   An appeal filed by the appellee from the same judgment, or some portion of the same judgment, as the appellant has appealed from. A cross appeal is generally made a part of the review proceedings set in motion by the original appeal.

notice of appeal   The process by which appellate review is initiated; specifically, written notice to the appellee advising him or her of the appellant's intention to appeal.

UNITED STATES DISTRICT COURT
FOR THE NORTHERN DISTRICT OF CALIFORNIA

JANET JONES,

    PLAINTIFF,   CIVIL NO. 98765

VS.

DAISY MARTIN AND THE

ELEGANT FLOWERS CORPORATION,

AN OREGON CORPORATION.

NOTICE OF APPEAL

Notice is hereby given that the Elegant Flowers Corporation, defendant herein, hereby appeals to the United States Court of Appeals for the _____ Circuit from the final judgment entered on this action on July 13, 1995.

Respectfully submitted,

TAYLOR MOORE

15 Plaza de Oro

Sacramento, CA 94813

(916) 555-1212

Attorney for Defendant

THE ELEGANT FLOWERS

CORPORATION

Notice of Appeal The notice of appeal is filed by the losing party in a lawsuit, seeking a review of the trial court's decision.

The appellant is also required to file an appendix to its brief, which includes the following parts:

1. Relevant docket entries in the lower court proceeding
2. Relevant portions of the pleadings, charge, findings, or opinion
3. Judgment, order, or decision in question
4. Any other parts of the record to which the parties wish to direct the attention of the court.

Ten copies of the appendix must be filed with the clerk. One copy is served on each counsel of record. Rule 30(d) of the Federal Rules of Appellate Procedure specifies the arrangement of the appendix, as follows:

1. List of parts of record contained in the appendix, in order, with page references
2. Relevant docket entries
3. Other parts of the record in chronological order.

Exhibits designed for inclusion in the appendix may be placed in a separate volume. Four copies of this separate exhibits volume must be filed with the appendix, and a copy served on counsel for each party.

The appellee's brief should follow the requirements of the appellant's brief, with the exception of the statement of issues in the case. This section is not necessary unless the appellee disagrees with the appellant's statement. No conclusion is required in the appellee's brief.

The reply brief permitted by Rule 28(c) of the Federal Rules of Appellate Procedure permits the appellant to file a brief in reply to the appellee's brief. The appellee may also file a cross-appeal based on a different legal rationale than the appeal filed by the appellant.

Oral argument is the presentation of the basis for the appeal before the court of appeals. Oral arguments are permitted in all appellate cases unless, pursuant to local rules, a three-judge panel, after examination of the briefs, unanimously decides that the oral argument is not needed.

After the court of appeals has rendered a decision, a dissatisfied party may seek to continue the appellate process. However, should the appellant eventually lose the case, the appellee may use certain posttrial judgment procedures to secure payment of the award.

Statutory remedies allow for the execution of a judgment within 30 days after the entry of a judgment. The party seeking to execute on the judgment is known as the **judgment creditor**. The party who must pay the judgment is known as the **judgment debtor**. It is often helpful for the judgment creditor to uncover details about the financial condition of the judgment debtor. To facilitate this process, the law permits postjudgment discovery. Postjudgment discovery procedures offer the judgment creditor a relatively simple and inexpensive method of determining the amount and location of the judgment debtor's assets.

A writ of **execution** may be issued 10 days after entry of a final judgment order. A writ of execution is a court order compelling the seizure of the judgment debtor's property to satisfy the judgment. Proper notice must be given to the public and to anyone who has an interest in that property before it can be sold at a public auction. In addition, the judgment debtor must be given the opportunity to pay the judgment creditor before the auction is held.

Another means by which the judgment creditor could collect is by posttrial **garnishment**, a separate but ancillary lawsuit filed in the court that rendered the judgment. The garnishment is brought against a third-party garnishee, that is, a person or company that is holding assets belonging to the judgment debtor. The judgment creditor must obtain a writ of garnishment. The garnishee is then served with the writ and a summons. The garnishee will be compelled to reveal how much of the judgment debtor's money or property is in his or her possession. Once this is known, the judgment creditor can seize the money or property. Bank accounts and wages can be the targets of posttrial garnishment. However, state and federal laws protect a certain percentage of a debtor's income so that he or she can still make a living, despite the garnishment.

BALLENTINESBALLENTINESBALLENTINESBALLENTINESBALLENTINESBALLENTINESBALLENTINESBALLENTINESBALLENTINESBALLENTINESBALLENTINESBALLENTINESBALLENTINES

judgment creditor   A creditor who has secured a judgment against his or her debtor which has not been satisfied.

judgment debtor   A person against whom a judgment, which has not been satisfied, has been entered.

execution   A writ or process for the enforcement of a judgment.

garnishment   A proceeding by a creditor to obtain satisfaction of a debt from money or property of the debtor which is in the possession of a third person or is owed by such a person to the debtor.

Summary Questions

1. Would a question involving proper service of process be a question of procedural law or substantive law?
2. If it does not appear to be practical to initiate litigation, what are some alternative methods of settling a dispute?
3. What are the primary sources for the law of civil litigation?
4. What is a cause of action?
5. What matters are generally contained in a complaint or petition?
6. What types of remedies may be requested from a court?
7. What is a summons?
8. What kinds of responses can a defendant make to the initial pleading?
9. What is an affirmative defense and why is it important?
10. What steps can be taken if the opposing party fails to respond to requests for discovery?
11. What are the major methods of discovery?
12. What are interrogatories?
13. What is a release? What types of releases are available?
14. What are some of the paralegal's duties in trial preparation?
15. What is an appeal?

Practical Paralegal Skills

To complete the following questions and tasks, assume that the facts in the law office scenario in this chapter are true, and that the accident described in the scenario took place in your home town.

1. In which court would you file the summons and complaint? What is the filing fee?
2. Prepare a complaint based on the local rules of court.
3. What is the procedure for requesting a court date in your jurisdiction? How long does it take to get a court date?

Notes

For further reference, see *Civil Litigation for the Paralegal,* by Peggy Kerley, Paul Sukys, and Joanne Banker Hames (Delmar Publishers Inc. and Lawyers Cooperative Publishing 1992).

[1] Milano, Carol, "1993 Legal Assistant Today Salary Survey," *Legal Assistant Today* 48 (May/June 1993).

CHAPTER 9

The Tort Paralegal and Personal Injury Litigation

A relatively small number of paralegals specialize exclusively in the personal injury law area, which is closely related to tort law. However, the work of most paralegals involves torts. Because all paralegals (especially personal injury paralegals) must be familiar with torts and tort law, this chapter discusses the role of the personal injury paralegal in detail, and then focuses on various aspects of tort law that are of particular concern to paralegals.

The Role of Personal Injury Paralegals in Tort Litigation

Personal injury paralegals, whose work almost exclusively concerns litigation based on tort law, represent approximately 10 percent of the paralegals in the United States. A 1993 *Legal Assistant Today* survey indicated that of all the respondents across the nation, 8.9 percent specialized in the area of person injury law. The salaries of personal injury paralegals ranked below average in comparison with paralegals in all areas of law. The national average salary for a personal injury paralegal in 1993 was $25,295. The highest reported salary of a personal injury paralegal was $55,000 and the lowest was $15,480.[1]

The Work of Personal Injury Paralegals in the United States

The work of personal injury paralegals often has a heavy emphasis on interviewing clients and witnesses. The litigation aspect of their positions is very similar to that of paralegals who specialize in any area of civil litigation.

The tasks performed by a personal injury law paralegal will vary greatly depending on whether the paralegal works for a plaintiff's firm or a defense firm (often an insurance company). The following lists some of the tasks most commonly included in the job description of tort or personal injury law paralegals.

Assisting the Defense

1. Interview clients to determine facts relating to their cases
2. Review accident reports and other reports provided by the police or investigators

3. Obtain statements from witnesses to the alleged tort
4. Assist with all aspects of discovery, including medical records, medical examinations, and interrrogatories
5. Assist with pretrial and trial procedures
6. Research legal and factual issues
7. Draft answers to the paintiff's complaints
8. Organize file and exhibits for trial
9. Assist with client preparation for trial
10. Assist the attorney during trial
11. Research and draft posttrial motions
12. Maintain tickler file to remind attorney and client of important court dates and other deadlines.

Assault	Battery
Attempt to make harmful or offensive contact with another person without consent	Unconsented physical contact
Placing the victim in reasonable apprehension for physical safety	Offensive or harmful contact
Threat of imminent contact	Intent to touch another person in offensive or injurious manner

Elements of a Cause of Action for Assault and Battery *Assault* is the threat of unwanted physical contact and *battery* is the actual unwanted physical contact.

Assisting the Plaintiff

1. Interview witnesses
2. Draft complaints, interrogatories, and pleadings
3. Assist with pretrial and trial processes
4. Assist client by giving referrals to appropriate government agencies
5. Draft subpoenas
6. Catalog and prepare exhibits for trial.

Many of these tasks are discussed throughout this chapter. Tasks that may not be performed by a personal injury law paralegal include appearing in court on behalf of a client and giving legal advice to a client.

Skills Important to Personal Injury Law Paralegals

Personal injury law paralegals need some very distinct skills. These paralegals must be able to communicate well, both orally and in writing. They must have the ability to communicate effectively with clients, witnesses, and opposing

Intentional Infliction	Reckless Infliction
Outrageous conduct	Outrageous conduct
Conduct intended to cause severe mental anguish	Conduct known (or reasonably should be known) to cause severe mental anguish
Victim suffers severe mental anguish as result	Victim suffers severe mental anguish as result

Elements of a Cause of Action for Infliction of Emotional Distress *Emotional distress* is a plaintiff's psychological harm caused by the actions of the defendant.

counsel, any of whom may be distraught, upset, or hostile. The paralegal must be able to conduct thorough interviews and investigations to obtain all the necessary facts, often under extraordinary circumstances. Finally, the personal injury law paralegal must possess the ability to perform detailed legal research and apply it with a thorough understanding of civil court systems and procedures.

An Introduction to Torts

A **tort** is a wrongful injury to a person or his or her property. The person inflicting the harm is called the **tortfeasor** (*feasor* meaning "doer"). The word *tort* is French, taken from the Latin *torquere* (meaning "to twist") to characterize behavior that warps or bends society's rules about avoiding harm to others. The French phrase *de son tort demesne* (meaning "in his own wrong") was used to describe grievous misconduct between individuals and to assign blame to the responsible party.

Tort law considers the rights and remedies available to persons injured through other people's carelessness or intentional misconduct. Tort law also holds persons in certain circumstances responsible for other people's injuries regardless of blame. Torts are commonly subdivided into three broad categories: intentional torts, negligence, and strict (or absolute) liability. Paralegals who work in the areas of personal injury or worker's compensation law are most often concerned with intentional torts and negligence. Paralegals who

BALLENTINESBALLENTINESBALLENTINESBALLENTINESBALLENTINESBALLENTINESBALLENTINESBALLENTINESBALLENTINESBALLENTINESBALLENTINESBALLENTINESBALLENTINESBALLENTINES

tort A wrong involving a breach of duty and resulting in an injury to the person or property of another. ... [A] tort is a violation of a duty established by law ... . [T]he tort is a private wrong that must be pursued by the injured party in a civil action.

tortfeasor A person who commits a tort.

specialize in products liability are often concerned with strict (or absolute) liability.

Intentional Torts

Intentional torts consist of actions designed to injure another person or that person's property. The tortfeasor intends a particular harm to result from the misconduct. There are several specific types of intentional torts: battery, assault, false imprisonment, infliction of emotional distress, fraud, misrepresentation, malicious prosecution, abuse of process, invasion of privacy, defamation (libel and slander), trespass, conversion, slander of title, commercial disparagement, and defamation by computer.

    Battery occurs when a tortfeasor touches another person without consent. *Assault* is an attempted battery. *False imprisonment* happens when an individual is intentionally confined against his or her will. *Infliction of emotional distress* results from someone's outrageous conduct that is designed to cause another to suffer anxiety, fright, or anguish. *Fraud* occurs when the tortfeasor intentionally makes false statements to entice someone to give up something of value to the tortfeasor. *Misrepresentation* exists when one person makes a false statement (or behaves so as) to deceive another individual. *Malicious prosecution* happens when a prosecutor purposefully and in bad faith files groundless criminal charges against a defendant. *Abuse of process* exists when a plaintiff maliciously uses the court system against a defendant to achieve some unlawful objective. *Invasion of privacy* occurs when someone publicly exploits another's private affairs in an unreasonably intrusive manner. *Defamation* is an injury to one's reputation in the community and may be inflicted by *libel,* which is written defamation, or *slander,* which is oral defamation. *Trespass* is unlawful or unreasonable interference with the use of someone's property. *Conversion* is wrongfully taking personal property from its rightful owner, either permanently or for an indefinite period of time. *Slander of title* happens when someone falsely and maliciously disparages the ownership rights that a legal owner has in his or her property. *Commercial disparagement* occurs when one makes a false or misleading statement about a business to discourage the public from patronizing that business. *Defamation by computer* exists when personal information about an individual that is kept in a computer system is misused or is incorrect and results in injury to that person's reputation or ability to obtain credit.

Negligence

Negligence is the failure to exercise reasonable care to avoid injuring others. It is distinguishable from intentional torts in that negligence does not require the *intent* to commit a wrongful action; instead, the wrongful action itself is sufficient to constitute negligence. Intentional torts, as the name indicates, require the tortfeasor to intend to commit the wrongful act. What makes misconduct negligent is that the behavior was not reasonably careful and someone was injured as a result of this unreasonable carelessness.

Strict, or Absolute, Liability

Strict (or **absolute**) **liability** is the tortfeasor's responsibility for injuring another regardless of intent, negligence, or fault. The most important type of strict liability is **products liability**, a theory under which the manufacturer or other seller of an unreasonably dangerous or defective product is held liable for injuries the product causes. Strict liability is different from intentional torts in that

---

negligence   The failure to do something that a reasonable person would do in the same circumstances, or the doing of something a reasonable person would not do. Negligence is a wrong generally characterized by carelessness, inattentiveness, and neglectfulness rather than by a positive intent to cause injury.

strict liability   Liability for an injury whether or not there is fault or negligence; absolute liability.

product liability   The liability of a namufacturer or seller of an article for an injury caused to a person or to property by a defect in the article sold.

|||| *Law Office Scenario*   **||||**

As an experienced personal injury paralegal, William was often asked to sit in on initial client conferences with the attorney he worked for, Anna Rosenthal. On this particular day, Anna was meeting with a new client, John Jacobson.

John had recently been involved in an automobile collision, and he was contemplating a lawsuit against the driver of the other vehicle. William was asked to attend the meeting with John to take notes. Later he would follow up with John to gather further details and explain the procedures that would be followed throughout the lawsuit (if one was to be initiated).

William went to the reception area to greet John. John's left arm was in a cast, his right hand was bandaged, and he was on crutches. William assisted him into the conference room, where he briefly described the automobile collision to Anna and William.

"I was going North on Elm Street across the intersection of Elm and Second Avenue, when the driver of a black pickup truck ran the red light and broadsided me. The driver's name was Steve Jensen," he said.

"The police arrived and took our statements. Steve Jensen admitted that the accident was completely his fault. I think he had been drinking," he continued. "I broke my left arm and sprained my right ankle."

"Was Mr. Jensen injured?" asked Anna.

"Well ..." John hesitated. "I guess I broke his nose when I punched him. That's how I hurt my right hand. I lost my temper when I got out of the car, and I punched him in the nose before he could even say anything. I didn't really mean to hurt him, I was just so upset about the accident. He could have killed me!"

William listened as John continued describing the incident to Anna. He then met with John alone to collect further details concerning his injuries, medical treatment, medical expenses, expected recovery, and other information concerning the accident.

---

intent to commit an absolute liability tort is irrelevant. Likewise, strict liability is distinguishable from negligence, because the tortfeasor is responsible under absolute liability regardless of how careful he or she might have been.

The Unique Elements of Each Tort

Each type of tort contains its own unique elements. For instance, battery may be readily distinguished from defamation because it carries its own definition and rules that separate it from other intentional torts. Likewise, the elements of negligence are different from strict liability's components, and so on. The key to understanding tort law is to identify the type of broad tort category involved in the case. Ask whether the problem contains intentional torts (and, if so, which

particular one[s]), negligence, or strict liability. Next, apply the appropriate rules of law to the specific facts of the case.

Paralegals who work in the personal injury area of law or other areas of law involving torts must be able to identify the type of tort category involved in each case to which they are assigned. In the law office scenario, William would probably be able to recognize negligence on behalf of the potential defendant, Steve Jensen. In addition, he would probably realize that John Jacobson committed an intentional tort when he punched Steve in the nose.

Sources of Tort Law

Tort law is derived from both common and statutory law. Legislatures often enact statutes to supplement, modify, or supersede common-law tort principles. Paralegals who are asked to perform tort law research often must research both the statutes and the case law in the pertinent jurisdiction. In addition, the American Law Institute has assembled the Restatements of Law for decades.

The *Restatement of Torts* and its successor, the *Restatement (Second) of Torts*, summarize the legal principles discussed in common-law decisions and are very valuable secondary sources concerning tort law.

Public Policy Objectives in Tort Law

Like every aspect of our legal system, there are several purposes underlying tort principles. These include (1) protecting persons and property from unjust injury by providing legally enforceable rights; (2) compensating victims by holding accountable those persons responsible for causing such harms; (3) encouraging minimum standards of social conduct among society's members; (4) deterring violations of those standards of conduct; and (5) allocating losses among different participants in the social arena.

Protecting Persons and Property: Accountability

Modern tort law strives to prevent unjustified harm to innocent victims. Tort law enables private citizens to use the legal system to resolve disputes in which one party claims that the other has acted improperly, resulting in harm. The system compels the tortfeasor to compensate the injured party for his or her losses. This **accountability** (or **culpability**) factor is crucial to our legal sense of fair play and equity. People should be held responsible for their actions, especially when they wreak havoc on others. Redress should be available for innocent victims of carelessness, recklessness, or intentional injury.

Minimum Standards of Social Conduct: Deterrence

To function meaningfully in American society, citizens must understand society's norms and values. One extremely important norm encourages

the public to behave so as to avoid hurting others or their belongings. Tort law is largely composed of minimum standards of conduct, and persons functioning below such thresholds are defined as tortfeasors, whereas individuals acting at or above such criteria are acceptable to the community. However, the intention is not to ensure conformity; rather, the ideal is to inspire people to respect the dignity and integrity each individual possesses. We should not infringe heedlessly upon another's activities unless we are willing to accept such interference with our own lives. Tort law discourages abuses by establishing a clear system of legal rights and remedies enforceable in court proceedings. We know that we can go to court when someone strikes us, invades our privacy, creates a nuisance, or acts negligently toward us. Likewise, we know that we might be hauled into court if we do these things to others. By establishing minimum standards of conduct, tort law sets the rules for living—those "rules of thumb" by which we try to get along with other people.

Allocating Losses among Different Individuals or Groups

In today's extended marketing chain, people buy canned fruit from a local grocery that bought it from a wholesaler that bought it from a manufacturer. If the fruit is spoiled, perhaps the purchaser's spouse or child, rather than the purchaser, will suffer the injury. The culpability lines become less clear as the producer of the defective item becomes more removed from the ultimate user. Tort law has evolved *products liability* to determine who is in the best position to bear the costs of defective products—the innocent user or the sellers and manufacturers. It is an economic decision that courts and legislatures have made in stating that industry can best afford the costs of injuries caused by dangerously made goods. In other words, the burden of shouldering the economic loss is placed upon commercial business instead of the individual suffering the harm. This illustrates how tort law can be used to assign the expenses associated with misfortune, even when fault is hazy at best. More commonly, though, a single tortfeasor can be identified and saddled with the financial obligation.

Intentional Torts

Intentional torts consist of conduct that is fashioned to harm another person or his or her property. The mischeif is directed with the purpose of inflicting injury. All intentional torts include two elements: intent and injurious behavior. **Intent** may be broadly defined as the desire to achieve a particular result. Specifically, the tortfeasor must intend to accomplish the harmful consequences of his or her actions. This does not require malice or ill will, however; the tortfeasor must simply intend to cause the consequences that give rise to the tort. Commonly, though, those consequences include some type of harm. Then these acts must actually conclude in the injury that was intended.

For certain peculiar intentional torts, intent, strictly speaking, is not required. For example, for reckless infliction of emotional distress, intent is not essential. The tortfeasor need only know (or reasonably should know) that his or her outlandish actions will produce emotional injury. This knowledge element acts as a substitute for intent.

Intent and Action Together

Intent reflects the tortfeasor's state of mind and must occur simultaneously with the misconduct. For example, assume that David and Linda are carpenters. Linda tosses a piece of wood across a room into a pile, but before it lands the wood strikes David in the throat. Linda would not be liable for battery, because, although the board struck David, Linda did not intend this to happen. Suppose David thought about throwing the board back at Linda but did nothing and walked away. David would not be liable for assault because no action accompanied his desire.

Intentional torts present a relatively black-and-white image of the law, in which it is fairly easy to distinguish the "good" person from the "bad." The victim seems truly exploited, and the tortfeasor is clearly responsible and to blame (from a moral or ethical point of view) for having purposefully injured the victim. Our sense of fair play is rewarded when intentional tortfeasors are held accountable for their mischief.

Types of Intentional Torts

This section describes the most common intentional torts by analyzing the legal definitions and elements of each. A tort law paralegal might be involved in researching the facts and the law for

BALLENTINESBALLENTINESBALLENTINESBALLENTINESBALLENTINESBALLENTINESBALLENTINESBALLENTINESBALLENTINESBALLENTINESBALLENTINESBALLENTINESBALLENTINESBALLENTINES

accountable   Responsible; liable.

culpable   Blameworthy; blameable; responsible; at fault.

intent   Purpose; the plan, course, or means a person conceives to achieve a certain result.

any of these torts, and in helping to apply legal theory to the facts of a given case.

Assault and Battery

The preceding example of the careless carpenters depicts two of the most common intentional torts: assault and battery. Of all torts, these are perhaps the most straightforward.

Assault

Assault is an attempt by one person to make harmful or offensive contact with another individual without consent. Actual physical contact is not necessary; in fact, contact converts an assault to a battery. Assault is distinguishable from battery in that no touching is required.

The rights being protected by recognition of this tort involve each person's right to control what touches his or her person. Assault is also intended to protect individuals from the fear or apprehension that unconsented contact will take place. **Apprehension** means that a person reasonably fears for his or her physical safety in anticipation of being struck by the unconsented harmful or distasteful contact. This apprehension must be **reasonable**, meaning that the anxiety must be rational given the perceived threat of contact. For example, if a four-year-old warns that she is going to punch her father's head off, her father probably would not be overly concerned, as it would be unreasonable for an adult to fear a child's threatened battery under such circumstances. Threats at a distance also do not present sufficient reason for alarm, because it is physically impossible for the threatening party to fulfill the threat. This states the next legal requirement for assault: immediate threat of contact.

Assault involves the imminent or immediate threat that unconsented contact is about to occur. The fear arises from the likelihood that someone or something unwanted is about to strike. For instance, Michelle's threat to hit George while talking to him on the telephone does not present an immediate risk, because the deed cannot be completed at the time the threat is made. Therefore, no assault has taken place.

Battery

A completed assault is called a battery. Strictly defined, a **battery** is the intentional, unconsented touching of another person in an offensive or injurious manner. There are three basic elements to this tort:

1. Unconsented physical contact
2. Offensive or harmful contact
3. The tortfeasor's intent to touch another person in an offensive or injurious manner.

John Jacobson from the law office scenario most certainly comitted the tort of battery when he punched Steve Jensen in the nose, as (1) the punch was unconsented physical contact that was (2) harmful to Steve and (3) it was John Jacobson's intent to punch Steve.

Actual touching is necessary for a battery to occur. However, contact need not be made with a person's body. It is sufficient for the tortfeasor to touch the victim's clothing, or an object that the victim is carrying, such as a purse, or an object in which the victim is sitting, such as a chair or automobile. These items are said to become *extensions* of the person which, if touched, translates into touching the person himself or herself.

Battery occurs only if the victim did not consent to the physical contact. Consent can be *expressed*

BALLENTINESBALLENTINESBALLENTINESBALLENTINESBALLENTINESBALLENTINESBALLENTINESBALLENTINESBALLENTINESBALLENTINESBALLENTINESBALLENTINESBALLENTINES

assault   An act of force or threat of force intended to inflict harm upon a person or to put the person in fear that such is imminent … . The perpetrator must have, or appear to have, the present ability to carry out the act.

apprehension   Anxiety.

reasonable   Rational; not arbitrary or capricious; sensible.

battery   The unconsented-to touching or striking of one person by another, or by an object put in motion by him or her, with the intention of doing harm or giving offense.

or *implied*. Expressed consent is relatively easy to identify. For example, participants in sporting events readily consent to physical contact routinely associated with the activity. Implied consent arises out of particular situations, in which individuals, by being involved, implicitly agree to some types of minor contact. For instance, people walking in crowds impliedly consent to incidental contact as they accidentally bump into passersby. It is reasonable and normal to expect that this will occur in crowded places, and those involved are (or should be) willing to tolerate some minor jostles.

Battery requires touching that is harmful or offensive. Although harmful contact should be relatively simple to perceive, offensive touching may present some surprises. Often, offensive contact may be intended as positive or complimentary, such as a pat on the back or kiss on the cheek from a co-worker. The recipient, however, may find these actions distasteful. This addresses the consent issue: people do not usually consent to touching that repulses them.

Whether or not the physical contact is offensive is judged by a **reasonable person test**. Would a reasonable person have been insulted by the contact, given the same or similar circumstances? Reasonableness is often based upon the victim's actions in conjunction with the tortfeasor's. For example, if two co-workers are accustomed to "goofing around" by jokingly touching one another (pats on the back, fake punches, tickling, etc.), then such behavior would not be reasonably offensive. In effect, the participants consented to the activity. On the other hand, a male supervisor touching a female employee in a sexually explicit fashion could reasonably be perceived as degrading and offensive.

Intent

Battery, like all intentional torts, includes an element of intent. The tortfeasor must have intended to make contact with another individual in a harmful or offensive manner. Thus, accidentally bumping into someone in an elevator as it jerked into motion would not be a battery, because the contact was unintentional. But pinching that person while leaving the elevator would be battery, as the act was purposefully designed to make offensive contact.

Sometimes the tortfeasor tries to strike someone but ends up hitting someone else. For instance, if Robert threw a stone at Stuart but struck Mark instead, then Robert has committed battery against Mark. Although Robert intended to strike Stuart, his intent is said to be carried along by the object he set into motion—the stone—and his intent is thus transferred with the stone onto whomever it reaches—in this case, Mark. Note, too, that Robert has assaulted Stuart by throwing the stone and missing, provided that Stuart was placed in reasonable apprehension, and so on.

Transferred intent is an effective tool for protecting persons from misdirected physical contacts. It holds the tortfeasor accountable for the consequences of his or her actions even though, strictly speaking, he or she did not desire to hit the third person involved.

False Imprisonment

False imprisonment occurs when the tortfeasor intentionally confines someone without his or her consent. This tort is meant to protect each individual's right to control his or her own freedom of movement. Essentially, there are four elements to false imprisonment:

BALLENTINESBALLENTINESBALLENTINESBALLENTINESBALLENTINESBALLENTINESBALLENTINESBALLENTINESBALLENTINESBALLENTINESBALLENTINESBALLENTINESBALLENTINESBALLENTINES

reasonable man (person) test   A standard for determining negligence, which asks: "What would a reasonable person have done in the same circumstances?" ... [I]t measures the failure to do that which a person of ordinary intelligence and judgment would have done in the circumstances, or the doing of that which a person of ordinary intelligence and judgment would not have done.

transferred intent   The doctrine that if a defendant who intends to injure one person unintentionally harms another, the intent is transferred to the person who is unintentionally harmed. This doctrine permits the defendant to be prosecuted as if he or she had intended to harm the person injured.

false imprisonment   The unlawful restraint of one person of the physical liberty of another.

1. Confinement without captive's consent
2. Tortfeasor's intent to confine victim
3. Confinement for an appreciable length of time
4. No reasonable means of escape.

Confinement

All methods of confinement include (1) a restriction of the victim's freedom of movement, (2) the captive's awareness or fear of the restriction, and (3) the victim's nonconsent to the restriction. The second element prevents the victim from escaping, either because no routes of escape are available, or because the victim is afraid to attempt escape for fear of the tortfeasor's reprisals.

There are several ways in which the tortfeasor may confine his or her captive. Physical barriers are the most common method of falsely imprisoning someone. Placing the captive in a locked room or a moving automobile (while refusing to stop) are common examples. However, the physical barriers need not be so small as a single room or vehicle. A captive may be restricted to the grounds of a series of adjacent buildings. It is even possible for the victim to be penned in by such unexpected blockades as an automobile blocking the victim's access from a driveway to a street. The physical barrier need only restrict the captive's freedom of movement. This essentially traps the victim, either by some actual physical obstruction, such as a locked door, fence, or wall, or by an object which the tortfeasor is using to restrain the captive, such as the automobile blocking the driveway or even the tortfeasor's own body obstructing a doorway.

Sometimes no locked door or wall is necessary to confine a person. Threats of physical or emotional violence can be quite effective. In this way, confinement is achieved by expressed **intimidation**. The victim is afraid to escape for fear of physical or emotional injury.

These types of threats need not be explicit, however. Implied threats also work effectively. For instance, if a store manager tells a shoplifting suspect to wait in a room for questioning "so that nobody has to telephone the police," the threat of arrest and criminal prosecution is clearly implied, and the suspect will probably comply out of fear.

Captive's Consent to Confinement

The intentional tort of false imprisonment cannot occur if the victim consents to the captivity. **Consent** includes awareness and acceptance of the confinement. Thus, if a shoplifting suspect agrees to remain in a room pending questioning by store security, this constitutes consent, because the patron knows and accepts the restriction to the room.

Intent to Confine

The tortfeasor must intend to confine the victim for false imprisonment to happen. Consider the example of an accidental lock-in at a department store, where a customer is inadvertently locked in the store after closing hours. There would be no false imprisonment, because the store management had no desire to confine the patron. Intent may be expressed or implied by conduct.

Confinement for Appreciable Time Period

Although no definite time period is required, false imprisonment occurs only if the confinement has existed for an appreciable length of time. This depends upon the specific facts of each case. Usually, *appreciable confinement* is defined as unreasonable under the circumstances. That could be a matter of seconds, if someone is restrained in an extremely hazardous situation, such as in a burning building; or it could be a question of an hour or two, such as during a shoplifting investigation.

BALLENTINESBALLENTINESBALLENTINESBALLENTINESBALLENTINESBALLENTINESBALLENTINESBALLENTINESBALLENTINESBALLENTINESBALLENTINESBALLENTINESBALLENTINESBALLENTINES

intimidation   The act of putting a person in fear by threatening to commit an unlawful act. Intimidation does not necessarily involve an act of violence or even a threat of violence.

consent   Agreement; approval; acquiescence; being of one mind.

No Reasonable Means of Escape

False imprisonment cannot happen if the captive has a reasonable avenue of escape. In other words, the confinement must be complete. If the victim could simply walk away from the situation, then no false imprisonment transpired. Reasonable means of escape depend upon the facts of each case, but usually they include any route that a reasonable person would use under the circumstances to flee. For example, if Roger makes improper advances upon Betty in his automobile, and Betty has only to open the door to leave, then she has a reasonable avenue of escape, and no false imprisonment has happened. However, if Roger made the same advances on Betty in a fourth-floor apartment, in which the only exits were one door (which Roger blocked) and the windows, then false imprisonment would have occurred. Betty could hardly be expected to escape by leaping from a fourth-story window.

Infliction of Emotional Distress

In the law of intentional torts, infliction of emotional distress has developed as a separate cause of action to protect injured parties from other people's efforts to cause shock, fright, or other psychological trauma. *Emotional distress* may be broadly defined as mental anguish caused by a tortfeasor. Synonyms such as fright, anxiety, shock, grief, mental suffering, or emotional disturbance are commonly used to describe this tort. The condition can include shame or embarrassment as well. The critical aspect of infliction of emotional distress is that the victim suffers from mental anguish rather than from some physical injury caused by the tortfeasor. It is the psychological harm that this tort intends to remedy.

Not just any insult or offensive behavior will result in this tort, however. The misdeed must be so outrageous that a reasonable person would suffer severe emotional injury as a consequence. This is the key element to all infliction of emotional distress cases. Minor annoyances or indignities are part of everyday life, and these are not included in this tort. If it were otherwise, the courts would overflow with lawsuits based upon the irritations we all encounter from other people almost daily. Obviously, the law cannot reshape the world into the loving, peaceful utopia we might prefer, but it can discourage flagrant actions tailored to cause mental suffering.

Intentional Infliction

Intentional infliction of emotional distress contains three elements:

1. Outrageous conduct by the tortfeasor
2. Conduct intended to cause severe mental anguish in the victim
3. The victim's suffering severe mental anguish as a consequence of the tortfeasor's behavior.

First, the tortfeasor's behavior must be sufficiently outrageous. The common test for outrageous conduct is one of reasonableness. Would a reasonable person suffer substantial emotional distress as a result of the tortfeasor's actions? Were these activities so outlandish as to shock the conscience of a reasonable person? Or, put another way, would a person of ordinary sensibilities suffer mental pain as a consequence? This generally excludes all but the most extreme types of egregious conduct.

Examples of outrageous conduct abound in the legal literature. Tasteless practical jokes often provide fodder for emotional distress litigation. Consider the person who places a dead mouse inside a soda pop bottle from which someone is drinking and then tells the drinker about the mouse. Or the heartless prankster who tells a parent that his or her child has just been struck and killed by an automobile when, in fact, this never occurred, as the joker knew perfectly well. These are clear instances of outrageous conduct that most people would agree are highly offensive and would cause intense emotional dismay to the victims.

Obviously, intentional infliction cases must include the element of intent. The tortfeasor must purposefully behave so as to create mental anguish in the victim; the tortfeasor desires to cause anguish. This separates intentional infliction from reckless infliction, which does not require that the tortfeasor tailor his or her acts to cause mental suffering.

Naturally, the victim must actually suffer emotionally as a result of the tortfeasor's antics. Again, the test for anguish revolves around the way a reasonable person of ordinary sensibilities would react to the tortfeasor's actions. Courts have often complained that determining genuine emotional suffering from faked distress is extremely difficult, because anyone can pretend to be upset by something. However, physical symptoms usually accompany mental distress, such as loss of sleep, weight, appetite, or vigor; illnesses brought on after the mental shock; or other signs of effect, such as tremors, twitches, or sensitivity to loud or sudden noises. It is important to note, though, that modern courts do not require physical manifestations in intentional infliction cases. Mental suffering alone, unaccompanied by physical effects, is sufficient, provided that the trier of fact is convinced of the authenticity of the distress.

Reckless Infliction

The elements of **reckless** *infliction of emotional distress* are the same as for intentional infliction, except that intent is not necessary. Instead, it is adequate that the tortfeasor knew or reasonably should have known that his or her deeds would cause severe emotional distress to the victim. The behavior must still be outrageous, but it is enough that the tortfeasor carelessly or wantonly acted so as to emotionally disturb the victim.

Many reckless infliction cases include the mishandling of the remains of deceased persons. Consider a common fact pattern: A funeral home cremates the deceased instead of following the family's clear and explicit instructions regarding burial. Even though the funeral home did not intend this error, the conduct could be construed as so reckless as to fall within this tort.

Another type of fact situation involves the unanticipated effect of a practical joke. Consider the pranksters who vandalized someone's automobile by smearing it with manure, knowing that the vehicle owner took enormous pride in the car's appearance. The jokers knew that the owner had a weak heart, but were only expecting to shake him up. When the owner saw his prize automobile, he collapsed from a heart attack. This illustrates wanton misconduct. Although the pranksters did not intend the victim to suffer heart failure as a consequence of their deed, the tortfeasors' behavior revealed utter disregard for the health and well-being of the victim, and accordingly they would be liable for reckless infliction of emotional distress.

Fraud and Misrepresentation

Fraud occurs when a tortfeasor makes false statements to entice the victim to give up something of value to the tortfeasor. **Misrepresentation** exists when the tortfeasor knowingly makes false statements or purposefully behaves in such a way as to deceive the victim. The two torts are quite similar. Both involve false statements or actions. Both include deception as the tortfeasor's objective. Yet fraud features the element of underhanded economic gain: the victim surrenders something valuable to the tortfeasor as a result of the spurious comments. As a practical matter, however, a tortfeasor who commits fraud also commits misrepresentation, although they technically are not the same tort. Still, many courts view them as synonymous.

The elements of each tort are practically interchangeable. For fraud, the following must exist:

reckless   [C]onduct demonstrating an indifference to consequences, particularly those involving danger to life or to the safety of others.

fraud   Deceit, deception, or trickery that is intended to induce, and does induce, another to part with anything of value or surrender some legal right.

misrepresentation   The statement of an untruth; a misstatement of fact designed to lead one to believe that something is other than it is; a false statement of fact designed to deceive.

1. The defrauder must intend to deceive by making false statements
2. The defrauder must know that the statements made are false
3. The purpose of the false statements must be to entice the victim into giving the tortfeasor something of value.

For misrepresentation, the first two elements of fraud must occur. Some courts, however, also add the third element to misrepresentation, making it identical to fraud. In such jurisdictions, the two concepts are thus redundant.

A tortfeasor commits fraud or misrepresentation by making false statements designed to delude the victim. For example, if Aaron tells Stephanie that he can repair her broken dishwasher for $100, when Aaron knows that he lacks the requisite skill and knowledge to do so, then Aaron has made false statements intended to mislead Stephanie into paying him the money for work he cannot perform.

The tortfeasor must know that the information given to the victim is false for fraud or misrepresentation to happen. For instance, if Henry sold Michelle a new computer with a defective floppy disk drive of which Henry was totally unaware, then Henry has not engaged in either fraud or misrepresentation, because he did not know about the product defect when he made the sale.

For fraud, the defrauder must make false statements tailored to encourage the victim to surrender something of value to the tortfeasor. In the preceding example, Aaron duped Stephanie in order to receive her money. This constitutes fraud.

Malicious Prosecution and Abuse of Process

Usually the law distinguishes malicious prosecution from abuse of process in this way: Malicious prosecution occurs in criminal prosecutions, whereas abuse of process happens in civil litigation. They are similar intentional torts.

Malicious Prosecution

Malicious prosecution arises when a private citizen files with the prosecutor a groundless criminal complaint against another person (who is named as the defendant in the subsequent criminal proceeding). The following elements comprise this tort:

1. Groundless criminal prosecution against the accused
2. The complainant's malice in filing the spurious charges
3. The accused's acquittal from, or dismissal of, the criminal charges
4. Injury to the accused as a result of the prosecution.

The individual registering a criminal complaint with the police or prosecutor is sometimes called the **complainant**. The complainant's actions are considered bogus if he or she prefers criminal charges without probable cause to think that the accused was guilty of the crime. **Probable cause** is routinely defined as the reasonable belief that the accused is guilty of the alleged crime. This belief need exist only at the time the criminal charges are initiated for probable cause to exist. However, if it later becomes obvious through investigation that the accused did not commit the alleged crime, then the complainant's insistence on continuing prosecution would be malicious prosecution.

Malice in filing spurious criminal charges may be inferred from the circumstances surrounding the case. If the complainant knew (or reasonably

malicious prosecution A criminal prosecution or civil suit commenced maliciously and without probable cause.

complainant A person who files a formal accusation of a crime. … A person who makes any formal complaint.

probable cause A reasonable amount of suspicion, supported by circumstances sufficiently strong to justify a prudent and cautious person's belief that certain alleged facts are probably true.

malice State of mind that causes the intentional doing of a wrongful act without legal excuse or justification; a condition of mind prompting a person to the commission of a dangerous or deadly act in deliberate disregard of the lives or safety of others.

should have known) that the accused did not commit the alleged crime, then malice is implied. Also, if the complainant is using the criminal prosecution to obtain some improper objective, such as intimidating the accused into settling a disputed civil claim or to extort money from the accused, then this likewise implies malice.

To recover successfully for malicious prosecution, the accused must have been acquitted of the groundless criminal charges initiated by the complainant, or the prosecution must have been otherwise disposed of in the accused's favor (dismissal of charges, for instance). Like all torts, the accused must prove actual injury as a consequence of the wrongful prosecution. This is most often accomplished by showing damage to the accused's reputation in the community or financial standing, mental anguish, or legal expenses associated with defending the criminal charges.

Abuse of Process

Abuse of process is the civil equivalent of malicious prosecution. It occurs when the tortfeasor misuses a legal proceeding against another person to achieve an unlawful objective. The elements of abuse of process are:

1. Misuse of a legal proceeding, or threat of such misuse
2. Misuse to achieve unlawful objectives
3. Injury to the victim as a result of the misuse.

The tortfeasor must intentionally misuse (or threaten to misuse) a legal proceeding against another person to accomplish an objective to which the process abuser is not legally entitled. The tortfeasor might threaten frivolous civil litigation in an attempt to frighten the victim into paying a disputed claim. For example, the process abuser might file a groundless lawsuit against an innocent defendant in an attempt to "scare up some quick money." This occasionally occurs in personal injury litigation when fault is difficult to assign and prove; the personal injury plaintiff abuses process by suing a convenient (but innocent) defendant (who usually has assets or insurance but seems unlikely to defend a frivolous lawsuit).

Litigation is not the only legal process that may be misapplied, however. Creditors filing improper mechanic's liens against debtors to collect on disputed debts, or debtors threatening to file bankruptcy to avoid creditors, are also guilty of abuse of process.

The pivotal aspect of abuse of process is the tortfeasor's misuse of a legal proceeding to gain some indirect benefit to which he or she is not legally entitled. The tortfeasor has an ulterior motive for manipulating the legal proceeding.

Invasion of Privacy

Invasion of privacy exists when someone publicly exploits another person's private affairs in an unreasonably intrusive manner. Perhaps no other intentional tort excites the public indignation more than invasion of privacy. However, the popular conception of the right to **privacy** does not always afford legal remedies. In tort law, there are four separate types of invasion of privacy:

1. Appropriation
2. Unreasonable intrusion
3. Public disclosure of private facts
4. False light in the public eye.

The United States Supreme Court also recognizes a fifth type of invasion of privacy protected under the United States Constitution. This includes actions by governmental agencies that infringe upon a citizen's life, liberty, or property interests safeguarded by the Constitution. However, this type is not covered by tort law.

BALLENTINESBALLENTINESBALLENTINESBALLENTINESBALLENTINESBALLENTINESBALLENTINESBALLENTINESBALLENTINESBALLENTINESBALLENTINESBALLENTINESBALLENTINESBALLENTINES

abuse of process The use of legal process in a manner not contemplated by the law to achieve a purpose not intended by the law.

invasion of privacy A violation of the right of privacy.

privacy [T]he right to be left alone.

Appropriation

Appropriation occurs when the tortfeasor uses a person's name or likeness without permission to gain some benefit. For example, if an advertising company uses a person's photograph to sell a product without that person's consent, then the firm would be liable to the person for invasion of privacy by appropriation. Most cases involving this variety of invasion of privacy consist of unauthorized use of photographs, artist's sketches, or quotations associated with names to sell someone else's goods or services.

Unreasonable Intrusion

Unreasonable intrusion involves an excessive and highly offensive assault upon one's seclusion or solitude. Several illustrations should clarify. If store security personnel demand that a suspected shoplifter disrobe, or if they rifle through the suspect's personal belongings in an illegal search, this would be considered unreasonable intrusion. Intentional eavesdropping upon a private conversation is another example. Searching another's mail or trash to discover private information, or obtaining unauthorized access to someone's bank account or tax records, are yet other instances. Courts have also found that illegal, compulsory blood tests equal unreasonable intrusion. Simple trespassing onto an individual's land to snoop also violates this version of privacy.

Public Disclosure of Private Facts

When a tortfeasor communicates purely private information about a person to the public without permission, and a reasonable person would find this disclosure extremely objectionable, then invasion of privacy by *public disclosure of private facts* has taken place. Truth is *not* a defense against this tort, because it is the unauthorized and offensive public revelation of private facts that is being protected against.

The most common example of such disclosure involves communications by the mass media. For example, if a newspaper article mentions an ordinary citizen by name and discusses in detail his or her drug dependency problems, and the person did not consent, then public disclosure of private facts has occurred. Public figures, however, generally do not succeed in lawsuits against the media when such disclosures are made without malice.

False Light in the Public Eye

Invasion of privacy by placing a person in a *false light in the public eye* happens if the tortfeasor publicly attributes to that individual spurious opinions, statements, or actions. For instance, if a magazine used, without permission, someone's photograph and name in an embarrassing fashion, this would place the victim in a false light publicly. One fact pattern repeated in many court cases concerns a plaintiff's photograph and name which appear in a newspaper adjacent to a negative story appearing on the same page, when the story and photograph appear in such a way as to suggest a connection between the two.

Defamation: Libel and Slander

Defamation consists of two varieties: libel and slander. **Libel** is a written false and disparaging statement about an individual that the tortfeasor communicates to a third person. **Slander** is an oral false and disparaging statement about a person that the tortfeasor communicates to a third party. Courts often refer to this communication element as **publication**. Publication of the

BALLENTINESBALLENTINESBALLENTINESBALLENTINESBALLENTINESBALLENTINESBALLENTINESBALLENTINESBALLENTINESBALLENTINESBALLENTINESBALLENTINESBALLENTINESBALLENTINES

defamation   Libel or slander; the written or oral publication, falsely and intentionally, of anything that is injurious to the good name or reputation of another person.

libel   A false and malicious publication, expressed either in printing, writing, or by signs and pictures, tending to harm a person's reputation and expose him or her to public hatred, contempt, or ridicule.

slander   A false and malicious oral statement tending to blacken a person's reputation or to damage his or her means of livelihood.

publication   The act of making something known to the public; the act of publishing. ... [T]he act of communicating a defamation to a person or persons other than the person defamed.

defamatory information must injure the victim's reputation in the community. The elements can be outlined as follows:

1. Written (libel) or oral (slander) statement
2. False and defamatory statement about a person
3. Tortfeasor's communication of the statement to a third party
4. Harm to the victim's reputation in the community.

Defamation is another intentional tort, like assault and battery, that virtually everyone has experienced, either as victim or tortfeasor (or both). One need only recall a recent imprudent remark to mentally invoke accusations of slander or libel. Nevertheless, the elements determine whether defamation has occurred.

Nature of the Statement

For libel, the statement must generally be written in some fashion. This does not necessarily mean writing, such as handwriting, or printed words, such as those appearing on this page. There are many forms of written expression, including such unusual methods as billboards, skywriting with smoke or banners pulled by an airplane, or placing objects such as stones into the shapes of letters. The critical element of writing is whether the information is communicated visually through means of an alphabet.

For slander, the statement must be orally delivered. But it does not have to be words. Gestures, particularly obscene ones, also qualify, provided that the meaning of the gestures is sufficiently clear to onlookers to be defamatory.

Harm to Reputation in the Community

A statement is considered *defamatory* if it causes the fourth element—namely, injury to the victim's reputation in the community. For purposes of libel

and slander, **community** is narrowly defined as a significant number of persons acquainted or familiar with the victim. Although some courts have held that "a community of one" is sufficient under certain circumstances, most courts maintain that larger numbers are required. Nevertheless, certain expressions, such as "a handful," "a closely associated group," and "associates in the neighborhood or workplace," suggest small numbers in most instances.

Many courts define the victim's injury in more emotional terms. For example, it has commonly been held that statements are libelous or slanderous if they ridicule, humiliate, or subject the victim to contempt or hatred from among his or her peers.

Publication

The tortfeasor must communicate the false and derogatory statement to a third party. That means that statements made by the tortfeasor directly to the victim are defamatory only if seen or heard by another or others.

Publication takes place through any means by which the false information is disseminated. This includes anything spoken, either in person or over amplification (megaphone or loudspeaker at a ballpark, for instance), radio, television, or telephone; or anything written, including letters, telegrams, scribbled messages, billboards, or printed and published works (such as a letter to the editor in the local newspaper, for instance).

Truth as Absolute Defense

Truth is considered an absolute defense in defamation cases. If the information the tortfeasor communicates is true, then no libel or slander occurred. To successfully use this defense, the tortfeasor must prove the veracity of the statement.

What is true is often a matter of opinion. It always depends upon the nature of the derogatory comments. For example, to call a person born out of wedlock a "bastard" is technically accurate, but in today's society the term is rarely used as defined

BALLENTINESBALLENTINESBALLENTINESBALLENTINESBALLENTINESBALLENTINESBALLENTINESBALLENTINESBALLENTINESBALLENTINESBALLENTINESBALLENTINESBALLENTINES

community   People living in the same place ... and subject to the same laws. ... Society in general.

in the dictionary. Courts have struggled with the elasticity of truth, and a variety of formulas for pinpointing truth have been posited in court opinions. The most common states that literal truth in every detail is unnecessary. If the statement is substantially true, so that a reasonable person would decide that the accusations were justified given these facts, then truth will operate as a defense to defamation actions.

Trespass to Land

Trespass is an ancient concept in tort law. *Trespass to land* occurs when a tortfeasor enters upon a landowner's real estate without consent. The tortfeasor trespasses when he or she intentionally acts in such a way as to violate the landowner's exclusive right to use the land. The elements of trespass to land are threefold:

1. Unauthorized entry upon another person's real estate
2. Tortfeasor's intent to enter without consent
3. Tortfeasor's actions interfering with the landowner's exclusive right to use the land (possession).

Entry

The tortfeasor must enter upon a landowner's real estate without permission. **Entry** occurs when the tortfeasor acts so as to interfere with the landowner's exclusive right to use the property. For example, walking across someone's front lawn constitutes *personal entry*, because the tortfeasor personally entered the land. Also, entry happens if a person throws trash in a neighbor's back yard. This is an example of *physical entry*, because the trash depositor placed an unwanted substance (trash) on the land. Both these examples include the interference element. The front lawn owner cannot utilize his or her property exclusively if someone is walking across it. The neighbor's use

of his or her back yard is severely hampered by the accumulation of another's trash. The tortfeasor's conduct in either case has disrupted the landowner's exclusive use of the real estate. This is the foundation of the tort of trespass to land.

The entry must be without consent. This essentially translates as a permission element. For instance, if a farmer allows a person to cross her fields to reach a lake in which to fish, then that person has not committed trespass—the entry was authorized. Similarly, homeowners may invite visitors onto their premises by extending an implied welcome, such as clearing sidewalks of snow up to a house door or placing doorbells outside the doors. This suggests that people may come upon the property to speak with the landowner. Consequently, door-to-door salespersons would not necessarily be trespassing if they had reason to believe that the homeowner welcomed their presence. However, if the yard were fenced in, with a "no soliciting" sign displayed, then salespersons would know that they did not have permission to enter the property.

Sometimes persons have a lawful right to enter upon another's land. For example, if the landowner gives an easement to a utility company to install utility lines across the property, then the utility company has the legal right to enter the premises to install and maintain the lines. Accordingly, no trespass to land could happen. Also, a process server, such as the county sheriff, generally has the legal right to enter the defendant's land to deliver a plaintiff's complaint and summons. No trespass to land would occur in such an instance.

One's lawful right to be upon another's premises may be withdrawn, however. Consider the example of the patron of a store. Customers are invited to come upon the premises to spend money. Suppose one such individual becomes disruptive, annoying other shoppers and employees. The store manager could demand that the agitator leave immediately. At this point, the

trespass   An unauthorized entry or intrusion of the real property of another.

entry   The act of going upon real property.

customer becomes a trespasser, because remaining means that he or she is present upon another's land without consent. Although the provocateur was originally invited into the store as a patron, once he or she was ordered to leave, trespass occurred.

The tortfeasor must have intended to enter the landowner's real estate without consent. Thus, if Twila is forced to cross a neighbor's front yard to escape a pursuing wild animal, she has not committed trespass to land. Twila did not intend to cross her neighbor's property without permission; rather, she was essentially forced across by the chasing animal. However, if she digs a hole in her neighbor's yard while searching for a water pipe, the entry was intentional.

No Actual Harm Required

It is important to note that, under trespass law, the unauthorized entry need not cause any damage to the real estate. It is sufficient that the transgression occurred. Trespass law presumes that injury has happened simply because the tortfeasor has interfered with the landowner's use of the realty. Thus, simply walking across someone's front lawn without permission is trespass to land, although no actual harm arises from the conduct. These types of trespasses to land are often called *technical trespasses*. Courts generally award only nominal damages in such cases, because no actual injury came from the trespass. The judgment award is ceremonial or symbolic of the technical invasion of the landowner's property rights.

Possession: Landowner's Exclusive Right to Use

To comprise trespass to land, the tortfeasor's unauthorized entry must interfere with the landowner's exclusive right to use his or her realty. This is sometimes called the **exclusive right of possession**, which entitles the landowner to use the property without anyone else's meddling. This exclusivity requirement may at first appear overly harsh. One might well ask what wrong has been done just by crossing someone's land, for example. Trespass intends to protect one's real estate in much the same way as assault and battery are intended to protect one's person. The objective is protection from undesired interferences. In this respect, trespass seeks merely to protect one's realty from other people encroaching upon it, just as assault and battery are meant to deter unwanted physical contact.

Trespass Above and Below Land

Trespass to land may occur not only upon the surface of the realty, but also above and below it. For instance, if a utility company erects wires across one's land without consent, this would constitute trespass to land, because the landowner owns the air above the soil. This could present insurmountable difficulties for aircraft. Fortunately, modern common law implies an exception for aircraft to fly over private property.

Similarly, one owns the resources under the earth. Although this enters into the complex area of oil, gas, and mineral law (within which special legal theories have evolved), it may be said generally that one owns the mineral resources beneath one's real estate. Accordingly, if someone mines under a person's land without permission, trespass to land has occurred.

Toxic Tort Actions

A significant percentage of modern tort litigation is devoted to actions involving toxic chemicals, pollution, hazardous waste disposal and transportation, and other environmentally sensitive issues. These are sometimes referred to as *toxic tort actions*. These lawsuits cover causes of action from all of the areas of tort law: trespass to land, negligence, absolute liability for ultrahazardous substances, products liability, and nuisance.

Trespass to land occurs when toxic substances enter upon another's property. The trespass elements remain the same:

BALLENTINESBALLENTINESBALLENTINESBALLENTINESBALLENTINESBALLENTINESBALLENTINESBALLENTINESBALLENTINESBALLENTINESBALLENTINESBALLENTINESBALLENTINESBALLENTINES

exclusive   Shutting out other occurrences or possibilities; not shared.

right of possession   A person's right to occupy and enjoy property.

1. Unauthorized entry upon another person's real estate
2. Tortfeasor's intent to enter without consent
3. Tortfeasor's actions interfering with the landowner's exclusive right to use the land (possession).

In the case of toxic substances, the unauthorized entry is seepage or accumulation of the hazardous material on the victim's land. Few owners consent to having toxins placed over, upon, or under their realty. Most people want such materials to be taken as far away from them as possible.

The tortfeasor's intent to enter without permission may be implied from the disposal method used. For instance, toxic waste buried in metal barrels will, over time, rust through and seep into the underground soil, unless the material is contained in an isolated fashion, such as an underground concrete crypt. If the tortfeasor failed to take sufficient precautions to prevent subterranean seepage, then the intent to trespass may be implied. Another example of implied intent is dumping toxic fluids into waterways. The tortfeasor desired the river or stream to carry the dangerous substances downstream, which would plainly deposit the gunk on the shores of other people's property.

The tortfeasor's interference with the plaintiff's exclusive possession of his or her land is equally clear. The toxic residues are a highly offensive and potent invasion, making some real estate uninhabitable. A more significant illustration of trespass would be difficult to imagine. Similarly, when landowners' underground water supplies are contaminated with buried toxic waste seepage, trespass to land occurs.

Trespass to Chattel

A tortfeasor commits *trespass to chattel* when he or she possesses someone's personal property without consent. A **chattel** is personal property, as opposed to real property, which is land. An automobile, a textbook, a pet dog or cat, and a desk are examples of chattels. Trespass to chattel has elements similar to those of trespass to land:

1. Unauthorized possession of, or interference with the use of, another individual's personal property
2. Intent to deprive (or interfere with) the owner's possession or exclusive use of his or her chattel.

Unauthorized Possession of Another's Chattel

Suppose Nadene takes a neighbor's textbook during class. Unless Nadene obtained the neighbor's consent before seizing the text, Nadene has engaged in unauthorized possession of another's personal property. The book's owner did not give Nadene permission to possess the chattel. When a tortfeasor takes possession of another's personal property without consent, there is an act of **dispossession**.

Consent may be implied under certain circumstances. For instance, if Alfred gives his car keys to a friend, the implication is that the friend may use Alfred's motor vehicle. Similarly, hotel guests may presume that the management intended them to use the electricity, water, soap, and tissues supplied to the rooms. However, if a patron takes the hotel's pillows, sheets, and towels, this would be unauthorized possession, as staying in a hotel does not implicitly entitle guests to such items.

Unauthorized Interference with Use

It is possible to commit trespass to chattel without actually wrenching possession of the personal property from its rightful owner. Interference with the chattel owner's use of the property is

---

BALLENTINESBALLENTINESBALLENTINESBALLENTINESBALLENTINESBALLENTINESBALLENTINESBALLENTINESBALLENTINESBALLENTINESBALLENTINESBALLENTINESBALLENTINESBALLENTINES

chattel   Personal property that is visible, tangible, and movable.

dispossession   A forced or fraudulent changing of possession … from one person to another.

sufficient. For instance, if a tortfeasor purposely fed Reggie's prize hogs a contaminated food, so that the hogs became ill and lost weight, then the tortfeasor engaged in unconsented interference with Reggie's use of the animals. If Cherrie's landlord shut off the electricity to her apartment without permission, then this would constitute unauthorized interference with the use of her personal property (provided, of course, that Cherrie had paid her electric bill).

Intent to Deprive or Interfere

To commit trespass to chattel, the tortfeasor must intend to interfere with or deprive the chattel owner of possession or the exclusive use of his or her personal property. Intent may be expressed, as it was when Nadene took her neighbor's book. It may also be implied under the circumstances. For example, assume that Cherrie's landlord changed the locks on her apartment door in order to lock her out, although she had paid her rent and had done nothing to violate her rental agreement. This would imply the landlord's intent to deprive Cherrie of possession of her personal property inside the apartment. Her use of the chattels would definitely be hindered.

Similarly, lack of intent may be implied. For example, assume Bud found his neighbor's cow grazing along a public highway and took the animal to his barn for safekeeping until he could telephone the neighbor. Although Bud took possession of the cow without his neighbor's consent, Bud did not intend to interfere with the neighbor's use of the cow. Nor did he wish to deprive his neighbor of possession. Bud simply wished to protect the animal from harm. This is emphasized by his efforts to contact his neighbor to come claim the cow. Thus, Bud lacked intent to trespass to chattel.

Conversion

Conversion occurs when a tortfeasor, without consent, deprives an owner of possession of the owner's chattel and puts or converts the property to the tortfeasor's own use. It is essentially a broader version of trespass to chattel. Conversion consists of three elements:

1. Depriving the owner of possession of a chattel
2. Intent to deprive possession and convert the property to one's own use
3. The owner's nonconsent to the tortfeasor's possession and use of the chattel.

Depriving of Possession

Under conversion, the tortfeasor must actually deprive the owner of possession of personal property. This means that the tortfeasor controls another's personal property so as to prevent the owner from using it. For example, suppose Nadene took her neighbor's textbook and refused to return it. Nadene's "dominion and control" over the book prevents the neighbor from using his or her chattel.

Normally, conversion is differentiated from trespass to chattel based upon the scope of the deprivation. With trespass to chattel, many courts have held that the deprivation need only be minor or temporary. With conversion, several courts have ruled that the deprivation must be so extensive as to suggest a desire to deprive the owner of possession permanently. There is considerable disagreement among different jurisdictions as to this issue, however. The majority of courts maintain that conversion has occurred simply because the tortfeasor deprived the owner of dominion and control over the chattel, regardless of length of time or permanent intent.

Deprivation of possession may occur in a variety of ways. *Physical possession* of the chattel is most common, although deprivation may happen through *damage or destruction* of the personal property. For instance, if someone plows under Kathy's garden to plant grass seed, this amounts to deprivation of possession, since Kathy can no longer use her vegetables. Similarly, if someone

conversion Control over another person's personal property which is wrongfully exercised; control applied in a manner that violates that person's title to or rights in the property.

opens a window during a thunderstorm, and rain soaks Sig's stereo, the injury has deprived Sig of the use of his chattel.

Deprivation may also take place simply through use. Some forms of personal property cannot be picked up and carried away. For instance, electricity, free-flowing liquids, and other intangible items are commonly defined as chattels under state commercial codes. One possesses such things by using them. If Morgan, Colleen's neighbor, plugs his garage heater into her electric outlet without permission, and Colleen's electric bill suddenly soars, Morgan has deprived her of dominion and control over her electricity. This translates as deprivation of possession.

Intent to Deprive and Convert to Own Use

Conversion requires that the tortfeasor intend to deprive the owner of possession of his or her chattel. This is comparable to trespass to chattel. However, unlike trespass to chattel, conversion also requires that the tortfeasor convert the personal property to his or her own use. For example, assume Joey and Lisa are acquaintances at school. Then suppose that Joey found Lisa's earrings on a bench at the mall. Joey might keep the earrings until he saw Lisa at school later in the week, but, because Joey did not intend to use the earrings himself, he is not guilty of conversion. However, if Joey wore the earrings to the school dance, he would have converted them to his own use.

It is important to note that the tortfeasor does not have to injure the chattel to convert it. Conversion occurs simply because the owner has been deprived of the use of the personal property without having given permission. Injury occurs to the owner's property rights to exclusively use the chattel.

Lack of Consent

Naturally, the owner must not have granted permission to someone to use or possess the chattel. If Victoria allows a classmate to borrow her text overnight to study, then the classmate has not converted the book. Consent may be expressed,

Libel	Slander
Written statement	Oral statement
False and defamatory statement	False and defamatory statement
Publication to third party	Publication to third party
Injury to victim's reputation in the community	Injury to victim's reputation in the community

Elements of Cause of Action for Defamation The major difference between libel and slander is the communication medium: libel is a written falsity and slander is verbal falsity.

as in the book-borrowing situation, or it may be implied. For example, suppose that Bob leaves his automobile at a mechanic's for an oil replacement. The mechanic did not convert Bob's property, because Bob impliedly gave the mechanic permission to possess the vehicle for repair purposes. However, if the mechanic went joy-riding in Bob's car after changing the oil, this would be conversion, because Bob did not implicitly consent to that use of his car.

Even though the chattel owner may have consented to a tortfeasor's possession, this permission may be revoked. This could result in a conversion. For example, Bob complains that he did not authorize any additional work done on his automobile, but he is willing to pay for the oil change, which he did request. The mechanic insists that Bob also pay for the unauthorized repairs and refuses to return Bob's car until he pays the extra amount. Because Bob did not agree to these additional charges, he insists that his vehicle be returned immediately. Thus, Bob has revoked the permission he originally gave the mechanic to possess the chattel. If the mechanic does not comply with Bob's demand, the mechanic will be liable for conversion.

Conversion as a Crime

Many state statutes define conversion as a criminal offense. Some statutes use the term *theft* instead.

Simultaneously, conversion is considered an intentional tort under the common law. This means that the chattel owner may sue in a civil action under the tort theory of conversion and may also contact the county prosecutor (or other local law enforcement authority) to file a criminal complaint for conversion. These separate legal actions are commonly pursued simultaneously in most jurisdictions.

Slander of Title, Commercial Disparagement, and Defamation by Computer

The intentional torts of slander of title, commercial disparagement, and defamation by computer involve defamed property interests. The trio has a common ancestry. All arose from the intentional tort of defamation, which concerns personal impugnation.

Slander of Title

Slander of title results when a tortfeasor makes false statements about an individual's ownership of property. The false statements are not designed to defame the owner personally; rather, the purpose of the aspersions is to injure the owner's ability to use the property. Slander of title contains three basic elements:

1. False statements regarding a person's ownership of property
2. Intent to hinder or damage the owner's use of the property
3. Communication (publication) of the falsehoods to third parties.

A tortfeasor commits slander of title by making false statements about a person's ownership of property. This usually occurs when the tortfeasor falsely impugns the title to another's property. Normally, cases involving this tort include real estate

and the filing of spurious liens. Often, businesses that provide services to customers who do not pay will file liens against the customers' real estate. The lien attaches to the title of the land so that the property cannot be leased or sold without the lien. Suppose a business threatens to file a lien against a customer who does not owe the business any money. If the lienholder wrongfully files a lien, then the lien has defamed the integrity of the landowner's title. The improper lien falsely suggests to the world that the landowner has not properly paid his or her debts to the lienholder, though in actuality the lienholder has no legal right to file the lien against the landowner. This improper lien filing constitutes making false statements about someone's ownership of property.

By making the false statements about ownership, the tortfeasor must intend to hamper or injure the owner's use of his or her property. This is demonstrated in the preceding lien example. The lienholder filed the lien to prevent the landowner from selling or using his or her realty without first paying the debt supposedly owed to the lienholder. But, in fact, no money was due, so the lien was falsely filed.

The false statements about another's property ownership must be transmitted to third parties in slander-of-title actions. The slander in the preceding lien example is communicated to the public when the lien is recorded at the county recorder's office. It then becomes a matter of public record.

Commercial Disparagement

Another type of slander focuses directly upon the chattel itself: commercial disparagement. *Commercial* **disparagement** may be defined as false statements communicated (published) to third parties about a person's goods, services, or business enterprise. The intentional tort of commercial disparagement includes three varieties: disparagement of goods, disparagement of services, and disparagement of business. Like slander of title, *disparagement*

BALLENTINESBALLENTINESBALLENTINESBALLENTINESBALLENTINESBALLENTINESBALLENTINESBALLENTINESBALLENTINESBALLENTINESBALLENTINESBALLENTINESBALLENTINES

slander of title   A false or malicious statement, oral or written, that brings into question a person's right or title to real or personal property, causing him or her damage.

disparagement   Discredit; detraction; dishonor; denunciation; disrespect.

of goods impedes the chattel owner's ability to use his or her personal property. *Disparagement of services* interferes with a service provider's ability to engage in provision of services. *Disparagement of business* occurs when the tortfeasor impugns the integrity of another's business venture. Commercial disparagement may be divided into three elements:

1. False statements about an individual's goods, services, or business
2. Intent to injure the victim's ability to use goods, furnish services, or conduct business
3. Communication (publication) to third parties.

The tortfeasor must express false statements about another's personal property, services, or business reputation (sometimes called **goodwill**). For example, if someone carries a sign in front of a grocery store declaring, "This store sells spoiled fruit!," when in fact the store carries fresh and wholesome fruit, then the sign carrier has made disparaging remarks about the quality of the grocery's foodstuffs. This impugns the integrity of both the goods themselves and the store's reputation. Similarly, if someone tells his or her friends that a particular dentist uses inferior materials to fill cavities when, in reality, the dentist uses professionally acceptable materials, then the dentist's services and reputation have been wrongfully impaired.

Disparagement of goods requires that the tortfeasor intend to injure the victim's capability to use chattels, provide services, or engage in business. Normally, cases involving goods relate to sales. In the preceding illustrations, the sign carrier obviously desired to discourage other shoppers from buying fruit at that particular grocery; the person criticizing the dentist wished to dissuade friends from seeking the dentist's services. The clear underlying objective in both examples is to hamper the ability of these enterprises to conduct business.

Like slander of title, commercial disparagement requires that the false statements be communicated to third parties. In the examples, the sign carrier transmitted the false complaints to anyone reading the sign. The friends of the disgruntled patient heard the falsehoods about the dentist. Like the intentional torts of slander and libel (defamation), publication may occur through oral or written means.

Defamation by Computer

Defamation by computer is a relatively recent intentional tort. Because of the proliferation of computerized databases that can store virtually any information about anyone, the likelihood of mistakes has increased. Further, as access to computerized material expands, the dissemination of inaccurate information can become enormously damaging to the victim.

Defamation by computer most frequently involves cases concerning erroneous credit information entered into a readily accessible computer database. A credit company reports to a national credit reporting agency that a particular individual has become delinquent in account payments. This bad credit rating can have alarming negative effects upon the person being reported. If the information reported is false, the injury is especially annoying, because future credit may hang in the balance of good credit reports.

Defamation by computer may be defined as the inclusion of false information about a consumer's credit rating, in a computer recordkeeping system, which harms the consumer's ability to secure credit. The tort includes four elements:

1. False information about a person's credit rating
2. Entering such erroneous data into a computerized recordkeeping system
3. Communication (publication) of the incorrect information to third parties
4. Injuring the victim's ability to obtain credit as a result of the false computerized data.

BALLENTINESBALLENTINESBALLENTINESBALLENTINESBALLENTINESBALLENTINESBALLENTINESBALLENTINESBALLENTINESBALLENTINESBALLENTINESBALLENTINESBALLENTINES

goodwill The benefit a business acquires, beyond the mere value of its ... tangible assets, as a result of having a good reputation and the respect of the public.

Defenses to Intentional Tort Actions

Persons accused of intentional torts may use any of several legal defenses, justifications, or excuses to defeat the claim. The tort law paralegal must keep these potential defenses in mind when investigating the facts of a case, regardless of which side he or she works for.

Self-Defense

Self-defense is probably the most familiar legal defense for the average person, and is perhaps the easiest legal justification to illustrate. It is most commonly applied to the intentional torts of assault and battery, but it may be used in cases involving false imprisonment. **Self-defense** is the exercise of reasonable force to repel an attack upon one's person or to avoid confinement. The nature of the action is simple: the victim of an assault or battery may use that degree of force necessary to prevent bodily injury (or offensive contact) from the attacker. Similarly, the victim of false imprisonment may use the force needed to prevent or escape confinement.

The elements of self-defense are (1) use of reasonable force (2) to counter an attacking or offensive force as (3) necessary to prevent bodily injury, offensive contact, or confinement.

The neutralizing force a person uses in self-defense is limited. The force cannot be greater than what is reasonably necessary to dispel the attacking force. This is called **reasonable force**. The reasonableness issue is difficult to reduce to clearly defined terms. Much depends upon the options available to the victim. Many courts hold that, in the face of deadly force, if a victim might reasonably escape from the attack, then this choice must first be selected before deadly force may be used

in self-defense. Several courts apply the same rule to situations involving threats of serious bodily injury. However, the majority of jurisdictions maintain that a person is not required to flee his or her home if threatened by an intruder. This is sometimes called the **castle doctrine**, in which a dweller is considered "king" or "queen" and may use any amount of force, including deadly force, to resist an intruder, such as a burglar. Nevertheless, the party exercising self-defense must be opposing an attacking or offensive force.

The force used in self-defense must be necessary to prevent bodily injury, offensive contact, or to avoid confinement. *Necessary force* is that which is reasonably perceived as required to rebuff an attack or confinement.

Defense of Persons or Property

As a legal justification for assault or battery, defense of other persons or defense of injury to property is similar to self-defense. A person who would otherwise have committed assault or battery may be excused if the action was taken to protect another individual or property from harm. This would include freeing someone subject to false imprisonment.

Defense of Persons: Elements

Defense of persons as a legal justification for assault or battery has the following elements: (1) use of reasonable force (2) to defend or protect a third party from injury (3) when the third party is threatened by an attacking force. For example, if Marie were about to throw a vase at Marjorie, Simon could use reasonable force to subdue Marie before she could complete the throw. Simon

---

BALLENTINESBALLENTINESBALLENTINESBALLENTINESBALLENTINESBALLENTINESBALLENTINESBALLENTINESBALLENTINESBALLENTINESBALLENTINESBALLENTINESBALLENTINES

self-defense   The use of force to protect oneself from death of imminent bodily harm at the hands of an aggressor. A person
  may use only that amount of force reasonably necessary to protect ... against the peril with which he or she is threatened.

reasonable force   Force that is appropriate in the circumstances.

castle doctrine   The doctrine that a person may use whatever force is required to defend his or her home and those in it.

would not have committed battery, because he grabbed Marie to prevent her from harming Marjorie. Simon would be entitled to the legal defense of defense of another person to avoid liability for battery.

The same principles used in self-defense to define reasonable force also apply to defense of persons. Thus, Simon could not use excessive force to repel Marie's attack against Marjorie. For instance, if Simon struck Marie sharply in the head with a two-by-four piece of lumber, this would be unnecessarily brutal force to subdue the vase attack.

Also, like self-defense, the repelling force must be used to counter an attacking force. If Marjorie telephoned Simon to complain that Marie had just thrown a vase at her, then Simon could not run over and clobber Marie and then claim defense of another as an excuse.

Defense of Property: Elements

Conduct that otherwise might be assault or battery may be vindicated if the action is taken to defend property from damage or dispossession. A property owner has the right to possess and safeguard his or her property from others. The elements of *defense of property* are (1) use of reasonable force (2) to protect property from damage or dispossession (3) when another person, the invader, attempts to injure or wrongfully take possession of the property. Defense of property is often used in situations in which sellers repossess property from defaulting buyers.

The reasonable force contemplated here is essentially identical to that discussed in regard to self-defense. Many courts, however, restrict the defensive force to the least amount necessary to protect the property from harm or dispossession. This is a narrower definition of reasonableness, suggesting that human well-being is more important than the safety of property. Under this theory, most courts would not allow deadly force or extreme force likely to cause serious bodily injury to be used to defend property under any circumstances.

The property owner or possessor uses reasonable force to repulse an attacking force that is attempting to harm or possess the property. The

Defense of Persons	Defense of Property
Use of reasonable force	Use of reasonable force
To defend or protect a third party from harm	To protect from damage or dispossession
Third person is threatened by attacking force	Someone attempts to harm or wrongfully possess property

Elements of Defense of Persons or Property
Courts generally place a greater importance on defending people rather than property.

use of reasonable force to expel a trespasser to land is called *ejectment*. Defense of real property cases frequently involves landowners who have placed dangerous traps for trespassers. The trespassers are often seeking to steal personal property and usually violate various criminal statutes involving theft or burglary. Nevertheless, landowners may not set up deadly traps to inflict serious bodily injuries upon such criminals. Springloaded guns have been the most common snares litigated. A landowner places a shotgun inside a barn or outbuilding which is triggered by a tripwire placed across a window or doorway. The thief steps upon the wire while trying to enter and is shot. Courts universally condemn this use of deadly force to defend property.

Rightful Repossession

An owner of personal property generally has the right to repossess, by force if necessary, a chattel that has been wrongfully taken or withheld. This is the defense of *rightful repossession*. The defense is generally applied to allegations of trespass to land, assault, battery, and sometimes conversion and trespass to chattel. However, the amount of force that may be used is extremely limited. Generally, the elements of rightful repossession include the following: (1) use of reasonable force (2) to retake possession of personal property (3) of which the owner has been wrongfully dispossessed (or to which the owner is denied possession), (4) provided the efforts to retake the chattel are made promptly after the original dispossession or denial of possession occurs. For this defense, reasonable force is defined along the same lines as for defense of property.

Retaking Possession of Personal Property

The chattel owner seeks to repossess personal property to which he or she is entitled. This is the crux of the defense. If someone has wrongfully dispossessed an owner of his or her chattel, then the owner is entitled to enter upon the dispossessor's land to recover the chattel. This provides a defense to trespass to land. Reasonable force may be applied to recover possession of the personal property.

Prompt Repossession Efforts

Older common law cases held that a chattel owner's efforts to repossess personal property must occur soon after the chattel was wrongfully taken away. Just how promptly this needed to occur, however, was not clearly defined. Many nineteenth-century opinions ruled that hot pursuit was necessary. Hot pursuit is usually defined for purposes of criminal law, but its meaning is the same for this tort defense. **Hot pursuit**, in this context, means a rapid chase as soon as possible after the owner has discovered that his or her chattel is missing. This presumes, of course, that the personal property owner knows who took the chattel.

Wrongful Denial of Possession

The chattel owner need not be dispossessed of the personal property for this defense to apply. Consider the example of someone who originally took possession of the chattel with the owner's consent, but later wrongfully refuses to return it. If the owner then attempted to retake possession and was accused of trespass to land, assault, or battery, the owner could apply rightful repossession as a defense.

Most cases involving denial of possession deal with bailments, in which the owner has delivered possession of the chattel to someone else for a specific purpose, with the explicit understanding that the chattel is to be returned at a certain time or upon demand. When an automobile is taken to a mechanic for repair, for instance, there is a bailment. The mechanic would have lawful possession of the vehicle, because the owner left it for repairs. Suppose, however, that the mechanic made unauthorized repairs and sought to charge the owner. If the owner demanded return of the car and the mechanic refused, then this refusal would constitute wrongful denial of possession. The owner could use reasonable force to enter the mechanic's premises to retake the chattel. The owner would not be liable to the mechanic for trespass to land because of the rightful repossession defense.

Note that this result would be different if there had been a dispute over authorized repairs. Most state statutes provide mechanics with possessory liens, which empower repair persons to keep possession of vehicles until repair charges have been paid. However, some statutes provide that the amounts due must be undisputed.

Wrongful Dispossession

For the defense of rightful repossession to apply, the owner's chattel must have been unlawfully dispossessed, or its return have been unlawfully denied. This means that the dispossessor or retainer must not have a legal right to possess (or deny return of) the chattel.

In the preceding bailment example, the mechanic did not possess the automobile unlawfully, because the owner had left it for repairs. However, when the mechanic performed unauthorized work and sought payment, and the owner demanded the car's return, then the mechanic wrongfully possessed the vehicle—specifically, the repair person committed trespass to chattel and

BALLENTINESBALLENTINESBALLENTINESBALLENTINESBALLENTINESBALLENTINESBALLENTINESBALLENTINESBALLENTINESBALLENTINESBALLENTINESBALLENTINESBALLENTINESBALLENTINES

fresh pursuit (hot pursuit)   The pursuit of a person ... to recover property from a thief, if [the owner] pursues and apprehends him or her immediately.

possibly conversion. Thus, the owner would be entitled to repossess with reasonable force and could use that defense against the mechanic's lawsuit for trespass to land, assault, or battery.

Consent

Consent is a broad defense applicable to every intentional tort and is clearly the most pervasive defense thereto. Consent occurs when the victim of an intentional tort voluntarily agrees to the tortfeasor's actions, provided that the victim understands (or reasonably should understand) the consequences of the tortfeasor's deeds. This knowledge factor is sometimes called **informed consent**.

The consent defense contains the following elements: (1) Voluntary acceptance of an intentionally tortious act (2) with full knowledge or understanding of the consequences. Actually, consent is not a legal defense at all. If consent existed, then the intentional tort could not have occurred.

Informed Consent: Voluntary Acceptance

Consent will be a successful defense to an intentional tort action only if the victim willingly and knowingly agreed to the tortfeasor's conduct. Accordingly, a victim who is coerced into tolerating an intentional tort cannot consent to it, because the victim was compelled to undergo the tort. Further, the victim must comprehend the implications of the tortfeasor's actions to consent to them.

Part of the **voluntary**, or *volition*, factor of consent is the victim's mental **capacity** to agree. Some persons simply lack sufficient mental abilities to understand the consequences of a tortfeasor's actions. Severely retarded or mentally incapacitated individuals, for example, might not grasp the implications of a tortfeasor's misbehavior. Intoxicated individuals may also have insufficient mental faculties to comprehend the results of an intentional tort. Children, particularly when very young, may lack cognitive development adequate to grasp the

ramifications of intentional torts. For such persons, consent could become virtually impossible.

Implied Consent

Consent may be expressed, either orally or in writing, or it may be implied by conduct or circumstances. For instance, public officials or famous persons are assumed to consent to adverse publicity merely by placing themselves in the public limelight. Consent to publicity is therefore implied, and public officials or celebrities cannot recover for libel or slander, unless malice is proven.

The most common example of implied consent involves emergency medical treatment. If a patient is unconscious and is taken to a hospital emergency room, the medical personnel may presume that the patient consents to treatment, at least to the extent of the emergency condition. Thus, if someone is found unconscious on the pavement, suffering from gastrointestinal bleeding, and an ambulance takes her to the hospital, the patient is presumed to agree to treatment of the emergency condition, in this case a "G.I. bleed," which is often life-threatening. Later, if the patient regains consciousness and protests against the treatment (perhaps upon religious grounds), the patient cannot sue for battery for the unauthorized emergency care. However, once conscious and clearminded, the patient could insist that further treatment be foregone. Failure to stop treatment would then constitute battery. Suppose, instead, that the medical personnel treated beyond the emergency condition, such as removing a portion of diseased skin while treating the intestinal bleeding. Implied consent does not apply to nonemergency treatment, and thus battery would have occurred.

Mistake

Sometimes people act based upon inaccurate information or incorrect interpretations of events.

BALLENTINESBALLENTINESBALLENTINESBALLENTINESBALLENTINESBALLENTINESBALLENTINESBALLENTINESBALLENTINESBALLENTINESBALLENTINESBALLENTINESBALLENTINESBALLENTINES

informed consent   Agreement to permit something to occur, after having been given as much information as necessary to make an intelligent and rational ("informed") decision.

voluntary   A word applied to an act freely done out of choice, not brought about by coercion, duress, or accident.

capacity   Competency in law ... . A person's ability to understand the nature and effect of the act in which he or she is engaged.

The actor intended the result of his or her conduct but behaved under false beliefs. Often, had a person known the true state of affairs, he or she would have behaved differently. Tort law recognizes this human tendency to err with the defense of mistake, which provides individuals with an escape route from intentional tort liability. As a legal defense, **mistake** is the good faith belief, based upon incorrect information, that one is justified in committing an intentional tort under the circumstances. The elements may be detailed as follows: (1) Good faith conviction that one's actions are justified (2) with the belief based upon faulty information; and (3) the conduct would otherwise be considered tortious but for the erroneous belief.

The actor must reasonably believe that, under the incorrect facts the actor thinks are true, the actor's conduct will be legally excused. The good faith conviction, like all elements of mistake, depends heavily upon the specific facts of each case. To use mistake as a defense to intentional torts, the actor must base his or her conviction upon erroneous details which, if they had been true, would have justified the conduct. It may seem apparent that the defense of mistake applies only if the actor has engaged in behavior which, except for the defense, would be considered tortious.

Privilege

As an intentional torts defense, **privilege** is a legal justification to engage in otherwise tortious conduct in order to accomplish a compelling social goal. For example, if a child is drowning in a swimming pool, one might wish to commit trespass to land to save the child's life. Comparatively speaking, the social value of saving a life outweighs the landowner's right to exclude trespassers from his or her property.

Privilege is most commonly a defense to trespass to land, trespass to chattel, conversion, assault, battery, and false imprisonment, although it may be applied against other intentional torts as well. Privilege includes the following considerations:

1. Do the actor's motives for engaging in an intentional tort outweigh the injury to the victim or his or her property?
2. Was the actor justified in committing the intentional tort to accomplish his or her socially desirable purposes, or could a less damaging action have been taken instead?

This formula shows how courts balance values between the socially acceptable motives of the tortfeasor (actor) and the tort victim's compensation for injury. Privilege presumes that the intentional tort is legally justified because of the higher purposes to be achieved.

Motive describes the goal which a participant wishes to accomplish by taking a particular action. Motive may be discovered by probing the mental state of the actor. This mind-reading occurs in many areas of law. For example, in criminal law, **mens rea** loosely translates from the Latin as "evil thoughts" and suggests a psychological component to criminal conduct. In tort law, motive is synonymous with *intent*, which is broadly defined as the desire to attain a certain result. For purposes of the privilege defense, motive must be socially advantageous to a point which excuses intentionally harming another person or his or her property.

With privilege defenses, courts frequently ask whether the tortfeasor's objectives could have been reached through behavior that would have been less harmful to the victim. Several distinct intentional tort defenses, such as rightful repossession,

BALLENTINESBALLENTINESBALLENTINESBALLENTINESBALLENTINESBALLENTINESBALLENTINESBALLENTINESBALLENTINESBALLENTINESBALLENTINESBALLENTINESBALLENTINES

mistake   An erroneous mental conception that influences a person to act or to decline to act; an unintentional act, omission, or error arising from ignorance, surprise, imposition, or misplaced confidence. … An error; a misunderstanding; an inaccuracy.

privilege   An immunity, exemption, right, or advantage possessed by an individual … which … exists by operation of law or … other permission; an exemption from a burden.

motive   The reason that leads the mind to desire a result; … that which causes the mind to form intent; the reason for an intention.

mens rea   An "answerable intent," i.e., an intent for which one is answerable.

Knight v. Jewett
232 Cal. App. 3d 1142,
275 Cal. Rptr. 292 (1990)
Review Granted, 278 Cal. Rptr. 203,
804 P.2d 1300 (Cal. 1991)

TODD, Acting Presiding Justice.

Kendra Knight appeals a summary judgment granted in favor of Michael Jewett in her lawsuit against Jewett for negligence and assault and battery stemming from a touch football game in which she was injured. Knight contends [...] it was error to apply the doctrine of assumption of risk to defeat the assault and battery cause of action and [...] there were triable issues of fact that should have precluded the granting of summary judgment.

On January 25, 1987, Knight and several other individuals, including Jewett, gathered at the Vista home of Ed McDaniels to observe the Super Bowl football game. Knight and Jewett were among those who decided to play a game of co-ed touch football during half-time using a "peewee" football often used by children. Apparently, no explicit rules were written down or discussed before the game, other than the requirement that to stop advancement of the player with the ball it was necessary to touch that player above the waist with two hands. Knight and Jewett were on different teams.

Previously, Knight had played touch football and frequently watched football on television. Knight voluntarily participated in the Super Bowl half-time game. It was her understanding that this game would not involve forceful pushing, hard hitting or hard shoving during the game. She had never observed anyone being injured in a touch football game before this incident.

About five to ten minutes after the game started, Jewett ran into Knight during a play and afterward Knight asked Jewett not to play so rough. Otherwise, she told him, she would stop playing.

On the next play, Knight suffered her injuries, when she was knocked down by Jewett and he stepped on her little finger of her right hand. Kendra had three surgeries on the finger, but they proved unsuccessful. The finger was amputated during a fourth surgery.

According to Jewett, he had jumped up to intercept a pass and as he came down he knocked Knight over. When he landed, he stepped back and onto Knight's hand.

According to Knight's version, her teammate, Andrea Starr had caught the ball and was proceeding up the field. Knight was headed in the same direction, when Jewett, in pursuit of Starr, came from behind Knight and knocked her down. Knight put her arms out to break the fall and Jewett ran over her, stepping on her hand. Jewett continued to pursue Starr for another 10 to 15 feet before catching up with her and tagging her. Starr said the tag was rough enough to cause her to lose her balance and fall and twist her ankle.

Jewett did not intend to step on Knight's hand and did not intend to hurt her. ... Knight contends her cause of action for assault and battery is viable and she should be allowed to proceed to trial on it. ... Jewett argued it must fail because Knight consented to the physical contact.

Consent is a viable defense to the tort of assault and battery. "A person may, by participating in a game, or by other conduct, consent to an act which might otherwise constitute a battery." Here, however, we need not dwell on whether Jewett can successfully interpose a defense of consent to Knight's assault and battery cause of action.

Inasmuch as this case reaches us on appeal from a summary judgment in favor of Jewett, it is only necessary for us to determine whether there is any possibility Knight may be able to establish her case.

A requisite element of assault and battery is intent. Here, however, there is no evidence that Jewett intended to injure Knight or commit a battery on her. Moreover, the record affirmatively show Knight does not believe Jewett had the intent to step on her hand or injure her. Without the requisite intent, Knight cannot state a cause of action for assault and battery.

self-defense, or defense of others or property, are simply particular types of privilege. Each has a social benefits component that justifies otherwise tortious misconduct.

Necessity

Necessity is another variety of privilege that excuses otherwise tortious misconduct. Under this defense, the tortfeasor is justified in engaging in an intentional tort to prevent more serious injury from an external force. **Necessity** contains three elements: (1) Committing an intentional tort (2) to avert more serious injury (3) caused by a force other than the tortfeasor (4) and the tortfeasor's actions were reasonably necessary to avert the greater harm. Necessity can be a puzzling defense. Its elements compel courts to balance competing interests, employing more value judgments than usual.

In a necessity situation, the tortfeasor is usually faced with having to choose between the lesser of two evils. On the one hand, the tortfeasor must inflict injury upon a victim or the victim's property. On the other hand, the tortfeasor could do nothing and watch a greater havoc occur.

For necessity to operate as a defense to an intentional tort, the more significant danger being averted must originate from a source other than the tortfeasor. The necessity defense cannot protect a tortfeasor who creates the catastrophic condition and then must engage in an intentional tort to resolve the crisis.

As is generally true with privilege, necessity requires that the tortfeasor's conduct be reasonably necessary to prevent the more substantial danger. Thus, the tortfeasor must use only that degree of force required to avert the greater risk. Fires illustrate this aspect of reasonably required action; many necessity cases involve burning buildings. Several 19th-century court opinions discussed "row" structures, which were many discrete buildings attached in long rows down a street. If one were to catch fire, it was likely that the entire block would burn to the ground. To avoid this calamity, the flaming building was often destroyed. There simply was no less damaging alternative when the building was fully ablaze. If the building owner sued for trespass to land, the courts routinely applied the necessity defense to protect the tortfeasor from liability to the building owner.

Public Officer's Immunity for Legal Process Enforcement

Public officials often engage in activity that normally would be considered intentionally tortious. However, because such persons are authorized by law to engage in such conduct, they are protected from liability. Several types of governmental action fall within this protected class. The most common include: (1) process serving; (2) execution sales; (3) attachment or replevin; and (4) arrest by warrant.

Service of Process

Service of Process is the method by which a defendant in a lawsuit is notified that a plaintiff has filed suit against the defendant. Service of process is the means used to notify the defendant. Most commonly, the court clerk either mails a copy of the summons and the plaintiff's complaint to the defendant (usually by certified or registered mail), or the sheriff delivers the summons and complaint directly to the defendant. It is the latter case of actual physical delivery that gives rise to litigation. The defendant might sue the sheriff for trespass to land when the sheriff arrived on the defendant's real estate to deliver the summons. However, the sheriff has the power, either by statute or common law, to enter another person's land to serve process. The landowner's lawsuit against the sheriff would fail as a result of this defense.

Execution Sales

When a plaintiff wins judgment against the defendant in a civil action, the defendant usually

---

BALLENTINESBALLENTINESBALLENTINESBALLENTINESBALLENTINESBALLENTINESBALLENTINESBALLENTINESBALLENTINESBALLENTINESBALLENTINESBALLENTINESBALLENTINESBALLENTINES

necessity   That which is necessary; that which must be done.

service of process   Delivery of a summons, writ, complaint, or other process to the opposite party, or other person entitled to receive it, in such manner as the law prescribes … .

has a certain period of time, often 30 days, within which to pay the judgment. If the defendant fails to pay, the plaintiff may return to court and file a writ of **execution** requesting the court to order the defendant's property sold to satisfy the judgment. These forced sales are often referred to as **execution sales** or **sheriff's sales**, because the sheriff is frequently the public official responsible for seizing and selling the defendant's property. The defendant might sue the sheriff for trespass to land, trespass to chattel, and conversion after the sheriff comes and gets the defendant's property. However, once again the sheriff is legally protected. Statutes and common law empower law enforcement officials to seize and sell property to satisfy judgments. Therefore, the sheriff would be immune from liability.

Attachment or Replevin

Attachment is a court-ordered remedy in a lawsuit. When a plaintiff is entitled to a remedy against the defendant in a lawsuit, and the defendant is likely to dispose of his or her property to avoid losing it in a subsequent execution action, the plaintiff may ask the court to attach the property on the plaintiff's behalf. The court then orders a law enforcement officer, such as the sheriff, to seize the defendant's property subject to attachment. The defendant might think to sue the sheriff for conversion or trespass to chattel, but the defendant should think again. The sheriff is authorized by statute or common law to take the defendant's property into custody under attachment, and the defendant's cause of action against the sheriff would fail.

Replevin is another court-ordered remedy. A plaintiff sues a defendant who wrongfully possesses the plaintiff's chattel and refuses to return it. The plaintiff asks the court for replevin, which means that the court would order the defendant to return the personal property to the plaintiff. If the defendant still refuses to comply, the court could instruct the sheriff to seize the chattel. The defendant's lawsuit for conversion or trespass to chattel against the sheriff would again be defeated by the law enforcer's defense of legal authority to act.

Arrest by Warrant

Police officers often arrest suspected criminals under the authority of a court-issued **arrest warrant**. Suppose the suspect were innocent of any crimes. Could the suspect sue the police department for false imprisonment, assault, battery, and infliction of emotional distress, for having been arrested? If the law enforcement personnel were acting pursuant to an arrest warrant properly ordered by a judge, and if they acted in good faith to apprehend the suspect named in the warrant, then they would not be liable for any intentional torts as a consequence of taking the suspect into custody.

Warrantless Arrest

Police officers, and sometimes even ordinary citizens, engage in **warrantless arrests**. Could they be liable for false imprisonment, battery, assault, trespass to land, and infliction of emotional distress?

Statutes and common law authorize law enforcement personnel to arrest criminal suspects even without court-issued warrants under certain circumstances. For example, when a police officer witnesses a felony, he or she may arrest the suspect immediately. This proper enforcement of a

BALLENTINESBALLENTINESBALLENTINESBALLENTINESBALLENTINESBALLENTINESBALLENTINESBALLENTINESBALLENTINESBALLENTINESBALLENTINESBALLENTINESBALLENTINESBALLENTINES

execution   A writ or process for the enforcement of a judgment.

execution sale (sheriff's sale)   A public sale by a sheriff or similar officer of property seized under a writ of execution ... .

attachment   The process by which a person's property is figuratively brought into court to ensure satisfaction of judgment ... rendered against him or her. ... [T]he property may be sold to satisfy the judgment.

replevin   An action by which the owner of personal property taken or detained by another may recover possession of it.

arrest warrant   Legal process issued by a court directing a law enforcement officer to arrest a named person on a specific charge.

warrantless arrest   The arrest of a person without an arrest warrant.

legal process would be a defense against the suspect's intentional torts lawsuit.

Private citizens, too, may take suspected criminals into custody under the theory of **citizen's arrest**. Under the common law, a private citizen may take a suspect into custody if the citizen has witnessed the suspect commit a felony or breach of the peace. This would include situations in which the citizen reasonably thinks that the suspect has committed a felony. Historically, this defense was often used to protect store owners who detained suspected shoplifters from liability for false imprisonment actions.

Reasonable Discipline

We are all familiar with the concept of discipline. Anyone who has either had or been a parent understands the exercise of authority to maintain order within the household. Students for centuries have exchanged horror stories about strict disciplinary teachers. Such authority figures have used discipline in both the home and schools, which usually involves inflicting several intentional torts, including assault, battery, false imprisonment, and infliction of emotional distress. The defense of reasonable discipline, however, protects the disciplinarian from tort liability. There are three elements of *reasonable discipline:* (1) Use of reasonable force (2) by a parent, guardian, or authorized individual against a child (3) to maintain order or punish unacceptable misconduct.

The force a parent or guardian applies against a child must be reasonable under the circumstances. Naturally, reasonableness depends upon the exact facts of each case, but a general principle may be gleaned from the court decisions. For purposes of this defense, *reasonable force* may be defined as that degree of force required to restore decorum or punish deviant conduct. Force that goes beyond this is deemed excessive.

When a child attends school, the law implies that the teacher assumes the role of parent or guardian while the child is present at the institution. The teacher is referred to as *in loco parentis,* which translates from Latin as "in place of the parent." This means that the teacher (or school principal) basically enjoys the same right to use reasonable force for discipline as do a child's parents. In recent times, however, courts have become antagonistic to this defense when applied to nonparents or guardians. In modern education, corporal punishment has been severely discouraged as a disciplinary technique. Occasionally, litigation arises after a child is struck by a teacher as punishment. Educators must be much more careful than in days past when inflicting corporal penalties, because courts are increasingly less tolerant of the discipline defense for nonparents or guardians.

The disciplinarian must be using reasonable force against a child to maintain decorum (such as in a school classroom) or penalize deviant conduct (such as punishing a child who has intentionally broken a window). However, these motives do not give the disciplinarian a free hand to inflict punishment beyond that which is reasonable. Courts and legislatures are becoming increasingly aware of the significant problem of child abuse, much of which involves parental misconduct that once was judicially protected under the reasonable discipline defense. As social problems become more public and prominent, courts and legislatures become more sensitive to these issues and the search for solutions. As a result, recent court decisions have upheld a child's right to sue parents in tort for using exorbitant force as punishment.

Statutes of Limitation

Statutes of limitation are statutes restricting the time within which a plaintiff may file his or her

BALLENTINESBALLENTINESBALLENTINESBALLENTINESBALLENTINESBALLENTINESBALLENTINESBALLENTINESBALLENTINESBALLENTINESBALLENTINESBALLENTINESBALLENTINESBALLENTINES

citizen's arrest   An arrest made by a person other than a police officer ... legal under certain circumstances.

in loco parentis   Means "in the place of parents." Describes a person who, in the absence of a child's parent or guardian, and without formal legal approval, temporarily assumes a parent's obligations with respect to the child.

statutes of limitations   Federal and state statutes prescribing the maximum period of time during which various types of civil actions and criminal prosecutions can be brought after the occurrence of the injury or the offense.

lawsuit for a particular cause of action against a defendant. All states have statutes of limitations for almost all tort actions, including intentional torts. The most common tort statutes of limitations are two years. This means that the plaintiff has two years from the date that an intentional tort occurred to file his or her lawsuit against the defendant. If the plaintiff fails to file within this statutory time period, then his or her cause of action against the defendant is barred forever.

Although two years is a common statute of limitations period for many torts, the exact time period varies among states and different types of torts. One should always research the specific statute of limitations for each cause of action, whether in tort or in other areas of law. This is a vital piece of information for both the plaintiff and the defendant. If the statute of limitations has expired, the defendant may respond with this defense and have the plaintiff's case dismissed or otherwise disposed of (usually by summary judgment). The plaintiff must be aware of the statute of limitations in order to file the lawsuit in a timely manner.

Negligence

Most people equate negligence with carelessness. The phrase conjures up images of actions that are slovenly, haphazard, heedless, or foolhardy. As a legal concept, negligence is much more precise, but it embodies all of these characteristics.

Negligence may be broadly defined as the failure to exercise reasonable care to avoid injuring others or their property. Reasonable care depends upon the exact circumstances of each case. This is the "shifting sands" aspect of negligence with which legal students—and the legal system—struggle. The key term is *reasonableness*. In any tort case in which negligence might exist, ask the threshold question: Did the tortfeasor act unreasonably under the circumstances? This is essentially all that negligence entails.

The tortfeasor can be negligent either by doing or by not doing something. When courts speak of *negligent acts or omissions* by the tortfeasor, they mean that the tortfeasor behaved unreasonably either by doing a specific careless activity or by failing to do something that the tortfeasor should have done.

Negligent actions are positive events; something is done. For instance, if Roger lit a fire in high winds that carried sparks onto a neighbor's roof and set the house ablaze, Roger's action (heedless burning) would be deemed unreasonable. Negligent omissions are usually phrased negatively;

the tortfeasor failed to do a reasonable act. For example, suppose Marie's front porch had a rotten step that she failed to repair. A salesperson visiting her home falls through the step and breaks a leg. Marie's omission (failure to repair the step) would be considered unreasonable.

Negligence may be specifically defined as the tortfeasor's failure to exercise reasonable care which causes a foreseeable injury to another person or that person's property. Negligence includes the following elements:

1. Duty of reasonable care and scope of duty (foreseeability of victim)
2. Breach of the duty by the tortfeasor
3. Causation of injury to the victim (cause-in-fact or substantial factor)
4. Proximate cause (foreseeability of injury)
5. Damages to the victim (recovery).

Each of these elements is required for negligence to exist, so each element is a threshold question. If "no" answers any single element, negligence does not exist. Paralegals who specialize in personal injury must be familiar with the elements of negligence. They must be able to ascertain from a review of the facts of a case whether the defendant may have acted negligently to cause the injury to the plaintiff. When asked to review a case for potential negligence, the personal injury paralegal should (1) review all the pertinent case facts; (2) list the elements of negligence; and (3) identify each element of negligence as it applies to the case at hand.

Scope of Duty and Standards of Reasonable Care

Negligence analysis begins with the duty of reasonable care. First, the scope of the duty must be determined. This focuses on the foreseeability of the victim.

Duty in tort law is the obligation either to do or not to do something. In negligence, the duty of **reasonable care** is the responsibility to act reasonably so as to avoid injuring others. This may also be stated negatively: the duty of reasonable care is the obligation *not* to behave *un*reasonably so as to avoid injuring others. For example, motor vehicle operators owe a duty of reasonable care to drive carefully and avoid injuring other drivers, their vehicles, or pedestrians. A driver who runs a red light and collides with another vehicle has not fulfilled the duty of reasonable care in operating his or her motor vehicle. Clearly, though, one does not owe a duty of reasonable care to everyone else in the universe. *Scope of duty* is a limitation on the persons to whom one owes the duty. Scope of duty is often described in terms of reasonable foreseeability.

Foreseeability

Foreseeability in tort law is the notion that a specific action, under particular circumstances, would produce an anticipated result. If an injury were **foreseeable**, then one could take precautions to avoid the behavior that might be expected to cause harm. If a tortfeasor failed to take such precautions, he or she breached the duty of reasonable care.

Scope of Duty	Foreseeable Plaintiffs Theory
The tortfeasor owes a duty of reasonable care to avoid injuring others or their property.	The plaintiff may recover from the defendant only if it were reasonably foreseeable that the defendant's actions would injure the plaintiff.
Duty includes persons for whom it is reasonably foreseeable that injury will occur as a result of the tortfeasor's actions.	Persons outside the defendant's scope of duty are considered unforeseeable plaintiffs.

Scope of Duty of Reasonable Care and Foreseeable Plaintiffs Theory Scope of duty refers to individuals who might foreseeably be injured as a result of the defendant's actions. The foreseeable plaintiffs theory states: if it were reasonably foreseeable that the plaintiff would be harmed as a consequence of the defendant's actions, the defendant's scope of duty includes the victim.

Foreseeability limits the scope, or extent, of the duty owed to others. One asks the threshold question: Was it reasonably foreseeable that the person injured would be harmed as a consequence of the tortfeasor's actions? If so, the scope of the duty of reasonable care includes the individual hurt. This is sometimes called the *foreseeable plaintiffs theory*, because it was reasonably foreseeable that the plaintiff (who is suing the tortfeasor for negligence) would be damaged because of the tortious conduct. Persons outside this range of duty are considered *unforeseeable plaintiffs*, because the tortfeasor could not reasonably have anticipated that they would be harmed by the tortfeasor's actions.

BALLENTINESBALLENTINESBALLENTINESBALLENTINESBALLENTINESBALLENTINESBALLENTINESBALLENTINESBALLENTINESBALLENTINESBALLENTINESBALLENTINESBALLENTINESBALLENTINES

duty   A legal obligation, whether imposed by the common law, statute, court order, or contract. … An obligation or responsibility.

due care (reasonable care)   That degree of care which a person of ordinary prudence would exercise in similar circumstances.

foreseeable   That which may be anticipated or known in advance; that which a person should have known.

Standards of Reasonable Care

Reasonable care is a most elusive concept in negligence law. It depends upon the particular facts of each problem. Still, tort law has developed an abstract measure of reasonable care, called the *reasonable person standard.*

The *reasonable person* is an imaginary individual who is expected to behave reasonably under a given set of circumstances to avoid harming others. The tortfeasor is alleged to have done something, or have failed to do something, that was unreasonable and that caused the victim's injuries. The tortfeasor's conduct is measured under the reasonable person standard in this fashion: In the same or similar circumstances, would the reasonable person have acted as the tortfeasor behaved? If so, then the tortfeasor did not violate his or her duty of reasonable care. If not, then the tortfeasor breached the duty.

The trier of fact in a negligence lawsuit determines whether the defendant acted as the reasonable person would have behaved in a specific case. This is usually a jury, but it could be the judge in a bench trial. In effect, the jurors decide what was reasonable by investigating how they, and others they know, would have behaved. Suddenly, the reasonable person standard becomes clear: it is what the jurors conclude was reasonable under the circumstances. This settles the question of whether the defendant breached the duty of reasonable care to the plaintiff.

At first glance, the reasonable person standard seems arbitrary, as each juror determines the defendant's negligence based upon his or her own personal, gut-level response. The judicial system, however, safeguards against one capricious definition of reasonableness by offering the option of a jury trial, which forces several persons to agree upon an appropriate measure of due care. Although a judge in a bench trial is the sole trier of fact, the judge's legal training is presumed to compensate for any bias in defining reasonableness.

The reasonable person is supposed to resemble the defendant as closely as possible in terms of

1. Ask: Would the reasonable person have acted as the defendant did, under the same or similar circumstances?
2. Match the skills or abilities of the reasonable person to those of the defendant (e.g., physician, attorney, plumber, rodeo rider) if these abilities were involved in the alleged negligent actions (professional community standard).
3. Trier-of-fact decides how the reasonable person would have acted in a particular situation.

The Reasonable Person Standard The reasonable person is an imaginary person who behaves reasonably under a given set of circumstances to avoid harming others.

special abilities. This enables the trier of fact to assess reasonableness more precisely in a specific case. For example, if the defendant was a plumber who was alleged to have negligently installed a leaking water line, the reasonable person would also possess the same training and knowledge as plumbers employed in the defendant's geographical area. This is sometimes called the *professional community* **standard of care**, which is based on the custom and practice among professionals working in the defendant's community. This measure is determined through expert testimony from members of the defendant's profession. Physicians, attorneys, accountants, veterinarians, electricians, beauticians, and the like are evaluated in negligence lawsuits by this standard of care.

The defendant's limitations also are important in shaping the reasonable person standard. For instance, if the defendant were physically handicapped, then the reasonable person would likewise share identical handicaps. The jury, in effect, must conceptualize how the reasonable person would have behaved in a wheelchair, with impaired hearing, or without certain limbs. The outcome of this empathy should be a more accurate reasonableness definition that best fits the defendant and the circumstances of the case. The result, ideally, is a just and equitable outcome in the litigation.

standard of care The standard by which negligence is determined in a particular situation.

Causation of Injury

Even if the defendant breaches his or her duty of care owed to the plaintiff, the defendant will not be legally negligent, nor liable for the plaintiff's injuries, unless the defendant's actions caused the harm.

Cause-in-Fact

Causation is a critical component of negligence. To be liable, the tortfeasor must have caused the victim's injuries. *Causation of injury* relates to the tortfeasor's actions that result in harm to the injured party. Courts frequently refer to this as *cause-in-fact*, meaning that, in negligence litigation, the defendant's misconduct produced the plaintiff's injuries.

Causation may be direct or indirect. *Direct causation* is often called *but-for causation*, a term often applied in the common law. The formula is straightforward: but for the tortfeasor's (defendant's) actions, the victim (plaintiff) would not have been harmed. But-for, or direct, causation is straight-lined, that is, the tortfeasor's behavior is usually the immediate cause of the victim's misfortune. In the example in our law office scenario, Steve Jensen's negligence would probably be considered the direct cause of John Jacobson's injuries because, had Steve not run the red light, John would not have been harmed.

Indirect causation occurs when several forces combine to produce injuries. To resolve the causation dilemma, the but-for test serves poorly. Instead, one needs a formula that satisfactorily accounts for the multiple factors that produced the injuries. For indirect causation, there is substantial factor analysis, which states that the tortfeasor is liable for injuries to the victim when the tortfeasor's misconduct was a substantial factor in producing the harm. When two or more defendants act together to produce the plaintiff's injury, the courts consider them to have acted in concert. All defendants are held liable for their combined conduct in such cases. This is called **joint and several liability**, another form of causation.

Joint and Several Liability

Multiple tortfeasors are each held individually accountable to the victim for the combined negligent behavior of all the tortfeasors. For instance, suppose that a surgical team, composed of two surgeons, three nurses, and an anesthesiologist, loses count of surgical sponges and leaves one in the patient's abdomen. The patient contracts peritonitis as a consequence. Because all of the medical personnel acted together in the operation, they are said to have functioned in concert. Their collective conduct produced harm to the patient. Thus, each individual would be personally liable for the patient's injuries. In other words, all of the personnel would be jointly and severally liable.

Multiple tortfeasors may injure a victim by acting in sequence, rather than simultaneously as in the medical malpractice example. The sequence of combined events produces the harmful results.

Proximate Cause

Joint and several liability is simple to discern when the chain of negligent events is relatively short and direct. However, when the sequence of activity is long, drawn-out, and complicated by peculiar twists and unexpected occurrences, then the three types of causation analysis (cause-in-fact, substantial factor analysis, and joint and several liability) become unreliable for determining whether the tortfeasor is liable to the victim. Another analytical tool must be applied to establish negligence in such circumstances. This approach is called proximate cause.

Proximate cause, or *legal cause* as it is sometimes called, exists when the tortfeasor's actions cause a foreseeable injury to the victim. Court opinions often refer to the plaintiff's injuries as

BALLENTINESBALLENTINESBALLENTINESBALLENTINESBALLENTINESBALLENTINESBALLENTINESBALLENTINESBALLENTINESBALLENTINESBALLENTINESBALLENTINESBALLENTINES

causation   A causing; the producing of a result.

joint and several liability   The liability of two or more persons who jointly commit a tort.

proximate cause   [T]hat cause which, unbroken by any intervening cause, produced the injury, and without which the result would not have occurred; the primary cause; the efficient cause.

THE TORT PARALEGAL AND PERSONAL INJURY LITIGATION

the natural and probable consequence of the defendant's misconduct. The key to proximate cause is foreseeable injury. Was the victim's injury the reasonably foreseeable result of what the tortfeasor did? If so, then the tortfeasor's actions proximately caused the plaintiff's harm. If not, then proximate cause did not exist, and the defendant will not be liable to the plaintiff under negligence theory.

Proximate cause is distinguishable from causation. The term *proximate cause* is unfortunate because it is a constant source of confusion with causation. *Causation* is the chain of events linking the tortfeasor's conduct to the victim's injury. *Proximate cause* is the zone within which the plaintiff's injury was reasonably foreseeable as a consequence of the defendant's behavior. Think of proximate cause as a circle. Actions inside the circle cause foreseeable injuries to victims. Actions outside the circle are beyond the *zone of foreseeability*.

Damages

Damages are the injury that the plaintiff suffered as a result of the defendant's tortious conduct. As in all torts, damages must be proven for negligence. Courts will not compensate a victim unless some documentable harm has been done.

Recall that, with certain intentional torts such as battery, assault, or trespass, no physical harm is required. In negligence law, however, some determinable injury must be proven for the tortfeasor to be held liable to the injured party. Normally, this involves monetary losses as a result of harm to a person or the person's property. For instance, if someone loses muscular control in the legs after an automobile accident with a careless driver, then the injured party could demonstrate economic loss as a consequence of the harm. The plaintiff could quantify the losses sustained through lost wages, inability to continue an occupation, loss of bodily function, emotional impairment, and related damages. The plaintiff must prove actual injury to recover. This harm may be physical or emotional, but it must exist.

Compensatory Damages

Compensatory damages are most common in negligence cases. As the name suggests, **compensatory damages** are designed to compensate the victim for the tortfeasor's negligence. Normally, the plaintiff proves monetary losses, such as out-of-pocket expenses (e.g., medical, property repair), lost income, pain and suffering, loss of property value, or loss of bodily function. Personal injury paralegals are often assigned the task of identifying and keeping track of certain types of the plaintiff's compensable damages. This job may include documenting medical expenses incurred by the plaintiff, as well as lost wages and other special expenses.

Punitive Damages

Punitive or **exemplary damages**, which are often awarded for intentional torts such as fraud or intentional infliction of emotional distress, are almost nonexistent in negligence cases, because negligence involves carelessness rather than wanton or intentionally tortious behavior. The punishment component of punitive damages would be excessive in most negligence cases, although exemplary damages are occasionally used in gross negligence cases. **Gross negligence** involves

BALLENTINESBALLENTINESBALLENTINESBALLENTINESBALLENTINESBALLENTINESBALLENTINESBALLENTINESBALLENTINESBALLENTINESBALLENTINESBALLENTINESBALLENTINESBALLENTINES

damages   The sum of money that may be recovered in the courts as financial reparation for an injury or wrong suffered as a result of ... a tortious act.

compensatory damages (actual damages)   Damages recoverable in a lawsuit for loss or injury suffered by the plaintiff as a result of the defendant's conduct.

punitive damages (exemplary damages)   Damages that are awarded over and above compensatory damages ... because of the wanton, reckless, or malicious nature of the wrong done to the plaintiff. Such damages bear no relation to the plaintiff's actual loss ... , because their purpose is to make an example of the plaintiff to discourage others from engaging in the same kind of conduct in the future.

gross negligence   Willfully and intentionally acting, or failing to act, with a deliberate indifference to how others may be affected.

carelessness that exceeds ordinary, reasonable care standards and approaches willful and wanton misconduct. If the negligence is sufficiently excessive, the court might allow punitive damages for the injured party. For instance, if a surgeon left a scalpel inside a patient during an operation, this might be considered gross negligence by the medical community. Such misconduct exceeds that degree of reasonable care ordinarily expected of doctors. Physicians simply are expected to avoid such slipshod surgical efforts.

Proving Negligence

Proof is an essential aspect of all litigation. Negligence claims are normally proven through the typical evidentiary processes. These include oral testimony, depositions, documentary evidence, and demonstrative evidence (such as photographs or computer simulations).

Burdens of Proof and Rejoinder

The plaintiff has the burden of proving that the defendant was negligent. This forces the plaintiff to prove by a preponderance of the evidence that all negligence elements existed (duty, breach, causation, proximate cause, and injury). The evidence must establish that the defendant's actions were negligent and caused the plaintiff's injuries.

Once the plaintiff has made a **prima facie case** (meaning that proof has been established by or beyond a preponderance), the burden shifts to the defendant, who must then counter the plaintiff's evidence with proof of his or her own. This is sometimes called the defendant's *burden of*

rejoinder or **rebuttal**. The defendant must disprove the plaintiff's case against him or her.

In some cases, however, the burden of proof is different. What if the plaintiff cannot prove the defendant's negligence? Consider an example. Suppose a patient were unconscious during an operation. Suppose the surgical nurse failed to remove all the sponges from the patient, and later the patient contracted peritonitis. How could the plaintiff prove that the defendants (nurse, surgeon, and hospital) were negligent in leaving the sponge inside the plaintiff? What witnesses could the plaintiff call to testify, other than the surgical team? The plaintiff was unconscious and unaware of the entire procedure. How could the plaintiff meet the burden of proof in such circumstances? Such unusual cases require a special burden of proof called res ipsa loquitur.

Res Ipsa Loquitur

Res ipsa loquitur (meaning "the thing speaks for itself") is used in negligence cases in which the plaintiff is in a disadvantaged position for proving the defendant's negligence. Under the doctrine of res ipsa loquitur, the defendant's negligence is presumed as a result of his or her actions. This shifts the burden of proof to the defendant. In other words, the defendant must disprove his or her negligence from the outset of litigation. The plaintiff's burden of proof is converted into the defendant's burden of rejoinder.

The plaintiff must prove only certain essential facts, such as what injury occurred, what the defendant was doing, and how the defendant's action (or inaction) related to the plaintiff's harm. To use res ipsa loquitur, the circumstances of the

BALLENTINESBALLENTINESBALLENTINESBALLENTINESBALLENTINESBALLENTINESBALLENTINESBALLENTINESBALLENTINESBALLENTINESBALLENTINESBALLENTINES

prima facie case   A cause of action or defense that is sufficiently established by a party's evidence to justify a verdict in his or her favor, provided the other party does not rebut that evidence; a case supported by sufficient evidence to justify its submission to the trier of fact and the rendition of a compatible verdict.

rejoinder   A reply; an answer; a retort.

rebut   To deny; to refute; to contradict; to contravene.

res ipsa loquitur   Means "the thing speaks for itself." When an instrumentality causes injury, an inference or rebuttable presumption arises that the injury was caused by the defendant's negligence, if the ... instrumentality was under the exclusive control or management of the defendant and the occurrence was such as in the ordinary course of events would not have happended if the defendant had used reasonable care.

case must strongly imply negligence by someone. Court opinions often quote the following elements:

1. The defendant (or his or her employee[s]) must have been in exclusive control of the object or action that produced the plaintiff's injury.
2. The plaintiff's injury must be of a type that ordinarily would not have happened unless negligence were involved.
3. The defendant must be in a better position to prove his or her lack of negligence than the plaintiff is to prove the defendant's negligence.

Certain courts and legal scholars add a fourth element, which states that the plaintiff cannot have contributed to his or her own injuries.

For res ipsa loquitur to apply, the events that led to the plaintiff's injury must have been under the defendant's exclusive control. This includes the defendant's employees. Res ipsa loquitur also insists that the plaintiff's injury be one that normally would not have happened unless negligence were involved. At least the court will make this presumption and allow the defendant to refute it by proving that reasonable care was used. Under res ipsa loquitur, the defendant must be in a better position to prove that he or she was not negligent than the plaintiff is to establish the defendant's negligence. This makes it easier for the defendant to prove that reasonable care was used. The plaintiff is at a disadvantage to prove the defendant's negligence. However, the defendant can more easily show that safeguards were used. In this fashion, the defendant could prove that reasonable care was used, and that therefore no negligence happened.

Premises Liability

Special negligence rules apply to owners and occupiers of land. *Occupiers* include individuals who do not own but use real estate, including tenants (lessees). As negligence law developed, American courts devised different standards of reasonable care for land owners or land users. The distinctions depended upon who the injured party (plaintiff) was, in terms of the victim's purpose for being on the land where the owner's negligence was alleged to have occurred.

For example, under old common law, the land owner owed a different duty of reasonable care to the injured party depending upon whether the victim was a trespasser, a licensee, or an invitee. Thus, the plaintiff's status as a trespasser, licensee, or invitee determined the scope of duty that the owner owed.

Courts and legal scholars for decades have complained that this three-tier analytical approach is arbitrary and unnecessary. After all, ordinary negligence theory appears adequately equipped to establish the land owner's duty of reasonable care. If an owner acted unreasonably in maintaining his or her realty, and as a result a victim was harmed, then the owner should be liable. Regular negligence theory works well to produce a just result, say these critics. Many courts have in fact abolished the three-tier land owner standards of care, although others continue to apply it.

Trespassers

Land owners owe no duty of reasonable care toward **trespassers**. Owners may not intentionally injure trespassers upon their real estate, but they need not search their realty and safeguard it for trespassers' unauthorized uses. Courts favoring this policy reason that a land owner should not be required to exercise ordinary reasonable care to protect a tortfeasor (i.e., trespasser) from harm. Because the trespasser is committing an intentional tort, negligence law insists only that real estate owners avoid intentionally injuring trespassers. Otherwise, the trespasser assumes the risk of entering someone else's land without permission.

Land owners owe a higher duty of reasonable care to trespassing children, however. The reasoning behind this special rule states that younger children are so inexperienced and naive that they may not fully appreciate dangers lurking upon

trespasser [A] person who enters the land of another without an invitation to do so and whose presence is not suffered.

the land. Therefore, owners must exercise ordinary, reasonable care to safeguard their realty for trespassing children who are enticed onto the land to investigate the dangerous condition that injured them. Young children are often attracted out of curiosity to investigate dangerous conditions on realty, such as abandoned wells, railroad tracks, swimming pools, or unused machinery. These alluring items are often hazardous, a fact that the trespassing child may not understand. The attraction element has given this special rule its name of **attraction theory** or, more commonly, **attractive nuisance**. If a trespassing child is injured as a result of having been enticed onto the land to investigate some dangerous condition, then the landowner is liable for such harm.

Many courts have discarded the attraction element to the theory. For these courts, it is sufficient that (1) the injury to the trespassing child was reasonably foreseeable; (2) the danger on the land presented an unreasonable risk of harm to trespassing children; (3) the danger on the land was artificial, meaning manmade rather than natural; (4) because of the child's youth, he or she could not appreciate the risks involved or did not discover (and understand) the threat; (5) the threatening condition was located at a place across which children were likely to trespass; and (6) the land owner failed to exercise reasonable care to protect trespassing children from the danger that caused the harm. Under this version of attractive nuisance, the danger did not have to entice the child onto the land. It is adequate that the child encountered and was hurt by a danger that he or she did not fully discern.

A number of jurisdictions depart from this artificial condition element. These courts would include natural dangers, such as streams, quicksand, or rock formations, as risks against which the land owner must take precautions to protect trespassing children.

Licensees

Licensees are persons who have permission to be upon another's land. They are distinguishable from trespassers in that the land owner has consented to their presence upon his or her realty. This consent may be expressed or implied. Examples of licensees include social guests, such as friends who gather at a person's house to study or neighbors coming over to borrow tools; door-to-door salespersons or charitable solicitors (when the land owner has not prohibited their entry by posting warning signs); and frequent trespassers to whose incursions the land owner implicitly consents (such as when trespassers frequently use shortcuts that the land owner does not discourage through fencing or sign-posting).

Owners owe licensees a duty of reasonable care in using the real estate. This includes the owner's obligation to correct known dangers (both artificial and natural) on the land. In other words, if the owner knows (or reasonably should know) that a hazardous condition exists on the realty, then he or she must exercise reasonable care in safeguarding licensees from these risks. For example, if an abandoned well has not been covered, and a travelling salesperson visits and falls into the well (which cannot be seen because of overgrown grass), then the land owner has breached his or her duty of reasonable care to the salesperson, assuming that the owner knew (or should have known) that the well was there and could not be detected. However, the owner is not required to discover and correct unknown threats on the land.

Invitees

Invitees are persons invited upon the land owner's premises. Originally, the common law restricted the term to individuals invited onto premises for business purposes, such as customers to a grocery, clothing store, amusement park,

attractive nuisance (attraction theory) An unusual mechanism, apparatus, or condition that is dangerous to young children but is so interesting and alluring as to attract them to the premises on which it is kept.

licensee A person who enters upon the property of another for his or her own convenience, pleasure, or benefit, uninvited but tolerated by the owner.

invitee A person who enters the premises of another at the latter's invitation, or for business purposes, or for their mutual advantage.

or tavern. Modern cases, however, state that an invitee need not be seeking any business-related purposes when he or she enters another's real estate. It is sufficient that the land owner encourage the invitee to visit.

Usually, invitees are persons coming onto the land for some purpose that the owner wishes to serve. Commonly, this includes any business, but could also include nonprofit organizations, such as churches, soup kitchens, charitable hospitals, or even colleges.

Land owners owe the highest duty of reasonable care to invitees. Owners must not only repair known dangers on the property but also must discover and correct unknown risks. This is a broader standard, requiring the land owner to take extra efforts to render his or her premises reasonably safe for invitees.

The logic underlying this stiffer standard of care suggests that an owner who invites someone onto his realty should be expected to exercise greater caution to insure that the premises are reasonably danger-free. After all, the invitee would not be on the land to begin with had it not been for the owner's invitation.

Invitees and Licensees Distinguished   *Invitee* is a subcategory of *licensee,* yet the terms are distinguishable. All licensees have the owner's implied or expressed permission to be on the land, but the land owner does not have to invite or encourage licensees to visit; rather, the owner may just passively tolerate the licensees' presence. With invitees, however, the owner impliedly or expressly invites them onto the real estate. This reflects the owner's active role in getting the invitees onto his or her land. Usually, the owner seeks customers for business; hence, courts often speak of *business invitees*.

Implicit or Express Invitation   The land owner's invitation to others to enter the premises may be expressed (e.g., a welcome sign outside a church, or a business posting its hours on its door) or implied (e.g., a business leaving its doors open during business hours).

Duty to Trespasser	Land owner/occupier owes no duty of reasonable care; is required only to avoid intentional (or willful and wanton) injury.
Duty to Licensee	Land owner/occupier owes duty of reasonable care to correct known dangers on premises.
Duty to Invitee	Land owner/occupier owes duty of reasonable care to discover and correct unknown dangers on premises.
Traditional Negligence Theory	Applies regular negligence standards to determine land owner/occupier liability.
Duty to Trespassing Children (Attractive Nuisance Theory)	Land owner/occupier owes duty of reasonable care to protect trespassing children from artificial dangers on premises, when (1) injury to child is reasonably foreseeable, (2) danger presented unreasonable risk of harm, (3) child could not appreciate dangerous condition, and (4) danger existed at place at which children are likely to trespass.

Land Owners' and Occupiers' Negligence Liability
The duty of care of the owner or occupier depends on the status of the visitor.

Limited Areas of Invitation   Obviously, most land owners do not invite people into every nook and cranny of their property. Certain regions are off-limits. For example, most businesses have storage rooms, manager's offices, or machinery rooms that patrons are specifically discouraged from entering. Virtually any business has door signs warning "private," "authorized personnel only," "keep out," and similar prohibitions. The owner's invitation to invitees does not include such areas. If an individual were injured while visiting an off-limits zone, then that person would be considered merely a licensee, or perhaps even a trespasser (depending upon how sternly the warning was phrased—such as "no trespassing—keep out!"), rather than an invitee.

Traditional Negligence Theory in Land Owner Cases

As noted earlier, many courts have elminated the trespasser/licensee/invitee approach in favor of regular negligence theory. Instead of forcing the injured party into one of these three categories, many courts simply ask the routine negligence questions: Was the injury reasonably foreseeable? Did the land owner's scope of duty include the victim? Did the owner cause the victim's injury? and so forth. Many courts, however, cling tenaciously to the older three-tier analysis. This demonstrates how entrenched precedent becomes: once a rule of law becomes settled, it is difficult to raze the monolith and renovate its concepts. The law changes at a snail's pace. More often than not, this provides valuable stability and predictability in legal problem solving. Nonetheless, it also makes legal principles slow to adapt to the rapid changes of our dynamic society.

Bailments

A *chattel* is personal property. Personal property includes everything that is not land, which is real property. Chattels include this textbook, a pet cat, and the chewing gum a classmate just borrowed from another student.

A **bailment** exists when the personal property owner, called the **bailor** delivers possession of his or her chattel to someone else, called the **bailee**, who keeps it until the bailor requests that the item be returned or delivered to someone else. Examples of bailments include attended pay parking garages, lockers at the college bookstore, dry cleaners, and commercial shippers. Any business in which the chattel owner transfers possession of the personal property to the bailee, who keeps it on the owner's behalf, creates a bailment relationship between owner and holder.

Historically, courts developed a three-tier approach to bailments, just as with land owners' negligence. First of all, the bailee must exercise reasonable care to safeguary the owner's personal property while the bailee possesses it. However, the standard of care differs depending upon who benefits from the bailment relationship.

The bailor and the bailee often do not benefit equally in a bailment relationship. In come cases, only the bailor benefits. This is called a *bailment for the bailor's sole benefit.*

What if only the bailee benefits? This is bailment for the bailee's sole benefit. Bailments that benefit only the bailor or bailee are often **gratuitous bailments**. This is because the nonbenefiting party does not receive any payment or compensation for his or her role in the bailment relationship.

Most often, both bailor and bailee benefit. This is called a *mutual benefit bailment* and is typical of **bailments for hire**, in which the bailee is in the bailment business. Examples include pawn shops, attended pay parking lots, pay storage lockers, and commercial shippers.

When a bailment is for the sole benefit of the bailor, the bailee owes only a duty of slight care to safeguard the personal property from harm. **Slight care** is that degree of caution one uses

---

BALLENTINESBALLENTINESBALLENTINESBALLENTINESBALLENTINESBALLENTINESBALLENTINESBALLENTINESBALLENTINESBALLENTINESBALLENTINESBALLENTINESBALLENTINES

bailment   The entrusting of personal property by one person … to another … for a specific purpose, with the understanding that the property will be returned when the purpose is accomplished, the stated duration of the bailment is over, or the bailor reclaims it.

bailor   The person who entrusts property to another in a bailment.

bailee   The person to whom property is entrusted in a bailment.

gratuitous bailment   A bailment for the sole benefit of the bailee; that is, one in which no compensation is involved.

bailment for hire   A bailment for compensation.

slight care   A very minimal degree of care; the least degree of care.

when involved in relatively unimportant activities in which damage is not a concern. With a mutual benefit bailment, the bailee owes a duty of ordinary, reasonable care to safeguard the chattel from damage.

When a bailment benefits only the bailee, the bailee owes a duty of great care to safeguard the personal property from injury. **Great care** is an extraordinary degree of caution one uses when involved in exceedingly important activities in which extreme care should be used to avoid injury.

In recent years, however, courts have begun to abandon the three-tier analysis for bailments, just as many have done for land owners' negligence liability. Instead, these modern courts apply regular negligence theory to decide if the bailee failed to exercise reasonable care in protecting the bailor's chattel from harm. This approach is easier to apply, because benefits analysis often is difficult to conceptualize. It is easier simply to ask whether the bailee used reasonable care in safeguarding the personal property.

Vicarious Liability

Vicarious liability is the liability of one person, called the **principal**, for the tortious conduct of another, subordinate individual, called the **agent**, who was acting on the principal's behalf. In negligence law, principal/agent relationships most often involve employers and employees. The situation is simple. The principal is the employer, who hires the agent (employee) to work on the employer's behalf.

The principal/agent relationship, however, does not have to be that of employer and employee. Nineteenth- and early twentieth-century cases spoke of *master and servant*. This older classification suggested that the servant could work for the master without being paid. Thus, whether the agent is compensated for acting upon the principal's behalf is largely irrelevant to the issue of vicarious liability. Instead, focus upon this inquiry: Was one person acting on behalf of another? If so, a principal/agent relationship is present, and vicarious liability could exist.

Respondeat Superior

The employer is responsible for the negligence (or, for that matter, any torts) that his or her employees commit while working. This doctrine of vicarious liability is called *respondeat superior*, a Latin phrase meaning, "Let the superior answer."

Not every employee activity gives rise to the respondeat superior doctrine, however. An employer is responsible only for an employee's actions that fall within the **scope of employment**, the range of conduct that the employer expects the employee to perform as part of his or her job. Employers are not liable for torts committed by employees that fall outside the scope of employment.

Employers are usually not vicariously liable for the negligence of their employees while the employees are coming to or going from work. This is called the *coming and going rule*. The only situation in which an employer would be liable in such circumstances is if the employee were performing work-related activities while on the way to or from the job.

Employers are also not vicariously liable for the negligence of their employees when employees go off on their own to handle personal matters, even though they might be performing work otherwise. Thus, if the employee were negligent while

BALLENTINESBALLENTINESBALLENTINESBALLENTINESBALLENTINESBALLENTINESBALLENTINESBALLENTINESBALLENTINESBALLENTINESBALLENTINESBALLENTINESBALLENTINESBALLENTINESBALLENTINES

great care   The degree of care a prudent person usually exercises concerning his or her own affairs of great importance.

vicarious liability   Liability imposed upon a person because of the act or omission of another.

principal   [T]he person for whom the agent acts and from whom the agent receives his or her authority to act.

agent   [O]ne who acts for and represents the other party, ... the principal.

respondeat superior   Means "let the master respond." The doctrine under which liability is imposed upon an employer for the acts of its employees committed in the course and scope of their employment.

scope of employment   A phrase referring to activities carried out by an employee in doing the work assigned to him or her by the employer.

pursuing activities unrelated to employment during ordinary working hours, this would be considered *frolic and detour*, and the employer would not be vicariously liable.

Independent Contractors

An **independent contractor** is someone who has entered into a contract with another person to perform a specific task. The independent contractor controls how he or she accomplishes the job. The individual hiring the independent contractor simply agrees to pay him or her for doing the chore. Independent contractors are distinguishable from employees in that the employer does not control how an independent contractor does the job. In contrast, employers do control how their employees perform their tasks.

Persons hiring independent contractors are not vicariously liable for the independent contractors' negligence. The reasoning is that the independent contractor is engaging in his or her own work and should be responsible for his or her own negligence. The hirer is simply buying the independent contractor's finished service, and has nothing to do with how the independent contractor achieves the desired results.

Negligent Infliction of Emotional Distress

Emotional distress consists of mental anguish caused by a tortfeasor. This condition includes fright, anxiety, shock, grief, mental suffering, shame, embarrassment, and emotional disturbance. The tort exists when the tortfeasor inflicts psychological injury on the victim, that is, when the tortfeasor acts negligently to produce a psychological harm. *Negligent infliction of emotional distress* consists of: (1) Outrageous conduct by the tortfeasor, which (2) the tortfeasor reasonably should have anticipated would produce (3) significant and reasonably foreseeable emotional injury to the victim; when (4) the tortfeasor

Bailment for Bailor's Sole Benefit	Bailee owes duty of slight care to safeguard chattel from harm.
Bailment for Mutual Benefit	Bailee owes duty of ordinary, reasonable care to protect chattel from injury.
Bailment for Bailee's Sole Benefit	Bailee owes duty of great care to guard personal property from damage.
Traditional Negligence Theory	Applies regular negligence elements to determine bailee's liability.

Bailee's Negligence Liability A bailment exists when the property owner (bailor) delivers possession of his or her personal property to another (bailee).

breached his or her duty of reasonable care to avoid causing such emotional harm to the victim; and (5) the victim was a reasonably foreseeable plaintiff.

Extra Elements in the Common Law

These generalized elements of negligent infliction of emotional distress are synthesized from those of many jurisdictions. Different courts apply various special requirements to negligent infliction cases, and it is always wise to check the rules and formulations of the particular jurisdiction in which your case lies.

A minority of courts insist that some physical impact accompany the emotional injury. Thus, the tortfeasor must negligently do something that physically touches the victim if the victim is to recover damages for negligent infliction of emotional distress. This is often called the *impact rule*, and it has been severely criticized in the legal literature and judicial decisions.

The purpose of the impact requirement is to protect against false claims of emotional distress. Because mental anguish is largely invisible, courts at the turn of the century felt that

independent contractor As distinguished from an employee, a person who contracts to do work for another person in his or her own way, controlling the means and method by which the work is done but not the end product.

the defendant had to make contact with the plaintiff to justify compensating something as easy to fake as mental harm. Modern courts utilizing the impact rule have seen impact in almost any physical touching. Something as casual as putting one's hand on a classmate's shoulder would be considered sufficient contact to satisfy the impact rule. Hence, it would seem that, as a safeguard against faked claims of emotional distress, the physical impact requirement does little or nothing to ensure honesty and sincerity for allegations of mental hurt.

The majority of courts have abandoned the impact rule in favor of the *physical manifestations rule*. This requires that, in addition to mental suffering, the plaintiff must experience physical symptoms as a result of the emotional distress. This rule is also thought to protect against bogus claims of emotional injury. After all, if a victim experiences some physical malady associated with an emotional harm, such as an ulcer, hives, sleeplessness, weight loss, or bowel dysfunction, then the probability is that the emotional harm is genuine.

What happens when the negligent action occurs to someone else, and the plaintiff is a bystander who witnesses a negligent injury to another person? Could the tortfeasor be liable to the bystander for negligent infliction of emotional distress? Consider an example. Suppose parents witnessed their child being struck by a negligent driver. Would the parents have a cause of action against the driver for negligent infliction of emotional distress?

No impact occurred to the parents, although they may suffer physical manifestations as a result of witnessing their child's injury. The proper question, however, may be phrased in ordinary negligence terms: Did the driver owe (and breach) a duty of reasonable care to the parents by injuring their child? Did the driver's actions cause the parents' emotional suffering? Does proximate cause exist? Were the parents injured?

Certainly, the driver could not reasonably anticipate that any bystander would suffer emotional distress as a result of the driver's negligent act of hitting a pedestrian. There must be some way to limit the scope of duty (and, hence, the range of

Vicarious Liability	Liability of principal for negligent actions of agent serving on principal's behalf. Commonly involves employer/employee relationships.
Respondeat Superior	"Let the superior answer": Doctrine through which employers may be held vicariously liable for employees' negligent actions committed within the scope of employment.
Scope of Employment	Range of conduct that employer expects of employee during performance of assigned employment responsibilities.
Coming and Going Rule	Employers are not vicariously liable for employees' negligence while employees are coming to and going from work, unless employer has specifically requested employee to carry out a specific work-related task during such times.
Frolic and Detour Rule	Employers are not vicariously liable for employees' negligence when employees deviate from assigned tasks within scope of employment. Usually involves employees going off on their own to pursue personal needs.
Independent Contractors	Employers are not liable for independent contractors' negligence, because I.C.'s act independently and are responsible for their own conduct.

Forms of Vicarious Liability Under the vicarious liability doctrine, the principal is liable for the tortious conduct of an agent who was acting on the principal's behalf.

foreseeable plaintiffs). Courts have attempted to establish such limits by creating the *zone of danger rule*. Under this rule, only bystanders who fall within the zone of danger can recover for negligent infliction of emotional distress. In other words, these individuals must have been threatened by the original negligent action (e.g., negligent driving of a vehicle) and have reasonably feared for their own safety.

Other courts have restricted recovery in negligent infliction cases to bystander plaintiffs who are related to the victim who they witnessed being injured. This may be called the *family relationships rule.*

Still other courts have insisted that the bystander perceive the traumatic, negligent event directly through the senses (e.g., seeing the collision; hearing the child's screams; feeling the heat of the car exploding; smelling the burning clothing). This may be labelled the *sensory perception rule.*

Defenses to Negligence

Always remember these basic analytical rules:

1. *Negligence defenses are used only by the defendant against the plaintiff.* The party alleged to have been negligent can use defenses against the party alleging negligence. In cases involving counterclaims, in which the defendant counter-sues the plaintiff, remember that the defendant becomes a counter-plaintiff against the original plaintiff, who becomes a counter-defendant, at least as far as the counterclaim is concerned. The same holds true for third-party complaints and answers.

2. *Negligence defenses are applied only in response to the plaintiff's allegations that the defendant acted negligently.* Again, in counterclaims and third-party claims, remember who is the alleging party and who is the alleged wrongdoer. In a counterclaim, the defendant might allege that the plaintiff acted negligently toward the defendant. Re-title the parties to reflect their new roles toward each other with respect to the counterclaim. The counterdefendant (i.e., the plaintiff) would be entitled to use negligence defenses against the counter-plaintiff (i.e., the defendant).

   The same is true for third-party claims. Defendants may become third-party plaintiffs, bringing third-party defendants into the litigation through cross-complaint. The scenario is this: A plaintiff sues a defendant, alleging that a tort has been committed. The defendant cross-sues a third-party defendant for that third party's participation in committing the tort. Negligence defenses are available to the third-party defendant against the third-party plaintiff's negligence claims.

3. *Ask who is alleging negligence and who is alleged to have been negligent.* The alleged tortfeasor is the person who may utilize defenses.

Contributory Negligence

Contributory negligence is the plaintiff's negligence that contributed to his or her injuries. The elements of contributory negligence include:

1. The plaintiff's duty of reasonable care to himself or herself

2. The plaintiff's breach of that duty

3. The plaintiff's actions (or failures to act) that contributed to his or her injuries (causation, proximate cause)

4. Resulting injuries to the plaintiff.

One has a duty of reasonable care to protect oneself from injury. If a person breaches this duty by causing injury to himself, then he has been negligent toward himself. Suppose a tortfeasor (defendant) also participated in causing the harm. Nonetheless, the victim (plaintiff) contributed to the resulting injury. This is contributory negligence.

BALLENTINESBALLENTINESBALLENTINESBALLENTINESBALLENTINESBALLENTINESBALLENTINESBALLENTINESBALLENTINESBALLENTINESBALLENTINESBALLENTINESBALLENTINES

contributory negligence   [A] failure by the plaintiff to exercise reasonable care which, in part at least, is the cause of an injury.

Common Elements (applying standard negligence theory to emotionally distressing conduct)	(1) outrageous conduct by tortfeasor, when (2) tortfeasor reasonably should have anticipated that behavior would produce (3) signifcant and reasonably foreseeable injury in plaintiff, (4) tortfeasor breached duty of reasonable care, and (5) victim was foreseeable plaintiff.
Impact Rule	Plaintiff must experience physical impact from defendant's actions to recover for negligent infliction of emotional distress.
Physical Manifestions Rule	No physical impact is required, but plaintiff must experience physical symptoms associated with mental anguish that defendant caused.
Zone of Danger Rule	Bystander witnessing negligent injury to third party must have been immediately threatened by negligent activity.
Family Relationships Rule	Bystander must be a family relative of the injured by the tortfeasor's negligent act.
Sensory Perception Rule	Bystander must perceive with his or her senses (sight, hearing, smell, touch, taste) the injury to another person as a result of the tortfeasor's negligent act.

Elements of Negligent Infliction of Emotional Distress

At common law, contributory negligence barred the plaintiff from recovering any damages from the defendant. Even if the defendant were negligent in causing 99 percent of the plaintiff's harm, and the plaintiff were only 1 percent contributorily negligent, the courts ruled that the plaintiff could collect nothing against the defendant.

Last Clear Chance

When a defendant uses the contributory negligence defense against a plaintiff, the plaintiff has a defensive weapon with which to respond. This is called **last clear chance** and is a rebuttal to a contributory negligence defense. Last clear chance theory states that, although the plaintiff was contributorily negligent in causing his or her own injuries, the defendant had the last opportunity to avert harm but, because of the defendant's negligence, the defendant failed to take advantage of this "last clear chance" to avoid hurting the plaintiff.

Last clear chance nullifies the contributory negligence defense. In other words, the defendant cannot escape liability for his or her negligence (by invoking the contributory negligence defense) if the defendant had the last clear chance to avoid the injury.

Unfairness of Contributory Negligence

Is the common law theory of contributory negligence fair and just? Even if the defendant was 99 percent responsible for the plaintiff's injury, the plaintiff's 1 percent of contributory negligence completely barred the plaintiff's claim. Would it not be more logical for the defendant's liability to reflect his or her share of responsibility for the injury?

Many legal scholars and judges criticized the common law rule for much of the twentieth century. It seemed unduly harsh to the plaintiff, who might have been only marginally involved in injuring himself or herself. Also, it allowed the defendant, who might have been significantly responsible for the plaintiff's harm, to completely avoid liability. Courts and legislatures have

BALLENTINESBALLENTINESBALLENTINESBALLENTINESBALLENTINESBALLENTINESBALLENTINESBALLENTINESBALLENTINESBALLENTINESBALLENTINESBALLENTINESBALLENTINESBALLENTINES

last clear chance doctrine A rule of negligence law by which a negligent defendant is held liable to a plaintiff who has negligently placed himself or herself in peril, if the defendant had a later opportunity than the plaintiff to avoid the occurrence that resulted in injury.

modified the common law rule by adopting comparative negligence theory.

Comparative Negligence

The comparative negligence defense has replaced contributory negligence in most states. The defense of comparative negligence enables the defendant's liability to be adjusted according to the extent of the plaintiff's contribution to his or her own injuries. **Comparative negligence** may be defined as a measurement and comparison of the plaintiff's and the defendant's negligence in causing the plaintiff's injuries.

The comparative negligence defense has three elements:

1. Negligence of the plaintiff in contributing to his or her own injuries.
2. Calculation of the percentage of the plaintiff's negligence that contributed to his or her injuries.
3. Calculation of the percentage of the defendant's negligence that produced the plaintiff's injuries.

In some jurisdictions, a fourth element is included: the defendant must have been more negligent than the plaintiff.

Comparative negligence balances the degrees of each party's negligence that produced the plaintiff's harm. In effect, the plaintiff's and defendant's negligence are compared to see which was more responsible for causing injury. This comparative negligence balancing is typically measured in percentages of negligence. This is sometimes called *culpability factoring* or *liability apportionment*. However, the paralegal may find this approach frustrating. What are the correct percentages?

There is no exact formula. It depends upon the facts of each case. The trier of fact decides the percentages in comparative negligence. Thus, the jury (or judge, in a bench trial) must closely examine the facts and assign negligence percentages to the plaintiff and the defendant. Whatever percentages are selected, triers of fact probably rely on intuition and gut feeling as much as anything.

Comparative negligence is used to calculate the amount of the defendant's liability to the plaintiff. Assume that the following percentages were selected: Defendant 75 percent negligent, plaintiff 25 percent negligent. What would be the outcome of the case? The defendant would be liable to the plaintiff for 75 percent of the amount plaintiff received in damages. If the plaintiff recovered judgment against the defendant, receiving a $100,000 damages award, under this percentage the defendant would be liable for $75,000.

The advantages of comparative negligence are immediately apparent. Instead of completely barring the plaintiff's recovery (as common law contributory negligence would have done), culpability factoring enables the plaintiff to recover damages for the defendant's share of responsibility in causing the injuries. Liability apportionment also protects the defendant from paying for the plaintiff's share in harming himself or herself. The result is a just and equitable outcome to the litigation.

Assumption of Risk

Assumption of risk is another defense to negligence. **Assumption of risk** means that the plaintiff assumed the risk of doing (or not doing) something that resulted in his or her injuries. Assumption of risk involves (1) the plaintiff's voluntary

---

BALLENTINESBALLENTINESBALLENTINESBALLENTINESBALLENTINESBALLENTINESBALLENTINESBALLENTINESBALLENTINESBALLENTINESBALLENTINESBALLENTINESBALLENTINESBALLENTINESBALLENTINES

comparative negligence   The doctrine adopted by most states that requires a comparison of the negligence of the defendant with the negligence of the plaintiff: the greater the negligence of the defendant, the lesser the level of care required of the plaintiff to permit him or her to recover. ... [T]he plaintiff's negligence does not defeat his or her cause of action, but it does reduce the damages he or she is entitled to recover.

assumption of risk   The legal principle that a person who knows and deliberately exposes himself or herself to a danger assumes responsibility for the risk, rather than the person who actually created the danger.

assumption of a known risk (2) with a full appreciation of the dangers involved in facing that risk.

For the assumption of risk defense to insulate the defendant from negligence liability, the plaintiff must have voluntarily decided to engage in an activity that the plaintiff knew (or reasonably should have known) was dangerous. In other words, the plaintiff must willfully face a known risk. The plaintiff must fully understand the dangerous nature of the activity that he or she voluntarily undertakes.

Assumption of risk is a complete defense to negligence. Like common law contributory negligence, it totally bars the plaintiff's recovery. If the plaintiff assumed the risk, the defendant cannot be liable for negligence.

Statutes of Limitations

Statutes of limitations are statutes restricting the time within which a plaintiff may file a lawsuit for particular causes of action against a defendant. State statutes of limitations vary in numbers of years and among the different types of negligence. The period for medical malpractice claims, for instance, may be two years in one state and three years in another. Similarly, lawsuits involving premises liability may have one-year statutes of limitations in one state and three-year statutes in another. Paralegals whose work often involves torts and personal injury cases must be familiar with the specific statutes of limitations in their own states for the various types of negligence causes of action.

Strict Liability

Under intentional torts and negligence, tortfeasors are held accountable for their wrongful actions. Fault is an essential part of the reasoning. What was the defendant's misconduct that hurt the plaintiff? Was it intentional, willful, and wanton, or was it negligent action? Placing the blame is second nature in negligence or intentional torts analysis.

Absolute or *strict liability,* in contrast, holds the tortfeasor responsible for his or her behavior regardless of fault. In other words, the tortfeasor could have used every possible degree of care to protect against injuring the victim, but this would not prevent liability. Fault is irrelevant to absolute liability. The tortfeasor is strictly liable just because he or she did something specific that hurt the plaintiff.

One's sense of fair play may rebel against strict liability; it may seem unfair to hold a defendant accountable even if he or she did not intentionally or negligently misbehave. This fault concept, which extends throughout every area of law, is why absolute liability is restricted to certain types of activities, such as abnormally dangerous tasks and defectively manufactured products. Under strict liability, society (through its courts and legislatures) has decided that the person engaged in certain ventures should bear the risk of liability to individuals innocently injured as a consequence of the dangerous or defective item or action. It is society's decision that persons owning wild animals, using fire or explosives, or manufacturing products are in the best economic position to pay for plaintiffs' injuries arising from these activities.

Absolute liability resembles insurance. Defendants are insuring, or guaranteeing, the safety of plaintiffs who come into contact with what tort law calls *abnormally dangerous* or *ultrahazardous instrumentalities*. These activities or objects are just plainly dangerous by their very nature.

Animal Owners' Liability

Modern absolute liability first arose in the common law involving private ownership of wild animals and the use of fire or explosives.

Wild Animals

The ancient common law cases use the Latin term *ferae naturae*, meaning "wild nature," to refer to wild animals. These are animals that have naturally wild dispositions, as opposed to tame animals, which are called *domitae naturae,* meaning "domesticated nature." Examples of *ferae naturae* include deer, bison, snakes, bees, tigers, gophers, or prairie dogs.

A person can claim ownership of a wild animal—the trick is to catch the beast. Once someone had control over a wild animal, it was considered to be his or her property until it escaped to its natural, free state. The common law cases call this ownership the exercise of *dominion and control* over the wild animal. American law holds that the state (or the federal government), under its police power, owns wildlife in trust for the benefit of all citizens. This is why one must obtain state or federal hunting or fishing licenses to take wildlife.

Wildlife ownership is important for purposes of absolute liability. If a wild animal injures someone, the victim cannot sue the beast (or, at the very least, cannot easily collect judgment). Instead, the plaintiff looks to the animal's owner for compensation. Owners are strictly liable for the injuries their wildlife inflicts. It does not matter that the owner exercised every precaution to safeguard others from being hurt by the wild animals. If the beast attacks and hurts someone, the owner must compensate the victim for the injuries. Because the common law presumes that wild animals are dangerous by nature, strict liability applies to any injuries they cause.

Domestic Animals

Domitae naturae are animals that the law presumes to be harmless. Examples of domestic animals include dogs, cats, or livestock such as pigs, horses, and sheep. When domesticated animals hurt someone, the common law states that the owner is liable if he or she were negligent in handling the animals. Liability would also arise if an owner intentionally used domestic animals to hurt someone. For example, suppose an attack dog's owner ordered the animal to attack a victim. This is a form of battery, because the animal is considered an extension of the tortfeasor's body.

Owners may be held absolutely liable for injuries caused by their domestic animals if the animals exhibit vicious tendencies. When a dog growls or snarls, when a bull paws the ground and snorts, or when a cat arches its back and hisses, these are all demonstrations of vicious propensities. When a domestic animal routinely displays these characteristics, so that it gets a reputation for viciousness, it is said to have *vicious propensities*. An owner of such an animal will be held strictly liable for any injuries the beast inflicts, under the so-called *vicious propensity rule*. All states except Indiana have adopted this common-law principle.

Defenses in Animal Absolute Liability Cases

Normally, negligence or intentional tort defenses are ineffective against strict liability. However, certain exceptions have arisen in the common law for particular types of absolute liability, such as cases involving animals. The following defenses can protect an animal owner from strict liability:

1. Assumption of risk
2. Contributory and comparative negligence
3. Consent
4. Self-defense and defense of others.

If the individual injured by a wild (or vicious-propensity domestic) animal voluntarily assumed a known risk, with full appreciation of the dangers involved, then the owner is not strictly liable for the inflicted injuries. Courts justify this defense on equitable grounds. It would be unfair to hold owners absolutely liable for harm their animals caused if the victims chose to subject themselves to the danger.

ferae naturae   Wild animals.

Courts often rule that the plaintiff's contributory or comparative negligence in an animal attack will prevent the owner's absolute liability. Some courts state that a plaintiff's contributory negligence bars strict liability altogether. This means that the plaintiff would have to prove that the defendant (owner) was negligent in keeping the animal that attacked and hurt the plaintiff. Other courts simply ignore absolute liability theory and reshape the case in a negligence mold, in which the plaintiff's and defendant's respective degrees of negligence are compared.

An injured plaintiff might also have consented to exposure to a dangerous animal. Consent is usually based upon a person's employment responsibilities while working around animals. When a wild or vicious domestic animal attacks a victim, but the owner used the animal as a means of self-defense or defense of other persons, then the owner would not be strictly liable for the inflicted injuries. Note, though, that most jurisdictions' statutes have changed the common law owner liability (and the available defenses) in dog-bite cases. These statutes can substantially affect a dog owner's liability and defenses.

Abnormally Dangerous Activities

Abnormally dangerous activities are inherently perilous because of the actions and the devices involved. Common examples include the use of explosives, poisons, hazardous wastes (the so-called *toxic torts*), or (in some jurisdictions) electricity, natural gas, and water supplied through unprotected utility lines. Many early 20th-century cases refer to *ultrahazardous activities*. Although some courts split hairs distinguishing ultrahazardous from abnormally dangerous, the expressions are essentially interchangeable.

A person engaged in abnormally dangerous activities shall be strictly liable for injuries caused by his or her actions. There are several criteria for absolute liability:

1. The abnormally dangerous activity created a high risk of substantial injury to an individual or his or her property.

2. This risk could not be removed through the use of reasonable care.

3. The activity is not commonly undertaken (the common usage principle).

4. The activity was inappropriately undertaken in the place in which the victim was harmed.

5. The hazards that the activity creates outweigh the benefits that the activity brings to the community.

Cases involving toxic substances often revolve around absolute liability theory, applying the abnormally dangerous activity analysis. Of all the causes of action usually associated with toxic torts (including trespass to land, negligence, nuisance, and strict liability), absolute liability offers the best common law avenue for plaintiffs to recover.

High Risk of Substantial Injury

To be abnormally dangerous, the defendant's activity must create a great threat of seriously injuring the plaintiff or the plaintiff's property. For instance, consider a highway construction company that uses dynamite to excavate rock and earth. Dynamite presents an enormous risk of injuring others nearby if it is not used properly.

Wildlife (ferae naturae)	Owner strictly liable for injuries caused by wild animals
Domestic Animals (domitae naturae)	Owner absolutely liable for injuries caused by domestic animals *only* if such animals display vicious propensities
Defenses	1. Assumption of risk 2. Contibutory negligence 3. Comparative negligence 4. Consent 5. Self-defense 6. Defense of others

Animal Owners' Absolute Liability and Defenses
The duty of care owed by animal owners depends on the nature of the animal.

The threat of harm is significant, as people could be killed or their property destroyed if the dynamite were not used correctly.

Reasonable Care

If the tortfeasor could have eliminated the risk of harm through the use of reasonable care, then the activity is not abnormally dangerous, and absolute liability does not apply. For example, a utility company could exercise reasonable care and protect citizens from the great threat posed by electricity or natural gas simply by using insulated wires or double-sealed underground pipelines. Reasonable care could easily eliminate the risks of electrocution or explosion. If the utility company actually used these (or other) reasonable precautions, but a victim nonetheless was somehow injured, then the activity (supplying electricity or natural gas) would not be ultrahazardous.

Note the hidden implication in this element, though. Failure to use reasonable care to safeguard others from the risks involved in the activity could make it abnormally dangerous. For instance, suppose a utility ran electricity through uninsulated wires. Many courts have held that this would make the activity ultrahazardous, so the utility company would be strictly liable for injuries. However, not all courts interpret the reasonable care standard in this way.

Common Usage and Inappropriate Use

Abnormally dangerous activities and substances are those not commonly undertaken or used in everyday life. This is sometimes called the *common usage principle.* For instance, consider explosives, toxic chemicals, or poisonous gases. How often does the average person use them? Does anyone in the reader's neighborhood? What about the manufacturing plant across town? But, it could be said, that is only one facility, and the vast majority of the public in the community does not use such substances. These, then, would be examples of abnormally dangerous substances, because they are not commonly used.

What about flammable substances? Many courts have included these as ultrahazardous items. But virtually everyone uses gasoline every day. Would gasoline not fall within common usage? Whether gasoline is abnormally dangerous depends upon how it is being used. The gas one keeps in his or her garage for the lawn mower would not be ultrahazardous; however, the huge storage tanks would be abnormally dangerous. Furthermore, to be ultrahazardous, the activity or substance must have been inappropriately performed or used in the place in which the victim was harmed.

Hazards Outweigh Benefits: Balancing Test

Courts often apply a balancing test to decide if an activity is abnormally dangerous. Such an analysis compares the dangers created by the activity with the benefits that the community derives from the activity.

For example, suppose the state government is building a new highway to improve access between hospitals and an isolated rural town. The construction crew uses dynamite to clear the area for the road. A nearby homeowner suffers structural damage to her house as a result of the blasting and sues the government under strict liability theory. Courts may balance the benefits derived against the risks involved. The highway would improve the community's access to hospital facilities. The dangers created by dynamite use, which in this case involved structural damage, are probably outweighed by these benefits.

Many courts have applied this approach throughout this century. Several jurisdictions, however, have rejected the rule, either in whole or in part.

Defenses

Many state legislatures have enacted statutes protecting certain abnormally dangerous activities from strict liability. These statutes usually shield public utilities distributing electricity and natural gas, private contractors performing construction (particularly highway) work for the government, and municipal zoos or parks that maintain wild animals. Under these statutes, the protected entities cannot be held absolutely liable for injuries caused by wild animals or ultra-hazardous activities. Instead, plaintiffs must prove that the protected defendants were negligent or committed intentional torts.

Legislatures often justify such immunity statutes on the grounds that government (and the private companies that often work under governmental contracts) must be protected from the harshness of strict liability if certain essential activities are to be performed. How, the argument goes, can governments build roads, operate zoos or parks, supply utilities, or enable private industry to satisfy energy demands, if these activities carry the burden of strict liability whenever someone inadvertently gets hurt? Because legislatures enact statutes, and the public can change the legislature (through voting) and thus change the statutes, citizens who disagree with the immunity laws can elect new legislators to modify these provisions.

Scope of Liability: Proximate Cause

Proximate cause in absolute liability cases is defined similarly to cause in negligence cases. Animals or abnormally dangerous activities must proximately cause the victim's injuries if the tortfeasor is to be held strictly liable. For absolute liability purposes, proximate cause has the following elements:

1. The plaintiff's injuries must have been a reasonably foreseeable consequence of the defendant's actions; and
2. The victim must have been a foreseeable plaintiff (meaning that it must have been reasonably foreseeable that the plaintiff would be injured as a result of the defendant's activities).

When applied to strict liability cases, proximate cause does not include the duty of reasonable care, which is an element of negligence theory. Nevertheless, some courts insist on including the duty when discussing proximate cause in absolute liability cases. But negligence is irrelevant to strict liability; therefore, the duty of reasonable care is also irrelevant.

Products Liability

Products liability was established as a distinct tort theory in the landmark case of *Greenman v. Yuba Power Products, Inc.,* 59 Cal. 2d 57, 377 P.2d 897, 27 Cal. Rptr. 697 (1962). In this case, the California Supreme Court completed more than 100 years of legal evolution that culminated in strict products liability.

Products liability is society's decision, through its courts and legislatures, that businesses manufacturing and selling defective products are in the best economic position to bear the expenses incurred when a faulty product injures an innocent user. The theory may be simply put: Why should the hapless victim shoulder the burdens (medical costs, permanent injuries, etc.) produced by a defectively made product? Instead, should not the manufacturer or seller of that product be liable for the resulting harms? If one has ever been hurt by a defective product, one might answer affirmatively. If one were a manufacturer or seller, however, he or she might feel differently.

Historical Development of Products Liability

In the early 19th century, English and American common law held that persons injured by defective products had to sue under contract law rather than tort law. These courts felt that the appropriate cause of action was breach of contract or, more precisely, breach of warranty. A **warranty** is a guarantee that a product or service meets certain quality standards. If a product fails to meet such standards, as is the case when a product is defective, then the warranty has been breached.

Under early 19th-century English and American common law, only persons who had made contracts with the manufacturer or seller of a defective

warranty   [A] promise, either express or implied by law, with respect to the fitness or merchantability of the article that is the subject of the contract.

product could recover damages for breach of warranty or breach of contract. This contractual relationship is called **privity of contract**. Privity exists when parties are directly engaged in an agreement between them. If Joseph contracts with Harris, in which Joseph agrees to sell Harris a product for a certain price, then there is privity of contract between them.

Privity of contract is unnecessary if the defective product (such as a mislabelled poison) is imminently dangerous. Courts characterized this as the *imminent danger exception* to the privity-of-contract rule. Throughout the 19th century, many courts expanded the imminent danger rule to include spoiled food, explosives, improperly assembled scaffolding, an exploding coffee urn, and defectively made automobile wheels. Many courts found liability in contract warranty law, but this still required privity of contract. The landmark case in this century, which is often said to have sparked modern products liability law, is *MacPherson v. Buick Motor Co.,* 217 N.Y. 382, 111 N.E. 1050 (1916). The court declared that privity of contract was obsolete. If a product, because of its defective manufacture, became unreasonably dangerous, then the manufacturer or seller would be liable for injuries caused by the defective product. Negligence theory was applied to determine whether the defective product was unreasonably dangerous. The manufacturer had to be negligent in making the faulty product.

Parties

Three classes of parties are involved in products liability cases: the product manufacturer, the seller, and the ultimate user.

The *product manufacturer* makes the defective product that gives rise to the entire products liability lawsuit. *Seller* includes anyone who is in the business of selling goods such as the one that is faulty. This includes the manufacturer as well as wholesalers and retailers. *Wholesalers* are businesses that buy and sell goods to *retailers,* which

in turn sell the products to customers, usually individual persons.

When we buy a product, we are *purchasers*. In products liability law, however, the party injured by flawed merchandise need not be the original buyer. Instead, a member of the purchaser's family, or a friend of the buyer, could recover damages if hurt by a defective product. The key is whether it is reasonably foreseeable that the user would have utilized the product. This individual is called the *ultimate user,* because that person eventually used the product that caused an injury.

In products liability litigation, the ultimate user becomes the plaintiff who sues various defendants: the retailer, the wholesaler(s), and the manufacturer. The plaintiff uses a shotgun approach to products liability—namely, sue all the sellers. This may seem excessive, but the plaintiff has a logical explanation. In the product distribution chain from manufacturers, sellers, purchasers, and ultimate users, the deficient product passes through many hands before reaching its unfortunate victim. The plaintiff sues all the sellers along the product distribution chain to ensure that one of them (probably the manufacturer) will have sufficient monies to pay a judgment. In tort law, this is called *"going for the deep pocket."* In other words, the plaintiff tries to sue defendants that have money and could satisfy a damages award. Paralegals may specialize in products liability law by working for corporate counsel of a manufacturer, wholesaler, or retailer, or by working for a law firm that specializes in representing either defendants or plaintiffs in products liability cases.

Elements

Products liability is defined as strict, or absolute, liability for the seller or manufacturer of a defectively made product that injures a user of the item. Privity of contract is not required in products liability. The ultimate user need not have purchased the merchandise directly from the seller

BALLENTINESBALLENTINESBALLENTINESBALLENTINESBALLENTINESBALLENTINESBALLENTINESBALLENTINESBALLENTINESBALLENTINESBALLENTINESBALLENTINESBALLENTINES

privity of contract   The legal relationship between the parties to a contract.

or manufacturer, although some states require that a sale of the product have occurred somewhere between the manufacturer and the ultimate user. However, it need not be a direct transaction between the two.

Remember also that the seller or manufacturer's negligence is irrelevant to strict liability. It does not matter how much care the seller or manufacturer used in making or maintaining the product. Every possible precaution could have been utilized, but that simply makes no difference. If the product was defective, and a user was harmed as a result, absolute liability applies—period.

There are five elements of products liability, as defined by most state courts or statutes:

1. The defect must render the product unreasonably dangerous to use.

2. The seller or manufacturer must be in the business of selling products such as the flawed one(s).

3. The product cannot have been substantially changed between the time it left the seller or manufacturer's hands and the time it reached the ultimate user.

4. The defect must have proximately caused the ultimate user's injuries.

5. The ultimate user must have used the product properly, i.e., in a way that the product was designed to be used.

In some jurisdictions, several additional elements are required:

6. The ultimate user must have been foreseeable (foreseeable plaintiffs theory).

7. The seller or manufacturer must have been responsible for the condition in which the product was maintained.

8. In a few states, a sale of the product must have occurred. This could be a sale between the manufacturer and a wholesaler, or a wholesaler to a retailer, or a retailer to a customer. Basically, someone at some point had to buy the defective thing.

Unreasonably Dangerous Products   The product must be unreasonably dangerous as a result of its defect. Courts look to see if the product has become unreasonably threatening because of its defect. There are four types of unreasonably dangerous defects: (1) fault in product design; (2) error in product manufacturer or assembly; (3) improper product maintenance; and (4) manufacturer/seller's failure to warn.

Products can be unreasonably dangerous if they have a defective design. Courts look to see whether the product is inherently dangerous because of a poor design but for which (that is, if such a defect did not exist) the product would have been safe to use. Courts decide faulty design (which make products unreasonably dangerous) in terms of three tests. A product is unreasonably dangerous if a consumer ordinarily would not appreciate the threat inherent in its design. This assumes that the ultimate user, like most people, understands that some products have dangers built in to their uses. The defect becomes unreasonably hazardous because the reasonable person would not be expected to anticipate the danger created by the faulty design. Courts have labelled this the *consumer contemplation test*. Another test to determine if a product is unreasonably dangerous by its design is called the *danger/utility test*. Under this standard, a product is unreasonably hazardous if the danger created by its design outweighs the benefits derived from its use. Finally, under the state-of-the-art discoverability test, if manufacturers could have discovered hazards created by defective product designs, using current, state-of-the-art technologies, then failure to do so makes a design-flawed product unreasonably dangerous.

Safely designed products may become unreasonably dangerous as a result of improper assembly or manufacture. This is sometimes called an *assembly defect*.

Sellers occasionally fail to maintain merchandise properly. When a buyer purchases the product, it might not function correctly because of a *maintenance defect*. Using the negligence formula, the seller of a product with a maintenance defect would also be liable under negligence theory, as well as products liability.

Sometimes products are unreasonably dangerous by their very nature. Lawn mowers, chain saws, poisons, and chemicals can be lethal if not cautiously used. However, purchasers may not always spot the obvious dangers in a product. Accordingly, manufacturers and sellers have an obligation to warn the ultimate user about inherent product dangers. Failure to warn could result in strict liability. For instance, look at almost any household appliance. Each one warns not to place hands or feet here or there, because of rotating knives, extremely hot surfaces, or the presence of scalding waters. If one uses rat poison or insect sprays, the containers warn not to ingest the contents or get them in one's eyes. These are common examples of warnings that manufacturers and sellers use to avoid absolute liability. If the user is warned, then the user knows the risks.

Business Requirement   Most common law and statutory versions of products liability insist that the manufacturer or seller be engaged in the business of selling products such as the defective item(s) that injured the ultimate user. This requirement is easily met in most cases involving manufacturers, wholesalers, or retailers. Its purpose is to exclude products liability for people who are not in the business of selling such goods.

Substantially Unchanged Condition Requirement   For products liability to apply, the product must reach the ultimate user without any substantial changes in its condition from the time it left the manufacturer or seller. This is a crucial requirement. If something happened along the product distribution chain to alter the product (perhaps creating the unreasonably dangerous condition), then it would be unfair to hold manufacturers or sellers accountable for something they did not cause.

In some states, products liability common law or statutes require that, for strict liability to exist, the manufacturer or seller must be responsible for how the defective product was maintained. This seems logical. If the seller was not in any way responsible for how the product was assembled or stored (until it was sold or used), then that seller would have no control over the products it distributed. Products liability attempts to place the blame on the party responsible for the defect, so this requirement attempts to protect innocent sellers from absolute liability for product defects caused by someone else.

Proximate Cause   The defective product must have been the proximate cause of the plaintiff's injury if liability is to attach.

Proper Use Requirement   The ultimate user must use the defective product properly in order for products liability to apply. In other words, the user must use the product for some function for which it was designed or intended to be used.

Foreseeable Plaintiffs Theory   In some jurisdictions, it must have been reasonably foreseeable that the ultimate user would use the defective product. This is called *foreseeable plaintiffs theory* in negligence. Some ultimate users are not reasonably foreseeable. For example, it is highly improbable that a one-year-old infant would come into contact with industrial cleaners used in manufacturing processes. Such a person could not be a reasonably foreseeable ultimate user of such a product. However, members of a product purchaser's family, or the buyer's neighbors, could be foreseeable users of defective goods.

Defenses

Several of the defenses to absolute liability also apply to products liability. Courts have generally held that contributory negligence is not a defense in products liability cases. This seems logical, because contributory negligence is a defense to negligence and negligence has no place in strict liability cases. Allowing the ultimate user's contributory negligence to bar absolute liability for a defective product would be the legal equivalent of mixing apples and oranges.

This is not to say, however, that the plaintiff (the ultimate user) can use a defective product

THE TORT PARALEGAL AND PERSONAL INJURY LITIGATION

irresponsibly or wantonly. The ultimate user is expected to use the product properly, as it was intended to be used. This is an element of products liability, although some courts consider product misuse to be a defense. If the ultimate user misuses a defective product and is injured as a consequence, his or her products liability claim against the manufacturer or seller will be denied, because the harm resulted from the plaintiff's misuse of the product. This defense is effective even though the misused product was defective.

Some product uses may be unusual, but are not actually misuses. For example, chairs are designed to be sat on, yet using a chair as a ladder is not a misuse of the product, because it is reasonably foreseeable that one might use a chair for such a purpose. In other words, reasonably foreseeable uses, even though the product may not originally have been intended or designed for such functions, are acceptable uses. A products liability claim would not be barred if the ultimate user used the product in a reasonably foreseeable fashion.

Assumption of risk, in contrast, is usually accepted as a defense. The ultimate user assumes the risk of being injured by a hazardous product in three ways: (1) by discovering the defect but disregarding it and using the product anyway; (2) by failing to properly maintain the product;

and (3) by failing to follow instructions or heed warnings for safe product use.

Assumption of risk is the plaintiff's voluntary assumption of a known risk with a full appreciation of the dangers involved in facing that risk. In products liability cases, the plaintiff is the ultimate user. The ultimate user assumes the risk by discovering a product defect and then ignoring the risks involved and using the product anyway.

Ultimate users cannot recover in products liability if they failed to properly maintain the product for safe uses. Courts often characterize this as an assumption-of-risk defense.

How often have you used a product without first reading the instructions? Surely everyone has done this. Most of the time the products we use are sufficiently simple that we can use them properly after a quick glance. With a complex product, however, following instructions could prevent injuries. Products liability plaintiffs often argue that defectively designed products are unreasonably dangerous. However, sometimes these plaintiffs did not follow the manufacturer's instructions for product use and as a consequence were hurt. Also, an ultimate user occasionally disregards manufacturer's warnings that specifically point out the dangers inherent in the product design. Both of these actions are types of assumption of risk.

Nuisances

A **nuisance** is an unreasonable or unlawful use of one's real property that injures another person or interferes with another person's use of his or her real property. There are two types of nuisances: private and public. Occasionally, the same activity constitutes both a private and a public nuisance. These are sometimes called *mixed nuisances*.

Private Nuisance

A **private nuisance** occurs when someone (1) uses his or her land in such a way as to (2) unreasonably and substantially interfere with (3) another person's use and enjoyment of his or her land. The tortfeasor (defendant) is the land user whose activities

nuisance   Anything a person does that annoys or disturbs another person in his or her use, possession, or enjoyment of his or her property, or which renders the ordinary use or possession of the property uncomfortable.

private nuisance   A nuisance that threatens injury to one or just a few persons; a nuisance that violates only private rights and produces damages to one or no more than a few persons.

offend his or her neighbors. The neighboring land user(s) (plaintiff[s]) sue the tortfeasor for engaging in a private nuisance. The second element in commission of a private nuisance, unreasonable and substantial interference, is the most susceptible of interpretation.

Whether the tortfeasor's use of real estate is unreasonable and substantially interferes with another's land use is usually defined in terms of offensiveness. The critical question is: How offensive is the tortfeasor's land use? Offensiveness is determined by applying the reasonable person standard. Would a reasonable person with ordinary sensitivities find the tortfeasor's land use unreasonably offensive? If so, then the tortfeasor has unreasonably and substantially interfered with the plaintiff's use and enjoyment of his or her land. Therefore, the tortfeasor has committed a private nuisance.

The reasonable person standard is normally a community standard. In other words, it asks how people living in the community in which the alleged nuisance is taking place would react to the activity. This *reasonable community* reaction supposedly evaluates whether the tortfeasor's land use is unreasonable and a substantial interference with neighboring land uses.

Use and enjoyment is a term of art in nuisance law. The two are always used together. The term **use** would be sufficient, but **enjoyment** imparts an emotional aspect to nuisance law. The alleged nuisance activity ruins the pleasure neighbors gain through the ways in which they use their real estate. This seems to make the tortfeasor's activities more blameworthy.

Examples

There are many common examples of private nuisances to which to apply the elements just explained. These situations can be classified in broad categories: (1) physical effects on land; (2) health hazards or offending sensibilities; and (3) unwanted associations with neighboring uses.

Physical Effects on Land Neighboring land users often complain if a tortfeasor's use of realty creates constant vibrations, pollutes water or soil, destroys crops, or creates flooding, excessive clutter, or unwanted excavations.

Health Hazards or Offending Sensibilities

People's sensibilities are ways in which their physical senses (sight, hearing, smell, taste, and touch) and their emotional senses (what they find disgusting, repulsive, threatening, etc.) are affected such as noxious odors, smoke and dust, or excessive noise and temperature. The disposal or transportation of hazardous wastes or toxic chemicals are frequently the ground for private nuisance actions. Underground or surface water supplies that are contaminated by leaking toxic chemical dumps, or air that is filled with poisonous dusts (such as uranium dust vented from a nuclear power plant) are excellent examples of private nuisances. Much of the toxic tort litigation brought today involves nuisance actions.

As for offending sensibilities, consider creditors who occasionally use intimidation tactics to coerce customers to pay delinquent accounts. A favorite technique is the late-night telephone call. The creditor might telephone a delinquent customer several times late at night, every day for weeks or even months, to try to persuade the patron to pay the overdue amount. Customers subjected to such harassment often suffer emotional distress and related physical manifestations. Courts routinely determine that such activity constitutes a private nuisance. It is an unreasonable interference with the customer's use and enjoyment of the privacy of his or her home life. In fact, plaintiffs besieged with incessant phone calling often sue the culprit under several causes of action—namely, the intentional torts of invasion of privacy

use The enjoyment of real property by occupying it or by otherwise putting it to use.
enjoyment The ability to exercise a right.

or intentional infliction of emotional distress—along with nuisance.

Unwanted Associations with Neighboring Uses

For decades, landowners have rushed to the courthouse to file private nuisance actions against the owners of houses of ill repute, X-rated movie theatres, adult bookstores, and liquor or gambling establishments. These cases illustrate clearly the personal nature of offensiveness. Some persons simply cannot abide living in the vicinity of these types of activities. They do not wish to be associated with these land uses. These persons typically become plaintiffs in nuisance lawsuits in an attempt to drive out activities that they find repugnant.

In cases such as these, courts often struggle with community standards to decide if the activities are private nuisances. Are the plaintiffs overreacting, or are their objections reasonable? Would reasonable persons agree that having to live adjacent to establishments engaged in these pursuits is an unreasonable and substantial interference with the use and enjoyment of the realty? This is not an easy question to answer.

"Coming to the Nuisance" Defense

Often, a person will move into a neighborhood in which an offensive activity is already situated. In many cases, the manufacturer, trash dump, junkyard, or adult bookstore has been doing business in the same location for years. The plaintiff came to the area after the alleged nuisance was already there. When this happens, and the plaintiff then sues for private nuisance, the defendant may plead the "coming to the nuisance" defense. The *coming to the nuisance defense* involves the plaintiff who owns or uses land at a location in which the alleged nuisance activity was already occurring. If the plaintiff came to the nuisance, then he or she cannot recover against the defendant. A reasonable person would not have chosen to buy or use land

adjacent to a known, present, and distasteful land use next door. In essence, the plaintiff assumes the risk of obnoxiousness from the nuisance activity by coming to the place while knowing that the nuisance is already there, waiting to offend the plaintiff.

Public Nuisance

A **public nuisance** is a land use that injures the public at large rather than just a single individual. A public nuisance unreasonably interferes with the public's enjoyment of legal rights common to the public. The elements of public are: (1) The tortfeasor's use of land that (2) unreasonably and substantially interferes with (3) the public's use and enjoyment of legal rights common to the public. The standard of unreasonable and substantial interference is identical to that used in private nuisances, except that the interference must be to the public rather than a sole plaintiff.

Unlike private nuisances, which can adversely affect a single person, a public nuisance must harm the general public. More than one person must always be affected (or, at least, potentially affected) by the alleged nuisance activity. This does not require a multitude of angry citizens. Residents of a single neighborhood would suffice.

Use and Enjoyment of Common Legal Rights

The use and enjoyment element in public nuisance is significantly different from the one discussed in private nuisances. With public nuisances, the tortfeasor's obnoxious land use interferes with the public's common legal rights, such as the right to peaceably assemble in public places, the right to use public streets and sidewalks without being subjected to offensive activities, or the right to safe and healthy conditions in one's neighborhood.

Although citizens often file public nuisance complaints with their local governmental agencies,

---

BALLENTINESBALLENTINESBALLENTINESBALLENTINESBALLENTINESBALLENTINESBALLENTINESBALLENTINESBALLENTINESBALLENTINESBALLENTINESBALLENTINESBALLENTINES

public nuisance   An act or omission that adversely affects the safety, health, or morals of the public, or causes some substantial annoyance, inconvenience, or injury to the public.

it is the government, through its municipal governing bodies or its prosecuting attorneys, that sues defendants alleged to be committing public nuisances. This is because the government represents the public at large and must enforce its citizens' legal rights against tortfeasors. At common law, or by statute or, in some states, by state constitutional provision, state and local governments have the authority to protect their citizens from public nuisances. The source of this power is the states' **police powers**, which give governments authority to file lawsuits or enact legislation to protect the public's health, welfare, safety, or morals. These are usually very broad powers that give governments considerable flexibility to forbid certain so-called offensive activities.

Types of Public Nuisances

Almost all public nuisances are defined by statute or ordinance. Many such laws focus on land uses which legislators believe a majority of the population would find offensive, unhealthy, or immoral. Of course, one may agree or disagree with what the government has labelled a public nuisance. Common targets of public nuisance laws include institutions devoted to (1) gambling, (2) prostitution, (3) distribution of sexually explicit materials, (4) sale of alcohol, or (5) toxic waste management. Other typical public nuisances include (1) allowing certain weeds or poisonous plants to grow on one's land; (2) failing to comply with health code provisions by keeping one's residence clean and vermin-free; and (3) keeping unrestrained wild or vicious animals on one's property.

"Coming to the Nuisance" Not a Defense

Generally, courts do not recognize the coming to the nuisance defense in public nuisance cases.

This defense focuses on the individual plaintiff who purchases or uses land next to a preexisting, private nuisance activity. Public nuisances, by definition, affect the public at large, and the very existence or continuation of the public nuisance activity is considered harmful, whether it was preexisting or not.

Mixed Nuisances

Often, the same activity can constitute both a private and a public nuisance. These are sometimes called **mixed nuisances**. Apply this rule of thumb in such cases: The greater the number of persons adversely affected by an allegedly offensive land use, the more likely it will be considered a public, as well as a private, nuisance.

Nuisances Per Se

Courts often consider activities violating public nuisance statutes to be **nuisances per se**. *Per se* is Latin, meaning "by itself." In tort law, it usually means that some behavior has violated a statute, and therefore the defendant is automatically liable. Sometimes courts, in the common law, decree that certain conduct is per se tortious. Negligence per se is an example. Per se nuisances have also been established by common law court decisions.

A public nuisance per se is an activity that violates the statute and is automatically considered a public nuisance. The tortfeasor thus loses from the start of litigation, simply by violating the statute. Statutes (and, rarely, common law) may also declare certain private nuisances to be per se nuisances.

BALLENTINESBALLENTINESBALLENTINESBALLENTINESBALLENTINESBALLENTINESBALLENTINESBALLENTINESBALLENTINESBALLENTINESBALLENTINESBALLENTINESBALLENTINESBALLENTINES

police power The power of government to make and enforce laws and regulations necessary to maintain and enhance the public welfare and to prevent individuals from violating the rights of others.

mixed nuisance A nuisance that is both public and private in its effects.

nuisance per se An act, occupation, or structure that is considered a nuisance at all times and under any circumstances, regardless of location or surroundings.

Remedies for Nuisances

When one has identified a private or public nuisance, what does one do about it? In other words, what remedies are available to plaintiffs against defendants? **Remedies** are the relief that plaintiffs receive against defendants in lawsuits. The most common remedy in tort actions is *money damages,* in which the defendant must pay the plaintiff a sum of money to satisfy the judgment. The trier-of-fact sets the amount owed after a trial has been held.

Other, nonmonetary remedies are also available for torts such as nuisance. These are called *equitable remedies.* Equitable remedies do not involve money damages; instead, the court orders the defendant to do (or, more commonly, *not* to do) something. When the court orders a defendant to do something, it issues a **mandamus** *order*. When the court orders a defendant not to do something, it issues an **injunction** or *restraining order.*

For centuries, money damages were considered inappropriate in nuisance cases. Courts would apply only equitable remedies. In nuisance law, the most common equitable remedies include (1) abatement and (2) injunction, although now money damages are occasionally permitted in nuisance cases.

Abatement

In nuisance cases, abatement is the most common remedy plaintiffs seek. With **abatement**, the defendant is ordered to cease, or *abate,* the nuisance activity. Abatement is often permanent. The defendant must desist from conducting the nuisance activity after a judgment for abatement is entered. This provides complete relief for the plaintiff, because the nuisance activity will be discontinued. Abatement can create harsh economic consequences for defendants, but the public policy behind abatement is clear: Nuisance tortfeasors have injured someone (or, if the public, many people). As long as the nuisance continues, the plaintiff(s) will continue to be hurt. The only certain solution is to stop the nuisance altogether.

Money Damages

When abatement could impose an unreasonably severe economic burden upon the nuisance tortfeasor, courts have broken with the ancient common law tradition and awarded plaintiffs money damages instead of abatement. This way, the plaintiffs can be compensated for their injuries produced by the nuisance activities, and the defendant can survive (economically) by staying in business, even though the nuisance also continues. Courts using this alternative are usually attempting to balance interests between conflicting land uses.

Injunctions

Courts enforce abatement through injunctive relief. *Injunctions* are court orders to defendants to cease and desist from engaging in nuisance activities. There are two types of injunctions: (1) temporary injunctions, including temporary restraining orders (T.R.O.s); and (2) permanent injunctions.

Temporary injunctions are often used from the time a plaintiff files suit until the first court hearing. The plaintiff, in his or her complaint, asks the court to issue a **temporary restraining order (TRO)**, forbidding the defendant from conducting an alleged nuisance activity until a court hearing can be held to determine if the activity constitutes

---

BALLENTINESBALLENTINESBALLENTINESBALLENTINESBALLENTINESBALLENTINESBALLENTINESBALLENTINESBALLENTINESBALLENTINESBALLENTINESBALLENTINESBALLENTINESBALLENTINESBALLENTINES

remedy   The means by which a right is enforced, an injury is redressed, and relief is obtained.

mandamus   A writ ... requiring the performance of some ... act.

injunction   A court order that commands or prohibits some act or course of conduct.

abatement of nuisance   The elimination of a nuisance.

temporary restraining order (TRO)   [I]njunctive relief that the court is empowered to grant, without notice to the opposite party and pending a hearing on the merits, upon a showing that failure to do so will result in "immediate and irreparable injury, loss, or damage."

a nuisance. Under most rules of civil procedure, TROs may be issued for up to 10 days, while the court convenes a hearing to decide if a nuisance has occurred. After the hearing, if the evidence convinces the judge that a nuisance is happening, the court may order further temporary injunctive relief, banning the defendant's nuisance activity until a trial on the merits may be held.

The purpose of temporary injunctions is to protect the plaintiff from further harm if a nuisance is in fact occurring. Plaintiffs often must post bond to compensate the defendant if the court or jury later decides that the defendant did not engage in a nuisance. This is to protect the defendant from economic losses suffered while the injunctions were in effect and the defendant was not permitted to conduct the nuisance activity (which could mean lost profits or extra expenses).

Permanent injunctions are abatement orders instructing the defendant to permanently stop doing the nuisance activity. They are usually issued after a trial on the merits, once the trier of fact has concluded that a nuisance exists. If the defendant fails to obey a permanent injunction by continuing the nuisance, the court can punish the defendant by holding him or her in **contempt**. This punishment may involve monetary fines or even imprisonment.

Other Torts

By statute or common law, many other actions may be classified as torts. The tort law paralegal may well become involved in cases concerning actions to which specific legal theories apply, and may find his or her research skills tested while trying to determine the current status of some of these causes of action in her or his jurisdiction.

Negligence Per Se

Negligence per se is behavior that is automatically negligent as a matter of law. When a statute defines certain conduct as negligent, and a tortfeasor violates the statute by engaging in that activity, then the tortfeasor is presumed to have been negligent by violating the statute. To meet the burden of proof, a plaintiff need only show that the defendant's actions violated the negligence statute. The defendant is then presumed negligent. This shifts the proof burden to the defendant, who must then present effective negligence defenses to avoid liability. A per se negligent defendant might also avoid liability by showing that he or she was not the proximate cause of the plaintiff's injuries. In other words, the defendant would have to prove that his or her violation of the statute did not proximately cause the plaintiff's harm.

The negligence defenses of contributory negligence, comparative negligence, and assumption of risk also apply to negligence per se cases. Also, not every statutory violation constitutes negligence per se. To recover under negligence per se theory, the plaintiff must be within the class of persons protected by the statute or ordinance.

Absolute Liability Mislabelled as Negligence Per Se

Courts occasionally equate negligence per se with strict, or absolute, liability. However, the two tort theories are distinct. Negligence per se simply presumes negligence because of the tortfeasor's violation of a statute. Negligence is based upon the tortfeasor's failure to exercise reasonable care. Absolute liability holds the tortfeasor accountable, regardless of fault, for doing an abnormally dangerous activity. No degree of care is sufficient to avoid strict liability.

permanent injunction   An injunction granted after a final hearing on the merits ... .

contempt   An act of disrespect toward a court ... ; deliberate disobedience of a court order.

This confusion between absolute liability and negligence per se occurs because of the outcomes in each type of case. If the defendant violates a negligence statute, he or she is presumed automatically negligent. Liability is almost as certain as in strict liability cases. Thus, the two concepts are often equated, although they are substantially different.

Toxic Torts

Statutes sometimes declare that violations of regulations regarding the transportation, disposal, or management of hazardous or toxic substances create a presumption of negligence as a matter of law. These statutory provisions support plaintiffs' causes of action against tortfeasors who carelessly control abnormally dangerous materials.

Wrongful Death

Wrongful death statutes give the surviving family members of a deceased tort victim a cause of action against the tortfeasor whose negligence or intentional torts resulted in the victim's death. The typical factual pattern in a wrongful death action is: (1) a tortfeasor commits a tort against the victim; (2) the victim dies as a result of the tortfeasor's actions; (3) the victim's spouse or children, or both, sue the tortfeasor for wrongfully causing the victim's death.

Under wrongful death statutes, the surviving family members, usually the victim's spouse or children, become the plaintiffs. However, some statutes allow the victim's parents or siblings to become plaintiffs. The victim's estate may also be permitted to sue the defendant for wrongful death damages under some statutes.

Damages

A tort victim's surviving family members may recover damages for the lost income that the victim would likely have earned had he or she not been killed by the tortfeasor. Wrongful death statutes usually define these damages in terms of the decedent's lost earnings potential based upon income at the time of death. This income base is projected over time. The future time period used is normally the victim's life expectancy, which is calculated from insurance actuarial tables. The projected earnings potential is normally adjusted for the victim's projected living expenses, had he or she survived.

Wrongful death statutes (or the common law) also frequently permit a tort victim's surviving family to recover damages for the lost love and companionship of the decedent. This is similar to pain and suffering damages. However, many statutes do not allow recovery of such damages. Wrongful death statutes (or courts interpreting them) often label this type of damages **loss of consortium**. Many statutes define *consortium* as both economic and intangible benefits lost to a victim's surviving family because of the victim's death. The intangible element could include lost love, companionship, and even the survivors' mental anguish upon losing a loved one.

Defenses

In wrongful death actions, the tortfeasor may use any defense applicable to the specific tort that produced the victim's injury. For example, suppose the victim had been contributorily or comparatively negligent, or assumed the risk, of the defendant's actions that killed the victim. Suppose the tortfeasor killed the victim while acting in self-defense or defense of others. The tortfeasor may escape liability for wrongfully causing the victim's death if any of the suitable tort defenses apply in the case. Defenses are available in a wrongful death action just as if the victim were still alive and, as plaintiff, were suing the defendant.

wrongful death   A death that results from a wrongful act.

loss of consortium   The loss of a spouse's assistance or companionship, or the loss of a spouse's ability or willingness to have sexual relations.

Wrongful Life

Wrongful life actions are lawsuits for the wrongful birth of a child. These are also called **wrongful birth** or **wrongful pregnancy** actions. The plaintiffs are usually the surprised parents, and the defendant is normally the physician who performed ineffective sterilization surgery upon either the mother or the father. Wrongful life, then, can be considered another form of medical malpractice, which is negligence.

The typical situation involving unwanted pregnancy is as follows: A couple visit a physician, wishing a vasectomy or tubal ligation to prevent future conceptions. The doctor performs the surgery. However, because of the surgeon's negligence, the operation fails. The couple end up conceiving a child and then end up suing the physician whose negligence "caused" the unexpected (or unwanted) birth of a child.

In certain cases, the plaintiffs (parents) sue the physician for the unwanted birth of a child born with birth defects or other congenital problems. This may occur when a doctor assures a couple that an unborn child will not be harmed by a disease the mother contracted during pregnancy, but when born, the child does in fact have substantial birth defects caused by the mother's infection. Another such situation involves a child who is born with genetic defects that a doctor assured the parents were not present or inheritable.

Wrongful life actions are a recent tort invention, having arisen within the last 25 years. This new tort has received mixed reviews from appellate courts across the United States. Some jurisdictions reject the tort altogether; others permit it in circumstances involving birth deformities; and still others allow the action even for healthy but unwanted children when sterilization has failed. Wrongful life litigation demonstrates the ingenuity of attorneys and legal scholars searching for new sources of recovery for harmed plaintiffs. Depending upon one's point of view, one may consider this tort just another form of "chiseling" against the medical profession, or one may find it a perfectly acceptable compensation for innocent parents who might be unprepared (or unable to afford) family additions. Certainly, the cases have involved much emotion and moral judgment.

In addition to the expenses incurred during pregnancy and delivery of the "wrongful life" child, plaintiffs seek (and sometimes recover) damages from the responsible physician(s) for the cost of raising the child until he or she reaches the age of majority, most often defined by modern statutes as 18 years of age. One can imagine the enormous judgments such plaintiffs might receive under these circumstances.

Tort Immunity

A tort law paralegal must be alert to potential defenses, no matter which side of the case he or she is working on. One may find, through research and investigation, that a tort has been committed, but certain defendants may have some form of immunity. Tort **immunities** are absolute defenses against a plaintiff's tort claims. If the defendant successfully invokes an immunity defense, he or she cannot be held liable for any torts committed. It is the reverse of absolute liability. Tort immunities absolutely protect the defendant from tort liability. There are many types of tort immunity,

BALLENTINESBALLENTINESBALLENTINESBALLENTINESBALLENTINESBALLENTINESBALLENTINESBALLENTINESBALLENTINESBALLENTINESBALLENTINESBALLENTINESBALLENTINESBALLENTINES

wrongful birth   When a ... child is born to parents who decided not to prevent or terminate the pregnancy because of erroneous medical advice ... .

wrongful conception (wrongful pregnancy)   When a child is born as the result of a negligently performed sterilization of either the father or the mother ... .

immunity   An exemption granted by law, contrary to the general rule; a privilege.

but the most common include sovereign (governmental) immunity and legal infirmities such as infancy or insanity.

Governmental, or Sovereign, Immunity

Sovereign (governmental) immunity has a long and storied history throughout the annals of tort law. To understand modern applications of this doctrine, one must trace its roots and development.

In the history of tort law, governments have held an enviable position. Until the 20th century, governments were immune from liability for torts committed by their employees. This immunity was called **sovereign immunity**, or (in modern times) **governmental immunity**. It stemmed from the ancient English (and Western European) legal tradition that the king could not be sued by his subjects unless he consented. Courts applied the legal maxim *The king can do no wrong*. This maxim traces its origins to pre-Roman times when the emperor was considered divine and, thus, incapable of errors that the law could remedy. Official tortfeasors thus enjoyed immunity from liability unless they agreed to be sued, which one would naturally not if one had committed any torts.

Many courts found the absolute defense of sovereign immunity to be unreasonably harsh on the plaintiffs. To avoid the full force of the immunity, early in the century American courts began distinguishing the different types of governmental activities that were or were not exempt from tort liability. There were two categories: governmental and proprietary.

Governmental/Proprietary Distinction

When governmental bodies perform certain public protection activities, such as providing fire, police, or ambulance services, they are considered to be undertaking *governmental functions*. Persons performing governmental functions are immune from tort liability, under the early 20th-century court decisions. Even if the fire, police, or ambulance departments committed torts against a citizen while performing their duties, the old case law defined these as governmental actions immune from liability.

Governmental bodies also perform certain business-like activities (usually associated with the private sector). These are defined as *proprietary actions* and do not carry immunity from tort liability. For example, a municipality may provide utility services to its residents, such as water, sewer, electric, or natural gas, but this activity more closely resembles a private business enterprise than a public, governmental function. If the governmental agency providing such services committed torts, the government would be liable, and the immunity defense would not prevent liability.

Courts have struggled with this governmental/proprietary distinction for decades. What about cities that provide garbage collection? What about public parks? Are these governmental or proprietary functions? Courts often decide based upon whether a fee is assessed to users of these services. If a fee is charged, then the activity is considered proprietary. If not, then it is governmental. This may be called the *fee standard.*

Similar to the fee standard is the *pecuniary benefit test.* When governments provide services for profit, then the activities are proprietary. If governments offer services for the common public good, without economic benefit to the governmental units themselves, then the activities are governmental.

Within the past 20 years, many state courts have abolished the governmental/proprietary distinction and with it the defense of sovereign immunity. These courts now focus upon whether the governments committed any torts—just as courts would handle any other tort lawsuit. Many state legislatures and Congress have enacted statutes eliminating or restricting sovereign

sovereign immunity (governmental immunity)   The principle that the government ... is immune from suit except when it consents to be sued ... .

Contributory Negligence	Not considered a defense in products liability cases
Assumption of Risk	Ultimate user's voluntary assumption of known risk with full appreciation of dangers involved
	Occurs when ultimate user ignores a discovered defect and uses the product while knowing of its dangerous condition
	Occurs when ultimate user fails to properly maintain product
	Occurs when ultimate user fails to follow instructions or heed warnings for safe product use
Product Misuse by Ultimate User	If ultimate user misuses the product, then he or she cannot recover under products liability
	Reasonably foreseeable uses are *not* misuses of products

Defenses to Products Liability Contributory negligence is not a defense in products liability cases. The other defenses generally focus on the actions and understanding of the ultimate user of the product.

immunity to particular types of services, such as public parks or utilities.

Statutes of Limitation

Statutes of limitation are statutes establishing time limits within which plaintiffs may file tort actions against defendants. There are statutes of limitations for tort lawsuits against governmental units. These often establish an elaborate written notification procedure that the plaintiff must follow to notify all the relevant governmental agencies (and their directors) that a lawsuit has been filed against them.

Public Officers

Somewhat different from sovereign immunity is the individual tort immunity granted to certain public employees engaged in their official capacities. Certain governmental officials are immune from personal liability for any torts committed while they were performing their public duties.

Legislators and judges enjoy an absolute immunity from tort liability for acts in their official governmental capacities. In performing legislative or judicial functions, it is possible that these public officials might commit torts against individual citizens. The common law protects judges and legislators from any liability whatsoever for having committed such torts. Executive branch officials, however, do not receive this blanket immunity, although administrative officers serving judicial or legislative functions do receive absolute immunity. For example, an agency adjudication officer, prosecutor, or county council legislator would be protected completely from tort liability.

Governmental official immunity is intended to ensure that legislators and judges may pursue their public duties without the chilling effect that fear of tort liability might have. Imagine how cautious legislators or judges would have to be in decision-making if, with each sensitive topic, they had to worry about tort liability. These officials might become paralyzed by second-guessing, and the liability spectre could influence their public policy decisions. This rationale for the immunity is often repeated in the common law. To encourage maximum public benefit from the services of the public's judges and legislators, the law must thus totally protect these officials from tort liability.

Children of Tender Years

For centuries, the common law has held that young children, often referred to as "children of tender years" in the court opinions, may be immune, or are subject to limited, tort liability. Children of **tender years** are usually defined as young children under the age of seven years. Under traditional common law, any person under the age of 21 (and in the past 20 years, 18) is classed as a **minor**. However, only very young children normally enjoy the tender-years immunity. Although many opinions, particularly older cases, have granted immunity to teenagers, most cases limit tender years to below age seven. A significant number of cases, however, include the eight-to-twelve age group within the immunity.

Absolute Immunity for Intentional Torts

Most states still follow the ancient common law rule that children of tender years are incapable of committing intentional torts, and are therefore immune from intentional tort liability. This immunity is based upon the concept that young children are mentally and emotionally incapable of having the proper intent to commit an intentional tort. Because they are so young, they lack the experience and development to appreciate fully the significance of their actions, which sometimes are tortious in nature.

Immunity from Negligence

Most courts do not grant absolute negligence immunity to young children. Instead, the child tortfeasor's age is merely one factor to be considered in determining the standard of reasonable care which the reasonable child of tender years would have used in a particular case. A minority of states have held that children below a certain age (usually seven years) cannot commit negligence and are therefore immune from liability. Most states, however, would agree that only extremely young children, often less than three or

Elements	Activity that unreasonably and substantially interferes with use and enjoyment of another's land
	Unreasonable and *substantial* defined by community standard (reasonable person standard) regarding offensiveness of activity
	Defendant's activity must proximately cause plaintiff's injuries
Examples	Physical effects on land (vibrations, pollution, crop destruction, flooding, junk clutter or excavations)
	Health hazards and offending sensibilities (noxious odors, smoke, dust, extreme noise or temperature, incessant telephone calling)
	Unwanted associations with neighboring uses (prostitution houses, distributors of explicit sexual material, gambling institutions)
Defense	Coming to the nuisance
	Plaintiff arrives to use land after nuisance activity already exists

Elements of a Cause of Action for Private Nuisance and its Defenses A private nuisance occurs when landowners use their property in a manner that unreasonably and substantially interferes with another's use and enjoyment of his or her own land.

four years of age, are incapable of negligence and thus immune.

tender years A term used to describe minors, particularly when they are very young.

minor A person who has not yet attained his or her majority; a person who has not reached legal age … .

Summary Questions

1. Suppose that a prominent local politician in your area reads about her "current extramarital affair" in the newspaper one morning. She has given no interviews to the reporter and certainly did not give permission for the story. If the story has no truth to it, what tort has been committed? What if the story is entirely true?

2. Suppose that Peter and Rob get into an argument over the telephone, and Peter tells Rob that he is going to "punch his lights out" and hangs up. Peter then gets in his car, drives over to Rob's house and barges in. He takes a swing at Rob, but misses him. When Rob ducks the swing, he inadvertently pushes his brother, Bud, who is standing nearby. Bud hits his head on the fireplace mantle, giving himself a concussion. Was an assault committed? By whom? When? Was a battery committed?

3. Suppose Theresa throws a punch at Amy, who grabs Theresa's wrist. Theresa's wrist gets sprained in the process. Has Amy committed a tort? What might her defense be?

4. What are the elements of negligence?

5. What is joint and several liability?

6. Can an employer be held responsible for his or her employee's negligent actions? Under what conditions?

7. What is the difference between contributory negligence and comparative negligence?

8. If Katherine's pet boa constrictor escaped from its cage and attacked someone, would Katherine be liable? What if Katherine could prove that she used due care to keep the pet in the cage and someone else accidentally set it free?

Practical Paralegal Skills

Look in your local newspaper and find an article concerning a lawsuit involving a tort to answer the following questions.

1. What type of tort is being alleged in the lawsuit?

2. Who is the alleged tortfeasor?

3. Can you identify each element of the tort as it applies in this case?

4. Can you think of any possible defenses that may be asserted by the alleged tortfeasor?

Notes

For further reference, see *Torts and Personal Injury Law,* by William Buckley (Delmar Publishers Inc., and Lawyers Cooperative Publishing © 1993).

[1] Milano, Carol, *Legal Assistant Today* 48 (May/June 1993).

CHAPTER 10

The Paralegal and Criminal Law and Procedure

Only a small percentage of paralegals work in the criminal law area, yet this area of law holds a certain fascination for many students and paralegals. This chapter discusses the role of the criminal law paralegal, focusing on various aspects of criminal law and criminal procedure that are of particular concern to paralegals.

The Role of Paralegals in Criminal Law

Criminal law paralegals represent only a small percentage of the paralegals in the United States. A 1993 *Legal Assistant Today* survey indicated less than 3 percent of paralegals across the nation specialized in the area of criminal law. The salaries of criminal law paralegals ranked slightly below average in comparison with paralegals in all areas of law. The national average salary for a criminal law paralegal in 1993 was $25,397. The highest reported salary of a criminal law paralegal was $41,000.[1]

The Work of Criminal Law Paralegals in the United States

The work of criminal law paralegals often has a heavy emphasis on interviewing clients and witnesses. The litigation aspect of their positions can be very similar to that of civil litigation paralegals; many of the same procedures followed by civil litigation paralegals for trial preparation are also used by criminal law paralegals. The tasks performed by the criminal law paralegal will vary greatly depending on whether the paralegal works for a prosecutor or a defense attorney. The following lists some of the more common tasks included in the job description of criminal law paralegals.

Assisting the Defense Attorney

1. Interview clients to determine facts relating to their case.
2. Review police reports and other reports provided by the prosecutor.
3. Obtain statements from witnesses to the alleged crime.
4. Assist with all aspects of discovery, including police reports and search warrants.
5. Assist with pretrial and trial procedures.
6. Research legal and factual issues.
7. Assist client with obtaining information concerning bail.
8. Organize file and evidence for trial.
9. Assist with client preparation for trial.
10. Assist the attorney during trial.
11. Research and draft posttrial motions.
12. Draft possible posttrial motions.
13. Maintain tickler file to remind attorney and client of important court dates and other deadlines.

Assisting the Prosecutor

1. Interview witnesses.
2. Draft complaints.
3. Assist with pretrial and trial processes.
4. Assist crime victims by giving referrals to appropriate government agencies.
5. Draft subpoenas.
6. Catalog and prepare exhibits for trial.

Tasks that may not be performed by a criminal law paralegal include appearing in court on behalf of a client and giving legal advice to a client.

Skills Important to Criminal Law Paralegals

Criminal law paralegals must be able to communicate well, both orally and in writing. The criminal law paralegal must communicate effectively with clients, witnesses, and crime victims who may be distraught and upset. The paralegal must be able to conduct thorough interviews and investigations to obtain all the necessary facts, often under the worst of circumstances.

The criminal law paralegal must also know how to perform detailed legal research on issues of law. In addition, the paralegal must have a thorough understanding of criminal court systems and procedures.

Criminal Law in the United States Legal System

Before you can discuss criminal law or criminal procedure, you must have a basic understanding of the legal system of the United States as it pertains to criminal law matters. Criminal law and procedure are significantly influenced by federal and state constitutional law, the common law, and statutory law at both the federal and state levels. This section focuses on proper jurisdiction of the courts and the United States court system.

Jurisdiction

Most crimes fall under the jurisdiction of the state governments. The U.S. Constitution gives the duty of protecting the general welfare of the people to the states. Deciding what acts should be criminal, and punishing individuals who commit those actions, is such a duty. Therefore, most crimes are state law crimes. Murder, rape, assault, and embezzlement are all crimes usually punished by the states, not the federal government.

Many crimes are prohibited by both state and federal law. These crimes fall under **concurrent jurisdiction**. In these instances, state and federal authorities share jurisdiction to bring charges against the accused. For example, drug dealers are subject to federal law if they transport or sell drugs in interstate commerce, and they are also subject to the laws of the state where the transaction occurred. Who will bring charges in these situations is more a political question than a legal one. Our discussion on double jeopardy later in

this chapter will give a clearer picture of the potential outcome in this example.

The states (as well as other jurisdictions, such as the District of Columbia), the federal government, and local governments each have a separate set of criminal laws. Because criminal law paralegals may work on cases in state and federal court systems, it is important that they be familiar with procedures for both of these court systems.

In **criminal law**, the executive branch investigates alleged violations of the law, gathers the evidence necessary to prove that a violation has occurred, and brings violators before the judicial branch for disposition. This is done through the various state and federal law enforcement and administrative agencies. When the law enforcement agency has completed its investigation, the case is turned over to a **prosecutor**. The prosecutor is the attorney responsible for representing the public's interests, who files the formal criminal charge, or conducts a grand jury investigatory indictment, and then conducts the prosecution through to fruition. In the federal system, the prosecutor is called a *United States Attorney*. In the states and localities, prosecutors may be known as *district attorneys, county attorneys, city attorneys*, or simply *prosecutors*.

Criminal Law in the Court Systems

Criminal law matters are heard in both the federal and the state court systems. In addition, many

concurrent jurisdiction   Two or more courts having the power to adjudicate the same class of cases or the same matter.

criminal law   Branch of the law that specifies what conduct constitutes crime and establishes appropriate punishments for such conduct.

prosecutor   A public official, elected or appointed, who conducts criminal prosecutions on behalf of her jurisdiction.

FUNCTIONS OF THE EXECUTIVE BRANCH IN CRIMINAL PROSECUTIONS	
Law Enforcement Agencies	Investigate criminal conduct; gather evidence to prove that a criminal violation has occurred.
Prosecutor	Files formal criminal charge or conducts a grand jury investigatory indictment; conducts prosecution through to conclusion.

The police detect alleged criminal law violators and the prosecution conducts the trial process for the government to determine guilt.

criminal matters may be heard in **inferior courts** within the state systems. Many municipal courts, police courts, and justices of the peace fall into this category. State inferior courts have limited jurisdiction; for example, municipal courts usually hear municipal ordinance violations and only minor state law violations. The amount of money that a person may be fined and the amount of time that a defendant may be sentenced to serve

in jail are also limited. Generally, juries are not used at the inferior court level.

Most inferior courts in the state system are not courts of record; therefore, no tape recording or stenographic recording of the trial or hearing at the inferior court is made. Thus, when an appeal is taken to the trial level, it is normally a **trial de novo**. This means that the trial level court conducts a new trial rather than reviewing a record, as most appellate courts do, because there is no record to review.

Because most state trial courts are **courts of general jurisdiction**, most criminal matters are heard within the state trial courts. However, some states have courts of limited jurisdiction designed specifically to hear criminal trials. Criminal cases in federal court are heard by district courts, and criminal appeals are heard by the circuit courts of appeals.

Criminal law paralegals who work for defense attorneys are often exposed to several different courts within the criminal law system. It is important that criminal law paralegals understand the different rules and procedures followed by each court system with which they are involved.

An Introduction to Criminal Law

At times, criminal law paralegals will be involved in a criminal case from the very beginning. Defense paralegals may be involved in arranging bail for a client and for reviewing the charges against the client. For that reason, it is important that criminal law paralegals understand the basics of crime and criminal law in the state in which they work.

Whereas civil law has as its primary purpose the compensation of those injured by someone else's behavior, the purpose of criminal law is twofold. First, it is intended to prevent behavior that society has determined is undesirable. A second purpose of criminal law is to punish those who do acts deemed undesirable by society. Arguably, there is only one purpose: to prevent

BALLENTINESBALLENTINESBALLENTINESBALLENTINESBALLENTINESBALLENTINESBALLENTINESBALLENTINESBALLENTINESBALLENTINESBALLENTINESBALLENTINESBALLENTINESBALLENTINES

inferior courts   1. A court of original jurisdiction, as distinguished from an appellate court; a trial court. 2. A court of limited jurisdiction.

trial de novo   A new trial, a retrial, or a trial on appeal from a justice's court or a magistrate's court to a court of general jurisdiction. A trial ... in which the matter is tried again as if it had not been heard before and as if no decision had previously been rendered.

court of general jurisdiction   Generally, another term for trial court; that is, a court having jurisdiction to try all classes of civil and criminal cases except those which can be heard only by a court of limited jurisdiction.

antisocial behavior; under this theory, punishment is only a tool to achieve the primary goal of preventing antisocial behavior. In any event, prevention and punishment are essential reasons why we have criminal law and a criminal justice system. In criminal law, the government, whether national, state, or local, is always the party that files criminal charges. The brief introduction to criminal law in this section includes discussions on the distinction between criminal law and criminal procedure, the power of the government to regulate the behavior of individuals in our society, the purposes of punishing criminal law violations, and the sources of American criminal law.

The Distinction Between Criminal Law and Criminal Procedure

Much like civil law and civil procedure, there is a distinction between criminal law and criminal procedure. Criminal law, as a field of law, defines what constitutes a crime. It establishes what conduct is prohibited and what punishment can be imposed for violating its mandates. Criminal law establishes what degree of intent is required for criminal liability. In addition, criminal law sets out the defenses that may be asserted to criminal charges. The alibi and insanity defenses, for instance, come under the umbrella of criminal law.

Criminal procedure, on the other hand, puts substantive criminal law into action. It is concerned with the procedures used to bring criminals to justice, beginning with police investigation and continuing throughout the process of administering justice. Criminal procedure addresses such questions as when and under what conditions a person may be arrested, and how long after charges are filed the accused must wait before a trial is held. Without criminal procedure, it would be impossible to administer criminal law.

In the following law office scenario, if Sandy Sherwood were asked to research the process for charging Mr. Jackson and how long Mr. Jackson could be held before he was formally charged or before bail was set, Sandy would be concerned with the rules of criminal procedure. If Sandy were researching the possible crimes that Mr. Jackson might be charged with and the possible penalties for those crimes, she would be concerned with criminal law.

The Power of Government to Regulate Behavior

Freedom and liberty are two concepts that pervade the American political being. *Freedom* generally means the ability to act without interference. In a political and legal sense, it means the ability to act free from the interference of government. However, even in the most free societies, personal behavior is limited because the actions of every member of society have the potential, at times, to affect other members. Without government, there is little control over the individual's behavior. No system would exist to punish those who intentionally injure others or to allow persons injured by the negligence of another to recover their losses. There would be no deterrent to wrongful behavior other than fear of retribution from the victim. To prevent anarchy, people establish governments. The people then invest their governments with certain authorities and powers, so that the government can control the behavior of all the people.

The Preamble to the United States Constitution recognizes this principle of providing some freedoms in an effort to secure other freedoms. It states:

We, the People of the United States, in Order to form a more perfect Union, establish Justice, insure domestic Tranquillity, provide for the common defence, promote the general Welfare, and secure the Blessings of Liberty to ourselves and our Posterity, do ordain and establish this Constitution for the United States of America.

Every government is different, but one trend that seems true of nearly all nations is that governmental involvement with the affairs of the people

criminal procedure The rules of procedure by which criminal prosecutions are governed.

Law Office Scenario

Sandy Sherwood was in the middle of drafting a motion when the receptionist called her on the intercom. "A Mr. Thomas Jackson is on the telephone," she said. "He wants to talk with Mr. Levinson, but he's at lunch. He said it's regarding a criminal matter, and there are no attorneys available—can you talk with him?"

"Sure," said Sandy. As a criminal law paralegal for a small law firm, she was accustomed to handling client calls when the attorneys were in court or otherwise unavailable.

"This is Tom Jackson," the caller said. "Your firm represented me on a drunken driving charge a few years ago. Now I need an attorney right away to come and get me out of jail!"

"What is the problem?" asked Sandy.

"Well, they think I assaulted someone—someone who might even die," said Mr. Jackson. "But I didn't do it. I was on my way to visit my friend Arnold Litchfield, to return the television set that I borrowed from him, when I was stopped in the alley near his home, handcuffed, and brought down here in a police car. They won't tell me the whole story, and they haven't charged me yet, but I guess someone hit Arnold over the head with something and stole some stuff out of his apartment. Arnold is in the hospital and they're not sure whether he's going to make it. When they saw me in the alley carrying his television set, and found other things in my car that I had borrowed from Arnold, they thought I was the one who did it! I've been down here since 1:00 this morning. This is my one telephone call, and I need someone to come and get me out of here right away!"

"I'll locate Mr. Levinson and someone will be down there as soon as possible, Mr. Jackson. Tell me exactly where they are holding you."

is continually increasing, in part because people are less independent. Members of society now depend on one another to provide goods and services that were once commonly self-provided. In addition, the staggering increase in world population has caused people to have much more contact with each other than they did 100 years ago. As the population and dependence of people increases, so does the likelihood that one person's actions may affect another. The greater the population, contact between, and dependence of people on one another, the greater the number of conflicts that will arise requiring government intervention.

As government involvement in private life increases, it becomes more difficult to protect individual rights, also known as **civil liberties**. Although we have bestowed upon our government certain powers which have the effect of limiting our behavior, we have also specifically created civil rights upon which the government may not encroach. Many of these rights are contained in the first 10 amendments to our Constitution, commonly known as the Bill of Rights. As the world becomes more populated and complex, the balance between permissible government involvement in the private lives of its citizens and impermissible encroachment upon those citizens' civil liberties becomes harder to maintain. As that line becomes thinner, the duty of the lawyer and legal assistant to be zealous in preparation of their defenses increases.

Control of people's behavior is achieved through both civil law and criminal law. Generally, society reserves only those acts that are perceived as serious moral wrongs or extremely dangerous for sanction under criminal law. Acts that are accidental

civil liberties Political liberties guaranteed by the Constitution and, in particular, by the Bill of Rights … .

or are not serious breaches of moral duty are usually not criminal, but may lead to civil liability. Thoughts about how acts should be classified are very subjective and often change.

For example, the 1980s saw an increased effort to stop people from driving while under the influence of alcohol. Many states enacted new laws increasing the penalty for violating their driving-under-the-influence statutes. In addition, a few states limited police discretion by requiring that violators be arrested. As public concern over alcohol-related automobile accidents increased, the focus turned to criminal law to prevent such behavior. Increased penalties, consistent arrest policies, and mandatory alcohol treatment for those convicted are now common. Extensive media coverage of particular cases has gotten the word out that one who drives while intoxicated risks arrest, conviction, and punishment, as well as civil liability for injuries to property and person. What this example shows is that society determines what acts will be treated as criminal based on public perceptions of morality, the importance of deterrence, and the danger posed to the public by the acts in question.

The Purposes of Punishing Criminal Law Violators

The criminal justice system uses punishment as a tool to prevent behavior determined by society to be undesirable. There are many theories that support punishing criminal law violators, including deterrence, incapacitation, rehabilitation, and retribution.

Specific and General Deterrence *Specific deterrence* seeks to deter individuals already convicted of crimes from committing crimes in the future. It is a negative reinforcement theory. By punishing Mr. X for today's crime, we teach him that he will be disciplined for future criminal behavior. The arrest and conviction of an individual shows that individual that society has the capability to detect crime and is willing to punish those who commit crimes.

General deterrence attempts to deter all members of society from engaging in criminal activity. In theory, when the public observes Ms. X being punished for her actions, the public is deterred from behaving similarly for fear of the same punishment.

Incapacitation *Incapacitation,* also referred to as *restraint*, is the third purpose of criminal punishment. Incapacitation does not seek to deter criminal conduct by influencing people's choices, but prevents criminal conduct by restraining those who have committed crimes. Criminals who are restrained in jail or prison, or who are executed, are incapable of causing further harm to the general public.

Rehabilitation *Rehabilitation* is another purpose for punishing criminals. The theory of rehabilitation maintains that if the criminal is subjected to various educational and technical programs, treatment, counseling, and other measures, it is possible to alter the individual's behavior to conform to societal norms.

Retribution *Retribution*, or societal vengeance, is the fifth purpose. Simply put, punishment through the criminal justice system is society's method of avenging a wrong.

Sources of Criminal Law

Sources of criminal law include common law, statutory law, ordinances, court rules, and constitutional law.

Common Law

The oldest form of criminal law in the United States is the common law, which still has a significant impact on criminal law in the United States. Even though approximately half of the states no longer recognize common-law crimes, common law continues to be important for many reasons.

First, many statutes mirror the common law in language; that is, legislatures often simply codify the common-law criminal prohibitions. Second, legislatures occasionally enact a criminal

PURPOSES OF PUNISHING CRIMINAL LAW VIOLATORS
1. Specific deterrence
2. General deterrence
3. Incapacitation
4. Rehabilitation
5. Retribution

Society cannot arrive at a general consensus of which purpose is most successful. However, most individuals involved with today's criminal justice system would argue that the emphasis is on punishment, not deterrence or rehabilitation.

prohibition without establishing the penalty for violation. In such cases, courts often look to the penalties applied to similar common-law crimes for guidance. Third, the common law not only provided a mechanism for creating new crimes, but also established many procedures used to adjudicate criminal cases. These procedures most often dealt with criminal defenses. What defenses can be raised? How and when may they be asserted? Such questions were often answered by the common law. For example, the various tests to determine whether a defendant was sane when an alleged crime was committed were developed under the common law. If a legislature has not specifically changed these procedural rules, they remain in effect, even if the power of courts to create common law crimes has been abolished.

Statutory Law

During the 19th century, states began a major movement away from the common law, toward codifying the criminal law. Today, nearly all criminal law is found in criminal codes.

Many states have modeled their criminal code after the **Model Penal Code**. The *Model Penal Code and Commentaries* was drafted by a group of experts in criminal law who worked for the American Law Institute, a private organization. The intent of the drafters of the Code was to draft a consistent, thoughtful code that could be recommended to the states for adoption. The code itself is not law until adopted and made into law by a legislature. By 1985, approximately 34 states had "enacted widespread criminal-law revision and codification based on its provisions; fifteen hundred courts had cited its provisions and referred to its commentary."[2]

Ordinances

Many cities have criminal ordinances that mirror state statutes, only they apply to acts that occur within the jurisdiction of the city. For example, many cities have assault and battery ordinances, just as their states have assault and battery statutes. Traffic and parking violations may also be criminal, although some cities pursue these as civil violations, which permits the state to pursue the criminal charge.

Court Rules

The United States Congress and all of the state legislatures have enacted some form of statute establishing general rules of civil and criminal procedure. However, to "fill in the gaps" left by legislatures, courts adopt court rules, which also govern criminal processes. Although court rules deal with procedural rather than substantive issues, they are important. Of course, court rules may not conflict with legislative mandates. If a rule does conflict with a statute, the statute is controlling. Because the work of criminal law paralegals is often centered around criminal procedure, it is important that criminal law paralegals be familiar with the court rules for the pertinent federal, state, and local court systems.

BALLENTINESBALLENTINESBALLENTINESBALLENTINESBALLENTINESBALLENTINESBALLENTINESBALLENTINESBALLENTINESBALLENTINESBALLENTINESBALLENTINESBALLENTINESBALLENTINESBALLENTINES

Model Penal Code   A proposed criminal code prepared jointly by the Commission on Uniform State Laws and the American Law Institute.

Constitutional Law

Finally, constitutional law is included as a source of criminal law, not because it defines what conduct is criminal, but because of its significant effect on criminal law generally. Particularly, the United States Constitution, primarily through the Bill of Rights, is responsible for establishing many of the rules governing criminal procedure. This has been especially true in the past few decades.

The Two Essential Elements of a Crime

Nearly every crime consists of two essential elements, the mental intent part and the physical part. It is common to distinguish between acts that are intentional and those acts that occur accidentally. Everyone has, at some time, caused injury to another person or another person's property accidentally. The fact that the injury was accidental and not intended often leads to a statement such as, "I'm sorry, I didn't mean to hurt you." In these situations, people often feel a social obligation to pay for any injuries they have caused, or to assist the injured party in other ways, but they probably do not expect to be punished criminally. As the late Supreme Court Justice Holmes once said, "Even a dog distinguishes between being stumbled over and being kicked." Making such a distinction between accidental and intentional acts that injure others appears to be natural and consistent with common notions of fairness. The criminal law often models this theory; that is, people are often held accountable for intentional behavior and not for accidental, even though the consequences may be the same. Under some circumstances, however, accidental behavior (negligent or reckless) may be the basis of criminal liability.

Mens Rea

Mens rea is the mental part of a crime, or the state of mind required to be criminally liable. It is often defined as "a guilty mind" or possessing a criminal intent. It is best defined as the state of mind required to be criminally liable for a certain act.

Mens Rea and the Common Law

One principle under the common law was that there could be no crime if there was no act accompanied by a guilty mind. If the defendant intended to cause the consequences of the act, he or she had a specific intent. If the defendant intended only the act, and not the result of that act, then the defendant possessed *general* **intent**. For instance, suppose that the facts of the Tom Jackson case in the law office scenario prove that Tom Jackson and Arnold Litchfield were arguing over the television set that Tom Jackson was found with when Tom pushed Arnold, who fell and hit his head, causing a fatal head wound. Tom probably possessed general intent, in that he meant to harm Arnold. However, Tom probably did not possess **specific intent** to kill Arnold. The distinction between general and specific intent is often an important one, as statutes usually require specific intent for a higher-level crime and general for a lower. In this example, many state statutes would allow Tom Jackson to be charged with first-degree murder if he intended to kill Arnold Litchfield, but only second-degree murder if he only intended to injure Arnold Litchfield.

BALLENTINESBALLENTINESBALLENTINESBALLENTINESBALLENTINESBALLENTINESBALLENTINESBALLENTINESBALLENTINESBALLENTINESBALLENTINESBALLENTINESBALLENTINESBALLENTINESBALLENTINES

mens rea An "answerable intent," i.e., an intent for which one is answerable; an evil intent; a guilty mind; a criminal intent.

intent Purpose; the plan, course, or means a person conceives to achieve a certain result. Intent is not … limited to conscious wrongdoing, and may be inferred or presumed.

specific intent The intent to commit the very act with which the defendant has been charged.

SUMMARY OF SOURCES OF CRIMINAL LAW

Source	Comment
Constitutions	The United States and every state have a constitution. The United States Constitution is the supreme law of the land. Amendment of the federal constitution requires action by both the states and the United States Congress.
Statutes	The written law created by legislatures. Also known as codes. State statutes may not conflict with either the state constitution or the federal constitution. State statutes are also invalid if they conflict with other federal law, and the federal government has concurrent jurisdiction with the states. Statutes of the United States are invalid if they conflict with the United States Constitution or if they attempt to regulate outside federal jurisdiction. Legislatures may change statutes at will.
Common Law	Law that evolved, as courts, through judicial opinions, recognized customs and practices. Legislatures may alter, amend, and abolish the common law at will. In criminal law, the common law is responsible for the creation of crimes and for establishing defenses to crimes.
Regulations	Created by administrative agencies under a grant of authority from a legislative body. Regulations must be consistent with statutes and constitutions and may not exceed the legislative grant of power. The power to make rules and regulations is granted to fill in the gaps left by legislatures when drafting statutes.
Ordinances	Written law of local bodies, such as city councils. Must be consistent with all higher forms of law.
Model Penal Code	Written under the direction of the American Law Institute. It was drafted by experts in criminal law to be presented to the states for their adoption. It is not law until a state has adopted it, in whole or part. More than half the states have adopted at least part of the Model Penal Code.
Court Rules	Rules created by courts to manage their cases. Court rules are procedural and commonly establish deadlines, lengths of filings, and the like. Court rules may not conflict with statutes or constitutions.

One means of proving specific intent, in some jurisdictions, is by showing that the defendant knew that by committing an act he or she would be violating the law. This requirement of knowledge is known as **scienter**. In jurisdictions that require such knowledge, if an individual violates a criminal law while believing that the act engaged in is lawful, then specific intent is lacking and only general intent can be proven. Without scienter, no crime may exist to punish. Consider the crime of receiving stolen property. If an individual received stolen property, but did so without knowledge that it was stolen, then no chargeable crime was committed.

General intent is much easier to define, as it is simply the desire to act. In most situations, if the prosecution can show that a defendant intended to commit the prohibited act, then general intent is proved. Generally, no desire to cause a particular consequence is required. So, if you fire a gun without a desire to kill someone, but the bullet does kill a person, you possess a general intent and may be prosecuted for a general-intent homicide.

Strict Liability

Strict liability, or liability without fault are exceptions to the common-law requirement that there be both an evil mind and an evil act to commit a crime. Strict liability crimes usually are minor violations, punished by fines but not incarceration. However, strict liability is permitted for felonies and may be punished with incarceration. There are many strict liability crimes in every state, and legislatures are increasingly using the strict liability standard when declaring acts illegal. Some typical strict liability crimes include running a stoplight, speeding, and statutory rape.

Vicarious Liability

The term **vicarious liability** applies in situations where one person is held accountable for the actions of another. Under vicarious liability, there is no requirement of mens rea, as is the case for strict liability; additionally, there is no requirement

for an act, at least by the defendant. The person who is liable for the actions of another need not act, encourage another to act, or intend any harm at all. As is true with vicarious liability in tort law, this situation is most common between employers and employees. Employers may be liable for the actions of their employees when criminal laws relating to the operation of the business are violated. Vicarious liability is often imposed on those who market food and drugs because of the significant public welfare interest in the quality of these products.

Corporate liability is a form of vicarious liability. Under the common law, corporations could not be convicted of crimes. However, this is no longer so. Corporations, partnerships, and other organizations can be held criminally accountable for the acts of their employees and agents. Obviously, companies cannot be incarcerated, so fines are usually imposed. In some instances, injunctions may be imposed. Finally, note that corporate liability does not free the agent from criminal liability. In most cases the agent or employee also remains criminally liable for his or her act.

Current Approaches to Mens Rea

The drafters of the Model Penal Code chose to reject most of the common-law terms when they addressed mens rea. The result is that the Model Penal Code recognizes four states of mind: (1) purposeful; (2) knowing; (3) reckless; and (4) negligent.[3]

To act purposely, a defendant must have a desire to cause the result. **Purposely** most closely equates with what the common law called specific intent.

To act **knowingly**, a defendant must be aware of the nature of the act and be practically certain that the conduct will cause a particular

BALLENTINESBALLENTINESBALLENTINESBALLENTINESBALLENTINESBALLENTINESBALLENTINESBALLENTINESBALLENTINESBALLENTINESBALLENTINESBALLENTINESBALLENTINESBALLENTINESBALLENTINESBALLENTINES

scienter Knowledge, particularly guilty knowledge; knowledge a person has that, as a matter of law, will result in his or her liability or guilt.

strict liability Liability for an injury whether or not there is fault or negligence; absolute liability.

vicarious liability Liability imposed upon a person because of the act or omission of another.

corporate liability The liability of a corporation for the acts of its directors, officers, shareholders, agents, and employees.

purposely Intentionally; knowingly.

knowingly With knowledge; deliberately; consciously; intentionally.

result, which is not the defendant's objective. The difference between purposeful acts and knowing acts is that to be purposeful, one must act intending to cause the particular result. To act knowingly, the defendant must be practically certain (nearly 100 percent positive) that the result will occur, but the defendant is not committing the act to cause that result. For example, if a legitimate moving company owner leases a van to an illegal drug dealer, knowing that the van will be used to transport drugs across the country, then the owner has acted knowingly. He has not acted with purpose because it is not his objective to transport the contraband.

The third state of mind recognized by the Model Penal Code is **recklessly**. A person acts recklessly when she consciously disregards a substantial and unjustifiable risk that the result will occur. The difference between a knowing act and a reckless act is in the degree of risk. The Code says that the risk taken must be one that involves a "gross deviation from the standard of conduct that the law-abiding person would observe in the actor's situation."[4]

The final state of mind recognized by the Code is negligence. The definition of **negligence** is similar to recklessness; that is, a "substantial and unjustifiable risk" must be taken by the defendant. However, a person acts negligently when he or she has no conscious awareness of the risk, when he or she should have. When a defendant has acted negligently, he or she has failed to perceive (be aware of) the risk altogether, and that failure is a gross deviation from a law-abiding person's standard.

Paralegals who are asked to research the law regarding a specific crime must know the mens rea of the crime, and they should be able to determine whether proof exists that the mens rea was present in the case at hand.

Actus Reus

Actus reus is the physical part of a crime: it is the act engaged in by the accused. An *act* is a physical movement. If Mr. Jackson from the law office scenario had taken a fireplace poker and hit Arnold over the head, the act would have been swinging the poker down on Arnold's head. The Model Penal Code states that a "person is not guilty of an offense unless his liability is based on conduct that includes a voluntary act … "[5]

Voluntariness

To be held criminally liable for one's actions, those actions must be voluntary. To be **voluntary**, an act must occur as a result of the actor's conscious choice. The person accused must have acted freely, or no liability attaches. The Model Penal Code requires that acts be voluntary and specifically lists the following as being involuntary:

1. Reflexes and convulsions
2. Bodily movements during unconsciousness or sleep
3. Conduct during hypnosis or resulting from hypnotic suggestion
4. Other movements that are not a product of the effort or determination of the actor.[6]

The concepts of mens rea and actus reus should not be confused. All that is required to have an act is a choice by the defendant to act. No evil intent is required to have an act; that is a question of mens rea. Say that Jim chooses to swing his arm. As a result he hits Terry. The intent required to prove battery, and whether Jim possessed that intent, are questions of mens rea. To establish actus reus, all that need be known is whether Jim voluntarily chose to swing his arm. His swing

---

BALLENTINESBALLENTINESBALLENTINESBALLENTINESBALLENTINESBALLENTINESBALLENTINESBALLENTINESBALLENTINESBALLENTINESBALLENTINESBALLENTINESBALLENTINESBALLENTINES

recklessly   [C]onduct demonstrating an indifference to consequences, particularly those involving danger to life or to the safety of others.

negligence   The failure to do something that a reasonable person would do in the same circumstances, or the doing of something a reasonable person would not do.

actus reus   An "answerable act," i.e., an act for which one is answerable; a guilty act.

voluntary   A word applied to an act freely done out of choice, not brought about by coercion, duress, or accident.

would be involuntary if Bill grabbed Jim's arm and moved it, causing it to strike Terry.

Thoughts and Statements as Acts

Thoughts alone cannot be criminal acts. People may think evil thoughts, but if there is no act furthering such a thought, there is no crime. Generally, people are also free to speak. The First Amendment to the United States Constitution protects freedom of speech. When the First Amendment applies, speech may not be made criminal. There are, however, limits to the First Amendment's protection of speech. Inciting riots, treason, solicitation, conspiracy, and causing imminent harm to others are examples of speech that may be prohibited or controlled.

Personal Status as an Act

Generally, a person's status cannot be declared criminal. Illness, financial status, race, gender, and religion are examples of human conditions. Some conditions are directly related to illegal behavior. For example, being addicted to illegal narcotics is a condition that cannot be punished because that status is generally not considered to be an act.

Possession as an Act

Possession of certain items, such as narcotics, burglary tools, or dangerous weapons, may be made criminal. Possession is not, strictly speaking, an act. Possession does not involve an active body movement; rather, possession is a passive state of being. Even so, most possession laws have been upheld.

Omissions as Acts

Generally, only acts are prohibited by criminal law. Rarely does criminal law require a person to act. However, there are some situations in which people have a duty to act, and failure to act is criminal. An *omission* is a failure to act when required to do so by criminal law.

It is often the case that a person who may have a *moral* duty to act does not have a *legal* duty to act. In most instances, people do not have a legal duty to assist one another in times of need. It would not be criminal in most jurisdictions for an excellent swimmer to watch another drown. Nor would it be criminal to watch another walk into a dangerous situation, such as a bank robbery in progress, if the observer had no connection with the criminal event. There are exceptions to this rule, though. To be liable for a failure to act, a person must have a "duty" to act, and this duty can arise in many different ways.

First, criminal statutes may impose a duty to act. For example, businesses that store or dispose of toxic materials are required to file certain documents; taxpayers are required to file tax returns; and those involved in automobile accidents are required to stop at the scene of the accident.

Second, a duty to assist another can be created by the existence of a personal relationship. The most common examples are parent to child and spouse to spouse. In such personal relationships, a level of dependence exists that gives rise to criminal liability for failure to assist the party who is in danger.

A duty to act can also be created in a third way, by contract. For example, physicians are hired to care for the health of their patients. If a doctor watches as a patient slowly dies, doing nothing to save the patient's life when he or she could have taken measures, the doctor is liable for homicide.

Finally, any time a person creates the circumstance that endangers a stranger, a duty to save the stranger is also created. This is so whether the danger was caused intentionally or negligently. Thus, if arsonists set fire to a house that they believe to be empty and then discover that it is not, the arsonists must attempt to save anyone inside. If not, the arsonists are also murderers. The same would be true if the fire were caused by negligence.

Causation

Some acts are criminal even though the prohibited result does not occur. For example, it is a crime to lie when testifying in court (the crime of perjury), even if no juror believes the testimony and the outcome of the trial is not changed because of it. For crimes that do require a particular result, the act must be the "cause" of the result. In criminal law, two forms of causation exist, factual and legal. An act is the *cause in fact* of the result if the result would not have occurred unless the act occurred. This is known as the *sine qua non test*, which means that "**but for**" the conduct, the harm would not have resulted. **Legal cause** must also be proved. Legal causation focuses on the degree of similarity between the defendant's intended result and the actual result. Legal cause is also commonly referred to as **proximate cause**. *Proximate* means nearly, next to, or close. In the context of criminal causation, it refers to the relationship between the act and the result. The result must be a consequence of the act, not a coincidence. A happening is proximately caused by an act if a reasonable person would have foreseen and expected the result. This is called **foreseeability**.

If either the cause in fact or the legal cause is missing, then a defense as to the intent of the crime exists. Even if so, the actor may be convicted of a lower, nonintent crime.

Concurrence

As discussed earlier, there are two primary components of crime, the mental and the physical. Although a showing of mens rea is not required for every crime, there must be a showing of some act or omission for each crimes.

For crimes that have both a mental and a physical element, an additional requirement of concurrence must be proved. *Concurrence* is the joining of mens rea and the act. The mens rea must be the reason that the act was taken. Stated another way, the mental state must occur first and set the act into motion. The mere fact that the mental state happens before the act does not mean that there is concurrence. There must be a connection between the intent and the act; the mens rea must set the act into motion.

Crimes Against the Person

Crimes are often categorized as crimes against the person, crimes against property, and crimes against the public. Although it is common to make these distinctions, they are used only for organizational purposes. In a sense, all crimes are offenses against the public, which is why the public prosecutes crimes and private individuals may not. Also, any offense "against property" actually injures a person, not the property; a stolen television set does not long to be returned to its owner. The classifications are accurate in that

they describe the focus of the criminal conduct. The focus of a thief's act is property; hence, a crime against property. The focus of a rapist's attack is a human; hence, a crime against the person.

Elements of a Crime

Almost every crime consists of separate parts. Each part of a crime is an *element* of that crime. At trial, every element of a crime must be proven

but-for rule   A rule of tort law … used to determine whether a defendant is legally responsible for a plaintiff's injuries.

legal cause   1. The proximate cause of an injury. 2. Probable cause. 3. Cause that the law deems sufficient.

proximate cause   As an element of liability in a tort case, that cause which, unbroken by any intervening cause, produced the injury, and without which the result would not have occurred; the primary cause; the efficient cause.

foreseeable   That which may be anticipated or known in advance; that which a person should have known. In the law of negligence, a person is responsible for the consequences of his or her acts only if they are foreseeable.

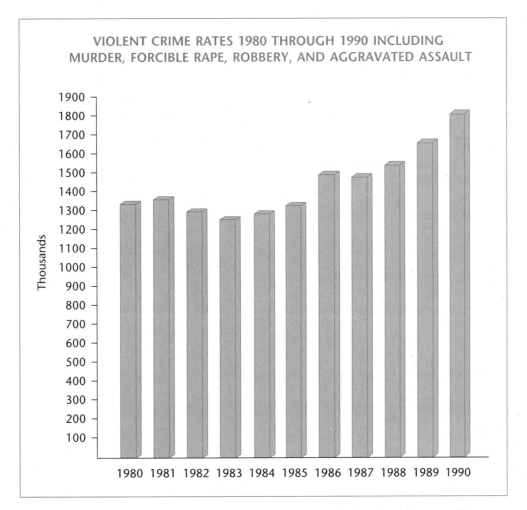

VIOLENT CRIME RATES 1980 THROUGH 1990 INCLUDING MURDER, FORCIBLE RAPE, ROBBERY, AND AGGRAVATED ASSAULT

Violent Crime Rates (1980–1990) Violent crimes include murder, forcible rape, robbery, and aggravated assault. Except for a few years, the trend is upward.

beyond a reasonable doubt by the prosecution. If any element is not proven beyond a reasonable doubt, the accused must be found not guilty. This rule requires that each element be proved individually. It is important for criminal law paralegals who assist both prosecuting attorneys and defending attorneys to understand the elements of each crime, so they can help to determine whether all elements of the crime are present in each particular case. If Tom Jackson from our law office scenario is actually charged with a crime, it may be Sandy Sherwood's task to research the crime in the pertinent state statutes to determine what the elements of the crime are and how they apply to Mr. Jackson's case.

Often, if one crime has been proven, all the elements of a related lesser crime can also be proven. For example, if a defendant is convicted

beyond a reasonable doubt The degree of proof required to convict a person of a crime. A *reasonable doubt* is a fair doubt based upon reason and common sense, not an arbitrary or possible doubt.

of murdering someone with a hammer, the defendant has also committed a battery of the victim. In such circumstances, the lesser offense merges into the greater offense. This is the **merger of offenses doctrine**. Under this doctrine, both crimes may be charged, but if the defendant is convicted of the more serious crime, the lesser is absorbed by the greater, and the defendant is not punished for both. If acquitted of the greater charge, the defendant may be convicted of the lesser.

Because each city and state has its own unique laws, this discussion of specific crimes is limited to the major crimes recognized, in some form, in most jurisdictions.

Homicide

Homicide is the killing of one human being by another. Not all homicides are crimes. It is possible to cause another person's death accidentally, that is, not accompanied by mens rea, but still to be subject to criminal liability. Under the Model Penal Code, purposeful, knowing, negligent, and reckless homicides may be punished. The mens rea part of the homicide is important. The determination of what mens rea was possessed by the defendant (actually, what mens rea can be proven by the prosecution) usually determines what crime may be punished.

Most states divide murder into degrees, most often into first and second degrees. **First-degree murder** is the highest form of murder and is punished more severely than second-degree murder. **Second-degree** murder is a higher crime than manslaughter.

For a murder to be of the first degree—the highest crime—it must be shown that the homicide was willful, deliberate, and premeditated. Generally, first-degree murder applies whenever the murderer has as a goal the death of the victim. Second-degree murder is commonly given a negative definition: "all murders that are not of the first degree are of the second." Second-degree murder differs from the first in that the defendant lacks the specific intent to kill or lacks the premeditation and deliberation element of first-degree murder.

This distinction is an area where inferences are important. Juries (or judges, if the court is acting as the finder of fact) are permitted to view the facts surrounding the murder and determine what the defendant's state of mind was at the time the act occurred. A jury may conclude from the facts that the defendant did not intend to cause the death of the victim, but that the defendant did intend to cause serious bodily injury. In that event, the crime is second-degree murder.

Corpus Delicti

Corpus delicti is a Latin phrase that translates as "the body of a crime." Every crime has a corpus delicti, or substance of the crime. For example, in murder cases the corpus delicti is the death of a victim and the act that caused the death. In arson, the corpus delicti is a burned structure and the cause of the fire. Prosecutors have the burden of proving the corpus delicti of crimes at trial. A confession of an accused is never enough to prove corpus delicti. There must be either direct proof or evidence supporting a confession.

Assault and Battery

Assault and battery are two different crimes, although they commonly occur together. As with homicide, all states have made assaults and batteries criminal by statute.

BALLENTINESBALLENTINESBALLENTINESBALLENTINESBALLENTINESBALLENTINESBALLENTINESBALLENTINESBALLENTINESBALLENTINESBALLENTINESBALLENTINESBALLENTINES

merger of offenses   The doctrine that when a lesser offense is a component of a more serious offense, prosecution can only be for the greater offense.

homicide   The killing of a human being.

first-degree murder   Murder committed deliberately with malice aforethought, that is, with premeditation.

second-degree murder   A murder that does not fall into the category of first-degree murder; a murder committed with intent to kill, but without premeditation or deliberation.

corpus delicti   Means the "body of the crime"; the fact that a crime has actually been committed.

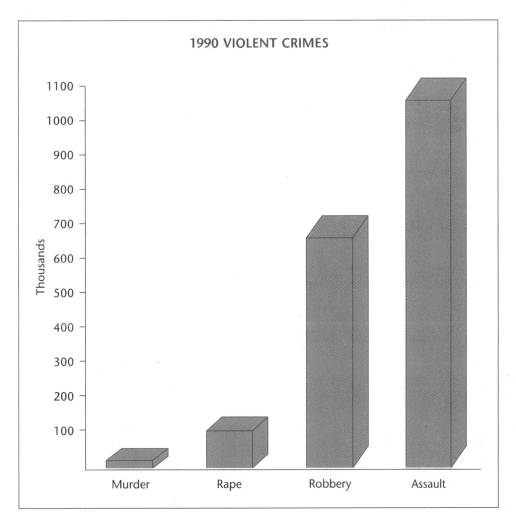

1990 Violent Crimes Assault, the threat of unwanted physical contact, accounted for more than one million cases in 1990 alone.

A **battery** is an intentional touching of another that is either offensive or harmful. The mens rea element varies among the states; however, most now provide for both intentional and negligent battery. The Model Penal Code provides for purposeful, knowing, and reckless batteries. In addition, if one uses a deadly weapon, negligence may give rise to a battery charge. Otherwise, negligence may not provide the basis for a battery conviction.

The actus reus of battery is a touching. An individual need not touch someone with his or her actual person to commit a battery. Objects that are held are considered extensions of the body. A touching must be either offensive or harmful to be a battery.

BALLENTINESBALLENTINESBALLENTINESBALLENTINESBALLENTINESBALLENTINESBALLENTINESBALLENTINESBALLENTINESBALLENTINESBALLENTINESBALLENTINESBALLENTINES

battery The unconsented-to touching or striking of one person by another, or by an object put in motion by him or her, with the intention of doing harm or giving offense.

There are two breeds of **assault**. First, when a person puts another in fear or apprehension of an imminent battery, then assault has been committed. The second type of assault is an attempted battery. Any unsuccessful battery is an assault, regardless of the victim's knowledge of the act. Of course, it must be determined that the act in question would have been a battery had it been completed.

Under special circumstances an assault or battery can be classified as aggravated and a higher penalty imposed. The crime is aggravated if the assault or battery is committed while the actor is engaged in the commission of another crime. It is also common to make assault and battery committed on persons of some special status more serious. Law enforcement officers or other public officials often fall into this category. The extent of injury to the victim may also lead to an increased charge. Usually a battery is aggravated if the harm rises to the level of "serious bodily injury." Some states specifically state that certain injuries, such as the loss of an eye, aggravate the crime of battery.

Sex Crimes

The term "sex crimes" actually encompasses a variety of sexually motivated crimes. Rape, sodomy, incest, and sexually motivated batteries and murders are included. Obscenity, prostitution, abortion, distribution of child pornography, and public nudity are examples of other sex-related offenses.

Although certain offenses are universally prohibited, other offenses vary by state. For example, rape is criminal in all states, but prostitution is not. However, many other sexual acts that have been considered "abnormal" are crimes in most states. Most states recognize the crimes of sodomy, incest, and several sex offenses against children.

Rape

Under common law, the elements of rape were (1) sexual intercourse with (2) a woman not the man's wife, (3) committed without the victim's consent and by using force. Most states have modernized the common-law definition of **rape** to permit minors and women to be charged with rape. Second, the marital rape exception has been abolished in most states. Finally, the last requirement has changed significantly: a person need not resist to the extent required under the common law. What is required now is proof that the victim did resist, although a victim need not risk life or serious bodily injury in an attempt to prevent the rape. The elements of rape under many new statutes are: (1) sexual intercourse (2) with another against that person's will or without that person's consent (3) by the use of force or under such a threat of force that a reasonable person would have believed that resistance would have resulted in serious bodily harm or death.

Nonforcible Rape

Under some circumstances, one may commit a rape even though the other party consented to the sexual contact. So-called **statutory rape** is such a crime. The actus reus of statutory rape is sexual intercourse with someone under a specified age, commonly 16. The purpose of the law is to protect those whom the law presumes to be too young to make a mature decision concerning sex. Hence, consent is not relevant; a statutory rape has occurred when a girl under 16 consents to sexual intercourse with an 18-year-old male.

In most states, statutory rape is a strict liability crime. The act of having sex with someone less than the specified age is in itself proof of guilt. No showing of mens rea is required. Similar to statutory rape, having sex with those who are

assault An act of force or threat of force intended to inflict harm upon a person or to put the person in fear that such harm is imminent; an attempt to commit a battery.

rape Sexual intercourse with a person by force or by putting the victim in fear or in circumstances in which he or she is unable to control his or her conduct or to resist.

statutory rape Sexual intercourse with a female under the age of consent, with or without her consent.

incapable of consenting due to mental or emotional disability is also rape.

Kidnapping and False Imprisonment

In recent years, the crime of **kidnapping** has received much publicity. Whether the kidnapper is a stranger or a noncustodial parent, kidnapping and false imprisonment are recognized as crimes in every state in the country.

Kidnapping

Kidnapping is a felony that carries a harsh penalty in most states. Additionally, if the kidnapping takes the victim across state lines, the crime is a violation of the Federal Kidnapping Act.[7] The federal government, usually the Federal Bureau of Investigation, may become involved in any kidnapping 24 hours after the victim has been seized, by the virtue of the Federal Kidnapping Act, which creates a presumption that the victim has been transported across state lines after that period of time. The elements of kidnapping are (1) the unlawful (2) taking and confinement and (3) asportation of (4) another person (5) by the use of force, threat, fraud, or deception. *Asportation* refers to movement of the victim.

Parental Kidnapping In recent years, "childnapping," or kidnapping of one's own child in violation of a custody order, has received much public attention. Because of the rise in the number of such acts, new statutes specifically aimed at parental kidnapping have been adopted. The federal government entered this arena in 1980 by enacting the Parental Kidnapping Prevention Act, which requires that all states respect child custody orders of other states.[8] Kidnapping of one's own child is normally punished less severely than other kidnapping.

False Imprisonment

The crime of **false imprisonment** is similar to kidnapping, and, in fact, all kidnappings involve a false imprisonment. The opposite is not true—not all false imprisonments are kidnappings. A false imprisonment occurs when (1) one person (2) interferes (3) with another's liberty (4) by use of threat or force (5) without authority. The primary distinction between the two crimes is the absence of asportation as an element of false imprisonment.

Today, some states have one statute that encompasses both false imprisonment and kidnapping. Such statutes are drafted so that the crime is graded, often elevating the crime if the motive is ransom, rape, serious bodily injury, or murder.

Crimes Against Property and Habitation

Arson, burglary, and the many forms of theft are all considered to be crimes against property. A special classification of crimes against habitation also exists in many states. Special crimes against habitation developed because the common law sought to protect the important sanctuary of a person's home.

Arson

Arson is both a crime against property, and a crime against habitation. In the common law, arson was defined very narrowly as the (1) malicious (2) burning of a (3) dwelling house of (4) another. Today, the definition of arson has been broadened

---

BALLENTINESBALLENTINESBALLENTINESBALLENTINESBALLENTINESBALLENTINESBALLENTINESBALLENTINESBALLENTINESBALLENTINESBALLENTINESBALLENTINESBALLENTINESBALLENTINES

kidnapping   The crime of taking and detaining a person against his or her will by force, intimidation, or fraud.

false imprisonment   The unlawful restraint by one person of the physical liberty of another.

arson   The willful and malicious burning of a building. In some jurisdictions, arson includes the deliberate burning of any structure.

by statute in most, if not all, states. It is now common to prosecute an owner of property for burning his or her own building, if the purpose was to defraud an insurer or to cause another injury. Also, the structure burned usually need not be a dwelling, although most statutes aggravate the crime if a dwelling is burned. The common law did not recognize explosions as a burning, but the Model Penal Code and most statutes now do. The mens rea for arson under the Model Penal Code is purposeful and reckless.

Arson is often graded. The burning of a dwelling is usually the highest form of the crime. The burning of uninhabited structures is usually the next highest form of arson; the burning of personal property, if treated as arson, is the lowest.

Burglary

The (1) breaking and entering (2) of another's dwelling (3) at night (4) for the purpose of committing a felony once inside, was **burglary** under the common law. A burglary, or entry of a dwelling, may be for the purpose of theft, rape, murder, or another felony. For that reason, burglary is a crime against habitation as well as against property and person.

Modern statutes have eliminated the breaking requirement, although most still require some form of "unlawful entry." Because trespasses, frauds, and breakings are unlawful, they all satisfy modern statutory requirements.

No jurisdiction continues to require that the structure entered be a dwelling. Most statutes now refer to all buildings or other structures.[9]

The third requirement under common law—that the burglary occur at night—is no longer an element of burglary. However, many states do aggravate the crime if it happened at night.

The fourth element, which required that the person entering have as a purpose the commission of a felony once inside, is the mens rea of the crime. Some statutes now provide that intent to commit any crime, whether misdemeanor or felony, is sufficient. However, many continue to require an intent to commit either a felony or any theft.

Most jurisdictions have changed the definition of burglary in such a way that the following elements are common: (1) an unlawful entry (2) of any structure or building (3) for the purpose of committing a felony or stealing from the premises (4) once inside. In cases where the acts of breaking and entering with an intent to commit a burglary are not completed, juries are permitted to infer intent from the actions of the defendant. A jury did just that in the *Lockett* case.

Theft Crimes

There are many types of theft. Some thefts are more violative of the person, such as robbery. Others are more violative of a trust relationship, such as an attorney absconding with a client's money. At common law, the theft crimes of larceny, embezzlement, receiving stolen property, robbery, false pretenses, and extortion were recognized.

Larceny involves the (1) trespassory taking (2) and carrying away (asportation) (3) of personal property (4) of another (5) with an intent to permanently deprive the owner of possession.

The elements of **false pretenses** are (1) a false representation of (2) a material present or past fact (3) made with knowledge that the fact is false (4) and with an intent to defraud the victim

BALLENTINESBALLENTINESBALLENTINESBALLENTINESBALLENTINESBALLENTINESBALLENTINESBALLENTINESBALLENTINESBALLENTINESBALLENTINESBALLENTINESBALLENTINES

burglary At common law, the offense of breaking and entering a dwelling at night with the intent to commit a felony. The crime of burglary has been broadened by statute to include entering buildings other than dwellings, with or without a breaking, and regardless of the time of day or night.

larceny The crime of taking personal property, without consent, with the intent to convert it to the use of someone other than the owner or to deprive the owner of it permanently. Larceny does not involve the use of force or the threat of force.

false pretenses The crime of obtaining the money or property of another by fraudulent misrepresentation. The essential elements of the offense are an intentional false statement concerning a material fact, in reliance on which title or possession is surrendered.

THE STATE OF ILLINOIS
V.
GERRY LOCKETT
196 Ill. App. 3d 981, 554 N.E.2d 566 (1990)

Justice O'CONNOR delivered the opinion of the court:

Gerry Lockett was charged with residential burglary (Ill. Rev. Stat. 1985, ch. 38, par. 19-3), convicted after a jury trial, and sentenced to 8 years imprisonment … .

At about 3:00 A.M. on November 27, 1987, Allan Cannon entered his apartment, which he shared with his sister, at 1057 West Berwyn in Chicago. Cannon noticed a broken window in his sister's bedroom. He then saw a man, whom he did not know, standing about six feet away from him in the apartment hallway. The only light came from the bathroom off the hallway. The man said to Cannon, "I know your sister." Cannon fled the apartment to call the police from the nearby El station. Outside his apartment, Cannon saw the man running down an alley. Cannon described the man to police as a dark black man with curly hair, about 5'5", weighing about 200 pounds.

Cannon returned to his apartment and noticed that his bicycle had been placed on his bed, and that his sister's baby clothes, which had been packed in bags, had been thrown all over. Although the apartment was in a general state of disarray, which Cannon admitted was not uncommon, nothing had been taken … .

Lockett also argues, without merit, that the evidence could not support an inference of his intent to commit a theft. But when Cannon entered his apartment, he found a broken window and later noticed a rock and broken glass on the floor, indicating that the window had been broken from outside. Cannon also discovered contents of the apartment had been rearranged and thrown about. Even assuming that Lockett was, as he said, an acquaintance of Cannon's sister, and that the Cannons, as defense counsel implied, were less than diligent housekeepers, Lockett's presence, without permission, in the dark, empty apartment, at 3:00 A.M., supported the jury's inference of intent to commit a theft.

---

(5) thereby causing the victim to pass title to property to the actor. Crimes involving fraudulent checks, **mail fraud,** and **forgery** are all closely related to false pretenses.

Embezzlement involves the (1) **conversion** (2) of personal property (3) of another (4) by one who has acquired lawful possession (5) with an intent to defraud the owner.

Not only is it a crime to steal another's property, but it is also a crime to receive property that one knows is stolen, if the intent is to keep that property. The elements of **receiving stolen property** are (1) receiving property (2) that has been stolen (3) with knowledge of its stolen character (4) with an intent to deprive the owner of the property.

Robbery is (1) a trespassory taking (2) and carrying away (asportation) (3) of personal property (4) from another's person or presence (5) using either force or threat (6) with an intent to steal the property. Robbery is actually a type of assault mixed with a type of larceny. Because of the

BALLENTINESBALLENTINESBALLENTINESBALLENTINESBALLENTINESBALLENTINESBALLENTINESBALLENTINESBALLENTINESBALLENTINESBALLENTINESBALLENTINESBALLENTINESBALLENTINES

mail fraud   The use of the mails to perpetrate a fraud.

forgery   The false making, material alteration, or uttering, with intent to defraud or injure, of any writing which, if genuine, might appear to be legally effective or the basis for legal liability.

embezzlement   The fraudulent conversion of property, including but not limited to money, with which a person has been entrusted.

conversion   Control over another person's personal property which is wrongfully exercised; control applied in a manner that violates that person's title to or rights in the property.

receiving stolen property   Receiving property with the knowledge that it is stolen property, and with fraudulent intent.

robbery   The felonious taking of money or any thing of value from the person of another, or from his or her presence, against his or her will, by force or by putting him or her in fear.

immediate danger created by the crime of robbery, it is punished more severely than either larceny or simple assault.

Extortion, more commonly known as *blackmail,* is similar to robbery because they both involve stealing money under threat. However, the threat in a robbery must be of immediate harm, whereas extortion involves a threat of future harm. The elements of extortion are (1) the taking or acquisition of property (2) of another (3) using a threat (4) with an intent to steal the property.

Consolidated Theft Statutes

The distinctions among common-law theft crimes are often hard to draw. This fact, coupled with the belief that there is no substantive difference between stealing by fraud or by quick use of the hands, has led many jurisdictions to do away with the common-law crimes and replace them with a single crime named *theft.* The Model Penal Code contains a comprehensive consolidation of theft offenses. Provided that a defendant is not prejudiced by doing so, the specification of one theft crime by the prosecution does not prohibit conviction for another. For example, if a defendant is specifically charged with larceny, he or she may be convicted of false pretenses or embezzlement by a jury. The Code recognizes the following forms of theft:

1. Theft by taking (includes common-law larceny and embezzlement)
2. Theft by deception (includes common-law false pretenses)
3. Theft by extortion
4. Theft of property known to be mislaid, misdelivered, or lost, if no reasonable attempt to find the rightful owner is made
5. Receiving stolen property
6. Theft of professional services by deception or threat
7. Conversion of entrusted funds
8. Unauthorized use of another's automobile

Destruction of Property

Destruction of property, commonly called **criminal mischief**, is normally a specific-intent crime which includes all types of destruction affecting the value or dignity of the property. Mischief is often graded so that offenses against public property, which result in damage in excess of a stated dollar amount, or which involve a danger to human life, are penalized more heavily than others. The most serious mischiefs are usually low-grade felonies; the remainder are classed as misdemeanors.

Crimes Against the Public

Certain crimes do not have individual victims. These crimes involve the public welfare, social order, and society's morals. In one sense, the victim of these crimes is the public as a whole, although, in a sense, all crimes injure society as a whole. It is often beneficial for criminal law paralegals to be familiar with the elements of the crimes against the public in the jurisdictions in which they work.

A thorough understanding of these crimes enables criminal law paralegals to better assist the defense attorneys or the prosecutors for whom they work. Crimes against the public can be divided into three categories: crimes against public morality, crimes against the public order, and crimes against the administration of government.

extortion   The criminal offense of obtaining money or other thing of value by duress, force, threat of force, fear, or color of office.

criminal mischief (malicious mischief)   The willful destruction of the property of another.

Crimes Against Public Morality

Religion has played a strong role in determining what acts are crimes against public morality and should be illegal. Of course, religious groups do not dictate such policy—such dictation would violate the First Amendment's prohibition against mixing church and state. Religion does, however, influence the moral values of the members of a society. This is one reason that some acts, which arguably harm no one directly, are prohibited. Some of these crimes include **prostitution**, **solicitation**, *deviate sexual conduct*, **indecent exposure**, **lewdness** and **obscenity**.

Crimes Against the Public Order

Crimes against the public order involve breaches of the peace. The phrase **breaches of the peace** refers to all crimes that involve disturbing the tranquillity or order of society. All jurisdictions prohibit breaches of the peace in some form by statute. These statutory crimes include **disorderly conduct, unlawful assembly, riot,** *inciting violence*, *unlawful threat*, and **vagrancy**.

Drug and Alcohol Crimes

Crimes that involve the use or sale of narcotics and alcohol are often classified as crimes against the public because of their impact on the order of society. Alcohol-related driving accidents are the cause of many fatalities. Drug addiction often is the cause of other crimes, such as theft, assault, and prostitution. Police report that a number of domestic problems are caused by alcohol and drugs and that much of the violence directed toward law enforcement officers is drug-related. Large cities have experienced a tremendous increase in the use and sale of drugs, which has led to more assaults, batteries, and drug-related homicides. In recent years, the federal government has played a larger role in drug-related law enforcement. The national government has made money available to localities for increased drug-related law enforcement, as well as intensifying its own law enforcement efforts.

Crimes Against the Administration of Government

Some of the crimes considered "crimes against the public" bear directly upon the administration of government and justice and less upon moral determinations. **Perjury, bribery**, tax crimes, **obstruction of justice**, and **contempt** are such crimes.

BALLENTINESBALLENTINESBALLENTINESBALLENTINESBALLENTINESBALLENTINESBALLENTINESBALLENTINESBALLENTINESBALLENTINESBALLENTINESBALLENTINESBALLENTINES

prostitution   Engaging in sexual intercourse or other sexual activity for pay.

solicitation   The crime of encouraging or inciting a person to commit a crime. The act of a prostitute in seeking clients; the act of a pimp.

indecent exposure   Exposing one's private parts in a manner, and at a time and place, which is offensive to public decency.

lewdness   Gross sexual indecency.

obscenity   Printed matter, visual material, or language that is obscene.

breach of the peace   Conduct that violates the public order or disturbs the public tranquillity.

disorderly conduct   An act that breaches the peace, grossly offends public morality, or endangers public safety or public health.

unlawful assembly   The acts of three or more persons assembled together with the intention of doing violent injury to the persons or property of others.

riot   The acts of three or more persons assembled together who threaten to do injury to the persons or property of others, or who, by means of violence, actually do damage to others or their property.

vagrancy   At common law, the offense of wandering about or going from place to place with no visible means of support.

perjury   Giving false testimony in a judicial proceeding or an administrative proceeding; lying under oath as to a material fact; swearing to the truth of anything one knows or believes to be false.

bribery   The crime of giving something of value with the intention of influencing the action of a public official.

obstruction of justice   The crime of impeding or hindering the administration of justice in any way.

contempt   An act of disrespect toward a court or legislative body; deliberate disobedience of a court order.

Parties and Inchoate Offenses

Not all crimes are committed by individuals. Not all planned crimes are completed. This section examines group criminal responsibility and uncompleted crimes. Those who participate in a crime are referred to as *parties*. Uncompleted crimes are referred to as *inchoate crimes*.

Parties to Crimes

As illustrated in the following law office scenario, individuals may participate in the commission of a crime in several different capacities. At common law, there were four parties to crimes: principals in the first degree, principals in the second degree, accessories before the fact, and accessories after the fact.

A principal in the first degree is the participant who actually committed the proscribed act. For example, Adam in the law office scenario would be considered a principal in the first degree.

A principal in the second degree is a party who aids, counsels, assists, or encourages the principal in the first degree during commission of the crime. This rule requires that a party be present during a crime to be a principal in the second degree. However, constructive presence is sufficient. Whenever a party is physically absent from the location of the crime, but aids from a distance, that party is a principal in the second degree. Thus, if Bob from our hypothetical case waits in the getaway car outside the bank, then Bob is a principal in the second degree. First-degree and second-degree principals are punished equally. Principals in the second degree are also referred to as **accomplices**, as are accessories before the fact.

Anyone who aids, counsels, encourages, or assists in the preparation of a crime, but is not physically present during the crime, is an **accessory before the fact**. If Carol, an expert in bank security, assisted in planning the robbery, then Carol is an accessory before the fact. The primary distinction between a principal in the second degree and an accessory before the fact is the absence during the crime of the accessory before the fact.

The mens rea of an accomplice (before and during a crime) is usually intent (specific) in common-law terms, or knowing or purposeful in Model Penal Code language. Negligent and reckless acts do not make a person a principal in the second degree or an accessory.

Accessories after the fact continue to be treated differently. A person is an **accessory after the fact** if: (1) he or she provides aid, comfort, or shelter to a criminal (2) with the purpose of assisting the criminal in avoiding arrest or prosecution (3) after the crime is committed, and (4) the accessory was not present during commission of the crime. If Adam and Bob in our example flee to Don's house, and Don hides them from the police, Don is an accessory after the fact. It is possible to be an accessory both before and after the fact. Hence, if Carol were to hide Adam and Bob from the police, Carol would be an accessory both before and after the fact. Accessories after the fact are not punished as severely as the other three classifications of parties.

The mental state required to prove that a person was an accessory after the fact is twofold. First, it must be shown that the defendant was aware of the person's criminal status. Second, it must be proven that the defendant intended to hinder attempts to arrest or prosecute the criminal.

BALLENTINESBALLENTINESBALLENTINESBALLENTINESBALLENTINESBALLENTINESBALLENTINESBALLENTINESBALLENTINESBALLENTINESBALLENTINESBALLENTINESBALLENTINES

accomplice   A person who knowingly and voluntarily helps another person commit a crime; one who acts as an accessory.

accessory before the fact   A person who helps another person plan or commit a crime but who is not present at the scene of the crime.

accessory after the fact   A person who, after a crime has been committed, assists the person who committed it to escape arrest.

Law Office Scenario

Theresa James is a criminal law paralegal with the firm of Brooks & Fleming. She has just been handed an assignment from Mr. Brooks.

"I just spoke over the telephone with a new client," Mr. Brooks informed Theresa. "Her name is Carol Lewis. An acquaintance of Carol's, Adam Kreiger, was recently arrested for a bank robbery and has implicated Carol as being involved. According to Adam, he and Bob Brewster and Carol agreed to rob a bank. Adam entered the bank, pointed a gun at a teller, and demanded that money be placed in the bag. Bob waited in the getaway car outside the bank and drove Adam away from the scene of the crime. Adam has said that Carol was not in the bank or the getaway car, but that she is an expert in bank security and she assisted in planning the robbery.

Carol has been brought in for questioning, and she called me from the police station. She has not been charged with any crime yet.

"Theresa, please research our federal statutes regarding robbery and let me know what possible charges may be brought against Carol."

Criminal law paralegals, both those working for the defense and those working for the prosecution, should be able to identify the criminal parties to a crime by reviewing the pertinent facts to a case. They may be asked to assist attorneys by identifying the criminal liability of each party involved in the crime.

Inchoate Crimes

Not all planned crimes are completed. Because of the danger posed by substantial planning, accompanied by an intent to carry out a plan, some uncompleted crimes may be punished. By punishing inchoate acts, the deterrent purpose of the criminal justice system is furthered. If the rule were otherwise, law enforcement officials would have no incentive to intervene in a criminal enterprise before it was completed. By punishing attempt, conspiracy, and solicitation, an officer may prevent a planned criminal act from occurring without the risk of losing a criminal conviction. The purposes of **attempt** laws are to deter people from planning to commit crimes, to punish those who intended to commit a crime but were unsuccessful, and to encourage law enforcement officers to prevent unlawful activity.

Conspiracy is (1) an agreement (2) between two or more persons (3) to commit an unlawful act or a lawful act in an unlawful manner. The agreement is the actus reus of the crime and the intent to commit an unlawful act or a lawful act in an unlawful manner is the mens rea.

Solicitation is much broader than trying to engage someone in prostitution. Solicitation is the (1) encouraging, requesting, or commanding (2) of another (3) to commit a crime. Solicitation is a specific-intent crime: the person must intend to convince another to commit an offense.

BALLENTINESBALLENTINESBALLENTINESBALLENTINESBALLENTINESBALLENTINESBALLENTINESBALLENTINESBALLENTINESBALLENTINESBALLENTINESBALLENTINESBALLENTINESBALLENTINES

attempt An act done with the intent to commit a crime, which would have resulted in the crime being committed except that something happened to prevent it.

conspiracy An agreement between two or more persons to engage in a criminal act or to accomplish a legal objective by criminal or unlawful means.

solicitation The crime of encouraging or inciting a person to commit a crime.

Defenses to Criminal Accusations

Criminal defendants usually claim they are innocent of the charges raised against them. A defendant's reason for asserting that he or she is innocent is called a *defense*. Defenses can be factual ("I didn't do it!"). They can also be legal ("I did it, but the case was filed after the statute of limitation had run"). Many defenses were developed under the common law; however, many others have been created by legislation, and some defenses even originated in the constitutions of the states and federal government. The basic purpose of all defenses is to avoid liability. Some defenses are complete (perfect); that is, if the defense is successful, the defendant goes free. Other defenses are partial; the defendant avoids liability on one charge but may be convicted of a lesser offense. Some of the more commonly used types of defenses are affirmative defenses, insanity, duress and necessity, and use-of-force defenses.

Affirmative Defenses

A special class of defenses known as **affirmative defenses** go beyond simple denial; they raise special issues. Defenses that raise the question of a defendant's mental state to commit a crime (i.e., insanity and intoxication) and whether justification or excuse existed to commit the crime (i.e., self-defense) fall into the affirmative defenses class.

As a general rule, criminal defendants may sit passively during trial, as the prosecution bears the burden of proving the allegations. In all instances, burden of proof refers to two burdens, the burden of production and the burden of persuasion. Because it is not practical to require prosecutors to prove that every defendant was sane, was not intoxicated, or did not have justification to use force, the burdens for affirmative defenses are different than for other defenses. First, defendants have the duty of raising all affirmative defenses. At trial, this means that defendants must produce some evidence to support the defense. This is known as the **burden of production**. Defendants do not have to convince the factfinder that the defense is valid. They are only required to bring forth enough evidence to establish the defense.

After defendants have met the burden of production, the **burden of persuasion** must then be met. There is a split among the states: some require the defendant to carry this burden, whereas others require it of the prosecution. If the defendant has the burden, then he or she must convince the factfinder that the defense is true. Defendants must prove their defenses by a preponderance of the evidence. In jurisdictions that require prosecutors to disprove an affirmative defense, there is again a split as to the standard of proof required. Some require proof by a preponderance; others require proof beyond a reasonable doubt.

Criminal law paralegals may be asked to research local law to determine which procedure is followed in a particular jurisdiction and what defenses are considered affirmative defenses.

Insanity

Insanity is a mens rea defense. If a defendant was insane at the time of the crime, it is unlikely that the requisite mens rea existed. It is generally held that one who is insane is incapable of forming a rational purpose or intent. In fact, in

BALLENTINESBALLENTINESBALLENTINESBALLENTINESBALLENTINESBALLENTINESBALLENTINESBALLENTINESBALLENTINESBALLENTINESBALLENTINESBALLENTINESBALLENTINESBALLENTINES

affirmative defense   A defense that amounts to more than simply a denial of the allegations in the plaintiff's complaint. It sets up new matter which, if proven, could result in a judgment against the plaintiff even if all the allegations of the complaint are true.

burden of going forward (burden of production)   The duty of a party, with respect to certain issues being tried, to produce evidence sufficient to justify a verdict before the other party is obligated to produce evidence to the contrary.

burden of persuasion   The ultimate burden of proof; the responsibility of convincing the jury or, in a nonjury trial, the judge, of the truth.

most jurisdictions defendants may put on evidence to establish that insanity prevented the requisite mens rea from being formed. This is the defense of **diminished capacity**. It is a direct attack on the mens rea element of the crime, separate from the defense of insanity. If successful, the result could be conviction of a lesser, general-intent crime. In the *Oricks* case, the defendant appealed his conviction of first-degree murder, claiming, among other things, that he lacked the capacity to form the mental state that is a requisite element of first-degree murder.

CHARLES ORICKS, Appellant,
v.
STATE OF INDIANA, Appellee
Supreme Court of Indiana
July 30, 1978
377 N.E.2d 1376 (Ind. 1978)

Appellant was convicted of first degree murder, Ind. Code § 35-13-4-1 (Burns 1975) (repealed October 1, 1977). On appeal he raises five issues:

(1) sufficiency of the evidence of appellant's capacity to form the mental states comprising elements of first degree murder … .

The facts giving rise to appellant's conviction are as follows. Appellant and his wife Linda Oricks separated in early October, 1976, over differences arising from appellant's abuse of alcohol and inability to maintain employment. Appellant stayed at his grandparents' home. On the evening of October 23, 1976, Mrs. Oricks brought appellant's infant son to visit appellant, according to the informal visitation arrangements which the couple had observed during the separation. During the visit appellant and his wife argued over appellant's suggestion that they reunite. Appellant picked up a shotgun, pointed it at Mrs. Oricks' face, and pulled the trigger. When the weapon failed to fire, appellant loudly asked where the shells were. Mrs. Oricks retreated to her automobile; appellant followed her, released the air from its tires, and again threatened to shoot her. Mrs. Oricks called the sheriff from a neighbor's house, and two deputies were dispatched to take Mrs. Oricks and her child home.

The next day, Mrs. Oricks returned to appellant's grandparents' home with her mother, Mrs. Martha Collins, and one Roland Hudson, the former husband of a friend of Mrs. Oricks, to retrieve the disabled vehicle. While Mrs. Oricks and Mr. Hudson were removing their tire tools form the trunks of their cars, appellant appeared on the porch with the shotgun and fired at them. Mrs. Oricks was struck and wounded by one of the first shots; Mrs. Collins was shot and killed as she tried to aid her daughter. A neighbor saw appellant reload the shotgun, walk down to Mrs. Collins and his wife as they lay on the ground, and fire it at one of the women at close range. Eight to ten shots were fired altogether, from a six-shot shotgun. After the shooting appellant walked by Mrs. Oricks and told her that she "deserved what she got." Mrs. Collins death resulted from a severe wound of the head caused by a shotgun blast.

I.

Appellant challenges the sufficiency of the evidence of premeditation and of "specific intent to kill." These mental states which appellant contends he could not form are two attributes of the element of the offense of first degree murder denominated "premeditated malice," which is often defined as follows:

"In order that there may be such premeditated malice as will make a killing murder in the first degree, the thought of taking life must have been consciously conceived in the mind, the conception must have been meditated upon, and a deliberate determination formed to do the act. Where the homicide has been preceded by a concurrence of will, with an intention to kill, and these are followed by deliberate thought or premeditation, although they follow as instantaneous as successive thoughts can follow each other, the perpetrator may be guilty of murder of the first degree." …

At trial appellant presented evidence that at the time of the slaying he was drunk, in a state of emotional anguish, an alcoholic, incapable of exercising control over his impulses and unable to form the intent to commit murder or to premeditate on that intent. The purpose of presenting this evidence was to persuade the jury that he had not, in fact, at the time of the slaying, entertained a purpose and an intention to shoot and kill Mrs. Collins or a premeditated malice, and should therefore be found not guilty as charged.

The jury nevertheless returned a verdict of guilty. In the appeal before us, appellant has drawn our attention to this same body of evidence. The manifest purpose of doing so is to support his appellate claim that his conviction should be reversed on insufficiency grounds. We cannot set aside a jury verdict because of the presence of such exculpatory evidence, but only upon the absence of substantial evidence of probative value upon one or more of the essential elements. ... Having considered the evidence supporting the verdict, including appellant's actions and verbal conduct leading up to and at the time of the shooting, and immediately thereafter while in custody of the police,

we are led to the conclusion that the jury was warranted in inferring beyond a reasonable doubt that appellant did, on the occasion of the offenses charged, in fact hold in his mind the purpose and intent to shoot and kill Mrs. Collins and did premeditate upon such thought. The strong and persuasive evidence so formidably arrayed before the jury by the defense that appellant could not and did not form these requisite mental status was for the jury to consider, and it was within the province of that body to interpret it and assess its weight in its decision making process.

Three tests are used to determine sanity in the criminal law context: *M'Naghten*; irresistible impulse; and the Model Penal Code. Each jurisdiction is free to use whichever test it wishes to determine insanity.

M'Naghten

In 1843, Daniel M'Naghten was tried for killing the British prime minister's secretary. M'Naghten was laboring under the paranoid delusion that the prime minister was planning to kill him, and he killed the minister's secretary, believing him to be the prime minister. The jury found M'Naghten not guilty by reason of insanity.[10] The decision created controversy, and the House of Lords asked the justice of the Queens Bench to specify the standard for acquittal on the grounds of insanity.[11] Those standards, which were attached to the decision, came to be known as the **M'Naghten test**:

1. At the time that the act was committed

2. the defendant was suffering from a defect of reason, from a disease of the mind, which caused

3. the defendant to not know
   a. the nature and quality of the act taken or
   b. that the act was wrong.

Irresistible Impulse

Under the *M'Naghten* test, a defendant who knew that his or her actions were wrong, but could not control his or her behavior because of a disease of the mind, is not insane. This conclusion has led a few jurisdictions, which basically follow *M'Naghten*, to supplement the rule. These states add that a defendant is not guilty by reason of insanity if a disease of the mind caused the defendant to be unable to control his or her behavior. This determination holds even if the defendant understood the nature and quality of the act or

BALLENTINESBALLENTINESBALLENTINESBALLENTINESBALLENTINESBALLENTINESBALLENTINESBALLENTINESBALLENTINESBALLENTINESBALLENTINESBALLENTINESBALLENTINES

diminished capacity The rule that a criminal defendant, although not sufficiently mentally impaired to be entitled to a defense of insanity, may have been so reduced in mental capacity ... that he or she was incapable of forming the mental state necessary, in law, for the commission of certain crimes.

M'Naghten rule A test employed in a number of jurisdictions for determining whether a criminal defendant had the capacity to form criminal intent at the time he or she committed the crime of which he or she is accused. Specifically, the M'Naghten rule is that an accused is not criminally responsible if he or she was laboring under such a defect of reason from disease of the mind that he or she either did not know the nature of his or her act or, if he or she did, that he or she did not know it was wrong.

knew that the behavior was wrong. This is known as **irresistible impulse**.

The Model Penal Code Test

The Model Penal Code contains a definition of insanity similar to, but broader than, the *M'Naghten* and irresistible impulse tests. This test, also referred to as the *substantial capacity test,* reads:[12]

> A person is not responsible for criminal conduct if at the time of such conduct as a result of mental disease or defect he lacks substantial capacity either to appreciate the criminality [wrongfulness] of his conduct or to conform his conduct to the requirements of law.

The Model Penal Code test has been adopted by a few jurisdictions. The federal courts used the test until Congress enacted a statute that established a test similar to the *M'Naghten* test. That statute places the burden of proving insanity, by clear and convincing evidence, on the defendant.

Disposition of the Criminally Insane

Contrary to popular belief, those adjudged insane by a criminal proceeding are not immediately and automatically released. In most jurisdictions, after a defendant has been determined "not guilty by reason of insanity," the court (the jury in a few states) must then make a determination of whether the person continues to be dangerous. If so, commitment to a mental institution is to be ordered. If the defendant is determined not to be dangerous, then release follows.

Insanity at the Time of Trial

The United States Supreme Court has held that a defendant who is insane at the time of trial may not be tried.[13] The Court found that the due process clauses of the Fifth and Fourteenth Amendments require that a defendant be able to assist in his or her defense and understand the proceeding against him or her. The test for determining insanity in this context is different from that previously discussed. Insanity exists when a defendant lacks the capacity to understand the proceedings or assist in defense. This simply means that defendants must be rational, possess the ability to testify coherently, and be able to meaningfully discuss their cases with their lawyers.

If defendants are unable to stand trial because they are insane, they are usually committed until they are competent. Many statutes have mandatory commitment of defendants determined incompetent to stand trial. However, indefinite confinement based solely upon a finding of incompetence to stand trial is unconstitutional.

Last, the Supreme Court has held that a person who has become insane after being sentenced to death may not be executed until his or her sanity is regained.[14] The constitutional basis of the Court's decision was the Eighth Amendment's prohibition of cruel and unusual punishment. Justice Marshall stated that "It is no less abhorrent today than it has been for centuries to exact in penance the life of one whose mental illness prevents him from comprehending the reasons for the penalty or its implications."[15]

Duress and Necessity

Consider these facts: Terry Teller is ordered by a bank robber, who is brandishing a gun, to place the money in her drawer in a bag and give it to the bank robber, or "she will be planted six feet under." Has Terry committed theft? Although the elements of theft may be satisfied, Terry may assert the defense of **duress**. To prove duress, one must show (1) that he or she was threatened (2) and that the threat caused a reasonable belief

irresistible impulse An impulse to commit an act that one is powerless to control. ... [T]he test used in some jurisdictions to determine insanity for purposes of a criminal defense.

duress Coercion applied for the purpose of compelling a person to do, or to refrain from doing, some act. ... Duress may be a defense to a criminal prosecution if the defendant committed the crime out of a well-grounded fear of death or serious bodily harm.

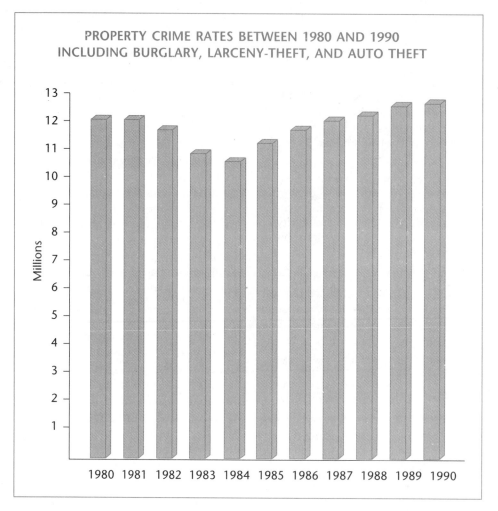

Property Crime Rates (1980–1990) Property crime includes burglary, larceny-theft, and auto theft. Since 1984, there has been an upward growth rate.

(3) that the only way of avoiding serious personal injury or death to himself, herself, or another (4) was to commit the crime. Duress was recognized at common law and continues to be a statutory defense today.

Necessity is similar to duress. However, whereas duress is created by human pressures, necessity comes about by natural forces. When a person is confronted with two choices, both causing harm, he or she is to choose the lesser harm. After making that choice, the actor may assert the defense of necessity to the act. For example, a person may be justified in breaking into a cabin to avoid freezing to death. A captain of a ship may be justified in a trespassory use of another's dock if setting ashore is necessary to save the ship and its passengers.

BALLENTINESBALLENTINESBALLENTINESBALLENTINESBALLENTINESBALLENTINESBALLENTINESBALLENTINESBALLENTINESBALLENTINESBALLENTINESBALLENTINESBALLENTINES

necessity That which is necessary; that which must be done. … Necessity is a defense in a criminal prosecution if the defendant committed the crime to prevent a more serious harm from occurring.

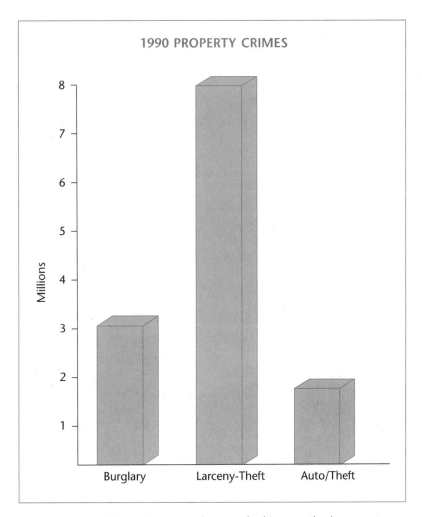

1990 Property Crimes Larceny, the act of taking another's property without consent, accounted for nearly eight million property crimes in 1990.

Duress and necessity are complete defenses. When valid, they result in acquittal on all related charges.

Use-of-Force Defenses

In some situations, the law permits actors to use physical force against others. Self-defense, defense of others, defense of property, and the use of force to make arrests fall into this class. Self-defense, defense of others, and defense of property, when successful, are complete defenses.

Self-Defense

To prove **self-defense** it must be shown that the actor (1) was confronted with an unprovoked, (2) immediate threat of bodily harm; (3) that force was

BALLENTINESBALLENTINESBALLENTINESBALLENTINESBALLENTINESBALLENTINESBALLENTINESBALLENTINESBALLENTINESBALLENTINESBALLENTINESBALLENTINESBALLENTINESBALLENTINESBALLENTINES

self-defense The use of force to protect oneself from death or imminent bodily harm at the hands of an aggressor. A person may only use that amount of force reasonably necessary to protect … against the peril with which he or she is threatened.

necessary to avoid the harm; (4) and that the amount of force used was reasonable. The most important point is that the force used to defend oneself be reasonable. It would be unreasonable to stab a person who is attempting to slap one's hand. Deadly force may be used to defend against an attack that threatens serious bodily injury or death, but not against other attacks.

Defense of Others

It is also a justified use of force to defend another. The rules are similar to that of self-defense: there must be a threat of immediate danger to the other person; the perception of threat must be reasonable; the amount of force used must be reasonable; and deadly force may be used only to repel a deadly attack.

Defense of Property and Habitation

At common law and by modern legislative enactment, one may use force to defend property. As with defending oneself, only reasonable force may be used. Because property is not as valuable as life, deadly force may not be used to protect property. Thus, one must allow another to take or destroy property before killing to defend it. No force is reasonable if other methods of protecting the property were available.

The basic rules concerning defense of property also apply to defense of habitation: one must have a reasonable belief that the property is threatened; only reasonable force may be used to protect the property; and other nonviolent remedies must be utilized before resorting to force. One difference between defending dwellings and defending other property is that deadly force may be used, under some circumstances, to protect one's home.

The Model Penal Code allows the use of deadly force if either (1) the intruder is attempting to take the dwelling (with no legal claim to do so) or (2) the intruder is there to commit a crime (arson, burglary, theft) and has threatened deadly force or poses a substantial risk to those inside.[16]

Some people choose to protect their property with manmade devices, such as electric fences and spring guns. Others have used natural protection, such as dogs and snakes. Regardless of which is used, the rules are the same. If the device employs nondeadly force, it is likely to be lawful. An electric fence that does not have sufficient electric current to kill is a justified use of force.

Infancy

At common law, it was a complete defense to any charge that the accused was a child under the age of seven at the time the crime was committed. It was irrebuttably presumed that children under seven were incapable of forming the requisite mens rea to commit a crime. A rebuttable presumption of incapacity existed for those between 7 and 14 years of age. The presumption could be overcome for those between 7 and 14 if the prosecution could prove that the defendant understood that the criminal act was wrong.

Few minors are charged with crimes today, because of the advent of juvenile court systems in the United States. Currently, all states have a juvenile court system that deals with juvenile delinquency and neglected children. Some states, however, allow certain minors to be charged and tried as adults in some circumstances. The criminal law paralegal may have to research state law in these situations, whether to assert or rebut the defense of infancy.

Intoxication

In this context, **intoxication** refers to all situations in which a person's mental or physical abilities are impaired by drugs or alcohol. It is generally said that voluntary intoxication is a defense if it has the effect of negating the required mens rea.

intoxication   A disturbance of mental or physical capacities resulting from the use of alcohol, drugs, or other substances; a substance-induced impairment of a person's judgment or sense of responsibility.

ELEMENTS OF COMMON-LAW THEFT CRIMES

Crime	Elements
Larceny	1. The trespassory taking 2. and carrying away 3. of personal property 4. of another 5. with an intent to permanently deprive the owner of possession
Embezzlement	1. Conversion 2. of personal property 3. of another 4. by one who has acquired lawful possession 5. with intent to defraud the owner
False Pretenses	1. False representation of 2. a material present or past fact 3. made with knowledge that the representation is false 4. and with an intent to defraud the victim 5. thereby causing the victim to pass title to property to the actor
Receiving Stolen Property	1. Receiving property 2. that has been stolen 3. with knowledge of its stolen character 4. with an intent to deprive the owner of the property
Robbery	1. A trespassory taking 2. and carrying away 3. of personal property 4. from another's person or presence 5. using either force or threat 6. with an intent to steal the property
Extortion	1. The taking or acquisition of property 2. of another 3. using a threat 4. with an intent to steal the property

For the defendant to be found guilty of these theft crimes, the prosecution must prove that the defendant acted with intent.

In common-law language, if intoxication prevents a defendant from being able to form a specific intent, then the crime is reduced to a similar general-intent crime. For the crime of murder, intoxication is a defense if it prevented the defendant from forming the premeditation, deliberation, or purposefulness element. In such cases the charge is reduced from first-degree to second-degree murder. Not all states recognize voluntary intoxication as a defense.

Mistake

People may be mistaken in two ways. First, one may believe that some act is legal when it is not. This is a *mistake of law*. Second, one may not understand all the facts of a given situation. This is a *mistake of fact*. As a general proposition, mistake of fact is a defense and mistake of law is not. However, many exceptions to each rule have been developed.

For the most part, unawareness that an act is illegal is not a defense. The law presumes that everyone knows what is legal and what is not. Mistakes that fall into the second group act to negate mens rea and are more likely to be successful. For example, when an officer believes that he or she has the authority to take a person into custody, and makes the arrest in good faith, but without probable cause, the officer is not guilty of kidnapping or criminal confinement.

Entrapment

To what extent should police officers be permitted to encourage others to commit a crime? This question underlies the defense of **entrapment**. Entrapment occurs when law enforcement officers encourage a person to commit a crime, intending to arrest and prosecute that person for commission of that crime.

The Model Penal Code adopted an objective method of determining whether a person was entrapped. The objective approach does not focus on the particular defendant's predisposition, but asks whether the police conduct creates a "substantial risk that an offense will be committed by persons other than those who are ready to commit it."17

In many states, entrapment may not be used to defend against crimes involving violence to the person, such as battery and murder. The Model Penal Code also takes this view.

Alibi and Consent

Alibi and consent are two factual defenses. An **alibi** is a claim by a defendant that he or she was not present at the scene of the crime at the time it was committed. Whenever a defendant asserts an alibi, he or she is simply refuting the government's claim of facts. Defendants are usually required to give the government notice that an alibi is claimed prior to trial. Of course, the government must prove the elements of the crime (i.e., presence at the crime) beyond a reasonable doubt. This means that the defendant bears no burden in an alibi defense.

Victim consent is a defense to some crimes, such as rape or larceny. That is, if a person consents to sex or to give away property, there is no crime. Consent is, however, not a defense to many crimes, such as statutory rape, incest, child molestation, battery, and murder.

Statutes of Limitation

Many crimes must be prosecuted within a specified time after being committed. A **statute of limitation** sets the time limit. If prosecution is initiated after the applicable statute has expired, the defendant is entitled to a dismissal.

Statutes vary in length, and high crimes such as murder have no limitation. Generally, the more serious the crime, the longer the statute. Statutes begin running when the crime occurs; however, statutes may be tolled in some situations. **Tolling** refers to stopping the clock. The time during which a defendant is a fugitive is commonly tolled.

BALLENTINESBALLENTINESBALLENTINESBALLENTINESBALLENTINESBALLENTINESBALLENTINESBALLENTINESBALLENTINESBALLENTINESBALLENTINESBALLENTINESBALLENTINES

entrapment   Inducing a person to commit a crime he or she is otherwise not inclined to commit, in order to bring a criminal prosecution against him or her.

alibi   The defense that the accused was elsewhere at the time the crime was committed.

statutes of limitations   Federal and state statutes prescribing the maximum period of time during which various types of civil actions and criminal prosecutions can be brought after the occurrence of the injury or the offense.

tolling the statute   A term referring to circumstances that, by operation of law, suspend or interrupt the running of the statute of limitations.

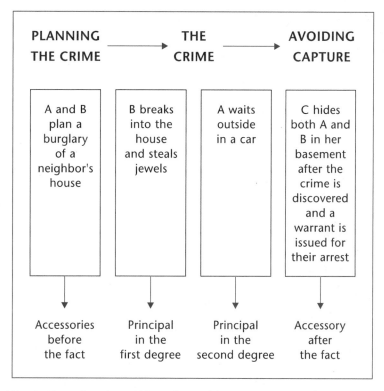

PLANNING THE CRIME	THE CRIME		AVOIDING CAPTURE
A and B plan a burglary of a neighbor's house	B breaks into the house and steals jewels	A waits outside in a car	C hides both A and B in her basement after the crime is discovered and a warrant is issued for their arrest
Accessories before the fact	Principal in the first degree	Principal in the second degree	Accessory after the fact

Parties to a Burglary When determining accessories and principals to burglary, it is important to know which stage of the crime they participated in and their role in execution of the crime.

Constitutional Defenses

A variety of defenses arise from the first nine amendments to the United States Constitution. A few constitutional defenses, such as the protection of expression by the First Amendment, should already be familiar to you. In addition, many procedural rights, such as the right to a speedy trial, are granted by the Constitution. Bear in mind that each state has its own constitution, which may provide greater protection than the United States Constitution.

The Fifth Amendment to the United States Constitution provides that "no person shall be subject for the same offense to be twice put in jeopardy of life or limb." This is the **double jeopardy** clause and it applies only to criminal proceedings. There are actually two prohibitions in the double jeopardy clause. It prevents (1) a second prosecution for the same offense and (2) a second punishment for the same offense.

The Fifth Amendment also states that no person "shall be compelled in any criminal case to be a witness against himself." This mandate against self-incrimination applies to all proceedings, whether civil or criminal.

The First Amendment contains a large number of protections, including freedom of the press; choice and practice of religion; freedom of speech; and freedom to peaceably assemble. Although the First Amendment is only directly applicable against

double jeopardy   A rule originating in the Fifth Amendment that prohibits a second punishment or a second trial for the same offense.

the national government, the Fourteenth Amendment extends its protections to the states. Whenever a statute conflicts with a constitutionally protected activity, the statute may be challenged and struck down.

Criminal Procedure

The phrase *criminal procedure* describes the method of enforcing substantive criminal law. To state it another way, criminal procedure puts substantive criminal law into action.

Each state and the federal government has its own procedural rules. In some instances, the variation is significant. Many federal procedural rules can be found in the United States Code. A good number of procedures are judicially created (and approved by Congress) and are found in the Federal Rules of Criminal Procedure (Fed. R. Crim. P.). However, basic criminal procedure is founded on the United States Constitution.

The United States plays a major role in defining the rights of criminal defendants in both federal and state prosecutions. The basis for federal involvement is the United States Constitution, and two developments account for its role in state criminal law. First, the reach of the Constitution has been extended to the states through what is known as incorporation.Second, the rights found in the **Bill of Rights** have been significantly expanded.

Incorporation

Prior to adoption of the Fourteenth Amendment, the Bill of Rights guarantees were interpreted by the Supreme Court as only restricting the power of the national government, which meant that rights such as the right to counsel or the right to be free from unreasonable searches and seizures were guaranteed only to defendants who were prosecuted in federal court. If a state did not have a constitutional or statutory provision granting the right, then the defendant was not entitled to that protection when prosecuted in state court.

In 1868, the Fourteenth Amendment to the United States Constitution was adopted. One goal of the Fourteenth Amendment was to extend constitutional protections to the states. Section One of that amendment reads:

> All persons born or naturalized in the United States, and subject to the jurisdiction thereof, are citizens of the United States and the State wherein they reside. No State shall make or enforce any law which shall abridge the privileges or immunities of citizens of the United States; nor shall any State deprive any person of life, liberty, or property, without due process of law; nor deny to any person within its jurisdiction the equal protection of the laws.

The language of the Fourteenth Amendment is similar to that found in the Fifth Amendment, insofar as they both contain a due process clause. It is through the due process and equal protection clauses that the powers of the states are limited. However, what is meant by *due process* has been the subject of great debate among jurists.

In the 1960s the Supreme Court adopted the selective incorporation doctrine. A right is incorporated under this doctrine if it is (1) a fundamental right and (2) essential to the concept of ordered liberty. Nearly the entire Bill of Rights has been incorporated under this doctrine, except the right to grand jury indictment and the requirement of a 12-person jury.[18] Currently, there is some debate concerning the right to be free from excessive bail. Once incorporated, a right applies against the states to the extent and in the same manner as it does against the United States.

BALLENTINESBALLENTINESBALLENTINESBALLENTINESBALLENTINESBALLENTINESBALLENTINESBALLENTINESBALLENTINESBALLENTINESBALLENTINESBALLENTINESBALLENTINESBALLENTINES

Bill of Rights   The first 10 amendments to the United States Constitution. The ... portion of the Constitution that sets forth the rights which are the fundamental principles of the United States and the foundation of American citizenship.

Expansion of Rights

Another major development in the area of constitutional criminal procedure has been the expansion of many rights. The language of the Constitution is concise. It refers to "unreasonable searches and seizures," "due process," "equal protection," "speedy and public trial," and the like. No further definition or explanation of the meaning of these provisions is provided. The process of determining the meaning of such phrases is known as *constitutional interpretation*. It is possible to make each right ineffective by reading it narrowly. The opposite is also true.

During the 1960s, many rights found in the Bill of Rights were expanded by court decisions. *Expansion* refers to extending a right beyond its most narrow reading. The effect of expansive interpretation is to increase the defendant's rights. An example of an expansive interpretation is the *Miranda v. Arizona*[19] decision, in which the Court determined that every person is entitled to be informed of his or her rights prior to questioning

by a law enforcement official. Although the language of the Fifth Amendment does not explicitly state that a defendant must be advised of the right to remain silent, to have the assistance of counsel, and so on, the Court now requires that such admonishments be given because of its expanded interpretation of the Fifth Amendment.

Exclusionary Rule

Another important constitutional development is the **exclusionary rule**. The rule is simple: Evidence obtained by an unconstitutional search or seizure is inadmissible at trial. The rule was first announced by the Supreme Court in 1914[20]; however, at that time, the rule had not been incorporated. Therefore, the exclusionary rule did not apply to state court proceedings. This status was changed in 1961, when the Supreme Court declared that evidence obtained in violation of the Constitution could not be used in state or federal criminal proceedings.[21]

Searches, Seizures, Arrests, and Interrogations

Searches, seizures, and arrests are vital aspects of law enforcement. Because they involve significant invasions of individual liberties, limits on their use are included in the constitutions, statutes, and other laws of the state and federal governments. The most important limitation on searches, seizures, and arrests is the Fourth Amendment to the United States Constitution, which reads:

> The right of the people to be secure in their persons, papers and effects, against unreasonable searches and seizures, shall not be violated, and no warrants shall issue but upon probable cause, supported by oath or affirmation, and particularly describing the place to be searched and the persons or things to be seized.

Two remedies are available to the defendant whose Fourth Amendment rights have been violated by the government. First, in a criminal prosecution he or she may invoke the exclusionary rule. Second, he or she may have a civil cause of action against the offending officer under a civil rights statute or for a "constitutional tort."[22]

Searches and Seizures

Law enforcement personnel must execute searches and seizures with the utmost care and respect for the defendant's rights. Evidence obtained through unlawful searches may not be admitted in court.

BALLENTINESBALLENTINESBALLENTINESBALLENTINESBALLENTINESBALLENTINESBALLENTINESBALLENTINESBALLENTINESBALLENTINESBALLENTINESBALLENTINESBALLENTINES

exclusionary rule   The rule of constitutional law that evidence secured by the police by means of an unreasonable search and seizure, in violation of the Fourth Amendment, cannot be used as evidence in a criminal prosecution.

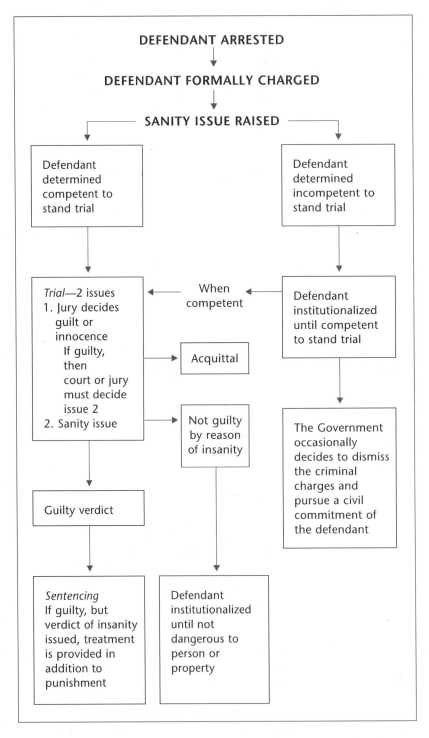

Insanity and Criminal Procedure The insanity defense is an affirmative defense, which means the defendant bears the burden of proof at trial.

Obtaining Warrants

Depending on the circumstances, a search may be conducted with or without a warrant. The Supreme Court has expressed a strong preference for the use of warrants, when possible, over warrantless actions.[23] The warrant preference serves an important purpose: it protects citizens from overzealous law enforcement practices.

A search conducted pursuant to a valid search warrant is reasonable per se. Warrantless searches are permitted only in special circumstances, and it is the responsibility of the government to prove that the facts of the case fit into one of the exceptions to the warrant requirement. The Fourth Amendment enumerates the requirements that must be met before a warrant can be issued. It is the responsibility of the law enforcement officer requesting the warrant to establish the following elements to the satisfaction of the judge making the warrant determination:

1. The evidence presented must establish probable cause to believe that, within the area to be searched, the items sought will be found.

2. There must be probable cause to believe that the items sought are connected to criminal activity.

3. The area to be searched and any item to be seized must be described with particularity. The amount of specificity required varies from case to case. A warrant that authorizes a police officer to search a particular home for unauthorized contraband clearly violates the Fourth Amendment, whereas a warrant authorizing a search of the same home for a "nine-inch knife with an ivory handle" is valid, provided the warrant is valid in all other respects.

4. The facts that are alleged to establish probable cause must be "supported by oath or affirmation." In the typical case, the government will produce one or more affidavits to prove that a warrant is justified.

5. The warrant must be issued by a neutral and detached magistrate. Although judges are most commonly given the authority to issue warrants, a state may grant this authority to others.

Warrants may be issued to search and seize any item that constitutes evidence of a crime, is the fruit of a crime, is contraband, or is used to commit a crime.[24] A particular officer, or an entire unit of officers, may be directed by the warrant to conduct the search. The language of the warrant itself contains the duties of the officers executing the warrant, as well as their limitations.

Exceptions to the Search Warrant Requirement

The general rule is that a warrant must be obtained before a search may be undertaken, but there are many exceptions, sometimes referred to as *exigent circumstances*. Exceptions to the search warrant requirement include:

1. Voluntary consent to the search validates the search.

2. Under the **plain view doctrine**, a warrantless seizure of evidence by an officer who is lawfully in a position to see the evidence is valid.

3. A warrantless search on a motor vehicle stopped on a public road is reasonable, provided that the officer had probable cause to believe that an object subject to seizure would be found in the vehicle.

4. An inventory search may be conducted of impounded vehicles whenever the driver or owner is arrested.

5. Searches at the border of the United States do not require probable cause or a warrant.

BALLENTINESBALLENTINESBALLENTINESBALLENTINESBALLENTINESBALLENTINESBALLENTINESBALLENTINESBALLENTINESBALLENTINESBALLENTINESBALLENTINESBALLENTINESBALLENTINES

plain view doctrine   An exception to the search warrant requirement of the Fourth Amendment, which allows warrantless seizure of evidence observed in "plain view" by an officer from a place where he or she has a legal right to be.

6. A defendant's person may be fully searched, without first obtaining a warrant, after a lawful arrest.

7. A warrantless search and seizure may be made to preserve evidence that might be destroyed before a warrant can be obtained.

8. Police officers are permitted to enter areas protected by the Fourth Amendment without a warrant if there is an emergency or if the officers are in hot pursuit.

9. The Supreme Court has held that the "open fields" around one's home are not protected by the Fourth Amendment, so officers are free to intrude upon such areas without first obtaining a warrant.

10. Under certain circumstances, police officers have the right to stop and frisk individuals if they have probable cause to believe that the person being stopped and frisked has committed or is about to commit a crime.

Arrest

One of the most serious interferences with a person's liberty is to be physically seized by the government. Equally, arrest plays an important role in effective law enforcement. Because of the significant impact arrest has on a person's life, the right to arrest is limited by the Fourth Amendment.

Generally, an *arrest* is a deprivation of freedom by a legal authority. Seizures by the police take on two primary forms. At the lower end of the spectrum is the *Terry v. Ohio*[25] seizure, which occurs whenever a person reasonably believes that he or she is not free to leave. In addition, the seizure must be as brief as possible and of limited intrusion to the person detained. Any seizure that goes beyond the *Terry* standard is an arrest. A *Terry* investigatory detention may be transformed into an arrest if the person is detained for an unreasonable length of time, or if the police use intrusive investigatory tactics.

Searches must be conducted pursuant to a valid warrant, unless an exception to the warrant requirement can be shown. Arrests, on the other hand, are quite different. Rather than a requirement for a warrant, in most instances, there is simply a preference for one.

Despite the preference, most arrests are made without first obtaining a warrant. However, the Fourth Amendment does require that probable cause exist before an arrest can be made. For a warrantless arrest in a public place to be upheld, it must be shown that the officer who made the arrest had probable cause (1) to believe that a crime was committed and (2) that the person arrested committed the crime. As with searches and seizures, probable cause can be established in a number of ways: statements from victims and witnesses, personal knowledge and observations of the officer, reliable hearsay, and information tips. If an arrest is to be made in an area protected by the Fourth Amendment, such as a person's home, a warrant must be obtained, unless an exception exists.

As discussed previously, an officer may search an arrestee fully as an incident to arrest. In addition, the area within the arrestee's immediate control may also be searched. The scope of a search incident to arrest, however, is limited to areas where a weapon may be obtained by the person arrested. Clearly, a search of any room other than the one where a defendant is being held is not supported by the search incident to arrest doctrine.

Criminal law defense paralegals may be asked to review arrest warrants after a client has been arrested to obtain information concerning the charges brought against a client. They may also learn important facts concerning the circumstances of an arrest or seizure during client interviews.

Interrogations, Confessions, and Admissions

Questioning by police officers is a commonly used law enforcement tool. An **interrogation** occurs whenever officers question a person they suspect has committed a crime. A **confession** is a statement made by a person claiming that he or she has committed a crime. If a person asserts certain facts, which are inculpatory but do not amount to a confession, an **admission** has been made.

Interrogations, confessions, and admissions are governed by the Fifth Amendment right to be free from self-incrimination and the Sixth Amendment right to counsel.

Miranda

Not all questioning by law enforcement officers must be preceded by the Miranda warnings. A defendant must be "in custody" and "interrogated" by police before *Miranda* has effect. This is known as the *custodial interrogation requirement.*

Before a person in custody may be interrogated, the required warning must be recited to the arrestee. Specific language need not be used as long as the defendant is fully and effectively apprised of each right. The Supreme Court stated in *Miranda v. Arizona*[26] that the following rights and facts must be conveyed to the defendant:

1. The right to remain silent.
2. Any statements may be used against the defendant to gain a conviction.
3. The right to consult with a lawyer and to have a lawyer present during questioning.
4. For the indigent, the right to a lawyer who will be provided without cost.

The warnings are to be read to all persons in custody who are to be interrogated. The law does not presume that any person, including an attorney, knows his or her rights. The warnings should be presented in a timely manner and read at a speed such that the arrestee can gain a full understanding of the impact.

Any statement obtained in violation of *Miranda* is inadmissible at trial to prove guilt. Further, any other evidence that is the fruit of such a statement must also be excluded from trial. The defendant ordinarily raises the issue prior to trial through a motion to suppress.

Voluntariness Requirement

As was true under the common law, all confessions must be made voluntarily. This is required by the due process clauses of the Fifth and Fourteenth Amendments. The totality of the circumstances must be examined when making the voluntariness determination.

Police officers do not have to physically coerce a confession for it to be involuntary. Mental or emotional coercion by law enforcement officers also violates a defendant's due process rights.

Pretrial Procedures

Both paralegals who work for criminal defense attorneys and those who work for the prosecution are often very involved in assisting with the pretrial process. It is very important that they become familiar with the pretrial procedures for the states and municipalities in which they work, as well as the Federal Rules of Criminal Procedure, because procedures vary significantly from jurisdiction to jurisdiction.

Discovery and Investigation of Criminal Activity

The pretrial process begins when law enforcement learns that a crime has been committed (or is to be committed). The police may discover criminal activity themselves, or a citizen may report such activity.

BALLENTINESBALLENTINESBALLENTINESBALLENTINESBALLENTINESBALLENTINESBALLENTINESBALLENTINESBALLENTINESBALLENTINESBALLENTINESBALLENTINESBALLENTINESBALLENTINESBALLENTINES

interrogation   The questioning of a criminal suspect by the police.

confession   A voluntary admission by a person that he or she has committed a crime.

admission   1. A statement of a party to an action which is inconsistent with his claim or position in the lawsuit and which therefore constitutes proof against him. 2. A voluntary statement that something asserted to be true is true.

Once the police are aware of criminal activity, the prearrest investigation begins. There are two objectives in this stage. First, the police must determine whether a crime has been committed. Second, if a crime has been committed, the police attempt to gather sufficient evidence to charge and convict the person believed to be guilty.

Arrest

Once adequate evidence exists, an arrest is made in most cases. However, in some misdemeanor cases a defendant is asked to come to the police station, and an arrest is not made unless the defendant refuses. The arrest may be made without an arrest warrant (an order of the court) in some situations. In other situations, an **ex parte** hearing may be held to determine whether probable cause exists to believe that the person under investigation committed the crime. If so, the judge may issue an arrest warrant.

At the time of arrest, the police ordinarily search the defendant. Once at the police station, the defendant is booked. Booking consists of obtaining biographical information about the defendant (name, address, etc.), fingerprinting the defendant, and taking a photograph, commonly known as a *mug shot*. The defendant is usually permitted to make a telephone call at this stage.

The defendant is then searched and held in jail until further arrangements are made. For minor offenses, the defendant may be able to post bail prior to appearing before a judge. In such cases, defendants are out of jail within hours. All others have to wait for a judge to set a bail amount at an initial appearance. Following the example in our law office scenario, if Carol is arrested as an accessory before the fact in an armed robbery, she would probably have to await a hearing before bail was set. During and after this stage, law enforcement investigation and gathering of evidence may continue.

The Complaint

The prosecutor must then review the evidence gathered by law enforcement and decide whether to charge the person held. If the prosecutor decides affirmatively, he or she will file a complaint. The **complaint** is the first document filed with the court, and it acts as the initial charging instrument. The Federal Rules of Criminal Procedure state: "The complaint is a written statement of the essential facts constituting an offense charged. It shall be made upon oath before a magistrate." The complaint need not be written upon personal knowledge, that is, an officer may use hearsay and circumstantial evidence in a complaint. Affidavits from those who have personal knowledge, such as witnesses and victims, are often attached to the complaint.

In cases where a warrant is sought to arrest a defendant, the complaint is often produced in support of the request for a warrant. This occurs at the ex parte hearing mentioned earlier. Federal law requires that a warrant be issued if probable cause is established by the complaint and its accompanying affidavits. Upon the request of the government, a summons (an order to appear) may be issued rather than an arrest warrant.[27]

If the defendant was arrested without a warrant, the complaint serves as the charging document at the initial appearance or preliminary hearing. Paralegals for the prosecution may be asked to draft complaints, for the prosecutor's review and approval, based on the available preliminary evidence in a case.

For traffic violations and some lesser misdemeanors, the complaint acts as both a summons to appear in court and the charging document. In such cases, the defendant appears in court on only one occasion and the ticket is used in place of an information or indictment.

The Initial Appearance

After arrest, the defendant is taken "without unnecessary delay" before the nearest available federal magistrate.[28] In most cases, this means that a defendant will be brought before the judge within 24 hours. However, if a defendant is arrested on a weekend, it may be the following Monday before the defendant has the initial appearance, unless a weekend session of court is held.

The first appearance is brief. It is the duty of the presiding judge to make sure that the person arrested is the person named in the complaint. The defendant is also informed of various rights, such as the right to remain silent and the right to the assistance of counsel. If the defendant is indigent, the court will appoint counsel. Finally, a preliminary hearing date is set. If the defendant is in jail, the court determines whether he or she should be released prior to trial.

Pretrial Release and Detention

In many cases, defendants are released prior to trial. A court may order many types of releases, but the predominant methods are cash bail, surety bond, property bond, and personal recognizance.

When the court opts to set bail, a defendant who has the resources may simply pay into the court the amount of the bail and be released prior to trial.

Whenever a third party, usually a professional bondsman, agrees to pay the bond for a defendant, a surety bond is created. The common practice is for the defendant to pay the surety 10 percent or more of the bond amount in exchange for the bondsman's making the defendant's bail. The 10 percent is not refunded to the defendant after the case is concluded. It is like an insurance premium. Some sureties require security (collateral) before they will issue a bond. Defendants may pledge cars, houses, or other property to obtain release under this type of bond, known as a property bond.

For many misdemeanors and a few felonies, a defendant may be released on personal recognizance. To gain such a release, a defendant need only promise to appear.

Regardless of the method used, courts frequently impose conditions for bail upon defendants. Defendants who are arrested, caught intimidating witnesses, or found interfering with the judicial process may be jailed until trial.

Pretrial detention may not be used to punish a person. To do so violates a person's due process right to be free from punishment without a fair trial. However, a defendant may be detained if there is reason to believe that he or she will not appear for trial, or if he or she poses a threat to others.

Criminal law paralegals working for the defense often keep files on available bail bondsmen in the area in which they work. Paralegals may be called upon to assist clients with obtaining the necessary bail.

At times, the bail set for defendants may be so high that they are unable to pay for the bail bond, and may be required to remain in jail. If the defendant's attorney feels that the bail is unreasonably high and prohibitive, he or she may bring a motion to have the bail reduced. Criminal law paralegals are often responsible for drafting the documents for the motion to reduce bail (see sample Notice of Motion to Reduce the Amount of Bail).

Preliminary Hearing

The defendant's second appearance before a judge is the **preliminary hearing**. How this stage is handled by the states varies significantly. Criminal law paralegals working for the defense must be familiar with the preliminary hearing procedures, or know where to locate the pertinent court rules of every jurisdiction in which they are involved. At the preliminary hearing, the court determines if probable cause to believe the accused committed the crime exists. If probable cause is found, the defendant is *bound over* to the next stage of the process, which is either trial or review by a grand jury. If probable cause is not established, the defendant is released.

BALLENTINESBALLENTINESBALLENTINESBALLENTINESBALLENTINESBALLENTINESBALLENTINESBALLENTINESBALLENTINESBALLENTINESBALLENTINESBALLENTINESBALLENTINESBALLENTINES

ex parte   Means "of a side," i.e., from one side or by one party. The term refers to an application made to the court by one party without notice to the other party.

complaint   A formal charge of a crime.

preliminary hearing   A hearing to determine whether there is probable cause to formally accuse a person of a crime; that is, whether there is a reasonable basis for believing that a crime has been committed and for thinking the defendant committed it.

AO 442 (Rev. 5/85) Warrant for Arrest

United States District Court

_____ DISTRICT OF _____

UNITED STATES OF AMERICA
V.

WARRANT FOR ARREST

CASE NUMBER

To: the United States Marshall
and any authorized United States Officer

YOU ARE HEREBY COMMANDED to arrest _____
                                                    Name

and bring him or her forthwith to the nearest magistrate to answer a(n)

☐ Indictment ☐ Information ☐ Complaint ☐ Order of Court ☐ Violation Notice ☐ Probation Violation Petition

charging him or her with (brief description of offense)

In violation of Title _____ United States Code, Section(s) _____

_____   _____
Name of Issuing Officer   Title of Issuing Officer

_____   _____
Signature of Issuing Officer   Date and Location

_____
(By) Deputy Clerk

Bail fixed at $_____   by_____
                                                    Name of Judicial Officer

RETURN
This warrant was received and executed with the arrest of the above-named defendant at _____ _____

DATE RECEIVED	NAME AND TITLE OF ARRESTING OFFICER	SIGNATURE OF ARRESTING OFFICER
DATE OF ARREST		

Warrant for Arrest For a warrant to be legitimate, it must be issued by an impartial judge upon a finding of probable cause, supported by oath.

The preliminary hearing can be quite lengthy compared to a defendant's initial appearance. The hearing is adversarial. Witnesses are called and the attorneys are allowed to make arguments. Rules of evidence are applied in modified form, so that hearsay and illegally obtained evidence

AO 442 (Rev. 5/85) Warrant for Arrest

THE FOLLOWING IS FURNISHED FOR INFORMATION ONLY

DEFENDANT'S NAME: _____

ALIAS: _____

LAST KNOWN RESIDENCE: _____

LAST KNOWN EMPLOYMENT: _____

PLACE OF BIRTH: _____

DATE OF BIRTH: _____

SOCIAL SECURITY NUMBER: _____

HEIGHT: _____   WEIGHT: _____

SEX: _____   RACE: _____

HAIR: _____   EYES: _____

SCARS, TATOOS, OTHER DISTINGUISHING MARKS: _____

_____

_____

FBI NUMBER: _____

COMPLETE DESCRIPTION OF AUTO: _____

_____

INVESTIGATIVE AGENCY AND ADDRESS: _____

_____

_____

_____

Warrant for Arrest *(Continued)*

are often considered. Defendants have a right to counsel, to cross-examine the prosecution witnesses, and to present defense witnesses.

The Federal Rules of Criminal Procedure require that the date for preliminary examination be scheduled at the defendant's initial appearance. It shall be held within 10 days of the initial appearance if the defendant is in custody and within 20 if the defendant has been released.

In 1991, the United States Supreme Court examined the need for prompt probable cause determinations in warrantless arrest situations. In *County of Riverside v. McLaughlin*,[29] the Court held that persons arrested without a warrant must have a probable cause determination within 48 hours after arrest, or sooner if reasonable. Time to gather additional evidence, ill will, or the fact that the defendant was arrested on a weekend are not sufficient to delay the probable cause determination longer than 48 hours.

If a grand jury has issued an indictment, the preliminary hearing may be dispensed with in the federal system.[30]

The Formal Charge

There are two formal charges: the information and the indictment. **Informations** are charges filed by prosecutors. Informations are often prepared by criminal law paralegals, for the approval of the prosecutor. **Indictments** are issued by **grand juries**. Once filed, an information or indictment replaces the complaint and becomes the formal charging instrument.

In early American history, grand juries were used to guard against unfair and arbitrary government prosecutions. The drafters of the United States Constitution believed grand jury review so important that they stated in the Fifth Amendment that "no person shall be held to answer for a capital, or otherwise infamous, crime, unless on a presentment or indictment of a Grand Jury."

Grand juries consist of 12 to 23 persons, who are usually selected in the same method as petit juries (juries which determine guilt or innocence). Grand juries sit for longer periods of time and are called to hear cases as needed. The purpose of grand jury review is the same as preliminary hearing: to determine whether there is probable cause to believe the defendant committed the alleged crime. The process used by a grand jury is quite different from that of the preliminary hearing, however.

First, grand juries are closed. The public, including the defendant, are not entitled to attend. Second, the prosecutor runs the show before the grand jury, and the defendant has no right to present evidence or to make a statement. Third, the actions of grand juries are secret. Those who attend are not permitted to disclose what transpires. Defendants have no right to know what evidence is presented to a grand jury, unless it is exculpatory (tends to prove the defendant's innocence). Fourth, those who testify before the grand jury are not entitled to have counsel in the jury room. In most states, witnesses are permitted to leave the proceeding to confer with counsel waiting directly outside. Because statements made to a grand jury can be used later, the Fifth Amendment right to be free from self-incrimination is available to witnesses. Grand juries can overcome Fifth Amendment claims (refusals to testify) by granting witnesses immunity from prosecution.

After a grand jury has completed its investigation, a vote on whether to charge is taken. In the federal system, grand juries consist of 16 to 23 people. At least 12 must vote for indictment.[31] In many cases, indictments are sealed until the indicted defendant is arrested.

The United States Supreme Court has ruled that grand jury review is not a fundamental right; therefore the Fifth Amendment requirement for indictment is not applicable against the states. Nonetheless, many states have grand juries and require that serious charges be brought by indictment.

Indictments must be written and state in "plain and concise" terms the essential facts constituting the offense charged.[32] The indictment must contain all the essential elements of the crime charged. If an indictment charges more than one crime, each crime must be a separate count.

BALLENTINESBALLENTINESBALLENTINESBALLENTINESBALLENTINESBALLENTINESBALLENTINESBALLENTINESBALLENTINESBALLENTINESBALLENTINESBALLENTINESBALLENTINES

information An accusation of the commission of a crime, sworn to by a district attorney or other prosecutor, on the basis of which a criminal defendant is brought to trial for a misdemeanor and, in some states, for a felony.

indictment A charge made in writing by a grand jury, based upon evidence presented to it, accusing a person of having committed a criminal act, generally a felony.

grand jury A body whose number varies with the jurisdiction, ... whose duty it is to determine whether probable cause exists to return indictments against persons accused of committing crimes.

AO 91 (Rev. 5/85) Criminal Complaint

United States District Court

_____ DISTRICT OF _____

UNITED STATES OF AMERICA
V.

CRIMINAL COMPLAINT

CASE NUMBER _____

(Name and Address of Defendant)

I, the undersigned complainant being duly sworn state the following is true and correct to the best of my knowledge and belief. On or about _____ in _____ county, in the _____ District of _____ defendant(s) did, (Track Statutory Language of Offense)

In violation of Title _____ United States Code, Section(s) _____

I further state that I am a(n) _____ and that this complaint is based on the following facts:
                                    Official Title

Continued on the attached sheet and made a part hereof: ☐ Yes   ☐ No

_____
Signature of Complainant

Sworn to before me and subscribed in my presence.

_____ at _____
Date   City and State

_____   _____
Name and Title of Judicial Officer   Signature of Judicial Officer

Criminal Complaint The complaint prepared by the police or prosecutors presents a statement before a judge alleging that the defendant violated criminal laws.

Jurisdiction must be noted, and the law upon which the charge is made must be cited.

The second formal method of charging a crime is by information. Informations are filed by prosecutors without grand jury review. The current trend is away from indictments and toward charging by information. Informations serve the same function as indictment. Under the federal rules, informations must take the same form as indictments. They must be plain, concise, and in writing. All essential elements, as well as the statute relied upon by the government, must be included.[33] As with indictments, informations must be filed with the appropriate court.

Arraignment

After the formal charge has been filed, the defendant is brought to the trial court for **arraignment**. This is the hearing at which the defendant is read the formal charge and asked to enter a **plea**.

Defendants may plead guilty, not guilty, or nolo contendere. By pleading guilty a defendant admits to all the charges contained in the charging document, unless a plea agreement has been reached with the government. A **plea agreement**, also known as a **plea bargain**, is the product of negotiations between the prosecutor and the defendant. It is common for the prosecution to dismiss one or more charges of a multicount charger to reduce a charge in exchange for a defendant's plea of guilty.

If a defendant enters a not guilty plea, the court will set a trial date. In some instances, courts will set a pretrial schedule, which includes a pretrial conference date and a deadline for filing pretrial motions.

Finally, a plea of nolo contendere or no contest may be entered. *Nolo contendere* is a Latin phrase that translates to "I do not contest it." The defendant who pleads nolo contendere neither admits nor denies the charges and has no intent of defending against them. Nolo contendere is treated as a plea of guilty. That is, the government must establish that a factual basis exists to believe the defendant committed the offense, and the court accepting the plea must be sure that the plea is made voluntarily and knowingly. In most jurisdictions, as in federal courts,[34] a defendant may plead nolo contendere only with the approval of the court.

The advantage of entering a no-contest plea over a guilty plea is that the no-contest plea cannot be used in a later civil proceeding against the defendant, whereas a guilty plea can. If the case is not disposed of by a plea of guilty or nolo contendere, the parties will begin preparing for trial.

Pretrial Discovery

The term *discovery*, as associated with criminal law, refers to a process of exchanging information between the prosecution and defense. Discovery is not as broad in criminal cases as in civil cases, and the methods used in criminal law discovery are significantly different.

Bill of Particulars

One method that defendants use to obtain information about the government's case is a **bill of particulars**. The purpose of a bill of particulars is to make general indictments and informations more specific. A bill of particulars is not a true discovery device. It is intended to provide a defendant with the details about the charges against him or her that are necessary for preparation of a defense and to avoid prejudicial surprise at trial.[35] The attorney for the defendant may demand a bill of particulars, typically by filing a motion for a bill of particulars, which may be drafted by the paralegal for the criminal defense attorney.

BALLENTINESBALLENTINESBALLENTINESBALLENTINESBALLENTINESBALLENTINESBALLENTINESBALLENTINESBALLENTINESBALLENTINESBALLENTINESBALLENTINESBALLENTINESBALLENTINESBALLENTINES

arraignment   The act of bringing an accused before a court to answer a criminal charge made against him or her and calling upon him or her to enter a plea of guilty or not guilty.

plea   At common law, the response or responses that the defendant in a civil action was required to file to state a defense to a complaint, petition, declaration, or bill in equity. In criminal cases, a response required by law of a person formally accused of crime, specifically, either a plea of guilty, a plea of nolo contendere, or a plea of not guilty.

plea agreement (plea bargain)   An agreement between the prosecutor and a criminal defendant under which the accused agrees to plead guilty, usually to a lesser offense, in exchange for receiving a lighter sentence than he or she would likely have received had he or she been found guilty after trial on the original charge.

bill of particulars   In criminal prosecutions, a more detailed statement of the offense charged than the indictment or information provides. A criminal defendant is entitled to a bill of particulars, as part of the discovery process, if the nature and extent of the offense are not alleged with sufficient particularity to allow the preparation of an adequate defense.

STATE OF NEW MEXICO
COUNTY OF _____

_____

State of New Mexico

vs.   NOTICE—MOTION TO REDUCE

Carol Lewis   AMOUNT OF BAIL

                                                        FILE NO. 1234567

_____

To: Samuel Brighton, Prosecuting Attorney of _____ County, State
of New Mexico:

   You are hereby notified that on May 5, 1995, at 2:00 P.M., or as soon
thereafter as counsel can be heard, at the courtroom 11 of the _____
County Courthouse, State of New Mexico, defendant will move the court for an
order reducing her bail. Said motion will be made on the grounds that the
offense with which the defendant is charged is a bailable offense, and that the
bail now set is excessive.

   Said motion will be based on this notice, the affidavit of Carol Lewis, a copy
of which is attached hereto and served herewith, and on the pleadings, papers,
records, and files in the above-entitled action.

   Dated May 1, 1995.

                                                _____
                                                Benjamin A. Brooks

Statements of the Defendant

Rule 16(a)(1)(A) of the Federal Rules of Criminal Procedure states that, upon request, the government must allow the defendant to inspect, copy, or photograph all prior relevant written and recorded statements made by the defendant. This includes testimony that defendants give before grand juries—an exception to the rule of secrecy of grand jury proceedings. Statements made by a defendant that are summarized by the police (or other government agent), but not verbatim or signed by the defendant, are also discoverable if the prosecution intends to use them at trial. This discoverability is not true of written and recorded statements of a defendant.

Criminal Record of the Defendant

Fed. R. Crim. P. 16 also requires prosecutors to furnish a copy of the defendant's criminal record to the defendant, including not only the records known to the prosecutor, but also those that can be discovered through due diligence.

Documents and Tangible Objects

Under Rule 16, defendants are entitled to inspect and copy photographs, books, tangible objects, papers, and buildings and places that are in the possession of the government if:

1. The item is material to preparation of the defendant's defense

2. The item will be used by the government at trial

3. The item was obtained from, or belongs to, the defendant.

This section of Rule 16 has a reciprocal provision. That is, defendants must allow the government to inspect and copy defense items. However, the rule is not as broad for government discovery. Defendants only have to permit inspection and copying of items intended to be used at trial.

Scientific Reports and Tests

All scientific reports and tests in the possession of the government (or which can be discovered through due diligence), including mental examinations of the defendant, autopsy reports, drug tests, fingerprint analysis, and other tests and examinations, must be turned over to the defendant, if requested. The defendant must accord the government reciprocity, if requested. For example, if a defendant undergoes an independent mental examination, the government is entitled to review the evaluator's report prior to trial.

Statements of Witnesses/Jencks Act

In the federal system, defendants are not entitled to inspect or copy statements of prosecution witnesses prior to trial. However, the Jencks Act, 18 U.S.C. § 3500, permits a defendant to review a prior written or recorded statement after the witness has testified for the government.

This procedure often causes trial delay, as defendants usually request time between direct examination and cross-examination to review such statements. For this reason, some federal prosecutors provide this information prior to trial. The Jencks Act is a matter of federal statutory law and does not apply to state criminal prosecutions.

Depositions

Whereas depositions are freely conducted under civil procedure, Fed. R. Crim. P. 15 allows depositions only when "exceptional circumstances" exist. Expected absence of a witness at trial is an example of an exceptional circumstance. If such a circumstance is shown, the deposition may be ordered by the trial court, and the deposition may be used at trial. Of course, both the defendant and government have the opportunity to question the witness at the deposition.

Motion Practice

In both civil and criminal practice, a *motion* is a request made to a court for it to do something. In most cases, a party who files a motion is seeking an order from the court. Whenever a person desires something from a court, a formal motion must be filed and copies sent to opposing counsel.

Motion to Dismiss If a defendant believes that the indictment or information is fatally flawed, the appropriate remedy is a motion to dismiss. In some jurisdictions the request would take the form of a motion to quash. Examples of fatal flaws in the charging instrument are that the court lacks jurisdiction, that the facts alleged do not amount to a crime, or that the defendant has a legal defense, such as double jeopardy.

Motion to Suppress As previously discussed, evidence obtained in an unconstitutional manner may not be used at trial. Objection at trial to the admission of such evidence is one method of excluding such evidence. Another is by way of a motion to suppress prior to trial.

Motion for Change of Venue As with civil litigation, *venue* means place for trial. In state criminal proceedings, venue usually lies in the county where the crime occurred. In federal proceedings, venue lies in the district where the crime occurred. Most federal crimes are interstate in character, and the charges may be filed in any district where the crime took place.

The Federal Rules of Criminal Procedure permit transfer of a case from one district to another if "the defendant cannot obtain a fair and impartial trial" at the location where the case is pending. In addition, a district judge may transfer a case if it is most convenient for the defendant and witnesses.

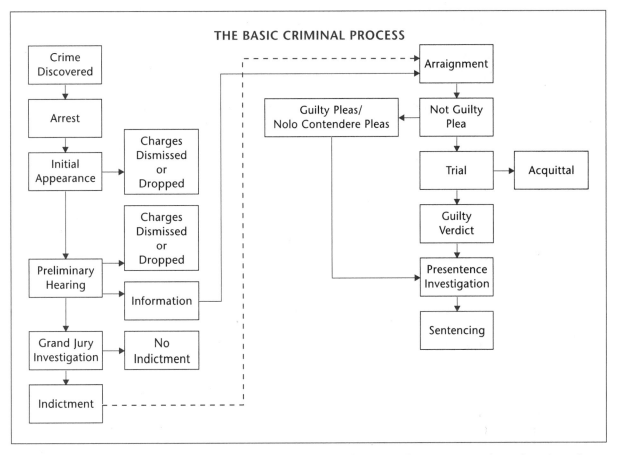

THE BASIC CRIMINAL PROCESS

The Criminal Law Process This chart illustrates the process of the criminal justice system from detection of a crime through the arrest, indictment, trial, and sentencing of the criminal law violators.

Pretrial publicity of criminal matters may be cause to transfer a case (change venue in state proceedings). If a defendant receives considerable negative media coverage, it may be necessary to try the defendant in another location.

Motion for Severance Fed. R. Crim. P. 8 permits two or more defendants to be charged in the same information or indictment if they were involved in the same crime. This rule also permits joinder of two offenses by the same person in one charging instrument, provided the offenses are similar in character or arise out of the same set of facts.

In some situations, severance of the two defendants may be necessary to assure fair trials. In other instances, if a defendant is charged with two or more offenses, it may be necessary to sever the offenses to ensure a fair trial. For example, if a defendant plans to testify concerning one charge and not the other, severance is necessary.

Motion in Limine Prior to trial, both the defendant and the prosecution may file motions in limine. This is a request that the court order the other party not to mention or attempt to question a witness about some matter. A motion in limine is similar to a motion to suppress except that it encompasses more than an admission of illegally seized evidence.

Other Motions A variety of other motions may be filed. If the prosecution fears that revealing

---

STATE OF NEW MEXICO
COUNTY OF _____

_____

State of New Mexico

vs.

Carol Lewis

MOTION FOR BILL OF

PARTICULARS

FILE NO. 1234567

_____

Comes now Carol Lewis, Defendant, and pursuant to [cite statute or rule], moves the court for an order directing the State of New Mexico to file a bill of particulars of the following matters embraced within the information:

The ground for this motion is that the defendant cannot adequately and properly prepare for trial without such particulars as to said matters.

Dated May 10, 1995.

_____

Benjamin Brooks

Attorney for Defendant

---

information required under a discovery rule will endanger the case or a person's life, they may file a motion for a protective order. In such cases, the trial court reviews the evidence and decides whether it is necessary to keep the evidence from the defendant. If granted, the judge will enter a protective order so stating.

Motions for continuance of hearings and trial dates are common. In criminal cases, courts must be careful to not violate speedy trial requirements.

Pretrial Conference

Sometime prior to trial, the court will hold a pretrial conference. This may be weeks or only days before trial. At this conference, the court will address any remaining motions and discuss any problems the parties have. In addition, the judge will explain his or her method of trying a case, such as how the jury will be selected. The next stage in the criminal proceeding is the trial.

Trial, Sentencing, and Appeal

Many criminal matters are not concluded until a trial is held and the defendant is sentenced (if found guilty). In some instances, even a resolution of the matter at trial does not conclude the matter, if a criminal conviction is appealed. This section examines the criminal trial process, including the rights of the defendant, the trial procedure, sentencing, and appeal.

Trial Rights of Defendants

A defendant who is to stand trial is afforded many rights. These rights may stem from the Constitution, the Bill of Rights, statutes, and rules of criminal procedure. Some of those rights include the right to a jury trial, the right to a public trial, the right to confrontation and cross-examination of witnesses, the presumption of innocence, the right to a speedy trial, and the defendant's right to be represented by counsel. It is often the task of defense attorneys (assisted by paralegals) to ensure that defendants receive all trial rights to which they are entitled.

The Right to a Jury Trial

A *trial* is a method of determining guilt or innocence. The Sixth Amendment to the United States Constitution reads, in part, "[i]n all criminal prosecutions, the accused shall enjoy the right to a speedy and public trial, by an impartial jury of the State and district wherein the crime shall have been committed … ." The Sixth Amendment is fully applicable against the states via the Fourteenth Amendment.

The Sixth Amendment has been interpreted to mean that defendants have a right to a jury trial for all offenses that may be punished with more than six months' imprisonment. Most crimes with less than six months as their maximum punishment are petty offenses, for which there is no right to trial by jury.[36]

Juries sit as factfinders. A defendant may be entitled to have a jury decide guilt or innocence, but there is no right to have a jury decide other matters, such as the proper sentence or what law to apply. Some jurisdictions have juries impose sentence or make a sentence recommendation to the trial court. However, this practice is not common and there is no federal constitutional mandate for it.

The Supreme Court has held that there is no constitutional requirement for 12 jurors.[37] Nor does the Constitution require juror unanimity, although there is a limit to how small a jury may be and how few jurors must concur in a verdict. In one case, the Supreme Court found a law unconstitutional that required trial by six jurors and permitted conviction with a vote of five to one.[38] It is common for six-person juries to be used for misdemeanors. However, a unanimous verdict is constitutionally required for conviction. If a 12 member jury is used, it is constitutional to permit a conviction upon a concurrence of 9 or more jurors.

The Right to a Public Trial

The Sixth Amendment also guarantees the right to a public trial. This applies throughout the trial, from opening to return of the verdict, and also applies to many pretrial hearings, such as suppression hearings. The presence of the public is intended to keep prosecutions "honest." As the Supreme Court stated in *Estes v. Texas*,[39] "History has proven that secret tribunals were effective instruments of oppression."

The defendant's right to a public trial is not absolute. Trial judges, acting with extreme caution, may order that a hearing be conducted in private. Facts that support excluding the public are rare. An example of when exclusion of the public may be justified is when an undercover law enforcement agent testifies and public exposure would put the officer's life in jeopardy.

The Right to Confrontation and Cross-Examination

The Sixth Amendment also contains a right to confront one's accusers, which means that a defendant has the right to cross-examine the witnesses of the prosecution. The confrontation clause restricts the government's use of hearsay evidence. *Hearsay* is a statement made by a person out of court. The Federal Rules of Evidence prohibit hearsay unless it falls within a recognized exception. For the prosecution to use hearsay, it must be shown that (1) the witness is unavailable at trial through no fault of the government and (2) the statement was made under circumstances wherein it appears reliable.

The confrontation clause implicitly includes the right of a defendant to be present at his or her trial. This right includes the entire trial, from selection of the jury to return of the verdict. It also includes many pretrial matters, such as suppression hearings. Of course, defendants have a right to be present at both sentencing and probation revocation hearings. Although the right to be present during one's trial is fundamental, it may be lost by disruptive behavior.

The Presumption of Innocence and Burden of Proof

One of the most basic rights underlying the right to a fair trial is the presumption of innocence. All those accused must be proven guilty by the government. Criminal defendants have no duty to defend themselves and may remain silent throughout their trials. In fact, the government is prohibited from calling defendants to testify, and defendants cannot be made to decide whether they will testify at the start of the trial.[40] The fact that a defendant chooses not to testify may not be mentioned by the prosecutor to the jury. Defendants may testify on their own behalf, but if they do, they are subject to full cross-examination by the prosecutor.

The standard imposed upon the government in criminal cases is to prove guilt beyond a reasonable doubt. A doubt that would cause a reasonable or prudent person to question the guilt of the accused is a reasonable doubt. Although not precisely quantified, the beyond a reasonable doubt standard is greater than the civil preponderance (51 percent likely) standard but and less than absolute (100 percent confidence of guilt). The prosecution must prove every element of the charged crime beyond a reasonable doubt. A juror must vote for acquittal if he or she harbors a reasonable doubt.

To further the presumption of innocence, judges must be careful not to behave in such a manner that implies to the jury that a defendant is guilty. Presenting a defendant at a jury trial in prison clothing, handcuffs, or shackles may be considered prejudicial to the defendant.

The Right to a Speedy Trial

All criminal defendants have a right to a speedy trial. The Sixth Amendment, as extended by the Fourteenth Amendment to the states, guarantees speedy trial. To date, the United States Supreme Court has not set a specific number of days within which a trial must be conducted. Rather, the Court has said that four factors must be considered when determining whether a defendant has enjoyed a speedy trial:

1. The length of the delay
2. The reason for the delay
3. Whether the defendant has asserted the right to a speedy trial
4. How seriously the defendant was prejudiced.[41]

The time for speedy trial begins once the defendant is arrested or formally charged.[42] If a defendant is charged by sealed indictment, the speedy trial countdown does not start until the indictment has been opened.

To avoid prejudice by having a trial before a defendant has had an opportunity to prepare a defense, the statute provides that trial shall not occur for 30 days, unless the defendant consents to an earlier date.

The Right to Counsel

The Sixth Amendment to the United States Constitution provides that "in all criminal prosecutions, the accused shall enjoy the right ... to have the Assistance of Counsel for his defense." The right to counsel is one of the most fundamental rights guaranteed to criminal defendants and is fully applicable to the states.

The right to the assistance of counsel is found not only in the Sixth Amendment, but also in the Fifth and Fourteenth Amendments. If the defendant does not have the financial means to pay an attorney, one will be appointed without cost to the defendant. To qualify for appointed counsel, the defendant does not have to be financially destitute; it need only be shown that the defendant's financial situation will prevent him or her from being able to retain an attorney. An indigent defendant does not have a right to choose the appointed attorney; this decision falls within the discretion of the trial court.

In *Faretta v. California*,[43] the right to self-representation was established. The Supreme Court recognized that the assistance of trained legal counsel was essential to preparing and presenting a defense. However, in balance, the Court found that a defendant's right of choice was of greater importance. As such, defendants may choose to act as their own counsel (*pro se*), even though the decision increases the probability of conviction.

The right of self-representation is not absolute. A defendant who engages in disruptive behavior during the proceeding may be relieved of pro se status. Standby counsel, if appointed, may be ordered to complete the trial.

Trial Procedure

Criminal law paralegals frequently assist defense attorneys at trial. They are often involved in every step of the trial procedure, from the jury selection to the final arguments.

Voir Dire

The first stage of trial is the **voir dire**. This is a French phrase that translates "to speak the truth." Voir dire is also known as *jury selection.*

The process of selecting a jury differs among the jurisdictions. In all jurisdictions, prospective jurors are asked questions bearing upon their individual ability to serve as fair and impartial jurors, but each state differs in how this information is obtained. In many states, the judge is responsible for asking most of the questions. In others, the

judge makes only a few brief inquiries and the lawyers do most of the questioning.

There are two ways of eliminating a juror. First, if one of the attorneys believes that a juror could not be fair and impartial, then the juror will be challenged for cause. If the judge agrees, the juror is released. An unlimited number of jurors may be eliminated for cause.

In addition to challenges for cause, a juror may be eliminated by a party using a peremptory challenge. Each party is given a specific number of peremptory challenges at the start of the trial and may strike jurors until that number is exhausted. A party is free to eliminate, without stating a reason, any potential juror. However, a juror may not be eliminated because of his or her race.[44]

In the federal system, both the defendant and prosecutor have 20 peremptory strikes in death cases, and 3 in misdemeanors; in noncapital felony cases, the defendant gets 10 and the government 6.[45] States have similar rules. As with civil law voir dire, criminal law paralegals are often involved in the jury selection process by drafting questions for the potential jurors, observing the questioning, and taking notes.

Preliminary Instructions

In the next stage in the trial proceedings, the judge gives preliminary instructions to the jury. The trial judge will explain to the jury what its obligation is and give a brief introduction to the law and facts of the case. The judge may read the formal charge verbatim to the jury or may summarize its contents. The presumption of innocence is explained, and the judge will admonish the jury to not discuss the case prior to deliberating. Jurors are told not to read newspaper articles or watch television reports concerning the trial.

Opening Statements

After the judge has given the preliminary instructions, the parties address the jury with what is

voir dire examination Examination of a potential juror for the purpose of determining whether he or she is qualified and acceptable to act as a juror in the case. A prospective juror who a party decides is unqualified or unacceptable may be challenged for cause or may be the subject of a peremptory challenge.

commonly known as opening statements. The purpose of opening statements is to acquaint the jury with the basic facts of the case. Opening statement is not the time for counsel to argue the law; only the facts expected to be presented should be mentioned.

In some cases, the defense attorney may be permitted to wait until after the prosecution has put on its entire case before presenting an opening statement. Because the purpose of opening statement is to present the facts surrounding the charge to the jury, opening statements are often waived in bench trials.

The Prosecution's Case in Chief

Because the government has brought the charges, it puts its case on first by calling witnesses to testify and producing exhibits.

All jurisdictions have rules of evidence that govern the admissibility of and procedure for admitting evidence. The Federal Rules of Evidence are used in the federal courts and many states have modeled their own state rules after them.

Many evidentiary questions can be resolved prior to trial through a motion in limine. Questions arising during trial are handled through "objections." If an attorney believes that a question, statement, or action of the opposing lawyer is improper, he or she may object. The court then rules on the objection and the trial continues.

The confrontation clause assures the defendant the right to cross-examine the prosecution's witnesses. Normally, cross-examination is limited to matters raised during the prosecution's direct examination. The defense also has the right to review an exhibit before it is shown to the jury.

Directed Verdict

After the government has rested (finished its case), the defendant may move for a directed verdict or, as it is also known, a *judgment of acquittal*. Upon such motion, the trial judge reviews the evidence presented by the government. If the evidence to support a conviction is insufficient, the judge will enter a directed verdict favoring the defendant.

A directed verdict may never be entered favoring the government.

The prosecution's evidence is insufficient if reasonable persons could not conclude that the defendant is guilty. If the trial court grants a motion for directed verdict, the jury never deliberates and is discharged. Directed verdicts are rarely granted, as most judges prefer to have the jury return a verdict.

The Defense Case

If the motion for directed verdict is denied, the defense may put on its case. The defendant is not required to put on a defense and juries are instructed to not infer guilt by the absence of a defense.

If a defendant chooses to present a defense, the rules are the same as for the prosecution. The defendant may call witnesses and introduce exhibits, as limited by the rules of evidence. Defense witnesses are subject to cross-examination by the prosecutor. Defendants do not have to testify, but may choose to do so. If a defendant does testify, he or she is subject to cross-examination by the prosecutor.

Rebuttal

After the defense has concluded, the prosecution may call rebuttal witnesses in an effort to disprove the defense's evidence. No new issues may be raised during rebuttal. The defense is then permitted to rebut the prosecution's rebuttal evidence.

Closing Arguments

After the evidentiary stage of the trial has concluded, the parties present their closing arguments. The length of closing arguments is left to the discretion of the trial judge.

Attorneys may argue both the facts and the law during closing arguments. However, an attorney may not argue law different from that which the judge will express to the jury as controlling in the case. Closing arguments give the parties an opportunity to summarize the evidence and explain their positions to the jury.

Attorneys must not make incorrect factual or legal statements to the jury. Objections to such statements may be made; if they are sustained, the jury will be instructed by the judge to disregard the statement. Prosecutors must be especially careful not to make inflammatory remarks about the defendant or defense counsel. Such remarks, if extreme, can lead to mistrial.

Final Instructions

After closing arguments are completed, the judge will instruct the jury. Through these instructions the judge explains the law to the jury. The information contained in the judge's instructions includes the prosecutorial burden, the standard of proof, the elements of the charged crime, how to weigh and evaluate evidence, and rules for reaching a verdict.

Jury Deliberations and Verdict

After instructions, the jury goes into deliberations. If necessary, when the court fears contamination of the jury, it may order the jury sequestered. In all cases, jury deliberations are secret.

Generally, no person has contact with the jury when it is deliberating. If the jury has a question for the judge, it is escorted into the courtroom where all the parties may hear the question. Some judges, but not all, permit juries to take the exhibits and instructions with them into the jury room.

On occasion, a jury may communicate to the judge that a verdict cannot be reached. Some courts then give the jury an *Allen* charge, an instruction encouraging any jurors in the minority to reexamine their position.[46] Although courts must be careful with such charges, they do not violate the United States Constitution. However, some states have banned the *Allen* charge.

Whenever a jury is hung, the court will declare a mistrial and set a new trial date. Because of the expense and inconvenience of trying cases a second time, plea bargains are often reached.

If a verdict is reached, the parties are summoned to the courtroom and the jury verdict is read. The parties may request that the jury be polled,

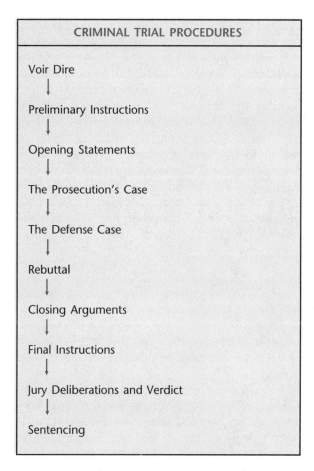

CRIMINAL TRIAL PROCEDURES

Voir Dire
↓
Preliminary Instructions
↓
Opening Statements
↓
The Prosecution's Case
↓
The Defense Case
↓
Rebuttal
↓
Closing Arguments
↓
Final Instructions
↓
Jury Deliberations and Verdict
↓
Sentencing

At each stage, the three primary participants in the trial (defense, prosecution, and judge) have significant roles to play which dramatically affect the outcome of the case.

that is, each juror is asked what his or her verdict was. If there has been an error, the judge may order the jury to return to deliberations or may declare a mistrial.

JNOV/New Trial

If the jury returns a verdict of guilty, the defendant may move for a judgment notwithstanding the verdict or JNOV. A JNOV is similar to a directed verdict in that the defendant is asserting that the evidence is insufficient to support a guilty verdict.

In addition to JNOV, a defendant may file a motion for a new trial. The common-law equivalent of a motion for a new trial was the writ of error coram nobis. Coram nobis is still recognized in a few states. This motion is different from the JNOV because the defendant is not claiming that the evidence was insufficient, but rather that the trial was flawed. For example, if a defendant believes that evidence was admitted that should have been excluded and that he or she was denied a fair trial because of its admission, he or she may file a motion for a new trial. A motion for new trial may also be made because of new evidence discovered after trial.

Sentencing

After conviction, sentence must be imposed. For many misdemeanors and nearly all infractions, sentence is imposed immediately. For felonies and some misdemeanors, a future sentencing date is set.

In most cases, sentence is imposed by the trial judge. A few jurisdictions provide for a jury sentence recommendation, and even fewer actually permit the jury to impose sentence. The jury always plays a role in deciding whether the death penalty should be imposed.

The legislature determines how a crime should be punished. Legislatures normally set ranges within which judges may punish violators. In recent years, there has been a substantial movement to limit the discretion of judges in the federal system and in many states. The right of the legislative branch in this area is curbed by the Eighth Amendment, which prohibits "cruel and unusual punishment." The protection of the Eighth Amendment has been extended to state proceedings through the Fourteenth Amendment. However, legislatures still retain wide discretion in deciding how to punish criminals.

The Death Penalty

Clearly, the most controversial punishment is the death penalty. In early American history, capital punishment was commonly used. During the 19th century, use of the death penalty greatly declined. Today, more than half the states provide for the death penalty, and its use has regained popular support. Although the number of inmates actually executed every year is small, the number is increasing.

Incarceration

Incarceration is an effective method of dealing with dangerous persons. In some cases, the offender is also rehabilitated. Incarceration is the most common method of punishing violent offenders. Offenders may be committed to prisons, camps, or local jails. Those sentenced to short terms (one year or less) are usually housed in a local jail; those with longer terms usually are committed to a prison.

For crimes with incarceration as their punishment, the sentencing judge is usually given a range of time by sentencing guidelines within which to sentence the defendant. For example, assault may be punished by one to three years in prison. The judge is vested with the discretion to decide what amount of time within that range best suits the particular facts of the case.

If a defendant is already serving a sentence on another crime, or is convicted of two related crimes, the sentencing judge may impose concurrent or consecutive sentences. If two sentences are *concurrent,* it is said that they "run together." That is, if a defendant receives two five-year sentences, he or she will actually spend five years incarcerated. If the sentences are **consecutive**, the defendant will spend a total of 10 years incarcerated.

---

consecutive sentences   Sentences of imprisonment for crimes in which the time of each is to run one after the other without a break.

After committing the defendant to a correctional institution, the judge loses responsibility for and control over him or her, unless state statute provides otherwise. In many states, parole is available to prison inmates. **Parole** is an early release from prison and is used to encourage inmates to stay out of trouble while in prison. Parole decisions are made by state corrections officials, such as parole boards. Similar to probation, an offender must comply with certain conditions while on parole. Conditions routinely include not possessing a gun; not contacting the witnesses, judge, jurors, or prosecutor involved with the offender's conviction; and not becoming involved in further criminal activity. Violation of a condition of parole may result in recommitment to prison.

Probation and Revocation

A popular alternative to incarceration is probation (also known as a *suspended sentence*). Probation is not always an alternative and is rarely available for crimes punishable by life imprisonment or death. While on probation, the defendant is released from custody, but must comply with conditions imposed by the court during the probationary period. Each defendant is placed under the supervision of a probation officer during this period. The probation officer is an officer of the court, not of the corrections system.

Typical conditions of probation include keeping steady employment, refraining from other unlawful conduct, not carrying a firearm or other weapon, and not leaving the jurisdiction of the court. A defendant who violates a condition of probation may be disciplined. Generally, the decision about whether any action should be taken for a violation is made by the probation officer. If a violation is extreme, the probation officer may file a petition to revoke probation.

Community Service

One alternative to incarceration for nonviolent offenders is community service. In such a program, a defendant's sentence is suspended and the completion of a stated number of community service hours is a condition of the defendant's probation. In most instances a probation officer works with the probationer to find an appropriate job. However, the judge may require that a specific job be performed.

Restitution and Fines

The purpose of restitution is to compensate the victim, not punish the offender. As such, restitution is not a substitute for other forms of punishment. Any amount of ordered restitution must, of course, be related to the actual losses sustained by the victim.

In contrast to restitution, the purpose of a fine is to punish the offender. Fines are a very common method of punishing misdemeanants. Serious crimes are often punished with both a fine and incarceration. Any fine imposed must be reasonable, that is, the amount must be within the financial means of the offender.

Other Sentencing Alternatives

In recent years, many new alternatives to incarceration have been developed. Such alternatives are actually forms of probation and are thus administered by courts and probation officers. Some of these alternatives include work release, alcohol and drug treatment, participation in a defensive/safe-driving school, periodic urinalysis or blood screening for drugs, house arrest, and residence in halfway houses.

Postconviction Remedies

A defendant who is found guilty may have the option of filing a motion for a new trial or appealing the decision of the court. The Constitution of the United States does not confer a right to appeal.[47] Regardless, every state provides for appeal by either statute or consitutional provision. Once a state establishes a right to appeal, the United

parole   The release of a person from imprisonment after serving a portion of his or her sentence, provided he or she complies with certain conditions.

States Constitution requires that appellate procedure not violate the Fourteenth Amendment's due process or equal protection clauses.

Because of the double jeopardy clause, defendants have a broader right to appeal than does the government. The prosecution has a limited right to appeal. Because of the prohibition of trying a person twice for the same offense, the government has no right to appeal acquittals. A defendant who is tried and convicted is free to appeal any factual or legal error. However, this right may be limited by a requirement of preservation. To satisfy this rule, the defendant must raise the issue at the trial level, to give the trial judge an opportunity to avoid error. Failure to raise the issue results in a waiver. For example, a defendant who does not challenge the sufficiency of an indictment at the trial level may not raise that issue for the first time before the appellate court.

Summary Questions

1. Henry and Frank argued over a poker game they were playing at Henry's house, and Frank left angry. On his way out, he broke the windows of a car in front of Henry's house, assuming that it was Henry's car. However, the car actually belonged to Henry's neighbor, Bruce. Frank is now charged with the purposeful destruction of personal property. He claims that his act was not purposeful because he did not intend to break the windows of Bruce's car. Discuss this defense.

2. You have just been given an assignment to research the elements of the crime of accessory to murder after the fact. Is this a question of substantive or procedural law?

3. Suppose that Brenda and Jane are roommates who get into an argument. If Brenda tells Jane, "You're going to be sorry," throws a pair of scissors at her, and misses, has Brenda committed any crime? If so, what is the crime and what are the elements of that crime?

4. What are mens rea and actus reus? Must both be present for the commission of a crime to occur?

5. Suppose that Gary drives home from the bar one evening and misses his driveway, running over his neighbor's lawn and fence. The police arrive and he is charged with driving while under the influence. At trial he is found guilty. As part of his sentence, Gary is ordered to repair his neighbor's fence. What theory of punishment has the court decided to follow? If Gary is also ordered to attend alcohol abuse treatment classes, what theory of punishment has the court decided to follow?

6. A person who helps principals prepare to commit a crime, but is not present during the commission, is called what?

7. Has Jan committed attempted murder if she decides to kill her sister and mentally works out the details of when, how, and where?

8. What happens if an officer fails to read a defendant his or her rights prior to obtaining a confession?

9. What is a bill of particulars?

10. Suppose that a prosecutor loses a murder case against a defendant. If the prosecutor can find grounds for appeal, can the defendant be tried again? Why or why not?

Practical Paralegal Skills

Assuming the facts in the second law office scenario in this chapter, locate the pertinent statutes for your state. What crimes might Adam Kreiger, Bob Brewster, and Carol Lewis be charged with in your state? What are the elements of those crimes?

Notes

For further reference, see *Criminal Law and Procedure,* by Daniel Hall (Delmar Publishers Inc., and Lawyers Cooperative Publishing © 1992).

1 Milano, Carol, "1993 *Legal Assistant Today* Salary Survey Results," *Legal Assistant Today* 48 (May/June 1993).

2 Samaha, J., *Criminal Law* (3d ed. 1990).

3 Model Penal Code § 2.02 (General Requirements of Culpability).

4 Model Penal Code § 2.02(2)(c).

5 Model Penal Code § 2.01.

6 *Id.*

7 18 U.S.C. § 1201.

8 28 U.S.C. § 1738A.

9 LaFave & Scott, *Criminal Law* 797 (1986).

10 *M'Naghten's Case*, 8 Eng. Rep. 718 (H.L. 1843).

11 LaFave & Scott, *Criminal Law* § 4.2A(a) (1986).

12 Model Penal Code § 4.01(1).

13 *Dusky v. United States*, 362 U.S. 402 (1960).

14 *Ford v. Wainwright*, 477 U.S. 399 (1986).

15 *Id.* at 417.

16 Model Penal Code § 3.06(d).

17 Model Penal Code § 2.13(2).

18 The Seventh Amendment's guarantee of a jury trial in civil cases also has not been incorporated.

19 *Miranda v. Arizona*, 384 U.S. 436 (1966).

20 The rule as applied in federal courts was announced in *Weeks v. United States*, 232 U.S. 383 (1914). However, it appears that the rule was applied in at least one case prior to that date. *See* LaFave & Israel, *Criminal Procedure* 78 (1985).

21 *Mapp v. Ohio*, 367 U.S. 643 (1961).

22 *Bivens v. Six Unknown Named Agents*, 403 U.S. 388 (1971).

23 *Beck v. Ohio*, 379 U.S. 89 (1964).

24 Fed. R. Crim. P. 41(b).

25 392 U.S. 1 (1968).

26 *Miranda v. Arizona*, 384 U.S. 436 (1966).

27 Fed. R. Crim. P. 4.

28 Fed. R. Crim. P. 5.

29 No. 89-1817, slip op. (U.S. May 13, 1991).

30 18 U.S.C. § 3060(e).

31 Fed. R. Crim. P. 6.

32 Fed. R. Crim. P. 7(c).

33 Fed. R. Crim. P. 7(c).

34 Fed. R. Crim. P. 11.

35 *United States v. Diecidue*, 603 F.2d 535 (5th Cir.), *cert. denied*, 445 U.S. 946 (1979).

36 *Baldwin v. New York*, 399 U.S. 66 (1970).

37 *Williams v. Florida*, 399 U.S. 78 (1970).

38 *Burch v. Louisiana*, 441 U.S. 130 (1979).

39 381 U.S. 532 (1965).

40 *Brooks v. Tennessee*, 406 U.S. 605 (1972).

41 *Barker v. Wingo*, 407 U.S. 514 (1972).

42 *United States v. Marion*, 404 U.S. 307 (1971).

43 422 U.S. 806 (1975).

44 *Batson v. Kentucky*, 476 U.S. 79 (1986).

45 Fed. R. Crim. P. 24(b).

46 The charge gets its name from *Allen v. United States,* 164 U.S. 492 (1896), wherein the Supreme Court approved its use.

47 *McKane v. Durston*, 153 U.S. 684 (1894).

CHAPTER 11
The Paralegal and Business Organizations

General Motors and the local corner store are both forms of business organizations. Our entire economy is dominated by business organizations of various types.

This chapter introduces the role of business organization paralegals in dealing with business organizations. Next, it focuses on the different types of business organizations in the United States, discussing sole proprietorships, partnerships, limited partnerships, and corporations. The chapter concludes with a discussion of the factors to be considered when choosing a type of business organization for a venture.

The Role of the Paralegal in Business Organization Matters

Paralegals who specialize in working with business organizations are typically considered to be *corporate paralegals* even though they may specialize in working with partnerships or other types of business organizations. In the fast-growing paralegal field, the number of corporate paralegals employed in the United States is second only to the number of litigation paralegals. In a 1993 survey performed by the staff at *Legal Assistant Today,* paralegals working in the corporate law area accounted for more than 10 percent of the respondents; 12 percent of the survey respondents reported that they were employed by a corporation (as opposed to a private law firm or the public sector).[1]

The average salary of corporate law paralegals was among the highest reported, at $33,799. The highest reported salary of a corporate law paralegal was $72,600. Average salaries of all responding paralegals employed by corporations was $31,485, whereas paralegals employed by law firms averaged $27,339, and those employed by the public sector in government positions was only $25,000.

The paralegal working in the corporate law area often specializes in one or more areas within the corporate law area, including incorporation and organization of business corporations or nonprofit corporations, corporate mergers and acquisitions, securities law, qualified retirement plans, or partnerships.

Specific tasks often performed by corporate paralegals may include:

1. Drafting all forms of corporate documents
2. Reviewing and updating corporate minute books
3. Incorporating and dissolving corporations
4. Preparing foreign corporation qualification documents
5. Assisting with mergers and acquisitions
6. Assisting in compliance with SEC rules and regulations
7. Researching blue sky laws
8. Researching partnership law
9. Drafting partnership agreements
10. Drafting partnership resolutions.

The Work of Corporate Paralegals in the United States

Short of giving legal advice to clients, corporate paralegals are able to assist with almost all areas and aspects of corporate law. Typically the paralegal's duties will be dominated by document drafting and research.

Skills Important to Corporate Paralegals

Possibly the most important skills to a successful corporate paralegal career are writing skills, organizational skills, and legal research skills. Corporate paralegals often spend much of their time drafting corporate documents, including agreements and corporate resolutions, which must be drafted with accuracy and precision.

In addition to drafting documents, corporate paralegals are often called upon to organize corporate files and documents for meetings and closings. Corporate mergers and acquisitions can involve hundreds of documents that must be reviewed and accounted for at all times during the process. Legal research skills are also very important to corporate paralegals, who must often familiarize themselves with the laws of several different states in which their corporate clients transact business.

Introduction to Business Organizations

The most prominent types of business organizations in the United States are the sole proprietorship, the partnership, the limited partnership, and the corporation. There is also a new form of business organization, often called the *limited liability company,* that is recognized in several states. The limited liability company is a business organization that has many features of both a partnership and a corporation, but the majority of states does not recognize the limited liability company at this time.

Every type of business organization recognized in the United States has a significant effect on our society and our economy. This impact is reflected both in the number of each type of business organization in the United States and in the income generated by each type of business organization.

Number of Business Organizations

The small business owned by a sole proprietor is the most common form of business organization in

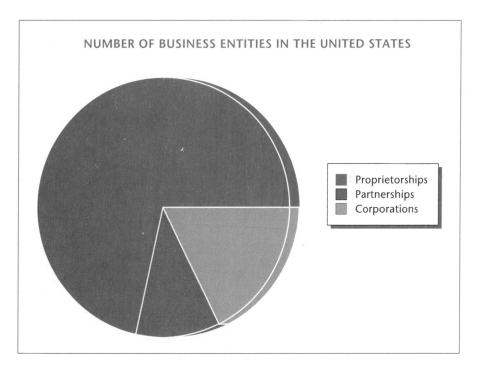

NUMBER OF BUSINESS ENTITIES IN THE UNITED STATES

- Proprietorships
- Partnerships
- Corporations

Business Entities in the United States   Nearly 75 percent of all business organizations in the United States are proprietorships.

the United States. During 1988, income tax returns indicated that there were more than 13.6 million sole proprietorships in the United States. There were about 10 million more sole proprietorships than corporations during 1987, which numbered just over 3.5 million and were the second most common type of business organization.

Partnerships ranked a distant third in number, with only 1.6 million in the United States during 1988.[2] The number of partners in these partnerships ranged from two to several hundred.

Income of Business Organizations

It is important to recognize the magnitude of the role that the corporation plays in the United States economy and in each of our lives. During 1988, United States corporations reported an excess of $9 trillion in business receipts, whereas sole proprietorships reported $672 billion, and partnerships reported $464 billion.[3] Most of us depend on corporations for our livelihoods, whether it be a small, family-owned corporation or a multi-million-dollar corporate conglomerate. We also cannot overlook the great influence that corporate marketing has over the consumer purchases we make and the prices we pay for those goods. The 1991 figures indicate that corporations report over $100 billion per year in advertising expenses.[4]

Although sole proprietorships make up the majority of business enterprises in this country, they report a much lower net income than corporations do. Although there were more than 10 million more sole proprietors than corporations during 1988, the sole proprietorships earned only $126.3 billion, in comparison to the $413 billion earned by corporations.[5] During 1988, the approximately 1.6 million partnerships in the United States had net income totaling $14.5 billion.

An Introduction to Sole Proprietorships

The **sole proprietorship** is the most common form of business organization in the United States, as well as the simplest. A sole proprietor is the sole owner of all of the assets of this type of business and is solely liable for all the debts of the business.

Unlike a corporation, the business of the sole proprietor is not considered a separate entity; rather, it is considered an extension of the individual. The sole proprietor is personally responsible for all legal debts and obligations of the business and is entitled to all profits of the business. The sole proprietor may delegate decisions and management of the business to agents, but all authority to make decisions must come directly from the sole proprietor, who is ultimately responsible for all business-related acts of employees.

Very few formalities must be observed for an individual to commence business as a sole proprietorship. Because a sole proprietorship is not considered to be a separate entity, there are no formalities involved in forming the sole proprietorship. Any formalities that do exist are not unique to sole proprietorships, but may be required of all types of business organizations. These may include filing a certificate of assumed name, trade name, or fictitious name; applying for tax identification numbers; and getting sales tax permits and licenses.

Using an Assumed Name, Trade Name, or Fictitious Name

Most states allow a sole proprietor to transact business under a name other than his or her own name, provided that the purpose for doing

sole proprietorship   Ownership by one person, as opposed to ownership by more than one person, ... a corporation, ... a partnership, etc.

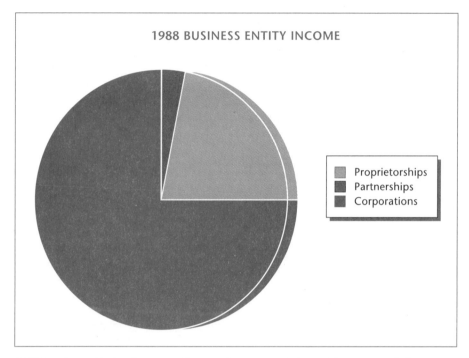

1988 Business Entity Income Corporations earned about 75 percent of the income reported by all business organizations in 1988.

so is not a fraudulent design or the intent to injure others.[6] Most state statutes set forth certain requirements that must be met before an individual may transact business under an **assumed name**, **trade name**, or **fictitious name**, as it may variously be called.

Typically, if the proposed name is available and otherwise complies with state statutes, an application for certificate of assumed name, trade name, or fictitious name, or similar document, is filed with the Secretary of State of the state in which the sole proprietor intends to do business. State statutes often require that a notice of intent to transact business under an assumed name be published. The intent of these statutes is to protect the public by giving notice or information as to the persons with whom the business

deals, and to afford protection against fraud and deceit.[7]

Application for Tax Identification Number

Applying for tax identification numbers is a task often delegated to corporate paralegals. Requirements for applying for state tax identification numbers vary by state. Generally, whenever a sole proprietorship acts as an employer, he or she must apply for a state tax identification number. In addition, any sole proprietor who hires one or more employees must apply for a federal employer identification number by completing Form SS-4 and filing it with the appropriate office of the Internal Revenue Service.

BALLENTINESBALLENTINESBALLENTINESBALLENTINESBALLENTINESBALLENTINESBALLENTINESBALLENTINESBALLENTINESBALLENTINESBALLENTINESBALLENTINESBALLENTINESBALLENTINES

assumed name   A fictitious name or an alias.
trade name   The name under which a company does business.
fictitious name   An artificial name that a person or corporation adopts for business or professional purposes.

An Introduction to Partnerships

Although **partnerships** are not as common as sole proprietorships or corporations, they are a significant form of business organization in the United States. Partnerships necessarily involve two or more people and are somewhat more complex than sole proprietorships. The formation of a partnership is often a viable alternative to incorporating.

Partnership Defined

The Uniform Partnership Act defines a partnership as an "association of two or more persons to carry on as co-owners a business for profit."[8] The five essential words or phrases in this definition that are elements of a partnership are "two or more persons," "carry on," "co-owners," "business," and "for profit."

The "two or more persons" element differentiates the partnership from the sole proprietorship. The word *persons*, as used in this definition, includes "individuals, partnerships, corporations and other associations."[9]

The "carry on" element implies that the partners must actively carry on the partnership business together, in addition to possessing co-ownership of the business or of property.

The "co-ownership" element refers to ownership of the business of the partnership, and requires that the business be a single entity owned by more than one person. Co-ownership also means that the partners have a right to participate in the management of the partnership and to share in the profits (and losses) of the partnership.

The "business" element, as defined in the Uniform Partnership Act, includes "every trade, occupation, or profession."[10]

Finally, the "for profit" element refers to the intention of the partnership. Not every partnership earns a profit, but earning a profit must be an objective of the partnership. Nonprofit organizations may not be partnerships.

Law Governing Partnerships

The primary source of law governing partnerships is state statute, which is derived at least in part from the Uniform Partnership Act. In 1914, the National Conference of Commissioners on United States Laws approved the Uniform Partnership Act and recommended it for adoption by all state legislatures. The American Bar Association approved the Uniform Partnership Act in 1915. Prior to that time, partnerships were governed by common and civil law. At this time, all states but Louisiana have adopted the Uniform Partnership Act or substantially similar versions of the Act. Louisiana partnerships are still governed by the civil law concerning partnerships in that state.

In August of 1992 the National Conference of Commissioners on Uniform State Laws approved the Revised Uniform Partnership Act, which is substantially different from the original Uniform Partnership Act. At the time this text was written, the approved Revised Uniform Partnership Act had not been adopted by any state.

In addition to the provisions of the Uniform Partnership Act, as modified by the state of domicile, partnerships are also governed by contract law, common law, and civil law.

BALLENTINESBALLENTINESBALLENTINESBALLENTINESBALLENTINESBALLENTINESBALLENTINESBALLENTINESBALLENTINESBALLENTINESBALLENTINESBALLENTINESBALLENTINESBALLENTINES

partnership An undertaking of two or more persons to carry on, as co-owners, a business or other enterprise for profit; an agreement between or among two or more persons to put their money, labor, and skill into commerce or business, and to divide the profit in agreed-upon proportions.

The Partnership as a Separate Entity

Whereas the sole proprietor's business is considered an extension of the individual, and the corporation is considered a separate entity, the exact nature of the partnership is not so readily defined. There are arguments to support both the *aggregate theory,* which suggests that a partnership is the totality of the persons engaged in the business rather than an entity in itself, and the *entity theory.* Under the entity theory, the partnership is considered to be an entity separate and distinct from its partners. Partnerships under common law were not considered to be a separate entities, but rather extensions of their partners.

IRS Form SS-4 This tax form is used to apply for a federal employer identification number.

Partners' Rights and Responsibilities

Partners have a unique relationship, both among themselves and in dealings with third parties on behalf of the partnership. Under the Uniform Partnership Act, a partner is entitled to the following separate and distinct property rights:

1. The partner's rights in specific partnership property
2. The partner's interest in the partnership
3. The partner's right to participate in management of partnership affairs.[11]

Partners' Specific Property Rights

Each partner is a co-owner with the other partners of specific partnership property. Partnership property is held as a *tenancy in partnership,* and each partner has an equal right with the other partners to possess specific partnership property for partnership purposes. However, the partner has no right to possess such property for any other purpose without the consent of the other partners.[12] The Uniform Partnership Act states that on the death of a partner, with the exception of the last surviving partner, the deceased partner's right in specific partnership property vests in the surviving partner or partners, who have the right to possess the property for partnership purposes.

Partners' Interest in the Partnership

The Uniform Partnership Act defines the nature of a partner's interest in the partnership as "his share of the profits and surplus, and the same is personal property."[13] Because this interest in the partnership is considered personal property, it is assignable, unless prohibited by the partnership agreement. An **assignment** of a partner's interest in the partnership does not necessarily dissolve the partnership, and the assignee does not become a new partner. The **assignee** of a partner's interest in a partnership is only entitled to receive the profits to which the partner would otherwise be entitled in accordance with the partner's contract.

Partners' Rights to Participate in Management

Each partner is granted by statute the right to participate in management of the partnership. Because full participation in management by every partner is often not practical or desirable, a partnership agreement may appoint a managing partner or a managing partnership committee. However, partners may not be denied the right to join in management of the partnership if it is their desire to do so and if there are no contradicting terms in the partnership agreement. The right to participate in management of the partnership must be specifically waived by any partner giving up that right.

The Relationship Among Partners

The relationship among partners is unique. Each partner has certain rights when dealing with other partners and each partner is subject to certain duties when dealing with the other partners.

Rights of Partners

The Uniform Partnership Act grants partners the following rights when dealing with each other, unless those rights are altered by a written agreement of the partners:

1. Each partner has the right to receive repayment of his or her contribution.
2. Each partner has the right to share equally in the profits and surplus of the partnership remaining after all liabilities are satisfied.
3. Each partner has the right to receive indemnification for payments and personal liabilities incurred on behalf of the firm.

assignment   A transfer of property, or a right in property, from one person to another.

assignee   A person to whom a right is assigned.

ESSENTIAL ELEMENTS OF A PARTNERSHIP
1. Two or more partners
2. Partners must carry on partnership business together
3. Partners must be co-owners
4. Partners must participate in a business
5. The partnership business must be operated with the intent of making a profit

A partnership is formed when more than one person forms a business with the intent of making a profit.

4. Each partner has the right to receive interest on advances and, under certain circumstances, on capital contributions from the date of the advance or payment of the contribution.
5. Each partner has the right to share equally in the management and conduct of the business.
6. Each partner has the right to have access to the firm's books.
7. Each partner has the right to receive reasonable compensation for services rendered in winding up the partnership affairs.[14]

In addition, the Uniform Partnership Act grants to partners the right to have a formal accounting of the partnership affairs whenever it is deemed "just and reasonable,"[15] and the right to have access to the partnership books for inspection and reproduction.[16]

Partners' Duties in Dealing with Each Other

Partners' duties are also prescribed by state statute. The Uniform Partnership Act provides that partners have the following duties, unless otherwise indicated in the partnership agreement:

1. The duty of partners to contribute toward losses sustained by the firm according to each partner's share in the profits.
2. The duty of partners to work for the partnership without remuneration.
3. The duty of partners to submit to a vote of the majority of the partners when differences arise among the partners as to any ordinary matters connected with the partnership affairs.[17]

Partners' Fiduciary Duty to Each Other

One of the most significant aspects of the partners' relationship is the **fiduciary duty** of the partners to each other, including a duty to exercise good faith and maintain the highest integrity in dealing with other partners.

Partners as Agents

The Uniform Partnership Act specifically states that the law of **agency** applies under the Act. Partners are generally agents for the other partners and for the partnership itself. This means that each partner can act on behalf of the partnership and on behalf of the other partners with regard to partnership matters.

Liability of Partners

Partners are jointly liable for all debts and obligations of the partnership, and creditors may look to the personal property of partners if partnership assets are insufficient to cover a debt. Partners are also jointly and severally liable for any loss or injury caused to any person who is not a partner in the partnership, or for any penalty incurred, due to the wrongful act or omission of any partner acting in the ordinary course of the business of the partnership or with the authority of co-partners. In the event of any such wrongful

BALLENTINESBALLENTINESBALLENTINESBALLENTINESBALLENTINESBALLENTINESBALLENTINESBALLENTINESBALLENTINESBALLENTINESBALLENTINESBALLENTINESBALLENTINESBALLENTINES

fiduciary duty   The duty to act loyally and honestly with respect to the interests of another; the duty the law imposes upon a fiduciary.

agency   A relationship in which one person acts for or on behalf of another person at the other person's request.

act or omission, the partnership is liable to the same extent as the partner so acting or omitting to act.[18] In addition, the partnership is bound to make good on any loss incurred from the misappropriation of funds of one or more partners.

The Relationship Between Partners and Others

Except as otherwise specified in the partnership agreement or by statute, each partner acts as an agent of the partnership when dealing with others concerning partnership business, and has **actual authority** to bind the partnership to contractual relationships with third parties. This authority may be **express authority** stemming from the partnership agreement, or it may be **implied authority** based on the nature of the partnership relationship.

Certain acts, however, require unanimous consent of the partners, unless otherwise specified in the partnership agreement. The unanimous consent of the partners is generally required to:

1. Assign the partnership property in trust for creditors or on the assignee's promise to pay the debts of the partnership
2. Dispose of the goodwill of the business
3. Do any other act that would make it impossible to carry on the ordinary business of the partnership
4. Confess a judgment
5. Submit a partnership claim or liability to arbitration or reference.[19]

Partners do not have **apparent authority** for the foregoing, and the act of an unauthorized partner to execute one of the foregoing does not constitute an act of the partnership.

Partnership Powers

Although a partnership is not considered a separate entity for all purposes, the partnership as an entity is granted certain powers under the Uniform Partnership Act. In many ways similar to a corporation, the partnership is granted the powers necessary for it to conduct business, including the power to enter into contracts, borrow money, act as agent for others, become a member of another partnership, become a shareholder of a corporation, and enter into a joint venture with a third party.

Organization and Management of a General Partnership

The organization and management of partnerships can vary significantly depending upon the individual partners and other circumstances. The parameters of the organization and management are defined by the statutes of the state of domicile and by the partnership agreement.

Management and Control

Although all partners are given equal rights to manage the partnership under the Uniform Partnership Act, this is not always a practical or desirable method of management, and these rights may be altered in the agreement among the partners. Often, especially with larger partnerships, the partners will delegate the management of the partnership to one or more managing partners. This delegation of the right to manage must be granted by all partners, and no partner can be denied the right to manage the partnership unless that right is waived.

Under the Uniform Partnership Act, the general rule regarding a dispute over the internal

BALLENTINESBALLENTINESBALLENTINESBALLENTINESBALLENTINESBALLENTINESBALLENTINESBALLENTINESBALLENTINESBALLENTINESBALLENTINESBALLENTINESBALLENTINESBALLENTINESBALLENTINES

actual authority   In the law of agency, the power of an agent to bind his or her principal. Although such authority must be granted by the principal to his or her agent, authority will be deemed to have been granted if the principal allows the agent to believe that the agent possesses it. Further, actual authority may be implied from the circumstances and need not be specifically granted.

express authority   Authority expressly granted to or conferred upon an agent or employee by a principal or employer.

implied authority   The authority of an agent to do whatever acts are necessary to carry out his or her express authority.

apparent authority   Authority which, although not actually granted by the principal, he or she permits his or her agent to exercise.

management affairs of the partnership is that the decision is to be made by a majority of the partners.[20] There are, however, many exceptions to that rule, including certain acts that must be approved by unanimous agreement of the partners. Acts contrary to the terms of the partnership agreement, as well as any amendments to the partnership agreement, also require the unanimous consent of all partners.

Oral Partnership Agreements

Although the partnership agreement is fundamental to the partnership, the agreement may be verbal. A partnership may also exist with no express agreement among the parties whatsoever, so long as all of the elements of a partnership are present.

Although an oral partnership may be legal and binding under certain circumstances, it has serious drawbacks. It is difficult to prove the terms of an oral partnership agreement, or even that a partnership exists, when there is no written agreement. Also, certain types of oral partnership agreements may be prohibited by law. For instance, under the **Statute of Frauds**, it is impossible to form an oral agreement for a period longer than one year.

Partnership Agreements

Corporate paralegals are often responsible for drafting the **partnership agreement**, or *partnership articles* as that document is sometimes referred to. The partnership agreement is the contract entered into by all partners setting forth the agreed-upon terms of the partnership. The partnership agreement is considered the "law of the partnership" and is enforced as such unless any of the terms of the partnership agreement are contrary to law. Because the partnership agreement is a contract between the partners, it is subject to contract law.

PARTNERS' RIGHTS	
Rights in Specific Partnership Property	Each partner is co-owner with the other partners of specific partnership property which is held as a tenancy in partnership. Each partner has an equal right to possess specific partnership property for partnership purposes only.
Interest in the Partnership	Each partner is entitled to a share of the profits and surplus. That share is considered personal property and is referred to as the partners' *interest*.
Partners' Rights to Participate in Management of the Partnership	Each partner is entitled to an equal right to participate in the management of the partnership, unless partners specifically waive that right by written agreement.

The paralegal may be involved with drafting partnership agreements.

Following is a checklist of items that should be considered for inclusion in the partnership agreement.

Partnership Agreement Checklist

- Names and addresses of partners
- Name of partnership
- Purpose of partnership
- Address of principal place of doing business
- Term of partnership agreement
- Partner contributions
- Requirements for additional contributions
- Partnership assets
- Goodwill evaluation on distribution of assets

Statute of Frauds   A statute, existing in one or another form in every state, that requires certain classes of contracts to be in writing and signed by the parties. Its purpose is to prevent fraud or reduce the opportunities for fraud.

partnership agreement   The agreement signed by the members of a partnership that governs their relationship. It is sometimes referred to as *articles of partnership*.

- Partners and partnership liability
- Distribution of profits and losses
- Partner indemnification
- Partners' duties
- Partners' powers and limitations thereon
- Partner compensation and benefits
- Partner and partnership expenses
- Management and control of business
- Life insurance on lives of partners
- Accounting procedures and record keeping
- Changes in partners
- Death of partner
- Sale or purchase of partnership interest
- Arbitration of differences among partners
- Partnership termination
- Dissolution and winding up
- Date of agreement
- Integration clause
- Signatures of all partners

Financial Structure of a Partnership

Partnerships have a unique financial structure that is often tailored to suit the needs of the partners. The partnership capital, which includes all of the assets of the partnership, consists of contributions from the partners and the undistributed income earned by the partnership.

Capital Contributions

The partnership capital, usually contributed by the partners, may be in the form of cash, real or personal property, or the personal expertise or services rendered by a partner. The partnership agreement should state the required capital contribution of each partner and the form of that contribution. In addition to the initial capital

contribution, the partnership agreement may require each partner to contribute additional capital to the partnership as needed for continuance of the partnership business.

Pursuant to the Uniform Partnership Act, no withdrawal of capital from the partnership is permitted until the partnership is dissolved. If this is not desirable, appropriate provisions may be made in the partnership agreement for the withdrawal of capital prior to dissolution.

Profits and Losses

Another of the more important characteristics of a partnership is a sharing of the profits and losses among the partners. Under the Uniform Partnership Act, the partners share the profits and losses of the partnership equally, regardless of each partner's capital contribution to the partnership. The partners may, however, set their own formula for sharing in the profits and losses of the partnership in the partnership agreement. That formula may be based on several factors, including the amount of each partner's initial capital contribution, additional capital contributions, and services rendered on behalf of the partnership by each partner. When partners' contributions to the partnership are unequal, their shares of the profits and losses may be unequal as well, so long as the appropriate provision is made in the partnership agreement. In any event, if it is not desirable for all partners to share all profits and losses equally, it is crucial that this matter be addressed in the written partnership agreement.

Dissolution, Winding Up, and Termination of the Partnership

The **dissolution** of a partnership is more of a process than an event. The term *dissolution*, when used in reference to general partnerships, does not mean the termination of the partnership.

BALLENTINESBALLENTINESBALLENTINESBALLENTINESBALLENTINESBALLENTINESBALLENTINESBALLENTINESBALLENTINESBALLENTINESBALLENTINESBALLENTINESBALLENTINESBALLENTINES

dissolution of partnership   The change in the relation of partners caused by any partner's ceasing to be associated in the carrying on of the business. Any such change brings about the dissolution of the partnership.

Under the Uniform Partnership Act, *dissolution* is defined as "the change in the relation of the partners caused by any partner ceasing to be associated in the carrying on as distinguished from winding up of the business."[21]

Upon dissolution of the partnership, the partnership relationship terminates with respect to all future transactions, and the authority of all partners to act on behalf of the partnership and on behalf of each other terminates, except to the extent necessary for winding up of the partnership. **Winding up** is the process by which the accounts of the partnership are settled and the assets are **liquidated** to make distribution of the net assets of the partnership to the partners and dissolve the partnership. Winding up may include the performance of existing contracts, the collection of debts or claims due the partnership, and payment of the partnership's debts.

Causes of Dissolution

The dissolution of a partnership may be either voluntary or involuntary (by decree of court). Voluntary dissolution of a partnership may be precipitated by:

1. The expiration of the term of the partnership or completion of a specific undertaking as set forth in the partnership agreement
2. The express desire of one or more of the partners when no definite term or event triggering dissolution is defined by agreement
3. The unanimous agreement of all partners
4. The expulsion of any partner pursuant to the terms of the partnership agreement
5. The express will of any partner at any time
6. Any event that makes it illegal for the partnership business to continue or for the partners to carry on in the partnership

7. The death of any partner
8. The bankruptcy of any partner or the partnership.[22]

In addition, upon application by or for any partner, the appropriate court may by decree order the partnership to dissolve for any of the following reasons:

1. Any partner is found to be insane
2. Any partner becomes incapable of performing his or her part of the partnership contract
3. Any partner is guilty of conduct that may prejudicially affect the carrying on of the business
4. Any partner willfully or persistently commits a breach of the partnership agreement, or conducts himself or herself in matters relating to the partnership business so that it is not reasonably practicable to carry on the business in partnership with him or her
5. The business of the partnership can only be operated at a loss
6. Any other circumstances that render a dissolution equitable.

Continuation of Partnership after Dissolution

When a partner dies, retires, or otherwise withdraws from a partnership pursuant to the partnership agreement, the partnership is dissolved and the winding-up process commences, unless one of the following conditions exists:

1. The partner who is withdrawing or retiring, or the legal representative of a deceased partner, consents to continuation of the partnership business
2. The partnership agreement contains provisions indicating that the remaining partners

winding up   The dissolution or liquidation of a corporation or a partnership.

liquidation   The winding up of a corporation, partnership, or other business enterprise upon dissolution by converting the assets to money, collecting the accounts receivable, paying the debts, and distributing the surplus if any exists.

have the option of continuing the business on the retirement, withdrawal or death of any partner

3. The partnership agreement contains provisions indicating that the partnership does not dissolve upon the retirement, withdrawal, or death of any partner.

If any of the foregoing conditions are met, and the remaining partners choose to continue the partnership, the winding-up process will not commence.

Wrongful Dissolution

When one partner dissolves the partnership in contravention of the partnership agreement, the innocent partners may elect to wind up the partnership and seek damages from the partner causing the wrongful dissolution. They may also continue the business under the same name, either by themselves or jointly with others; or they may continue the business and seek damages from the partner causing the wrongful dissolution.[23]

Dissolution Agreement

A written dissolution agreement among the partners of a dissolving partnership can help alleviate any disputes as to the method and timing of the dissolution, as well as any disputes that may arise subsequent to winding up. In the dissolution agreement, the partners who have the right to wind up the partnership generally appoint a liquidating partner or partners and delegate the authority to liquidate the partnership and settle the partnership affairs.

Distribution of Assets

Unless otherwise specified in the partnership agreement, the rules for distribution of the partnership assets are set by statute. Pursuant to § 40

of the Uniform Partnership Act, the assets of the partnership are:

1. The partnership property
2. Any necessary contributions of the partners to pay the liabilities of the partnership.

The liabilities of the partnership rank in order of payment, as follows:

1. Liabilities owing to creditors other than partners
2. Liabilities owing to partners other than for capital and profits
3. Liabilities owing to partners in respect of capital
4. Liabilities owing to partners in respect of profits.

In settling the accounts of the partnership, the partnership property is first used to pay the liabilities in order of rank. If the partnership property is insufficient to cover all of the partnership liabilities, the partners are required to make contributions to cover the liabilities. If any, but not all, of the partners are insolvent, or otherwise unable or unwilling to contribute to payment of the liabilities, the liabilities of the partnership must be paid by the remaining partners in the same proportion as their share of the profits of the partnership. Any partner, or the legal representative of any partner, who is required to pay in excess of his or her fair share of the liabilities to settle the affairs of the partnership, has the right to enforce the contributions of the other partners pursuant to statute and the partnership agreement, to the extent of the amount paid in excess of his or her share of the liability.

The exact method of distribution should be set forth clearly in the partnership agreement. Generally, the partners are entitled to a distribution of the assets in the same percentage as their contribution of capital to the partnership, with adjustments made for subsequent contributions in the form of capital contributions and services rendered on behalf of the partnership.

An Introduction to Limited Partnerships

Limited partnerships are a special type of partnership that offer certain partners limited liability. Limited partnerships share many of the characteristics of general partnerships, with a few important differences.

Limited Partnership Defined

A **limited partnership** is a partnership created by statute with one or more **general partners** and one or more **limited partners**. The status of general partners of a limited partnership is very similar to that of the partners of general partnerships, and they have many of the same rights, duties, and obligations. Limited partners, in contrast, are in many ways more like investors than partners, because their risk is limited to the amount of their contributions and they are not entitled to manage the business of the limited partnership. As with a general partnership, a partner may be a "natural person, partnership, limited partnership (domestic or foreign), trust, estate, association, or corporation."[24]

Law Governing Limited Partnerships

Limited partnerships are governed by state statutes, which are almost all derived from uniform law. All states except Louisiana, Alaska, and Vermont have adopted the Revised Uniform Limited Partnership Act (RULPA), which was approved in 1976 and substantially amended in 1985. Alaska and Vermont have adopted the Uniform Limited Partnership Act (ULPA), which was approved in 1916.

The Limited Partnership as a Separate Entity

Much like the general partnership, a limited partnership may be treated as a separate entity for certain purposes, and as an aggregate of the individual partners for other purposes. When dealing with certain matters, including real estate ownership and the capacity to sue, the limited partnership is considered a separate entity. For other purposes, such as income taxation, the limited partnership is still considered an aggregate of the individual partners. Under common law, no partnership was ever considered a separate entity, and many states still subscribe to the common law approach when dealing with limited partnerships.[25]

Partners' Rights and Responsibilities

Limited partnerships include more than one type of partner, and those partners are subject to different statutory rights and responsibilities. The relationship between limited partners and general partners is also unique.

General Partners' Rights and Responsibilities

Except as otherwise provided by statute and the limited partnership agreement, the rights and responsibilities of a general partner in a limited partnership are very similar to those of a partner in a general partnership. Unlike limited partners, general partners are personally responsible for

---

BALLENTINESBALLENTINESBALLENTINESBALLENTINESBALLENTINESBALLENTINESBALLENTINESBALLENTINESBALLENTINESBALLENTINESBALLENTINESBALLENTINESBALLENTINES

limited partnership   A partnership in which the liability of one or more of the partners is limited to the amount of money they have invested in the partnership.

general partner   A partner in an ordinary partnership, as distinguished from a limited partnership.

limited partner   A partner in a limited partnership whose liability is limited to the sum he or she contributed to the limited partnership as capital. A limited partner is not involved in managing or carrying out the business of the partnership.

the liabilities and obligations of the limited partnership. Section 9(1) of the original Uniform Limited Partnership Act specifically limited the powers of general partners, by enumerating certain forbidden acts, but no such restrictions on general partners are contained in the Revised Uniform Limited Partnership Act.

Limited Partners' Rights and Responsibilities

The limited partner is often seen as more of an investor than an actual partner to the partnership. The limited partner has few of the rights granted to partners in a general partnership and few of the responsibilities. One of the most important characteristics of limited partners is that they have limited personal liability. Their risk is limited to the amount of their investment in the limited partnership.

The interest of a limited partner in a partnership is considered to be personal property. The limited partner holds no title to the assets of the partnership, but has only his or her interest in the partnership.[26]

Unlike the partners in a general partnership, limited partners have no right to participate in management of the partnership, and may actually lose their limited liability status if they are found to be "taking part in the control of" the partnership business. In that event, the limited partner may be held personally liable for the debts and obligations of the limited partnership.

Exactly what constitutes "taking part in control" of the business has been the focus of many a court case, and is still subject to debate. However, in the Revised Uniform Limited Partnership Act, some guidance is given by a list of "safe harbor" activities:

A limited partner does not participate in the control of the business ... solely by doing one or more of the following:

(1) being a contractor for or an agent or employee of the limited partnership or of a general partner or being an officer, director, or shareholder of a general partner that is a corporation;

(2) consulting with and advising a general partner with respect to the business of the limited partnership;

(3) acting as surety for the limited partnership or guaranteeing or assuming one or more specific obligations of the limited partnership;

(4) taking any action required or permitted by law to bring or pursue a derivative action in the right of the limited partnership;

(5) requesting or attending a meeting of partners;

(6) proposing, approving, or disapproving, by voting or otherwise, one or more of the following matters:

   (i)   the dissolution and winding up of the limited partnership;

   (ii) the sale, exchange, lease, mortgage, pledge, or other transfer of all or substantially all of the assets of the limited partnership;

   (iii) the incurrence of indebtedness by the limited partnership other than in the ordinary course of its business;

   (iv) a change in the nature of the business;

   (v)   the admission or removal of a general partner;

   (vi) the admission or removal of a limited partner;

   (vii) a transaction involving an actual or potential conflict of interest between a general partner and the limited partnership or the limited partners;

   (viii) an amendment to the partnership agreement or certificate of limited partnership; or

   (ix) matters related to the business of the limited partnership not otherwise enumerated in this subsection ... , which the partnership agreement states in writing may be subject to the approval or disapproval of limited partners;

(7) winding up the limited partnership pursuant to Section 803; or

(8) exercising any right or power permitted to limited partners under this Act and not specifically enumerated in this subsection.[27]

The RULPA further states that the possession or exercise of any powers not included in this list does not necessarily constitute participation of the limited partner in the partnership business.

The Relationship Between General Partners and Limited Partners

Because limited partners are prohibited from participating in the control of the business, the relationship between general partners and limited partners differs significantly from the relationship among partners in a general partnership. General partners owe a fiduciary duty to limited partners, and the sole general partner of a limited partnership owes to limited partners an even greater duty than that normally imposed on partners, especially when the general partner holds a majority interest.[28]

One person may be both a general partner and a limited partner in the same partnership. In that event, the partner will have all of the rights and responsibilities of a general partner. However, his or her contribution to the partnership as a limited partner will be protected in the same manner as the contribution of any other limited partner.

Organization and Management of a Limited Partnership

The organization and management of a limited partnership is generally similar to that of a general partnership, with two important distinctions. First, the limited partnership is formed by filing a limited partnership certificate for public record. Second, the general partners of the limited partnership control the partnership business.

Corporate paralegals are often responsible for several aspects of the organization and management of limited partnerships. Most importantly, paralegals are often delegated the task of drafting and filing limited partnership certificates and limited partnership agreements. To draft certificates and agreements effectively, paralegals must be familiar with state statutory requirements. In addition, office form files and formbooks containing sample limited partnership certificates and limited partnership agreement provisions are often helpful.

The Limited Partnership Certificate

The limited partnership does not exist until the limited partnership certificate is filed with the Secretary of State or other designated state official according to state statute. This document may include the entire agreement between the partners, but more commonly it contains the minimum amount of information required by state statute, with the full agreement of the partners contained in a limited partnership agreement or in other documents that are not filed for public record.

Whereas the original Uniform Limited Partnership Act required that the limited partnership certificate contain a great deal of information, including information concerning the partners' contributions, the Revised Uniform Limited Partnership Act allows many of those required provisions to be included in the limited partnership agreement or records kept by the limited partnership. The information contained in these records need not be made public in the limited partnership certificate. In states where the RULPA has been adopted, the certificate of limited partnership need contain only the following:

1. The name of the limited partnership
2. The office address and the name and address of the agent for service of process
3. The name and the business address of each general partner
4. The latest date upon which the limited partnership is to dissolve
5. Any other matters the general partners determine to include in the certificate.[29]

When any significant information in the limited partnership certificate changes, or when an error in the certificate is detected, a certificate of amendment must be filed pursuant to state statutes. Under most circumstances, any amendment to the limited partnership certificate must be approved and executed by all partners.

LIMITED PARTNERSHIP CERTIFICATE
(Revised Uniform Limited Partnership Act)

1. The name of the limited partnership is ABC Real Estate Development Limited Partnership.

2. The office address of the principal place of business of the limited partnership is:

123 Main Street
Hometown, NY 12345.

3. The name and office address of the agent for service of process is:

Alexander Anderson
123 Main Street
Hometown, NY 12345.

4. The name and business address of each general partner is as follows:

Name	*Address*
Alexander Anderson	123 Main Street, Hometown, NY 12345
Benjamin Brown	123 Oak Court, Hometown, NY 12345
Cathy Collins	123 Oak Court, Hometown NY 12345.

5. The latest date upon which the limited partnership is to dissolve is December 31, 1999.

Signed this _____ day of _____ , 19___ .

GENERAL PARTNERS:

_____

_____

_____

Required Limited Partnership Records

In addition to the information set forth in the limited partnership certificate, in states following the Revised Uniform Limited Partnership Act, the following records must be kept at a partnership office designated for partnership record-keeping:

1. A current list of the names and business addresses of all partners. This list must identify the general partners in alphabetical order and separately list in alphabetical order the limited partners.

2. A copy of the certificate of limited partnership and all certificates of amendment

thereto, together with executed copies of any powers of attorney pursuant to which any certificate has been executed.

3. Copies of the limited partnership's federal, state and local income tax returns and reports, if any, for the three most recent years.

4. Copies of any effective written partnership agreements.

5. Copies of any financial statements of the limited partnership for the three most recent years.[30]

The following information must be set out in a writing kept at the partnership office, unless it is contained in the limited partnership agreement:

1. The amount of cash and a description and statement of the agreed value of any other property or services contributed by each partner and which each partner has agreed to contribute.

2. The times at which or events on the happening of which any additional contributions agreed to be made by each partner are to be made.

3. Any rights of partners to receive, or of a general partner to make, distributions to a partner, including a return of all or any part of the partner's contribution.

4. Any events upon the happening of which the limited partnership is to be dissolved and its affairs wound up.[31]

These records must be kept subject to inspection and copying at the reasonable request and at the expense of any partner during ordinary business hours.

Limited Partnership Agreement

The limited partnership agreement should encompass the entire agreement among all partners. This document usually goes into much more detail than the limited partnership certificate, because it is not a document of public record, and it is more easily amended than the limited partnership certificate.

Limited Partnership Agreement Checklist

- Name and address of each limited partner and each general partner and a designation of their partnership status
- Name of the limited partnership
- Purpose of the limited partnership
- Address of the limited partnership's principal place of business
- Duration of the limited partnership agreement
- Contributions of both general partners and limited partners
- Limited partnership assets
- Liability of general partners and limited partners to each other and third parties
- Distribution of profits and losses to general and limited partners
- Indemnification of partners
- Duties of general partners
- Duties of limited partners
- Limited partners' rights of substitution
- Limitation on powers
- General partner compensation
- Partnership expenses
- Management and control of business by general partners
- Limited partners' rights in review of business policies
- Business policies
- Accounting practices and procedures
- Changes in general or limited partners by withdrawal, expulsion, retirement, or death
- Sale or purchase of limited partnership interest
- Arbitration provisions
- Termination of limited partnership
- Dissolution and winding up
- Date of agreement
- Signatures of all general partners and limited partners.

Changes in the Limited Partnership

Many types of changes in the limited partnership may affect its continuance, including the admission of new general partners, the admission of new limited partners, and the withdrawal of general and limited partners.

Admission of New General Partners   The requirements for admitting new general partners vary from state to state and depend especially upon which form of the Uniform Limited Partnership Act the state has adopted. In general, in states following the original ULPA, the limited partnership may admit general partners only by the unanimous written consent of all general and limited partners. Typically, in states following the RULPA, general partners may be admitted with the written consent of all partners, or by another means set forth in the limited partnership agreement.

Admission of New Limited Partners   States following the original ULPA generally require that an amendment to the limited partnership certificate be filed before new limited partners can be added.[32] In states following the Revised Act, amendment of the limited partnership certificate is not necessary.

Withdrawal of General Partners   As with the general partnership, the death or withdrawal of a general partner generally causes the dissolution of a limited partnership. However, there are many exceptions to this rule. A general partner may withdraw from a limited partnership at any time by giving written notice to the other partners. If a general partner withdraws from the partnership in violation of the terms of the limited partnership agreement, the limited partnership may recover damages from the withdrawing partner for breach of the partnership agreement, and those damages may be used to offset any distribution to which the withdrawing general partner is otherwise entitled.

Withdrawal of Limited Partners   The limited partnership is not dissolved upon the death or withdrawal of a limited partner. In the event of the death of a limited partner, the executor or administrator of the deceased limited partner's estate succeeds to all of the decedent's rights for the purpose of settling his or her estate.

Financial Structure of a Limited Partnership

The financial structure of a limited partnership is more complex than that of either a sole proprietorship or a general partnership. A basic concept of the limited partnership is that a limited partner must "make a stated contribution to the partnership, and place it at risk."[33] Under the original Uniform Limited Partnership Act, limited partners are allowed to contribute cash or other property, but not services.[34] This restriction does not appear in the Revised Uniform Limited Partnership Act.

Withdrawal of Contributions

Terms and conditions for disbursements and the withdrawal of contributions prior to dissolution of the limited partnership are typically set forth in either the limited partnership certificate or the limited partnership agreement. However, there are certain statutory restrictions on the withdrawal of contributions. Under the ULPA, no disbursements or withdrawals of contributions are allowed to limited partners unless all liabilities of the partnership, except those to general partners and those to limited partners on account of their contributions, have been paid or there remains property of the partnership sufficient to pay them.[35] Under the RULPA, distributions to partners are forbidden except to the extent that, after giving effect to the distribution, all liabilities, other than those to partners on account of their interests, do not exceed the fair value of the partnership assets.

Profits and Losses

The profits and losses of a limited partnership are shared among the partners pursuant to the partnership agreement or certificate. If the partnership agreement does not specify a manner for allocating the profits and losses, they are allocated on the basis of the value, as stated in the partnership records, of the contributions made by each partner, to the extent they have been received by the partnership and have not been returned.[36]

Dissolution, Winding Up, and Termination

The termination of a limited partnership is a process that involves several steps, including cancellation of the certificate of limited partnership, winding up the affairs of the limited partnership, and settling and distributing the partnership's assets.

Causes of Dissolution

The original Uniform Limited Partnership Act states that dissolution of the limited partnership occurs on the retirement, death, or insanity of a general partner, unless the business is continued by the remaining general partners under a right to do so stated in the certificate of limited partnership or with the consent of all members.[37] The Revised Uniform Limited Partnership Act provides that a limited partnership is dissolved, and its affairs must be wound up, when the first of the following events occurs:

1. The time period specified in the certificate expires
2. Specific events specified in writing in the certificate occur
3. The partners all consent in writing to dissolve the partnership
4. An event of withdrawal of a general partner occurs
5. The entry of a decree of judicial dissolution.

An "event of withdrawal" of a general partner, as the term is used in the RULPA, includes the general partner's voluntary withdrawal, removal, insolvency, incompetency, and assignment of the general partner's interest. An event of withdrawal does not cause dissolution if there is at least one other general partner and the certificate allows the business to be carried on, or if, within 90 days after such an event, all partners agree in writing to continue the business. If all partners agree to continue the business, they may appoint one more additional general partner if necessary or desirable.

A limited partner may have the right to have the partnership dissolved and wound up by court decree when the limited partner's rightful demand for return of contribution is not met or when it is not reasonably practicable to carry on the business of the limited partnership in conformity with the partnership agreement.

Cancellation of Certificate of Limited Partnership

Because a limited partnership is created by the certificate of limited partnership filed with the state authority, the certificate must be cancelled before the limited partnership can be terminated. The certificate is cancelled by means of a certificate of cancellation containing all the information required by state statute filed with the Secretary of State.

Winding Up the Limited Partnership's Affairs

Under the Revised Uniform Limited Partnership Act, "the general partners who have not wrongfully dissolved a limited partnership or, if none, the limited partners, may wind up the limited partnership's affairs."[38] Any partner or any partner's legal representative or assignee may also make application to an appropriate court to wind up the limited partnership's affairs.

Settlement and Distribution of Assets

Under § 23 of the original Uniform Limited Partnership Act, the accounts of the partnership are settled in the following order after a dissolution:

(a) Those to creditors, in the order of priority as provided by law, except those to limited partners on account of their contributions, and to general partners,

(b) Those to limited partners in respect to their share of the profits and other compensation by way of income on their contributions,

(c) Those to limited partners in respect to the capital of their contributions,

(d) Those to general partners other than for capital and profits,

(e) Those to general partners in respect to profits,

(f) Those to general partners in respect to capital.

Unless the certificate or a subsequent agreement provides otherwise, limited partners share in the assets in respect to their claims for capital and for profits on their contributions in proportion to the respective amounts of such claims.

Under § 408 of the Revised Uniform Limited Partnership Act, the assets of the limited partnership are distributed in the following order upon dissolution:

(1) to creditors, including partners who are creditors, to the extent permitted by law, in satisfaction of liabilities of the limited partnership other than liabilities for distributions to partners …;

(2) except as provided in the partnership agreement, to partners and former partners in satisfaction of liabilities for distributions …; and

(3) except as provided in the partnership agreement, to partners first for the return of their contributions and secondly respecting their partnership interests, in the proportions in which the partners share distributions.

An Introduction to Corporations

The **corporation** is one of the most complex forms of business organization. There are many types of corporations, but this section focuses on the business corporation, which is the predominant form.

Corporation Defined

An early Supreme Court decision defined the corporation as "an artificial being, invisible, intangible, and existing only in contemplation of law."[39] This definition has been used frequently over the years. Another definition that is popular in the courts defines the corporation as a "creature of the law, with an identity or personality separate and distinct from that of its owners, and which, by necessity, must act through its agents."[40] Whatever the exact definition, the corporation possesses the following characteristics that distinguish it from other types of business organizations:

1. The corporation is an artificial entity created by law

2. The corporation is an entity separate from its owners or managers

3. The corporation has certain rights and powers which it exercises through its agents

4. The corporation has the capacity to exist perpetually.

The Corporation as a Separate Legal Entity

In contrast to the sole proprietorship and general partnership, which are extensions of the individual owner or owners, the corporation is considered "an entity distinct from its individual members or stockholders, who, as natural persons, are merged in the corporate identity, and remains unchanged and unaffected in its identity by changes in its individual membership."[41] In many respects,

BALLENTINESBALLENTINESBALLENTINESBALLENTINESBALLENTINESBALLENTINESBALLENTINESBALLENTINESBALLENTINESBALLENTINESBALLENTINESBALLENTINESBALLENTINES

corporation   An artificial person, existing only in the eyes of the law, to whom a state or the federal government has granted a charter to become a legal entity, separate from its shareholders, with a name of its own, under which its shareholders can act and contract and sue and be sued.

corporations are treated as "artificial persons" under law. As an artificial person, a corporation is subject to many of the same rights and obligations under the law as a natural person.

Because the corporation is a separate entity, the corporation itself is liable for any debts and obligations it incurs. The shareholders, directors, and officers of a corporation are generally not personally liable for the corporation's debts and obligations.

Piercing the Corporate Veil

Although the **shareholders** of a corporation are generally free from personal liability for the corporation's obligations, there are certain circumstances under which the corporate entity may be disregarded and shareholders held personally liable for the debts and obligations of the corporation. This is referred to as *piercing the corporate veil.* Courts generally are reluctant to pierce the corporate veil, but may do so when the corporation is used to avoid a clear legislative purpose[42]; when it is necessary to preserve, protect, and enforce the rights of others; or to prevent an injustice.[43] The corporate veil of a small or closely held corporation may be pierced when the corporation is found to be an "alter ego" of an individual and if doing so will help secure a just determination of the action.[44] Courts have found that the "corporate entity may be disregarded where there is such unity of interest and ownership that the separate personalities of the corporation and the individual no longer exist and where, if the acts are treated as those of the corporation alone, an inequitable result will follow."[45]

Although courts usually pierce the corporate veil only to prevent inequity, injustice, or fraud, other factors are also considered. The corporation is scrutinized to determine if it is actually operated as a corporation and whether the statutory formalities for incorporating and operating the corporation have been followed. The following factors often support piercing the corporate veil:

1. Improper or incomplete incorporation
2. Commingling of corporate and shareholder funds
3. Failure to follow statutory formalities
4. Failure to hold regular shareholders' and directors' meetings
5. Failure of shareholders to represent themselves as agents of a corporation, rather than individuals, when dealing with outside parties
6. Undercapitalization.

The fact that it is possible for the corporate veil to be pierced under certain circumstances makes it imperative that all corporate formalities be followed by the corporation and that those formalities be properly documented. In the *Hormel* case, which follows, the corporate veil was pierced and the corporation's shareholders were found liable for a corporate debt when the court found that the shareholders had depleted the corporate checking account for the specific purpose of avoiding payment of a check issued to a creditor.

Law Governing Corporations

As a separate entity, the corporation must be in compliance with all laws concerning it. The source of most law regarding corporations is state statute. The statutes of every state in the country are derived, at least in part, from the Model Business Corporation Act, first published in 1950, or the 1984 Revised Model Business Corporation Act. The Model Act continues to be revised through the date of this publication.

Corporations are created by and generally governed by the statutes of the state of **domicile** (the state in which the corporation is incorporated).

shareholder (stockholder)   The owner of one or more shares of stock in a corporation; a person who appears on the books of a corporation as the owner of one or more shares of its stock. The terms *shareholder* and *stockholder* are used interchangeably.

domicile   The relationship that the law creates between a person and a particular locality or country.

A corporation that transacts business in a foreign state, however, subjects itself to the statutes of that state for certain purposes.

Corporate Rights and Powers

As a separate entity, the corporation enjoys certain rights and powers separate from those of its shareholders, directors, or officers. Corporations, as artificial persons, are entitled to many of the same rights as natural persons, including many of the same constitutional rights.

Many powers granted to corporations by state statute may be limited or enhanced by the corporation's articles of incorporation. State statutes generally grant corporations perpetual duration and succession in its corporate name and the same powers as an individual to do all things necessary or convenient to carry out its business and affairs.[46] This includes such powers as the right to buy, own, and sell property, both real and personal.

Special Types of Corporations

There are many types of corporations, distinguished by their financial structure, ownership, and purpose. Some of the more common types of corporations include business corporations, professional corporations, nonprofit corporations, S corporations, limited liability companies, and statutory close corporations.

Business Corporations

Business corporations, which include large, publicly held corporations and smaller, closely held corporations, are by far the most numerous type in this country. They may be formed for the purpose of engaging in any lawful business, unless a more limited purpose is desired.

Professional Corporations

Under common law, professionals were only allowed to practice individually or as partners. However, in recent years most states have adopted statutes providing for the formation of professional corporations, or professional service corporations, as they are sometimes called. The Model Professional Corporation Act provides that professional corporations may be formed "only for the purpose of rendering professional services and services ancillary thereto within a single profession."[47] An exception to the single profession rule permits one or more professions to be combined to the extent permitted by the licensing laws of the state of domicile.

Nonprofit Corporations

A nonprofit corporation, or not-for-profit corporation as it is sometimes referred to, may be formed only for certain nonprofit purposes, including charitable, civic, educational, and religious purposes. Incorporating as a nonprofit corporation does not ensure exemption from federal income taxation. To qualify for tax exemption, the corporation must meet the requirements of Internal Revenue Code § 501(c) and obtain approval from the Internal Revenue Service.

S Corporations

The Internal Revenue Service recognizes a special category of corporations, referred to as S corporations, for federal income tax purposes. An eligible small business corporation may elect to be treated as an S corporation if all its shareholders agree. There is usually no distinction between S corporations and other types of corporations at the state level.

Unlike a business corporation, the income of an S corporation generally is not taxed at the corporate level, but is passed through to the shareholders of the corporation, much like income is passed through to the partners of a partnership. S corporations must meet the specific eligibility requirements set out in I.R.C. § 1361.

Limited Liability Companies

The limited liability company offers both the tax advantages of a partnership and the limited liability advantages of a business corporation. Rather than a type of corporation, the limited liability company is actually a new form of business organization that is recognized in fewer than 15 states in the country.[48] Limited liability companies are organized as such at the state level. This type of business organization closely resembles the S corporation, but fewer restrictions apply to its owners. Currently, several states are considering the adoption of legislation permitting this new type of business organization.

George A. Hormel & Company
V.
James Wesley FORD, Ruthie Belcher Ford, and
Ford Wholesale Pizza Products, Inc.
No. CA 85 1545.
[486 So. 2d 927 (La. Ct. App. 1986)]
Court of Appeal of Louisiana, First Circuit
March 25, 1986.

PONDER, Judge.

Defendants James Wesley Ford and Ruthie Belcher Ford appealed the judgment holding them personally liable for the price of meat products purchased by the defendant corporation.

The issue on appeal is the liability of the individual defendants for a corporate debt.

We affirm.

The Fords, husband and wife, were the owners of Ford Wholesale Pizza Products, Inc. of which Mr. Ford was the sole director and officer. On January 11, 1982, he telephoned the Shreveport offices of plaintiff, George A. Hormel & Company, and contracted to purchase a quantity of meat products for $5,194.82. The next day at the Fords' direction, a corporate employee drove to Shreveport, picked up the meat and delivered a check, drawn upon the corporate bank account and signed by Mrs. Ford, to Hormel in the amount of the purchase price. However, the driver failed to deliver the meat to the corporation in Baton Rouge.

Upon learning of this fact, the Fords decided to and did deplete the corporate account so that the check issued to Hormel would be returned for insufficient funds. Thereafter, Hormel's demand for the amount due was ignored, and this suit followed.

After trial on the merits, the trial court ruled in Hormel's favor against the Fords individually, finding that a disregard of the corporate entity was justified based on the Fords' act of depleting the corporate account with the intent of depriving Hormel of the purchase price ... . The Fords appealed ... .

Defendants contend that the trial court erred in ruling that the factual circumstances herein justified a finding of individual liability for a corporate debt.

A corporation is a distinct legal entity, separate from the individuals who comprise it. As a general rule, individual shareholders are not liable for the debts of the corporation. However, in a few limited situations, a court may ignore the corporate fiction, "pierce the corporate veil," and hold the individual liable for debts incurred by the corporation. ... This can be done when a shareholder practices fraud or other misconduct upon a third person through the corporation or disregards the corporate entity to such an extent that the corporation is indistinguishable from its shareholders. ...

The decision to pierce the corporate veil must be made based upon the totality of the circumstances present in each case. ... Whether imposition of individual liability is justified under particular circumstances is primarily a factual finding to be made by the trial court. ...

Mr. and Mrs. Ford testified that they used the money withdrawn from the corporate account to pay other corporate creditors, including Mr. Ford, but offered no proof of the legitimacy or amount of these other corporate debts, nor could they specify how much of the amount withdrawn was paid to Mr. Ford. Both essentially admitted that they intentionally depleted the corporate account with the specific purpose in mind to avoid payment of the check issued to Hormel.

The trial court, in its reasons for judgment, concluded that the acceptance by Mr. Ford of monies withdrawn from the corporate account for the purpose of avoiding a corporate debt amounted to an appropriation of corporate funds "to the disadvantage of" or in defraud of a corporate creditor; and this amounted to misconduct of such a nature as to justify imposition of personal liability upon Mr. and Mrs. Ford. We find no manifest error in this conclusion. ...

AFFIRMED.

[Citations omitted.]

Statutory Close Corporations

Statutory close corporations generally have no more than 50 shareholders and have elected close corporation status. Such a corporation must specifically state in its articles of incorporation that it is a close corporation.[49] Because statutory close corporations are allowed to place certain restrictions on the transfer of corporate shares, the corporation's stock certificates must contain specific language on their face to indicate that the corporation is a statutory close corporation and that the shareholder's rights may differ from those of other corporations. All state statutes have some type of provision regarding notification of an election to become a statutory close corporation.

Statutory close corporations are generally allowed to operate without many of the statutory formalities imposed on other types of corporations. Because the shareholders and directors are often the same individuals, statutory close corporations are usually permitted to operate without a board of directors, leaving the management and operation of the corporation to the shareholders. In addition, the shareholders of a statutory close corporation need not adopt bylaws if the required provisions are included in the corporation's articles of incorporation or a separate shareholder agreement.

Forming the Business Corporation

One of the duties most often assigned to corporate paralegals is the incorporation of businesses. The corporation is an entity that cannot exist until it has been properly incorporated by the filing of articles or a certificate of incorporation with the Secretary of State or other appropriate state official. Like Michael in the following law office scenario, corporate paralegals must be familiar with every aspect of forming a corporation in their state.

Incorporators

The *incorporator* is the individual who actually signs the articles or certificate of incorporation to form the corporation. The role played by the incorporator is usually minor, and his or her involvement typically ceases after the articles or certificate are filed or after the organizational meeting electing the first board of directors is held. At times, the attorney for the corporate client serves as the incorporator and signs and files the articles of incorporation on behalf of the client.

Articles of Incorporation

The document actually filed with the appropriate state authority to form the corporation is typically called the **articles of incorporation**, although in some states it may be referred to as the *certificate of incorporation* or *charter*. The articles of incorporation contain essential information regarding the corporation and must comply with the statutory requirements of the proposed corporation's state of domicile. Most state provisions are similar to the Model Business Corporation Act, which requires only four items to be set forth: (1) the name of the corporation, (2) the number of shares the corporation is authorized to issue, (3) the street address of the corporation's initial registered office, and (4) the name of the initial registered agent at that office, and the name and address of each incorporator.[50]

The name chosen by the corporation must comply with the statutes of the state of domicile. Most states require that the name of the corporation contain a word or words indicating that the corporation is a corporate entity; the name of a corporation domiciled in a state following the Model Business Corporation Act must include the word "corporation," "incorporated," "company," or "limited," or the abbreviation "corp.," "inc.," "co.," or "ltd.," or words or abbreviations of like import in another language. In addition, the name of the corporation must not be the same as or deceptively similar to the name of any other corporation or entity of record in the office of the Secretary of State of the state of domicile, and it must not mislead as to the purpose of the corporation.

The articles of incorporation must set forth the number of shares of each class of stock that the corporation is authorized to issue. State statutes

articles of incorporation   The charter or basic rules that create a corporation and by which it functions.

Law Office Scenario

Michael Longtree, a corporate paralegal at the Simmons & Simmons law firm, was called into attorney Diane Peterson's office early one Wednesday morning.

"Michael," she said, "I met with a new client last evening regarding the formation of a new corporation. They want to form a new corporation for their marketing consulting business. It will be a Minnesota business corporation. I

had my secretary type up the information you will need to form the corporation. Please prepare all of the necessary incorporation documents. I would also appreciate it if you would prepare a memo for our client, advising them of the formalities that must be followed to operate as a Minnesota business corporation. Let me know if you have any questions."

---

may require additional information regarding the corporation's authorized stock as well.

The articles of incorporation must also include the registered office of the corporation and registered agent located in the state of domicile to receive service of process on behalf of the corporation. Finally, the name and address of each incorporator must be set forth. The incorporators also must sign the articles of incorporation in the method prescribed by state statute.

The articles of incorporation may include any additional information that the incorporators choose to include regarding the management and administration of corporate affairs.

The articles of incorporation must be filed with the appropriate state authority within the state of domicile to become effective. In addition, any other incorporation requirements imposed by the state of domicile, such as publishing a notice of incorporation, must be complied with for effective incorporation.

Organizational Meetings

After the articles of incorporation are filed, the organizational meeting of the corporation is usually held. The requirements for this organizational meeting, and the organizational actions that must be taken, vary greatly from state to state. Either the incorporators or a majority of the directors named in the articles of incorporation may be required

to call the organizational meeting and give notice to the directors and/or shareholders of the corporation. As a practical matter, the organizational meeting is usually attended by the incorporators, the initial board of directors, and shareholders, which often total only a very few people.

The purpose of the organizational meeting is to organize the corporation. This usually involves the election of officers, the subscription and payment of the capital stock, the adoption of bylaws, and any other steps necessary to create the capacity to transact the legitimate business for which the corporation was created.

The following items listed below are often considered for action at the organizational meeting. Depending on state statute, some of these actions may also require shareholder approval:

1. Approval and acceptance of articles of incorporation
2. Acceptance of stock subscriptions
3. Ratification of the acts of incorporator(s)
4. Election of officers
5. Adoption of bylaws
6. Approval of accounting methods
7. Approval of form of stock certificate
8. Banking resolutions
9. Recommendation of S corporation election to the shareholders
10. Adoption of employee benefit plans.

ARTICLES OF INCORPORATION
OF
ANDERSON AND CROWN MARKETING, INC.

The undersigned, acting as Incorporators of a corporation under the Minnesota Business Corporation Act, Minn. Stat. § 302(a), adopt the following Articles of Incorporation for such corporation.

I. NAME

The name of this corporation is Anderson and Crown Marketing, Inc.

II. AUTHORIZED STOCK

The number of shares that the corporation is authorized to issue is 10,000 shares of common stock, without par value.

III. INITIAL REGISTERED OFFICE AND AGENT

The name and address of the initial registered agent and office of this corporation are as follows:

Joan L. Anderson
123 Main Street
Bigtown, MN 12345

IV. INCORPORATORS

The names and addresses of the Incorporators signing these Articles of Incorporation are:

Name	Address
Joan L. Anderson	123 Main Street Bigtown, MN 12345
Elizabeth M. Crown	1234 1st Avenue Minneapolis, MN 50505.

IN WITNESS WHEREOF, the undersigned Incorporators have executed these Articles of Incorporation this _____ day of _____ , 19___ .

Articles of Incorporation Articles of Incorporation may be drafted by the paralegal. This document generally includes the name of the corporation and information on stock, registering agent, and incorporators. It is filed with the Secretary of State within the state of domicile.

The shareholders may be required by statute to attend the organizational meeting or to hold a different meeting referred to as the "first meeting of shareholders." This meeting is often a part of, or held immediately following, the organizational meeting or the first meeting of the board of directors. The following items are often considered for action at the first shareholder meeting:

_____

Joan L. Anderson

_____

Elizabeth M. Crown

STATE OF MINNESOTA

COUNTY OF WASHINGTON

   BEFORE ME, the undersigned authority, personally appeared Joan L. Anderson and Elizabeth M. Crown, to me known to be the persons who executed the foregoing Articles of Incorporation, and they acknowledged to and before me they executed such instrument.

   IN WITNESS WHEREOF, I have hereunto set my hand and seal this _____ day of _____ , 19___ .

_____

Notary Public, State of MN

My Commission Expires:

(Notarial Seal)

Articles of Incorporation _(Continued)_

1. Election of directors
2. Approval of S corporation election
3. Approval of bylaws.

All actions taken at the organizational meeting must be recorded by meeting minutes, which are filed in the corporation's minute book. In the alternative, under more recent law, the required resolutions may be made without the formality of a meeting if they are recorded by a **unanimous** written consent in lieu of organizational meeting. The unanimous writing must be signed and dated by all individuals entitled to notice and attendance at a meeting of the directors and/or shareholders. State statutes must be consulted and followed carefully if a unanimous writing is used.

Bylaws

Bylaws are the "rules and guidelines for the internal government and control of a corporation."[51] The bylaws, which are typically adopted by the board of directors, prescribe the rights and duties of the shareholders, directors, and officers with regard to the management and governance of the corporation The following provisions are commonly included in corporate bylaws:

1. The address of the corporation's principal office and any other significant offices to be used by the corporation
2. Requirements for shareholder meetings, including the time, place, and notice

---

unanimous   Complete approval or concurrence; the concurrence of everyone.

requirements for the annual meetings and the requirements for calling and holding special shareholder meetings, and who is entitled to receive notice of the shareholder meetings

3. The number of directors and their terms of office

4. Details regarding the requirements for board of director meetings, including the time, place, and notice requirements for the annual meetings and the requirements for calling and holding other director meetings

5. Provisions for the removal and resignation of directors

6. Provisions for director compensation

7. Provisions limiting or expanding director liability, within statutory limits

8. Provisions for the required officers of the corporation, including the officers' titles, their powers and duties, and the compensation for each officer

9. Approval of a form of stock certificate for each class or type of stock to be used, including the required signatures, and the means for transfer of stock and replacement of lost, stolen, or destroyed certificates

10. The method for determining the dividends to be paid on the corporation's stock, and the timing and method for the payment of dividends

11. The corporation's fiscal year

12. A reproduction of the corporate seal, if one is to be used

13. Provisions for keeping the corporate records, including a statement regarding which records that are to be kept, their location, and the inspection rights of officers, directors, and shareholders

14. Procedures for amending the corporation's bylaws.

The bylaws are typically dated and signed by the secretary of the corporation and filed in the corporate minute book.

Organization and Management of the Business Corporation

A corporate entity must act through its agents, the most visible of which are its officers and directors. The roles of the officers, directors, and shareholders can be very different, but each functions as an integral part of the operation of the business corporation.

Authority of the Board of Directors

Directors are given the statutory authority to make most decisions regarding the operation of the corporation. Although it may appear that they have free rein to operate the corporation as they see fit, directors are elected by the corporation's shareholders. A director who does not act in the shareholders' best interests could be voted out of office at the next election, or even removed before his or her term expires.

State statutes generally grant full authority to the **board of directors** to manage the business and affairs of the corporation. However, that authority may be limited in the articles of incorporation. In addition, certain corporate acts, if not within the ordinary business and administration of the corporation, may require approval of the shareholders.

The following actions often require shareholder approval:

1. Amendment and restatement of the articles of incorporation

2. Enactment, amendment, or repeal of bylaws

3. Issuance of stock of the corporation

4. Dissolution of the corporation

5. Calling of shareholder meetings

BALLENTINESBALLENTINESBALLENTINESBALLENTINESBALLENTINESBALLENTINESBALLENTINESBALLENTINESBALLENTINESBALLENTINESBALLENTINESBALLENTINESBALLENTINESBALLENTINES

board of directors   The directors of a corporation or association who act as a group in representing the organization and conducting its business.

UNANIMOUS WRITTEN CONSENT TO ACTION TAKEN
IN LIEU OF ORGANIZATIONAL MEETING
OF
ANDERSON AND CROWN MARKETING, INC.

The undersigned, being all of the incorporators, shareholders, and directors of Anderson and Crown Marketing, Inc., hereby consent to and ratify the action taken to organize the corporation as hereafter stated:

The Articles of Incorporation filed on October 24, 1995, with the Secretary of State of Minnesota, is hereby approved and it shall be inserted in the corporate minute book of the corporation.

The persons whose names appear below are hereby duly appointed directors of the corporation to serve for a period of one year and until their successors are appointed or elected and shall qualify:

> Joan L. Anderson
>
> Elizabeth M. Crown.

The persons whose names appear below are hereby duly appointed officers of the corporation to serve for a period of one year and until their successors are appointed or elected and shall qualify:

Chief Executive Officer:	Joan L. Anderson
Chief Financial Officer:	Elizabeth M. Crown
Secretary:	Elizabeth M. Crown.

Bylaws regulating the conduct of the business and affairs of the corporation, as prepared by Diane Peterson, counsel for the corporation, are hereby adopted and inserted in the record book.

The corporation shall have no corporate seal.

The directors are hereby authorized to issue the unsubscribed stock of the corporation at such times and in such amounts as they shall determine, and to accept in payment therefor cash, labor done, personal

Unanimous Written Consent to Action Taken in Lieu of Organizational Meeting
This document allows corporate directors and shareholders to agree to management decisions without the need for calling a formal meeting.

6. Approval of merger and consolidation plans
7. Sale of corporate assets other than in the regular course of business.

Duties of the Board of Directors

The duties of a corporate director are several and complex. They are based on longstanding property, real property, or leases therefor, or such other property as the board may deem necessary for the business of the corporation.

The Chief Financial Officer of the corportion is hereby duly authorized to open a bank account with First National Bank, located at Bigtown, Minnesota, and is authorized to execute a resolution for that purpose on the printed form of said bank.

The Chief Executive Officer is hereby duly authorized to designate the principal office of the corporation in this state as the office for service of process on the corporation, and to designate such further agents for service of process within or without this state as is in the best interests of the corporation. The president is hereby further authorized to execute any and all certificates or documents to implement the above.

Dated _____

_____

_____

Unanimous Written Consent to Action Taken in Lieu of Organizational Meeting   *(Continued)*

common law, as well as specific statutes. In general, directors owe the following to the corporation and its shareholders:

1. A fiduciary duty
2. A duty of care
3. A duty of loyalty.

The director's duty to the corporation and its shareholders resembles a fiduciary duty, in that the entire management of corporate affairs is often entrusted to the directors of the corporation, who are responsible for acting in the best interests of the corporation and the shareholders. This "quasi-fiduciary" duty has been defined as follows:

They are required to act in the utmost good faith, and in accepting the office, they impliedly undertake to give to the enterprise the benefit of their care and best judgment and to exercise the powers conferred solely in the interest of the corporation or the stockholders as a body or corporate entity, and not for their own personal interests.[52]

In addition to their fiduciary duty to shareholders, directors must use "due care" and be diligent in the management and administration of the corporation's affairs and in the use or preservation of its property.[53] The exact measure of this degree of care is impossible to define, although one test often used is the "ordinarily prudent person test," which means acting with the diligence and care that would be exercised by an ordinarily prudent person in like circumstances.

Directors have a duty of loyalty to the corporation and its shareholders. They must at all times act in a manner that serves the best interest of the corporation, as opposed to the directors' other interests or the directors' personal interests.

Individuals who are directors of related corporations or have interests in related businesses may find themselves in a potential conflict of interest. Directors should abstain from participating in corporate decisions that may give even the appearance of a conflict of interest. Some statutes require that directors disclose the existence and nature of potential conflicting interests and all known material facts with regard to the proposed transaction.

Personal Liability of Directors

The imposition of personal liability on corporate directors for poor business decisions would be impractical, if not impossible. Directors generally cannot be held personally liable for any damages caused to the corporation as the result of their good faith decisions. However, personal liability may be imposed in several instances.

A director who fails in his or her fiduciary duty, duty of due care, and duty of loyalty to the corporation may be subject to personal liability for any damages caused to the corporation and/or its shareholders. When directors clearly act beyond the scope of their authority, personal liability may be imposed upon them for losses caused by the unauthorized acts. Directors acting beyond the scope of their authority may be required to make good any losses out of their personal assets.

Directors are also personally liable for their negligent acts that involve injury or loss to the corporation or to third parties. This liability is based on the common-law rule "which renders every agent liable who violates his authority or neglects his duty to the damage of his principal."[54]

Directors may also be personally liable to the corporation and to third parties for any fraudulent or other tortious acts committed by them, or by the corporation to their knowledge. Corporate directors are not personally liable for fraud involving the corporation of which they were unaware, or of which they should not have reasonably been expected to be aware.

Director Compensation and Reimbursement

Directors are often called upon to serve the corporation in several different ways, and they may or may not be directly compensated by the corporation. Director compensation is usually set by the board of directors, unless the right to set director

[STATE NAME]

This Certifies that ___Jane Doe_____ is the owner and
registered holder of _____one hundred (100)_____ Shares of
the authorized capital stock of the ABC Corporation, no par value

transferable only on the books of the corporation by the holder hereof in person or by duly authorized attorney upon surrender of this certificate property endorsed.
IN WITNESS WHEREOF, the said corporation has caused this certificate to be signed by its duly authorized officers and to be sealed with the seal of the corporation
this __31st_____ day of __December_____, 19_92__.

CORPORATE SEAL

_____ Secretary   _____ President

Stock Certificate The stock certificate must include the following information: name of the issuing corporation, state of corporate domicile, name of the stockholder, and number and class of shares.

compensation is limited to the shareholders by the statutes of the state of domicile or the corporation's articles of incorporation or bylaws. A director generally has a right to be reimbursed for advances made or expenses incurred on behalf of the corporation. A director, however, has no right to be reimbursed for expenses incurred by his or her own wrongdoing.

Election and Term of Directors

The directors of a corporation are elected by the shareholders to operate and manage the affairs of the corporation, usually for one-year terms. With the possible exception of close corporations, all corporations are generally required to elect a board of directors and to have a board of directors at all times. Modern corporate law typically provides no restrictions on either the number or qualifications of directors other than those in the corporation's articles of incorporation or bylaws.

The term of each director expires at the next annual meeting of shareholders following the election, when the director's successor is elected and qualifies, or when the number of directors decreases. It is generally the shareholders' right to remove any director, with or without cause, by a majority vote at a special shareholders' meeting called specifically for that purpose. The requirements and procedures for removing a director may be set by the articles of incorporation or the bylaws, so long as those provisions comply with state statutes.

Board of Director Meetings and Resolutions

Most actions of the board of directors are taken through resolutions passed at board meetings. Modern corporate law recognizes the impracticality of mandatory, formal director's meetings for all board of director actions and three changes to the Model Business Corporation Act have been followed almost uniformly by the states to make it easier for boards of directors to act:

1. Annual board of directors meetings are optional

2. Action may be taken by the board of directors by a unanimous written consent, signed by each director

3. Telephonic meetings by the board of directors are generally acceptable.

Notice requirements for board meetings also have been relaxed in most states. The directors of the corporation must be aware of and follow all requirements for annual and special meetings, as prescribed by statute and by the corporation's articles of incorporation and bylaws.

A typical agenda for an annual board of directors meeting may include:

1. Approve the minutes from the last meeting of the board of directors

2. Approve dividends to be paid to the corporation's shareholders

3. Approve an annual report to be filed with appropriate state authority (if required)

4. Review the corporation's financial reports

5. Elect corporate officers to serve until the next annual meeting or until their successors are duly elected and qualify

6. Set the compensation of corporate officers for the succeeding year

7. Approve bonuses for officers and directors

8. Ratify the acts of officers and directors for the past year

9. Deal with any other matters of concern regarding the operation and business of the corporation.

Corporate Officers

Officers are, in the broadest sense, agents of the corporation.[55] They are individuals elected by the board of directors to oversee the business of the corporation, under the authority of the directors. An individual may be an officer and a director at the same time. In small corporations, all the officers are usually directors as well.

Generally, the officers of a corporation have the titles, duties, and responsibilities assigned to them under the statutes of the state of domicile, the articles of incorporation or bylaws of the corporation, or by resolution of the board of directors. Statutes may be very specific regarding the required officers of a corporation, naming the titles and duties that they must assume. More often, however, in modern corporate law the corporation is given much latitude regarding the officers it chooses and the duties assigned to those officers.

Officers are generally elected by a majority of the board of directors at the board's annual meeting. Traditionally, officers hold office for one year and are either re-elected or replaced at the next annual meeting of the board of directors. In recent years, however, many key corporate officers have negotiated contracts with the board of directors that extend well beyond the traditional one-year term.

Shareholder Rights and Responsibilities

A *shareholder,* or *stockholder,* is the owner of one or more shares of the corporation's stock. Each shareholder is, in effect, at least part owner of the corporation itself. Generally, shareholders of business corporations need not meet any qualifications. A shareholder may be an individual or an entity. Unless the corporate veil is pierced, or the shareholder gives a personal guarantee, the shareholder's liability is limited to the consideration to be paid for the shareholder's own shares.

The shareholders are the owners of the corporation and, as such, they are entitled to certain rights, including the right to inspect the corporate records. These rights are usually set forth in the statutes of the state of domicile, and may be extended in either the bylaws or the articles of incorporation.

Preemptive rights give shareholders the opportunity to protect their position in the corporation by allowing them to purchase newly issued shares of the corporation's stock in an amount proportionate to their current stock ownership. Special consideration must be given to the statutory

treatment of preemptive rights in the corporation's state of domicile, so that the incorporation documents can be drafted appropriately.

The freedom to transfer corporate stock without restriction has always been considered a basic shareholder right. However, courts have found that "restrictions may be imposed for the mutual convenience and protection of the parties, so long as such restrictions are not unreasonable and do not constitute an impairment of the stockholder's contractual rights."[56] Certain restrictions on transfer may be desirable to protect shareholders' status in the corporation and to monitor the inclusion of new shareholders. Shareholders of a **closely held corporation** may wish to have the option to purchase shares of a withdrawing shareholder before the shares are sold to an outsider. Also, shareholders looking toward the future may desire to ensure a market for their stock when they decide to sell.

Restrictions on the transfer of stock may be placed in the articles of incorporation, in the bylaws, or in a separate shareholder agreement or *buy-sell agreement.* Restrictions on the transfer of stock of statutory close corporations may also be prescribed by the close corporation act or business corporation act of the state of domicile.

Personal Liability of Shareholders

One of the greatest advantages to incorporating is that the corporate entity shelters individual shareholders from personal liability for the corporation's debts and obligations. A shareholder's liability generally consists of no more than the consideration paid for the shareholder's own stock in the corporation. The two most common exceptions to the rule of nonliability occur when the corporate veil is pierced, or when the individual shareholder grants a personal guarantee of some obligation of the corporation.

BALLENTINESBALLENTINESBALLENTINESBALLENTINESBALLENTINESBALLENTINESBALLENTINESBALLENTINESBALLENTINESBALLENTINESBALLENTINESBALLENTINESBALLENTINESBALLENTINES

preemptive right   The right or privilege of a stockholder of a corporation to purchase shares of a new issue before persons who are not stockholders. This entitlement allows a shareholder to preserve his or her percentage of ownership in the corporation.

closely held corporation   A corporation in which all the stock is owned by a few persons or by another corporation.

Shareholder Meetings

Shareholder meetings are often the forum for the most important decisions regarding the future of the corporation. Annual meetings of shareholders are often required under state statutes, although the statutes generally allow the time and place for holding the annual meeting to be set in the corporation's bylaws.

It is sometimes necessary or desirable to hold special shareholder meetings in between the regularly scheduled annual meetings. Specific requirements as to who may call a special meeting are prescribed by statute and may be elaborated on in the articles of incorporation or bylaws of a corporation.

For an action to be taken at a meeting of the shareholders, (1) a quorum must be present, and (2) a sufficient number of shareholders present must vote in favor of the proposed action. Voting at meetings held by smaller corporations may be done by a voice vote properly noted in the minutes of the meeting. However, votes are cast by ballot at most formal shareholder meetings. Those ballots, along with the proxies received from shareholders not in attendance, are tallied to determine whether a quorum is present and whether enough votes were received to adopt the proposed resolutions.

Shareholders who are unable to attend shareholder meetings may vote through the use of a **proxy**, "an authority given by the holder of the stock who has the right to vote it to another to exercise his voting rights."[57] The term *proxy* is often used both for the person who votes in place of the shareholder and for the document that transfers the voting power to that person.

Annual shareholder meetings are held for the purpose of electing directors of the corporation. In addition, shareholders typically vote to ratify the acts of the directors taken during the past year, and vote on any other business that may require shareholder approval, such as the amendment of the articles of incorporation, issuance of stock, acquisitions and mergers involving the corporation, the sale of corporate assets outside the normal course of business, or the dissolution of the corporation. State statutes or the corporation's articles of incorporation or bylaws may set forth other or different actions which require shareholder approval.

The Model Business Corporation Act, and the statutes of most states, allow shareholders to take action without a meeting through means of a written consent signed by all shareholders entitled to vote on the action. For smaller corporations, this written consent or "Unanimous Writing of the Shareholders in Lieu of Meeting" has become an invaluable tool for approving matters that require shareholder consent, especially matters that require attention between the regularly scheduled shareholder meetings.

Corporate Minute Books

The minutes or unanimous written consents from both director and shareholder meetings are kept in a corporate minute book, as are other important documents regarding the corporation. The contents of the corporate minute book often include the articles or certificate of incorporation, the corporate charter, the corporate bylaws, the minutes of the organizational meeting, minutes of all meetings of the board of directors and shareholders, or unanimous written consents of all board of director and shareholder resolutions.

Corporate minute books are often kept in the office of the corporate attorney, and the task of keeping the corporate minute book in order and up-to-date often falls to the paralegal. The corporate paralegal may be responsible for contacting corporate clients annually to remind them of the need for annual meetings or the advisability of preparing unanimous writings in lieu of annual meetings. They may then follow up by attending

BALLENTINESBALLENTINESBALLENTINESBALLENTINESBALLENTINESBALLENTINESBALLENTINESBALLENTINESBALLENTINESBALLENTINESBALLENTINESBALLENTINESBALLENTINES

proxy   1. A person who holds an authorization to act in the place of another. 2. An authorization, usually in writing, under which one person acts for another. 3. Authority given in writing by one shareholder in a corporation to another shareholder to exercise his or her voting rights for him or her.

annual meetings and preparing minutes or by preparing unanimous writings in lieu of meetings.

Qualification as a Foreign Corporation

The state or jurisdiction of the corporation's charter or incorporation is considered to be the corporation's state of domicile, regardless of where the corporation's headquarters are located or where it transacts the majority of its business. A corporation is considered to be a **foreign corporation** in every state or jurisdiction other than its state of domicile. Because corporations are subject to the jurisdiction of the courts in any state in which they transact business, they must qualify or register to do business as a foreign corporation in any state in which they transact business, and they must provide an agent to receive service of process in the foreign state in accordance with the laws of the foreign state.

The penalties for transacting business in a foreign state without first qualifying vary from state to state. One of the most severe is prohibition from commencing legal action to enforce contracts in the foreign state. This penalty is enforced under state "door-closing statutes." Foreign corporations that transact business without the proper authority may also be subject to substantial fines.

Although the requirements for qualifying to do business vary from state to state, in general, the corporation must obtain a **certificate** of authority or similar document from the proper state authority before it begins transacting business in the foreign state. The certificate of authority is usually obtained by filing an application, along with any other required documents, with the Secretary of State in the foreign state. Many states require that the application be made on a prescribed form.

After a corporation has qualified to do business in a foreign state, it must remain in compliance with the statutes of the foreign state with regard to filing annual reports, paying the prescribed taxes and fees, and all other statutory formalities imposed on qualified foreign corporations. The statutes of the foreign state will also prescribe procedures for withdrawing from doing business in that state.

The Financial Structure of the Corporation

Three main concerns must be addressed regarding a corporation's financial structure: (1) its ability to raise and maintain the necessary level of capital with which to operate the business; (2) the distribution of earnings and profits to its shareholders; and (3) the division of its assets upon dissolution. Paralegals are not responsible for advising corporate clients on their financial structures. However, a basic understanding of corporate financial structure greatly aids paralegals, who are often responsible for drafting articles of incorporation, minutes and other corporate documents that are affected by the design of a corporation's financial structure.

Capital

Before a corporation can begin transacting business, it must have the necessary capital with which to work. The directors typically rely on the issuance of equity and debt securities, loans from third parties, and loans from shareholders to raise the initial capital for the corporation. After formation, income generated by the corporation's business is also a major source of capital.

Equity securities are shares of stock in the corporation that are sold to shareholders. Debt securities represent loans to the corporation or other interests that must be repaid. Capital generated by the issuance of equity securities is often referred to as *equity capital,* and the issuance of debt securities generates *debt capital.* The corporation's capital typically consists of a mixture

BALLENTINESBALLENTINESBALLENTINESBALLENTINESBALLENTINESBALLENTINESBALLENTINESBALLENTINESBALLENTINESBALLENTINESBALLENTINESBALLENTINESBALLENTINESBALLENTINESBALLENTINES

foreign corporation   A corporation incorporated under the laws of one state, doing business in another.

certificate   A formal or official written declaration intended as an authentication of the fact or facts set forth therein.

of debt and equity capital, and it is usually a function of the incorporators or the board of directors to determine the best mix and the best sources for the required capital.

Equity Financing

Equity financing involves the issuance of shares of stock of the corporation in exchange for cash or other consideration which will become corporate capital. The most common method of equity financing is the issuance of common stock in exchange for cash. However, many variations are available. The issuance of equity securities means granting certain rights to those who have given consideration for the securities, including the shareholder's proportionate right with respect to the earnings, assets, and management of the corporation. Unlike debt security holders, the holders of equity securities are not guaranteed a return on their investment in the corporation, and therefore place at risk their entire investment in the equity securities.

When a corporation is formed, the articles of incorporation must set forth the number and type of shares of stock which the corporation is authorized to issue, and any other information required by statute. These shares are referred to as the **authorized shares**. The board of directors may not issue equity shares in excess of the authorized shares. If the directors deem it appropriate to increase the number of authorized shares, the articles of incorporation must be amended.

Common Stock The ownership of almost all corporations is represented, at least in part, by *common stock*. If no designation is made in the articles of incorporation, the authorized stock is considered to be common stock if only one class is authorized. Common stockholders usually have unlimited voting rights and are entitled to receive the net assets of the corporation upon its dissolution.

Preferred Stock *Preferred stock* is "stock which enjoys certain limited rights and privileges (usually dividend and liquidation priorities) over other outstanding stock but which doesn't participate in corporate growth in any significant extent."[58] The terms of preferred stock vary and may be restricted by state statute. Typically, preferred stockholders are granted a dividend preference over the common stockholders in a fixed amount per share or in a certain percentage. Preferred stockholders may also be granted voting rights, redemption rights, conversion rights, and priority to the assets of the corporation on dissolution.

Consideration for Shares of Stock Unless the right is granted to the shareholders under statute or the articles of incorporation, the board of directors is typically responsible for the issuance of stock for adequate consideration. The price per share of stock for the initial issue is determined by the amount of capital required to begin the business, the number of initial investors, and the number of shares to be issued. Under the Model Business Corporation Act, consideration for shares of stock may be in the form of "any tangible or intangible property or benefit to the corporation."[59] Consideration may include cash, promissory notes, services or contracts for services to be performed on behalf of the corporation, or other securities of the corporation.

Stock Certificates Although the Model Business Corporation Act prescribes the minimum form and content for stock certificates, it also allows corporations to issue stock without the formality of a stock certificate so long as the prescribed information is included in a written statement sent to the shareholder within a reasonable time after the issue or transfer of the shares without a certificate.[60] The information printed on stock certificates includes the name of the issuing corporation, the corporation's state of domicile, the name of the person to whom the stock is issued,

BALLENTINESBALLENTINESBALLENTINESBALLENTINESBALLENTINESBALLENTINESBALLENTINESBALLENTINESBALLENTINESBALLENTINESBALLENTINESBALLENTINESBALLENTINESBALLENTINESBALLENTINES

authorized capital stock (authorized shares)   The maximum amount of capital stock that a corporation is authorized to issue under its charter or articles of incorporation.

the number and class of shares, and a designation of the series, if any, the certificate represents. Stock certificates must also contain a summary of the designations, relative rights, preferences, and limitations applicable to the class of shares which the certificate represents when the corporation is authorized to issue more than one class or series of shares. Certificates generally must be signed by two officers of the corporation.

Dividends   Once the business of the corporation has net earnings, the profits of the corporation are usually distributed to the appropriate shareholders in an equitable manner in the form of dividends. A **dividend** is a "payment to the stockholders of a corporation as a return on their investment."[61] Generally, dividends are paid on a regular basis in the ordinary course of business without reducing the stockholders' equity or their position to enjoy future returns of the corporation. These dividends are generally payable only out of the surplus or profits of the corporation, and may be in the form of cash, stock, or other property of the corporation.

Debt Financing

Debt financing refers to obtaining capital through loans to the corporation, which must be repaid with interest in accordance with the terms agreed to by contract between the corporation and lender or the holder of the debt securities. Debt financing refers to anything from a simple loan represented by a promissory note to the issuance of bonds.

The control of the existing shareholders is not diluted by the issuance of debt securities. Also, the issuance of debt securities offers certain tax advantages to the corporation, because the payment of interest is generally tax deductible as an expense, whereas dividends paid to equity shareholders are not. However, interest must generally be paid on debt securities, whether or not the corporation has any income for a particular period.

Also, too high a debt/equity ratio may hinder the corporation's ability to obtain short-term loans, and may increase the likelihood of insolvency.

The board of directors typically decides what type of debt capital will suit the corporation's needs: short-term, intermediate-term, long-term, or any combination thereof. One of the most significant factors influencing this decision is the applicable state and federal securities regulations.

For instance, they must consider the possible impact of the federal Securities Act of 1933, the federal Securities and Exchange Act of 1934, and the securities acts of the corporation's state of domicile. Although most small stock issuances are exempt from registration under these acts, certain stock issuances are regulated by the Securities and Exchange Commission, and it is important to be aware of these acts' effects.

Corporate Dissolution

Corporations are given life by the statutes of their state of domicile, and that life must be terminated in accordance with those statutes. Although articles of incorporation may generally provide for a date or event that will trigger dissolution, most corporations exist perpetually and must be dissolved when there is no further reason for their existence. **Dissolution** generally refers to termination of the corporation's legal existence. However, the corporate existence continues after dissolution for certain purposes. In addition to dissolving the corporation in accordance with the statutes of its state of domicile, the corporation must surrender its certificate of authority to transact business in any state in which it is qualified to transact business and must file the appropriate forms and returns with the Internal Revenue Service.

Corporations are dissolved for many reasons, including bankruptcy or insolvency, cessation of the corporation's business, the sale of all or substantially all of the corporation's assets, or the death of key shareholders, directors, or officers.

BALLENTINESBALLENTINESBALLENTINESBALLENTINESBALLENTINESBALLENTINESBALLENTINESBALLENTINESBALLENTINESBALLENTINESBALLENTINESBALLENTINESBALLENTINESBALLENTINESBALLENTINES

dividend   A payment made by a corporation to its shareholders, either in cash, in stock, or out of surplus earnings.

dissolution of corporation   The termination of a corporation's existence and its abolishment as an entity.

Extensive planning by the corporation's management, board of directors, attorneys, and accountants is usually necessary to execute the dissolution, winding up, and liquidation in the manner most beneficial to shareholders.

Voluntary Dissolutions

The most common type of corporate dissolution is the voluntary dissolution, which is approved by the directors and shareholders of the corporation. The procedures for voluntarily dissolving a corporation depend on the statutes of the state of domicile, but generally involve obtaining the appropriate approval by the directors and shareholders, filing articles of dissolution or another appropriate document with the proper state authority, and winding up the affairs of the corporation by liquidating its assets, paying creditors' claims, and distributing the balance to shareholders.

Articles of Dissolution and Notice of Intent to Dissolve   In states following the Model Business Corporation Act, the first and only state filing required to dissolve a corporation is the articles of dissolution. After the articles of dissolution are filed, the corporate existence continues, but the corporation is considered to be a dissolved corporation and may continue its business only for the purpose of winding up its affairs. The articles of dissolution usually include:

1. The name of the corporation
2. The date dissolution was authorized
3. The number of votes entitled to be cast on the proposal to dissolve, and a statement that the number cast for dissolution was sufficient for approval
4. The effective date of the dissolution.

The articles of dissolution must be submitted with the appropriate filing fee in accordance with state statute.

In other jurisdictions, a notice of intent to dissolve must be filed with the appropriate state authority prior to the winding-up process. The articles of dissolution are generally filed in these jurisdictions only after all of the corporation's debts (including any tax liabilities) have been paid and all of the corporation's assets have been distributed. In addition to the filing with the Secretary of State, these states often require that the notice of intent be published in a legal newspaper in the county in which the registered office of the corporation is located.

Winding Up and Liquidation

The statutes of virtually every state provide for the complete and orderly winding up of the affairs of dissolved corporations and for protection of the creditors and shareholders of liquidating corporations.[62] The following activities may be appropriate:

1. Collection of assets
2. Disposition of properties that will not be distributed in kind to shareholders
3. Discharge or making provision for discharge of liabilities of the corporation
4. Distribution of remaining property among shareholders according to their interests
5. Every other act necessary to wind up and liquidate the business and affairs of the corporation.

Liquidation of a corporation refers to the "winding up of the affairs of the corporation by reducing its assets, paying its debts, and apportioning the profit or loss."[63] Corporations may be liquidated either before or after they are dissolved.

As a part of the winding-up and liquidation process, state statutes may require that creditors of the corporation be given notice and that they be allowed to submit claims for payment of any debt owed by the corporation. Often, notification must be sent to each individual creditor, or notice must be given to the public, or both. Under the Model Business Corporation Act, claims against a dissolved corporation are barred if the claimant was given proper notice but did not submit a claim by the deadline. The claim may also be barred if the claim is rejected and the claimant does not commence a proceeding to enforce the claim within 90 days.

The statutes of several states provide dissolving corporations with the option of giving notice to creditors. However, if the dissolving corporation does not give proper notice, it will be liable to its creditors for a substantially longer time.

Distributions to Shareholders As a part of the winding-up and liquidation process, the assets remaining after the corporation's debts are paid must be distributed to the shareholders of the dissolved corporation. The assets may be reduced to cash prior to distribution, or they may be distributed in kind. The shareholders receive a pro rata portion of the assets based on the number of shares owned and the rights of each particular class of shares. Preferred shareholders may have a priority right to the assets upon dissolution of a corporation.

Involuntary Dissolution

Whereas most corporate dissolutions are voluntary, under certain circumstances a corporation may be forced into dissolving by its state of domicile, by its shareholders, or by unsatisfied creditors. State statutes generally require that involuntary dissolutions be accomplished through judicial proceedings. However, several states provide for administrative dissolution by the appropriate state official, without the necessity of a judicial proceeding.

Administrative Dissolution In an administrative dissolution, the corporation forfeits its right to exist, usually by failing to pay income taxes, failing to file annual reports, or failing to provide a registered agent or office in compliance with state statutes. The state of the corporation's domicile dissolves the corporation. Although state statutes often provide several different grounds for dissolution, the corporation is generally given several opportunities to rectify the situation that creates the grounds for involuntary dissolution.

Even after the corporation has been administratively dissolved, statutes typically provide a time period within which it may be reinstated. However, once a corporation is dissolved, it may lose the right to use its name in the state, and that name may be taken by another corporation. If the corporation is reinstated, its corporate name must be available or it must use a different name. If the reinstatement is determined to be effective, it relates back to the effective date of the administrative dissolution and the corporation resumes its business as if the administrative dissolution had never occurred.

Judicial Dissolutions Judicial dissolutions are supervised by the proper court. Although in some instances the shareholders and directors of a dissolving corporation request judicial supervision over a voluntary dissolution, judicial dissolutions are usually involuntary. Judicial proceedings for dissolution are usually initiated by a petition of the state attorney general, by minority shareholders, or by an unsatisfied creditor.

After it is determined that grounds for a judicial dissolution exist, the court may enter a decree dissolving the corporation and directing commencement of the winding up of the corporation's affairs and the liquidation of its assets. The court often appoints a receiver to manage the business and affairs of the corporation during the winding-up process. This court-appointed receiver typically has rights and powers, assigned by the court, to sell and dispose of the corporation's assets and to distribute any remaining assets to the shareholders as directed by the court.

Choosing a Form of Business Organization

Before a business venture begins, the founders of the business must decide, often with the advice of their legal counsel, which type of business organization will best meet their needs and the needs of the business.

There are several factors in choosing the best form of business organization, including the amount of personal risk the founders of the business are willing to take, the desired management structure, and the need for capital to begin the business. Continuity of the business and statutory formalities for each type of business organization must also be considered.

Limitation on Liability

One of the key factors to be considered when choosing a form of business organization is the liability to be assumed by the founders and future investors of the business. Often, a decision as to business organization will be made on this factor alone.

Sole Proprietor's Liability

One of the most significant disadvantages to doing business as a sole proprietor is the unlimited liability faced by the business owner. The owner is solely responsible for all debts and obligations of the business, as well as any torts committed personally by the sole proprietor or by employees acting within the scope of their employment. There is no protection for the sole proprietor's personal assets. Creditors may look to both the business and the personal assets of the sole proprietor to satisfy their claims.

Insurance can help to prevent a personal catastrophe to the sole proprietor, but insurance is not available to cover every potential type of liability. Individuals who operate certain types of business that have a high, uninsurable liability risk will almost always do best to incorporate.

Partners' Liability

Unlimited personal liability of the owners is also one of the strongest arguments against doing business as a general partnership. Partners are personally liable for the debts, obligations, and torts committed by or on behalf of the partnership. This disadvantage is compounded by the fact that all partners are liable for the acts of any one partner who is acting on behalf of the partnership. Wealthy partners may be at a disadvantage when the liabilities of the partnership exceed the partnership assets and creditors turn to the individual partners for payment.

As with sole proprietorships, the partnership may purchase insurance to cover many potential liabilities. In addition, third parties may agree in their contracts with the partnership to limit their recovery to partnership assets. However, not all liabilities are insurable, and lenders may not work with a partnership without the personal guarantees of the partners.

Limited Partnership Liability

One of the more attractive features of a limited partnership is the limited liability offered to its limited partners. Limited partners can invest money without becoming liable for the debts of the firm as long as they do not participate in control of the business or hold themselves out to be general partners.

The limited liability offered to limited partnerships does not extend to all partners, however. A limited partnership cannot exist without at least one general partner who has unlimited liability for the debts and obligations of the limited partnership.

Corporate Liability

One of the most prevalent reasons for forming a corporation is the limited liability that the corporate structure offers to its shareholders, directors, and officers. Theoretically, the corporation is responsible for its own debts and obligations, leaving the shareholders, directors, and officers free from personal liability.

The limited liability benefit of incorporating does have its boundaries, however. The corporate veil may be pierced under certain circumstances, leaving the individual shareholders exposed to personal liability for the corporation's debts and obligations. Also, as a practical matter, shareholders of a new or small corporation are often required to give their personal guarantees to obtain financing on behalf of the corporation. If the corporation has few assets in its own name, banks and

Type of Entity	Advantages	Disadvantages
Sole Proprietorship		Owner personally responsible for all debts, obligations, and torts of the business.
General Partnership		All partners have unlimited personal liability for the debts and obligations of the partnership. Partners are personally liable for partnership debts and obligations and torts committed by each partner on behalf of the partnership.
Limited Partnership	Limited partners' liability is limited to their investment in the partnership. Limited partners have no personal liability for limited partnership debts and obligations or torts committed by the limited partnership.	General partners have unlimited personal liability. General partners are personally liable for partnership debts and obligations and for torts committed by the limited partnership.
Corporation	Shareholders, directors, and officers generally have no personal liability for the debts, obligations, or torts of the corporation.	Corporate veil may be pierced under certain circumstances.

Limitation on Liability Individuals who are interested in forming a business organization should be fully aware of the advantages and disadvantages of each type of entity.

other lenders often will refuse financing to the corporation without the personal guarantee of individual shareholders who have an adequate net worth to secure the corporation's loan.

Desired Management Structure

Each type of business organization offers a unique management structure with unique advantages and disadvantages. The form of business organization chosen should offer a management structure that fits the preferences of the individual founders of the business.

Sole Proprietorships

The most obvious advantage of a sole proprietorship is that the sole proprietor has full authority to manage the business in any way he or she sees fit, without having to obtain permission from a partner or a board of directors. Also, because the sole proprietor is not required to document decisions or obtain permission from others, the sole proprietorship is not subject to the bureaucracy and delays in the decision-making process that are often associated with partnerships and corporations. The sole proprietor may hire any number of employees or agents and delegate any authority desired. However, as the only owner of the business, the sole proprietor is always in command.

The sole proprietorship management structure can have its drawbacks, too. Although it may be very appealing to an individual starting a new business to be able to make all the business decisions, there are many instances where diversity in management can be equally appealing. The sole proprietor does not have the experience and expertise of other partners, directors, or shareholders to rely on.

General Partnerships

One of the most distinct management advantages offered by partnerships is that all partners have the right to full participation in management. Partners of smaller partnerships may find this appealing if they have varied backgrounds and areas of expertise and all wish to actively participate. All partners are allowed to act freely on behalf of the partnership, with few restrictions. Larger partnerships, in contrast, are allowed the flexibility of putting the management of the partnership into the hands of the best individual or group of individuals for the job.

Although the loosely structured management of a partnership may be an advantage under certain circumstances, it also may work as a definite disadvantage. The number and personalities of the partners can greatly affect the success or failure of the management prescribed for partnerships by statute. Because the majority rules, in the event of disagreement regarding management decisions, a stalemate can result if the partnership consists of an even number of partners. The fact that each partner can act on behalf of the partnership also can cause problems when partners disagree on fundamental issues. A carefully constructed partnership agreement delegating the authority to make management decisions can alleviate some of these problems when there is disagreement among the partners, but the partnership agreement cannot account for all possible contingencies.

Limited Partnerships

Although every partner is entitled to an equal share of the management of a general partnership, limited partners must relinquish all control over partnership matters to maintain their status and enjoy limited liability. Limited partners must place their full trust in the general partners for successful management and control of the business. In effect, limited partners trade their right to partnership management for limited personal liability.

Corporations

Corporations have the advantage of centralized management. Shareholders generally participate in management of the corporation by voting for the directors of the corporation who will manage the corporation's business.

In small, closely held corporations, the shareholders often operate without a board of directors, or the shareholders elect themselves to be the directors and officers of the corporation. In effect, the smaller corporation is often run by its owners. In contrast, directors and officers of larger corporations may own little or no stock in those corporations.

Tax Considerations

Taxation of the business organization can have a significant economic impact on the business's success or failure. The successful business organization must not allow taxation to cause an undue burden. In addition, the income tax implications of investing in the business must not be prohibitive to potential investors.

Sole Proprietorships

The income of the sole proprietorship is reported on a schedule to the sole proprietor's individual income tax return. The profit or loss of the business is added to the sole proprietor's other income, if any, and taxed at the taxpayer's individual rate. This can be particularly advantageous for startup businesses, which often incur a loss in the first year or so. If a sole proprietorship experiences a net loss during a particular year, the sole proprietor can use that loss to offset other income. Another income tax benefit to the sole proprietor is that there is no double taxation of the business income. However, because the sole proprietorship's income is taxed at the sole proprietor's personal income tax rate, individuals who run very profitable businesses or who have a large income from other sources will pay taxes at a higher rate.

Partnerships

The principal tax benefit to partners is that the partnership itself is not liable for income tax; only a single tax is paid by the partners on income derived from the partnership. Partnerships are required to file only an informational tax return with the Internal Revenue Service. Also, because the income of the partnership flows through to the individual partners, if the partnership experiences a net loss, each partner's share of that loss may be written off on the partner's individual income tax return, offsetting any other income. Again, as with the sole proprietorship, because of this income flow-through, if the partnership is earning a substantial income, partners with other income who are already in a high income-tax bracket may be at a disadvantage.

Limited Partnerships

Like general partnerships, the limited partnership itself is generally not subject to income taxation.

The ability of the limited partnership to pass profits and especially losses directly to the limited partners, without the limited partners risking anything more than their investment, can be a significant advantage over the corporate and general partnership tax structures.

Corporations

Although the corporate structure can offer advantages under certain circumstances, in other instances the tax disadvantages may be enough reason to choose another form of business organization. The most serious corporate tax drawback is double taxation of the corporate income. Unlike sole proprietorships, partnerships, S corporations, and limited liability companies, most corporations are taxed as entities separate from their shareholders and must pay income tax on their earnings. In addition, the shareholders of the corporation must pay income tax on income or dividends received from the corporation.

Entity	Advantages	Disadvantages
Sole Proprietorship	Sole proprietor has full authority to manage business. Not subject to bureaucracy and delays of partnerships and corporations.	Lack of diversity in management experience and expertise.
General Partnership	All partners have right to full participation in management business. Flexibility in management exists when management provisions are included in partnership agreement.	Loosely structured management may be a detriment in larger partnerships. Consent of all partners must be obtained on certain matters.
Limited Partnership	General partners have authority to act on behalf of limited partnership without obtaining permission from limited partners on most matters.	Limited partners may not participate in the management of the partnership. Approval of limited partners must be obtained on certain matters.
Corporation	Centralized management. Shareholders can participate in management through voting for directors.	Consent of all members of the board of directors and consent of the shareholders may be rquired to take certain actions.

Management Structure Each type of business organization has a unique management structure with its own advantages and disadvantages.

The income of the corporation is, in effect, taxed twice.

In addition to income tax, corporations may be subject to special state taxes, including incorporation taxes and franchise taxes. Corporations are also subject to fees and taxes in any foreign states in which they transact business.

Corporations do have the advantage of having many available income tax writeoffs unique to the corporation. Many corporate expenses, including employees' salaries, can be itemized and subtracted from the corporation's earnings to reduce its taxable profits.

The owners of a corporation may be in a position to take advantage of several employee benefit plans which can be used to compensate employees and reduce the company's income tax liability. These benefits may be in the form of contributions to qualified pension and profit-sharing plans, group term life insurance, medical care insurance, medical reimbursement plans, and other employee benefits. Many of these benefits are in the form of nontaxable income to the employee-shareholders of the corporation and are used as a means to pass tax-free income through to the shareholders of the corporation while giving the added bonus of a tax deduction to the corporation.

With the exception of S corporations, corporations may freely choose their fiscal tax year, which may be different from the calendar year. The corporation can choose the tax year that is most advantageous to its business and that best fits its natural business cycle.

Potential for Raising Business Capital

No business organization can exist for long without the ability to raise working capital. Each type of business organization has distinct advantages and disadvantages in raising capital for the business.

Sole Proprietorships

A wealthy entrepreneur starting a second or third business may not have a problem with lack of capital. However, most individuals must overcome the barrier created by their own financial circumstances. The amounts they are able to borrow, based on their own financial wealth and the business plan, may not be sufficient to fund the type of business they desire to run.

Partnerships

Although partnerships are generally restricted to the personal capital of the partners, and the capital the partners are able to borrow based on their personal wealth, the partnership does have an advantage over a sole proprietorship because there is a broader base from which to obtain capital. Unlike a corporation, a partnership may not sell shares of stock to raise capital to run its business. The capital of the partnership usually consists of contributions from the partners and any loans that can be obtained based on the partners' personal wealth and the partnership assets. This can be a great deterrent to businesses with substantial initial capital requirements.

Limited Partnerships

In addition to the capital resources typically available to general partnerships, limited partnerships can raise initial capital by attracting limited partners who are passive investors. In addition, the limited partnership may raise additional capital when required by adding new limited partners.

Corporations

Compared to sole proprietorships or partnerships, the corporation has the best potential for raising capital. Investors may be enticed by the tax benefits and limited liability offered by corporate investments. The flexible nature of the corporate capital structure allows corporations to appeal to a wide variety of investors with varying needs. The corporation may sell shares of stock of different classes to meet the needs of investors.

Continuity of Business

If the business organization ceases to exist when the founder or management dies, it can be a distinct disadvantage to the investors.

Entity	Advantages	Disadvantages
Sole Proprietorship	Income is only taxed once, at personal income tax rate of sole proprietor. Business losses may be used to offset other income of owner.	Sole proprietors who are in a high personal income tax bracket may be at a disadvantage.
Partnership	Income is only taxed once, at the personal income tax rate of partners. Partnership losses may be used to offset other income of partners.	Partners who are in a high personal income tax bracket may be at a disadvantage.
Limited Partnership	Income is only taxed once, at the personal income tax rate of partners. Partnership losses may be used to offset other income of partners.	Partners who are in a high personal income tax bracket may be at a disadvantage.
Corporation	Many available income-tax writeoffs unique to the corporation. Corporations can usually choose their own fiscal year end. Employee benefit plans available to corporations offer unique benefits.	Double taxation of corporate income. Special state taxes, including incorporation taxes and franchise taxes.

Tax Considerations Each business organization has tax requirements that must be considered.

Sole Proprietorships

Because the sole proprietorship is in many ways merely an extension of the individual, when the individual owner dies or ceases to do business, the business itself usually terminates. Although the sole proprietor may have employed several employees or agents, that agency relationship terminates upon the death of the sole proprietor. If all of the assets of the business are transferred to another individual, and the business is kept intact, another sole proprietorship is formed.

Partnerships

Under the Uniform Partnership Act, unless otherwise specified in the partnership agreement or other written agreement between the partners, the partnership dissolves whenever one partner ceases to be a partner, for whatever reason. This can be a definite disadvantage for a going concern,

because the dissolution may be untimely and costly to the remaining partners.

Upon the death of a partner, the deceased partner's right to specific partnership property will pass to the remaining partners, who have the right to possess the property for partnership purposes. However, the deceased partner's interest in the partnership will pass to the deceased partner's heirs. Unless this issue is addressed in a carefully worded agreement, the remaining partners often have to liquidate the partnership assets to distribute the deceased partner's interest to his or her heirs.

The partnership agreement, a separate written agreement, or the will of a deceased partner may provide for the continuance of a partnership upon the death or withdrawal of a partner; it may also provide for a substitution of the deceased or withdrawing partner. Not all partnership rights are assignable, however, and the partnership without the deceased or withdrawing partner is actually a different partnership.

Limited Partnerships

Although the limited partnership does not enjoy continuity of business to the same extent as a corporation, it is not always necessary for a limited partnership to dissolve upon the death, retirement, or withdrawal of a partner. Under the Revised Uniform Limited Partnership Act, the limited partnership need not necessarily dissolve upon the withdrawal of a general partner if at the time there is at least one other general partner and the written provisions of the partnership agreement permit the business to be carried on by the remaining general partner and that partner does so. In any event, the limited partnership need not be dissolved and is not required to be wound up by reason of any event of withdrawal if, "within 90 days after the withdrawal, all partners agree in writing to continue the business of the limited partnership and to the appointment one or more additional general partners if necessary or desired."[64]

Corporations

An important advantage to doing business as a corporation is that the corporation has the ability to exist perpetually. Unlike the sole proprietorship or partnership, the corporation does not dissolve upon the death or withdrawal of any of its shareholders, officers, or directors. Shares of stock may be sold, gifted, or bequeathed to others without affecting the continuity of the corporation or its business.

Formalities, Regulatory Requirements, and Cost of Organization

The required formalities, the regulatory requirements, and the cost of organization vary significantly for each type of business organization. For instance, the formalities associated with the sole proprietorship are few, but the formalities associated with a publicly held corporation can be prohibitive.

Sole Proprietorships

Sole proprietorships are not created nor governed by statute, so very few formalities must be observed by a sole proprietor. A sole proprietor must, however, comply with the licensing and taxation regulations that are imposed on all forms of businesses. A sole proprietor must be aware of and obtain any necessary licenses, sales tax permits, and tax identification numbers before commencing business. Also, if the business is to be transacted under a name other than the sole proprietor's own name, the state where the business is transacted will probably require that an application for certificate of assumed name, trade name, or fictitious name be filed.

There are no qualification requirements for transacting business in a foreign state as a sole proprietorship. Unlike a corporation, a sole proprietor may transact business in a neighboring state without having to qualify and pay a fee to the appropriate state authority. The sole proprietor must, however, be sure to comply with any licensing and taxation requirements peculiar to that foreign state.

Costs for starting up and maintaining a sole proprietorship are relatively low. There are no minimum capital restrictions, and few, if any, state filing fees. Some possible start-up expenses include attorneys' fees for legal advice, and filing and publishing fees for a certificate of assumed name, trade name or fictitious name.

General Partnerships

Although partnerships are governed by statute, the required statutory formalities are few. Although a concise, written partnership agreement is a good investment in almost any circumstance, it is not required, and a partnership may be formed by a verbal agreement between two or more people.

State statutes vary with regard to partnership filing requirements and other formalities, and the pertinent state statutes must always be reviewed and complied with. Most states do not require partnership registration with the Secretary of State or other state official before commencing business. However, a certificate of assumed name or other similar document is usually required when the partnership will be transacting business under an assumed name, trade name, or fictitious name. A number of states require the registration of every partnership with the appropriate state official, regardless of whether the business is using a fictitious name.

Whereas a corporation must qualify to do business as a foreign corporation in any state other than its state of domicile, in which it transacts business, historically it has not been necessary to register to do business as a foreign partnership. State laws concerning this may change, however, and must be checked for newly imposed requirements.

Typically, no special licensing requirements are imposed on a partnership because it is a partnership; rather, the licensing requirements are imposed due to the nature of the business transacted by the partnership.

Partnerships are required to file a U.S. Partnership Return of Income, which reports their income and distributions. A tax return also may be required at the state level.

There are no minimum capital requirements for starting a partnership, and the startup costs, including any required state filing fees, tend to be significantly lower than those for corporations. Although the legal and organizational expenses involved with forming and operating a partnership are usually significantly less than those involved with forming and operating a corporation, they can still be substantial. In addition to state filing fees for the partnership certificate and a certificate of assumed or fictitious name, significant legals fees are typically associated with the drafting of a partnership agreement. Because of the diverse nature of partnerships, a good partnership agreement will usually require careful, individual drafting, so the initial legal fees can be considerable.

Limited Partnerships

The limited partnership is a creature of statute, and as such must be created by documentation

Entity	Advantages	Disadvantages
Sole Proprietorship		Capital is limited to the personal funds of the sole proprietor and the funds he or she can borrow.
Partnership	Several individual partners may contribute to the partnership capital.	Capital is limited to the personal funds of the partners and the funds they can borrow.
Limited Partnership	Limited partnership may attract passive investors as limited partners.	Capital is limited to the personal funds of the general and limited partners and the funds they can borrow.
Corporation	Shares of stock may be sold. Investors may be enticed by limited liability offered by the corporation. Flexible nature of the corporate capital structure allows corporations to appeal to a wide variety of investors with varying needs. Corporation may borrow funds in its own name.	

Potential for Raising Capital The need for capital is essential for any business organization. The paralegal can help explain the advantages and disadvantages to individuals interested in forming a business entity.

Entity	Advantages	Disadvantages
Sole Proprietorship		The sole proprietorship terminates upon the death of the owner.
Partnership	Under certain circumstances, the partnership may continue after the death of a partner.	Under certain circumstances, the death of any partner will cause a dissolution of the partnership.
Limited Partnership	Typically, the limited partnership will continue after the death of a limited partner.	Typically, the limited partnership will dissolve after the death of a general partner.
Corporation	The corporate entity does not dissolve upon the death or withdrawal of a shareholder, officer, or director. Shares of stock may be sold, gifted or bequeathed to others without affecting the continuity of the corporation.	

Continuity of Business How and whether a business entity can continue after the death of the founder may be important to law office clients.

filed with the proper state authority. The certificate of limited partnership must be executed and filed before the limited partnership's existence begins. Therefore, there are many more formalities associated with the creation of a limited partnership as compared to a sole proprietorship or a general partnership. Limited partnerships are also often subject to many of the same reporting requirements imposed on corporations. A limited partnership may be required to register or qualify to do business as a foreign limited partnership in any state, other than its state of domicile, in which it proposes to transact business.

The legal and organizational expenses of a limited partnership can be substantial. The founders of a limited partnership usually incur legal fees for preparation of a limited partnership agreement and certificate, and filing fees for the certificate of limited partnership and possibly a certificate of assumed name.

Corporations

Numerous formalities and reporting requirements are associated with the formation and maintenance

of the most complex type of business entity, a corporation. First, articles of incorporation must be filed and all other incorporation formalities imposed by the corporation's state of domicile must be followed before the corporate existence begins. Once the corporation is formed, several ongoing statutory requirements must be complied with. Annual meetings of the shareholders and directors may be required, and annual reports often are required by the state of domicile. Publicly held corporations may be subject to the registration and reporting requirements imposed by federal and state securities laws. The corporation, as a separate entity, must also file a corporate income tax return and pay income tax each year to the Internal Revenue Service and (often) the state of domicile and states in which it transacts business. Also, unlike sole proprietorships and most partnerships, if a corporation is to transact business in any state other than its state of domicile, it must qualify with the proper state authority in the foreign state.

All of these requirements can be time-consuming and costly. However, as mentioned previously, it is important that a corporation comply with all corporate formalities to ensure that there is no cause for the corporate veil to be pierced.

Transferability of Ownership Interest

An ownership interest in a business organization may be of little value to the retiring owner if he or she cannot easily sell or transfer that interest for a fair price. The transferability of an ownership interest varies considerably among the different forms of business organizations.

Sole Proprietorship Interest

When it comes time to sell the business, transferring the full proprietary interest of a sole proprietor may be difficult. Because the business is linked closely with the identity of the owner, the business may be worth much less when broken into its tangible assets. There may be no available buyer for the business, and the sole proprietor may have to take a loss by selling off the business's assets.

Unlike stock of a publicly traded corporation, which can be sold on an exchange for a broker's fee, selling a sole proprietorship can be a difficult, time-consuming and expensive ordeal. Many sales require extensive appraisals of the business's assets. It may be difficult to place a fair dollar value

Entity	Advantages	Disadvantages
Sole Proprietorship	No formation formalities. Few other formalities and low cost of organization.	
Partnership	Few statutory formalities.	Written partnership agreement recommended. Some states require partnership registration before commencing business.
Limited Partnership		Must be formed by documentation filed with the proper state authority. Often subject to same reporting requirements as corporations. Must register or qualify to do business in foreign states.
Corporation		Numerous formalities and reporting requirements associated with formation and maintenance of corporation, including incorporation filing and fee and annual reports filed with state authorities. Publicly held corporations may be subject to numerous registration and reporting requirements. Must register or qualify to do business in foreign states.

Formalities, Regulatory Requirements, and Cost of Organization The costs of starting a business entity and keeping it solvent are very important to clients.

Entity	Advantages	Disadvantages
Sole Proprietorship		Because business is linked closely with the identity of the owner, the business may be worth much less when broken down by tangible assets. Transfer of assets may be expensive. The "sole proprietorship" itself is not transferable.
Partnership	Partner's interest may be sold or assigned.	Partner's entire right is not freely transferable. The right to specific partnership property and the right to management of the partnership may not be freely sold or assigned.
Limited Partnership	Limited partner's interest is generally transferable with fewer restrictions than those imposed on partners of a general partneship.	There are restrictions on the transfer of a general partner's interest. Certain assignments may be considered an event of withdrawal.
Corporation	Restrictions on transfer of stock may exist if provided for in the corporation's articles of incorporation or in the pertinent statutes.	Generally, shares of stock of a corporation are freely transferable by the shareholders of the corporation.

Transferability of Ownership Interest Because owning a business is tantamount to owning property, the paralegal should have an understanding of how property is transferred through wills and trusts.

on some assets, including the **goodwill** and name of the business.

Partnership Interest

Unlike corporate shareholders, who may generally sell their shares of stock without restriction, a partner's entire right to the partnership is not freely transferable. Although a partner's interest may be sold or assigned as far as the assigning partner's rights to receive the profits and surplus of the partnership are concerned, the right to specific partnership property may not be sold or assigned unless sold or assigned by all partners.

In addition, a partner's right to management of the partnership is not assignable. Therefore, a partner's share of the partnership may not simply be sold to another individual who will become a partner. Under certain circumstances, though, if the remaining partners consent, a partner's entire right to the partnership may be sold. In this situation, a new partnership will be formed.

If a partner dissolves the partnership by withdrawing before expiration of the term of the partnership set forth in the partnership agreement, the withdrawing partner may be liable to the remaining partners for any damages caused by the dissolution.

goodwill   The benefit a business acquires, beyond the mere value of its capital stock and tangible assets, as a result of having a good reputation and the respect of the public.

Limited Partnership Interest

Although a partner's interest in a limited partnership is not as easily transferred as a corporate interest, the limited partner's interest is generally assignable with fewer restrictions than those imposed on the partners of a general partnership. The assignment of a limited partner's interest does not necessarily cause a dissolution of the limited partnership; in some instances, the entire interest of the limited partner may be assigned, with the assignee becoming a substitute partner.

General partners also have certain rights to assign their interests in a limited partnership. Under the Revised Uniform Limited Partnership Act, a general partner may have all of the same rights of assignability as a limited partner, although certain assignments may be considered an event of withdrawal. In any event, the limited partnership offers much more flexibility with regard to transfer of partnership interests than a general partnership does.

Corporate Interest

In contrast to the sole proprietorship and partnership, an ownership interest in a corporation is easily transferred. Barring a prohibitive agreement among the shareholders, or restrictions in the corporation's articles of incorporation or bylaws, shares of stock may be bought and sold freely. Because a shareholder's interest in the corporation is represented by stock certificates, the transfer of unrestricted stock may be as simple as an endorsement by the shareholder to the purchaser or transferee of the stock.

In many cases, however, restrictions are placed on the transfer of shares of closely held corporations, either by statute, the articles of incorporation, bylaws, or an agreement between the shareholders. These agreements often give the corporation or the existing shareholders the first option to purchase the shares of any shareholder who wants to sell. An agreement by the shareholders may also provide for the purchase of shares of deceased shareholders by the corporation and/or the other shareholders. Unless addressed in a written agreement, a deceased shareholder's shares of stock are passed on to his or her heirs like any other asset.

 Summary Questions

1. Which is the most prevalent form of business organization in the United States? Which reports the highest annual business receipts and the highest income?

2. Why might an individual who is the sole owner of a business decide to operate as a corporation instead of as a sole proprietorship?

3. What is piercing the corporate veil, and how can it be avoided?

4. If the ABC Corporation wants to do business under the name of "ABC Machine Repair," what must it do?

5. What are the three distinct rights of partners in a general partnership?

6. David Harrison is a limited partner in the Advanced Enterprises Limited Partnership, but he is unhappy with the way the business is being operated. David begins attending management meetings and contributes his input on all major decisions. He has now asked the managing partner for the right to vote on all matters concerning management of the business. What are the risks to David if management should decide to allow his continued participation in control of the business?

7. What document must be filed with the proper state official to form a business corporation? What are the minimum requirements for this document under the Model Business Corporation Act?

8. What type of business organization offers the greatest protection from personal liability? Is this protection absolute?

9. What is double taxation, and what form of entity is subject to double taxation?

10. What are some advantages corporations have when it comes to raising capital for the business?

Practical Paralegal Skills

Assume the facts in the law office scenario regarding Anderson and Crown Marketing, Inc. are true. Based on that information, and the following notes concerning the proposed new corporation, prepare Articles of Incorporation that would be appropriate for forming a business corporation in your home state. Also, prepare a cover letter for filing that document with the Secretary of State or other appropriate state official. Include in the letter the Articles of Incorporation, the appropriate filing fee, and any other documentation that may be required in your home state.

NOTES

Name:	Anderson and Crown Marketing, Inc.
Place of Business:	194 Oak Terrace Center City, MN 55123
Registered Agent:	Joan L. Anderson
Registered Office:	194 Oak Terrace Center, City, MN 55123
Duration:	Perpetual
Authorized Shares:	10,000 shares of common stock, without par value
Issued Shares:	1,000 to Joan L. Anderson 1,000 to Elizabeth M. Crown
Board of Directors and Incorporators:	Joan L. Anderson 194 Oak Terrace Center City, MN 55123 and Elizabeth M. Crown 1327 1st Avenue Minneapolis, MN 12345

Officers:		
	Chief Executive Officer:	Joan L. Anderson
	Chief Financial Officer	Elizabeth M. Crown
	Secretary:	Elizabeth M. Crown

Notes

For further reference, see *The Law of Corporations, Partnerships, and Sole Proprietorships,* by Angela Schneeman (Delmar Publishers Inc., and Lawyers Cooperative Publishing 1993).

[1] Milano, Carol, "1993 *Legal Assitant Today* Salary Survey Results," *Legal Assistant Today* 48 (May/June 1993).

[2] U.S. Bureau of the Census, *Statistical Abstract of the United States: 1992* at 520 (112th ed. 1992).

[3] *Id.* at 520.

[4] U.S. Bureau of the Census, *Statistical Abstract of the United States: 1991* at 529 (111th ed. 1991).

[5] *Id.* at 525.

[6] 57 Am. Jur. 2d *Name* § 64 (1988).

[7] *Id.*

[8] Uniform Partnership Act § 6.

[9] *Id.* § 2.

[10] *Id.*

[11] Uniform Partnership Act § 24.

[12] *Id.* § 25.

[13] *Id.* § 26.

[14] *Id.* § 18.

[15] *Id.* § 22.

[16] *Id.* § 19.

[17] *Id.* § 18.

[18] Uniform Partnership Act § 13.

[19] *Id.* § 9(3).

[20] *Id.* § 18(h).

[21] *Id.* § 29.

[22] *Id.* § 32.

[23] 59A Am. Jur. 2d *Partnership* § 891 (1987).

[24] Revised Uniform Limited Partnership Act § 101(11).

[25] 59A Am. Jur. 2d *Partnership* § 1246 (1987).

[26] *Id.* § 1345.

[27] Revised Uniform Limited Partnership Act § 303(b).

[28] 59A Am. Jur. 2d *Partnership* § 1333 (1987).

[29] Revised Uniform Limited Partnership Act § 201.

[30] *Id.* § 105.

[31] *Id.*

[32] Uniform Limited Partnership Act § 8.

[33] 59A Am. Jur. 2d *Partnership* § 1354 (1987).

[34] Uniform Limited Partnership Act § 4.

[35] *Id.* § 16.

[36] Revised Uniform Limited Partnership Act § 503.

[37] Uniform Limited Partnership Act § 20.

[38] Revised Uniform Limited Partnership Act § 803.

[39] 18 Am. Jur. 2d *Corporations* § 1 (1985).

[40] *Id.*

[41] 18 Am. Jur. 2d *Corporations* § 42 (1985).

[42] *Id.* § 43.

[43] *Id.* § 44.

[44] *Id.* § 45.

[45] *Id.*

[46] 1984 Revised Model Business Corporation Act § 3.02.

[47] Model Professional Corporation Act § 3.

[48] The states of Colorado, Florida, Indiana, Iowa, Kansas, Minnesota, Nevada, Texas, Utah, Virginia, and Wyoming currently recognize the limited liability company.

[49] Statutory Close Corporation Supplement § 3(a).

[50] 1984 Revised Model Business Corporation Act § 2.02(a)(1).

[51] 18A Am. Jur. 2d *Corporations* § 310 (1985).

[52] 18B Am. Jur. 2d *Corporations* § 1689 (1985).

[53] *Id.* § 1695.

[54] *Id.* § 1700.

[55] *Id.* § 1342.

[56] 18A Am. Jur. 2d *Corporations* § 683 (1985).

[57] *Id.* § 1069.

[58] *Id.* § 438.

[59] 1984 Revised Model Business Corporation Act § 6.21(c).

[60] *Id.* § 6.26.

[61] *Id.* § 6.31.

[62] 19 Am. Jur. 2d *Corporations* § 2828 (1985).

[63] *Id.* § 2733.

[64] Revised Uniform Limited Partnership Act § 10.

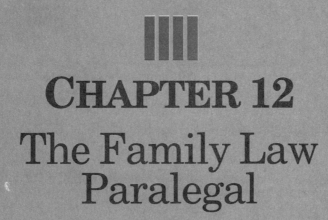

CHAPTER 12
The Family Law Paralegal

CHAPTER OUTLINE

The Role of the Paralegal in Family Law

An Introduction to Family Law

The Marriage Relationship

Terminating the Marriage Relationship

Antenuptial Contracts

Cohabitation, Marriage Alternatives, and Nontraditional
Relationships

Parent and Child Relationships

Family law in the United States is concerned with many aspects of the family and the relationship of the family members. Not only does it encompass marriage and divorce, but it also includes child custody, adoption, child abuse and neglect, and juvenile delinquency.

The role of the paralegal in family law in the United States cannot be overestimated. Family law paralegals can perform most functions that were previously performed exclusively by family law attorneys. Of equal importance, the family law paralegal often works closely with the client, who may be an individual going through a divorce, a couple adopting a child or seeking a prenuptial agreement, or even an entire family.

This chapter introduces the role of paralegals in family law, followed by an introduction to family law. Next, its focus is on the marriage relationship, termination of the marriage relationship, and antenuptial agreements. The discussion then turns to the ever-changing areas of cohabitation, marriage alternatives, and nontraditional relationships. This chapter concludes with a look at certain aspects of parent and child relationships.

The Role of the Paralegal in Family Law

Although the number of paralegals employed in the family law area is not overwhelming, their impact on the practice of family law in this country cannot be overlooked. Paralegals play an important role in performing tasks traditionally performed by family law attorneys, and in acting as liasons between attorney and client. Communication with the client is a very significant part of the family law paralegal's job.

According to a 1993 *Legal Assistant Today* survey,[1] 4.8 percent of the respondents indicated that family law was their specialty. Paralegals employed by general practice firms are also often involved in family law work from time to time.

Family law paralegals most often work in private law firms, whether it be for a sole practitioner or a firm with several hundred attorneys. However, some family law paralegals are also employed by federal, state, or county agencies. Most often these paralegals act as advocates for those who are experiencing financial hardship.

The 1993 average salary of a family law paralegal was $24,753, slightly below the national average of all paralegals. The highest reported salary for family law paralegals during 1993 was $39,270.

The Work of Family Law Paralegals in the United States

The work of family law paralegals often requires considerable time in meeting with clients and interviewing them over the telephone. Performing legal research and drafting legal documents and correspondence are also significant parts of the family law paralegal's work. Following is a list of some of the more common tasks that may be included in the job description of a family law paralegal:

1. Interviewing clients
2. Completing client questionnaires from information garnered during initial interview
3. Researching law and procedures
4. Coordinating service of process
5. Reviewing pleadings received on behalf of client
6. Drafting pleadings and other legal documents, including summonses, petitions, motions, orders, stipulations, and decrees
7. Preparing for and attending depositions
8. Preparing deposition summaries

9. Preparing interrogatories

10. Assisting with preparation of answers to interrogatories

11. Assisting with pretrial preparation

12. Assisting with trial preparation.

Paralegals may specialize in many different subareas of family law, including divorce, adoption, and prenuptial agreements. Paralegals may specialize in any type of family law that is practiced.

Skills Important to the Family Law Paralegal

Possibly more than any other area of law, excellent interpersonal skills are important to the family law paralegal. There is an old saying in divorce law to the effect that divorce attorneys see "good people at their worst." Under the extreme stresses of divorce, people do and say things that they would not do or say under any other circumstances. Divorce is so common today that we sometimes fail to realize the emotional roller-coaster on which divorcing couples ride. Unfortunately, lawyers and family law paralegals all too often feel the full brunt of divorce clients' stresses. Clients frequently regard paralegals as more approachable and less intimidating than the attorneys for whom the paralegals work. Family law paralegals must handle clients with a mix of empathy, objectivity, and professionalism.

In addition to interpersonal skills, paralegals must have excellent organizational skills and the ability to communicate well in writing. Much of the family law paralegal's job involves keeping track of important court dates and other deadlines and drafting documents and correspondence.

An Introduction to Family Law

In our society, perhaps more than any in the world, we turn to the law and lawyers for resolution of our social problems. The high frequency of divorce in American society makes family law practice an important area of the legal profession. This brief introduction to family law explores the history of family law, the adversarial nature of family law, and the sources of family law in the United States.

The History of Family Law

In the three centuries since English colonization of America, no area of law has undergone more change than family law. Family and family life have changed radically and the law has changed accordingly. At the outset, it is important to note that regulation of the family by legislatures and courts has always been problematic. There has always been a lack of consensus over the extent to which the state should intercede in family relationships. For example, we are inclined to feel that the state should protect children from abuse, neglect, and even economic misfortune. At the same time, we feel that parental authority is essential to the integrity of the family and that the state should intrude upon or limit this authority only when absolutely necessary.

Family law as it exists today bears little resemblance to the law governing the family at the time of American independence. Although other areas of law, such as the law of property, may be seen as a logical evolution from ancient English roots, family law is an American creation, consciously departing from English legal traditions. For example, Connecticut allowed absolute divorce long before England did so. Divorce is really an American legal institution.

The moral basis of family law was formalized when the church assumed responsibility for regulating domestic relations in the late Middle Ages. At that time, marriage became a sacrament, subjecting the marital relationship to church regulation. Our family law originated in the

canon law, the law of the ecclesiastical courts. Because America did not employ ecclesiastical courts or canon law, domestic relations were subsumed under the courts of equity, except in colonies, such as Connecticut and Massachusetts, that refused to adopt courts of equity. At the founding of the American Republic, the division between courts of equity and common-law courts was still very strong. There was no common-law tradition of family law except for property rights, and the common law was most appropriately charged with formal legal matters such as the remedies for injury to person or property, for crimes, and for breach of contract. Although the sacred relationships of status within the family ultimately shifted from canon law to equity, the common law had nevertheless built a law of the family pertaining to property rights, and these form an important feature of modern family law.

The History of Divorce

Divorce as we know it is a purely modern development in our legal system. Under English law, divorce was an ecclesiastical matter governed by canon law. In 1765, Blackstone described two forms of divorce: total divorce, *a vinculo matrimonii* (from the bond of matrimony), and divorce from bed and board (legal separation), *a mensa et thoro*. **Divorce a vinculo matrimonii** was based on some impediment to the marriage in the beginning, making the marriage invalid and its offspring illegitimate. **Divorce a mensa et thoro** arose from a valid marriage suffering from some cause, such as adultery, that justified a legal separation. Divorce a mensa et thoro allowed the award of alimony to the wife. At the time of his writing, Blackstone noted a recent development—the granting of total divorce by Parliament.

Toward the end of the 17th century, parliamentary divorce was established in England and copied in some colonies. Legislative divorce continued in the American states in the 19th century without the cumbersome procedure required in England. In England, parliamentary divorce was grounded exclusively in adultery (of the wife only until 1801) and was preceded by divorce a mensa et thoro from an ecclesiastical court and a successful suit for criminal conversation against the wife's lover.

With independence from England, America expressed a strong antipatriarchal attitude, which was reflected in the views of family law. In this country, husband and wife were partners to a family contract of their own choosing, and the laws governing this contract were similar to but distinct from those regarding other sorts of contracts. Although quite naturally borrowing from the traditional concepts to be found in canon law, lawyers, lawmakers, and judges also argued about the enforceability of the terms of the marriage contract. For example, the courts early rejected premarital (antenuptial) contracts because they encouraged divorce; courts, as protectors of the family, could not countenance this development. Cohabitation agreements were also unenforceable because they were seen as having an illegal purpose (fornication).

Family Law and the Adversarial Process

American legal procedure has developed around an **adversarial process** in which disputing parties arm themselves with legal representatives and ultimately try their cases before an impartial judge if the lawyers and the parties cannot reach an agreement. The sides are viewed as hostile and the lawyers are duty-bound to fight for the interests

BALLENTINESBALLENTINESBALLENTINESBALLENTINESBALLENTINESBALLENTINESBALLENTINESBALLENTINESBALLENTINESBALLENTINESBALLENTINESBALLENTINESBALLENTINES

canon law   Christian religious law, particularly that of the Roman Catholic church.

divorce   A dissolution of the marital relationship between husband and wife.

divorce a vinculo matrimonii   A decree that dissolves the marriage because of matrimonial misconduct. Also called *absolute divorce*.

divorce a mensa et thoro   A decree that terminates the right of cohabitation, and adjudicates matters such as custody and support, but does not dissolve the marriage itself. A divorce a mensa et thoro is often referred to as *legal separation*, *judicial separation*, or *limited divorce*.

adversary proceeding (adversarial process)   A trial or other proceeding in which all sides have the opportunity to present their contentions; a process involving a contested action.

TYPICAL MARRIAGE REQUIREMENTS
■ Minimum age requirements
■ Prohibition of marriages between certain blood relatives
■ Prohibition of bigamous marriages
■ Prohibition of homosexual marriages
■ Capacity to consent requirements
■ Solemnization of marriage requirements

Failure to abide by these requirements can result in a void or voidable marriage.

of their clients. Because this model quite naturally tends to focus and intensify the dispute, many states have attempted to soften the process by adopting no-fault divorce statutes. Another way of attempting to neutralize the effects of the adversarial process is the growing use of **mediation** services to attempt to resolve disputes between divorcing couples in a more friendly atmosphere. At times, the family law paralegal may be asked to assist clients through the mediation process.

Divorcing couples with minor children pose a serious problem for the legal system. We assume that the parents' primary concern is for the best interests of their children, but divorcing parents often aggravate the damage that divorce causes children by drawing them into an ongoing conflict. The presence of minor children also usually means that the divorcing parents will continue to come into contact, and many will unfortunately continue to fight in such a way as to do additional harm to the children. The dilemma of the adversarial system in this context can thus be summarized: Because our legal system is premised on an adversary contest and because divorce requires the official adjudication of rights and duties between divorcing parties, the legal system inevitably tends away from an amicable, toward a hostile, settlement of divorce.

We also must note that the disputing parties are often consumed by poorly controlled anger, jealousy, and self-reproach, which tend to intensify the warlike aspect of the underlying legal dispute. Perhaps in no other area of practice do attorneys receive the sorts of client demands that are common to divorce law.

Sources of Family Law

Family law is primarily a product of state legislation. However, the United States Constitution, federal legislation, and federal courts are also sources of family law.

State Law and the Uniform Marriage and Divorce Act

State law is the predominant source of all family law, and each state has adopted its own unique family laws. Paralegals who work in this area are often asked to research both state statutes and state case law.

The Uniform Marriage and Divorce Act (UMDA) is a product of the National Conference of Commissioners on Uniform State Laws. Like other uniform laws published by this body, the UMDA is unofficial unless and until adopted by a state legislature. Nevertheless, as a general proposal for family law, it represents an up-to-date view of the law of this area and is persuasive authority in situations where existing statutes and cases do not cover the issue confronting a court.

The United States Constitution

An unprecedented volume of new family law has been established under the United States Constitution in recent years. Cases arguing a constitutional basis, including the right to privacy and the equal protection clause of the Fourteenth Amendment, have been used to make sweeping changes to family law and, in some instances, overturn existing state laws. In 1979 the Supreme Court

mediation   The voluntary resolution of a dispute in an amicable manner.

of Louisiana overturned the conviction of a defendant under a state criminal neglect-of-wife statute. The statute made it a crime for a husband, but not a wife, with financial means to intentionally fail to support his destitute spouse. In that case, the court held that the gender-based scheme of the statute violated the equal protection clause of the Fourteenth Amendment to the United States Constitution.[2] Courts in several other states, including California, Maryland, Massachusetts, Pennsylvania, and Georgia, have also found similar gender-based statutes to be unconstitutional, either under the Fourteenth Amendment to the United States Constitution or under the constitutions of their respective states.

Federal Courts and Legislation

Traditionally, federal legislation and federal courts have not been a source of family law, and their role in family law is still minimal. However, in recent years, federal legislation has been adopted in an attempt to combat nationwide problems concerning child support. Also, with increasing frequency, federal courts have used their authority to enforce both state and federal child support laws.

The Marriage Relationship

Until quite recently, marriage was predicated on a motivation to procreate. Marriage in our society has always been monogamous, at least as far as the law is concerned. Basically, our law provides that male-female pairs may establish an enduring legal bond that allows sexual intimacy, while banning sexual relations outside of marriage. In addition, the marriage laws in our society secure property and inheritance rights for legal spouses under certain conditions. In earlier societies in which rank and status were largely determined by family relations, limitations on sexual relations assured legitimacy and paternity, and presented the family as a stable unit within the community and society.

Our society has always deemed laws regulating the marriage relationship to be important and necessary. This section examines the marriage relationship from a legal standpoint, beginning with creation of the marriage relationship and then moving on to marriage contracts. This section concludes with a look at the modern view of marriage as a partnership.

Creation of the Marriage Relationship

Regulations governing the creation of a valid marriage are established by state statutes and vary significantly from state to state. The statutes of most states set both substantive and formal requirements for a valid marriage. For example, most states have laws regulating the age of the individuals wishing to be married. Typically, those under the age of 16 are strictly prohibited from marrying and those under the age of 18 are prohibited from marrying without parental consent. States also have laws barring marriage between certain blood relatives (such as uncle and niece). In addition, homosexual marriages and **bigamous** marriages are prohibited under state laws.

Formal requirements imposed by state law require that both parties have the capacity to consent to marriage. Those seeking a marriage license must generally be "of sound mind." In addition, states have specific formalities with regard to the **solemnization** of the marriage. Typically, a recognized civil or religious authority, such as a judge, justice of the peace, or minister, must solemnize the marriage of the parties. Failure to comply with state statutory requirements for a valid marriage may cause the marriage to be either void or voidable.

Marriage Contracts

The fundamental unit of society is the family. Although it may be the primary building block of

STATE STATUTES SETTING GROUNDS FOR DIVORCE

Alabama	Ala. Code § 30-2-1*
Alaska	Alaska Stat. § 25.24.050
Arizona	Ariz. Rev. Stat. Ann. § 25-312*
Arkansas	Ark. Code Ann. § 9-12-301
California	Cal. Civ. Code § 4506 et seq.*
Colorado	Colo. Rev. Stat. § 14-10-102*
Connecticut	Conn. Gen. Stat. § 46b-40*
Delaware	Del. Code Ann. tit. 13, § 1505
District of Columbia	D.C. Code Ann. §§ 901–924
Florida	Fla. Stat. ch. 61.502*
Georgia	Ga. Code Ann. § 19-5-3*
Hawaii	Haw. Rev. Stat. § 580-41*
Idaho	Idaho Code § 32-601-616*
Illinois	Ill. Rev. Stat. ch. 40, para. 401
Indiana	Ind. Code § 31-1-11.5-3*
Iowa	Iowa Code § 598.17*
Kansas	Kan. Stat. Ann. § 60-1601
Kentucky	Ky. Rev. Stat. Ann. § 403.140*
Louisiana	1990 La. Act 1009
Maine	Me. Rev. Stat. Ann. tit. 19, § 691*
Maryland	Md. Fam. Law Code Ann. § 7-103
Massachusettes	Mass. Gen. L. ch. 208, § 1*
Michigan	Mich. Comp. Laws. § 25.81*
Minnesota	Minn. Stat. § 518.06*
Mississippi	Miss. Code Ann. § 93-5-1
Missouri	Mo. Rev. Stat. § 452.305*

State Statutes Setting Grounds for Divorce Every state has different rules pertaining to divorce, so paralegals should become familiar with their own state's rules.

society, our own society in recent decades has demonstrated that the bonds between husband and wife are often fragile. All human societies, including ours, regulate and ritualize marriage and

bigamy The crime of marrying while married.
solemnization of marriage The performance of the marriage ceremony.

Montana	Mont. Code Ann. § 40-4-104*
Nebraska	Neb. Rev. Stat. § 42-347*
Nevada	Nev. Rev. Stat. § 125.010*
New Hampshire	N.H. Rev. Stat. Ann. § 458.7*
New Jersey	N.J. Stat. Ann. § 2A:34-2
New Mexico	N.M. Stat. Ann. § 40-4-1*
New York	N.Y. Dom. Rel. Law § 170
North Carolina	N.C. Gen. Stat. § 50-7
North Dakota	N.D. Cent. Code § 14-05-03*
Ohio	Ohio Rev. Code Ann. § 3105.17*
Oklahoma	Okla. Stat. tit. 12, § 1271*
Oregon	Or. Rev. Stat. § 107.025*
Pennsylvania	23 Pa. Cons. Stat. § 3301
Rhode Island	R.I. Gen. Laws § 15-5-2*
South Carolina	S.C. Code Ann. § 20-3-10
South Dakota	S.D. Codified Laws Ann. § 25-4-2*
Tennessee	Tenn. Code Ann. § 36-4-101 *et seq.* *
Texas	Tex. Fam. Code Ann. § 3.01 *et seq.*
Utah	Utah Code Ann. § 30-3-1*
Vermont	Vt. Stat. Ann. tit. 15, § 551
Virginia	Va. Code Ann. § 20-91
Washington	Wash. Rev. Code § 26.09.040*
West Virginia	W. Va. Code § 48-2-4*
Wisconsin	Wis. Stat. § 767.07*
Wyoming	Wyo. Stat. § 20-2-101 *et seq.* *

* Grounds for divorce need only be an "irretrievable breakdown of the marriage relationship," a "breakdown of the marriage to the extent that the objects of marriage have been destroyed and there remains no reasonable likelihood that marriage can be preserved," or "incompatibility."

State Statutes Setting Grounds for Divorce *(Continued)*

procreation and the relations created through marriage. What may be remarkable about our society is that, like so many other areas of American endeavor, we look to legal institutions to resolve family conflicts rather than to purely social or religious institutions. This means not only that courts order family rights and duties, but also that family matters are ultimately turned over to lawyers.

To establish rights and duties that can be enforced (i.e., recognized and ordered by courts), lawyers cast disputes in terms of property rights

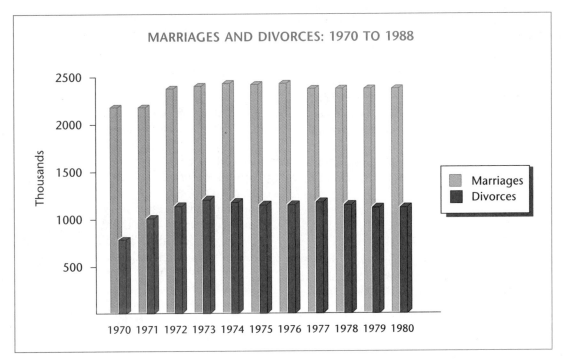

Marriages and Divorces (1970–1988) There are nearly half as many divorces each year as there are marriages.

that are determined by mutual agreement (contract) and rights which the law imposes independent of contract, usually the area of torts. The marriage itself is traditionally viewed as a contractual arrangement because the parties voluntarily assume the relationship of husband and wife, but the most important duties are those imposed by law rather than the agreement of the parties. For example, husband and wife are obligated to provide mutual support for each other and support and nurture for their children. Individuals may avoid these duties by agreement only under special circumstances allowed by the law.

Although marriage has long been described as a contract, throughout most of the history of Anglo-American law, it has not been an ordinary contract, one that could be freely made, altered, and broken. In recent decades, the states, which in America assumed responsibility for domestic regulation, have moved in the direction of making the marriage contract much more like other contracts,

in which the contracting parties control the relationship. Many of the features of family law can be explained by the tension between the special regard with which we view marriage and the family and the objective contractual rights and duties which the law imposes on family relationships.

Marriage as a Partnership

The partnership model of the family appears to be a powerful trend in the 20th century. It provides a useful legal perspective in two ways. First, viewing the husband and wife as partners conforms to modern values regarding intimate relations. Understood in the term *partners* is "equal partners," a concept found explicitly and implicitly in modern cases and statutes. Second, the partnership is a metaphor for a business enterprise for profit. Partnerships are business arrangements of close, mutual, and trusting individuals who have decided to pool their talents and resources to succeed in a chosen enterprise. Husband and wife fit this model, with the additional features of a sexual relationship and procreation as traditional goals.

Like a business partnership, a marriage may now be dissolved without the need to show either side at fault, in many instances. The only issue is a fair and proper division of the resources. When children are involved, their interests may be paramount for the court, but the dissolution of partnership viewed in material terms remains the model for the breakup.

The Duty to Support

Spousal support during the marriage has changed from the unilateral duty of the husband to support the wife to duties of mutual support. The intricacies of these obligations are revealed by the liability for **necessaries**, which has shifted along with the duty to support.

A common-law rule imposed liability on a husband for debts incurred by his wife if the debts were for necessaries, namely, food, clothing, and shelter. Many states have enacted legislation, referred to as family-expense statutes, aimed at protecting the creditors of either husband or wife. The state of Washington provides an unexceptionable example:

> The expenses of the family and the education of the children including stepchildren, are chargeable upon the property of both husband and wife, or either of them, and in relation thereto they may be sued jointly or separately. Provided, that with regard to stepchildren, the

obligation shall cease upon the termination of the relationship of husband and wife.[3]

Marriage Partners or Business Partners?

The business partnership model of marriage has always been implied in **community property** states, where property acquired during the marriage is owned equally. **Equitable distribution** states have reached a similar position with a presumption of the equal value and contribution of both spouses, regardless of their economic contribution. Both these schemes, however, are economic, concerned with the distribution of assets without consideration of fault. **No-fault divorce** minimizes the noneconomic relationship so that dissolution of marriage very much resembles the dissolution of a business partnership.

A business partnership is an organization in which a duty of loyalty is owed among the partners. Partners may not act against the interests of the partnership nor the interests of the other partners. When the partnership breaks up, it is assumed that the assets were equally shared, unless the partnership agreement indicated otherwise. If we accept these underlying principles as the general rules or customs of business partnerships, we can see that they could readily apply to a marriage partnership. The most important feature of this model concerns the meaning of being a partner, in regard to equality of authority, responsibility, and ownership. The marital partnership has evolved from a master-servant model toward one of equality.

BALLENTINESBALLENTINESBALLENTINESBALLENTINESBALLENTINESBALLENTINESBALLENTINESBALLENTINESBALLENTINESBALLENTINESBALLENTINESBALLENTINESBALLENTINESBALLENTINES

necessaries Things reasonably necessary for maintaining a person in accordance with his or her position in life. Thus, depending upon the person's economic circumstances, "necessaries" may not be limited simply to those things required to maintain existence, i.e., shelter, food, clothing, and medical care.

community property A system of law under which the earnings of either spouse are the property of both the husband and the wife, and property acquired by either spouse during the marriage (other than by gift, under a will, or through inheritance) is the property of both. States that have adopted this system are called *community property states*.

equitable distribution Some jurisdictions permit their courts, in a divorce case, to distribute all property obtained during the marriage on an "equitable" basis, that is, without regard to whose name the property is in. In deciding what is equitable, the court takes into consideration factors such as the length of the marriage and the contributions of each party, including homemaking.

no-fault divorce A term for the requirements for divorce in jurisdictions in which the party seeking the divorce need not demonstrate that the other party is at fault. The requirements differ from state to state.

Law Office Scenario

When Lynn Anderson agreed to conduct the preconference interview with her firm's new client, Brenda Bane, she didn't know what she was getting into. As a paralegal for a law firm that specialized in family law, Lynn often conducted initial interviews with clients who wanted to retain an attorney for a divorce. It was Lynn's responsibility to collect the standard information from clients regarding their family situation, their assets, and their wishes with regard to divorce. Lynn would collect all of this information on a client interview sheet and pass it on to an attorney, who would then have an advance perspective of the case at hand. This procedure was very cost-effective for both Lynn's firm and its clients.

When Lynn met with Brenda Bane, however, she knew immediately that this would be anything but a routine divorce. Brenda came in wearing a scarf and dark glasses that she did not remove until after she and Lynn were alone in the conference room. Lynn could then see that she was dealing with a very young woman.

"I need to get a divorce from my husband," Brenda said quietly. "Here is his name and address."

Lynn took the paper handed to her and recorded Brenda's husband's name. Before she could say anything else, Brenda poured out her story.

"I met this guy at a party last week when I was on spring break. We fell in love at first sight, drove out of town, and got married in one of those chapels. We spent the night in a hotel. When I woke up the next morning, he was gone! We had so much to drink the night before, I don't even think we slept in the same bed!" Brenda began to cry.

"I haven't heard from my husband since the night we were married, and I realize now that it was a mistake. I don't know how I am going to pay for a divorce. My parents have been supporting me while I'm in school. I'm only 17, and they will have a fit when they find out what I did."

"Okay," said Lynn. "Your attorney will know how to help you. Let me just get a little more information from you, and I'll call in your attorney, Ms. Benson."

Terminating the Marriage Relationship

The family law paralegal is often the first person from a law firm to meet with a new family law client. It is usually the paralegal's responsibility to collect the pertinent information from a new client either prior to or during the client's first meeting with the attorney. The family law paralegal must be patient, understanding, and professional while listening to the client's story.

The information gathered by the family law paralegal during the first meeting is usually collected with the aid of a client interview form. The exact nature of the information that must be obtained from the client will depend on state law, but often includes the material in the following sample.

CLIENT INTERVIEW FORM

Personal Data

I. Client

    a. Name (maiden and other names)

    b. Age

c. Telephone numbers

d. Employer

e. Earnings

f. Address, including county and length of time resided there

g. Dates of prior marriages, if any, including dates of dissolution

h. Social Security number.

II. Spouse

a. Name (maiden and other names)

b. Age

c. Address, including county, length of time at residence, and whether residence is owned or rented

d. Employer

e. Earnings

f. Length of residence in state

g. Dates of prior marriages, if any, including date of dissolution

h. Social Security number

i. Physical description, and place and time for service of process.

Marriage Data

a. Date and place of marriage

b. Age of client and spouse at time of marriage

c. Date of separation

d. Name, age, sex, date and place of birth of each child born or adopted to present marriage

e. Name, age, sex, date and place of birth of all children of previous marriages of either spouse

f. Is wife pregnant? Expected date of birth?

g. Reason for divorce?

h. Is there a possibility of reconciliation?

Property

a. Property owned by client at time of marriage, including real property, personal property, cash, stocks, and bonds

b. Property received by client as gift or bequest during marriage

c. Property acquired by parties during marriage, including real property, personal property, cash, stocks, bonds, and other property

d. Insurance policies in effect for client, spouse, and children, including life, health, and disability

e. Pension plans in which client or spouse are participants

f. Nature of any ownership in businesses

g. Debts.

Allowances Requested

a. Alimony

b. Child support

c. Property settlements

d. Monthly expenses.

Custody of Children

a. Does client want custody?

b. Does spouse want custody?

c. Is there any dispute over custody?

d. Where have the children been living since separation?

e. Suggested visitation.

The information that must be gathered at the initial meeting with a client may seem overwhelming. Depending on office policy, the client may be sent a questionnaire to complete prior to his or her first office appointment at the law firm, to expedite the collection of this information. It may also be helpful to send to the client a list of documents to bring to the first meeting, including:

1. Deeds, mortgages, and other documents relating to real estate owned by the parties

2. A list of outstanding debts

3. A list of the credit cards owned by the parties, who has each credit card in his or her possession, and what the current balance is on each credit card

4. An inventory of household items, including any antiques or collections

5. Financial statements

6. Insurance policies, including medical, life, and disability

7. Copies of any pension plan documents to which either party is a participant

8. Income tax returns

9. Financial statements and any other pertinent information concerning businesses owned by the parties.

The family law paralegal's task at this point is more to listen and gather information than to advise. In the example in the law office scenario, it may occur to Lynn Anderson that Brenda Bane's marriage might be annulled, avoiding a costly divorce. However, the question of an annulment may have to be researched, and Brenda's attorney will be in the best position to advise her of that possibility.

Because of the number of divorces in this country, the bulk of family law in this country concerns the dissolution of marriage and the child support and property settlements often stemming from dissolution of marriage. Marriages are terminated in one of two ways: by annulment or by marriage dissolution. The dissolution of a marriage raises several issues that must be resolved, including child custody, property settlement, and alimony.

Annulment

When used in family law, **annulment** refers to the legal process of invalidating a marriage. This is to be distinguished from divorce or dissolution of marriage, which terminates a valid marriage.

Annulment and Divorce Distinguished

Conceptually, the most important difference between annulment and divorce relates to the grounds for ending the marriage. Annulment is based on a defect in existence when the marriage was contracted. Divorce is based on grounds that arise after the marriage. For instance, it is often possible to obtain an annulment if one of the parties to the marriage was impotent or sterile at the time of the marriage (assuming this fact was unknown to the other party). However, impotence or sterility developing after the marriage contract would not ordinarily be grounds for annulment; the complaining party would be forced to resort to divorce to get out of the marriage. (Impotence and sterility are features special to the law of domestic relations because the law traditionally viewed the purpose of the marriage contract as the procreation of legitimate offspring.)

Whereas divorce is effective when the decree terminating the marriage is final, annulment operates retroactively to invalidate the marriage from its beginning. This is so because the cause of action for annulment is some impediment to the formation of the marriage contract itself—if the contract was invalid, no marriage resulted. A divorce, in contrast, is based on a valid marriage contract and a valid marriage.

Void and Voidable Marriages

Marriages that may be annulled may be either void or voidable. Under traditional contract theory, some contracts are deemed void and some are merely voidable. A *void* contract is not considered enforceable at any time; a *voidable* contract is valid until a court declares it invalid, even though that declaration operates retroactively to the inception of the contract. Because of the passage of time and removal of the impediment to validity, a voidable contract may become enforceable.

Marriage contracts are similarly subject to the void-voidable distinction. Although a void marriage theoretically may be ignored by all parties, because it has no existence, often a declaration of nullity or its equivalent should be sought to avoid future complications. Because of the special nature of the marriage contract, the grounds for invalidity are somewhat different from those in other contracts. Marriages are generally considered void if certain statutory requirements were not met at the time of the marriage.

annulment of marriage　The act of a court in voiding a marriage for causes existing at the time the marriage was entered into. Annulment differs from divorce in that it is not a dissolution of the marriage but a declaration that no marriage ever existed.

Marriages generally considered void

1. Bigamous marriage (i.e., one of the parties is already married)

2. Incestuous marriage; each state specifies what relationships may not marry (e.g., parent-child, brother-sister, aunt-nephew)

3. Marriage by **mental incompetent**, (i.e., one of the parties lacked mental capacity to contract to marry)

4. Marriage under the minimum age, if at least one of the parties was below the minimum age to marry (as distinguished from parties old enough to marry with parental consent who did not obtain parental consent, which would be voidable).

Examples of marriages merely voidable

1. Failure to meet formal requirements for a licensed marriage

2. Fraud with regard to essentials of marriage

3. Fraud with regard to inability or unwillingness to have children

4. Fraud on the court or legal process.

Brenda Bane, in the law office scenario, would probably have a void marriage, depending on the pertinent state law. Her marriage could be void because she was underage and did not have parental consent. In addition, even if marrying at 17 is legal in the state in which Brenda was married, her marriage could be voidable if her husband did not know that she was underage, or if they did not have a valid marriage license. In some states, this marriage may be voidable because it was apparently never consummated.

Consequences of Annulment

Historically, annulment treated the marriage as if it had never occurred, but the harshness of this has been softened in recent times. In particular, annulment should not bastardize the offspring of an annulled marriage. The Uniform Marriage and Divorce Act § 207(c) states: "Children born of a prohibited marriage are legitimate."

Quite different is the situation with regard to alimony. Under the common law, it was the duty of the husband to provide for the wife, and this extended to legal separations. This duty, however, depended upon a valid marital contract and was therefore inconsistent with an annulment. A number of states have passed legislation allowing alimony following annulment under restricted circumstances, such as when the receiving spouse is an innocent party.

Marriage Dissolution

Our modern laws concerning divorce have evolved from the laws concerning separation (divorce a mensa et thoro), which established grounds for the court to order separate living, such as adultery, cruelty, abandonment, and long absence. Divorce, or its modern counterpart, dissolution, which took on the features of tort suit, was brought on the basis of fault, and the allocation of assets resembled compensation for injuries.

The movement toward *no-fault divorce*—divorce granted without the necessity of proving one of the parties at fault—was induced by an acceleration in the divorce rate and the inadequacy of traditional procedures. Many states allowed divorce on the grounds of cruelty or incompatibility, which permitted couples to obtain divorces on flimsy allegations uncontested by the other party. The result was essentially judgment by default, a process in which most judges were willing to participate. In states like New York, which limited divorce grounds to adultery or were otherwise quite restrictive, or when one of the parties was uncooperative, a vacation to Reno could result in a Nevada divorce.

Lawyers, judges, and others also came to realize that the adversarial process of divorce was harmful to the survivors and inimical to reconciliation. State intrusion into the family to keep

BALLENTINESBALLENTINESBALLENTINESBALLENTINESBALLENTINESBALLENTINESBALLENTINESBALLENTINESBALLENTINESBALLENTINESBALLENTINESBALLENTINES

mental incapacity (mental incompetence)   The inability to understand the nature and character of the transaction in which one is involved.

it together or set its standards was a miserable failure, and each state set about to extricate itself from this unseemly process. Although different statutes were written for different states, the basic divorce process today is probably more uniform in practice than at any time in American history.

Obtaining a divorce is theoretically easy, because all states have some form of no-fault divorce, meaning one party may get a divorce even if the other party objects. The procedures for obtaining a divorce are established by state statute and by the rules of the pertinent court. Typically, a divorce is initiated when a petition is served on one spouse by the other. There may be pretrial orders to set temporary child custody and support and other matters that must be addressed before trial. Discovery, negotiations, pretrial hearings, and a trial typically conclude a divorce proceeding.

The Petition

Most often, a divorce is initiated when one spouse contacts an attorney, who prepares a **petition** for dissolution of marriage and has it served upon the other spouse. The petition is drafted in accordance with state statutes and with the wishes of the client initiating the proceeding. The petition is served upon the other spouse and filed with the appropriate court to request a decree of dissolution of the marriage. Although the exact contents of the petition will depend on state statute, petitions typically include the following:

1. Residence or domicile of plaintiff

2. Existence of the marriage relation

3. Facts showing the nature of the statutory offense on which the action is based, with the time and place of the commission stated with reasonable certainty. In some states it is permissible to simply state the permissible grounds from the state statutes, such as an "irretrievable breakdown of the marriage relationship."

4. Statistical matters such as name, age, sex and residence of any dependent minor children, if required.

5. Description of property owned by the parties, either separately or jointly, if a property settlement is sought as part of the decree.

6. Prayer for relief.[4]

Following is a sample Petition for Dissolution of Marriage form that would be acceptable in several jurisdictions.[5]

Family law paralegals who are asked to prepare petitions for the dissolution of marriage often use the law office's form files, state statutes and rules of court, and state-specific formbooks. After the petition is drafted, the paralegal also typically prepares a summons and sees to the filing and service of the summons and petition in accordance with state statutes and local court rules.

The respondent typically has a period of 20 to 30 days to serve and file an **answer** to the petition. If the respondent does not serve and file an answer, the petitioner may use procedures in the pertinent state statutes and court rules for default proceedings.

Temporary Hearings

Unless both parties to a divorce proceeding are in complete agreement concerning child custody, the payment of debts, and the distribution of assets, a temporary hearing is usually held. Often, the summons and petition for dissolution of marriage are served with a notice of a temporary hearing. At the temporary hearing, the judge or family court referee grants an order establishing the manner in which the divorcing couple's affairs will be managed until the divorce becomes final. Some of the matters addressed in a temporary order may include:

1. Temporary child custody

2. Temporary possession of the homestead

BALLENTINESBALLENTINESBALLENTINESBALLENTINESBALLENTINESBALLENTINESBALLENTINESBALLENTINESBALLENTINESBALLENTINESBALLENTINESBALLENTINESBALLENTINESBALLENTINES

petition   The name given in some jurisdictions to a complaint or other pleading that alleges a cause of action.

answer   A pleading in response to a complaint.

3. Liability for current debts, including car and mortgage payments

4. Restraining orders prohibiting either party from interfering with the other party

5. Orders prohibiting either party from selling assets belonging to both parties.

A temporary hearing that includes a **restraining order** may be crucial if there has been any domestic abuse during the marriage, or if child custody is in dispute. The family law paralegal may be responsible for drafting the documents connected with the temporary hearing with the

---

COURT CAPTION

In Re: the Marriage of:

Patricia Smith,

     Petitioner

vs.

Raymond Smith,   PETITION FOR THE

     Respondent.   DISSOLUTION OF

                                      MARRIAGE

This petition is filed by Patricia Smith, wife, who alleges as follows:

I.

Irreconcilable differences have caused the irremediable breakdown of the marriage of Patricia Smith, Petitioner and Raymond Smith, Respondent.

II.

The residence of wife is 123 Beta Avenue, City of Anytown, County of Alpha, State of Iowa. Wife has been a resident of the State of Iowa for a period of 10 years.

III.

The residence of the husband is at 12345 5th Street, Apt. 2, City of Anytown, County of Alpha, State of Iowa. Husband has been a resident of the State of Iowa for a period of 15 years.

IV.

Wife is not pregnant.

V.

Husband and wife were married on June 5, 1985, in the City of Anytown, County of Alpha, State of Iowa, and separated on or about May 12, 1993.

VI.

The living children of the marriage are as follows:

Name	Age	Address
Linda Patricia Smith	4	123 Beta Avenue Anytown, Iowa
Brandon Laurence Smith	2	123 Beta Avenue Anytown, Iowa.

VII.

An agreement dated July 5, 1993, has been entered into between the parties providing for custody of the minor children of the parties with the wife, with visitation rights of the husband as further set forth in that agreement. Per that agreement, husband has agreed to pay to the wife $350 per month per child, payable on the 15th of each and every month until each child reaches the age of 18 years.

Wherefore, petitioner prays for judgment as follows:

1. For dissolution of the marriage of Patricia Smith and Raymond Smith.

2. That the custody of the above-named children be awarded to Patricia Smith;

3. That Raymond Smith be required to pay to Patricia Smith the sum of $350 per month per child for the support and maintenance of the children, until each child reaches the age of 18 years; and

4. That the court grant such other and further relief as it may deem proper.

[Signature and Verification]

---

aid of office forms and formbooks. He or she may also be responsible for scheduling the temporary hearing with the attorney, the clerk of court, and the client.

Discovery

Like other civil court proceedings, divorce proceedings may involve discovery, including interrogatories,

restraining order An order of court equivalent to a preliminary injunction or a temporary restraining order.

demands for production of documents, and depositions to ascertain financial information from the other party. Often, after gathering the financial information from the client, it becomes apparent that discovery is needed to get financial information that is in the possession of the other party. Family law paralegals assist with the divorce discovery process in much the same way that all civil litigation paralegals participate in the discovery process. They may aid in drafting and serving interrogatories and in assisting clients with preparing answers to interrogatories. When depositions are used, paralegals often are responsible for scheduling the deposition, for serving the notice of deposition, and for reviewing and digesting the depositions.

Negotiation and Mediation

Rarely are the terms of a divorce settlement actually ordered by a court. More often, the parties agree to a settlement prior to the final hearing and the judgment issued by the court encompasses their agreement. For that reason, negotiations between the attorneys for the petitioner and respondent are a big part of the divorce procedure. Paralegals do not take responsibility for negotiating on behalf of a client, although at times they may be asked to draft correspondence setting forth settlement proposals, and they may be asked to assist with mediation.

Mediation, a relatively new step in divorce proceedings, is mandatory in some instances. Mediation services are offered through the family court services of some court systems, and private mediation services are available in nearly every major community throughout the United States. Private mediators have a knowledge of local family law, and they work to assist the divorcing couple in reaching an agreement regarding property settlement and child custody. They may even prepare a settlement agreement based on the conclusions the couple reaches. Mediation does not replace the court procedure for obtaining a divorce. Even when a couple has reached a full agreement concerning every aspect of the dissolution of their marriage, it must still be approved by a court. Often the attorney will assist a couple who has sought mediation

services by reviewing their settlement agreement and representing one party in court.

Mediation has earned favor in recent years for many of the following reasons:

1. Mediation provides the divorcing couple with a forum for resolving their disputes
2. Mediation is often seen as less hostile than the traditional divorce procedures
3. Mediators take a problem-solving approach rather than an adversarial approach
4. Mediators often offer creative solutions to the problems faced by divorcing couples
5. Mediation may cause less trauma for the children of the divorcing couple
6. Mediation is not of public record.

Some of the drawbacks to mediation include the fact that the couples do not relay information under oath (there is no penalty for perjury). Private mediation can also be expensive. Furthermore, both parties must be willing to participate and cooperate for the process to be successful, and there is no guarantee that the mediators will be fair and unbiased.

The Pretrial Hearing

Most jurisdictions require a pretrial hearing. In some jurisdictions, the court sets the date for the hearing; in others, the attorney or paralegal may be responsible for scheduling it. The purposes of the pretrial hearing are to define the issues upon which the parties are in disagreement, to determine how long it will take to try the case, and to encourage the parties to settle, or to set a trial date. In uncontested divorces, some jurisdictions may waive the pretrial hearing or use it simply to set a date for the final hearing. In jurisdictions where the family court judge or referee will be reviewing information concerning the dissolution, it is often the paralegal's responsibility to see that all pertinent documents are assembled for the attorney to bring to court, and that the client is notified of the hearing date and prepared for attendance at the pretrial. Clients will undoubtedly feel more comfortable about attending the pretrial hearing if the typical procedures have been explained to them.

COURT CAPTION

In Re: the Marriage of:

Patricia Smith,

      Petitioner

vs.   DECREE OF

Raymond Smith,   DISSOLUTION OF

Respondent.   MARRIAGE

_____

      This cause came on to be heard by this court December 19, 1995, on Petitioner's Petition for Dissolution of Marriage, default having been duly entered against Defendant. The court heard the testimony of Petitioner and received as evidence a Property Settlement, Custody, and Child Support Agreement entered into by the Petitioner and Respondent on the 5th day of July, 1995, attached hereto as Exhibit A.

      This court has found that Petitioner and Respondent have entered into an agreement respecting their personal property rights, division of custody of their minor children, and provisions for child support and visitation, a copy of which is on file in this action.

      It is hereby ordered, adjudged, and decreed that the marriage relationship between the parties is hereby dissolved.

      It is hereby ordered, adjudged, and decreed that, pursuant to the agreement between the parties, the permanent custody of the minor children be with the Petitioner, subject to the Respondent's right of visitation as set forth in the agreement between the parties.

      It is further hereby ordered, adjudged, and decreed that, pursuant to such agreement, Respondent shall contribute the sum of $350.00 per child per month to Petitioner for the maintenance, care, and education of their minor children, payable on the 15th of each and every month hereafter.

      It is further ordered, adjudged, and decreed that the property settlement of the parties set out in the agreement be, and it is hereby, approved, confirmed, and ratified.

      Dated: _____ .

_____ Signature [by the Court]

Divorce Decree The decree of divorce is the judgment of the court dissolving the marriage relationship and establishing the terms for the care of minor children and distribution of property.

The Trial

After the pretrial hearing, preparation will begin for the trial, if one is to be held. Witnesses must be contacted and scheduled, all documentation must be organized and gotten ready for presentation, and the client must be prepared and kept informed of any developments. Witnesses called in a divorce trial may include experts to testify concerning the fitness of one spouse to be a custodial parent, including psychiatrists, psychologists, and other experts on mental health and children. Lay persons may also be called to testify as character witnesses and as to what they have observed concerning the fitness of one parent or the other. Expert witnesses such as accountants and appraisers may also be called to testify concerning valuation of the couple's property and other financial matters.

If the parties have reached agreement on all issues prior to trial, the family law paralegal is often asked to prepare findings of fact, conclusions of law, and a **decree of divorce** or dissolution to be entered by the court. The decree dissolves the marriage between the parties, awards alimony (if any is awarded), determines the ownership of the parties' property, and establishes the custody and support of any minor children of the parties.

In addition to preparing the witnesses and necessary documentation, family law paralegals often attend the trial to assist the attorney with the presentation of exhibits, to contact and greet witnesses, and take to notes.

Even after the trial has concluded, the family law paralegal may have many tasks to complete for the client. The paralegal may be responsible for assisting the client with property transfers, including the preparation of deeds and transfers of real and personal property. The client should also be sent a copy of the decree of divorce when it is received by the law firm, and should be advised to keep it in a safe deposit box or other secure place for safekeeping.

Child Custody

In the majority of marriage dissolutions, the custody of any minor children of the marriage is not in dispute. The divorcing parents usually agree on which parent will have custody of the minor children without court intervention. At times, divorcing couples may even agree to joint custody.

Child Custody Disputes

Child custody disputes arise when both natural parents want custody of their children upon dissolution of their marriage (or termination of their relationship). Only in very rare instances is there ever a custody battle between a natural parent and a stepparent. In almost all instances, the natural parent is assumed to have custody over his or her natural children.

Traditionally, the mother of the children was given custody unless she was deemed an unfit parent. Today, mothers are granted custody in the vast majority of cases, although more and more fathers are asking for and being granted custody of their children.

In any child custody dispute, the purpose of the proceedings is to place the children in the situation that suits their own best interests. It is defining those "best interests" that creates problems. Section 402 of the Uniform Marriage and Divorce Act prescribes the following factors to be taken into account to determine what is in the child's best interests:

> "(1) the wishes of the child's parent or parents as to his custody; (2) the wishes of the child as to his custodian; (3) the interaction and interrelationship of the child with his parent or parents, his siblings and any other person who may significantly affect the child's best interests; (4) the child's adjustment to his home, school and community; (5) the mental and physical health of all individuals involved. The court shall not consider conduct of a present or proposed custodian that does not affect his relationship to the child."

Whatever statutory guidelines followed by the courts, the child custody dispute is often decided by the family court judge's opinion of what is in the child's best interests. A claim of abuse of discretion is often grounds for an appeal of child custody orders, as was the situation in the *Sellers* case.

TOMMY LEE SELLERS
V.
VERNELL D. SELLERS
555 So. 2d 1117
(Ala. Civ. App. 1989)

[T]he Circuit Court of Russell County entered a final divorce decree dividing the parties' property and awarding the mother the custody of the minor son and daughter. The father appeals, contending that the trial court abused its discretion by failing to award permanent custody of the minor son to the father.

The father's primary contention is that the trial court abused its discretion because the minor son testified that it was his desire and preference to reside with his father.

The preference of a child involved in a divorce with regard to its custody is entitled to much weight .... The wishes of the child, however, are not controlling. The primary consideration in a child custody case is the best interest and welfare of the child involved. ... In determining what is in the best interest of the child, the trial court should consider a variety of factors, including the sex and age of the child, its emotional, social, moral, material, and educational needs, and the characteristics of those seeking custody including age, character, stability, mental and physical health, and their respective home environments. ... In an initial custody determination, there is no presumption in favor of either party—the parties stand on equal footing. ...

Here, the trial court reviewed the evidence and determined that it was in the child's best interest to award custody to the mother. ... [T]he judgment of the trial court is presumed to be correct and will not be reversed on appeal unless it is unsupported by the evidence so as to be plainly and palpably wrong. ...

Our review of the evidence in the record shows that it does support the trial court's decision to award custody to the mother.

At the time of the hearing, the parties were in their middle thirties and had been married for approximately sixteen years. The son is fifteen years old, and the daughter is twelve years old. Both parties are employed on a full-time basis.

At the time of the hearing, the father was living in the marital home. The son testified that he had lived in that home since he entered kindergarten and that he wished to remain there and live with his father "for school" purposes. The son had lived with the father off and on since the parties separated. At the time of the hearing, however, he was residing with his mother at his request.

The evidence further reflects that the father "brutally beat" the mother, gambled on occasion, and, at the time of the hearing, was under psychiatric care and on medication for his "nerves."

In view of the evidence, we cannot say that the trial court's judgment is unsupported by the evidence so as to be plainly and palpably wrong. Accordingly, this case is affirmed.

AFFIRMED.

Joint Custody

A relatively recent custody development that gained popularity during the 1970s is **joint custody**. When a divorcing couple decide to share the legal custody and responsibility for a child, they may agree to joint custody. Although this solution to the problem of custody battles won favor initially, many critics have charged that it often puts too much stress on the child to be juggled between two households with such frequency.

Property Settlements

The rules and policies regarding distribution of marital assets at divorce show inconsistency among different states, within each state, and over

BALLENTINESBALLENTINESBALLENTINESBALLENTINESBALLENTINESBALLENTINESBALLENTINESBALLENTINESBALLENTINESBALLENTINESBALLENTINESBALLENTINESBALLENTINESBALLENTINES

decree of divorce   A final judgment granting a divorce.

joint custody   An arrangement whereby both parties to a divorce retain legal custody of their child and jointly participate in reaching major decisions concerning the child's welfare.

time. Perhaps courts and legislatures are attempting to do the impossible—introduce fairness to relationships in which the partners themselves have despaired of fairness, however hard they tried to achieve it. In addition, courts and legislatures are attempting to establish general rules to allocate family wealth in a society in which values with regard to both family and wealth are highly fragmented. The disarray in which we find statutes and decisions echoes the confusion characterizing the contemporary marriage relationship; family law seems to be driven by issues rather than consensus. The area of **property settlements** shows this issue orientation in the evolving law of pension rights for the nonemployee spouse, for reimbursement to one spouse for contribution to the education and professional career of the other spouse, and in equal value placed on homemaking and breadwinning.

Although some issues are politically sponsored, as with many women's issues, much of the law is initiated through litigation. This has significant ramifications. First, rules and policies are based on the particular qualities of individual cases. Second, the absence of consensus and rule requires that judges continue to exercise great discretion, creating uncertainty in each case, which in turn threatens to lead to litigation because lawyers cannot make accurate predictions of outcomes.

Attorneys and their clients must examine both property distribution and alimony as part of the whole settlement scheme. The goal of property distribution at divorce is fairness to the parties. The modern phrase *equitable distribution* embodies the principle of fairness. As values change, the perception of fairness also changes. In earlier times, when women had very limited opportunities to produce income, it seemed fair that the husband assume the duty of economic support for the family. This continued after divorce because the former wife was likely to be impoverished without alimony, and entitlement to permanent alimony was necessary because the wife acquired property while married. Even after divorce, she was likely to receive only support during her lifetime, with little else in the way of property rights. Today this scheme is hopelessly antiquated, but not long ago it fit the model of family and society.

Judicial Discretion

Traditionally, because domestic relations cases arose in equity, judges enjoyed great discretion in molding their decisions to be fair to the parties. In recent years, state legislatures have been active in divorce legislation, frequently establishing specific guidelines for the distribution of property and thus intruding on judicial discretion. As these laws become more specific, they naturally diminish the degree of discretion enjoyed by the judiciary. Courts as well have often sought to encourage consistency by treating certain matters as governed by established rules.

The effect of rules is influenced by our appellate process. When a party to a divorce case is dissatisfied with the decree of the trial court, appeal may be grounded on two possible errors of the lower court:

1. If the decision was within the discretion of the judge, the appellant may claim that there was an abuse of discretion.

2. If the judge followed a principle of law, the appellant may argue that the law was incorrectly stated or applied.

Community Property States and Common Law

Throughout the history of family law, lawyers have been accustomed to dividing the states into jurisdictions with community property principles or the so-called common-law jurisdictions. Actually, only Louisiana can legitimately claim to be a non-common-law jurisdiction, tracing its roots directly to the civil law systems of Spain and France.

BALLENTINESBALLENTINESBALLENTINESBALLENTINESBALLENTINESBALLENTINESBALLENTINESBALLENTINESBALLENTINESBALLENTINESBALLENTINESBALLENTINESBALLENTINESBALLENTINESBALLENTINES

property settlement (postnuptial agreement; postmarital contract)   An agreement between husband and wife settling property rights between them as part of a divorce action. Court approval may or may not be required.

Equitable distribution means that the courts may distribute the property acquired during the marriage on an equitable basis, that is, without regard to whose name the property is in. In deciding what is equitable, the court takes into consideration factors such as the length of the marriage and the contributions of each party, including homemaking. One of the major motivations for enacting equitable distribution legislation was to give official recognition to noneconomic contributions of homemakers. The differential in economic contribution, then, gives way to an assumption of equality of effort by the partners to a marriage, in much the same way that business partners are treated as equal partners.

Equitable distribution today is a legislative product that evolved in many instances from judicial decisions. The statutes stress equity over equality, providing guidelines for judicial division of property.

In *community property* states, the income and earnings of both husband and wife during the marriage are owned equally and acquisitions made with this income are owned equally. In these states, the general rule is that property acquired during the existence of the community (i.e., the marriage) is jointly owned unless received by gift, will, or inheritance. Property owned before the marriage is separate property, as are gifts and bequests. Important problems still arise, though, regarding separate property, such as the allocation of any increase in value of separate property; whether separate property has been commingled with community property in such a way as to lose its separate property status; whether a spouse contributed to enhance the value of separate property; and whether income from the separate property is itself separate property. Unfortunately, the various states have chosen to answer these issues in different ways.

Upon divorce, the couple's assets (with some exceptions) ought to be divided roughly equally under both schemes. In fact, equitable distribution borrowed the partnership model from the community property states. In 1984 Wisconsin became the first state to adopt a community property law modeled on the Uniform Marital Property Act (UMPA). The UMPA was designed to apply to property during marriage rather than divorce and elected a community property scheme. The UMPA was a product of the National Conference of Commissioners on Uniform State Laws, the entity that constructed the UMDA (Uniform Marriage and Divorce Act), which in § 307 devised equitable distribution and community property alternatives. It is worthy of note that this group chose a community property scheme as the model proposed for all states. This is a reflection of the nearly universal acceptance of the partnership model of marriage.

The role of the paralegal in assisting with property settlements begins with the initial client interview. The family law paralegal is usually instrumental in collecting the information concerning the property of the parties, its current ownership, and its acquisition. After an agreement has been reached, the family law paralegal is often responsible for drafting the property settlement agreement for the signature of both parties and, at times, for incorporating the agreement into the judgment and decree when the petitioner is the client.

Alimony

Alimony (maintenance) originated from the husband's lifelong duty to support his wife, whether married or divorced. Today, either husband or wife may receive alimony. In recent times, courts and legislatures have come to disfavor permanent alimony. Most awards now come in the form of periodic payments lasting a few months or years, designated as *rehabilitative alimony* and designed to return a homemaker to the job market (i.e., to help a dependent spouse get through the post-divorce period of adjustment to self-sufficiency). Lump-sum alimony is occasionally awarded, often to provide compensation for contributions by one

---

BALLENTINESBALLENTINESBALLENTINESBALLENTINESBALLENTINESBALLENTINESBALLENTINESBALLENTINESBALLENTINESBALLENTINESBALLENTINESBALLENTINESBALLENTINES

alimony   Ongoing court-ordered support payments by a divorced spouse, usually payments made by an ex-husband to his former wife.

spouse, such as a wife working to put her husband through professional education. Alimony is part of a more comprehensive plan dividing the resources and obligations of the spouses; the distribution of assets and child support are the other two important economic ingredients of this plan.

Alimony is characterized by a high degree of discretion on the part of the judiciary, although most states have now provided more or less detailed guidelines for judges to weigh when awarding alimony. Alimony is based principally on the need of the recipient and the ability to pay of the spouse making support payments. Need is a relative concept, depending to a large degree on the standard of living enjoyed during the marriage. Alimony is usually terminated by the death of either party or by remarriage of the recipient. Depending on the jurisdiction, termination may be waived in the property settlement agreement.

A postdivorce procedure in the form of a petition for modification is available to increase or decrease alimony or to extend or shorten the period during which payments are made. The key element in a successful suit for modification is proof of changed circumstances justifying modification. For the recipient of alimony to obtain an upward modification, it must be shown also that the payor has the ability to pay the increased amount.

Postmarital Contracts

Written agreements between a divorcing couple setting forth their agreement with regard to the disposition of any property owned by either of them; maintenance of either of them; and support, custody, and visitation of their children are referred to as *postnuptial agreements*, *separation agreements*, or *property settlement agreements*. Postnuptial agreements should be executed when divorce or permanent separation is imminent, lest they be voided for promoting divorce. Postmarital agreements are becoming more acceptable to the courts and legislatures, but considerable variation continues among the states. Because of changing law and different traditions, different jurisdictions run the gamut of rules in these matters. Careful draftsmanship is essential.

Section 306 of the Uniform Marriage and Divorce Act addresses postnuptial agreements as follows:

Section 306(a) To promote amicable settlement of disputes between parties to a marriage attendant upon their separation or the dissolution of their marriage, the parties may enter into a written separation agreement containing provisions for disposition of any property owned by either of them, maintenance of either of them, and support, custody, and visitation of their children.

(b) In a proceeding for dissolution of marriage or for legal separation, the terms of the separation agreement, except those providing for the support, custody, and visitation of children, are binding upon the court unless it finds, after considering the economic circumstances of the parties and any other relevant evidence produced by the parties on their own motion or on request of the court, that the separation agreement is unconscionable.

Antenuptial Contracts

Some couples elect to put the terms of their marriage contracts into a written contract before their marriage. These contracts are called by the alternative names *antenuptial*, *premarital*, and *prenuptial agreements* or *contracts*. The **antenuptial agreement** describes the relative statuses of husband and wife; it redefines to a greater or lesser extent the rights and duties of the spouses that

antenuptial agreement (prenuptial agreement)   An agreement between a man and a woman who are to be married, governing the financial and property arrangements between them in the event of divorce, death, or even during the marriage. Such an agreement may override obligations or rights provided by statute.

are otherwise expressed or implied by law. Although formerly rejected by the courts because such agreements contemplated divorce, in recent years the courts have reversed themselves and accepted antenuptial arrangements much like other contracts. Courts and legislatures vary considerably, however, in the requirements they impose to find such agreements valid and enforceable. The contents of antenuptial agreements, as well as who should enter into an antenuptial agreement, are both important considerations.

The Contents of an Antenuptial Agreement

The contents of an antenuptial agreement will depend on the character of the parties and their intended relationship. Many agreements contain great detail concerning the expectations of the parties to the marriage. Some details may seem quite practical: "Husband will be in charge of financial record-keeping, paying household bills promptly on a monthly basis." Some may seem unduly trivial: "Wife will prepare dinner on Monday, Wednesday, and Friday evenings while the Husband will prepare dinner on Tuesday, Thursday and Sunday evenings, Saturday being reserved for dining out or whatever arrangement is made by mutual agreement." Some couples have even attempted to set a minimum frequency of sexual contact. All of these terms are permissible, yet none of them appears to be enforceable—no court is likely to use its powers to require compliance. Nonetheless, highly detailed agreements do present a picture of the relationship envisioned by the couple and may be used later, if the relationship has soured, to show that one of the spouses lived up to the conditions while the other failed. Presumably, in no-fault divorces, such lapses merit little attention with regard to severing marital bonds, but fault remains a negotiating weapon when property settlement, custody of children, and support payments are discussed in the pretrial process.

As a concrete example, it might be apparent from the premarital agreement that it was intended that the wife would return to finish her education when the children had all entered elementary school. If the marriage terminated before she was able to accomplish this goal, the agreement would make a powerful argument in favor of rehabilitative alimony for this purpose. This would be particularly true if the agreement divided rights and duties and the wife had performed her part of the bargain.

The overriding concern of the law and the legal practitioner with regard to premarital agreements is the disposition of property rights upon death or divorce. It goes without saying that one of the spouses would be materially better off if the antenuptial agreement were invalid or unenforceable. More than greed is involved. At death, enforcement of the agreement usually means that persons close to the deceased but not close to the surviving spouse will get a share that would otherwise be reserved to the surviving spouse. At divorce, enforcement means that a disliked, despised, or even hated spouse will get the lion's share of property that was once enjoyed by both. Under such circumstances, it is essential that the antenuptial agreement be properly drafted.

An antenuptial agreement presents special problems uncommon in other contracts. Here we have a very special contract, which may not take effect for decades. In some respects it is like a will, especially in making distribution of property at death. A will, however, is not a contract—it is a unilateral disposition of property and may be unilaterally revoked until the death of the testator. Nor is an antenuptial agreement a contract in the usual sense of an exchange of promises to be performed—it is really a mutual denial of rights and duties that would otherwise be imposed by law. For example, all states provide for a surviving spouse to receive a share of the decedent's estate if there is no will, or to elect to take a share of the estate if dissatisfied with the will. An antenuptial agreement is the only way to circumvent this law and provide a lesser share.

As another example, California is a community property state, so property earned and acquired during the marriage is deemed community property owned equally by husband and wife. A couple could provide in an antenuptial agreement to keep their respective properties separate, thus circumventing the law of community property.

The fact that the property distributions described by antenuptial agreement commonly do not go into effect until many years after the agreement is signed presents two problems. First, the law may change; it has been changing for several decades and is likely to continue to change as antenuptial agreements become ever more popular and used in more situations. Second, regardless of the state in which the contract was made or in which the couple lived, married, and were domiciled, divorce or death may take place in a state with a very different attitude toward antenuptial agreements than the one in which the contract was signed. Some protection may be afforded by including a clause requiring application of the law of the state where the contract was finalized (presumably the intended domicile of the couple). Although most states are inclined to honor such a clause, antenuptial agreements fall in an area (namely, family law) where public policy considerations are heavy, and the court may choose to ignore the clause on policy grounds.

Who Should Have an Antenuptial Agreement?

Certain circumstances suggest the advisability of an antenuptial agreement, but the character of the relationship of the bride and groom decides whether an agreement is actually executed. The antenuptial agreement introduces harsh economic consideration into what is presumably a romantic relationship; it suggests that one of the parties has second thoughts about the permanence of the relationship or the sincerity of the other party. For this reason, many who think an antenuptial agreement desirable will nonetheless refuse to raise the subject.

In the past, antenuptial agreements were sought in two kinds of situations. Older persons marrying for companionship or convenience without the intention of building a family (commonly with their respective children already self-supporting) often chose to keep their property separate, having planned for some time for the disposition of their property at death. When both parties were affluent, one did not take advantage of the other. The antenuptial agreement gave some assurance that the May member of a May-December marriage was not a golddigger by limiting the property to be gained in death or divorce. (If this seems unfair, note that the wealthy partner could always express generosity through gift or will.)

Persons contemplating second marriages, who have children by prior marriages, should seriously consider drawing up an antenuptial agreement. The demands on family resources can be great when second marriages are involved, and nearly everyone will feel unfairly treated. When the couple plans through an antenuptial agreement for the allocation of resources, they will be forced to confront these problems and make a reasonable attempt to head off the worst scenario.

Typically, the burdens of antenuptial agreements are concerned with fairness, disclosure, and conscionability. Voluntariness, consent, and fraud are basic features of contractual validity which apply to antenuptial agreements as well.

Cohabitation, Marriage Alternatives, and Nontraditional Relationships

A legal marriage is often thought of in technical terms: a couple is married who have the capacity to marry and who register their marriage at the courthouse. However, many couples engage in relationships which have all the attributes of marriage except the license. Some couples make no pretense of their lack of a license, whereas others hold themselves out as husband and wife and are perceived as such. Still others fall somewhere in between.

Form Drafting guide—Checklist—Matters to be considered in drafting an antenuptial agreement [9A Am. Jur. *Legal Forms 2d* (Rev.)]

Checklist of matters that should be considered in drafting an antenuptial agreement:

- Name and address of prospective husband

- Maiden name, married name, if any, and address of prospective wife

- Description of property owned by each

- Approximate value of property

- Statement of complete disclosure

- Consideration

- Description and value of property to be transferred

- Provision defining ownership of after-acquired property

- Provisions in event of death of parties
  — Transfer of property
  — Effect on terms of agreement
  — Third-party considerations

- Benefits for children of marriage or of prior marriages

- Release of marital property rights

- Effect of termination of marriage, other than by death

- Effective date of agreement

- Revocation, termination, or modification provisions

- Evidence of independent representation by counsel for each party

- Date of agreement

Checklist of Items to Be Included in Antenuptial Agreements An antenuptial agreement is a written arrangement made before marriage.

At an earlier period in American history, consensual unions were quite common, especially on the frontier where clergy and courts were few and far between. This gave rise to the **common law marriage**, which, once established, was just as legally binding as a licensed marriage. The law favors marriage; that is, it will presume that a marriage exists whenever feasible. The law also favors legitimacy, which bolsters the presumption of marriage to avoid making offspring illegitimate.

common law marriage A marriage entered into without ceremony, the parties agreeing between themselves to be husband and wife, followed by a period of cohabitation.

It is no wonder, then, that in an era of consensual unions and erratic or nonexistent recordkeeping, a legal vehicle for establishing marriage and legitimating children would arise.

Perhaps it is not surprising, either, that in the modern era of careful recordkeeping most states have abolished common law marriage and rely more on licenses and records. Thus, many cases which would in former times have been common law marriages no longer qualify. Judges are frequently faced with situations begging for some recognition of marital status. For example, a couple maintain a long-term relationship, have children, and are believed by their community to be married. When he dies, however, technically his "widow" is not entitled to any widow's or survivor's property or benefits. Judges have used a number of means to provide an equitable result in such cases.

In contrast, in recent years, many couples have deliberately chosen not to marry even though their relationship has a character resembling most marriages. Still others seem to be engaged in what was formerly called "trial marriage," i.e., living together as an experiment in contemplation of marriage. A countless number of other living arrangements have also developed.

All of these relationships present the problems that occur in marriage when they end by design or death. What property belongs to whom? What happens to any children born of the relationship? The law and the decisions in this area tell us much about our society's vision of marriage and family, at least in legal terms. This section focuses on common law marriages, cohabitation agreements, and nontraditional relationships.

Common Law Marriage

As the name suggests, common law marriage was largely a creation of custom and the courts, although some legislatures established the requirements for common law marriages. The basic requirements were fourfold:

1. Capacity to marry

2. A present, mutual agreement to permanently enter the marriage relationship to the exclusion of all other relationships

3. Public recognition of the relationship as a marriage; "holding oneself out as husband and wife" (repute)

4. Public assumption of marital duties and **cohabitation** (cohabitation).

Of these, repute and cohabitation distinguished common law marriage from other forms of marriage. Agreement could be inferred from repute and cohabitation; in the common law of England, the agreement to take each other as husband and wife was the basis for establishing a marriage.

A common law marriage may take time to establish by repute and cohabitation. Some states that codified the requirements gave a specific time period, such as cohabitation for four or seven years. Once the common law marriage has been established, however, it relates back, that is, the couple is deemed married from the outset of the period in which the marriage was established. This is a good way of establishing the legitimacy of children born to the relationship, but presents problems with ownership of property acquired during the period in which the marriage was germinating. Because common law marriages are informal arrangements lacking official documentation, the existence of a common law marriage may not be discovered through record searches. This lack of formality may cause problems at a later date when the transfer of property, especially real estate, is involved.

Modern Equivalents to Common Law Marriage

As most states abolished common law marriage, unions that would formerly have been granted marital status were put in limbo. Although in many instances, the parties disdained family values or merely neglected to obtain a license, many others had a good faith belief that they were married.

cohabitation   Living together as husband and wife, although not married to each other.

Putative Marriage   A **putative marriage** is a marriage that is invalid for some reason but which is given some effects of a valid marriage. Although the requirements for a putative marriage vary from state to state, the principle requirements are (1) a good faith belief in the validity of the marriage by at least one of the partners, and (2) an attempted ceremonial marriage. Under the early canon law, the concept seems to have evolved to protect those who went through what they believed to be a valid church wedding which turned out to be invalid. In the United States, putative marriage was first associated with states having some civil law background from Spain or France, earliest in Louisiana, but also notably in California and Texas. Although it is commonly associated with community property states, it has spread in recent years to a number of common-law, separate property states, such as Illinois, Colorado, Minnesota, and Montana. This popularity is due in large part to Uniform Marriage and Divorce Act § 209, which encourages the statutory adoption of putative marriage.

> Section 209. Any person who has cohabited with another to whom he is not legally married in the good faith belief that he was married to that person is a putative spouse until knowledge of the fact that he is not legally married terminates his status and prevents acquisition of further rights. A putative spouse acquires the rights conferred upon a legal spouse. ... If there is a legal spouse or other putative spouses, rights acquired by a putative spouse do not supersede the rights of the legal spouse or those acquired by other putative spouses, but the court shall apportion property, maintenance and support rights among the claimants as appropriate in the circumstances and in the interests of justice.

Cohabitation Agreements

The final set of situations involving unofficial unions concerns cohabiting partners who have no intention of either the pretense or the actuality of marriage. These are couples who do not qualify for marital status and do not seek marital rights, but who nevertheless become involved with the law in a dispute over property to which both partners have contributed but only one is apparent holder of title or property. The legal arguments in such cases include those who attempt to obtain marital rights to such items as pensions, worker's compensation, or Social Security by arguing a broad definition of *spouse*, *widow*, or *family*. These latter are often decided on dependency status or simple equity, because they do not involve interfering with the distribution of assets among competing claimants. Nevertheless, some couples may belong in the first category (cohabitants) who believed they were, or pretended to be, married but were domiciled in a state hostile to recognizing informal marriages (common law, putative, or presumption of marriage).

Cohabitants do not have a marital agreement, but they may have, or at least argue they had, a contractual arrangement. This could consist of an actual cohabitation agreement in writing, which the parties executed when they began to live together. In the alternative, they might have an oral agreement or an implied agreement. They might have cooperated in a business venture in such a way as to suggest some sort of business partnership remedy. In relationships that last for many years, funds inevitably become **commingled** so that it is difficult to attribute individual ownership of specific assets. When the relationship fails or terminates because of death, the partner who appears to have been shortchanged may well seek a legal remedy.

Litigants face two principal hurdles in bringing suit. First, cohabitation is illegal in most states, assuming the term includes illicit sexual activity. Courts are disinclined to put their blessings on these relationships. Second, the court—the traditional protector of marriage and family—hesitates to create a marriage-like relationship when the couple has defied social convention and

BALLENTINESBALLENTINESBALLENTINESBALLENTINESBALLENTINESBALLENTINESBALLENTINESBALLENTINESBALLENTINESBALLENTINESBALLENTINESBALLENTINESBALLENTINESBALLENTINES

putative marriage   A marriage that, although invalid because of some impediment, ... was nonetheless entered into in good faith.

commingle   To merge; to mix.

legal procedure. Thus, courts are not inclined to resolve issues when the parties voluntarily declined the appropriate legal means to establish their respective rights and duties. Only when the inequities indicate a clear injustice will the courts be likely to interfere.

American society, however, seems to have chosen to accept wide freedom in intimate relationships, and shows a new tolerance toward alternative lifestyles. The law inevitably follows social mores. In addition, cohabiting partners should be free to make contracts. In most states the laws against fornication and adultery are rarely, if ever, enforced; cohabitation is only technically a crime. As long as compensation is not sought for sexual services, and the substance of the claim is independent of the sexual aspects of the relationship, a contract between the parties should be honored by the courts. If someone hired a maid or a cook, the contract would be honored without regard to incidental sexual activity.

Marvin and Its Progeny

Marvin v. Marvin,[6] the first "palimony" case, ran through many appeals. *Marvin* involved the termination of a seven-year relationship between the movie star Lee Marvin and Michelle Triola Marvin. Michelle sued on an alleged oral contract under which Lee and Michelle had agreed to share their earnings during their relationship. The California Court of Appeals and the California Supreme Court accepted the proposition that cohabitants could contract in such a fashion if the contract was not grounded in illicit sexual services. Without condoning such relationships, the courts held that contracts independent of such consideration were enforceable. The California court also went through a list of equitable remedies or devices designed to remedy unjust enrichment or compensate a cohabitant for services rendered. This case broke new ground, and set new standards, for many later decisions, including many outside the state of California.

Nontraditional Relationships

Certain traditional attributes of the family, such as sexual intimacy, partnership based on love and affection, and procreation and nurture of children, are presently assumed by persons who do not fit the traditional legal definition of *family*, specifically single persons and homosexuals. In addition, advances in medicine and science have opened new possibilities for procreation through artificial insemination and the implantation of fertilized eggs. Meanwhile, the number of illegitimate births appears to be reaching new peaks. Whereas in the past the courts relied on the fact or the appearance of marriage to establish rights and duties between husband and wife and parent and child, today many who appear to fall clearly outside even a broad definition of *family* are claiming such rights, including pension benefits, parental leave, or even the right to marry, as well as the right to adopt.

Because the Fourteenth Amendment to the U.S. Constitution prohibits the states from denying any person equal protection of the laws, those who are deemed ineligible to marry or to be classified as a family may raise Fourteenth Amendment arguments. For example, may a state lawfully restrict adoption to heterosexual couples? Assuming for the sake of argument that homosexual couples, as well as single men and women, can be shown to provide a healthy, nurturing environment for children, how can the law discriminate against them? These questions are fraught with controversy and raise powerful emotions; their legal resolution is not yet clearly delineated.

Parent and Child Relationships

Children add a dimension to family law that distinguishes it from other areas of law. Family law commonly deals with the welfare of human beings who have not reached the age of legal competence (*majority*), who are frequently the subjects of abuse or exploitation, and who must be protected by society through its legal institutions when the family, the primary social institution, fails. Problems in other areas of law are often neatly handled by the transfer of wealth from one pocket to another; family law involves issues that are not readily measured in dollars and cents.

Family law paralegals are often involved in the legal aspects of parent and child relationships, including the rights of children, child support, and adoption. They may be exposed to these areas of law through their work in private law firms, or they may work for federal, state, or county social agencies that deal with the welfare of children.

The Rights of Children

Although child abuse and neglect have been prohibited by the law since early times, the protection afforded children came in the guise of **parens patriae**, a doctrine which gives the state authority over those suffering legal disabilities, including children. This principal is paternalistic in tradition—the state acts as the parent when the legal parents are unable or unwilling to carry out their parental duties. The state protects the child. Recently, however, many have argued that children should have rights. Unfortunately, this creates a legal anomaly: How can children, who are without legal capacity, have rights as against the very persons, namely their parents, who are ultimately responsible for enforcing their rights? The *Gregory K.* case may be prophetic in this regard.

On September 27, 1992, an Orlando, Florida court permitted a 12-year-old boy to terminate the parental rights of his natural parents and allow his foster parents to adopt him (his natural father did not oppose the adoption). The news media branded this a "divorce" brought by a child against his mother. Many observers concluded that the case was significant only because the media gave it

significance. Although this may be technically true, when the media focuses its attention on a case, legal issues become social and political issues. In this instance, the case not only underlined the plight of neglected children, but also suggested the woeful inadequacies of the social service programs that deal with them. What was unusual about the termination of parental rights in this case was the lack of involvement of a social service agency. Typically an action for termination of parental rights is brought by an agency and often initiated by the court. The *Gregory K.* case was unique in giving a minor legal status to bring an action against a parent to terminate parental rights.

Parental authority is buffeted between the concern over adolescent freedom, as represented by teen-age pregnancy and juvenile crime on the one hand, and serious abuse and neglect by parents, on the other. The legal system will inevitably be asked to resolve this clash. It is difficult to predict the exact outcome, but the atmosphere changed from the 1970s, when money was steadily increased for social programs, to the 1980s and beyond, when the answer to social problems elicited criminalization of misbehavior. For instance, Florida has a law under which a parent driver may receive serious jail time for injury or death to a young child who is not buckled into the car. It is becoming a crime to be a bad parent.

At times, determining who is or is not the child's parent presents an entirely different set of problems. The Uniform Parentage Act defines a parent-child relationship as the legal relationship existing between a child and his or her natural or adoptive parents, incident to which the law confers or imposes rights, privileges, duties, and obligations. The following states have adopted the Uniform Parentage Act:

Alaska	Hawaii
California	Illinois
Colorado	Kansas
Delaware	Minnesota

BALLENTINESBALLENTINESBALLENTINESBALLENTINESBALLENTINESBALLENTINESBALLENTINESBALLENTINESBALLENTINESBALLENTINESBALLENTINESBALLENTINESBALLENTINES

parens patriae doctrine   The doctrine that dependent and incompetent persons are under the protection and control of the state. This concept empowers the state, within the limits imposed by the Constitution, to institutionalize orphans, individuals with serious mental defects, and others who are unable to care for themselves.

Missouri   North Dakota
Montana   Ohio
Nevada   Rhode Island
New Jersey   Washington
New Mexico   Wyoming

Child Support

When a child's parents are unmarried and one parent is responsible for the physical custody of the children more than the other, the primary caretaker is entitled to compensation for providing more than her or his share of support.

Parental Duty to Support

The English common law was surprisingly silent about a father's duty to support his children. Perhaps it was felt that this is a fundamental element of natural law that did not require restatement. Some have argued that the duty of support as found in the law evolved from the English poor laws, which were designed to prevent the poor from becoming a burden on the state. During the marriage, failure to support could be remedied by child neglect and abuse statutes, but postdivorce support echoes this early origin in enforcing a private welfare system.

Like spousal support during marriage, parental support extends only to necessaries. In fact, contemporary controversy over parental support for a college education has been argued in some courts as whether a college education is a necessary.

As the duty of support was first legally recognized, it applied only to the father. In the 20th century, the duty of support was extended to mothers as secondarily liable for support. This concept was destined to fail, as the equal protection clause of the Fourteenth Amendment was applied with greater force to legal distinctions based on gender.

Unmarried fathers are also obligated to support their offspring. Adoptive parents are legally bound to support their adoptive children. Adoption servers the legal bond between a child and its natural parents and treats the child as having the same legal relationship to its adoptive parents as a natural child would have. There is even a trend toward recognizing stepparents' legal obligations to support their stepchildren.

Need and Ability to Pay

Like alimony, child support is based on the children's need for support and the parent's ability to pay. If the mother has custody of the minor children, her resources may be considered in the amount ordered to be paid by the father. Similarly, when the father has custody of the children, the mother may be ordered to pay child support to the father.

Unlike alimony, the resources of the beneficiary have only a limited impact on the award. A child's resources (e.g., a trust set up by grandparents) would not ordinarily reduce the parental obligation for furnishing necessaries.

The relation between child support and the marital settlement agreement also differs from alimony. Some jurisdictions honor a waiver of future right to modify the amount of alimony, but the child has neither negotiated nor agreed to the support terms of the agreement. If the parents act in concert against the interests of the child, the court is responsible for protecting the child. If need increases, the court will not be bound by a waiver in an agreement.

Child Support and Remarriage

Divorced parents remarry, often to other divorced parents, and often bear more children, thereby creating step relationships and half-siblings. The person paying child support faces the dilemma of too many demands on his or her resources. Society and the law hold Dad and Mom morally responsible for all their children: If they could not support the children of their first marriage, they should not have remarried, much less continued procreating. Phrased neutrally, the "first family first" doctrine argues that the level of support established for children of a prior marriage should not be diminished by the parent's choice to have additional children. Although support is normally modifiable based on changed circumstances of the parties, this is an apparent exception. It is difficult to defend a principle which penalizes children who are innocent of the "fault" of their parents; a trend may be developing toward apportioning the resources in a humane and rational way to serve the interests of all the children. Stepchildren traditionally had little claim on the stepfather's or stepmother's resources, presumably because they were supported by their natural fathers and mothers.

The Enforcement Problem

Both law and society have been unforgiving in the pursuit of those who are in arrears in their child support payments. In 1992, the popular media suddenly became aroused by the "deadbeat dad" problem, after many years of federal and state action designed to step up enforcement of child support orders. The motivation for government action was not a simple and direct response to the woeful record of support payments, although statistics in that regard demanded attention and action. The state's and especially the federal government's attention is aimed at reducing the government's share in welfare payments to single-parent families. In many instances, public assistance provided support when parents failed to meet their legal support obligations. New laws provided means for collecting arrears that could then be credited to amounts paid, mostly through Aid to Families with Dependent Children (AFDC), in the form of welfare.

These efforts were begun primarily through the Office of Child Support Enforcement (OCSE) of the U.S. Department of Health and Human Services, beginning in 1974, and are presently collecting several billion dollars yearly. The federal government furnishes funds for state enforcement programs at the same time that it imposes requirements on them in order to receive the funds. Amendments to the law (the Federal Enforcement Initiative of 1974) in 1984 and 1988 added more requirements and made more drastic the means of enforcement. AFDC applicants assign their uncollected support rights to the state and must assist efforts to collect. The states must maintain records and the federal government maintains records to assist in locating parents who are in arrears.

Under the new requirements imposed on the state, new laws must require employee withholding of child support from paychecks of those in arrears. Arrears in excess of $1,000 must be deducted from state and federal income tax refunds. Under the 1988 amendments, new orders for support or orders modifying support will cause support payments to be automatically deducted from paychecks whether the payor is in arrears or not. The 1988 amendments also provide new standards for paternity and provide federal funds for paternity testing, in an obvious effort to go after unwed fathers.

From time to time, family law paralegals may be asked to use their investigative skills to locate parents who have not paid child support. The State Parent Locator Service may be useful to contact a sister state with regard to out-of-state driver's licenses, vehicle registrations, and welfare and social services files. The Federal Parent Locator Service may assist with information possessed by the IRS, Social Security Administration, Veterans Administration, National Personnel Records Center, and the Labor Department.

Adoption

Most adoptions take place through specialized state or private adoption agencies. Some states have prohibited private placement adoptions between adults and nonrelated children. Others require approval by social workers for such adoptions. Many paralegals specialize in the area of adoption, working either for social service agencies or private law firms.

Eligibility of Potential Parents to Adopt

State statutes generally provide that any adult may petition for adoption. This includes both married couples and single individuals. Because of the large number of adults wishing to adopt children, and the shortage of "desirable" children waiting to be adopted, parents wishing to adopt a child are often subject to stringent state criteria which

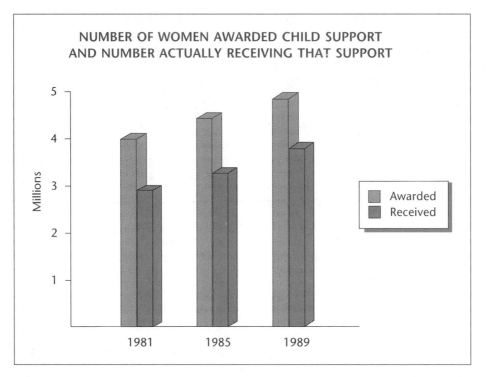

Number of Women Awarded Child Support versus Number Actually Receiving Support (1981, 1985, 1989) Only about 75 percent of the women who are awarded child support by the courts actually receive any. This is a fact that the federal and state governments are trying to remedy.

must be met before they are considered eligible to adopt a child. Adults wishing to adopt a child are often required to meet certain tests concerning their personal and financial qualifications, which can be very restrictive. Certain adoption agencies also consider the adoptive parents' religion and race as a factor when determining their eligibility.

Blood Relatives

Intuition suggests that blood relatives make the best caretakers of children. By custom, orphans become the wards of their close relatives; someone is expected to come forward to take charge of the children. For divorced parents with minimal resources or for working single mothers, parental duties may be overwhelming, so children are often placed in the care of grandparents or aunts and uncles. Even if it is a purely temporary placement,

with legal custody remaining with the parent or parents, the desire to adopt may arise for many reasons. With orphans, de facto adoption may be followed by legal adoption. The courts or agencies look for the same factors applicable to custody disputes—wholesome environment, continuity of care (same home, school, neighborhood, etc.), keeping siblings together, and so on. Divorce raises an added complication, because the natural parents may fight the adoption. Assuming consent to the adoption, however, blood relatives are highly favored.

Foster Parents

Children who have been placed in the care of strangers may remain with them via adoption even though the foster care administered through the state is commonly conditioned on the foster parents not attempting to become adoptive parents.

Stepparents

One of the most common relations involved in adoption is the stepparent. The typical scenario features a stepfather who is actively involved in raising his wife's children by a former marriage, with the natural father mostly or completely absent and perhaps totally neglecting support obligations. Adoptions seem most appropriate when the child or children have developed a relationship with their stepparent which is based on affection and support. The greatest stumbling block to such an adoption is the denial of consent by the natural parent. This may be overcome by a court finding that abandonment or neglect has severed the bonds between parent and child, but the law so strongly favors continuance of the biological bond as a legal bond that lack of consent in many instances is fatal to the adoption process.

Unwed (Nonmarital) Fathers

Until recent years, fathers of illegitimate offspring had no rights or legal relationship with their children. With the advent of financial responsibility through paternity suits, though, such fathers could expect to have rights as well. Visitation rights were forthcoming, and custody was possible if the mother died or her custody was detrimental to the child. Still, because the father had not married the mother and usually had not otherwise acknowledged paternity, his rights inevitably threatened the maternal bond. Courts and legislatures have created a balancing act between recognition of the special place of the mother without depriving the father of rights.

Surrogacy

Because of the *Baby M* case in 1988, much public attention was directed at so-called *surrogacy contracts*. Adoption by strangers may involve contracts and negotiations, but surrogacy contracts have the added element that the natural father will take custody of the child while the surrogate mother relinquishes custody in favor of adoption by the natural father's wife. Conception is ordinarily produced by artificial insemination with the contracting father's sperm or by implanting a fertilized ovum in the surrogate mother. In the former case, the child-bearer is the biological mother, but not in the latter. The problem with surrogacy arrangements arises from the fact that they appear to be simple contracts enforceable in the courts by traditional contract remedies—but their subject matter is unique. From one point of view, surrogacy contracts appear to be agreements to sell babies, which is clearly illegal. In contrast, because the natural fathers are assuming custody, they cannot be said to be buying something to which they already have a right. These contracts have also been considered offensive because they imply that women's bodies may be rented for a period of time, and may encourage exploitation of the poor by the rich. Additionally, surrogacy involves the psychobiology of rending an infant from its natural mother, whose feelings and state of mind have undoubtedly changed considerably from the time of contracting. For all of these, and perhaps other reasons, the *Baby M* case, in which the surrogate mother changed her mind after birth of the child, awakened a diversity of intense emotional and intellectual responses, and many states jumped to pass special legislation to regulate surrogacy contracts.

Children Available for Adoption

The law in this country has always favored natural families and blood relationships. The rights of the natural parent are not taken lightly. Only under the most unusual circumstances may a child be adopted without the natural parent's consent to the adoption. Consents of the natural parents must usually be in writing, signed, and acknowledged or notarized. Some states require that consent may not be given until after the child's birth.

A child may be put up for adoption upon a parent's death or extreme disability, or the parents' inability or unwillingness to care for a child. However, much of the emphasis on adoption in recent years has focused on children with special needs, whose only alternative to adoption may be long-term institutionalization or foster care. In many instances, the adopting parents of these hard-to-place children may be eligible for subsidies

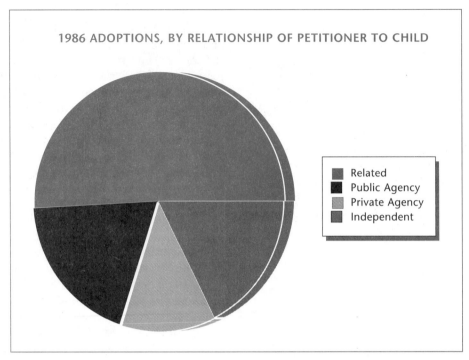

1986 ADOPTIONS, BY RELATIONSHIP OF PETITIONER TO CHILD

- Related
- Public Agency
- Private Agency
- Independent

Adoptions by Relationship of Petitioner to Child (1986) Half of all adoptions are by relatives of the child.

from the state or federal government. The aim of these subsidies is twofold. First, it assists in finding homes for hard-to-place children with special needs. Second, it assists the adoptive family with the additional expense often associated with caring for children with special needs.

Adoption Procedures

The procedures for adoption will depend on state law and the agencies and children involved. Following is a list of some state statutory references relating specifically to procedures for the adoption of minors:

Ala. Code § 26-01-1 *et seq.*

Alaska Stat. § 20.15.010 *et seq.*

Ariz. Rev. Stat. Ann. § 8-102 *et seq.*

Cal. Civ. Code § 221 *et seq.*

Conn. Gen. Stat. §§ 45–63

Del. Code Ann. tit. 13, § 901 *et seq.*

D.C. Code Ann. § 16-301 *et seq.*

Fla. Stat. Ann. § 63.011 *et seq.*

Ga. Code Ann. § 19-8-1 *et seq.*

Haw. Rev. Stat. § 578-1

Ill. Rev. Stat. ch. 40, para. 1501 *et seq.*

Ind. Code § 31-1-1 *et seq.*

Iowa Code § 600.1 *et seq.*

Kan Stat Ann. § 59-2101 *et seq.*, 59-2277 to 59-2279

Ky. Rev. Stat. Ann. § 199.470 *et seq.*

La. Rev. Stat. Ann. § 9.421 *et seq.*

Me. Rev. Stat. Ann. tit. 19, § 531 *et seq.*

Md. Cts. & Jud. Proc. Code § 3-601 *et seq.*

Mass. Gen. L. ch. 210, §§ 1–11A

Minn. Stat. § 259.21 *et seq.*

Miss. Code Ann. § 93-17-3 *et seq.*

Mo. Rev. Stat. § 453.010 *et seq.*

Mont. Code Ann. § 40-8-103 *et seq.*

Neb. Rev. Stat. § 43-101 *et seq.*

Nev. Rev. Stat. § 127.010 *et seq.*

N.H. Rev. Stat. Ann. § 170-B:1 *et seq.*

N.Y. Dom. Rel. Law § 109 *et seq.*

N.D. Cent. Code § 14-15-01 *et seq.*

Ohio Rev. Code Ann. § 3107.01 *et seq.*

Okla. Stat. tit. 10, §§ 55, 60.1 *et seq.*

Or. Rev. Stat. § 109.310 *et seq.*

R.I. Gen. Laws § 15-7-1 *et seq.*

S.C. Code Ann. § 15-45-120

S.D. Codified Laws Ann. § 15-6-1 *et seq.*

Utah Code Ann. § 78-30-1 *et seq.*

Vt. Stat. Ann. tit. 15, § 431 *et seq.*

Va. Code Ann. § 63.1-220 *et seq.*

Wash. Rev. Code § 26.32.010 *et seq.*

W. Va. Code § 48-4-1 *et seq.*

Wis. Stat. § 48.81 *et seq.*

Wyo. Stat. § 1-22-101 *et seq.*

(Always examine local statutes or rules.)

Paralegals are often instrumental in working with the adopting adults (petitioners) to collect information from them and prepare the necessary documentation. Petitioners may assist with the following procedures common to adoptions:

1. Obtaining necessary information concerning petitioners, including certified copies of marriage documents, and dissolution of marriage documents (if applicable)

2. Preparing release documents for the signature of natural parents

3. Drafting the document initiating the adoption proceeding, the petition for adoption, the decree of the court approving the adoption, and the decree of adoption.

To ensure compliance with statutory requirements in adoption proceedings, attention should be given to consideration such as the following:

- Period of petitioner's residence in state before filing petition

- Ages of petitioner and child

- Relationship of petitioner to child, if any

- Race and relation of natural parents, child, and petitioner

- Person or persons having legal custody of child

- Necessary consent to the adoption

- Parties entitled to notice of adoption proceedings

- Property owned by child

- Placement of child in petitioner's home and residence therein for required period before filing petition

- Favorable recommendation by person or agency charged with informing court as to propriety of adoption

- Circumstances bearing on adoption as being in best interests of child, such as petitioner's good moral character and financial status

Adoption Checklist [1A Am. Jur. *Pld. & Pr. Forms* (Rev.)] The paralegal may be given the responsibility of ensuring that this type of checklist is completed.

Summary Questions

1. What are the main sources of family law in the United States?
2. Where would you look to find information on the required contents of a petition for dissolution of marriage?
3. What are some things that may make a marriage void?
4. Under what circumstances may a marriage be voidable?
5. What are the differences between an annulment and a divorce?
6. Why is the awarding of alimony less common now than it was in the past?
7. What is the major factor courts consider when ruling on child custody?
8. What is a putative marriage?
9. Why might an antenuptial agreement be advisable when the engaged couple have children from previous marriages?

Practical Paralegal Skills

Based on the excerpts from the following client information sheet, prepare a petition for dissolution of marriage that would be appropriate for initiating a dissolution proceeding for Mary Smith in the state and county in which you live.

CLIENT INFORMATION SHEET

1. Client Name: Mary K. Smith, Petitioner

2. Date of Birth: August 12, 1958

3. Address: 156 Main Street
[Home town], [Home state] [Zip Code]

4. Length of time in state: _____

5. Occupation: Customer Relations Manager

6. Social Security Number: 123-45-6789

7. Spouse's Name: John T. Smith, Respondent

8. Date of Birth: February 12, 1957

9. Address: 840 Oak Drive
[Home town], [Home state] [Zip Code]

10. Length of time in state: _____

11. Children:
Leslie Margaret Smith   April 5, 1987
Thomas James Smith   July 23, 1989

12. With whom and where do children reside: Presently residing with petitioner at 156 Main Street

13. Previous marriages of parties: None.

14. Any written agreements as to custody, visitation, etc.? No written agreements have been entered into. However, respondent has agreed that the children should reside with their mother and that he should be allowed visitation every other weekend, two weeks during the summer months, Christmas Eve, the Saturday preceding Easter, the Fourth of July, and the Friday following Thanksgiving.

15. Relief: The Petitioner requests the following relief:

a. A dissolution of the marriage relationship

b. Custody of the minor children

c. Child support in the sum of $500 per month

d. The property at 123 Main Street, subject to the mortgage and all other encumbrances on the property

e. No alimony is requested

f. The Petitioner would like an equal division of all outstanding mutual debts of the parties.

16. Grounds for Dissolution: The grounds for dissolution are an irretrievable breakdown of the marriage relationship [or other grounds as permitted in your state].

 ## Notes

For further reference, see *Family Law*, by Ransford C. Pyle (Delmar Publishers Inc., and Lawyers Cooperative Publishing 1994).

[1] Milano, Carol, "1993 *Legal Assistant Today* Salary Survey Results," *Legal Assistant Today* 48 (May/June 1993).

[2] *State v. Fuller*, 377 So. 2d 355, 14 A.L.R 4th 711 (La. 1979).

[3] Wash. Rev. Code § 26.16.205.

[4] 8a Am. Jur. *Pld. & Pr. Forms* (Rev.), at 238.

[5] 8a Am. Jur. *Pld. & Pr. Forms* (Rev.), at 239.

[6] 18 Cal. 3d 660, 557 P.2d 106, 134 Cal. Rptr. 815 (1976).

CHAPTER 13
The Wills, Trusts, and Estates Paralegal

As the baby-boom generation begins to age, more attention is being given by society to wills, trusts, and estates. Paralegals play a very significant role in this area, and attorneys are relying heavily on paralegals to keep their services affordable.

The Role of Paralegals in Working with Wills, Trusts, and Estates

According to a 1993 *Legal Assistant Today* survey, 3 percent of the legal assistants who responded indicated that their specialty was estates and probate. The average salary of these respondents was $28,689, with the highest reported salary of an estate and probate legal assistant being $43,750.[1]

The Work of Estate Planning and Probate Paralegals in the United States

Most paralegals who specialize in estate planning work for private law firms, and their work focuses on drafting wills and trusts under the direction of an attorney. Paralegals who specialize in probate administration are also most often employed by private law firms. However, some probate paralegals are employed by probate courts. The work of probate paralegals often focuses on assisting the personal administrators or the executors of estates. Their work involves accounting for assets, completing probate forms, and distributing assets. The following list contains a description of some of the more common tasks performed by the wills, trusts and estates paralegal.

Estate Planning

1. Interview clients to determine facts relating to their potential estates
2. Review financial information submitted by clients and prepare checklists for attorney's review
3. Prepare drafts of wills, trusts, and related documents

4. Obtain information regarding insurance policies, and see that proper beneficiaries are designated to complement estate plan
5. See to the proper execution of wills by client and witnesses.
6. Prepare summaries of wills and other documents for clients.

Probate

1. Attend client conferences to explain proper procedures following the death of a client or family member
2. Prepare and file (when necessary) probate forms
3. Assist with collection and inventory of the assets of the deceased, including contents of safety deposit boxes, bank accounts, and all real and personal property
4. Assist with the clerical, bookkeeping and accounting functions relating to the estate
5. Prepare estate tax returns
6. Review claims against the estate
7. Assist with the liquidation of assets
8. Maintain communications with clients to advise them of the progress of settling the estate.

Skills Important to Wills, Trusts, and Estates Paralegals

In addition to having a good understanding of the pertinent law of the state in which the paralegal is employed, the wills, trusts, and estate paralegal must possess several other skills to excel in this area of law. The estate planning paralegal must have effective interviewing skills to help gather all pertinent information regarding the client's estate. In addition, the estate planning paralegal must possess the concise writing skills associated with drafting wills, trusts, and other estate planning documents.

With regard to the probate area of law, the paralegal must be able to communicate effectively with individuals who may be experiencing considerable grief. The probate process can often take several months and sometimes even years. Constant delays, which are often unavoidable, can be a great source of frustration to the probate client. Because the paralegal may be the probate client's main link to the law firm, it is important that the paralegal communicate often and effectively with the client to ensure that there are no misunderstandings. Often, the best policy to is to follow up most telephone conversations with written confirmation. The probate paralegal must also be able to work with numbers. Paralegals are often responsible for the day-to-day bookkeeping matters concerning the estate, as well as the more complex accounting matters concerning estate taxes.

An Introduction to Estate Planning and Probate

The significance of quality legal advice and appropriate will drafting for disposition of individuals' assets in the manner they desire upon death cannot be overemphasized. The right to leave property by **will** is not an inherent right, but a privilege permitted by law. Property not disposed of by a valid will passes to the **decedent's** heirs (if any) in accordance with the intestacy statutes of the decedent's state of domicile.

Each state has its own laws, passed by its legislature, setting forth precise rules for the disposition of property by will. Without such laws, one could not make a will. The following is an example of a state statute permitting the making of a will:

> Every person eighteen years of age or older and of sound mind may by his last will in writing signed by him or by a person in his presence and by his express direction, and attested and subscribed in his presence by two or more competent witnesses, dispose of his property, real and personal ... .

Mass. Gen. L. ch. 191, § 1.

Wills are **ambulatory**; that is, they are movable or subject to change. They can be revoked or changed at any time before the death of the maker. People may change their wills as often as they wish, and it is not uncommon for a person to have several wills during his or her lifetime. People should review their wills about every five years to adjust for changes in their assets. They may also need to change guardians, executors, and trustees as their circumstances change. In addition, it is often necessary, especially in view of today's high divorce rate, to change one's **beneficiaries**.

The exact language used in a will becomes particularly significant when the court interprets the meaning of a will and determines the intention of the person who made the will (the **testator**). The testator's intention must be ascertained from the particular words used in the will itself, from the context in which those words are used, and from the general scope and purpose of the

will   An instrument by which a person (the testator) makes a disposition of his or her property, to take effect after his or her death.

decedent   A legal term for a person who has died.

ambulatory   Changeable; capable of alteration; revocable.

beneficiary   1. A person who receives a benefit. 2. A person who has inherited or is entitled to inherit under a will.
3. A person for whom property is held in trust.

testator   A person who dies leaving a valid will.

will, read in the light of the surrounding and attending circumstances.

As mentioned earlier, when someone dies without a will, his or her property passes according to a specific scheme adopted by the state legislature. That scheme, known as the *law of intestate succession*, may or may not carry out the wishes of the decedent. **Intestate succession** is the process whereby the heirs become beneficially entitled to the property of one who dies without a will. In general, real property passes according to the law of intestate succession in the state where the property is located. In contrast, personal property passes according to the law of intestate succession in the state where the decedent was **domiciled** at the time of death. State laws of intestate succession are not identical. People often die thinking their property will pass one way, when in fact it passes in a different way altogether. Some of the major implications of dying without a will include the fact that there are no named heirs, guardians, or personal representatives. In addition, benefits that could be realized through a testamentary trust will not be available.

A Bundle of Rights

Paralegals need a basic understanding of property in its various forms—bank accounts, stock certificates, life insurance, and so on—because property is the basic element underlying wills, estates, and trusts. Without property, there would be nothing to give anyone in a will, nothing to plan about, and nothing to put in trust.

In the following law office scenario, Ms. Schmidt seemed to place little importance on the fact that the estate she owned with her brother was held in joint tenancy, but Amy certainly did. Details concerning how property that is co-owned is held at the time of one owner's death are of the utmost importance when interviewing a client regarding a probate.

Property is generally considered anything that people own, such as houses, cars, furniture, bank accounts, stocks, bonds, and money. Indeed, property is sometimes defined as everything that is the subject of ownership. In a legal sense, however, property is not considered to be the item itself. More properly, it consists of the various rights or interests that people have in it. Thus, property, in the eyes of the law, is considered to be a bundle of rights.

This bundle of rights can be considerable and can be spread among various people. For example, many people may have rights to a house and the land that goes with it. The owner (there is often more than one) has the exclusive right to possess the property unless it is leased to someone else, along with the right to bring a trespass action against a trespasser. If someone else has a **life estate** in the property, that person has the exclusive right to possession for his or her life, and a third person may have a future interest—the right to possession when the life tenant dies. The bank that holds a mortgage on the property has the right to prevent the person in possession from committing waste (that is, damaging the property). The bank also has the right to take the property or sell it if the owner does not pay

BALLENTINESBALLENTINESBALLENTINESBALLENTINESBALLENTINESBALLENTINESBALLENTINESBALLENTINESBALLENTINESBALLENTINESBALLENTINESBALLENTINESBALLENTINESBALLENTINES

intestate succession   Inheritance from a person who dies intestate.

domicile   The relationship that the law creates between a person and a particular locality or country. Domicile is a person's permanent home or permanent abode.

property   Real property and personal property; tangible property and intangible property; corporeal property and incorporeal property.

life estate   An estate that exists as long as the person who owns or holds it is alive. Its duration may also be the lifetime of another person.

Law Office Scenario

Amy Wendell, a paralegal at Goodman and Lewis, was informed that Dolores Schmidt had arrived for her first probate appointment. As a paralegal specializing in the probate area, Amy often attended the initial meeting with the responsible attorney or met with the client prior to the meeting with the attorney to collect information from the client. This morning James Sanders, Ms. Schmidt's attorney, was tied up at a meeting, so Amy was meeting with Ms. Schmidt first.

After Amy greeted Ms. Schmidt, an elderly woman who was apparently quite distraught, she explained the situation to Ms. Schmidt and asked what she could do to help.

"My brother passed away the day before yesterday," said Ms. Schmidt. "He was 80 years old and his heart just gave out. He was on his honeymoon in Hawaii at the time, and now the little golddigger who married him is going to get everything that we worked so hard for."

"I'm very sorry about your brother, Ms. Schmidt," said Amy. "Did he leave a will?"

"No. He had one but he tore it up when he got married," said Ms. Schmidt. "He was going to prepare a new one but he hadn't gotten around to it yet."

"What can you tell me about his assets?" asked Amy.

"Well, his biggest asset was the rather large estate that we purchased in 1940. We bought it for $50,000, but now it is valued at over $5 million. Here is a copy of the deed. Now my brother's wife wants me to sell it and pay to her half of the value."

Amy looked at the deed quickly. It was in fact a deed transferring a property to "Dolores and Lowell Schmidt, as joint tenants." Amy set the deed aside and continued her interview with Dolores Schmidt. Ms. Schmidt had brought several other deeds and purchase agreements with her evidencing her co-ownership with her brother of several pieces of real estate, as well as several items of personal property. Some were transferred to Ms. Schmidt and her brother as tenants in common, some were transferred to them as joint tenants, and some were transferred to them with no designation.

---

the mortgage. An attaching creditor who wins a suit against a property owner may have the right to have the property sold by a sheriff to obtain the amount of the judgment. Cities and towns have similar rights to sell private property to satisfy liens for overdue taxes.

These varied rights that persons may have make up the bundle of rights usually referred to as **real property**. Similar rights relating to **personal property** are also applicable. When people die owning such rights, the rights pass to others according to the applicable state laws.

Probate Property

When an estate is settled, the probate court deals only with what is commonly referred to as *probate property* or the **probate estate**. This is the real and personal property that was owned by the decedent either solely or with others as a

BALLENTINESBALLENTINESBALLENTINESBALLENTINESBALLENTINESBALLENTINESBALLENTINESBALLENTINESBALLENTINESBALLENTINESBALLENTINESBALLENTINESBALLENTINESBALLENTINES

real property   Land, including things located on it or attached to it directly or indirectly; real estate.

personal property   All property other than real property.

probate estate   The estate of a decedent subject to the jurisdiction of the probate court.

tenant in common. Title to real property owned by a decedent vests in the decedent's heirs immediately upon death but is subject to divesting. The probate process is necessary to prove the heir's title. In contrast, title to personal property owned by a decedent passes to the executor or administrator of the decedent's estate; the probate process is necessary to have the executor or administrator appointed and to safeguard the rights of all interested parties.

Real Property

People can own real property either solely or concurrently with others as tenants in common, joint tenants, or, in some states, as tenants by the entirety. To determine the type of ownership that a decedent had in real property, it is necessary to examine the decedent's deed to the property. If the decedent inherited the property, it is necessary to examine the probate court records to determine the decedent's extent of ownership.

Real property that was owned **severally** by the decedent is part of the probate estate and must be included in the list of probate assets. Similarly, the decedent's interest in real property that was owned with others as a **tenant in common** is also part of the probate estate. For example, following our law office scenario, although the estate owned by Ms. Schmidt and her brother would not be considered probate property, all pieces of real estate held by Ms. Schmidt and her brother as tenants in common would be.

Personal Property

Title to both tangible and intangible personal property owned by the decedent must be examined to determine whether it is probate property. Items such as household furniture, jewelry, silverware, china, crystal, books, televisions, and personal effects are examples of **tangible** personal property that are commonly part of a decedent's estate. Certificates of title must usually be examined to determine the decedent's title to automobiles, boats, and motor homes.

Stocks, bonds, and negotiable instruments are examples of **intangible** personal property; they are evidence of the right to property but not the property itself. Documents such as stock certificates, bond certificates, promissory notes, bank books, insurance policies, and written contracts may be used to prove title to intangible personal property.

Nonprobate Property

Some things that people own are not part of their estates when they die. Such nonprobate property includes jointly owned property, community property, life insurance with named beneficiaries, property held in a living trust, pension plan distributions, and individual retirement accounts with named beneficiaries. Although these items pass outside of probate directly to the surviving joint owner or beneficiary, they are part of the decedent's gross estate for estate tax purposes.

As part of their work, paralegals often assist the attorney in gathering the information needed to settle an estate and to complete tax returns. A detailed list of nonprobate property, together with its value, must be obtained by the personal representative of the estate to determine whether the estate is large enough for an estate tax return to be filed. If the gross estate (total of all taxable items) is $600,000 or more, a federal estate tax return must be filed.

Jointly Owned Property

Real property that was owned by a decedent and another as joint tenants is not part of the decedent's

---

BALLENTINESBALLENTINESBALLENTINESBALLENTINESBALLENTINESBALLENTINESBALLENTINESBALLENTINESBALLENTINESBALLENTINESBALLENTINESBALLENTINESBALLENTINES

severally   Distinctly; separately; apart from others.

tenancy in common   A tenancy in which two or more persons own an undivided interest in an estate in land ... or in personal property. As opposed to joint tenants, tenants in common have no right of survivorship; when a tenant in common dies, his or her interest passes to his or her heirs rather than to the cotenant or cotenants.

tangible property   Property ... that has physical substance; property that can be physically possessed.

intangible property   An incorporeal right unrelated to a physical thing; a right to inherit property.

probate estate. Joint property remains the property of the surviving joint owner or owners when one of the owners dies. For example, in the law office scenario, the estate owned by Ms. Schmidt and her brother as joint tenants would not be considered part of her brother's estate. Ms. Schmidt's new sister-in-law would not be entitled to any part of that estate, regardless of what claim she may have on her husband's probate property.

Joint tenancy is not limited to real property. Bank accounts, stocks, bonds, and automobiles are commonly owned by two or more people as joint tenants. Unless it can be shown that a bank account was opened in joint names only for convenience, the account will pass to the surviving depositor when one depositor dies and will not be part of the decedent's estate.

Community Property

A form of ownership by spouses, called **community property**, is used in eight states in the United States. Community property is property (except a gift or inheritance) that is acquired by the personal efforts of either spouse during marriage and which, by law, belongs to both spouses equally. In community property states, a spouse can leave his or her half of the community property by will to whomever he or she chooses.

In some community property states, when a spouse dies intestate, all the community property passes to the surviving spouse. In such a situation, the surviving spouse retains his or her half-interest and inherits the deceased spouse's half-interest, thereby obtaining full title to the entire property.

Life Insurance with Named Beneficiary

A life insurance policy with a named, living beneficiary is not part of the probate of the decedent. The proceeds of the policy are paid directly to the beneficiary, bypassing probate altogether. Like jointly owned property, however, life insurance owned by a decedent is part of the decedent's gross estate for estate tax purposes, and must be included on the estate tax return.

Pay-on-Death Accounts

A *pay-on-death (POD) account*, also known as a **Totten trust**, is a savings-bank account in the name of the depositor as trustee for another person called a *beneficiary*. The depositor may withdraw money from the account at any time during the depositor's lifetime. When the depositor dies, however, the money in the account belongs to the beneficiary. Totten trust accounts pass directly to the named beneficiary and are not considered to be part of the depositor's estate.

Living Trusts

A **living trust** or **inter vivos trust** becomes effective during the lifetime of the person who establishes it. A living trust is not under the control and supervision of the probate court, and property held by such a trust is not part of a decedent's probate estate, although it is considered part of the decedent's gross estate for federal estate tax purposes, unless it is an irrevocable trust.

BALLENTINESBALLENTINESBALLENTINESBALLENTINESBALLENTINESBALLENTINESBALLENTINESBALLENTINESBALLENTINESBALLENTINESBALLENTINESBALLENTINESBALLENTINES

joint tenancy An estate in land or in personal property held by two or more persons jointly, with equal rights to share in its enjoyment [and] ... the right of survivorship, which means that upon the death of a joint tenant the entire estate goes to the survivor[s].

community property A system of law under which the earnings of either spouse are the property of both the husband and the wife, and property acquired by either spouse during the marriage (other than by gift, under a will, or through inheritance) is the property of both.

Totten trust A trust created by a bank deposit which a person makes with his or her money in his or her own name as trustee for another person. ... [I]t is revocable at will until the depositor dies or completes the gift in his or her lifetime by some unequivocal act or declaration.

inter vivos trust (living trust) A trust that is effective during the lifetime of the creator of the trust.

Life Estates

A *life estate* is an ownership interest that is limited in duration to either the life of the owner or the life of another person. When the life tenant dies, the property belongs to whomever owns the remainder interest, without the necessity of probate.

Intestate Succession

Paralegals learn quite early in their careers that people often delay making wills, for many and various reasons. Some people may want to avoid the expense of consulting a lawyer. Others may dread any discussion of death, or may assume that their assets are not worth enough to require a will. Still others may be well intentioned, but too busy or too preoccupied with the responsibilities of daily life.

When people die without a will, it is said that they die **intestate**. The law of the state where the decedent is domiciled determines how the personal property will pass. In contrast, the law of the state where the property is located will determine how the real property will pass. Thus, because state laws differ, it is possible for an intestate's real property located within the state to pass differently from real property located outside the state. Intestate property passes pursuant to the law of intestate succession or **intestacy**.

The Passing of Intestate Property

It is important for paralegals to know how intestate property passes. This knowledge will be useful when assisting the law firm in settling testate as well as intestate estates, because in all estates, the heirs must be listed on the court petition for probate of a will or administration of an estate. In addition, the heirs must be notified of the court procedure and be given an opportunity to appear if they wish to do so.

Probate property passes according to the law of intestate succession when the owner dies without a will. In contrast, nonprobate property passes directly to the joint owner or owners and does not pass according to the law of intestate succession.

Even when someone dies with a will, some property may not be included under its terms. That property passes as intestate property according to state law. This may also be the case when the individuals named in the testator's will predecease him or her, when children are unintentionally omitted from their parent's will, or when someone named to receive a gift in a will refuses to accept it. This refusal may seem strange, but death taxes can sometimes be reduced when property passes to a family member other than the one named in the will to receive it. The gift is renounced or disclaimed and passes by intestacy to other family members in a way that results in a tax savings to the family as a whole.

Simultaneous Death

Sometimes a husband and wife, a parent and child, or other relatives die in a common disaster, and it is impossible to determine who died first. The Uniform Simultaneous Death Act, which has been adopted by almost every state, allows the property of each person to be distributed as if he or she had survived, unless a will or trust provides otherwise. For example, if a husband and wife die together in a car accident and each owns separate property, (1) the husband's property will pass to his heirs as though his wife was not living at the time of his death, and (2) the wife's property will pass to her heirs as though her husband was not

intestate Pertaining to a person, or to the property of a person, who dies without leaving a valid will.

intestacy The status of the estate or property of a person who dies without leaving a valid will.

living at the time of her death. Property owned jointly by both decedents is distributed equally. Thus, in the preceding example, half of the husband's jointly owned property will pass to the husband's heirs and the other half will pass to the wife's heirs as though her husband was not living at the time of her death.

In states that have adopted the Uniform Probate Code (UPC), a specific time period must pass to establish that someone has "survived" an intestate. If someone does not survive the intestate by 120 hours (5 days), he or she is considered to have died *before* the intestate.[2]

Homicide by Heir or Devisee

A murderer inheriting from his or her victim is a repulsive thought. To ensure that people do not benefit from their own wrongdoings, state laws provide that whomever is convicted of murdering another cannot inherit from the victim's estate. Some states, including those which have adopted Uniform Probate Code § 2-803, have passed laws, called *slayer statutes,* to this effect. Other states reach the same conclusion through court decision. Some courts use a constructive trust theory to prevent killers from inheriting from their victims.

Rights of Surviving Spouse

The amount that a surviving spouse inherits from a spouse who dies without a will differs widely from state to state. Some states give only **dower** or **curtesy rights**; others merely allow a life estate in real and personal property; still others give property to the widow and children during widowhood and afterward to children. Some states give the surviving spouse an absolute interest in the property up to a specified amount;

Probate Property	■ Real and personal property owned solely by the decedent
	■ Interests in property held as a tenant in common
Nonprobate Property	■ Property owned in joint tenancy
	■ Community property
	■ Life insurance with named beneficiaries
	■ Pension plan distributions and individual retirement accounts with named beneficiaries
	■ Money held in pay-on-death accounts
	■ Property held in a living trust

Items Typically Considered to be Probate Property and Nonprobate Property Probate property is any property that reverts to the estate of someone who has died.

other states deduct an amount from the surviving spouse's share, depending upon the extent of his or her separately owned assets.

The portion of the estate given to a surviving spouse depends upon who else is alive; that is, if parents, children, grandchildren, or other decedents of the deceased are still living. States adjust the amount given to the surviving spouse according to the existence or absence of parents, children, grandchildren, and decedents of the deceased spouse.

Rights of Other Heirs

Years ago, under common law, when someone died intestate, the **heirs** were those who inherited

dower The legal right or interest that a wife acquires by marriage in the property of her husband. ... Dower ... has been substantially modified in most states, but every state retains aspects of the concept for the protection of both spouses.

curtesy The rights a husband had under the common law with respect to his wife's property. Today these rights have been modified in every state in various ways, but all states that retain curtesy in some form extend the same rights to both spouses.

heirs Persons who are entitled to inherit real or personal property of a decedent who dies intestate; persons receiving property by descent.

the real property, and the **next-of-kin** inherited the personal property. In most jurisdictions today, heirs are these persons, including the surviving spouse, entitled under the statutes of intestate succession to the property of a decedent.[3] Sometimes the term *heirs* is used in an even broader sense, referring to anyone who inherits property, whether by will or by intestate succession. In contrast, next-of-kin are these persons who are nearest of kindred to the decedent; that is, most nearly related by blood. Spouses are not related by blood and are therefore not considered next of kin.

Consanguinity and Affinity

Kindred—people related by blood—are said to be related by **consanguinity**, which means kinship or blood relationship. The relationship may be either lineal or collateral. **Lineal consanguinity** is the relationship between people who are related in a direct line either downward, as between child, grandchild, and great-grandchild; or upward, as between parent, grandparent, and great-grandparent. **Collateral consanguinity**, on the other hand, is the relationship between persons who have the same ancestors but who do not ascend or descend from each other. Collateral relatives include brothers and sisters, aunts and uncles, nieces and nephews, and cousins.

People who are related by marriage are said to be related by **affinity**. They include stepparents, stepchildren, parents-in-law, and daughters- and sons-in-law. Because they are not related by blood to a decedent, they do not inherit from the decedent under the laws of intestate succession.

Half Blood

Persons who are related by **half blood**, such as a half-brother or half-sister, have the same mother or father in common, but not both parents. The laws of intestate succession differ among the states as to relatives of the half blood.

Degrees of Kindred

Determining how closely people are related can be a complex process. The method most commonly used in the United States to determine the relatives most nearly related by blood is the civil-law method. Under this method, each relationship to the decedent is assigned a degree. The degree of kinship of a relative is calculated by counting upward from the decedent to the nearest common ancestor, then downward to the nearest relative. Each generation represents one degree. For example, parents and children of a decedent are related to the decedent in the first degree. Grandparents, grandchildren, brothers, and sisters are related to the decedent in the second degree. Uncles, aunts, nephews, nieces, and great-grandparents are third-degree relatives. First cousins, great-uncles, great-aunts, and great-great-grandparents are fourth-degree relatives.

Within the degrees of kindred, certain priorities are recognized. For example, the decedent's children receive preference over the decedent's parents, although they are both in the same degree. Similarly, the decedent's brothers and sisters are favored over the decedent's grandparents.

next of kin   A person's next of kin may be either his or her blood relatives, or those persons who would inherit from him or her under the laws of intestate succession.

kin (kindred)   Relatives; persons related by blood or consanguinity.

consanguinity   Relationship by blood; having the blood of a common ancestor.

lineal consanguinity   The blood relationship between individuals from whom a person is descended in a direct line of ascent (EXAMPLE: father; grandfather; great-grandfather) or between individuals descended from a person in a direct line of descent (EXAMPLE: daughter, granddaughter; great-granddaughter).

collateral consanguinity   A blood relationship based upon a common ancestor.

affinity   The relationship existing by virtue of marriage.

half blood   A person who shares one parent in common with another person.

Lineal Descendants

As discussed earlier, a lineal relationship exists between a person's children, grandchildren, and great-grandchildren. They all descend from a common ancestor and are referred to as **issue**. When someone dies intestate, the decedent's children receive what remains after the surviving spouse receives his or her share. If no surviving spouse exists, the children share the entire estate.

Grandchildren take their parent's share **per stirpes**, that is, by right of representation, when their parents are dead; the children stand in place of their deceased parents for purposes of inheritance. Under some state laws, when all of the intestate's children have predeceased the intestate, grandchildren inherit **per capita** (by the heads) rather than per stirpes. In this method, the number of grandchildren is counted and each receives an equal share.

Adopted Children

For inheritance purposes, modern state statutes generally treat adopted children as kindred or blood relatives of the adopting parents and as strangers to their former blood relatives. Under the Uniform Probate Code, for the purposes of intestate succession, an adopted person is the child of the adopting parent and not of his or her natural parent.

Illegitimate Children

In contrast to the English common law, most states in the United States have traditionally had statutes allowing **illegitimate (nonmarital) children** to inherit from their mothers and their maternal ancestors. The rationale was that it is

unjust to "visit the sins of the parents upon their unoffending offspring." The right of illegitimate children to inherit from their fathers, however, was not widely acknowledged until 1977. In that year, the U.S. Supreme Court held that an Illinois law allowing children born out of wedlock to inherit by intestate succession only from their mothers and not their fathers violated the equal protection clause of the Fourteenth Amendment to the U.S. Constitution. Since then, most state laws allow nonmarital children to inherit from and through their fathers who have either acknowledged paternity or who have been adjudicated to be their fathers in paternity proceedings, as well as from and through their mothers.

Lineal Ascendants

Lineal descendants include a person's children, grandchildren, great-grandchildren, and so on. Lineal ascendants, who "ascend" from the individual and include parents, grandparents, and so forth, and have their own distinctive inheritance rights under intestate succession. When no issue of an intestate are alive, both parents, or the surviving parent if one is deceased, inherit what remains after the surviving spouse receives his or her share.

Brothers and Sisters

When someone dies intestate survived by no issue and no father or mother, the part of the estate not passing to the surviving spouse usually passes to the decedent's brothers and sisters equally. The children of deceased brothers and sisters (i.e., nieces and nephews) take their parents' share by right of representation. As in the case of

BALLENTINESBALLENTINESBALLENTINESBALLENTINESBALLENTINESBALLENTINESBALLENTINESBALLENTINESBALLENTINESBALLENTINESBALLENTINESBALLENTINESBALLENTINESBALLENTINES

issue All persons who are descendants of one ancestor, including all future descendants. … [W]hen used in a will, "issue" will be taken to mean children or grandchildren, or all *living* descendants, if that is the testator's clear intention. "Issue" may or may not include adopted children, depending upon state law.

per stirpes Means "by the root"; according to class; by representation. *Per stirpes* describes the method of dividing or distributing an estate in which the heirs of a deceased heir share the portion of the estate that the deceased heir would have received had he or she lived.

per capita Means "by the head"; by the individual.

illegitimate child A child born to parents who are not married to each other.

grandchildren, some state laws provide that when all of the intestate's brothers and sisters have predeceased the intestate, their issue inherit per capita rather than per stirpes. The number of nieces and nephews are counted and each receives an equal share.

If the Deceased is Survived by	A Surviving Spouse Receives	In These States
Children of the marriage	All*	AZ, IA, MT, VA, WI
	$100,000 + 1/2*	CT
	$70,000 + 1/2*	MN
	$60,000 + 1/2*	MI
	$50,000 + 1/2*	AL, AK, ID, ME, NE, NH, NJ, ND, NY, UT
	$30,000 + 1/2*	OH**, PA*
	$25,000 + 1/2*	CO
	$20,000 + 1/2*	FL, MO
	$15,000 + 1/2	MD, NC**
	$5,000 + 1/2	DE+
	1/2	CA**, HI, IL, IN**, KS, KY+, MA, NV**, OK, OR, RI+, SC, SD**, VT**, WA, WY
	1/3	AR+, TX, VT+, WV
	1/4	NM
	Life estate + 1/3	AR, KY
	Life estate	DE, IN, RI
	Equal with children	GA, MS
	Homestead + 1 yr. allow.	TN
No children but by parents	All	AZ, AR++, CO, FL, GA, IL, IA, KS, MN, MS, MT, NM, NY, OH, OK, OR, SC, TN, VA, WI, WV, WY
	$200,000 + 1/2	MA
	$100,000 + 3/4	CT
	$100,000 + 1/2	AL, SD, UT
	$60,000 + 1/2	MI
	$50,000 + 1/2	DE+, ID, ME, NE, NH, NJ, ND, RI+
	$30,000 + 1/2	PA

Rights of the Surviving Spouse of One Who Dies Intestate This summary of state laws illustrates the differences in the laws of intestacy. The paralegal must be aware of the tendency of these laws to change: up-to-date statutes must be checked when you are looking up a state's intestacy laws.

If the Deceased is Survived by	A Surviving Spouse Receives	In These States
No children but by parents	$25,000 + 1/2	NC, VT
	$20,000 + 1/2	MO
	$15,000 + 1/2	MD
	$5,000 + 1/2	AK
	3/4	IN, WA
	1/2	CA, HI, KY, NV, TX
	Life estate + $75,000	RI
	Life estate	DE
No children and no parents but by brothers or sisters	All	AL, AK, AZ, AR++, CO, CT, DE+, FL, GA, HI, ID, IL, IN, IA, KS, MD, MI, MN, MS, MO, MT, NE, NC, ND, NM, NH, NJ, NY, OH, OK, OR, PA, SC, TN, UT, VA, WI, WV, WY
	$200,000 + 1/2	MA
	$100,000 + 1/2	SD
	$50,000 + 1/2	ME, RI+
	$25,000 + 1/2	VT
	3/4	WA
	1/2	CA, KY, NV, TX
	Life estate + $75,000	RI
	Life estate	DE
No children, parents, brothers, or sisters	All	In many states

*The surviving spouse receives half when the deceased is survived by children who are not of the marriage, except in Virginia, where the surviving spouse receives one-third.

**One-third when the deceased is survived by two or more children.

+Personal property.

++If married three years.

Rights of the Surviving Spouse of One Who Dies Intestate   *(Continued)*

Next of Kin

When someone dies intestate survived by no issue, no father or mother, and no brothers or sisters or children of deceased brothers or sisters, the part of the estate not passing to the surviving spouses passes to the decedent's closest kindred, according to state statute. These include grandparents, aunts and uncles, and cousins.

Escheat

When people die intestate survived by no spouse and no ascertainable kindred, their property

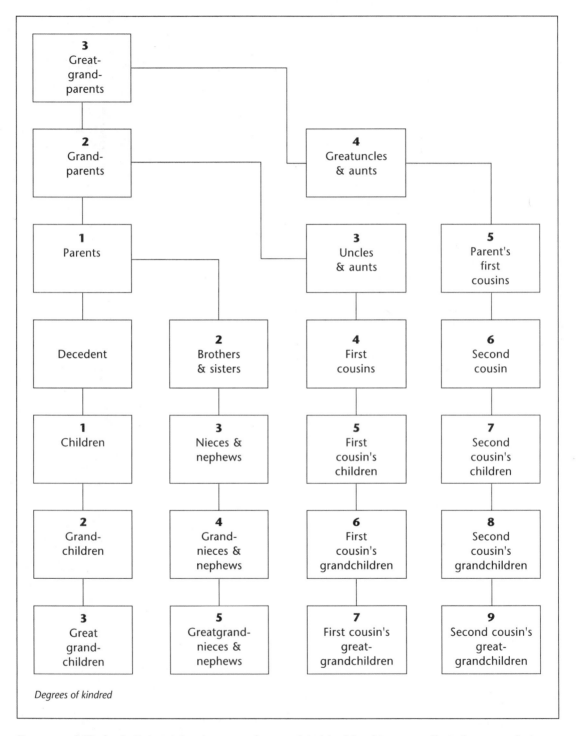

Degrees of kindred

Degrees of Kindred   Determining how people are related by blood is a complicated process, but essential when someone dies intestate.

escheats, that is, passes to the state. Some state laws provide that personal property escheats to the state in which the deceased was domiciled and real property escheats to the state in which the property is located. Other state laws provide that both real and personal property escheat to the state in which the property is located.

Some state laws provide that an inheritance escheats to the state when the beneficiary under a will cannot be located.

The Last Will and Testament

Paralegals need good judgment and interpersonal skills when interviewing clients for preparation of the clients' wills. A testator must be of **sound mind** at the time of execution of the will for the will to be valid. Being able to assess whether a client is of sound mind becomes crucial when the paralegal is asked to witness the will: witnesses may later be asked to vouch for the mental stability of the testator if the will is contested. Mrs. Jensen from the following law office scenario obviously was not of sound mind when Jena went to visit her. It would have been irresponsible to prepare a new will for her, and the will certainly would not have been valid.

Besides dealing with the testator, paralegals must be familiar with specific requirements of the legal document itself: for example, that wills must be in writing in most cases; that specifically two witnesses must be present; that witnesses must sign in each other's presence or in the presence of the person making the will; and that real estate is treated differently from personal property.

The law of wills, estates, and trusts of today has its roots in the feudal system that prevailed in England in the 11th, 12th, and 13th centuries. In those days, it was considered a disgrace to die without a **testament**, which was a will of personal property; wills of real property were not generally allowed. Technically, the term *will* refers to an instrument that disposes of real property and the term *testament* refers to an instrument that disposes of personal property. A *will and testament* refers to an instrument that disposes of both real and personal property. This distinction is not made in practice in the United States today.

State Statutory Formalities

Paralegals who work in the field of wills, estates, and trusts need to become familiar with their own state's statutes governing the formalities of executing a will, because each state in the United States has its own statutes setting forth these requirements. Except for states that have adopted the Uniform Probate Code, the laws are not uniform. State statutes generally address age requirements, testamentary capacity, the necessity of a writing, the will's execution, and witness requirements.

Age Requirements

Under the laws of most states, a person must have reached the age of 18 to make a will. Some state variations exist on the general age requirement. For example, in Oregon and Texas married people under the age of 18 may also make a will. In Idaho, emancipated minors may do so as well. Members of the armed forces and the Merchant Marines may make a will at any age in the states of Indiana and Texas.

BALLENTINESBALLENTINESBALLENTINESBALLENTINESBALLENTINESBALLENTINESBALLENTINESBALLENTINESBALLENTINESBALLENTINESBALLENTINESBALLENTINESBALLENTINES

escheat   The right of the state to take title to property after the death of a person who has not disposed of the property by will and has left no heirs to inherit it.

sound mind   A term referring to the mind of a person who is sane and mentally competent.

testament   A will.

Law Office Scenario

|||| Law Office Scenario ||||

Jena Stevens, a paralegal at Martins & Brandon, was given the assignment of interviewing an elderly client, Mrs. Jensen, in the nursing home for the purpose of preparing a new will for her. Jena was looking forward to the assignment. She had worked with Mrs. Jensen in the past, and she was one of Jena's favorite clients. When she got to the nursing home, however, she noticed immediately that something was wrong.

"Who are you?" Mrs. Jensen asked quietly.

"Jena Stevens, a paralegal from Martins & Brandon," Jena replied. "Do you remember me?"

Mrs. Jensen clutched Jenna's arm and looked into her eyes for a few seconds. "I just wasn't sure if it was really you," she said. "They have gotten to so many people."

"What?" asked Jena.

"You know, Them!" said Mrs. Jensen, pointing upward, "From Mars. I'm sure they've taken over my daughter's mind, so I want to change my will to leave everything to my husband, Rex. They tried to tell me that he died five years ago, but I know they're lying."

Jena just smiled and listened to Mrs. Jensen for a while. Jena was able to steer the conversation away from the Martians and soon they were able to have a lucid conversation. Mrs. Jensen seemed to forget all about changing her will, and Jena left promising that she would come and visit again sometime.

Testamentary Capacity

For a will to be valid, the person making the will must have **testamentary capacity**. This means that he or she must be of sound mind at the time of execution of the will. There is a four-part test to determine soundness of mind. Testators must: (1) know, in a general way, the nature and extent of their bounty (i.e., riches); (2) know, in a general way, who would be the natural objects of their bounty (although they need not leave anything to them); (3) know that they are making a will; and (4) be free from delusions that would influence the disposition of their property.

As suggested earlier, paralegals are often called upon to witness wills and may have to determine if an unfamiliar testator is of sound mind. Conversation is the natural way to explore someone's mental capacities, especially when dealing with elderly clients. Asking questions about the testator's family, occupation, places of residence, travels, and leisure-time activities can be an effective way to get to know the testator in the short time available. In the law office scenario example, it did not take Jena much conversation at all with Mrs. Jensen to realize that Mrs. Jensen was experiencing delusions and was not of sound mind.

Necessity of a Writing

With the exception of certain **nuncupative** (oral) wills allowed by many states, wills must be in writing. Many states recognize nuncupative wills of personal property made by soldiers in the military service and mariners at sea. Some states also recognize nuncupative wills of very

BALLENTINESBALLENTINESBALLENTINESBALLENTINESBALLENTINESBALLENTINESBALLENTINESBALLENTINESBALLENTINESBALLENTINESBALLENTINESBALLENTINESBALLENTINES

testamentary capacity   The mental capacity of a testator, at the time of making his or her will, to be able to understand the nature of his or her act and, generally if not precisely, the nature and location of his or her property and the identity of those persons who are the natural objects of his or her bounty.

nuncupative will   A will declared orally by a testator during his or her last illness, before witnesses, and later reduced to writing by a person who was present during the declaration.

small amounts of personal property or of personal property made during a lasting illness when witnesses are present.

A **holographic will** is a will that is entirely in the handwriting of the testator, and signed by the testator, but not witnessed. About half of the states in the United States recognize holographic wills as valid. The rest of the states do not allow them because of the lack of witnesses. Under the UPC, a holographic will is valid if the signature and the material (i.e., important) portions of the document are in the testator's handwriting.[4]

In the *Reed* case (which follows), the Supreme Court of Wyoming rejected a tape-recorded statement that was purported to be a decedent's last will and testament on the grounds that it did not fall under the definition of a *holographic will.*

The Will's Execution

Paralegals working in law offices often play key roles in the execution of wills. It is important that they be thoroughly familiar with their state law on signing and witnessing requirements, because wills can be contested if they are not properly executed. Wills must be signed, attested, and witnessed in accordance with the precise rules of the state where the will is executed. This is one of the reasons why it is dangerous for lay persons to make their own wills. Most lay persons are not aware of the technical rules that must be followed when executing a will.

Written wills must be signed either by the testator or by someone else in the testator's presence who is directed to do so by the testator. A **signature** may be any mark that the testator intends to be a signature. Thus, a barely discernible signature written by an elderly person's shaking hand or an *X* made by someone who cannot write are accepted as signatures if the intent of the person writing it was to authenticate the instrument. In some states, the testator's signature must be written at the end of the will; most states, however, do not have this requirement.

Witness Requirements

Nonholographic wills must be witnessed in the presence of the testator by competent witnesses. With the exception of Louisiana and Vermont (which require three witnesses), all states in the United States require two witnesses to a will. Some state laws stipulate that the witnesses be in each other's presence when they sign. Paralegals who work in one of these states must be aware of the rule, because a violation can cause a will to be invalid.

The act of witnessing a will consists of two parts, attesting and subscribing. To **attest** means to see the signature or take note mentally that the signature exists as a fact. To **subscribe** means to write beneath or below. Usually courts hold that witnesses to wills must do both. Thus, some cases have held that a will was improperly executed, and therefore void, when the testator refused to allow the witnesses to see his signature which he had previously written. Some states avoid problems with attestation by suitable statutory language.

In some states, witnesses who are named as beneficiaries under the will lose the inheritance unless there are two other witnesses who inherit nothing under the will. Even spouses of witnesses often lose their inheritances, unless there are extra witnesses who do not inherit under the will. Many states, however, protect witnesses who make

holographic will   A will that is entirely written and signed by the testator in his or her own handwriting. In many states, the requirement that the signing of a will be witnessed is not imposed in the case of a holographic will, because a successful counterfeit of another person's handwriting is very difficult; the requirement that the will be entirely in handwriting is therefore thought to be sufficient protection against forgery.

signature   The name of a person as affixed by him or her, in his or her own handwriting, to an instrument, document, or other writing, or to any surface.

attest   To swear to; to bear witness to; to affirm to be true or genuine.

subscribe   To sign; literally, to "sign under" one's name at the end of a document.

In the Matter of the ESTATE of Robert G. REED, Deceased
Margaret F. BUCKLEY, Appellant (Petitioner)
v.
R. Brooke HOLSTEDT and Wilhelmina M. Kelly, Appellees
(Contestants)
Supreme Court of Wyoming
December 1, 1983
672 P.2d 829, 42 A.L.R.4th 167 (Wyo. 1983)

BROWN, Justice.

The issue here is whether a tape recorded statement made by a deceased person can be admitted to probate as a will. We agree with the trial court that it cannot, and will affirm.

Robert G. Reed died on March 2, 1982. On April 23, 1982, the court appointed appellees co-administrators, finding that Mr. Reed died intestate. On October 29, 1982, appellant filed a petition for probate of will, alleging that a tape recording found by the police in Mr. Reed's home was the valid will of the deceased. The tape recording was found in a sealed envelope on which was handwritten "Robert Reed. To be played in the event of my death only! (signed) Robert G. Reed."

Appellant requested that the letters of administration issued to appellees be revoked and that she be appointed executrix of decedent's will. The trial court refused to revoke the letters of administration and refused to admit into probate the tape recording and its transcript.

Appellant argues that 1) a voice print complies with the "handwriting" requirement of a holographic will, 2) a sound recording clearly expresses the intent of the decedent, and 3) the rules of evidence require a sound recording be admitted as a sufficient writing.

… The right to make a will did not exist at common law, at least with respect to real property. It is a statutory right, subject to control by the legislature. … Therefore, before a will may be admitted to probate it must comport to the state's statutory scheme. Appellant must demonstrate that the recorded statement offered as a will complies with Wyoming statutes governing wills.

Section 2-6-112, W.S. 1977, provides in part:

"Except as provided in the next section [§ 2-6-113], all wills to be valid shall be in writing, or typewritten, witnessed by two (2) competent witnesses and signed by the testator or by some person in his presence and by his express direction … ."

Section 2-6-113, W.S. 1977, provides:

"A will which does not comply with W.S. 2-6-112 is valid as an holographic will, whether or not witnessed, if it is entirely in the handwriting of the testator and signed by the hand of the testator himself."

Appellant contends that the tape recording should be admitted to probate as a form of holographic will. … According to appellant the major difference in magnetic tape recording and hand print is that the former writing is done through voice print while the latter is done through hand print. Appellant reasons, therefore, that in this age of advanced electronics and circuitry the tape recorder should be a method of "writing" which conforms with the holographic will statute.

The Wyoming statutes are clear and unambiguous in their description of an holographic will. A holographic will must be entirely in the handwriting of the decedent. …

The use of a tape recording or other type of voice print as a testamentary instrument is a decision for the legislature to make. We will not enlarge, stretch, expand or extend the holographic will statute to include a testamentary devise not falling within the provisions of the statute.

Affirmed.

the mistake of witnessing a will under which they are also beneficiaries. These states' laws provide that if the witness would have inherited had the testator died intestate, the witness may inherit the amount in the will, but not more than the intestate share. The 1990 revision of the UPC gives full protection to witnesses when they inherit under the will; it states that the signing of a will by an interested witness does not invalidate the will or any provision of it.[5]

Witnesses to a will must be *competent*, which, in general, means competent to be a witness in a court of law. Massachusetts has defined competency as being of "sufficient understanding," meaning that the witness understands what a will is and what is taking place when a will is executed. Although most states have no age requirements for witnesses to wills, Arkansas and Utah require witnesses to be at least 18 years old; Iowa requires them to be at least 16, and Texas requires them to be at least 14.

Relaxation of Formalities

The 1990 revision of the UPC contains a section that relaxes the strict, formal requirements for executing wills if the proponent of the document establishes by clear and convincing evidence that the decedent intended the document to be a will.[6]

Professional Guidelines

To avoid the pitfalls of an improperly executed will, this procedure is recommended:

1. The testator is asked to read the will carefully, being certain that it is accurate; that it expresses the testator's will; and that all aspects of the will are understood.

2. The proper number of witnesses are brought into the room and introduced to the testator. The door is closed, and the group should not be interrupted.

3. The testator declares to the witnesses that the instrument before them is his or her will and requests them to act as witnesses to its execution. The witnesses do not read the will.

4. The testator signs the will at the end, making sure that all witnesses observe the signature.

5. The testator initials or signs the margin of each page of the will for purposes of authenticity.

6. One witness reads the attestation clause (the clause preceding the witness's signature) aloud. The witnesses then sign their names

and write their addresses while the testator and other witnesses observe.

7. If a self-proof clause is used, a notary public, who must also be present, takes the oaths and acknowledgments of the testator and the witnesses.

Changing and Revoking Wills

Just as making a will involves technicalities, changing or revoking a will also requires certain formalities. Paralegals should encourage testators to seek competent legal advice whenever they want to alter their wills in any way.

Altering the terms of a will is most effectively done through a **codicil**. A codicil must refer specifically to the will being changed and must be executed with the same formalities as required for execution of a will. A properly executed codicil has the effect of **republishing**, that is, reestablishing, the will. It is said that a codicil breathes new life into a will. Thus, a will with only one witness or a will that has been revoked is reestablished with a properly executed codicil. Additions to a will following its execution have no legal effect unless the will is re-signed by the testator and re-attested by the proper number of witnesses. Making a new will or adding a codicil to the existing will are the best ways to avoid future problems.

Revoking a Will

State statutes set forth precise methods for **revoking** (canceling) a will. The act of revoking a will must be accompanied by the testator's intent to revoke the will. There are four principal methods of revoking a will:

1. The English Statute of Frauds declared that a will could be revoked by "burning, canceling, tearing, or obliterating." The English Wills Act prescribed "burning, tearing, or otherwise destroying." Most American

codicil   An addition or supplement to a will, which adds to or modifies the will without replacing or revoking it.

republication   The reinstatement of a will that has been revoked.

revocation   A nullification, cancellation, or withdrawal of a power, privilege, or act.

statutes use the language of one of these acts.

2. In general, the execution of a new will revokes a prior will. To revoke a prior will in some states, however, the new will must either expressly state that it revokes an earlier will or it must be inconsistent with the old will; otherwise, the new will is treated as a supplement to the old will (like a codicil). The 1990 revision of the UPC says that the "testator is presumed to have intended a subsequent will to replace rather than supplement a previous will if the subsequent will makes a complete disposition of the testator's estate."[7]

3. The subsequent marriage of a person who has made a will revokes the will in some states unless the will declares that it is made in contemplation of marriage to a particular person.

4. Under the laws of many states, a divorce or dissolution of marriage revokes bequests and devises to a former spouse—but not the will itself—unless the will specifically provides otherwise. In addition, a divorce revokes the appointment of the former spouse as an executor or trustee under the will.

Grounds for Contesting a Will

To **contest** a will, a person must have *standing*—that is, some beneficial interest that will be lost if the will is allowed. This usually means that the person contesting would inherit either under an earlier-made will or under the law of intestacy. Wills may be contested on the grounds of improper execution, unsound mind, fraud, and undue influence.

To successfully contest a will on the ground of fraud, it must be shown that the testator relied on false statements when making the will. To contest a will on the grounds of undue influence, it must be shown that the testator's free will was destroyed and, as a result, the testator did something contrary to his or her true desires. The burden is on the person alleging fraud or undue influence to prove that those conditions existed. When there is fraud or undue influence, the court may disallow only part of the will, instead of the entire will as in the case of improper execution and unsound mind.

Structure of a Model Will

Wills come in a fascinating variety of shapes, sizes, and sorts. Even a handwritten will written on a greeting card may actually be valid in some states under certain circumstances. Wills have been written on the backs of envelopes, restaurant place mats, prescription blanks, hospital charts, tractor fenders, and jailhouse walls. In this section, we examine the structure of a model will and the parts of the will that make it valid and effective, including the introductory paragraphs, the main body, the fiduciary and tax provisions, and the ending paragraphs.

Common Elements

Names, addresses, burial directions—these are among the many details that attorneys and paralegals will discuss with clients when preparing the clients' wills. No required form for a valid will exists, other than the placement of the signature in some states. However, carefully drawn wills often follow a similar pattern.

Wills and trusts are drafted with the aid of a computer or word processor in the modern law office. Most of the clauses in wills and trusts are

BALLENTINESBALLENTINESBALLENTINESBALLENTINESBALLENTINESBALLENTINESBALLENTINESBALLENTINESBALLENTINESBALLENTINESBALLENTINESBALLENTINESBALLENTINESBALLENTINES

contest   An attempt to defeat the probate of a will, commonly referred to as an attempt to "set aside the will."

IIII   *Law Office Scenario*   IIII

Michael Bauman, a paralegal, had just arrived at the Dow & Engel Law firm early one morning and was turning on the lights when a woman walked through the door.

"Is attorney Engel in this morning?" she asked.

"He's not in now," Michael answered. "I think he'll be in court this morning. Can I schedule an appointment for you?"

"Yes," answered the woman. "My name is Helen White, and I would like to talk with him about my father's estate. He died leaving no will, although I'm sure that he intended to leave everything to us kids. Look, on the back of this get-well card that I sent to him in the hospital, he wrote 'I leave everything in equal shares to my three children.' He didn't know that my brother had passed away the week before. I didn't have the heart to tell him."

Michael looked at the card. It was signed "Edward White," two other names were signed below, and the word witnesses was written under their names.

---

stored in the computer's memory for use when needed; then they are pulled up and tailored to fit the particular situation at hand. Paralegals today must be computer-literate and able to create documents when called upon to do so. Despite our constant reliance on computers, it is important to remember that they cannot think. All wills must be carefully reviewed and proofread before clients are asked to sign them. Each provision must be carefully considered to ensure its relevance and accuracy in the case at hand.

Introductory Paragraphs

The introductory paragraphs of a will often include the exordium clause, directions for funeral arrangements, and instructions to pay debts.

Exordium Clause

The *exordium clause,* or *publishing clause* as it is sometimes called, is the opening paragraph of a will. Its purposes are (1) to identify the testator, (2) to state the testator's domicile or residence, (3) to declare the instrument to be the testator's last will, and (4) to revoke all prior wills and codicils made by the testator.

Exordium Clause

I, (name of testator), also known as (other names if any), [or formerly known as (maiden name)] of (street address), City of _____, County of _____, State of _____, declare this to be my last will and testament, hereby revoking all wills and codicils heretofore made by me.

When naming the testator in a will, it is important to include all names that the testator uses in the ownership of all types of property, including real property, personal property, securities, and bank accounts, which is often done by writing the words "also known as … " after the testator's name.

The testator's domicile establishes the court in which the estate will be settled. The probate court in the place where the testator was domiciled at the time of death has primary jurisdiction to administer the decedent's estate.

The exordium clause should also contain a specific revocation of any prior wills. In some states, for a revocation to be effective, it is necessary to mention in the new will that it revokes the old one. In other states, a later will revokes an earlier one even though nothing is mentioned in the new will about revocation. By stating in a will that it revokes all prior wills, there can be no question about the testator's intent when wills with different dates are found after the testator's death.

Funeral Arrangements

Clients often request that their preferences concerning funeral, burial, or cremation be placed in their wills. Usually a brief statement regarding their wishes is sufficient.

Including funeral and burial arrangements or cremation instructions in a will is not always advisable because such matters must be taken care of immediately, and the will may not be found or allowed by the court for several weeks. In addition, the courts in some states do not treat the testator's wishes regarding funeral and burial arrangements as binding, deferring instead to the wishes of the surviving spouse or next of kin. Attorneys sometimes advise their clients to write a separate letter of instructions about funeral arrangements rather than to include them in a will. The letter can be placed in the envelope with the will, with copies given to close family members and to a funeral director.

Instructions to Pay Debts

Because the executor is required by law to pay the debts of the decedent, it is not necessary to put a clause in the will instructing the executor to do so. Any instructions to pay debts should be used with caution. Such instructions might require the payment of otherwise uncollectible debts (such as debts that were extinguished by bankruptcy or a statute of limitations) as well as the payment of mortgages on the decedent's real property. If no such clause is included in the will, though, the executor might have to pay off existing mortgages from other assets of the estate so that real property will pass to the devisees free and clear of all debt. If such a clause is included, real property

will pass to the devisees subject to any existing mortgages on the property.

Main Body

The main body of a will consists of the dispositive provisions, the residuary clause, and sometimes other miscellaneous clauses. The dispositive provisions of a will dispose of the testator's property. These provisions vary considerably because they are drafted to meet the needs of the individual client. Gifts under a will may be specific, general, or demonstrative.

Specific Legacies

In states that have not adopted the UPC, a **specific legacy** (often called a *specific bequest*) is a gift in a will of an identifiable item of property (other than real estate), such as a car, a diamond ring, a bank account, or a stock certificate. In states that have adopted the UPC, a legacy or bequest is referred to as a devise.

Specific Legacies

I give and bequeath the following items of personal property if owned by me at the time of my death to the individuals listed below:

(a) To my daughter, (name), if she shall survive me, the portrait of my husband's grandmother.

(b) To my daughter, (name), if she shall survive me, my diamond-ruby-sapphire ring, my Korean Satsuma vase, and all pieces of my Friendly Village China.

I may leave a memorandum stating my wishes with respect to the disposition of other articles of tangible personal property, but such memorandum will be simply an expression of my wishes and shall not create any trust or obligation nor shall they be offered to probate as a part of this will.

---

specific legacy   A bequest of specific personal property.

One advantage of a specific legacy is that it is used for the payment of debts only after the general legacies (money from the general assets of the estate) have been depleted. On the other hand, a specific legacy is subject to **ademption**. If the testator does not own the item at the time of death, the person named to receive it receives nothing. A common type of specific legacy is a gift of all of one's tangible personal property.

Specific Devises

A gift of real property in a will is known as a *devise*. A **specific devise** is a gift in a will of an identifiable parcel of real property. The term includes personal property in states that have adopted the UPC.

When a person dies owning real property solely, or with others as a tenant in common, title to the decedent's share passes to his or her heirs at the moment of death. This passing contrasts with title to personal property, which passes to the personal representative, who distributes it to the heirs after paying the estate's debts, taxes, and expenses. Real property can, however, be taken from the heirs and sold by the executor under a power-of-sale clause in the will or under a license to sell from the court to pay debts of the estate. Unless a will provides otherwise, real property is usually the last asset to be used for the payment of estate debts.

Devise of Real Property

To my (relationship), (name), I give my real property consisting of a residence and lot located at (street address), City of _____, County of _____, State of _____, and more particularly described as follows: (insert full legal description), if (he or she) survives me; but if (he or she) fails to so survive me, I give the above-described property to (relationship), (name), if (he or she) survives me.

General Legacy

A **general legacy** is a gift of money from the general assets of the estate. Gifts given under a residuary clause in a will are also considered to be general. A gift of money in a will, in addition to being a general legacy, is known as a **pecuniary bequest**.

Demonstrative Legacy

A **demonstrative legacy** is a gift of a specific sum of money with a direction that it be paid out of a particular fund. It differs from a specific legacy in that the gift is not taken away, i.e. adeemed, if there is no money in the fund. Instead, the general assets of the estate are used to fund the gift. Thus, a demonstrative legacy is a special kind of general legacy.

Residuary Clause

A will should be written so that it allocates all of the testator's property; thus, the will must contain a **residuary clause**. The residuary clause distributes all of the testator's property that is not disposed of in other clauses of the will. It is a crucial clause because it acts as a safety net, catching any property that falls through the cracks or that is inadvertently omitted from the will.

BALLENTINESBALLENTINESBALLENTINESBALLENTINESBALLENTINESBALLENTINESBALLENTINESBALLENTINESBALLENTINESBALLENTINESBALLENTINESBALLENTINESBALLENTINESBALLENTINESBALLENTINES

ademption   Disposition by a person, during his or her lifetime, of property which is the subject of his or her will. An ademption revokes the legacy or devise.

specific devise   A devise of specific real estate.

general legacy   A legacy of personal property or money that may be satisfied out of the general estate of the testator, as opposed to a legacy of a particular item of personal property or of money from a specific fund.

pecuniary legacy (pecuniary bequest)   A legacy consisting of a sum of money.

demonstrative legacy   A legacy that specifies a particular fund or particular property of the testator as the primary source of payment of a sum of money given in a will.

residuary clause   A clause in a will that disposes of the part of the estate that is left after all other legacies and devises have been paid and all claims against the estate are satisfied.

No particular language is necessary in a residuary clause. It may begin, "I give, devise, and bequeath the rest, residue, and remainder of my estate to ..." or it may simply say, "I give the residue of my estate to ..." Similar variations are acceptable as well.

Residuary Clause

I direct that all the rest, residue, and remainder of my estate, real, personal, and mixed, of whatever kind and wherever situated, of which I may die seized and possessed, or in which I may have any interest or to which I may be entitled or over which I may have any power of appointment, including any lapsed or adeemed legacies (herein called my "residuary estate"), shall be divided into ___ equal shares, to be disposed of as follows:

Miscellaneous Clauses

Wills are drawn to meet the particular needs of individuals, so there is no limit to the variety of clauses that can be included in a will. Also, new clauses are continually written to keep up with changes in state inheritance laws and federal tax laws. Miscellaneous clauses within the main body of the will may include clauses that specifically address the issues of adopted children, community property, and disinheritances.

Fiduciary and Tax Provisions

Wills commonly have provisions naming fiduciaries, giving them special powers, and allowing them to serve without furnishing a surety on their official bond. In addition, many wills contain a clause establishing the source for payment of death taxes.

Fiduciaries

Paralegals have many opportunities to deal with fiduciaries in the course of their work because the nature of a fiduciary's responsibility often requires working with a law firm. **Fiduciaries** are persons who are appointed to oversee property that belongs to others and who, therefore, serve in a position of trust. In the case of a will, fiduciaries include executors, guardians, and trustees.

The Executor

An important advantage of having a will is that the testator is allowed to select the person who will eventually settle the testator's estate. An **executor** (male) or an *executrix* (female) is a person named in a will to serve as the personal representative of the estate. His or her principal task is to gather the assets, pay the debts (including taxes and expenses of administration), and distribute the remainder according to the terms of the will.

Appointment of Executor or Executrix

I nominate and appoint my (relationship), (name), as executor of this will. If he (or she) shall fail to qualify or cease to serve, I nominate and appoint my (relationship), (name), to serve as executor in his (or her) place.

The Guardian

Another advantage of having a will, and perhaps the most important one for parents with young children, is that parents can name one or more **guardians** for their children if they die while the children are minors. There are two kinds of guardians: a guardian of the person and a guardian of the property. A *guardian of the person* has the care and custody of the child, which is given

BALLENTINESBALLENTINESBALLENTINESBALLENTINESBALLENTINESBALLENTINESBALLENTINESBALLENTINESBALLENTINESBALLENTINESBALLENTINESBALLENTINESBALLENTINESBALLENTINES

fiduciary A person who is entrusted with handling money or property for another person.

executor A person designated by a testator to carry out the directions and requests in the testator's will and to dispose of his or her property according to the provisions of his or her will.

guardian A person empowered by the law to care for another who, by virtue of age or lack of mental capacity, is legally unable to care for himself or herself. Guardianship may also involve the duty to manage the estate of the incompetent person.

as a natural right to parents unless they are found to be unfit. In contrast, a *guardian of the property* has the responsibility of caring for the child's property until the child becomes an adult. Such a guardianship is not a natural right of a parent and may be given by a court to someone other than a parent. Language in a will naming a surviving spouse as guardian of the person and property of minor children, however, is usually followed by the court.

Appointment of Guardian

I appoint my spouse, (name), as guardian of the person and property of my minor children. If for any reason my spouse fails to qualify or ceases to serve as guardian of the person of any minor child of mine, I appoint my friend (or other relationship), (name), as such guardian in my spouse's place. If for any reason my spouse fails to qualify or ceases to serve as guardian of the property of any minor child of mine, I appoint my friend (or other relationship), (name), as such guardian in my spouse's place. No guardian of the person or property appointed in this will need furnish any surety on any official bond.

The Trustee

When a will contains a trust, the trust is known as a **testamentary trust**. The will appoints one or more trustees to administer the trust and often provides for the appointment of successor trustees if the first-named trustees are unable to serve.

Powers of Fiduciaries

The power of a fiduciary to act without court approval is somewhat limited. Unless the will provides otherwise, fiduciaries must seek court approval to do whatever is necessary for proper administration of the estate. To eliminate the need for fiduciaries to seek court approval, and thereby reduce administration costs, include a powers clause in the will.

Powers of Executor

My executor shall have full power of management and authority to sell, either at public or private sale, or to exchange, lease, pledge, or mortgage, in such manner and on such terms as such executor deems advisable, any or all property, real or personal, in my estate and to execute all deeds, assignments, mortgages, leases, or other instruments necessary or proper for these purposes; to compromise claims in favor of or against my estate on such terms as such executor deems advisable; to retain any securities or other property owned by me at the time of my death, although the same may not be considered a proper investment; to make distribution of property in kind, and for such purposes to determine the value of such property; and generally to do any and all such acts and things and execute any and all such written instruments with respect to such property as if the absolute owner thereof.

No Surety on Bond

Executors are required to post a bond before they can be appointed. By doing so, they become personally liable up to the amount of the bond in the event the estate is mishandled. In some states, unless the will provides otherwise, there must be a **surety** on the bond. The cost of a surety can be saved by providing in the will that the executor be exempt from giving surety on his or her bond.

Tax Provision

The purpose of the tax provision in a will is to establish a source for the payment of death taxes. The tax clause apportions the burden of federal and state death taxes among the estate assets.

BALLENTINESBALLENTINESBALLENTINESBALLENTINESBALLENTINESBALLENTINESBALLENTINESBALLENTINESBALLENTINESBALLENTINESBALLENTINESBALLENTINESBALLENTINESBALLENTINES

testamentary trust   A trust created by will.

surety   A person who promises to pay the debt or to satisfy the obligation of another person (the principal). As opposed to the obligation of a guarantor, the obligation of a surety is both primary and absolute; that is, it does not depend upon a default by the principal.

Ending Paragraphs

The ending paragraphs of a will include the testimonium clause, the attestation clause, and the self-proof clause.

Testimonium Clause

The **testimonium clause** (sometimes called the *signature clause*) comes immediately before the testator's signature. It is used to establish the end of the will, to introduce the testator's signature, and to fix the date of execution on the instrument. Some attorneys like to have the testator read the testimonium clause aloud to the witnesses before signing it, as a declaration that the instrument being signed is the testator's will.

Testimonium Clause

In Witness Whereof, I, the undersigned (name of testator or testatrix), do hereby declare that I willingly sign and execute this instrument as my last will, in the presence of each of the witnesses, who also sign below, and that I execute it as my free and voluntary act for the purposes herein expressed, this ___ day of _____, 19 ___.

Besides signing on the signature line below the testimonium clause, the testator should either sign or initial each of the other pages of the will. Although not a requirement, signing every page helps to prevent the substitution or loss of pages preceeding the testimonium clause.

Attestation Clause

The **attestation clause** follows the testator's signature and precedes the witnesses' signatures. The clause is not required, but it is customary and helps to ensure compliance with the law of will execution. A will is usually executed properly when the directions in the attestation clause are followed precisely.

Attestation Clause

On this ___ day of _____, 19 ___, at (address), City of _____, County of _____, State of _____, the above-named testator signed the foregoing instrument in our presence, and at the same time declared it to be his last will and testament, and we do now at his request, and in his presence and in the presence of each other, hereto subscribe our names as witnesses hereof.

After the testator has signed the will in the witnesses' presence, it is customary to have one of the witnesses read the attestation clause aloud. The witnesses then sign below the attestation clause and write their home addresses beside their signatures.

Self-Proof Clause

In many states, if all of the heirs at law of a decedent do not assent to the allowance of a will, the testimony (or sworn affidavit) of one of the witnesses is required for the will to be allowed. This condition sometimes creates problems: heirs at law cannot always be located, and witnesses may have moved or died. To alleviate these complications, some states have enacted statutes allowing a will to be proved without testimony if it is self-proved by affidavits of the testator and the witnesses made before an officer authorized to administer oaths (usually a notary public). The clause, located at the end of the will, is called a *self-proof clause*.

Self-Proof Clause

I, (name), the testator, sign my name to this instrument this ___ day of _____, 19 ___, and being first duly sworn, do hereby declare to the undersigned authority that I sign and execute this instrument as my last will and that I sign

---

BALLENTINESBALLENTINESBALLENTINESBALLENTINESBALLENTINESBALLENTINESBALLENTINESBALLENTINESBALLENTINESBALLENTINESBALLENTINESBALLENTINESBALLENTINES

testimonium clause A clause at the end of a deed, which recites that the parties have "set their hands and seals" to the deed on the date specified.

attestation clause A clause, usually at the end of a document such as a deed or a will, that provides evidence of attestation.

it willingly (or willingly direct another to sign for me), that I execute it as my free and voluntary act for the purposes therein expressed, and that I am eighteen years of age or older, of sound mind, and under no constraint or undue influence.

_____
Testator

We, _____ and _____, the witnesses, sign our names to this instrument, being first duly sworn, and do hereby declare to the undersigned authority that the testator signs and executes this instrument as his last will and that he signs it willingly (or willingly directs another to sign for him), and that each of us, in the presence and hearing of the testator, hereby signs this will as witness to the testator's signing, and that to the best of our knowledge the testator is eighteen years of age or older, of sound mind, and under no constraint or undue influence.

_____
Witness

_____
Witness

The State of _____
County of _____

Subscribed, sworn to and acknowledged before me by _____, the testator and subscribed and sworn to before me by _____ and _____, witnesses, this ___ day of _____, 19 ___.

(Seal)   _____
                Notary
                Public

_____

Will Drafting

Estate planning paralegals are often assigned the task of drafting wills for the approval of attorneys and clients. Given the information collected from the client during the initial client interview, instructions from the attorney, and office forms, the paralegal who is familiar with the requirements for each type of will is well equipped to draft wills. Most law offices prepare lengthy wills in their word processing departments. The paralegal will be responsible for completing the proper form for the word processing department, drafting any language unique to the particular will he or she is preparing, and for proofreading and revising the will as necessary after it is returned from word processing.

Most well-designed word processing systems for the preparation of wills have various forms to complete for several different types of wills. The forms include several options for alternative paragraphs to suit each particular client's needs. However, under many circumstances, the clients' preference may be for nonstandard will provisions, so additional drafting of unique language must be done.

Trusts

Paralegals who work with trusts must be familiar with terminology that reflects the complexities of trust arrangements. Simply stated, a **trust** is an agreement whereby a person called the settlor gives property to a trustee (one or more individuals or entities), who holds the property in trust for the benefit of the beneficiary (one or more individuals) according to the terms of the trust instrument. The property held in trust is known by different names, including the _trust res,_ the _trust corpus,_ the _trust principal,_ the _trust property,_ and the _trust fund._ It may include cash, securities, real estate, or other property.

BALLENTINESBALLENTINESBALLENTINESBALLENTINESBALLENTINESBALLENTINESBALLENTINESBALLENTINESBALLENTINESBALLENTINESBALLENTINESBALLENTINESBALLENTINES

trust A fiduciary relationship involving a trustee who holds trust property for the benefit or use of a beneficiary. Property of any description or type ... may properly be the subject of a trust. The trustee holds legal title to the trust property ... ; the beneficiary holds equitable title.

Clause	Function
Exordium Clause	To identify the testator, state the domicile, declare the instrument to be a will, and revoke prior wills
Funeral Directions	To specify the funeral and burial conditions desired by the testator
Instructions to Pay Debts	To instruct the executor to pay debts (use cautiously)
Dispositive Provisions	To dispose of specific property
Residuary Clause	To distribute all property not otherwise disposed of
Appointment of Fiduciaries	To appoint the executor, guardian, and trustee
Powers of Fiduciaries	To provide special powers to the fiduciaries
No Surety on Bond	To avoid a surety on the bond
Tax Clauses	To establish the source for payment of death taxes
Testimonium Clause	To establish the end of the will, introduce the testator's signature, and fix the date of execution of the instrument
Attestation Clause	To introduce witnesses' signatures and ensure compliance with the law of execution of wills
Self-Proof Clause	To prove the will without testimony

Principal Clauses in a Will The paralegal may be responsible for drafting wills. With guidance from a supervising attorney, each of these clauses should be reflected in the will.

Parties to a Trust

The parties to a trust are the settlor (also known as the trustor, grantor or donor), the trustee, and the beneficiary (or cestui que trust).

The Settlor

To be a **settlor** of a trust, a person must be competent, which means, generally, that the person must be capable of making a will or entering into a contract. A minor or someone who is insane, for example, would not have the capacity to be the settlor of a trust. In addition to being competent, a settlor must own the property to be placed in trust. When property is already held in trust, only the beneficiary has the power to establish another trust in the property.

The Trustee

A valid trust must have a provision for the office of **trustee**, but it is not necessary that someone be nominated for that position. The court will not allow a trust to fail for lack of a trustee. When no one is nominated or the nominee is deceased, incompetent, or declines the position, and no provision for a replacement is provided, the court has the power to appoint a trustee.

Generally, anyone having the capacity to manage his or her own affairs can be a trustee. This usually excludes someone under a legal disability. However, the sole trustee of a trust cannot be the sole beneficiary of that trust, although a trustee can be a beneficiary by combining with other trustees or other beneficiaries. For example, a sole trustee can be a beneficiary if one or more additional beneficiaries are included. Similarly, a trustee can be a sole beneficiary if an additional person serves as a co-trustee.

Trustees have a **fiduciary relationship** with their beneficiaries. This is a relationship of trust and confidence requiring the exercise of a high degree of honesty and good faith. Trustees must be loyal to their trust at all times: they cannot profit personally from the trust property; they cannot commingle trust property with their own property; they must treat their beneficiaries fairly, and they cannot delegate the management of the trust to others. Trustees must also keep accurate accounts, showing receipts and disbursements of principal and income. In addition, trustees must exercise reasonable care and prudence in management of the trust property.

Although trustees have some implied powers and various powers provided by state statutes, the principal powers of a trustee are found in the powers clause of the instrument that created the trust. For this reason, trustees should be familiar with the trust instrument under which they operate. Similarly, persons dealing with trustees may wish to examine the trust instrument to determine the extent of the trustees' power, especially when purchasing real property from a trustee.

The Beneficiary

A *beneficiary* is an essential party to a trust. Without one, a trust cannot exist. It is not necessary that a particular person be named as beneficiary; it is merely necessary that a beneficiary be capable of being identified and ascertained. At all times during the life of the trust, it must be possible to determine the person or persons for whose benefit the trust was created. The beneficiary need not be in existence at the time of creation of a trust. Thus, trusts for the benefit of unborn children are valid. Any person who is capable of owning property may be a beneficiary of a trust. Individuals of any age or capacity, corporations, and governmental bodies fall in that category.

Creation of a Trust

When a trust is established, the trustee receives the **legal title** to the property—that is, full and absolute ownership, but without a beneficial interest (i.e. without any personal gain or profit). The beneficiary, in contrast, holds the **equitable title** (also known as *beneficial title*), which is the right to profit or benefit from the property.

A trust can be created by either a **conveyance** in trust or a **declaration of trust**. In a conveyance in trust, the legal title moves away from the settlor to the trustee. In a declaration of trust, the legal

---

BALLENTINESBALLENTINESBALLENTINESBALLENTINESBALLENTINESBALLENTINESBALLENTINESBALLENTINESBALLENTINESBALLENTINESBALLENTINESBALLENTINESBALLENTINESBALLENTINES

settlor   The creator of a trust; the person who conveys or transfers property to another (the trustee) to hold in trust for a third person (the beneficiary).

trustee   The person who holds the legal title to trust property for the benefit of the beneficiary of the trust, with such powers and subject to such duties as are imposed by the terms of the trust and the law.

fiduciary relationship   A relationship between two persons in which one is obligated to act with the utmost good faith, honesty, and loyalty on behalf of the other.

legal title   Title that evidences apparent ownership, as distinguished from equitable title, which indicates a beneficial interest.

equitable title   Title recognized as ownership in equity, even though it is not legal title or marketable title; title sufficient to give the party to whom it belongs the right to have the legal title transferred to him or her.

conveyance   The transferring of title to real property from one person to another. ... Any transfer of title to either real property or personal property.

declaration of trust   1. A voluntary statement by which an owner of property acknowledges that he or she holds the property in trust for someone else. 2. The document creating a trust.

title is retained by the settlor, who becomes the trustee.

Conveyance in Trust

When a trust is created by a conveyance in trust, the settlor transfers legal title to someone else—a trustee. The settlor may either retain the equitable title to the property or transfer it to someone else. By definition, whoever has equitable title is the beneficiary of the trust. A conveyance in trust is usually created by a *trust agreement* (a contract) between the settlor and the trustee. The trust agreement describes the trust property, gives directions for distribution of the principal and income, and spells out the duties and powers of the trustee.

Declaration of Trust

A *declaration of trust* is a trust in which the settlor transfers the equitable title to the trust property to someone else and retains the legal title. It is often referred to as a *one-party trust*. The settlor declares that he or she is now holding the property in trust for the benefit of someone else—the beneficiary. The settlor becomes the trustee.

Trust Formalities

Although trusts are usually created by written documents, such as a deed, a will, a trust agreement, or some other instrument, a writing is not always necessary to create a trust. **Parol** (oral) trusts dealing with personal property are generally enforceable. Some states require that notice be given to the beneficiary by the grantor when an informal, oral declaration of trust for personal property is made, to establish the intent necessary to create a trust. In contrast, trusts dealing with real property must be in writing under many state laws.

Rule Against Perpetuities

Under the **rule against perpetuities**, every interest in property is void unless it must vest, if at all, not later than 21 years after some life in being at the time of creation of the interest. A private trust cannot exist for more than 21 years after the life of the person named in the trust or other instrument that initially transferred the property. For example, if a settlor left money in trust for the settlor's children and then for the lives of the settlor's grandchildren, the rule would be violated because the grandchildren could include children of an as-yet unborn child of the settlor and this could occur more than 21 years after the death of all currently living beneficiaries. The rule against perpetuities does not apply to charitable trusts.

Express Trusts

Express trusts, sometimes referred to as *voluntary trusts*, are created in explicit terms, either oral or written. No particular words, such as *trust* or *trustee*, are required to create an express trust. However, the intent to create a trust by the settlor is essential and must be evident. The intention that legal title be vested in one person to be held in some other manner or for some purpose on behalf of another must be apparent. To be valid, an express trust must include the following elements: (1) a competent settlor, (2) a provision for a trustee, (3) a trust res, and (4) one or more designated beneficiaries. The testamentary trust and the living trust are the most common forms of express trusts.

Testamentary Trusts

A *testamentary trust* is a conveyance in trust created by will, in which the trust property is bequeathed or devised in a will to a trustee for the benefit of a beneficiary. It has no effect until the

BALLENTINESBALLENTINESBALLENTINESBALLENTINESBALLENTINESBALLENTINESBALLENTINESBALLENTINESBALLENTINESBALLENTINESBALLENTINESBALLENTINESBALLENTINES

parol   Oral; by word of mouth; spoken, as opposed to written.

rule against perpetuities   The common law rule that prohibits the creation of a future interest or a future estate that has the possibility of not vesting within 21 years, plus nine months, of some life in being at the time of creation of the interest.

express trusts   A trust created by a direct or positive declaration of trust.

testator dies. The will must clearly express the testator's intent to create a trust by separating the legal title from the equitable title and by conveying the legal title to a trustee for the beneficiary's benefit. Like the will itself, a testamentary trust is under the control and supervision of the probate court after the testator's death. The trust becomes a matter of public record, and the trustee is required to file annual accounts with the probate court.

For a testamentary trust to become operative, the will must first be proved and allowed, and **letters testamentary** must be issued by the court. Next, the assets of the estate must be gathered by the executor, and the debts, taxes, and costs of administration paid. Meanwhile, the person named in the will as trustee, or someone else if none is named, files a petition with the court to be appointed trustee. Many states require the filing of a bond when the trustee is appointed. Finally, the executor makes distribution of the estate assets. He or she turns over to the trustee the appropriate property that is to be held in trust according to the directions in the will. Thus, when there is a testamentary trust, the trustee's job begins when the executor's job ends.

Living Trust

A *living trust,* also known as an *inter vivos trust,* becomes effective during the settlor's lifetime. It is created by either a conveyance in trust or a declaration of trust. Unlike a testamentary trust, a living trust is not under the control and supervision of the probate court, and is not a matter of public record unless the trust must be recorded to establish title to real property. The lack of court supervision and the element of privacy are considered important advantages of a living trust. Living trusts may be either revocable or irrevocable.

Revocable Living Trust

In a **revocable living trust**, the settlor retains the right to alter, amend, or revoke the trust during the settlor's lifetime. When the settlor dies, the dispositive provisions of the trust take effect, and the trust then becomes irrevocable. The right to revoke a trust does not survive the settlor's death. Because of its flexibility, the revocable living trust is commonly used by estate planners. Such a trust has no tax advantages, however.

A trust can be altered, amended, or revoked only if the power to do so is expressed in the trust instrument. For that reason, a specific clause so stating is essential to make a living trust revocable. When the settlor of a revocable living trust wishes to revoke it, he or she must so notify the trustee in writing.

Settlors can put all of their property into a revocable living trust, receive the income during their lifetime, and give the principal, through the trust instrument, to whomever they designate upon their death. Property that is held in trust does not belong to the settlor's estate; it is owned by the trust and the trustee has legal title to it. By using trusts in some states, people can avoid homestead awards and prevent other types of family allowances from being taken from their estates.

Irrevocable Living Trust

An **irrevocable** living trust cannot be revoked or amended by the settlor once it has been established. A trust is irrevocable unless the trust instrument contains a statement that it can be revoked. To make the intent of the settlor clear, however, practitioners usually put this clause in an irrevocable trust:

This trust shall be irrevocable and shall not be revoked or terminated by trustor or any other

BALLENTINESBALLENTINESBALLENTINESBALLENTINESBALLENTINESBALLENTINESBALLENTINESBALLENTINESBALLENTINESBALLENTINESBALLENTINESBALLENTINESBALLENTINESBALLENTINES

letters testamentary   A document issued by the probate court appointing the executor of the estate of a decedent who died leaving a will.

revocable trust   A trust in which the settlor does not give up the right to revoke.

irrevocable trust   A trust in which the settlor permanently gives up control of the trust property.

person, nor shall it be amended or altered by trustor or any other person.[8]

The principal advantage of an irrevocable trust is the elimination of the trust property from the settlor's gross estate for federal estate tax purposes. In addition, income from trust property may be shifted from the settlor to the trust itself, which may be in a lower tax bracket than the settlor. The principal disadvantage of an irrevocable trust is that it cannot be changed once it has been established.

TESTAMENTARY TRUST FOR SUPPORT, MAINTENANCE, AND EDUCATION OF CHILDREN
[17 AM. JUR. *Legal Forms* 2d § 251:239]

I give the residue of my estate, in trust, to [name of trustee], of [address], City of _____, County of _____, State of _____. If [he or she] should fail or refuse to serve, or cease to serve, as trustee, then to [name of alternate or successor trustee], of [address], City of _____, County of _____, State of _____. The trust hereby created shall be held, administered, and distributed in the following manner:

1. *Trustee's Discretionary Payment among Beneficiaries.* I direct trustee to pay or apply so much of the net income [if desired, add: and principal] of this trust to the support, maintenance, and education of any of my children who have not reached twenty-two (22) years of age as in the discretion of trustee seems necessary for the proper support, maintenance, and education of such children.

   In making any payment or application, I direct that trustee take into consideration other resources and income of my children. I direct trustee to accumulate all undistributed net income of the trust property and add it to the principal.

   In exercising [his or her] discretion in making such payments of net income [if appropriate, add: or principal], trustee is not limited to making equal distribution to all the beneficiaries, but may make such distributions, considering the balance remaining in the trust and the estimated future requirements of the beneficiaries, as appear necessary under the circumstances.

   Trustee shall charge support payments made under this provison against the trust estate, rather than against the ultimate distributive share of the beneficiary for whose benefit the support payments are made.

2. *Division of Trust Estate When All Children Have Reached Twenty-two Years of Age.* When all my children have either attained twenty-two (22) years of age or died prior thereto, I direct trustee to divide the trust estate into a number

Sample Testamentary Trust A testamentary trust is found within a will and is executed upon death of the testator.

of shares equal to the number of my living children and deceased children having surviving issue. I direct trustee to divide the shares, giving one share to each living child, and one share to the surviving issue of each deceased child, per stirpes.

3. *"Education" Defined.* The term "education" as used in the trust provisions of this will includes both college and post-graduate study by the beneficiary concerned at an accredited institution of his or her choice. Distribution by trustee from the trust of amounts for "education" shall include reasonable living and travel expenses of the beneficiary concerned.

4. *Disposition of Trust Principal When All Beneficiaries Die Before Time Prescribed for Distribution.* If when I die, or if at any time before distribution of my trust estate as herein otherwise provided, my [wife or husband] and all my issue are deceased, and no provision has been made in this will governing the disposition in such case of the trust estate herein established, I direct that such trust, or whatever portion of it remains, be distributed to those who are at that time my heirs.

5. *Saving Clause Avoiding Rule Against Perpetuities.* Each trust provided for in this will shall in any event terminate 21 years after the death of the last to survive of [my wife or my husband or other named beneficiaries] and my issue living at the time of my death. On such termination, the trust estate, both income and principal, shall be distributed among the income beneficiaries of the trust in the proportions in which they are entitled to receive the income. If the respective amounts of income which the beneficiaries are at that time entitled to receive are not definite, I direct trustee to distribute the trust estate to such of my issue as are entitled to receive income at that time, per stirpes. If at that time I have no issue surviving, the trust estate shall be distributed to the benficiaries than entitled to the trust income, in equal shares.

Sample Testamentary Trust *(Continued)*

Pour-over Trust

A *pour-over trust* is a provision in a will in which the testator leaves a gift (often the residue of the estate) to the trustee of an existing living trust. When the testator or testatrix dies, the assets of the estate "pour" into the existing trust and are distributed according to the directions contained in the living trust. Although a pour-over trust receives its assets from a will after the death of the settlor, such a trust is considered to be a living trust rather than a testamentary trust because the trust comes into existence when the settlor is alive. In addition, the details of the trust, including the trustee's rights and duties, are contained in the trust instrument rather than the will.

Specialized Trusts

Paralegals who work with trusts must be familiar with a variety of trusts and need to know what type of trust is most suitable in a particular situation. Some of the specialized trusts with which paralegals often work include Totten trusts, spendthrift and sprinkling trusts, marital deduction trusts, charitable trusts, and life insurance trusts.

Totten Trust

A *Totten trust* is a savings bank account in the name of the depositor as trustee for another person. The depositor may withdraw money from the account at any time during the depositor's lifetime. When the depositor dies, the money in the account belongs to the beneficiary.

Spendthrift Trust

A **spendthrift trust** contains a provision that protects the trust assets from creditors and from the beneficiary's reckless spending. With such a provision, the principal and interest of the trust cannot be reached by creditors until they are received by the beneficiary, and the beneficiary cannot assign the principal and interest before receiving them. Without such a provision, a beneficiary for whom money is being held in trust could take the trust instrument to a bank, borrow on it, and assign the rights to the trust to the bank as collateral for the loan.

Sprinkling Trust

A **sprinkling trust**, also known as a **spray trust**, gives the trustee the power to determine how the trust's income or principal or both are to be allocated among a group or class of beneficiaries. Trustees have the power to distribute the trust income and principal among the persons who are most needy or in a way that will minimize taxes.

Marital Deduction Trusts

Under federal estate tax laws, property passing from a decedent to a surviving spouse is not taxable. Instead, it is deductible from the decedent's taxable estate and is known as the **marital deduction**. A trust that is designed to make optimal use of the marital deduction is called a *marital deduction trust*. Such a trust may distribute property to a surviving spouse in various ways, including: (1) an outright gift; (2) a life estate with a general power of appointment; (3) a credit-shelter trust; and (4) a QTIP trust.

Sometimes settlors wish to give the entire trust corpus outright to a surviving spouse when they die. This can be done through a simple clause, such as the following, in the trust:

Upon the settlor's death, the trustee shall distribute all principal and income, outright and free of trusts, to the settlor's surviving spouse.

Another way to qualify for the marital deduction is to leave property in trust to the surviving spouse for life, and upon the spouse's death, to whomever the surviving spouse appoints in a will. This can be done by granting a *life estate* with power of appointment in either a living trust or a testamentary trust.

In a *credit-shelter trust*, also known as an *A-B trust,* a *bypass trust,* or an *exemption equivalent trust,* a deceased spouse's estate passes to a trust rather than to the surviving spouse. This strategy reduces the possibility of the surviving spouse's estate being taxable, which is one drawback to outright distribution.

A *QTIP trust* (qualified terminable interest property trust) also qualifies for the marital deduction. This third type of trust is used when the settlor wants to pass the entire principal of the trust to someone other than the surviving spouse, but wants the spouse to have income from the trust for life. A QTIP trust gives all trust income to the surviving spouse for life, payable at least

---

spendthrift trust   A trust that provides a fund for the maintenance of a spendthrift, protecting him or her against his or her own wastefulness and recklessness. A spendthrift trust prevents the beneficiary from voluntarily selling or conveying his or her entitlement and bars his or her interest from seizure by his or her creditors as well.

sprinkling trust (spray trust; discretionary trust)   A trust whose income the trustee may distribute among its beneficiaries as, when, and in the amounts he or she chooses.

marital deduction   [A] deduction allowed under both the federal estate tax and gift tax with respect to property passing from one spouse to the other.

annually. Upon the death of the surviving spouse, the principal of the trust is transferred to other beneficiaries named within the trust.

Charitable Trusts

A **charitable trust**, sometimes called a *public trust,* requires the property held by the trustee to be used for public charitable purposes. A charitable trust is created for the benefit of a part of the general public rather than for an individual or designated group of individual persons.

Life Insurance Trust

If carefully prepared, a *life insurance trust* may be used to pass money to heirs tax-free. An irrevocable trust is first established, and then the trustee purchases a life insurance policy on the settlor's life. The settlor contributes a certain amount of money each year to pay premiums on the policy. When the settlor dies, the proceeds of the insurance policy are paid to the trust. If the trust contains certain powers, the settlor's spouse may receive the income from the trust for life. Upon the spouse's death, the principal passes tax-free to the settlor's heirs.

Estate Planning

Paralegals need to know the general purpose of estate planning in order to appreciate their specific role and tasks in the process. *Estate planning* is the positioning of a person's assets to most effectively maintain and protect the family, both during and after the person's life. The main purpose of all family estate planning is to obtain the maximum benefits of principal and income for the family and to pass on the family property intact (i.e., without any losses). Also important is the disposition of the property according to the client's desires, while also maintaining family harmony.

The general goal of estate planning is to protect the family unit and to provide financial and psychological security. The proper positioning of a person's assets may generate a larger proportion of available after-tax income. A thoughtful insurance program may help to create a cash reserve and an estate that would otherwise be nonexistent. Assets that might be depleted or reduced in value may be preserved by appropriate planning. The use of gifts, trusts, marital deductions, powers of appointment, pension and profit-sharing plans, and other business arrangements are additional methods used by the estate-planning team to ensure the family's security and to maximize the assets ultimately shared by the beneficiaries.

The Planning Team

Individuals with different training and abilities, including the paralegal, form the estate-planning team. An attorney who specializes in estate planning plays a key role, as many legal issues must be addressed. The client's accountant can provide information about the client's income taxes, details of assets and liabilities, and realistic appraisals of those assets. A life insurance underwriter can determine the client's need for life insurance, suggest the type and amount required, and prepare an overall, cost-effective life insurance plan for the client. If a bank is appointed as executor or trustee, a trust officer of the bank will also be a team member.

An important member of the estate-planning team is the well-trained paralegal, who can provide much-needed assistance to the attorney. Paralegals can relieve the attorney of many of the routine details of the estate-planning process and thereby reduce the cost and time involved.

charitable trust   A trust established for a charitable purpose.

With proper training, paralegals can assist the attorney in many ways, including the following:

1. Working with clients to assure that necessary estate-planning information is gathered

2. Assisting with the preparation of estate-planning questionnaires

3. Analyzing client assets and financial information

4. Drafting legal documents, such as deeds, wills, and trusts

5. Preparing summaries of provisions of wills and trust agreements

6. Preparing tax calculations

7. Monitoring state statutes to ensure that estate plans conform to state law

8. Reviewing and analyzing insurance policies

9. Preparing change-of-beneficiary forms

10. Recording instruments appropriately.

Gathering Information

Paralegals are frequently involved in the first, and probably most important, step of the estate-planning process: gathering facts. Without these facts, the process cannot continue. Obtaining all the necessary data requires persistence and is the basis for all other procedures. The needed facts can be classified as: (1) domicile, (2) property, (3) beneficiaries, and (4) the individual's objectives.

Domicile   The probate court in the place where the testator was domiciled at the time of death has primary jurisdiction to administer the decedent's estate. This jurisdiction is also where the estate is taxed, and this state's law is followed to determine the distribution of personal property. Thus, the estate planner must establish and make clear the client's domicile.

Property   All property should be listed in detail, including automobiles, household effects, objects of art, stamp collections, books, and similar possessions. The estate planner must determine the location of all real estate, the form in which title is held, its cost, its fair market value, and the amount of any mortgages on the property. All insurance must be listed, with the cost, age, present value, face value, cash surrender value, type of policy, and beneficiaries noted for each policy. Balance sheets and income statements of all businesses and partnerships must be reviewed. Stocks, bonds, and bank accounts should all be listed individually, and pension plans, profit-sharing plans, and stock option agreements should also be noted. All jointly owned property must be listed, as well as information about gifts made during the client's lifetime.

Beneficiaries   A family tree is a helpful device to visualize a family and all its members. Such a diagram pinpoints the often complex lineal relationships discussed previously in this chapter. Besides this visual aid, however, detailed information about all family members is essential to acknowledge or locate all heirs.

Objectives   The individual objectives of the client are the main focus of estate planning. The client's desires must be clarified and fulfilled in whatever way the client determines. The client may wish to endow the surviving spouse primarily or to favor one child, despite possible family resentment. The legal ramifications of such decisions must be discussed, but ultimately the client's personal preferences determine the specific aspects of the estate plan.

These four categories of facts—domicile, property, beneficiaries, objectives—point to general kinds of information needed in the estate-planning process. The following checklist is a helpful guide to the more specific information required.

**Family Estate Plan
Checklist**

[Harris, *Family Estate Planning Guide*, § 20 (1st ed. Lawyer's Cooperative Publishing Co).]

1. Name in full—other names or initials

2. Residence—domicile

3. Age and medical history

4. Family tree

5. Is there a safe-deposit box? Where? Where is key? Form in which held?

6. Is there a will? Where kept?

7. Is there an antenuptial agreement?

8. Has there been a divorce or separation?

9. Beneficiaries—names, addresses, relationship, age, marital status, financial status, financial needs, prospects, character traits

10. Personal property—auto, boat, airplane, objects of art, jewelry, household effects, stamp or coin collection, library

11. Real estate—domestic, foreign, record owner

12. Insurance—cost, value, age, amount, kind, beneficiary

13. Business interests—sole proprietor, partner, shareholder

14. Securities—bonds, mortgages, stock; cost, present market value, ownership

15. Trading accounts—broker, securities, balance, cost, present market value, ownership

16. Pledged property—value, cost, amount due, agreement

17. Joint property

18. Trust accounts

19. Custodian accounts

20. Pension rights

21. Profit-sharing plan rights

22. Stock options

23. Deferred compensation agreement

24. Social Security benefits

25. Power of appointment

26. Possible testamentary benefits

27. Settlor of trust

28. Beneficiary of trust

29. Previous gifts—dates, amounts, donees, income tax returns

30. Cash, savings accounts, checking accounts, accounts receivable

31. Patents

32. Copyrights

33. Wasting assets

34. Contract rights

35. Liabilities—secured, unsecured, contingent

36. Community property.

Even more detailed is the questionnaire that experienced family estate planners normally request clients to complete before the initial interview with the attorney. Completion of the questionnaire in advance reduces the attorney's time and legal fees. Many items in the questionnaire may not apply to a particular client; however, using so detailed a questionnaire ensures that all facts will be considered when formulating the best plan for the client.

Estate Planning Tools

Estate planning is sometimes called an art rather than a science, because it involves a considerable amount of creativity. Every client's unique situation requires an individualized approach by the estate planner. The tools available to the estate planner are limitless, but the principal ones are wills, trusts, gifts, powers of appointment, and insurance. The living will and the durable power of attorney are also often used by estate planners to ensure that clients' wishes are carried out should they become too ill to make those wishes known.

Wills

A will is considered the single most important estate-planning instrument. Without a will, state law rather than the wishes of the decedent determines disposition of the decedent's property. A will has no effect prior to the testator's death.

A well-organized will should be outlined before it is drafted. An outline forces the drafter to think through the entire document before focusing on specific details. It provides an overview of what has to be done and shows whether the planned document includes all necessary provisions. An outline also helps weed out potential inconsistencies in the document and furnishes a fail-safe checklist to make sure that everything required has been included.

Trusts

Trusts are used by estate-planning specialists to reduce problems created by joint ownership, to avoid the expenses and publicity of probate, and to reduce death taxes. Trusts are also used to pass assets on to future generations, to provide income for persons during their lives, and to prevent family assets from being mismanaged or spent unwisely.

Gifts

The use of gifts during one's lifetime is an important estate-planning device that offers tax-saving advantages. Death taxes can be reduced by giving property away while one is alive, but the gift must be completed. A *completed* gift is a donation that is placed beyond the dominion and control of the donor. *Dominion and control* means retention by the donor of the power to direct the disposition or manner of enjoyment of the property that was given away.

A donor can give $10,000 a year to each of any number of donees (people who receive gifts) without any tax consequences. Under the split-gift provision of the Internal Revenue Code, spouses may consent to treat gifts of one spouse as if made one-half by each spouse, and thereby double the amount that may be given away tax-free each year. For example, one parent of three children can give as much as $30,000 annually to the children ($10,000 to each) without filing a gift tax return,

and both parents, by consenting, could increase the amount to $60,000.

Powers of Appointment

When making a will or a trust, people sometimes do not know who their beneficiaries should be. They cannot predict which family members will be most needy at the time of their death. A **power of appointment** in a will or trust allows flexibility in determining who will inherit from a decedent's estate. It allows someone besides the decedent to decide, after the decedent's death, who will be the beneficiaries and to what extent.

Insurance

Insurance performs many roles in a family estate plan. Most important is its ability to furnish liquidity to an estate. As part of an integrated business plan, insurance may be used to finance the sale of a business interest, thereby guaranteeing sufficient cash to prevent a forced liquidation and the accompanying losses. Insurance may also create an estate that would not otherwise exist.

The Living Will

The **living will** is a written expression of one's wishes concerning health care during a terminal condition. At least 80 percent of the states have enacted living will laws. Even in states which have not, lawyers are sometimes asked to draft living wills for people who wish to have their desires known. Living will laws generally provide a procedure for people to leave instructions that they be allowed to die naturally and not kept alive by artificial means. If properly executed, the instructions are binding on health-care providers in most instances. Often, paralegals are asked to assist with the drafting of living wills, with the use of state-required forms, office forms and formbooks.

BALLENTINESBALLENTINESBALLENTINESBALLENTINESBALLENTINESBALLENTINESBALLENTINESBALLENTINESBALLENTINESBALLENTINESBALLENTINESBALLENTINESBALLENTINES

power of appointment   A power given by a person (the grantor) to another person (the donee or grantee) to select (appoint) a person or persons to receive an estate or to receive interest or income from an estate. A power of appointment may be given by deed or similar instrument, or by will.

living will   A document in which a person sets forth directions regarding medical treatment to be given if he or she becomes unable to participate in decisions regarding his or her medical care.

Advantages of Inter Vivos Gifts
[Harris, *Family Estate Planning* 189 (3rd ed., Hoops ed.)]

1. $10,000 per donee per year is excluded from the federal estate and gift tax.

2. Lifetime gifts reduce the assets which could otherwise pass through probate, thereby reducing the delays and expenses attendant to probate administration.

3. Removal of assets from the jurisdiction of the probate court serves also to remove such assets from public scrutiny.

4. A testamentary expression of intent can be challenged and successfully attacked more easily than a completed lifetime gift.

5. The donor may be relieved of the responsibilities of managing assets.

6. A gift in trust may furnish skilled investment advice to inexperienced investor, although the same result could be achieved by retention of an investment counsellor.

7. A gift in trust could provide for management and preservation of the assets in the event of the donor's incompetency, without the necessity for judicial intervention.

8. A gift in trust can fend off importuning relatives.

9. Speculatively inclined donors can protect their families against their own business reverses and assure themselves of future financial security.

10. If accumulation is prohibited by the law of the donor's domicile, a gift in trust permits the donor to select the law by which the trust will be governed.

11. A gift may create financial maturity and indepence among family members.

An inter vivos gift is given to the beneficiary while the donor is alive.

Durable Power of Attorney

Prior to the 1960s, when someone became incapacitated, the only option was to have a guardian or conservator appointed by a court to handle the person's affairs. Obtaining such an appointment was time-consuming and expensive, requiring affidavits by attending physicians and court appearances by attorneys. To make it easier and less expensive for someone to act on behalf of an incompetent, all states in the United States have enacted legislation authorizing the **durable power of attorney**.

BALLENTINESBALLENTINESBALLENTINESBALLENTINESBALLENTINESBALLENTINESBALLENTINESBALLENTINESBALLENTINESBALLENTINESBALLENTINESBALLENTINESBALLENTINESBALLENTINES

durable power of attorney   A power of attorney that remains effective even though the grantor becomes mentally incapacitated. Some durable powers of attorney become effective *only* when a person is no longer able to make decisions for himself or herself.

An ordinary **power of attorney** is a written instrument authorizing another person to perform certain specified acts on one's behalf. One who authorizes another to act on one's behalf is called a **principal**. One who is authorized to act on another's behalf is called either an **agent** or an **attorney-in-fact**. A durable power of attorney contains language indicating that the power is to survive the maker's incapacity or become effective when the principal becomes incapacitated. The durable power of attorney must be executed by the principal when he or she is in good mental health and still capable of handling his or her own affairs.

Concluding the Estate Planning Process

Even after all the necessary estate-planning documents have been prepared and executed by the client, the estate-planning process is not complete. The matters of storage and safekeeping of estate-planning documents, the periodic review of the estate-planning documents, and the changes of beneficiaries on life insurance policies and pension plans required by the estate plan must still be attended to. Often, these items are addressed in a closing letter, drafted by the paralegal, to the estate-planning client. This closing letter may do the following:

1. Address the storage and safekeeping of wills and other estate-planning documents prepared for the client, by stating specifically where those documents will be kept. Often they are kept in a safe or vault at the law firm. Other clients may choose to keep them in a safe or safe deposit box.

2. The client should be reminded of the need to review the estate plan periodically, in light of changing laws and changing family circumstances.

3. The client should be reminded to change beneficiaries on life insurance policies or pension plans (if necessary). At times this is done prior to or during the final meeting with the client. If not, the paralegal may want to offer his or her assistance with obtaining the necessary forms to change beneficiaries.

Most of these items are typically discussed during the last meeting with the estate-planning client. However, putting this information in a letter serves as a permanent record regarding the location of the client's wills and other important matters concerning the client's estate plan.

Family Protection, Lapses, and Ademption

At times clients may feel that their security and actual survival are threatened by the death of a spouse or income provider. Fortunately, state laws have been enacted for the protection of family members.

Protection of Widows and Children

Knowledge of the protection provided by state laws enables paralegals to offer reassurance to fearful

---

BALLENTINESBALLENTINESBALLENTINESBALLENTINESBALLENTINESBALLENTINESBALLENTINESBALLENTINESBALLENTINESBALLENTINESBALLENTINESBALLENTINESBALLENTINESBALLENTINES

power of attorney   A written instrument by which a person appoints another as his or her agent or attorney in fact and confers upon him or her the authority to perform certain acts.

principal   In an agency relationship, the person for whom the agent acts and from whom the agent receives his or her authority to act.

agent   One of the parties to an agency relationship, specifically, the one who acts for and represents the other party, who is known as the principal.

attorney in fact   An agent or representative authorized by his or her principal, by virtue of a power of attorney, to act for [the principal] in certain matters.

TO MY FAMILY, MY PHYSICIAN, MY LAWYER AND ALL OTHERS WHOM IT MAY CONCERN

Death is as much a reality as birth, growth, maturity, and old age—it is the one certainty of life. If the time comes when I can no longer take part in decisions for my own future, let this statement stand as an expression of my wishes and directions while I am still of sound mind.

If at such a time the situation should arise in which there is no reasonable expectation of my recovery from physical or mental disability, I, JOHN P. DOE, of N. Main Avenue, Mytown, Wisconsin, direct that I be allowed to die and not be kept alive by medications, artificial means, or heroic measures. I do, however, ask that medication be mercifully administered to me to alleviate suffering even though this may shorten my remaining life. I do not fear death as much as I fear the indignity of deterioration, dependence, and hopeless pain.

This statement is made after careful consideration and is in accordance with my strong convictions and beliefs. I want the wishes and directions here expressed carried out to the extent permitted by law. Insofar as they are not legally enforceable, I hope that you will regard yourselves as morally bound by these provisions. I recognize that it places a heavy burden of responsibility upon you, and it is with the intention of sharing that responsibility and of mitigating any feelings of guilt that this statement is made this ___ day of _____, 199 ___ .

_____   _____

Witness   John P. Doe

_____

Witness

SUBSCRIBED AND SWORN to before me this ___ day of _____, 199 ___ .

_____

Notary Public

Sample Living Will Living wills outline one's wishes to be allowed to die a natural death and not be kept alive by heroic measures or artificial means. Not all states recognize living wills.

clients. Attorneys can provide specific suggestions to address their needs. Some available options include a family allowance, homestead protection, exempting property from creditors' claims, dower and curtesy, a spouse's elective share, and pretermitted children laws.

SAMPLE ESTATE PLANNING CLOSING LETTER

April 25, 1995

Mr. and Mrs. John Doe
123 Main Street
Hometown, ID 45678

Dear Mr. and Mrs. Doe:

I am enclosing for your information photocopies of your wills that were executed by you in our office on April 20, 1995. The originals of these wills will be kept in our office vault for safekeeping.

As we discussed during our last meeting, it is an important part of your estate plan to change the beneficiary designation on John's life insurance policy with Great American Life Insurance Company to "The Trustees Named in the Last Will and Testament of John Doe." If you would like any assistance with making this beneficiary change, please contact my paralegal, Brian Harding.

As we also discussed, I would recommend that you review the enclosed wills and all other estate-planning documents at least every five years and call me if you have any questions or if you feel that any changes may be appropriate. Changes in tax laws, probate laws, and your family situation may make changes to your estate plan desirable in the future.

It has been a pleasure working with you to complete your estate plan. If you have any questions, please feel free to contact Brian or me.

Sincerely,

Cynthia Clark
Attorney at Law

Enclosures

Family Allowance

To provide for the immediate support of the family when a breadwinner dies, state laws generally contain a mechanism for immediate access to money from the decedent's estate. Probate courts have authority to grant an allowance from the estate to the surviving spouse and children to provide for their immediate needs after the death of the decedent. This allowance is known as the **family allowance** or **widow's allowance**. The amount of the allowance is discretionary with the court depending on the size of the estate, its debts, and the needs of the surviving spouse and children.

BALLENTINESBALLENTINESBALLENTINESBALLENTINESBALLENTINESBALLENTINESBALLENTINESBALLENTINESBALLENTINESBALLENTINESBALLENTINESBALLENTINESBALLENTINESBALLENTINES

family allowance   An amount paid out of the assets of a decedent's estate for the necessary expenses of the widow and children until final settlement of the estate.

widow's allowance   Same as elective share.

Homestead Protection

An important protection for families who own their residences is the **homestead exemption**, available under many state laws whether or not there is a death in the family. The homestead exemption is designed to place the family residence beyond the reach of creditors, and it allows the head of a family to keep the family home regardless of the amount of family debt.

In states that have adopted the Uniform Probate Code, a surviving spouse is entitled to a homestead allowance up to a certain amount of money; if there is no surviving spouse, minor children qualify for the allowance. The homestead allowance is exempt from and has priority over all claims against the estate and is in addition to any share passing to the surviving spouse or minor children by will of the decedent, intestate succession, or by way of an elective share.[9]

Although the homestead exemption applies in most states only to real property, a few states allow a homestead exemption on personal property as well. Some states put a limit on the value of the homestead exemption, but others do not.

Exempt Property

Under the laws of some states, certain property of a decedent, called *exempt property,* passes to the surviving spouse or children and is not subject to the claims of general creditors. For example, in states that have enacted the Uniform Probate Code, a surviving spouse is entitled to $3,500 worth of personal property comprising any combination of household furniture, automobiles, furnishings, appliances, and personal effects.[10] If there is no surviving spouse, children of the decedent are entitled jointly to the same value. These rights are in addition to the homestead allowance, as well as any benefits or share passing to the surviving spouse or children by the will of the decedent, by way of an elective share, or by intestate succession.

Dower and Curtesy

The rights of dower and curtesy originated in early England to provide surviving spouses with a means of support after the death of a spouse. *Dower,* under English law, was the right of a widow to a one-third life estate in all real property owned by her husband during the marriage. *Curtesy* was the right of a widower to a life estate in all real property owned by his wife during the marriage, but only if issue of the marriage were born alive.

Dower and curtesy rights arise only upon the death of the other spouse. In addition, these rights do not apply to real property owned by the deceased spouse as a joint tenant with someone else, or to property as to which the surviving spouse has released the right of dower or curtesy.

Spouse's Elective Share

To protect surviving spouses from being disinherited, state laws allow them to renounce the provisions made for them in the deceased spouse's will. Instead of inheriting under the terms of the will, surviving spouses may elect to *take against* (i.e., waive) the will and inherit an amount set forth in their state's statutes, which is often referred to as a *forced share* or an **elective share**.

In some jurisdictions, the forced share is tied to the amount that the survivor would have received if the deceased spouse had died without a will. In other states, a different formula is used to determine the amount of inheritance when a surviving spouse decides to renounce the provisions of a will and become a **forced heir**.

BALLENTINESBALLENTINESBALLENTINESBALLENTINESBALLENTINESBALLENTINESBALLENTINESBALLENTINESBALLENTINESBALLENTINESBALLENTINESBALLENTINESBALLENTINESBALLENTINES

homestead exemption   [T]he immunity of real property from execution for debt, provided the property is occupied by the debtor as the head of the family.

elective share   In some states, the share a surviving spouse may elect to take in the estate of the deceased spouse. In such jurisdictions, it replaces dower. ... [A]lso referred to as a *statutory share* or *forced share.*

forced heir   A person who cannot be disinherited by a testator ... , except when there is a legal cause for disinheritance.

Pretermitted Children

Generally, parents may disinherit children as long as they do so intentionally. If a **pretermitted child** (a child omitted from a parent's will) can prove that the omission was unintentional, the omitted child may be able to inherit an intestate share of the parent's estate. This rule also applies to the issue (lineal descendants) of deceased children who are omitted from a parent's will. The Uniform Probate Code sets forth specific circumstances under which pretermitted children may claim and specific indications of when an omission is intentional. Careful drafting of the will is essential to avoid questions in this area.

Lapsed Legacies and Devises

It is common for testators to outlive the persons to whom they leave gifts in their wills. When legatees or devisees die before the testator, gifts to them in the testator's will are known as **lapsed legacies** or **lapsed devises**. With some exceptions, such gifts become part of the residuary estate and are inherited by the residuary legatees and devisees named in the residuary clause of the will.

Many states have laws, known as **antilapse statutes**, that minimize the effects of lapse. The typical antilapse statute provides that if a gift is made to a relative of the testator who dies before the testator and leaves issue surviving the testator, the issue will receive the gift. Some state antilapse statutes apply to gifts given to anyone at all.

Ademption

Frequently, property that is specifically bequeathed or devised in a will is not owned by the testator at death. Either the testator disposed of the property after executing the will or the property became extinct. A specific legacy or devise is adeemed if the property is not in existence or does not belong to the testator at the time of death. The item is said to **adeem** by extinction. When an item of property adeems, the legatee or devisee of that property simply does not receive it, and he or she receives nothing in its place.

Probate Courts and Uniform Laws

Probate paralegals must be familiar with the probate court systems in the states in which they work. In addition, they must be conversant with the probate law of their states, which may be based on the Uniform Probate Code as well as other uniform laws.

Probate Jurisdiction

In their research, paralegals often locate state statutes that apply to specific situations and determine what court has jurisdiction. **Jurisdiction** is the power or authority that a court has to hear

BALLENTINESBALLENTINESBALLENTINESBALLENTINESBALLENTINESBALLENTINESBALLENTINESBALLENTINESBALLENTINESBALLENTINESBALLENTINESBALLENTINESBALLENTINESBALLENTINESBALLENTINES

pretermitted child   A child of a testator who is omitted from the testator's will. Generally the right of such a child to share in the decedent's estate depends upon whether the omission was intentional or unintentional.

lapsed legacy   A legacy that was good when the will was made but that has failed since then because of the death of the legatee before the death of the testator.

lapsed devise   A devise that was good when the will was made but that has failed since then because of the death of the devisee before the death of the testator.

antilapse statute   A statute providing that, if a person named to receive property in a will dies before the person who made the will, his or her share will not lapse, but will take effect as if he or she had died immediately after the death of the testator. The effect of such a statute is to ensure that a beneficiary's share will go to his or her heirs and not to others.

adeem   To take away; to make an ademption.

jurisdiction   In a general sense, the right of a court to adjudicate lawsuits of a certain kind.

a case and make a decision. Without jurisdiction, any decision by a court would be meaningless.

Federal Courts

Federal courts have no jurisdiction to probate wills or to administer estates. Federal court cases usually involve **in personam jurisdiction**, whereas probate proceedings are **in rem** proceedings to determine title to, or the extent of a person's interest in, specific property located within a state court's jurisdiction.

State Courts

Specific state courts have jurisdiction to **probate** wills or to administer estates. This jurisdiction derives from either the state constitution or acts of the state legislature. Many states have established a separate court and empowered it with **probate jurisdiction**. In most states, this separate court is referred to as the **probate court**. However, some states designate this same court as the *court of chancery,* the *surrogate court,* or the *orphan's court.* States that have not established separate courts give the authority to probate wills and to administer estates to courts of general jurisdiction, such as superior courts, district courts, circuit courts, county courts, and courts of common pleas. Some of these courts of general jurisdiction create separate internal divisions, one of which is empowered to probate wills and to administer estates.

Probate Records

In some states, the records of all probate activities are kept in an office called the *Registry of Probate.* In these states, an official, called the *Register*

of Probate, is either elected or appointed to administer the office. The Register of Probate is responsible for the care and custody of all books, documents, and papers filed with the probate court. He or she must maintain the probate records, compile indexes, and make the records available to the public upon request. In other states, this recordkeeping function is performed by the clerk of court. The Register or clerk keeps a docket of all cases that come before the court and, in general, handles all clerical matters necessary for the probate court's operation.

Uniform Laws

Uniform laws are laws that have been proposed by the National Conference of Commissioners of Uniform State Laws (a body with representatives from every state) for adoption by state legislatures. These recommendations are not requirements; states may adopt the uniform laws or pass their own laws. Some uniform laws have been adopted, either in whole or in part, by many state legislatures; others have been adopted by only a few state legislatures. The version adopted by a state is often amended by the state legislature, thereby making the "uniform" law no longer uniform. Using the index to your state statutes will help you find your own state's version of any uniform laws.

Uniform Probate Code

The Uniform Probate Code (UPC) was designed to modernize and standardize the laws relating to the affairs of decedents, minors, and certain others who need protection. The law developed in response to growing dissatisfaction with the high

BALLENTINESBALLENTINESBALLENTINESBALLENTINESBALLENTINESBALLENTINESBALLENTINESBALLENTINESBALLENTINESBALLENTINESBALLENTINESBALLENTINESBALLENTINESBALLENTINESBALLENTINES

jurisdiction in personam   The jurisdiction a court has over the person of a defendant.

in rem action   A legal action brought against property ... , as opposed to an action brought against the person.

probate   The judicial act whereby a will is adjudicated to be valid.

probate jurisdiction   Matters with respect to which a probate court has both the right and the duty to exercise its authority.

probate court   A court with jurisdiction to probate wills and to supervise the administration of decedents' estates.

Uniform Laws   Model legislation prepared and proposed jointly by the American Law Institute and the Commission on Uniform State Laws, the purpose of which is to promote uniformity throughout the country with respect to statutes governing significant areas of the law. Many Uniform Laws are adopted by many, most, or all of the states, with variations from state to state.

cost, long delays, and unnecessary formalities involved with old-fashioned probate procedures. Some people resented the judicial control and interference by the court in what they considered family matters. For some states, the UPC offered welcome changes.

For example, the UPC gives heirs and devisees the option of selecting supervised or unsupervised administration. Supervised administration occurs under the continuing authority of the court. In contrast, unsupervised administration occurs without court action unless requested by an interested

Name of Uniform Act	States That Have Adopted Uniform Act
Absence as Evidence of Death and Absentees' Property Act	TN, WI
Anatomical Gift Act (1987 Act)	AR, CA, CT, HI, ID, MT, NV, ND, RI, UT, VT, VA, WI
(1968 Act)	AL, AK, AZ, CO, DE, DC, FL, GA, GU, IL, IN, IA, KS, KY, LA, ME, MD, MA, MI, MN, MS, MO, NE, NH, NJ, NM, NY, NC, OH, OK, OR, PA, SC, SD, TN, TX, VT, VI, WA, WV, WY
Ancillary Administration of Estates Act	WI
Disclaimer of Property Interests Act	AL, IL, ME, MD, VT, WV
Multiple-Person Accounts Act	CO
Probate Code	AL, AZ, CO, FL, HI, ID, ME, MI, MN, MT, NE, NM, ND, SC, UT
Probate of Foreign Wills Act	TX, WI
Simultaneous Death Act	All states except LA, MT, and OH
Statutory Form Power of Attorney Act	CA
Statutory Rule Against Perpetuities	CT, FL, GA, MA, MI, MN, MT, NE, NV, OR, SC
Statutory Will Act	MA
Testamentary Additions to Trusts Act	All states except AL, LA, RI, VA, and WI
TOD Security Registation Act	CO, WI
Transfers to Minors Act	AL, AK, AZ, AR, CA, CO, DC, FL, GA, HI, ID, IL, IN, IA, KS, KY, LA, ME, MD, MA, MN, MO, MT, NV, NH, NJ, NM, NC, ND, OH, OK, OR, RI, SD, UT, VA, WV, WI, WY
Unclaimed Property Act	AL, AZ, CO, HI, FL, GA, ID, IA, LA, ME, MD, MN, MT, NV, NH, NJ, NM, ND, OR, RI, SC, TN, UT, VT, VI, VA, WA, WI
Veterans' Guardianship Act	AR, CO, IN, KY, LA, MO, NC, OH, OK, RI, SD, TN, VT, VI, WA, WI

Uniform Laws Relating to Wills, Estates, and Trusts A paralegal must be aware of any changes in these laws.

Name of Uniform Act	States That Have Adopted Uniform Act
Disclaimer of Transfers by Will, Intestacy or Appointment Act	DE, IL, KS, KY, ME, MN, NJ, NC, OR
Disclaimer of Transfers Under Nontestamentary Instruments Act	DE, KS, KY, ME, ND, OR
Disposition of Community Property Rights at Death Act	AK, AR, CO, CT, HI, KY, MI, MT, NY, OR, VA, WY
Disposition of Unclaimed Property Act (1966 Act)	AL, AR, DC, IL, IN, IA, KS, MN, MS, MO, NE, NV, OK, OR, SD, TN
(1954 Act)	MD, VT, WV
Durable Power of Attorney Act	AL, AZ, CA, CO, DE, DC, HI, ID, IN, KS, KY, ME, MA, MI, MN, MO, MT, NE, NM, ND, OK, PA, SC, TN, UT, WV, WI
Estate Tax Apportionment Act (1964 Act)	HI, ID, MD, ND, OR, RI, VT, WA
(1958 Act)	AL, MI, MT, NH, WY
Gifts to Minors Act (1966 Act)	CT, DE, MS, NE, NJ, NY, PA, SC, TN, TX, VT, WA
(1956 Act)	MI, VI
Guardianship and Protective Proceedings Act	AL, AZ, CO, DC, HI, ID, ME, MI, MT, NE, NM, ND, SC, UT
Interstate Arbitration of Death Taxes Act	CA, CO, CT. ME, MD, MA, MI, MN, NE, PA, SC, TN, VT, WV, WI
Interstate Compromise of Death Taxes Act	CA, CO, CT, ME, MD, MA, MI, MN, NE, NH, NJ, NY, PA, SC, TN, VT, WV

Uniform Laws Relating to Wills, Estates, and Trusts *(Continued)*

person. Although there is no court supervision, the Registrar of Probate is given the authority to process any necessary documents and to decide whether they are complete. In unsupervised administration, an interested person can petition the court to resolve a question, such as the validity of the will or appointment of the personal representative. The court does not become involved unnecessarily—only to settle controversies or doubts.

The purposes of the Uniform Probate Code are:

1. To simplify and clarify the law concerning decedents, missing persons, protected persons, minors, and incapacitated persons

2. To discover and make effective the intent of a decedent in the distribution of his or her property

3. To promote a speedy and efficient system for liquidating the estate of the decedent and making distribution to its successors

4. To facilitate use and enforcement of certain trusts

5. To make uniform the law among the various jurisdictions.[11]

Other Uniform Laws

Several other uniform laws may affect the probate and administration of estates. One of the most significant is the Uniform Simultaneous Death Act, which sets forth rules to be followed when the passage of property depends upon the time of death and no sufficient evidence can establish which person died first.

Also significant are the Uniform Transfers to Minors Act, which allows any kind of property to be transferred to a custodian for the benefit of a minor, and the Uniform Anatomical Gift Act, which provides for an easy way to make a testamentary donation of vital organs for medical research or transplant.

Probating a Will and Administering an Estate

Paralegals often work with attorneys and clients from the very beginning of a probate, helping to perform the multitude of tasks that arise when an estate is settled. Their assistance may begin with research, as in the following law office scenario, or it may begin with the initial office conference with a probate client. When a client contacts a law office concerning a probate, an initial appointment with the attorney and paralegal who will be working on the file is often scheduled immediately. At times, as when the decedent owned a business, some matters concerning the decedent's estate must be dealt with as soon as possible. In addition, out-of-town relatives who have come to attend the funeral often want to attend the meeting with the attorney. If the deceased is a former client of the law firm, the paralegal is often asked to pull the client's past files for review before the initial meeting with the family. If the firm has prepared the decedent's will, at least a copy of the will will be in the file, as well as financial information and useful information concerning family members.

At the first meeting, the following matters are typically addressed:

1. If the decedent died with a valid will, a determination is made with regard to the personal representative named in the will. Is this person willing and able to serve? If not, has an alternate been named?

2. If the decedent died without a valid will, a determination should be made with regard to which family members are best qualified to serve as administrators of the estate and whether they are willing to do so.

3. A list of all living and deceased heirs of the decedent should be made, including their full legal names, addresses, and relation to the deceased.

4. A plan should be made for keeping the family informed of the progress in handling the estate. Do all family members wish to be notified of all actions taken on behalf of the estate, or do they only wish to be notified of major events during the probate process?

5. The attorney should explain the probate process to the family, including what role each involved individual will fulfill. At this point, a preliminary decision should be made as to the extent of the personal representative's involvement in the probate process. The personal representative may wish to take a very active part in completing and filing all the paperwork necessary to probate the estate, or he or she may defer those duties to the attorney and paralegal.

6. A determination should be made as to any assets that may require immediate attention, such as insurance that may lapse if not paid, or a business that must be run.

|||| *Law Office Scenario* ||||

Mary Abrams had just returned from her lunch break when she was called into the office of Attorney Jennifer Bryant.

"Did you hear about that small plane that went down in Whitewater last night, Mary?" Jennifer asked. "Three people got killed in the crash, including two of our clients, Clyde and Thelma Powell."

"I did hear about that," Mary answered. "I heard that they all died instantly."

"That's right. Clyde and Thelma were both dead when the ambulance arrived at the scene. We have their estates to settle, and I'm on my way over to their house now to talk with the children's grandparents."

"How many children did they have?" Mary asked.

"Well, Clyde had a four-year-old daughter from a former marriage and Thelma had a seven-year-old son from a former marriage," Jennifer explained. "Plus, they had a two-year-old daughter from their marriage."

"What a shame. Those poor children."

"Neither parent had a will," Jennifer continued. "They owned a house together as joint tenants, and they had a joint bank account. I've written some details here in the file. Clyde owned his own car, and a large amount of AT&T stock. Thelma owned her own car and quite a few stocks and bonds. Thelma was the beneficiary of Clyde's life insurance policy. I'd like you to check the simultaneous death statute to see who will inherit their property."

"Okay," Mary replied as Jennifer put on her coat, preparing to leave the office.

"And while you're at it, see if our state allows an estate to transfer money to minors," Jennifer said as she walked out of her office. "Those children are going to inherit quite a bit of property."

"I'll look into that, too," Mary replied, thinking about where she would begin her research.

---

7. The paralegal should record the pertinent information gathered from the family members with regard to the decedent's debts and assets, and give the family a list of items that must be furnished to the paralegal or attorney when they can be located.

The information to be gathered includes:

1. Information concerning bank accounts held by the decedent, including their location and the amount of cash in each account

2. Information concerning real estate in which the decedent held an interest, including deeds, owner's duplicate certificates of title, abstracts, mortgages, and leases

3. Information concerning stocks and bonds held by the decedent

4. Information concerning insurance policies on the life of the decedent or owned by the decedent

5. Copies of the decedent's income tax returns

6. Copies of gift tax returns filed by the decedent

7. List of the decedent's debts at his or her date of death

8. Information concerning any pension or profit-sharing plans in which the decedent was a participant

9. Information on any pending estate or trust in which the decedent had an interest

10. Any other information concerning assets, debts, and financial matters of the decedent.

When someone dies owning property, the property must be protected. The decedent's debts must be paid, the individuals who should own the remainder of the property after the debts are paid must be identified, and the remainder must be distributed accordingly. The term *probate* is often used to describe this procedure. *Probating a will* is the process of proving or establishing before the probate court that the document being offered for official recognition as the will of the decedent is in fact genuine. **Administering an estate** means settling and distributing the estate of a deceased person.

The probate process includes the appointment of a **personal representative**, giving him or her the legal authority to: (1) collect and preserve the assets owned by the decedent; (2) pay the decedent's debts and taxes; and (3) distribute the remainder of the assets according to the terms of the will or the law of intestate succession. The probate process protects the decedent by seeing that his or her wishes are carried out. It protects the heirs by ensuring that all of the decedent's property is collected and accounted for by determining the lawful heirs. It also establishes title to property that has been inherited.

Protection of Decedent

When someone dies, it must first be determined whether he or she left a will. If a will is found, it must be turned over to the probate court in which the decedent was domiciled within the time period after death (often 30 days) set by state statute. Failure to give a will to the probate court can be a criminal offense.

Protection of Heirs

Another important function of the probate procedure is the protection of heirs and next-of-kin. The names of heirs and next-of-kin must be listed on the petition for probate. They are notified of the probate proceeding and allowed to present any legally sound objections.

Establishing Title

The probate process also protects heirs by providing a system for establishing title to inherited property. This assures heirs, legatees, devisees, and future buyers that title is good. If the decedent left a will, legatees and devisees cannot prove their title to the property unless the will is probated. Similarly, in estates, heirs must have the authority of the probate court to establish their title to property they inherit.

The Personal Representative

Paralegals may be asked to assist the personal representative, the individual assigned to manage the affairs and settle the estate of someone who dies while owning property. Because his or her duties involve good faith, trust, and special confidence, a personal representative is a type of fiduciary and acts in a fiduciary capacity. The law imposes an unusually high standard of ethical and moral conduct on a fiduciary because he or she holds property interests for the benefit of others.

When someone dies testate, the person nominated in the will as personal representative, or some other interested person, petitions the court to have the will allowed and to be appointed personal representative. When someone dies intestate, one of the heirs, next-of-kin, or a creditor files a petition with the court requesting the appointment. With variations from state to state, notice of a hearing on the petition is given to all interested parties either by service of process, mail, or publication in a newspaper. A time period of about three to four weeks is established for interested parties to respond to the notice. The hearing may

administration of estate   The management of a decedent's estate by an administrator or executor so that all the decedent's assets are collected, all debts, administration expenses, and taxes are paid, and all remaining assets are distributed to the persons entitled to receive them.

personal representative   [T]he executor or administrator of a decedent's estate … .

be dispensed with if no one objects to the petition. If no contest arises, the court allows the will or grants the administration and appoints the personal representative. When a contest does occur, a judge or jury decides the question in dispute.

Personal Representative's Bond   In some states, the appointment of a personal representative is not complete until the representative has given bond. A *bond* is a written promise by the personal representative and the sureties (if any) to pay the amount of the bond to the court if the representative does not faithfully perform his or her duties.

Duties of Personal Representative   The duties of a personal representative are to collect and preserve the assets of the estate; pay the debts, taxes, and expenses of administration; and distribute the remainder according to the terms of the will or the law of intestate succession if there is no will. Specific rules and regulations for carrying out the duties of a personal representative are set forth in each state's statutes.

Formal Probate Proceedings

Formal probate proceedings are instituted when someone dies owning assets above a specific value set by state statute, or when the court is to supervise all aspects of the estate's settlement. The UPC defines *formal proceedings* as those conducted before a judge with notice to interested persons.[12] In some states, formal probate proceedings are known as *probate in solemn form*.

Formal probate proceedings involve the following steps:

1. A petition is filed with the court
2. Notice is given to interested parties
3. In a testate estate, the will is proved
4. A bond is given by the personal representative, unless waived

5. Letters are issued by the court
6. An inventory is filed
7. Notice or a time period is given to creditors to make claims
8. Debts, taxes, and expenses of administration are paid
9. Distribution is made to the beneficiaries
10. An account is filed with the court

Under the UPC, formal probate proceedings can be either supervised or unsupervised. In supervised administration, the estate is settled under continuous court surveillance from beginning to end. Unsupervised administration begins formally but becomes less supervised by the court once the personal representative is appointed.

Petition for Probate or Administration

In testate cases, probate proceedings begin when the executor named in the will files a **petition** for probate with the court. This is a formal, written application asking the court to prove and allow the will and to appoint the petitioner, who is nominated in the will, as executor. If someone other than the person nominated as personal representative in the will is the petitioner seeking the appointment, a different form, called a *petition for administration with the will annexed*, must be filed with the court. Each state has its own forms for these purposes, which can be obtained from the particular court involved.

Notice to Interested Parties

Upon receiving the will and the petition for probate or the petition for administration, the court issues an order, sometimes called a **citation**, requiring the petitioner to notify all heirs at law, devisees, and legatees, either by personal service, newspaper advertising, or both, that the petition has been filed.

BALLENTINESBALLENTINESBALLENTINESBALLENTINESBALLENTINESBALLENTINESBALLENTINESBALLENTINESBALLENTINESBALLENTINESBALLENTINESBALLENTINESBALLENTINESBALLENTINES

petition   An application made to a court *ex parte*.

citation   A writ issued by a judge, ordering a person to appear in court for a specified purpose.

Proof of Will

The procedure for proving a will varies from state to state. Even within a state, several different methods may be used. One method is to have one or more of the attesting witnesses testify before the judge or the clerk of court as to how the will was executed and the testator's competence.

A second method is to have one or more of the attesting witnesses sign a written affidavit before the Register of Probate stating facts about the execution of the will. When witnesses have died or cannot be found, their handwriting may have to be proved. A third method is to obtain written approval of the surviving spouse and the heirs at

---

[31 Am. Jur. 2d § 379]
[UPC § 3-715]

With some exceptions, a personal representative may do the following:

1. Retain assets, including those in which the representative is personally interested or which are otherwise improper for trust investment.

2. Receive assets from fiduciaries or others.

3. Perform, compromise, or refuse to perform the decedent's contracts.

4. Satisfy written charitable pledges, even if not binding or not properly presented as claims, if in the representative's judgment the decedent would have wanted this done under the circumstances.

5. Deposit or invest liquid assets in prudent investments reasonable for trustees.

6. Acquire or dispose of assets for cash or on credit, at public or private sale; and manage, develop, improve, exchange, partition, change the character of, or abandon assets.

7. Make ordinary or extraordinary repairs or alterations in buildings and erect or demolish buildings.

8. Subdivide, develop, or dedicate land or easements to public use; vacate plats and adjust boundaries; or adjust differences in valuation on exchange or partition by giving or receiving consideration.

9. Lease (as lessor or lessee), with or without option to purchase or review, for a term within or extending beyond administration.

10. Enter into a mineral lease or similar agreement.

11. Abandon property.

12. Vote securities in person or by proxy.

13. Pay calls, assessments, and other sums chargeable or accruing against or on account of securities, unless barred by the claims provisions.

14. Hold a security in the name of a nominee or other form without disclosing the estate's interest.

Authorized Transactions of a Personal Representative

15. Insure assets against damage, loss, and liability, and himself or herself against liability to third persons.

16. Borrow money, with or without security, to be repaid from estate assets or otherwise; and advance money to protect the estate.

17. Compromise with any debtor or obligor; or extend, renew, or modify any obligation to the estate; or accept a transfer in lieu of foreclosure.

18. Pay taxes, assessments, the representative's own compensation, and other expenses.

19. Sell or exercise stock subscription or conversion rights and consent to the reorganization, consolidation, merger, dissolution, or liquidation of a business.

20. Allocate items of income or expense to income or principal, as permitted or provided by law.

21. Employ people.

22. Prosecute or defend claims or proceedings in any jurisdiction to protect the estate and himself or herself in performance of duties.

23. Sell, mortgage, or lease property or any interest in it for cash, credit, or both, with or without security.

24. Continue (with limitations) an unincorporated venture in which the decedent was engaged at death.

25. Incorporate any business or venture in which the decedent was engaged at death.

26. Provide for exoneration of the personal representative from personal liability in any contract made on behalf of the estate.

27. Satisfy and settle claims and distribute the estate.

Authorized Transactions of a Personal Representative *(Continued)*

law. If all interested parties agree to the allowance of a will, neither testimony of witnesses nor affidavits are necessary. Under the laws of many states, a will containing a self-proof clause may be admitted to probate without the testimony or affidavit of witnesses.

Allowance of Bond and Issuance of Letters

Some states require all personal representatives to have a bond. In addition, they require a surety on the bond unless the will provides otherwise or unless all heirs agree to the appointment without sureties. In other states, a bond is not required when the will contains a clause to that effect. In those states, unless the will indicates that a bond is required, the bond can be waived if all beneficiaries named in the will assent to the waiver in writing.

Once the personal representative's bond is allowed, the court issues a certificate of appointment known as *letters testamentary* in a testate estate and

letters of administration in an intestate estate. These letters serve as evidence of the fiduciary's right to take possession of the estate property. In some states, the letters remain in full force and effect until completion of the estate or until resignation or removal of the personal representative. In other states, a time limit (such as 15 months) applies to the appointment, after which an extension must be obtained. An authenticated copy of the letters, issued by the court, may be used to establish their validity.

The Inventory

One of the duties of a personal representative after receiving letters of appointment is to file an inventory with the probate court. This task may also be assigned to the paralegal. An **inventory** is a detailed list of property owned by the decedent, together with its estimated value as of the decedent's date of death. All property in the estate should be listed in detail on the inventory, including serial numbers of automobiles, stock certificates, certificates of deposit, savings bond and savings account numbers, legal descriptions of real property, and the book and page where any deed is recorded at the Registry of Deeds. States have different time limits within which the inventory must be filed, ranging from one to six months from the date of the personal representative's appointment.

Payment of Debts, Taxes, and Expenses

After gathering the assets and preparing an inventory, the next task of the personal representatives is to determine the extent of claims against the estate. Here again the paralegal may assist, particularly with preparing correspondence and maintaining records of creditors' claims. Creditors are responsible for bringing claims to the personal

representative's attention within a specific time period. Once the deadline has passed, creditors will not be able to collect the money due them. Time periods are established so that personal representatives will know by a specific date the exact amount owed to creditors. This knowledge enables the personal representatives to make decisions regarding the allocation of estate assets.

Taxes and Expenses

Preparing and filing estate tax returns can be a major part of the work of a personal representative. The paralegal is often asked to help complete various types of tax returns. State and federal individual income tax returns (Form 1040) often must be prepared for the decedent's last year of life up to the date of death. After that, if the estate has income, state and federal estate income tax returns (Form 1041) may have to be prepared from the date of death until the year's end. Finally, if the value of the estate exceeds certain limits, state and federal estate tax returns (Form 706) must be prepared. Federal estate taxes must be paid within nine months after death.

Decedent's Debts

After the expiration of a time period set by state statute, the personal representative pays the claims against the estate. If the estate is **insolvent**, the personal representative pays claims according to the priorities established by state statute.

Sale of Real Property

In most states, title to real property owned by a decedent vests in the decedent's heirs immediately upon death. In contrast, title to personal property vests in the personal representative when he or she is appointed. Therefore, although real property

---

BALLENTINESBALLENTINESBALLENTINESBALLENTINESBALLENTINESBALLENTINESBALLENTINESBALLENTINESBALLENTINESBALLENTINESBALLENTINESBALLENTINESBALLENTINESBALLENTINESBALLENTINESBALLENTINES

letters of administration   A document issued by the probate court appointing the administrator of the estate of a person who has died without leaving a will.

inventory   An itemized list or schedule of assets, property, or other articles, sometimes with notations of their value.

insolvency   The status of a person when his or her total assets are of insufficient value to pay his or her debts. The inability of a person to pay his or her debts as they become due or in the ordinary course of business.

is included in the inventory of the estate, it is not usually included in the final account, because the personal representative has no control over it. When the debts exceed the value of the personal property, however, the personal representative may sell the real property to obtain the money to pay the debts. Such a sale is done under the court's supervision (often by the issuance of a license to sell) unless the will gives the personal representative the power to sell real property without court supervision. The proceeds from sale of real property are included in the personal representative's final account.

Distribution

After the time has expired for creditors to make claims, and the debts and taxes have been paid, the remaining assets of the estate are distributed according to the terms of the will or the law of intestate succession. Some states have special rules allowing the distribution of property in kind, which avoids having to sell the property to distribute cash.

When there are not enough assets to pay the legacies and devises in a will, the rules of abatement are applied. First, specific legacies and devises are paid in full. Next, general or pecuniary legacies and devises are paid: these abate pro rata if the assets are insufficient to pay them in full.

Final Account

The last task of the personal representative is to prepare and file the personal representative's final account (called a *final return* in some states) with the court. Usually, only one account is filed; however, if an estate is open longer than a year, many states require an account to be filed annually, with a final account at the end.

The account is a listing of everything that the fiduciary has received and disbursed during the period covered by the account. With variations from state to state, a typical account lists receipts in one schedule, disbursements in another schedule, and the balance in a third schedule. If the account is final, no third schedule is necessary.

In some states, allowance of the final account by the court formally closes the estate. In other states, the personal representative files a petition for discharge which, when allowed, formally closes the estate. Even after an account is allowed, however, the court may correct manifest error in a judgment or revoke a judgment altogether if the judgment was obtained through fraud.

Informal Probate Proceedings

Informal probate proceedings may be used in most states when someone dies owning assets below a specific value set by state statute, or when there is no reason to have the court supervise all aspects of the estate's settlement. The UPC defines *informal proceedings* as those conducted without notice to interested persons by an officer of the court acting as a registrar for probate of a will.[13] Informal proceedings, sometimes referred to as *unsupervised administration*, are relatively simple, with a minimum amount of paperwork and bureaucratic involvement.

Ancillary Administration

A resident of one state often owns real and personal property in another state. After the decedent's death, the property in the other state must be recovered for the benefit of the decedent's estate and arrangements must be made for the payment of debts in that state. The term applied to this process is **ancillary administration**, meaning the administration of an estate in a state where a decedent owns property but is not domiciled.

ancillary administration   The administration of a decedent's estate in a state other than the one in which he or she lived, for the purpose of disposing of property he or she owned there.

Summary Questions

1. How is it decided who will inherit when the deceased did not have a will?
2. What are some advantages to having a will?
3. What are some types of property that are not considered to be part of the probate estate?
4. For inheritance purposes, how do modern state statutes treat adopted children?
5. In what ways may a will be revoked?
6. What court has primary jurisdiction to administer a decedent's estate?
7. What are one advantage and one disadvantage of a specific legacy?
8. What are the principal advantages and disadvantages to an irrevocable trust?
9. What is the primary purpose of all estate planning?
10. What is the purpose of the homestead exemption, and what does it do?
11. Why is a personal representative known as a fiduciary?
12. In general, what are the duties of a personal representative?

Practical Paralegal Skills

Use the facts from the following client information sheet to prepare a simple will for Sandra Jones that would meet the requirements of the statutes in your state.

Client Information Sheet

1. Name in full: Sandra K. Jones, also known as Sandra Kay Jones.
2. Residence: 123 Main Street, [Hometown], [Homestate] [Zip code].
3. Family information:
   Mother and Father—both deceased
   Husband—deceased
   Children:

   1. Andrea Jones   Seattle, Washington   Single, no children
   2. Marcia Cole   Boston, Massachusetts   Married, three children:
      Brian Cole, age 10
      James Cole, age 4
      Sarah Cole, age 2
   3. Elizabeth Hanson   Miami, Florida   Divorced, one child:
      Brian Hanson, age 9

   Brothers and Sisters: One brother, Henry Henderson   St. Paul, Minnesota
4. Type of Will: Simple will.
5. Specific Legacies: Wedding ring and engagement ring to Andrea Jones, if she survives.
6. Specific Devises: None.
7. General Legacy: None.

8. Demonstrative Legacy: None.

9. Residuary Clause: To three daughters, or to the children of deceased daughter, per stirpes.

10. Executor: Henry Henderson, St. Paul, Minnesota.
    Alternate: Andrea Jones.

11. Disposition of estate: Entire estate should be left to three daughters, equally, and to the grandchildren, per stirpes.

12. Personal property—auto, boat, airplane, objects of art, jewelry, household effects, stamp or coin collection, library.

Notes

For further reference, see *Administration of Wills, Trusts, and Estates,* by Gordon W. Brown (Delmar Publishers Inc. and Lawyers Cooperative Publishing 1993).

[1] Milano, Carol, "1993 *Legal Assistant Today* Salary Survey Results," *Legal Assistant Today* 48 (May/June 1993).

[2] UPC § 2-104.

[3] UPC § 1-201(17).

[4] UPC § 2-502.

[5] UPC § 2-505.

[6] UPC § 2-503.

[7] UPC § 2-507(c).

[8] 17 Am. Jur. *Legal Forms* 2d 251:122.

[9] UPC § 2-401.

[10] UPC § 2-402.

[11] UPC § 1-102.

[12] UPC § 1-201(15).

[13] UPC § 1-201(19).

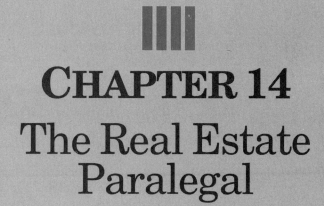

CHAPTER 14
The Real Estate Paralegal

The Role of Paralegals in Real Estate

Real estate law affects all of us at one time or another. Whether you are purchasing a new home or renting an apartment, the law of real estate will affect you. Real estate paralegals must be familiar with real estate law in their states, and with procedures affecting the transfer of real estate within the counties in which they work.

Real estate paralegals may work for law firms that specialize in commercial real estate transactions, or they may work for smaller firms that handle the transfer of residential real estate. They may also be employed by corporations that often deal in real estate, real estate development companies, title companies, or government agencies that transfer and record the titles to real estate.

Real Estate Paralegals in the United States

A significant number of paralegals in the United States specialize in the area of real estate. According to a 1993 *Legal Assistant Today* survey, approximately 6.5 percent of the respondents indicated that they work in real estate law. The salaries of those respondents who specialized in real estate law averaged $30,156, slightly above the average salary of all paralegals responding to the survey. The highest paid real estate paralegal responding to the survey had an annual salary of $58,000 during 1993.[1]

The Work of Real Estate Paralegals in the United States

The work of the real estate paralegal often involves title research, document preparation and review, and attendance at real estate closings. The real estate paralegal may also specialize in mortgage foreclosures. The following lists of some of the more common tasks that may be included in the job description of a real estate paralegal:

1. Research zoning ordinances and other laws relating to the transfer and use of real estate

2. Prepare land sales contracts
3. Order title work from title company
4. Review abstract or certificate of title
5. Research titles
6. Prepare maps of property based on legal description of property
7. Prepare draft of title opinions
8. Schedule closings
9. Prepare deeds
10. Prepare notes
11. Prepare mortgage
12. Review all documents prepared by other parties
13. Provide lender with necessary documentation
14. Attend closing to assist with document review and execution and the transfer of funds
15. Review title work
16. Disburse funds
17. File necessary documentation after closing.

Skills Important to the Real Estate Paralegal

Besides having a familiarity with the real estate law and customs in his or her area, the real estate paralegal must be very detail-oriented and have the ability to communicate very effectively and precisely. Because the real estate paralegal cannot be familiar with the pertinent law in all situations, legal research skills are also very important. The real estate paralegal must be able to properly define the situation and question at hand, and find an answer to that question.

Organizational skills can be equally important to real estate paralegals, who often find themselves working on commercial real estate transactions that involve numerous documents. The real estate paralegal is often responsible for orchestrating the commercial real estate closing and ensuring that all documents are properly prepared, executed, and filed. Paralegals working in the area of mortgage foreclosures are often responsible for keeping track of (and meeting) important deadlines.

Although attention to detail is important for every paralegal, it is of particular importance to the real estate paralegal, who is often asked to review legal descriptions and other title documentation that could be ineffective due to the slightest error.

Finally, real estate paralegals must know their way around the real estate recording systems in the state and counties in which they work. They should know where and how to file real estate documentation in the appropriate government authority's office.

An Introduction to Real Property

The discussion in this chapter is not confined to the statutes, codes, and ordinances concerning real property. It also takes a broader look at many aspects of real property in the United States. This section begins by defining real property, discussing the physical aspects of real property, and investigating the differences between real and personal property. It then explores the economic aspects of real property, the supply and demand of real property, and the uses of real property in the United States.

Real Estate and Real Property Defined

Real estate has two principal meanings. First, the term **real estate** means a piece of land that can be used for some purposes. It is usually referred to as a **parcel**. Note that when the term is used this way, it means the land. This piece of land can be used for farming, mining, ranching, an industrial plant, a shopping center, a school, a home, an apartment complex, or any other acceptable purpose. This way of referring to real property is the most common, colloquial way. There is a more technical meaning for the term *real estate*, however. In this meaning, *real estate* is a bundle of legal rights in relation to a particular parcel of land. Sometimes a distinction is made between the term *real property*, and the term *real estate*. When that distinction is being used, *real estate* means the land and *real property* means the bundle of legal rights. Most often, as in this chapter, they are used interchangeably.

The owner of real estate has several distinct rights, including:

1. The right to possess and occupy the property
2. The right to control the property, including determining how others can use it (such as by a lease or an easement)
3. The right to enjoy the property (*enjoy* means to make any legal use of the property, from planting flowers to drilling for oil)
4. The right to dispose of the property, such as by giving it away or selling it.

This bundle of legal rights applies to surface rights, subsurface rights, and **air rights**. In addition, there are also **water rights**. Water rights have become increasingly important because water is a scarce commodity in the western United States, where there is comparatively little rainfall, and it is important everywhere because of consumer and industrial use.

BALLENTINESBALLENTINESBALLENTINESBALLENTINESBALLENTINESBALLENTINESBALLENTINESBALLENTINESBALLENTINESBALLENTINESBALLENTINESBALLENTINESBALLENTINESBALLENTINES

real estate (real property)   1. Land, including things located on it or attached to it directly or indirectly. ... 2. [T]he interest a person has in land or his or her rights with respect to it.

parcel   A lot or tract of real estate.

air rights   The right to use the airspace above one's land.

water rights   An easement for the use of water or for the right to use another's premises to transport water over or through.

The Physical Aspects of Real Estate

Real estate has three important physical aspects. First, it does not move, so it is referred to as being *immobile*. Second, it is always there and cannot be destroyed, so it is referred to as *indestructible*. Third, each piece of real property is different from every other—if only because it is at a different location than any other piece—so it is referred to as having *uniqueness*, or the parcels are said to be *heterogeneous*, (all different from one another). Although the land cannot be moved, parts of it can be removed through the process of mining. However, even if the mining process produces the world's largest manmade hole, the land on which mining occurs does not actually go anywhere. Small pieces of land can disappear by a gradual wearing away (*erosion*) or by a catastrophic event like an earthquake or tidal wave (*avulsion*), but these events happen so infrequently that for our purposes land is permanent.

Real versus Personal Property

Property law began as law of real property. Originally, all property was real property. As time passed, however, important distinctions were made between real property and what came to be called **personal property**. Essentially, real property became whatever was land and whatever was permanently attached or affixed to the land; personal property became anything that was not real property. The original concept of personal property was that it was movable. Although that concept remains important in distinguishing **tangible** goods (things that can be touched, moved, bought, and sold, from computers to cars) from real property, the concept of personal property has gone beyond distinctions based on mere mobility.

A newer concept in personal property is **intangible** (cannot be touched) personal property.

DEFINING REAL ESTATE
Real estate is:
▪ Immobile
▪ Indestructible
▪ Unique
▪ Permanent

This aspect of personal property deals with property that cannot be seen or touched, but that carries ownership rights, usually represented by pieces of paper such as stock certificates, bonds, or letters patent issued by the Patent Office. For convenience, we speak as if those pieces of paper were the actual property. However, they are only the symbols of the property rights and claims to money.

Another important concept to recognize is that property can change in either direction between real property and personal property. If trees or crops are growing on land, they are part of the land—part of the real property. When they are **severed**, or disconnected from the land, they cease to be real property and become personal property. A distinction is made, however, between the plants growing on the real property over a period of more than a year—trees, bushes, grasses—and vegetation that is planted annually, such as crops. Plants growing on real property over a period of more than a year are considered to be a part of the real estate. Plants that are planted by someone's labor, usually annually, though considered part of the real property until their harvest, are the personal property of the planter, because everyone knows they will be severed and removed from the property. If the land is sold, crops may be disposed of separately from the real property, but any trees on the land would pass to the new owner without any question. If crops are not separately disposed of by

BALLENTINESBALLENTINESBALLENTINESBALLENTINESBALLENTINESBALLENTINESBALLENTINESBALLENTINESBALLENTINESBALLENTINESBALLENTINESBALLENTINESBALLENTINESBALLENTINESBALLENTINES

personal property   All property other than real property, including … tangible … and intangible property.

tangible property   Property, real or personal, that has physical substance; property that can be physically possessed.

intangible property   Property that has no intrinsic value, but evidences something of value.

severance   The act of detaching things affixed to the land.

contract, they are transferred with the real property. Another example of real property becoming personal property is the mineral deposit that is brought to the surface. For instance, the pool of oil underground is real property, but when it comes to the surface and into the pipeline, it becomes personal property.

Clearly, the distinction here is between being attached to—being part of the land—and being severed or separate from the land. That change is the point at which an item of real property becomes personal property. This process can occur in the other direction as well. A piece of personal property can come onto the real property and become permanently attached to the land and thereby become real property. When a building is constructed, it comes onto the property in its component parts—such as concrete mix for the foundation, water, lumber, nails, screws, electrical wiring, and plumbing pipes—as personal property. When the building is finished, all these elements have become part of the real property. The completed building is permanently attached to the real estate and is a permanent improvement on real estate.

The Economic Aspects of Real Property

Real estate has traditionally been an abundant resource in America. With millions of square miles and billions of acres, the sheer amount of land in the United States is staggering. It was considered abundant and cheap when there were few people wanting it. During the westward expansion (1600–1900), historians have noted that most land was originally taken up for speculative purposes. It was not originally settled by pioneer families. Instead, speculators bought it from the government and resold it to settlers, many of whom were simply smaller scale speculators who later resold the land to someone who may have cleared it of trees or put up the first buildings. In most of these transactions, the purpose of acquiring the

land was to make money on the resale of the land, not to occupy it as a home, farm, or business site.

Much of the development of American real estate has had its basis in turnover and resale for a profit. This use is one of the major economic aspects of the real estate business. Many prominent and great Americans, including George Washington, have been involved in this business. Today, however, undeveloped land is not readily available for speculative purposes, because the good land has already been settled. What remains is mostly desert, mountain, or far from desirable jobs and cities. Most of today's speculation is in and around cities.

During 1989, more than 1.3 million people in this country were employed in real-estate-related jobs, including many paralegals employed by companies whose sole purpose is investment in real estate and/or its development. Real estate investment and development are incredibly big businesses in this country.

This business is founded in certain qualities of real estate. First, it is a *scarce commodity*, because it is unique. Second, its value is affected by the use to which it can be put. That use many times is determined by the **improvements** that have been added to the real property. A house, an apartment building, a factory, or a shopping center change the nature of the land's use and thus its value. The term *improvement* has two meanings. First, it refers to anything that is a permanent addition to the real property, from a fence to a skyscraper. Second, *improved property* means that the parcel of property has access to utilities and roads; such items as water, electricity, gas, and sewerage are available for the owner or user of that parcel of land. *Unimproved land*, sometimes called *raw land,* lacks access to these elements; its value is generally less than that of improved land.

Another aspect of real property is that it takes a lot of money to buy it and to make improvements on it. Because the land and improvements will remain unchanged for a long time, a land investment

improvement   Anything that enhances the value of real property permanently.

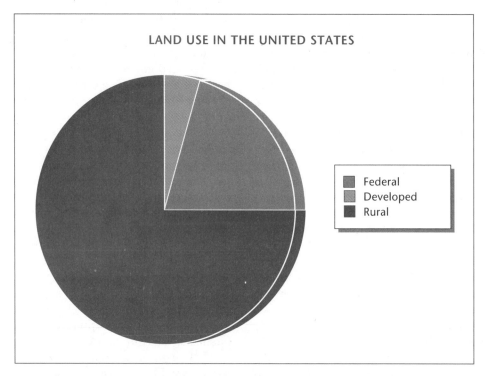

LAND USE IN THE UNITED STATES

■ Federal
■ Developed
■ Rural

About 75 percent of the land in the United States is devoted to rural uses.

is considered a permanent investment. Frequently buyers increase both their investment and the value of the property. The land itself rarely **depreciates** (declines in value), because it does not change; it is always there, immobile and indestructible. The improvements to the land (usually buildings) will depreciate over a long time, usually 10 to 50 years or even longer. Nevertheless, land can **appreciate** (increase in value) and demand, speculation, scarcity, a growing population, or other economic factors or conditions can affect the value of real property so that its current price rises or falls.

A final basic aspect of real estate economics is site preference. The traditional real estate sales rule expressing the importance of site preference is: "What are the first three rules of selling real estate? Location, location, and location." There are desirable ("hot") areas to live in and to build in.

Since 1950, the industrial heartland of the Northeast and the Great Lakes areas have not been hot, but the states of California, Texas, and Florida have been. These three states now comprise close to a quarter of America's population, its largest cities, its greatest industrial strength, and some of its worst pollution problems.

This type of population shift because of site preference is on the largest scale, but home purchase decisions are often determined by the availability of schools, churches, transportation, inexpensive water, and a myriad of other factors. For businesses, site preference can be determined by many other factors, such as taxation, labor force cost and quality, support systems, transportation, and proximity to markets. Of all the individual factors involved in a selection, site preference is considered the single most important one.

BALLENTINESBALLENTINESBALLENTINESBALLENTINESBALLENTINESBALLENTINESBALLENTINESBALLENTINESBALLENTINESBALLENTINESBALLENTINESBALLENTINESBALLENTINESBALLENTINES

depreciation   The lessening in worth of any property caused by wear, use, time, or obsolescence.
appreciate   To rise in value.

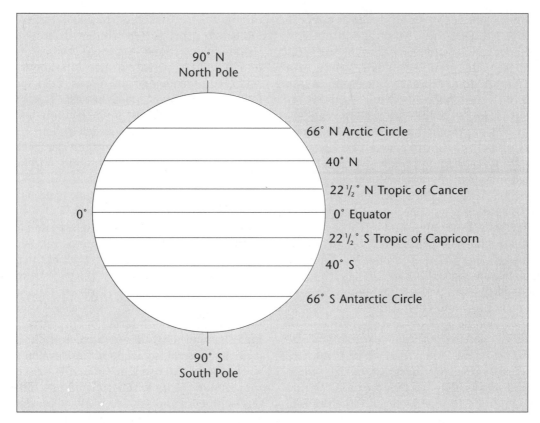

Parallels Parallels run horizontally across the globe.

There are five basic types of real estate:

1. Residential, ranging from single-family residences to condominium units in a high rise

2. Business real estate, which can be either (a) commercial (generally for investment purposes) or (b) industrial, which can range from mining to manufacturing to warehousing

3. Rural land uses, such as farming, grazing, forest and lumber production, and sometimes recreational facility use

4. Special purpose land uses, such as churches, hospitals, and many educational institutions

5. Public uses, ranging from water purification plants to courthouses.

Evaluations of real property, called **appraisals**, are based on these different land uses. Each different use requires a different evaluation method, because the objectives of the owners differ substantially. Differences in appraisal methods also reflect the different types of interests that real estate owners may have in their property.

Real Estate Transactions: Supply and Demand

If you work in real estate, your job will depend upon the economics of the real estate business. Although it is not a technical legal matter, economics often determines what can be done and the direction the law will take.

appraisal Valuation; a determination of the worth or value of something.

Economics has a number of laws that apply to real estate transactions, including supply and demand laws and pricing rules. For instance, increased real estate demand usually produces a greater supply, and decreased demand causes the supply to go down—albeit quite slowly, because real estate properties are relatively inflexible. If a lot of people have a lot of money available and they want to spend it on housing, the supply of housing will expand to meet that demand. Sometimes, a greater supply can expand demand. For instance, large amounts of cheap, affordable housing may stimulate buyer demand. Price often reflects supply. The less there is of an object, the higher the price. That rule explains why homes costing $10 million have fewer buyers than homes that cost $100,000.

Outside factors can control or stimulate the real estate market as well. One of these, the cost of money, has long been a key factor in slowing or encouraging the construction business and the entire real estate industry. When interest rates are low, real estate sales are much better than when the cost of funds is high. Another factor is speculative buying and selling, which can force the real estate market up. However, the consequence of such speculation usually is that the market suffers a severe fall, because the prices have risen beyond any economic basis for such high prices.

Another factor that affects the real estate market is the number of people who can afford to buy the product. High-paying jobs, ample disposable income, and an interest in home ownership all stimulated the home construction and resale market from 1945 to the 1980s. With fewer high-paying jobs, and with monthly mortgage payments representing an enormous proportion of the would-be owners' disposable income, the nature of the business is bound to change significantly.

The Uses of Real Estate in the United States

The real estate industry has been a very large one and a key component of economic prosperity in America since the end of World War II. It is seen by many economists as a bellwether for the economy in general, so that what happens in real estate often is a precursor of what will happen in the economy as a whole. America's real estate is primarily held in private ownership (about 60 percent), and various governments, principally the federal government, hold the rest. The large proportion of government land holdings is because much land in the West is desert and has little economic use. Agricultural land use is the largest by far. Crop land, grazing land, and forest account for close to 75 percent of the land usage. Only 2–3 percent of our land use is accounted for by cities and urban development.

The vast variety of real estate uses and activities has created a real estate business that is complex and diverse in its activities. Think of the multiple types of skills required to perform certain needed activities in real estate. First, one must know where the land is. A surveyor meets that need by measuring the boundaries of the parcel of land and placing the results on a piece of paper called a *survey*. Second, someone has to develop the land so that it can be used, or subdivide existing land into smaller units for specialized use. Then various engineers and architects are necessary to design a building and tie it into the society's social systems and services, which range from water and sewerage to electronics and pollution control.

All these elements cost money. Multiple types of financing may be used. The range of financing possibilities runs from banks, savings and loan associations, and secondary mortgage market placements to sophisticated syndications and financings arranged in the bond, stock, and other financial markets. Afterward, the actual construction work must be done under the guidance of a general contractor, usually with the assistance of a number of specialized subcontractors. The variety of construction workers involved in creating multiple types of buildings seems almost endless. Common to many construction activities are carpenters, roofers, electricians, plumbers, concrete workers, and general laborers, who do a variety of tasks from putting up wallboard to cleaning up afterward. After construction is completed, specialized property managers or caretakers may be needed if the owner does not occupy the premises.

The number of paralegals employed in the real estate industry also depends on the real estate market. When real estate sales are high, many more paralegals are needed, especially in title insurance companies, real estate development companies, and law firms that handle a high volume of real estate transactions.

The Legal Description of Real Property

Because real estate paralegals are often responsible for drafting documents to transfer real property, they must have a precise means for describing that property. Real property is described by one of several methods.

Legal descriptions can sometimes appear confusing. However, the crucial point to keep in mind is that precise location is the essence of what the law and the land owner want to achieve. With this precision, the amount of land and the location of land can be determined so exactly that there should be no need for a later dispute of the matter. This result permits greater public peace and fewer legal actions to clog our courts.

This section focuses on how the system of surveying and describing land came about and how and why it developed. It also explains the commonly used American surveying systems. It is important that real estate paralegals be familiar with legal descriptions and the methods commonly used for legal descriptions in the areas in which they work. Often paralegals will review legal descriptions from a client's deed or property title. They may be asked to map out the property being described to better illustrate the property for the client.

Introduction

The purpose of legal description is to determine, precisely, where one property begins and the next one ends. In other words, the legal description establishes boundaries that all parties can agree upon, that are easily identified, and that are unlikely to create a basis for later dispute.

In medieval England, where our body of real estate law began, one of the original units of property was called a *hyde* or a *hide*. A *hyde* was an area adequate to support a minor noble who had a manor house. This area included sufficient people to work the land and do all the things necessary to produce the crops to support the fighting men who were essential to protect the people from domestic gangs, robbers, and foreign invaders. The actual amount of land varied by its fertility and productivity.

Another medieval method of land description set boundaries by natural objects. This method would set a description from the "large oak tree to the middle of the creek and down to where the creek turns and then to the top of the hill and then back to the oak tree." Although roughly accurate, this system encountered a number of problems, such as the movement of natural objects. What happens when the oak tree dies or the creek bed changes direction?

These simple and natural methods were usually adequate, but they were imprecise, and by the 18th century, scientific developments had progressed so that various surveying methods replaced the natural methods. To understand the precision that surveying can provide for legal description, it is necessary to know some basics about our globe and what surveying does.

Our planet is roughly a sphere with a circumference of approximately 25,000 miles at the equator. Although it is a three-dimensional object, we are dealing with its surface in the measurements we want to make. We think of the surface

BALLENTINESBALLENTINESBALLENTINESBALLENTINESBALLENTINESBALLENTINESBALLENTINESBALLENTINESBALLENTINESBALLENTINESBALLENTINESBALLENTINESBALLENTINESBALLENTINESBALLENTINES

legal description   In deeds and mortgages, a description of the real estate that is the subject of the conveyance, by boundaries, distances, and size, or by reference to maps, surveys, or plats.

as circular because standing on the earth and viewing an unobstructed horizon (as at sea on a calm day) lets the viewer see the circular curve of the earth. Like a circle, our earth has 360 degrees. Each degree going north or south is about 70 miles, and each degree unit is called a *parallel*. New York and Chicago are close to 40 degrees north of the equator. With this scheme we can find ourselves anywhere on a north–south line on the earth. How can we find ourselves on an east–west line? Eventually, a fixed point (Greenwich, England, for the English-speaking peoples of the world; Paris, France, for the French) was agreed upon as 0 degrees. One set of lines went west from Greenwich 180 degrees and the other set went east from Greenwich 180 degrees. Thus, the 360 degrees of a circle are achieved. These lines are called *meridians*.

This pattern of parallels and meridians sets a grid over the face of the earth. However, the area included in any rectangle made by one degree of a parallel and a meridian is thousands of square miles and is not very precise. Each degree, symbolized by an °, can be broken down into 60 minutes, symbolized by ′, and each minute can be broken down into 60 seconds, symbolized by ″. Thus, a *minute* is about one mile, 293 yards; a *second* becomes about 34.22 yards, or a little more than one-third the length of a football field. This precision allows ships to sail and planes to fly across the oceans without worrying about where they are when out of sight of land. Today, increased precision allows ships to be pinpointed by satellite to within a few feet and allows intercontinental missiles to arrive at their targets with almost pinpoint accuracy, regardless of whether they were launched from land, air, or beneath the sea.

Commonly Used American Surveying Systems

In modern real estate descriptions, three basic methods are used for land that is not covered in a plat of survey. The first is the metes and bounds system; the second is the government or rectangular survey system; the third is a subcategory for smaller areas or developments and is called the plat method.

Metes and Bounds

The **metes and bounds** method gets a very precise result in the hands of a competent surveyor. The surveyor takes a point of beginning (POB) and determines the line of due north—south that runs through it. Then a straight line, called a *bearing,* is determined to the next point. This bearing is a reading from a compass and is also called a *compass direction* or *compass bearing*. The direction (called an *angle*) of that line is described in terms of the compass direction in which it goes and in terms of its length. Thus, a line could go at (have a bearing of) an angle of 36 degrees, 25 minutes, and 15 seconds west of due south for 275.51 feet. That statement is abbreviated as "S. 36°x25′, and 15″ W. 275.51." This process is repeated from point to point around the perimeters of the property until the point of beginning is reached again. (Note that the abbreviation for a foot of distance (′) is the same as the abbreviation for a minute of surveying direction (′). Don't confuse them; you must rely upon context to tell the difference. This technique is somewhat similar to the connect-the-dots game that children play. Originally, the points were often natural objects, such as "the big boulder." Once the surveyor has established that the line is a certain angle and runs a certain distance, the physical points do not have to be maintained, because they can be recreated at any time by any other surveyor. The following is a sample metes and bounds legal description:

> All that tract or parcel of land situated in the town of Bigge City, County of Alpha, State of Wisconsin, bounded and described as follows: Beginning at the junction of the easterly line of Main Street and the southerly line of Elm Street and running thence north 60 degrees east 535 and 87/100s feet; thence, 90 degrees due east 847 and 79/100s feet along the land of the Town of Bigge City to the land of Karen C. Anderson;

BALLENTINESBALLENTINESBALLENTINESBALLENTINESBALLENTINESBALLENTINESBALLENTINESBALLENTINESBALLENTINESBALLENTINESBALLENTINESBALLENTINESBALLENTINESBALLENTINES

metes and bounds   A property description, commonly in a deed or mortgage, that is based upon the property's boundaries and the natural objects and other markers on the land.

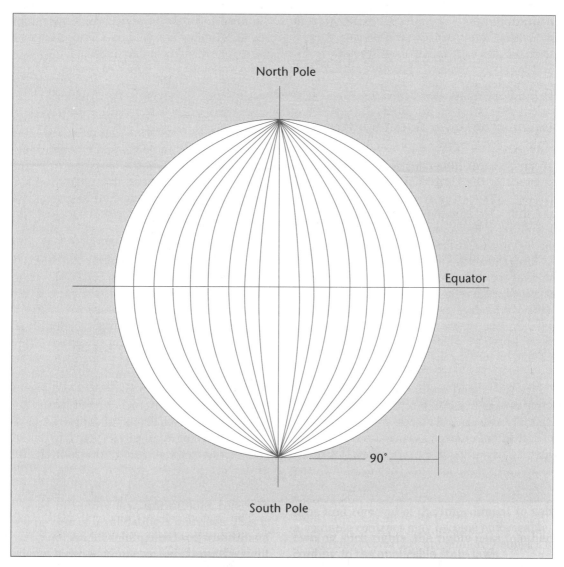

Meridians Meridians run from pole to pole on the globe. Measurements are made up of 180 degrees east and 180 degrees west of the 0 degree location.

then, south 30 degrees east 575 and 92/100s feet along the land of the aforesaid Karen C. Anderson to the land of Robert E. Smith; thence south 59 degrees 59 minutes 48 seconds 1023 and 88/100 feet along the land of the aforesaid Robert E. Smith to Main Street; thence north 39 degrees 59 minutes 57 seconds 864 feet along Elm Street to the point or place of beginning.

Containing an hypothetical measurement per a fictional survey dated January 15, 1995, of Daniel John Stevens 18.6589 acres. Anytown, Wisconsin.

Today, artificial objects, such as streets, fences, or stakes, have been added to natural objects as points of reference. Both types together are referred to as **monuments**. The main drawback to this method is that it does not remain precise. Monuments can change. It is not used frequently today and is used primarily when the value of the property is not great.

Rectangular or Government Survey System

The *rectangular* or **government survey** system covers much of the United States. Our national government created this system to encourage settlement in the old Northwest Territories (parts of Ohio, and all of Indiana, Illinois, Michigan, and Wisconsin) in the early 1780s. The area was immense, and the settlement was done slowly over the next 50 years. To ensure that the hundreds of thousands of settlers had clear title to their property, this system had to be accurate, precise, and verifiable by a surveyor at any time.

The rectangular survey system is based upon the standard global grid that consists of parallels and meridians. The survey system determines the base lines (parallels) and meridians. The intersection of a base line and a principal meridian is selected. The system is laid out as follows: Starting at that initial intersection point, the surveyors measure 24 miles north, 24 miles west, 24 miles south, and 24 miles east until they have enclosed an area of 576 square miles. This largest of the surveying boxes is called a *check* or a *quadrangle*. It is broken down into 16 **townships** of 6 miles on a side or 36 square miles each. Each township is broken down into 36 **sections** of one square mile each. Each section is broken down into 640 **acres**.

The meridians, as can be seen on the global grid, all converge on the poles, so their lines curve toward each other. To avoid the problem of declining distance toward the poles, guide meridians are set at 24-mile intervals east and west from the principal meridian and are adjusted at every standard parallel north or south of the base line. In this manner, each check is corrected at its boundaries so that it remains close to square.

Each section is designated by its position in relation to the base line and principal meridian. The designation in north–south terms is by *tiers*, as in "Tier 1 North of the base line"; the designation in east–west terms is by *ranges*, as in "Range 4 West of the Third Principal Meridian." "Tier 1 North of the base line" simply means that the townships that sit directly north of the base line are in the first tier or layer north of it. Tier 2 North would be the second layer north; Tier 3 South would be the third layer south of the base line. The same process works for the ranges east and west of the principal meridian.

A legal description begins by identifying the smallest possible area that describes the property and then shows its placement in successively larger patterns. For instance, "the northern one-half of the northeast one-quarter of the northeast one-quarter of Section 3, Tier 3 South, Range 3 East of the Third Principal Meridian, in Smith County, State of Minnesota." Note how the section, range, and tier are used to describe the general area. Now that the section can be identified, a different system is used within the section. That system is based on the 640 acres in the section.

The first step is to quarter the 640 acres into 160-acre units. These are simply described as the northwest, northeast, southeast, or southwest quarters of the section. Each quarter-section is then broken down into quarters again or into halves. A half of a quarter-section would have 80 acres in it, whereas a quarter of a quarter-section

---

BALLENTINESBALLENTINESBALLENTINESBALLENTINESBALLENTINESBALLENTINESBALLENTINESBALLENTINESBALLENTINESBALLENTINESBALLENTINESBALLENTINESBALLENTINES

monument   With respect to real estate, a physical object, whether natural or artificial, on the ground that establishes a boundary line.

government survey   The survey of lands in the public domain, conducted by the federal government, under which land is laid out in townships, sections, and quarter sections.

township   As laid out by government survey, a tract of land six miles square.

section   A ... parcel of land consisting of 640 acres as laid out by government survey.

acre   Measure of land containing 160 square rods, 4,840 square yards (160 square rods or 43,560 square feet).

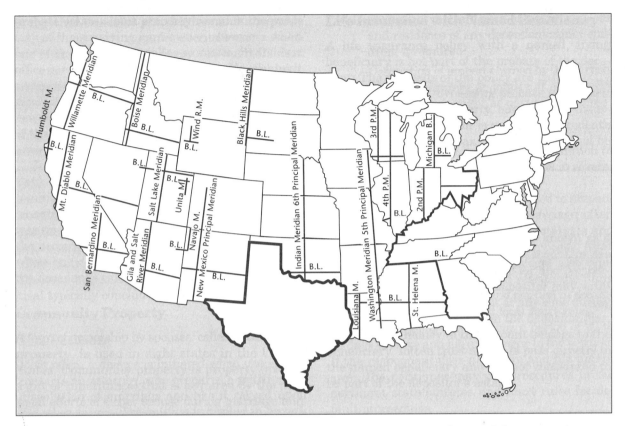

Rectangular or Government Survey System Map of the United States showing layout of the rectangular method. Not all meridians are shown.

would have 40 acres. Those quarter-sections of quarter-sections can themselves be divided into quarters, in the same manner, so that there are 10-acre units. One-half of one of those units would be five acres. Note the logic of the progression to smaller units.

Although the government survey system works well for large areas such as farms and ranches, it is very awkward to use in urban areas because of the tiny portions of real estate owned by one person. This problem is met by using both the government survey system and an additional device called a plat of survey.

Plat of Survey

The **plat** of survey is extremely useful for further subdividing under the government survey system. For example, a large area of land, say 40 acres, that can be identified on the government survey system as the SE ¼ of the SE ¼ of an identified section is going to be developed into homes. The developer buys that parcel of land and hires a surveyor, who lays the 40 acres out into *blocks* that are bounded by streets. Within each block, *lots* for the homes are surveyed and their boundaries are established. The surveyor identifies the

plat A map of a tract of land, showing the boundaries of the streets, blocks, and numbered lots.

blocks and the lots by a numbering system. The developer names the area "Green Acres." The surveyor prepares a map that shows the preceding information, plus where the sewers, power lines, gas pipes, and other utilities will be placed, and other information that will be needed for this development. This map is called a *plat of survey*. The plat is recorded in the local office where deeds are recorded. The legal description of a particular lot might be "Lot 6 in Block 5 in Green Acres, a subdivision of the SE 1/4 of the SE 1/4 of Section 12 of Township 4 … ."

The plat of survey (sometimes also called the *lot and block method*) becomes the final breakdown of area unless there is vacant land in this plat that can be further subdivided. The plat will often assign numbers to lots and a name to the subdivision, and will include the date of the survey, the name of the surveyor, and the subdivider.

Fixtures

When drafting documents to transfer real property, it is important for all parties to be in complete understanding regarding exactly what is included in the transfer. Fixtures are supposed to be included, but deciding what is a fixture and whether it is part of the deal are common problems.

Fixtures are sometimes difficult to understand because they blur the distinction between real and personal property. Technically, a *fixture* is a piece of personal property that is so closely attached to real property that it ceases being personal property and becomes an inseparable part of the real property. A fixture begins its life as a piece of personal property, but through its use, it becomes a part of the real property. Thus, the law governing that particular item starts out as the law of personal property, but once the item has been attached to or associated with the piece of real estate, it becomes subject to the law of real estate. The legal issue usually is whether the item of personal property has become so irrevocably attached to the real property that it has become part of the real property and is now itself real property. It is easy to see why there are many conflicts in this area.

The parties in conflict are those who claim an interest in the disputed piece of property; the dispute concerns whether it is a fixture. These parties are often (1) the financier–lender who supplied the money to purchase the fixture item or to purchase the building, and (2) the landlord–building owner, and (3) the tenant. Residential examples of fixtures are the new, wall-to-wall carpeting or the under-the-counter dishwasher that the tenant has installed. Most fixture disputes deal with commercial items, usually equipment, because these items have a higher value. Ultimately, the question is whether the item must be left behind as a fixture when the tenant leaves, or whether the tenant may take it along as an item of personal property.

Consider the following example. Jane Carter leases a building to make industrial equipment. A tool and die machine is brought into the factory dismantled and is then assembled in place and bolted to the floor. The cost of the machine was $575,000, and it has a 25-year life span. After five years, Jane finds a better location and plans to remove the machine, but the landlord sues her, claiming that the machine is a fixture and a permanent part of the building. Who wins? Now, add to the complexity the fact that Jane is financing the machine through her bank or some other long-term commercial financier on an installment

BALLENTINESBALLENTINESBALLENTINESBALLENTINESBALLENTINESBALLENTINESBALLENTINESBALLENTINESBALLENTINESBALLENTINESBALLENTINESBALLENTINESBALLENTINES

fixture An article, previously personal property, that, by being physically affixed to real estate, has become part of the real property; something so connected to a structure for use in connection with it that it cannot be removed without doing injury to the structure.

loan and that that party has a perfected security interest in the machine. Finally, add the element that the landlord is buying the building through a commercial loan and its mortgagee regards the machine as an asset that belongs to the building. The mortgagee's recorded mortgage on the property covers any additions to the real property as assets included in the mortgage. The case of *C.I.T. Financial Services v. Premier Corp.*[2] demonstrates just this type of complicated situation, and shows that disputes concerning the nature of property that may be considered either real or personal can be very complex and often lead to litigation.

C.I.T. FINANCIAL SERVICES,
Appellee,
v.
PREMIER CORPORATION,
DEFENDANT,
and
BancOklahoma Agri-Service, Corporation,
Third-Party Defendant/Appellant.
No. 63504.
Supreme Court of Oklahoma.
Oct. 20, 1987.

The occupant of a double-wide mobile home went bankrupt. This lawsuit is between two creditors, each claiming a lien against the mobile home. If we determine the mobile home to be personal property, then the original purchase money lender will prevail unless its lien has lapsed. If we determine it to be a part of the real estate, then the later mortgagee (who had no notice of the earlier transaction) can get in ahead of the original lender. We hold as a matter of law upon the undisputed facts of this case that the mobile home became a part of the realty, and that the later mortgagee is not bound by the original purchaser's agreement that the property would remain as personal property.

The essential facts are these. On December 29, 1978 Premier Corporation purchased a mobile home in which C.I.T. Financial Services (plaintiff and appellee) took a security interest by assignment of the installment sales contract. In that contract Premier agreed not to make the mobile home a part of any real estate. C.I.T. recorded its financing statement (U.C.C. 1) in the county treasurer's office, but it did not record the sales contract (with the above mentioned provision) nor did it attempt to comply with the filing requirements where one takes a security interest in fixtures.

Premier placed the mobile home on land which it owned. It affixed it to a foundation of poured cement footings, cinder blocks, and metal skirting. It was so attached with bolts and steel straps, and, according to plaintiff's witness, an anchor in the ground. The wheels were removed. Front and back concrete steps were attached. The home was hooked up to gas, electricity, water, and telephone lines, and to a septic tank. It contains 1960 square feet, and has never been removed from its foundation.

The legal status of a pre-fabricated home under these circumstances is a question of first impression for this court. The basic question is simply this: Must the law treat this mobile home as real property or as personal property?

[Okla. Stat. tit. 60, § 7 (1981)]

> A thing is deemed to be affixed to land when it is attached to it by roots, as in case of trees, lines, or shrubs, or embedded in it, as in the case of walls, or permanently resting upon it, as in the case of buildings, or permanently attached to what is thus permanent, by means of cement, plaster, nails, bolts or screws.

This court has identified three factors to consider in determining whether an item is a fixture and thus not removable: (1) The actual or constructive annexation to the realty, or something appurtenant thereto, (2) the appropriateness to the use or purpose of that part of the realty with which it is connected, and (3) the intention of the party making the annexation to make it a permanent accession to the freehold.

Although there are no Oklahoma decisions determining whether a mobile home affixed to a permanent foundation is a fixture, other courts, applying the three-part test applicable in Oklahoma, have found such homes to be fixtures. ...

Reexamination of the three-part test mentioned at the outset shows that the first two are easily satisfied here: (1) the actual annexation to the realty was done in a seemingly permanent fashion, and (2) the appropriateness of the use of the annexed property to the land is met by its use as a farm house on the land being farmed. The third item required for consideration is the intent of the annexer, in this case, Premier Corporation, the original purchaser.

On the intent question C.I.T. places great reliance on the words appearing in the original sales contract: "The commodity will remain personal property and will not become part of my real estate." ... Although a court would normally enforce such a provision as between the parties to the agreement, such provision is of de minimis effect in determining an issue between third parties not bound thereby.

That the provision is not binding on the parties here is abundantly clear.

Considering (1) the manner by which the mobile home was affixed to the foundation and the earth, (2) the use to which it was put, and (3) what we perceive to have been objective, physical actions present in securing the property to the land, we conclude that as a matter of law the test is met, and the mobile home must be adjudged a fixture to the real estate, and not a mere chattel.

At times, even when the building owner and the possible fixture owner are the same person, it can be important to determine whether the item is a fixture or personal property, for property tax or accounting purposes. The primary tests of whether a piece of personal property (usually equipment) has become a fixture are (1) how it is attached; (2) the manner of its adaptation; (3) the removability of the item; and (4) the intent the parties indicated at the time of attachment. The *attachment issue* concerns whether the item has become so much a part of the building that it is essential to the building's use. Windows and heating ducts are examples of fixtures in buildings; a building cannot be used without them. The *adaptation issue* is how specifically tailored the piece of equipment is to the building. Screen and storm windows and curtains cut for that particular window both serve as examples of fixtures. In addition, if a building was constructed around a particular piece of heavy industrial equipment, that equipment would appear to be a fixture. The *removability issue* refers to the ease with which the item can be removed from the premises and the potential damage to the premises due to removal of the item. The *intention issue* deals with what the parties thought would be the use of the piece of property. This is the most important single determinant of whether an item is a fixture. Whatever the parties agreed upon—one hopes in writing—will settle the issue. Risks arise when no one agrees upon what that piece of personal property will be before it is installed.

It is important not to confuse a true fixture with a **trade fixture**. Trade fixtures are the property of a business tenant who places them in the building, but their method of attachment is so much less permanent that they are not fixtures. Generally, trade fixtures are personal property and remain the tenant's property. A true fixture added or affixed to the building by a tenant, however, becomes the property of the landlord and remains behind when the tenant moves out at the end of the lease.

Recording Real Estate Documents in the Public Records

Real estate paralegals are often involved in several aspects of real estate transfers. They may research the title to the property to ensure that the buyer will be purchasing a clear title; prepare the proper deeds to transfer the property; and record the transfer documents with the appropriate city, county, or state authority. Depending on the jurisdiction, real estate transfers may have little meaning until the necessary documentation is recorded with the proper authority.

Even when a parcel of land is properly described, it is necessary that no other party who might be interested in that parcel of property or the owner of any adjacent property be misled. Parties who have a need to know about a parcel include government authorities, for taxing, zoning, and other public purposes; prospective creditors; prospective buyers; utility companies; and a number of others. To protect an interest in a property, it is **recorded**. This action provides others with **constructive notice** of the interests being claimed.

The first document commonly recorded is the one giving the owner his or her rights in the property, a **deed**. If there is a plat of survey, that document is also recorded by the developer who had the plat created to define the boundaries of the property being developed. The plat of survey may contain restrictions that place limitations on the use of land in the subdivision. The claims of third parties are also recorded. These are usually the claims of creditors, and range from persons who do work on the property and file notices of **mechanic's liens** to the lenders who financed the purchase of the home with a note and mortgage. The list of other documents that may be filed is endless.

A number of different recording systems must be checked to determine who has claims on the real property. There is a system called the *grantor-grantee index* (also called a *cross index* because it cross-references various parties with claims to the property). It shows who has had the title to and interests in the searched parcel of real estate up to the present. Thus, a title search can be done from this system. The grantor gives title to the grantee; in the next transfer, that grantee becomes the grantor to the subsequent grantee. This system is arranged alphabetically by the last names of the grantor and the grantee.

▪ Garden bulbs, plants, shrubs, and trees
▪ Storm sashes, storm doors, screens, and awnings
▪ Window shades, blinds, traverse and curtain and drapery rods
▪ Attached lighting fixtures and bulbs
▪ Plumbing fixtures, water heater, heating plants, furnaces
▪ Built-in air conditioning equipment, electronic air filter
▪ Attached television antenna, cable television jacks and wiring
▪ Built-in dishwashers, garbage disposals, trash compactors, ovens, cooktop stoves, microwave ovens, hood fans, intercoms
▪ Attached carpeting, mirrors, garage door openers and all controls, smoke detectors, and fireplace screens, doors, and heatilators

Items Commonly Considered to be Residential Fixtures Fixtures are any personal property that has been permanently affixed to real property.

The *tract system* is based on legal descriptions. Each transaction is tied to a specific legal description. Often, under a subdivision with various numbered lots, each lot will have a separate entry. Each successive owner is listed under that entry.

Creditors' mortgages are usually filed in a *mortgagor-mortgagee index*, although sometimes they are filed directly in the grantor-grantee index. First the lien document is filed, and then, when the lien is satisfied, the satisfaction or release is filed. Often, the mortgagee-creditor returns the satisfaction or release to the mortgagor-debtor and lets the former debtor file the document.

BALLENTINESBALLENTINESBALLENTINESBALLENTINESBALLENTINESBALLENTINESBALLENTINESBALLENTINESBALLENTINESBALLENTINESBALLENTINESBALLENTINESBALLENTINESBALLENTINES

trade fixtures Articles attached to leased premises by the tenant to aid him or her in carrying on his or her trade or business. Unlike residential fixtures, the tenant is free to remove trade fixtures upon termination or expiration of the lease.

record To file or deposit a document or instrument for recording.

constructive notice Circumstances such that the law considers that actual notice took place, regardless of whether it did; a substitute for actual notice based upon a presumption of notice which is so strong that the law does not permit it to be contradicted.

deed A document by which real property, or an interest in real property is conveyed from one person to another.

mechanic's lien A lien created by law for the purpose of securing payment for work performed or materials furnished in constructing or repairing a building or other structure.

Another real estate recordkeeping system in urban areas shows all the plats of survey and the plans for development in each area. It can be closely tied into a tract system, and it has the advantage of allowing one to determine what the boundaries of the property are, what buildings are on it, and what easements affect the property.

Finally, there are *fixture filings* in the real property records. Under Article 9 of the Uniform Commercial Code (the UCC), filings for fixtures are to be made in the real estate records where a mortgage would be filed.

In addition to these title records, there are additional records that can affect real property rights. There are various taxing authorities, ranging from the federal and state governments to local authorities, that can include a number of governmental agencies. There can be special assessments for special projects affecting the parcel of real property. There can be pending suits in courts that have jurisdiction over the owner or over the property, and one must make a **lis pendens** search to determine the existence of those suits. In addition, there can be special property use restrictions from zoning boards, construction and building codes, land use plans, environmental requirements, and subdivision limitations and regulations. Checking these records is referred to as *searching the record*. It is essential to search and to have searches brought current at the time of any transfer. Most times title is "brought down" one last time on the day of closing to ensure that there are no new impediments to the closing or surprises occurring after the prior search but before the actual closing and transfer of title.

The Torrens System

Where documentation for a certain piece of real estate is filed may depend on whether the property is considered to be abstract property or Torrens property. In the late 19th century, an Australian, Sir Robert Torrens, invented a new system of providing public, constructive notice about real estate transactions. That system, named for him, is called the **Torrens System**. It is used principally in large metropolitan areas such as New York City, Boston, Chicago, and Minneapolis-St. Paul, but Torrens statutes have been adopted in a number of states.

Property is initially transferred to the Torrens System through a court proceeding wherein the landowner applies to the court for title transfer. To obtain the transfer, the landowner presents to the court an application listing all the parties that have interests in the land. Any party to the suit may contest it. If the applicant proves that he or she is the owner, the court so finds, lists the encumbrances and restrictions on the title, and orders an official called a Registrar of Titles to register the title and issue a **Certificate of Title**.

Subsequent transfers of Torrens property occur when the proper documentation is filed with the Registrar of Titles, who then destroys the previous Certificate of Title and issues a new Certificate of Title in the name of the new owner. The owners of Torrens property customarily are issued an Owner's Duplicate Certificate of Title, which serves as proof of their ownership of the property.

Recording Priority

Timely filing of documents after a real estate closing can be of the utmost importance. In some instances, it may be necessary to file documents proving ownership of the property before another claim on the property can be recorded. Recording priority is decided by state statute. There are three main types of statutes regarding priority

BALLENTINESBALLENTINESBALLENTINESBALLENTINESBALLENTINESBALLENTINESBALLENTINESBALLENTINESBALLENTINESBALLENTINESBALLENTINESBALLENTINESBALLENTINES

lis pendens   A pending suit or pending action. Refers to the jurisdiction, power, or control a court has over the property involved in a suit during litigation. The *doctrine of lis pendens* states that a pending suit is notice to all the world, and therefore a person who purchases real property involved in the pending litigation will be bound by the judgment in the case.

Torrens title system   A system for the registration of titles to land, which exists in several states. Under the Torrens system, ... the name of the owner of the land appears on a certificate of title that is conclusive evidence of ownership.

certificate of title   [A] document that shows the name of the owner of land identified in the document in jurisdictions.

over filings. These statutes are known as the no-tice, race, and notice-race statutes.

Notice Statutes

Under a *notice statute*, one must give public notice—by recording the document(s) that reflect the trans-action—to be protected against the superior claim of a subsequent good faith purchaser. In theory, the person who did not record his or her interest could still win if the other party actually knew of that prior interest, but proving that the other party had this knowledge can be very difficult, whereas the facts of recording are public information.

Race Statutes

Under a *race statute*, protection is based upon who filed first; first to file wins. There is no issue about good faith and knowledge. Only a few states have these statutes, however.

Notice-Race Statutes

The *notice-race statute*, as its name implies, has elements of both notice statutes and race statutes. A good faith checking requirement is imposed on a subsequent purchaser, but "the race to the court-house" element is involved as well. Not only must the party concerned record the pertinent docu-ments, but he or she must also record prior to other parties to have priority and protection against a subsequent good faith purchaser for value.

Real estate paralegals are often given the re-sponsibility for filing real estate documents. It is important that they be familiar with the customs and procedures for filing real estate documentation in the areas in which they work. It is often a good practice to keep a file, conveniently located, with the telephone numbers of the county authorities in charge of real estate recordings, as well as their addresses, filing procedures, and filing fees.

The Legal Rules for Owning Real Property

As illustrated in this law office scenario, the rules for owning real property, especially for multi-ple ownership of real estate, can be extremely im-portant, especially when transferring property. Real estate paralegals must be familiar with these basic rules and with the resources for researching questions concerning the legal rules for real estate ownership.

This section examines various rules and forms of real estate ownership, including freehold in-terests, leasehold estates, multiple owners of a parcel of real estate, and easements.

Law Office Scenario

A client of your law firm, Judy Barnes, has come to Jerry Jefferson, one of the attorneys in your firm, with a real estate question. It seems that her father deeded the old family home-stead to her and her brother—"To Jim Barnes and Judy Barnes, forever"—before he died. Now Judy's brother, Jim, has passed away and Jim's children are claiming a half share of the prop-erty. Judy is sure that her father intended for her to be the sole owner of the property upon her brother's death and that his children have no valid claim. Attorney Jefferson does not nor-mally work in the real estate area and he has asked that you conduct the necessary research to determine if Judy has the right of survivor-ship to the property she owned with her brother.

Freehold Interests: Fee Estates and Life Estates

A **freehold** interest in real estate gives the owner the title to the property and the right to possess the property. The fee simple absolute and the life estate are both considered freehold interests.

Fee Simple Absolute

The greatest interest one can own in real estate is called a **fee simple absolute**. This term refers to the land itself; the land is called the *fee*. The rest of the term means that the owner has all of the bundle of rights belonging to that particular piece of land. *Fee simple absolute*, *fee simple*, or just *fee* all mean that the possessor of that set of rights can sell or dispose of the land in any way he or she chooses. The most common ways in which this transfer can be done are (1) by sale (the owner moves), (2) by gift (to a family member during the owner's lifetime or at death by the owner's will), (3) by failure to pay an obligation such as a debt (such as the mortgage), or (4) by government seizure for failure to pay taxes.

Language in the deed (the document used to transfer the property) to create a fee simple is something like "I convey Blackacre to John Doe in fee simple" or "I give Blackacre to Jane Doe forever." Traditionally, a grant required language like "to John Doe and his heirs."

Conditional Fees

One's interest in real property is called an *estate*. An estate that has at least one of any number of conditions attached to it is referred to as a **conditional fee**. The concept of the conditional fee is straightforward. The property is transferred in fee simple, but the transfer is subject to a condition. With a conditional fee, the transferee will lose title to the property if a condition specified in the deed granting the title occurs or if an existing condition specified in the deed ceases to exist.

This type of estate involves two parties. The first party is a *fee holder*, who owns the real property until the condition in the granting language is violated. The second party (usually the grantor) *may* get it back, and is said to have a **possibility of reverter**. For example, consider Alex Michaels, who owns the Shady Ranch in fee simple. He wants to give it to a charity that does medical research, but he is concerned that the charity uses too large a percentage of its funds to pay its top executives. Alex could, therefore, give Shady Ranch to the charity "so long as the top ten executives of the charity receive no more than 10% of the annual receipts of the charity for their compensation." The charity could own Shady Ranch for years, but if the earnings of the top 10 executives ever exceeds 10 percent of annual receipts, the property could revert back to Alex Michaels. The charity in this example owns a conditional fee to the property and Alex Michaels is said to have a possibility of reverter.

Another type of estate closely related to the conditional fee is referred to as a *fee simple upon condition subsequent*. This is a fee granted with a condition attached to the grant. Instead of having the grantor's interest be a possibility of reverter, though, the grantor's interest is called a *right of entry* or a *power of termination*. Unlike a conditional fee, the fee simple upon condition subsequent requires the reversionary interest holder to take some action to retrieve the property. It does not automatically return to the grantor if the condition is violated.

BALLENTINESBALLENTINESBALLENTINESBALLENTINESBALLENTINESBALLENTINESBALLENTINESBALLENTINESBALLENTINESBALLENTINESBALLENTINESBALLENTINESBALLENTINESBALLENTINESBALLENTINES

freehold   An estate in fee or a life estate in real property.

fee simple absolute (fee simple)   [T]he most complete estate in land known to the law. It signifies total ownership and control. It may be inherited free of any condition, limitation, or restriction by particular heirs.

conditional fee   An estate in land, also known as a fee conditional or fee simple conditional, which is limited to particular heirs. If the grantee has no heirs of the type described in the condition, the estate reverts to the grantor.

possibility of reverter   A type of future interest that remains in a grantor when, by grant or devise, he or she has created an estate in fee simple determinable or fee simple conditional, the fee automatically reverting to him or her or his or her successors upon the occurrence of the event by which the estate is limited.

The Life Estate

A **life estate** may exist (1) for the life of the holder of the estate or (2) for the life of another person. Literally, the life estate exists so long as the person who has the named life is alive. After that party dies, the property often reverts (goes back to) the grantor or his or her heirs. Here, again, two parties are involved: the estate holder, called the **life tenant**, and the party to whom the property goes afterward, the holder of a reversion or a **remainderman**. The future estate holder is said to have a **future interest** in the property.

The holder of a reversion is the original grantor or that grantor's heirs. In essence, the estate goes back to the same party who granted it. A *remainderman* is another party whom the grantor designated as the person to take the property after the life estate ends.

Leasehold Estates

The fee simple, conditional, and life estates are called *freehold estates*. As noted, they represent the greatest set of rights for the longest period of time. There are, obviously, lesser interests in land. Generally, these interests are called **leasehold estates**. They are usually created by a written agreement or a contract, normally called a **lease**, between a **landlord** and a **tenant**. The estate that the landlord grants and the tenant receives is a *leasehold*, and the tenant's interest is called a **tenancy**. The landlord usually retains a reversion, and in most cases, the property is involved in repeated rentals over the years. Both the landlord and the tenant have rights that can be transferred to third parties under certain circumstances.

A leasing arrangement generally involves a business activity by the landlord done for profit; the tenant is given certain rights to use the property for a certain period. In return, the tenant pays rent, which may be a fixed amount or a variable payment based on a variety of commercial factors.

Most commercial leases are governed by the law of contracts that relate to real estate, and in many urban areas these leases are now governed by local ordinances and regulations. Commercial leases can have, among other things, allocations of expenses (such as maintenance), tax benefits, and risks between the parties, as well as standard leasing terms.

Types of Tenancies

The duration of the tenancy may be for a specified period of time, and a lease for that period creates an **estate for years**. Note, however, that the time period need not be as long as a year. It is normal to lease property for different time periods—an overnight hotel leases by the day or the hour; a

---

BALLENTINESBALLENTINESBALLENTINESBALLENTINESBALLENTINESBALLENTINESBALLENTINESBALLENTINESBALLENTINESBALLENTINESBALLENTINESBALLENTINESBALLENTINES

life estate An estate that exists as long as the person who owns or holds it is alive. Its duration may also be the lifetime of another person.

life tenant A person who holds a life estate.

remainderman A person entitled to receive a **remainder**.

remainder An estate in land to take effect immediately after the expiration of a prior estate, created at the same time and by the same instrument.

future interest An estate or interest in land or personal property, including money, whether vested or contingent, that is to come into existence at a future time.

leasehold (leasehold estate) The interest or estate of a lessee under a lease.

lease A contract for the possession of real estate in consideration of payment of rent, ordinarily for a term of years or months, but sometimes at will. The person making the conveyance is the landlord or lessor; the person receiving the right of possession is the tenant or lessee.

landlord (lessor) An owner of real property who leases all or a portion of the premises to a tenant.

tenant (lessee) A person who occupies realty under a lease with a landlord.

tenancy 1. The right to hold and occupy realty or personalty by virtue of owning an interest in it. 2. Possession of realty under a lease; the relationship existing between a landlord or lessor and a tenant or lessee.

estate for years An estate that terminates after a specific number of years.

skyscraper may have a lease for 99 years. It is also possible to lease for 999 years (but many courts would treat that as a transfer of a fee simple). The amount of time to be given and the process for notice of termination of the lease is usually specified within the lease itself.

A different type of duration occurs with a lease for a **periodic** tenancy. This arrangement is a

---

Dated this 13th day of April, 1995.

Received of James A. Arnold and Dorothy D. Arnold, husband and wife, the sum of One Thousand Dollars and No/100 ($1,000.00), by cash as earnest money to be deposited upon acceptance of Purchase Agreement by all parties. Said earnest money is part payment for the purchase of the property located at:

123 Shady Lane, in the City of Anytown, County of Alpha, State of Illinois, legally described as:

The Northern one-half of the Northeast One-quarter of the Northeast One-Quarter of Section 3, Tier 3 South, Range 3 East of the Third Principal Meridian, in Cottonwood County, State of Illinois

including the following property, if any, owned by Seller and used and located on said property: garden bulbs, plants, shrubs, and trees; storm sashes, storm doors, screens, and awnings; window shades, blinds, traverse and curtain and drapery rods; attached lighting fixtures and bulbs; plumbing fixtures, water heater, gas furnace, attached television antenna, built-in dishwasher, garbage disposal, gas range and oven, and all carpeting, all of which property Seller has this day agreed to sell to Buyers for the sum of Two Hundred Twenty-Five Thousand and 00/100 Dollars ($225,000.00), which Buyers agree to pay in the following manner: Earnest money of One Thousand Dollars ($1,000.00) cash on or before the date of closing, and the balance of Two Hundred Twenty-Four Thousand and 00/100 Dollars ($224,000.00) by financing in accordance with the attached addendum.

Upon performance by Buyers Seller shall deliver a Warranty Deed conveying marketable title subject to:

(A) Building and zoning laws, ordinances, state and federal regulations; (B) Restrictions relating to use or improvement of the property without effective forfeiture provisions; (C) Reservation of any mineral rights by the State of Illinois; and (D) Utility and drainage easements which do not interfere with existing improvements.

Seller shall be responsible for and pay all real estate taxes due and payable in the year 1994 and all prior years. Buyer shall be responsible for and pay all real estate taxes due and payable in the year 1995 and all subsequent years.

Real Estate Sales Contract The sales contract includes the names of the buyer and the seller, the location and boundary of property, the offer, the price (if the sale is not for cash), and signatures.

Seller shall, within a reasonable time after acceptance of this agreement, furnish an abstract of title, or registered property abstract, certified to date to include proper searches covering bankruptcies, state and federal judgments and liens, and levied and pending special assessments. Buyer shall be allowed 10 business days after receipt of abstract for examination of title and making any objections which shall be made in writing or deemed waived. If any objection is so made, Seller shall have 10 business days from receipt of Buyers' written objections to notify Buyers of Seller's intention to make title marketable within 120 days from Seller's receipt of such written objection. If notice is given, payments hereunder required shall be postponed pending correction of title, but upon correction of title and within 10 days after written notice to Buyers the parties shall perform the Purchase Agreement according to its terms. If no such notice is given or if notice is given but title is not corrected within the time provided for, this Purchase Agreement shall be null and void, at option of buyers; neither party shall be liable for damages hereunder to the other and earnest money shall be refunded to Buyers.

Seller warrants that buildings are constructed entirely within the boundary lines of the property, and that there is a right of access to the property from a public right of way. Seller further warrants that prior to the closing, payment in full will have been made for all labor, materials, machinery, fixtures, or tools furnished within the 120 days immediately preceding the closing in connection with construction, alteration, or repair of any structure on or improvement to the property.

If there is any risk of loss or damage to the property between the date hereof and the date of closing, for any reason, including fire, vandalism, flood, earthquake, or act of God, the risk of loss shall be on Seller. If the property is destroyed or substantially damaged before the closing date, this Purchase Agreement shall become null and void, at Buyers' option, and earnest money shall be refunded to Buyers.

This Purchase Agreement, any attached exhibits, and any addenda or amendments signed by the parties shall constitute the entire agreement between Seller and Buyers, and supersedes any other written or oral agreements between Seller and Buyers. This Purchase Agreement can be modified only in writing signed by Seller and Buyers.

Real Estate Sales Contract   *(Continued)*

tenancy that is repeated again and again for the same time period. This tenancy may be created by a lease or by implication from the actions of the parties. For instance, a tenant moves into an apartment with no lease. As long as the tenant pays his or her rent monthly and it is accepted monthly, this relationship creates a periodic tenancy with a monthly duration.

BALLENTINESBALLENTINESBALLENTINESBALLENTINESBALLENTINESBALLENTINESBALLENTINESBALLENTINESBALLENTINESBALLENTINESBALLENTINESBALLENTINESBALLENTINESBALLENTINES

periodic   Occurring at regular intervals.

If Buyers default in any of the agreements herein, Seller may terminate this Purchase Agreement, and payments made hereunder may be retained by Seller and Agent as liquidated damages, as their respective interests may appear. If this Purchase Agreement is not so terminated, Buyers or Seller may seek actual damages for breach of this Agreement or specific performance of this Agreement; and, as to specific performance, such action must be commenced within six months after such right of action arises.

As of the date of this Agreement, Seller represents that he has not received a notice of hearing for a new public improvement project from any governmental assessing authority, the costs of which project may be assessed against the property. If a notice of pending special assessment is issued after the date of this Agreement and on or before the date of closing, Buyers shall assume payment of all such amounts. If any such special assessments shall exceed Five Thousand Dollars ($5,000.00), this Purchase Agreement shall be null and void.

Seller shall deliver possession of the property not later than _____ after closing.

Seller warrants that the property is directly connected to city sewer and city water.

The Buyers set forth herein agree to purchase the property for the price and on the terms and conditions set forth above.

Buyers:

_____

James A. Arnold

_____

Dorothy D. Arnold

The owner of the property accepts this agreement upon the terms and conditions set forth above.

Seller:

_____

Brian Lewis

Real Estate Sales Contract *(Continued)*

A third type of estate is called a **tenancy at will**. With this type of tenancy, there is no agreement regarding rent, and either party may end the tenancy at any time.

tenancy at will   A tenancy that continues only as long as both parties wish it to, i.e., "at the will of" the parties. The duration of such a tenancy is uncertain and indefinite.

Finally, a **tenancy at sufferance** describes the estate that a wrongful occupant of property has. Usually, the tenant has held over after originally being there properly, but now there is no lease. Common law gave the landlord the right to hold the tenant to a new lease at the same terms or to evict the tenant. Until the landlord makes this election, a tenancy at sufferance exists between the parties.

The Landlord's Duties

The landlord has the duty to provide the tenant with **quiet enjoyment** of the property. This means that the landlord has a duty to do nothing that will make possession by the tenant difficult. The landlord may not, for instance, try to evict the tenant wrongfully. Note that it is the actions of the landlord that count, not the actions of third parties. Howling dogs and loud music are not problems of the landlord, because the term *quiet* has no reference to sound or noise in this use of the word; it means undisturbed.

Another obligation of the landlord, which is changing, is the obligation to be certain that the premises are fit for use. Modern law often requires that the residential landlord maintain the premises under the theory of an implied warranty of habitability. Much of this law has arisen from problems with slumlords and their failure to maintain the premises of their buildings. Various other government rules, requirements, and regulations may also create additional duties for the landlord when there is a consumer residential relationship. The basis for these imposed duties is the government's interests in zoning, health, environmental, or public safety laws.

The landlord's duty to keep the premises in good condition or safe repair depends upon whether that part of the property is under the control of the landlord. Common areas such as halls, steps, and the like are under the control of the landlord, and they must be maintained. Areas inside leased premises, however, are under the control of the tenant.

The Landlord's Rights

In addition to the duties imposed on landlords, they are entitled to certain rights; for instance, the right to receive the agreed-upon rent for their premises from the tenant, and the right to have their property maintained in a nondestructive manner. The landlord also has the right to repossess the property upon termination of the lease period. Several remedies are available to landlords with tenants who hold over after the term of the lease has expired. Many of these remedies are set by statute and may include the collection of damages of up to two or three times the regular rent from the tenant, the right to increase the tenant's rent, and the right to evict the tenant. The landlord also has certain statutory rights when the tenant fails to pay the rent according to the lease. These remedies often include the landlord's right to evict the tenant after giving proper notice. Finally, the landlord has the right to recover damages from the tenant when the tenant damages the premises in a manner contrary to the lease agreement.

The Tenant's Duties

The tenant's obligations are those specified in the lease as well as the general obligations imposed by law. The most important ones are the obligation to pay rent and not to damage the premises in any way beyond normal wear and tear. If the landlord evicts the tenant for noncompliance with a clause in the lease, the tenant may not be liable for any further rent payments. Similarly, after the tenant has moved out and breached the leasing contract without cause, the rent payments usually remain an obligation, unless the landlord

---

BALLENTINESBALLENTINESBALLENTINESBALLENTINESBALLENTINESBALLENTINESBALLENTINESBALLENTINESBALLENTINESBALLENTINESBALLENTINESBALLENTINESBALLENTINESBALLENTINES

tenancy at sufferance   The tenancy of a person who continues in possession after his or her right of possession has ended; the tenancy of a holdover tenant.

covenant for quiet enjoyment   A covenant that title is good and that therefore the grantee will be undisturbed in his or her possession and use of the property.

rents the property to another at a comparable rent. Many leases have clauses to settle what the obligations of the parties are under most possible circumstances.

The Tenant's Rights

Tenants enjoy the possessory right to quiet enjoyment of the property. This gives the tenant the right to recover damages from the landlord and from others who trespass or otherwise disturb the tenant's possession of the property. The tenant is also granted the right to have the common areas of the premises maintained by the landlord pursuant to the lease and building and housing codes. The tenant also usually has the statutory right to terminate the lease upon destruction of the premises. For example, in many jurisdictions, if Charlie Timms is a tenant in an apartment building that burns down in an accidental fire, caused through no fault of Charlie's, Charlie has the right to abandon the property and pay no further rent.

Multiple Owners of a Parcel of Real Estate

A fee simple, fee conditional, life estate, estate for years, and a periodic estate are all possible with multiple owners. Generally, multiple ownership of real estate is called **concurrent** ownership. In most states, there are two basic ways to have concurrent ownership. These are joint tenancy with the right of survivorship and tenancy in common.

Joint Tenancy

Property owned in **joint tenancy** is subject to the **right of survivorship**. Therefore, if Adam, Bob, and Cathy own a piece of property as joint tenants, and Adam dies, Adam's share does not go to his estate or his heirs. Rather, Adam's share goes to Bob and Cathy. Bob and Cathy would then each own a full half-share in the property as joint tenants (rather than their former one-third share each). Under most circumstances joint tenancy is characterized by the "four unities" of time, title, interest, and possession. *Unity of time* means that the owners must receive the title as joint tenants at the same time, by the same conveyance. *Unity of title* means that the title must be granted to all joint owners from the same source. *Unity of interest* means that all joint owners have an equal interest in the property. Finally, *unity of possession* means that each joint owner has an equal right to possess all the property. If the land owned by Adam, Bob, and Cathy consists of three acres, each of the joint owners has the right to possess the entire property. They are not each assigned one acre for their sole possession. Joint tenancy is difficult to create and easy to destroy by conveying (transferring) the interest or mortgaging it. Either of these acts severs or breaks the joint tenancy as far as the party acting. It does not, however, affect the relationship between the other joint tenants. For example, if Cathy severs her interest in the property by mortgaging it, Adam and Bob remain joint tenants in two-thirds of the property, while Cathy becomes a tenant in common with them.

Tenants in Common

The owners of property in **tenancy in common** have a right to possession of the entire property and cannot claim a specific piece of it, but they need not be equal owners of the property. Upon the death of a tenant in common, his or her interest passes in his estate. This tenancy has no right of survivorship.

BALLENTINESBALLENTINESBALLENTINESBALLENTINESBALLENTINESBALLENTINESBALLENTINESBALLENTINESBALLENTINESBALLENTINESBALLENTINESBALLENTINESBALLENTINES

concurrent   1. Having the same jurisdiction or authority. 2. Occurring at the same time.

joint tenancy   An estate in land … held by two or more persons jointly, with equal rights to share in its enjoyment. … [U]pon the death of a joint tenant the entire estate goes to the survivor[s].

right of survivorship   In the case of a joint tenancy or a tenancy by the entirety, the entitlement of the surviving tenant, upon the death of the other, to hold in his or her own right whatever estate or interest both previously shared.

tenancy in common   A tenancy in which two or more persons own an undivided interest in an estate in land … . [W]hen a tenant in common dies, his or her interest passes to his or her heirs rather than to his or her cotenant[s].

If there is any question as to which type of ownership exists, the courts generally resolve the issue in favor of tenancies in common. It appears that the rationale for favoring the tenancy in common (which goes back centuries) is based on at least two theories. First, the tenancy in common is much simpler and easier to create. Second, the tenancy in common allows property to pass by will, and does not lock it up as tightly as the joint tenancy. In addition, death duties may apply to the asset in the tenancy in common, but not to the property held in joint tenancy.

As illustrated by the law office scenario at the beginning of this section, the distinction between joint tenancy and tenants in common is an important one to make when transferring property to two or more individuals. In the law office scenario, because the deed to Jim and Judy did not specify that the property was to be held in joint tenancy, it would probably be considered a tenancy in common in most jurisdictions. Jim's children would be entitled to Jim's share of the property, even if that was not Jim and Judy's father's intent.

Paralegals are often involved in drafting transfer documents. They must be aware of the formalities for transferring property to multiple owners in their states to avoid any future problems. Often, property that is to be transferred to two or more owners as joint tenants must include specific language, such as "to Jim and Judy Barnes, as joint tenants," to be valid.

Easements

A type of property right, which concerns the rights of a third party to use the land of another, is called an **easement**. Easements are the right to use the land of another for a limited, usually specific, purpose. The most frequent easements are those of utility companies for the lines that go into buildings to provide gas, electrical, telephone, and similar services. These companies must use the property of others for their business. However, because what they provide is something that most people want, this set of easements is more of an enhancement than a restriction on ownership rights.

Another typical situation arises when one property owner has the right to use the property of an adjacent property owner. This may occur when one party sells part of his or her property to another and grants an easement to the purchaser so that the purchaser may reach his or her property. This kind of easement is typically specified in the deed by which the property was transferred. The easement relationship of these two parcels is described with two technical terms. The piece of property that has attached to it the right of using another piece of property is called the **dominant tenement**; the piece of property which is being used is called the **servient tenement**. The right to use the other piece of property is an easement. Because one property would have no value without it, the easement might also be described as a *necessary easement*; it is said to be created by necessity.

An easement may be created by (1) necessity or by (2) legal language in a deed or sales contract. It may also be created by (3) implication, (4) dedication, or (5) prescription. An easement can be created by implication when Jane Jones, who owns adjacent parcels of property, does two things. First, she adds some improvement (perhaps a sidewalk) that overlaps both parcels of land; second, she conveys one of the parcels to someone else, say Steve, and mentions this easement. Both Steve and Jane have an easement. Jane is said to have granted one to Steve and reserved one for herself. Easement by dedication is common for contractors to do. *Dedication* means committing

BALLENTINESBALLENTINESBALLENTINESBALLENTINESBALLENTINESBALLENTINESBALLENTINESBALLENTINESBALLENTINESBALLENTINESBALLENTINESBALLENTINESBALLENTINESBALLENTINESBALLENTINESBALLENTINESBALLENTINES

easement   A right to use the land of another for a specific purpose.

dominant tenement   Real property that benefits from an easement which burdens another piece of property, known as the servient tenement.

servient tenement   Real property that is subject to an easement that benefits another piece of property, known as the dominant tenement.

land to the public use. It occurs many times with streets, alleys, and parks. Easement by *prescription* is like **adverse possession**, in which a party uses another's land for a period specified by state law (often 10 to 20 years), the use is hostile to the owner's interest, and the practice is open and notorious. When all of these elements are complied with, the easement by prescription makes it impossible for the landowner to deny the easement holder the right to continue to use the land.

Title Determination and Protection

Real estate paralegals must have an understanding of the public records kept regarding real estate to properly obtain information about (1) who has (2) certain rights in (3) a particular piece of property. Paralegals are often given the task of ordering searches to determine the owner of a specific piece of property and any claims against the owner or against the property itself. The paralegal who works in this area must understand the different ways of determining who has title. He or she must also have a basic understanding of the process of searching to determine who has claims on the title and the ways in which title insurance is used to protect the owner's or lender's interests in the parcel of real property.

This section includes a discussion of what constitutes marketable title, the types of documents that may be recorded for a given piece of property, and the process of examining the title to a specific piece of property.

Marketable Title

Any buyer of real estate wants to be certain that the title he or she is receiving is good, clear title. In other words, the buyer wants to be sure that the title being purchased is **marketable title**. For title to be marketable, the buyer (or the buyer's agent, such as his or her attorney) must be able to find out if other persons have claims on the property—who has claims, what they claim, when the claim began, and how much money the claim amounts to. If there are no claims that affect the prospective buyer's use of the property or which would affect the buyer's ownership rights, the property is said to have **clear title**.

Clear title, however, need not be perfect title, in which there are no claims of any sort on the property. Clear title often includes certain claims for roads, utilities, and other claims by local, state, or federal governmental agencies.

The problems for title determination lie primarily in two areas: (1) prior parties in the **chain of title** and (2) creditors who have filed claims against the seller (or a prior holder of the property) by placing a lien on the property for an unpaid obligation. The first group consists of persons with ownership claims; the second group is creditors of someone who owns or has owned the property.

A search of the documents in the public records affecting a particular parcel of real property is done in the local government's real estate office (usually at the county level; often referred to as the County Recorder of Deeds or Register of Deeds or simply the Recorder's Office). This process is

adverse possession   The act of occupying real property in an "open, notorious, and hostile manner," under a claim of right, contrary to the interests of the true owner. Such possession over a period of years is a method for acquiring title.

marketable title   A title free from encumbrances for which a person of reasonable prudence and intelligence, who is well informed as to the facts and their legal significance, would be willing to pay fair market value.

clear title   Good title; marketable title; title to land or other property that is free from doubts or defects.

chain of title   The succession of transactions through which title to a given piece of land was passed from person to person from its origins to the present day.

referred to as a **title search**, and it determines the quality of the title that the seller is offering to the buyer. **Title insurance** is often available to cover any mistakes in the title search.

Types of Documents to Be Recorded

When researching the title to real estate, one may encounter several types of documents on the record. The first category of documents that may be recorded generally reflect the transfer of real estate or some interest in it. The following lists some of the most common transfer documents:

1. A deed of transfer of some interest in the real property
2. The will of a decedent transferring the real property
3. A sales agreement or memorandum of sale
4. An assignment of a mortgage
5. A lease
6. The assignment of a lease
7. A map or plat of subdivision
8. Condominium documents
9. Homeowners' associations documents
10. An easement
11. A divorce decree affecting the real estate
12. Options to purchase the property.

The second most common type of document recorded relates to credit transactions in some manner. The most common of these are:

1. A mortgage on the property
2. A satisfaction of mortgage
3. A release of mortgage
4. A bankruptcy decree affecting the ownership of the property

5. A security agreement
6. A financing statement filed under the Uniform Commercial Code
7. A purchase money mortgage or a second mortgage
8. A mechanic's lien for work done on the property but not paid for.

The paperwork evidencing legal actions in court is another type of document that is often recorded. These include:

1. Judgments
2. Court decrees that directly affect the land
3. Sheriff's deeds reflecting the sheriff's sale of the property
4. Lis pendens
5. Tax liens
6. Probate court documents.

Trust agreements, and powers of attorney that include in them the power to take actions affecting real estate or transferring an interest in real property, may also be recorded.

Most recording statutes require that any document that is to be recorded must be acknowledged. The process of acknowledgment generally occurs this way: the party signing the document goes to an official who is an impartial party, proves who he or she is, and states that he or she is aware of the contents of the documents, and that the execution of the document is his or her voluntary act. Some jurisdictions may also require the witnessing of documents to be recorded.

The Process of Examining Title

Today, in most urban areas and in the closely related rural areas around them, there are business corporations called **title companies** or *abstract*

BALLENTINESBALLENTINESBALLENTINESBALLENTINESBALLENTINESBALLENTINESBALLENTINESBALLENTINESBALLENTINESBALLENTINESBALLENTINESBALLENTINESBALLENTINES

title search   An examination of all documents of record relating to the status or condition of the title to a given piece of real estate (including deeds reflecting past ownership and outstanding mortgages and other liens) in order to verify title.

title insurance   An insurance policy in which the insurer agrees to indemnify the purchaser of realty, or the mortgagee, against loss due to defective title.

title company   A company that conducts title searches and sell title insurance.

companies. These businesses cover two functions. First, they have personnel who do the actual searching and provide a written report of the status of the title. Second, for what is usually a minimal fee, they provide insurance against any errors in the information provided in that title search. One is said to "order title" or to "bring down title" for the first process and to "buy a title policy" for the second process. Much of the work involved in preparing for the title search process is handled through the buyer's attorney or through the paralegal who works for the buyer's attorney. To request a title search, the legal description of the property, the name of the property owner, and any other information or documents that might affect the search (such as the names of any creditors or the dates of transactions) must be made available to the title company or the individual examining the title.

The grantor-grantee index and, at times, the tract index must be searched. Circumstances may also warrant a search of other public records, such as the separate mortgage index, a judgment index, and a lis pendens index. By checking the proper indexes at the county level, one can check back up the chain of title from the party presently claiming title or any other interest in the real property.

These indexes are not simply lists of the names of the buyers and sellers, but of all the parties who have any interest or claim in real property, such as creditors (such as mortgagees), transferees (such as lessees or life tenants), or any assignor or assignee. The names of the grantor, seller, creditor, etc. are listed alphabetically in one set of books and those of the other party to the transaction, such as the grantee, buyer, debtor, etc., are listed alphabetically in the other set of books. For each transaction, each index also includes the date, name of the other party, location where the document is recorded, and a description of the property.

These indexes often go back to the original grant of the property from the government. Because such a complete search would involve an enormous amount of work in areas that have been settled for several hundred years and have rapid turnover in ownership, most jurisdictions have placed time limits on how far back a party must go in searching the chain of title; the most common number of years appears to be 40. One should be aware of the details of the local statute regarding what must be checked.

There are two methods to determine the status of title and protect the prospective transferee: preparing an abstract of title or obtaining title insurance.

First, an attorney may be employed to examine an **abstract of title** and prepare a legal opinion that will evidence the status and quality of the title to the property. The term *abstract of title* frequently refers to the work of the attorney or abstract company that examines the documents and makes a list of factors affecting the chain of title. This abstract not only lists the documents, and explains what has and has not been examined, but also provides a synopsis of what the documents mean. The abstract, however, does not tell the purchaser the status of the title or the risks that he or she may face. To have that evaluation, an attorney must prepare a legal opinion based on the abstract of title or upon the attorney's own independent evaluation of the documents. Usually, the owner of the property or a local title company will have an existing abstract, which can be updated each time the property changes hands.

A legal opinion of the title of Torrens property may be made based on a search at the Registrar of Titles' office to determine the proper issuance of the Certificate of Title to the property, in addition to a search of the other indexes if indicated.

Second, one can use a title insurance company. In most parts of the country, this method is the most common, because the document search and evaluation are combined and done by the company issuing title insurance that will protect the policy holder from defects in the title. Essentially, the company has trained staff, some of whom are

---

abstract of title   A short account of the state of the title to real estate, reflecting all past ownership and any interests or rights, such as a mortgage or other liens, which any person might currently have with respect to the property.

attorneys, do the same work in preparing the abstract and title opinion. If the company is satisfied that the title is in proper order, it will also issue an insurance policy to protect the buyer's title.

In many instances, an experienced real estate paralegal, working for the buyer's attorney, does the title search. The attorney for the buyer then prepares a title opinion based on the paralegal's search. In addition, the buyer often purchases title insurance through the attorney for the lender.

The Acquisition and Transfer of Real Property

Land is acquired or transferred in one of four basic ways. First, one can transfer it by a deed. This document is usually accompanied by a real estate sales contract. It is also possible that the property could be transferred by deed as a gift. Second, one can transfer real property at death by will or by intestacy, so that the property passes by the law of descent. A third way to transfer real property is by adverse possession. Finally, one can acquire title to real estate by various legal actions, which frequently involve a foreclosure by court order. The documents frequently used for transferring real estate usually include a sale or purchase contract, a deed, a land contract, and various financial documents, all of which are discussed in this section. Regardless of the type of transfer and the documents used, nearly all real estate transfers are concluded at a closing, discussed at the end of this chapter.

Transfers by Deed

A *deed* is the legal document containing the language necessary to transfer a parcel of real property from one person to another. Usually, a sales contract is involved in this transaction as well. The setting is a sale, frequently for profit. The parties involved are the buyer and the seller, with their support teams. Usually, the seller has an attorney, a banker (who provided any existing mortgage on the property), and a real estate agent or broker. The buyer may not have a broker, but usually does have an attorney and a financier who is providing the money to pay off the seller, and may have an insurance agent ready to issue a binder for a new policy to cover the property. Large commercial real estate transactions can involve even more people, including escrow agents, appraisers, surveyors, taxing authorities, and a number of other parties who act at some point in the transfer process.

Transfer by Death of Owner

The second method is transfer of real property because of death. This transfer is done in one of two ways. First, it can be achieved by a **will**. Second, real property can be transferred under the law of **intestacy**. A person dying without a will is said to die **intestate**, or in the condition of intestacy. Each state has laws governing the distribution of all types of property, and they must be consulted when real property is transferred after the owner's death without a will. The parties involved in the transfer of property on the death of the owner may include the **decedent**, the surviving spouse, the decedent's children, other family members, friends, charities, attorneys, and the **probate court**.

BALLENTINESBALLENTINESBALLENTINESBALLENTINESBALLENTINESBALLENTINESBALLENTINESBALLENTINESBALLENTINESBALLENTINESBALLENTINESBALLENTINESBALLENTINESBALLENTINES

will   An instrument by which a person (the testator) makes a disposition of his or her property, to take effect after his or her death.

intestacy   The status of the estate or property of a person who dies without leaving a valid will.

intestate   Pertaining to a person, or to the property of a person, who dies without leaving a valid will.

decedent   A legal term for a person who has died.

probate court   A court with jurisdiction to probate wills and to supervise the administration of decedents' estates.

Transfer by Adverse Possession

Transfer of property by adverse possession is a different situation. This process involves one party taking away the real property of another, or a portion of that property. The standard requirements for adverse possession are that the claimant has held the property for a statutory length of time, the claim has been open, notorious, clearly against the other party's interest, and actual. As the phrase *adverse possession* indicates, the activity is one that is against the interests of the other party. This type of transfer is quite rare, and it is not favored in the law. It can occur, but it causes a forfeiture of a legal owner's interest in his or her land.

Other Types of Transfers

In addition to adverse possession, there are several other types of transfers that may be involuntary, including escheat, eminent domain, and foreclosure transfers.

Escheat

Escheat occurs when a property owner dies without leaving the property to a beneficiary by a will, and the owner has no heirs, so the property returns to the state. In some states, real property passes to the local government and personal property passes to the state government.

Eminent Domain

Eminent domain is the right of the government to take private property for public purposes. The government sometimes permits agencies or quasi-public organizations to exercise its right of eminent domain. To exercise this right, the state must file a suit of condemnation and establish that (1) the property is needed for public use, that (2) the owner will be paid a fair amount for his or her property, and (3) that the rules of due process have been observed. The basis for determining that the compensation is fair is usually official estimates, which may be countered by landowner estimates or appraisals of higher value. These disputes are heard in administrative and subsequent judicial proceedings. The land taken by eminent domain in a process that complies with all due process requirements may be used for a variety of public purposes, such as a highway, a school, or a park, or for semi-public use, such as a utility property like a railroad right-of-way.

Foreclosure

Several methods of **foreclosure** exist. The two most common methods are the foreclosure suit and foreclosure under a power-of-sale clause. A mortgage foreclosure suit is initiated when the mortgagee sues the mortgagor in a civil suit after a default on the mortgage by the mortgagor. The mortgagee sues for a judgment to be executed by a sale of the mortgaged property by the sheriff.

State statues usually provide that a mortgagor may reinstate the mortgage by paying to the mortgagee a specified sum of money as set forth in the statues. That sum typically includes the amount due under the mortgage, plus interest, costs, disbursements, and attorney fees. Even after the foreclosure sale has occurred, state statutes usually provide a time period during which the mortgagor has the right of redemption, during which the mortgagor may pay a specified amount to the party who purchased the property at the sheriff's sale. The redemption amount typically includes the amount bid at the sheriff's sale plus interest to the date of redemption.

In a foreclosure under a power-of-sale clause, the foreclosure process is private and does not

BALLENTINESBALLENTINESBALLENTINESBALLENTINESBALLENTINESBALLENTINESBALLENTINESBALLENTINESBALLENTINESBALLENTINESBALLENTINESBALLENTINESBALLENTINES

escheat   The right of the state to take title to property after the death of a person who has not disposed of the property by will and has left no heirs to inherit it.

eminent domain   The power of the government to take private property for a public use or public purpose without the owner's consent, if it pays just compensation.

foreclosure   1. A legal action by which a mortgagee terminates a mortgagor's interest in mortgaged premises. 2. The enforcement of a lien, deed of trust, or mortgage on real estate, ... by any method provided by law.

involve using the courts. The mortgage document itself contains a power-of-clause, which permits the mortgagee to foreclose by following statutory procedure when there has been a default under the terms of the mortgage. The statutory procedures involved in this type of foreclosure often involve:

1. Publication of a notice of foreclosure in a legal newspaper
2. Service of notice of foreclosure on the mortgagor or occupants of the property
3. Sale of the property by the county sheriff

Real estate paralegals often conduct foreclosure procedures under power-of-sale clauses. Paralegals who work in this area must be very familiar with state statutes for mortgage foreclosure procedures. In addition, they must be aware of and meet the deadlines set by statute and the terms of the mortgage documents.

Even in foreclosure, the property owner—if the property contains a home—retains certain rights called **homestead** rights. These rights are defined and limited by statute, but generally serve as property exemptions which put the property beyond the reach of creditor. For example, in some states, the limit may be a dollar amount, such as $5,000; in another state, it may be the amount of land protected, say, one-half acre. These amounts, in dollars or land, cannot be sold to satisfy debts. They have been designed to protect the family from outside problems and provide it with a minimum for its survival.

Private creditors typically resort to the foreclosure process only after all other remedies have been exhausted. It is usually much easier to get repaid in the regular manner than to go through the lengthy, expensive, and potentially harmful process of foreclosure.

When mortgages are guaranteed by the Federal Housing Administration or the Veterans Administration, foreclosures require special procedures.

The extensive regulation on this subject generally contemplate several months' default and mandate complete fair play to the debtor.

Paralegals who work on mortgage foreclosures often have established systems within their offices for complying with the procedures for both types of foreclosure in a timely manner. Aids include forms, checklists, and tickler systems for meeting important deadlines.

Documents for Transferring Real Estate

Several documents are usually involved in the transfer of real property. Real estate paralegals are often responsible for drafting these documents for the approval of the responsible attorney and the client's signature. The three most important and common documents are (1) the sales contract, (2) the deed, and (3) financial documents, such as a note together with a mortgage or a deed of trust.

The Sales or Purchase Contract

In order for real estate to be sold—whether this transaction involves buying a home or a factory or an office building—the parties need a document that specifies what they are agreeing to do. In this way, no one gets confused, there are fewer misunderstandings, and the path of the true transaction is less litigious. This document is referred to as the **real estate sales contract** or the **purchase agreement**.

The following elements are usually necessary in a real estate sales contract. First, the parcel of land must be identified. This identification is achieved by using a formal legal description to locate the property precisely. An ordinary street address is completely inadequate; it can be changed.

Other items usually included in the real estate sales contract are (2) the identity of the buyer

---

BALLENTINESBALLENTINESBALLENTINESBALLENTINESBALLENTINESBALLENTINESBALLENTINESBALLENTINESBALLENTINESBALLENTINESBALLENTINESBALLENTINESBALLENTINESBALLENTINESBALLENTINESBALLENTINES

homestead   [T]he right to own real property free and clear of the claims of creditors, provided the owner occupies the property as his or her home.

real estate contract   A contract for sale of land.

agreement of sale (purchase agreement)   [A]n agreement which obligates the seller to sell and the buyer to buy ... .

and the seller; (3) the consideration to be given, that is, the price of the property, to be paid at closing; (4) the amount of earnest money to be deposited to show good faith; (5) the time, place, and manner of closing or settlement; (6) the date of the sales contract; (7) the type of deed the seller will deliver at closing; (8) the type of title that the parties have agreed to transfer between one another; (9) the method of transferring possession from the seller to the buyer; and (10) the division between buyer and seller of certain overlapping elements such as taxes, utility payments, interest, or special assessments. This splitting between the parties is called *apportionment* and is negotiable between the parties, but it generally follows the customs of the area. In addition, the sales contract may specify what personal property items will and will not be included in the transfer. These items could include anything from the window coverings in a home to chandeliers, stoves, and dishwashers to the pieces of equipment in a factory that are fixtures and stay with the building. The sales contract may also indicate who is responsible for paying the transfer tax to record the deed of transfer.

The purpose of the sales contract is to specify the areas of agreement between the parties. To be absolutely clear and safe, the contract must identify and include every area in which a dispute could arise and all arguments between the parties. It is essential to identify everything that could be a risk to the client and to find a way to agree about it in the contract so that there are no questions, doubts, or attempts to take advantage at a later date by either party.

The sales contract has some historical formalities with which to comply. This sales contract must, under the Statute of Frauds, be in writing. The **Statute of Frauds** provides that the transfer of any interest—at all—in real estate must be in writing. This writing must have, minimally, (1) the names of the parties (the buyer and the seller); (2) a land description; (3) the signatures of the parties who will be bound by the contract; (4) the price; and (5) if the sale is not for cash, the terms of the financial arrangements. Some states require further technical formalities, such as witnessing or attesting the signatures of the parties to the contract.

It should be noted that all the parties who own the property should sign the sales agreement. If this simple requirement is not met, there may be problems in enforcing the contract later. This problem is particularly acute when a home is being sold and one spouse does not sign. Later, it will probably be impossible to force the sale to go through, because the spouse has certain rights in the property that cannot be taken away; the spouse must consent to sell. If the property is owned by a corporation or a partnership, the appropriate signature requirements should be observed. Forms for sales agreements that include state-specific requirements are commonly available at stationery stores and other stores that sell legal forms.

After the sales contract has been properly executed, the attorneys for the buyers of the property typically have a title search performed by a title company or otherwise research the title to the real property to assure that the title to the real property is clear.

The Deed

There are a number of types of deeds, but the four most common are the warranty deed, a special warranty deed, a quitclaim deed, and a bargain and sale deed. A warranty deed provides the greatest protection for the buyer, the special warranty substantially less, and the quitclaim virtually no protection. A bargain and sale deed conveys the land without any protective covenants to the buyer from the seller.

In essence, a **warranty deed,** sometimes also called a *general warranty deed,* has the seller (the

BALLENTINESBALLENTINESBALLENTINESBALLENTINESBALLENTINESBALLENTINESBALLENTINESBALLENTINESBALLENTINESBALLENTINESBALLENTINESBALLENTINESBALLENTINESBALLENTINES

statute of frauds　A statute, existing in one or another form in every state, that requires certain classes of contracts to be in writing and signed by the parties. Its purpose is to prevent fraud or reduce the opportunities for fraud.

warranty deed　A deed that contains title covenants.

For valuable consideration, Brian Lewis, a single man, Grantor, hereby conveys and warrants to James A. Arnold and Dorothy D. Arnold, husband and wife, Grantees, as joint tenants, real property located at 123 Shady Lane, in the City of Anytown, County of Alpha, State of Illinois, legally described as:

The Northern one-half of the Northeast One-Quarter of the Northeast One-Quarter of Section 3, Tier 3 South, Range 3 East of the Third Principal Meridian, in Alpha County, State of Illinois

together with all hereditaments and appurtenances belonging thereto.

_____
Brian Lewis

STATE OF ILLINOIS)
)SS
COUNTY OF ALPHA)

The foregoing instrument was acknowledged before me this ___day of _____ , 199___ , by Brian Lewis, Grantor.

_____
Notary Public

Warranty Deed The warranty deed is a document that transfers real property in which the seller guarantees clean title to the buyer.

grantor under the deed) provide the buyer (the grantee under the deed) with a promise that is very close to a guaranty. Not only does the seller promise that he or she has valid title to the property, but he or she promises to protect the buyer from any harm that may occur to the buyer from any defect in the title, regardless of when it occurred or who created it. The most common language that creates a warranty deed is "convey and warrant," but other language is also used.

The second type of deed, a **special warranty deed**, is a warranty deed, but its promises and buyer protections are not nearly as extensive as those of the general warranty deed. This deed, sometimes called a *grant deed*, only promises protection to the buyer (grantee) from anything that the seller (grantor) has done. There is no climbing back up the chain of title if the problem originates in a situation that occurred before the seller acquired the property. The seller only warrants that

BALLENTINESBALLENTINESBALLENTINESBALLENTINESBALLENTINESBALLENTINESBALLENTINESBALLENTINESBALLENTINESBALLENTINESBALLENTINESBALLENTINES
special warranty deed A deed that contains a **special warranty** rather than a general warranty.
special warranty [A] warranty by which the grantor promises to protect the grantee and his or her heirs only against the claims of those claiming "by, through or under" him or her.

he or she has not done anything that will cause the buyer problems with the title. The language for this deed is special. The words are "bargain, grant and sale." Further, any particular jurisdiction may require other special language to create a special warranty deed.

The **quitclaim** deed does literally what its name says: the grantors give up any claims they have to the property. They make no promise that they have any rights in the property at all. It is a simple, bare conveyance of the seller's interest in the property, and provides the buyer with no recourse against the seller under the deed. The language for this deed is usually "quitclaims any and all interest" or it could be "I transfer all my right, title, and interest." Frequently this deed is used as a transfer release.

The final type of deed, the **bargain and sale deed**, simply transfers the land itself, as opposed to the seller's title. It contains no covenants and is not frequently used.

The deed is the transfer document in a sale of real estate, and some formalities concerning deeds must be recognized and observed. Although consideration is often recited, it usually is not necessary for the deed itself. But for the existence of a sales contract, consideration is needed. Note that a grantor can give the property as well as sell it. Donating the property does not require any consideration if the deed is properly executed and delivered.

Further, it is necessary to have a proper description of the land. It is best to have a legal description, but the courts have permitted vaguer land descriptions when they were clear. If the grantor referred to the property as "my home," this identification of the property *in some states* would be clear enough if the grantor had only one home.

The deed must also indicate the type of estate being granted, whether that estate be a fee simple, a fee conditional, or a life estate. There may also be various promises about the title, referred to as **covenants**.

Another formal requirement is *execution*. This need is met by the grantor signing the document, in some cases sealing it, and often having someone attest his or her signature. Many states have a prescribed form of attestation for deeds.

Execution of the deed must be followed by its **delivery** to the grantee. This aspect is rarely a problem in commercial transactions, but when the grantor is giving (as opposed to selling) the property to the grantee, delivery can be important; delivery is the final evidence of the grantor's intent to transfer the property.

The final step in making the transfer safe for the grantee is the recording of the deed. Although recordation is not necessary for the grantee's protection vis-à-vis the grantor, it is usually necessary to protect against a special type of possible subsequent purchaser.

The Land Contract

In contrast to the cash sale that has traditionally been the standard for the home sale industry, there is another device that permits the sale of property over a period of time. This type of device can also be used outside the home real estate market. It is an *installment sales contract*, under which monthly (or periodic) payments are made by the buyer to the seller. This arrangement has several other names as well, such as *installment contract* and *contract for deed*. It should be noted that the buyer does not obtain a formal transfer of the property by deed until the final payment is made. In some jurisdictions, the buyers are seen

---

BALLENTINESBALLENTINESBALLENTINESBALLENTINESBALLENTINESBALLENTINESBALLENTINESBALLENTINESBALLENTINESBALLENTINESBALLENTINESBALLENTINESBALLENTINESBALLENTINES

quitclaim deed A deed that conveys whatever interest the grantor has in a piece of real property, as distinguished from the more usual deed which conveys a fee and contains various covenants, particularly title covenants.

bargain and sale deed A deed conveying real property without covenants.

covenant In a deed, a promise to do or not to do a particular thing, or an assurance that a particular fact or circumstance exists or does not exist.

delivery A handing over; the surrender of possession to another.

as having equitable title because of the payments they have made and their commitment to making all of them. Some states have decided, though, that there is no title in the buyer at all until the final payment is made.

A clause that appears in all land contracts provides that breach of the contract, particularly nonpayment of the installments, creates a *forfeiture*. This seller's remedy permits the seller to end the contract, keep the payments made, and regain possession of the property. Forfeitures are not favored in the law, and a clause providing for forfeiture must be written into the land contract as a remedy to which the parties have agreed upon in their bargaining. State laws often provide specific and strict requirements for forfeitures under land contracts.

The Financial Documents

Almost all real estate sales involve some type of financing. Few people or businesses have the cash available to make a purchase outright, and frequently it is not desirable to do so for cash flow and tax reasons. Consequently, at least one financier is usually involved in the transaction.

The credit transaction involves a series of documents. The first document is the **note**, the evidence of the debt owed and the promise to repay the debt. Because the borrower-debtor might not be able to repay the loan on time (or sometimes at all), the creditor-lender usually wants to have another way of getting repaid. What the creditor does is obtain the right to sell the real property for which it has advanced the loan if the borrower does not repay it. Be aware that there are two types of transactions here: a credit-debt transaction, where one party borrows and the other lends an agreed-upon amount of money for the purchase of real estate, and a collateral transaction, whereby the real property secures the debt.

The **mortgage** is one of the principal ways of documenting a real estate collateral transaction. The mortgage gives the lender (the party making the loan—doing the act of lending) the right to take the property if certain events happen. The most common event triggering the retaking (called a foreclosure) is the nonpayment, when due, of installments on the loan. The mortgage theory begins with the buyer of the real property taking the title to the land. When the buyer possesses the title, the buyer can give someone a lien on the property—in this case, the lender, in the form of a mortgage. The mortgagor (borrower) is the title holder.

The formalities for mortgages are essentially the same as those for deeds. The mortgage must be in writing, signed, have a proper legal description of the real property, and be sealed, acknowledged, and delivered. The document usually takes the form of a transfer from the debtor to the creditor. Although the form appears absolute, it is only conditional—upon nonpayment. Finally, the mortgage form should be recorded as soon as possible.

It is frequently necessary for one of the parties to a mortgage to transfer his or her interest in the mortgage. Most frequently, this event occurs when the **mortgagor** (borrower) needs to move. However, a mortgage transfer can also happen when the **mortgagee** (lender) sells off the note and mortgage. The latter situation is not difficult, because the mortgagee is assigning its right to be paid, but the mortgagor is delegating a duty. Transferring rights is not difficult, but transferring duties can create several problems.

If the new party becomes obligated on the note and mortgage, he or she is said to have assumed the mortgage. If the new party does not become obligated on the original note and mortgage, he or she is said to take the property subject to the mortgage.

hoberman

BALLENTINESBALLENTINESBALLENTINESBALLENTINESBALLENTINESBALLENTINESBALLENTINESBALLENTINESBALLENTINESBALLENTINESBALLENTINESBALLENTINESBALLENTINES

note A written promise by one person to pay another person a specified sum of money on a specified date; a term used interchangeably with *promissory note*.

mortgage A pledge of real property to secure a debt.

mortgagor A person who mortgages his or her property; the borrower.

mortgagee The person to whom a mortgage is made; the lender.

> For valuable consideration, Brian Lewis, a single man, Grantor, hereby conveys and quitclaims to James A. Arnold and Dorothy D. Arnold, husband and wife, Grantees, as joint tenants, real property located at 123 Shady Lane, in the City of Anytown, County of Alpha, State of Illinois, legally described as:
>
> The Northern one-half of the Northeast One-Quarter of the Northeast One-Quarter of Section 3, Tier 3 South, Range 3 East of the Third Principal Meridian, in Alpha County, State of Illinois
>
> together with all hereditaments and appurtenances belonging thereto.
>
> _____
> Brian Lewis
>
> STATE OF ILLINOIS   )
>   )SS
> COUNTY OF ALPHA)
>
> The foregoing instrument was acknowledged before me this ___day of _____ , 199___ , by Brian Lewis, Grantor.
>
> _____
> Notary Public

Quitclaim Deed The quitclaim deed is a document that transfers the seller's title and interest in real property. The document contains no warranties.

The Real Estate Closing

The *real estate closing* is the meeting that usually takes place between the buyer and seller of a property and their representatives. At the closing, the buyer typically pays the seller the agreed-upon price and, in turn, the seller gives the deed conveying the property. Paralegals are often instrumental at real estate closings. They may be responsible for reviewing the documents received from the other party and the documents to be signed by the attorney's client, and for overseeing the proper execution and exchange of documents and of the property proceeds. A settlement statement, often the one prepared by the U.S. Department of Housing and Urban Development (HUD) is often used to facilitate closings.

After the real estate closing, the paralegal will often be responsible for any follow-up work, including the proper recording of deeds.

Summary Questions

1. Margery James is selling her farm to John Brown. On that farm is an apple tree that grew from a seedling planted 10 years ago by Margery's son. Margery would like to take the

tree with her to transplant in the yard of her new home. Is the tree considered real property or personal property? Under what circumstances can Margery take the tree with her?

2. What are some reasons that it is important to promptly record real estate transfer documents?

3. What is the greatest type of ownership interest one can have in real property?

4. If property is deeded from Mary, for the life of Paul, then to Craig, what type of an interest does Paul have in the property? What type of interest does Craig have?

5. The carpeting on the hallway stairs in Janet's apartment building is worn, torn, and hazardous. Janet has asked her landlord to fix the carpeting, fearing that one of her guests may be injured. Her landlord has told her that she is responsible for it, because it is directly outside her apartment and the wear and tear were obviously caused by her and her frequent guests. Who is responsible?

6. If 123 Oak Street was deeded to "Ben Johnson and Brian Johnson," would they be considered joint tenants or tenants in common of the property in most states?

7. What is the main reason that married couples often prefer to hold property in joint tenancy?

8. As a purchaser of a piece of property, would you rather receive a warranty deed or a quitclaim deed to the property? Why?

Practical Paralegal Skills

Following the law office scenario in this chapter, draft a warranty deed from Jim and Judy Barnes's father, Thomas J. Barnes, a single man, to transfer the property from Thomas J. Barnes to Jim and Judy Barnes in the manner in which he intended according to Judy Barnes. The address of the property is 439 Elm Drive, Sherwood, Pennsylvania. It is legally described as:

The Northern One-Half of the Northeast One-Quarter of the Northeast One-Quarter of Section 3, Tier 3 South, Range 3 East, of the Third Principal Meridian, in Cottonwood County, State of Pennsylvania.

Notes

For further reference, see *The Law of Real Property* by Michael P. Kearns (Delmar Publishers Inc. & Lawyers Cooperative Publishing Co. 1994).

1 Milano, Carol, "1993 *Legal Assistant Today* Salary Survey Results," *Legal Assistant Today* 48 (May/June 1993).

2 747 P.2d 934 (Okla. 1987).

CHAPTER 15
The Intellectual Property Paralegal

Intellectual property is a unique area of law, and the work of the intellectual property paralegal is also unique. This chapter examines the three basic areas of intellectual property—patents, trademarks, and copyrights—by focusing on the paralegal's role in each of these areas.

The Role of the Paralegal in Intellectual Property Law

Intellectual property is a new but promising area of law for paralegals. Although few paralegals currently specialize in this area, the paper-intensive and administrative nature of intellectual property fits well with paralegal skills and training. Intellectual property paralegals often work for large law firms, for smaller law firms that specialize almost exclusively in intellectual property law, and for corporations that are frequently involved in intellectual property matters. This section includes a brief look at the role of the intellectual property paralegal, including the number of paralegals who specialize in this area, the work typically performed by them, and the skills important to the intellectual property paralegal.

Intellectual Property Paralegals in the United States

The intellectual property paralegals in this country are a rather small, well-paid group of individuals. According to a 1993 annual salary survey in *Legal Assistant Today*, approximately 2 percent of the paralegals surveyed reported that they specialized in the intellectual property area. However, those paralegals had one of the highest reported average salaries. According to the survey, the average salary for intellectual property paralegals during 1993 was $35,719. The highest reported salary among the paralegals specializing in intellectual property was $50,000.[1]

The Work of Intellectual Property Paralegals in the United States

Paralegals who work in intellectual property deal mainly with copyrights, trademarks, and patents. Much of the work in this area, though rather complex, can be performed by a competent paralegal. Although paralegals cannot give legal advice to intellectual property clients or represent a client in a copyright, trademark, or patent infringement lawsuit, they can perform almost every other duty in this area of law.

Following is a list of some of the tasks typically performed by paralegals who specialize in the area of intellectual property:

Copyrights

1. Assist with the preparation and filing of copyright applications
2. Research pertinent copyright laws
3. Research current copyrights
4. Research possible copyright infringements
5. Assist with all aspects of copyright infringement litigation.

Trademarks

1. Research existing trademarks
2. Assist with the preparation and filing of trademark registration applications
3. Research pertinent state and federal trademark laws
4. Assist with all aspects of possible litigation dealing with trademarks.

Patents

1. Research existing patents
2. Assist with the preparation and filing of patent applications
3. Assist with any potential patent infringement litigation.

Skills Important to the Intellectual Property Paralegal

The intellectual property paralegal must possess excellent communication skills, both written and verbal. The paralegal specializing in this area is often asked to communicate with the client and with state and federal agencies, and must be able to do so in a professional and accurate manner. Forms completed by the paralegal must communicate with great detail and accuracy the exact intent of the client.

The intellectual property paralegal must also be a very organized individual. He or she is often responsible for handling numerous reports, applications, and exhibits for several clients at one time. Critical deadlines must be kept track of precisely. Finally, the intellectual property paralegal must have the ability to accurately research both federal and state laws dealing with copyrights, trademarks, and patents.

An Introduction to Patents

In 1849, Walter Hunt registered a **patent** for a small metal device—a pin that fastened pieces of cloth together. What was remarkable about Hunt's device was that it could be used without leaving a protruding point (e.g., enabling parents to diaper babies without fear that the infant would be injured). Hunt's safety pin is now taken for granted but at the time of its debut, it was innovative. In order to encourage new inventions, a limited monopoly is granted to a patent owner, officially known as the *grant of* **letters patent**. In the United States, this grant of patent rights only occurs upon registration of the invention with the U.S. Patent and Trademark Office (which acts under the authority of the U.S. patent statutes). Unlike copyright and trademark law, no rights are granted under patent law until the invention or discovery has been registered. Assuming the patent owner pays certain maintenance fees, the patent expires after 17 years from the date of registration. After that time, the public is free to make, use, or sell the invention. The grant of patent rights has been compared to an agreement between the United States and an inventor. The inventor discloses the

invention and for a limited time (17 years) the inventor can monopolize the rights to it. However, when the patent expires, the invention enters the **public domain**, where any person may freely make, sell, or use it. The laws protecting U.S. patent rights are derived from the Constitution, and the patent owner may resort to litigation in the federal courts to enforce these rights.

The remainder of this section addresses some particular areas with which the intellectual property paralegal who works with patents must be familiar, including federal law and preemption, the Patent and Trademark Office, registered attorneys and agents, the subject matter of patents, rights under patent law, patent requirements, and patent ownership.

Federal Law and Preemption

Article 1, § 8, clause 8 of the U.S. Constitution grants Congress the power "to promote the progress of science and useful arts, by securing for a limited time to authors and inventors the exclusive right to their respective writings and discoveries."

BALLENTINESBALLENTINESBALLENTINESBALLENTINESBALLENTINESBALLENTINESBALLENTINESBALLENTINESBALLENTINESBALLENTINESBALLENTINESBALLENTINESBALLENTINESBALLENTINES

patent   The exclusive right of manufacture, sale, or use granted by the federal government to a person who invents or discovers a device or process that is new and useful.

letters patent   The document issued by the government granting a patent.

public domain   [A] literary composition or other [invention] that has not been copyrighted [or patented] or with respect to which the copyright [or patent] has expired.

Based upon this constitutional grant, Congress passed several patent acts, the most recent of which was the Patent Act of 1952, codified at Title 35 of the United States Code (35 U.S.C. § 1 *et seq.*). There have been various amendments to the Patent Act of 1952, and various proposals also have been made to modify the patent laws to conform to the laws of other countries. Regulations regarding patent law and operation of the Patent and Trademark Office are established in Title 37 of the Code of Federal Regulations (C.F.R.).

Although the states may create laws regarding ownership and transfer of ownership of patents, only the federal government can create laws regarding the standards of validity of patents and the grant of patent rights. The federal courts interpret patent laws and are the proper forum for filing patent infringement actions. The resulting judicial precedents are set forth in case reports such as the *Federal Supplement, Federal Reporter, U.S. Supreme Court Reports*, and *United States Patent Quarterly*. The federal government preempts state law regarding patent validity and infringement. **Preemption** is the authority of the federal government to preclude the states from exercising powers granted solely to the federal government.

The Patent and Trademark Office

The **Patent and Trademark Office** (PTO) is responsible for determining patentability and issuing federal registration of patents. The Patent and Trademark Office is part of the Department of Commerce, and is under the direction of the Commissioner of Patents and Trademarks. The Patent and Trademark Office is located in Virginia, but its postal address is "Commissioner of Patents and Trademarks, Patent and Trademark Office,

Washington, DC 20231." Rules and regulations for PTO activities are established in Title 37 of the Code of Federal Regulations. Other rules are provided in special Patent and Trademark Office publications such as the *Manual of Patent Examining Procedure*.

Registered Attorneys and Agents

An inventor is free to prepare his or her own patent application. However, most inventors prefer to use the services of a certified patent specialist with a scientific or technical background. To represent an inventor, an attorney or agent must be able to converse with the inventor in the technical language of the invention. For this reason, the Patent and Trademark Office established a licensing process. Both attorneys and nonattorneys may take an examination (the patent agent's exam), provided they have a college degree or the equivalent in one of the physical sciences. A *patent agent* is a nonattorney licensed by the Patent and Trademark Office to prepare and prosecute patent applications. Patent agents cannot represent parties in litigation or perform any activity amounting to the practice of law. For example, if Brian is a paralegal with a college degree in one of the physical sciences, he may take an examination to become a patent agent. If he passes the exam, he can prepare and file Jane's patent application. He can respond to letters (also known as *office actions*) from the examiners at the Patent and Trademark Office and participate in the amendment of the application. However, he cannot advise Jane as to the legal consequences of Jane's ownership of the invention (e.g., in a divorce or for purposes of making a will).

A *patent attorney* is an attorney licensed by the Patent and Trademark Office to prepare and prosecute patent applications and to perform

---

BALLENTINESBALLENTINESBALLENTINESBALLENTINESBALLENTINESBALLENTINESBALLENTINESBALLENTINESBALLENTINESBALLENTINESBALLENTINESBALLENTINESBALLENTINESBALLENTINESBALLENTINES

preemption   The doctrine that once Congress has enacted legislation in a given field, a state may not enact a law inconsistent with the federal statute.

Patent and Trademark Office   Authorized by the Constitution and established by Congress, this office of the federal government registers all trademarks and grants all patents issued in the United States. Its duties also include examining patents, hearing and deciding appeals from inventors and trademark applicants, and publishing the *Official Gazette*.

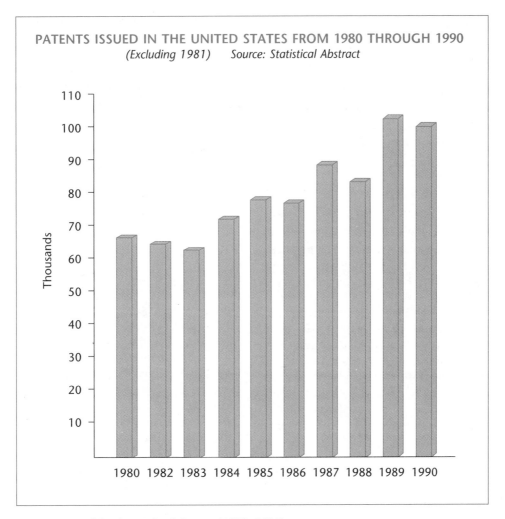

PATENTS ISSUED IN THE UNITED STATES FROM 1980 THROUGH 1990
(Excluding 1981)   Source: Statistical Abstract

Patents Issued in the United States (1980–1990)

other legal tasks. When employing a patent attorney, the inventor executes a **power of attorney**. When employing a patent agent, the inventor executes an *authorization of agent*. These documents must be filed on an application-by-application basis with the Patent and Trademark Office.

The patent attorney or patent agent prepares the application and responds to objections from the examiner, but often the inventor's assistance is required. The process of guiding a patent application through the Patent and Trademark Office is known as **prosecution** of the patent application.

power of attorney   A written instrument by which a person appoints another as his or her agent or attorney in fact and confers upon him or her the authority to perform certain acts.

prosecution   The act of pursuing or carrying forward an undertaking that has been started.

Subject Matter of Patents

Congress has established the subject matter that can be protected under U.S. patent law. This subject matter includes processes, machines, articles of manufacture, and compositions of matter, all of which are considered **utility patents**. In addition to utility patents, the statutory subject matter also includes ornamental **design patents** and **plant patents**.

Rights under Patent Law

The rights granted under patent law are *exclusionary*. That is, the owner of a patent may exclude others from making, using, or selling the patented subject matter (i.e., the invention, design or plant) throughout the United States. Patent rights are *divisible*. The owner of a patent may split these exclusionary rights and assign or license various rights to different parties. If a party, without authorization from the patent holder, makes, sells, or uses the patented subject matter, that is an **infringement of the patent**. It also is an infringement if a party makes an immaterial variation of the patented invention. Unlike other forms of intellectual property law, patent law can prevent use of the infringing device by a consumer. For example, if a consumer buys and uses an infringing device, the patent owner has the right to sue the consumer for infringement. This right is not usually asserted against consumers of mass produced devices, but it may be exercised in the case of expensive or limited-production inventions.

First to Invent

Thomas Edison once stated, "invention is 1 percent inspiration and 99 percent perspiration." The "inspiration" of which Edison spoke is the conception of the mental idea for the invention. The "perspiration" results from physical acts—the developing, testing, or revising of the mental concept so that a useful working invention is created. In patent law, this latter process is known as **reduction to practice**. In addition to the building and testing of an invention, the act of preparing and filing a patent application is also considered a reduction to practice (known as *constructive reduction to practice*). The date of invention is either the date the invention was conceived (providing that the applicant diligently reduced the invention to practice) or the actual date of reduction to practice.

In the United States, patents are granted to the first person to invent; (it is a "first to invent" system). The first person to invent has **priority** of invention and, assuming all other statutory requirements are met, is granted a patent. Under United States law, the party who first files a patent application is presumed to be the first inventor. However, disputes may arise as to which party was the first to invent. When an application is made for a patent that, in the opinion of the Commissioner of the Patent and Trademark Office, would interfere with any pending application, a proceeding known as a *patent interference* is instituted in the Patent and Trademark Office and held before the Board of Patent Appeals. Similar issues regarding priority of invention may also arise in a patent infringement lawsuit.

Patent Claims

The rights granted under patent law extend only to the invention as defined in the claims published in the patent. 35 U.S.C. § 112 states that the patent application specification must "conclude with one or more claims particularly pointing out and distinctly claiming the subject matter which

utility patent   The most common type of patent, granted on the basis that the invention is of benefit to society.

design patent   A patent of a design that gives an original and pleasing appearance to an article.

plant patent   A patent granted on a manmade, multicellular living vegetable organism that does not exist in nature.

infringement of patent   The manufacture, use, or sale of a patent or process patent without the authorization of the patent owner.

reduction to practice   In patent law, completing the patenting process by putting an invention to use or into practice on a demonstration basis.

priority   The status of that which is earlier or previous in point of time, degree, or rank; precedence.

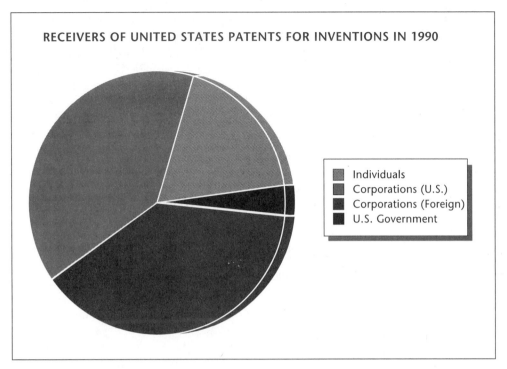

RECEIVERS OF UNITED STATES PATENTS FOR INVENTIONS IN 1990

Individuals
Corporations (U.S.)
Corporations (Foreign)
U.S. Government

Receivers of United States Patents for Inventions (1990)   Corporations, both U.S. and foreign, accounted for about 70 percent of all patents issued in 1990.

the applicant regards as his invention." *Patent claims*, therefore, are the legal description or definition of the invention.

Doctrine of Equivalents

The patent owner has the right to exclude anyone from literally infringing the claims of the patent. Even if the competing method or thing is not a literal copy, the patent owner has the right to prevent the sale, use, or manufacture of a competing method or thing if it employs substantially the same means to achieve substantially the same results in substantially the same way as that claimed. Consider a company, Lightco, that owns a patent on a device that detects lightning and displays its location and distance. Another company, Brightco, manufactures a similar device, without authorization from Lightco. Brightco's device achieves the same result in the same manner. Lightco sues for patent infringement. Brightco

argues that its device receives data from a wider frequency range, processes the data in a special way, and employs a more sophisticated display than Lightco's device. The court however, finds that these elements are equivalent to the elements disclosed in Lightco's patent specifications and recited in the patent claim. Lightco wins because the owner of a utility patent may prohibit the use, sale, or manufacture of an invention or discovery that is substantially similar even though it does not correspond literally to what is called for by the claims of the patent.

Patent Requirements

The four requirements for a utility patent are: (1) the invention falls within one of the classes described in the statute; (2) the invention is useful; (3) the invention, when made, is novel; and (4) the invention, when made, is nonobvious.

Statutory Classes

To qualify for utility patent rights, an invention or discovery must fall within one of the statutory classes provided in 35 U.S.C. § 101. Those categories are: (1) useful processes; (2) machines; (3) manufacture or composition of matter; or (4) any new and useful improvement of such items. These broad categories may include, as established by the Supreme Court, "anything under the sun that is made by man," provided that it meets the statutory requirements. It is possible that an invention or discovery may overlap two categories.

Useful Invention

The Patent and Trademark Office is only empowered to grant utility patents on useful inventions or discoveries. To be **useful**, an invention must have a use or purpose and must work (i.e., be capable of performing its intended purpose). Usefulness is generally the easiest requirement to establish, because most inventions are created or discovered for some useful purpose.

Novelty and Prior Art

Novelty is a statutory requirement of U.S. patent law. The invention or discovery must differ in some way from the prior art (the publicly known or existing knowledge in the field). When assessing the prior art, the patent examiner or courts will consider:

1. Prior patents that issued more than one year before the filing date of the patent or before the date of invention

2. Prior publications having a publication date more than one year before the filing date of the patent or before the date of invention

3. U.S. patents that have an effective application filing date prior to the date of invention of the patent at issue

4. Anything in public use or on sale in the United States more than one year before the effective filing date of the patent application at issue

5. Anything that was publicly known or used by others in this country before the date of invention of the invention defined in the claims in question

6. Anything that was made or built in this country by another person before the date of invention of the invention defined in the claims in question, if the thing made or built by the other party was not abandoned, suppressed or concealed.

Nonobviousness

All inventions must meet a requirement of *nonobviousness*. This requirement demands an inquiry into whether persons working in the field would consider the invention obvious. When the question of nonobviousness arises, the examiner at the Patent and Trademark Office inquires of experts in the field as to whether the subject matter of the patent application is sufficiently different from what had previously been used or described. In other words, would the invention or discovery be obvious to a person having ordinary skill in the pertinent science or technology?

Patent Ownership

Like other intellectual property, a patent is a form of personal property that can be assigned, sold, licensed, pledged as collateral, transferred, or left in a will. The application for the patent must be made in the name of the inventor. However, the inventor does not always become the owner of the patent. Employees of companies, as a consequence of employment agreements or company policies, routinely assign their inventions to their employers.

BALLENTINESBALLENTINESBALLENTINESBALLENTINESBALLENTINESBALLENTINESBALLENTINESBALLENTINESBALLENTINESBALLENTINESBALLENTINESBALLENTINESBALLENTINESBALLENTINES

useful   To be patentable, an invention must be new and useful. An invention is "useful" if it is capable of performing the functions for which it was intended and its use is not contrary to law, morality, or public policy.

novelty   In patent law, a requirement for the patentability of an invention; namely, that it be a thing of distinct individuality not previously known or used.

Patent rights may be licensed. Some legal experts view the **license** as an agreement by the patent owner not to use and for the licensee's use. The payment for this right may be in the form of an up-front payment or by way of royalties. There may be minimum and maximum royalties for a year, and there also may be engineering fees for continued improvements or maintenance of the patented invention. It is common to license rights to an invention prior to issuance of a patent. Because the patent application process is so lengthy,

PATENT REQUIREMENTS
▪ Must fit into statutory classes
▪ Must be a useful invention
▪ Must be a novelty
▪ Must be nonobvious

a company will want a head start on advertising and manufacturing plans.

The Patent Application Process

The patent application process usually begins with research of the prior art. The attorney or intellectual property paralegal examines previous patent records and other publications about prior inventions and forms an opinion as to patentability. If the search results indicate that a patent is likely to be granted (if promptly applied for), the application, text, and drawings are drafted. In addition, the attorney, if requested, may perform research as to the potential for commercial exploitation of the invention.

The topics addressed throughout the rest of this section are those with which intellectual property paralegals must be familiar to assist with the patent application process. These topics include the novelty search, the patent application, and patent infringement.

The Novelty Search

Before drafting an application, a patent attorney usually orders a *patent search* (sometimes known as a *novelty search*). The purpose of the search is to try to determine whether the invention may be novel and nonobvious, and therefore whether to file a patent application. If the determination is made to file the application, the search also offers background and provides technical and commercial information regarding similar inventions. Some patent practitioners distinguish the novelty search from a more comprehensive search used by patent attorneys to assess the facts in patent litigation or patent licensing contexts.

The average cost for a novelty search is about $1,000, depending on the complexity of the invention, and it is usually performed by a professional searcher familiar with the area of technology of the invention. The searcher reviews the published patents (and often other publications) at the Patent and Trademark Office or elsewhere, identifies the documents that seem to be relevant, obtains copies of these documents, and furnishes them to the patent attorney or inventor. Most patent attorneys maintain a listing of searchers in different technologies; others refer to the *Directory of Registered Patent Attorneys and Agents Arranged by States and Countries*. Because the searching is often performed at the Patent and Trademark Office in Arlington, Virginia, an attorney or paralegal may be able to locate a suitable person located in that area to perform a search. A suitable searcher generally has knowledge in a specific field (for

license Authorization by the owner of a patent to make, use, or sell the patented article; permission by the owner of a trademark or copyright to use the trademark or to make use of the copyrighted material.

example, computer, electrical, or chemical sciences) as well as familiarity with the search room, library, or database that is to be searched.

After the results of the novelty search are received, the patent attorney reviews them and advises the inventor of the potential for patentability. If the opinion of the attorney is that the invention would not have been obvious, and if there appears to be a potential for commercialization of the product, the attorney will likely advise proceeding with the preparation and filing of a patent application.

Independent Patent Searching

Although generally not recommended, it is possible for anyone to perform a novelty search without the aid of a professional searcher. There may be occasions when an attorney or inventor needs patent information other than for a novelty search. There are various procedures for performing patent research, including travel to the Patent and Trademark Office in Arlington, Virginia, to perform the research there.

Patent searching can also be accomplished by computer with an *online database*, a collection of information that is accessed by a person using a computer connected to a telephone line. Each online database has a system of searching, storing, and printing information. The content of each online database is different.

The Patent Application

The drafter of a patent application must possess a relevant scientific or technical background as well as skillful application-drafting style. A patent application is typically not prepared by an unsupervised paralegal unless that paralegal is also a patent agent. The inventor, a patent attorney, or a patent agent is usually the drafter of the patent application. Even though the paralegal is not usually solely responsible for preparation of the application, it is helpful to have knowledge of the process, because paralegals often perform related activities, including the assembly of the elements of the application package and assistance in patent searching.

The application itself usually includes the following:

1. A summary of the background of the invention
2. The objectives and advantages of the invention
3. A description of the drawings
4. An explanation of how the invention works
5. A conclusion
6. Discussion of ramifications and the aspects claimed for patent protection.

The application and drawing are submitted with the appropriate fees, and supporting statements, petitions, and declarations. Fees depend on the size of the entity registering the patent (smaller companies can pay lower fees, providing they also file a necessary declaration regarding their small size).

The *transmittal letter* is more than a cover letter listing the enclosed documents—it is a formal requirement of the application and must include the name of the inventor, the title of the invention, the total number of pages of specifications and claims, and the number of sheets of drawings. If a small entity declaration is enclosed, that should also be noted.

Documents or fees filed with the Patent and Trademark Office should include a Certificate of Mailing. This statement may be appended to any document and should be signed and dated.

Certificate Of Mailing

I hereby certify that this document is being deposited with the United States Postal Service, as first class mail on the date indicated above in an envelope addressed to the Commissioner of Patents and Trademarks, Washington, DC 20231.

Application Processing

It takes approximately 18 months for the Patent and Trademark Office to process a patent application. On the average, the PTO issues two *office actions* during the processing period. In a large

J. Sheldon, *How to Write a Patent Application*
[One-Volume treatise with detailed analysis of all types of patent applictions as well as applicable references from C.F.R., U.S.C., and MPEP.] Available from Practising Law Institute, 810 Seventh Avenue, New York, NY 10102-0105.

Kramer & Brufsky, *Patent Law Practice Forms*
[A multivolume treatise that includes all of the forms and rules used for patent applications, prosecution, and litigation.] Available from Clark Boardman Callaghan, 155 Pfingsten Road, Deerfield, IL 60015-4998.

Manual of Classification
[A loose-leaf book containing the classes and subclasses of inventions of the Patent and Trademark Office.] Available from the Superintendent of Documents, U.S. Government Printing Office, Washington, DC 20402; also available on many database services.

Classification Definitions
[Contains the changes in classification of patents as well as definitions of new and revised classes and subclasses]. Available from the Patent and Trademark Office, Washington, DC 20231.

Manual of Patent Examining Procedure
[Also known as the MPEP, a loose-leaf reference work used by patent examiners.] Available from the Superintendent of Documents, U.S. Government Printing Office, Washington, DC 20402.

Horwitz, *Patent Office Rules and Practice*
[Nine-volume treatise (forms volumes are available separately) which includes complete copy of *MPEP*, all statutes and regulations, PTO Notice, and rules.] Available from Matthew Bender, 11 Penn Plaza, New York, NY 10001.

Additional Information Sources on Patent Applications

number of cases, the patent examiner initially finds some fault in the application (e.g., the examiner determines that the claims are too broad and requests that the applicant amend the claims to more narrowly define the invention).

Notice

During the *pendency period* (between filing and issuance of the patent), the inventor may use the notice "Patent Pending," "Pat. Pend.," "Patent Applied For", or similar variations. The notice informs the public that the inventor is seeking a patent.

However, there is no enforcement power behind such notice. That is, the inventor cannot sue under the patent law because a patent has not yet been issued. The patent pending notice simply informs the public that if a patent is issued, the inventor will enforce his or her rights. After the patent has been issued, the owner should mark the invention with "Pat." or "Patent" and the number of the patent. If this notice is used, the owner may recover damages from an infringer from the time that the infringement began. The notice must be applied to the patent owner's products that embody the patented invention, not merely to advertising or promotional materials. If the notice is not used, the owner can only recover damages as of the date the infringer is informed of the patent and charged with infringing it—usually by a cease-and-desist letter from the patent owner's attorney.

Patent Infringement

There are two ways in which a patent can be infringed. In a *literal infringement*, the defendant has made, used, or sold all of the components of a patent claim exactly as the claim is stated. The alleged infringement is a duplicate of the claim in the patent. The second type of infringement, *infringement under the doctrine of equivalents*, occurs if the defendant makes, sells, or uses a substantially similar device which varies from the exact wording of the patent claim. The infringing invention employs substantially the same means to achieve substantially the same results in substantially the same way as the plaintiff's invention. A suit for patent infringement often triggers a defensive attack on the validity of the patent. The litigation becomes two separate battles, one in which the plaintiff claims damage from infringement and the other in which the defendant attempts to invalidate the plaintiff's patent rights. The pursuit and defense of patent infringement is expensive and often risky.

An Introduction to Trademarks

Trademark laws are derived from common-law principles that prohibit companies from competing unfairly. Certain common-law principles regarding competition are grouped together under the title of **unfair competition**. The general purpose of unfair competition laws is to prevent one company from passing off its goods or business as another's. For example, Smith is a popular cloth maker in 18th-century England. Another cloth maker fraudulently claims that its cloth was made by Smith, too. Under common-law rules, the English courts would have prohibited the second company from competing unfairly—that is, attempting to pass off its goods as that of Smith's. Trademark law is a part of this broad law of unfair competition, but with a more specific purpose—to prevent the unauthorized use of any word, symbol, design, device, logo, or slogan that identifies and distinguishes one product from another.

Trademarks and Service Marks

The use of trademarks is based on a simple principle of commerce. When two businesses are competing for the same consumers, each business will attempt to attract the consumer's attention and gain the purchaser's loyalty. For example, if Kellogg's and Nabisco, two food companies, each sell corn flakes, they will attempt to distinguish their cereals with distinctive names, packages, and logos. They will attempt to create a brand loyalty based upon these trademarks. For this reason, manufacturers create special names, logos, and other devices to distinguish one product from another and to avoid consumer confusion. Any word, symbol, design, device, logo, or slogan that identifies and distinguishes one product from another is a **trademark**. A mark that is used in the sale or advertising of services, to identify and distinguish

---

BALLENTINESBALLENTINESBALLENTINESBALLENTINESBALLENTINESBALLENTINESBALLENTINESBALLENTINESBALLENTINESBALLENTINESBALLENTINESBALLENTINESBALLENTINESBALLENTINES

unfair competition   In business, the use or imitation of another firm's name, mark, logo, design, or title for the purpose of creating confusion in the public mind and inducing the public to believe that a competitor's business or product is one's own. Such practices are illegal.

trademark   A mark, design, title, logo, or motto used in the sale or advertising of products to identify them and distinguish them from the products of others. A trademark is the property of its owner and, when registered under the Trademark Act, is reserved for the exclusive use of its owner.

services performed for the benefit of others, is known as a **service mark**. The same principles of law govern trademarks and service marks. Throughout this section, all comments about trademark law also apply to service marks, unless a specific exception is noted.

Goodwill

A trademark, separated from goods and services, has little value. There is no property right, for example, in the words, *Coca-Cola*. The value or property rights associated with a trademark are connected to the goodwill created by the trademark. **Goodwill** is the tendency or likelihood of a consumer to repurchase goods based upon the name or source. It is an expectation of continued public patronage. If a company uses a distinctive mark or logo and the consumer establishes a loyalty or association to that product, the company earns goodwill. For example, a waitress at a restaurant may inform Andre, a customer, that the only available cola is *Pepsi Cola*. Andre is a loyal drinker of *Coca-Cola* and will not purchase Pepsi. In other words, *Coca-Cola* has established goodwill with Andre. A transfer of rights of a trademark has little value unless the goodwill is also transferred.

Trade Names

A **trade name** is the name of a business or company. For example, DiskCo is the trade name of a company that owns the right to the trademark *Brontosaurus* for a computer game. When the term *DiskCo* is used to identify the business (e.g., on company stationery, business cards, and in business directories), the name functions as a trade name and not as a trademark. It identifies the business, but is not used to create a consumer

association with specific goods or services. Although *DiskCo* may be protected under state statutes or principles of unfair competition as a trade name, it will be protected as a trademark only if the company uses *DiskCo* to identify and distinguish its goods.

Many trade names do also function as trademarks. For example, *Sony* is both a trade name and a trademark for consumer electronics goods and services. When *Sony* is used on company letterhead (for example, the Sony Corporation of America), it is a trade name, but when *Sony* is used on consumer electronics goods, it is a trademark.

Trade Dress

Often a business uses other identifying features for a product or service besides a trademark. For example, *Advil* is a registered trademark for pharmaceutical pain relievers. However, in addition to the trademark *Advil*, the product is packaged in a distinctive dark blue box with yellow lettering. The total image and overall appearance of a product or service is its *trade dress*. Trade dress may include the shape, size, color or color combinations, texture, graphics, or even particular sales techniques. Although trade dress cannot be registered like a trademark, federal and state laws regarding unfair competition protect trade dress under principles similar to trademark law. In 1992, for example, the U.S. Supreme Court interpreted the Lanham Act, a federal statute, to protect the distinctive trade dress of a chain of Mexican restaurants. One chain of Mexican restaurants had adopted decor and design elements similar to those of a competitor. In order to avoid consumer confusion, the chain that had imitated the decor and design was barred from further use of such similar elements.

service mark   A mark, design, title, or motto used in the sale or advertising of services to identify the services and distinguish them from the services of others. A service mark is the property of its owner and, when registered under the Trademark Act, is reserved for the exclusive use of its owner.

goodwill   The benefit a business acquires, beyond the mere value of its capital stock and tangible assets, as a result of having a good reputation and the respect of the public.

trade name   The name under which a company does business. The goodwill of a company includes its trade name.

DIRECT MARKETING OF VIRGINIA, INC.,
Plaintiff

v.

E. MISHAN & SONS, INC. and R.B.M. LTD.,
Defendants
No. 90 Civ. 5947 (RPP)
United States District Court, S.D. New York.
December 10, 1990.

This is a diversity action alleging copyright infringement and unfair competition. Plaintiff Direct Marketing of Virginia, Inc. ("DMV") has moved for a preliminary injunction pursuant to Fed.R.Civ.P. 65 enjoining defendant E. Mishan & Sons, Inc. ("Mishan") from the manufacture, importation, distribution, sale and display of its product and enjoining defendant's use of any trade dress confusingly similar to plaintiff's trade dress. For the reasons set forth below, plaintiff's motion is granted.

Over the past eight months, a bona fide catfight has erupted between DMV and Mishan. DMV claims in this action, filed on September 14, 1990, that the watch face design on defendant's PLAYFUL KITTY WRIST WATCH ... infringes the copyrighted design on DMVs CAT AND MOUSE WATCH, ... in violation of 17 U.S.C. § 501(a). DMV also claims that Mishan is marketing its PLAYFUL KITTY WRIST WATCH in packaging so confusingly similar to plaintiff's packaging as to constitute trade dress infringement in violation of section 43(a) of the Lanham Act, 15 U.S.C. § 1125(a).

It is undisputed that plaintiff DMV is the owner of two copyrights ... both showing a pictorial design for a watch face. The work underlying the first registration is a drawing of a short-haired, striped gray cat with green eyes. ... There is a tiny stylized black mouse just outside the green panel. The mouse is positioned to move around the watch face as the second hand. ...

Registration No. VA 415-270, issued to DMV on September 27, 1990, is for a derivative work entitled "Cat and Mouse II" based on the first copyrighted design and shows a new rendition of the cat. ...

Plaintiff's CAT AND MOUSE WATCH is a novelty item retailing for about $20. The design on the watch face uses the rotating black mouse of the first copyright registration and the long-haired gray tabby cat of the second registration. ...

DMV markets the CAT AND MOUSE WATCH wholesale to retail stores and through mail order. DMV began to advertise its watch in April 1990 and filled its first orders in June 1990. DMV has spent approximately $2 million on print advertising ... as well as nearly $3 million on television advertising and several thousand dollars on syndication pieces distributed with credit card billing statements, both beginning in June 1990. ... DMV has sold approximately one million CAT AND MOUSE WATCHES, grossing nearly $20 million, since June 1990.

In July or August 1990, defendant E. Mishan & Sons, an importer and wholesaler of giftwares, housewares and toys, began selling a PLAYFUL KITTY WRIST WATCH. The watch face sports a short-haired, gray tabby cat with blue-green eyes, a white face, chest and paws but no whiskers. A tiny black mouse identical in size and design to plaintiff's mouse acts similarly as the second hand on the Misham watch. ... Mishan has sold approximately 200,000 PLAYFUL KITTY WRIST WATCHES to date.

... It is well-settled in this Circuit that in order to obtain a preliminary injunction, a party must show (1) irreparable harm and (2) either (i) a likelihood of success on the merits or (ii) sufficiently serious questions going to the merits to make them fair ground for litigation and a balance of hardships tipping decidedly in that party's favor. ... The issue before the Court is whether DMV has satisfied the second prong of the ... test for either of its claims.

COPYRIGHT INFRINGEMENT

DMV has demonstrated a likelihood of success by offering proof of the two elements of a claim for copyright infringement: (1) ownership of a valid copyright and (2) unauthorized copying by defendant.

... Defendants do not dispute the ownership or validity of the copyright in question. ... The idea of designing a watch face to show a full-bodied cat which appears to "see" a mouse as the mouse circles the cat in the manner of a second hand is an unprotectible idea. However, plaintiff's expression of that idea—using "America's favorite cat, the Tabby" in a sitting position facing to the left with a stylized rather than realistic rendering of a mouse—is, in this Court's view, protectible expression.

... Where direct evidence of copying is unavailable, plaintiff in a copyright infringement action can prove copying indirectly by proving access and substantial similarity. ... This is the rare copyright infringement case in which there is some direct evidence of copying. Edward Mishan testified that he supplied his Hong

Kong manufacturer with advertisements showing a watch bearing the copyrighted design of Registration No. VA 406-808. Although Mishan claims to have instructed the manufacturer to use Mishan's cat artwork, he offers no credible explanation for switching to the same colors a used on DMV's CAT AND MOUSE WATCH or for using an identical background and mouse.

DMV also proved copying indirectly. Mishan had a reasonable opportunity to view the design on the CAT AND MOUSE WATCH beginning with DMV's print advertising in April 1990 and its television advertising prior to June 12, 1990.

The court finds defendant's design to be substantially similar to the copyrighted design belonging to plaintiff. The test for substantial similarity is "whether an average lay observer would recognize the alleged copy as having been appropriated from the copyrighted work." ...

Accordingly, because DMV has shown a likelihood of success of its copyright infringement claim, it is entitled to preliminary injunctive relief.

TRADE DRESS INFRINGEMENT

The unregistered trade dress of a product may be protected ... if it is nonfunctional and has acquired secondary meaning in the marketplace. The trade dress of a product has sufficient secondary meaning if the plaintiff establishes that the purchasing public associates that dress with the goods from a single producer or source rather than just with the product itself. ... A claim for trade dress infringement then arises when the plaintiff alleges that a competitor's packaging is so similar as to create a likelihood of consumer confusion about the product's source. ...

Plaintiff has demonstrated (1) the strength of its trade dress among consumers based on its $5 million advertising budget and its $20 million in gross sales; (2) that the products are similar; (3) that the trade dress is similar; (4) that there is no credible explanation for the similarity of Mishan's packaging but that it was Mishan's intent to copy and that Mishan's use of the words "AS NATIONALLY ADVERTISED" when only plaintiff's product had been advertised is not only misleading but demonstrates a clear attempt to palm off the product as plaintiff's and to create confusion between them; (5) that the products are in direct competition; and (6) that the low cost ($10–$20) and novelty nature of the watches indicate that consumers will make swift, unpondered purchasing decisions. In addition, there is evidence (7) of at least one instance of actual confusion. Accordingly, plaintiff is entitled to preliminary injunctive relief on its trade dress infringement claim. ...

IT IS SO ORDERED.

Sources of Trademark Law

If another company were to copy the distinctive lettering and use a similar name such as *Coco Cola*, consumers would likely be confused when purchasing soft drinks. By using a similar name and style of lettering, *Coco Cola* is trading off *Coca-Cola*'s goodwill with consumers and has infringed the trademark of *Coca-Cola*. This is an unfair method of competing. When a substantially similar trademark is used on similar goods or services and is likely to cause consumer confusion, **trademark infringement** occurs.

Federal law provides a means of protecting and registering marks for goods or services that are in commerce regulated by the federal government (i.e., generally any product or service sold in interstate commerce), or that are intended to be used in interstate commerce. However, unlike copyright law and patent law, trademarks are not

BALLENTINESBALLENTINESBALLENTINESBALLENTINESBALLENTINESBALLENTINESBALLENTINESBALLENTINESBALLENTINESBALLENTINESBALLENTINESBALLENTINESBALLENTINESBALLENTINES

infringement of trademark A use or imitation of a trademark in such manner that a purchaser of goods is likely to be deceived into believing that they are the goods of the owner of the trademark.

exclusively within the control of the federal government. Each state also has its own trademark registration process.

This section focuses on particular sources of trademark law, including federal trademark law and the Lanham Act, the Trademark Law Revision Act of 1988, state trademark law and the Model Trademark Act, and the Patent and Trademark Office.

Federal Trademark Law and the Lanham Act

Unlike protection granted to copyrights and patents under § 8 of the U.S. Constitution, there is no specific authorization in the Constitution regarding trademarks. However, the Constitution authorizes Congress to regulate **interstate commerce**. Therefore, under its authority to regulate commerce, Congress passed the Lanham Trademark Act in 1946, codified at 15 U.S.C. § 1051 *et seq.* One of the primary purposes of the Lanham Act is to protect the public from confusion or deception by enabling purchasers to identify and obtain desired goods or services. The Lanham Act provides for a registration system and establishes remedies for infringement of federally registered trademarks. A trademark or service mark that is federally registered is identified by the symbol ® or language noting federal registration. In addition to federal trademark protection, the Lanham Act is also used to protect against other forms of unfair competition. The Lanham Act has been the basis for lawsuits regarding trade dress infringement, false advertising, or other forms of consumer deception.

Regulations regarding federal trademark practice appear in the Code of Federal Regulations in Titles 35 and 37. If there is a clash between federal and state trademark laws, federal law will preempt state trademark law. Even if a trademark is not registered with the federal government (or under state law), it may still be protected under these common-law principles of unfair competition. This is because the Lanham Act does not create trademark rights—it merely provides a registration scheme and certain remedies for the owners of valid trademarks.

Trademark Law Revision Act of 1988

Under the Lanham Act, as it was originally enacted in 1946, a trademark owner could only apply for registration *after* the mark was used in interstate commerce. In 1988, the Lanham Act was overhauled. The effective date of this trademark revision was November 16, 1989. Among the changes was a provision for a new system under which a trademark owner can apply for registration prior to using the mark, based upon the owner's bona fide intent-to-use the mark. The intent-to-use (ITU) provision was very important for companies seeking protection. For example, prior to ITU, a company might invest a large amount of money preparing labels and advertising even though an application for registration could not be made until after the product was released in commerce. If, for some reason, the trademark could not be federally registered, the owner would have wasted a great deal of money. With the ITU provision, there is some predictability for a business introducing new products, because it can acquire an assurance as to whether registration will occur prior to the preparation of advertising and labels.

As originally passed, the Lanham Act protected federally registered marks for an initial period of 20 years. Because many trademarks were abandoned before the 20 years ended, the Patent and Trademark Office files contained a great deal of deadwood. The 1988 revision of the Lanham Act also revised the period of protection for federally registered marks. Marks registered after November 16, 1989 are protected for an initial ten year period, after which the registrant may renew the mark for subsequent 10-year periods.

interstate commerce   Commerce between states; that is, from a given point in one state to a given point in another.

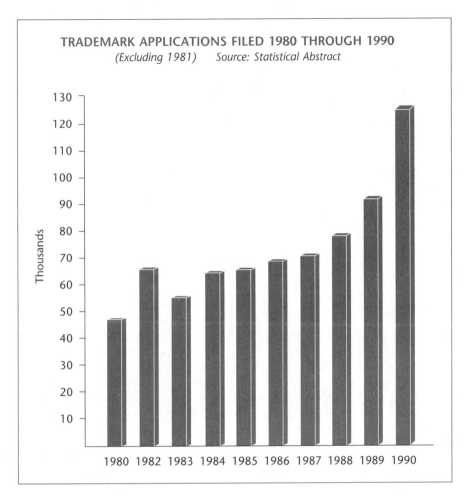

Trademark Applications Filed (1980–1990)

State Trademark Law and the Model Trademark Act

Some trademarks will not qualify for federal registration because the mark is not used on goods in interstate commerce, commerce between the United States and a foreign country, or any other commerce regulated by the federal government. For example, the owner of a floor-polishing business in New York City uses the trademark *Big Apple Polisher.* There is no interstate commerce involved in advertising or providing the floor waxing services. The business is only concerned about protecting its rights within the state of New York. Therefore, the owner will register the mark in New York under state law.

If the floor-waxing business advertises in New Jersey, begins performing services in New Jersey, or intends to do either of these things, the owner may apply for federal registration. There is an advantage to federal registration. For example, the owner of the New York state registration for *Big Apple Polishers* will not be able to stop a similarly named floor-polishing business from registering in the state of Washington. However, with a federal registration, the owner will be able to stop the subsequent Washington user.

Each state has its own trademark law. Most of these laws are patterned on the Model State Trademark Bill, which in turn, is based upon principles in the Lanham Act. Generally state registrations occur through the office of the respective Secretary of State. If a dispute arises as to state trademark rights, the litigation is usually brought in the state where the mark is registered.

The Patent and Trademark Office

The Patent and Trademark Office is responsible for the federal registration of trademarks. Rules and regulations for PTO activities are established in the Lanham Act, in the Code of Federal Regulations, and in special Patent and Trademark Office publications such as the *Trademark Manual of Examining Procedure* (TMEP). If there is a conflict between trademark owners regarding the federal registration, cancellation, or use of a federally registered mark, the parties may resolve the conflict through the Trademark Trial and Appeal Board (TTAB).

Acquiring Trademark Rights

Unlike copyright and patent laws, trademark laws do not reward creativity. That is, trademark rights do not arise from invention, discovery, or creativity. Trademark laws grant protection to the person who first uses the mark in commerce. Consider the trademark *Cracker Jack*. In the 1880s, two German immigrants, the Ruekheim brothers, sold a snack food consisting of popcorn and peanuts covered with molasses. A customer eating the snack supposedly remarked, "This is crackerjack," an expression meaning that the product was excellent. The brothers decided to use the term *Cracker Jack* as the trademark for their snack food. A few years later, another customer supposedly told the brothers, "The more you eat, the more you want." This became the slogan (and another trademark), for the *Cracker Jack* snack food. It does not matter who first created the term *Cracker Jack* or the slogan, "The more you eat, the more you want." What matters is who *first* used it on goods in commerce. That person acquires trademark rights. Why? Because trademark law is based upon the principle of protecting the consumer and allowing companies to compete fairly. The first user of the mark on goods in commerce creates an association with consumers. Subsequent users are likely to confuse consumers as to the source of the product. To avoid confusion and encourage fair competition, trademark laws grant rights to the first user of the mark in commerce. The extent of trademark rights is affected by five factors: (1) the distinctiveness of the mark, (2) the goods or services, (3) the date of first use in commerce, (4) the geographic area in which the mark is used, and (5) the registration of the mark, if any.

The Distinctiveness of the Mark

One factor that affects trademark rights is the distinctiveness of the mark. If a mark is inherently **distinctive**, it is considered to be *strong,* and trademark protection begins upon its use in commerce. The owner of an inherently distinctive mark will be able to stop subsequent users of similar marks on similar goods and services immediately. However, if a mark is not inherently distinctive, and if it merely describes a product or its nature, quality, characteristics, ingredients, or origin, it is considered *weak* because it is only descriptive. A descriptive mark will not acquire trademark protection until the owner can demonstrate that consumers associate the term with the goods or services. This proof of consumer association is known as *secondary meaning.*

distinctive   Characteristic; distinguishing; particular; uncommon; idiosyncratic.

The Goods or Services

One of the cornerstones of trademark law is that protection for a mark extends only to the particular goods or services with which the mark is used, intended to be used, or likely to be used. The rationale is that the purpose of trademark is to avoid consumer confusion among competitive or related goods.

Date of First Use in Commerce

When two trademark owners use a substantially similar mark on goods in commerce, the first party to adopt and use a particular mark in connection with its goods or services is known as the **senior** *user*. A party who adopts and uses a trademark similar to the mark previously adopted and used by the senior user is known as a **junior** *user*. With few exceptions, a senior user has priority over junior users.

To be considered a senior user, a company must establish that it was the first user of a mark in commerce. In addition to its prior use, the company must be able to establish that the use has been continuous. A long period of nonuse may result in the loss of trademark rights.

Selecting a Trademark

There are innumerable methods of selecting a trademark or service mark. Very often, a company will survey its market to determine consumer reaction and response. In addition, there are numerous books and articles, as well as computer programs, that have been written to aid in the process of choosing a competitive trademark. Selecting the mark often involves identifying the market for the goods or services and examining the competition.

After selection of a mark, it is important that the mark be screened and evaluated for use as a trademark and for its registrability. If a company rushes to market, unaware that a similar trademark is already being used, the effect can be devastating. At worst, a court may issue a preliminary injunction and the company will have to cease and desist from any further use of the infringing mark, as well as pay damages and attorney fees to the competitor. At best, the two companies will reach an agreement that permits mutual use. In either case, there will be considerable expense and aggravation in attempting to sort out the trademark dispute—generally at a time when a company wishes to put all its efforts into marketing instead of into legal wrangling.

Experienced paralegals within a law office can guide a company through the selection process and assist in searching the marketplace to determine if competitors are using a similar mark. In addition, the law office can determine the extent of trademark protection required. For example, is federal registration anticipated, or will state registration suffice? All of these considerations and expert guidance can help to avoid unnecessary problems and confusion.

Preliminary Screening Methods: Locating Conflicting Marks

After identifying the marks that a company may want to use, research must be done to determine if there is a potential conflict. The most complete analysis of possible trademark conflicts is offered by professional trademark searching firms. However, these firms often charge several hundred dollars to report on one mark. If a company

senior   Of primary importance, rank, or right.

junior   Of secondary importance, rank, or right.

is considering multiple marks, the cost could quickly run into the thousands of dollars. Therefore, before hiring a professional trademark searching firm, it is a good idea to perform preliminary searches. To keep costs to a minimum, the client may wish to perform some of the preliminary investigations itself (e.g., investigating trade publications or reviewing the marketplace).

Trade Publications and Directories

One simple method of evaluating marks is to have the client or the paralegal review trade publications. Almost every trade or business has a journal, publication, or directory published for the benefit of the companies competing within the trade. Directories are particularly helpful because they contain indexes that allow fast cross-referencing of product or service titles. By reviewing these publications, it may be possible to determine if a similar mark is already being used in the field.

Online Computer Databases

An *online database* is a collection of information that can be accessed by a person using a computer connected to a telephone line. Online databases such as *CompuServe, American On-line, NEXIS,* and *The Knowledge Index* contain articles from news magazines, trade publications, and journals. Each online database has its own system of searching, storing, and printing information. Various fees may be involved when using an online database. Initially, most services charge an annual or subscription fee (which includes the introductory software). There may also be a monthly fee. Some systems charge a fee for each search as well for the total time on the system during each session.

If the results of an online database search turn up numerous articles with matching terms, the attorney supervising the trademark evaluation should review the materials to determine if there are any conflicts or if the terms are used as descriptive designations within the trade. The supervising attorney may then want to eliminate such terms from further evaluation.

International Considerations

Another concern in the process of evaluating a mark is the possible worldwide use of the mark. Does the client intend to use the mark in countries other than the United States? If so, it is now possible to search online for marks in certain foreign countries. The trademark applicant also may need the assistance of an international trademark agent, located in each country. Such agents are often necessary if the U.S. applicant wishes to register the trademark in a foreign country.

Trademark Search Reports

A few companies perform extensive trademark research functions, including trademark searches. These companies may search federal and state registrations as well as international and common-law marks. After performing the research, they provide an extensive written report to the client. The report breaks the information into sections, and includes reproductions of potentially conflicting marks. The professional searching companies use sophisticated searching techniques and computer software. Using these methods, the companies can find matching marks that are phonetically similar or that share similar root words, prefixes suffixes or variants. For example, a search for the mark *Jam Session* for computer software would locate marks identical or similar to *jam,* such as *Jam Factory, Jam/Reportwriter, Jamis, James, ITC Jamille, Vam, Bam,* and *Jims.* Similarly, the search would locate matches and similar terms for *session,* such as *Business Session, Color Session, Conversessions, Supersession,* and *Sessionnet.*

The analysis of a trademark search report should always be carefully performed by both the paralegal and the supervising attorney. The paralegal may initially examine and review the results, but it is important that an attorney review the search for any potential conflicts. The purpose of the trademark search is to determine if there are any potential conflicts that could affect the registration process, not to determine whether a mark can be registered.

Federal Registration

Although registration of trademarks is strongly recommended, it is important to remember that registration, whether state or federal, does not create a trademark and is not essential to proving that the trademark is valid. The ownership and right to the exclusive use of a trademark derive from the owner's adoption and use of the mark, not from registration of the mark. These are principles of common law, and the owner of a valid mark can always enforce these common-law rights regardless of whether a trademark registration has been issued.

The process to achieve registration includes three major steps: (1) filing of the application; (2) examination by the Patent and Trademark Office; and (3) publication for opposition in the *Official Gazette* of the Patent and Trademark Office. If all of these steps are achieved and there is no opposition preventing registration, the Patent and Trademark Office issues a Certificate of Registration.

The Application

Since 1990, the Patent and Trademark Office has processed approximately 120,000 trademark applications per year. Because of this vast number of applications, it is important to prepare the application and attached documentation properly. An application for registration based upon use in commerce should include (in addition to the application form) a drawing, the proper fee, and three specimens of the mark as used in connection with the goods or services. The specimens are not required for intent-to-use applications. This package of materials is delivered to the Patent and Trademark Office, where the application is given a number and assigned to a PTO examining attorney (also known as the *trademark examiner*). If the examining attorney has no objections, the mark is published in the *Official Gazette*. After publication, the public then has 30 days to object to registration of the mark. If there is no opposition, a trademark registration will be issued.

The various federal trademark application forms are reproduced in the publication *Basic Facts About Trademarks,* available from the U.S. Department of Commerce, Patent & Trademark Office, Washington, DC 20231. This publication is also available through the Government Printing Office.

There is no requirement that the "official" form be used. Instead of filling out a trademark application form, many applicants create their own applications by typing all the information. The Patent and Trademark Office prefers typewritten, double-spaced applications, one side only of 8.5-by-11-inch paper, with a 1.5-inch margin on the left and top of the page.

The Registers

The drafters of the Lanham Act created two registers for marks, the Principal Register and the Supplemental Register. Registration of a mark on the Principal Register conveys numerous substantive rights, and as a result, it is the preferred method of federal trademark protection. Registration on the Supplemental Register does not convey the bundle of rights and protections granted on the Principal Register. For example, registration on the Supplemental Register is not prima facie evidence of the registrant's exclusive right to use the mark in connection with the goods or services, and the owner of a mark on the Supplemental Register cannot utilize the power of the U.S. Customs Service to stop importation of infringing goods.

Examination by the Patent and Trademark Office

A trademark registration will be rejected if the mark is merely descriptive or deceptively misdescriptive of the goods or services it represents; if it is immoral or scandalous; if it creates a false representation; if it is confusingly similar to a registered mark; or if it involves the unauthorized use of the name or image of a living person or a deceased president. In addition, there are several other less common reasons for rejection of a trademark registration. The paralegal working in this area should be familiar with the statutes and regulations governing these matters.

An Introduction to Copyrights

Copyright is the right, granted by federal statute, of an author to exclusively control the reproduction, distribution, and sale of his or her literary, artistic, or intellectual productions for the period of the copyright's existence. Copyright law is one of the most prominent subareas of intellectual property law. It is a very complex area of law and some attorneys and paralegals are exclusively copyright specialists. This section introduces the subject of copyrights by examining the sources of copyright law, discussing exactly what is protectible under copyright law, the eight categories of works of authorship, and derivative works and compilations. It concludes with a look at materials that may not be copyrighted.

Sources of Copyright Law

The drafters of the U.S. Constitution established authors' rights in Article 1, § 8, clause 8 of the Constitution. This copyright clause granted Congress the power "to promote the progress of science and useful arts, by securing for a limited time to authors and inventors the exclusive right to their respective writings and discoveries." This constitutional grant became the basis for America's copyright laws. Modern copyright law stems from several sources, primarily federal acts and regulations.

The Copyright Act of 1909

Although the Copyright Act of 1909 has been superseded, it is still significant. All works published between 1909 and 1978 are still covered by its provisions. For example, the book "The Catcher in the Rye," by J.D. Salinger, was published in 1951. If Mr. Salinger were to sue an infringer of his book today, the federal district court would use the Copyright Act of 1909 to determine the rights of the parties.

The Copyright Act of 1909 only protects published works. Under copyright law, a work is **published** if copies or phonorecords (in the case of sound recordings) are distributed to the public by sale or other transfer of ownership, or by rental, lease, or lending.

The Copyright Act of 1976 and Amendments

The Copyright Act of 1976 is a complete revision of the Copyright Act of 1909. It protects all works of authorship created between 1978 and the present, whether published or unpublished. It also protects unpublished works created before 1978 that are registered after January 1, 1978. Under copyright law, there is a difference between creation and **publication** of a work. A work is *created* when it is fixed in a tangible form for the first time. The Copyright Act of 1976 is codified at 17 U.S.C. §§ 101–181.

Although the Copyright Act of 1976 was intended to encompass new technologies, disputes arose as to the protectability of computer software programs under copyright law. In 1980, Congress amended the Copyright Act to include computer programs as protected works. A *computer program* was defined as a "set of statements or instructions

BALLENTINESBALLENTINESBALLENTINESBALLENTINESBALLENTINESBALLENTINESBALLENTINESBALLENTINESBALLENTINESBALLENTINESBALLENTINESBALLENTINESBALLENTINESBALLENTINESBALLENTINES

copyright   The right of an author, granted by federal statute, to exclusively control the reproduction, distribution, and sale of his or her literary, artistic, or intellectual productions for the period of the copyright's existence.

publish   To issue; to distribute; to disseminate; to circulate.

publication   With respect to copyright and the law of literary property, the act of making a writing, voice recording, musical score, or the like available to the public by sale or other form of distribution.

to be used directly or indirectly in a computer in order to bring about a certain result."

The Code of Federal Regulations

Copyright Office Rules of Practice and related copyright regulations are located in the Code of Federal Regulations at Title 37 (37 C.F.R. §§ 201.1–211.6).

The Berne Implementation Amendments

Approximately 80 nations belong to the Berne Convention for the Protection of Literary and Artistic Works. This union of countries adheres to a treaty covering categories of works. By joining the Berne Convention, the United States benefits from mutual regulations among member nations. Because various aspects of the Copyright Act of 1976 were in conflict with the Berne rules, Congress amended the Copyright Act of 1976 with the Berne Implementation Amendments, which became effective on March 1, 1989.

The Copyright Office

The Copyright Office is a division of the Library of Congress. It is an administrative agency directed by the Register of Copyrights. Its purpose is to determine if submitted materials constitute copyrightable subject matter and then either issue a registration or explain the reason for the refusal of copyright. If an applicant disagrees with a decision of the Copyright Office, the Copyright Act of 1976 provides that such decisions may be reviewed by the federal courts. The Copyright Office also issues numerous circulars and other publications, performs searches of Copyright Office information, records transfers of copyright ownership, and regulates certain compulsory licenses and royalties.

The Federal Courts

The federal courts interpret and enforce the copyright laws. Because the federal government has exclusive jurisdiction over copyright cases, lawsuits involving copyright law can be brought only in the federal courts. The most common issue litigated in copyright cases is **copyright infringement**, which occurs when an authorized party with access to a work has copied it or interfered with a right granted under copyright law.

What Is Protectible under Copyright Law?

Copyright protects the literary, musical, graphic, or other artistic form in which an author expresses intellectual concepts. If the author's creation meets the standards of copyright law, it is considered a work of authorship protectible under copyright law. When drafting the Copyright Law of 1976, Congress specifically chose not to limit the definition of a *work of authorship,* realizing that authors are continually finding new ways of expression. Section 102 of the Copyright Act of 1976 states that "copyright protection subsists ... in original works of authorship fixed in any tangible medium of expression, now known or later developed, from which they can be perceived, reproduced, or otherwise communicated, either directly or with the aid of a machine or device."

Originality

Originality under copyright law does not mean aesthetic worthiness, uniqueness, novelty, or a degree of creativity. It generally means that the work is original to the author and is more than a trivial variation on any preceding work. Originality requires only a modest degree of intellectual labor. For example, two photographers take pictures of a landscape. One uses expensive equipment and creates a magnificently composed picture, whereas the other uses a simple camera with a fixed lens. Each photograph would be original to its author and more than a trivial variation on the preceding photographs of the landscape. Therefore, despite aesthetic issues, there would be sufficient

infringement of copyright Using any portion of copyrighted material without the consent of the copyright owner.

originality to satisfy the copyright requirement for both photographs.

Fixation in a Tangible Medium of Expression

A work is **fixed** when it is embodied in a tangible form that is perceptible by the human senses, either directly or with the aid of a machine. The Copyright Act of 1976 requires that the work be embodied in a form that is "sufficiently permanent or stable so as to permit it to be perceived, reproduced or otherwise communicated for a period of more than transitory duration."

Under copyright law, the author's expressions must be manifested in a concrete form. Examples of works that are fixed are a song that is recorded on audiotape, a story that is printed on paper, or a visual image that is captured on photographic film. Works that are not fixed include a speech that is not transcribed, a live performance of a song, or a live broadcast of a television program that is not simultaneously recorded. The requirement of fixation does not mean that a work must be manufactured or published. A handwritten diary is fixed and thus meets the requirement for copyrightability.

Copyright law protects fixed works of authorship. It is important to understand the difference between the protectible work and the physical form (copies or phonorecords) in which the work may be embodied. For instance, if a photographer captures an image on photographic film, there is a distinction between the visual image and the physical object known as the photograph. The photograph is a **copy**, a material object that incorporates the image. The same visual image may be fixed on other items besides photographic film, such as on a T-shirt, on a cup, or on the cover of a magazine. Each of these reproductions is a copy of the visual image. There may be many copies of a work, but only one protectible work.

The Eight Categories of Works of Authorship

The first U.S. copyright act granted protection to the creators of books, maps, and charts—all the necessary works of authorship for forging a new country. During the past two centuries, Congress has passed various copyright laws expanding the protection of copyright to include new technologies such as motion pictures, sound recordings, and computer programs. When the Copyright Act of 1976 was drafted, Congress listed seven broad categories of works. In 1990, the Copyright Act of 1976 was amended to include an eighth category, architectural works. The fact that a work does not fit into one of these categories does not disqualify it from protection, however. Congress intended that the act be "illustrative and not limitative." At issue in determining protectibility is not whether a work falls into one of the categories, but whether it satisfies the requirements of § 102 of the 1976 Copyright Act.

Literary Works

The textbook you are reading is a copy of a literary work. So is *Gone with the Wind,* a Corvette repair manual, an employee directory, or an advertisement. The Copyright Act of 1976 defines **literary works** as works "expressed in words, numbers, or other verbal or numerical symbols or indicia, regardless of the nature of the material objects, such as books, periodicals, manuscripts, phonorecords, film, tapes, disks, or cards, in which they are embodied."

Computer software programs such as *Windows* and *WordPerfect* are considered literary works because they can be expressed in computer languages that use letters, words, and numbers. Certain works are not considered literary works, though expressed in words. Lyrics for a song would be part

---

BALLENTINESBALLENTINESBALLENTINESBALLENTINESBALLENTINESBALLENTINESBALLENTINESBALLENTINESBALLENTINESBALLENTINESBALLENTINESBALLENTINESBALLENTINESBALLENTINES

fixed   Established or set. ... Permanent; definite; stable.

copy   A reproduction of an original work.

literary work   In copyright law, "works, other than audiovisual works, expressed in words, numbers, or other verbal or numerical symbols or indicia, regardless of the nature of the material objects, such as books, periodicals, manuscripts, phonorecords, film, tapes, disks, or cards, in which they are embodied."

of a musical work copyright, and the script for a play would be a dramatic work.

Dramatic Works

A *dramatic work* is usually a play (and any accompanying music) prepared for stage, cinema, radio, or television. Although a dramatic work does not have to have dialogue or plot, it is generally a narrative presented by means of dialogue and action. *Death of a Salesman, A Streetcar Named Desire,* and *A Chorus Line* are examples of dramatic works. A dramatic work provides directions for performance. A play can be embodied either in its manuscript form, or in video or another form of fixation.

Pictorial, Graphic, and Sculptural Works

The Copyright Act of 1976 defines *pictorial, graphic, and sculptural works* as works that "include two-dimensional and three-dimensional works of fine, graphic, and applied art, photographs, prints and art reproductions, maps, globes, charts, diagrams, models, and technical drawings, including architectural plans." This list is neither conclusive nor all-inclusive. Generally a *pictorial, graphic, and sculptural work* is considered any visual arts work that is fixed and meets standards of copyrightability. It can range from the fine art of Mary Cassatt, Henry Moore or Pablo Picasso to the finger paintings produced by school children.

Motion Pictures and Audiovisual Works

An image of a horse embodied on a photographic slide is considered to be a pictorial work. But when that same image is presented as part of a slide show with a series of related slides (for example, the horse in the stages of making a jump), the result is an audiovisual work. *Audiovisual works* are related images in a series (together with accompanying sounds) which are shown by a machine or device.

Architectural Works

An architectural work is the design of a building as embodied in any tangible medium of expression,

EIGHT CATEGORIES OF WORKS OF AUTHORSHIP
▪ Literary works
▪ Dramatic works
▪ Pictorial, graphic, and sculptural works
▪ Motion pictures and audiovisual works
▪ Architectural works
▪ Musical works
▪ Sound recordings
▪ Phonorecordings

Copyright law defines each category of work differently; the paralegal must be able to discern these differences.

including a building, architectural plans, or drawings. The building constructed from the architectural work is a copy. If the building is located in a place that is ordinarily visible to the public, the owner of the underlying architectural work cannot prevent others from making, distributing, or publicly displaying pictures or other pictorial representations of the building. In addition, the owners of a building embodying an architectural work do not have to obtain the consent of the copyright owner of the architectural work to make alterations to the building or to authorize destruction of the building.

Musical Works

A *musical work* is a musical composition. For example, the song "Happy Birthday" is a musical work published in 1935. The authors receive compensation when the song is performed in plays, movies, or other works. A musical work also may be an orchestral work or music produced by traditional or electronic means. Most harmonic embellishments or rhythmic variations are considered to be in the public domain and free for all to use.

Lyrics are words (or nonsense sounds) that accompany music and form a component of the composition. The copyright for the musical composition protects both the words and the melody, and the composer can control or limit the use of either element. For example, if someone were to print the words to the rock song *Satisfaction* without permission of the songwriters, that would infringe the copyright on the musical composition, even though only the lyrics were used. Certain music is not protected in the musical works category. Music that accompanies a dramatic work or an audiovisual is protected and registered under those respective categories.

Sound Recordings

A *sound recording* is a work resulting from the fixation of a series of musical or other sounds (including narration or spoken words). The performer, producer, or recording company usually claims copyright in the sound recording. It is necessary to have copyright protection for both musical works and sound recordings because each form of protection is different: a musical work copyright protects the musical composition; a sound recording copyright protects the way the composition is performed.

For example, John Lennon and Paul McCartney are the composers of the song *Yesterday*. Frank Sinatra recorded the song *Yesterday*. Mr. Sinatra did not write the song, so he is not entitled to claim copyright for the musical work. However, his unique arrangement and performance of *Yesterday,* is entitled to sound recording copyright. Therefore, the compact disc containing Frank Sinatra's performance contains two copyrightable works: the Sinatra sound recording and the underlying Lennon-McCartney musical work.

Phonorecords

Unlike other works of authorship, sound recordings are not embodied in copies, but are embodied in phonorecords, a term that can include records, cassettes, compact discs, or other recording media. Because the method of recording and selling music is constantly evolving, a *phonorecord* is considered to be a material object, other than a copy of an audiovisual work, in which sounds are fixed by any method, whether the method is now known or later developed. For instance, compact discs are considered phonorecords, even though they were not available at the time the Copyright Act of 1976 was enacted.

Derivative Works and Compilations

A work need not be entirely original to be copyrightable. Derivative works and compilations are both forms of work which are separately copyrightable.

Derivative Works

The drafters of the Copyright Act of 1976 defined a *derivative work* as a work based upon one or more preexisting works, such as a translation, musical arrangement, dramatization, fictionalization, motion picture version, sound recording, art reproduction, abridgment, condensation, or any other form in which a work may be recast, transformed, or adapted. A work consisting of editorial revisions, annotations, elaborations, or other modifications which, as a whole, represent an original work of authorship is also a **derivative** work.

A derivative work is separately copyrightable. However, the copyright in the derivative only protects the new material. That is, the new material must be sufficiently original to qualify for protection by itself. For example, if an artist created a new work by painting a coat and hat on the Mona Lisa, only the new material (the hat and coat) would be protected. Any other artist may create a new derivative work with a substantially different hat and coat.

Artists often create derivatives from their own work. During the 20th century, the creation of derivative works has proved a lucrative source of income for authors who have had their literary works turned into feature films and made-for-television movies.

BALLENTINESBALLENTINESBALLENTINESBALLENTINESBALLENTINESBALLENTINESBALLENTINESBALLENTINESBALLENTINESBALLENTINESBALLENTINESBALLENTINESBALLENTINES

derivative Something not original; something arising from another thing.

Fictional literary or visual characters may become derivative works. For example, Walt Disney created the animated cartoon *Steamboat Willie,* in which the Mickey Mouse character first appeared. The character of Mickey Mouse is still widely recognized, even though the original cartoon is remembered solely for its historical significance. Under copyright law, characters such as Mickey Mouse may be protected apart from the work from which they are derived or in which they first appeared.

Compilations and Collective Works

Often an author creates a work by selecting various components and grouping them together in a unique manner. For example the owners of copyright in *Bartlett's Familiar Quotations* have chosen famous sayings. The manner in which the authors of *Bartlett's* selected and arranged the quotation is protectible as a *compilation.*

Many compilations group facts or data which would be not protectible, but the manner of arrangement and selection of material, if it meets the standard of originality, is protectible. A compilation will not be protected simply because an author has worked hard to gather the information. The selection and arrangement of the facts must be original. In *Feist Publications v. Rural Telephone Service Co.,*[2] the U.S. Supreme Court denied protection to a telephone directory which alphabetically listed names and addresses. Justice Sandra Day O'Connor stated, "Copyright rewards originality, not effort."

The term *compilation* includes collective works. A *collective work* is a work, such as a periodical issue, anthology, or encyclopedia, in which a number of contributions, constituting separate and independent works in themselves, are assembled into a collective whole. Unlike other compilations, such as a directory or book of quotations, the underlying elements assembled into a collective work can be separately protected; for example, the components of a collection of short stories by John Updike or a collection of "greatest hits" recordings from the 1970s are protectible. Other examples of collective works include a magazine or newspaper, a group of film clips, or a poetry anthology.

What Is Not Protectible under Copyright Law?

Section 102 of the Copyright Act of 1976 defines what is copyrightable, but it also specifically excludes certain things from copyright protection. Section 102(b) states, "In no case does copyright protection for an original work of authorship extend to any idea, procedure, process, system, method of operation, concept, principle, or discovery, regardless of the form in which it is described, explained, illustrated, or embodied in such work." These exclusions are further discussed in the Code of Federal Regulations.

37 C.F.R. § 202.1
Material Not Subject to Copyright

The following are examples of works not subject to copyright and applications for registration of such works cannot be entertained:

(a) Works and short phrases such as names, titles, and slogans; familiar symbols or designs; mere variations of typographic ornamentation, lettering or coloring; mere listing of ingredients or contents;

(b) Ideas, plans, methods, systems, or devices, as distinguished from the particular manner in which they are expressed or described in a writing;

(c) Blank forms, such as time cards, graph paper, account books, diaries, bank checks, scorecards, address books, report forms, order forms and the like, which are designed for recording information and do not in themselves convey information;

(d) Works consisting entirely of information that is common property containing no original authorship, such as, for example: Standard calendars, height and weight charts, tape measures and rulers, schedules of sporting events, and lists of tables taken from public documents or other common sources.

Material that is not protected under copyright (or other proprietary laws) is free for the public use and is considered to be in the public domain.

Short phrases and ideas, for example, are in the public domain. Works of authorship that are otherwise copyrightable may fall into the public domain, in one of several ways. For instance, if the copyright has expired or has been forfeited, or if the material in question was created by U.S. government employees in the course of their employment, the material is considered to be in the public domain.

Determining whether a work is in the public domain requires research. The Copyright Office does not maintain a list of public domain works. However, private companies can perform searches and furnish public domain reports.

Copyright Ownership

The author initially acquires all rights to a copyrightable work. This means that the author is the original owner of copyright. The owner of copyright holds the title to copyright and any of the rights granted under copyright law. Ownership of copyright, like ownership of real or personal property, enables the owner to transfer, license, sell, or grant rights to another person.

This section examines the bundle of rights associated with copyright ownership. It also examines some of the exceptions to the author owner rule, such as works made for hire. Next, it focuses on the incidents of copyright ownership, such as the duration and transfer of copyright. This section concludes with a brief look at researching copyright status.

The Bundle of Rights

Section 106 of the Copyright Act of 1976 provides a bundle of rights to the author of a copyrightable work. This bundle includes the exclusive rights of reproduction, adaptation, publication, performance, and display—all of the means of commercially exploiting a copyrightable work. If one of these rights is exercised without the authorization of the author of the work, an infringement has occurred. The bundle of rights is granted to authors regardless of whether copyright protection was secured under the current copyright act or the Copyright Act of 1909. Each right granted under copyright is separate and divisible and can be transferred, licensed, or otherwise granted to a third party who becomes the owner of copyright as to that specific grant.

Right to Reproduce the Work

A work is *reproduced* when it (or a substantial portion of it) is copied and fixed in a material form such as a copy or phonorecord. The right to reproduce a work is the most elementary power of copyright because it controls the right of duplication.

Right to Distribute the Work to the Public

The author controls distribution of the work to the public, whether by sale, gift, loan, lease, or rental. This is also known as the right to publish the work, or publication right.

Right to Adapt the Work: Right to Prepare Derivative Works

Prior to the 20th century, authors had difficulty securing adaptation rights. For instance, a novelist could not stop a playwright from adapting a novel for the stage. It was not until 1870 that Congress granted authors the right to control the dramatization or translation of their books. This was the origin of derivative rights, also known as the right to adapt a work. The adaptation right is particularly important to authors because it controls the making of derivative works.

Right of Public Performance

To perform a work publicly has a much broader meaning than the common concept of a **performance**. For example, the playing of a phonorecord in a nightclub is public performance. Other examples of a public performance may include the following: a novelist reads aloud from her work; a dancer presents a ballet; a motion picture company authorizes a showing of its latest film; a songwriter performs an original composition at a nightclub; a radio station plays a record containing a copyrighted song; a television station broadcasts a television show; or a cable TV company receives the television station broadcast containing a copyrighted program and rebroadcasts it via cable transmission.

To perform a work publicly may mean that a performance of a work is transmitted to the public by means of a device or process. For example, the playing of a copyrighted musical work over the public address system at a dance club also would be a performance. Similarly, any transmission of a work by a radio or television station is a performance.

If a company provided seating, charged admission, and played a motion picture for the public, that unauthorized showing would clearly violate the right to control public performance. But what if the company rented videotapes and provided viewing rooms for the public? According to several court decisions, the showing of rented films in private booths is a public performance, and permission must be acquired from the author. The rental of videotapes for viewing in a hotel room, however, is not an infringement of the public performance right.

The performance right does not extend to sound recordings. This does not mean that radio stations may freely perform recordings without any authorization, however. As discussed previously, an audio recording usually contains two separate copyrightable works: a sound recording copyright protects the arrangement or production of a song, and a musical works copyright protects the underlying song being performed. By way of example, a radio station plays a recording of *Born in the U.S.A.*, an original song by Bruce Springsteen. Authorization is not required from the record company that owns the sound recording. However, some form of authorization is required from Mr. Springsteen, who is the author of the musical composition. Such authorization usually comes from performing rights societies acting on behalf of individual owners.

Right to Display the Work

The right to display a work refers to the public showing of a copyrighted work. For example, a painter has a right to control the public exhibition of a work prior to the sale of that work. The Copyright Act of 1976 states that to *display publicly* means to show a copy of a work, either directly or by means of a film, slide, television image, or any other device or process.

In the case of a motion picture or other audiovisual work, the nonsequential showing of individual images is a display. Therefore, if individual images from the film, Sleeping Beauty, were projected at a public theater, that showing would infringe the right to display the work. If the complete film was shown in sequence, that would infringe the performance right. In both cases, the permission of the copyright owner should be acquired.

Fair Use

It was the intent of the drafters of the Constitution that copyright law should encourage creativity. However, creativity could be severely hampered if there were no limitations on authors' rights. Imagine if a music reviewer could not quote lyrics or if the owner of a painting could not display the work in a museum. Such uses would be considered an infringement unless the bundle of rights were limited. The Copyright Act of 1976 includes several limitations in §§ 107 through 118. Each of these limitations serves as a defense to a claim of infringement. The most commonly asserted defense is fair use.

Fair use is a right to use copyrighted materials for limited purposes and without the consent of

---

BALLENTINESBALLENTINESBALLENTINESBALLENTINESBALLENTINESBALLENTINESBALLENTINESBALLENTINESBALLENTINESBALLENTINESBALLENTINESBALLENTINES

performance   In copyright law, publicly giving or presenting a play, musical work, dance, film, or the like.

fair use doctrine   The principle that entitles a person to use copyrighted material in a reasonable manner, including a work's theme or idea, without the consent of the copyright owner.

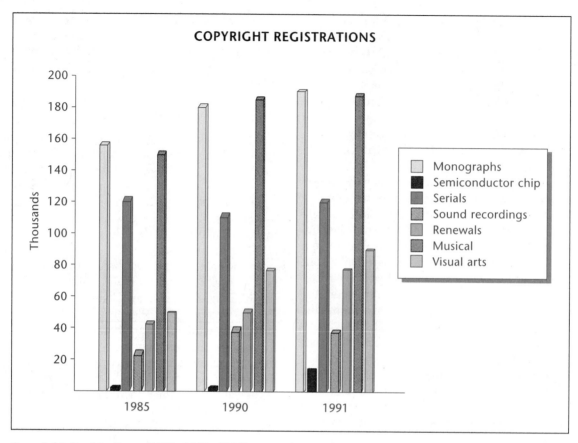

Copyright Registrations (1985, 1990, 1991) In each time period, monographs and musical works account for the majority of copyright registrations.

the author. Supreme Court Justice Blackmun wrote that the intent of fair use is "to encourage users to engage in activities the primary benefit of which accrues to others." In other words, fair use is intended to promote a benefit to the public by permitting the borrowing of portions of a work. Traditionally, this has meant the right to comment upon, criticize, or parody copyrighted works. The application of fair use principles also means to incorporate and balance the right of free speech granted under the U.S. Constitution.

The Copyright Act of 1976 offers several examples of fair use, including copying for "purposes such as criticism, comment, news reporting, teaching (including multiple copies for classroom use), scholarship, or research." Other examples were presented in the legislative history of the Copyright Act of 1976, including quotation of excerpts in a review or criticism for purposes of illustration or comment; use in parody of some of the content of the work parodied; summary of an address or article, with brief quotations in a news report; and reproduction of a work in legislative or judicial proceedings or reports.

Works Made for Hire

Intellectual property paralegals like Stephanie in the following law office scenario must be familiar with certain aspects of copyrights, including works made for hire. *Works made for hire* are creations by authors and creators who do not own the copyright to their own work.

Normally, the person who creates the work is the author and owner of copyright, but under certain circumstances, someone who employs or supervises the work of another is considered the author and owner of copyright. This principle, known as the *work made for hire doctrine,* shifts ownership of the copyright from the creator of the work to the employer. Determining whether a work is made for hire is very important. Consider the following scenario: A charitable organization hires a public broadcasting crew to videotape the Mardi Gras in New Orleans. The video crew later licenses portions of the video for use in a sexy movie. The charity is unable to stop the second use because a court has determined that the video crew retained rights of ownership in the videotape and could license it freely. This result could have been avoided if the persons hiring the crew had been familiar with the concept of works made for hire. If the work is created as work made for hire, the hiring party (whether individual or business entity) is considered the author and should be so named in the application for registration.

The case in the law office scenario points out the importance of having a detailed written agreement when a work for hire is involved. As the scenario now stands, the ABC Games and Toy Corporation would probably be entitled to the copyright, but it may take an expensive lawsuit to prove it.

Duration of Copyright

Under the 1909 Act, copyright protection lasted for an initial term of 28 years from the date that it was secured. If the copyright was renewed during the last year of the term (i.e., the 28th year),

---

Law Office Scenario

Stephanie Smith, an intellectual property paralegal for a small law firm, has been asked to sit in on a meeting between attorney Jim Hanson and the president of the ABC Games and Toys Corporation, one of the firm's larger clients.

"We have a problem with two of our former employees," begins the president of the company, Tony Albright. "We hired two computer software technicians to write software for computer games for us. Now they have left the corporation and are competing with us by selling the software they created to our customers."

"What kind of an arrangement did you have with these two employees?" asked attorney Hanson.

"These two employees were hired to write software for a new line of nonviolent computer games for 6- to 12-year-olds. They did most of their work at home, on computers that we loaned to them. Twice a week they came into the office to report on their progress and to demonstrate their product. They were paid $1,000 per week each, plus a $5,000 bonus after they completed the project. Their work with us was terminated after they turned in the finished computer game per our specifications.

"We are in the process of applying for a copyright for the software, but last week we heard from one of our customers that our former employees were offering essentially the same software they designed for us to our competitors for sale," said Tony. "What can we do?"

"Well," said attorney Hanson, "I'd like to get a little more specific information from you on this matter. We also have that other merger and acquisition matter to discuss.

"Stephanie," attorney Hanson continued, "Could you please start researching this possible copyright infringement matter?"

WHAT IS *NOT* COPYRIGHTABLE?
■ Ideas
■ Useful articles
■ Inventions, methods, and processes
■ Facts
■ Names, titles, or short phrases
■ Typefaces
■ Material considered to be in the public domain

protection would continue for an additional 28-year period. The second 28-year period of the copyright term was known as the *renewal term*. Therefore, if renewed, the total time for protection under the Copyright Act of 1909 was 56 years. If the copyright was not renewed, protection ended after 28 years and the work would fall into the public domain. Many well-known works, such as the film *It's a Wonderful Life,* fell into the public domain because the proprietors failed to renew copyright.

Effect of the Copyright Act of 1976

The Copyright Act of 1976 modified the duration of copyright for works protected under the earlier act. The purpose of the modification was to extend the total length of copyright for works published under the previous act to 75 years. If a work was in its renewal term when the Copyright Act of 1976 went into effect, the renewal term was extended to 47 years. Alternatively, if a work registered under the Copyright Act of 1909 was in its first term as of January 1, 1978, the work could be renewed for a period of 47 years. This 47-year period is known as the *extended renewal term*. For example, if a work was created in 1940 and renewed in 1968, the duration of copyright would automatically be extended to 2015 (47-year renewal term).

Congress amended the Copyright Act in 1991 to provide for automatic renewal. Owners of copyright for works protected under the Copyright Act of 1909 no longer have to renew copyright. The protection is automatically extended for an additional 47-year period. However, certain incentives are offered to authors who voluntarily register for renewal during the 28th year.

Researching Copyright Status

It is often important to determine the copyright status of a particular work, especially if permission to copy that work may be required. Researching copyright status is an important task often performed by paralegals. Individuals may research Copyright Office records at the Library of Congress; the Copyright Office may perform searches; computer databases may be accessed for copyright information, or private search companies can be hired to perform these services. Copies of records can be ordered directly from the Copyright Office. Sometimes it is necessary to use a variety of methods to fully research copyright status.

Obtaining Copies of Copyright Office Records

Copies of registration and records can be acquired directly from the Copyright Office if certain information is available. If the necessary information is already known, a search of Copyright Office records is not necessary to acquire copies.

All requests for certified or uncertified copies of Copyright Office records or deposits should be made to the Certifications and Documents Section, LM-402, Copyright Office, Library of Congress, Washington, DC 20559. This section may be contacted by telephone at (202) 707-6787.

THE BUNDLE OF RIGHTS
■ The right to reproduce the work
■ The right to distribute the work to the public
■ The right to adapt the work; right to prepare derivative work
■ The right of public performance
■ The right to display the work

These rights are listed in § 106 of the Copyright Act of 1976.

Published between 1909 through 1921	Initial term of copyright of 28 years. If renewed during the 28th year, copyright is extended for an additional 28-year period.
Published between 1922 and 1963	Initial term of copyright of 28 years. If renewed during the 28th year, copyright is extended for an additional 47-year period.
Published between 1964 and 1978	Initial term of copyright of 28 years and automatically renewed for an additional 47-year period. Incentives exist for voluntary renewal during 28th year.
Created on or after January 1, 1978	(a) Sole author—life of author plus 50 years. (b) Joint authors—life of surviving author plus 50 years. (c) Works made for hire—75 years from first publication or 100 years from creation, whichever is less. (d) Anonymous and pseudonymous works—75 years from first publication or 100 years from creation, whichever is less.
Created before 1978 but published on or after January 1, 1978	(a) Sole author—life of author plus 50 years. (b) Joint authors—life of surviving author plus 50 years.

Duration of Copyright Protection It is important to know when copyright protection ceases.

Obtaining Copies of Deposits

Under certain circumstances, the Copyright Office will provide certified or uncertified reproductions of published or unpublished works deposited in connection with a copyright registration. In order for such reproductions to be made, one of the following three conditions must be met:

1. Written authorization from the copyright claimant, his or her agent, or the owner of any exclusive right as demonstrated by written documentation of the ownership transfer.

2. Written request from the attorney for a plaintiff or a defendant in copyright litigation involving the copyrighted work, which must include (1) the names of all parties and the nature of the controversy; (2) the name of the court where the case is pending; and (3) satisfactory assurance that the reproduction will be used only in connection with the litigation.

3. A court order for a reproduction of a deposited article, facsimile, or identifying portion of a work which is the subject of litigation in its jurisdiction.

A fee should not be submitted unless the requesting party is certain of the amount. The Copyright Office will review each request and quote a fee. Write to the Certifications and Documents Section, LM-402, Copyright Office, Library of Congress, Washington, DC 20559.

Investigating Copyright Status

The first place to begin any copyright investigation is by examining the work at issue. Looking at a book, computer program, or phonorecord may provide certain information, such as the date of publication, copyright claimant, and author. After acquiring this information, the person performing the investigation must plan a strategy for further investigation. What funds are available for the investigation? If money is limited, the investigating party may wish to examine the Copyright Office Catalogs at a local library; contact the Copyright Office for a search; or, if residing near Washington, D.C., search the Copyright Office records personally. If more funds are available, a private search firm may be hired or an online copyright database may be accessed.

The Copyright Office publishes the *Catalog of Copyright Entries (CCE)*, which is divided according to the classes of works registered. Portions of the *CCE* are available in microfiche form. The *CCE* contains essential facts about registrations but does not include verbatim reproductions of the registration record. In addition, there is a time lag of approximately one year, so more recent registrations may not be included. Finally, the *CCE* cannot be used for researching the transfer of rights, because it does not include entries for assignments or other recorded documents. Many libraries have a copy of the *CCE*.

Upon request, the Copyright Office will search its records at a fee of $20 per hour (or fraction of an hour). This search is usually initiated by submission of a Search Request Form, which can

- Copyright notice on the source
- The Copyright Office
- The *Catalog of Copyright Entries*
- Online computer databases

Sources for Investigating Copyright Status A paralegal working in a law office specializing in copyright law must become familiar with these resources.

be obtained by a telephone call to the office at (207) 707-6850. The Copyright Office may quote a fee for such services, and this estimate should be provided to the Copyright Office prior to initiation of the search. A search may be expedited for an expedited searching fee of $30 per hour (or fraction of an hour). A Copyright Office search may not always be conclusive because not all works are registered and recent works may not have been cataloged.

Copyright searches may also be performed by online computer databases and private search companies. In addition to searching Copyright Office records, private search companies also may be able to provide additional information, such as tracing the copyright history of fictional characters or special title reports (showing similarly titled works).

Computers and the Law:
The Rights of Software Program Owners

Anyone who has used a personal computer is aware of the ease with which programs can be copied from disk to disk. In the 1970s, the manufacturers of computer software became concerned about the loss of revenue from unlawfully made copies. Computer users also were concerned about copyright law, because each act of copying a program, even for purposes of backup or installation, technically amounted to an infringement.

Copyright lawyers created a solution. Instead of selling the programs, these software products

would be licensed. The difference is that a *license* is a contract that grants rights or permission to do something under certain conditions. If the person licensing the software, the licensee, violates the terms of the grant, an infringement has occurred. These agreements are known as *shrink-wrap agreements*, because the consumer enters into the license by breaking the shrink-wrapped plastic that seals the diskettes.

On the outside of the shrink-wrap there is usually a warning to the effect that, by breaking the seal, the consumer agrees to be bound by the terms and conditions of the licensing agreement. The consumer is granted certain rights and warranties in exchange for the right to use the program. If the consumer does not wish to enter into the shrink-wrap agreement, a method is provided by which the program can be returned for a full refund. Sometimes the shrink-wrap agreement is triggered when the consumer signs and mails in the warranty/registration card.

Registration of Copyright and Copyright Notice

Registration is not necessary to obtain copyright protection. Under the Copyright Act of 1976, copyright protection begins once the work is created. Although registration is permissive and not mandatory under the current copyright act, it is strongly recommended. If a work has been registered prior to an infringement lawsuit, the copyright owner may be entitled to statutory damages and attorney fees. In any case, the plaintiff in a copyright infringement lawsuit must acquire a Certificate of Registration in order to file the lawsuit. For example, if the owner of a copyrighted photograph wants to sue a magazine for copying the photograph without authorization, the owner must register the work before filing the lawsuit.

Registration of copyright is an administrative process. The applicant submits an application, a fee, and deposit materials. An examiner at the Copyright Office determines whether: (1) the material deposited constitutes copyrightable subject matter and (2) the legal and formal requirements of copyright law have been met. Then the Register of Copyrights registers the claim to copyright and issues a Certificate of Registration to the applicant. The certificate contains the information given in the application, together with the number and effective date of the registration. If the Copyright Office determines that material deposited does not constitute copyrightable subject matter, or that the claim is invalid for any other reason, the Register of Copyrights will refuse registration and notify the applicant in writing of the reasons for the refusal.

The remainder of this section addresses topics of particular concern to an intellectual property paralegal when assisting with a copyright registration, including the basic registration, preparation of a copyright application, and notice of copyright.

The Basic Registration

The Copyright Office permits one basic registration to be made for each version of a particular work. For example, one basic registration would be filed for the novel *The Shining*, written by Stephen King. This basic registration serves as the primary copyright record. If this registration must be corrected or amplified, a separate Form CA must be filed. If the ownership is transferred, a new basic registration would not be made; instead, documents or records regarding the transfer of ownership would be filed separately.

Each version of a work is entitled to its own basic registration. For example, if the novel *The Shining* were revised, along with a new introduction and additional text, a basic registration would be made for the new version.

Preparing the Copyright Application

The Copyright Office receives more than half a million registrations for copyright each year. The Copyright Office examines each registration and determines its registerability. To proceed rapidly through the registration process, knowledge of registration procedures is essential. The copyright application has been designed for use by lay persons, and additional information is often furnished with the application to help guide the applicant through the process. However, despite the simplicity of the copyright form, many of the decisions that must be made have serious effects on protection of the work. The person preparing the registration must be aware of many issues and nuances of copyright law, including the correct application to use, the nature of the work being registered, information about the copyright claimant, and information about the components or origin of the work. In addition, materials must be deposited with the registration. It is also important that the person assisting in preparation of the registration avoid the use of any untrue or fraudulent statement or representation. When in doubt, a paralegal or legal assistant should actively seek supervision in the preparation of copyright applications or other copyright forms. If additional assistance is necessary in the registration process, the Copyright Office provides guides for filling out each application, as well as circulars dealing with the registration of particular types of works.

Notice of Copyright

The most visible sign of copyright ownership is the notice—the © symbol (or the word "Copyright") followed by the year of first publication and the name of the copyright claimant. For two centuries of federal copyright law, Congress required that every visually perceptible published copy or phonorecord contain a notice of copyright ownership. If the notice was omitted, the law prescribed drastic penalties such as the loss of copyright rights. Many works fell into the public domain simply because the owner failed to include the proper copyright notice. The rationale for requiring copyright notice was that it informed the public that the work was protected. The laws regarding copyright notice changed in the 1980s, though. Works first published on or after March 1, 1989 do not have to include notice. Despite this change, the voluntary use of copyright notice is recommended and certain incentives exist for continued use.

The copyright notice has three elements: the symbol © or word "Copyright"; the year of first publication; and the name or abbreviation of the owner of copyright. Although the order is not set forth in the Copyright Act of 1976, the elements are traditionally presented as follows:

> © 1989 Softco or
> Copyright 1989 Softco Company

The Register of Copyrights has prescribed certain regulations regarding notice placement at 37 C.F.R. § 201.20. The complete regulations may be obtained from the Copyright Office by requesting Circular 96 § 201.20. In addition, Circular 3 explains the basics of copyright notice.

Copyright Infringement

Infringement is the unauthorized use of a work protected by copyright law. Infringement occurs when a party with access to a work has copied it or interfered with a right granted under copyright law. For example, infringement may occur when someone copies several chapters of a book or performs a copyrighted song without authorization of the owner.

There are two steps in proving infringement. First, the person claiming infringement must prove ownership and validity of the copyright. Second, the copyright owner must demonstrate that the defendant violated one of the exclusive rights.

Copying does not have to be an exact duplication to qualify as an infringement. Copying is proven by introducing evidence that the defendant had access to the copyrighted material and that the material in question is substantially similar to the copyrighted material.

Copyright Litigation

Like all litigation, a copyright lawsuit requires a great deal of preparation and attention to procedural details. Missing a filing deadline, failing to respond to a document request, or making a misrepresentation to the court can have disastrous effects for a litigant. Intellectual property paralegals are often instrumental in all aspects of copyright litigation.

The federal district courts have exclusive jurisdiction over any lawsuit arising under the copyright statute, and the Federal Rules of Civil Procedure govern the parties in federal litigation.

Summary Questions

1. If an author decides to write a second edition of his or her book, does the original copyright cover the second edition? Can a new copyright be issued?
2. What are some of the rights that go with copyright ownership?
3. What is "fair use" as associated with copyright ownership?
4. What is the difference between a trademark and a service mark?
5. If a corporation uses a unique trademark to identify its products, but does not register the trademark, does it have any rights to the trademark?
6. What are the four basic patent requirements?
7. In what ways do the qualifications for and duties of patent attorneys and patent agents differ?

Practical Paralegal Skills

Locate and cite the statute in your state that concerns trademark registration. What are the basic requirements for trademarks in your state? Where are trademark applications filed?

Notes

For further reference, see *Intellectual Property: Patents, Trademarks, and Copyrights,* by Richard Stim (Lawyers Cooperative Publishing and Delmar Publishers Inc. 1994).

[1] Milano, Carol, "1993 *Legal Assistant Today* Salary Survey Results," *Legal Assistant Today* 48 (May/June 1993).

[2] 499 U.S. 340 (1991).

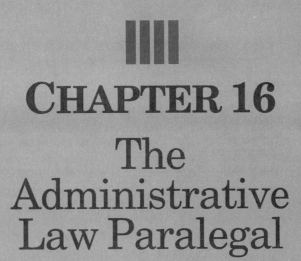

CHAPTER 16
The Administrative Law Paralegal

CHAPTER OUTLINE

Administrative Law Paralegals in the United States

An Introduction to Administrative Law

Administrative Rulemaking

Due Process and Fairness

Agency Investigations

Informal Action and Discretion

Formal Adjudication

Judicial Review

Public Rights

Administrative Law Paralegals in the United States

Thousands of paralegals in the United States work in the area of administrative law. According to the 1993 *Legal Assistant Today* salary survey, the average 1993 salary of all administrative and legislative paralegals responding to the survey was $44,750. The average annual salary of paralegals who work for the federal government in 1990 was $32,164.[1]

The Work of Administrative Law Paralegals in the United States

Administrative law is the body of law that controls the way in which **administrative agencies** operate. Considering the number of administrative agencies in our government, and all the areas of our lives that are regulated by administrative agencies, it is not difficult to imagine the numerous areas in which administrative law paralegals can specialize. Administrative law paralegals are most often employed by administrative agencies, although they may also be employed by law firms that specialize in representing citizens in administrative law matters and by corporations that are concerned with complying with administrative rules and regulations.

Paralegals often play an instrumental role in the federal agencies and law firms in which they work. Many administrative law paralegals are given a tremendous amount of responsibility, including the authority to appear on behalf of clients at administrative hearings. Many administrative law paralegals work for government agencies such as the following:

1. The United States Department of Health and Human Services
2. The United States Department of Justice
3. The United States Department of Treasury
4. The United States Department of Transportation
5. The United States Department of State
6. The United States Department of Labor

The specific functions performed by administrative law paralegals are dictated by the law firm or agency for which they work. The following duties are performed by most administrative law paralegals, wherever they work:

1. Collect information from citizens
2. Handle complaints and questions from citizens
3. Research pertinent statutes and administrative rules and regulations
4. Appear at administrative hearings
5. Draft numerous types of legal documents.

Skills Important to Administrative Law Paralegals

The skills that allow administrative law paralegals to succeed on the job will vary depending on the agency or law firm that employs them. Certainly, administrative law paralegals must be proficient at legal research. They must be familiar with all of the aids that are available for assisting with research in their area of law, including the periodicals that publish administrative law decisions.

Not only must administrative law paralegals be proficient at research, but they must also be able to effectively communicate what they learn through their research. Administrative law paralegals must be able to communicate with attorneys who are very well versed in that area of law. In addition, they are often called on to simplify the

BALLENTINESBALLENTINESBALLENTINESBALLENTINESBALLENTINESBALLENTINESBALLENTINESBALLENTINESBALLENTINESBALLENTINESBALLENTINESBALLENTINESBALLENTINESBALLENTINESBALLENTINES

administrative law   The body of law that controls the way in which administrative agencies operate.

administrative agency   A board, commission, bureau, office, or department, of the executive branch of government, that implements the law which originates with the legislative branch.

results of their research in terms that the general public can clearly understand.

Investigating skills may be very important to administrative law paralegals, who often must collect data and investigate the facts concerning possible violations of administrative law. Excellent verbal communication is also a necessity for many administrative law paralegals, especially those who appear at administrative hearings from time to time.

An Introduction to Administrative Law

Federal and state administrative agencies have become important vehicles for the implementation of governmental work in the United States. Because the number of agencies in the United States has grown significantly in recent years, as has the authority these agencies possess, a body of law has developed to control and administer their behavior and function. This body of law is known as *administrative law*. More specifically, administrative law defines the powers, limitations, and procedures of administrative agencies. Of particular concern are the rights of individuals when dealing with administrative agencies.

Administrative Agencies

Administrative agencies come in many forms and sizes. This is due, in large part, to the fact that agencies are created to confront an array of problems. In addition, agencies exist at all levels of government. The primary focus of this chapter is on federal administrative agencies, although many of the principles apply to all agencies.

Administrative agencies have many names, including departments, commissions, bureaus, councils, groups, services, divisions, and agencies. Agencies may also have subunits bearing one of these designations.

Not all agencies are of great concern to the study of administrative law. The study of administrative law focuses on agencies that affect the rights of individuals, also known as **civil rights**. The National Labor Relations Board is an example

of an agency that establishes policies which often affect the rights of individuals.

The Need for Agencies

In the United States the operations of government are split among three branches: legislative, executive, and judicial. Administrative agencies are generally considered a part of the executive branch of government, although at times they serve functions typical of all three branches of government.

There are two important reasons that we have agencies. First, the job of government has become too large for Congress, the courts, and the executive branch to handle. Congress simply does not have time to make all the laws, the president to enforce all the laws, or the courts to adjudicate all the cases.

Second, agencies possess expertise. Every year Congress must deal with a large and diverse group of issues. Discrimination, environmental concerns, military and national security matters, and the funding of science and art are but a few of the issues Congress must address. It is impossible for Congress to be expert in all the areas it regulates. However, agencies can and do specialize in an area. Agencies possess technical knowledge and expertise in their respective specialties, and can hire whomever they need to complete their tasks. They benefit from continuous involvement with the same policy area.

Because of agency expertise, many believe agencies are in a better, more informed position

civil rights 1. All the rights the law gives a person. 2. Constitutional or statutory guaranties against discrimination by reason of race, religion, national origin, gender, age, or disability.

to make many decisions. Others assert that continued exposure to the same problems and issues makes an agency indifferent and uncaring.

Types of Agencies

Nearly all administrative agencies are characterized as either (1) social welfare or (2) regulatory. *Social welfare agencies* are responsible for promoting the general welfare of the people. This often includes providing services or cash distributions to persons who qualify for assistance. The Social Security Administration, Department of Veterans Affairs, and Department of Housing and Urban Development are examples of federal social welfare agencies.

Regulatory agencies are responsible for proscribing or requiring certain behavior; determining compliance with the law; and prosecuting, and occasionally, punishing those who have violated the law. For example, state departments of motor vehicles may write the regulations concerning the licensing of vehicles, monitor compliance with the licensing rules, and punish those who operate motor vehicles without proper licensing.

Regulatory agencies possess a wide range of powers. Many agencies control licensing in a particular arena, such as the Federal Communications Commission, which determines who may hold a license to broadcast communications.

Regulatory agencies also set rates in certain industries. For example, a state may have a body that must approve rate changes for utilities, such as gas and electricity companies.

Finally, regulatory agencies often have the authority to regulate business practices. For example, the Occupational Safety and Health Administration sets standards for safety in the workplace.

Agencies are also characterized as either executive or independent. *Executive agencies* are organs of the executive branch. The highest officer in such an agency is the *secretary*. The president nominates this person, who is confirmed by the Senate of the United States. This person sits on the president's Cabinet and may be fired at the will of the president.

Other agencies are referred to as *independent* because the president exerts less control over them. The Securities Exchange Commission (SEC), the Federal Communications Commission (FCC), and the National Labor Relations Board (NLRB) are examples of independent agencies. These agencies are often headed by a group of persons, usually referred to as a *board*. Although the heads of independent agencies may undergo the same selection process (nomination and confirmation), as heads of executive agencies, the statutes governing independent agencies may provide that the agency heads are appointed for a fixed number of years. The time fixed typically does not correspond to the president's term of office, and such agency heads may not be fired by the president for political reasons. Congress usually requires some nonpolitical cause before a board member of an independent agency may be fired. This political independence allows agency heads to make decisions and policies that are unpopular with the president, but correct in the agency heads' determination, without fear of losing their jobs.

Administrative Procedure Act

In 1946, the Congress of the United States enacted the **Administrative Procedure Act** (APA), a comprehensive law governing the procedures agencies must use in the performance of their functions. The APA was enacted to curb the power of agencies. Because agencies are not always neutral participants in the administrative process, but possess great authority, Congress established rules to prevent abuses of agency power. The federal APA applies only to federal agencies.

In addition to the federal APA, the National Conference on Uniform State Laws and the American Bar Association approved a Uniform State APA in 1946. That act has been amended twice, first in 1961 and then again in 1981. A total of 30 states

---

BALLENTINESBALLENTINESBALLENTINESBALLENTINESBALLENTINESBALLENTINESBALLENTINESBALLENTINESBALLENTINESBALLENTINESBALLENTINESBALLENTINESBALLENTINESBALLENTINESBALLENTINESBALLENTINES

Administrative Procedure Act A statute enacted by Congress that regulates the way in which federal administrative agencies conduct their affairs and establishes the procedure for judicial review of the actions of federal agencies.

and the District of Columbia have adopted the Model State APA, and the remaining 20 states have enacted some other form of administrative procedure statute.

Because the federal government and state governments often regulate different areas, all must establish their own agencies to effect their own laws and policies. Accordingly, there are a multitude of agencies, each with its own particular rules and procedures. In addition to federal and state agencies, many local governments have their own agencies.

Administrative law paralegals must be somewhat familiar with both the APA and the pertinent state and local laws governing administrative agencies in the states in which they work.

Delegation of Authority

The power **delegated** to agencies can be very broad, and it often reflects the authority of the three branches of government. For example, many agencies have authority similar to the legislative branch of government, in that they have the power to issue rules that affect and control the behavior of citizens and businesses. In addition, these same agencies may have powers similar to the executive branch, in that they can investigate and prosecute offenders or violators of the rules they have set. Further, agencies often have powers similar to the judicial branch of government, in that they can adjudicate particular disputes concerning the rules set by the agency. Because of the broad powers afforded to agencies, the power delegated must meet with certain judicial tests to be valid.

Delegation of authority to administrative agencies is not new. Delegation has been common throughout the history of the federal government. Prior to 1935, delegation of authority was consistently upheld against challenges that it was

THE 10 LARGEST EXECUTIVE BRANCH AGENCIES BY EMPLOYEES (1990)
▪ Department of Defense
▪ Department of Veterans Affairs
▪ Department of Treasury
▪ Department of Housing & Urban Development
▪ Department of Agriculture
▪ Department of Justice
▪ Department of Interior
▪ Department of Commerce
▪ Department of Transportation
▪ Department of State

violative of the doctrine of **separation of powers**. In the 1930s, the Great Depression led to the creation of many new agencies, each with a broad delegation of authority. Because of the need to confront the serious economic crisis quickly, legislation was often hurriedly drafted and many of the **enabling statutes** poorly written. This led to several judicial invalidations of delegation of authority to the agencies. In recent years, though, nearly all delegations have been upheld. This does not mean that the delegation doctrine has been rendered a dead letter. Modern courts have specific tests to use when determining if the doctrine has been violated.

One test to determine if a delegation is lawful is the *standards* test. Congress must be sure to provide sufficient standards to guide agencies in the administration of the power they are delegated. That is, Congress must establish the policy within which an agency must work.

BALLENTINESBALLENTINESBALLENTINESBALLENTINESBALLENTINESBALLENTINESBALLENTINESBALLENTINESBALLENTINESBALLENTINESBALLENTINESBALLENTINESBALLENTINES

delegation   The act of conferring authority upon, or transferring it to, another.

delegation of powers (delegation of authority)   The transfer of power from the president to an administrative agency.

separation of powers   A fundamental principle of the Constitution, which gives exclusive power to the legislative branch to make the law, exclusive power to the executive branch to administer it, and exclusive power to the judicial branch to enforce it. The authors of the Constitution believed that the separation of powers would make abuse of power less likely.

enabling act (enabling statute)   A statute that gives the government the power to enforce other legislation or that carries out a provision of a constitution ... a clause in a statute granting the government the power to enforce or carry out that statute.

Another test commonly used is the *intelligible principle* test. This was the approach used by the Supreme Court in 1989 in *Mistretta v. United States,*[2] which involved a delegation to the United States Sentencing Commission. The Commission was established by Congress to research sentencing in the federal courts and to establish a set of guidelines from which federal judges would have to sentence those convicted of crimes. The law was challenged as an unlawful delegation of a legislative function, namely, determining what punishment should be imposed for criminal behavior. The delegation was upheld because (1) the Commission was mandated to use current sentence averages as a "starting point"; (2) the purposes and goals of sentencing (the policy issues) were determined by Congress; and (3) the Commission had to work within statutory prescribed minimums and limits when setting the guideline ranges. That is, the guidelines could not sentence an individual to more or less time than Congress set out by statute. The Court held that Congress had provided the Commission with an "intelligible principle" from which to act.

This case, as well as other recent cases, stress the importance of agency accountability. Courts now examine delegations more closely, often looking beyond the text of the statute into legislative history and related laws. Simple determinations of whether a delegated function is legislative, judicial, or executive are no longer dispositive. The question is whether the delegatee is accountable to the appropriate branch of government. Although most delegations today would survive judicial scrutiny under both the intelligible principle and sufficient standards tests, recent decisions show that the delegation doctrine is alive and well.

Delegation and Criminal Law

Administrative agencies do not delve into criminal law to a great extent. Because a number of constitutional safeguards are afforded to criminal defendants (such as the right to a jury trial before a competent court), criminal cases must be heard by courts of law. An agency may, with sufficient guidance from Congress, establish a rule declaring an act criminal, but it may not determine what punishment should be imposed for violation of the rule. In addition, delegations of judicial authority are limited to hearing infractions or similar wrongs and to assessing monetary fines. Any crime that is more serious, or involves a more severe punishment, must be heard by a competent court of law.[3]

In some communities, certain misdemeanors or infractions have been recharacterized as civil wrongs, and agencies have been given the authority to adjudicate them. Parking and traffic violations are an example. In such cases, the agency's authority must be limited to levying small fines. Constitutional protections intended for criminal defendants cannot be circumvented by calling a crime a civil wrong.

Although money penalties may be imposed (but not created) by an administrative agency, imprisonment may not. The authority to impose incarceration is reserved exclusively to the judiciary. This is likely true of all forms of punishment more severe than fines. Agencies may be delegated certain penal rulemaking responsibilities; the authority to promulgate penal regulations to an agency has been upheld.

The executive branch is responsible for enforcement of the law. Therefore, law enforcement

THE 10 LARGEST INDEPENDENT AGENCIES BY EMPLOYEES (1990)
▪ U.S. Postal Service
▪ Tennessee Valley Authority
▪ National Aeronautics and Space Administration
▪ General Services Administration
▪ Federal Deposit Insurance Corporation
▪ Environmental Protection Agency
▪ U.S. Information Agency
▪ Office of Personnel Management
▪ Small Business Administration
▪ Smithsonian Institution, Summary

agencies are responsible for ferreting out and prosecuting criminal conduct. Agency authority over the legislative and judicial aspects of penal law is limited.

Arrest and Detention

Although agencies may not imprison individuals as punishment, they may arrest and detain persons if justified by extreme circumstances. Generally, public health officials may be given the authority to arrest and detain (*quarantine*) persons who pose a threat to the community. Similarly, persons who pose a threat to themselves or others may be detained for psychiatric evaluation and treatment.

United States immigration officers have been delegated the authority to detain illegal aliens under warrants issued not by a court, but by the Attorney General. This delegation was upheld despite the fact that a neutral magistrate was not interposed between the government and the alien. The Supreme Court stressed that there was a long-standing history of alien detention without judicial approval and that this justified continuing the practice.[4] Hence, an alien may not be imprisoned by an agency for being present in the United States illegally, but may be arrested and detained pending deportation. The latter is not viewed as punishment. Rather, it is a method of enforcing the INS mandate to exclude illegal aliens.

Administrative Rulemaking

All actions taken by an agency can be classified as executive, judicial, or legislative. When an agency acts in its judicial capacity, its behavior is referred to as **adjudicatory**. When acting in its legislative capacity, its behavior is referred to as *rulemaking*. The distinction between **adjudication** and **rulemaking** is important, as the APA imposes different responsibilities upon agencies depending upon which function is being performed.

Rulemaking is the process whereby agencies establish law to implement a statutory duty. For example, the Fair Labor Standards Act, 29 U.S.C. § 201 *et seq.*, establishes minimum wages and maximum hours for employees. The statute does not, however, detail how the law is to be applied. For example, the statute exempts certain employees from its coverage, such as bona fide executive, administrative, and professional personnel.

Today, the bulk of laws is made by agencies, not legislative bodies. In 1989 the **Code of Federal Regulations** was 196 volumes long and contained more than 60 million words, far larger than the United States Code.[5] The Code of Federal Regulations (C.F.R.) is a compilation of federal administrative regulations. Its numbering system parallels the United States Code. The C.F.R. is one tool of extreme importance to the research performed by administrative law paralegals.

Although regulations are subordinate to statutes, they have equal weight with statutes when applied, provided they are soundly created. The rulemaking authority must stem from an enabling statute. Congress may delegate the authority to create rules consistent with its statutes, but an agency may not assume this authority without such permission. In other words, the creation of

BALLENTINESBALLENTINESBALLENTINESBALLENTINESBALLENTINESBALLENTINESBALLENTINESBALLENTINESBALLENTINESBALLENTINESBALLENTINESBALLENTINESBALLENTINESBALLENTINES

adjudicatory   Refers to the decision-making or quasi-judicial functions of an administrative agency, as opposed to the judicial functions of a court.

adjudication   The final decision of a court, usually made after trial of the case; the court's final judgment.

rulemaking   The promulgation by an administrative agency of a rule having the force of law, i.e., a regulation.

Code of Federal Regulations   An arrangement, by subject matter, of the rules and regulations issued by federal administrative agencies.

an agency and an assignment of duties to it does not implicitly create the right to promulgate rules; the legislative body must specifically authorize the agency to promulgate rules.

In addition to being within the legislative delegation, rules must also be reasonable. That is, a rule must rationally relate to its enabling statute. If a rule does not so relate, it may be invalidated by a reviewing court.

Rulemaking and Adjudication Defined

Section 551(4) of the APA defines a *rule* as the "whole or a part of an agency statement of general or particular applicability and future effect designed to implement, interpret, or prescribe law or policy or describing the organization, procedure, or practice requirements of an agency." It is sometimes hard to distinguish between rulemaking (a legislative function) and adjudication (a judicial function). This rule attempts to distinguish "decisions" and "orders" from "rules" and "regulations" by stating that if the action is intended to have future effect, it is a rule. Additionally, rules "implement, interpret, or prescribe law or policy" or describe the "organization, procedure, or practice requirements" of agencies. In this regard, rulemaking and adjudication parallel statutory legislation and common law. If an agency decides upon a policy which is to be followed from that date forward, or issues a rule explaining how it will perform some function (e.g., claims for unemployment compensation benefits must be filed within 30 days of leaving one's job), it has created a rule.

Justice Holmes defined *adjudication* as a process that "investigates, declares and enforces liabilities as they stand on present or past facts and under laws supposed already to exist. That is the purpose and end. Legislation on the other hand looks to the future and changes existing conditions by making a new rule to be applied thereafter to all or some part of those subject to its power."[6] Generally, adjudications involve individual claims, whereas rules are directed at large groups of people. Adjudications can result in an immediate sanction against an individual; a rule does not. An adjudication must be taken to enforce a rule before a person or company can be sanctioned.

Often, however, the issues are similar. For example, if an agency announces that to be eligible for unemployment benefits, one must file his or her application within 30 days of leaving the job, a rule has been announced. If a claimant is denied benefits because he or she filed the claim 31 days after leaving his or her job and appeals that decision, an adjudication has been started.

Types of Rules

There are two types of rules: legislative and interpretive.

Legislative Rules **Legislative rules** can be further divided into those which are *procedural* and those which are *substantive*. As a general proposition, a legislative delegation of authority carries with it an implicit right to establish necessary procedural rules to enforce and implement the agency's delegated authority. Agencies are normally bound by their own procedural rules, as are those who deal with agencies.

The other form of legislative rule is substantive. Substantive rules affect the rights of individuals; they are the functional equivalent of substantive statutes. If promulgated properly, rules have the effect of statutes; they require or prohibit actions and may impose penalties for violations of their mandates. Although a rule must be consistent with the agency's enabling statute, it may declare something that the statute does not. The APA uses the phrase "substantive rules" rather than *legislative rules*.

A court may not substitute its judgment for that of a substantive agency rule. That is, a reviewing court cannot declare that a better standard or procedure must be used. A substantive rule has the force and effect of law.

BALLENTINESBALLENTINESBALLENTINESBALLENTINESBALLENTINESBALLENTINESBALLENTINESBALLENTINESBALLENTINESBALLENTINESBALLENTINESBALLENTINESBALLENTINESBALLENTINES

legislative rule   [A] regulation having the force of law, promulgated by an administrative agency carrying out a statutory mandate empowering or requiring it to regulate.

Interpretative Rules *Interpretative rules* do not declare something new; they do not "fill in the gaps" of legislation. Rather, they represent an agency's interpretation of a statute's meaning. Interpretative rules are used to inform the public of how the agency intends to implement and enforce a statute, based upon its understanding of the statute's meaning and purpose. An interpretative rule may be issued even when no express authority to make rules was delegated by Congress. Whether a rule is interpretative or substantive often depends upon whether Congress has given the agency the authority to promulgate rules. If rulemaking authority has been granted, the rule is more likely substantive than interpretive.[7]

Unlike substantive rules, interpretative rules do not have the force of statutes. Courts will interpret statutes on their own and are not bound by agency interpretations. However, great weight is often given to agency interpretative rules by courts. The reason courts value agency interpretations is that agencies are considered "expert" and "experienced" in their respective specialties, whereas courts are not.[8]

Rulemaking Procedure

Rulemaking is the administrative equivalent of the legislative process of enacting statutes. Agencies are not subject to stricter constitutional requirements in the rulemaking process than are legislatures in enacting statutes. Because legislatures are not required to conduct hearings or provide notice of proposed legislation, neither are agencies. However, Congress has established procedures that agencies must follow when adopting rules. Also, many agencies have adopted rules that increase their procedural obligations, in an effort to make the process fair. In most cases, agency failure to comply with these requirements invalidates a rule. The APA recognizes three procedural forms of rulemaking; formal, informal, and exempted.

Formal Rulemaking

Formal rulemaking is the most time-consuming, expensive, and procedurally involved method of

TYPES OF RULEMAKING	
Formal Rulemaking	Prescribed by statute
	Notice published
	Formal hearing
	Time-consuming
	Expensive
Hybrid Rulemaking	Notice published
	Written comments submitted and reviewed
	Oral testimony may be permitted
	Statement of decision issued
	Less expensive
	Less time-consuming
Informal Rulemaking	Exists by default
	Notice published
	Written comments submitted and reviewed
	Oral testimony may be permitted
	Statement of decision issued
	Less expensive
	Less time-consuming

Administrative agencies have three ways in which they may promulgate rules and regulations. Each way is established by law in the Administrative Procedures Act.

rulemaking for agencies. It is not used as often as informal rulemaking. Section 553(c) of the APA requires formal rulemaking whenever "rules are required by statute to be made on the record after an opportunity for an agency hearing." Therefore, formal rulemaking is required only when mandated by Congress in a separate statute. The APA alone never mandates formal rulemaking. When formal rulemaking is required, the agency must follow the APA adjudicatory procedures; that is, a trial-type hearing must be held.

Before the hearing is conducted, an agency contemplating a new rule must give notice to the public. This is normally done by publishing the date of the hearing in the *Federal Register*, in what is sometimes referred to as a *notice of proposed rulemaking* or NPR.

The APA requires that the notice include "either the terms or substance of the proposed rule or a description of the subjects and issues involved," as well as a reference to the legal authority upon which the agency has been delegated the authority to enact the proposed rule. There is no rule requiring an agency to publish the text of the proposed rule, although this is sometimes done.

Once the agency has satisfied its notice requirements, it must conduct an evidentiary or trial-type hearing on the date announced in its notice. At this hearing, interested persons must be given an opportunity to present evidence and cross-examine witnesses. A full court-style hearing need not be conducted to satisfy this requirement. Rules of evidence are relaxed, there is no right to rebuttal, and concerns about disqualification, bias, and related matters are given less scrutiny than in the judicial context. However, § 554(d) of the APA does prohibit **ex parte** communications by the agency decision makers.

Finally, the agency must issue its rule. APA § 553(d) requires that an agency publish a final rule at least 30 days before it becomes effective. This time period gives those affected by the rule an opportunity to come into compliance before the rule becomes effective. Also, it provides those who wish to challenge the rule an opportunity to do so before it is enforced. Challenges may be pursued in a court or before the agency. APA § 553(e) provides that agencies "shall give an interested person the right to petition for the issuance, amendment, or repeal of a rule."

Formal rulemaking has been criticized as being too costly and time-consuming. Proponents of this view point to the Food, Drug, and Cosmetic Act as an example of the problem inherent in formal rulemaking. One hearing which had a transcript of nearly 8,000 pages dealt with one question: whether peanut butter should be comprised of 87.5 or 90 percent peanuts. For this reason, many people prefer informal rulemaking.

Informal Rulemaking

Under the APA, informal rulemaking exists by default. If a statute does not require formal rulemaking, and an exemption does not apply, then informal rulemaking may be used.

Three simple requirements are imposed upon an agency when using informal rulemaking. First, as with formal rulemaking, the agency must publish a notice of proposed rulemaking, normally in the *Federal Register*. Also as with formal rulemaking, reference to the legal authority granting the agency the power to enact the rule is required, as is a description of the proposed rule.

Second, the agency must give interested persons the opportunity to participate in the process. No trial-type hearing is required, though. Rather, interested persons have the right to submit to the agency written comments containing data, views, or arguments.

Although not required to do so, agencies occasionally permit interested persons to testify orally. The notice of proposed rulemaking will state whether oral testimony will be allowed, as well as the date of the hearing. If the agency decides to have all information and testimony submitted in written form, the notice will recite the address where the information is to be sent and the date by which it must be received.

This process is important to rulemaking. Through public participation, an agency educates itself. It is exposed to various thoughts, methods, and alternatives, and it is supplied with information that it would otherwise have had to pay for or pay to have produced. Also, it becomes aware of prevailing public attitudes. All are important and enhance the quality of an agency's decision-making.

Finally, APA § 553(c) requires the agency to issue its final rules with a "concise statement of

ex parte   [A]n application … by one party without notice to the other party.

their basis and purpose." This requirement is not as strict as the findings requirement of adjudication and formal rulemaking. However, a rule may be invalidated by a reviewing court if the purpose for its enactment or the basis upon which it is issued is so vague that there can be no meaningful judicial review. This requirement is twofold. First, the agency must articulate the basic rationale underlying its decision. The major policy issues must be identified, as well as the reasons the agency reacted to them as it did. Second, the agency must identify the essential facts upon which the decision rests. It need not be detailed, but a decision that recites no facts may be overturned.

As is true with formal rulemaking, an agency must publish a final rule at least 30 days before it becomes effective. APA § 553(e) provides interested persons the opportunity to petition for issuance, amendment, or repeal of the rule.

Exempted Rulemaking

The APA contains a number of exemptions from rulemaking procedures. If an exemption applies, an agency need not comply with either formal or informal rulemaking, and may issue a rule without giving interested persons an opportunity to participate. Again, agencies *may* permit interested persons to participate in some manner beyond what the APA requires, and this is sometimes done.

All rulemaking relating to the military and foreign affairs is exempted from the procedural requirements of the APA. Presumably, this is largely due to the need for secrecy in such matters.

Personnel matters of the government are also exempted, as are agency management issues. For example, an agency may enact a rule concerning the process for disciplining its employees without having to give public notice. Government grant and contract matters are also exempted.

Section 553(b)(3) contains an important exemption: an agency need not allow public participation when developing interpretative or procedural rules. This includes statements of "policy, or rules of agency organization, procedure, or practice." Remember that interpretative rules do not state anything new; they are an agency's interpretation of existing legislation.

Finally, § 553(b)(3), the catchall provision, permits an agency to bypass the notice and comment procedure whenever it is "impracticable, unnecessary, or contrary to the public interests" to use that procedure. An agency relying on this provision must have "good cause" to skip the procedure and must explain its reasons for doing so in its final rule. This decision may be appealed to a court.

Hybrid Rulemaking

Although formal rulemaking provides for participation of interested persons, it has been criticized as being too costly and time-consuming. Informal rulemaking, in contrast, is quicker and less expensive, but is criticized for not providing interested persons enough participation.

In an effort to cure these problems, courts, Congress, and the president have created "hybrid" procedures. Hybrid rulemaking adds a procedural step beyond what is required for informal rulemaking. A common hybrid is the requirement that interested persons be permitted to present their comments orally. Another is to require testimony and permit interested persons the opportunity cross-examine witnesses.

Congress may create hybrids by specifying a particular procedure for a particular agency. It has done so on many occasions. The president may also impose a rule on an executive branch agency to increase its procedural steps. The president cannot, however, lessen the requirements of the APA.

Due Process and Fairness

The Fifth Amendment to the Constitution of the United States provides that "no person shall be deprived of life, liberty, or property without due process of law." The Fifth Amendment applies against the federal government. The Fourteenth Amendment contains identical language and applies against the states.

Due process is a broad concept. It is intended to protect people from arbitrary government conduct. The due process clauses mandate that a government treat persons with a certain minimum amount of fairness when taking life, liberty, or property from those persons. Due process has two aspects: procedural and substantive.

Procedural due process describes the minimum steps that must be taken by a government before it can deprive a person of life, liberty, or property. It is not concerned with exactly what the agency does, but rather how the agency does it. Whether a person is entitled to notice or a hearing are questions of procedural due process.

Substantive due process is concerned not with the procedures used to make a rule or adjudicate an individual case, but with the substance of a rule or adjudication. It is possible for constitutional procedures to be used to implement a rule, but for the rule itself to be violative of the Constitution. Substantive due process protects people from arbitrary laws.

For example, assume that a law provides that businesses serving food may not schedule female employees to work after dark. Suppose that a restaurant did schedule female employees to work after dark. If a violating restaurant is provided with notice of a hearing and an opportunity to present its case at that hearing, procedural due process has been satisfied. However, the substance of the law can be questioned on both substantive due process and equal protection grounds.

At one time, the federal courts of the United States were active in reviewing legislation and rules under substantive due process analysis. No deference was given to rulemakers. A law would not be upheld unless a court determined that its goal was lawful and the means to achieve the goal were reasonable. Today, however, reviewing courts give legislatures and agencies deference when reviewing most laws. So long as a statute or rule is rationally related to a lawful governmental objective, it is upheld. Most laws, when reviewed under the rational basis test, are upheld.

Courts are more active, though, when a fundamental right or suspect class is being regulated. Examples of fundamental rights include the freedom of travel, the right to vote, and freedom of the press. Suspect classes are groups who have historically been discriminated against, such as those discriminated against because of race or national origin. Whenever the government regulates a fundamental right or suspect class, the regulation must pass a stricter test than rational relationship—the law must survive **strict scrutiny**. For a regulation in this area to be valid, it must further a compelling or overriding governmental interest. Most laws subjected to strict scrutiny fail.

In recent years, an intermediate test has begun to develop. This test requires that a regulation bear a substantial relationship to an important governmental interest to be valid. The exact boundaries of this classification have not been defined. Illegitimate children constitute a group which the United States Supreme Court has refused to protect with strict scrutiny, but has required the government to show more than a mere rational relationship when legislation is aimed at the group.

In administrative law, due process affects more than just rulemaking. Every day administrative officials make decisions that affect the lives of many persons. Often these actions are not easily characterized as rulemaking or adjudicatory. Regardless,

---

BALLENTINESBALLENTINESBALLENTINESBALLENTINESBALLENTINESBALLENTINESBALLENTINESBALLENTINESBALLENTINESBALLENTINESBALLENTINESBALLENTINESBALLENTINESBALLENTINES

due process of law   Law administered through courts of justice, equally applicable to all under established rules that do not violate fundamental principles of fairness.

procedural due process   [A right] grounded in the Fifth Amendment and the Fourteenth Amendment ... [which] implies a proceeding in which a person has a full opportunity to protect his or her rights.

substantive due process   A right grounded in the Fifth Amendment and the Fourteenth Amendment. ... [T]he concept that the government may not act arbitrarily or capriciously in making, interpreting, or enforcing the law.

strict scrutiny test   A term the Supreme Court uses to describe the rigorous level of judicial review to be applied in determining the constitutionality of legislation that restricts a fundamental right or legislation based upon a suspect classification.

such actions may have to comply with the fairness requirements imposed by the due process clauses.

To determine if agency action (governmental action) must satisfy due process, two questions must be asked and answered. First, is state action (governmental action) being taken? Second, does the action deprive a person of life, liberty, or property? If both of these questions are answered in the affirmative, then a decision as to what procedures are required must be made.

Cost-Benefit Analysis

To decide what procedures must be followed, a cost-benefit analysis is performed. In all instances, due process requires notice and an opportunity to respond. What must be determined is whether a person is entitled to notice before or after some governmental action is taken, and the nature of the required response. That is, will a simple informal presentation to an agency official satisfy due process, or must a full evidentiary-type hearing be conducted? These are not easy questions to answer in all instances. The interests of the individual in receiving extended procedural protections are weighed against the interests of the government in minimizing the process.

Life, Liberty, and Property

The three interests protected by the due process clauses are life, liberty, and property. Rarely do agencies affect a person's interest in life. Therefore, we begin this examination with property interests.

A person may have a *property interest* in tangible or intangible property. Automobiles, houses, money, and jewelry are examples of tangible property. Obviously, if an agency attempts to take a person's tangible property (such as by forfeiture or condemnation proceedings), due process must be afforded by the agency.

Less obvious are the many intangible property interests people hold, such as the interest a person may have in receiving government benefits or entitlements. For example, does an individual have a property interest in receiving welfare benefits? At one time, due process did not stretch to such matters. If a person did not have an express constitutional right to something, then the government could take it almost at will. Government entitlements were viewed as privileges or gratuities. Because benefits and grants were "gifts" from the government, they could be revoked at will. Not until a right was encroached upon did the government have to comply with due process. However, the rights versus privileges distinction is no longer used to analyze such issues.

The Supreme Court of the United States examined the rights versus privileges doctrine in *Goldberg v. Kelly*,[9] and therein stated that "[i]t may be realistic today to regard welfare entitlements as more like 'property' than a 'gratuity.' Much of the existing wealth in this country takes the form of rights that do not fall within traditional common-law concepts of property." The Court stated that a person has a protected property interest in a benefit if he or she has a "legitimate claim or expectation to that benefit." In short, the Court rejected the rights versus privileges analysis. The question now is whether a person has an *entitlement*, or a legitimate expectation of receiving a benefit.

Government employment may also be considered protected intangible property, under certain circumstances, as may licenses to engage in a profession, and a driver's license if that license is necessary to earn one's livelihood. Utility service may be protected. When the government provides electricity or gas to the public at large, service cannot be terminated without providing the customer an opportunity to contest the charges or prove that payment has been made. A person may also have a protected interest in attending a public school, college, university, or other educational program.

Liberty interests are also protected by the due process clauses. Liberty encompasses a multitude of personal freedoms. The right to move about as one pleases, without government interference, is protected. This is not particularly relevant to administrative law, as agencies do not normally restrain or incarcerate people. However, a few exceptions should be noted. For example, state parole boards must provide due process before revoking the parole of a convict. Similarly, a probationer is entitled to a hearing before his or her probation is revoked.

Also, the Immigration and Naturalization Service has the authority to detain illegal aliens.

Liberty interests are not only physical in nature; rights that are more metaphysical may also be protected. For example, a person's interests in his or her good name and reputation have also been determined to be protected as liberty interests. Therefore, agencies must consider due process concerns before publicly accusing an individual of something that is humiliating, stigmatizing, or damaging to the reputation.

Once it is determined that a life, property, or liberty interest is being affected, then due process must be afforded. What does that mean? Generally, due process requires that the affected person or entity be provided with notice of a possible deprivation and a hearing. What is required varies depending on the facts of each case. Courts employ the cost-benefit analysis when deciding what procedure must be afforded.

Notice

The right to notice is central to due process. The notice aspect of due process has two prongs. First, an interested person is entitled to notice of what the agency is about to do. This may include the basic facts and charges upon which the agency is going to act. For example, a notice to appear before the Bureau of Motor Vehicles for "disciplinary action" is not sufficient, whereas a notice to appear for "potential license revocation for driving while intoxicated" is. Second, consistent with the constitutions, the APA requires that a person receive notice of the law and facts at issue and the legal authority under which the hearing is being conducted. Notice of a hearing must be *timely*. This means that notice must simply be sufficient to allow a person to prepare for the hearing.

Administrative law paralegals responsible for giving notice under the APA must be sure that all requirements are complied with. Failure to give proper notice can have serious consequences.

Hearing

Hearings take many forms. Courts use the cost-benefit analysis when determining what exactly must be done to satisfy due process. Hearings must be held in such a place that those interested will not be severely burdened by appearing. The APA permits an agency to conduct its hearings at its office in Washington, D.C., or elsewhere, taking into consideration the convenience of parties. However, the due process clauses may mandate that a hearing be conducted near a party's residence if he or she has no money or method of getting to Washington, D.C.

The due process clauses do not require trial-type hearings in all cases. In fact, what is required differs depending upon the type of case. In all cases, though, the procedure must be fair. In some circumstances a person is entitled to an oral hearing before an administrative law judge, although in some the interested parties may be limited to submitting written arguments. Even when oral hearings are held, the due process clause does not require that trial-like procedures be used. In reality, many administrative hearings are informal.

The APA provides that all persons compelled to appear before an agency (i.e., witnesses) and all parties are entitled to the assistance of counsel.[10] The due process clauses also mandate that agencies permit persons counsel in some administrative hearings. However, the right to have retained counsel has not been extended to a right to have counsel appointed, as in the criminal context.

Agency Investigations

Administrative law paralegals can be involved on either side of an administrative agency investigation. They can be working with a law firm, like Karen

in the following law office scenario, to ensure that the client's rights are protected, or they can be working with the agency, conducting or assisting

Law Office Scenario

The law firm's telephone was already ringing when Karen Clark unlocked the door and turned on the lights. As a legal assistant in a busy law firm specializing in administrative law, Karen was often the first one present in the morning.

"May I speak to attorney Jones, please?" asked the voice on the other end of the line. "My name is James Grunge, of Grunge Manufacturing, Inc., and I was referred to attorney Jones by Brian Williams. He told me that attorney Jones specializes in administrative law matters."

"That's correct," said Karen. "I'm sorry, but she isn't in yet this morning. I expect her soon. Can I take a message?"

"Yes. Please tell her that it's urgent that she call me as soon as possible at 555-1234," said Mr. Grunge. "I am the owner of a plastic products manufacturing company. This morning when I arrived at work, there were five men here who said they are from the State Environmental Protection Agency. I said they could come in and look around, but they are inspecting my entire factory, including the grounds out back where we dump our refuse. They are conducting some sort of tests back there. I need to know if this is legal! Should I demand that they produce a warrant?"

"I'll try to reach attorney Jones at home or in her car," said Karen. "I'll have her call you as soon as possible."

with the investigation. In either event, it is important that administrative law paralegals know the rules for administrative agency investigations—specifically, that they know what is permissible and what is not.

Information is the lifeblood of agency decision-making. Agencies depend on information when promulgating rules and conducting adjudications, and in all other aspects of regulating an industry. The public benefits from an educated agency, because its actions are informed and the agency is more likely to be successful in its objective.

Nevertheless, it is a basic tenet of American political ideology that individuals should be free from excessive governmental interference in their lives. Agency inspections usually involve two competing interests: the administrative agency's need to acquire information and enforce its mandate versus the individual's right to be free from excessive governmental interference.

Administrative law paralegals participate in nearly all aspects of agency investigations, including gathering data, interviewing citizens and heads of businesses, and preparing reports. Administrative law paralegals may also be responsible for conducting certain authorized inspections. The administrative law paralegal who is responsible for investigations has two main concerns. First, the inspection must be authorized, necessary, and legal. Second, information collected from the investigation must be assembled into meaningful and useful reports. Important aspects of agency investigations include recordkeeping and reporting; Fourth and Fifth Amendment concerns; inspections, tests, and searches; subpoenas; and parallel proceedings.

Recordkeeping and Reporting

One method used by administrative agencies to acquire information is to require individuals and businesses to keep records or report information to the agency. Most agencies, especially regulatory agencies, possess broad authority to require recordkeeping and reporting.

The APA itself does not require particular recordkeeping or reporting, in keeping with the theory that the APA is intended to be a procedural rather than a substantive statute. The APA does, however, provide that reporting may be required as provided for by other law.[11]

The authority of agencies to require reporting is not limited to instances when a violation of law is suspected. Agencies may require members of a group or industry over which the agency has jurisdiction to report information to the agency, in an effort to educate itself and monitor compliance with the law. In general, an agency may require the disclosure of information, or it may require that records be kept if the following requirements are met: (1) the agency has jurisdiction over the subject and individual concerned; (2) the requirement must be reasonable and not overly burdensome; (3) and the information must not be privileged. For example, in the law office scenario, it would not be unreasonable for the Environmental Protection Agency to require Grunge Manufacturing, as a manufacturer of plastic products that uses toxic materials, to keep records accounting for the disposal of its hazardous waste.

Fifth Amendment Aspects

Recordkeeping and reporting requirements raise important constitutional issues, usually involving the Fifth Amendment to the Constitution of the United States, which contains the privilege against **self-incrimination**. The privilege against self-incrimination means that persons cannot be forced to give evidence against themselves, whether oral or written. The provision is important to recordkeeping and reporting requirements because a person may be required by an agency to provide information that could prove the person had committed a crime. For example, the Internal Revenue Service requires individuals to file tax returns. Federal tax law requires that taxpayers claim all income, whether derived from legal or illegal activity.

Hence, a person engaged in prostitution is required to report all income from that enterprise to the Internal Revenue Service. May that information then be used to prosecute the individual for prostitution? The privilege against self-incrimination is applicable to such reporting requirements.

A person may not be forced to provide information that could be used to prove his or her guilt. However, for a claimed privilege to be valid, a person must have a reasonable belief that the information provided may be later used in a criminal prosecution. If a person has a reasonable concern that the information may be used in a criminal prosecution, it does not matter that the information is sought in a civil context.

As to the earlier example, Congress has avoided the Fifth Amendment problem by providing that information provided by taxpayers may not be passed on to law enforcement officials. The privilege against self-implication is not applicable; therefore, the Fifth Amendment need not be invoked because no reasonable belief that a prosecution will result exists.

There are several limitations upon the Fifth Amendment's privilege against self-incrimination in the administrative context. Business entities such as corporations may not claim the privilege against self-incrimination. This privilege is reserved to natural persons.

The privilege applies only to compelled information, that is, communications which are testimonial in nature, not previously recorded information. For example, if Steven voluntarily maintains records and is later required to produce those records, the privilege is inapplicable, even if the records are incriminating. This is because Steven is not being compelled to produce the information contained in the record (which would be testimonial); he has already done that voluntarily. Rather, he is being compelled by the order to take the physical act of providing the records to the agency, which is not a testimonial act.

BALLENTINESBALLENTINESBALLENTINESBALLENTINESBALLENTINESBALLENTINESBALLENTINESBALLENTINESBALLENTINESBALLENTINESBALLENTINESBALLENTINESBALLENTINESBALLENTINESBALLENTINES

self-incrimination   Testimony, or any other act or statement, by which a person incriminates himself or herself; i.e., implicates himself or herself in the commission of a crime.

In addition, the privilege does not apply to information in the possession of a third party. For example, Jane may not claim the Fifth Amendment privilege for tax information that her accountant has concerning her. Once the information is given up to a third party, then the government may compel that party to produce the information.

Finally, a privilege may be overcome with a grant of **immunity** from the government. There are two types of immunity: transactional immunity and derivative use. Before an agency can offer immunity, it must get the approval of the Attorney General of the United States and determine that the information is necessary to the public interest.[12]

Transactional immunity shields the witness from prosecution of all offenses related to his or her testimony. For example, if a witness testifies concerning a robbery, the government may not prosecute the witness for that robbery, even if the government has evidence of guilt independent of the witness's testimony. Transactional immunity gives more protection to the citizen than is required by the Constitution, so when it is granted a witness may be ordered to testify.

For a witness to be compelled to testify (or produce information to an agency), *derivative use immunity* must be provided. This prohibits the government from using the witness's testimony or any evidence derived from that testimony to prosecute the witness. However, any and all evidence that is independently obtained may be used against the individual. Use immunity only prohibits the government from using the witness's testimony against him or her.

Inspections, Tests, and Searches

Administrative agencies conduct inspections and tests regularly. For example, the United States Environmental Protection Agency (EPA) conducts tests at toxic disposal facilities to ensure compliance with the environmental laws of the United States. The United States Nuclear Regulatory Commission inspects nuclear facilities for the same purpose. A host of federal and state agencies are responsible for inspecting business premises to protect the health and welfare of employees, customers, and the public. An inspection may be conducted to view records, conditions, and/or premises.

As with recordkeeping and reporting requirements, the APA does not specifically authorize inspections, but it provides for inspections "as authorized by law."[13] The APA also provides that no hearing is necessary when adjudicative decisions rest solely on tests, inspections, or elections.[14] Thus, an agency need not conduct a hearing if it relies only on tests, inspections, or elections when making a decision in a case. If any other evidence is relied upon, normal notice and hearing requirements must be satisfied.

Fourth Amendment Aspects

Most administrative inspections do not have as a purpose the discovery of crimes. Rather, they are usually intended to discover civil violations. Despite the purpose underlying an administrative inspection or test, the Fourth Amendment to the United States Constitution must be considered.

The Fourth Amendment reads:

The right of the people to be secure in their persons, houses, papers, and effects, against unreasonable searches and seizures, shall not be violated, and no warrants shall issue, but upon probable cause, supported by Oath or affirmation, and particularly describing the place to be searched and the persons or things to be seized.

Although it was not true at one time, today the law regards most administrative inspections as searches, and hence subject to the Fourth Amendment's warrant, probable cause, and reasonableness

BALLENTINESBALLENTINESBALLENTINESBALLENTINESBALLENTINESBALLENTINESBALLENTINESBALLENTINESBALLENTINESBALLENTINESBALLENTINESBALLENTINESBALLENTINESBALLENTINES

immunity from prosecution   A guaranty to a person that if he or she testifies against others, he or she will not be prosecuted for his or her own criminal conduct.

transactional immunity   A guaranty given a person that if he or she testifies against others he or she will not be prosecuted for his or her own involvement in the crime to which the testimony relates.

requirements. However, the application of the Fourth Amendment to administrative inspections is different from its application to searches in the criminal context. This is because the courts have recognized that administrative inspections differ from searches in criminal cases in several respects.

First, administrative searches usually do not have as their purpose the securing of evidence to support a criminal prosecution. If it can be shown that the purpose of an administrative inspection was to obtain evidence in support of a criminal prosecution, a full search has been conducted and the Fourth Amendment applies in the same manner as it would in a criminal case.

Second, there is recognition that in today's complex, urbanized society, agencies must be given broad authority to enforce their mandates. With the large number of social problems and issues that agencies must confront, courts have come to realize that if the requirements of the Fourth Amendment were not relaxed, administrative agencies would in many respects be ineffective.

Even though its requirements are relaxed, the Fourth Amendment does apply to administrative agency actions that constitute searches. Not all inspections amount to searches. Agency officials may enter a public place and make observations. Such observations are not considered searches for Fourth Amendment purposes.

Generally, a search has been conducted when an agency official has inspected an area within which the owner, possessor, or occupant has a reasonable expectation to privacy. For example, an inspector may visually observe the dining room of a restaurant. Because the restaurant owner has no reasonable expectation of privacy in such an area, there has been no search and the Fourth Amendment is inapplicable. However, if the inspector demanded entry into the owner's private office in the back of the restaurant, or into a closed kitchen area, then a search has been conducted.

Once it has been determined that there has been a search, then the Fourth Amendment must be satisfied. In the majority of cases this involves probable cause, warrant, and reasonableness requirements.

The Fourth Amendment requires that a warrant authorizing a search be obtained before the search is conducted. A warrantless search by an administrative officer is unreasonable and void unless some exception to the warrant requirement exists. Many exceptions have been recognized in the criminal law context, but the most important in administrative law is consent. A person may agree or consent to a warrantless search. Consent must be given voluntarily.

Although the Fourth Amendment speaks only of "dwellings," it has been interpreted as extending protection to other structures as well, including businesses. However, it has been held that there is a lesser reasonable expectation of privacy in businesses than there is in one's home.

In administrative cases, the nature of the potential violation, the likelihood that a violation will be found in the area to be searched, and similar facts may be considered when applying the Fourth Amendment. A warrant may be issued, therefore, authorizing the inspection of a number of houses in a neighborhood consisting of old structures which are likely to have health and safety violations, even though there is no probable cause to believe that specific violations exist.

Subpoenas

Most agencies possess the authority to issue **subpoenas** to compel production of information from an individual or business that refuses to provide required information. In general, four requirements must be met before an authorized agency may issue a subpoena:

1. The investigation undertaken must be authorized by statute, and the investigation must be undertaken for legitimate purposes

2. The information sought must be relevant to the investigation

subpoena   A command in the form of written process requiring a witness to ... testify.

3. The information sought must not be overly burdensome
4. The information sought must not be privileged.

Without subpoena power, agencies would have no method of requiring compliance with reporting or other production-of-information requirements.

Agencies do not have an inherent power to issue subpoenas. Congress must expressly grant that power in the enabling statute. Some statutes specify who has the authority to issue subpoenas (often the head of the agency). Because it is impracticable to have every subpoena issued by a large agency to be signed by the agency head, a practice has developed where the agency head signs and provides blank subpoenas to lower agency officials for use. In some instances, the authority to sign subpoenas has been delegated to subordinates.

In federal court proceedings, subpoenas must be issued by the clerk of court upon the request of a party. The subpoena may be issued in blank, to be filled out later by the requesting party. The requesting party need not show materiality or relevance to obtain a subpoena.

The same is not true in administrative proceedings. The APA does not itself confer the power to issue subpoenas; it does provide that agency subpoenas authorized by another statute may be issued upon the request of a party. It further states that an agency may require the requesting party to submit a statement showing "general relevance and reasonable scope of the evidence sought."[15] An agency may, if these are not proved, deny a request for subpoena.

Parallel Proceedings

The civil or administrative laws often overlap with the criminal laws. In some instances, a single statute may have both a criminal and a civil (often administrative) aspect. In such cases, parallel civil and criminal proceedings are possible. Generally, parallel proceedings are constitutionally sound.

Courts may, however, suspend an administrative proceeding if necessary to preserve a constitutional or statutory right. For example, **discovery** is more broad in civil cases than in criminal. It would be inappropriate for the government to initiate a civil case parallel to a criminal case in hopes of benefiting from the broader discovery rules. Likewise, the same theory could be used to prevent the disclosure of prosecution or defense strategy, violate the Fifth Amendment's privilege against self-incrimination, or otherwise prejudice a case.[16]

Informal Action and Discretion

A great majority of agency actions are informal. It is the exception and not the rule, in both rule-making and adjudication, that formal procedures must be used. In addition, agencies perform many functions that fall outside the rulemaking or adjudication models. These acts are governed by the rules concerning informal procedures. However, these actions constitute the bulk of administrative actions, and so informal procedures have been called the "lifeblood of the administrative process."

Generally, informal actions are not governed by statute. Accordingly, agencies exercise significant discretion when performing these functions. There is little judicial review of such discretion.

An agency has **discretion** when it has choices. Whenever an agency is permitted to choose from

BALLENTINESBALLENTINESBALLENTINESBALLENTINESBALLENTINESBALLENTINESBALLENTINESBALLENTINESBALLENTINESBALLENTINESBALLENTINESBALLENTINESBALLENTINESBALLENTINES

discovery   A means for providing a party, in advance of trial, with access to facts that are within the knowledge of the other side, to enable the party to better try his or her case.

discretion   The power conferred upon an official to act according to his or her own judgment and conscience, within general rules of law only … .

more than one action or decision, the agency is exercising its discretion. Decisions not to act can rarely be successfully challenged. It is when an agency takes some affirmative act that it is most at risk of reversal or liability.

Often when agencies act informally, there is little or no procedure to protect individuals. Discretion may be unfettered or hampered by only minimal constraints. Therefore, questions of fairness are common in this area, and due process is often at issue.

Be aware, however, that the law (as enforced by the judiciary) is not the only limitation upon agency discretion. Political accountability is also a limitation. Angering Congress, the president, or the public can lead to detrimental consequences for an agency.

This introduction to informal actions and discretion includes a discussion of prosecutorial discretion, discretion to settle cases, protective action, advisory opinions and declaratory orders, and other informal actions.

Prosecutorial Discretion

Generally, the Department of Justice, through its offices of United States Attorneys, is responsible for enforcing criminal statutes, even when the subject matter of such a criminal prohibition falls within the jurisdiction of another agency. Agencies, however, prosecute the civil aspect of such violations. While performing such functions, they exercise the same discretion that federal prosecutors do when enforcing criminal laws. *Prosecutorial discretion* includes deciding who to investigate and prosecute; whether to settle such a case before, during, or after a prosecution; and related decisions.

Why must agencies decide who to investigate? Because not all persons and businesses can be investigated for compliance with the law. Agencies do not have the resources to embark upon such an endeavor. Therefore, agencies investigate select cases.

Many factors affect these decisions, such as the likelihood of discovering a violation and the expense and convenience of conducting a particular investigation. Generally, administrators are empowered with the discretion to decide who should be investigated for a violation. Accordingly, a party subject to an investigation may not object by claiming selective prosecution.

Agencies also exercise the discretion to decide who shall be prosecuted. As mentioned earlier, agencies do not possess the resources to prosecute every discovered violator. Factors in such a decision include the likelihood of victory at trial, the seriousness of the violation, the expense of the prosecution, the deterrent effect of such a prosecution, and the need to resolve presented legal or factual issues.

Discretion to Settle Cases

Because agencies have huge caseloads, negotiation and settlement of cases are common agency practices. This avoids the time and expense of trial and pretrial procedures. Settlement may occur before a case has been filed, while a case is pending, or later (to avoid appeal).

The APA requires that agencies give respondents in complaint cases the chance to settle "when time, the nature of the proceeding, and the public interest permit."[17] Although agencies must consider settlement proposals, there is no limitation on their authority to accept or reject proposals. When contemplating settlement, an agency must consider the public interest, as well as how consumers, regulated parties, and others will be affected. Many agencies have established rules governing settlement.

Protective Action

Some statutes authorize agencies to take actions to protect the health, safety, and economic well-being of individuals or the public at large. Recalls, seizures by agencies of goods or other items, suspensions of licenses, and cease-and-desist orders are all forms of protective action. For example, the Food and Drug Administration may seize or recall contaminated food, drugs, or cosmetics; a state licensing board may suspend a physician's right to practice medicine; an attorney general's office may issue a cease-and-desist order to a company that engages in deceptive consumer practices. In *Dixon v. Love*, it was decided that an agency could properly summarily revoke a person's driver's license in order to remove a threat to the public.

DIXON V. LOVE
431 U.S. 105 (1977)

The issue in this case is whether Illinois has provided constitutionally adequate procedures for suspending or revoking the license of a driver who repeatedly has been convicted of traffic offenses. The statute and administrative regulations provide for an initial summary decision based on official records, with a full administrative hearing available only after the suspension or revocation has taken effect.

The case centers on § 6-206 of the Illinois Driver Licensing Law (c. 6 of the Illinois Vehicle Code). The section is entitled "Discretionary authority to suspend or revoke license or permit." It empowers the Secretary of State to act "without preliminary hearing upon a showing by his records or other sufficient evidence" that a driver's conduct falls into any one of 18 enumerated categories. Pursuant to his rulemaking authority under this law, § 6-211(a), the Secretary has adopted administrative regulations that further define the bases and procedures for discretionary suspensions. These regulations generally provide for an initial summary determination based on the individual's driving record. ...

Appellee Love, a resident of Chicago, is employed as a truck driver. His license was suspended in November 1969, under § 6-206(a)(2), for three convictions within a twelve-month period. He was then convicted of a charge of driving while his license was suspended, and consequently another suspension was imposed in March 1970 pursuant to § 6-303(b). Appellee received no further citations until August 1974, when he was arrested twice for speeding. He was convicted of both charges and then received a third speeding citation in February 1975. On March 27, he was notified by letter that he would lose his driving privileges if convicted of a third offense. On March 31 appellee was convicted of the third speeding charge.

On June 3, appellee received a notice that his license was revoked effective June 6. ...

It is clear that the Due Process Clause applies to the deprivation of a driver's license by the State. ...

Moreover, the risk of an erroneous deprivation in the absence of a prior hearing is not great. Under the Secretary's regulations, suspension and revocation decisions are largely automatic. Of course, there is the possibility of clerical error, but written objection will bring a matter of that kind to the Secretary's attention. In this case appellee had the opportunity for a full judicial hearing in connection with each of the traffic convictions on which the Secretary's decision was based. Appellee has not challenged the validity of those convictions or the adequacy of his procedural rights at the time they were determined. Since appellee does not dispute the factual basis for the Secretary's decision, he is really asserting the right to appear in person only to argue that the Secretary should show leniency and depart from his own regulations. Such an appearance might make the licensee feel that he has received more personal attention, but it would not serve to protect any substantial rights. We conclude that requiring additional procedures would be unlikely to have significant value in reducing the number of erroneous deprivations.

Finally, the substantial public interest in administrative efficiency would be impeded by the availability of a predetermination hearing in every case. Giving licensees the choice thus automatically to obtain a delay in the effectiveness of a suspension or revocation would encourage drivers routinely to request full administrative hearings. Far more substantial than the administrative burden, however, is the important public interest in safety on the roads and highways, and in the prompt removal of a safety hazard ... . [T]he Illinois statute at issue in the instant case is designed to keep off the roads those drivers who are unable or unwilling to respect traffic rules and the safety of others.

We conclude that the public interests present under the circumstances of this case are sufficiently visible and weighty for the State to make its summary initial decision effective without a predecision administrative hearing.

The decision on whether protective actions should be taken falls within the discretion of agency officials. There are, of course, conditions which must exist before such an action can be taken. For example, a state medical licensing board must have some measure of credible evidence to believe that a physician is incompetent before issuing a suspension. Summary protective action, if factually supported, is not per se violative of due process, although due process does require that an immediate postaction hearing be conducted.

Advisory Opinions and Declaratory Orders

Laws can be ambiguous and vague. How a statute or regulation will be applied to particular facts may be unknown. This is problematic to those who desire to comply with the law but do not know exactly what the law is. To remedy this problem, some agencies issue **advisory opinions**.

Upon request from a person regulated, an agency may issue an advisory opinion expressing its interpretation of a law or explaining its policy, practices, or procedures. For example, if a taxpayer is not sure if a particular deduction is valid, an advisory opinion from the taxing authority may be sought.

Advisory opinions are a good tool for assuring compliance with the law. It is often easier to comply with requirements before engaging in a practice than it is to cease the practice at a later date. Further, the use of advisory opinions assists small businesses that do not have the resources to master applicable regulations. An advisory opinion is less time-consuming and expensive than conducting an investigation and prosecution to gain compliance at a later date. Also, it is appealing to those regulated as being more fair.

Many agencies have established procedures governing the issuance of advisory opinions. In some circumstances, an agency may wish to promulgate a regulation to respond to a recurring problem. In others, an advisory opinion may be issued.

A similar tool is the *declaratory order*. The APA provides that an agency "in its sound discretion, may issue a declaratory order to terminate a controversy or remove uncertainty."[18] The declaratory order is the administrative equivalent of the judicial **declaratory judgment**. Its purpose is to resolve questions of law that have arisen but are not currently being contested.

Declaratory orders have the same effect as orders issued after adjudications. They differ from adjudications, however, because they may be issued before a controversy arises, which is why they are similar to advisory opinions. The APA limits the issuance of declaratory orders to situations in which a formal adjudication is required. Therefore, in most situations a declaratory order may not be issued.

Other Informal Actions

Every day, agency officials make decisions that are vested to their sound discretion. As administrators, agencies manage public projects, lands, and other property. Decisions concerning purchases, leases, sales, employee concerns, and the like must be made.

Agencies must also deal with the media. Decisions concerning the release of information and the issuance of statements must be made by agency officials. Publicity may be used to inform the public, warn the public of a danger, or to sanction offenders of the law.

In summary, most agency action is informal. Most informal action is discretionary, and there is little judicial review. Familiarity with a particular agency's informal rules and procedures is important to the successful representation of a client who is dealing with that agency.

BALLENTINESBALLENTINESBALLENTINESBALLENTINESBALLENTINESBALLENTINESBALLENTINESBALLENTINESBALLENTINESBALLENTINESBALLENTINESBALLENTINESBALLENTINES

advisory opinion   A judicial interpretation of a legal question requested by the legislative or executive branch of government.

declaratory judgment   A judgment that specifies the rights of the parties but orders no relief. ... [I]t is a binding judgment and the appropriate remedy for the determination of an actionable dispute when the plaintiff is in doubt as to his or her legal rights.

Formal Adjudication

The APA provides that any proceeding which results in an "order" is an adjudication.[19] **Order** is defined to include all actions, including licensing, that are not rulemaking. As a result, a great number of agency actions are considered adjudications.

A proceeding involving a charge by an agency that a person or business has violated a regulation or statute is an adjudication. It is an adjudication for an agency to consider issuing, suspending, or revoking a permit or license. Most government employees are entitled to adjudicatory procedures when suspended or fired from government employment.

The introduction to formal adjudication in this section includes a discussion of proper notice, participation, intervention, consolidation, class actions, and discovery.

Notice

Adjudications are the administrative equivalent of court trials. Although the procedures and formalities are more relaxed than in court trials, the theme is the same: adversarial parties present evidence, examine and cross-examine witnesses, and make statements to a presiding official.

For this process to work, all parties must receive notice of an impending adjudication. The APA requires that all parties be "timely informed" of the time, place, and nature of the hearing.[20] These requirements are central to fairness, and the due process clauses, as well as the APA, require such disclosures.

Administrative law paralegals are often involved in all aspects of formal administrative hearings. Whether they work for the attorney who represents the citizen or for the agency, they are often called on to participate in all prehearing and hearing matters. Many agencies allow paralegals to represent clients at hearings.

Participation, Intervention, Consolidation, and Class Actions

All parties in interest must receive notice and be permitted to participate in the hearing. Those who are not obvious parties may seek to intervene.

All parties are entitled to make opening and closing statements, call witnesses, cross-examine witnesses, and otherwise participate. The joinder of a party is, therefore, an act which will cost significant time at a hearing.

Being a party is not the only way one can participate in a hearing. A person may be called as a witness. For many who are interested in a case, but do not want to go so far as intervening, having the opportunity to testify may be satisfactory. Such an individual must, however, have information relevant to the proceeding. A mere narrative or opinion is not likely to be permitted.

A person or group may also seek to file an *amicus curiae* brief. Amicus briefs are most common at the appellate stage of court proceedings, although they are sometimes used in administrative proceedings. Amicus briefs are an efficient tool, as they permit a person or group to express a perspective or opinion without becoming a party.

Class actions are sometimes filed against administrative agencies also. For example, all those persons overcharged by a public utility may bring a class action to recover overpayments or enjoin the agency from collecting.

BALLENTINESBALLENTINESBALLENTINESBALLENTINESBALLENTINESBALLENTINESBALLENTINESBALLENTINESBALLENTINESBALLENTINESBALLENTINESBALLENTINESBALLENTINESBALLENTINESBALLENTINES

order   A determination made by an administrative agency.

amicus curiae   "Friend of the court." A person who is interested in the outcome of the case, but who is not a party, whom the court permits to file a brief for the purpose of providing the court with a position or a point of view which it might not otherwise have.

class action   An action brought by one or several plaintiffs on behalf of a class of persons.

Discovery

The rules of civil procedure of all United States courts provide for discovery after a case has been initiated. *Discovery* is the pretrial process whereby the parties in a case exchange information. The purpose of discovery is to allow the parties to prepare for trial in an informed manner. Discovery prevents "trial by surprise" and encourages settlement; it also makes trials more fair and efficient.

The rules of discovery in administrative proceedings are much different from those used in courts. First, the APA does not mention discovery, except in the context of the Freedom of Information Act. The APA therefore does not require agencies to disclose information prior to the hearing. Similarly, it has been determined that the Constitution of the United States does not require prehearing discovery in administrative proceedings.

Many agencies, such as the Federal Trade Commission, have adopted a set of discovery rules. Some are similar to the rules used in the federal courts. Additionally, many agencies provide information even though they are not required to do so. Therefore, it is a good practice always to make a request.

Another discovery device which may be used by those charged by an agency is the **Jencks** Act, 18 U.S.C. § 3500. Under this statute, attorneys for the government who are performing a prosecutorial function must disclose prior statements of government witnesses after the witness has testified. Because this causes delays in hearings, the government often provides this information in advance of the hearing.

Finally, a nondiscovery device, the **stipulation**, is often used in connection with formal adjudications. A stipulation is an agreement between the parties that a particular matter is true. Stipulations expedite trial, as they eliminate testimony and other evidence from having to be presented. For example, the parties to a hearing may agree that a company used a particular procedure in disposing of toxic materials, but may disagree as to whether that procedure is lawful. To save time, the parties can stipulate to the particular disposal procedure used. Once stipulated, it is treated as true at the hearing, and the parties are bound by their agreement.

Prehearing Conference

APA § 556(c)(6) states that "employees presiding at hearings may hold conferences for the settlement or simplification of the issues by consent of the parties." The prehearing conference is the administrative equivalent of a judicial pretrial conference. Because of the issues discussed during the conference, it is a good source of discovery for the parties. At the prehearing conference, the parties may discuss and identify the issues, discuss stipulations, review exhibits and other evidence, provide lists of witnesses expected to be called, and consider settlement. Also, the presiding official will review with the attorneys the format and procedure of the hearing. The presiding officer decides when the prehearing conference is to take place, and may conduct the conference days, weeks, or even months before the date of hearing.

The Hearing

Simply because a proceeding qualifies as an adjudication under the APA does not mean that trial-type procedures must be used. The APA only mandates trial-type procedures whenever specifically required by another statute. Section 554 of the APA, entitled "Adjudications," only applies to adjudications "required by statute to be determined on the record after opportunity for an agency hearing."

A congressional mandate for a hearing is not likely to be construed as requiring a trial-type hearing; Congress must clearly state that the right to a trial-type hearing is granted.

BALLENTINESBALLENTINESBALLENTINESBALLENTINESBALLENTINESBALLENTINESBALLENTINESBALLENTINESBALLENTINESBALLENTINESBALLENTINESBALLENTINESBALLENTINES

Jencks rule   The rule that a defendant in a federal criminal prosecution has the right to examine government papers to be better able to cross-examine or impeach government witnesses.

stipulation   An agreement by the parties to a lawsuit with respect to certain uncontested facts. A stipulation avoids the need to present evidence regarding the matters it covers; it is entered into to save time and expense.

If a full trial-type hearing is not required, an agency may use any other form of hearing within the limits of due process. In rare circumstances the due process clauses may require that some form of evidentiary hearing be held, regardless of whether a hearing is required by statute.

As in trial-type evidentiary hearings, the parties to formal adjudications may make opening and closing statements, call and cross-examine witnesses, and present other evidence. Objections may be made. An administrative law judge or other officer presides at the hearing. However, some important differences exist between judicial trials and administrative adjudications.

Evidence

The Federal Rules of Evidence do not apply in federal administrative hearings. The APA merely states that "[a]ny oral or documentary evidence may be received, but the agency as a matter of policy shall provide for the exclusion of irrelevant, immaterial, or unduly repetitious evidence."[21] Thus, agencies must establish policies concerning the exclusion of irrelevant, immaterial, or unduly repetitious evidence, but they are not bound by common law or statutory rules of evidence.

A presiding officer of an administrative hearing may admit hearsay or other evidence which would be excluded from a judicial trial, unless the agency has a rule of evidence requiring otherwise. As a result, it is common for administrative law judges to take a liberal approach to evidence and admit nearly all evidence, often with the qualification "for what it's worth." This means that the factfinder will consider not only the substance of the evidence when making its decision, but the reliability of the evidence as well.

Standards of Proof

As in judicial trials, the standard of proof in an administrative hearing is usually a **preponderance**

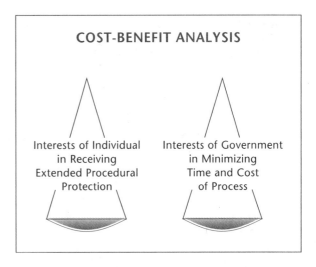

COST-BENEFIT ANALYSIS

Interests of Individual in Receiving Extended Procedural Protection

Interests of Government in Minimizing Time and Cost of Process

Cost Benefit Analysis The interests of the individual (entities separate from the government) are weighed against the interests of the government when determining which type of rulemaking procedure is required.

of the evidence. The preponderance of the evidence standard is met when the trier of fact believes that the fact asserted is more likely true than not. In terms of percentages, this means 51 percent or greater.

When Congress has not specified what standard should be applied, courts have imposed a higher standard in some cases, such as when civil liberties are threatened. Courts may impose a clear and convincing standard, which falls between the lower preponderance and higher beyond a reasonable doubt standards.

Administrative Law Judges

The right to a hearing does not equate with the right to have one's case heard by any particular individual, such as the head of an agency. Nor does the right to be heard carry with it the right to be heard by the agency official who will ultimately make the final decision. It is common practice for

BALLENTINESBALLENTINESBALLENTINESBALLENTINESBALLENTINESBALLENTINESBALLENTINESBALLENTINESBALLENTINESBALLENTINESBALLENTINESBALLENTINESBALLENTINESBALLENTINES

preponderance of the evidence The degree of proof required in most civil actions. It means that the greater weight and value of the credible evidence, taken as a whole, belongs to one side in a lawsuit rather than to the other side. ... [T]he party whose evidence is more convincing has a "preponderance of the evidence" on its side and must, as a matter of law, prevail in the lawsuit because it has met its burden of proof.

an agency to have a case heard by one official and decided by another, because some statutes require that final adjudicative decisions be made by agency heads. This is, of course, impossible in every case. Therefore, agency heads delegate the responsibility to other agency officials, often called administrative hearing officers, hearing examiners, referees, presiding officers, or administrative law judges, to name a few. Today, most are titled **administrative law judges** (ALJs) at the federal level.

The APA empowers ALJs with the authority to: administer oaths and affirmations; issue subpoenas authorized by law; make decisions concerning the evidence offered at hearings; take or cause depositions to be taken; control the hearing presided at; hold settlement and other conferences with the consent of the parties; dispose of procedural requests and similar matters; make or recommend the decision, as provided for elsewhere in the APA; and take other actions authorized by the agency that are consistent with the APA.[22]

The Decision

The final stage in the adjudicative process is the issuance of a decision. The APA requires that the parties to an adjudication be permitted to submit proposed findings and conclusions before any decision (initial, recommended, or final) is rendered. Once these documents are filed, the decision is issued.

The decision process is much different in administrative adjudications than in judicial trials. Courts issue personal decisions. The judge, maybe with the aid of a law clerk, hears the evidence and the arguments of counsel, reads the filings of the parties, considers the evidence and law, and then issues his or her decision. If an agency head presides over a hearing, a final decision can be rendered from that official in a manner similar to a judge issuing an opinion after conducting a trial. The same is not true when another person presides over a hearing.

If an ALJ presides over a hearing, APA § 557(b) provides that the ALJ shall issue either an initial or a recommended decision. The difference between the two decisions is significant. The initial decision becomes the final decision absent an appeal from the decision, whereas recommended decisions must be certified and transmitted to the agency for it to act upon.

Finally, in formal rulemaking and applications for initial licenses, the APA permits the ALJ to certify and transmit the record to the agency, which may then issue a tentative decision or have one of its "responsible employees" issue a recommended decision. The parties may then comment on the tentative decision.

Findings

The APA requires that all "decisions, including initial, recommended, and tentative decisions, are a part of the record and shall include a statement of findings and conclusions, and the reasons or basis therefor, on all the material issues of fact, law, or discretion presented on the record."[23] This requires much more than a bare decision; a statement of "granted," "denied," "suspended," "revoked," or the like is not adequate and will be remanded by a reviewing court to the agency to make findings. An agency must issue its findings in writing. An oral decision is proper as long as it is followed by a written decision containing the findings and conclusions supporting the decision.

The APA requires that findings and conclusions be rendered on all material issues of fact. **Material** means not only relevant, but also important to the outcome of the case. If a fact is material, an agency must address it by making a finding and conclusion in its decision. In addition, the decision must recite the reasons and basis underlying the agency's decision. This is a requirement of reasoned opinions, which forces the agency to tie its findings in with its decision. Thus, the agency must find the facts, reach a conclusion, render a

administrative law judge   A person, generally a civil servant, who conducts hearings held by an administrative agency.

material   Important; relating to substance rather than form; going to the merits; relevant.

decision, and explain why the facts and conclusions reached led it to the decision it rendered.

There are no findings requirements for informal adjudications (hearings).

Judicial Review

In certain circumstances, judicial review of agency orders, decisions, rules, or other actions is available. It is the duty of the courts to review agency actions. Without judicial review, constitutional, statutory, and other limitations upon agency action would be valueless. The availability of judicial review is limited by a number of doctrines, some of which are statutory and some of which have been developed at common law.

Statutory Authority for Review

In the federal system, most reviewing authority is derived from a statute. The common-law system of review has been largely replaced by legislative declarations concerning the availability of review. Congress enjoys great discretion when legislating in the area of judicial review: it may provide for when the review must be sought, where it must be sought, and other limitations upon review when properly brought.

Generally, when a statute provides for review, no other method may be used to establish a court's authority to hear the case, with the possible exception of cases in which a constitutional issue is raised. Hence, in most cases, the statute is the exclusive method for obtaining judicial review.

Nonstatutory Review

If a statute does not provide for review, nonstatutory review may be available. There is a strong preference in the courts for review. Similarly, there is a strong presumption that Congress does not intend to preclude review when a statute is silent on the subject.

At common law, agency courts could issue various writs which were not specifically provided for by statute, such as certiorari, mandamus, habeas corpus, and prohibition. The authority of federal courts to issue such writs continues today, as Congress has provided for certain of them by statute.

However, in the federal system certiorari is no longer available. It has been replaced by the injunction and declaratory judgment. Similarly, the writ of prohibition is a dead letter in federal administrative law.

Review is different in every state. Although many, if not all, have a statutory form of review, some continue to recognize all the common-law writs as well. Other states do not recognize the writs as an alternative to statutory review.

As mentioned previously, review of agency actions that encroach upon constitutional rights may be had without the approval of Congress. This theory is premised upon concepts of due process and judicial power.

Finally, at common law agency orders were not self-enforcing. To enforce one of its orders, an agency had to seek the assistance of a court. Under this system, courts reviewed orders for lawfulness. In the federal system today, most orders become final unless appealed within a certain period of time. Failure to comply with an order can result in a fine or penalty.

Public Rights

Informed participation of the public is the hallmark of democracy. Citizens should be aware of what their government is doing, plans on doing, and has done. Citizens should be permitted, in most situations, to participate in governmental decisionmaking. This section examines the rights of the public to obtain information from the government and to observe its operations. The discussion begins with the Freedom of Information Act, the primary tool for obtaining information from the United States government. Ironically, a discussion of the rights of the public would be incomplete without a discussion of the Privacy Act, a law that prevents governmental disclosure of information in special circumstances. Finally, we close with an examination of the Government in the Sunshine Act.

Freedom of Information Act

Congress enacted the **Freedom of Information Act** (FOIA) in 1966.[24] That law is not part of the APA. The purpose of the FOIA is to make information held by the government available to the public. "The basic purpose of the FOIA is to ensure an informed citizenry, vital to the functioning of a democratic society, needed to check against corruption and to hold the governors accountable to the governed."[25]

The statute creates a presumption that documents should be available to the public. Only if a document clearly fits into one of nine exceptions set out in the FOIA may the government deny a request for disclosure. The FOIA provides for three forms of disclosure: publication; inspection and copying; and production upon request.

Publication Requirement

The first form of disclosure is publication in the *Federal Register*. FOIA § 552(a)(1) requires the following information to be published by every agency:

A. A description of its central and field organizations. A statement of to whom, and the method whereby, the public may obtain information, make submittals or requests, or obtain information; and

B. A statement of general course and method by which its functions are channeled and determined, including requirements of formal and informal procedures; and

C. Its rules of procedure, descriptions of forms available to the public, where to get those forms, and instructions as to the scope of all papers, reports, or examinations; and

D. Its substantive rules and regulations of general applicability, including statements of general policy and interpretations of law; and

E. All amendments, revisions, or repeals of any of the above.

Personnel and other internal administrative matters do not have to be published. Parties dealing with an agency are not bound, nor may they be adversely affected, by any information or rule for which there is a publication requirement that has not been complied with, unless actual and timely notice of the information or rule has been made upon the party.

Inspection and Copying Requirement

The second form of disclosure entails making information available for public inspection and copying. FOIA § 552(a)(1) requires that agencies make the following information available for inspection and copying:

A. All orders, final opinions (including concurring and dissenting) made during adjudication; and

B. Those statements of policy and interpretation adopted by the agency but not published in the *Federal Register*; and

C. Administrative staff manuals and instructions to staff that affect a member of the public.

This provision is sometimes referred to as the "reading room" requirement, because it is satisfied by providing a location for people to inspect and copy documents. As an alternative to providing a reading room, an agency may promptly publish the information and provide copies for sale.

In addition to making these documents available to the public, the FOIA requires that all agencies "maintain and make available for public inspection and copying a current index" of materials required

Freedom of Information Act A federal statute that requires federal agencies to make available to the public, upon request, material contained in their files, as well as information on how they function. The Act contains various significant exemptions from disclosure ... .

to be made available or published. Each agency is required to publish, at least quarterly, and distribute copies of each index and its supplements. If this is impracticable, an agency may issue an order stating that the index and supplements, if any, will not be published or distributed; such an order must be published in the *Federal Register*. If this is done, the agency must provide the index upon request at a cost no greater than the actual cost of duplication.

If an agency fails to make information available or fails to index documents, the FOIA provides that those orders, opinions, statements of policy, or the like may not be used against a party, unless the party has been given actual and timely notice of the terms thereof.

Production upon Request Requirement

The first two requirements provide that agencies must take affirmative steps toward disclosure before a request is made. For information not covered by either the publication or inspection and copying requirements, an agency is to make it promptly available, upon request, if two requirements are met. First, a request for information must reasonably describe the records desired; second, the request must comply with the agency's procedures concerning the time, place, and fees.

This provision is the catch-all. All documents other than those specified for publication or inspection and copying fall into this category. When one speaks of filing a request for information under the FOIA, it is upon this provision that the requester relies.

Exemptions

The FOIA contains nine exemptions. These exemptions are exclusive; that is, no others exist. Further, the nine expressly provided for are narrowly construed by the courts. This is consistent with the fundamental policy underlying the FOIA: disclosure in government, not secrecy.

The exemption provisions are permissive. An agency does not *have* to withhold information just because it falls within one of the FOIA exemptions. The agency has the discretion to decide whether to produce such records. This is true of all information, including that which is private or confidential. The nine exemptions recognized under the FOIA are:

1. Certain information concerning the national defense and foreign policy
2. Agency personnel matters
3. Information covered under other statutes authorizing the withholding of records from disclosure
4. Trade secrets and financial information
5. Agency memoranda
6. Personnel and medical files
7. Certain law enforcement records
8. Financial institution information
9. Geological information.

The FOIA exempts from disclosure records concerning national defense and foreign policy. To qualify under this exemption, the president must issue an executive order requiring that the documents sought be kept classified.

The second exemption applies to internal agency personnel rules and practices. Rules concerning vacation leave and lunch breaks are examples of the rules exempted.

Many other statutes authorize withholding records from disclosure, and the FOIA incorporates these exemptions by reference. However, Congress may not grant an agency unlimited power to withhold records, because the FOIA also requires that the other statute "leave no discretion on the issue" or that it establish "particular criteria for withholding or refer ... to particular types of matters to be withheld."

Another exemption permits withholding trade secrets and other "commercial or financial information obtained from a person and privileged or confidential."

The fifth exemption applies to "inter-agency or intra-agency memorandums or letters which would not be available by law to a party other than [one] in litigation with the agency."

The sixth exemption allows an agency to withhold personnel and medical files and similar files which would constitute a clearly unwarranted invasion of privacy if disclosed. As part of the administration of agencies, applications for employment, medical records of employees, and the like are acquired. Similarly, an agency may acquire records of nonemployees which contain personal information. This exemption has been interpreted broadly. In one case, disclosure of the results of a study of housing loans was determined to be within the scope of this exemption because the names of the loan recipients, their marital status, the legitimacy of their children, their welfare payments, and other private information were included.

The seventh exemption allows law enforcement records to be withheld, provided that disclosure would:

    A. interfere with enforcement proceedings; or

    B. deprive a person of a right to a fair trial or an impartial adjudication; or

    C. constitute an unwarranted invasion of personal privacy; or

    D. disclose the identity of a confidential source; or

    E. disclose investigative techniques and procedures; or

    F. endanger the life or physical safety of law enforcement personnel.

This exemption applies to administrative and civil proceedings as well as criminal ones. Investigatory records are not protected forever, though. Once an enforcement proceeding is completed, the records are to be made available, unless some other exemption applies.

The eighth exemption applies to records that are "contained in or related to examination, operating, or condition reports prepared by, on behalf of or for the use of an agency responsible for the regulation or supervision of financial institutions." It is believed that public access to financial institution information may unnecessarily result in decreasing public confidence in financial institutions, or even cause a panic.

"Geological and geophysical information, and data, including maps, concerning wells" constitutes the ninth exemption.

Congressional Monitoring

In an effort to monitor administration of the FOIA, Congress requires that each agency submit a yearly report to the Speaker of the House of Representatives and President of the Senate, which reports are then referred to the appropriate committees. The agency report must include: the number of times the agency refused to produce records and the reasons therefor; the number of appeals of agency refusals and the results thereof; the names and titles of each person denying a request and the number of denials each issued; the results of each disciplinary proceeding against agency employees for noncompliance with the FOIA; a copy of each rule promulgated concerning the FOIA; a copy of each agency's fee schedule and total fees collected; and other such information concerning administration of the FOIA. In addition to each agency's report, the Attorney General is directed to report the number of cases arising under the FOIA, the exemptions involved in each case, the disposition of each case, the costs, fees, and penalties imposed, and an explanation of any efforts the Department of Justice has taken to encourage agency compliance with the FOIA.

Privacy Act

The antithesis of the FOIA is the Privacy Act.[26] Whereas the purpose of the FOIA is to make governmental records available to the public, the purpose of the Privacy Act is to withhold sensitive documents from public disclosure. The Privacy Act is a section entitled "Records maintained on individuals" within the APA. This reflects the Act's goal of protecting individual records, not other governmental records. *Records* are defined as "any item, collection, or grouping of information about an individual that is maintained by an agency, including, but not limited to, his education, financial transactions, medical history, and criminal and employment history and that contains his name, or the identifying number, symbol, or other identifying particular assigned to the individual, such as finger or voice print or a photograph."

The heads of some agencies may promulgate rules exempting certain records from the requirements of the Privacy Act. The agency must include in such rules a statement of reasons for the exemption. Specifically, records maintained by the Central Intelligence Agency are exempted, as are records concerning the enforcement of criminal laws, protection of the president and other individuals, the armed services, and other materials.

Collection of Information

The FOIA does not prohibit agencies from collecting information about people. The Privacy Act does, however, restrict an agency's authority to collect information. The Act limits the collection of information, by agencies maintaining a "system of records," about individuals to that information "necessary to accomplish a purpose of the agency required to be accomplished by statute or executive order of the President." *Individual* has been interpreted to not include businesses.

The Privacy Act also requires that, to the greatest extent practicable, personal information be collected directly from the individual if the information may adversely affect the individual. In its request for information, the agency must inform the individual of its authority to make the request, whether disclosure is voluntary or involuntary, for what purpose the information will be used, the routine uses which may be made of the information, and the consequences of not providing the information. The Act defines *routine use* as the use of a record for a purpose which is compatible with the purpose for which it was collected. The term *system of records* means a group of records under the control of an agency from which information may be retrieved by the name of an individual or by some other number or symbol assigned to an individual.

An individual must be given access to his or her records or to information about him or her contained in an agency's records, upon request.

Government in the Sunshine Act

A fundamental tenet of democracy is openness of government. The more open and available government is, the greater the public's confidence and participation in government will be. This is the foundation of the FOIA. It is also the basis of the Government in the Sunshine Act,[27] another part of the APA.

The Sunshine Act generally requires that agency meetings be open to public observation. The Act applies only to "collegial" agencies, that is, agencies headed by more than one person. There is no requirement that a single agency head make his or her deliberations public.

Agencies do not have to conduct open meetings when such openness will result in the disclosure of specific types of information. The matters exempted are similar to those exempted from the coverage of the FOIA. Meetings are presumed to be open and may be closed only if one of the exemptions applies. In some circumstances, the public interest may demand that a meeting remain open even though one of the exemptions applies. If a separate statute requires that a meeting remain open, it may not be closed. The reason for closing a meeting must be certified by the agency. The decision to close a meeting must be made by majority vote of the agency heads.

Summary Questions

1. The state of Minnesota regulates fishing in its more than 10,000 lakes, partly by issuing fishing licenses. These licenses are issued by the Department of Natural Resources. Is the Department of Natural Resources a social welfare agency or a regulatory agency?

2. In what way do agencies possess power similar to that of the legislative branch of government, the executive branch of government, and the judicial branch of government?

3. What are some of the limitations on the powers of agencies?

4. How are legislative rules different from interpretative rules?

5. What are three interests protected by the due process clause?

6. Why aren't all violations of agency rules and regulations dealt with through formal adjudication?

7. What is the main purpose of the FOIA?

8. What is the main purpose of the Government in the Sunshine Act?

Practical Paralegal Skills

Has your state adopted the Model State Administrative Procedure Act? Find and cite the Administrative Procedure Act for your state. Also, locate the Code of Federal Regulations within your law library.

Notes

For further reference, see *Administrative Law*, by Daniel E. Hall (Delmar Publishers Inc. & Lawyers Cooperative Publishing Co. 1994).

[1] *Occupational Outlook Handbook* (1992–1993 ed.).

[2] *Mistretta v. United States*, 488 U.S. 361 (1989).

[3] *United States v. Widdowson*, No. 90-1639 (U.S. Oct. 7, 1991).

[4] *Abel v. United States*, 362 U.S. 217 (1960).

[5] Schwartz, *Administrative Law* (3d ed. 1991).

[6] *Prentis v. Atlantic Coast Line Co.*, 211 U.S. 210, 226 (1908).

[7] K. Davis, *Administrative Law* § 5.02 (Hornbook Series, West Publishing Co. 1972).

[8] *Skidmore v. Swift & Co.*, 323 U.S. 134 (1944).

[9] *Goldberg v. Kelly*, 397 U.S. 254 (1970).

[10] APA § 555(b).

[11] APA § 555(c).

[12] 18 U.S.C. § 6004.

[13] APA § 555(c).

[14] APA § 554(a)(3).

[15] APA § 555(d).

[16] Modjeska, *Administrative Law, Practice and Procedures* 32–33 (Lawyers Cooperative Publishing Co., 1982).

[17] APA § 554(c).

[18] APA § 554(d).

[19] APA § 551(6).

[20] APA § 554(b).

[21] APA § 556(d).

[22] APA § 556(c).

[23] APA § 557(c)(A).

[24] 5 U.S.C. § 552.

[25] *NLRB v. Robbins Tire & Rubber Co.*, 437 U.S. 314 (1978).

[26] APA § 552(a).

[27] APA § 552(b).

CHAPTER 17

The Bankruptcy Paralegal

Bankruptcy becomes a big business during an economic recession. In addition to the average working person, corporate conglomerates file for bankruptcy or reorganization at an increasing rate. Bankruptcy filings in the United States have increased more than 140 percent during the past six years.

This introduction to bankruptcy law begins with a look at the role of the bankruptcy paralegal in the United States. Next, the focus of this chapter is on the bankruptcy estate, bankruptcy courts, and voluntary bankruptcy proceedings. After a brief introduction to involuntary bankruptcies, this chapter concludes with discussion of alternatives to bankruptcy.

The Role of the Paralegal in Bankruptcy Law

When there is a downturn in the economy, fewer new paralegal jobs are created. The bankruptcy business thrives, however. Jobs for bankruptcy paralegals grow at an increasing rate. The economic adversity faced by many individuals and businesses in the past few years has meant an increase in bankruptcies and an increase in positions for bankruptcy paralegals.

Bankruptcy paralegals most often work for law firms that specialize in bankruptcy law, usually representing the debtor or creditor or acting as a bankruptcy trustee. Other bankruptcy paralegals may work for the bankruptcy court systems.

This section includes a brief look at the role of the bankruptcy paralegal, including the number of paralegals who specialize in this area, the work they typically perform, and the skills important to the bankruptcy paralegal.

Bankruptcy Paralegals in the United States

Although the number of bankruptcy paralegals in the United States is increasing, their number is still relatively small. According to a 1993 annual salary survey in *Legal Assistant Today,* approximately 3 percent of the paralegals surveyed reported that they specialized in the bankruptcy area. The responding bankruptcy paralegals had an average 1993 salary of $28,721, with the highest reported salary among bankruptcy paralegals being $53,000.[1]

The Work of Bankruptcy Paralegals in the United States

Paralegals who work in the bankruptcy area for attorneys representing debtors spend the majority of their time interviewing clients, collecting information regarding the client's debts and assets, and completing bankruptcy forms. Paralegals who work in the bankruptcy area for attorneys representing creditors may spend time investigating the debtors' property and property values. Paralegals working for creditor attorneys may also be called on to attend creditors' meetings to question the debtor concerning his or her assets and debts. Following is a list of some of the tasks typically performed by bankruptcy paralegals:

Acting as Trustee

1. Preparing notices to banks and financial institutions requesting the release of debtors' funds
2. Coordinating appraisals of debtors' assets
3. Preparing newspaper notices regarding sale of debtors' assets
4. Preparing accounts of property sold
5. Reviewing claims for distribution of funds.

Debtor

1. Interviewing clients regarding their financial situation

2. Drafting bankruptcy petitions
3. Preparing for first meeting of creditors
4. Attending hearings in bankruptcy.

Creditor

1. Preparing claims of creditor
2. Filing claims of creditor with bankruptcy court.

Skills Important to the Bankruptcy Paralegal

The bankruptcy paralegal must have a thorough knowledge of bankruptcy court procedures and must be familiar with the forms required for bankruptcies. In addition, the bankruptcy paralegal must have excellent interviewing and organizational skills.

An Introduction to Bankruptcy

Bankruptcy is the system under which a debtor may come into court or be brought into court by his or her creditors, either seeking to have his or her assets administered and sold for the benefit of creditors and to be discharged from his or her debts (a *straight bankruptcy*), or to have his or her debts reorganized. Bankruptcy proceedings suspend the normal operation of rights and obligations between the debtor and his or her creditors.[2] Bankruptcy proceedings must follow the applicable laws, and the debtor must be eligible for either a voluntary or involuntary bankruptcy proceeding. The two major goals of bankruptcy are (1) to convert the debtor's assets into cash and distribute it to unsatisfied creditors, and (2) to give the debtor a fresh start, free from many prior obligations, with certain assets intact.

Bankruptcy Law

Bankruptcy is a creation of federal law, specifically Title 11 of the U.S. Code under the authority of the U.S. Constitution. The U.S. Constitution, art. I, § 8, clause 4, grants Congress the power "to establish … uniform rules on the subject of bankruptcies throughout the United States." Title 11 provides for straight bankruptcy proceedings under Chapter 7, which is entitled "Liquidation." In the context of the statute, **liquidation** refers to the process of collecting the debtor's nonexempt assets and distributing the assets, or proceeds from their sale, to unsatisfied creditors. In return, the debtor receives a discharge releasing him or her from liability from certain prebankruptcy debts.

Chapter 7 bankruptcy typically means a cancellation of most debts in exchange for the debtor's nonexempt property. In addition, Chapters 9, 11, 12, and 13 are considered rehabilitative chapters that provide for alternatives to straight bankruptcy by restructuring the debtor's debt. Because most bankruptcies are filed under Chapter 7, Chapter 7 bankruptcies are the main focus of this chapter. Proceedings under Chapters 9, 11, 12, and 13 are later discussed as alternatives to bankruptcy.

The main source of law governing bankruptcies is the Bankruptcy Reform Act of 1978, but bankruptcy proceedings must also conform to the Bankruptcy Rules and to state bankruptcy law.

The Bankruptcy Reform Act of 1978

Title 11 of the United States Code is the Bankruptcy Reform Act of 1978 (also referred to as the

---

BALLENTINESBALLENTINESBALLENTINESBALLENTINESBALLENTINESBALLENTINESBALLENTINESBALLENTINESBALLENTINESBALLENTINESBALLENTINESBALLENTINESBALLENTINES

bankruptcy The system under which a debtor may come into court … or be brought into court by his or her creditors … , either seeking to have his or her assets administered and sold for the benefit of the creditors and to be discharged from his or her debts … , or to have his debts reorganized … .

liquidation 1. The extinguishment of a debt by payment. 2. The ascertainment of the amount of a debt or demand by agreement or by legal proceedings.

Bankruptcy Code). Title 11 includes the following chapters:

Chapter 1: General Provisions, Definitions and Rules of Construction

Chapter 3: Case Administration

Chapter 5: Creditors, the Debtor, and the Estate

Chapter 7: Liquidation

Chapter 9: Adjustment of the Debts of a Municipality

Chapter 11: Reorganization

Chapter 12: Adjustment of Debts of a Family Farmer with Regular Annual Income

Chapter 13: Adjustment of the Debts of an Individual with Regular Income

Chapter 15: United States Trustees

The two major amendments to the Bankruptcy Reform Act of 1978 are the Bankruptcy Amendments and Federal Judgeship Act of 1984 and the Bankruptcy Judges, United States Trustees, and Family Farmer Bankruptcy Act of 1986.

Bankruptcy Rules

In addition to the Bankruptcy Reform Act of 1978, the Federal Rules of Bankruptcy Procedure govern the practice and procedure of bankruptcy law. The Bankruptcy Rules, not the Federal Rules of Civil Procedure, govern procedure in bankruptcy courts.

State Bankruptcy Law

Although bankruptcies are authorized and governed by federal law, state law also plays a significant role. Many issues determined by bankruptcy courts depend on the laws of the debtor's state of domicile. State courts create and define property interests.

Eligibility

Most individuals who reside in, or have a domicile, a place of business, or property in the United States, are eligible to file for bankruptcy in the United States Bankruptcy Courts. Most United States partnerships and corporations are also

---

|||| *Law Office Scenario* ||||

Pamela Brooks, a bankruptcy paralegal at the Carson & Powell law firm, was just getting ready to lock up the office and leave for the evening when the phone rang.

"This is Maggie Paulson," the caller identified herself. Pamela recognized the name as that of a prior divorce client of the firm's.

"I have just had it with these creditors," said Maggie. "Day and night they are calling me, demanding to know when I'm going to pay my bills. One even came to my house the other night.

"I'm doing my best to pay them off, but since my hours got cut to part-time, I'm really having trouble making ends meet. I think I need to file for bankruptcy."

"Let me schedule an appointment for you to meet with one of the attorneys," said Pamela. "I can get you in tomorrow afternoon."

"Well, I think before I come in tomorrow, I'm going to go shopping," said Maggie. "I've had my eye on a few gorgeous things that aren't really necessities. If I'm going to file for bankruptcy and get out of paying my debts, I might as well go out in style. I think I'll charge this diamond necklace that I saw at Winston's the other day, and then perhaps I'll go over and pick out a new car ... "

"Perhaps you should talk to one of the attorneys before making any major purchases," suggested Pamela. "Maybe I can get you in tomorrow morning?"

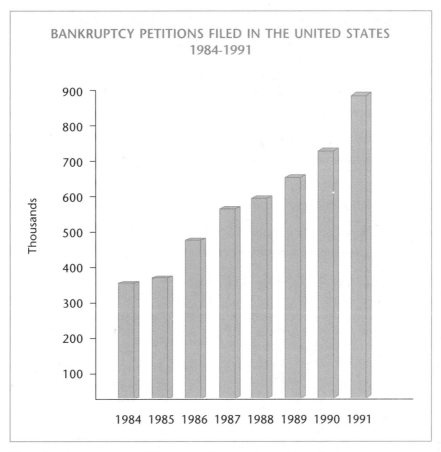

There has been a nearly 300 percent increase in petitions filed over an eight-year period.

eligible. A husband and wife may file a joint petition for bankruptcy.

Those specifically excluded from being considered debtors under Chapter 7 bankruptcies include:

1. Estates or executors or administrators of a deceased individual
2. Banking institutions
3. Insurance companies
4. Railroads
5. Those who have filed for bankruptcy proceedings and received a discharge within the previous six years.

In addition, debtors who have filed within the previous 180 days and have had their cases dismissed are not eligible if the dismissal was by the court for failure to abide by court orders or appear before the court, or if the case was dismissed pursuant to a motion of the debtor following a request for relief from the automatic stay.

Voluntary Bankruptcy

Most bankruptcies are **voluntary bankruptcies**. They are initiated by petition of the debtor.

voluntary bankruptcy   A bankruptcy that the debtor himself or herself initiates … .

Involuntary Bankruptcy

Involuntary bankruptcy occurs when one or more unsatisfied creditors files a petition to force a debtor into bankruptcy. Creditors may file a petition for involuntary bankruptcy under Chapters 7 and 11. Involuntary bankruptcy proceedings are not allowed under Chapters 12 or 13. Insurance companies, banking institutions, farmers, and charitable corporations are not subject to involuntary bankruptcy proceedings.

The Bankruptcy Estate

In a bankruptcy proceeding, the debtor has the benefit of having certain debts forgiven. However, in return, he or she may have to give up certain **assets**. The debtor's nonexempt assets will be seized by the bankruptcy trustee to be sold for the benefit of the creditors.

The debtor's assets as of the date of filing of a petition for bankruptcy are often collectively referred to as the **bankruptcy estate**. The bankruptcy estate includes "all legal or equitable interests of the debtor in property as of the commencement of the case."[3] Assets acquired after the bankruptcy petition is filed are typically not considered part of the bankruptcy estate.

An important part of working with a debtor who is petitioning for bankruptcy is ascertaining the nature, value, and location of all assets in the bankruptcy estate. A checklist is typically used during the initial client interview to prepare a list of the debtor's assets. The assets generally considered to be part of the bankruptcy estate include:

- Both tangible and intangible property
- Both real and personal property
- Property owned by the debtor in his or her possession
- Property owned by the debtor in the possession of others
- Certain property that the debtor has recently given away

- Property that has recently been repossessed
- Property (or cash) that has recently been paid to certain creditors
- Property not yet in the debtor's possession that he or she is entitled to receive
- Property inherited within 180 days after filing for bankruptcy
- Property received from a marital settlement agreement or divorce decree within 180 days after filing for bankruptcy
- Death benefits or life insurance policy proceeds received within 180 days after filing for bankruptcy.

Exempt Property

The debtor is entitled to keep certain exempt property. Both federal and state law provide for exemptions under certain circumstances. In some states, the debtor may choose either the federal list of exemptions *or* the state list of exemptions, whichever is more beneficial to him or her. In other states, the debtor must follow the state exemption laws.

Residents of the following states may choose to follow either state or federal laws regarding bankruptcy exemptions:

Connecticut	Hawaii
District of Columbia	Massachusetts

BALLENTINESBALLENTINESBALLENTINESBALLENTINESBALLENTINESBALLENTINESBALLENTINESBALLENTINESBALLENTINESBALLENTINESBALLENTINESBALLENTINESBALLENTINESBALLENTINES

involuntary bankruptcy   A bankruptcy initiated by one's creditors.

asset   Anything of value owned by a person or an organization. Assets include not only all real property and personal property, but intangible property … .

bankruptcy estate   All of the property of the debtor at the time the petition in bankruptcy is filed.

Michigan
Minnesota
New Jersey
New Mexico
Pennsylvania
Rhode Island

South Carolina
Texas
Vermont
Washington
Wisconsin

Residents of all other states must follow their state exemption laws. State exemptions vary from state to state. In general, they include:

- A portion of the equity in the debtor's residence
- Motor vehicles, not to exceed a set value
- Reasonably necessary clothing
- Household appliances
- Jewelry, not to exceed a set value
- Personal effects
- Life insurance, not to exceed a set value
- Public employee pensions
- Tools of the trade or profession of the debtor, not to exceed a set value
- A portion of the debtor's earned but unpaid wages
- Public benefits, such as welfare, Social Security, or unemployment compensation accumulated in a bank account.

Section 522(d) of the Bankruptcy Code is a list of property that can be considered exempt under the Code. The list pertains to debtors and their **dependents**, which includes spouses. Following is a summary of the items in that list:

1. The debtor's interest, not to exceed $7,500 in value, in real property or personal property that the debtor or a dependent of the debtor use as a residence, or in a burial plot for the debtor or a dependent of the debtor.

2. The debtor's interest, not to exceed $1,200 in value, in one motor vehicle.

3. The debtor's interest, not to exceed $200 in value in any particular item or $4,000 in aggregate value, in household furnishings, household goods, wearing apparel, appliances, and the like.

4. The debtor's interest, not to exceed $500 in value, in jewelry.

5. The debtor's interest, not to exceed $750 in value, in any implements, professional books, or tools, of the trade of the debtor or the trade of a dependent of the debtor.

6. Any unmatured life insurance contract owned by the debtor, other than a credit life insurance contract.

7. Professionally prescribed health aids for the debtor or a dependent of the debtor.

8. The debtor's right to receive
   a. a Social Security benefit, unemployment compensation, or a local public assistance benefit;
   b. a veterans' benefit;
   c. a disability, illness, or unemployment benefit;
   d. alimony, support, or separate maintenance, to the extent reasonably necessary for the support of the debtor and any dependent of the debtor;
   e. a payment under certain stock bonus, pension, profit-sharing, annuity, or similar plans or contracts on account of illness, disability, death, age, or length of service, to the extent reasonably necessary for the support of the debtor and any dependent of the debtor,

9. The debtor's right to receive, or property that is traceable to
   a. an award under a crime victim's reparation law
   b. A payment on account of the wrongful death of an individual of whom the debtor was a dependent, to the extent reasonably necessary for the support of the debtor and any dependent of the debtor;

dependent   One entitled to support, as a spouse or child.

c. a payment under a life insurance contract that insured the life of an individual of whom the debtor was a dependent on the date of such individual's death, to the extent reasonably necessary for the support of the debtor and any dependent of the debtor;

d. a payment in compensation of certain losses of future earnings of the debtor or an individual of whom the debtor is or was a dependent, to the extent reasonably necessary for the support of the debtor and any dependent of the debtor.

Nonexempt Property

Items that are usually considered nonexempt, and may be sold for the benefit of creditors, include:

- Cash, bank accounts, stocks, bonds, and other investments
- Second motor vehicles
- Second homes
- Expensive musical instruments not used by a professional musician
- Stamp, coin, and other collections
- Family heirlooms.

Homestead

Even if the debtor has kept current with mortgage payments on his or her **homestead**, the debtor's home is still at risk of being sold for cash to distribute to creditors, under certain circumstances. Under the federal exemption laws and the exemption laws of most states, equity in a homestead to a limited amount is exempt. Therefore, if the debtor has minimal equity in the homestead and if there are no delinquent payments on the homestead, the trustee would not attempt to sell the homestead. For example, under the federal exemption, up to $7,500 in equity in the residence of the debtor is exempt. If the debtor had just $3,000 in equity, the trustee would not attempt to sell the homestead for the benefit of creditors, because there would be no funds available for the creditors after the sale. If, in contrast, the debtor has $200,000 of equity in his or her residence, and the debtor owes creditors in excess of $200,000, an attempt may be made by the trustee to sell the homestead to pay the creditors.

If the debtor's home is not sold, the debt owed on the home will not be forgiven. The debtor must maintain payments on the homestead per any mortgage agreements in order to prevent mortgage foreclosure proceedings by the mortgagee. Filing for bankruptcy does not prevent the mortgagee from initiating foreclosure proceedings.

Bankruptcy Courts

Because bankruptcies are governed by federal law, bankruptcy proceedings are heard in special federal **bankruptcy courts**. Bankruptcy courts are not really separate courts, but are a part of the federal district courts. Bankruptcy petitions are typically filed in the federal judicial district in which the debtor has resided for the 180 days immediately preceding the filing.

Filing procedures for bankruptcy courts vary from court to court. The correct bankruptcy court should be consulted for specific rules on filing bankruptcy petitions, such as how many copies

BALLENTINESBALLENTINESBALLENTINESBALLENTINESBALLENTINESBALLENTINESBALLENTINESBALLENTINESBALLENTINESBALLENTINESBALLENTINESBALLENTINESBALLENTINESBALLENTINES

homestead exemption   [T]he immunity of real property from execution for debt, provided the property is occupied by the debtor as the head of the family.

bankruptcy courts   Federal courts that hear and determine only bankruptcy cases.

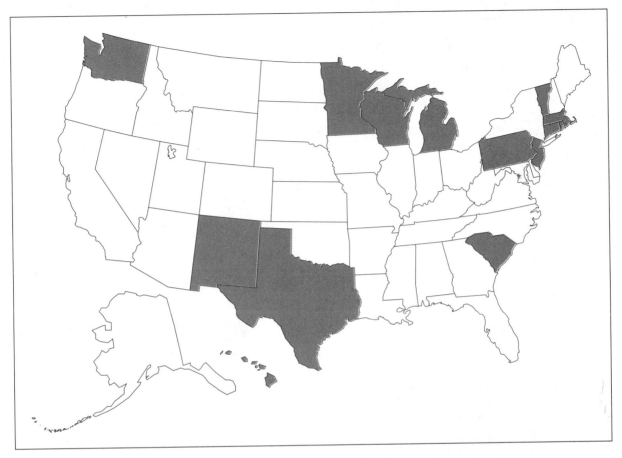

States in Which Residents May Choose Either State or Federal Bankruptcy Exemption Laws

are required, and to obtain local forms (if any are required).

United States Trustees

The 1986 amendments to the Bankruptcy Code provide for United States Trustees on a nation-wide basis. The function of the United States Trustees is to perform administrative duties, such as appointing bankruptcy trustees, that were previously performed by bankruptcy judges.

The U.S. Attorney General has the authority to appoint 21 United States Trustees, each for a specific geographical region of the United States. In addition, the Attorney General may also appoint one more assistant trustee in regions where the case load warrants it.

Initiating Voluntary Bankruptcy Procedures

There is often a sense of urgency on the client's part to begin bankruptcy proceedings. Aside from the debtor's desire to "get it all over with," filing for bankruptcy is one way to get creditors off one's back. After the debtor has filed the petition for bankruptcy, the bankruptcy court assumes control over the debtor's property. The debtor may not sell his or her assets or pay creditors without the permission of the bankruptcy court. During the bankruptcy procedure, the debtor's assets and debts will be managed by a trustee appointed by the bankruptcy court.

Filing the Petition and Other Required Documents

The bankruptcy procedure is begun with the filing of a petition and several other forms with the proper bankruptcy court, along with the required filing fee. Currently the filing fee is $120.

The Petition

The first form that must be filed with the bankruptcy court is the **petition**, which requests the bankruptcy court to discharge the debts of the debtor. The petition is Form 1.

Form 6

Form 6 consists of a number of schedules relating to the debtor's current assets and debts. Form 6 includes the following schedules:

1. Schedule A—Real Property
2. Schedule B—Personal Property
3. Schedule C—Property Claimed as Exempt
4. Schedule D—Creditors Holding Secured Claims
5. Schedule E—Creditors Holding Unsecured Priority Claims
6. Schedule F—Creditors Holding Unsecured Nonpriority Claims
7. Schedule G—Executory Contracts and Unexpired Leases
8. Schedule H—Codebtors
9. Schedule I—Current Income
10. Schedule J—Current Expenditures.

In addition, a summary of schedules A through J must be filed with Form 6, as well as a declaration concerning the debtor's schedules.

Form 7

Form 7, entitled Statement of Financial Affairs, provides information concerning the debtor's economic affairs for several years prior to the filing.

Form 8

Form 8 concerns the collateral listed for secured loans. It is a debtor's statement of intention, in which the debtor declares to the bankruptcy court and to secured creditors what plans he or she has for the listed collateral.

Mailing Matrix

A *mailing matrix* is a form used for mailing labels, for notices to creditors. It is a blank page with approximately 30 boxes to be completed with creditors' names and mailing addresses. It may or may not be required by the bankruptcy court. The matrix is used by the trustee to make mailing labels.

Bankruptcy Trustees

Soon after the petition is filed with the court, the court appoints a **bankruptcy trustee** to review the petition and other documents and to give notice to the creditors. Trustees are paid by the court and often a receive a fee based on a percentage of the assets distributed to the creditors. Bankruptcy attorneys may be appointed by the court to serve as bankruptcy trustees if they are not otherwise involved in the bankruptcy case. The trustee is considered the representative of the bankruptcy estate.

Trustee Duties

The main duty of the bankruptcy trustee is to collect the nonexempt assets of the debtor for sale

BALLENTINESBALLENTINESBALLENTINESBALLENTINESBALLENTINESBALLENTINESBALLENTINESBALLENTINESBALLENTINESBALLENTINESBALLENTINESBALLENTINESBALLENTINES

petition in bankruptcy   A document filed in a bankruptcy court initiating bankruptcy proceedings.

trustee in bankruptcy   A person appointed by a bankruptcy court to collect any amounts owed the debtor, sell the debtor's property, and distribute the proceeds among the creditors.

and to distribute the proceeds to the creditors pursuant to applicable law. For this reason, the trustee assumes responsibility for the debtor's assets as soon as bankruptcy proceedings begin.

The trustee may also challenge property that the debtor has claimed as being exempt, and certain transfers made just prior to or subsequent to initiation of the bankruptcy proceedings. The trustee must also challenge invalid creditor claims. If any lawsuits are initiated or defended on behalf of the bankruptcy estate, the trustee will represent the bankruptcy estate with regard to such litigation.

Official Form No.1. Voluntary Petition
UNITED STATES BANKRUPTCY COURT FOR THE
. . . . DISTRICT OF . . . .

```
_____x
In re                              :
. . . . . . . . . . . . . . . . . . ,     :
Debtor [set forth here all names   :
including trade names used by      :     Case No. . . . .
Debtor within last 6 years].       :
Social Security No. . . . .         :
and Debtor's Employer's Tax        :
Identification No. . . . ..         :
_____x
```

Voluntary Petition

1. Petitioner's mailing address, including county is . . . .

2. Petitioner has resided [or has been domiciled or Petitioner's principal place of business has been or the principal assets of the petitioner have been] within this district for the preceding 180 days [or for a longer potion of the preceding 180 days than in any other district].

3. Petitioner is qualified to file this petition and is entitled to the benefits of title 11, United States Code as a voluntary debtor.

4. [If appropriate] A copy of petitioner's proposed plan, dated . . . ., is attached [or Petitioner intends to file a plan pursuant to chapter 11 or chapter 13] of title 11, United States Code.

5. [If petitioner is a corporation] Exhibit "A" is attached to and made part of this petition.

6. [If petitioner is an individual whose debts are primarily consumer debts.] Petitioner is aware that [he or she] may proceed under chapter 7, 11, 12, or 13 of title 11, United States Code, understands the relief available under each such chapter, and chooses to proceed under chapter 7 of such title.

7. [If petitioner is an individual whose debts are primarily consumer debts and such petitioner is represented by an attorney.] A declaration or an affidavit in the form of Exhibit "B" is attached to and made a part of this petition.

WHEREFORE, petitioner prays for relief in accordance with chapter 7 [or chapter 11 or chapter 13] of title 11, United States Code.

Signed: . . . . ,
Attorney for Petitioner.

Address: . . . . ,
. . . .
[Petitioner signs if not represented by attorney.]
. . . . ,
Petitioner.

I, ..., the petitioner named in the foregoing petition, declare under penalty of perjury that the foregoing is true and correct.
Executed on . . . .

Signature: . . . .
Petitioner.

Form 1 A petition requests a bankruptcy court to discharge the debts of the debtor.

Exhibit "A"

[If petitioner is a corporation, this Exhibit "A" shall be completed and attached to the petition pursuant to paragraph 5 thereof.]

[Caption as in Form No. 1]

FOR COURT USE ONLY

. . . .
Date Petition Filed

. . . .
Case Number

. . . .
Bankruptcy Judge

1. Petitioner's employer identification number is . . . .

2. If any of petitioner's securities are registered under section 12 of the Securities and Exchange Act of 1934, SEC file number is . . . .

3. The following financial data is the latest available information and refers to petitioner's condition on . . . .

    a. Total assets: $ . . . .
    b. Total liabilities $ . . . .

		Approximate number of holders
Secured debt, excluding that listed below	$	. . . .
Debt securities held by more than		
100 holders	$	
Secured	$	. . . .
Unsecured	$	. . . .
Other liabilities, excluding contingent or		
unliquidated claims	$	. . . .
Number of shares of common stock	$	. . . .

Comments, if any: . . . .

4. Brief description of petitioner's business: . . . .

5. *[If presently available, supply the following information]* The name of any person who directly or indirectly owns, controls, or holds, with power to vote, 20% or more of the voting securities of petitioner is . . . .

6. *[If presently available, supply the following information]* The names of all corporations 20% or more of the outstanding voting securities of which are directly or indirectly owned, controlled, or held, with power to vote, by petitioner are . . . . . .

    [If petitioner is an individual whose debts are primarily consumer debts, this Exhibit "B" shall be completed and attached to the petition pursuant to paragraph (7) thereof.]

[Caption as in Form No. 1]

For Court Use Only.

. . . .
Date Petition filed

. . . .
Case Number

. . . .
Bankruptcy Judge

Form 1 *(Continued)*

Notifying the Creditors

There may be a significant delay between the time the petition is filed and the time the trustee mails notice to the creditors. In such instances, the attorney for the debtor may send notices to the creditors to ensure that they will not continue contacting the debtor.

Bankruptcy paralegals are often responsible for mailing these letters of notice to each creditor listed in the petition. The letter should notify all

"I, ..., the attorney for the petitioner named in the foregoing petition, declare that I have informed the petitioner that [he or she] may proceed under chapter 7, 11, 12, or 13 of title 11, United States Code, and have explained the relief available under each such chapter.

. . . .
"Executed on

. . . .
"Signature

. . . .
Attorney for Petitioner".

Form 1   *(Continued)*

creditors that the debtor has filed a petition for voluntary bankruptcy under Chapter 7 of the U.S. Bankruptcy Code.

Examination of Assets and Debts

Soon after the bankruptcy trustee is appointed, he or she will review the petition and other documents submitted to the bankruptcy court to make a determination as to whether there are sufficient nonexempt assets to sell to raise cash for the debtor's creditors. If there are sufficient assets, the trustee will determine that it is an *asset case*. If not, the bankruptcy will be determined to be a *no-asset case.*

In the notice of bankruptcy sent to the creditors, the trustee notifies the creditors of the date and place for the meeting and whether the bankruptcy is an asset case or a no-asset case. If it is an asset case, the creditors will be directed to file claims. Creditors have 90 days after the date of the meeting of creditors to file claims. The trustee then reviews the claims and sells the nonexempt bankruptcy assets. The funds from sale of the nonexempt assets are then distributed to the creditors according to their claims.

Stay of Collection

An automatic stay is triggered when the bankruptcy petition is filed, to protect the debtor from further collection efforts by creditors during the bankruptcy proceedings. Section 362(a) of the Bankruptcy Code lists the activities that are stayed by commencement of a bankruptcy case. It includes almost all typical creditor collection activity. The stay does not apply to collection efforts for spousal maintenance or child support, nor to efforts to collect for assets acquired after the petition for bankruptcy is filed. The automatic stay ends when the bankruptcy case is dismissed or when the debtor receives a discharge.

Meeting of Creditors

The meeting of the creditors is attended by the bankruptcy trustee, the debtor, the debtor's attorney, and possibly the debtor's creditors. If the debtor is married, his or her spouse must also attend. At times, a bankruptcy paralegal may attend the meeting with the attorney or in place of the attorney.

Although creditors receive notice of the meeting, most creditors typically do not attend. Secured creditors occasionally attend the meeting to obtain more information from the debtor. The meeting is usually spent clarifying information concerning the debtor's situation for the trustee. It is permissible at the creditors' meeting for a new trustee to be elected by creditors holding at least 20 percent of the amount of certain unsecured claims. This, however, is rarely done. If a new trustee is not elected at the meeting, the interim trustee becomes the permanent trustee for the duration of the case.

At the first meeting of creditors, the debtor's nonexempt assets are collected by the trustee to be sold for the benefit of the creditors. If the trustee does not agree with the assets listed as exempt, the trustee may file an objection with the bankruptcy court, and a hearing will be held. At the hearing, the bankruptcy judge makes the final determination as to the exempt and nonexempt property of the debtor.

If the debtor wishes to keep certain nonexempt property, and has been able to raise cash since the petition was filed, he or she may choose to purchase the assets from the trustee. The trustee will then distribute the cash to the creditors in lieu of the property.

Collecting and Disbursing the Debtor's Assets

Paralegals working for those employed as bankruptcy trustees often become very involved in collecting, evaluating, and disbursing the assets of the debtor. The trustee must consider the priorities set by law for disbursing the assets of the debtor.

Official Form No.6 Schedules of Assets and Liabilities

[Caption as in Form No.1]
Schedule A.—Statement of All Liabilities of Debtor.

Schedules A-1, A-2 and A-3 must include all the claims against the debtor or the debtor's property as of the date of the filing of the petition by or against the debtor.

Schedule A-1.—Creditors having priority.

(1)	(2)	(3)	(4)	(5)
Nature of claim	Name of creditor and complete mailing address including zip code	Specify when claim was incurred and the consideration therefor; when claim is subject to setoff, evidenced by a judgment, negotiable instrument, or other writing, or incurred as partner or joint contractor, so indicate; specify name of any partner or joint contractor on any debt	Indicate if claim is contingent, unliquidated, or disputed	Amount of claim

a. Wages, salary, and commissions, including vacation, severance and sick leave pay owing to employees not exceeding $2,000 to each, earned within 90 days before filing of petition or cessation of business (if earlier specify date). $ . . . .

b. Contributions to employee benefit plans for services rendered within 180 days before filing of petition or cessation of business (if earlier specify date) $ . . . .

c. Claims of farmers, not exceeding $2,000 for each individual, pursuant to 11 U.S.C. § 507(a)(5)(A). $ . . . .

d. Claims of United States fishermen, not exceeding $2,000 for each individual, pursuant to 11 U.S.C. § 507(a)(5)(B). $ . . . .

e. Deposits by individuals, not exceeding $900 for each for purchase, lease, or rental of property or services for personal, family, or household use that were not delivered or provided. $

f. Taxes owing [itemize by type of tax and taxing authority]
   (1) To the United States $ . . . .
   (2) To any state $ . . . .
   (3) To any other taxing authority $ . . . .
          Total $ . . . .

Form 6

Schedule A-2.—Creditors holding security

(1) Name of creditor and complete mailing address including zip code	(2) Description of security and date when obtained by creditor	(3) Specify when claim was incurred and the consideration therefor; when claim is subject to setoff, evidenced by a judgment, negotiable instrument, or other writing, or incurred as partner or joint contractor, so indicate; specify name of any partner or joint contractor on any debt	(4) Indicate if claim is contingent, unliquidated, or disputed	(5) Market Value	(6) Amount of claim without deduction of value of security
			Total		$. . . . .

Schedule A-3.—Creditors having unsecured claims without priority.

(1) Name of creditor [including last known holder of any negotiable instrument] and complete mailing address including zip code	(2) Specify when claim was incurred and the consideration therefor; when claim is contingent, unliquidated, disputed, subject to setoff, evidenced by a judgment, negotiable instrument, or other writing, or incurred as partner or joint contractor, so indicate; specify name of any partner or joint contractor on any debt	(3) Indicate if claim is contingent, unliquidated, or disputed	(4) Amount of claim
		Total	$. . . . .

Schedule B—Statement of All Property of Debtor

Schedules B-1, B-2, B-3, and B-4 must include all property of the debtor as of the date of the filing of the petition by or against the debtor.

Schedule B-1.—Real Property

Description and location of all real property in which debtor has an interest [including equitable and future interests, interests in estates by the entirety, community property, life estates, leaseholds, and rights and powers exercisable for the debtor's own benefit]	Nature of interest [specify all deeds and written instruments relating thereto]	Market value of debtor's interest without deduction for secured claims listed in Schedule A-2 or exemptions claimed in Schedule B-4
	Total	$. . . . .

Form 6   *(Continued)*

Secured Claims

Secured claims, or **secured debts**, are debts guaranteed by some particular items of property (often referred to as **collateral** or **security**). Under the debtor's agreement with the creditor, the creditor has the right to possess the collateral or security or to sell the collateral or security to pay for the debts if the debtor defaults in his or her obligations. Within a prescribed amount of time after the debtor files a bankruptcy petition, the debtor must

Schedule B-2.—Personal Property

Type of Property	Description and Location	Market value of debtor's interest without deduction for secured claims listed on Schedule A-2 or exemptions claimed in Schedule B-4
		Total $ . . . .
a. Cash on hand		$ . . . . . .
b. Deposits of money with banking institutions, savings and loan associations, brokerage houses, credit unions, public utility companies, landlords and others		. . . . . .
c. Household goods, supplies and furnishings		. . . . . .
d. Books, pictures, and other art objects; stamp, coin and other collections		. . . . . .
e. Wearing apparel, jewelry, firearms, sports equipment and other personal possessions		. . . . . .
f. Automobiles, trucks, trailers and other vehicles		. . . . . .
g. Boats, motors and their accessories		. . . . . .
h. Livestock, poultry and other animals		. . . . . .
i. Farming equipment, supplies and implements		. . . . . .
j. Office equipment, furnishings and supplies		. . . . . .
k. Machinery, fixtures, equipment and supplies [other than those listed in Items j and l] used in business		. . . . . .
l. Inventory		. . . . . .
m. Tangible personal property of any other description		. . . . . .
n. Patents, copyrights, licenses, franchises and other general intangibles [specify all documents and writings relating thereto]		. . . . . .
o. Government and corporate bonds and other negotiable and nonnegotiable instruments		. . . . . .
p. Other liquidated debts owing debtor		. . . . . .
q. Contingent and unliquidated claims of every nature, including counterclaims of the debtor [give estimated value of each]		. . . . . .
r. Interests in insurance policies [name insurance company of each policy and itemize surrender or refund value of each]		. . . . . .
s. Annuities [itemize and name each issuer]		. . . . . .
t. Stock and interests in incorporated and unincorporated companies [itemize separately]		
u. Interests in partnerships		. . . . . .
v. Equitable and future interests, life estates, and right or powers exercisable for the benefit of the debtor (other than those listed in schedule B-1) [specify all written instruments relating thereto]		. . . . . .
	Total	$ . . . . . .

Form 6 *(Continued)*

inform the court of his or her intention for dealing with secured claims by completing a form entitled the "Individual Debtor's Statement of Intention." Although a bankruptcy discharge can discharge the

secured debt A debt for which security or collateral has been given.

collateral Stocks, bonds, or other property that serve as security for a loan or other obligation; property pledged to pay a debt.

security Collateral; a pledge given to a creditor by a debtor for the payment of a debt or for the performance of an obligation.

Schedule B-3.—Property not otherwise scheduled

Type of Property	Description and Location	Market value of debtor's interest without deduction for secured claims listed Schedule A-2 or exemption claimed in Schedule B-4
a. Property transferred under assignment for benefit of creditors, within 120 days prior to filing of petition [specify date of assignment, name and address of assignee, amount realized therefrom by the assignee, and disposition of proceeds so far as known to debtor]		$ . . . . . .
b. Property of any kind not otherwise scheduled		. . . . . .
	Total	$ . . . . . .

Debtor selects the following property as exempt pursuant to 11 U.S.C. § 522(d) [or the laws of the State of . . . .]

Schedule B-4.—Property claimed as exempt

Type of Property	Location, description, and so far as relevant to the claim of exemption, present use of property	Specify statute creating the exemption	Value claimed exempt
			$ . . . . . .
			. . . . . .
		Total	$ . . . . . .

Summary of debts and property.
[From the statements of the debtor in Schedules A and B]

Schedule		Total
Debts		
A-1/a,b	Wages, etc. having priority	$ . . . . . .
A-1(c)	Deposits of money	. . . . . .
A-1/d(1)	Taxes owing United States	. . . . . .
A-1/d(2)	Taxes owing states	. . . . . .
A-1/d(3)	Taxes owing other taxing authorities	. . . . . .
A-2	Secured claims	. . . . . .
A-3	Unsecured claims without priority	. . . . . .
	Schedule A total	$ . . . . . .
Property		
B-1	Real property [total value]	$ . . . . . .
B-2/a	Cash on hand	. . . . . .
B-2/b	Deposits	. . . . . .
B-2/c	Household goods	. . . . . .
B-2/d	Books, pictures, and collections	. . . . . .

Form 6   *(Continued)*

debt owed to a secured creditor, it cannot eliminate the secured creditor's rights to the collateral in most instances, unless additional steps are taken. If the secured property is exempt property, the debtor may be able to have the debt discharged without giving up the collateral.

Secured claims for nonexempt property can generally be handled in one of three ways. First, the

B-2/e	Wearing apparel and personal possessions	. . . .
B-2/f	Automobiles and other vehicles	. . . .
B-2/g	Boats, motors, and accessories	. . . .
B-2/h	Livestock and other animals	. . . .
B-2/i	Farming supplies and implements	. . . .
B-2/j	Office equipment and supplies	. . . .
B-2/k	Machinery, equipment, and supplies used in business	. . . .
B-2/l	Inventory	. . . .
B-2/m	Other tangible personal property	. . . .
B-2/n	Patents and other general intangibles	. . . .
B-2/o	Bonds and other instruments	. . . .
B-2/p	Other liquidated debts	. . . .
B-2/q	Contingent and unliquidated claims	. . . .
B-2/r	Interests in insurance policies	. . . .
B-2/s	Annuities	. . . .
B-2/t	Interests in corporations and unincorporated companies	. . . .
B-2/u	Interests in partnerships	. . . .
B-2/v	Equitable and future interests, rights, and powers in personalty	. . . .
B-3/a	Property assigned for benefit of creditors	. . . .
B-3/b	Property not otherwise scheduled	. . . .
	Schedule B total	$ . . . .

Unsworn Declaration under Penalty of Perjury
of Individual to Schedules A and B

I, ..., declare under penalty of perjury that I have read the foregoing schedules, consisting of . . . . sheets, and that they are true and correct to the best of my knowledge, information and belief.

Esecuted on . . . .

Signature: . . . .

Unsworn Declaration under Penalty of Perjury
on Behalf of Corporation or Partnership
to Schedules A and B

I, ..., [the president *or other officer* or an authorized agent of the corporation] *[or a* member *or an authorized agent of the partnership]* named as debtor in this case, declare under penalty of perjury that I have read the foregoing schedules, consisting of . . . . sheets, and that they are true and correct to the best of my knowledge, information, and belief.

Executed on . . . .

Signature: . . . .

Form 6   *(Continued)*

debtor can **surrender** the property. In that event, the creditor collects the collateral that was put up for the debt in return for cancellation of the debt. Second, the debtor may choose to **redeem** the property. In that event, the debtor keeps the collateral and pays to the creditor its fair market value. Third, the creditor may choose to *reaffirm* the debt with the creditor. In that event, the debtor must sign a reaffirmation agreement with the creditor within 45 days after filing the bankruptcy petition. The debt will thus survive the bankruptcy, and the debtor will continue to make payments to the creditor per their agreement.

Section 521(1)(A) of the Code specifies the following duty on the part of the debtor with regard to secured assets:

BALLENTINESBALLENTINESBALLENTINESBALLENTINESBALLENTINESBALLENTINESBALLENTINESBALLENTINESBALLENTINESBALLENTINESBALLENTINESBALLENTINESBALLENTINESBALLENTINES

surrender   To give up; to give back; to give back possession; to yield.
redeem   To buy back; to pay off.

(A) within thirty days after the date of the filing of a petition under chapter 7 of this title or on or before the date of the meeting of creditors, whichever is earlier, or within such additional time as the court, for cause, within such period fixes, the debtor shall file with the clerk a statement of his intention with respect to the retention or surrender of such property and, if applicable, specifying that such property is claimed as exempt, that the debtor intends to redeem such property, or that the debtor intends to reaffirm debts secured by such property.

Priorities

When disbursing the debtor's nonexempt assets and proceeds from the sale of nonexempt assets, the bankruptcy trustee must adhere to the priorities set by statute. Section 507 of the Bankruptcy Code provides that the following expenses and claims have priority, in the following order:

1. Administrative expenses allowed under § 503(b) of the Bankruptcy Code, and any fees and charges assessed against the bankruptcy estate under chapter 123 of title 28.

2. Unsecured claims allowed under § 502(f) of the Bankruptcy Code.

3. Certain allowed unsecured claims for wages, salaries, or commissions, including vacation, severance, and sick leave pay.

4. Certain allowed unsecured claims for contributions to an employee benefit plan.

5. Certain allowed unsecured claims of persons engaged in the production of raising grain, against a debtor who owns or operates a grain storage facility, or persons engaged as United States fishermen against a debtor who has acquired fish or fish produce from a fisherman through a sale or conversion, and who is engaged in operating a fish produce storage or processing facility. These claims have priority to the extent of $2,000 for each such individual.

6. Allowed unsecured claims of individuals, to the extent of $900 for each, arising from the deposit, before the commencement of the bankruptcy case, of money in connection with the purchase, lease, or rental of property, or the purchase of services, for the personal, family, or household use of such individuals, that were not delivered or provided.

7. Certain allowed unsecured claims of governmental units, to the extent that such claims are for:
   a. certain income taxes
   b. certain property taxes
   c. taxes required to be collected or withheld and for which the debtor is liable in whatever capacity
   d. employment taxes
   e. excise taxes; and
   f. customs duties arising out of the importation of merchandise, penalties related to claims of a kind specified in this paragraph and in compensation for actual pecuniary loss.

8. Certain allowed unsecured claims based upon any commitment by the debtor to the Federal Deposit Insurance Corporation, the Resolution Trust Corporation, the Director of the Office of Thrift Supervision, the Comptroller of the Currency, or the Board of Governors of the Federal Reserve System, or their predecessors or successors to maintain the capital of an insured depository institution.

A debtor's attorney fees are considered administrative expenses allowed under item 1 of the foregoing list. This ensures that attorneys who represent debtors in bankruptcy proceedings will in fact get paid a reasonable amount for their services.

The Discharge

The end result of most bankruptcy proceedings is a **discharge**. The discharge voids most of the creditors' prebankruptcy debts and prohibits further collection efforts as to those debts. There are certain grounds for withholding a discharge; not all debtors who file for bankruptcy are entitled to receive a discharge. In addition, not all debts of the debtor will be discharged.

Grounds for Withholding Discharge

The grounds for withholding a discharge include:

1. Being a corporation or partnership. Corporations and partnerships may not receive discharges under Chapter 7 bankruptcies.
2. Making fraudulent conveyances
3. Failing to keep or preserve financial records
4. Depriving the trustee of property or information by:
   a. making a false oath or account in connection with the bankruptcy case
   b. presenting or using a false claim against the estate
   c. receiving or giving consideration for action or inaction in the bankruptcy proceeding; or
   d. withholding books and records from the bankruptcy trustee
5. Failing to explain loss of assets
6. Refusing to testify
7. Committing a prohibited act in connection with the bankruptcy of the debtor's relatives, partners, partnership, or corporation
8. Receiving a discharge in a Chapter 7 or 11 case within the past six years
9. Receiving a discharge in a Chapter 13 case in the past six years under most circumstances
10. Making a waiver of discharge, signed by the debtor.

Exceptions to Discharge

As mentioned previously, certain debts are considered nondischargeable under § 523 of the Bankruptcy Code. The debtor will remain liable for these debts after other debts have been discharged and the bankruptcy case has been closed. Debts that may not be discharged include:

1. Certain taxes or customs duties.
2. Money, property, services, or an extension, renewal, or refinancing of credit, to the extent obtained by false pretenses or fraudulent written statements.
3. Debts to creditors who were not listed in the bankruptcy petition or given timely notice pursuant to the Bankruptcy Code.
4. Debts for fraud or defalcation while acting in a fiduciary capacity, embezzlement, or larceny.
5. Debts to a spouse, former spouse, or child of the debtor, for alimony to, maintenance for, or support of such spouse or child, in connection with a separation agreement, divorce decree, or other order of a court of record, determination made in accordance with state or territorial law by a governmental unit, or property settlement agreements.
6. Debts incurred for willful and malicious injury by the debtor to another entity or to the property of another entity.
7. Debts for fines, penalties, or forfeitures payable to and for the benefit of a governmental unit, which are not compensation for actual pecuniary loss, other than a tax penalty.
8. Debts for an educational benefit overpayment or loan made, insured, or guaranteed by a governmental unit, or made under any program funded in whole or part by a governmental unit or nonprofit institution, or for an obligation to repay funds received as an educational benefit, scholarship, or stipend unless such debt became due more than seven years prior to the time of the bankruptcy filing or unless excepting such debt from discharge will impose an undue hardship on the debtor and the debtor's dependents.
9. Debts incurred due to death or personal injury caused by the debtor's operation of a motor vehicle if such operation was unlawful

because the debtor was intoxicated from using alcohol, a drug, or another substance.

10. Debts for which the discharge was waived by the debtor in a prior bankruptcy case concerning the debtor

11. Debts arising from acts of fraud or defalcation while acting in a fiduciary capacity

committed with respect to any depository institution or insured credit union.

12. Debts incurred for malicious or reckless failure to fulfill any commitment by the debtor to the federal depository institutions regulatory agency to maintain the capital of an insured depository institution.

Involuntary Bankruptcy Proceedings

Involuntary bankruptcy proceedings are initiated when creditors file a petition for bankruptcy of a debtor with the bankruptcy court. After that time, the debtor has a chance to respond to the petition by filing an answer. If no answer is filed by the debtor, the court will enter relief for the creditors.

Involuntary Bankruptcy Petitions

The involuntary bankruptcy proceeding is also commenced with the filing of a petition in bankruptcy court. The petition must be filed by a prescribed number of creditors, typically three, with unsecured claims totaling at least $5,000. If the debtor has fewer than 12 unsecured creditors, any one unsecured creditor with an unsecured claim of $5,000 or more may sign the petition.

Appointing a Trustee for Involuntary Bankruptcy Proceedings

If necessary, the bankruptcy court may appoint an interim trustee to take possession of or manage the debtor's assets or business prior to the time an order for relief is issued. Section 303(g) of the Bankruptcy Code provides that an interim trustee may be appointed "if necessary to preserve the property of the estate or to prevent loss to the estate."

When the Order for Relief Is Not Granted

When the debtor files an answer to the petition for involuntary bankruptcy and the court finds that involuntary bankruptcy is not necessary or warranted, the debtor may be entitled to relief from the petitioning creditors under certain circumstances. The debtor may be granted relief for any costs and attorney fees, as well as for any damages caused by the taking of the debtor's property by the interim trustee. In certain cases, if the petition was filed in bad faith, the court is permitted to award damages to the debtor, including punitive damages.

Alternatives to Bankruptcy

Whereas Chapter 7 bankruptcies are considered full liquidation bankruptcies, the Bankruptcy Reform Act of 1978 also provides less drastic remedies. Chapters 11, 12, and 13 are considered rehabilitative proceedings, and are designed to permit the debtor to retain assets and restructure and repay most debts over an extended period of time. Chapter 9 proceedings are designed for the adjustment of debts of municipalities. In addition to the bankruptcy alternatives under the Bankruptcy Code, many debtors opt for out-of-court workouts to repay their debts.

February 1, 1994

Winston's Department Store
Attention: Credit Department
1234 Main Street
Anytown, WA 98765

Re: The account of Maggie Paulson
        Account # 123456789

Dear Sir or Madam:

Please be advised that our firm represents Maggie Paulson with regard to a bankruptcy proceeding. On January 17, 1995 we filed a voluntary petition under Chapter 7 of the U.S. Bankruptcy Code on behalf of Ms. Paulson. The case number is 34-675675-95.

Pursuant to 11 U.S.C. § 362(a), you are prohibited from taking any of the following actions with regard to the account of Maggie Paulson (the "debtor"):

1.   Taking any action against the debtor to collect any debt owed to you

2.   Enforcing any lien on debtor's real or personal property

3.   Repossessing any property in the possession of debtor

4.   Discontinuing any service or benefit currently being provided to debtor; or

5.   Taking any action to evict debtor from her place of residence.

A violation of these prohibitions may be considered to be contempt of court and may be punished accordingly.

If you have any questions concerning the bankruptcy proceeding, please contact me or attorney Samuel Smith from our office.

Sincerely,

Pamela Brooks

Pamela Brooks

Paralegal

Letter of Notice to Creditors Listed in the Petition

Chapter 11

Chapter 11 of the Bankruptcy Reform Act of 1978 is entitled "Reorganization." In general, most individuals and entities that are eligible to file bankruptcy proceedings under Chapter 7 may file for a reorganization under Chapter 11. Unlike eligibility requirements for Chapter 7, railroads are eligible for Chapter 11 and stockbrokers and commodity brokers are not. Chapter 11 is, however, primarily intended for the benefit of corporations and partnerships. Chapter 11 provides for a reorganization of the corporation's or partnership's debts pursuant to a plan proposed by the debtor and approved by a bankruptcy court. Chapter 11 proceedings do not liquidate the corporation or partnership.

Chapter 11 proceedings are often initiated by corporations whose management wishes to maintain as much control over the company's assets as possible. At times, Chapter 11 proceedings are conducted without the appointment of a trustee, leaving the corporation or partnership to make many of the decisions normally left to bankruptcy trustees.

Chapter 11 proceedings are also used to buy time or stall unsatisfied creditors. A plan of reorganization under Chapter 11 need not be filed for 120 days after the filing of the petition. The petition can be withdrawn during that time.

Chapter 12

Chapter 12 was a temporary provision of the Bankruptcy Code that expired on October 1, 1993. Chapter 12 of the Bankruptcy Reform Act of 1978 was entitled "Adjustment of Debts of a Family Farmer with Regular Annual Income." As the title suggests, Chapter 12 proceedings were designed for the benefit of family farmers, to give them a chance to reorganize their debts and keep their land in situations where the family farm might otherwise be lost.

Chapter 13

Chapter 13 of the Bankruptcy Reform Act of 1978 is entitled "Adjustment of Debts of an Individual with Regular Income." The intent of Chapter 13 is to allow individual debtors with regular income to voluntarily restructure their debt for full repayment, while retaining their assets. Chapter 13 proceedings are available only to individuals who meet the following criteria:

1. The debtor must have a regular income, and
2. The debtor must have noncontingent, liquidated, unsecured debts of less than $100,000 and noncontingent liquidated, secured debts of less than $350,0000.

Individuals whose spouses meet these requirements are also eligible.

An individual is considered to have a regular income if he or she has an income sufficiently stable and regular to enable such individual to make payments under a plan under Chapter 13.[4] A *contingent debt* is one which the debtor will be obligated for only upon the occurrence or happening of some event that will trigger the liability of the debtor.

Chapter 13 proceedings depend on a plan that is drafted by the debtor, or the debtor's attorney, which must be approved by the creditors and the bankruptcy court. Chapter 13 proceedings are generally considered more flexible and less expensive than Chapter 11 proceedings.

Workouts

Bankruptcy attorneys often participate in facilitating an out-of-court workout between the debtor and his or her creditors. A *workout* is a private, negotiated adjustment of creditor-debtor relations. In a workout agreement, the debtor and all creditors negotiate and agree to terms for repayment of the debts that would probably have an effect similar to that of bankruptcy proceedings. Workouts have the advantage of being flexible, and they can generally be completed much quicker than a bankruptcy court proceeding.

Summary Questions

1. What is the main difference between Chapter 7 bankruptcies and proceedings under Chapters 11 and 13?
2. When does the bankruptcy proceeding commence?
3. Who must bring a petition for an involuntary bankruptcy?

4. Are laws concerning exempt property set by the Bankruptcy Code or state law?

5. Would a luxury automobile be considered exempt under the Bankruptcy Code?

6. How are creditors named and notified of a bankruptcy?

7. What is a stay of collection, and when does it go into effect?

8. Are all debts automatically discharged in a Chapter 7 bankruptcy?

9. Whose job is it to collect and disburse the assets of the debtor?

10. What are some grounds for withholding a discharge?

Practical Paralegal Skills

1. Where are bankruptcies filed for individuals residing in your city? Prepare a sample cover letter to the proper bankruptcy court for Maggie Paulson. Be sure the letter is addressed properly and includes the following:

    a. The correct number of copies of the pertinent forms for a Chapter 7 bankruptcy

    b. The proper filing fee

    c. Any other pertinent information.

2. What property is exempt from Chapter 7 bankruptcies in your state? Find the pertinent bankruptcy statute for your state and make a list of the exempt property listed therein.

Notes

[1] Milano, Carol, "1993 Legal Assistant Today Salary Survey Results," *Legal Assistant Today,* 48 (May/June 1993).

[2] 9 Am. Jur. 2d § 1.

[3] 11 U.S.C. § 524(a).

[4] 11 U.S.C. § 101(29).

CHAPTER 18

Every Paralegal Is a Contracts Paralegal

This chapter on contracts is an appropriate one with which to conclude an exploration of paralegals in American law. After reviewing other substantive areas, it must be apparent that contract matters cut across every area of law. Students and paralegals must have a firm understanding of the basic elements of a contractual relationship if they wish to succeed in real estate, corporate law, intellectual property, wills and trusts, bankruptcy, litigation, or any other area of law. This chapter discusses the role of the paralegal in all matters of contract law.

The Role of Paralegals in Contract Matters

Although the 1993 *Legal Assistant Today* survey did not survey paralegals as to their association with contract matters, every area of practice includes some work in contracts. The criminal law paralegal may investigate white-collar crime involving contract fraud. The tort law or personal injury law paralegal may look at contracts containing warranties that give rise to products liability. The real property paralegal may draft contracts binding parties to the transfer or distribution of real estate. In short, contract law is an integral part of every area of legal practice and symbolic of American culture.

Contracts are used in virtually every segment of human interaction. For example, contracts, in some form, are used in employee–employer relationships, when buying a meal at a favorite restaurant, when buying or selling corporate assets, when selling or purchasing a house, or when marrying or divorcing another person. Therefore, a paralegal must have a working knowledge of the basic elements of a contractual relationship. For example, for a contract to be binding, the parties must be legally capable of entering into a contractual relationship. One party must make another an offer, which must then be considered. Only then can the offer be accepted, thus creating a binding and enforceable contract.

A paralegal may be responsible for the following tasks:

1. Drafting and proofreading contracts, agreements, and memoranda
2. Interviewing clients
3. Researching relevant statutes, case law, and regulations
4. Reviewing existing contracts to evaluate claims of breach
5. Assisting in pretrial activities, including pleadings, motions, discovery, interrogatories, and investigation
6. Drafting correspondence to clients, courts, attorneys, and so on
7. Maintaining client files
8. Preparing or reviewing financial affidavits
9. Drafting corporate or governmental policies
10. Attending meetings, administrative hearings, and trials.

Paralegals who work in the contracts area must be familiar with the basic requirements for contracts and with the pertinent statutes concerning contracts. In addition, they must be familiar with the resources commonly used to assist in the drafting of contracts, including office form files and formbooks.

BALLENTINESBALLENTINESBALLENTINESBALLENTINESBALLENTINESBALLENTINESBALLENTINESBALLENTINESBALLENTINESBALLENTINESBALLENTINESBALLENTINESBALLENTINES

contract   An agreement entered into, for adequate consideration, to do, or refrain from doing, a particular thing. The Uniform Commercial Code defines a contract as the total legal obligation resulting from the parties' agreement. ... [T]he transaction must involve an undertaking that is legal to perform, and there must be mutuality of agreement and obligation between at least two competent parties.

Formation of a Contract:
Offer, Consideration, and Acceptance

A contract can be as informal as a spoken agreement between two individuals, or as complex as a several-hundred-page written agreement between two corporations. Regardless of the nature of the contract, a valid contract must be between two or more parties, with capacity, who reach an agreement involving the exchange of valid consideration to do or refrain from doing some lawful act.

The legal rules for formation of a valid contract are definite and fairly strict. No matter what its subject matter, a contract, to be valid, must be initiated by an offer concerning valid consideration that is accepted.

Paralegals who are asked to determine if a valid contract has been made between two or more parties with capacity to contract should first determine the following:

1. Was an offer made?
2. Did the offer involve the exchange of valid consideration?
3. Was the offer accepted?

Offer or Preliminary Negotiation

The first stage of the contracting process is the offer. An **offer** is a communication by the **offeror** to a willing party, the **offeree**, of an intent to be bound to a contract. Critical to the definition is the **intent** of the party making the initial offer. Unless the offeror has the requisite intent to be bound to the proposed bargain, there is no true offer.

Intent

The first question that must be asked is whether the offeror has serious intent or is simply testing the waters through *preliminary negotiations*. Preliminary negotiations suggest a tentative nature by the offeror; they are considered a form of a solicitation and normally do not constitute an offer. Lacking is the commitment of a promise by the offeror to be bound to the offer. For example, assume that a woman is considering selling an old car. She places an ad in the newspaper stating, "Am interested in selling my old car, would consider $500." Another woman contacts the advertiser and says that she will buy the car for $500. This situation does not create an offer. The first woman was only soliciting bids, and a firm promise or commitment does not exist. There is no intent.

Common-law rules suggest that an offeror must intend to be bound to the contract. If the intent of the offeror is lacking, the assumption is that an offer did not exist. The tricky part is determining a party's intent to make a contract, as opposed to a mere proposal or even making an offer in jest. Courts will apply an objective standard rather than a subjective standard to determine whether an offer exists, based upon a reasonable person test. That is, would a reasonable person in the offeree's position believe that the offeror intended to be bound to a contract? The key to this test is not what the offeror considers reasonable; rather, it is an objective third party's impression of the seriousness of the offer and the manifestations of intent communicated by the offer.

Caution should be used when making offers that are not intended to be taken seriously. The courts will enforce a contract based upon the objective intent, and may enforce an agreement even if that was not the true intention. The effect upon the offeree's understanding of the communication, along with a court's application of the objective test, is what determines whether an offer exists.

BALLENTINESBALLENTINESBALLENTINESBALLENTINESBALLENTINESBALLENTINESBALLENTINESBALLENTINESBALLENTINESBALLENTINESBALLENTINESBALLENTINESBALLENTINESBALLENTINES

offer A proposal made with the purpose of obtaining an acceptance, thereby creating a contract.

offeror A person who makes an offer.

offeree A person to whom an offer is made.

intent Purpose; the plan, course, or means a person conceives to achieve a certain result.

|||| *Law Office Scenario* ||||

As a paralegal at the Williams law firm, Katherine Lawrence had been asked to attend the initial interview with her law firm's new client, Rachel Evert, who had scheduled an appointment to see attorney Williams regarding a possible contract dispute.

Katherine was given a copy of the contract to review two days prior to the meeting with Rachel. Attorney Williams asked her to review the contract to determine if it was in fact a valid contract. She was then to outline the terms of the contract for attorney Williams.

The contract was between Rachel and the Country Oak Furniture Company. The contract specified that for the sum of $10,000, Rachel, a furniture maker, was to deliver ten three-tier shelving units to the Country Oak Furniture Company on or before December 31, 1995.

After the delivery of just three shelving units, Rachel's workshop caught on fire and destroyed all of her materials and tools. Delivery of the remaining shelving units prior to December 31 will be impossible. Country Oak has threatened to sue her for breach of contract.

Definite Terms

Not only must an offeror have intent, but the **terms** of the offer must also be sufficiently certain and definite, so that the offeree knows what to accept. The more specific the terms, the higher the likelihood that an offer exists. If terms are left out or the parties are still haggling over terms, the transaction will probably constitute a preliminary negotiation rather than an offer. Unfortunately, what constitutes definite, clear, and certain terms is a question of fact that often must be decided by a judge or a jury. Sometimes the law sets out specific requirements, such as with real estate contracts, as to how definite an offer must be to be effective, but this is the exception and not the rule.

To be safe, an offer should specify, at minimum, the **material** terms:

1. The parties
2. The price
3. The subject matter of the contract
4. The time of performance of the contract.

Parties   Persons who intend to be bound to a contract should be clearly identified. There should be no question as to who the offeror and offeree are and, thus, who will ultimately be responsible under the contract. Failure to identify the parties in an offer is fatal to the contracting process.

Price   The specific price the parties intend to pay for the subject matter of the contract is important. Under the common law of contracts, the law does not permit the price term to be uncertain and negotiated at a later date. The offer must contain the specific price, or the offer will be considered an invitation to negotiate or merely a preliminary negotiation. Note, though, that price terms under the Uniform Commercial Code (UCC) need not be certain for a definite offer to exist.

Subject Matter   Certainty of the subject matter is a requirement for an effective offer. The subject matter must be easily identifiable and not subject to question. How specific the identity of the subject matter must be depends on the nature of

---

BALLENTINESBALLENTINESBALLENTINESBALLENTINESBALLENTINESBALLENTINESBALLENTINESBALLENTINESBALLENTINESBALLENTINESBALLENTINESBALLENTINESBALLENTINESBALLENTINES

term   A portion of an agreement relating to a particular matter.

material   Important; relating to substance rather than form; going to the merits; relevant.

the subject matter. Real estate requires substantial detail, whereas an offer for the purchase of a compact disc player does not. Statutes may dictate how definite the subject matter of the offer must be. The best rule is to be at least detailed enough so that reasonable persons will not differ in their understanding of the subject matter of the offer.

Time of Performance   When the parties perform their obligations could be critical to the transaction. Often parties specify a date for performance and set conditions if the performance date is not met. Under common law, if a contract's time of performance is not specified, a reasonable time period will be implied. Each transaction will dictate what is considered reasonable. The time of performance must be understood by the parties if there is to be a valid offer.

Communication of Offer

An offer cannot be valid unless it is communicated to the offeree. The offeree must know of the offer for there to be a power of acceptance. This observation may seem silly, but look at it in the context of a reward. Assume that there has been a surge of arsons in Southern California. The state's Attorney General posts a reward of $10,000 for anyone who catches the arsonist. One afternoon, a tourist, who knows nothing about the arson, spots a man running out of the woods holding a gasoline can. Flames are visible in the woods, so the tourist contacts the police, who subsequently arrest the arsonist based upon information provided by the tourist. Can the tourist claim the $10,000? Probably not, because he knew nothing of the offer, which makes him ineligible to receive the reward. The law requires that the offeror communicate the offer and that the offeree know of the offer for there to be acceptance.

If Rachel from the law office scenario received the contract from Country Oak Furniture in the mail with a letter asking her to consider the contract and sign and return it within two weeks if the terms were acceptable, a valid offer would have been made to Rachel.

Consideration

With few exceptions, **consideration** must exist if there is to be a binding contract. In understanding consideration, a few ground rules must be laid. First, rid yourself of the notion that consideration is only money. Second, consideration deals with **value**; it is what the parties think is valuable, even though others may not. Consequently, think of consideration as something personal between the parties. Finally, consideration may be something of great value or little value; the amount does not matter. The most important point is that consideration is a necessary element in a valid contract.

Consideration is a benefit to the promisor or a detriment to the promisee which is bargained for and given in exchange for a promise. For consideration to exist in a contract, there must be an exchange of something of value. *Value* is defined as something of worth to the parties. In addition, there must be a bargained exchange between the parties. The parties must suffer a legal benefit or legal detriment, that is, something must be given up in exchange for the promise. Lastly, the consideration must be legal. Therefore, for consideration to exist, there must be:

1. A detriment or benefit
2. A bargained exchange between the parties
3. Value
4. A promise
5. Legality.

BALLENTINESBALLENTINESBALLENTINESBALLENTINESBALLENTINESBALLENTINESBALLENTINESBALLENTINESBALLENTINESBALLENTINESBALLENTINESBALLENTINESBALLENTINESBALLENTINES

consideration   The reason a person enters into a contract; that which is given in exchange for performance or the promise to perform; the price bargained and paid; the inducement.

value   1. Monetary worth. 2. The worth of a thing in money, material, services, or other things for which it may be exchanged. 3. Estimated worth.

Paralegals often assist attorneys in analyzing contracts for consideration. Is consideration present? (Contracts are usually full of provisions showing the element of consideration which binds the agreement between the parties.) Is there an exception if consideration is not found? Case law will be your guide in answering these questions.

Elements of Consideration

The required existence of consideration proves the serious intent of the parties to bind themselves to the promises exchanged. If consideration was not needed, one could walk away from a contract, suggesting that the promise was merely a **gift**

General Form

(1) In consideration of the sum of TEN THOUSAND DOLLARS AND NO CENTS paid to John Doe by Jane Roe, the receipt of which is acknowledged, Doe agrees as follows:

For Value Received

(2) For value received, Allen Alpha agrees with Betty Beta to do the following:

Mutual Promises

(3) The parties in consideration of their mutual promises to each other agree as follows:

(4) NOW, THEREFORE, for and in consideration of the premises and the mutual promises, covenants, and agreements set forth in this Agreement, Jane Roe and John Doe agree as follows:

Services Rendered

(5) In consideration of the performance by Allen Alpha of BigCo Services at 1234 Main Street, Any City, U.S.A., Betty Beta agrees to pay the total sum of $400.00.

(6) In consideration of the services to be rendered under this Agreement, John Doe shall be entitled to compensation in the amount of TEN THOUSAND DOLLARS AND NO CENTS to be paid on completion of performance under this Agreement.

Love and Affection

(7) In consideration of the natural love and affection that Karen White has for Alicia Black, Karen White agrees to:

Release of Claim Provision

(1) In consideration of the release of the claim brought by Jane Roe against John Doe regarding the alleged defects in construction of her garage, John Doe to pay the amount of $4,000.00 to Jane Roe on or before June 15, 1995, as full and final payment of all claims.

General Consideration Provisions

(2) In consideration of the cancellation of the claim of Jane Roe against John Doe for alleged defects in construction of a garage in the sum of FOUR THOUSAND DOLLARS AND NO CENTS, and of the release of John Doe in the settlement of this case, and in consideration of the payment this day made by Jane Roe to John Doe of the sum of FOUR THOUSAND DOLLARS AND NO CENTS, receipt of which is acknowledged, John Doe agrees to release and forever discharge Jane Roe from all claims or causes of actions arising from the construction of the garage.

Settlement Provision

(1) In consideration of the mutual promises, covenants, and agreements set forth in this settlement agreement, the parties agree as follows:

Real Estate Provision

Purchase and sale of property

(1) In consideration of the mutual promises and covenants set out, Jane Roe agrees to sell and does sell, and John Doe agrees to buy and pay for, and does buy, the property located at 123 Main Street, Bigcity, State.

Conveyance of real property

(2) In consideration of the conveyance by Jane Roe to John Doe of the real property situated in the County of Dallas, State of Texas, more particularly described below, John Doe agrees to pay FIVE HUNDRED THOUSAND DOLLARS AND NO CENTS for the property located at 1234 Main Street, Dallas, Texas, more particularly set forth herein:

Devise of real property

(3) In consideration of the agreement by Jane Roe, contemporaneously with this agreement, to make a will and provide therein for the devise to John Doe of the real property situated in the County of Dallas, State of Texas, more particularly described below, and the agreement not to revoke the devise contained in such will, and further agreement not to sell, transfer, convey, mortgage, or otherwise dispose of such property to any other person, John Doe agrees as follows:

General Consideration Provisions *(Continued)*

and therefore unenforceable. This would allow individuals to abandon their contracts and probably spur even more lawsuits than presently exist. Consequently, consideration is a valuable and necessary part of the process.

BALLENTINESBALLENTINESBALLENTINESBALLENTINESBALLENTINESBALLENTINESBALLENTINESBALLENTINESBALLENTINESBALLENTINESBALLENTINESBALLENTINESBALLENTINESBALLENTINESBALLENTINES

gift A voluntary transfer of property by one person to another without any consideration or compensation.

Provision for a Gift

Gift of Household Goods

(1) Know all men by these presents, that I, Nancy David of City, State, in consideration of natural love and affection, give to my daughter, Serena Davis, all the household furniture and effects, books, pictures, and all other tangible personal property whatsoever in my dwelling house at 123 Main Street, City, State.

Gift of Real Property

(2) This deed, made this 5th day of July, 1995, between Howard Davis of City, State, herein called the Donor, and his daughter, Serena Davis of City, State, herein called the Donee.

(3) Witnesseth, that the Donor, in consideration of his natural love and affection for the Donee, does hereby give, grant, and convey to the Donee, her heirs and assigns, all the following described real property in the City of _____ State of _____ :

General Consideration Provisions *(Continued)*

Detriment or Benefit The definition of consideration states that there must be a benefit or detriment to the parties. Each party to the contract gains something or gives up something in the contracting process. When a party gains, a legal benefit exists; when a party sacrifices, a legal detriment exists. Legal detriment is usually found when parties do something or act in some way they do not legally have to or refrain (forbear) from doing something that they have a legal right to do.

Bargained Exchange of the Parties There must be a bargained-for exchange by the parties. A promise may be exchanged for another promise, as in a bilateral contract; or for an act, as in a unilateral contract; or for the forbearance of an act. The focus is on the exchange of promises between the parties of benefits and detriments. This concept is known as **mutuality**. Mutuality exists between the parties, furnishing each with some form of detriment or benefit.

For Value Critical to the concept of consideration is that the exchange of the benefit and detriment be something of value to the parties. Note that only the parties decide on the value. It is the value upon which the parties agree. In addition to money or property, value attaches to services rendered or the act of forbearing. Each type of value is valid as consideration.

The most typical kind of value (consideration) is money. In most contracts the consideration bargained for is the exchange of money.

Exchanges of property between the parties also constitute value and therefore consideration. For example, assume Susan owns only a computer and needs a printer. She finds Katie, who has a printer but no computer. Susan and Katie could contract as follows:

I promise to allow you to use my printer three times a week in exchange for the use of your

---

BALLENTINESBALLENTINESBALLENTINESBALLENTINESBALLENTINESBALLENTINESBALLENTINESBALLENTINESBALLENTINESBALLENTINESBALLENTINESBALLENTINESBALLENTINES

mutuality Two persons having the same relationship toward each other with respect to a particular right, obligation, burden, or benefit; the condition of being mutual.

computer every morning from 9:00 a.m. to 11:00 a.m., Monday through Friday.

The consideration in the example is the exchange of property and, therefore, the value to each party.

Another thing of value to parties is services, so an exchange of services between parties is also valid consideration. Courts will look for an exchange, not necessarily what the exchange entails. Suppose that a farmer needs workers, but does not have much money to pay them. The farmer offers to give them free food and lodging in exchange for working 30 hours per week. The value is the exchange of services for property. Courts have held this to be value because it is a bargained-for exchange between the parties.

Acts of Forbearance   Requesting someone to refrain from doing something that he or she has a legal right to do is also considered value. The value may be unique or personal to the parties, but it is nevertheless something of value.

Promise Between the Parties   The parties must have made a promise to each other for something of value, or consideration will not be found. For example, I promise to give you my ring. You take it. What is the promise *between* the parties? Nothing. Giving up a ring in exchange for nothing is gratuitous, and is therefore a gift. There is no promise between the parties, no exchange, no benefit or detriment, no value. If I promise to give you a bracelet in exchange for $100, then that is a promise between us, the parties, and is enforceable. In the law office scenario, the promises between the parties were Country Oak's promise to pay $10,000 to Rachel and Rachel's promise to deliver the furniture.

Value Must Be Legal   The value exchanged must be legal. If the parties exchange something that they do not have the legal right to exchange, the consideration is nonexistent. For example, Lillie offers to sell cocaine to Rachel for $1000. The consideration is illegal and thus unenforceable in court.

Adequacy of Consideration

Courts do not have a predetermined set of rules to decide how much consideration is enough to make a contract binding. In fact, courts shy away from inquiring into the **adequacy** of the consideration bargained for in a contract. The reason behind this arm's-length approach is that courts encourage freedom of the bargaining process and believe that the responsibility for deciding how much consideration is sufficient rests with the parties to the contract. Even if the value bargained for seems inadequate or unfair, courts generally do not inquire into the reasons as to why the parties agreed on a particular amount or type of consideration.

Courts, however, will inquire as to adequacy if the consideration appears to be nominal and perpetuating a **sham**. In these situations, the indications are that there was no bargain at all, and therefore no true consideration. When sham consideration is found, courts will not enforce the promises between the parties. Inquiries into the adequacy of the consideration are few, but they exist. When issues of fraud, misrepresentation, mistake, duress, undue influence, and unconscionability are raised, the adequacy of the consideration may become an issue. However, these instances are the exception and not the rule.

Absence of Consideration

When consideration is absent, courts will not enforce the alleged contract made between the parties. Because consideration is a necessary element in contract formation, the lack of it renders the contract invalid, unless an exception exists. Instances in which courts have found consideration absent involve gifts, illusory promises, moral consideration, past consideration, and contracts under the pre-existing duty rule. Each is important.

BALLENTINESBALLENTINESBALLENTINESBALLENTINESBALLENTINESBALLENTINESBALLENTINESBALLENTINESBALLENTINESBALLENTINESBALLENTINESBALLENTINESBALLENTINESBALLENTINES

adequate consideration   A fair and reasonable price or value for the subject matter of the contract in question; a sufficient price in law.

sham   A deception; a trick; a fraud.

Gifts The promise of a gift is unenforceable for lack of adequate consideration. If someone promises to bequeath a gift in a will, but does not fulfill that promise, a court will not find that a contract existed between the parties, as there was no consideration. In a gift situation, there is neither a bargained-for exchange nor a benefit or detriment to the parties. The exchange is one-sided, with only one party benefiting and no legal detriment being suffered. No expectation of a bargained-for exchange occurs, and therefore there is no enforceable contract.

Illusory Promises Promises based upon one party's wish, desire, or hopes is not sufficient to create an adequate basis for a contract. Expressions that create such indefiniteness are considered **illusory promises**. An illusory promise is one that gives a false impression of a contract but in reality does not obligate the party making the promise to anything. There is no bargained-for exchange between the parties. Words suggesting an illusory promise are:

- We will order your products when we need them.
- We will order the product as we may want from time to time.
- We will order the product as demand dictates.
- We will request shipment of your product when we wish.

None of this language creates a mutuality of obligation between the parties; therefore, the necessary consideration for a binding contract is lacking. Illusory promises lack consideration and are unenforceable contracts.

Moral Consideration A promise to compensate for a past moral obligation is unsupported by consideration and hence unenforceable. There is no bargained-for exchange between the parties, as one performs the act gratuitously without regard to contractual considerations. Courts generally will not find consideration for a past moral obligation.

Past Consideration A valid contract cannot be based on past consideration; that is, an act performed or detriment suffered prior to the time the contract is formed. With past consideration, a pretext appears to exist for a contractual relationship, but mutuality is lacking. The key is that a promise to give value for goods or services previously rendered is not past consideration and does not create the basis of a new, enforceable contract.

The Preexisting Duty Rule Closely related to past consideration is the preexisting duty rule. When a person has a preexisting responsibility to do or not to do something, there is no bargained-for exchange. If the obligation exists either by law or prior agreement, the law will not infer consideration, as no detriment is suffered. Under this preexisting duty rule, consideration cannot be bargained for between the parties, as the responsibility to act or refrain from acting is already a duty.

The area in which the preexisting duty rule has been most heavily litigated deals with public service. Firefighters and police officers, for example, cannot extract benefits from a citizen for tasks that they are hired to perform. The preexisting duty rule also is often applied to construction contracts. Typically, a contractor agrees to provide services for a specific amount. While performing the service, the contractor realizes that the sum contracted for is insufficient to complete the work. The contractor threatens to walk off the job unless a higher price is paid for the service. The other party may pay the additional sum to avoid a work stoppage, but courts will not enforce payment of the additional sum, as a preexisting duty exists.

Exceptions: Contracts Enforceable Without Consideration

In the law, there are always exceptions to every rule. Under certain circumstances, contracts will

illusory promise A promise whose performance is completely up to the promisor … . Because the carrying out of such a promise is optional, there is no mutuality, and therefore the promise cannot form the basis of a valid contract.

be enforceable even though there is no consideration. Some of these exceptions are found in the doctrine of promissory estoppel, promises made after the statute of limitations has run, discharge in bankruptcy, or promises to pay for benefits received.

Promissory Estoppel   The concept of **promissory estoppel** is based on principles of justice and fairness. Although no consideration is apparent from the promises, if a party changes his or her position in reliance on a promise, courts may imply that consideration exists and find that a contract was created. Promissory estoppel focuses on the need for fairness and the avoidance of injustice in the contracting process. The doctrine may be applied when consideration is challenged and in other areas of contract law.

Promissory estoppel contemplates that the promisee relied to his or her detriment and also that the reliance was reasonably foreseeable by the promisor. **Foreseeability** is one of the keys in finding promissory estoppel.

Promissory estoppel has also been used as a means to enforce a contract when charities are involved. Often individuals or entities make charitable pledges and then fail to fulfill them. Because charities rely upon contributions, courts have held that a contract exists based upon the principles of promissory estoppel. Although a convincing argument can be made that a charitable pledge is merely a gift, charitable organizations rely to their detriment when they plan their organizations' functions, such as staff and supply expenses, around pledges. Courts have used promissory estoppel as a means to enforce otherwise invalid contracts.

Statutes of Limitation   **Statutes of limitation** impose time periods within which a party must file a lawsuit or lose its right to sue. Once a statute of limitation passes, parties cannot validly exercise their rights to pursue a claim. Statutes of limitation vary from state to state depending on the cause of action, but it is clear that a party cannot attempt to enforce a prior obligation (such as a debt) once the statute of limitations has passed, unless the party owing the debt puts the promise in writing. Simply saying "I will pay the debt I owe you" after the statute of limitation has run is not a contract because there is no consideration.

Bankruptcy   When a party files bankruptcy, creditors have real difficulty in collecting on contracts made prior to the bankruptcy. Through the laws in the Bankruptcy Code, debtors have the opportunity to reaffirm their debts. If the court accepts the new promise by the debtor, the contract will be enforceable even though no consideration exists between the parties.

Benefits Received   When a party has received a benefit, such as emergency medical care, whether a contract exists between the parties depends upon whether consideration is found. If the party did not agree to pay for the medical treatment, is there consideration for an enforceable contract? The answer depends upon whether the services were requested by the receiving party. When the answer is yes, consideration often will be found to bind the parties to a contract. If the services were not requested, courts will not find consideration present. So, when emergency medical services are rendered but not requested, should the doctor have to be the good samaritan and not receive payment for the services performed? Although consideration may not exist, under the doctrine of **quasi-contract** (implied-in-law contracts) the court

BALLENTINESBALLENTINESBALLENTINESBALLENTINESBALLENTINESBALLENTINESBALLENTINESBALLENTINESBALLENTINESBALLENTINESBALLENTINESBALLENTINESBALLENTINESBALLENTINESBALLENTINES

promissory estoppel   The principle that a promisor will be bound to a promise (that is, estopped to deny the promise), even though it is without consideration, if he or she intended that the promise should be relied upon and it was in fact relied upon, and if a refusal to enforce the promise would result in an injustice.

foreseeable   That which may be anticipated or known in advance; that which a person should have known.

statutes of limitations   Federal and state statutes prescribing the maximum period of time during which various types of ... actions ... can be brought after the occurrence of the injury or the offense.

quasi contract   An obligation imposed by law to achieve equity, usually to prevent unjust enrichment. A quasi contract is a legal fiction that a contract exists where there has been no express contract.

would create a contract based upon principles of fairness and justice.

Consideration in Dispute

Often disputes arise as to the amount of the consideration in a contract. When this happens, a settlement between the parties may occur. However, for a settlement to be upheld, courts rule on whether the disputed amount is a liquidated or an unliquidated claim.

Liquidated Claims A **liquidated claim** is a specific sum owed to a party. The amount owed is undisputed and known by the parties to the contract. If the person who owes the amount attempts to tender part payment of the amount as full payment of the obligation, does new consideration exist to discharge the prior debt? No. The party has a pre-existing duty to pay the entire debt, and part payment will not constitute new consideration for a new contract to cancel the claim.

Unliquidated Claims With an **unliquidated claim**, the sum is either not specifically known or is disputed. Suppose that Samantha agrees to pay $500 to get her car repainted. However, a chemical reaction with the car's front left bumper causes it to rust within a week. Samantha quickly stops payment on her check and writes to the repair shop. The amount is now unliquidated and disputed.

To remedy the situation, the parties may agree on a specific amount to satisfy the amount owed or in dispute, through a compromise and settlement agreement. It is not uncommon for parties to agree on a negotiated, compromise amount. They are, in effect, executing what is known as an **accord and satisfaction**. The compromise or agreement between the parties is known as the *accord* and the payment of the agreed amount is known as the *satisfaction*. This solves the problem of consideration. Accord and satisfaction must always go together.

Acceptance

Once an offer is communicated and the offeree considers it, it can be accepted. The **acceptance** is the response by the offeree to the offeror of an intent to be bound to the terms set out in the offer. Only the person to whom the offer is directed has the power to accept. Unless a party knows of the offer, there is no power of acceptance.

An acceptance by the offeree of the offer may be written, oral, or implied. Each mode of communication has a common thread: it must be unconditional and unequivocal—there can be no question as to the offeree's intent.

Written Acceptance

The offeree may respond to the offeror in a written communication. This form of acceptance is usually appropriate, although an offer may state a specific manner of acceptance. If the offer states a particular manner of acceptance, then to be effective the acceptance must comply with the terms of the offer. This is a **stipulation**, which effectively sets limitations on the acceptance.

The Mail Box Rule

When an offer is communicated by mail, the acceptance can be made through the same medium—the mail. The *mail box rule* states that when an offer is communicated in the mail, the acceptance is effective upon deposit in the mail, regardless of

BALLENTINESBALLENTINESBALLENTINESBALLENTINESBALLENTINESBALLENTINESBALLENTINESBALLENTINESBALLENTINESBALLENTINESBALLENTINESBALLENTINESBALLENTINESBALLENTINES

liquidated claim A claim the amount of which is agreed upon by the parties or which can be determined by applying rules of law or by mathematical calculation.

unliquidated claim A claim whose existence or amount is not agreed upon by the parties; a claim whose amount cannot be determined by applying rules of law or by mathematical calculation.

accord and satisfaction An agreement between two persons, one of whom has a cause of action against the other, in which the claimant accepts a compromise in full satisfaction of the claim.

acceptance [T]he assent, by the person to whom an offer is made, to the offer as made by the person making it.

stipulation A mandate; a requirement; a condition.

receipt by the offeror. This rule can have chaotic results, as the offeror may not know that an offer has been accepted and revoke the offer prior to receiving the acceptance. The **revocation** is effective upon receipt by the offeree, but the acceptance is effective upon deposit in the mail regardless of receipt by the offeror. Therein lies the problem with the mail box rule. Because the mail is often an unpredictable mode of communication, it is wise for the offeror to set out conditions or a stipulation in the acceptance. A better method to control or completely obviate the mail box rule is to state in the offer that the acceptance must be received by a specific date to be effective.

Communicating the acceptance by the same mode used by the offeror is effective when delivered to that same medium (e.g., offer by telegram and acceptance by telegram; the acceptance is effective when transmitted). However, if the acceptance is by a different medium than that used by the offeror, the acceptance is effective upon receipt by the offeror. Suppose an offer did not stipulate a manner of acceptance. If the offer was faxed and the acceptance was mailed, the mail box rule would not apply, and the acceptance would be effective only upon receipt by the offeror, not dispatch. For an offeror, controlling the method of acceptance can be critical.

Oral Acceptance

An acceptance may be communicated orally as well as in writing. When negotiating face-to-face, a verbal acceptance of an offer is effective. When the offeror hears the words "I accept" or a similar expression of assent, the acceptance is effective. This proposition also applies when the telephone is used. The acceptance is effective at the moment the offeree utters words of assent. Suppose that an offer is communicated by telephone and the offeree contacts the offeror within the time period specified and responds affirmatively to an answering machine or voice mail. Is that considered the same mode of communication? The courts have not yet decided that issue, but arguably it is the same mode of acceptance.

Implied Acceptance

An offeree's actions or conduct can indicate acceptance of an offer. Some believe that lack of communication or silence means assent to an offer, but this is not so. Unless both parties agree, silence is not normally considered an acceptance of an offer. However, there are three exceptions to this rule:

1. When an offeree takes the benefit of offered services with reasonable opportunity to reject them and reason to know that they were offered with the expectation of compensation
2. When the offeror has stated or given the offeree reason to understand that assent may be manifested by silence or inaction, and the offeree in remaining silent and inactive intends to accept the offer
3. When, because of previous dealings or otherwise, it is reasonable that the offeree should notify the offeror if he or she does not intend to accept.

Unilateral and Bilateral Contracts Distinguished

When all that is required of the offeree is performance, a **unilateral contract** is formed. The mode of acceptance is the conduct or actions of the offeree. No exchange of responses is necessary to indicate assent to the offer; rather, performance indicates the acceptance. Courts do not favor acceptance of an offer by a later action, as this means that the contract lacks a critical element—communication to the offeror. Acceptance of an offer through performance causes uncertainty. Courts favor a clear assent by the offeree to the offeror, creating a

BALLENTINESBALLENTINESBALLENTINESBALLENTINESBALLENTINESBALLENTINESBALLENTINESBALLENTINESBALLENTINESBALLENTINESBALLENTINESBALLENTINESBALLENTINESBALLENTINES

revocation A nullification, cancellation, or withdrawal of a power, privilege, or act.

unilateral contract A contract in which there is a promise on one side only, the consideration being an act or something other than another promise. ... [A]n offer that is accepted not by another promise, but by performance.

bilateral contract. An exchange between the parties is clear. Until communicated, an acceptance is ineffective, which leaves less room for uncertainty as to the offeree's actions.

The Mirror Image Rule

Whether an acceptance is communicated through a writing, orally, or impliedly, under common law the acceptance must be the same as the offer. The rule, known as the *mirror image rule,* states that an offer and acceptance must match exactly—they must mirror each other. Any deviation in the terms of the offer is a **counteroffer**, a new offer. Under the mirror image rule, it does not matter how slight the deviation or qualification is between the acceptance and offer. The rule is interpreted strictly and unless the counteroffer is in turn accepted by the original offeror, an agreement is not formed. In effect, the counteroffer terminates the original offer and substitutes itself as a new offer.

Terminating the Offer

There are a number of ways to end the formation process, thereby terminating the offer. Depending upon the circumstances, offers can terminate upon the happening of certain events, by action of the parties, or by operation of law. Each method results in the same thing—**termination** of the offer.

Action of the Parties

Various actions of the parties can terminate an offer. Typical actions terminating an offer are a counteroffer, rejection, revocation, and expiration of time.

Counteroffer A change in the terms, however slight, of the original offer creates a counteroffer. The power of acceptance is now switched, with the offeror having the power to accept the new offer. The common law is strict in its interpretation of deviations from the original offer: any change in the terms of the original offer terminates the offer. Virtually no exceptions exist under this common-law rule.

Rejection **Rejection** occurs when an offeree does not accept the stated terms of an offer. The negotiating terminates unless a new offer is communicated. In effect, a counteroffer is a rejection of the offer. Rejection is a typical method to terminate an offer. An acceptance can be written, oral or implied, and so can the rejection. A rejection can also be verbally communicated, either face-to-face or by telephone. Finally, a rejection may occur when the offeree's behavior suggests nonacceptance. This is a more difficult and more equivocal situation. Suppose that an attorney offers to sell you her services for $100 an hour. However, you go out and hire another attorney. That action is in effect an implied rejection.

Revocation Before an offer is accepted, an offeror may withdraw it at any time. This act is know as *revocation.* Some acts or events invite a revocation. Suppose that an offer is communicated, but the offerer receives no acceptance. The offeror withdraws the offer by mail and the offeree receives the withdrawal prior to the offeree's acceptance. This constitutes revocation. However, assume that Samantha has mailed an offer to Henry on the 1st of the month that arrives on the 16th. Henry mails his acceptance on the 27th. On the 30th, Samantha mails a revocation, which does not arrive until the middle of the following month. Because Henry mailed his acceptance before he received Samantha's revocation, the acceptance stands.

bilateral contract A contract in which each party promises performance to the other, the promise by the one furnishing the consideration for the promise from the other.

counteroffer A position taken in response to an offer, proposing a different deal.

termination 1. An end of something in time. 2. The act of bringing an end to something.

rejection Any act or word of an offeree, communicated to an offeror, conveying refusal of an offer.

The Option Contract   When an offeree pays the offeror money to keep an offer open for a specified period of time, an **option contract** is created. The offeror cannot revoke the offer, because the payment creates an **irrevocable offer**. The value paid restricts the rights of the offeror and enhances the power of the offeree. As long as the option is in effect, the offeror cannot revoke the offer, even if someone makes a better offer.

Expiration or Lapse of Time

Another means of revocation may come into effect automatically if a time limit has been set on the offer. If the offeror states in the offer that the acceptance must be received by a specific date, the offer automatically terminates unless acceptance is received by the specific time. If the offeree does not accept within the specified time period, the offer is automatically revoked—it **expires** or **lapses** due to the time limitation. This method of revocation is useful, as it sets restraints on an offeree's power to accept. Offerors usually do not want to leave offers open indefinitely.

Although case law suggests that an offer without a specific time deadline will expire upon the reasonable passage of time, this rule leaves open the age-old question of what is reasonable. The courts will review each circumstance to determine reasonableness. When time appears to be an important factor, the court will imply a shorter time period. Unfortunately, there is no exact time period for a "reasonable period of time." Therefore, to be safe, a definite termination date is the best protection.

Operation of Law

Offers also can be revoked due to some intervening factor over which neither party has control. The law guards against these circumstances when it would be improper to hold a party to an offer through no fault of its own. Typical methods of terminating an offer by operation of law are illegality, death, insanity, and destruction of the subject matter.

Illegality   When legislation is enacted that makes the subject of the offer illegal, the offer is terminated. Suppose that a produce company offers a supplier 1,000 pounds of Nicaraguan bananas. The U.S. government then determines that Nicaragua has committed too many human rights violations, and an embargo on Nicaraguan goods is signed into law. The offer would not stand because it would be illegal to import the goods into this country. The offer is terminated by a superseding illegality. Neither party has control over the circumstances, and therefore it would be inappropriate to hold the offeror to the offer.

Death   Death of the offeror automatically terminates the offer. No communication to the offeree is necessary, but, as a practical matter, it makes good business sense to let an offeree know that an offeror has died. Note that if the offeree dies, the power to accept by the intended offeree is terminated.

Insanity   Persons who have been declared by a court to be of unsound mind or insane do not have the power to create an offer. The logic behind this mode of termination holds that an insane offeror does not have the **legal capacity** to make an offer.

Destruction of the Subject Matter   When an offer is communicated and the subject matter of that offer is then destroyed, the offer is terminated. This often occurs when the subject matter and the

---

BALLENTINESBALLENTINESBALLENTINESBALLENTINESBALLENTINESBALLENTINESBALLENTINESBALLENTINESBALLENTINESBALLENTINESBALLENTINESBALLENTINESBALLENTINESBALLENTINES

option (option contract)   An offer, combined with an agreement supported by consideration not to revoke the offer for a specified period of time; a future contract in which one of the parties has the right to insist on compliance with the contract, or to cancel it, at his or her election.

firm offer (irrevocable offer)   Under the Uniform Commercial Code, an offer to buy or sell goods made in a signed writing which, by its terms, gives assurance that it will be held open. A firm offer is not revocable for want of consideration during the time it states it will be held open … .

expiration   Coming to an end; termination due to lapse of time.

lapse   To cease; to expire; to terminate.

legal capacity   The ability to execute binding contracts, deeds, wills, etc.; capacity.

acts are out of the offeror's control. "Acts of God," such as tornadoes, hurricanes, and floods, can all terminate an offer if they destroy the subject matter of an offer. Termination, under these circumstances, occurs because the thing or entity essential to the subject of the contract is destroyed.

Mutual Assent of the Parties

One of the most important parts of a contract is the parties' agreement to the terms and conditions set forth in the offer and acceptance. The parties must willingly and genuinely assent to the terms of contract, or the contract may be invalid. This is known as **mutual assent**.

Mutual assent can be defined as "the meeting of the minds." Under the law, this concept signifies that all parties have been open and honest in their dealings and that all understand the basis of the bargain. There are no hidden terms or meanings; each term is clearly stated and is only what it says. The communication of the offer and acceptance leads to an agreement between the parties which is a necessary element to a contract.

To determine whether mutual assent exists, the court will apply an objective standard of conduct. Did the parties to the contract act in such a way that it could be reasonably concluded that they agreed to the same terms and conditions, or did the acts of the parties show a contrary intent? The essence of mutual assent hinges on the parties having a mutual understanding of the terms and conditions of the contract. As with an offer, the intent of the parties, as viewed by an objective third party, is critical to the concept of mutual assent. Most terms must be clearly identified so that, objectively, a conclusion can be reached that a contract has been consummated.

Methods of Destroying Mutual Assent

A problem arises when the parties are not honest and genuine in their contractual negotiations. When terms are deliberately missing, or mistakes occur, or parties are placed under undue pressure, mutual assent is destroyed and the contract will fail. The most common ways to destroy mutual assent are fraud, misrepresentation, mistake, duress, and undue influence. If one of these issues (or, as they are more commonly know, defenses) is shown, an important element of the contract is destroyed, potentially terminating or voiding the contract.

Another method of destroying mutual assent that has developed over the years is based in public policy. Protecting the public from unfair contracts has become a method of destroying mutual assent and forms a basis for **rescinding** a contract. A common public policy argument used by attorneys and courts is that the contract is **unconscionable**. Often this occurs when one party to a contract takes advantage of another party by using terms that are patently unjust or unfair. Whatever the means, any of these methods may terminate a contract and destroy the meeting of the minds.

Fraud

Fraud is a common method of destroying mutual assent. By definition, it is a wrongful statement of

---

BALLENTINESBALLENTINESBALLENTINESBALLENTINESBALLENTINESBALLENTINESBALLENTINESBALLENTINESBALLENTINESBALLENTINESBALLENTINESBALLENTINESBALLENTINES

mutual assent   A meeting of the minds; consent; agreement.

rescission   The abrogation, annulment, or cancellation of a contract by the act of a party. … More than mere termination, rescission restores the parties to the status quo existing before the contract was entered into.

unconscionable   Morally offensive, reprehensible, or repugnant. An unconscionable contract is a contract in which a dominant party has taken unfair advantage of a weaker party, who has little or no bargaining power, and has imposed terms and conditions that are unreasonable and one-sided.

fraud   Deceit, deception, or trickery that is intended to induce, and does induce, another to part with anything of value or surrender some legal right.

fact or omission of fact knowingly made by a party with the intent to induce another party to enter into a contract. Critical to establishing fraud as a means of destroying mutual assent is that the party *knew* that his or her representation or statement was false.

When fraud is proven, the contract is usually voidable by the injured party, because a critical element of the contract—the mutual assent—has been destroyed. To this end, a court will award a party damages (money) or rescind the contract (cancel it) and put the parties back in the same positions they would have been in prior to consummating the contract.

Misstatement of Fact   To establish fraud, a party must show that the party initiating the contract knowingly misstated a fact or omitted to state a fact.

Fact Is Material   The misstatement or omission of fact must be material to the contract, that is, it must be critical to a party's decision to enter into the transaction. It goes to the heart of the contract.

Knowledge of False Statement   Also central to proving fraud is that the party making the statement had knowledge of its falsity. At the time the statement was made, the party must have known it was false.

Intent to Deceive   To prove fraud, a person must prove that the statement was made falsely and that the person who made the statement had the intent to deceive the party to whom the statement was made. This contemplates deliberate intent with total disregard for the actual facts. In establishing a claim for fraud, the party making any statement or omission must be shown to have had the intent to deceive another person to induce that person to enter into a contract.

Reliance on Misstated Fact or Representation
In addition to showing intentionally false representations made by the party committing the fraud, it must be shown that the person to whom the communication was made relied to his or her detriment on the false representations of that party. If it can be shown that the person accepted the contract, that he or she relied on the representations made, and that the representations were deceptive, a case for fraud is virtually assured.

Representation Caused Damage   The final point to be proven in a fraud claim is that a party relied to his or her detriment on the misstatement or omission of fact. This element goes directly to the issue of injury. To successfully establish a case for fraud, a party must show that he or she was injured or damaged by the representation of another party. This element is usually easy to show when the other elements are present.

Misrepresentation

Fraud and misrepresentation have similar characteristics. **Misrepresentation** is a misstatement of fact or omission of fact made innocently without the intent to deceive. The key difference between fraud and misrepresentation is the element of intent. In misrepresentation, the statement is made innocently without the knowledge necessary to establish deliberate conduct.

Duty to Disclose

An issue that is a constant source of debate is the extent of a party's duty to disclose. Must all facts be disclosed? Must a party correct another's false assumption? The answer, unfortunately, is, it depends. The law requires that parties act honestly in their dealings. Withholding vital or material information can give rise to a claim of misrepresentation. For example, assume that a seller puts a house on the market. Prior to putting the house up for sale, the seller notices a water stain on the ceiling, indicating a possible leak in the roof. The seller paints over the stain. A prospective buyer asks about the condition of the roof. Does the seller

BALLENTINESBALLENTINESBALLENTINESBALLENTINESBALLENTINESBALLENTINESBALLENTINESBALLENTINESBALLENTINESBALLENTINESBALLENTINESBALLENTINESBALLENTINESBALLENTINES

misrepresentation   The statement of an untruth; a misstatement of fact designed to lead one to believe that something is other than it is; a false statement of fact designed to deceive.

have a duty to disclose that the roof may have a leak? The answer is probably yes, because the seller does have reason to suspect a leak in the roof. Could a negative response to the buyer's question result in a claim for misrepresentation? Probably so.

Understanding the duty to disclose means understanding what constitutes a material fact. If a party misstates a basic assumption in the contract, the duty to disclose exists. Here the issue is not only the materiality of the information, but also the fact that the party is relying on a misplaced assumption. Did the representation induce the party to enter into a contract? If the answer is yes, misrepresentation exists. Giving only part of the truth creates a misleading impression and may constitute misrepresentation. The duty to disclose is clear.

Mistake

Mistake is a common means of destroying mutual assent. Mistake occurs when the parties to a contract are wrong about some act or event that is material to the transaction. As with fraud or misrepresentation, one of the critical elements is the materiality of the mistaken facts. Ignorance of the law or illiteracy will not form a basis of claim of mistake; the courts will hold those parties responsible for the content of the agreement.

Courts distinguish two types of mistakes: mutual mistakes and unilateral mistakes. For a contract to be set aside or rescinded, a mistake normally must be mutual. In a unilateral mistake situation, courts usually hold the parties to their duties and obligations and will not rescind the contract.

Mutual Mistake In a **mutual mistake**, both parties are wrong about the existence of a material fact to the transaction, and thus the courts often allow rescission of the contract. Because there has

not been a meeting of the minds, in that the parties to the contract have not agreed on the terms and conditions of the contract, the contract cannot be consummated. When mutual mistake is asserted, either party may renounce the contract, thus making the contract voidable.

Unilateral Mistake The situation is different for a **unilateral mistake**, a common ground alleged as a reason to set aside a contract. In a unilateral mistake case, only one party is mistaken about a material fact to the transaction. Traditionally, a court will not rescind a contract based on unilateral mistake, although there are a few exceptions to this rule.

Duress

Duress is another means of avoiding a contract. **Duress** is wrongful pressure on a person that deprives him or her of free will. For a duress action to be sustained, specific elements must be proven. The party alleging duress must show that the pressure or force asserted was extreme and that had the pressure not been exerted, the party would not have entered into the transaction. Duress is difficult to prove because it must go beyond a mere threat to overcome a party's free will. The pressure must be so extreme that coercion exists; it is not sufficient that the party was merely vulnerable.

Four situations generally give rise to a duress case. First, when a party threatens another person with violence, duress exists. If someone holding a knife to your spouse's throat stated, "Unless you sign this contract, I will kill him," duress would exist. Second, threats of imprisonment can create inordinate pressure on someone, destroying his or her free will. Assume that your spouse threatens that if you do not sign this decree of divorce giving

---

BALLENTINESBALLENTINESBALLENTINESBALLENTINESBALLENTINESBALLENTINESBALLENTINESBALLENTINESBALLENTINESBALLENTINESBALLENTINESBALLENTINESBALLENTINESBALLENTINESBALLENTINES

mistake An erroneous mental conception that influences a person to act or to decline to act; an unintentional act, omission, or error arising from ignorance, surprise, imposition, or misplaced confidence. … An error; a misunderstanding; an inaccuracy.

mutual mistake A mistake of fact that is reciprocal and common to both parties to an agreement, each laboring under the same misconception with respect to a material fact.

unilateral mistake A misconception by one, but not both, parties to a contract with respect to the terms of the contract.

duress Coercion applied for the purpose of compelling a person to do, or to refrain from doing, some act.

up custody of your children, she will file assault charges against you. This form of coercion may constitute duress. Thirdly, a claim for duress arises when a party threatens to take or keep a person's property. In this situation a party wrongfully asserts a claim against a person's property in order to extract a contractual advantage. Finally, duress can be alleged when one party threatens to breach a contract. This might occur when a party is dissatisfied with a contract and attempts to use wrongful leverage to modify or change the contract terms by threatening a breach.

A new form of duress, known as *economic duress,* has developed, but it is very difficult to prove. Economic duress occurs when (1) wrongful or unlawful conduct (2) causes financial hardship that (3) forces the injured party to act against his or her free will, which (4) causes economic detriment to the injured party; and (5) no immediate legal remedy exists. Courts find economic duress only in limited situations.

Undue Influence

Undue influence is another method of destroying mutual assent. Closely aligned with duress, the significant difference between undue influence and duress is that the former arises out of a confidential relationship. Undue influence occurs when a party who is in a position of trust unduly uses that position to gain an advantage over another person. Undue influence is a common problem with the sick and elderly. Quite often, caretakers can unduly influence weakened persons and extract monetary advantages from them. This can also occur in family relationship, as, for example, when a sibling attempts to influence a parent to disinherit another sibling so as to extract monetary gain from the parent's will. Courts look very closely at the relationships between the parties when undue influence is alleged. They consider the method used by the dominant person and the circumstances surrounding the contract. How weakened or susceptible was the influenced person? What is the relationship between the parties?

Unconscionability

All contracts impose upon each party the duties of good faith and fair dealing. When contracts are not fair in their performance or enforcement, the issue of unconscionability may arise. An **unconscionable contract** is one that shocks public sensibilities and is unreasonably oppressive. They usually occur when the parties' bargaining positions are so unequal that the public is best protected by invalidating the contract, because of the oppressive and shocking nature of the bargain. The key element in proving that a contract is unconscionable is a showing of lack of meaningful assent to the contract by the party claiming the defense. The party affected must show that he or she truly did not understand the terms and conditions of the contract, destroying mutual assent. Two types of unconscionability may be found: procedural unconscionability and substantive unconscionability.

Procedural Unconscionability When there is no meaningful choice by one party who enters into a contract, *procedural unconscionability* may exist. The key is in the party's assent to the contract. In forming the contract, the party is forced to enter into the contract without the ability to change, alter, or modify its terms. Nonnegotiable clauses, often referred to as *boilerplate provisions,* may appear in a contract as to which the weaker party is in a "take it or leave it" position. Sometimes procedural unconscionability can occur with high-pressure salespeople.

As with most cases involving mutual assent, a judge or jury must determine whether procedural unconscionability exists. Courts look closely at the effect of the contract on the party who was restricted in the bargaining process.

BALLENTINESBALLENTINESBALLENTINESBALLENTINESBALLENTINESBALLENTINESBALLENTINESBALLENTINESBALLENTINESBALLENTINESBALLENTINESBALLENTINESBALLENTINES

undue influence Inappropriate pressure exerted on a person for the purpose of causing him to substitute his or her will for the will or wishes of another.

unconscionable contract A contract in which a dominant party has taken unfair advantage of a weaker party, who has little or no bargaining power, and has imposed terms and conditions that are unreasonable and one-sided.

Substantive Unconscionability   Oppressive or overly harsh contracts are *substantively unconscionable*. This type of unconscionability often occurs with excessive price terms or unfair alterations in a party's remedies for breach of contract.

Substantive unconscionability is prevalent in installment contracts, in which a party pays, over a period of time, a purchase price with accrued interest and charges. Often the interest charges and fees are three to four times the actual price paid or actual value of the items purchased. Courts have held that such terms are unconscionable and void the contract.

The other area in which substantive unconscionability becomes a factor is in the remedies afforded a purchaser upon default under a contract. In this situation, the individual or entity who controls the terms of the contract expand its rights while diminishing the other party's rights. Courts have deemed this unfair and often refuse to enforce such contracts. Courts also have the option of excising the unconscionable clauses to balance the effect of the contract on the parties. The court's actions are always based upon principles of fairness.

Adhesion Contracts

Some courts have called unconscionable contracts **contracts of adhesion**. In an adhesion contract, one party to the contract is able to impose its will on another party, leaving no mutuality of assent. Some have termed this a method of **overreaching**. These kinds of contracts violate public policy and are usually set aside to protect the public good. The crucial point in understanding adhesion contracts is that they are not open to negotiation—the offeree must take the terms as they are or forgo entering into the contract. This clearly puts the offeror at an unfair advantage and basically removes any mutual assent from the contract.

Adhesion contracts are often standardized. They are preprinted, nonnegotiated contracts whose terms are set except for the parties, price, quantity, and length of payment time. Characteristics found in some adhesion contracts are very small print, unclear or ambiguous terminology, or overly complex language that clearly favors the drafter. Not all adhesion contracts are unconscionable, however. The court will review the totality of the circumstances surrounding the contract. Was there a gross disparity of bargaining powers? Did the party claiming an adhesion contract make any contribution to the bargaining process? Was there really mutual assent? If the answers to these questions are negative, a contract of adhesion may be found.

The common element causing adhesion and unconscionable contracts to be disfavored is the courts' attempt to protect the public welfare. Public policy is served by not allowing one party to benefit unfairly from a contract when the other party had no real participation in the process.

The Paralegal's Role

In the contracting process, facts may suggest that the parties have not been honest in their dealings. As a paralegal, you may be asked to investigate situations in which fraud or misrepresentation may have occurred. Similarly, duress or undue influence issues require analysis and examination. Along with your attorney, always ask questions of the parties to the contract to determine if mutual assent has been destroyed. Often, it is a slow, deliberate process.

Mistake is a bit different. Mistake often appears on the face of the contract, such as in the price or quantity term. These mistakes are usually clerical errors. To avoid this problem, carefully check all contracts for mathematical, typographical, and spelling errors. If it is your job to check figures and proofread, do so carefully. Any legal professional's nightmare is missing a critical word (like omitting the "not" from "shall not"), thus changing the entire meaning of the contract.

BALLENTINESBALLENTINESBALLENTINESBALLENTINESBALLENTINESBALLENTINESBALLENTINESBALLENTINESBALLENTINESBALLENTINESBALLENTINESBALLENTINESBALLENTINESBALLENTINESBALLENTINESBALLENTINES

adhesion contract (contract of adhesion)   A contract prepared by the dominant party (usually a form contract) and presented on a take-it-or-leave-it basis to the weaker party, who has no real opportunity to bargain about its terms.

overreaching   Taking unfair advantage in bargaining.

The paralegal should focus substantial attention on provisions that appear too one-sided and may be rendered unconscionable. Provisions that should be closely watched (and are often litigated) are default, remedy, and interest provisions. The keys to evaluating such provisions are whether their effect is a punishment and whether the parties had freedom in the negotiating process.

Default Provisions   When a party does not perform its obligations under a contract, that party is in **default**. Virtually all contracts have provisions setting forth the consequences of default. When analyzing the validity of a default provision, determine its effect on the defaulting party. Is the provision harsh and offensive and therefore unconscionable?

Examine the following default provisions:

---

1. In the event of a default of any kind, I hereby agree that the entire lease shall be accelerated and I shall be liable thereon for all past due principal payment, all accelerated payments, interest thereon at the rate of 10 percent per annum, costs, all other related charges, together with attorney fees in the amount of one-third of the total accelerated amount under the lease.

---

2. Upon the occurrence of an event of default and at any time thereafter, Lessor, in addition to any other rights and remedies he may have, shall have the right to take possession of the equipment, whereupon Lessee's right to use the same under and subject to the terms and provision of this Lease, and any other right or interest of Lessee to or in the equipment, shall absolutely cease, but such taking by Lessor shall not relieve Lessee of its obligations and liabilities hereunder.

The effect of these sample clauses is that a default, no matter how minor, will have an unconscionable result. Courts have held that such default provisions are invalid. When drafting, pay close attention to the cumulative effects of a default provision.

Interest Provisions   Provisions charging interest are standard in contracts, but the interest charged or the cumulative effect of an interest charge must be analyzed closely to determine if the interest charged is too high. State laws set limits on the rates that can be charged; excessive interest rates are usurious and unenforceable. Review interest provisions carefully and look at their total effect.

Remedy Provisions   When one party's remedies are limited, courts often rendered those provisions unenforceable as unconscionable. When one party excludes all possible remedies for another party who has been unable to perform its contractual obligations, the contract is too one-sided and thus likely invalid. Examine the following provisions:

---

1. The buyer's limit for breach of performance by the seller shall be limited to the difference between the contract price and the fair market value at the time of the breach and in no event is the buyer entitled to lost profits or consequential or punitive damages of any kind.

---

2. In the event of a breach of performance, the party shall only be entitled to a refund of the purchase price of the product purchased. This shall be the buyer's sole remedy and shall be in lieu of any other claims for incidental or consequential damages.

Most of these provisions unduly limit the possible recovery for one party to the contract and could be held unconscionable by a court. When provisions are too oppressive, the party preparing the contract will often suffer the consequences.

---

default   The failure to perform a duty or obligation. ... Fault; neglect; omission.

Capacity: The Ability to Contract

In contract law, agreeing or understanding the terms and conditions of a contract is not sufficient to bind the parties. An additional element must be present. **Capacity** is the legal ability to enter into a contract. This concept is defined as being over the legal age (which means 18 or 21 years of age, depending on your state statute) and being of sound mind (which means mentally competent).

Most individuals who enter into contracts have capacity, but occasions do arise when the parties to a contract lack the legal capacity to bind themselves to it. Individuals in this category are mentally handicapped, legally insane, intoxicated, or drugged persons, and minors. In addition, aliens and convicted felons in some instances lack capacity. Depending upon how the law views the person, those who lack capacity create either **void** or **voidable contracts**.

Determining the capacity of the parties may be another step in the paralegal's review of a contract. In the law office scenario, Rachel most certainly has the capacity to enter into the contract if she is an adult. Paralegal Katherine might want to check on the capacity of the Country Oak Furniture Company, though. Is that entity a valid corporation? Did the individual signing the contract have the authority to sign on behalf of the corporation?

Minors

State statutes determine when a person legally becomes an adult. Usually majority is reached at the age of 18 or 21 years old. Prior to reaching the age of majority, **minors**, or **infants** as the law sometimes refers to them, lack the capacity to create binding contracts.

Under the law, minors create voidable contracts and generally cannot be held responsible for the contracts they create. Minors who contract with adults can avoid contracts they enter into by disaffirming those contracts. **Disaffirmance** is a method of rejecting a contract through cancellation. A minor usually can disaffirm a contract prior to reaching majority and for a reasonable time after reaching majority, although courts differ as to what is a reasonable time. Courts look to the subject matter, the parties, and when the disaffirmance took place to determine if it is reasonable. However, the adult who contracts with a minor does not have the same luxury. When an adult contracts with a minor, the contract is binding unless the minor disaffirms or releases the adult from the contract. The law clearly protects the minor.

A method of holding a minor to a contract is to insist that an adult co-sign the contract. This effectively eliminates the minor's ability to disaffirm, as the adult will remain responsible for the contract. In addition, if a minor's **guardian** enters into a contract on the minor's behalf, this contract will generally be valid. Contracts made by a guardian often have a court's approval, negating the minor's right of disaffirmance, and thus are enforceable.

BALLENTINESBALLENTINESBALLENTINESBALLENTINESBALLENTINESBALLENTINESBALLENTINESBALLENTINESBALLENTINESBALLENTINESBALLENTINESBALLENTINESBALLENTINESBALLENTINES

capacity   Competency in law. ... A person's ability to understand the nature and effect of the act in which he or she is engaged.

void contract   A contract that creates no legal rights; the equivalent of no contract at all.

voidable contract   A contract that may be avoided or disaffirmed by one of the parties because it is defective.

minor   A person who has not yet attained majority; a person who has not reached legal age; a person who has not acquired the capacity to contract.

infancy   The status of a person who has not reached the age of majority and who therefore is under a civil disability; nonage; minority.

disaffirmance   The refusal to fulfill a voidable contract. ... Disclaimer; repudiation; disavowal.

guardian   A person empowered by the law to care for another who, by virtue of age or lack of mental capacity, is legally unable to care for himself or herself.

Exception for Necessities

Exceptions exist to every rule. When minors contract for **necessities**, such as food, clothing, shelter, and medical services, they, along with their parents, become responsible for the reasonable value of those items or services. For example, if a physician provides medical services and the minor does not pay, the parents will be responsible for the charges. Note that the law states that the minor or parents will be responsible for the *reasonable* value of those services. If someone attempts to take advantage of a minor by charging an exorbitant fee for a service, a court will determine what a customary and standard amount is for the service rendered and impose only that charge.

Further, courts examine the party's ability to pay. Generally, courts look to parents to pay for contracts for necessities. If the parents cannot afford to pay, courts have held children responsible for the contract.

The age-old question is what is a *necessity?* How do courts define this word, which imposes liability on minors or their families? Courts look to a child's needs, social status, and economic ability. Determining exactly what a child needs is very difficult and is usually analyzed on a case-by-case basis. Are shoes a necessity? A bicycle? A stereo system? Although a stereo system appears clearly not to be a necessity, suppose that the minor is a linguist who needs the equipment to practice languages and speech patterns. Perhaps then a stereo would be a necessity. Courts look closely at each particular situation.

Exception for Misrepresenting Age

More than ever, minors look and act like adults. It can be very difficult to tell a 15-year-old from a 20-year-old. With false identification easily obtainable, misrepresenting one's true age is not difficult. Thus, the law says that when a minor misleads another party into entering into a contract, either party can disaffirm the contract.

Ordinarily, an adult cannot disaffirm a contract made with a minor, but when misrepresentation is proven, the law will not hold the unsuspecting party to the contract. The rules vary from state to state, but it is clear that minors cannot benefit from their own wrongdoing.

Furthermore, although courts firmly maintain the minor's right to disaffirm a contract, they also require misrepresenting minors to put the adults back in the same position they had before making the contract (that is, prior to the misrepresentation). Courts thus attempt to prevent **unjust enrichment** and to act fairly and equitably. Consequently, when a contract is voided based upon misrepresentation, the law forces the minor to return any property gained through the contract; it does not allow them to profit from their own wrongdoing.

Although courts try to be fair, the tendency is still to lean toward the side of the minor. Chances are that if a minor cannot return the item, or if it is damaged, the minor will probably be allowed to disaffirm the contract, with virtually no consequences.

Ratification: Validating a Contract

When a minor accepts benefits form a contract, **ratification** occurs. The key to ratification is when it happens: for ratification to be effective, a minor must show some act of approval or some benefit from the contract after majority. Any other result would not protect the minor.

Ratification can elevate a voidable contract to the status of a valid one. When a minor becomes an adult and shows a willingness to abide by the terms of a contract made as a minor, ratification may be found. Implied *ratification* can be made by

---

necessities (necessaries) Things reasonably necessary for maintaining a person in accordance with his or her position in life.

unjust enrichment The equitable doctrine that a person who unjustly receives property, money, or other benefits that belong to another may not retain them and is obligated to return them.

ratification The act of giving one's approval to a previous act, either one's own or someone else's, which, without such confirmation, would be nonbinding. ... Ratification may be implied from a person's conduct; it may also take place as a result of accepting the benefits of a transaction. ... [T]he confirmation of an act that has already been performed.

a subtle act, such as continuing to make payments on a car after reaching majority. Ratification may also occur from an express act, which may be oral or written. No matter what the form of ratification, attaining majority effects the enforceability of the contract and erases any prior disability.

Insane and Mentally Ill Persons

Persons who lack mental capacity generally create voidable contracts or void contracts. The law distinguishes a person's capacity based on the degree of mental inability. Suppose that an individual's mental ability is impaired temporarily. This mentally infirm person may, however, have moments of lucidity in which he or she can understand the terms of a contract. If it can be proven that this person understood the contract and was competent when it was made, the contract may be enforced; but if the party was not competent or was mentally insane when the contract was created, it is void. If the condition of infirmity worsens, the disabled party may disaffirm the contract.

Determining whether a contract by a mentally disabled person is void or enforceable is a very difficult task. Each situation has to be evaluated independently to determine whether the person understood the terms of the contract and the consequences of his or her acts relating to the contract.

An easier case arises when a person has been legally declared by a court to be insane, or *non compos mentis*. For such persons, the right to contract is denied and thus any contracts they create are void. The only person who can enter into a contract on behalf of a declared incompetent person is the court-appointed guardian, whose acts must always have court approval. There are no exceptions to this rule, as courts will protect insane persons from themselves and society.

As with minors, society is also protected when necessities are provided to mentally incapacitated persons. A mentally incapacitated person is liable for contracts created for necessities under the theory of quasi-contract. However, only the reasonable value of the services provided will be allowed. Courts will not let the mentally incapacitated be taken advantage of.

Other Persons Lacking Capacity

In some other situations, persons may be legally incapable of forming a contract. This occurs when a person is intoxicated or drugged, an alien, or a convicted felon.

Intoxicated or Drugged Persons

Persons who are under the influence of alcohol or drugs often lack the capacity to contract. Capacity is determined by the degree of the intoxication. If the intoxication was to such a degree that the party had no ability to understand the nature of the contract, a court may not enforce the contract. The contract created is void. As with mentally incapacitated persons, courts evaluate these cases individually. Unless the facts are clear, courts generally do not like to void contracts based upon intoxication by alcohol or drugs.

Persons who are intoxicated may disaffirm or ratify a contract upon reattaining sobriety. If disaffirmance is desired, it must be total and complete and the party must return all consideration. Unless disaffirmance occurs soon after the disability is removed (e.g., when sobriety returns), the assumption will be that the party has ratified the contract, and it may thus be enforced.

Aliens

Persons who are not citizens of the United States are known as **aliens**. As a general rule, aliens have the capacity to contract, with very few restrictions. One exception concerns contracting with an alien whose country is at war with the United States. While hostilities continue, that alien lacks the capacity to contract and may create a voidable contract.

BALLENTINESBALLENTINESBALLENTINESBALLENTINESBALLENTINESBALLENTINESBALLENTINESBALLENTINESBALLENTINESBALLENTINESBALLENTINESBALLENTINESBALLENTINES

non compos mentis   Mentally incompetent; of unsound mind.

alien   Any person present within the borders of the United States who is not a U.S. citizen.

Classification	Status of Contract
Minors	Voidable
Mentally Incapacitated	
1. Lucid moment	Valid
2. Competent but not so judicially declared	Voidable
3. Declared incompetent by court	Void
Intoxicated Persons	Voidable
Aliens	Voidable
Convicts	
1. During imprisonment	Voidable
2. After release	Valid

Contract Status According to Party's Capacity

Convicted Felons

Upon imprisonment, many prisoners have restrictions placed not only on their freedom, but also on their ability to contract. Consequently, contracts created by incarcerated persons are unenforceable and void. However, once prisoners are freed, their contractual rights are restored, and they enjoy virtually the same rights they had prior to imprisonment.

Legality in Contracts

Even if parties accept an offer, provide the consideration, understand the terms for mutual assent, and have the capacity to contract, one more element must be present for a contract to be enforceable. That final element necessary to complete the formation of a contract is **legality**. The contract must have a legal purpose and legal subject matter to be enforceable between the parties. If a contract is deemed illegal, it is void.

Sometimes contracts that appear to be legal are later deemed by a court to be illegal. Parties may not know whether the contract they created is illegal or enforceable; a contract can be formed and then be deemed illegal when challenged in court. Consequently, the parties may not be able to predict the outcome of their contractual agreement. Legality can be a difficult issue to identify when no legal guidance exists.

In addition, an illegal contract can be formed when a party violates a statute or public policy. These are common grounds on which to void an existing contract.

Contracts Violating a Statute

A common type of illegal contract is created when the parties' agreement or conduct is prohibited by law. The most obvious example is a contract to kill someone for money. Common sense tells us that if you hire someone to kill your parents, promise

legality   The condition of conformity with the law; lawfulness.

the killer the proceeds of a life insurance policy as payment, and then renege on the agreement, no court in this country will enforce the contract. That kind of activity is criminal and an agreement to engage in unlawful activity is unenforceable and void. Agreements to engage in tortious activity, such as a deliberate scheme to defraud unsuspecting investors, are also void. These acts are illegal and thus any contract concerning those acts would be illegal and unenforceable.

Contracts Violating Public Policy

Courts have the discretion to void a contract when the contract is unfair, offends the public's moral sensibilities, or is oppressive. Unconscionable contracts fall into the category of oppressive and unfair transactions. An unconscionable contract can be avoided based upon lack of mutual assent and also on the basis of legality. The focus for a court is the public good and the public interest.

One type of contract that has received a great deal of public attention and court scrutiny is the *surrogacy contract,* which involves the hiring of a woman to bear an unrelated woman's or couple's child for a fee. Normally these contracts provide for a substantial fee to the surrogate for her services, as well as the payment of medical fees. Upon the birth of the child, the surrogate gives the child to the genetic parent or couple and terminates all her right to the child. The legality of such contracts has been challenged on several bases, including violation of child-selling laws as well as violation of public policy. Neither state statutes nor case law are clear on these issues.

Covenants Not to Compete

Contracts governing business relationships often include provisions that restrict the right to competition. In many circumstances, parties agree not to engage in a competitive business endeavor for

a period of time or within a specific geographical area. These clauses are normally used to protect one party from unfair competition when there is a high likelihood that the other party's competition could substantially affect the first party's business. These provisions are known as *restrictive covenants* or **covenants not to compete**. Restrictive covenants can be categorized as those incident to the sale of a business and those incident to an employment relationship. Each restricts the ability to compete under very specific circumstances. Because we live in a free market economy, where competition is encouraged, any restrictions on competition raise issues of unfairness.

Covenants Incident to a Business

When two parties contract for the sale of a business, it is very common, as part of the conditions of sale, to restrict or limit the seller's ability to compete in the same field for a specified period of time within a specified geographic area. The noncompetition provision is important because it effectively prohibits the seller from going into the same business, using the same contacts or suppliers, or engaging in other behavior that, in effect, undermines the value of the agreement for sale. Laws allow reasonable restrictions and reasonable restraints on competition when the provision is incident to the sale of a business. Whether a particular covenant not to compete is legal or illegal depends on its scope, however.

Many courts have set restrictions as to the extent of the geographic area and the time period in which a covenant may be enforced. What the court looks to is the type of business involved, the general geographic area in which the business operates, and the overall restriction on the seller's right to engage in business. If the covenant goes beyond what is reasonable and necessary, the court could sever the provision and enforce the contract with the noncompetition provision, or it

covenants not to compete   A provision in an employment contract in which the employee promises that, upon leaving the employer, he or she will not engage in the same business, as an employee or otherwise, in competition with the former employer. Such a covenant ... must be reasonable with respect to its duration and geographical scope.

could **reform** the provision to limit the clause and make it reasonable.

For example, suppose that you are selling a business in California. Your business involves the sale of seashell art and is limited to the counties of Los Angeles and Orange. However, when the covenant not to compete is drafted, it provides that you, the seller, may not sell seashell art anywhere in the entire state for a period of seven years. This would most likely be considered an unreasonable restraint of trade and competition. It would probably be declared void, because it extends for too long a period of time and covers a larger geographic area than is reasonable and necessary.

Critical to the analysis of a noncompetition clause is its reasonableness. Many states have statutes regulating the reasonableness of covenants not to compete. Such statutes generally have strict requirements. Courts do not look kindly upon contracts that restrict trade.

Covenants Incident to Employment

Similarly, employers can restrict the right of employees to compete in the same business after employment has terminated. The same standards apply as for business noncompetition covenants, in that the restrictions must be reasonable. The restrictions may include both geographic and time constraints. Such covenants are common in employment contracts, especially in industries such as computers and manufacturing. Employers attempt to protect the investment they have in their employees, especially persons with knowledge of and access to confidential proprietary information and trade secrets. Courts have allowed restrictive covenants in employment contracts as a method of protection for employers, if all the usual elements for contract formation are present, but they strictly construe such clauses. Again,

the courts look to the extent of the provision and its effect on the employee.

Exculpatory Clauses

Clauses that limit liability are known as **exculpatory clauses**. Exculpatory clauses are closely monitored by courts, which use essentially the same analysis as for unconscionable and adhesion contracts. Courts will attempt to determine (1) whether the bargaining powers of the parties were equal and (2) whether one party had any bargaining powers at all.

Exculpatory clauses are common. For example, when you park your car in a parking lot, there is often a limitation of liability on the claim ticket. Usually the claim ticket states that management will not be held responsible for any items stolen or damage to the car while it is in the lot or garage.

Exceptions to Illegality

Courts provide limited exceptions for enforcement of illegal contracts. The concept known as *in pari delicto* (equally at fault) focuses on the illegal acts of the parties. A court will not reward one party for illegal acts by allowing a case against another illegal actor. However, through a court's evaluation, if it is determined that the parties to the contract were not equally blameworthy, or if one party was guilty of **moral turpitude**, the court may enforce the contract against the person who is less guilty. In this situation, the parties are not in pari delicto—but this is the exception to the rule.

Connected to the pari delicto idea is *locus poenitentiae* (a time in which to repent). Under this theory, a party can withdraw from the contemplated illegal act before liability attaches. Thus, courts allow the parties to an illegal contract a time to repudiate the contract prior to

BALLENTINESBALLENTINESBALLENTINESBALLENTINESBALLENTINESBALLENTINESBALLENTINESBALLENTINESBALLENTINESBALLENTINESBALLENTINESBALLENTINESBALLENTINESBALLENTINESBALLENTINESBALLENTINES

reform   To correct; to make better; to modify.

exculpatory clause   A clause in a contract or other legal document excusing a party from liability for his or her wrongful act.

in pari delicto   Equally at fault.

moral turpitude   Depraved conduct; immoral conduct.

performance of the illegal contract. A court may allow recovery in the form of **restitution** from the party who has rescinded an illegal bargain, if that is appropriate.

Doctrine of Divisibility

To avoid the injustice that voiding an illegal contract may cause, courts can apply the doctrine of **divisibility**. By dividing a contract into sections, a court can remove the illegal portion and enforce the remaining, legal, provisions of the contract.

Before the doctrine can be applied, the contract and the circumstances surrounding its formation must meet certain requirements. First, the contract must be divisible into corresponding pairs of performances which the parties treated as equivalent exchanges. If the illegal performance is severable, the remainder of the contract can be enforced. Second, the illegality cannot affect the entire contract; if it does, the contract cannot be divisible. Last, the party seeking enforcement of the contract must not have engaged in serious misconduct.

If a case meets these requirements, the doctrine of divisibility applies and the illegal part may be severed from the contract. Courts often find that this method yields a more equitable result when the illegality issue is raised.

Summary Questions

1. What are the necessary elements for every binding contract?

2. Suppose that Tom mails to Janet an offer to purchase her truck, stating that if she wants to sell it on the proposed terms, she must respond by June 10. On June 9, Janet decides to accept the offer, and she mails her acceptance to Tom, who does not receive it until June 11. Is this a valid offer and acceptance?

3. Suppose that Jessica, who is 17 years old, decides to buy a car from Steve. She agrees to pay Steve $100 per month for four years. Jessica keeps up her end of the bargain for one year, until she decides she has paid enough for the car. She then tells Steve that they never had a binding contract because she was a minor when she entered into the contract. She tells Steve that she has the right to keep the car and discontinue payments now that she is an adult. Is she right?

4. Suppose that Ed enters into a contract with Terry for the purchase of 150 television sets. Terry delivers the television sets and Ed collects payment from Terry. If the television sets are faulty, might Terry be guilty of misrepresentation or fraud? Under what circumstances?

5. What is the difference between mutual mistake and unilateral mistake? Which mistake is more likely to make a contract voidable?

6. What is the difference between duress and undue influence?

7. What is an unconscionable contract?

restitution   [A] remedy that restores the status quo. Restitution returns a person who has been wrongfully deprived of something to the position he or she occupied before the wrong occurred; it requires a defendant who has been unjustly enriched at the expense of the plaintiff to make the plaintiff whole, either … by returning property unjustly held, by reimbursing the plaintiff, or by paying compensation or indemnification.

divisible contract   A contract whose parts are capable of separate or independent treatment; a contract that is enforceable as to a part which is valid, even though another part is invalid and unenforceable.

Practical Paralegal Skills

1. Assuming the facts in the law office scenario, do you think Rachel is guilty of breach of contract? What provisions in the contract may define her responsibility to Country Oak Furniture Company, considering her inability to deliver the shelving units?

2. Assuming the facts in the law office scenario, and using a sample contract from a formbook, draft a contract between Rachel Evert and The Country Oak Furniture Company. Considering Rachel's inability to deliver all of the shelves on time, what would the consequences be to her under the contract the way you have written it?

APPENDIX A

DIRECTORY OF PARALEGAL ASSOCIATIONS

NFPA Member Associations

Region I

Alaska Association of Legal Assistants
P.O. Box 101956
Anchorage, AK 99510-1956

Arizona Association of Professional Paralegals, Inc.
P.O. Box 25111
Phoenix, AZ 85002

Central Coast Legal Assistant Association
P.O. Box 93
San Luis Obispo, Ca 93406

Hawaii Association of Legal Assistants
P.O. Box 674
Honolulu, HI 96809

Juneau Legal Assistants Association
P.O. Box 22336
Juneau, AK 99802

Los Angeles Paralegal Association
P.O. Box 241928
Los Angeles, CA 90024
(213)251-3755

Oregon Legal Assistants Association
P.O. Box 8523
Portland, OR 97207
(503)796-1671

Sacramento Association of Legal Assistants
P.O. Box 453
Sacramento, CA 95812-0453
(916)763-7851

San Diego Association of Legal Assistants
P.O. Box 87449
San Diego, CA 92138-7449
(619)491-1994

San Francisco Association of Legal Assistants
P.O. Box 26668
San Francisco, CA 94126-6668
(415)777-2390

Washington State Paralegal Association
P.O. Box 232
Ardenvoir, WA 98811
(509)784-9772

Region II

Dallas Association of Legal Assistants
P.O. Box 12533
Dallas, TX 75225
(214)991-0853

Gateway Paralgegal Association*
P.O. Box 50233
St. Louis, MO 63105

Illinois Paralegal Association
P.O. Box 8089
Bartlett, IL 60103-8089
(708)837-8088

Kansas City Association of Legal Assistants
P.O. Box 13223
Kansas City, MO 64199
(913)381-4458

Kansas Legal Assistants Society
P.O. Box 1675
Topeka, KS 66601

Legal Assistants of New Mexico
P.O. Box 1113
Albuquerque, NM 87103-1113
(505)260-7104

Manitoba Association of Legal Assistants, Inc.*
22-81 Tyndall Avenue
Winnipeg, Manitoba R2X 2W2

Minnesota Association of Legal Assistants
2626 E. 82nd Street, Suite 201
Minneapolis, MN 55425
(612)853-0272

New Orleans Paralegal Association
P.O. Box 30604
New Orleans, LA 70190

Northwest Missouri Paralegal Association*
Box 7013
St. Joseph, MO 64507

Paralegal Association of Wisconsin, Inc.
P.O. Box 92882
Milwaukee, WI 53202
(414)272-7168

Rocky Mountain Legal Assistants Association
P.O. Box 304
Denver, CO 80201
(303)369-1606

West Central Texas Association of Legal Assistants
P.O. Box 6902
Abilene, TX 79608

Region III

Baltimore Association of Legal Assistants
P.O. Box 13244
Baltimore, MD 21203
(301)576-BALA

Bay Area Paralegal Association
P.O. Box 453
Severna Park, MD 21146

Cincinnati Paralegal Association
P.O. Box 1515
Cincinnati, OH 45201

Cleveland Association of Paralegals
P.O. Box 14247
Cleveland, OH 44114
(216)575-6090

Columbia Legal Assistants Association
P.O. Box 11634
Columbia, SC 29211-1634

Georgia Association of Legal Assistants
P.O. Box 1802
Atlanta, GA 30301
(404)433-5252

Greater Dayton Paralegal Association
P.O. Box 515, Mid-City Station
Dayton, OH 45402

Indiana Paralegal Association
P.O. Box 44518
Indianapolis, IN 46204

Legal Assistants of Central Ohio
P.O. Box 15182
Columbus, OH 43215-0182
(614)224-9700

Lexington Paralegal Association, Inc.
P.O. Box 574
Lexington, KY 40586

Louisville Association of Paralegals
P.O. Box 962
Louisville, KY 40201

Memphis Paralegal Association
P.O. Box 3646
Memphis, TN 38173-0646

Michiana Paralegal Association
P.O. Box 11458
South Bend, IN 46634

Middle Tennessee Paralegal Association
P.O. Box 198006
Nashville, TN 37219

Mobile Association of Legal Assistants
P.O. Box 1852
Mobile, AL 36633

National Capital Area Paralegal Association
P.O. Box 19124
Washington, DC 20036-9998
(202)659-0243

Northeastern Ohio Paralegal Association
P.O. Box 9236
Akron, OH 44305

Plaintiff Paralegal Association (Palm Beach)
P.O. Box 3115
Palm Beach, FL 33480

Roanoke Valley Paralegal Association
P.O. Box 1505
Roanoke, VA 24006

Region IV

Central Connecticut Association of Legal Assistants
P.O. Box 230594
Hartford, CT 06123-0594

Central Massachusetts Paralegal Association
P.O. Box 444
Worcester, MA 01614

Central Pennsylvania Paralegal Association
P.O. Box 11814
Harrisburg, PA 17108

Connecticut Association of Paralegals, Inc.
(Fairfield County)
P.O. Box 134
Bridgeport, CT 06601

ANGELA SCHNEEMAN

"Upon completing *The Law of Corporations, Partnerships,
and Sole Proprietorships,* I was driven to write this book because
I wanted students to understand the paralegal roles within
government, firms, or corporations. With this insight students
may choose the directions that are right for them and I will
have realized my goal as an author."

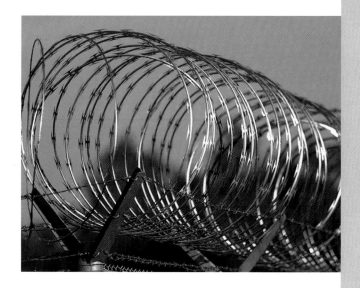

"Cellular telephones allow me to be reached while I'm working anywhere away from the office. In life and death cases our criminal defense attorneys wear pagers to be in constant contact with paralegals, the courts, and clients."

About 13 percent of paralegals work in criminal law. The national average salary for a criminal law paralegal is over $25,000 and can be as high as

$41,000. The criminal law paralegal spends a great deal of time interviewing clients and witnesses, preparing for trial, and assisting the attorney during trial and post-trial procedures. ||||

Approximately 6.5 percent of paralegals work in real esta law. The average annual sala is over $30,000, with a high of $58,000. The occupation c a real estate paralegal may involve title research, document preparation and review attendance at real estate clos ings, and mortgage foreclosur The paralegal must be familia with the local, state, and federal laws governing real estat transactions. ▐▐▐

More paralegals work in the litigation area than any other area of law, nearly 53 percent. These paralegals earn at or above the national average annual salary: between $28,000 and $30,000 depending on whether employed by defense or plaintiff attorneys. Litigation paralegals are set apart from other paralegals by the fact that they work with cases that involve trial courts and thus must fully understand the nuances of judicial procedures. ▐▐▐

The federal government reports that it has more than 30,000 law-related positions for which paralegals may be qualified. The average annual salary of administrative and legislative paralegals is nearly $45,000. Paralegals are most often employed by administrative agencies, although many may be employed by law firms which represent clients in administrative law matters or by corporations that are concerned with administrative rules and regulations. ▐▐▐

Nearly 9 percent of all employed paralegals work in the personal injury field. The national annual salary of personal injury paralegals is $26,000 and has been reported to be as high as $55,000. Personal injury and tort law include such diverse areas as products liability, defamation of character, nuisance, and false imprisonment. The tasks performed by the paralegal depend greatly on whether one works for the plaintiff or the defendant.

Approximately 2 percent of all paralegals are employed by law offices engaged in intellectual property matters. The average annual salary of an intellectual property paralegal is well over $35,000, with a high of $50,000+. The paralegal is often responsible for registering patent applications and renewals, researching current laws and filings, investigating possible copyright infringements, and working directly with musicians, authors, and scientists.

"I never thought my days would start in Dallas and end in Boston, L.A., or Miami. While sometimes exhausting, the pace of corporate mergers and acquisitions is really the reason I'm a paralegal."

Corporate paralegals account for over 10 percent of the employed legal assistants. The average annual salary is reported to be well over $33,000, but depends on the kind of law office (corporation, law firm, or government) hiring the paralegal. The paralegal assists attorneys in the formation, merger, legal management, acquisition, and dissolution of business entities (from proprietorships to partnerships to corporations). ▊▊▊

BANKRUPTCY PARALEGAL

About 3 percent of paralegals work on bankruptcy matters. The average annual salary is under $29,000, but can be as high as $53,000. The bankruptcy paralegal prepares notices to creditors, coordinates appraisals, prepares an accounting of assets sold, reviews claims for the distribution of funds, interviews clients, drafts petitions, attends hearings, and files claims with the bankruptcy court. ▐▐▐▐

"At a first meeting of creditors working smart beforehand yields significant time savings for the trustee, creditors, the firm, and the client. You can truly shine professionally."

Connecticut Association of Paralegals (New Haven)
P.O. Box 862
New Haven, CT 06504-0862

Delaware Paralegal Association
P.O. Box 1362
Wilmington, DE 19899

Erie County Paralegal Association*
4013 Cochran Street
Erie, PA 16508

The Greater Jersey Paralegal Association, Inc.*
P.O. Box 55
Flanders, NJ 07836

Legal Assistants of Southeastern Connecticut
P.O. Box 409
New London, CT 06320

Long Island Paralegal Association
P.O. Box 80
Kings Park, NY 11754

Manhattan Paralegal Association, Inc.*
521 Fifth Ave., 17th Floor
New York, NY 10175

Massachusetts Paralegal Association
P.O. Box 423
Boston, MA 02102
(617)469-7077

Paralegal Association of Rochester, Inc.
P.O. Box 40567
Rochester, NY 14604

Philadelphia Association of Paralegals
1411 Walnut Street, Suite 200
Philadelphia, PA 19102
(215)564-0525

Pittsburgh Paralegal Association
P.O. Box 2845
Pittsburgh, PA 15230
(412)642-2745

Rhode Island Paralegal Association
P.O. Box 1003
Providence, RI 02901

South Jersey Paralegal Association
P.O. Box 355
Haddonfield, NJ 08033

Southern Tier Association of Paralegals
P.O. Box 2555
Binghamton, NY 13902

Western Massachusetts Paralegal Association
P.O. Box 3005
Springfield, MA 01102

Western New York Paralegal Association, Inc.
P.O. Box 207, Niagara Square Station
Buffalo, NY 14202

West/Rock Paralegal Association
P.O. Box 101 - 95 Mamaroneck Ave.
White Plains, NY 10601

NALA Affiliated Associations
As of November 8, 1993

For Addresses contact NALA Headquarters, 1516 S. Boston, Suite 200, Tulsa, OK 74119 (918)587-6828; fax (918)582-6772.

Alabama

Legal Assistant Society of Southern Institute/PJC
Douglas Ingram, President
Birmingham, AL

Alabama Association of Legal Assistants
Miriam Rosario, CLA, President
Birmingham, AL
Michael C. Ivey, NALA Liaison
Birmingham, AL

Samford Paralegal Association
Rebecca King, President
Birmingham, AL

Marcia Jill Timbes, NALA Liaison
Birmingham, AL

Alaska

Fairbanks Associations of Legal Assistants
Helena L. Schreder, CLA, President
Fairbanks, AK
Sally G. Lowery, CLA, NALA Liaison
Fairbanks, AK

Arizona

Arizona Paralegal Association
Karin M. Scheehle, CLAS, President

Phoenix, AZ
Marian R. Johnson, CLA, NALA
Liaison
Tempe, AZ

Legal Assistants of Metropolitan Phoenix
Ruth M. Murphy, CLA, President
Phoenix, AZ
Helen L. Wertsching, CLA, NALA
Liaison
Phoenix, AZ

Tucson Association of Legal Assistants
Shirley L. Duran, CLA, President
Tucson, AZ
Mary E. Butera, CLA, NALA Liaison
Tucson, AZ

Arkansas

Arkansas Association of Legal Assistants
Patrice Carey, President
Little Rock, AR
Deborah J. Moon, NALA Liaison
Pine Bluff, AR

California

Legal Assistants Association of Santa Barbara
Helga Schmidt Metzler, President
Santa Barbara, CA
Carol W. Berg, CLA, NALA Liaison
Santa Barbara, CA

Paralegal Association of Santa Clara County
Jean M. Cushman, CLA, President
San Jose, CA
Jo Ellen Floch, CLA, NALA Liaison
San Jose, CA

Ventura County Association of Legal Assistants
Cynthia J. Adams, CLA, President
Ventura, CA
Pamela K. Jansz, CLA, NALA Liaison
Oxnard, CA

Colorado

Association of Legal Assistants of Colorado
Donna L. Coble, CLAS, President
Greeley, CO

Florida

Florida Legal Assistants, Inc.
Donnajeanne B. Hakler, CLAS,
President

St. Petersburg, FL
Carol D. Holler, CLAS, NALA
Liaison
Fort Lauderdale, FL 33308

Bay Area Legal Academy Student Association
George House, Jr., President
Tampa, FL
Dr. Darline Root, NALA Liaison
Tampa, FL

Dade Association of Legal Assistants
Joanne M. Del Campo, CLA,
President
Miami, FL
Lori Allen, CLA, NALA Liaison
Bay Harbor Island, FL

Gainesville Association of Legal Assistants
Beth A. Hoffman, President
Gainesvelle, FL
Theresa D. Becks, CLA, NALA
Liaison
Gainesville, FL

Jacksonville Legal Assistants
Tana J. Stringfellow, CLA
Jacksonville, FL
Mary Cathy Cassels, CLA, NALA
Liaison
Jacksonville, FL

Orlando Legal Assistants
Jennifer H. Cooper, CLA, President
Orlando, FL
Lisa Vander Weide, NALA Liaison
Orlando, FL

Pensacola Legal Assistants
Carol G. Skipper, President
Pensacola, FL
Catherine M. Kaiser, NALA Liaison
Pensacola, FL

Volusia Association of Legal Assistants
Mary J. Harrington, President
Ormond Beach, FL
Rosemary E. Hallman, CLA, NALA
S. Dayton, FL

Georgia

Georgia Legal Assistants
Elaine H. Hall, CLA, President
Alma, GA
Phyllis H. Driver, CLA, NALA

Liaison
Waycross, GA

Professional Paralegals of Georgia
Judith W. McCutcheon, CLA,
President
Atlanta, GA
Donita C. Berckemeyer, CLA, NALA
Liaison
Atlanta, GA

Southeastern Association of Legal Assistants of
Georgia
Angie H. Porter, CLA, President
Savannah, GA
Kathy J. Ulmer, NALA Liaison
Savannah, GA

South Georgia Association of Legal Assistants
Penny D. Wendel, CLA, President
Valdosta, GA
Michelle Adkins, CLA, NALA Liaison
Valdosta, GA

Idaho

Gem State Association of Legal Assistants
Suzanne M. Campbell, CLA,
President
Hailey, ID
Susan Carlson, CLA, NALA Liaison
Ketchum, ID

Illinois

Central Illinois Paralegal Association
Darlene G. Johnson, CLA, President
Bloomington, IL
Carolyn S. Pitts, CLA, NALA Liaison
Champaign, IL

Heart of Illinois Paralegal Association
Amy DeTrempe-Williams, President
Peoria, IL
Sharon R. Moke, NALA Liaison
Peoria, IL

Indiana

Indiana Legal Assistants
Tina M. Keller, President
Terre Haute, IN
Dorothy M. French, CLA, NALA
Liaison
Evansville, IN

Kansas

Kansas Association of Legal Assistants
Stephanie G. Rahm, CLA, President
Wichita, KS
Vicki R. Walton, CLA, NALA Liaison
Wichita, KS

Kentucky

Western Kentucky Paralegals
Kathy L. Grentzer, CLA, President
Paducah, KY

Louisiana

Louisiana State Paralegal Association
Sandra A. Smith, CLAS, President
Alexandria, LA
Karen L. McKnight, CLA, NALA
Liaison
Alexandria, LA

Northwest Louisiana Paralegal Association
Karen M. Greer, CLA, President
Shreveport, LA
Cindy L. Vucinovich, NALA Liaison
Shreveport, LA

Maine

Maine State Association of Legal Assistants
Linette C. George, President
Portland, ME
Nicole S. Hoglund, NALA Liaison
Portland, ME

Michigan

Legal Assistants Association of Michigan
Darcy L. Dustin, President
Kalamazoo, MI
Charlotte G. Curiston, NALA
Liaison
Dearborn, MI

Minnesota

Minnesota Paralegal Association
Monica Sveen-Ziebell, President
Rochester, MN
Muriel L. Hinrichs, NALA Liaison
Rochester, MN

Mississippi

Mississippi Association of Legal Assistants
Debra D. Hammack, President

Jackson, MS
Sharon S. Gowan, NALA Liaison
Macon, MS

Mississippi College Society of Legal Assistants
Becky Merrill, CLA, President
Jackson, MS
Dawn C. Crosby, CLA, NALA Liaison
Clinton, MS

Society for Paralegal Studies
Laura Lilly, President
Hattiesburg, MS
Ronald G. Marquardt, NALA Liaison
Hattiesburg, MS

Missouri

St. Louis Association of Legal Assistants
Stacia Sanders, President
St. Louis, MO
Shirley A. Bettis, NALA Liaison
St. Louis, MO

Montana

Montana Association of Legal Assistants
Barbara Jo Wilson, CLA, President
Missoula, MT
Myrna L. O'Hare, NALA Liaison
Missoula, MT

Nebraska

Nebraska Association of Legal Assistants
Mary K. Bronson, President
Lincoln, NE
Lorrie C. Dahl, NALA Liaison
Lincoln, NE

Nevada

Clark County Organization of Legal Assistants, Inc.
Madolynn R. Oliverius, CLAS,
President
Las Vegas, NV
Betsy Branyan Kidder, CLAS, NALA
Liaison
Las Vegas, NV

Sierra Nevada Association of Paralegals
Merrilyn Marsh, CLAS, President
Reno, NV
Candace R. Jones, CLAS, NALA
Liaison
Reno, NV

New Hampshire

Paralegal Association of New Hampshire
David A. Tucker, President
Manchester, NH
Susan Janes, NALA Liaison
Concord, NH

New Jersey

The Legal Assistants Association of New Jersey, Inc.
Stephanie A. Danelson, President
Clark, NJ
Joan T. Shufro, CLA, NALA Liaison
Caldwell, NJ

North Carolina

Coastal Carolina Paralegal Club
Nadine Nash, President
Jacksonville, NC
Col. Robert E. Switzer, NALA
Liaison
Jacksonville, NC

North Carolina Paralegal Association, Inc.
Mary F. Haggerty, CLA, President
Charlotte, NC
Linda H. Waldrop, CLA, NALA
Liaison
Hudson, NC

North Dakota

Red River Valley Legal Assistants
Linda Brastrup Johnson, CLA,
President
Moorhead, MN
Eileen Trones Nelson, CLA, NALA
Liaison
Grand Forks, ND

Western Dakota Association of Legal Assistants
Candy L. Pederson, CLAS, President
Minot, ND
Connie L. Sundby, CLA, NALA
Liaison
Williston, ND

Ohio

Toledo Association of Legal Assistants
Cathy L. Redford, President
Maumee, OH
Cynthia L. Getzinger, CLA, NALA
Liaison
Toledo, OH

Oklahoma

Oklahoma Paralegal Association
    Lennis D. Ailey, CLA, President
    Ponca City, OK
    Stephanie K. Mark, CLAS, NALA
    Liaison
    Tulsa, OK

Rose State Paralegal Association
    Judy Shaw, President
    Midwest City, OK

Student Association of Legal Assistants Roger State
    College
    Leah Vile, President
    Claremore, OK
    George R. Kennedy, Faculty Advisor
    Claremore, OK

TJC Student Association of Legal Assistants
    Judy Tucker, President
    Tulsa, OK

Tulsa Association of Legal Assistants
    Toni Goss Hammerton, CLAS,
    President
    Broken Arrow, OK
    Dianne M. Shelton, CLA, NALA
    Liaison
    Tulsa, OK

Oregon

Pacific Northwest Legal Assistants
    Sandra D. H. Stearns, CLA,
    President
    Bend, OR
    Gayla K. Austin, CLA, NALA Liaison
    Albany, OR

Pennsylvania

Keystone Legal Assistant Association
    Catrina L. Nuss, President
    Harrisburg, PA
    JoAnna M. Sarnosky, CLA, NALA
    Liaison
    Pottsville, PA

South Carolina

Central Carolina Technical College Paralegal
    Association
    Fay Steigerwalt, President
    Sumter, SC

Jim Curzan, Faculty Advisor
    Sumter, SC

Greenville Association of Legal Assistants
    Debbie S. Massingill, CLA,
    President
    Greenville, SC
    Pamela M. Kincaid, NALA Liaison
    Greenville, SC

Tri-County Paralegal Association
    Sylvia D. Pratt, CLA, President
    Charleston, SC

South Dakota

South Dakota Legal Assistants Association, Inc.
    Pamela M. Van Engelenhoven, CLA,
    President
    Sioux Falls, SD
    Deborah L. Flynn, NALA Liaison
    Pierre, SD

Tennessee

Greater Memphis Legal Assistants, Inc.
    Laurie B. Fee, CLA, President
    Memphis, TN
    Carol A. Scoggins, CLA, NALA
    Liaison
    Memphis, TN

Tennessee Paralegal Association
    Janet Davey, President
    Chattanooga, TN
    Ann S. Burns, CLAS, NALA Liaison
    Jackson, TN

Texas

Capital Area Paralegal Association
    Linette A. Edwards, CLAS,
    President
    Austin, TX
    Lynn C. Cox, NALA Liaison
    Austin, TX

El Paso Association of Legal Assistants
    Dianna L. Cutts, CLA, President
    El Paso, TX
    Cheryl Sellers-Lay, CLAS, NALA
    Liaison
    El Paso, TX

Legal Assistant Association/Permian Basin
    Lee Bell Ulvestad, CLA, President
    Midland, TX

Jo Taylor Behrends, CLA, NALA
Liaison
Odessa, TX

Northeast Texas Association of Legal Assistants
Javan Johnson, CLA, President
Longview, TX
Diane Hall, CLA, NALA Liaison
Longview, TX

Nueces County Association of Legal Assistants
Rose Phelps, President
Corpus Christi, TX
Belinda J. Damerow, NALA Liaison
Corpus Christi, TX

Wichita County Student Association
Kathy M. Parker, CLA, President
Wichita Falls, TX
Billie Ruth Goss, NALA Liaison
Wichita Falls, TX

Southeast Texas Association of Legal Assistants
Brenda E. Jenkins, CLA, President
Beaumont, TX
Lucinda (Cindy) Wagner, NALA
Liaison
Beaumont, TX

Texarkana Association of Legal Assistants
Diane Plunkett, CLA, President
Texarkana, TX
Myra Jean Conaway, CLA, NALA
Liaison
Texarkana, AR

Texas Panhandle Association of Legal Assistants
Sheila H. Liedtke, CLA, President
Amarillo, TX
Vanessa W. Baker, CLA, NALA
Liaison
Amarillo, TX

Tyler Area Association of Legal Assistants
Carolyn S. Burton, CLA, President
Tyler, TX
Kathy C. Geoffrion, CLA, NALA
Liaison
Tyler, TX

West Texas Association of Legal Assistants
Ruth H. Bagwell, CLA, President
Lubbock, TX
Juanita Fortenberry, CLA, NALA
Liaison
Littlefield, TX

Utah

Legal Assistants Association of Utah
Marilu Peterson, CLAS, President
Salt Lake City, UT
Jan S. Mahoney, CLA, NALA Liaison
Salt Lake City, UT

Virginia

Peninsula Legal Assistants, Inc.
Phyllis T. Anderson, CLAS,
President
Newport News, VA
Susan O'Connell Fawcett, NALA
Liaison
Virginia Beach, VA

Richmond Association of Legal Assistants
Lucy D. Strange, President
Richmond, VA
Patricia S. Stout, CLA, NALA
Liaison
Chester, VA

Tidewater Association of Legal Assistants
Carla L. Nagel, CLA, President
Poquoson, VA
Susan N. Bawtinhimer, NALA Liaison
Norfolk, VA

Virgin Islands

Virgin Islands Paralegals Association
Eula J. Castleberry-Hymes,
President
St. Thomas, VI
Jonetta Darden-Vincent, NALA
Liaison
St. Thomas, VI

Washington

Association of Paralegals and Legal Assistants of
Washington State
Sheila M. White, CLAS, President
Spokane, WA

Columbia Basin Paralegal Association
Regina A. Stevens, President
Kennewick, WA
Kerri Wheeler Feeney, CLAS, NALA
Liaison
Richland, WA

West Virginia

Legal Assistants of West Virginia, Inc.
   Joyce A. Wilson, President
   Charleston, WV
   Joanna W. Rini, CLA, NALA Liaison
   Charleston, WV

Wisconsin

Madison Area Legal Assistants Association
   Beverly A. Potts, CLA, President
   Madison, WI
   Kristine Caldwell, CLA, NALA
   Liaison
   Madison, WI

Wyoming

Legal Assistants of Wyoming
   Anita K. Schroeder, CLA, President
   Casper, WY
   Carol D. Martin, CLAS, NALA
   Liaison
   Rawlins, WY

---

* *Affiliate Member*

APPENDIX B

ASSOCIATIONS OF INTEREST TO PARALEGALS

American Association of Law Libraries
    53 West Jackson Boulevard, Suite 940
    Chicago, IL 60604

American Association for Paralegal Education (AAf PE)
    P.O. Box 40244
    Overland Park, KS 66204
    (913) 381-4458

American Bar Association (ABA)
    Standing Committee on Legal Assistants
    750 North Lake Shore Drive
    Chicago, IL 60611
    (312) 988-5000

Association of Legal Administrators (ALA)
    104 Wilmot Road, Suite 205
    Deerfield, IL 60015-5195
    (312) 940-9240

Legal Assistant Management Association (LAMA)
    P.O. Box 40129
    Overland Park, KS 66204
    (913) 381-4458

National Association for Independent Paralegals
    585 Fifth Street West
    Sonoma, CA 95476

APPENDIX C

REFERENCES FOR FINDING A PARALEGAL POSITION

Allen, Jeffrey G. *How to Turn an Interview Into a Job*, Simon & Schuster, Inc. (1983).

Bernardo, Barbara. *Paralegal—An Insider's Guide to the Fastest Growing Occupation of the 1990s*, Peterson's Guides, Inc. (1990).

Bolles, Richard Nelson. *What Color Is Your Parachute?*, Ten Speed Press (1991).

Estrin, Chere B. *Paralegal Career Guide*, John Wiley & Sons, Inc. (1992).

Estrin, Chere, and Andrea Wagner. *Where Do I Go From Here?*, Estrin Publishing (1992).

Figler, Howard. *The Complete Job Search Handbook*, Henry Holt & Co. (1988).

Jackson, Tom. *The Perfect Résumé*, Anchor Books (1981).

Kaplan, Robbie Miller. *Sure-Hire Résumés*, AMACOM Books (1990).

———*The Whole Career Sourcebook*, AMACOM (1991).

Kisiel, Marie, Ph.D. *How to Find a Job as a Paralegal: A Step-by-Step Job Search Guide*, West Publishing Co. (2d ed. 1992).

Krannich, Caryl Rae, and Ronald L. Krannich. *Interview for Success*, Impact Publications (1990).

Parker, Yana. *Damn Good Résumé Guide*, Ten Speed Press (1989).

Rosenberg, Arthur D., and David V. Hizer. *The Résumé Handbook*, Bob Adams, Inc. (1990).

Wagner, Andrea, *How to Land Your First Paralegal Job*, Estrin Publishing (1991).

APPENDIX D

THE CONSTITUTION OF THE UNITED STATES OF AMERICA

We the People of the United States, in Order to form a more perfect Union, establish Justice, insure domestic Tranquility, provide for the common defence, promote the general Welfare, and secure the Blessings of Liberty to ourselves and our Posterity, do ordain and establish this Constitution for the United States of America.

ARTICLE I

Section 1   All legislative Powers herein granted shall be vested in a Congress of the United States, which shall consist of a Senate and House of Representatives.

Section 2   (1) The House of Representatives shall be composed of Members chosen every second Year by the People of the several States, and the Electors in each State shall have the Qualifications requisite for Electors of the most numerous Branch of the State Legislature.

(2) No Person shall be a Representative who shall not have attained to the age of twenty-five Years, and been seven Years a Citizen of the United States, and who shall not, when elected, be an Inhabitant of that State in which he shall be chosen.

(3) Representatives and direct Taxes shall be apportioned among the several States which may be included within this Union, according to their respective Numbers, which shall be determined by adding to the whole Number of free Persons, including those bound to Service for a Term of Years, and excluding Indians not taxed, three fifths of all other Persons. The actual Enumeration shall be made within three Years after the first Meeting of the Congress of the United States, and within every subsequent Term of ten Years, in such Manner as they shall by Law direct. The Number of Representatives shall not exceed one for every thirty Thousand, but each State shall have at Least one Representative; and until such enumeration shall be made, the State of New Hampshire shall be entitled to chuse three, Massachusetts eight, Rhode Island and Providence Plantations one, Connecticut five, New York six, New Jersey four, Pennsylvania eight, Delaware one, Maryland six, Virginia ten, North Carolina five, South Carolina five, and Georgia three.

(4) When vacancies happen in the Representation from any State, the Executive Authority thereof shall issue Writs of Election to fill such Vacancies.

(5) The House of Representatives shall chuse their Speaker and other Officers; and shall have the sole Power of Impeachment.

Section 3   (1) The Senate of the United States shall be composed of two Senators from each State, chosen by the Legislature thereof, for six Years; and each Senator shall have one Vote.

(2) Immediately after they shall be assembled in Consequence of the first Election, they shall be divided as equally as may be into three Classes. The Seats of the Senators of the first Class shall be vacated at the Expiration of the second Year, of the second Class at the Expiration of the fourth Year, and of the third Class at the Expiration of the sixth Year, so that one third may be chosen every second Year; and if Vacancies happen by Resignation, or otherwise, during the Recess of the Legislature of any State, the Executive thereof may make temporary Appointments until the next Meeting of the Legislature, which shall then fill such Vacancies.

(3) No Person shall be a Senator who shall not have attained to the Age of thirty Years, and been nine Years a Citizen of the United States, and who shall not, when elected, be an Inhabitant of that State for which he shall be chosen.

(4) The Vice President of the United States shall be President of the Senate, but shall have no Vote, unless they be equally divided.

(5) The Senate shall chuse their other Officers, and also a President pro tempore, in the Absence of the Vice President, or when he shall exercise the Office of the President of the United States.

(6) The Senate shall have the sole Power to try all Impeachments. When sitting for that Purpose, they shall be on Oath or Affirmation. When the President of the United States is tried, the Chief Justice shall preside: And no Person shall be convicted without the Concurrence of two thirds of the Members present.

(7) Judgment in Cases of Impeachment shall not extend further than to removal from Office, and

disqualification to hold and enjoy any Office of honor, Trust or Profit under the United States: but the Party convicted shall nevertheless be liable and subject to Indictment, Trial, Judgment and Punishment, according to Law.

Section 4 (1) The Times, Places and Manner of holding Elections for Senators and Representatives, shall be prescribed in each State by the Legislature thereof; but the Congress may at any time by Law make or alter such Regulations, except as to the Places of chusing Senators.

(2) The Congress shall assemble at least once in every Year, and such Meeting shall be on the first Monday in December, unless they shall by Law appoint a different Day

Section 5 (1) Each House shall be the Judge of the Elections, Returns and Qualifications of its own Members, and a Majority of each shall constitute a Quorum to do Business; but a smaller Number may adjourn from day to day, and may be authorized to compel the Attendance of absent Members, in such Manner, and under such Penalties as each House may provide.

(2) Each House may determine the Rules of its Proceedings, punish its Members for disorderly Behaviour, and, with the Concurrence of two thirds, expel a Member.

(3) Each House shall keep a Journal of its Proceedings, and from time to time publish the same, excepting such Parts as may in their Judgment require Secrecy; and the Yeas and Nays of the Members of either House on any question shall, at the Desire of one fifth of those Present, be entered on the Journal.

(4) Neither House, during the Session of Congress, shall, without the Consent of the other, adjourn for more than three days, nor to any other Place than that in which the two Houses shall be sitting.

Section 6 (1) The Senators and Representatives shall receive a Compensation for their Services, to be ascertained by Law, and paid out of the Treasury of the United States. They shall in all Cases, except Treason, Felony and Breach of the Peace, be privileged from Arrest during their Attendance at the Session of their respective Houses, and in going to and returning from the same; and for any Speech or Debate in either House, they shall not be questioned in any other Place.

(2) No Senator or Representative shall, during the Time for which he was elected, be appointed to any civil Office under the authority of the United States, which shall have been created, or the Emoluments whereof shall have been encreased during such time; and no

Person holding any Office under the United States, shall be a Member of either House during his Continuance in Office.

Section 7 (1) All Bills for raising Revenue shall originate in the House of Representatives; but the Senate may propose or concur with Amendments as on other Bills.

(2) Every Bill which shall have passed the House of Representatives and the Senate, shall, before it become a Law, be presented to the President of the United States; If he approve he shall sign it, but if not he shall return it, with his Objections to that House in which it shall have originated, who shall enter the Objections at large on their Journal, and proceed to reconsider it. If after such Reconsideration two thirds of that House shall agree to pass the Bill, it shall be sent, together with the Objections, to the other House, by which it shall likewise be reconsidered, and if approved by two thirds of that House, it shall become a law. But in all such Cases the Votes of both Houses shall be determined by Yeas and Nays, and the Names of the Persons voting for and against the Bill shall be entered on the Journal of each House respectively. If any Bill shall not be returned by the President within ten Days (Sunday excepted) after it shall have been presented to him, the Same shall be a Law, in like Manner as if he had signed it, unless the Congress by their Adjournment prevent its Return, in which Case it shall not be a Law.

(3) Every Order, Resolution, or Vote to which the Concurrence of the Senate and House of Representatives may be necessary (except on a question of Adjournment) shall be presented to the President of the United States; and before the Same shall take Effect, shall be approved by him, or being disapproved by him, shall be repassed by two thirds of the Senate and House of Representatives, according to the Rules and Limitations prescribed in the Case of a Bill.

Section 8 (1) The Congress shall have Power To lay and collect Taxes, Duties, Imposts and Excises, to pay the Debts and provide for the common Defence and general Welfare of the United States; but all Duties, Imposts and Excises shall be uniform throughout the United States;

(2) To borrow Money on the credit of the United States;

(3) To regulate Commerce with foreign Nations, and among the several States, and with the Indian Tribes;

(4) To establish an uniform Rule of Naturalization, and uniform Laws on the subject of Bankruptcies throughout the United States;

(5) To coin Money, regulate the Value thereof, and of foreign Coin, and to fix the Standard of Weights and Measures;

(6) To provide for the Punishment of counterfeiting the Securities and current Coin of the United States;

(7) To establish Post Offices and post Roads;

(8) To promote the Progress of Science and useful Arts, by securing for limited Times to Authors and Inventors the exclusive Right to their respective Writings and Discoveries;

(9) To constitute Tribunals inferior to the supreme Court;

(10) To define and punish Piracies and Felonies committed on the high Seas, and Offenses against the Law of Nations;

(11) To declare War, grant Letters of Marque and Reprisal, and make Rules concerning Captures on Land and Water;

(12) To raise and support Armies, but no Appropriation of Money to that Use shall be for a longer Term than two Years;

(13) To provide and maintain a Navy;

(14) To make Rules for the Government and Regulation of the land and naval Forces;

(15) To provide for calling forth the Militia to execute the Laws of the Union, suppress Insurrections and repel Invasions;

(16) To provide for organizing, arming, and disciplining, the Militia, and for governing such Part of them as may be employed in the Service of the United States, reserving to the States respectively, the Appointment of the Officers, and the Authority of training the Militia according to the discipline prescribed by Congress;

(17) To exercise exclusive Legislation in all Cases whatsoever, over such District (not exceeding ten Miles square) as may, by Cession of particular States, and the Acceptance of Congress, become the Seat of the Government of the United States, and to exercise like Authority over all Places purchased by the Consent of the Legislature of the State in which the Same shall be, for the Erection of Forts, Magazines, Arsenals, dock-Yards, and other needful Buildings;—And

(18) To make all Laws which shall be necessary and proper for carrying into Execution the foregoing Powers, and all other Powers vested by this Constitution in the Government of the United States, or in any Department or Officer thereof.

Section 9   (1) The Migration or Importation of such Persons as any of the States now existing shall think proper to admit, shall not be prohibited by the Congress prior to the Year one thousand eight hundred and eight, but a Tax or Duty may be imposed on such Importation, not exceeding ten dollars for each Person.

(2) The Privilege of the Writ of Habeas Corpus shall not be suspended unless when in Cases of Rebellion or Invasion the public Safety may require it.

(3) No Bill of Attainder or ex post facto Law shall be passed.

(4) No Capitation, or other direct, Tax shall be laid, unless in Proportion to the Census or Enumeration herein before directed to be taken.

(5) No Tax or Duty shall be laid on Articles exported from any State.

(6) No Preference shall be given by any Regulation of Commerce or Revenue to the Ports of one State over those of another; nor shall Vessels bound to, or from, one State, be obliged to enter, clear or pay Duties in another.

(7) No Money shall be drawn from the Treasury, but in Consequence of Appropriations made by Law; and a regular Statement and Account of the Receipts and Expenditures of all public Money shall be published from time to time.

(8) No Title of Nobility shall be granted by the United States: And no Person holding any Office of Profit or Trust under them, shall, without the Consent of the Congress, accept of any present, Emolument, Office, or Title, of any kind whatever, from any King, Prince or foreign State.

Section 10   (1) No State shall enter into any Treaty, Alliance, or Confederation; grant Letters of Marque and Reprisal; coin Money; emit Bills of Credit; make any Thing but gold and silver Coin a Tender in Payment of Debts; pass any Bill of Attainder, ex post facto Law, or Law impairing the Obligation of Contracts, or grant any Title of Nobility.

(2) No State shall, without the Consent of Congress, lay any Imposts or Duties on Imports or Exports, except what may be absolutely necessary for executing its inspection Laws: and the net Produce of all Duties and Imposts, laid by any State on Imports or Exports, shall be for the Use of the Treasury of the United States; and all such Laws shall be subject to the Revision and Controul of the Congress.

(3) No State shall, without the Consent of Congress, lay any Duty of Tonnage, keep Troops, or Ships of War in time of Peace, enter into any Agreement or Compact with another State, or with a foreign Power, or engage in War, unless actually invaded, or in such imminent Danger as will not admit of Delay.

ARTICLE II

Section 1   (1) The executive Power shall be vested in a President of the United States of America. He shall hold his Office during the Term of four Years, and, together with the Vice President, chosen for the same Term, be elected, as follows:

(2) Each State shall appoint, in such Manner as the Legislature thereof may direct, a Number of Electors, equal to the whole Number of Senators and Representatives to which the State may be entitled in the Congress: but no Senator or Representative, or Person holding an Office of Trust or Profit under the United States, shall be appointed an Elector.

The Electors shall meet in their respective States, and vote by Ballot for two Persons, of whom one at least shall not be an Inhabitant of the same State with themselves. And they shall make a List of all the Persons voted for, and of the Number of Votes for each; which List they shall sign and certify, and transmit sealed to the Seat of the Government of the United States, directed to the President of the Senate. The President of the Senate shall, in the presence of the Senate and House of Representatives, open all the Certificates, and the Votes shall then be counted. The Person having the greatest Number of Votes shall be the President, if such Number be a Majority of the whole Number of Electors appointed; and if there be more than one who have such Majority, and have an equal Number of Votes, then the House of Representatives shall immediately chuse by Ballot one of them for President; and if no Person have a Majority, then from the five highest on the List the said House shall in like Manner chuse the President. But in chusing the President, the Votes shall be taken by States, the Representation from each State having one Vote; a quorum for this Purpose shall consist of a Member or Members from two thirds of the States, and a Majority of all the States shall be necessary to a Choice. In every Case, after the Choice of the President, the Person having the greatest Number of Votes of the Electors shall be the Vice President. But if there should remain two or more who have equal Votes, the Senate shall chuse from them by Ballot the Vice President.

(3) The Congress may determine the Time of chusing the Electors, and the Day on which they shall give their Votes; which Day shall be the same throughout the United States.

(4) No Person except a natural born Citizen, or a Citizen of the United States, at the time of the Adoption of this Constitution, shall be eligible to the Office of President; neither shall any Person be eligible to that Office who shall not have attained to the Age of thirty five Years, and been fourteen Years a Resident within the United States.

(5) In Case of the Removal of the President from Office, or of his Death, Resignation, or Inability to discharge the Powers and Duties of the said Office, the Same shall devolve on the Vice President, and the Congress may by Law provide for the Case of Removal, Death, Resignation or Inability, both of the President and Vice President, declaring what Officer shall then act as President, and such Officer shall act accordingly, until the Disability be removed, or a President shall be elected.

(6) The President shall, at stated Times, receive for his Services, a Compensation, which shall neither be increased nor diminished during the Period for which he shall have been elected, and he shall not receive within that Period any other Emolument from the United States, or any of them.

(7) Before he enter on the Execution of his Office, he shall take the following Oath or Affirmation:—"I do solemnly swear (or affirm) that I will faithfully execute the Office of President of the United States, and will to the best of my Ability, preserve, protect and defend the Constitution of the United States."

Section 2   (1) The President shall be Commander in Chief of the Army and Navy of the United States, and of the Militia of the several States, when called into the actual Service of the United States; he may require the Opinion, in writing, of the principal Officer in each of the executive Departments, upon any Subject relating to the Duties of their respective Offices, and he shall have Power to grant Reprieves and Pardons for Offenses against the United States, except in Cases of Impeachment.

(2) He shall have Power, by and with the Advice and Consent of the Senate, to make Treaties, provided two thirds of the Senators present concur; and he shall nominate, and by and with the Advice and Consent of the Senate, shall appoint Ambassadors, other public Ministers and Consuls, Judges of the supreme Court, and all other Officers of the United States, whose Appointments are not herein otherwise provided for, and which shall be established by Law: but the Congress may by Law vest the Appointment of such inferior Officers, as they think proper, in the President alone, in the Courts of Law, or in the Heads of Departments.

(3) The President shall have Power to fill up all Vacancies that may happen during the Recess of the Senate, by granting Commissions which shall expire at the End of their next Session.

Section 3 He shall from time to time give to the Congress Information of the State of the Union, and recommend to their Consideration such Measures as he shall judge necessary and expedient; he may, on extraordinary Occasions, convene both Houses, or either of them, and in Case of Disagreement between them, with Respect to the Time of Adjournment, he may adjourn them to such Time as he shall think proper; he shall receive Ambassadors and other public Ministers; he shall take Care that the Laws be faithfully executed, and shall Commission all the Officers of the United States.

Section 4 The President, Vice President and all Civil Officers of the United States, shall be removed from Office on Impeachment for, and Conviction of, Treason, Bribery, or other high Crimes and Misdemeanors.

ARTICLE III

Section 1 The judicial Power of the United States, shall be vested in one supreme Court, and in such inferior Courts as the Congress may from time to time ordain and establish. The Judges, both of the supreme and inferior Courts, shall hold their Offices during good Behaviour, and shall, at stated Times, receive for their Services, a Compensation, which shall not be diminished during their Continuance in Office.

Section 2 (1) The judicial Power shall extend to all Cases, in Law and Equity, arising under this Constitution, the Laws of the United States, and Treaties made, or which shall be made, under their Authority;—to all Cases affecting Ambassadors, other public Ministers and Consuls;—to all Cases of admiralty and maritime Jurisdiction;—to Controversies to which the United States shall be a party;—to Controversies between two or more States;—between a State and Citizens of another State;—between Citizens of different States;—between Citizens of the same State claiming Lands under Grants of different States, and between a State, or the Citizens thereof, and foreign States, Citizens or Subjects.

(2) In all Cases affecting Ambassadors, other public Ministers and Consuls, and those in which a State shall be Party, the supreme Court shall have original Jurisdiction. In all the other Cases before mentioned, the supreme Court shall have appellate Jurisdiction, both as to Law and Fact, with such Exceptions, and under such Regulations as the Congress shall make.

(3) The Trial of all Crimes, except in Cases of Impeachment, shall be by Jury; and such Trial shall be held in the State where the said Crimes shall have

been committed; but when not committed within any State, the Trial shall be at such Place or Places as the Congress may by Law have directed.

Section 3 (1) Treason against the United States, shall consist only in levying War against them, or in adhering to their Enemies, giving them Aid and Comfort. No Person shall be convicted of Treason unless on the Testimony of two Witnesses to the same overt Act, or on Confession in open Court.

(2) The Congress shall have Power to declare the Punishment of Treason, but no Attainder of Treason shall work Corruption of Blood, or Forfeiture except during the Life of the Person attainted.

ARTICLE IV

Section 1 Full Faith and Credit shall be given in each State to the public Acts, Records, and judicial Proceedings of every other State. And the Congress may by general Laws prescribe the Manner in which such Acts, Records and Proceedings shall be proved, and the Effect thereof.

Section 2 (1) The Citizens of each State shall be entitled to all privileges and Immunities of Citizens in the several States.

(2) A Person charged in any State with Treason, Felony, or other Crime, who shall flee from Justice, and be found in another State, shall on Demand of the executive Authority of the State from which he fled, be delivered up, to be removed to the State having Jurisdiction of the Crime.

(3) No Person held to Service of Labour in one State, under the Laws thereof, escaping into another, shall, in Consequence of any Law or Regulation therein, be discharged from such Service or Labour, but shall be delivered up on Claim of the Party to whom such Service or Labour may be due.

Section 3 (1) New States may be admitted by the Congress into this Union; but no new State shall be formed or erected within the Jurisdiction of any other State; nor any State be formed by the Junction of two or more States, or Parts of States, without the Consent of the Legislatures of the States concerned as well as of the Congress.

(2) The Congress shall have power to dispose of and make all needful Rules and Regulations respecting the Territory or other Property belonging to the United States; and nothing in this Constitution shall be so construed as to Prejudice any Claims of the United States, or of any particular State.

Section 4 The United States shall guarantee to every State in this Union a Republican Form of Government, and shall protect each of them against Invasion; and on Application of the Legislature, or of the Executive (when the Legislature cannot be convened) against domestic Violence.

ARTICLE V

The Congress, whenever two thirds of both Houses shall deem it necessary, shall propose Amendments to this Constitution, or, on the Application of the Legislatures of two thirds of the several States, shall call a Convention for proposing Amendments, which, in either Case, shall be valid to all Intents and Purposes, as Part of this Constitution, when ratified by the Legislatures of three fourths of the several States, or by Conventions in three fourths thereof, as the one or the other Mode of Ratification may be proposed by the Congress; Provided that no Amendment which may be made prior to the Year One thousand eight hundred and eight shall in any Manner affect the first and fourth Clauses in the Ninth Section of the first Article; and that no State, without its Consent, shall be deprived of its equal Suffrage in the Senate.

ARTICLE VI

(1) All Debts contracted and Engagements entered into, before the Adoption of this Constitution, shall be as valid against the United States under this Constitution, as under the Confederation.

(2) This Constitution, and the Laws of the United States which shall be made in Pursuance thereof; and all Treaties made, or which shall be made, under the Authority of the United States, shall be the supreme Law of the Land; and the Judges in every State shall be bound thereby, any Thing in the Constitution or Laws of any State to the Contrary notwithstanding.

(3) The Senators and Representatives before mentioned, and the Members of the several State Legislatures, and all executive and judicial Officers, both of the United States and of the several States, shall be bound by Oath or Affirmation, to support this Constitution; but no religious Test shall ever be required as a Qualification to any Office or public Trust under the United States.

ARTICLE VII

The Ratification of the Conventions of nine States, shall be sufficient for the Establishment of this Constitution between the States so ratifying the Same.

ARTICLES IN ADDITION TO, AND AMENDMENT OF, THE CONSTITUTION OF THE UNITED STATES OF AMERICA, PROPOSED BY CONGRESS, AND RATIFIED BY THE SEVERAL STATES, PURSUANT TO THE FIFTH ARTICLE OF THE ORIGINAL CONSTITUTION

AMENDMENT I (1791)

Congress shall make no law respecting an establishment of religion, or prohibiting the free exercise thereof; or abridging the freedom of speech, or of the press; or the right of the people peaceably to assemble, and to petition the Government for a redress of grievances.

AMENDMENT II (1791)

A well regulated Militia, being necessary to the security of a free state, the right of the people to keep and bear Arms, shall not be infringed.

AMENDMENT III (1791)

No Soldier shall, in time of peace be quartered in any house, without the consent of the Owner, nor in time of war, but in a manner to be prescribed by law.

AMENDMENT IV (1791)

The right of the people to be secure in their persons, houses, papers, and effects, against unreasonable searches and seizures, shall not be violated, and no Warrants shall issue, but upon probable cause, supported by Oath or affirmation, and particularly describing the place to be searched, and the persons or things to be seized.

AMENDMENT V (1791)

No person shall be held to answer for a capital, or otherwise infamous crime, unless on a presentment or indictment of a Grand Jury, except in cases arising in the land or naval forces, or in the Militia, when in actual service in time of War or public danger; nor shall any person be subject for the same offence to be twice put in jeopardy of life or limb; nor shall be compelled in any criminal case to be a witness against himself, nor be deprived of life, liberty, or property, without due process of law; nor shall private property be taken for public use, without just compensation.

AMENDMENT VI (1791)

In all criminal prosecutions, the accused shall enjoy the right to a speedy and public trial, by an impartial jury of the State and district wherein the crime shall have been committed, which district shall have been previously ascertained by law, and to be informed of the nature and cause of the accusation; to be confronted with the witnesses against him; to have compulsory process for obtaining witnesses in his favor, and to have the Assistance of Counsel for his defence.

AMENDMENT VII (1791)

In Suits at common law, where the value in controversy shall exceed twenty dollars, the right of trial by jury shall be preserved, and no fact tried by a jury, shall be otherwise re-examined in any Court of the United States, than according to the rules of the common law.

AMENDMENT VIII (1791)

Excessive bail shall not be required, nor excessive fines imposed, nor cruel and unusual punishments inflicted.

AMENDMENT IX (1791)

The enumeration in the Constitution, of certain rights, shall not be construed to deny or disparage others retained by the people.

AMENDMENT X (1791)

The powers not delegated to the United States by the Constitution, nor prohibited by it to the States, are reserved to the States respectively, or to the people.

AMENDMENT XI (1798)

The Judicial power of the United States shall not be construed to extend to any suit in law or equity, commenced or prosecuted against one of the United States by Citizens of another State, or by Citizens or Subjects of any Foreign State.

AMENDMENT XII (1804)

The Electors shall meet in their respective states and vote by ballot for President and Vice-President, one of whom, at least, shall not be an inhabitant of the same state with themselves; they shall name in their ballots the person voted for as President, and in distinct ballots the person voted for as Vice-President, and they shall make distinct lists of all persons voted for as President, and of all persons voted for as Vice-President, and of the number of votes for each, which lists they shall sign and certify, and transmit sealed to the seat of the government of the United States, directed to the President of the Senate;—The President of the Senate shall, in the presence of the Senate and House of Representatives, open all the certificates and the votes shall then be counted;—The person having the greatest number of votes for President, shall be the President, if such number be a majority of the whole number of Electors appointed; and if no person have such majority, then from the persons having the highest numbers not exceeding three on the list of those voted for as President, the House of Representatives shall choose immediately, by ballot, the President. But in choosing the President, the votes shall be taken by states, the representation from each state having one vote; a quorum for this purpose shall consist of a member or members from two-thirds of the states, and a majority of all the states shall be necessary to a choice. And if the House of Representatives shall not choose a President whenever the right of choice shall devolve upon them, before the fourth day of March next following, then the Vice-President shall act as President, as in the case of the death or other constitutional disability of the President—The person having the greatest number of votes as Vice-President, shall be the Vice-President, if such number be a majority of the whole number of Electors appointed, and if no person have a majority, then from the two highest numbers on the list, the Senate shall choose the Vice-President; A quorum for the purpose shall consist of two-thirds of the whole number of Senators, and a majority of the whole number shall be necessary to a choice. But no person constitutionally ineligible to the office of President shall be eligible to that of Vice-President of the United States.

AMENDMENT XIII (1865)

Section 1   Neither slavery nor involuntary servitude, except as a punishment for crime whereof the party shall have been duly convicted, shall exist within the United States, or any place subject to their jurisdiction.

Section 2   Congress shall have power to enforce this article by appropriate legislation.

AMENDMENT XIV (1868)

Section 1   All persons born or naturalized in the United States and subject to the jurisdiction thereof, are citizens of the United States and of the State wherein they reside. No State shall make or enforce any law which shall abridge the privileges or immunities of citizens of the United States; nor shall any State deprive any person of life, liberty, or property, without due process of law; nor deny to any person within its jurisdiction the equal protection of the laws.

Section 2   Representatives shall be apportioned among the several States according to their respective numbers, counting the whole number of persons in each State, excluding Indians not taxed. But when the right to vote at any election for the choice of electors for President and Vice-President of the United States, Representatives in Congress, the Executive and Judicial officers of a State, or the members of the Legislature thereof, is denied to any of the male inhabitants of such State, being twenty-one years of age, and citizens of the United States, or in any way abridged, except for participation in rebellion, or other crime, the basis of representation therein shall be reduced in the proportion which the number of such male citizens shall bear to the whole number of male citizens twenty-one years of age in such State.

Section 3   No person shall be a Senator or Representative in Congress, or elector of President and Vice-President, or hold any office, civil or military, under the United States, or under any State, who, having previously taken an oath, as a member of Congress, or as an officer of the United States, or as a member of any State legislature, or as an executive or judicial officer of any State, to support the Constitution of the United States, shall have engaged in insurrection or rebellion against the same, or given aid or comfort to the enemies thereof. But Congress may by a vote of two-thirds of each House, remove such disability.

Section 4   The validity of the public debt of the United States, authorized by law, including debts incurred for payment of pensions and bounties for services in suppressing insurrection or rebellion, shall not be questioned. But neither the United States nor any State shall assume or pay any debt or obligation incurred in aid of insurrection or rebellion against the United States, or any claim for the loss or emancipation of any slave; but all such debts, obligations and claims shall be held illegal and void.

Section 5   The Congress shall have power to enforce, by appropriate legislation, the provisions of this article.

AMENDMENT XV (1870)

Section 1   The right of citizens of the United States to vote shall not be denied or abridged by the United States or by any State on account of race, color, or previous condition of servitude.

Section 2   The Congress shall have power to enforce this article by appropriate legislation.

AMENDMENT XVI (1913)

The Congress shall have power to lay and collect taxes on incomes, from whatever source derived, without apportionment among the several States, and without regard to any census or enumeration.

AMENDMENT XVII (1913)

The Senate of the United States shall be composed of two Senators from each State, elected by the people thereof, for six years; and each Senator shall have one vote. The electors in each State shall have the qualifications requisite for electors of the most numerous branch of the State legislatures.

When vacancies happen in the representation of any State in the Senate, the executive authority of such State shall issue writs of election to fill such vacancies: *Provided,* That the legislature of any State may empower the executive thereof to make temporary appointments until the people fill the vacancies by election as the legislature may direct.

This amendment shall not be so construed as to affect the election or term of any Senator chosen before it becomes valid as part of the Constitution.

AMENDMENT XVIII (1919)

Section 1   After one year from the ratification of this article the manufacture, sale, or transportation of intoxicating liquors within, the importation thereof into, or the exportation thereof from the United States and all territory subject to the jurisdiction thereof for beverage purposes is hereby prohibited.

Section 2   The Congress and the several States shall have concurrent power to enforce this article by appropriate legislation.

Section 3   This article shall be inoperative unless it shall have been ratified as an amendment to the Constitution by the legislatures of the several States, as provided in the Constitution, within seven years from the date of the submission hereof to the States by the Congress.

AMENDMENT XIX (1920)

The right of citizens of the United States to vote shall not be denied or abridged by the United States or by any State on account of sex.

Congress shall have power to enforce this article by appropriate legislation.

AMENDMENT XX (1933)

Section 1　The terms of the President and Vice President shall end at noon on the 20th day of January, and the terms of Senators and Representatives at noon on the 3d day of January, of the years in which such terms would have ended if this article had not been ratified; and the terms of their successors shall then begin.

Section 2　The Congress shall assemble at least once in every year, and such meeting shall begin at noon on the 3d day of January, unless they shall by law appoint a different day.

Section 3　If, at the time fixed for the beginning of the term of the President, the President elect shall have died, the Vice President elect shall become President. If a President shall not have been chosen before the time fixed for the beginning of his term, or if the President elect shall have failed to qualify, then the Vice President elect shall act as President until a President shall have qualified; and the Congress may by law provide for the case wherein neither a President elect nor a Vice President elect shall have qualified, declaring who shall then act as President, or the manner in which one who is to act shall be selected, and such person shall act accordingly until a President or Vice President shall have qualified.

Section 4　The Congress may by law provide for the case of the death of any of the persons from whom the House of Representatives may choose a President whenever the right of choice shall have devolved upon them, and for the case of the death of any of the persons from whom the Senate may choose a Vice President whenever the right of choice shall have devolved upon them.

Section 5　Sections 1 and 2 shall take effect on the 15th day of October following the ratification of this article.

Section 6　This article shall be inoperative unless it shall have been ratified as an amendment to the Constitution by the legislatures of three-fourths of the several States within seven years from the date of its submission.

AMENDMENT XXI (1933)

Section 1　The eighteenth article of amendment to the Constitution of the United States is hereby repealed.

Section 2　The transportation or importation into any State, Territory or possession of the United States for delivery or use therein of intoxicating liquors, in violation of the laws thereof, is hereby prohibited.

Section 3　This article shall be inoperative unless it shall have been ratified as an amendment to the Constitution by conventions in the several States, as provided in the Constitution, within seven years from the date of the submission hereof to the States by the Congress.

AMENDMENT XXII (1951)

Section 1　No person shall be elected to the office of the President more than twice, and no person who has held the office of President, or acted as President, for more than two years of a term to which some other person was elected President shall be elected to the office of the President more than once. But this Article shall not apply to any person holding the office of President when this Article was proposed by the Congress, and shall not prevent any person who may be holding the office of President, or acting as President, during the term within which this Article becomes operative from holding the office of President or acting as President during the remainder of such term.

Section 2　This Article shall be inoperative unless it shall have been ratified as an amendment to the Constitution by the legislatures of three-fourths of the several States within seven years from the date of its submission to the States by the Congress.

AMENDMENT XXIII (1961)

Section 1　The District constituting the seat of Government of the United States shall appoint in such manner as the Congress may direct:

A number of electors of President and Vice President equal to the whole number of Senators and Representatives in Congress to which the District would be entitled if it were a State, but in no event more than the least populous State; they shall be in addition to those appointed by the States, but they shall be considered, for the purposes of the election of President and Vice President, to be electors appointed by a State; and they shall meet in the District and perform such duties as provided by the twelfth article of amendment.

Section 2   The Congress shall have power to enforce this article by appropriate legislation.

AMENDMENT XXIV (1964)

Section 1   The right of citizens of the United States to vote in any primary or other election for President or Vice President, for electors for President or Vice President, or for Senator or Representative in Congress, shall not be denied or abridged by the United States or any State by reason of failure to pay any poll tax or other tax.

Section 2   The Congress shall have power to enforce this article by appropriate legislation.

AMENDMENT XXV (1967)

Section 1   In case of the removal of the President from office or of his death or resignation, the Vice President shall become President.

Section 2   Whenever there is a vacancy in the office of the Vice President, the President shall nominate a Vice President who shall take office upon confirmation by a majority vote of both Houses of Congress.

Section 3   Whenever the President transmits to the President pro tempore of the Senate and the Speaker of the House of Representatives his written declaration that he is unable to discharge the powers and duties of his office, and until he transmits to them a written declaration to the contrary, such powers and duties shall be discharged by the Vice President as Acting President.

Section 4   Whenever the Vice President and a majority of either the principal officers of the executive departments or of such other body as Congress may by law provide transmit to the President pro tempore of the Senate and the Speaker of the House of Representatives their written declaration that the President is unable to discharge the powers and duties of his office, the Vice President shall immediately assume the powers and duties of the office as Acting President.

Thereafter, when the President transmits to the President pro tempore of the Senate and the Speaker of the House of Representatives his written declaration that no inability exists, he shall resume the powers and duties of his office unless the Vice President and a majority of either the principal officers of the executive department or of such other body as Congress may by law provide, transmit within four days to the President pro tempore of the Senate and the Speaker of the House of Representatives their written declaration that the President is unable to discharge the powers and duties of his office. Thereupon Congress shall decide the issue, assembling within forty-eight hours for that purpose if not in session. If the Congress, within twenty-one days after receipt of the latter written declaration, or, if Congress is not in session, within twenty-one days after Congress is required to assemble, determines by two-thirds vote of both Houses that the President is unable to discharge the powers and duties of his office, the Vice President shall continue to discharge the same as Acting President; otherwise, the President shall resume the powers and duties of his office.

AMENDMENT XXVI (1971)

Section 1   The right of citizens of the United States, who are eighteen years of age or older, to vote shall not be denied or abridged by the United States or by any State on account of age.

Section 2   The Congress shall have power to enforce this article by appropriate legislation.

AMENDMENT XXVII (1992)

No law varying the compensation for the services of the senators and representatives shall take effect, until an election of representatives shall have intervened.

TABLE OF CASES

GLOSSARY

abatement of nuisance The elimination of a nuisance.

abstract of title A short account of the state of the title to real estate, reflecting all past ownership and any interests or rights, such as a mortgage or other liens, which any person might currently have with respect to the property.

abuse of process The use of legal process in a manner not contemplated by the law to achieve a purpose not intended by the law.

acceptance [T]he assent, by the person to whom an offer is made, to the offer as made by the person making it.

accessory after the fact A person who, after a crime has been committed, assists the person who committed it to escape arrest.

accessory before the fact A person who helps another person plan or commit a crime but who is not present at the scene of the crime.

accomplice A person who knowingly and voluntarily helps another person commit a crime; one who acts as an accessory.

accord and satisfaction An agreement between two persons, one of whom has a cause of action against the other, in which the claimant accepts a compromise in full satisfaction of the claim.

accountable Responsible; liable.

acre Measure of land containing 160 square rods, 4,840 square yards (160 square rods or 43,560 square feet).

actual authority In the law of agency, the power of an agent to bind his or her principal. Although such authority must be granted by the principal to his or her agent, authority will be deemed to have been granted if the principal allows the agent to believe that the agent possesses it. Further, actual authority may be implied from the circumstances and need not be specifically granted.

actus reus An "answerable act," i.e., an act for which one is answerable; a guilty act.

adeem To take away; to make an ademption.

ademption Disposition by a person, during his or her lifetime, of property which is the subject of his or her will. An ademption revokes the legacy or devise.

adequate consideration A fair and reasonable price or value for the subject matter of the contract in question; a sufficient price in law.

adhesion contract (contract of adhesion) A contract prepared by the dominant party (usually a form contract) and presented on a take-it-or-leave-it basis to the weaker party, who has no real opportunity to bargain about its terms.

adjudication The final decision of a court, usually made after trial of the case; the court's final judgment.

adjudicatory Refers to the decision-making or quasi-judicial functions of an administrative agency, as opposed to the judicial functions of a court.

administration of estate The management of a decedent's estate by an administrator or executor so that all the decedent's assets are collected, all debts, administration expenses, and taxes are paid, and all remaining assets are distributed to the persons entitled to receive them.

administrative agency A board, commission, bureau, office, or department, of the executive branch of government, that implements the law which originates with the legislative branch.

administrative law The body of law that controls the way in which administrative agencies operate.

administrative law judge A person, generally a civil servant, who conducts hearings held by an administrative agency.

Administrative Procedure Act A statute enacted by Congress that regulates the way in which federal administrative agencies conduct their affairs and establishes the procedure for judicial review of the actions of federal agencies.

admission 1. A statement of a party to an action which is inconsistent with his claim or position in the lawsuit and which therefore constitutes proof against him. 2. A voluntary statement that something asserted to be true is true.

advance sheets Printed copies of judicial opinions published in loose-leaf form shortly after the opinions are issued. These published opinions are later collected and published in bound form with other reported cases which are issued over a longer period of time.

adversary proceeding (adversarial process)   A trial or other proceeding in which all sides have the opportunity to present their contentions; a process involving a contested action.

adverse possession   The act of occupying real property in an "open, notorious, and hostile manner," under a claim of right, contrary to the interests of the true owner. Such possession over a period of years is a method for acquiring title.

advisory opinion   A judicial interpretation of a legal question requested by the legislative or executive branch of government.

affidavit   Any voluntary statement reduced to writing and sworn to or affirmed before a person legally authorized to administer an oath.

affidavit of service   An affidavit that certifies that process has been served. Also referred to as a *return of service* or *proof of service*.

affinity   The relationship existing by virtue of marriage.

affirm   In the case of an appellate court, to uphold the decision or judgment of the lower court after an appeal.

affirmative defense   A defense that amounts to more than simply a denial of the allegations in the plaintiff's complaint. It sets up new matter which, if proven, could result in a judgment against the plaintiff even if all the allegations of the complaint are true.

agency   A relationship in which one person acts for or on behalf of another person at the other person's request.

agent   One of the parties to an agency relationship, specifically, the one who acts for and represents the other party, who is known as the principal.

agreement of sale (purchase agreement)   [A]n agreement which obligates the seller to sell and the buyer to buy … .

air rights   The right to use the airspace above one's land.

alibi   The defense that the accused was elsewhere at the time the crime was committed.

alien   Any person present within the borders of the United States who is not a U.S. citizen.

alimony   Ongoing court-ordered support payments by a divorced spouse, usually payments made by an ex-husband to his former wife.

ambulatory   Changeable; capable of alteration; revocable.

American Association for Paralegal Education   A national organization of paralegal teachers and educational institutions, which provides technical assistance and supports research in the paralegal field, promotes standards for paralegal instruction, and cooperates with the American Bar Association and others in developing an approval process for paralegal education.

American Bar Association   The country's largest voluntary professional association of attorneys. Its purposes include enhancing professionalism and advancing the administration of justice.

amicus curiae   "Friend of the court." A person who is interested in the outcome of the case, but who is not a party, whom the court permits to file a brief for the purpose of providing the court with a position or a point of view which it might not otherwise have.

ancillary administration   The administration of a decedent's estate in a state other than the one in which he or she lived, for the purpose of disposing of property he or she owned there.

annotation   A notation, appended to any written work, which explains or comments upon its meaning.

annulment of marriage   The act of a court in voiding a marriage for causes existing at the time the marriage was entered into. Annulment differs from divorce in that it is not a dissolution of the marriage but a declaration that no marriage ever existed.

answer   A pleading in response to a complaint.

antenuptial agreement (prenuptial agreement)   An agreement between a man and a woman who are to be married, governing the financial and property arrangements between them in the event of divorce, death, or even during the marriage. Such an agreement may override obligations or rights provided by statute.

antilapse statute   A statute providing that, if a person named to receive property in a will dies before the person who made the will, his or her share will not lapse, but will take effect as if he or she had died immediately after the death of the testator. The effect of such a statute is to ensure that a beneficiary's share will go to his or her heirs and not to others.

apparent authority   Authority which, although not actually granted by the principal, he or she permits his or her agent to exercise.

appeal   The process by which a higher court is requested by a party to a lawsuit to review the decision of a lower court. Such reconsideration is normally confined to a review of the record from the lower court, with no new testimony taken or new issues raised.

appellant   A party who appeals from a lower court to a higher court.

appellate jurisdiction   The authority of one court to review the proceedings of another court or of an administrative agency.

appellee   A party against whom a case is appealed from a lower court to a higher court.

appraisal   Valuation; a determination of the worth or value of something.

appreciate   To rise in value.

apprehension   Anxiety.

arraignment   The act of bringing an accused before a court to answer a criminal charge made against him or her and calling upon him or her to enter a plea of guilty or not guilty.

arrest warrant   Legal process issued by a court directing a law enforcement officer to arrest a named person on a specific charge.

arson   The willful and malicious burning of a building. In some jurisdictions, arson includes the deliberate burning of any structure.

articles of incorporation   The charter or basic rules that create a corporation and by which it functions.

assault   An act of force or threat of force intended to inflict harm upon a person or to put the person in fear that such harm is imminent; an attempt to commit a battery. The perpetrator must have, or appear to have, the present ability to carry out the act.

asset   Anything of value owned by a person or an organization. Assets include not only all real property and personal property, but intangible property … .

assignee   A person to whom a right is assigned.

assignment   A transfer of property, or a right in property, from one person to another.

assignor   A person who assigns a right.

assumed name   A fictitious name or an alias.

assumption of risk   The legal principle that a person who knows and deliberately exposes himself or herself to a danger assumes responsibility for the risk, rather than the person who actually created the danger.

attachment   The process by which a person's property is figuratively brought into court to ensure satisfaction of a judgment that may be rendered against him or her. In the event judgment is rendered, the property may be sold to satisfy the judgment.

attempt   An act done with the intent to commit a crime, which would have resulted in the crime being committed except that something happened to prevent it.

attest   To swear to; to bear witness to; to affirm to be true or genuine.

attestation clause   A clause, usually at the end of a document such as a deed or a will, that provides evidence of attestation.

attorney in fact   An agent or representative authorized by his or her principal, by virtue of a power of attorney, to act for [the principal] in certain matters.

attorney-client privilege   Nothing a client tells his or her attorney in connection with his or her case can be disclosed by the attorney, or anyone employed by the attorney or the attorney's firm, without the client's permission.

attractive nuisance (attraction theory)   An unusual mechanism, apparatus, or condition that is dangerous to young children but is so interesting and alluring as to attract them to the premises on which it is kept.

authorized capital stock (authorized shares)   The maximum amount of capital stock that a corporation is authorized to issue under its charter or articles of incorporation.

bailee   The person to whom property is entrusted in a bailment.

bailment   The entrusting of personal property by one person … to another … for a specific purpose, with the understanding that the property will be returned when the purpose is accomplished, the stated duration of the bailment is over, or the bailor reclaims it.

bailment for hire   A bailment for compensation.

bailor   The person who entrusts property to another in a bailment.

bankruptcy   The system under which a debtor may come into court ... or be brought into court by his or her creditors ... , either seeking to have his or her assets administered and sold for the benefit of the creditors and to be discharged from his or her debts ... , or to have his debts reorganized ... .

bankruptcy courts   Federal courts that hear and determine only bankruptcy cases.

bankruptcy estate   All of the property of the debtor at the time the petition in bankruptcy is filed.

bar association   A voluntary organization of members of the bar of a state or county, or of the bar of every state, whose primary function is promoting professionalism and enhancing the administration of justice.

bargain and sale deed   A deed conveying real property without covenants.

battery   The unconsented-to touching or striking of one person by another, or by an object put in motion by him or her, with the intention of doing harm or giving offense.

beneficiary   1. A person who receives a benefit. 2. A person who has inherited or is entitled to inherit under a will. 3. A person for whom property is held in trust.

beyond a reasonable doubt   The degree of proof required to convict a person of a crime. A *reasonable doubt* is a fair doubt based upon reason and common sense, not an arbitrary or possible doubt. To convict a criminal defendant, a jury must be persuaded of his or her guilt to a level beyond "apparently" or "probably." Proof beyond a reasonable doubt is the highest level of proof the law requires.

bicameral   Two-chambered, referring to the customary division of a legislature into two houses (a Senate and a House of Representatives).

bigamy   The crime of marrying while married.

bilateral contract   A contract in which each party promises performance to the other, the promise by the one furnishing the consideration for the promise from the other.

bill of particulars   In criminal prosecutions, a more detailed statement of the offense charged than the indictment or information provides. A criminal defendant is entitled to a bill of particulars, as part of the discovery process, if the nature and extent of the offense are not alleged with sufficient particularity to allow the preparation of an adequate defense.

Bill of Rights   The first 10 amendments to the United States Constitution. The ... portion of the Constitution that sets forth the rights which are the fundamental principles of the United States and the foundation of American citizenship.

billable hour requirements   Number of hours required of each attorney, paralegal, or other timekeeper to be billed to a client on behalf of the law firm.

board of directors   The directors of a corporation or association who act as a group in representing the organization and conducting its business.

breach of contract   Failure, without legal excuse, to perform any promise that forms a whole or a part of a contract, including the doing of something inconsistent with its terms.

breach of the peace   Conduct that violates the public order or disturbs the public tranquillity.

bribery   The crime of giving something of value with the intention of influencing the action of a public official.

brief   A written statement submitted to a court for the purpose of persuading it of the correctness of one's position. A brief argues the facts of the case and the applicable law, supported by citations of authority.

burden of going forward (burden of production)   The duty of a party, with respect to certain issues being tried, to produce evidence sufficient to justify a verdict before the other party is obligated to produce evidence to the contrary.

burden of persuasion   The ultimate burden of proof; the responsibility of convincing the jury or, in a nonjury trial, the judge, of the truth.

burden of proof   The duty of establishing the truth of a matter; the duty of proving a fact that is in dispute. In most instances the burden of proof, like the burden of going forward, shifts from one side to the other during the course of a trial as the case progresses and evidence is introduced by each side.

burglary   At common law, the offense of breaking and entering a dwelling at night with the intent to commit a felony. The crime of burglary has been broadened by statute to include entering buildings other than dwellings, with or without a breaking, and regardless of the time of day or night.

but-for rule   A rule of tort law ... used to determine whether a defendant is legally responsible for a plaintiff's injuries.

canon law   Christian religious law, particularly that of the Roman Catholic church.

capacity   Competency in law … . A person's ability to understand the nature and effect of the act in which he or she is engaged.

case law   The law as laid down in the decisions of the courts in similar cases that have previously been decided.

castle doctrine   The doctrine that a person may use whatever force is required to defend his or her home and those in it.

causation   A causing; the producing of a result.

cause of action   Circumstances that give a person the right to bring a lawsuit and receive relief from the court.

certificate   A formal or official written declaration intended as an authentication of the fact or facts set forth therein.

certificate of title   [A] document that shows the name of the owner of land identified in the document in jurisdictions.

Certified Legal Assistant   A legal assistant who has been certified by the National Association of Legal Assistants.

chain of title   The succession of transactions through which title to a given piece of land was passed from person to person from its origins to the present day.

change of venue   Moving the trial of a case from one county or judicial district to another … . A motion may be made requesting that the court transfer the case to a proper court when one party believes that the action has been commenced in the wrong judicial district, or when one party feels that there are extenuating circumstances concerning the venue, such as publicity concerning the case.

charitable trust   A trust established for a charitable purpose.

chattel   Personal property that is visible, tangible, and movable.

circumstantial evidence   Facts and circumstances from which a jury or a judge may reason and reach conclusions in a case.

citation   1. A writ issued by a judge, ordering a person to appear in court for a specified purpose. 2. Reference to authority on a point of law, by name, volume, and page or section of the court report or other book in which it appears.

citizen's arrest   An arrest made by a person other than a police officer … legal under certain circumstances.

civil law   Law based upon a published code of statutes, as opposed to law found in the decisions of courts. Body of law that determines private rights and liabilities, as distinguished from criminal law.

civil liberties   Political liberties guaranteed by the Constitution and, in particular, by the Bill of Rights … .

civil procedure   The rules of procedure by which private rights are enforced; the rules by which civil actions are governed.

civil rights   1. All the rights the law gives a person. 2. Constitutional or statutory guaranties against discrimination by reason of race, religion, national origin, gender, age, or disability.

class action   An action brought by one or several plaintiffs on behalf of a class of persons.

clear and convincing evidence   A degree of proof required in some civil cases, higher than the usual standard of preponderance of the evidence.

clear title   Good title; marketable title; title to land or other property that is free from doubts or defects.

closely held corporation   A corporation in which all the stock is owned by a few persons or by another corporation.

Code of Federal Regulations (C.F.R.)   An arrangement, by subject matter, of the rules and regulations issued by federal administrative agencies.

codicil   An addition or supplement to a will, which adds to or modifies the will without replacing or revoking it.

cohabitation   Living together as husband and wife, although not married to each other.

collateral   Stocks, bonds, or other property that serve as security for a loan or other obligation; property pledged to pay a debt.

collateral consanguinity   A blood relationship based upon a common ancestor.

commingle   To merge; to mix.

common law   Law found in the decisions of the courts rather than in statutes; judge-made law.

common law marriage   A marriage entered into without ceremony, the parties agreeing between themselves to be husband and wife, followed by a period of cohabitation.

community   People living in the same place ... and subject to the same laws. ... Society in general.

community property   A system of law under which the earnings of either spouse are the property of both the husband and the wife, and property acquired by either spouse during the marriage (other than by gift, under a will, or through inheritance) is the property of both. States that have adopted this system are called *community property states*.

comparative negligence   The doctrine adopted by most states that requires a comparison of the negligence of the defendant with the negligence of the plaintiff: the greater the negligence of the defendant, the lesser the level of care required of the plaintiff to permit him or her to recover. ... [T]he plaintiff's negligence does not defeat his or her cause of action, but it does reduce the damages he or she is entitled to recover.

compensatory damages (actual damages)   Damages recoverable in a lawsuit for loss or injury suffered by the plaintiff as a result of the defendant's conduct.

complainant   A person who files a formal accusation of a crime. ... A person who makes any formal complaint.

complaint   1. A formal charge of a crime. 2. The initial pleading in a civil action, in which the plaintiff alleges a cause of action and asks that the wrong done be remedied by the court.

concurrent   1. Having the same jurisdiction or authority. 2. Occurring at the same time.

concurrent jurisdiction   Two or more courts having the power to adjudicate the same class of cases or the same matter.

concurring opinion   An opinion issued by one or more judges which agrees with the result reached by the majority opinion rendered by the court, but reaches that result for different reasons.

conditional fee   An estate in land, also known as a fee conditional or fee simple conditional, which is limited to particular heirs. If the grantee has no heirs of the type described in the condition, the estate reverts to the grantor.

conference committee   A meeting of representatives of both houses of a legislature to resolve differences in the versions of the same bill passed by each, by working out a compromise acceptable to both bodies.

confession   A voluntary admission by a person that he or she has committed a crime.

conflict of interest   The existence of a variance between the interests of the parties in a fiduciary relationship.

consanguinity   Relationship by blood; having the blood of a common ancestor.

consecutive sentences   Sentences of imprisonment for crimes in which the time of each is to run one after the other without a break.

consent   Agreement; approval; acquiescence; being of one mind.

consent decree   1. A judgment in an action brought by an administrative agency, in which the defendant declines to admit wrongdoing but agrees not to engage in the conduct alleged, in exchange for which the government's suit is dropped. 2. A decree entered in an equitable action suit upon the consent of the parties. Such a decree is binding on the parties; they cannot subsequently appeal it or go to trial on the matter.

consideration   The reason a person enters into a contract; that which is given in exchange for performance or the promise to perform; the price bargained and paid; the inducement.

conspiracy   An agreement between two or more persons to engage in a criminal act or to accomplish a legal objective by criminal or unlawful means.

constructive notice   Circumstances such that the law considers that actual notice took place, regardless of whether it did; a substitute for actual notice based upon a presumption of notice which is so strong that the law does not permit it to be contradicted.

contempt   An act of disrespect toward a court or legislative body; deliberate disobedience of a court order.

contest   An attempt to defeat the probate of a will, commonly referred to as an attempt to "set aside the will."

contingent fee   A fee for legal services, calculated on the basis of an agreed-upon percentage of the amount of money recovered for the client by the attorney.

contract   An agreement entered into, for adequate consideration, to do, or refrain from doing, a particular thing. The Uniform Commercial Code defines a contract as the total legal obligation resulting from the parties' agreement. ... [T]he transaction must involve an undertaking that is legal to perform, and there must be mutuality of agreement and obligation between at least two competent parties.

contributory negligence   [A] failure by the plaintiff to exercise reasonable care which, in part at least, is the cause of an injury.

conversion   Control over another person's personal property which is wrongfully exercised; control applied in a manner that violates that person's title to or rights in the property.

conveyance   The transferring of title to real property from one person to another. ... Any transfer of title to either real property or personal property.

copy   A reproduction of an original work.

copyright   The right of an author, granted by federal statute, to exclusively control the reproduction, distribution, and sale of his or her literary, artistic, or intellectual productions for the period of the copyright's existence.

corporate liability   The liability of a corporation for the acts of its directors, officers, shareholders, agents, and employees.

corporation   An artificial person, existing only in the eyes of the law, to whom a state or the federal government has granted a charter to become a legal entity, separate from its shareholders, with a name of its own, under which its shareholders can act and contract and sue and be sued.

corpus delicti   Means the "body of the crime"; the fact that a crime has actually been committed.

corroborating evidence   Evidence from another source which tends to show the probability that the testimony of a prior witness is truthful.

counterclaim   A cause of action on which a defendant in a lawsuit might have sued the plaintiff in a separate action. Such a cause of action, stated in a separate division of a defendant's answer, is a counterclaim.

counteroffer   A position taken in response to an offer, proposing a different deal.

court of general jurisdiction   Generally, another term for trial court; that is, a court having jurisdiction to try all classes of civil and criminal cases except those which can be heard only by a court of limited jurisdiction.

court of limited jurisdiction   A court whose jurisdiction is limited to civil cases of a certain type or which involve a limited amount of money, or whose

jurisdiction in criminal cases is confined to petty offenses and preliminary hearings.

court reporter   A person who stenographically or by "voice writing" records court proceedings, from which he or she prepares a transcript that becomes a part of the record in the case.

court reports   Official, published reports of cases decided by courts, giving the opinions rendered in the cases, with headnotes prepared by the publisher.

court rules   Rules adopted by courts to govern civil and criminal processes.

covenant   In a deed, a promise to do or not to do a particular thing, or an assurance that a particular fact or circumstance exists or does not exist.

covenant for quiet enjoyment   A covenant that title is good and that therefore the grantee will be undisturbed in his or her possession and use of the property.

covenants not to compete   A provision in an employment contract in which the employee promises that, upon leaving the employer, he or she will not engage in the same business, as an employee or otherwise, in competition with the former employer. Such a covenant ... must be reasonable with respect to its duration and geographical scope.

criminal law   Branch of the law that specifies what conduct constitutes crime and establishes appropriate punishments for such conduct.

criminal mischief (malicious mischief)   The willful destruction of the property of another.

criminal procedure   The rules of procedure by which criminal prosecutions are governed.

cross-appeal   An appeal filed by the appellee from the same judgment, or some portion of the same judgment, as the appellant has appealed from. A cross appeal is generally made a part of the review proceedings set in motion by the original appeal.

cross-claim   A counterclaim against a coplaintiff or a codefendant.

culpable   Blameworthy; blameable; responsible; at fault.

cumulative evidence   Additional evidence of the same kind, or from the same source, to the same point; evidence proving that which has already been proven. Cumulative evidence is to be contrasted with corroborating evidence, which always comes from a different source and is often different in kind or character.

curtesy The rights a husband had under the common law with respect to his wife's property. Today these rights have been modified in every state in various ways, but all states that retain curtesy in some form extend the same rights to both spouses.

damages The sum of money that may be recovered in the courts as financial reparation for an injury or wrong suffered as a result of … a tortious act.

decedent A legal term for a person who has died.

declaration of trust 1. A voluntary statement by which an owner of property acknowledges that he or she holds the property in trust for someone else. 2. The document creating a trust.

declaratory judgment A judgment that specifies the rights of the parties but orders no relief. … [I]t is a binding judgment and the appropriate remedy for the determination of an actionable dispute when the plaintiff is in doubt as to his or her legal rights.

decree of divorce A final judgment granting a divorce.

deed A document by which real property, or an interest in real property is conveyed from one person to another.

defamation Libel or slander; the written or oral publication, falsely and intentionally, of anything that is injurious to the good name or reputation of another person.

default The failure to perform a duty or obligation. … Fault; neglect; omission.

default judgment A judgment rendered in favor of a plaintiff based upon a defendant's failure to take a necessary step in a lawsuit within the required time.

defendant The person against whom an action is brought.

delegation The act of conferring authority upon, or transferring it to, another.

delegation of powers (delegation of authority) The transfer of power from the president to an administrative agency.

delivery A handing over; the surrender of possession to another.

demonstrative evidence Physical evidence offered for viewing by the judge or jury.

demonstrative legacy A legacy that specifies a particular fund or particular property of the testator as the primary source of payment of a sum of money given in a will.

demurrer A method of raising an objection to the legal sufficiency of a pleading. A demurrer says, in effect, that the opposing party's complaint alleges facts which, even if true, do not add up to a cause of action and that, therefore, the case should be dismissed.

dependent One entitled to support, as a spouse or child.

deponent A person who gives a deposition. A person who gives sworn testimony in any form.

deposition The transcript of a witness's testimony given under oath outside of the courtroom, usually in advance of the trial or hearing, upon oral examination or in response to written interrogatories.

depreciation The lessening in worth of any property caused by wear, use, time, or obsolescence.

derivative Something not original; something arising from another thing.

design patent A patent of a design that gives an original and pleasing appearance to an article.

digest A series of volumes containing summaries of cases organized by legal topics, subject areas, and so on.

diminished capacity The rule that a criminal defendant, although not sufficiently mentally impaired to be entitled to a defense of insanity, may have been so reduced in mental capacity … that he or she was incapable of forming the mental state necessary, in law, for the commission of certain crimes.

direct evidence Proof that speaks directly to the issue, requiring no support by other evidence; proof based solely upon the witness's own knowledge, as distinguished from evidence from which inferences must be drawn if it is to have value as proof.

disaffirmance The refusal to fulfill a voidable contract. … Disclaimer; repudiation; disavowal.

discharge 1. A release from an obligation … . 2. The release of a debtor in a bankruptcy proceeding.

discovery A means for providing a party, in advance of trial, with access to facts that are within the knowledge of the other side, to enable the party to better try his or her case.

discretion The power conferred upon an official to act according to his or her own judgment and conscience, within general rules of law only … .

dismiss To order a case, motion, or prosecution to be terminated.

disorderly conduct An act that breaches the peace, grossly offends public morality, or endangers public safety or public health.

disparagement Discredit; detraction; dishonor; denunciation; disrespect.

dispossession A forced or fraudulent changing of possession ... from one person to another.

dissenting opinion A written opinion filed by a judge of an appellate court who disagrees with the decision of the majority of judges in a case, giving the reasons for his or her differing view. Often a dissenting opinion is written by one judge on behalf of one or more other dissenting judges.

dissolution of corporation The termination of a corporation's existence and its abolishment as an entity.

dissolution of partnership The change in the relation of partners caused by any partner's ceasing to be associated in the carrying on of the business. Any such change brings about the dissolution of the partnership.

distinctive Characteristic; distinguishing; particular; uncommon; idiosyncratic.

dividend A payment made by a corporation to its shareholders, either in cash, in stock, or out of surplus earnings.

divisible contract A contract whose parts are capable of separate or independent treatment; a contract that is enforceable as to a part which is valid, even though another part is invalid and unenforceable.

divorce A dissolution of the marital relationship between husband and wife.

divorce a mensa et thoro A decree that terminates the right of cohabitation, and adjudicates matters such as custody and support, but does not dissolve the marriage itself. A divorce a mensa et thoro is often referred to as *legal separation*, *judicial separation*, or *limited divorce*.

divorce a vinculo matrimonii A decree that dissolves the marriage because of matrimonial misconduct. Also called *absolute divorce*.

docket number Number assigned to a case by the clerk of court when the case is initially filed with a court; useful for identifying and tracking cases within the court system.

documentary evidence A document or other writing that tends to establish the truth or falsity of a matter at issue. When oral evidence is given, it is the person (i.e., the witness) who speaks; when documentary evidence is involved, it is the document that "speaks."

domicile The relationship that the law creates between a person and a particular locality or country. Domicile is a person's permanent home or permanent abode.

dominant tenement Real property that benefits from an easement which burdens another piece of property, known as the servient tenement.

double jeopardy A rule originating in the Fifth Amendment that prohibits a second punishment or a second trial for the same offense.

dower The legal right or interest that a wife acquires by marriage in the property of her husband. ... Dower ... has been substantially modified in most states, but every state retains aspects of the concept for the protection of both spouses.

due care (reasonable care) That degree of care which a person of ordinary prudence would exercise in similar circumstances.

due process of law Law administered through courts of justice, equally applicable to all under established rules that do not violate fundamental principles of fairness.

durable power of attorney A power of attorney that remains effective even though the grantor becomes mentally incapacitated. Some durable powers of attorney become effective *only* when a person is no longer able to make decisions for himself or herself.

duress Coercion applied for the purpose of compelling a person to do, or to refrain from doing, some act. ... Duress may be a defense to a criminal prosecution if the defendant committed the crime out of a well-grounded fear of death or serious bodily harm.

duty A legal obligation, whether imposed by the common law, statute, court order, or contract. ... An obligation or responsibility.

easement A right to use the land of another for a specific purpose.

elective share In some states, the share a surviving spouse may elect to take in the estate of the deceased spouse. In such jurisdictions, it replaces dower. ... [A]lso referred to as a *statutory share* or *forced share*.

embezzlement   The fraudulent conversion of property, including but not limited to money, with which a person has been entrusted.

eminent domain   The power of the government to take private property for a public use or public purpose without the owner's consent, if it pays just compensation.

enabling act (enabling statute)   A statute that gives the government the power to enforce other legislation or that carries out a provision of a constitution ... a clause in a statute granting the government the power to enforce or carry out that statute.

enjoyment   The ability to exercise a right.

entrapment   Inducing a person to commit a crime he or she is otherwise not inclined to commit, in order to bring a criminal prosecution against him or her.

entry   The act of going upon real property.

equitable distribution   Some jurisdictions permit their courts, in a divorce case, to distribute all property obtained during the marriage on an "equitable" basis, that is, without regard to whose name the property is in. In deciding what is equitable, the court takes into consideration factors such as the length of the marriage and the contributions of each party, including homemaking.

equitable relief   A remedy available in equity rather than at law; generally relief other than money damages.

equitable title   Title recognized as ownership in equity, even though it is not legal title or marketable title; title sufficient to give the party to whom it belongs the right to have the legal title transferred to him or her.

escheat   The right of the state to take title to property after the death of a person who has not disposed of the property by will and has left no heirs to inherit it.

estate for years   An estate that terminates after a specific number of years.

ethics   A code of moral principles and standards of behavior for people in professions such as law or medicine.

evidence   The means by which any matter of fact may be established or disproved. Such means include testimony, documents, and physical objects. The law of evidence is made up of rules that determine what evidence is to be admitted or rejected in the trial of a civil action or a criminal prosecution and what weight is to be given to admitted evidence.

ex parte   Means "of a side," i.e., from one side or by one party. The term refers to an application made to the court by one party without notice to the other party.

exclusionary rule   The rule of constitutional law that evidence secured by the police by means of an unreasonable search and seizure, in violation of the Fourth Amendment, cannot be used as evidence in a criminal prosecution.

exclusive   Shutting out other occurrences or possibilities; not shared.

exclusive jurisdiction   Jurisdiction when only one court has the power to adjudicate the same class of cases or the same matter.

exculpatory clause   A clause in a contract or other legal document excusing a party from liability for his or her wrongful act.

execution   A writ or process for the enforcement of a judgment.

execution sale (sheriff's sale)   A public sale by a sheriff or similar officer of property seized under a writ of execution ... .

executor   A person designated by a testator to carry out the directions and requests in the testator's will and to dispose of his or her property according to the provisions of his or her will.

expert witness   A person who is so qualified, either by actual experience or by careful study, as to enable him or her to form a definite opinion of his or her own respecting a subject about which persons having no particular training, experience, or special study are incapable of forming accurate opinions.

expiration   Coming to an end; termination due to lapse of time.

express authority   Authority expressly granted to or conferred upon an agent or employee by a principal or employer.

express trusts   A trust created by a direct or positive declaration of trust.

extortion   The criminal offense of obtaining money or other thing of value by duress, force, threat of force, fear, or color of office.

fair use doctrine   The principle that entitles a person to use copyrighted material in a reasonable manner, including a work's theme or idea, without the consent of the copyright owner.

false imprisonment The unlawful restraint by one person of the physical liberty of another.

false pretenses The crime of obtaining the money or property of another by fraudulent misrepresentation. The essential elements of the offense are an intentional false statement concerning a material fact, in reliance on which title or possession is surrendered.

family allowance An amount paid out of the assets of a decedent's estate for the necessary expenses of the widow and children until final settlement of the estate.

Federal Register An official publication, printed daily, containing regulations and proposed regulations issued by administrative agencies, as well as other rulemaking and other official business of the executive branch of government. All regulations are ultimately published in the Code of Federal Regulations.

Federal Rules of Civil Procedure A comprehensive set of rules governing procedure in civil cases in United States District Courts.

federalism The system by which the states of the United States relate to each other and to the federal government.

fee simple absolute (fee simple) [T]he most complete estate in land known to the law. It signifies total ownership and control. It may be inherited free of any condition, limitation, or restriction by particular heirs.

ferae naturae Wild animals.

fictitious name An artificial name that a person or corporation adopts for business or professional purposes.

fiduciary A person who is entrusted with handling money or property for another person.

fiduciary duty The duty to act loyally and honestly with respect to the interests of another; the duty the law imposes upon a fiduciary.

fiduciary relationship A relationship between two persons in which one is obligated to act with the utmost good faith, honesty, and loyalty on behalf of the other.

firm offer (irrevocable offer) Under the Uniform Commercial Code, an offer to buy or sell goods made in a signed writing which, by its terms, gives assurance that it will be held open. A firm offer is not revocable for want of consideration during the time it states it will be held open ... .

first-degree murder Murder committed deliberately with malice aforethought, that is, with premeditation.

fixed Established or set. ... Permanent; definite; stable.

fixed fee A standardized fee used by attorneys for performing routine legal tasks.

fixture An article, previously personal property, that, by being physically affixed to real estate, has become part of the real property; something so connected to a structure for use in connection with it that it cannot be removed without doing injury to the structure.

forced heir A person who cannot be disinherited by a testator ... , except when there is a legal cause for disinheritance.

foreclosure 1. A legal action by which a mortgagee terminates a mortgagor's interest in mortgaged premises. 2. The enforcement of a lien, deed of trust, or mortgage on real estate, ... by any method provided by law.

foreign corporation A corporation incorporated under the laws of one state, doing business in another.

foreseeable That which may be anticipated or known in advance; that which a person should have known. In the law of negligence, a person is responsible for the consequences of his or her acts only if they are foreseeable.

forgery The false making, material alteration, or uttering, with intent to defraud or injure, of any writing which, if genuine, might appear to be legally effective or the basis for legal liability.

fraud Deceit, deception, or trickery that is intended to induce, and does induce, another to part with anything of value or surrender some legal right.

Freedom of Information Act A federal statute that requires federal agencies to make available to the public, upon request, material contained in their files, as well as information on how they function. The Act contains various significant exemptions from disclosure ... .

freehold An estate in fee or a life estate in real property.

freelance paralegal A self-employed paralegal who offers his or her services to law firms, corporate legal departments, or the public.

fresh pursuit (hot pursuit)   The pursuit of a person ... to recover property from a thief, if [the owner] pursues and apprehends him or her immediately.

future interest   An estate or interest in land or personal property, including money, whether vested or contingent, that is to come into existence at a future time.

garnishment   A proceeding by a creditor to obtain satisfaction of a debt from money or property of the debtor which is in the possession of a third person or is owed by such a person to the debtor.

general damages   Damages that are the natural and probable result of the wrongful acts complained of.

general jurisdiction   The type of jurisdiction possessed by a trial court; that is, a court having jurisdiction to try all classes of civil and criminal cases except those which can be heard only by a court of limited jurisdiction.

general legacy   A legacy of personal property or money that may be satisfied out of the general estate of the testator, as opposed to a legacy of a particular item of personal property or of money from a specific fund.

general partner   A partner in an ordinary partnership, as distinguished from a limited partnership.

gift   A voluntary transfer of property by one person to another without any consideration or compensation.

goodwill   The benefit a business acquires, beyond the mere value of its capital stock and tangible assets, as a result of having a good reputation and the respect of the public.

government survey   The survey of lands in the public domain, conducted by the federal government, under which land is laid out in townships, sections, and quarter sections.

grand jury   A body whose number varies with the jurisdiction, ... whose duty it is to determine whether probable cause exists to return indictments against persons accused of committing crimes.

gratuitous bailment   A bailment for the sole benefit of the bailee; that is, one in which no compensation is involved.

great care   The degree of care a prudent person usually exercises concerning his or her own affairs of great importance.

gross negligence   Willfully and intentionally acting, or failing to act, with a deliberate indifference to how others may be affected.

guardian   A person empowered by the law to care for another who, by virtue of age or lack of mental capacity, is legally unable to care for himself or herself. Guardianship may also involve the duty to manage the estate of the incompetent person.

guardian ad litem   A person appointed by the court to represent and protect the interests of a minor or an incompetent person during litigation.

half blood   A person who shares one parent in common with another person.

headnote   A summary statement that appears at the beginning of a reported case to indicate the points decided by the case.

hearing   A proceeding in which evidence is introduced and witnesses are examined so that findings of fact can be made and a determination rendered. Although, in a general sense, all trials can be said to be hearings, not all hearings are trials. The difference is in the degree of formality each requires, the rules of procedure being more relaxed in hearings.

hearsay   The testimony of a witness as to a statement made to him or her outside of court, or made to someone else who told the witness what was said, that is offered in court to prove the truth of the matter contained in the statement.

heirs   Persons who are entitled to inherit real or personal property of a decedent who dies intestate; persons receiving property by descent.

higher courts   Any court that is above a lower court, usually an appellate court.

holographic will   A will that is entirely written and signed by the testator in his or her own handwriting. In many states, the requirement that the signing of a will be witnessed is not imposed in the case of a holographic will, because a successful counterfeit of another person's handwriting is very difficult; the requirement that the will be entirely in handwriting is therefore thought to be sufficient protection against forgery.

homestead   [T]he right to own real property free and clear of the claims of creditors, provided the owner occupies the property as his or her home.

homestead exemption   [T]he immunity of real property from execution for debt, provided the property is occupied by the debtor as the head of the family.

homicide   The killing of a human being.

illegitimate child   A child born to parents who are not married to each other.

illusory promise   A promise whose performance is completely up to the promisor … . Because the carrying out of such a promise is optional, there is no mutuality, and therefore the promise cannot form the basis of a valid contract.

immunity   An exemption granted by law, contrary to the general rule; a privilege.

immunity from prosecution   A guaranty to a person that if he or she testifies against others, he or she will not be prosecuted for his or her own criminal conduct.

implied authority   The authority of an agent to do whatever acts are necessary to carry out his or her express authority.

improvement   Anything that enhances the value of real property permanently.

in loco parentis   Means "in the place of parents." Describes a person who, in the absence of a child's parent or guardian, and without formal legal approval, temporarily assumes a parent's obligations with respect to the child.

in pari delicto   Equally at fault.

in rem action   A legal action brought against property …, as opposed to an action brought against the person.

incompetent person   A person who is not legally qualified for a specific activity (such as giving testimony or entering into a contract) by reason of … mental incapacity.

indecent exposure   Exposing one's private parts in a manner, and at a time and place, which is offensive to public decency.

independent contractor   As distinguished from an employee, a person who contracts to do work for another person in his or her own way, controlling the means and method by which the work is done but not the end product.

indictment   A charge made in writing by a grand jury, based upon evidence presented to it, accusing a person of having committed a criminal act, generally a felony.

infancy   The status of a person who has not reached the age of majority and who therefore is under a civil disability; nonage; minority.

inferior courts   1. A court of original jurisdiction, as distinguished from an appellate court; a trial court. 2. A court of limited jurisdiction.

information   An accusation of the commission of a crime, sworn to by a district attorney or other prosecutor, on the basis of which a criminal defendant is brought to trial for a misdemeanor and, in some states, for a felony.

informed consent   Agreement to permit something to occur, after having been given as much information as necessary to make an intelligent and rational ("informed") decision.

infringement of copyright   Using any portion of copyrighted material without the consent of the copyright owner.

infringement of patent   The manufacture, use, or sale of a patent or process patent without the authorization of the patent owner.

infringement of trademark   A use or imitation of a trademark in such manner that a purchaser of goods is likely to be deceived into believing that they are the goods of the owner of the trademark.

injunction   A court order that commands or prohibits some act or course of conduct. It is preventive in nature and designed to protect a plaintiff from irreparable injury to his or her property or other rights by prohibiting or commanding the doing of certain acts.

injunctive relief   Relief resulting from an injunction.

insolvency   The status of a person when his or her total assets are of insufficient value to pay his or her debts. The inability of a person to pay his or her debts as they become due or in the ordinary course of business.

intangible property   1. An incorporeal right unrelated to a physical thing; a right to inherit property. 2. Property that has no intrinsic value, but evidences something of value.

intent   Purpose; the plan, course, or means a person conceives to achieve a certain result. Intent is not … limited to conscious wrongdoing, and may be inferred or presumed.

intentional tort   An injury inflicted by positive, willful, and aggressive conduct, or by design, as opposed to an injury caused by negligence or resulting from an accident.

inter vivos trust (living trust)   A trust that is effective during the lifetime of the creator of the trust.

interpret   To construe; to explain; to draw out meaning.

interrogation   The questioning of a criminal suspect by the police.

interrogatories   Written questions put by one party to another, or ... to a witness in advance of trial.

interstate commerce   Commerce between states; that is, from a given point in one state to a given point in another.

intestacy   The status of the estate or property of a person who dies without leaving a valid will.

intestate   Pertaining to a person, or to the property of a person, who dies without leaving a valid will.

intestate succession   Inheritance from a person who dies intestate.

intimidation   The act of putting a person in fear by threatening to commit an unlawful act. Intimidation does not necessarily involve an act of violence or even a threat of violence.

intoxication   A disturbance of mental or physical capacities resulting from the use of alcohol, drugs, or other substances; a substance-induced impairment of a person's judgment or sense of responsibility.

invasion of privacy   A violation of the right of privacy.

inventory   An itemized list or schedule of assets, property, or other articles, sometimes with notations of their value.

investigate   To inquire; to look into; to make an investigation.

invitee   A person who enters the premises of another at the latter's invitation, or for business purposes, or for their mutual advantage.

involuntary bankruptcy   A bankruptcy initiated by one's creditors.

irresistible impulse   An impulse to commit an act that one is powerless to control. ... [T]he test used in some jurisdictions to determine insanity for purposes of a criminal defense.

irrevocable trust   A trust in which the settlor permanently gives up control of the trust property.

issue   All persons who are descendants of one ancestor, including all future descendants. ... [W]hen used in a will, "issue" will be taken to mean children or grandchildren, or all *living* descendants, if that is the testator's clear intention. "Issue" may or may not include adopted children, depending upon state law.

Jencks rule   The rule that a defendant in a federal criminal prosecution has the right to examine government papers to be better able to cross-examine or impeach government witnesses.

joint and several liability   The liability of two or more persons who jointly commit a tort.

joint custody   An arrangement whereby both parties to a divorce retain legal custody of their child and jointly participate in reaching major decisions concerning the child's welfare.

joint tenancy   An estate in land or in personal property held by two or more persons jointly, with equal rights to share in its enjoyment [and] ... the right of survivorship, which means that upon the death of a joint tenant the entire estate goes to the survivor[s].

judgment creditor   A creditor who has secured a judgment against his or her debtor which has not been satisfied.

judgment debtor   A person against whom a judgment, which has not been satisfied, has been entered.

judgment notwithstanding the verdict   A judgment rendered by the court in favor of a party, notwithstanding the fact that the jury has returned a verdict against that party.

judicial decision   A decision by a court.

judicial review   Review by a court of a decision or ruling of an administrative agency; review by an appellate court of a determination by a lower court.

junior   Of secondary importance, rank, or right.

jurisdiction   In a general sense, the right of a court to adjudicate lawsuits of a certain kind.

jurisdiction in personam (personal jurisdiction)   The jurisdiction a court has over the person of a defendant. It is acquired by service of process upon the defendant or by his or her voluntary submission to jurisdiction.

jurisdiction in rem   The jurisdiction a court has over property situated in the state.

jurisdiction quasi in rem   The jurisdiction a court has over the defendant's interest in property located within the jurisdiction.

kidnapping   The crime of taking and detaining a person against his or her will by force, intimidation, or fraud.

kin (kindred)   Relatives; persons related by blood or consanguinity.

knowingly With knowledge; deliberately; consciously; intentionally.

labor laws Federal and state statutes and administrative regulations that govern such matters as hours of work, minimum wages, unemployment insurance, safety, and collective bargaining.

landlord (lessor) An owner of real property who leases all or a portion of the premises to a tenant.

lapse To cease; to expire; to terminate.

lapsed devise A devise that was good when the will was made but that has failed since then because of the death of the devisee before the death of the testator.

lapsed legacy A legacy that was good when the will was made but that has failed since then because of the death of the legatee before the death of the testator.

larceny The crime of taking personal property, without consent, with the intent to convert it to the use of someone other than the owner or to deprive the owner of it permanently. Larceny does not involve the use of force or the threat of force.

last clear chance doctrine A rule of negligence law by which a negligent defendant is held liable to a plaintiff who has negligently placed himself or herself in peril, if the defendant had a later opportunity than the plaintiff to avoid the occurrence that resulted in injury.

lay witness A witness, other than an expert witness, who possesses no expertise in the field about which he or she testifies. Except in limited circumstances in some jurisdictions, a lay witness is not permitted to testify as to his or her opinion, but only as to things he or she actually observed.

lease A contract for the possession of real estate in consideration of payment of rent, ordinarily for a term of years or months, but sometimes at will. The person making the conveyance is the landlord or lessor; the person receiving the right of possession is the tenant or lessee.

leasehold (leasehold estate) The interest or estate of a lessee under a lease.

legal capacity The ability to execute binding contracts, deeds, wills, etc.; capacity.

legal cause 1. The proximate cause of an injury. 2. Probable cause. 3. Cause that the law deems sufficient.

legal description In deeds and mortgages, a description of the real estate that is the subject of the conveyance, by boundaries, distances, and size, or by reference to maps, surveys, or plats.

legal ethics The code of conduct among lawyers which governs their moral and professional duties toward one another, toward their clients, and toward the courts.

legal technician A self-employed paralegal who offers services directly to the public, without the supervision of an attorney.

legal title Title that evidences apparent ownership, as distinguished from equitable title, which indicates a beneficial interest.

legality The condition of conformity with the law; lawfulness.

legislation Laws enacted by a legislative body (such as Congress, a state legislature, or a city council).

legislative rule [A] regulation having the force of law, promulgated by an administrative agency carrying out a statutory mandate empowering or requiring it to regulate.

letters of administration A document issued by the probate court appointing the administrator of the estate of a person who has died without leaving a will.

letters patent The document issued by the government granting a patent.

letters testamentary A document issued by the probate court appointing the executor of the estate of a decedent who died leaving a will.

lewdness Gross sexual indecency.

libel A false and malicious publication, expressed either in printing, writing, or by signs and pictures, tending to harm a person's reputation and expose him or her to public hatred, contempt, or ridicule.

license 1. A special privilege, not a right common to everyone. 2. A privilege conferred on a person by the government to do something he or she otherwise would not have the right to do. 3. Authorization by the owner of a patent to make, use, or sell the patented article; permission by the owner of a trademark or copyright to use the trademark or to make use of the copyrighted material.

licensee A person who enters upon the property of another for his or her own convenience, pleasure, or benefit, uninvited but tolerated by the owner.

life estate   An estate that exists as long as the person who owns or holds it is alive. Its duration may also be the lifetime of another person.

life tenant   A person who holds a life estate.

limited partner   A partner in a limited partnership whose liability is limited to the sum he or she contributed to the limited partnership as capital. A limited partner is not involved in managing or carrying out the business of the partnership.

limited partnership   A partnership in which the liability of one or more of the partners is limited to the amount of money they have invested in the partnership.

lineal consanguinity   The blood relationship between individuals from whom a person is descended in a direct line of ascent (EXAMPLE: father; grandfather; great-grandfather) or between individuals descended from a person in a direct line of descent (EXAMPLE: daughter, granddaughter; great-granddaughter).

liquidated claim   A claim the amount of which is agreed upon by the parties or which can be determined by applying rules of law or by mathematical calculation.

liquidation   1. The extinguishment of a debt by payment. 2. The ascertainment of the amount of a debt or demand by agreement or by legal proceedings. 3. The winding up of a corporation, partnership, or other business enterprise upon dissolution by converting the assets to money, collecting the accounts receivable, paying the debts, and distributing the surplus if any exists.

lis pendens   A pending suit or pending action. Refers to the jurisdiction, power, or control a court has over the property involved in a suit during litigation. The *doctrine of lis pendens* states that a pending suit is notice to all the world, and therefore a person who purchases real property involved in the pending litigation will be bound by the judgment in the case.

literary work   In copyright law, "works, other than audiovisual works, expressed in words, numbers, or other verbal or numerical symbols or indicia, regardless of the nature of the material objects, such as books, periodicals, manuscripts, phonorecords, film, tapes, disks, or cards, in which they are embodied."

litigation   A legal action; a lawsuit.

living will   A document in which a person sets forth directions regarding medical treatment to be given if he or she becomes unable to participate in decisions regarding his or her medical care.

long arm statutes   State statutes providing for substituted service of process on a nonresident corporation or individual. Long arm statutes permit a state's courts to take jurisdiction over a nonresident if he or she has done business in the state, or has committed a tort or owns property within the state.

loss of consortium   The loss of a spouse's assistance or companionship, or the loss of a spouse's ability or willingness to have sexual relations.

lower court   An inferior court, usually a trial court; a court of limited jurisdiction.

mail fraud   The use of the mails to perpetrate a fraud.

majority opinion   An opinion issued by an appellate court that represents the view of a majority of the members of the court.

malice   State of mind that causes the intentional doing of a wrongful act without legal excuse or justification; a condition of mind prompting a person to the commission of a dangerous or deadly act in deliberate disregard of the lives or safety of others.

malicious prosecution   A criminal prosecution or civil suit commenced maliciously and without probable cause.

malpractice   The failure of a professional to act with reasonable care; misconduct by a professional person in the course of engaging in the profession.

mandamus   A writ … requiring the performance of some … act.

marital deduction   [A] deduction allowed under both the federal estate tax and gift tax with respect to property passing from one spouse to the other.

marketable title   A title free from encumbrances for which a person of reasonable prudence and intelligence, who is well informed as to the facts and their legal significance, would be willing to pay fair market value.

material   Important; relating to substance rather than form; going to the merits; relevant.

material evidence   Evidence that goes to the substantive matters in dispute or has legitimate bearing and effective influence on the decision of the case; evidence which is pertinent.

mechanic's lien A lien created by law for the purpose of securing payment for work performed or materials furnished in constructing or repairing a building or other structure.

mediation The voluntary resolution of a dispute in an amicable manner.

mens rea An "answerable intent," i.e., an intent for which one is answerable; an evil intent; a guilty mind; a criminal intent.

mental incapacity (mental incompetence) The inability to understand the nature and character of the transaction in which one is involved.

merger of offenses The doctrine that when a lesser offense is a component of a more serious offense, prosecution can only be for the greater offense.

metes and bounds A property description, commonly in a deed or mortgage, that is based upon the property's boundaries and the natural objects and other markers on the land.

minor A person who has not yet attained majority; a person who has not reached legal age; a person who has not acquired the capacity to contract.

misrepresentation The statement of an untruth; a misstatement of fact designed to lead one to believe that something is other than it is; a false statement of fact designed to deceive.

mistake An erroneous mental conception that influences a person to act or to decline to act; an unintentional act, omission, or error arising from ignorance, surprise, imposition, or misplaced confidence. ... An error; a misunderstanding; an inaccuracy.

mixed nuisance A nuisance that is both public and private in its effects.

M'Naghten rule A test employed in a number of jurisdictions for determining whether a criminal defendant had the capacity to form criminal intent at the time he or she committed the crime of which he or she is accused. Specifically, the M'Naghten rule is that an accused is not criminally responsible if he or she was laboring under such a defect of reason from disease of the mind that he or she either did not know the nature of his or her act or, if he or she did, that he or she did not know it was wrong.

Model Penal Code A proposed criminal code prepared jointly by the Commission on Uniform State Laws and the American Law Institute.

monument With respect to real estate, a physical object, whether natural or artificial, on the ground that establishes a boundary line.

moral turpitude Depraved conduct; immoral conduct.

mortgage A pledge of real property to secure a debt.

mortgagee The person to whom a mortgage is made; the lender.

mortgagor A person who mortgages his or her property; the borrower.

motion An application made to a court for the purpose of obtaining an order or rule directing something to be done in favor of the applicant.

motive The reason that leads the mind to desire a result; ... that which causes the mind to form intent; the reason for an intention.

moving party A party who makes a motion.

mutual assent A meeting of the minds; consent; agreement.

mutual mistake A mistake of fact that is reciprocal and common to both parties to an agreement, each laboring under the same misconception with respect to a material fact.

mutuality Two persons having the same relationship toward each other with respect to a particular right, obligation, burden, or benefit; the condition of being mutual.

National Association of Legal Assistants A national organization of legal assistants and paralegals whose purpose is to enhance professionalism and the interests of those in the profession, as well as to advance the administration of justice generally.

National Federation of Paralegal Associations An association of paralegal and legal assistant organizations nationwide whose purpose is to enhance professionalism and the interests of those in the profession, as well as to advance the administration of justice.

necessities (necessaries) Things reasonably necessary for maintaining a person in accordance with his or her position in life. Thus, depending upon the person's economic circumstances, "necessaries" may not be limited simply to those things required to maintain existence, i.e., shelter, food, clothing, and medical care.

necessity That which is necessary; that which must be done. ... Necessity is a defense in a criminal prosecution if the defendant committed the crime to prevent a more serious harm from occurring.

negligence The failure to do something that a reasonable person would do in the same circumstances, or the doing of something a reasonable person would not do. Negligence is a wrong generally characterized by carelessness, inattentiveness, and neglectfulness rather than by a positive intent to cause injury.

new trial A trial that may be ordered by the trial court itself, or by an appellate court on appeal, when prejudicial error has occurred or when, for any other reason, a fair trial was prevented.

next of kin A person's next of kin may be either his or her blood relatives, or those persons who would inherit from him or her under the laws of intestate succession.

no-fault divorce A term for the requirements for divorce in jurisdictions in which the party seeking the divorce need not demonstrate that the other party is at fault. The requirements differ from state to state.

non compos mentis Mentally incompetent; of unsound mind.

note A written promise by one person to pay another person a specified sum of money on a specified date; a term used interchangeably with *promissory note*.

notice of appeal The process by which appellate review is initiated; specifically, written notice to the appellee advising him or her of the appellant's intention to appeal.

notice of deposition Written notice that a party to a lawsuit must give to all other parties before taking a deposition.

novation The extinguishment of one obligation by another; a substituted contract that dissolves a previous contractual duty and creates a new one. Novation, which requires the mutual agreement of everyone concerned, replaces a contracting party with a new party who had no rights or obligations under the previous contract.

novelty In patent law, a requirement for the patentability of an invention; namely, that it be a thing of distinct individuality not previously known or used.

nuisance Anything a person does that annoys or disturbs another person in his or her use, possession, or enjoyment of his or her property, or which renders the ordinary use or possession of the property uncomfortable.

nuisance per se An act, occupation, or structure that is considered a nuisance at all times and under any circumstances, regardless of location or surroundings.

nuncupative will A will declared orally by a testator during his or her last illness, before witnesses, and later reduced to writing by a person who was present during the declaration.

obscenity Printed matter, visual material, or language that is obscene.

obstruction of justice The crime of impeding or hindering the administration of justice in any way.

offer A proposal made with the purpose of obtaining an acceptance, thereby creating a contract.

offeree A person to whom an offer is made.

offeror A person who makes an offer.

on all fours Refers to a judicial opinion in a case that is very similar to another case, both with respect to the facts they involve and the applicable law.

on point Refers to a judicial opinion that, with respect to the facts involved and the applicable law, is similar to but not on all fours with another case.

option (option contract) An offer, combined with an agreement supported by consideration not to revoke the offer for a specified period of time; a future contract in which one of the parties has the right to insist on compliance with the contract, or to cancel it, at his or her election.

oral argument A party, through his or her attorney, usually presents his or her case to an appellate court on appeal by arguing the case verbally to the court, in addition to submitting a brief. Oral argument may also be made in support of a motion.

order A determination made by an administrative agency.

ordinance A law of a municipal corporation; a local law enacted by a city council, town council, board of supervisors, or the like. A rule established by authority.

original jurisdiction The jurisdiction of a trial court, as distinguished from the jurisdiction of an appellate court.

overreaching Taking unfair advantage in bargaining.

paralegal   A person who, although not an attorney, performs many of the functions of an attorney under an attorney's supervision.

parcel   A lot or tract of real estate.

parens patriae **doctrine**   The doctrine that dependent and incompetent persons are under the protection and control of the state. This concept empowers the state, within the limits imposed by the Constitution, to institutionalize orphans, individuals with serious mental defects, and others who are unable to care for themselves.

parol   Oral; by word of mouth; spoken, as opposed to written.

parol evidence rule   Rule under which evidence of prior or contemporaneous oral agreements that would change the terms of a written contract are inadmissible.

parole   The release of a person from imprisonment after serving a portion of his or her sentence, provided he or she complies with certain conditions.

partnership   An undertaking of two or more persons to carry on, as co-owners, a business or other enterprise for profit; an agreement between or among two or more persons to put their money, labor, and skill into commerce or business, and to divide the profit in agreed-upon proportions.

partnership agreement   The agreement signed by the members of a partnership that governs their relationship. It is sometimes referred to as *articles of partnership*.

patent   The exclusive right of manufacture, sale, or use granted by the federal government to a person who invents or discovers a device or process that is new and useful.

Patent and Trademark Office   Authorized by the Constitution and established by Congress, this office of the federal government registers all trademarks and grants all patents issued in the United States. Its duties also include examining patents, hearing and deciding appeals from inventors and trademark applicants, and publishing the *Official Gazette*.

pecuniary legacy (pecuniary bequest)   A legacy consisting of a sum of money.

per capita   Means "by the head"; by the individual.

per stirpes   Means "by the root"; according to class; by representation. *Per stirpes* describes the method of dividing or distributing an estate in which the heirs of a deceased heir share the portion of the estate that the deceased heir would have received had he or she lived.

performance   In copyright law, publicly giving or presenting a play, musical work, dance, film, or the like.

periodic   Occurring at regular intervals.

perjury   Giving false testimony in a judicial proceeding or an administrative proceeding; lying under oath as to a material fact; swearing to the truth of anything one knows or believes to be false.

permanent injunction   An injunction granted after a final hearing on the merits … .

personal property   All property other than real property, including … tangible … and intangible property.

personal representative   [T]he executor or administrator of a decedent's estate … .

personal service of process   The actual or direct delivery of process (such as a writ or a summons) to the person to whom it is directed or to someone authorized to receive it on his or her behalf.

petition   1. An application made to a court *ex parte*. 2. The name given in some jurisdictions to a complaint or other pleading that alleges a cause of action.

petition in bankruptcy   A document filed in a bankruptcy court initiating bankruptcy proceedings.

plain view doctrine   An exception to the search warrant requirement of the Fourth Amendment, which allows warrantless seizure of evidence observed in "plain view" by an officer from a place where he or she has a legal right to be.

plaintiff   A person who brings a lawsuit.

plant patent   A patent granted on a manmade, multicellular living vegetable organism that does not exist in nature.

plat   A map of a tract of land, showing the boundaries of the streets, blocks, and numbered lots.

plea   At common law, the response or responses that the defendant in a civil action was required to file to state a defense to a complaint, petition, declaration, or bill in equity. In criminal cases, a response required by law of a person formally accused of crime, specifically, either a plea of guilty, a plea of nolo contendere, or a plea of not guilty.

plea agreement (plea bargain)   An agreement between the prosecutor and a criminal defendant under which the accused agrees to plead guilty, usually to a lesser offense, in exchange for receiving a lighter sentence than he or she would likely have received had he or she been found guilty after trial on the original charge.

pleadings Formal statements by the parties to an action setting forth their claims or defenses.

police power The power of government to make and enforce laws and regulations necessary to maintain and enhance the public welfare and to prevent individuals from violating the rights of others.

possibility of reverter A type of future interest that remains in a grantor when, by grant or devise, he or she has created an estate in fee simple determinable or fee simple conditional, the fee automatically reverting to him or her or his or her successors upon the occurrence of the event by which the estate is limited.

power of appointment A power given by a person (the grantor) to another person (the donee or grantee) to select (appoint) a person or persons to receive an estate or to receive interest or income from an estate. A power of appointment may be given by deed or similar instrument, or by will.

power of attorney A written instrument by which a person appoints another as his or her agent or attorney in fact and confers upon him or her the authority to perform certain acts.

prayer Portion of a bill in equity or a petition [complaint] that asks for ... relief and specifies the relief sought.

precedent Prior decisions of the same court, or a higher court, which a judge must follow in deciding a subsequent case presenting similar facts and the same legal problem, even though different parties are involved and many years have elapsed.

preemption The doctrine that once Congress has enacted legislation in a given field, a state may not enact a law inconsistent with the federal statute.

preemptive right The right or privilege of a stockholder of a corporation to purchase shares of a new issue before persons who are not stockholders. This entitlement allows a shareholder to preserve his or her percentage of ownership in the corporation.

preliminary hearing A hearing to determine whether there is probable cause to formally accuse a person of a crime; that is, whether there is a reasonable basis for believing that a crime has been committed and for thinking the defendant committed it.

preliminary injunction An injunction granted prior to a full hearing on the merits. Its purpose is to preserve the status quo until the final hearing.

preponderance of the evidence The degree of proof required in most civil actions. It means that the greater weight and value of the credible evidence, taken as a whole, belongs to one side in a lawsuit rather than to the other side. In other words, the party whose evidence is more convincing has a "preponderance of the evidence" on its side and must, as a matter of law, prevail in the lawsuit because it has met its burden of proof.

pretermitted child A child of a testator who is omitted from the testator's will. Generally the right of such a child to share in the decedent's estate depends upon whether the omission was intentional or unintentional.

prima facie case A cause of action or defense that is sufficiently established by a party's evidence to justify a verdict in his or her favor, provided the other party does not rebut that evidence; a case supported by sufficient evidence to justify its submission to the trier of fact and the rendition of a compatible verdict.

principal In an agency relationship, the person for whom the agent acts and from whom the agent receives his or her authority to act.

priority The status of that which is earlier or previous in point of time, degree, or rank; precedence.

privacy [T]he right to be left alone.

private law The rules of conduct that govern activities occurring among or between persons, as opposed to the rules of conduct governing the relationship between persons and their government.

private nuisance A nuisance that threatens injury to one or just a few persons; a nuisance that violates only private rights and produces damages to one or no more than a few persons.

privilege An immunity, exemption, right, or advantage possessed by an individual ... which ... exists by operation of law or ... other permission; an exemption from a burden.

privity of contract The legal relationship between the parties to a contract.

probable cause A reasonable amount of suspicion, supported by circumstances sufficiently strong to justify a prudent and cautious person's belief that certain alleged facts are probably true.

probate   The judicial act whereby a will is adjudicated to be valid.

probate court   A court with jurisdiction to probate wills and to supervise the administration of decedents' estates.

probate estate   The estate of a decedent subject to the jurisdiction of the probate court.

probate jurisdiction   Matters with respect to which a probate court has both the right and the duty to exercise its authority.

procedural due process   [A right] grounded in the Fifth Amendment and the Fourteenth Amendment ... [which] implies a proceeding in which a person has a full opportunity to protect his or her rights.

procedural law   The law governing the manner in which rights are enforced; the law prescribing the procedure to be followed in a case.

product liability   The liability of a namufacturer or seller of an article for an injury caused to a person or to property by a defect in the article sold.

promissory estoppel   The principle that a promisor will be bound to a promise (that is, estopped to deny the promise), even though it is without consideration, if he or she intended that the promise should be relied upon and it was in fact relied upon, and if a refusal to enforce the promise would result in an injustice.

property   Real property and personal property; tangible property and intangible property; corporeal property and incorporeal property.

property settlement (postnuptial agreement; postmarital contract)   An agreement between husband and wife settling property rights between them as part of a divorce action. Court approval may or may not be required.

prosecution   The act of pursuing or carrying forward an undertaking that has been started.

prosecutor   A public official, elected or appointed, who conducts criminal prosecutions on behalf of her jurisdiction.

prostitution   Engaging in sexual intercourse or other sexual activity for pay.

proximate cause   As an element of liability in a tort case, that cause which, unbroken by any intervening cause, produced the injury, and without which the result would not have occurred; the primary cause; the efficient cause.

proxy   1. A person who holds an authorization to act in the place of another. 2. An authorization, usually in writing, under which one person acts for another. 3. Authority given in writing by one shareholder in a corporation to another shareholder to exercise his or her voting rights for him or her.

public domain   [A] literary composition or other [invention] that has not been copyrighted [or patented] or with respect to which the copyright [or patent] has expired.

public law   Body of law dealing with the relationship between the people and their government, the relationship between agencies and branches of government, and the relationshp between governments themselves.

public nuisance   An act or omission that adversely affects the safety, health, or morals of the public, or causes some substantial annoyance, inconvenience, or injury to the public.

publication   1. The act of making something known to the public; the act of publishing. ... 2. [T]he act of communicating a defamation to a person or persons other than the person defamed. 3. With respect to copyright and the law of literary property, the act of making a writing, voice recording, musical score, or the like available to the public by sale or other form of distribution.

publish   To issue; to distribute; to disseminate; to circulate.

punitive damages (exemplary damages)   Damages that are awarded over and above compensatory damages or actual damages because of the wanton, reckless, or malicious nature of the wrong done by the plaintiff. Such damages bear no relation to the plaintiff's actual loss and are often called exemplary damages, because their purpose is to make an example of the plaintiff to discourage others from engaging in the same kind of conduct in the future.

purposely   Intentionally; knowingly.

putative marriage   A marriage that, although invalid because of some impediment, ... was nonetheless entered into in good faith.

quasi contract   An obligation imposed by law to achieve equity, usually to prevent unjust enrichment. A quasi contract is a legal fiction that a contract exists where there has been no express contract.

quitclaim deed   A deed that conveys whatever interest the grantor has in a piece of real property, as distinguished from the more usual deed which conveys a fee and contains various covenants, particularly title covenants.

rape   Sexual intercourse with a person by force or by putting the victim in fear or in circumstances in which he or she is unable to control his or her conduct or to resist.

ratification   The act of giving one's approval to a previous act, either one's own or someone else's, which, without such confirmation, would be nonbinding. … Ratification may be implied from a person's conduct; it may also take place as a result of accepting the benefits of a transaction. … [T]he confirmation of an act that has already been performed.

real estate (real property)   1. Land, including things located on it or attached to it directly or indirectly. … 2. [T]he interest a person has in land or his or her rights with respect to it.

real estate contract   A contract for sale of land.

real evidence   Physical evidence, as opposed to testimony; demonstrative evidence.

real property   Land, including things located on it or attached to it directly or indirectly; real estate.

reasonable   Rational; not arbitrary or capricious; sensible.

reasonable force   Force that is appropriate in the circumstances.

reasonable man (person) test   A standard for determining negligence, which asks: "What would a reasonable person have done in the same circumstances?" … [I]t measures the failure to do that which a person of ordinary intelligence and judgment would have done in the circumstances, or the doing of that which a person of ordinary intelligence and judgment would not have done.

rebut   To deny; to refute; to contradict; to contravene.

receiving stolen property   Receiving property with the knowledge that it is stolen property, and with fraudulent intent.

reckless   [C]onduct demonstrating an indifference to consequences, particularly those involving danger to life or to the safety of others.

recklessly   [C]onduct demonstrating an indifference to consequences, particularly those involving danger to life or to the safety of others.

record   To file or deposit a document or instrument for recording.

redeem   To buy back; to pay off.

reduction to practice   In patent law, completing the patenting process by putting an invention to use or into practice on a demonstration basis.

reform   To correct; to make better; to modify.

regulation   A rule having the force of law, promulgated by an administrative agency.

rejection   Any act or word of an offeree, communicated to an offeror, conveying refusal of an offer.

rejoinder   A reply; an answer; a retort.

release   [noun] A document or writing stating that a right or claim is given up or discharged. [verb] The act of giving up or discharging a claim or right to the person against whom the claim exists or against whom the right is enforceable.

relevant evidence   Evidence that proves or disproves a fact, or that tends to prove or disprove a fact. Relevance is the basic measure of the admissibility of evidence.

remainder   An estate in land to take effect immediately after the expiration of a prior estate, created at the same time and by the same instrument.

remainderman   A person entitled to receive a *remainder*.

remedy   The means by which a right is enforced, an injury is redressed, and relief is obtained.

replevin   An action by which the owner of personal property taken or detained by another may recover possession of it.

reply   1. In pleading, the plaintiff's answer to the defendant's setoff or counterclaim. 2. A response; an answer.

republication   The reinstatement of a will that has been revoked.

request for admissions   Written statements concerning a case, directed to an adverse party, that he or she is required to admit or deny. Such admissions or denials will be treated by the court as having been established, and need not be proven at trial.

res ipsa loquitur   Means "the thing speaks for itself." When an instrumentality causes injury, an inference or rebuttable presumption arises that the injury was caused by the defendant's negligence, if the … instrumentality was under the exclusive control or management of the defendant and the occurrence was such as in the ordinary course of events would not have happended if the defendant had used reasonable care.

rescind   To annul a contract from the beginning, not merely to terminate the contract as to future transactions.

rescission   The abrogation, annulment, or cancellation of a contract by the act of a party. … More than mere termination, rescission restores the parties to the status quo existing before the contract was entered into.

residuary clause   A clause in a will that disposes of the part of the estate that is left after all other legacies and devises have been paid and all claims against the estate are satisfied.

respondeat superior   Means "let the master respond." The doctrine under which liability is imposed upon an employer for the acts of its employees committed in the course and scope of their employment.

restitution   [A] remedy that restores the status quo. Restitution returns a person who has been wrongfully deprived of something to the position he or she occupied before the wrong occurred; it requires a defendant who has been unjustly enriched at the expense of the plaintiff to make the plaintiff whole, either … by returning property unjustly held, by reimbursing the plaintiff, or by paying compensation or indemnification.

restraining order   An order of court equivalent to a preliminary injunction or a temporary restraining order.

reversed   A term used in appellate court opinions to indicate that the court has set aside the judgment of the trial court.

reversed and remanded   An expression used in appellate court opinions to indicate that the court has reversed the judgment of the trial court and that the case has been returned to the trial court for a new trial.

revocable trust   A trust in which the settlor does not give up the right to revoke.

revocation   A nullification, cancellation, or withdrawal of a power, privilege, or act.

right of possession   A person's right to occupy and enjoy property.

right of survivorship   In the case of a joint tenancy or a tenancy by the entirety, the entitlement of the surviving tenant, upon the death of the other, to hold in his or her own right whatever estate or interest both previously shared.

riot   The acts of three or more persons assembled together who threaten to do injury to the persons or property of others, or who, by means of violence, actually do damage to others or their property.

robbery   The felonious taking of money or any thing of value from the person of another, or from his or her presence, against his or her will, by force or by putting him or her in fear.

rule against perpetuities   The common law rule that prohibits the creation of a future interest or a future estate that has the possibility of not vesting within 21 years, plus nine months, of some life in being at the time of creation of the interest.

rulemaking   The promulgation by an administrative agency of a rule having the force of law, i.e., a regulation.

rules of court (court rules)   Rules promulgated by the court, governing procedure or practice before it.

scienter   Knowledge, particularly guilty knowledge; knowledge a person has that, as a matter of law, will result in his or her liability or guilt.

scope of employment   A phrase referring to activities carried out by an employee in doing the work assigned to him or her by the employer.

second-degree murder   A murder that does not fall into the category of first-degree murder; a murder committed with intent to kill, but without premeditation or deliberation.

section   A … parcel of land consisting of 640 acres as laid out by government survey.

secured debt   A debt for which security or collateral has been given.

security   Collateral; a pledge given to a creditor by a debtor for the payment of a debt or for the performance of an obligation.

self-defense   The use of force to protect oneself from death of imminent bodily harm at the hands of an aggressor. A person may use only that amount of force reasonably necessary to protect … against the peril with which he or she is threatened.

self-incrimination   Testimony, or any other act or statement, by which a person incriminates himself or herself; i.e., implicates himself or herself in the commission of a crime.

senior   Of primary importance, rank, or right.

separation of powers A fundamental principle of the Constitution, which gives exclusive power to the legislative branch to make the law, exclusive power to the executive branch to administer it, and exclusive power to the judicial branch to enforce it. The authors of the Constitution believed that the separation of powers would make abuse of power less likely.

service mark A mark, design, title, or motto used in the sale or advertising of services to identify the services and distinguish them from the services of others. A service mark is the property of its owner and, when registered under the Trademark Act, is reserved for the exclusive use of its owner.

service of process Delivery of a summons, writ, complaint, or other process to the opposite party, or other person entitled to receive it, in such manner as the law prescribes, whether by leaving a copy at his or her residence, by mailing a copy to his or her attorney, or by publication.

servient tenement Real property that is subject to an easement that benefits another piece of property, known as the dominant tenement.

session laws The collected statutes enacted during a session of a legislature.

settlement The ending of a lawsuit by agreement.

settlor The creator of a trust; the person who conveys or transfers property to another (the trustee) to hold in trust for a third person (the beneficiary).

severally Distinctly; separately; apart from others.

severance The act of detaching things affixed to the land.

sham A deception; a trick; a fraud.

shareholder (stockholder) The owner of one or more shares of stock in a corporation; a person who appears on the books of a corporation as the owner of one or more shares of its stock. The terms *shareholder* and *stockholder* are used interchangeably.

shepardizing Using a citator.

signature The name of a person as affixed by him or her, in his or her own handwriting, to an instrument, document, or other writing, or to any surface.

slander A false and malicious oral statement tending to blacken a person's reputation or to damage his or her means of livelihood.

slander of title A false or malicious statement, oral or written, that brings into question a person's right or title to real or personal property, causing him or her damage.

slight care A very minimal degree of care; the least degree of care.

slip law Printed copies of a legislative enactment published in loose-leaf or pamphlet form shortly after the legislation is passed.

slip opinion A single judicial decision published shortly after it has been issued by the court and well before it is incorporated into a reporter.

sole proprietorship Ownership by one person, as opposed to ownership by more than one person, ... a corporation, ... a partnership, etc.

solemnization of marriage The performance of the marriage ceremony.

solicitation The crime of encouraging or inciting a person to commit a crime. The act of a prostitute in seeking clients; the act of a pimp.

solicitation The crime of encouraging or inciting a person to commit a crime.

sound mind A term referring to the mind of a person who is sane and mentally competent.

sovereign immunity (governmental immunity) The principle that the government ... is immune from suit except when it consents to be sued ... .

special damages Damages that may be added to the general damages in a case, and arise from the particular or special circumstances of the case.

special warranty [A] warranty by which the grantor promises to protect the grantee and his or her heirs only against the claims of those claiming "by, through or under" him or her.

special warranty deed A deed that contains a *special warranty* rather than a general warranty.

specific devise A devise of specific real estate.

specific intent The intent to commit the very act with which the defendant has been charged.

specific legacy A bequest of specific personal property.

specific performance The equitable remedy of compelling performance of a contract, as distinguished from an action at law for damages for breach of contract due to nonperformance. Specific performance may be ordered in circumstances where damages are an inadequate remedy.

spendthrift trust   A trust that provides a fund for the maintenance of a spendthrift, protecting him or her against his or her own wastefulness and recklessness. A spendthrift trust prevents the beneficiary from voluntarily selling or conveying his or her entitlement and bars his or her interest from seizure by his or her creditors as well.

sprinkling trust (spray trust; discretionary trust)   A trust whose income the trustee may distribute among its beneficiaries as, when, and in the amounts he or she chooses.

standard of care   The standard by which negligence is determined in a particular situation.

stare decisis   Means "standing by the decision." ... [T]he doctrine that judicial decisions stand as precedents for cases arising in the future. It is a fundamental policy of our law that, except in unusual circumstances, a court's determination on a point of law will be followed by courts of the same or lower rank in later cases presenting the same legal issue, even though different parties are involved and many years have elapsed.

Statute of Frauds   A statute, existing in one or another form in every state, that requires certain classes of contracts to be in writing and signed by the parties. Its purpose is to prevent fraud or reduce the opportunities for fraud.

Statutes at Large   An official publication of the federal government, issued after each session of Congress, which includes all statutes enacted by the Congress and all congressional resolutions and treaties, as well as presidential proclamations and proposed or ratified amendments to the Constitution.

statutes of limitations   Federal and state statutes prescribing the maximum period of time during which various types of civil actions and criminal prosecutions can be brought after the occurrence of the injury or the offense.

statutory rape   Sexual intercourse with a female under the age of consent, with or without her consent.

stipulation   1. A mandate; a requirement; a condition. 2. An agreement by the parties to a lawsuit with respect to certain uncontested facts. A stipulation avoids the need to present evidence regarding the matters it covers; it is entered into to save time and expense.

strict liability   Liability for an injury whether or not there is fault or negligence; absolute liability.

strict scrutiny test   A term the Supreme Court uses to describe the rigorous level of judicial review to be applied in determining the constitutionality of legislation that restricts a fundamental right or legislation based upon a suspect classification.

subject matter jurisdiction   The jurisdiction of a court to hear and determine the type of case before it.

subpoena   A command in the form of written process requiring a witness to come to court to testify.

subpoena duces tecum   A ... written command requiring a witness to come to court to testify and at that time to produce for use as evidence the papers, documents, books, or records listed in the subpoena.

subscribe   To sign; literally, to "sign under" one's name at the end of a document.

substantive due process   A right grounded in the Fifth Amendment and the Fourteenth Amendment. ... [T]he concept that the government may not act arbitrarily or capriciously in making, interpreting, or enforcing the law.

substantive law   Area of the law that defines right conduct, as opposed to procedural law, which governs the process by which rights are adjudicated.

summons   In a civil case, the process by which an action is commenced and the defendant is brought within the jurisdiction of the court.

supreme court   In most states, the highest appellate court of the state.

surety   A person who promises to pay the debt or to satisfy the obligation of another person (the principal). As opposed to the obligation of a guarantor, the obligation of a surety is both primary and absolute; that is, it does not depend upon a default by the principal.

surrender   To give up; to give back; to give back possession; to yield.

syllabus   The headnote of a reported case.

tangible property   Property, real or personal, that has physical substance; property that can be physically possessed.

temporary restraining order (TRO)   [I]njunctive relief that the court is empowered to grant, without notice to the opposite party and pending a hearing on the merits, upon a showing that failure to do so will result in "immediate and irreparable injury, loss, or damage."

tenancy   1. The right to hold and occupy realty or personalty by virtue of owning an interest in it. 2. Possession of realty under a lease; the relationship existing between a landlord or lessor and a tenant or lessee.

tenancy at sufferance   The tenancy of a person who continues in possession after his or her right of possession has ended; the tenancy of a holdover tenant.

tenancy at will   A tenancy that continues only as long as both parties wish it to, i.e., "at the will of" the parties. The duration of such a tenancy is uncertain and indefinite.

tenancy in common   A tenancy in which two or more persons own an undivided interest in an estate in land ... or in personal property. As opposed to joint tenants, tenants in common have no right of survivorship; when a tenant in common dies, his or her interest passes to his or her heirs rather than to the cotenant or cotenants.

tenant (lessee)   A person who occupies realty under a lease with a landlord.

tender years   A term used to describe minors, particularly when they are very young.

term   A portion of an agreement relating to a particular matter.

termination   1. An end of something in time. 2. The act of bringing an end to something.

testament   A will.

testamentary capacity   The mental capacity of a testator, at the time of making his or her will, to be able to understand the nature of his or her act and, generally if not precisely, the nature and location of his or her property and the identity of those persons who are the natural objects of his or her bounty.

testamentary trust   A trust created by will.

testator   A person who dies leaving a valid will.

testimonium clause   A clause at the end of a deed, which recites that the parties have "set their hands and seals" to the deed on the date specified.

third-party complaint   A complaint filed by the defendant in a lawsuit against a third person whom he or she seeks to bring into the action because of that person's alleged liability to the defendant.

title company   A company that conducts title searches and sell title insurance.

title insurance   An insurance policy in which the insurer agrees to indemnify the purchaser of realty, or the mortgagee, against loss due to defective title.

title search   An examination of all documents of record relating to the status or condition of the title to a given piece of real estate (including deeds reflecting past ownership and outstanding mortgages and other liens) in order to verify title.

tolling the statute   A term referring to circumstances that, by operation of law, suspend or interrupt the running of the statute of limitations.

Torrens title system   A system for the registration of titles to land, which exists in several states. Under the Torrens system, ... the name of the owner of the land appears on a certificate of title that is conclusive evidence of ownership.

tort   A wrong involving a breach of duty and resulting in an injury to the person or property of another. A tort is distinguished from a breach of contract in that a tort is a violation of a duty established by law, whereas a breach of contract results from a failure to meet an obligation created by the agreement of the parties. ... [T]he tort is a private wrong that must be pursued by the injured party in a civil action.

tortfeasor   A person who commits a tort.

Totten trust   A trust created by a bank deposit which a person makes with his or her money in his or her own name as trustee for another person. ... [I]t is revocable at will until the depositor dies or completes the gift in his or her lifetime by some unequivocal act or declaration.

township   As laid out by government survey, a tract of land six miles square.

trade fixtures   Articles attached to leased premises by the tenant to aid him or her in carrying on his or her trade or business. Unlike residential fixtures, the tenant is free to remove trade fixtures upon termination or expiration of the lease.

trade name   The name under which a company does business. The goodwill of a company includes its trade name.

trademark   A mark, design, title, logo, or motto used in the sale or advertising of products to identify them and distinguish them from the products of others. A trademark is the property of its owner and, when registered under the Trademark Act, is reserved for the exclusive use of its owner.

transactional immunity A guaranty given a person that if he or she testifies against others he or she will not be prosecuted for his or her own involvement in the crime to which the testimony relates.

transferred intent The doctrine that if a defendant who intends to injure one person unintentionally harms another, the intent is transferred to the person who is unintentionally harmed. This doctrine permits the defendant to be prosecuted as if he or she had intended to harm the person injured.

trespass An unauthorized entry or intrusion of the real property of another.

trespasser [A] person who enters the land of another without an invitation to do so and whose presence is not suffered.

trial A hearing or determination by a court of the issues existing between the parties to an action; an examination by a court of competent jurisdiction, according to the law of the land, of the facts or law at issue in either a civil case or a criminal prosecution, for the purpose of adjudicating the matters in controversy.

trial court A court that hears and determines a case initially, as opposed to an appellate court; a court of general jurisdiction.

trial de novo A new trial, a retrial, or a trial on appeal from a justice's court or a magistrate's court to a court of general jurisdiction. A trial … in which the matter is tried again as if it had not been heard before and as if no decision had previously been rendered.

trust A fiduciary relationship involving a trustee who holds trust property for the benefit or use of a beneficiary. Property of any description or type … may properly be the subject of a trust. The trustee holds legal title to the trust property … ; the beneficiary holds equitable title.

trust account A bank account created by a depositor for the benefit of a person or persons other than the depositor. The money in a trust account may not be commingled with other funds of the depositor or of the bank.

trustee The person who holds the legal title to trust property for the benefit of the beneficiary of the trust, with such powers and subject to such duties as are imposed by the terms of the trust and the law.

trustee in bankruptcy A person appointed by a bankruptcy court to collect any amounts owed the debtor, sell the debtor's property, and distribute the proceeds among the creditors.

unanimous Complete approval or concurrence; the concurrence of everyone.

unauthorized practice of law Engaging in the practice of law without the license required by law.

unconscionable Morally offensive, reprehensible, or repugnant. An unconscionable contract is a contract in which a dominant party has taken unfair advantage of a weaker party, who has little or no bargaining power, and has imposed terms and conditions that are unreasonable and one-sided.

unconscionable contract A contract in which a dominant party has taken unfair advantage of a weaker party, who has little or no bargaining power, and has imposed terms and conditions that are unreasonable and one-sided.

undue influence Inappropriate pressure exerted on a person for the purpose of causing him to substitute his or her will for the will or wishes of another.

unfair competition In business, the use or imitation of another firm's name, mark, logo, design, or title for the purpose of creating confusion in the public mind and inducing the public to believe that a competitor's business or product is one's own. Such practices are illegal.

Uniform Commercial Code (UCC) One of the Uniform Laws, which has been adopted in much the same form in every state. It governs most aspects of commercial transactions including sales, leases, negotiable instruments, deposits and collections, letters of credit, bulk sales, warehouse receipts, bills of lading and other documents of title, investment securities, and secured transactions.

Uniform Laws Model legislation prepared and proposed jointly by the American Law Institute and the Commission on Uniform State Laws, the purpose of which is to promote uniformity throughout the country with respect to statutes governing significant areas of the law. Many Uniform Laws are adopted by many, most, or all of the states, with variations from state to state.

unilateral contract A contract in which there is a promise on one side only, the consideration being an act or something other than another promise. … [A]n offer that is accepted not by another promise, but by performance.

unilateral mistake A misconception by one, but not both, parties to a contract with respect to the terms of the contract.

United States Code The official codification of the statutes enacted by Congress.

unjust enrichment The equitable doctrine that a person who unjustly receives property, money, or other benefits that belong to another may not retain them and is obligated to return them.

unlawful assembly The acts of three or more persons assembled together with the intention of doing violent injury to the persons or property of others.

unliquidated claim A claim whose existence or amount is not agreed upon by the parties; a claim whose amount cannot be determined by applying rules of law or by mathematical calculation.

use The enjoyment of real property by occupying it or by otherwise putting it to use.

useful To be patentable, an invention must be new and useful. An invention is "useful" if it is capable of performing the functions for which it was intended and its use is not contrary to law, morality, or public policy.

utility patent The most common type of patent, granted on the basis that the invention is of benefit to society.

vagrancy At common law, the offense of wandering about or going from place to place with no visible means of support.

valid Effective; sufficient in law; legal; lawful; not void; in effect.

value 1. Monetary worth. 2. The worth of a thing in money, material, services, or other things for which it may be exchanged. 3. Estimated worth.

venue The county or judicial district in which a case is to be tried. In civil cases, venue may be based on where the events giving rise to the cause of action took place or where the parties live or work. The venue of a criminal prosecution is the place where the crime was committed.

vicarious liability Liability imposed upon a person because of the act or omission of another.

void Null; without legal effect.

void contract A contract that creates no legal rights; the equivalent of no contract at all.

voidable Avoidable; subject to disaffirmance; defective but valid unless disaffirmed by the person entitled to disaffirm.

voidable contract A contract that may be avoided or disaffirmed by one of the parties because it is defective.

voir dire examination Examination of a potential juror for the purpose of determining whether he or she is qualified and acceptable to act as a juror in the case. A prospective juror who a party decides is unqualified or unacceptable may be challenged for cause or may be the subject of a peremptory challenge.

voluntary A word applied to an act freely done out of choice, not brought about by coercion, duress, or accident.

voluntary bankruptcy A bankruptcy that the debtor himself or herself initiates ... .

warrantless arrest The arrest of a person without an arrest warrant.

warranty [A] promise, either express or implied by law, with respect to the fitness or merchantability of the article that is the subject of the contract.

warranty deed A deed that contains title covenants.

water rights An easement for the use of water or for the right to use another's premises to transport water over or through.

widow's allowance Same as elective share.

will An instrument by which a person (the testator) makes a disposition of his or her property, to take effect after his or her death.

winding up The dissolution or liquidation of a corporation or a partnership.

work product rule The rule that an attorney's work product is not subject to discovery.

writ of certiorari A writ issued by a higher court to a lower court requiring the certification of the record in a particular case so that the higher court can review the record and correct any actions taken in the case which are not in accordance with the law.

wrongful birth When a ... child is born to parents who decided not to prevent or terminate the pregnancy because of erroneous medical advice ... .

wrongful conception (wrongful pregnancy) When a child is born as the result of a negligently performed sterilization of either the father or the mother ... .

wrongful death A death that results from a wrongful act.

INDEX